The history of Medway, Mass., 1713-1885

Ephraim Orcutt Jameson, George James La Croix

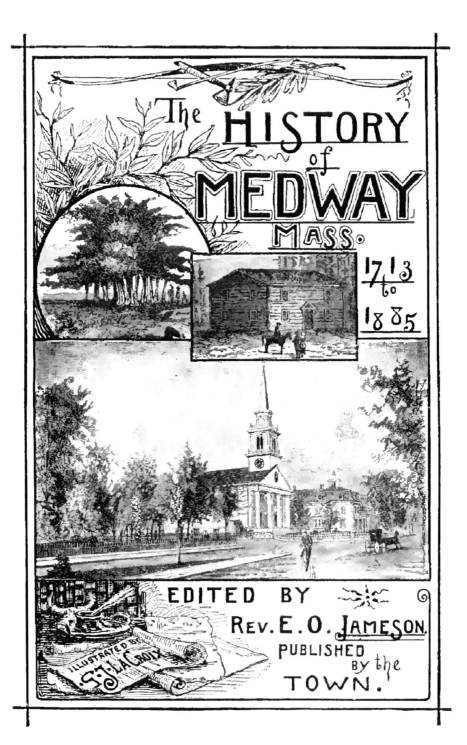

The History of MEDWAY MASS.

$17\frac{13}{60}$

1885

EDITED BY
Rev. E. O. Jameson.

ILLUSTRATED BY G. F. LACROIX

PUBLISHED
BY the
TOWN.

J. A. & R. A. REID, PRINTERS.
PROVIDENCE, R. I.

THIS VOLUME

IS

DEDICATED TO THE MEMORY OF THE EARLY SETTLERS,

TO

THEIR DESCENDANTS, WHEREVER RESIDING,

AND TO

THE PRESENT INHABITANTS

OF

MEDWAY, MASS

————

BY THE AUTHOR

The Action of the Town.

—•—

"Medway, Mass., 4 April, 1881.

"At a meeting of the inhabitants of Medway this day, it was

"Voted, To publish a History of the Town, and the following committee was chosen, to whom the matter was committed:

"Hon. M. M. Fisher, Dea. Anson Daniels, Dea. William Daniels, Rev. A. W. Ide, Rev. E. O. Jameson, Rev. R. K. Harlow, O. A. Mason, A. M. B. Fuller, E. N. Holbrook.

"O. A. Mason, Town Clerk."

THE PREFACE.

———•———

THE HISTORY OF MEDWAY given to the public in this volume, embodies the results of five years of cooperative effort and research to bring together all matters of local record and interest, by the members of the Committee of Publication, besides the more distinctive editorial work, which has been in hand for nearly two years   The editor has received valuable assistance from many persons interested in the undertaking, and for the genealogical data has depended very largely upon representatives of the different families in the town, who were duly invited to cooperate, and in many instances have generously responded.   Any seeming omissions, however, from the pages of genealogy and from other parts of the book, are due to the neglect of those solicited to make the desired returns.   Some errors will doubtless be found.   Among those who have contributed data, records, papers, biographical sketches, and materials of various kinds, most largely, may be mentioned the Hon. M. M. Fisher, the late lamented Dea. Anson Daniels, Orion A. Mason, Esq., Dea. William Daniels, A. M B. Fuller, Esq , George L. Richardson. A M , and William S Tilden, Esq

The ready cooperation and valuable contributions of these gentlemen. and of others not particularly named. are hereby gratefully acknowledged.

This volume covers the entire period of local history, embracing two hundred and twenty-five years, from 1660 to 1885 , or, from the first appearance of a white settler within the territory, to the recent date of the incorporation of the town of Millis.   The book is divided into ten sections, and gives, in consecutive order, an account of the first settlement, the municipal doings, the churches, the schools and other institutions, the industries, the military service, the miscellaneous matters, the cemeteries, the biographies of many persons, and the genealogies of numerous families.

The volume is printed on paper of excellent quality, and in mechanical execution is a model of skill and neatness.   It is embellished with twelve steel engravings by different artists. and nearly one hundred fine wood engravings, largely executed by a native of the town, George J. La Croix, Esq. No labor or expense has been spared to make the book attractive and valuable as a volume of local history, and it is given to the public with the best wishes of the compiler.

E. O JAMESON.

MILLIS, MASS , June 10, 1886

THE COMMITTEE OF PUBLICATION,

ELECTED BY THE TOWN,

APRIL 4, 1881

——•——

MILTON M FISHER,	WILLIAM DANIELS,
ANSON DANIELS.	ORION A MASON,
A. M. B. FULLER,	E. H. HOLBROOK,
R K. HARLOW,	ALEXIS W. IDE,

E O JAMESON.

——

The Organization of the Committee.

M. M. FISHER, *Chairman.*

O· A MASON, *Secretary.*

E. O. JAMESON, *Editor.*

——

THE ILLUSTRATIONS

BY

GEORGE J. LA CROIX

ASSISTED BY

FRANK MYRICK and F CHILDE HASSAM.

——

THE ENGRAVINGS

BY

J. C. BUTTRE, S. H. RITCHIE,

AND

GEORGE J LA CROIX.

THE CONTENTS.

— . —

The Wood Engravings.

The Steel Engravings.

THE REGION AND ITS SETTLEMENT.

1643 — 1713.

THE territory embraced within the limits of Medway was included in the patent granted in 1628 of " that part of New England lying between three miles to the north of the Merrimac and three miles to the south of Charles River, and of every part thereof in the Massachusetts Bay : and in length between the described breadth from the Atlantic Ocean to the South Sea." The settlements projected by these patentees became the " Massachusetts Bay Colony."

The Massachusetts Indians were divided into several tribes, each holding a claim to territory within prescribed limits ; and though the crown gave the right and title to their lands without consulting the original owners, yet, when settlements were formed, it was made a condition, in order to avoid difficulty afterward, that the settlers should see that the Indian titles were extinguished by purchase or otherwise. A small sum generally sufficed to effect this object.

The lands lying between the Charles and Neponset rivers were claimed by the tribe of the Neponsets ; and were purchased of their sachem, Chicka-tawbut, by William Pynchon, soon after the settlement of Boston. The country west and north of Charles River was the seat of various small tribes, and was not included in Mr. Pynchon's purchase.

The Charles River was called at first the Massachusetts River, and is mentioned by Captain John Smith in the account of his memorable voyage of discovery in 1614. But its name was soon after changed by him in honor of the second son of James, afterward known as Charles I.

The first town organized in the Chickatawbut purchase was Roxbury ; the next, in 1636, was Dedham, which included all the towns now lying along the southerly and easterly side of Charles River. Boggastow was the

2

Indian name for the valley of Charles River and the lands immediately north and west of it, from Natick to near the present site of Medway Village; and it was without doubt the domain of the tribe called the " Natick Indians." The first distinct mention of Boggastow in the Dedham records is in 1640, when Edward Alleyne, a prominent citizen of that town, received, as an acknowledgment of his public services, a grant of land " to lie in or about that place called Boggastow." The fact that this grant was made by the town of Dedham, which embraced no lands west of the river, shows that the name was applied to meadows lying on both sides of Charles River. West of the river at that time was " country land," the property of the Colony of Massachusetts Bay, having no town limits, civilization not having, as yet, pushed so far inland.

NATURAL SCENERY.

Medway has little to boast of beyond its neighbors in picturesque scenery. But there lies all about much of that quiet loveliness of landscape which abounds in this part of Massachusetts, and especially along the banks of the sleepy Charles. There are no mountains, no abrupt and rugged hills, no dashing, clamoring waterfalls, no singing brooks and broad, silvery lakes, such as give a wonderful charm to some towns in New England. But gentle elevations, beautiful valleys, the meandering river, broad, far-reaching meadow-lands skirted by forests of evergreen, the quiet flow of Boggastow and Chicken brooks, the waters of Popolatick, Winthrop, and Boggastow ponds furnish the elements of a scenery not destitute of beauty.

In approaching the town from the northeast, one is struck with the extent of the broad meadows stretching several miles to the south and southwest, with the silent and sedate Charles winding gracefully through them, without at any point sufficient fall to produce a perceptible current. This flat, unbroken plain is so near a dead level that an unusually heavy rainfall converts it into a broad lake. A circumstance especially inconvenient to the early farmers, who relied upon the grass to sustain their cattle during the winter, if it occurred in the early summer before the hay crop was gathered, as it not infrequently happened. In consequence of this we find that as early as 1673 the town of Medfield voted to tax the owners of the meadows upon the Charles and Stop rivers three pence per acre, to be expended in clearing the channels of these rivers, that their lands might be more perfectly drained. The proprietors afterward spent much money and labor in blasting rocks, and digging a canal below the meadows for the same purpose. But the sluggish Charles still remained about the same, preferring to lie quiet and stretch out into a broad lake whenever tempted by the melting of the snow or a great fall of rain, rather than fret and worry and dash about in a sparkling torrent, or become a moderately brisk stream. The owners of the meadows were naturally extremely jealous of any influence that even remotely might encourage this inactivity of the river. Therefore, in 1723, they petitioned the General Court not to grant Mr. Thomas Sawing leave to build a dam at Natick, lest it should hinder the slow-paced Charles and cause the flooding of the lands still more widely. At a later period, in 1753, the owners brought a suit for damages against Matthew Hastings, the owner of a dam at Natick, which resulted only in expense and in a suit brought by Hastings for malicious prosecution, which was, however, stayed by order of the court. The commissioners of sewers, upon the petition of the owners, attempted some measures of relief; this, too, ended in a tax to defray charges. The river has not improved in energy, but still winds gracefully along, and lingers as if enamored of the green meadow-lands.

Following the stream along upward there are found many quiet bits of picturesque landscape, where the wood lands from the hills jut out in points and groups of trees, invading the level meadow. Some of the bridges, too, of which there are twelve crossing from Medway, are structures of interest for their quaintness. At Rockville, so called, and above, the river changes its character and becomes more rapid. The Popolatick Pond, stretching out upon the Franklin side and surrounded by woods, deserves more attention than it receives. While at the arched bridge and along the mill-pond above Medway Village are scenes of great beauty, the masses of foliage on the opposite hill-sides adding greatly to the effect.

In the midst of the town, stretching almost from one side to the other, is the Black Swamp. The felling of the pine forest with which it was formerly covered has shorn it of much of its original weird blackness, but still it remains the most remarkable natural feature of the town, dividing it territorially, and depriving it of a municipal centre

Its dark, sullen, and persistent occupation of so central a position has been the cause of sectional jealousies and petty rivalries in the town, that might otherwise have been avoided. It would afford no site for a town hall, although one might have been located upon its borders. A permanent high school was a dream originating in the ardent desires of some of the more intelligent of the citizens, which for many years seemed uncertain of realization for the same cause. Nothing but the railroad could flank the swamp and make such a school practicable.

Parties, both in church and state, have sprung up on either side, having their party feelings intensified, perhaps, in being kept apart by this passive, silent, dogged intermeddler, until dangerous discussions were held upon the propriety of dividing the town, which, at least in one instance prior to our day, almost led to such a result. And yet Black Swamp has not proved an unmitigated evil, for it has no doubt prevented the centralization which so often in other towns has led to extravagant expenditure and so to burdensome indebtedness. And at last it served an excellent argument for establishing the new town of Millis.

To the east of the swamp is a range of sandy and not very productive hills, some of which are still crowned with pines, the principal of which was formerly called Bare Hill, and more recently Meeting-house Hill, on which was built the first meeting-house, and where the oldest burying-ground· in the town is located. Still farther east, lying between hills and meadows bordering upon the Boggastow Brook and Charles River, is a plain extending from the brook on the north almost to the river on the south, called in the early records the "Long Plain," upon which the meeting-house now stands. On the middle and southern portion of this plain the soil is light and sandy, while the northern portion and parts adjacent are very fertile and productive. Several hills springing out of the swamps and meadows with which they are surrounded, and still covered with wood, are called Great Island, Bridge Island, and Poorduck Island. These add much to the beauty of this part of the town.

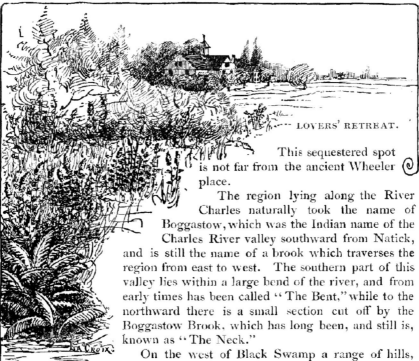

LOVERS' RETREAT.

This sequestered spot is not far from the ancient Wheeler place.

The region lying along the River Charles naturally took the name of Boggastow, which was the Indian name of the Charles River valley southward from Natick, and is still the name of a brook which traverses the region from east to west. The southern part of this valley lies within a large bend of the river, and from early times has been called "The Bent," while to the northward there is a small section cut off by the Boggastow Brook, which has long been, and still is, known as "The Neck."

On the west of Black Swamp a range of hills, the highest in town, stretches across its entire width from north to south. The soil on this swell of land is heavy and strong, and in some parts encumbered with boulders. This region produces good crops of grass and fruitful orchards. The views from many elevated points are worthy the attention of the lover of nature, especially that to the east and southeast, embracing the Blue Hills in Milton and the Moose Hills in Sharon in the distant horizon, and nearer the Noon Hill in Medfield, with a wide stretch of country to the northeast; also to the southwest, including the villages of West Medway and Caryville, and the town of Bellingham, and to the northwest the beautiful valley of the Chicken Brook, bounded by forest-crowned hills on the opposite side, dotted with farm buildings and variegated by orchards and growing crops, and with many single trees and groups, elms, oaks, hickories, and maples, scattered here and there. There are few quiet rural scenes more lovely. From the north end of this elevation the view of Winthrop Pond and the village of Holliston beyond, is very beautiful.

On the west of the Chicken Brook valley is another elevation, consisting of a heavy, wet, rocky soil, mingled with clay, which in its natural state produces chestnut, oak, maple, and hickory trees with surprising rapidity, and under cultivation is the best grass producing land in the town. To the waters of Chicken Brook belong the honor of being the motive power of the first carpet-loom in New England.

Duncan Wright commenced in his woolen mill on Chicken Brook to weave carpets. He subsequently became the founder of the Lowell Carpet Works, of world-wide reputation.

That part of the town west of the New Grant which formerly belonged to Holliston has a rough, broken surface, requiring much labor for its cultivation. It is crossed by Hoppin River, a small stream flowing to the southeast and falling into Charles River, forming at its mouth the boundary between Medway and Bellingham.

The region to the northward, lying on the south side and bordering upon Winthrop Pond, was called " Squit," from the Indian name of this region, which was Mucksquit. The large number of stone implements discovered and dug up in this vicinity seems to indicate that near this beautiful pond, which they called Winnekening — the Smile of the Great Spirit — was an Indian settlement. The early settlers named this sheet of water after the son of Governor Winthrop, who received a grant of land upon its borders.

Dinglehole lies a little to the northeast of the present residence of C. W. Emerson, M. D., and is embraced in Oak Grove Farm. In the olden times it was supposed to be the rendezvous of witches and of the evil one, the place where Satan met with his disciples, who there pledged themselves to his service. Unearthly sounds were heard, and strange lights were seen glancing about in this uncanny place. A tall pine tree, with its topmost branches strangely woven and twisted together into a fantastic crown, was supposed to mark the trysting-place.

This Dinglehole is like a large pit, with black, stagnant water of uncertain depth at the bottom, a scary place and famous in the legends of the neighborhood on account of the many curious incidents and marvelous adventures which have happened there. It is reported that in the early days many strange apparitions were seen and noises heard in and about Dingle-hole, to the great annoyance and disquietude of the good people of Boggas-tow in their lawful callings and accustomed avocations. Dinglehole, in its form, is thought very much to resemble a goose-yoke, but its name is un-doubtedly derived from the dingling or tinkling of a bell, which was fre-quently heard there on dark, misty summer evenings, and by the neigh-boring inhabitants supposed to be rung by the hobgoblins of the place, and thence called the "spirit's bell." Formerly this enchanted ground was bounded on all sides by a circular road, but more recently a highway has been built through it.

In this same vicinity, and within the limits of Oak Grove Farm, is a beautiful thicket of pines, whose fragrance and shade in summer render this spot an attractive resort.

The Pine Grove.

On a dark, moonless night, when the spirit's bell was always most sonorous, strange lights and globes of fire were fre-quently seen playing about Dinglehole, and the benighted traveler was astonished and almost petrified by the apparition of a man without a head, who would most uncere-moniously lead him around all night in the circular road without advancing him a step on his intended journey. It was anciently the custom of the good people in the vicin-ity of this terrific glen, on approaching it in the night, to say their prayers, and it was believed that on the pronunciation of cer-tain words the bell would cease its tinkling, the lights vanish, and the man without a head disappear in the deepest recesses of the woods, and there wait the arrival of a more ignorant or less pious traveler.

But mysterious bells, nocturnal fire-balls, and grim spectres of headless men were not the only terrors of this gloomy region. The place is said to have been infested with witches, in the shape of 'coons, weasels, and other little odoriferous animals, none of which could be caught or slain by the ordinary means. One day, as a famous modern Nimrod was hunting on this enchanted ground, he espied a large raccoon, sitting with the utmost dignity and composure upon the limb of an old pine tree. He leveled his gun with the most accurate aim, and discharged it at the object, within point-blank distance, without producing the least visible effect upon the creature at which he aimed. After repeatedly loading and discharging his piece with the same ill success, he cut a young witch-hazel, and with great acuteness of thought sharpened and fitted it to the bore of his gun, and " let off " full upon the countenance of his adversary. The unfortunate 'coon was never seen after this final shot, and it was rumored at the time that Mrs. Murkey Mullen, an elderly and somewhat unpopular lady in the neighborhood, was badly wounded in the face by some unaccountable accident, which had well-nigh terminated her sublunary existence. It was customary in olden times among the goodly dames of Boggastow and its vicinity, on the long winter evenings, to go out singly or in groups to spend a cheerful hour among their friends in knitting woolen stockings of divers colors, and chatting upon such subjects as most naturally engage the attention of the fair. Some of the most expert knitters, by making it a rule to form a stitch every time their tongues uttered a syllable, would knit up a prodigious long yarn in the course of an evening, and by this wise regulation the boys and girls of the neighborhood were most abundantly supplied with black, blue, and red stockings, manufactured with various taste by the skillful management and industry of their mothers. It was on one of these occasions that Mrs. Catherine Cabbage was returning home through Dinglehole from a winter evening visit. She had a large ball of black yarn and an unfinished stocking of the same material suspended from the waist and fastened to her dress by a pin, when she suddenly heard immediately behind her upon the snow-crust a noise like a step. She looked round with great trepidation, and saw, close to her heels, a small black creature, which seemed intent on overtaking her, and which at every new look seemed to increase both in size and speed. Her walk soon became a trot, next a run at full speed, but the frightful animal still kept at nearly the same distance, and continued to increase in size till it become as large as a bear. Mrs. Cabbage was in the greatest trepidation, but being favored by nature with the means of rapid locomotion, she soon reached home, almost breathless with terror and fatigue, and just enough in advance of her rabid pursuer to close and bolt the door upon his bearship. After she had recovered in some degree from her terror and confusion, and related with all proper exaggeration the story of her adventures, she examined her waist for her knitting-work, and was surprised to find that stocking and needles were missing, though the ball of yarn still remained appended to her person.

The probability of the case is that the fall of her knitting-work with a dingle was the cause of her fright, and the noise of the needles upon the snow-crust was mistaken for the tread of a wild beast, and that the tenacity of the yarn which held the stocking continued the pursuit by drawing it after her. In closing the door she shut in and broke the yarn, as the innocent cause of her trepidation was discovered next morning upon the door-step.

A story is told of an adventure somewhat serious in its consequences, and which illustrates the superstitions of those days. A team was unable to draw its load along this same way, when the driver, believing the hindrance to be the result of witchcraft, instead of whipping his cattle bestowed his blows upon the wheels of the cart. Soon the team drew the load without further trouble, and it was afterwards ascertained that the old woman who did the witch business in the neighborhood was covered with wales from the driver's whip.

THE OLD STONE BRIDGE AT THE NECK.

BOGGASTOW BROOK is not without its scenes of interest. In its upper part the stream is of considerable vivacity, but as it approaches the broad meadows it becomes sluggish like the Charles. It runs through the Boggastow Pond, a sheet of water whose surface lies hardly below the level of the Broad Meadow, and a quarter of a mile further east it falls into or rather unites with, the Charles River near the northeast corner of the town.

Thus Lovers' Retreat, Dinglehole, Pine Grove, Boggastow Brook, and The Old Stone Bridge, are some of the rural haunts of the region celebrated in legendary story, objects of curiosity and the scenes of many pleasurable and sentimental rambles.

Indian Claims and Early Grants.

Originally the territory of which Medway forms a part belonged to the Nipmuck Indians. The Charles River seems to have formed the eastern and southern boundary of their country, separating it from the dominion of the Massachusetts. The Nipmucks were once a powerful tribe, holding dominion over the greater portion of Middlesex and Worcester counties, with their capital near Wachusett Mountain, where their sachem resided. But before King Philip's war they became divided into several independent tribes, of which one was the Natick. While, therefore, the deed of Josias, a chief of the Massachusetts, acknowledging the grant of his grandfather, Chickatawbut, and confirming to Medfield her territory, related only to that part on the east side of the river, the Nipmucks claimed all that was on the west and north sides. Accordingly, on the 25th of January, 1672, the town of Medfield chose a committee consisting of Thomas Wight, Sen., John Frary, Sen., John Ellice, John Medcalf, and George Barber, " To treat and conclud with John of Boggastow, we mene John a Wasameg of Natick for the interest and right he claims in the Lands within our Towne Bownes on the west side of Charlles River." Under date of March 1st, 1672, the record is as follows : " This day the rate for the Endians pay was Drawen up it being 21£ 7s. there was all most a fifth part raised on the New Grant."

It was the custom of the Colonial Government to make grants of " country land " to eminent citizens. In 1643 the General Court of Massachusetts Bay granted to the Rev. John Allin two hundred acres of wild land lying in the forest beyond the west bounds of the town of Dedham. This is the earliest intimation that civilization was about to lay her hand upon the wilderness on the west side of the Charles River.

It is probable that the Rev. Mr. Allin never took the trouble even to visit his landed possessions, and it might have puzzled the godly man to tell the exact locality of his " farm," so called. Subsequently his rights of ownership were purchased by one of his parishioners, whose name will appear on a subsequent page as the first settler in these parts.

In 1649 Captain Robert Kayne, of Boston, received a grant of one thousand and seventy-four acres of meadow and upland upon Pawsett or Pocassett Hill, bounded south by Mr. Allin's farm ; and we learn from the records that the line between Medfield on the south and Sherborn on the north corresponded with the line between these two grants ; and also that the Broad Meadows were bounded north by Mr. Allin's land.

The Old Grant.

In 1649 the inhabitants of Dedham petitioned for a grant of land west of the river. The reason they gave was, " because we are streightened at our own doores by other towns and by rocky lands." At this day one naturally wonders how much of what they already possessed was under cultivation. But as they lived in a territory, as described by patent granted in 1628 as that part of New England extending from a point three miles north of the Merrimac to three miles south of the Charles, and from the Atlantic Ocean to the Pacific, with the illimitable wilderness around them as yet unoccupied, why should not their utmost wishes for room be gratified! Such seems to have been the view of the case taken by the General Court; for they responded to the petitioners by granting them a tract three miles from east to west and four miles from north to south, on condition that they should erect a distinct village thereon, within one year from the twenty-second day of October following. Captain Kayne, Mr. Edward Jackson, and the surveyor-general were appointed to lay it out, upon a week's notice being given by Dedham. Accordingly, May 22, 1650, " the new village in Dedham" was laid out. " The line," say the commissioners in their report, " beginning at a small hill or island in the meadow, on the west side of Charles River, and running thence about west three miles, then turning south three and a quarter miles and ending at Charles River, the river to be the bound to the place where the line began." The petitioners accepted this territory, though it did not embrace as much as was specified in the grant.

The town of Dedham granted the territory on the east side, and at their request the new village was called Medfield. Thirteen families having located on the east side, it became a town May 23d, 1651. In 1660 Samuel Maverick wrote *A Briefe Description of New England*, in which he says : " Five or Six Miles from Deadham is a Small in-land Towne called Medifield handsomely Seatted for Farming and breading of Cattle."

The small hill or island mentioned in the foregoing report is about a quarter of a mile north of Boggastow Pond; and the line running thence west, so far as is known, corresponds with the present line between Medway on the south, and Sherborn and Holliston on the north, the west end of it being at present the corner of the town of Millis. From this point the line ran south along the westerly border of Black Swamp, and came to the river at Medway village, passing a little to the west of the spot now occupied by Christ Church. The meadows along the banks of the Charles and its tributaries furnished, no doubt, a leading motive for the location of a town at this point. The grass procured without tillage, requiring only the labor of the haying, though inferior to that of the upland, produced by cultivation, was still a great boon to a people beginning to live in the wilderness, who had at once dwellings to provide, fields to clear, roads to make, and institutions to found, besides supplying the daily needs of life. By a wise forethought, this advantage was secured by grants on both sides of the river. Of so much importance was it considered that we find the first land on the west side divided among the new citizens of Medfield was that portion still called the Broad Meadows, lying north of the point where the railroad crosses the river. In 1652-3 a highway, the first in Medway, probably that still used for carting the hay, was laid out one rod and a half wide from the entrance of the Broad Meadows at the south, and running through the whole to the north end, crossing each lot. There were twenty-two lots, containing about ninety acres. These lots were bounded " on the north by a little river and by the meadow of Mr. John Wilson, of Dedham."

About the same time thirty-three acres of meadow were laid out " before Bridge street." These seven lots were bounded east by the river, and formed the tract now crossed by the turnpike.

In 1653 Abraham Harding and Peter Adams had grants in Grape

Meadow, a tract lying east of Black Swamp, and west of the farms of the late Andrew Morse and J. Willard Daniels, Esq.

At this time the record mentions the Great bridge. This spanned the river near where the railroad now crosses, and soon after mention is made of Dwight's bridge, both of which must have been constructed to gain access to the grass in the meadows, and the pasturage in the woods on the west side. Several grants were made "13 : 11 : 1655" to Benjamin Alby, Alexander Lovell, and others, of meadow-lands, by "Henry Adams, Dept."

These facts show the importance then attached to the meadows, while the uplands had as yet received little or no attention.

The neighboring town of Mendon found their territory so deficient in meadows that they petitioned the General Court to give them leave to take such as lay in adjoining territory not claimed by other towns, so that each farm of thirty acres might have at least ten acres of meadow, or in that proportion.

It was not until about the end of 1658 that the town voted to lay out some uplands on the west side of the Charles River. The localities are thus described : "On the longe plain to begin next to Boggistow River on that end" ; "At the furder Corner of our bounds By Charles river to begin next the town" ; "In pine valley to begin at north end and go throf it" ; "At the end of pine valley on a persell of land that the path goeth throfe."

"The longe plain" was the level land stretching southward from the mills to the meeting-house of the First Church of Christ, or perhaps farther south. Fifteen lots were granted in the spring of 1659, containing nearly one hundred and eighty acres, and a highway was reserved on the east end of the lots, running nearly north and south. These lots were bounded east and west by the waste land, and were taken up, beginning at the Boggastow Brook, according to the vote of the town, in the following order :

1.	Benjamin Alby,	15 acres.	9.	John Frary, Sen.,	14+ acres.
2.	Heirs of Joseph Morse,	15 "	10.	Robert Hinsdale,	9+ "
3.	Thomas Wright, Sen.,	15 "	11.	Joshua Fisher,	15+ "
4.	John Thurston,	10+ "	12.	Thomas Thurston,	11+ "
5.	Samuel Bullen,	13 "	13.	Thomas Ellis,	9+ "
6.	Peter Adams,	10+ "	14.	Mr. Wilson,	13+ "
7.	Nicholas Rockwood,	11+ "	15.	James Allen,	7+ "
8.	Thomas Wright, Jun.,	6 "			

173 acres.

With perhaps a single exception, those men who drew these lands never resided on this side of the river. The only one who became an inhabitant was Nicholas Rockwood, who in his old age came to reside with his son, John Rockwood. It was for their sons to become the first settlers.

Benjamin Alby, whose name is first in the above list, and whose lot was next to Boggastow Brook, received another grant in 1669, of twenty-five acres of upland, bounded northwest by his meadow, southwest by the waste land, southeast by a swampy brook, and in part on the northeast by Boggastow Brook ; a highway three rods broad to go through it to the mill. It seems that the two lots, consisting together of forty acres, were joined, and the description seems to point to the farm occupied by the late Mr. Richard Richardson, including some of the land on the northwest side of the road, now belonging to H. M. Collins, Esq., and others. Mr. Alby was a member of the first board of selectmen in Medfield. Afterward he disposed of his lands here, and in 1664 took part in the settlement of the town of Mendon. He made an agreement with the superintending committee to erect and maintain a corn-mill for the plantation, on Mill River, near the boundary between Mendon and Milford. His mill was probably started in 1664 or 1665. The authorities afterwards voted him a bounty of fifty acres, in consideration of his building and maintaining a mill. *The History of Milford* says: "Benjamin Albie was a very enterprising man, a public-land surveyor, and much employed in numerous layings-out of ways, lots, and common lands in early times. When Mendon became an incorporated town in 1667, he was made one of its first selectmen, and intrusted with other responsible offices. When King Philip's war broke out, in 1675, he fled eastward with the Mendon fugitives, and all his buildings were burnt by the savages. He was now an old man, and never returned farther than Medfield. There he probably died. All his Mendon property passed into the hands of his son James."

It appears that January 25, 1659, John Fussell received a grant of eight acres of upland lying on a little plain above the corner of the great swamp west of Charles River. This is the field on the south side of Union Street, near the railroad crossing. It formed a part of the Sylvanus Adams farm, now occupied by Cyrus Daniels. Mr. Fussell settled here afterward, and when the Indians destroyed Medfield his house was burned with him in it. Jonathan Adams, who married Mr. Fussell's daughter, afterwards rebuilt the house in which he resided.

In the latter part of 1659 it was ordered "that there shall be a highway to lie over the small brook west of Charles river which shall be for a driveway to pass between the land of John Fussell on the south of the way and the land of John Plimpton on the north of the highway, so to pass on west and up into the wilderness by a stony ridge hill where lieth a path; also that there is a highway laid out which turneth out of the aforesaid highway at the west end of John Plimpton's lot, and so throfe the other lots where it was at first drawn, to run two rods wide unto Boggastow brook for a leading way for such as have occasion to make use of it, but not for an open driveway."

The highway which was "to pass on west and up into the wilderness by a stony ridge where lieth a path" was doubtless that leading over the neck and so on by the Lyman Adams place. The other road mentioned as laid out and reserved at the east end of the Long Plain lots was that which ran directly from the house of Sylvanus Adams to that of the late Deacon Paul Daniell, and passed the residence of the late Richard Richardson, Esq., to Collins's mill. Along the woods there are still marks which show this ancient highway, although the traces in the open fields which existed a few years since are now quite obliterated.

The small stream, sometimes called "Spring Brook," is crossed by the old road to Medfield not far from the residence of the late Deacon Paul Daniell, and empties into Boggastow Brook a little distance to the eastward. Spring Brook in the early days swarmed with trouts and was a great resort for fishing. So famous was this brook for these speckled prizes that it became known as Trout Brook. But in later years this is a misnomer, except in a historic sense, and trout-fishing is one of the lost arts, for the best of reasons,— no trouts to be fished.

"The land at the furder Corner of our bounds By Charles river to begin next the town" is not easily located. "Pine valley" was perhaps the valley through which the road passes from the Great Bridge to the "Harding place," now the residence of Mr. Hosley. The end of pine plain might have been that around and west of the house of Moses Adams, Esq. The "persell of land that the path goeth throfe," is described in the grants as Boggastow plain. Ten lots were laid out containing ninety acres, a cart-way two rods wide to cross them all. The direction of this highway was northwest and southeast. It may have been that leading from Dwight's bridge to the Great bridge.

THE NEW GRANT.

In the Acts of the Provincial Government for 1659 it is recorded, "In ans⋅ to the peticon of the inhabitants of Meadfield, the Court judgeth it meete to graunt unto them as an addition unto their former bounds & at the west ends thereof two miles east & west & fower miles north & south provided it intrench not upon former graunts & ye Capt. Lusher & Left. Fisher are hereby appointed to make return thereof to the next session of

Court." This grant was made May 11, 1659, a day memorable for the execution in Boston of three Quakers, Stephenson, Dyer, and Henderson. It was laid out by Captain Lusher and Lieutenant Fisher, and formed a regular parallelogram, embracing eight square miles, afterward known as the New Grant. The north line was an extension of the north line of the first grant two miles to the west; thence running south, parallel with west line of the Old Grant to the river, which formed its southern boundary. To the east it was bounded by the Old Grant line. It embraced within its borders one-half of Winthrop Pond, the Indian name of which was Winnekening, or the Smile of the Great Spirit; also the territory now occupied by the little village at Metcalf Station, and even extended beyond the northwest side of the road leading from Holliston to Milford. These lines remained unchanged, and all this territory belonged to Medfield, and later to Medway, until 1829, when the northern portion of it was given to Holliston in exchange for a part of Holliston which lay to the west of Medway.

At the annual town-meeting, February 6, 1660, it was ordered that the New Grant be divided to all the inhabitants of the town that were proprietors, according to the common rules of division of land by the numbers of persons and estates, each member of the family being reckoned the same as ten pounds of estate.

As there was no large tract of meadow which could be so divided as to give each proprietor a share of sufficient size to justify a separate division, it was ordered that the meadow should be divided with the rest of the land as the lot might determine.

It was the practice, in order to prevent disputes and ill-feeling, to draw lots for the individual grants. The numbers were put in a hat and each man drew out and took his land where the lot fell, or, as it is expressed in the record, "where the providence of God shall direct."

April 20, 1660, it was ordered, "that highways be laid out on the New Grant four rods wide or more if it be needful in the judgment of those that lay them out."

One of the highways was to enter it from the Old Grant, half a mile north of Charles River, and to run westerly across the same to its west side; another to lie through the midst of the tract of land from the way just described, running northerly to the north end of the New Grant.

Neither of these roads was ever made and used in its entire length for public travel. The old discontinued road called Vine Lane, now unused and overgrown with bushes, which runs west from Holliston Street near the house of Edward Fennessy, and that past the north end of West Medway Cemetery, where it is called Evergreen Street, and on farther west the road past the house of A. P. Thayer, Esq., and up through the woods, now Mechanics and Oak streets, form a part of the first of these highways and now occupy the land which was originally left for that purpose. The other highway which was to lie through the midst of the New Grant, running northerly to the north end of the grant, was formerly called the Pond road, from the fact that it terminated at Winthrop Pond. That portion of it that is now in use as a public highway forms a part of Elm Street, the whole of Pond Street, a part of Lovering Street, and Allen Lane. The part not practicable for a road, with other such lands, was subsequently sold by the town.

These two highways divided the New Grant into three sections. The southern one next the river, containing about one thousand and seventy-nine acres, was divided into twelve farm lots by lines running north from the river to the first of these highways. The other two sections, each a mile wide, on the east and west sides of the pond road were divided into lots by lines running east and west. The west section, containing eighteen hundred and ninety-six acres, was divided into nineteen lots; on the west side of this section, land was left for a road now occupied by Summer Street. Of the east section, sixteen hundred and fifty-eight acres were divided into sixteen lots, and two hundred acres at the north end lying east of Winthrop Pond were left undivided, making eighteen hundred and fifty-eight acres.

It was ordered, "that the lots to be drawn shall take their place successively as they are drawn forth, the first lot to begin at the hither side of the grant on the division next the river, and to pass on through that division to the west side of it, and then to begin on the south end of the west division, and so to go through that tract to the north end of it; and then next, the lots shall take place on the south end of the tract of land on the east of the highway, and so to go successively through the same."

The following are the names of the proprietors of the New Grant in the order in which the lots were drawn, and the number of acres in each:

No.	NAMES.	A.	No.	NAMES.	A.
			23	Isaac Chenery	77
			24	Joseph Clark	161
	SECTION NEXT THE RIVER.		25	Robert Hinsdell	157
1	Ralph Wheelock	156	26	John Fisher	61
2	John Metcalf	117	27	Nicolas Rockwood	85
3	Robert Mason	57	28	Samuel Bullen	136
4	John Pratt	39	29	Abiel Wight	38
5	Widow Sheppard	51	30	John Frairy, Jr	177
6	Thomas Wight, Jr.	56	31	Mr. Wilson	147
7	Timothy Dwight	146			
8	John Turner	120		EAST SECTION.	
9	Alex. Lovell	94			
10	John Ellis	126	32	Gershom Wheelock	36
11	James Allen	102	33	Joshua Fisher	78
12	Joseph Thurston	15	34	Benjamin Alby	138
			35	John Frairy, Sen	147
	WEST SECTION.		36	Henry Adams	148
			37	Thomas Wight, Sen.	166
13	Heirs of Joseph Morse	141	38	Thomas Mason	73
14	Henry Smith	158	39	Francis Hamant	87
15	John Bullard	100	40	John Partridge	69
16	Sampson Frairy	68	41	John Warfield	22
17	Edward Adams	102	42	Thomas Ellis	77
18	John Fussell	24	43	John Bowers	102
19	William Partridge	61	44	Thomas Thurston	72
20	Jonathan Adams	84	45	John Thurston	191
21	Daniel Morse	12	46	Peter Adams	101
22	John Plimpton	107	47	George Barber	149

The cost of laying out this grant, paid by the town, was £19, 6s., 5d. The first lot, drawn by Ralph Wheelock, was that on which Medway Village now stands. It is recorded August 31, 1661: "Whereas the way leading through the new grant from east to west is found not passable nor capable of being made so; it is therefore agreed on, and also layed out by the men that were deputed thereunto that the way is to assent the hill by the river and from thence to cross the lot of Mr. Ralph Wheelock to the side line of John Medcalff's, by a little pine standing on a stony ridge and so to turn down by John Medcalff's side line, to the other way at the head of his lot, which is a matter of 40 rods and to be 4 rods wide."

At this early period there was no road from the Great bridge westward excepting that which is described as "the path up into the wilderness," which had been staked out and reserved for a highway, and which afterward became the country road to Mendon and so on further west. Here a portion of it is described as ascending the hill by the river, across Ralph Wheelock's lot. The little pine standing on the stony ridge has long since passed away, but the highway that turned by it "down by John Medcalff's side line to the other way at the head of his lot" is, no doubt, now represented in part by the street called "Lover's Lane," John Medcalff's lot lying on the west side of it.

The heirs of Joseph Morse took the lot including the farm of Addison P. Thayer, Esq., and the site of the Baptist church and Plainville. Henry Smith took the next lot to the north.

Mr. Wilson, who drew the lot at the northwest corner of the New Grant, was the Rev. Mr. Wilson, first minister of Medfield. His lot embraced the land on which stands the little village of Metcalf Station in Holliston, and the nursery of S. M. Cutler; it was bounded east by Winthrop Pond.

The first lot at the south end of the east division was taken by Gershom Wheelock. Upon it now stands the house of Edward Fennessy, Esq. This lot was but eighteen rods wide. The next was taken by Joshua Fisher. The lots were laid so regularly, and the record is so complete, that the situation of each of them can now be determined with very great certainty. It is safe to say that not one of the original owners ever occupied these lands; indeed more than one generation passed away before there was a settlement within the New Grant. In some cases the descendants of these men afterwards settled upon them.

The Rev. Abner Morse, in his *History of Sherborn and Holliston*, says: "Henry Morse, born June 14, 1703, and died April 5, 1766, settled ¼ mile southwest of Winthrop Lake, on a lot of 177 acres, assigned by the proprietors of Medfield, in 1659, to John Frairy, his great grandfather."

While the people of Medfield were engaged in acquiring a title to new lands, and extending their territory, hoping thereby to benefit posterity, if not themselves, settlements were actually begun on the west side of the river, a number of farms occupying the territory extending from the Farms bridge, now in Sherborn, to the northern border of Boggastow Pond. They were settled by men who had come up from towns nearer the coast, largely from Dorchester and Dedham. Indeed, nearly all the early settlers of the town were sons of the immigrants to America, members of the proverbially large families who were crowded out of the first family homestead by force of numbers, and were, as they then thought, obliged to seek for room and new homes farther west in the wilderness. Religious persecution in England had ceased, and the edicts of Star Chamber no longer drove men into exile. The Puritans had long been the dominant party at home. Laud, Strafford, and Charles had perished on the scaffold, and Cromwell was the ruler of England.

Prior to 1640, twenty-one thousand British subjects had settled in New England, the largest portion of whom had arrived between the years 1628 and 1638. After the latter date immigration nearly ceased, and the settlement of the interior towns progressed slowly. Boston and Cambridge, at the mouth of the Charles, were already old towns, and it was but natural that as population increased, the settlements should advance up the course of the river. Watertown, Brookline, Dedham, including Needham and Medfield, followed in succession. In those early days the fish furnished by the streams was an important item of food, easily obtained. Shad and alewives are said to have run up as far as Popolatic Pond before the dams rendered it impassable. The wild game of the forest was more abundant along the water-courses, while some amphibious animals were found only in the swamps and meadows along the margins of the streams. The springs that gushed out at the foot of the hills along the edge of the lowlands furnished water for the cattle and for the family, without the cost and labor of digging. These, together with the grass produced by the open meadows, were important motives inviting to these locations.

In 1652, within one year or a little more after the settlement of Medfield was fairly begun, Nicholas Wood and Thomas Holbrook, both of Dorchester, settled on the west side of the river, between Death's Bridge and Holbrook's Mills. They were beyond the limits of any town, one-half mile from each other, and four miles from their nearest English neighbors. The same year, or soon after, Hopestill Layland, a man of seventy years, also of Dorchester, with Henry, his son, came to the same neighborhood. He was undoubtedly an exile from the old country, as his age shows that he was born before there was any settlement in New England. In 1658 John Hill and Thomas Breck located a little to the southwest of the others, a third of a mile to the north of Boggastow Pond. These, too, were from Dorchester. About the same time came Benjamin Bullard and George Fairbanks from Dedham, and built very near the northerly border of the pond. There were some others joined them that did not become permanent settlers, but after a few years left. These daring spirits, so far isolated from the rest of the civilized world, attended public worship in Medfield, that being the nearest town, paid their taxes there, and took care of themselves in an independent way as best they could, being but little beholden to the rest of the world. They were all relatives by marriage. Wood and Layland married sisters; Holbrook married a sister of Henry Layland. Breck married a sister of Hill, and Bullard a sister of Fairbanks. Thomas Bass also appeared among them about 1660, and married the daughter of Nicholas Wood.

These constituted what was then called the Boggastow Farms. None of the owners lived in the territory of Medfield, except George Fairbanks: yet they were all enrolled as citizens, and births, deaths, and marriages in their families were recorded there until 1675, when Sherborn was incorporated, and they became citizens of that town.

3

THE FIRST SETTLERS.

GEORGE FAIRBANKS was undoubtedly the first to settle within the territory of Medway. It would be interesting to know the exact date of his arrival on the west side of the river, at least the year, but this we are not permitted to know. It is equally uncertain where he was born or who was his father. He married, August 26, 1646, Mary A. Harris in Dedham, where he resided, and had five children, the last recorded in Dedham being born December 23, 1656. The town of Medfield granted, February 6, 1660, to Mr. Fairbanks "such timber for fencing as shall make three hundred rails, with posts for it, as shall be set out by brother Wight, and John Medcalf shall appoint him with what he has already fallen to make up three hundred rails." This is the first mention made of him on the town records. It must have been between these two dates that he established himself within the territory of Medway. There can be no mistake about the locality of his farm, as his descendants to the seventh generation resided upon it, and it is within the recollection of many persons still living, that it was sold and went into other hands. It was originally bounded on the north by that of Benjamin Bullard, recently owned and occupied by the late Daniel Bullard, Esq., and embraced probably what is called the Mason Farm, now owned by Patrick Crowley. His dwelling was the famous Stone House near the north border of the pond. That which has been more recently known as the Fairbanks farm, was the southern portion of his large landed estate. The inventory after his death mentions three hundred acres adjacent to his homestead, and a small lot lying between the three hundred acres and the homestead. It may seem unaccountable that his name does not occur among the proprietors of Medfield in the division and distribution of the New Grant lands; but his house was near the Sherborn line, which was at that early time not very well defined, and his farm was reckoned one of the Boggastow farms beyond the limits of the town, and did not entitle its owner to town rights. In 1662 he, with thirteen of his neighbors, petitioned for the incorporation of Sherborn; and again in 1674. After the formation of the town he seems to have been an active citizen, engaged in public affairs. For four years he was selectman, and was chosen on a committee to engage and settle a minister. He drew land in Sherborn, and seems to have received all the privileges of a citizen. A committee of the General Court appointed to consider Sherborn affairs in 1677, say in their report: "As to the farms adjacent we conceive all those in Medfield bounds that were granted by this Court and received nothing of Medfield shall be accounted and liable to all charges and take up privileges in Sherborn." This explains Fairbanks' anomalous position. Soon after the organization of the town it was proposed to build a meeting-house and a spot was selected and agreed upon near the south part of the town, but after a delay of several years, it was voted to change the spot and build farther north, where the old meeting-house now stands. Upon which, Fairbanks became dissatisfied and, in 1681 "proposed to resign up to the Town all his rights and Interests in Sherborn with his former charges from the first petitioning, provided they would free him from Sherborn." His relations to Sherborn remained, however, unchanged till the time of his death, January 10, 1682.

The town of Medfield voted, June 5, 1683: "That as the farm of George Fairbanks, Sen., lies within the bounds of Medfield it is liable by law to bear public charge, and that it is expected that the Selectmen should put it into the Rates." Sherborn, still anxious to retain the taxes, continued to levy them on the farm until the inhabitants of Medfield petitioned the General Court to break off the arrangement between Fairbanks and the town of Sherborn. His son George, who inherited the southerly part of his father's farm, was considered a citizen of Medfield and allowed rights in the common lands with other proprietors.

JOSEPH DANIELL was the second settler within the territory of Medway. He was the son of Robert Daniell of Cambridge or Watertown, and the progenitor of all in Medway who bear the name of Daniell or Daniels, and of many in the neighboring towns, and throughout the commonwealth. He was born probably near the site of the United States Arsenal in Watertown, about the year 1635. When or whence the family immigrated are equally unknown; though there is a widely received opinion that they came from Wales. In 1655 his father died, leaving him at the age of twenty to share his estate with an older brother and three sisters, none of whom were married except the eldest, Elizabeth Daniell. In 1660, Mary married Samson Frary, of Medfield. Some years afterwards she and her husband removed to Deerfield, where she was murdered by the Indians. The marriage of his sister was probably the reason of the coming of Joseph Daniell to Medfield. February 3, 1662, he was accepted as a townsman by vote of the people, and in October of the same year was present at a town-meeting and drew lands, which fact indicates that he was already the possessor of a farm. His signature is attached to the articles of agreement of the town of Medfield, and his hand-writing is still preserved in old deeds. In 1663 his estate was valued £63; and in 1669 it had gone up to £106, 10s.

He probably built his house before 1665. It stood eight or ten rods east of the residence of the late Deacon Paul Daniell. The cellar was still to be seen as late as 1825, but the plow has since obliterated all trace of it. Joseph Daniell was voted, in 1662, a townsman, and Mary Fairbanks, eldest daughter of George Fairbanks, was a mere school girl, if that may be said of a girl that was living where there were no schools. She was hardly fifteen. It would therefore be absurd to suppose that her smiles had any influence in inducing him to secure a farm alongside of her father's in the wilderness, on the very border of civilization. There is a delightful uncertainty surrounding almost everything that occurred more than two hundred years ago. But one thing is quite sure: Joseph Daniell and Mary Fairbanks were married on the sixteenth day of November, 1665, and it is nearly certain that this was the first wedding that occurred within the bounds of what became Medway. One other occurred probably the same year, that of Jonathan Adams and Elizabeth Fussell.

Perhaps that 16th of November, 1665, was one of the early Thanksgiving days! Who would not like to know how weddings were conducted so long ago? Were the neighbors invited for miles around? Was hilarity prevalent, or solemnity and decorum? It is related that on a similar occasion which occurred in the same neighborhood many years after, some young men, out of revenge for not having received an invitation, stole the wedding pudding out of the oven, which happened to be on the outside of the house, while the ceremony was being performed within. Which circumstance clearly shows that the Puritanic principles of the fathers had not entirely subdued the love of fun and mischief in the young people.

It would be gratifying to know what kind of an outfit these young couples carried to their new homes ; what comforts and conveniences they possessed ; how they passed the dull, cold November days and the long dreary winter that followed ; what were their recreations when gossiping friends were shut off by unbroken snow-fields ; with no musical instruments, no newspapers, and no books save the old Bible   The grand old Bible furnished them with entertainment and instruction, and above all with comfort and courage to endure the hardships and privations of pioneer life   They had abundance of fuel for the winter, abundance of work for all seasons, and, no doubt, a superabundance of young. joyous, hopeful animal spirits that made the old woods resound with songs of gladness.

> " More lovely far such scenes of bliss
> Than monarchs ever saw
> E'en angels might delight to dwell   •
> Beneath my roof of straw "

The roof under which they dwelt was literally a roof of straw, covering a single apartment, with walls of logs, which was sitting-room, kitchen, pantry, and sleeping-room, all in one.   The big stone fire-place with its wide chimney was its grand feature.   How the great pile of pine, and maple, and oak blazed and roared and sent its red glare through and through the room, shedding warmth, and comfort, and joy to the loving hearts within !   Such were undoubtedly some of the features of those early homes

One other circumstance which has been overlooked till now, shows that George Fairbanks was the only settler in Medfield on the west side of the river until after 1660.   In that year the town came in possession of several " law books," of which one copy was placed in each neighborhood. One book was designated " to Georg Fairbanks and all the other inhabitants on that side the river."   In the case of the other neighborhoods every man's name was mentioned, which certainly renders it probable that the " other inhabitants " were prospective, and that George Fairbanks was the only dweller in that part of the town   One copy was assigned to the " farms, to Nicholas Woods, for him and Daniel Morse, Henry Lealand, Thomas Holbrook, and Thomas Bass."   These were Fairbanks' neighbors in 1660, the other families early at " The Farms " not having yet settled there.

JOHN FUSSELL and his son-in-law, JONATHAN ADAMS, were among the earliest settlers on this side the river.   They lived near the present residence of Mr. Henry M. Daniels

WILLIAM ALLIN settled probably on the place of the late Dr. Abijah Richardson about the year 1668, when he married Elizabeth Twitchell, daughter of Benjamin Twitchell.   His house stood several rods to the northeast of the present site, upon the old road which ran upon the north side of the hill. He seems to have been a citizen of Sherborn, having a relation to that town similar to that of George Fairbanks.   His wife was in full communion with the church in Medfield in 1667.   He died in 1736, aged, according to the best accounts, upwards of ninety years.   After his death his farm was purchased by Ebenezer Daniell, who was the grandfather of Mercy Daniell, the wife of Dr. Abijah Richardson, to whom it descended by inheritance, and in whose family it still remains.

PETER CALLEY also settled near the Boggastow mill before 1669.

THE STONE HOUSE.

In the early days of the settlement the residents of the Farms unitedly built a stone garrison house on the north border of the Boggastow Pond, a

THE SITE OF THE STONE HOUSE.

place of refuge and defense, to which they could flee in times of danger. They occupied one of the very outposts on the frontier of civilization. To the southwest Mendon had advanced a little beyond them, while to the west and northwest there was nothing but the unbroken wilderness between them and the Pacific Ocean, excepting some towns far away on the Connecticut River. To the east they were separated from their nearest neighbors by the river and wide reaches of swamp and country difficult to pass. Thus isolated, they were obliged to provide for their own safety with little hope of aid from others. The Indians, though at first friendly, were never desirable neighbors, nor was their character such as to inspire confidence. Under these circumstances the Stone House was an important feature of the settlement.

Though it was built by the united labors of the neighborhood for the benefit of all, tradition, supported by some recorded facts, renders it probable that it was occupied as a dwelling by George Fairbanks.

The Rev. Mr. Wilson, in a letter written the day after the burning of Medfield, speaks of it as "George Fairbanks' palisade."

The stones of which it was built were flat, and somewhat regular shaped, brought, probably, over the snow and ice of winter, from a field a mile distant to the northwest, where such stones are still found. The walls were laid in clay mortar. Morse, in *The History of Sherborn*, says: "It was sixty-five or seventy feet long, and two stories high. It had a double row of port holes on all sides, lined with white oak plank, and flaring inward, so as to require no one to expose himself before them, while the besieged, by taking cross aims, could direct their fire to any point of the compass. This fortress was lighted and entered at the south end, overlooking the pond, where the bank was so low that the assailants from that quarter, in leveling at the high windows, would only lodge bullets in a plank chamber floor, or among the furniture of the garret. The upper story was appropriated to the women and children, and had a room petitioned off for the sick."

As early as 1671 the English had become convinced that the Indians were plotting against them, and had tried to disarm them by requiring them to give up their guns, which had resulted in exasperation, and had also persuaded them to join in new treaties in which neither party appears to have put much faith. It was not, however, until June 28, 1675, that hostilities commenced; on that day one man was shot by the Indians at Swansea, and on the next day six or seven more were killed at the same place, and others in the neighborhood. A part of Taunton, Middleborough, and Dartmouth, in the vicinity of Pocasset, upon Narragansett Bay, soon followed the destruction of Swansea, which was burnt immediately after the 24th of June, on being abandoned by the inhabitants. Soldiers were ordered from Boston, an expedition was sent against the Indians, and the whole country was thoroughly alarmed. Imagination cannot picture a situation more trying, or more to be dreaded, than that in which the dwellers at "The Farms" were now placed. Exposed to the attacks of an enemy whose approach was stealthy, sudden, and when least expected, who kept no faith and knew no mercy, to fall into their hands was worse than death,—for it was death amid the fiercest insults, and by tortures the most protracted and excruciating that cruelty could devise. Murders were perpetrated at no great distance, and rumor was rife with threats of attack and destruction. Men slept with their weapons at hand, and carried them to their work in the field, and prayed holding on to their muskets. The narrow bridle-paths which served for highways, winding through the forest, were full of peril, and the stealthy tread of the Indian, more than a wild animal, was a source of constant terror. How could they leave their homes for the house of worship? Who of the loved ones could be left behind amid perils so appalling?

As the danger became more imminent the women and children were gathered into the Stone House, and after the labors of the day the men spent their nights with them. Such must have been the situation during the latter part of the summer and autumn of 1675 and the winter following. In September and October there were frequent battles at Hadley, Hatfield, Deerfield, and Springfield, and on December 19 occurred the great Narragansett Swamp fight.

On the 10th of February, 1676, Lancaster, a town not far off, was surprised with complete success, and eleven days later, on the 21st of February, about three hundred Indians attacked Medfield, led, according to his own word, by Monoco, a chief who lived near Lancaster and who was engaged in the destruction of that place, and afterwards of other towns. About half the buildings on the east side of the river were burned and seventeen persons killed or mortally wounded. The savages were frightened by the firing of the cannon, and fled across the "Great Bridge" which they burned; and it was not rebuilt until 1686. They held a savage feast or pow-wow of exultation the following night, on the high ground in full view of the ruined town.

The spot of this savage pow-wow after the burning of Medfield, February 21, 1676, is marked by a peculiar clump of trees which have become monumental.

THE KING PHILIP TREES.

Dr. Saunders, in his *Historical Sermon of 1817*, says: "At length the savages were compelled to retire over a bridge in the southwest part of the town. Burning the bridge in order to cut off pursuit, they retired to a savage feast on the top of the nearest hill in view of the ruins they had occasioned. Philip had been seen riding upon a black horse, leaping fences and exulting in the havoc he was making."

He says further, that "on the sixth of May following, the Indians met with a *notorious repulse* at the stone house near Medfield in the northeast corner of Medway; and on the second of July following there was near this a new conflict in the woods and more execution was done upon the enemy." About these trees cluster historical incidents in the early settlement of Medway, and thus they became monumental of the somewhat tragical events of those early times. These trees impress one as in themselves a great natural curiosity. In the first place the genus of the trees — the Nyssa — is very rare in this region. Flagg, in *The Woods and By-ways of New England*, says: "This tree has I believe no representation in the old continent, and though there are several species in the United States, only one is found in New England." He gives an illustration of one in the old town of Beverly. He says: "It has received a variety of names in different parts of the country, being called 'Swamp Hornbeam,' from the toughness of its wood; 'Umbrella Tree,' from a peculiar habit of some individuals to become flattened and slightly convex at the top. The name Inpelo was given it by the original inhabitants."

It assumes a greater variety of shapes than most other trees, sometimes grotesque and sometimes very symmetrical. "The foliage of the Inpelo is remarkable for its fine glossy verdure. The leaves are oval, narrowing toward the stem and rounded at the extremity." The most remarkable feature about these trees is their great number in close proximity within a very small space. Were thirty trees from eight to eighteen inches in diameter and thirty feet in height ever before seen standing in a circle not exceeding fifteen feet in diameter, making a top which at a little distance resembles but one tree? Is it probable that these can be the original trees or tree standing here two hundred years ago? Their size would seem to forbid the supposition. Are they a growth from the seeds of the ancient tree, or sprouts from the roots of a decayed stump? The junction of several at the ground with each other rather indicates a common origin from roots beneath the soil. These trees in their traditional and historical associations — in their rarity as a species and genus in New England, in their origin from a parent stock and their wonderful proximity and conformation — present so many points of interest as to justify their preservation from decay or accident, some commemorative structure upon the grounds near them, and deservedly have a place among the more enduring memorials on the page of our local history.

As nearly as can now be ascertained there were at that time in what is now Medway, but six families : those of George Fairbanks, Sen., George Fairbanks, Jr., Joseph Daniell, John Fussell, Jonathan Adams, William Allen, and Peter Calley, numbering thirty persons. On the Sherborn side were six more : Benjamin Bullard, Thomas Breck, John Hill, Henry Lealand, Jonathan Wood, his brother Eleazar Wood, and Thomas Holbrook, embracing thirty-eight persons, making sixty-eight in all. Not all these were present at the "Stone House" on this occasion, as will be seen further on, but there were probably as many as twenty men over sixteen years of age, eighteen women, seventeen children, and four persons between ten and sixteen years ; making a large family of at least fifty-nine persons.

Lovers there might have been among them, young men and maidens whose hopeful hearts were not especially depressed by the dangers around them, but rather rejoiced in circumstances which brought them together under the same roof, and gave them opportunity to show their heroic devotion. But who can imagine what must have been the emotions of the fathers and mothers who gathered their little ones here for safety? They must have seen the smoke of the burning town across the meadows, and have heard the boom of the cannon that frightened the Indians, but could not have known in those fearful hours of suspense the extent of the ruin which imagination would be sure to exaggerate. And in the keen winter night that followed, while the red glare of the pow-wow fire was seen shining on the tall trees of the forest in the southern horizon, the fierce war-whoop of the savage in the dance of triumph might have been borne over the silent fields and added a new pang to the hearts already overburdened. Nothing but their trust in God could have sustained them in such an hour.

But to render the situation still more trying, death was in their midst. During the attack upon Medfield, Jonathan Wood was killed on the east side of the river, near Death's Bridge, and his brother Eleazar who was with him was struck down, scalped and left for dead, though he afterward recovered. When the tragic news was brought to the Stone House the wife of Jonathan Wood was immediately seized with the pains of labor and soon after delivered of a daughter, her only child, and a few hours later died. This doubly-orphaned daughter, born under such peculiar circumstances, afterward became the wife of John Holbrook, who was an infant of between two and three years old, and in the same place of safety at the time.

The savages, in the morning, still bent upon the work of destruction, pressed on towards the stronghold   They apparently followed the highway, and when they came to Jonathan Adams' house set it on fire, and John Fussell, then nearly a hundred years old, was burned in it.   It seems probable that the family fled at the approach of the Indians and escaped, but were unable to take the old man with them.   Tradition says that Joseph Daniell was at home that morning looking after his cattle, but with his eyes open to the dangers around him.   Looking toward the south across the fields, he saw the heads of Indians rising out of a hollow and rapidly approaching.   He left his cattle and fled to the Stone House, where his family were already in safety.   The Indians came up and burned his buildings.   The house of William Allen was also burned ; and it seems probable that Peter Calley's shared the same fate.   We hear no more of his house, nor indeed of him. The perils of the situation, together with his losses, may have induced him to remove about this time to some more secure place.

The Stone House did not readily yield to the attack of the savages   Musket balls had little effect, and the keen fire of the defenders kept the assailants at a safe distance.   How early the attack commenced, how long it continued, or how persistently it was pressed, there are no means of knowing.   Nor do we hear anything of the killed and wounded   Probably the thick stone walls fully protected those within, and the Indians only were sufferers, of whose losses little could be known.   Their own exposure and want of success soon disheartened them.   But, not content with this repulse, they came again two months later, on the 6th of May, and with no better success.   On one of these occasions, unable to take the place by direct assault, they resorted to stratagem, which had been tried in other cases. They filled a farmer's cart with burning combustibles, hay, flax, and similar material, and pushed it down the hill at the foot of which the house stood, with the expectation that it would set the thatched roof on fire   After being well started on its way, it was left to its own direction, and with that perversity of disposition always apparent in wheeled carriages when left to themselves, instead of going directly to accomplish the mischief for which it was designed, it turned aside and rested against a friendly rock on the hill-side An Indian more heroic than the rest volunteered to turn it away from the obstacle, and give it a fresh impulse.   But a good Providence watched over the imperiled, and " the poor Indian " never returned to his comrades.   He had not calculated the danger, and paid the forfeit with his life.

On the 2d of July following, a band of savages were found in the woods near the same place.   They were attacked by the men from Medfield with such vigor and success that they met with another " notorious repulse." This was the last hostile attempt in the vicinity.

Though Philip's war broke the power of the Indians, yet the people along the frontier lived long after in a state of feverish anxiety which naturally resulted from their many and narrow escapes from danger, and from the proximity of savages, who, though subdued, were still hostile in feeling, and noted for their treachery and for the little value they set upon human life.   There were occasions for alarm for many years, when the Stone House was found a place of refuge.   On one of these occasions, when the neighbors were gathered within its friendly walls, the wife of John Richardson, who lived where Silas Richardson, Esq., lives, was, by the absence of her husband, alone in the house till evening stole upon her. In the dusk she was afraid to traverse the lonely mile and a half of mingled forest and clearing that lay between her and safety. After arranging the things in her house so as to give the impression that no one was at home, she descended into the cellar, shut the trap-door overhead, and sat upon the stairs, with her babe in her arms, all night. Who can imagine the agony of that long night, when imagination magnified every sough of the wind into a distant war-whoop, and every movement of the cattle into the stealthy tread of a savage.

At a still later period, the daughter-in-law of Mrs. John Richardson, the wife of that very infant which was held in the arms during that fearful night, and who was a daughter of Thomas Breck, when almost ninety-six years of age could remember having fled in her childhood to the Stone House for safety.

George Fairbanks was drowned in 1682. His son Jonathan appears to have inherited the northern and eastern part of his farm, including the Stone House. He, too, was drowned in attempting to cross the river from Medfield in 1719. The farm then fell into the hands of his two sons, Samuel and Jonathan, a part of which was sold to their uncle George, who occupied the southwestern portion of the original homestead, the place now owned by Mr. Frank E. Cook, and another part to Benjamin Bullard. Thus it is believed the site of the Stone House was transferred to Mr. Bullard, who afterward sold it to Abner Mason, of Medfield, in whose family it remained for three generations. It ceased to be necessary for safety and went to ruins. Its fallen walls were still to be seen within the memory of some who were living less than fifty years ago. But the last stone has since been carried away, so that there is nothing left to mark the exact spot where it stood. The ancient boulder that stayed the burning cart still lifts its head up on the hill-side, but it bears no mark to distinguish it from its numerous brethren crouching around ; so among the combatants, we have at this day no means of knowing whose heroism was especially instrumental in saving the little community. So peaceful is the scene, that no one looking upon it can realize the privations, anxieties, and dangers of those early days, or the sufferings that have hallowed this quiet and charming spot.

After the close of the war the population on the west side increased, but slowly. There are no means of ascertaining the exact date of arrivals, but from hints in the records the following may be considered approximately true :

ABRAHAM HARDING was building his house at the time of the burning of Medfield. It stood where the old " Country Road " is crossed by the Turn-pike, the place occupied recently by the late Theodore Harding, Esq., a descendant. The frame was raised, though uncovered. It escaped the fury of the savages, and tradition says it was the first framed house erected on the west side of the river.

JOSIAH ROCKWOOD, in 1677, settled on the place known as Oak Grove Farm. William Burgess married Bethiah Rockwood, and inherited the place. It was afterwards sold and remained in the Lovell family for one hundred years, and was purchased in 1880, by the late Lansing Millis, Esq.

JOHN ROCKWOOD, about the same time, built a house at the corner of the roads, nearly in front of the house of Mr. John M. Crane. He gave it to his son Hezekiah, who divided it at his death between his widow Esther and his sons, Josiah and Seth   The sons died soon after, without heirs. The widow Esther's estate was settled in 1681, when the place was sold to John Harding and Oliver Adams.

JOHN RICHARDSON is first mentioned in 1678   He settled where Silas Richardson, Esq., lives. His son John afterwards settled where Mr. Moses Richardson lives.   These farms have remained in the family ever since.

DEACON PETER ADAMS was probably on the west side before 1680. His house was near where Mrs. Appleton Foster's house now stands. Joseph, a son of Deacon Peter, gave it by deed to his nephew, Nathan Daniels, who sold it to Jonathan Adams.   It was here the first public worship was held after the incorporation of the town.

SAMUEL DANIELL, a brother of Joseph Daniell, settled in 1680 where Mr. Richard Richardson lived.   After his death, in 1695, the farm was sold to Jasper Adams, a brother of Jonathan Adams, to whom it afterwards fell, and in whose family it remained until purchased by Mr. Richardson.

VINCENT SHUTTLEWORTH came in 1681   His house stood forty or fifty rods to the southeast of that of the late Deacon Paul Daniell. Mr. Shuttleworth was a deserter in the Indian war, for which he was fined £5.   He afterwards became chargeable to the town, being Medfield's first pauper

JOHN PARTRIDGE, JOHN ADAMS, and JOHN CLARK also came in 1681.

JOHN PARTRIDGE was the first settler on the farm which has long been known as the home of the late Oliver Phillips. A grand-daughter of his married Abner Ellis, who came in possession of the farm, which was afterwards sold, before they removed to Ohio, then the far-off West   This place was the home of the Rev. Luther Wright during his pastorate in Medway.

JONATHAN ADAMS, son of Edward, in 1688, had settled on the turnpike near the Medfield meadows, where Mr. William Adams now lives.

SAMUEL HILL is first mentioned as being at town-meeting in 1693   He settled on The Neck, upon the farm lately owned by Lyman Adams, which remained in the family until purchased by Mr. Adams

JONATHAN FISHER, in 1693, was living upon the farm now owned by Mr. John M Crane. John Anderson married a daughter of Jonathan Fisher, and was the next owner.   From him it passed by sale into the hands of Jeremiah Daniell, who gave it to his grandson Jeremiah Daniell.

JOSEPH DANIELL, JR., in 1693, was living at the upper mill, at the place now occupied by Mr. Michael Hagerty, which remained in the ownership of his family until recently.

JOHN ADAMS, a son of Edward Adams, of Medfield, settled near the Medway pound, which at that date must have been not far from The Neck

---

THE MILLS.

ROBERT HINSDELL was one of the earliest proprietors of Medfield.   In 1659 he received a grant on Long Plain, and in 1660 a lot of one hundred and fifty acres in the New Grant.   But that which is most interesting at present is a grant of forty-six acres " lying on the other side of Boggastow Brook," made to him in payment for " the Bell."   This lot, which was afterward called the " bell land," is described as being divided by the highway leading over the brook, " forty acres being on the northwest side of the way and six acres on the southeast side, over against the forty acres." These facts prove that Robert Hinsdell was a man of remarkable public spirit and unusual enterprise. We are told that the early congregations were called to worship by the roll of the drum, or the firing of a gun. But Robert Hinsdell's ears were wounded, perhaps, by the use of such warlike sounds to preface the proclamation of " Peace on earth, good will toward men," so he procured for the Medfield meeting-house, the silver-tongued bell, for which he paid some foreign manufacturer, no doubt, the hard cash, and received as recompense wild land on the other side of Boggastow Brook.

He certainly showed sagacity in choosing his land alongside the most important mill site on this little stream. In 1659 the highway had been laid out across the Long Plain lots to the only convenient fording-place in the vicinity, but at the time this grant was made, December 11, 1661, it could have been little more than indicated by marked trees, and a very vague description in the records, for there were no inhabitants on the west side of the brook but Indians, and on the east side none nearer than George Fairbanks at the Boggastow Pond and the farms that lay beyond. The highway on that side was an Indian trail used by the inhabitants of the farms, leading up from Natick at no great distance from the river, across Pauset or Pocasset hill, as the elevation of land was called where the farms were situated north of the pond, thence crossing the brook it run westward to Mucksquit on the border of Winthrop Pond. The " bell land " lay on both sides of this highway.

Although there is no proof that Hinsdell ever lived on this side the river, yet we are assured that his love of enterprise did not expend itself in merely choosing an elegible farm lot, for in 1663 the ancient record speaks of the Boggastow mill dam, and two years later a committee was chosen to consider the complaint of George Fairbanks and view the cartway over Boggastow Brook, at Robert Hinsdell's mill. The mill was then built; the Indian trail had become a cartway; George Fairbanks' daughter had married and settled on the south side of the brook, and he, like a kind-hearted parent, desired to have a good cartway between their homes.

In 1669 Hinsdell sold his property in Medfield and removed to Hatfield, or Hadley, on the Connecticut River, where his sons were already established. In 1670 Joseph Daniell and Peter Calley were " desired and empowered to build a bridge over the southward most branch of the brook at Peter Woodward's mill." The same year the town granted Peter Calley " a parcel of rocky land that lyeth between his house and the mill of Peter Woodward." Three interesting facts are established by this record : that Peter Woodward had become owner of the mill ; that the mill stood where the brook is still divided into two channels by a long narrow island, and that Peter Calley, who is first mentioned as attending town-meeting in 1669, had a house in this vicinity. But it is difficult to determine on which side of the brook.

We hear nothing more of the mill until June 10, 1675, when a committee was chosen " to clear out the way formerly laid out on the north side of what was Peter Woodward's mill, to George Fairbanks' line and to see all incumbrances and annoyances by any person or persons removed." Some malicious persons had obstructed the road, and the language seems to imply that the mill had been destroyed. The letter of the Rev. Mr. Wilson to the governor of Massachusetts immediately after the destruction of Medfield speaks of two mills being destroyed by the Indians. As only one is known to have existed on the east side of the river, the other must have been Woodward's, the only one on the west side. The record already quoted seems to imply that the mill was destroyed some months before the burning of Medfield, and indeed before the outbreak of Philip's war, which seems not improbable, as the enmity of the Indians had long been gathering force, and depredations upon property were not infrequent. The temptation was great, the risk of detection small, and the annoyance of their enemy very considerable, who depended upon the mill to prepare material for their daily bread. There is little doubt the Indians burned the mill and obstructed the road. But once destroyed it was not soon rebuilt. In 1677, in a grant of land to William Allen, the highway is spoken of as leading from the place of Robert Hinsdell's mill, the name of the original owner being still sometimes associated with it, and nearly thirty years after, in 1705, when the road north of Boggastow Brook needed repairing again, it was described as leading from the place where Peter Woodward's mill stood, to the line between Medfield, and Sherborn.

At first there was, perhaps, no one bold enough to invest in such hazardous property in those troublous times. The inhabitants were few and the profits of the mill must have been small, but the inconvenience of being without a mill was very great.

At length, in 1680, the town voted "to give fifty acres of land where it may be most convenient for the encouragement of any that would adventure to build a grist mill upon Charles River, the mill to be builded and maintained every way sufficient for the town's use." The town promised on its part "not to build or suffer any other mill to the damage of this mill"; and also to "acquit said mill for seven years next after it is set to work of all town charges." The persons who accepted this offer were John Metcalf, Sen., John Partridge, Sen., Samuel Morse, Edward Adams, Joseph Allen, John Metcalf, Jr., Nathaniel Allen, George Barber, Ephraim Wight, Samuel Barber, John Plimpton, and Benjamin Wheelock.

This was the first mill built at Rockville, and the land, which was for many years after called the "New-mill-land" is described in the grant as "up stream of the mill, bounded with the river southward according to the various turnings thereof, by common land westward and northward by a varying line and with the land of George Barber, eastward." The road now called Green Street crossed this land.

It was not long before this mill, too, was burned, for in 1685 "Gamaliel Hinsdell was appointed by the selectmen to prosecute John Sunchamaug, an Indian, upon suspicion of firing the new mill." There is some other evidence pointing to the same fact. Exactly when the mill on Boggastow Brook was rebuilt does not appear. But in the records of Medfield mention is made of a meeting of the freeholders, as follows:

"168$\frac{5}{6}$. At a general meeting of y^e Freeholders of Medfield on y^e 7th day of February, 1686, the following action was taken: —

" VOTED — That there shall be five men, and but five chosen Selectmen for y^e management of y^e prudential affairs of y^e Town for the year ensuing.

" VOTED — That the Selectmen to be chosen for ye prudential affairs of ye Town for yᵉ year ensuing, shall have the whole power of yᵉ Town, excepting in yᵉ cases restrained in yᵉ year 1684 viz. granting lands — receiving inhabitants — granting liberty to any person to sel wood and timber out of town, taken off yᵉ common lands.

"GRANTED to Joseph Daniell the *stream* of *Boggastow Brook* so far as shall be needful for yᵉ advantage of his mill, and not to endanger any prᵖrietee on the sᵈ Brook, provided he maintain a good mill on yᵉ said stream for yᵉ supply of yᵉ Town."

The year following there was a meeting of the freeholders, whose names were as they appear in the following record:

"168⅞ At a general meeting of the Freeholders of Medfield, on the 6th day of February, Anno Dom. 168⅞, assembled the persons whose names are under written:

Mr. John Wilson, Sen.,	John Metcalf, Sen.,	John Turner, Sen.,
Ens. Edward Adams,	Jos. Clark, Sen.,	Samuel Smith, Sen.,
Sergt. John Harding,	Gam'l Hinsdale,	John Plimpton,
Sergt. Samuel Barber,	Jno. Thurston,	John Bullin,
Benj. Clark,	Joseph Allin,	Jos. Cheney,
Peter Adams, Sen.,	Benj. Fisk,	Jos. Plimpton,
Tho. Ellice,	John Fisher, Sen.,	Mich. Metcalf,
Elea. Adams,	Peter Adams, Jr.,	Jona. Adams, Jr.,
Jos. Mors,	Jos. Warren,	Jos. Daniels,
Samuel Wheelock,	Jos. Bullin,	John Metcalf, Jr.,
John Barber,	Jona. Boyden,	John Fisher, Jr.,
Samuel Bullin,	Ephr. Clark,	Jos. Ellice, Sen.,
Samuel Rockett,	Benj. Wheelock,	John Partridge, Sen.,
Ephr. Wight,	John Turner, Jr.,	Jer. Mors,
Elish. Bullin,	Samuel Smith, Jr.,	John Partridge, Jr.,
Will'm Allin,	Jos. Ellice,	Elea. Ellice."

At this meeting were granted further privileges, as appears in the following attested copy of the record made, in 1744, by Nathan Plimpton, Town Clerk of Medfield. The following is a fac-simile of the copy:

At a General Meeting of the Free holders of Medfield on the sixth day of February Anno Domini 1687 ⅞

Granted to Joseph Daniels Liberty to Land a Dam On the Common Land on Boyggetow Brook where he intends to set a mill and also liberty to Flood the Coman. Land there so far as shell be Convenient For a mill at all times for ever

A True Coppy taken Out of Medfield Town Book

Medfield June 4th 1744.

Attest — Nathan Plimpton Town Clerk of Medfield

After obtaining these grants, Joseph Daniell formed a partnership with Zachariah Buckminster, who resided in Sherborn, not very far away, and built the grist mill, which was afterwards owned by Joseph Daniell, Jr.

In 1692 Joseph Daniell gave to his son Joseph, who was about twenty-six years of age and recently married, one-half of the grist mill, and as appears not long after, in 1694, Joseph Daniell, Jr., came into possession of the other half by purchase of Zachariah Buckminster, of Sherborn. He subsequently erected a saw mill near the upper dam.

Joseph Daniel, Jr., in 1728, distributed to his three sons, Samuel, Joseph, and Ezra, his mill property, reserving to himself one-half of the grist mill. Both mills remained in the family for several generations, though the ownership was generally divided between two or more members of it, until both became the property of Amos Daniels, who died in 1823. His father, Moses Daniels, for the name had now changed from Daniell to Daniels, owned the upper mill, and was drowned October 20, 1800, in the flume while attempting to shut the gate.

Joseph Daniell, in 1693, appears to have owned "the place where Peter Woodward's mill stood," for in the deed to his son he conveyed half the grist mill; he gave also "the land where the old mill stood being two acres more or less a highway to lie through the same." Many years after, in 1729, Joseph Daniel, the son of Joseph, gave to his son Samuel one-half the saw mill and the ancient mill site, with what appears to have been the same "two acres of land." Joseph Daniell, Jr., appears to have had certain rights in lands granted by the General Court to a company of soldiers who went on an expedition to Canada under Captain Gardner. These rights are mentioned in his will. He died May 23, 1751. *Vid.* Genealogies

Timothy Daniell, who was the son of Samuel and the grandfather of Deacon Timothy Daniels, of Holliston, Mass., sold to Thaddeus Broad, in 1751, "two acres of land more or less with a grist mill thereon." This mill undoubtedly occupied the site of the first mill, built by Robert Hinsdell. Thaddeus Broad, June 23, 1781, deeds the mill to Adam Bullard, which was called Bullard's Mill.

Samuel Daniell, son of Joseph Daniell, Jr., sold out, in 1742, his homestead and real estate received from his father, to Jonathan Fuller, and removed to that part of Holliston which afterward became Medway. He owned the farm and lived where Cyrus Hill, Esq., now resides. He erected a mill on the stream passing near his house. He was called in ancient deeds, "Samuel Daniell, the miller."

At the close of the seventeenth century the population within the province afterward Medway, must have been quite small, as may be judged from the tax-list, which embraces the names of the householders who occupied lands at that time on the west side of the river Charles which afterward were within the limits of the town of Medway

---

The Tax-List of 1693.

John Adams,	John Clark,	George Fairbanks,	John Partridge,
Jonathan Adams, Sen.,	Joseph Daniell,	Jonathan Fisher,	John Richardson,
Jonathan Adams, Jun.,	Joseph Daniell, Jun.,	Abraham Harding,	John Rockett,
Peter Adams,	John Ellis,	Samuel Hill,	Josiah Rockett.

BLACK SWAMP LAID OUT IN 1702.

MARCH, 1702.—"Voted that the Black Swamp shall be laid out with such necks of upland and Ilands as shall make it formable by our former Rules of laying out Lands." The Black Swamp lots were laid out long and narrow; the lines ran east and west.

On the "west end of all the lots" a way two rods wide was reserved. This cartway is said in the records "to lie parallel to and adjoining to the line of the new Grant, or great grant." There were also two rods in width reserved on the east end of the lots, to lie common forever.

The division of Black Swamp began at the southerly part, near land of Theophilus Clark. All the lots were bounded by the highway at the west end. The width of each lot is here given:

NO.	NAMES.	RDS.	FT.	NO.	NAMES.	RDS.	FT.
1.	GEO. FAIRBANKS,	8	3	42.	Heirs Michael Metcalf,	5	0
2.	John Thurston,	17	9	43.	TIMOTHY CLARK,	1	12
3.	JOSEPH DANIELL, SEN.,	19	5	44.	Joshua Morse,	3	0
4.	JONATHAN FISHER,	9	4	45.	Eleazar Wheelock,	8	9
5.	Eleazar Adams,	9	8	46.	Samuel Clark,	1	8
6.	SAMUEL PARTRIDGE,	5	6	47.	Heirs Joseph Clark,	8	8
7.	Joshua Wight,	3	6	48.	Samuel Adams,		15
8.	John Hamant,	3	5	49.	Joseph Clark,	6	0
9.	Solomon Clark,	8	10	50.	John Turner, Jr.,	5	8
10.	BENJ. ALLEN, SEN.,	1	11	51.	Ichabod Harding,	3	9
11.	Jonathan Boyden, Sen.,	16	10	52.	John Bullen,	7	4
12.	Sarah Smith,	6	9	53.	EBENEZER THOMPSON,	3	0
13.	VINCENT SHUTTLEWORTH,	1	0	54.	Isaac Wheeler,	5	0
14.	Joseph Warren,	5	10	55.	JOSEPH DANIELL, JR.,	3	8
15.	Joseph Ellis,	10	11	56.	John Fisher, Jr.,	7	8
16.	JOHN ROCKETT,	9	11	57.	REBECCA RICHARDSON,	2	9
17.	Ephraim Wight, Jr.,	2	11	58.	THEOPHILUS CLARK,	4	14
18.	Samuel Ellis,	8	1	59.	Samuel Rockett,	4	6
19.	Priscilla Morse,	7	10	60.	JOHN PARTRIDGE,	5	4
20.	Joseph Baxter,	6	2	61.	Samuel Smith,	4	5
21.	Joseph Wight,	3	3	62.	Wm. Partridge,	3	9
22.	Henry Adams,	15	7	63.	JOHN ADAMS, Ed; son,	4	8
23.	Alex. Lovell,	9	4	64.	Joseph Allen, Sen.,	8	12
24.	JASPER ADAMS,	5	12	65.	Joseph Adams,	1	12
25.	EBENEZER DANIELL,	3	5	66.	John Thurston, Jr.,	6	0
26.	JOSIAH ROCKETT,	6	2	67.	John Dwight,	5	6
27.	Daniel Thurston,	4	8	68.	Elisha Bullen,	7	0
28.	Eleazar Leland,	8	0	69.	Joseph Bullen,	4	0
29.	John Fisher, Sen.,	8	0	70.	Heirs John Barber,	2	4
30.	Samuel Wight, Sen.,	5	7	71.	Mary Clark,	2	9
31.	Joseph Allen, Jr.,	2	8	72.	Heirs Jos. Plimpton,	5	9
32.	John Pratt,	5	0	73.	Timothy Hamant,	5	12
33.	Ephraim Wight, Sen.,	7	4	74.	JONATHAN ADAMS, JR.,	5	12
34.	Joseph Metcalf,	7	8	75.	Sarah Partridge,	4	8
35.	Jonathan Boyden, Jr.,	3	5	76.	Henry Smith,	1	5
36.	Henry Harding,	4	12	77.	William Allen,	6	4
37.	John Plimpton,	8	15	78.	ABRAHAM HARDING,	15	1
38.	Noah Clark,	1	13	79.	SAMUEL HILL,	8	8
39.	Nathaniel Clark,	4	14	80.	Jonathan Plimpton,	3	4
40.	Benjamin Clark,	7	7	81.	John Bowers,	2	8
41.	JONATHAN ADAMS, SEN.,	3	6	82.	Mary Adams,		11

NO.	NAMES.	RDS.	FT	NO.	NAMES	RDS	FT
83.	John Metcalf, ...	7	14	104.	Joseph Cheney, . .	8	0
84	John Fisher, min., . . .		11	105.	John Richardson, . .	2	8
85.	Nehemiah Sabin, ...	1	6	106.	Jeremiah Morse, Sen ,	7	4
86	John Harding, . .	6	6	107	John Adams, miller, . .	2	11
87	Jos. Plimpton, . . .	3	0	108	Henry Adams, Jr , .		4
88.	Sarah Wheelock, ...	3	0	109	John Bullard, . . .	2	7
89.	John Ad Pet. Son., . .	7	0	110.	Zechariah Partridge, . .	2	3
90.	Joseph Morse, ...	4	4	111.	John Turner, Sen , . . .	2	3
91.	Jeremiah Morse, ...	3	0	112.	Benj Allen, Jr , . .	3	0
92.	Ebenezer Mason, . . .	9	0	113	Eleazar Wight, . . .	4	2
93.	Nath'l Partridge, ...	9	4	114	Daniel Smith, . .	1	5
94.	Abigail Smith, . . .	2	12	115.	Eleazar Ellis, . . .	6	12
95.	Edward Adams, . .	3	12	116	John Ellis, ...	6	7
96	Samuel Wight, Jr., .	4	12	117	Nathaniel Allen, Sen , .	7	14
97.	Samuel Morse, ...	7	3	118	Return Johnson, . . .	2	14
98	Bethshuer Fisk, . . .	2	0	119.	Eleazar Partridge, .	5	15
99	Matthias Evans, heirs, . .	7	4	120.	Henry Guernsy, . . .	2	7
100.	Peter Adams, ...	6	12	121.	Samuel Bullen, ...	6	14
101.	Zachary Barber, . . .	7	0	122.	Isaac Turner, . .	2	12
102.	Nath'l Lovell, ...	4	7	123.	John Clark, . . .	7	0
103	Samuel Barber, . . .	7	12				

The largest of these lots was that of Abraham Harding, containing twenty-three acres. The smallest was that of Henry Adams, Jr., son of Edward Adams, whose lot was *four feet* wide, and about two hundred and fifty rods long, containing sixty-five square rods of land

The names of dwellers on the west side of Charles River at this date are indicated in the above list in small capitals. Ten new families had been added to the population since 1693.

EDUCATION IN THE EARLY TIMES.

In 1678 some of the inhabitants of Medfield contributed towards the "new college in Cambridge." Among the contributors were George Fairbanks, Jr., who gave one shilling and one bushel of Indian corn, and Joseph Daniell, who gave two shillings sixpence and two bushels of corn. Nicholas Rockwood, who was afterwards on the west side of the river, was also a contributor. He had been burned out in the Indian war. It seems that the subscription was made before the destruction of Medfield, though the collection was not made till afterwards, and in some cases the sums promised were not required on account of the losses of the subscribers.

This is the first mention made, showing an interest in education by the people on the west side of the Charles River.

It was not, however, until 1698 that any systematic effort was made to educate the children. One is, very naturally, curious to know how the children were taught during the forty years that had intervened since the first settlement was made. The old deeds show that some could not write, while the old records leave no doubt that the art of composition was but little understood. The instruction must have been very scanty, confined to the rudiments of reading, writing, and arithmetic. This year, twelve pounds and ten shillings were raised for schooling the children in the town, fifty shillings of which was to be expended on the west side of the river. Two years after, three pounds was raised for the same purpose, and the selectmen "agreed with Sergt. Joseph Danill to take care of the schooling." What is meant by taking care of the schooling is not quite clear. It probably meant providing a school-room and teaching the school, for under date of March 19, 1700, Sergt. Joseph Daniell was paid for teaching school in the year 1699.

The next record regarding this subject is as follows: "Feb. 21, 1700 payd unto peter Adams for his wives keeping school on that side of the River it being the full of his Due 2—9—11." It thus appears that in those early days, husbands received their wives' wages, and that ladies, long before the days of modern reform, were sufficiently educated to teach school, and were sometimes employed for that purpose. Mrs. Adams was the FIRST FEMALE TEACHER whose name has come down to us. She was already the mother of seven children, the oldest a daughter of twenty years, the youngest hardly two years of age. Her maiden name was Experience Cook.

September 13, 1704, "The town voted that the schools be kept on both sides the river proportionally to the charges of the inhabitants on either side. The inhabitants on the west side to provide a convenient room for a school this year for such time as shall be needful." No school-house had yet been built and the above vote, evidently, only contemplated hiring a room. Mrs. Adams had, before this, gathered the children into one of those large old-fashioned kitchens, perhaps in her own house.

Again, March 29, 1710, John Partridge, Sen., was paid for keeping school on the west side one month, one pound twelve shillings. It is apparent that the school privileges of those days were very scanty, but the records are still more scanty.

THE NEW MEETING-HOUSE.

The first meeting-house in Medfield was built before there were any inhabitants on the west side of the river. In 1705 it was proposed to build a new one, for what reason we are not told. Perhaps the old one was too small to accommodate the increasing population or it had become dilapidated in its more than fifty years of service. There is no doubt there were good and sufficient reasons, as the circumstances of our fathers did not allow any extravagance for the gratification of taste. It was November 13, 1705, when the vote was passed to build. It appears that the people on the west side objected to being taxed to build a house of worship so far from home, and presented their claim for one themselves. This was not an unreasonable view to take of the matter.

At a town-meeting a few days afterward it was "Voted that the inhabitants on the west side the river shall have one-half the sum they pay towards building the new meeting-house refunded, if they build a meeting-house on that side within twenty years." Subsequently, December 15, 1714, this promise was fulfilled, and twenty-two pounds and nine shillings refunded.

December 12, 1705, the town was again assembled, this time at the petition and request of the families on the west side, but after much debate the meeting was broken up without acting anything. What was the nature of the request does not appear from the records; we can only conjecture that the selfishness of human nature still objected to being taxed for a meeting-house so far away.

The meeting-house was built in 1706. It stood on the site of the first house, and remained till 1789. John Richardson and Henry Guernsey, carpenters from the west side, worked on the building, Joseph Daniell furnished shingles for which he was paid £12, 14s., 6d., and boards to the amount of 18s., 9d. And after it was completed he, with George Fairbanks, was placed upon an important committee, whose duty was no less than appointing seats for the people according to their titles, station, and estates.

Before this, several offices had been held by the west side men. Samuel Daniell and Joseph Daniell had held the important office of tithing men; and in 1693 George Fairbanks and Joseph Daniell were chosen selectmen, being the first that had been so honored west of the river.

But the people on this side of the river as they increased in numbers, were not accommodated by the new meeting-house. They were dissatisfied, and therefore petitioned the town for relief. As the petition was not recorded it is now uncertain whether they asked for a division of the town or for a meeting-house of their own. At a town-meeting, May 7, 1712, it was voted that the petition be left for further consideration. Three weeks later, the town refused to grant the petition.

The petitioners were not to be silenced so easily. Obtaining no relief from the town, it appears they applied to the Legislature, July 12, 1712. The town chose Captain Jonathan Boyden, Lieutenants Samuel Morse, Nathaniel Partridge, Jonathan Plimpton, and Samuel Barber to give reasons to the Great and General Court why the petition of the inhabitants of the west side of Charles River should not be granted. This committee were prohibited by vote of the same meeting from acting in any way for the division of the town.

The General Court recommended that the town raise money towards building another meeting-house on the west side of Charles River, and some other things, but the town was not willing to accept the recommendation, so, on the 9th of March, 1713, voted to petition the General Court, declaring their inability to build another meeting-house, and bear the charges attending it, and further voted to raise ten pounds to pay charges for promoting the petition, and to pay Mr. Paul Dudley three pounds to manage the town case.

Notwithstanding the opposition, a committee sent out by the Court to look over the ground, reported in favor of a division of the town; accordingly, on the twenty-fifth day of October, 1713, a bill was passed by the General Court, for the incorporation of Medway, and it became a town.

THE TOWN AND ITS DOINGS.

1713 — 1885.

THE INCORPORATION.

THE incorporation of the town of Medway came about when a considerable number of settlers had become permanently established as residents on the westerly side of the Charles River, to whom a meeting-house and a minister in their midst, became important. And to have these, a new town must be established. In those days it was, primarily, that the inhabitants of any locality might have a meeting-house and a "learned Orthodox minister" among them, that municipal powers were sought and granted. It was to make ready for the establishment of local Christian institutions, that the Great General Court was petitioned, and an act of incorporation passed, by which was established, in 1713, the town of Medway. Thus the state furnished a cradle to the early settlers of old Boggastow in which to rock the infant church; and for years the town, by its recorded votes, its officers, and its appropriations, nourished the childhood of the Church of Christ growing up within its limits.

The Rev. Joseph Baxter, the second pastor of Medfield, was in the seventeenth year of his ministry, when those of his flock living beyond the river, became a town and parish by themselves.

Medway was incorporated October 25, 1713, in the twelfth year of the reign of Queen Anne, Hon. Joseph Dudley being Provincial Governor of Massachusetts. An attested copy of this Act of Incorporation, a yellow and time-stained document, is still preserved with the records of the town, and reads as follows:

ANNO REGNI ANNÆ REGINÆ DUODECIM.

An Act for Dividing the Township of Medfield and erecting a new Town there by the name of Medway.

Whereas the Lands of the Township of Medfield within the County of Suffolk lye fituate on Charles River to wit on both fides of the faid River being divided by the fame and the town plat and principal fettlement, as alfo the meeting houfe for the Public Worfhip of God being feated on the Eaft fide for Accommodation of the firft and Ancient Inhabitants who are now much increafed many Iffued forth and fettled on the Weft fide of the River to a Competent number for a diftinct town of themfelves and labour under many hardfhips and Difficulties by reafon of Separation by the River to Enjoy Equal benefit and town privileges with others of their fellow townfmen and neighbors and have therefore made Application to the town as alfo addreffed this Court to be made a diftinct Town, Committees appointed by this Court having been upon the Ground viewed the land and reported in their favor for proper bounds to be fet them:

Be it Enacted by his Excellency the Governour, Council and Reprefentatives in General Court affembled and by the Authority of the Same That all those Lands Lying on the Weft Side of Charles River now part of the Townfhip of Medfield be Erected and made into a Diftinct and Separate Town by the name of Medway the River to be the Bound betwixt the Two Towns And that the Inhabitants of Medway have, ufe, Exercife and Enjoy So that they procure and Settle a Learned Orthodox Minifter of good Converfation among 'em and make provifion for an Honl fupport and maintenance for him and that in Order thereto they be Difcharged from further payment to the Miniftry in Medfield from and after the laft day of February next.

Provided alfo that all Province and Town Taxes that are already Levied or Granted be Collected and paid And all town Rights and Common undivided Lands remain to be divided among the interefted as if no separation had been made And Mr. George Fairbanks a principal Inhabitant of the faid Town of Medway is hereby Directed and Impowered to Notify and Summon the Inhabitants duly Qualified for Voters to Affemble and meet together for the choofing of Town Officers to ftand until the next Annual Election According to Law.

A true Copy — examined   Isᴬ Addington, *Secry*

— —

The Founders of the Town.

Daniel Adams,	Timothy Clark,	Samuel Hill, Jun.,
Jasper Adams,	Edward Clark,	Ephraim Hill,
John Adams,	Joseph Curtis,	Michael Metcalf,
Jonathan Adams, Sen ,	Ebenezer Daniell,	Samuel Metcalf,
Jonathan Adams, Jun ,	Jeremiah Daniell,	Benoni Partridge,
Joseph Adams,	Joseph Daniell, Sen.,	John Partridge,
Obadiah Adams,	Joseph Daniell, Jun ,	Zachariah Partridge,
Peter Adams,	Samuel Daniell,	Jonathan Partridge,
James Allen,	John Ellis,	Samuel Partridge,
William Allen,	George Fairbanks,	Daniel Richardson,
John Barber,	Jonathan Fisher,	John Richardson,
Joseph Barber,	Henry Guernsey,	John Rockwood,
John Bullard,	Abraham Harding,	Josiah Rockwood,
Malachi Bullard,	Abraham Harding, Jun.,	Ebenezer Thompson,
William Burgess,	John Harding,	Nathaniel Whiting,
John Clark,	Thomas Harding,	Nathaniel Wight.
Theophilus Clark,	Samuel Hill,	

The names of the above, not found located on the accompanying map of 1713, were aged men residing with their sons, or young men who, as yet, had not left the paternal roof to establish homes for themselves, except in two instances, viz.: Ebenezer Thompson, at this period, resided "Northeast of Black Swamp, near the road that runs on the line of swamp lots"; and Zachariah Partridge resided "on a road running east and west." Just where the localities thus described were, it is left for the reader to determine.

THE FIRST TOWN-MEETING.

In pursuance of the Act of Incorporation, a meeting of the new town was called, of which the following record appears:

"MEDWAY, November y^e 23, 1713.

At a Town meeting of the inhabitants of this Town apointed by virtue of an order of the Generall Court to choose town officers to stand untill the next annuall ellection or choise which will be in March 17$\frac{1}{3}$.

Voted, John Rocket is chosen Town Clark and to be one of the select men allso Serj Sam^ll Partridge Jonathan Adams Jun. Serj Jonathan Adams and Edward Clark are chosen select men

Voted, that Jonathan Fisher stands constabel for Medway till the next general meeting which be in March next ensuing.

Voted, That John Rockett and Jonathan Adams Jun. Serg^t Samuell Partridge and Serj Jonathan Adams and edward Clark be a comittee to take care to procure the meeting house built." *Vid* THE CHURCHES.

Voted, "that abraham harding sen^r John partridge and Theophilus clark to procure and cary in a petition to the Town Clerk of Medfield in order to the procuring of accommodations for the setting of the metting hous upon the place commonly called bare hills, and some conven't acomodations for the ministry near ther abouts.

Voted, that John Rockett and Zechariah partridge are chosen to go down and Recon with the honnerable comity which the genneral court sent to vew ye ground and report bounds for the Town of Medway and the charges to be leved in a town tax."

At a subsequent meeting it was

" *Voted*—That all the Town charges that hath ben expended for the giting of, and erecting of a township on the west sid of Charls river and naming it by the name of Midway is all sunk and never to be brought to the town any more except to paye and make the comitie satisfaction for their time which is acording to repoart Three pound and Fifteen Shillings."

One hundred pounds were granted by the town for the work of building a meeting-house, in addition to the amount due the town for its right in the Medfield meeting-house, which amounted to £22, 9s., 4d. The work was at once commenced, and the committee reported June 7th, that they had reckoned with the carpenter and made the first payment to him of thirty pounds.

The location of the meeting-house on Bare Hill was on the south side of the cemetery in East Medway. It was an elevated spot, and the meeting-house was a conspicuous object for miles around.

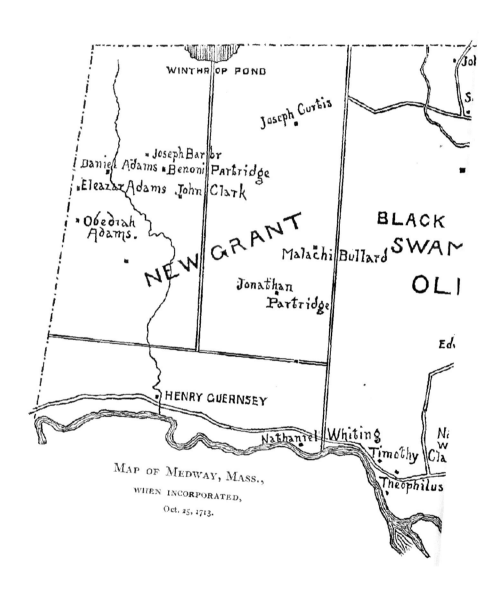

MAP OF MEDWAY, MASS.,

WHEN INCORPORATED,

Oct. 25, 1713.

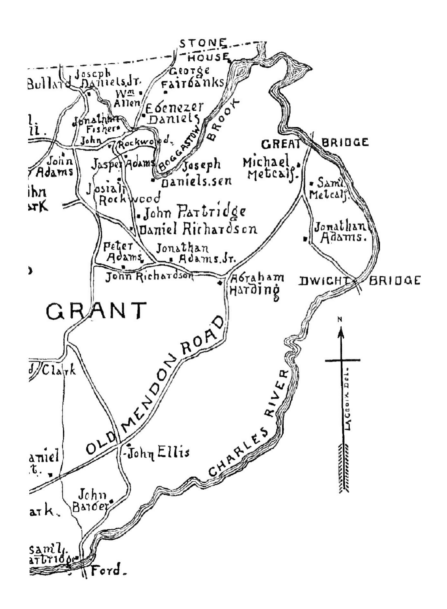

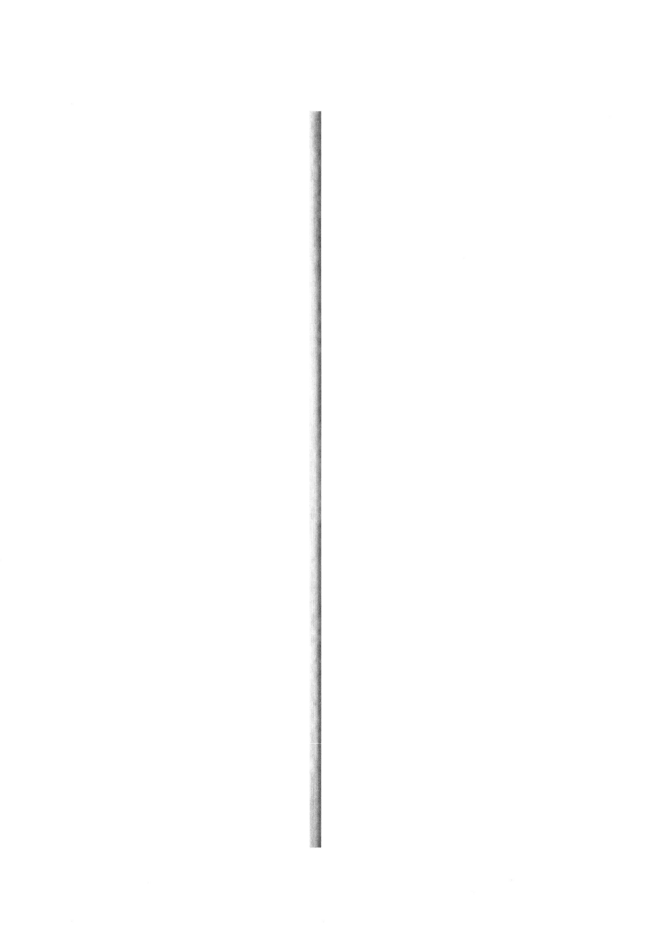

"October 15, 1714 The selectmen being present, finished the Town tax being drawn up into two lists, the one containing £61-8-0 for Ebenezer Thomson constabel to collect and the other list containeth £15-12-8 for John Clark constabel to collect and have granted A warrant two them to colect and pay in the same to the selectmen at or before the 15 of november next "

October 29 the town voted "that the buring place should be upon bare hill sumwhare with in forty Rods of the meeting house and a commity was chose by the vote of the Town to joyn with the commity yt Medfield have chose to lay out the buriing place who are Cpt george fairbanks and Zackari Partridge and John Richardson "

As it was one of the conditions of the incorporation of the town that it should provide itself with a minister, this duty came up early for settlement. It was then a matter of far graver importance than now. The minister of those times was looked up to with great reverence. He stood almost alone among his people in learning and literary attainments ; his influence, if judiciously exercised, was almost unbounded Hence, it was proper that great care should be exercised in the selection of one who was expected to remain during life in that relation, and the fitness of the candidate was carefully considered. All the people, whether church-goers or not, were obliged to contribute by their taxes to his support, and the receipts of the minister for the payment of his salary, were, from year to year, duly recorded. It appears that until about 1750, the civil and ecclesiastical history of the town were almost identical, and all matters relating to the settlement of a minister and his support, came before the inhabitants at the town-meeting, in the same way as highways, bridges, schools, and other town matters

Accordingly, at a town-meeting January 31, 1715, it was proposed to invite the Rev David Deming to settle here and "carry on the work of the ministry," at a salary of fifty-two pounds yearly.

The pastorate of Mr. Deming and those of his successors, are more fully considered elsewhere. *Vid.* THE CHURCHES.

THE FIRST ROAD laid out after the incorporation of the town was that crossing Stony Plain, and is so well described that it is easy to identify it. "June the 4th, 1715 The selectmen met at the house of Nathaniel Wight to lay out high wais for the benefit of this Town and for the Conveniency of travelers to pass from town to town as foloweth, begun in the Country Rhode that leds to Mendon near twenty rods east from Nat. Wights upon a straight line across part of the plain known by the name of Stony plain, and cross a swamp place comonly called pardice island, and by the south east side of Ebenezer Thompsons field on to bare hill, along at the south west end of the meeting house, to the laid out high way through the plain comonly known by the name of hills."

The first mention of schools in the doings of the town is as follows ·

" Assembled the inhabitants of Medwy on My ye 13, 1717, to chuse a [deputy] and grant mony for the building of a pound and keeping of a scool. No choyse for a deputy but by ye vote of them that was then and thear Assembled Granted four pounds of money to be raised as and put into the ministers Rate for to build a pound and keep a Scool."

The town seems then to have entered fully upon its corporate existence ; a church had been erected, a minister settled, a school established, roads laid out, and a pound had been built. The officers of the town appear to have been nearly the same as now, viz. : a clerk, or book-keeper as he is sometimes called, five selectmen, two constables, two highway surveyors, one fence-viewer, two tithing men, a field driver, a deer reeve, one or two persons to see "that the law relating to swine be kept and observed," and a sealer of weights and measures.

March 2, 1719, "Voted that the pew next to yᵉ pulpit should be for the ministers family to sit in," also "voted that there should be a pair of casements provided by the selectmen at the Town cost against the middel pew, them not to exceed four foot of glas." In 1725 the town voted that no person should "fall or cutt Down any young tree or shrub" within twenty rods of the meeting-house under penalty of ten shillings, to be paid for the use of the town. March 7, 1726, "At yᵉ Request of Lieut. Bullard and Sergt. Samuel Hill for liberty to Erect a smal Building for their particular use and Conveniency near the meeting house," the town voted "in Answer to this Request of yᵉ afore named Bullard and Hill that they should have liberty to erect the said smal building provided they set yᵉ said building not within Seven Rods. of yᵉ sᵈ Meeting House." This was a noon-house, such as were common in the vicinity of meeting-houses, where the worshipers could spend the time comfortably between the services in cold weather, as in those days the churches were not warmed. It required more endurance than worshipers of the present day possess, to sit out, in a freezing church, the long doctrinal discourses so highly prized by our forefathers.

THE FIRST REPRESENTATIVE to the Provincial Court, Jonathan Adams, was chosen in 1726. There had been several meetings previously called for that purpose but the voters had not thought it best to send, as the record of a meeting, December 3, 1713, shows, "the town concluded by a vote to send none, accounting ourselves not obliged by law to send any."

But in 1729 it appears that the law had been changed, so that a fine was imposed on a town for delinquency in this regard of their duty to the Province of Massachusetts Bay. The following original document is still preserved by Edson W. Barber, Esq., a lineal descendant of Mr. Joseph Barber:

"PROVINCE OF MASSACHUSETTS BAY.

JEREMIAH ALLEN, ESQ.,

Treasurer & Receiver General for His Majesties said Province.

To MR. JOS. BARBER, *Constable or Collector of the Town of Medway.*

GREETING : Assessment to you to collect   Amounting in the whole sum of sixteen pounds eleven shillings & seven pence.

This was the apportionment of a Tax assessed by the General Court of £8000 and of a further Tax of £240–1⅜ laid on several towns *for not sending a Representative as by Law they are obliged* and also for further tax of £2351 ₁⁵₆ paid the Representatives Anno 1729. Issued Nov. 11 1730. 4ᵗʰ year of George 2ᵈ. Signed by

JER. ALLEN."

In the year 1726, "ten pounds was granted for a moving school to be divided into three parts thus prescribed, that is five pounds for yᵉ body or East part of yᵉ town and fifty shillings for yᵉ inhabitants where yᵉ bent of yᵉ River so called and fifty shillings to yᵉ inhabitants of yᵉ New Grant so called or otherwise Mucksquit."

"March the 4, 172⅞, yᵉ selectmen being present Paid all the Known town dues and discharged the constables and there was found £1 1s. 9d in the treasury."

March 9, 1730, "Voted that there should be sufficient sum of mony Drawn out of the interst of the first bank to bye a buring cloath yt is deacent for the Town. Voted William Burgess should bye and make sd cloth and Commit to Deacon Thompson to Keep."

The next year at a town-meeting " the moderator by the Request of several of the inhabitants of the town proposed whether they would come to an agrement about the way of singing . . . and it appeared that the major part were for singing yt which is usually called the ' old way,' then the town proposed to chuse a man to lead the psalm for the Congregation and the vote fell upon Ensign Whiting, sd Whiting Refused in open meeting; and upon a second tryall of the vote it fell upon Jonathan Partridge."

To JONATHAN HILL, CONSTABLE

The sd we in his majestie's Name to will and Require you forth with to Notify the Inhabitants of this Town these and Every of them, such of them as are qualified by Law to vote in Town affairs so many of them as belong to your part to warn that they meet at the meeting house of this Town on Monday the fifth day of March next at nine o'clock in the morning, then and there to chuse Your officers to mannige the prudential affairs of the Town and to consider the circumstance of time and things and Grant Mr bucknam sum thing more for his Encurgement in the work of ye ministry Among us, if the Town think fitt

fail not and make Return of your so doing at or before the time above namd

Medway,	Edward Clark	
Feb. 9, 1732–3	Jeremiah Daniell	Select-
	John Adams	men
	Jonathan Adams	

I have warned the Inhabitants according to the Directions of the within written warrant

(Signed)   Jonathan hill,
Consble.

TOWN EXPENDITURES.

For Year 1734-5

	£	s.	d
" Book of Records,	0	12	0
for the Selectmn's charges,		11	6
To Edward Clark for Keeping Scool,	3	0	0
To John Richardson for sweeping meeting house,		16	0
Simon Plimpton for Runing line on Stony Plain betwen the land of Medfield and Medway,		2	0
Paid Mr. Salter of Borston for half barral of powder,	10	0	0
for one hundred weight of bulits and one hund flints,	5	15	0
to Edward Clark for bying the amunition,		5	0
To Timothy Clark for bringing powder and bulits,		3	6
Paid to Michael Medcalf for building the pound,	7	0	0
To John Childs for mending and making glas for ye meeting house,	1	13	

And Mr. Bucknam the minister acknowledges the receipt of one hundred pounds for his Salary for the year 1734. Total amount of expenditures, ... £129–18 – 0"

In 1744 the town chose two persons "to take care that the law be kept relating to Deer," and for many years thereafter at the annual meeting "deer reves" were chosen with other town officers. The law referred to forbids the killing of any deer between the tenth day of December and the first of August. The inhabitants seem to have suffered from the depredations of birds and animals, as it is recorded in February, 1742, that the selectmen completed a list of those interested in the premiums for killing squirrels and blackbirds, from which it appeared that eight hundred and seventeen squirrels and six hundred and eighty-four blackbirds had been destroyed, and nineteen pounds eleven shillings and sixpence ordered to be paid as bounties for the same. And in 1737 Seth Harding was paid one pound for "Killing a wild Catt." Professor Abner Morse says the last deer killed in Sherborn was about 1747. Bears were troublesome about Winthrop Pond as late as 1730, and the last panther made his appearance in Medway about 1790. Foxes at the present time are occasionally shot, and at long intervals an otter is captured in this vicinity, and raccoons were not, until within a few years since, entirely exterminated. The crow is still as troublesome to the farmer as he was one hundred and forty years ago, but insists upon his right to life and liberty in defiance of all efforts to the contrary.

As the population increased the meeting-house seems to have become too small to accommodate the worshipers, and as the two parts of the town were separated by long miles of swamp and unsettled territory, rendering the communication in winter inconvenient and sometimes difficult, the people of the New Grant began to agitate the question of a separation and the formation of a new society. This discussion was kept up for many years, until the establishment of a second religious society was secured.

"May 20 1731 It was proposed whether yᵉ town would fix and have the meeting house in the senter of the town or the most convenient place near the senter." This proposal, the clerk records, was "Knegatived."

In 1737 eight persons requested to be set off from the New Grant and annexed to Holliston. This was refused. The question was asked if the town would free the said eight inhabitants from paying any part of the minister's tax. This also was refused.

In 1738 the town met to act on the following articles: "To try the minds of yᵉ town whether they would take down yᵉ meeting house in sᵈ town and make it larger, or build a new meeting house and set it on yᵉ west side of Black Swamp by yᵉ Gravel Pit or on yᵉ Candle wood Island" and if not granted "to set off yᵉ inhabitants of yᵉ New Grant by yᵉ line that parts between yᵉ Old Grant and the New." The town refused, and the next January voted to enlarge the house where it then stood. In 1743 seventeen petitioners from the New Grant ask the town to allow them twelve weeks' preaching in the winter, which was negatived; but having, during the year, petitioned the General Court, the town came together in December, in a different state of mind, and voted to build a meeting-house in the centre of the town, or on the nearest upland should that point prove to be in the swamp; and a committee was chosen to superintend the matter, and Edward Turner, of Medfield, a surveyor, was appointed to designate this centre spot, which was probably not far from the present junction of Oakland and Main streets.

In May, 1744, a meeting was called to meet at this place, and to decide whether "the town judge it suitable to set a meeting house for yᵉ Public worship of God," and it was voted by a "great majority not suitable." A proposition was then made that it be set on land of Timothy Clark, about sixty rods west of Edward Clark's house, but this was decided not to be

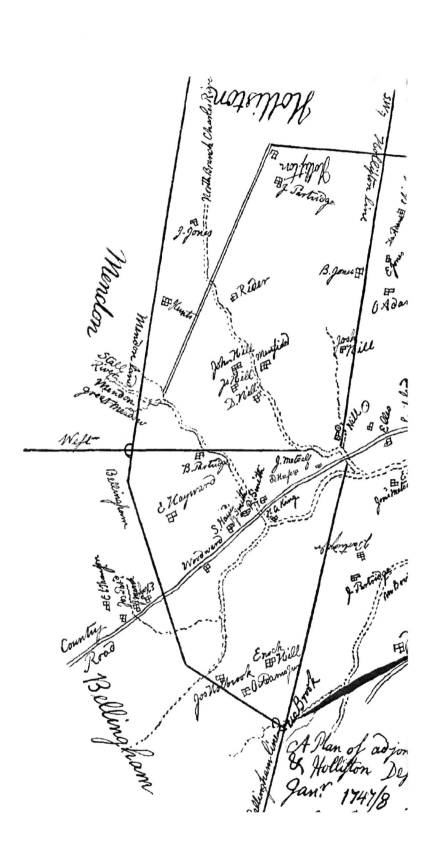

Holliston

Mendon

North Branch Charles River

Holliston Line

J. Jones

J. Partridge

Holliston

E. Jones

B. Jones

Rider

O. Adams

Kents

Josh Hill

John Hill

Mayfield

Mendon Line

Stall River

Mendon Great Meadow

Jos. Hill

D. Nell

Nell

E. Ellis

West

Bellingham

B. Partridge

J. Metcalf

E. Hayward

S. Hayes

B. Hayes

Smith

Jona Metcalf

Smith

H. A. King

Woodward

S. Emerson

E. Howard

J. Partridge

Jos. Hall

Iron Works

Enoch Hill

Jos. Holbrook

O. Adams Jun.

Country Road

Bellingham

Bellingham Line

Mill Brook

A Plan of adjoin
& Holliston De
Jan.r 1747/8

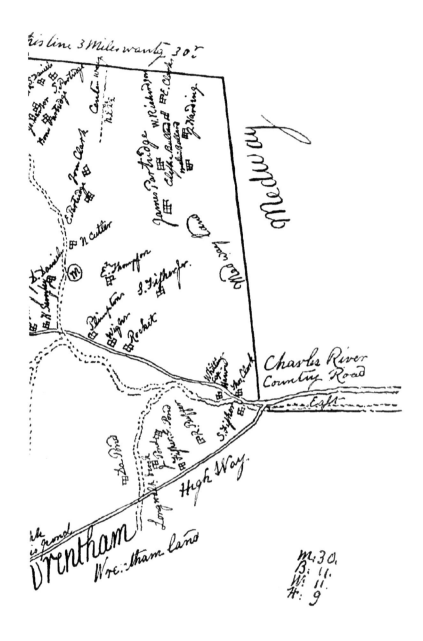

this line 3 Miles wanty 30°

Medway

Charles River
Country Road

East

High Way

Wrentham

Wrentham land

M: 30.
B: 11.
W: 11.
H: 9

2 Corners of Medway Wrentham Bellingham
ring to made a Distinct Preceinct
rawn by John Metcalf Surveyer
Inch

suitable. In December of this year the General Court ordered the payment of thirty pounds yearly from the town treasury to the people of the New Grant, but this does not seem to have proved a satisfactory settlement of the difference. In 1747 the town voted " whether the town will maintain two ministers in a general way that ye west part of ye town might enjoy equal privileges with the other parts of the town — Passed in the negative — Therefore put to vote whether ye town would set off ye west part of the town at ye center line, to be a separate Precinct — Passed in the negative — Then put to vote whether the town would free the inhabitants of the New Grant from ye present ministerial charges in Medway that they might maintain preaching amongst themselves in ye New Grant — Passed in the negative."

The matter was finally settled by the incorporation of the West Precinct by the General Court, December 29, 1748, and the next year a meeting-house was built, the Second Church of Christ formed, and in March, 1753, the town-meeting was first held there The establishment of this church seems, so far as the records are concerned, to have severed the union of church and state before existing. From this time the records contain only the usual town matters, and the meeting-house and minister disappear. The following receipt from the Rev. Nathan Bucknam is the last recorded.

" March ye 22 Anno Dom. 1748–49 Received of Dea John Barber town treasurer the sum of four Hundred Pounds old Tenor Bills in full satisfaction for my salary the past year, and I do hereby acquitt and discharge the said Town of Medway from all Debts, Dues, or demands whatsoever on the account of my yearly salary from the time of my first settling with them in the work of the ministry to the first day of this instant March as witness my hand — NATHAN BUCKNAM."

In the warrant for a meeting September 4, 1780, is the following article : " 5th To hear the proceedings of the Westerly Precinct of Medway relating to being formed into a distinct town. And to hear and act upon a petition of Lieut. Nathan Whiting and others to see if the town will set off the inhabitants of the New Grant to be a distinct town." " Passed in the negative."

February 2, 1764, an order was passed by the General Court directing the selectmen of each town and district to " take an exact account of the number of dwelling-houses, families and people in their respective towns and districts including as well Indians civilized, negroes and mulattos, as white people and females, as well as males," and the following is the result in Medway :

CENSUS OF 1765.

Houses 123   Families 138   Males under 18 years . . . 165
Females under 18 years. . . . 178   Males over 18 years 215
Females over 18 years 210   Negroes 17
    Total population 785

This was the first census of Massachusetts. This, together with that of 1775, was made by order of the Provincial Government, since which time a census has been ordered by the General Court once in ten years.

"To The Constable or Constables of the Town of Medway."

This List Contains Each Person's name Together with the office to which he was chosen on the 5th of March instant, for you to Warn and Summon to appear before Lawful authority in order to be Sworn to the faithful discharge thereof.

SAMUEL HAYWARD, *Warden.*

OLIVER ADAMS
SETH PARTRIDGE } *Surveyors of Highways.*
SAMUEL HILL Jun.

MOSES RICHARDSON *Surv. of Shingles & Clapboards of Boards & Lumber.*

TIMOTHY CLARK *Fence Viewer.*

JOHN CUTLER, JONATHn CUTLER
NATHANIEL PARTRIDGE } *Hogreeves.*
URIAH MORSE

LIEUT. JOHN HARDING *Sealer of Leather.*

Given under my hand at Medway, this 6 day of March, 1764. By order of the Selectmen.

(Signed)   ELIJAH CLARK, *Town Clk*

THE TROUBLOUS TIMES.

1765—1783.

The feeling of anxiety and alarm that existed in the colonies at what was deemed the oppressive acts of the British Government for several years before the Revolution, is indicated by the action of the town in 1765. After electing Elisha Adams for Representative to the General Court, a committee of five was chosen to draw up suitable instructions for his guidance, which were as follows:

"It need not surprise any thinking person that the colonies in North America should be greatly alarmed at the late stamp act from Great Britain as it effects their estates and liberties. It fills us with very great concern to find that measures have been adopted by the British ministry and acts of parliament made which press hard upon our invaluable rights. It is thought by your constituents that at this critical season you would not be unwilling to know their mind on this important affair. We look upon the said stamp act to be a burden, grievous, distressing and insupportable not only likely to enslave the present, but future generations. The great and heavy load of debt lying upon us at present arising from the late expensive war and the defence and support of his Magisties government here, has sunk us so low already that the addition of the weight of the stamp act will sink us into final ruin. We think it is our indispensable duty in justice to ourselves and posterity, as it is our undoubted privilege in the most open and unreserved, but decent and respectful terms to declare our greatest dissatisfaction with this law and we think it incumbent upon you by no means to join in any public measure for countenancing and assistance in the execution of the same, but to exercise your utmost endeavor in a modest, becoming manner to prevent said act taking place in this government and that you would with a watchful eye and great diligence, guard and protect the properties and liberties of your country, and charter in particular against all incroachments whatsoever made upon them and likewise desire you to oppose every attempt to raise by way of tax any sum or sums of money or dispose of any already in the treasury in any other way than has been the customary practice, or in short for any thing except defraying the necessary expense of the government. You may also signify our abhorance and detestation at every unruly outrage that has been or may be committed on persons or property anywhere in his Majesties Province of the Massachusetts Bay in New England."

In May, 1766, Jonathan Adams being the Representative, the town gave him instructions "relating to making up the losses to his Honor the Lieut. Governor and other gentlemen sustained by a riotous outrage in Boston last year, which we bear public testimony against, yet notwithstanding the Province as a Province were no actors in s⁰ riot, or accessory to it, therefore we do not think it just their losses should be made up by a province tax"; and in November of the same year he is directed to act "as he shall think most safe and prudent relating to the proposed act of compensation and of pardon and indemnity to the offenders in the the late times of confusion"

In January, 1768, the town voted "to concur with the vote passed in the town of Boston on the 28 October 1767 relating to taking all prudent and legal measures to encourage the produce and manufactures of the Province and to lessen the use of superfluities imported from afar."

In September, 1768, Captain Jonathan Adams was chosen "to join with a committee to be convened in Boston on September 22, to act for, and represent this town in advising and consulting such measures as his Majesties service, the peace and safety of his subjects in this Province may require."

These votes, with others following, indicate the state of public feeling, and show that the people of Medway were not idle spectators of the great drama about to open, but that they felt a deep interest in these events that were transpiring, and were prepared to resist the encroachments of the government, and bear their share of the burdens that might fall upon them

At the March meeting in 1770, the town voted that the inhabitants "will forbear the purchasing of Tea and wholly restrain themselves from the use of it, upon which there is a duty laid by the Parliament of Gr. Britian," and also that they will "forbear the purchasing of any goods knowingly, directly or indirectly of any importer or trader until the revenue acts shall be repealed," and a committee was chosen who recommended to the town "to frown upon all who may endeavor to frustrate the good design of the above vote, and to deem all who may at any time counteract it, no better than enemies to our Constitution and Banes to the commonwealth," and "that said town should not for the future knowingly choose any such person or persons into any place of office, either of honor or profit, in said town." The report of the committee was "unanimously" adopted, and the moderator was directed to transmit a copy of the proceedings to the committee of merchants in Boston.

In January, 1773, the town came together "to hear and consider the opinion of the inhabitants of the town of Boston manifested at a legal meeting of the said inhabitants on the 20 Nov. last relating to the rights of the Colonies." And it was voted that the several acts of Parliament pointed out "are subversive and violent infringements of those rights"; "that if peradventure our happy and glorious constitution may be rescued from impending ruin—that our representative in General Assembly should use his utmost influence at all times to recover and support the constitutional rights of the

Province"; that "nothing perhaps of a secular nature more excites our admiration and bespeaks our attention than the vigilence discovered of late by the inhabitants of the town of Boston to do all that in them lies to preserve our constitutional rights inviolate when threatened with destruction."

A committee of five, Elijah Clark, Moses Richardson, Uriah Morse, Daniel Pond, and Captain Jonathan Adams, was chosen to communicate the doings of this meeting to the people of Boston.

In December the town voted "that if any head of a family in this town shall buy any tea or permit any to be used or consumed in his family while subject to duties ought to be viewed as enemies to the Country and will be treated with disrespect by this town — that the selectmen of this town for the time being are directed and desired to withhold and forbear their approbation for inn holders and retailers of strong liquors in this town from all such persons that shall buy use and consume any tea in their houses while subject to duties for the purposes and payable as aforesaid."

In 1774 it is recorded "that there be an addition of 100 pounds of powder, 200 pounds of bullets, and 200 flints to the town stock of ammunition."

"Pursuant to the Precept within written the Freeholders and other Inhabitants of the Town of Medway qualified as is therein directed upon due Warrant given, assembled and met together the 27th Day of Septemr 1774 and did then elect and depute Captn Jonathan Adams to serve for and represent them in the Session or Sessions of the Great and General Court or Assembly, appointed to be convened, held, and kept for His Majesty's Service at the Court-House in Salem, upon Wednesday the Fifth Day of October, 1774: The said Person being chosen by the major Part of the Electors present at said Meeting.

Dated in Medway aforesaid, the 27th Day of Septemr Annoque Domini, 1774.
The person chosen as above said
notified thereof, and summoned
to attend accordingly by me
Asa Partridge Richardson,
      Constable of Medway.

Eleazr Adams Jnr } *Select-Men*
James Penniman } *of Medway.*"
Elijah Clark }

In August the town came together to consider "a letter from a committee of a convention of delegates of the several towns in the County of Suffolk to attend a meeting to be held in Dedham on the 6 of Sept next to deliberate on such matters as the disastrous circumstances of our public affairs may require, and to consult and advise what was prudent to be done at this present alarming situation of affairs," and a committee of five was chosen to attend the meeting. It was also voted to raise "some relief for the poor industrious people of the town of Boston — suffering — being put out of their ordinary business by an act of the British Parliament for blocking up the said harbor." At a meeting in September of this year, there being some doubt as to the legality of electing representatives, a committee of two was chosen to attend a meeting to be held at the house of Captain John Starrs, of Holliston, to confer upon the matter; the town also voted to purchase "two iron field pieces for better security and defence against the attempts or invasion of his Majesties enemies and to choose a committee of three men to procure the said field pieces as soon as may be of such bigness as the committee shall think most proper and to mount the same on carriages fit for execution provided the said

pieces may be had for a reasonable price." These field-pieces were purchased, and caused the town a great deal of trouble, as the next year they appear to have been lost, and much anxiety was manifested for their recovery.
They were probably taken by the troops for the defenses about Boston, and
were not recovered for some years

"At a meeting of the inhabitants of the Town of Medway legally assembled by adjournment the 27th day of Septem^r 1774 —

"The following Instructions being duly considered the s^d Inhabitants,
Voted the same to be Delivered to Capt Jon^a Adams as the rule of his conduct as Representative of the s^d Town in the Gene^rl Assembly:

"To Capt Jon^a Adams Representative of the Town of Medway

Sir, you being Elected to represent this Town in a great & Gen^{al} Court appointed
to be convened, held and kept for his majesty's service at Salim on the 5th day of
Octo^r Inst.

Your Constituents, the Inhabitants of the Town of Medway being sensibly affected
with Divers violent Infringements on our Charter rights and constitution^l Privileges, think it our Duty at this Critical, unhappy situation of Publick affairs, to express to you our sentiments and expectations.

And as we are not acquainted of what Particular Business will be laid Before you
in the General Assembly, Therefore we Expect that you will on all Proper occasions
Exert yourself in opposing all unconstitutional measures and appointments, and in
no way to adhere to any unconstitutional method, Councel or Proceeding.

And as we apprehend, Sir, you are not insensible of the unhappy and Distressed
circumstances of this Province, We depend on your Firm and Steady atteachment
in Promoting all such measures as shall be thought Salutary for the recovery and
Preservation of our Charter^d and Constitutional rights, and also all such measures as
shall be thought conducive to Promote His Majesty's real service and true Interest,
the peace, welfare, and Prosperity of the Province

And Whereas, the Late Convention of several counties having Taken under consideration the Precarious State and unhappy situation of Publick Affairs deem that a
Provincial Congress is Absolutely Necessary.

Therefore we instruct you that if the house of representatives, when assembled
shall deem such a Congress to be Necessary or Expedient and shall form or resolve
themselves into such a Congress that you represent this Town therein, and attend at
such time and place as shall be appointed for that purpose, in Order to Consult and
Determine on such measures as they shall judge will tend to Promote the real and
true interest of his majesty, the peace, good order and Prosperity of this Province.

  True Copy Attest.   Elijah Clark, *Town Cl^r*

                 Medway, August 9 1775

Gent^m

In observance of the Resolve of Congress on the 29 of June last, The Selectmen
of this Town are making Provision for the Coats for the Soldie^{rs} in the Massachusetts Service, and are determined to Supply you with the full Number of 43 Coats set
for this Town's Proportion by the first of Octr Next, Or as Soon as Possibly may be.

            By Order of the Selectmen

                Elijah Clark, *Ck.*

To The Gent Committ of Supplies
 for the Massachusetts forces

In January, 1775, the town voted thirty pounds "to encourage the enlisting of a number of able bodied men to the number of one quarter of the
military soldiers to complete and hold themselves in readiness to march at

the shortest notice"; and each man was allowed nine shillings bounty, and the treasurer was instructed to borrow a sufficient sum of money to meet this expense. These were "minute men," so often mentioned in the history of those times, and who were so prompt to rally at the commencement of hostilities a few months later, and who, raw and undisciplined, and scantily equipped, rose as one man, and taught the British in the first engagements of the war, that brave and loyal hearts beat under their homespun garb, and it was to be no holiday work to subdue a people ready and willing to fight for their homes and their rights.

Two representatives, Jonathan Adams and Moses Adams, were this year chosen to meet with the Provincial Congress at Watertown, in consequence of the "unhappy situation of affairs." They were instructed "on all proper occasions to promote peace and good order and that you will be ready to make suitable provision for the support of civil government and the just constitutional rights of the colony and at the same time oppose all extravagant or oppressive measures and that you promote just measures for a reconciliation between the parent state and the colonies and subserve the real interest, peace and welfare of both."

In the warrant for March meeting, 1776, "His Majesty's Name," in which all warrants heretofore were issued, was omitted, the town calling the meeting on its own responsibility; and the May warrant was issued in the name of the "Government and People of Massachusetts."

In 1776 Elijah Clark was chosen Representative to the General Court at Watertown, and in the instructions given him he is advised that if the "Honorable Continental Congress should for the safety of the colonies declare them independent of Great Britain that we will support them in the measure with our lives and fortunes."

Town Officers for 1776.

Chosen at the Annual Meeting, March 4, 1776, Moses Richardson, Moderator; Elijah Clark, Town Clerk.

CAPTAIN JONATHAN ADAMS, LIEUTENANT MOSES ADAMS, JOSEPH PARTRIDGE, JR., ENSIGN NATHANIEL PARTRIDGE, ENSIGN JOSEPH LOVELL, LIEUTENANT ASA CLARK, CAPTAIN JAMES PENNIMAN, } Selectmen.

SAMUEL HILL, JUN., HENRY ELLIS, AND STEPHEN ADAMS, } Assessors.   HENRY ELLIS, Treasurer.

ELIJAH CLARK, MAJOR JOSIAH FULLER, JOSHUA PEABODY, SIMEON CUTLER, AND JAMES BOYDEN, } Committee of Correspondence, Inspection and Safety.

JOHN WHEELER, GEORGE BARBER, AND AMOS RICHARDSON, } Constables.   STEPHEN CLARK AND NATHANIEL PARTRIDGE, } Wardens.

DANIEL RICHARDSON AND LIEUTENANT MOSES THOMPSON, } Tithingmen.

JOHN MORSE, CAPTAIN JOB PLIMPTON, HENRY DANIELS, CAPTAIN THOMAS METCALF, LIEUTENANTS NATHANIEL CLARK AND ABRAHAM HARDING, } Surveyors of Public Highways.

ELIJAH CLARK, whose name appears frequently in the records, represented the town in the General Court for five years. He was clerk of the town for twenty-four years, and the neat penmanship and methodical manner of his keeping of the books is in marked contrast with some portions of the records. Mr. Clark was a prominent man in the town during the Revolution. His father, Edward Clark, came to Medway in 1710, and built the house, still standing, but as presented here much larger than it was originally.

CLARK HOUSE — ERECTED IN 1710.

The oaken timbers of this dwelling have withstood the storms of one hundred and seventy-five years, and seem stout enough to last as many more. Here Elijah Clark was born in 1727, and succeeded to the farm. He was married to Bathsheba Harding in 1751, and having reared a large family died in 1801, honored and respected, at the age of seventy-four years. This ancient dwelling is now occupied by Putnam R. Clark, Esq. *Vid.* GENEALOGIES.

CAPTAIN JONATHAN ADAMS, who was another prominent man in the town, was born in 1704. He was sent as representative for eleven years, and was on the board of selectmen for fourteen years. He married Patience Clark in 1732, and died in 1804 at the age of ninety-six years.

At the March meeting in 1777, the taxes of the following persons were abated, "In consideration of the suffering and hardnesses endured in the Continental service the year past":

Lieutenant Joshua Gould,	Joel Morse,	Paul Holbrook,
Joshua Bullard,	Jonathan Graves,	Joshua Morse,
Joseph Clark,	John Hill,	Abiel Pratt,
Jonas Brick,	Jotham Ellis,	Ichabod Hawes, Jr.,
Jedediah Phillips,	John Barber,	Samuel Partridge,
David Hager,	Seth Mason,	James Barber,
Simpson Jones,	Jesse Richardson,	John Allen.

Vid. THE WAR OF THE REVOLUTION.

In August, 1779, the Rev. David Sanford was chosen to represent the town in a convention to be held at Cambridge, for the purpose of framing a "constitution and form of government for the state of Massachusetts Bay." The work of this convention was submitted to the town the next year, which in some of its provisions was not satisfactory, and there seems to have been another convention called, as in June, 1780, the town " put to vote to see if it be the minds of this town to choose a man in the name and stead of the Rev. David Sanford to sit in the next convention, and it passed in the negative by a great majority."

THE CURRENCY DEPRECIATED.

The depreciation of the currency during these years of the war may be inferred by the amounts raised, from time to time, for the payment of men and provisions furnished to the army.

In 1778 the town granted the sum of £2,735, 17s., 10d. " for the purpose of making an Everage in this town and to encourage men to engage in the Continental & state service "; in 1779, £4,436, 10s. was raised, and in 1780, £6,466, 13s., and £13,000 to purchase 9,120 pounds of beef, and in 1781 the expenditures of the town for the year before foot up £92,909, 10s., 3d. In one instance the town voted to pay those " who marched & served in the late alarm in Rhode Island," the sum of twenty-five pounds per day for their services. These sums, which in hard money must have rendered the town bankrupt, show us that an irredeemable currency brought the same evils in its train then, as in these days. The war had now lasted for six years; the burden had been bravely borne, but it weighed heavily, especially in the towns where there was but little wealth except in land and the ordinary produce of the farm; money was hard to get, and the difficulty of raising taxes, which to us seem light, required a great amount of self-denial and effort among the sparse population of that time. Draft after draft of the best blood of the town had been called for, and tax after tax paid, but we do not find any signs of faltering or submission, although the future must have looked dark and discouraging.

MEDWAY MAY 6th, 1781.

Rec^d of Capt. Moses Adams by the hand of Ralph Mann the sum of six hundred and fifty one Pounds Ten shillings and six pence in part of the money Produced by his pay-roll to recompence the Militia who march^d for the Defence of Rhode Island at the alarm in July Last.   p^r me   ELIJAH CLARK, *Town Treas.*"
651, 10, 6.

" To the Honr^{ble} the Treas^s of the Common Wealth of Massachusetts

Sir: Please to pay to Elijah Clark Treas^r of the Town of Medway all Such Sum or Sums of money as are or may be allowed and made up to us for wages &c on the pay roll of Capt John Baxter to recompence the Militia for service at Nantaskit in Octr 1782, and this shall be your Discharge for the *sums so paid.*

Witness our hands,   WILLIAM JACKSON,
                                       ELI ELLIS."

MEDWAY, MARCH 24, 1783.

The following report was adopted by the town May 30, 1781:

" The Committee chosen by the Inhabitants of the Town of Medway at their meeting upon adjournment the 22^d Day of May 1781 in order to Instruct Capt. Jonathan Adams the Representative of s^d Town.

And s^d committee being favored with the Instructions of the Town of Weymouth bearing Date Jan^{ry} 20th 1781 and finding them so well calculated and agreeable as to recommend their being adopted by the said Town of Medway with some little variation or alteration as follows viz.

To Capt Jonathan Adams, *Representative of the Town of Medway*

Sᴿ : Much uneasiness hath arisen in the minds of the People from an apprehension that Sums of money have been misspent during the war, and that monies and effects of one kind and another to a great amount are not this day accounted for. Whether these, or the neglect of early taxation, inattention to order and government, mistaken notions of inability or aversion of our enemies to maintain and continue the war, a fluctuating currency or a fluctuating system of politicks, are the causes of many of the misfortunes we have suffered, the evils we feel, and the Burthens arising from extraordinary taxes in quick succession laid upon us demand a serious enquiry and nothing short of an impartial enquiry into the State of our public affairs will satisfy the minds of people and open the way to the reformation of abuses and correction of errors It is therefore expected that you will use your utmost endeavours that no pains be spared to bring public defaulters to justice and that every measure that human wisdom can devise and known justice support be persued for restoring the public credit, removing the complaints of the injured and for conducting public Business with order, despatch economy and firmness so as to give dignity to government and content to the people and in a particular manner that all militia naval, or other military officers who have been intrusted with public money for expeditions or any other military purposes, committees for erecting powder mills, fortifications, building of vessels, of sequestration of purchases, for the sale of forfeited estates or of whatever name or denomination, treasurers of the board of war, commissioners, Agents of all sorts in short that all persons intrusted with public moneys, be required to account for them.

If upon reasonable notice given and a proper time allowed, they should refuse or neglect to account · that without favor or partiality, they be prosecuted, and that those who have been negligent in their public trusts be dismissed, and those guilty of fraud be punished with infamy. A steady and determined pursuit of such measures will do much to remedy our evils and render the government respectable, but they fall very short of a radical cure if similar measures be not adopted by Congress It is necessary, therefore, that the Delegates to Congress be instructed immediately to enter upon this just and necessary work, and officially to demand of their foreign ministers, commissioners and agents a faithful account of their management of public business and expence of public money, and that no character, however great, be screen'd from public scrutiny. Instruct the Delegates to insist on this and not to give over till they have fully accomplished the end proposed.

You will also use your endeavors that a remonstrance be made to Congress against the establishment of half pay to the Continental Officers after they are dismissed the Service, and disapprove of every such measure in this Common-Wealth, as it is a measure unreasonable, partial, and pernicious in its consequences. Have they not been promised large tracts of Land at the expiration of the war as an encouragement of their perseverance and as a future reward for their services? Have not the Militia officers accompanied them in their campaigns, fought by their Sides, and Shed their blood with them? Have not many of these sustained equal dangers and done equal Services, and for whom no pension is provided, nor one farthing for the Depreciation of their wages has been allowed? Have the Continental Officers been kept out of their just due? Have they not been supported equal to their merit? If not, let justice be done them. To this we willingly bind our estates But privileg'd officers with pay for life either civil or military, are repugnant to every Idea of a well regulated Common-Wealth, and have been found to introduce corruption, idleness, and luxury, discontent and factions In short pensions are the entering wedge to the ruin of a State, and we need not look further than that country once fondly called our mother country to read our own fate. Her pensioned tribes have already swarmed like the locusts of Egypt, and like them will devour the land

It is with extreme sorrow that we hear of the continental soldiers not being furnished with the clothing that has been provided for them, until they are almost naked, and the clothing almost rotten. Does this arise from the negligence of the General Court, of Agents or delinquency of Towns, or from what cause needs an immediate enquiry · also whether a less expensive and more certain method of procuring clothing, than levying them upon Towns cannot be adopted? Whether the late mode of laying fines on Towns for delinquencies will not in most instances operate directly contrary to the end designed? And in some be productive of great injustice to Individuals are questions worthy of consideration.

As a member of the General Court and as a friend to liberty truth and justice you will bear testimony against all public proceedings inconsistent with either, and endeavour that the Government be cautious in promising, faithful in performing, and at no time assume the power of postponing the performance or altering the nature of a promise, at will and pleasure.

You are too sensible of the importance of virtue and good manners, to the well being of a Common-Wealth to need our urging your utmost endeavours for the encouragement of these, and that every rational method be adopted by Government for suppressing profligacy of manners, extravagance in dress, luxury and dissipation, vice and immorality too much reigning amongst us.

We apprehend that among other measures the laying an Excise on Spirituous liquors and impost Duties, especially on articles of luxury and Superfluity will contribute to this end as well as to render the frequency of Taxes less necessary.

Your abilities and integrity leave us no room to doubt of your Strenuous endeavours to promote the public good: to support you in the exercise of them is the aim of these instructions, and may Heaven crown all your endeavours with success."

" The foregoing instructions being diligently read and duly considered were passed in the affirmative."

"*Attest,* DANIEL POND, *Moderator.*"

COMMISSION OF THEODORE CLARK, GENT^m.

Commonwealth ⎫
    of ⎬
Massachusetts. ⎭

BY HIS EXCELLENCY
JOHN HANCOCK, ESQ.,

Governor and Commander in chief in and over the Commonwealth of Massachusetts.

To THEODORE CLARK Gent^n, Greeting.

[SEAL.] You being appointed second Lieutenant of a company commanded by Capt. John Ellis in the Fourth Regiment of Militia in the County of Suffolk in said Commonwealth whereof Laban Mann Esqr is Colonel.

By virtue of the Power vested in me I do by these Presents (reposing special Trust and Confidence in your Loyalty Courage and good conduct) commission you accordingly,— You are therefore carefully and diligently to discharge the Duty of 2d Lieut. in leading, ordering and exercising said Company in Arms, both inferior Officers and Soldiers; and to keep them in good Order and Discipline. And they are hereby commanded to obey you as their 2^d Lieut. and you are yourself to observe and follow such Orders and Instructions as you shall from Time to Time receive from me or your superior officers.

Given under my hand and the seal of the said Commonwealth the First day of July in the Year of our LORD 1781, in the fifth Year of the Independence of the United States of America.

               (Signed)

                              JOHN HANCOCK.

By His Excellency's Command,
  JOHN AVERY jun. *Sec^y.*

In 1782 the town instructed its Representative, Moses Adams, as follows: " That he use his influence that the General Court lessen the prices of salary men and days' men that draw pay from the state at this day of public calamity, so that the people may not have just reason to complain of oppression, and that all persons not absolutely necessary for managing the affairs of this state that are paid by the government be dismissed, so that such heavy burthens by reason of such immense taxes laid upon this commonwealth to support the administration be relinquished. Your constituents advise to use your influence that a law be made to restrain the attorneys in our commonwealth from demanding excessive fees, and that the General Court be removed out of Boston into some other town . . . that there may be an immediate settlement made with the treasurer of this commonwealth, and all other public boards . . . and that for future there be a descriptive list transmitted to the several towns in this commonwealth annually giving a just account of the state of the treasury."

Scattered through the records of this period, and especially during the war, whole pages are filled with notices to strangers to depart out of the town, in order to prevent their gaining a settlement and thus possibly adding to the burdens of taxation for the support of poor, of which the following is a specimen:

"Whereas we have been informed that Job Puffer and Cloe Puffer came into this town some time in the month of November last from Wrenthan, and as we find ourselves unwilling to admit the said persons as inhabitants of this town — therefore in the name of the commonwealth you are hereby required forthwith to warn the said Job Puffer and Cloe Puffer to depart and leave this town within fourteen days, or give security to the selectmen to indemnify and save the town from all charges that may happen to accrue to the town by any means or cause of their continuing their residence here."

Signed by the selectmen and directed to Abijah Fairbanks, Constable.

In 1783 the town voted:

"If the absentees who have left this or any of the United States with their own particular interest therein, and sought to take protection under the British arms which invaded the same, and who have since the commencement of the late war joined or in any way assisted the British forces in destroying or subduing this or any part of the United States, ought to be prevented from returning, or possessing their own estates again from which they fled, and that sd absentees, being rightly termed conspirators and traitors ought to be wholly excluded the right or privilege of inhabitancy or residence in this or any of the United States of America for the future."

Great dissatisfaction appears to have existed in reference to the acts of Congress in granting half pay to the officers of Continental army and laying an impost on the states for this purpose, which they consider " a real grievance in its nature and unconstitutional." The instructions to the representative for this year, which are recorded in the clear and careful hand-writing of Elijah Clark, town clerk, were as follows:

"The Inhabitants of the Town of Medway. At a Legal Town Meeting held on adjournment the 28th day of May A. D. 1783

Voted, that the following Instruction be given to the Representative of this Town for his rule of Conduct in the General Court the Ensuing year viz.

To Capt. Moses Adams

Sir, Notwithstanding the Confidence this Town has placed in your Integrity and Abilities to Represent them in the General Court the Ensuing year and having no cause to Suspect your attachment to the Interest of this Town and the Prosperity and Welfare of this Commonwealth in General. Yet your constituents viewing the present Situation of Public Affairs think themselves in Duty bound to Express to you their Sentiments for the Regulation of your Conduct, Relating to the following Subjects viz. While we place Our attention to the Late Treaty we cannot but feel ourselves much concerned for the event of the 5th Article, which Respects those persons who have not Only fled from this Country when the Liberties thereof were Invaded, But also have Taken Protection under the Armes that Invaded the Same, and united their whole Efforts in Subjugating this Country and their Own fellow Citizens to their Cruel unnatural Designs. And being Apprehensive that Persons who have Exerted all their Power and Malice to overturn our Government Can never again make peaceable Subjects in it And without mentioning Every Perticular Objection which might be offerrd against the return of these persons who are Described by the Laws of this Commonwealth as Conspirators and Absentees and being fully convinced of the Dangerous Consequences which will attend the admitting them to regain their forfeitd estates, or place of Residence within this Commonwealth. We instruct you to use your Endeavours by all Proper means to prevent any Person of the aforesaid Description from Ever Returning to this State, or Regaining their justly forfeited Estates within this Commonwealth

Whereas it appears that by some means or other an undue Proportion of the Continental Old Bills of Credit have been Entroduced into this Commonwealth, whereby the Publick and Individuals of this State have Sufferd great Damages and Disappointments by reason that the sd Bills have not been Redeemed or Exchanged by the United States,

Therefore, that you use your Endeavours at all Proper Occasions that Some measures may be Adopted and Prosecuted which will Effect the Exchange or Redemption of the sd Bills on Some Just Principle, by the united States as Soon as may be.

That you Exert yourself at the most Early and favorable opportunity that shall Present To Revive a Petition Preferd to the General Court in 1781 By the Agents of a number of Towns in the Counties of Suffolk and middlesix Praying that a New County may be incorporated and to use your Endeavours that the prayer thereof may be Granted.

We Earnestly Recommend to you the greatest Economy and frugality with regard to the Expenditure of Publick monies and that you Oppose all Extravigrant unreasonable Grants, Salaries and half pay to the continental officers.

Attest   ELIJAH CLARK *Town Clk* "

The tax-list for 1783 fills a manuscript of fourteen pages about eight inches square, and contains the names of 216 residents and 98 non-residents. The poll-tax is 2s., 6d. ; the largest real estate tax-payers were Captain Joseph Lovell, £1, 3s., 8d. ; Asa P. Richardson, £1, 2s., 9d., and Nathaniel Lovell, £1, 0s., 8d.

MEDWAY ONE HUNDRED YEARS AGO.

" COPPY OF THE DESCRIPTION OF ye TOWN COMPOSED BY Mr BUCKNAM & HENRY ELLIS, 1785.

" Medway was Set off from medfield Containing all that was medfield on ye West Side of Charls River Bounded East & South on Charles river Southwest on Bellingham, West on Holliston & north on Sherburn till it comes to Charls river first mentioned.

" The Town in Length is about 6 miles & in Bredth on an Everage is about 3 miles & ½. The Surface of ye Town rough & unsightly By reason of woods & Swamps, that are Uncultivated & one Especially in ye Center of ye Town more than a mile from East to west & about 3 miles from North to South. & as for the Soil where it is Cleared Tolerable Grazing for Cattle & where menured Produces Plentiful Crops of Grain many Times more than is sufficient for ye Inhabitants. The air is clear & Healthy the Inhabitants Subsist Chiefly upon Husbandry. Buildings, Contains 2 meeting houses & about

137 Dwelling houfes, none Very Eligant But in Common Comfortable Habi-
tations, 144 other Buildings of Several Denom^{on}. N^{o}. of Inhabitants about
850. Divifions, the Town is Divided into 2 Parrifhes of ye Congregational Denominations. N^{o} of Births Deaths & marriages in ye Town of medway annually for 6 years paft upon an Everage are 22 Births 6 Deaths & 12 marriages,
Mills 4 Grift mills 5 Saw mills & one fulling Mill, 2 Grift mills & 2 Saw
mills on Charls river 2 Grift mills & 2 Saw mills on Boggeftow, and one
Saw mill on Chicking Brook So Called. Roads One a Country road Extending from Eaft to weft Called ye middle road from Bofton to Hartford,
& a County road Extending from South to North Leading to watertown &
the Eaftward parts. The Town of medway from the Center of s^{d} Town is
25 miles from Bofton & Lyeth Nearly Southweft from ye Town, & is in
ye County of Suffolk."

"DESCRIPTION of MEDWAY,
MR. BUCKNAM
Draft by E Clark, 1786 "

In 1787 Moses Richardson was chosen to represent the town in the General Court and his compensation was fixed at 4s., 6d per day, and he was directed to " deliver to the treasurer for the use of the town all sums he may
receive from the public treasury for his services, above that amount "

In the year 1789, by the perambulation of the line between Medway and
Holliston, it appears that it ran in a westerly direction from near the house of
Henry Bullard through Winthrop Pond, and across the road leading from
West Medway to Holliston, to a heap of stones in Ash Swamp, and then
southerly to Charles River ; Holliston bounding it on the north and west, this
included a considerable tract on the north now in Holliston, and left out about
as much, which is now in Medway, on the west. An exchange was made,
and the present boundary line between Medway and the town of Holliston
was established March 3, 1829. The boundary between Medway, Bellingham, and Franklin was straightened February 23, 1832 ; and March 13, 1839,
the boundary between Medway and the town of Franklin was changed ; and
February 23, 1870, a part of Medway was taken to constitute the new town
of Norfolk.

In 1792 a portion of Franklin was set off to this town, including what is
now known as Deanville, and the next year the estates of Peter Bullard and
Abner Mason, formerly a part of Sherborn, were added to Medway, and
March 3, 1792, the present boundary line between the two towns was established

The present Norfolk County was constituted March 22, 1793. The act
was approved March 26, 1793, by JOHN HANCOCK, Governor

The towns included were Bellingham, Braintree, Brookline, Cohasset,
Dedham, Dorchester, Dover, Foxborough, Franklin, Hingham, Hull, Med-
field, Medway, Milton, Needham, Quincy, Randolph, Roxbury, Sharon,
Stoughton, Walpole, Weymouth, and Wrentham.

Originally, May 10, 1643, the Colony of Massachusetts Bay was divided
into four counties, viz.: Essex, Middlesex, Suffolk, and Norfolk. The latter embraced the towns of Haverhill, Salisbury, Hampton, Exeter, Dover, and
Portsmouth, the last four were set off to New Hampshire in 1680 ; the other
towns were afterward included in Essex County, so that February 4, 1680,
the original Norfolk County in Massachusetts, ceased to exist.

The warrants of 1794 define the qualifications for voting for state officers to be, a residence in the state one year, twenty-one years of age, having an estate, the annual income of which is three pounds, or any estate of the value of sixty pounds ; and for town affairs, such as pay a single tax besides a poll, equal to two-thirds of the poll-tax.

Federal money began to appear on the records, and in the year 1795 the town expenditures were put down in dollars, cents, and mills, and thereafter pounds, shillings, and pence, disappeared from the books.

In 1795 the town directed the selectmen to set up guide-posts in accordance with an act of the Legislature, and the price for labor on the highways was fixed at six cents an hour for a man or a good team.

In one of the warrants for 1803, an article " to see if the town will give their suffrage for a turnpike road to be laid out through said town " was dismissed. This was the Hartford Turnpike built some two or three years after, running from Medfield meadows westerly the whole length of the town, nearly in a direct line. It was deemed a most important undertaking, and its construction was watched with as much, perhaps more, interest than the building of a railroad would now excite. It has proved a great convenience to the town, but the hopes of its projectors in regard to its financial results were doomed to disappointment and failure. It was used as a turnpike until about 1835, when it became a town way and has since been supported as other highways are.

The following petition was addressed to the selectmen with the view of constituting the two parishes of the town into one :

" MEDWAY, APRIL 6th 1803."

" To The Selectmen of Medway,"

" Gentlemen : Please to Insert an Article in your warrant for your next Town Meeting, viz :

To see if the East and West Parrishes of our said Town of Medway will agree to be formed into one distinct Town " (i. e. Parish) " or act any thing on the Subject as the said two Parrishes shall think proper.

In doing which you will oblege your

Humle Servts.

(Signed) Nathaniel Lovell, Ezekiel Plimpton, Simpson Jones, Stephen Clark, Ebenezer Ellis, Jeduthan Bullen, Elisha Fisher, Elijah Bridges, Sylvanus Adams."

This matter, as subsequently appears, had been under discussion for the past ten years in town-meetings, and various committees were appointed from time to time, to report to the town, but still the two parishes continued to remain distinct and separate.

In Pursuance to an " Act of the General Court of the Common Wealth of Massachusetts, for regulating elections. The following is an alphabitical list of the Inhabitants of the Town of Medway, as appear to the Subscribers, by the Valuation of said Town, to be Quallified by the Constitution of said Common Wealth, and of the United States, to Vote for Governor, Lieut. Governor, Senator, Representatives in General Court, & Representatives in Congress, viz :

A.	Hezekiah Adams	John Abbee	Oliver Adams
	Eliakim Adams	Jonathan Adams	Silvanus Adams
Nathaniel Allen	Moses Adams	Micah Adams	Jasper Adams
Ezra Adams	Aaron Adams	Silas Adams	Elijah Allen
Obediah Adams	Amos B. Abbee	Moses Adams Jur	Horatio Adams

B.	Jeremiah Daniels 3ᵈ	I.	Darius Partridge
	Elias Daniels		Ziba Partridge
Moses Bullen	Moses Daniels	Daniel Ide	Joseph Partridge
Mathia Bullard		Daniel Ide Jur	Moses Pond Junr
Joseph Barber			Nathan Plimpton
Joseph Barber Junr	E.	J.	
Isaac Bullard			R.
George Barber	Oliver Ellis	Simpson Jones	
Seneca Barber	Ebenezar Ellis	Nathan Jones	Simeon Richardson
George Barber, Jur	John Ellis		Ezra Richardson
Jeduthan Bullen	John Ellis Junr	K.	Elisha Richardson
Liberty Bullard	Henry Ellis Junr		Amos Richardson
Timothy Bullard	Henry Ellis	Isaac Kibbey	Abijah Richardson
Ralph Bullard	Samuel Ellis	Zebina Kingsbury	Abijah Richardson Jr
Jonathan Bullen	Moses Ellis		Joseph Richardson
Adam Bullard		L.	Asa P. Richardson
Elijah Bridges	F.		Prince Royal
Amos Bullard		David Lawrence	Moses Richardson
David Bullen	William Feltt	Joseph Lovell	Moses Rockwood
	Moses Feltt	Nathaniel Lovell	Moses Rockwood Jur
C.	Joel Fisk	Thaddeus Lovering	Amos Richardson Jur
	Silas Fairbank	Peter Lewitt	Artemus Richardson
Elisha Cutler	Elihu Fisher	Amos Lovering	Aaron Rockwood
Nathaniel Cutler			Amos Rockwood
Simon Cutler	G.	M.	Marcus Richardson
Simon Cutler Junr			
Samuel Clark	James Gibbs	Thomas Morse	S.
Asa Clark	William Greene	Ralph Mann	
Timothy Clark		Benoni Morse Jur	Jabez Shumway
Theodore Clark	H.	Luther Metcalf	Philo Santford
Joseph Clark		Abner Morse	Timothy Smith
Samuel Cleaveland	Theodore Harding	Abner Mason	
Calvin Cutler	Joel Haws	Simon H. Mason	T.
Stephen Clark	Reuben Hixson		
John Clark Jur	John Harding Jur	N.	Nathan Thayer
Phillips Clark	Timothy Hill		Amos Turner
	Thomas Harding	Joseph Newell	Hezelton Tafft
D.	Stephen Harding		Samuel Twiss
	Moses Hill	P.	Aaron Thayer
Henry Daniels	Isaac Hixson		
Lemuel Daniels	Seth Hixson	Elijah Partridge	W.
Asa Daniels	Asa Hixson	Ezekiel Plimpton	
Asa Daniels Jur	Samuel Hill	Simeon Partridge	Elias Whiting
Israel Daniels	Abram Harding	Job Plimpton	Joseph Ware
Amos Daniels	Simon Hill	Jedediah Phillips	James Wight
Henry Daniels Jur	Timothy Hammond	Ezekiel Partridge	Lewis Wheeler
Sabin Daniels	Asa Harding	Joel Partridge	Timothy Whiting
Jesse Daniels	Reuben Hill	Samuel Partridge	Aaron Wight
Jeremiah Daniels Jur	Abner Holbrook	Seth Partridge	Comfirt Walker
			Joshua Whiting

MEDWAY, December 12ᵗʰ 1804.   THEODORE CLARK, } *Assessors*
JABEZ SHUMWAY, } *of*
LEWIS WHEELER, } *Medway.*

Gentlemen: Selectmen of the Town of Medway."

In 1805 Ezekiel Plimpton petitioned the town that liberty might be granted to the owners of land to set out and cultivate various kinds of trees along the highways against their own premises. This article was referred to another meeting and dismissed. Mr. Plimpton was a hundred years in advance of his time. If his plan had been adopted, we should to-day be enjoying great benefits.

It was in 1805 that the limits of the school districts were defined, and the districts were numbered from one to six.

A survey was made in October, 1806, by Samuel Bullard, Esq., with a view to the division of the town. The new town was to include the westerly part of Medway, *i e.*, the New Grant, also parts of Bellingham, Holliston, and Franklin, 10,310 acres in area. On the basis of this survey Job Plimpton and others petitioned for a division of the town ; a committee to whom the matter was referred, reported in 1807 that they "are of opinion that the great and heavy expense which would fall on the remaining part of the town, by reason of the great number of bridges over Charles River which falls into that part of the said town, are powerful objections against the division, also the limited situation, both as to territory and population of that part of the town which is to remain being unable and thereby being deprived for a great number of years, if not forever, of any representation in the legislature." Not being able to separate, the next year an effort was made to consolidate the two parishes and build a church in the centre of the town, and in 1809 a committee was chosen, who reported that they had located the centre of the town "on the westerly side of Black Swamp on land of Thomas Wight, 132 rods due north from the turnpike road." This was not a satisfactory place, and several other spots east and west of this were proposed, and the matter was adjourned from meeting to meeting for a year or two, and finally dropped until 1813, when it was taken up and a committee of thirteen, after carefully examining the subject, reported that "we are of the opinion that the two societies should unite" and recommended the building of a meeting-house "on the rising ground which is on the land of Timothy Hammond and the Widow Bathsheba Clark's dower, south of the Hartford and Dedham turnpike, and southerly of the centre of said town," and that the town should petition the General Court to be incorporated as one parish, and that the town should purchase of the society in the west parish any material which had been provided for a new house there. On the 24th of May the town, in accordance with this report, voted to build on a site near that selected by the committee, but after reconsideration in two or three adjourned meetings the whole matter seems to have been dismissed.

In 1814 the town voted not to send a representative to the legislature "by reason of the town being at great expense by building meeting-houses, and also for an additional number of poor newly thrown upon the town." A vote was also passed "that all soldiers who shall be called into the United States service the present year shall receive from the town such a sum as with their pay will amount to sixteen dollars per month."

It had been the custom to choose two tithing men annually, but in 1815 four were chosen, and the following vote passed :

" Whereas the profanation of the Lord's Day by many inconsiderate persons has become notorious and is incompatible with a due regard to the christian sabbath, it being the ardent wish of this town that the tything men should use their vigilant exertions in order to put a stop to all unnecessary traveling on the Sabbath, and in all things cause the laws for the due observance of the Lord's Day to be duly executed according to the tenor and intent of their solemn oath."

The practice of choosing tithing men at the March meeting continued until the year 1845. Samuel Force and Anson F. White being the last incumbents of that office.

In 1818 the town voted "hereafter to hold the town meetings two out of every three years at the east parish and one year in the west parish also voted that it is expedient to build a convenient house for the holding of town meetings and for the storage of the town ammunition." A parish house, as it was called, was soon after built in each part of the town where town-meetings were afterwards held. In 1823, voted to hold the meetings alternately in East and West Medway; this was continued until 1842 when it was decided to hold the meetings every third year at the Village, as is the custom at the present time.

A Subscription for Bunker Hill Monument.

"Bunker Hill Monument Association.

Received of Mr. Joseph L. Richardson *One hundred fourteen &* $\frac{25}{100}$ Dollars, being the amount subscribed in the town of Medway toward the erection of a Monument on Bunker Hill.

114 $\frac{25}{100}$

   (Signed)   For Nathl. D. Russell, Treasurer.

                                         Isaac C. Brewer.

Boston, 30th May, 1825."

Previous to 1826 the few town paupers had been boarded by individuals at the expense of the town, but the increasing number of them led to the appointment of a board of overseers of the poor, and a committee was chosen to select a farm suitable for accommodating the poor of the town; and the same year the "old poor farm" on Farm Street, now occupied by Mr. Edward O'Donnell, was purchased and used for that purpose until 1865.

THE ALMSHOUSE. 1865-1885.

It appears that a reliable keeper was hired and an elaborate code of regulations was adopted, by which nothing stronger than beer or cider was to be allowed the inmates; no inmate could leave the place without permission from the master; fires and lights were to be extinguished by nine o'clock in the evening; no inmate was allowed to find fault with the master except to the overseers; a reasonable amount of labor was required of such as were able, and a " room of correction " was provided where transgressors were confined on a diet of bread and water.

For almost forty years the town's poor were provided with a comfortable home on these highlands of Medway, overlooking all parts of the town, and having a view of more distant landscapes, and enjoying a scenery nowhere surpassed in the region.

Afterward one of the finest residences at that time in the town was purchased in 1865, at an expense of nearly ten thousand dollars, as a home for the poor. It was located on the ancient homestead of Joseph Lovell, Esq., who for many years was the most prominent and honored citizen of the town. The dwelling-house was comparatively new, and near it stood, as sentinels, several majestic elms of more than a century's growth. These are still standing in vigorous life, and continue to give their own peculiar charm to the place, which is owned by Professor C. W. Emerson, M. D., Principal of the Monroe Conservatory of Oratory, in Boston. The house is being fitted up for a private residence, and will doubtless become one of the most attractive in the new town of Millis. Dr. Emerson has devoted the farm to the production of milk and stock.

In 1831 the time of the sitting of the legislature was changed to January, and, in consequence, the annual election of state officers and representatives took place in November. The observance of Election Day on the last Wednesday of May, which had heretofore been kept as a holiday, after this gradually fell into disuse. The next year a board of health was chosen on account of the prevalence of the cholera, and vigorous sanitary measures were adopted; the dwellings and surroundings of citizens were inspected, cellars cleaned out, offal removed, and measures that it would have been wise to have continued, were taken to ward off the dreaded scourge. Fortunately, very few cases occurred in this vicinity.

By act of Congress in 1836, the surplus revenue in the treasury was ordered to be distributed to the several states in proportion to the number of electors to which each was entitled. The amount received by Massachusetts was divided among the towns, and it was voted by this town that its share should be invested and the income devoted to educational purposes, and Warren Lovering, Luther Metcalf, Joseph L. Richardson, James Lovering, and Eleazar Daniels were chosen to take charge of it, and at a following meeting they reported that about three-quarters of the amount expected had been received, amounting to $2,560.31, and that this was all, probably, that would be received, and this amount had been loaned to individuals secured by mortgage and the interest applied as voted by the town. This arrangement was continued until 1843, when the larger part of it was used to pay the town debt.

In 1840 the expense for the support of the poor was unusually large, owing to some special expenditures that were deemed necessary, and the overseer of the poor recommended "that hereafter a detailed account of the expense of the poor be drawn up and printed for the use of the tax-payers," and at the meeting following it was voted " that the accounts of the select-men be included in the foregoing, and that a copy be furnished to each voter on the first of March."

THE FIRST PRINTED TOWN REPORT.

" EXPENSES OF THE TOWN OF MEDWAY, FOR THE YEAR ENDING FEBRUARY 25, 1841.

Expenditures and Receipts connected with the support of the Poor at the Alms House for the year ending February 13, 1841.

Expenditures.

For Grain............................	$36 43
" Flour and Bread................	17 06
" Butter and Cheese............	45 95
" Sugar and Molasses...........	20 39
" Coffee and Tea.................	21 36
" Fresh and Salt Meat..........	41 65
" Fresh and Salt Fish...........	15 35
" Potatoes........................	19 05
" Cider, Vinegar and Apples....	9 46
" Clothing and Shoes...........	49 50
" Sundries........................	40 13
" Grass and Garden Seeds......	11 01
" Pasturing and Grass..........	24 07
" Neat Stock.....................	108 00
" Swine...........................	10 05
" Blacksmith work...............	5 92
" Farming Utensils..............	8 12
" Repairs of Buildings..........	7 49
" Labor and Team Work........	9 16
" Sawyers Bill....................	9 23
" Medical Attendance...........	8 30
" Salary of J. Gould, Keeper....	215 00
" Services of Overseers.........	21 00
	$753 68

Receipts and Credits.

For Neat Stock....................	$23 25
" Swine	12 50
" Beef............................	25 91
" Pork and Lard.................	6 57
" Fowls...........................	4 46
" Knitting and Straw Braid.....	8 88
" Sundry Articles...............	13 31
" Lumber.........................	15 61
" Labor and Team Work.........	53 52
" State for support of Pauper....	2 17
	$166 18

Whole Expense of Poor..........$587 50

Amount due to sundry persons prior to March 1, 1840..........	543 45
Interest on the same.............	19 20
	$562 65

Amount due from sundry persons prior to March 1, 1840, considered good..................	$59 17

Leaving a balance due of.........$503 48

Agreeable to a vote of the Town the subscribers herewith present a Statement of the Poor House Expenditures and Receipts for the last year, and also the amount due prior to that time, which we believe to be substantially correct.

All which is respectfully submitted.

NATHAN HARDING,
SILAS RICHARDSON.

Expense of Schools.

Paid for District No. 1	$214 50
" " " " 2..	270 06
" " " " 3..	86 62
" " " " 4..	236 06
" " " " 5..	142 52
" " " " 6..	106 33
" " " " 7..	201 14
" " " " 8..	124 39
" S. H. Mason and Son................	6 33 $1,387 95

Expense of Town Officers.

Paid J. L. Richardson, Collector for 1839...................	$28 59
" J. L. Richardson, Collector for 1840...................	32 26
" A. Cole, Selectman, 1840..	10 00
" Jos. Adams, " "..	7 00
" O. Mason, " "..	5 00
" Assessors, "..	130 86
" School Committee "..	45 00
" " " 1839 .	64 00
	$322 71

Miscellaneous Expenses.

Paid for		1,941 feet of Plank for Bridges...............	$33 78
"	"	270 feet of Timber for Bridges	11 16
"	"	Labor on Bridges.....	21 74
"	"	Labor on Roads........	1 25
"	"	Bridge Materials, including Irons..............	10 15
"	"	Labor repairing Milford road....	11 35
"	"	Building a Bridge on said road...................	26 50
"	"	Expenses of repairs of West road............	623 00
"	"	Expenses of repairs of East road..............	243 75
"	"	Building Stone Bridge, &c. by S. Cutlers....	157 00
"	"	Building a temporary Bridge, by A. Daniel's saw-mill	34 67
"	"	School Books..........	30 76
"	"	2 Guide Boards.........	1 00
"	"	Discount on Taxes......	159 48
"	"	Military Services.......	25 00

Paid for		Repairs on Turnpike road....................	$16 00
"	"	Interest on Money accruing against the town	132 00
"	"	Expenses of borrowing said money and paying Interest..............	9 00
"	"	Court Fees on 2 Indictments......	22 78
"	"	Taxes abated on W. Cushing's 2 bills......	7 33
"	"	Taxes abated on J. L. Richardson's 4 bills...	56 90
"	"	services and labor on Turnpike road in 1839	15 75
"	"	Printing Town Expenses &c	7 50
			$1,657 85
			$3,368 51

All of which is submitted.

JOSEPH ADAMS, ⎱ Selectmen.
ORION MASON, ⎰

Medway, Feb. 25, 1841."

THE TOWN REPORT OF EXPENSES above, was printed on a single sheet and distributed in accordance with the foregoing vote.

It was found so convenient that two years later, in 1843, there was a town report, still more in detail, issued for the first time by an auditor appointed to examine and certify to the accounts of the different boards of town officers. The auditor for that year, and several years following, was Christopher Slocomb; the charge made by him for service was four dollars per annum. The bill for printing three hundred copies was six dollars.

From so small a beginning, the auditor's annual report has grown from year to year to its present elaborate form, which includes a statement of the whole receipts and expenditures of the town, together with reports and statements from the different departments of the town administration, births, marriages, and deaths, and numerous other matters interesting to the citizens.

In 1844 a proposal was made that the towns of Medway and Franklin should replace, by one of stone, the bridge leading over Charles River at the Village, near the Medway cotton manufactory; the existing bridge being insecure, and from its position a difficult one to maintain. As this necessarily involved very great expense, it met with considerable opposition, but the town finally decided to build a stone arch bridge of thirty-six feet span, just below the location of the old one. The next year a plan having been made by Mr. Whiting, and proposals called for, the estimated cost, $6,000, was so great that the subject was for a time postponed. In 1846 it was taken up, and the selectmen were directed to contract for the building of the bridge, provided it could be done for the sum of $4,000. This proved to be an unwise restriction which eventually involved the towns in considerable additional expense, as the structure was not firm enough, and in a short time partially fell down. In 1847 it was rebuilt in a more thorough manner, and still stands, and bids fair to be permanent.

In 1845 it began to be evident that the population and size of the villages in town imperatively demanded a fire department, the means of subduing fires being exceedingly primitive and inefficient; and a committee was chosen to take the matter into consideration, but the necessary expense involved caused considerable delay. An account of the formation of this department may be found in another place.

November, 1853, " Voted that the town clerk be authorized to deposit in the library of the Massachusetts Historical Society for preservation a volume of the Old Colony Laws commencing July 19 1775 the same containing 207 pages to be kept by said society for said town and subject to the order of said town at any future time." In 1855 it was voted that the above volume be deposited in the State Library for preservation.

The progress of the town is indicated by the following report of a committee in 1857 : " The public good requires a lock-up, or some place for confinement of disturbers of the peace, and your committee recommend that the town authorize the selectmen to procure some suitable place for the same and fit the same up in a convenient manner."

This year the state was divided into representative districts. Medway was in the Twelfth Norfolk District, which included also the towns of Foxboro, Wrentham, and afterwards Norfolk, and was entitled to send two representatives. In 1876 the state was re-districted, and Medway was in the Eighth Norfolk District, which included also the towns of Foxboro, Wrentham, Franklin, and Bellingham, and sent two representatives.

The record of the town in the great War of the Rebellion will be found elsewhere. The 29th of April, 1861, a town-meeting was called " To see if the town will adopt measures to raise and equip a military company for the service of the government and to raise and appropriate any sums of money necessary for that purpose." This meeting was a large and enthusiastic one; a military committee was chosen to furnish needful supplies for soldiers, and to provide for the families of those who enlisted.

During the four years of the war the town furnished its quota of troops as they were called for. Money was freely voted and expended, leaving the town at its close with a debt of about $30,000.

In 1865, the old almshouse having become too small for the accommodation of the poor, it was proposed to build a new one of sufficient size to accommodate the present and prospective needs of the town, and the board of overseers were authorized to procure a plan and provide materials for such a house; but before this was carried out it was thought best to dispose of the old farm and purchase a new one. Committees were chosen and lengthy reports made which resulted, finally, in the purchase of a suitable place.

In 1865 a code of by-laws containing directions for the government of town-meetings, police regulations, the collection of taxes, and other matters connected with the administration of town affairs, was adopted, printed, and circulated among the voters of the town ; this was afterward superseded by the present code, adopted in 1871.

In 1867 the streets of the town were named and copied into the records ;

and all streets and ways laid out since that time have received a name at the time of their acceptance by the town.

In 1868 a committee consisting of Granville E. McCullum, A. S. Harding, William Daniels, M. M. Fisher, D. A. Partridge, Amos H. Boyd, and W. P. Clarke, made a report recommending the erection of a monument to the memory of the soldiers from this town who fell in the war, to stand in or near Oakland Cemetery in the Village, and that the sum of $3,500 be granted for that purpose. This report was accepted, but no further action has been taken by the town.

In the latter part of 1868 a fire occurred which consumed the town clerk's office. The records were saved with the exception of a portion of the births, marriages, and deaths, which have since been copied from the lists at the State House in Boston. The library of the town was destroyed, but has since been replaced by a donation from the State of such law reports and documents as were lost.

The Warrant for the March Meeting 1871, contained the following article, viz. :

"To see what action the Town will take in regard to the code of By-Laws which were presented to them at the last November meeting by a Committee appointed for that purpose, or act any matter or thing concerning the same."

On which article the following action was taken, viz.:

Voted to accept the Report of the Committee as amended.
Voted to adopt the Report of the Committee as amended.

A true copy of Record, Attest: GEO. P. METCALF,
NORFOLK, SS. TOWN CLERK.
Approved. Superior Court, Sept. 7, 1871.
LINCOLN F. BRIGHAM,
C. J. S. Court.

A true copy of the By-Laws as approved.
Attest: ERASTUS WORTHINGTON, CLERK.

RULES AND BY-LAWS.

ADOPTED APRIL 3d, 1871.

ARTICLE I. — TOWN MEETINGS.

Sec. 1. Town Meetings shall be held in East Medway in the year A. D. 1871, West Medway in the year A. D. 1872, Medway Village in the year A. D. 1873, alternating at each of said places, once in three years.

Sec. 2. All Town Meetings shall be notified by posting a copy of the warrant calling the same at each of the Churches and Post Offices in Town, at least seven days before the day appointed for the meeting.

Sec. 3. The Annual Meeting for the election of Town Officers shall be held on the first Monday of March.

ARTICLE II. — GOVERNMENT OF TOWN MEETINGS.

Sec. 1. At the Annual Election of Town Officers the polls shall remain open for at least one hour, after which a vote may at any time be passed to close them in not less than ten minutes.

Sec. 2. The Presiding Officer of town meetings may require motions to be submitted to the town in writing

Sec. 3 No final vote shall be reconsidered unless the intention to do so shall be declared at the time of its adoption, and no article in any warrant shall be again considered after it has been disposed of, unless ordered by two thirds of the voters present.

Sec 4 All motions may be debated excepting the motion to adjourn, and motions to adjourn, to lay on the table, the previous question to postpone or to amend shall have precedence over all others in the foregoing order

Sec. 5 The duties of the Presiding Officer, not otherwise provided for by law, or by the foregoing rules, shall be determined by the rules of parliamentary law as laid down in Cushing's Manual as far as they are applicable to town meetings .

ARTICLE III — FINANCES.

Sec. 1 The financial year shall begin with the first day of February in each year, and close with the last day of January next following.

Sec. 2. The Selectmen may authorize the Treasurer to borrow money temporarily, in anticipation of the collection of taxes, should the same in their judgment be necessary, and to give the note or notes of the town therefor, signed by such Treasurer and countersigned by the Selectmen, and all town notes authorized by the vote of the town and given by the Treasurer shall be countersigned by the Selectmen

Sec. 3. The assessment of all taxes shall be completed and a list thereof delivered to the Collector on or before the first day of September in each year, excepting the assessment of poll taxes against those persons who only pay a poll tax, a list of which shall be completed and delivered to the Collector on or before the first day of July in each year, and shall be payable to the Collector at his Office, on or before the first day of August next following, and all of said taxes remaining unpaid on said last mentioned day shall be immediately put into the hands of an Officer for collection.

Sec. 4 All taxes assessed in each year, excepting the list of poll taxes referred to in section three of this article, shall be payable on or before the first day of December in the same year, and interest at the rate of one per cent per month shall be charged and collected from said first of December, on all taxes remaining unpaid on that day; and the Collector is required immediately after the first day of January in each year to exert all the powers vested in him by law for the collection of all unpaid taxes.

Sec 5 The Collector shall within thirty days after receiving the tax list, send or deliver to every tax payer his tax bill, excepting those who pay poll taxes only, on which shall be printed the rate of taxation, with the conditions of the same as herein provided.

Sec. 6 The Collector shall report to the Selectmen the list of taxes remaining unpaid on the first of February in each year, and said list shall be published in the Selectmen's Report.

Sec. 7 One Auditor shall be annually chosen by the town, whose duty shall be to audit the vouchers and accounts of the Selectmen, Town Treasurer, School Committee, Collector of Taxes, and all other Town accounts, at the close of the fiscal year, and they shall report the result of their examination to the Selectmen, who shall report to the town

Sec. 8. All Town Officers shall present their accounts for settlement for services rendered, with proper vouchers for all moneys paid by them on account of the town, at the close of the financial year in which they were elected, and the same shall appear duly audited in the report for that year

Sec. 9. The School Committee, Overseers of the Poor, Surveyors of Highways, and the Board of Engineers of the Fire Department, shall make up their annual reports and estimates of monies needed in their several departments the coming year, and deliver a copy to the Selectmen on or before the first day of February in each year; which reports, with their own and other matters usually published, with the amount of taxes collected, and the amount uncollected, with a list of delinquents, the Selectmen shall cause to be printed and distributed to the tax payers at least one week previous to the annual meeting.

6

ARTICLE IV.— STREETS, POLICE, ETC.

Sec. 1. No person shall move a building on any public street or way without written permission from the Selectmen, to be granted upon such terms and conditions as in their opinion the public safety may require; and if such removal would occasion injury to any shade, fruit, or ornamental tree overhanging or standing within the limits of said street or way, full damages shall be paid to the owners thereof by the parties removing said building, to be awarded by the Selectmen, with the right of appeal to a jury as in the matter of laying out town roads and highways.

Sec. 2. No person who has by law a right to cut down or remove any ornamental or shade tree standing in any highway, town way or street, shall exercise such right without first giving notice of his intention to one of the Selectmen; and if the Selectmen desire to retain the tree they shall give notice thereof to such person within ten days after his notice to them, and they may award damages to such person, who shall have the right to appeal to a jury, as in the matter of laying out town roads and highways.

Sec. 3. No person shall break or dig up the grounds in any street or public place for any purpose whatever, or hang any gate or door swinging into, or set or place any fence, post, tree, edgestone or other obstruction in, or change the grade or width of any public way, without the written license of the Selectmen, which shall prescribe the limitations and restrictions of such license.

Sec. 4. No person shall trim, lop, prune, or cut in any manner to the injury thereof, any shade, fruit, or ornamental tree planted in any of the streets of this town, without the consent of one of the Selectmen, or hitch or fasten any horse or other animal thereto, or to the boxing thereof.

Sec. 5. No person shall pasture any cattle or other animals, either with or without a keeper, upon any of the streets or ways of said town of Medway; providing that nothing in this By-Law shall affect the right of any person to the use of land within the limits of such street or way adjoining his own premises.

Sec. 6. No person shall coast, with a sled or runners, kick football, or play at any game in which a ball of any kind is used, or throw any stones, in any of the streets of said town.

Sec. 7. No person shall at any time fire crackers, torpedoes, or other explosive articles, or discharge fire-arms or cannon, in any street or other place where the public have a right to pass.

Sec. 8. No person shall swim or bathe in any of the waters within the limits of said town, so as to be exposed in a nude state to the view of any person passing or being on any street or in any dwelling house in this town.

Sec. 9. No person shall engage in hunting or fishing, or play at ball or other games, or discharge any fire-arms on the Sabbath day.

ARTICLE V.— TRUANCY.

Sec. 1. There shall be appointed at the annual meeting three Truant Officers, whose duty it shall be to see that the laws in regard to truancy are duly enforced, and make and prosecute to final judgment all complaints under the same, and they shall receive for their services such compensation as the School Committee shall deem reasonable.

Sec. 2. Any child between the ages of six and fifteen years who, without reasonable cause, does not attend school at least twelve weeks in each year, may be deemed a truant.

Sec. 3. Any child shall be deemed a truant who, while a member of any school, shall be absent from such school without the consent of said child's teacher, parent or guardian.

Sec. 4. A child guilty of truancy shall be reported by the teacher to one of the School Committee having charge of the schools; who shall, if he deems the offence sufficiently aggravated to deserve punishment, forthwith notify the parent or guardian of such child, who shall be allowed to prevent summary punishment by such pledges for the good conduct of the child as shall be satisfactory to the School Committee;

and if such pledges are not given or kept, the School Committee, or one of them, may forthwith notify one of the Truant Officers, who shall at once make the complaint required by law against such child before any Trial Justice or tribunal having jurisdiction of the case

Sec. 5   The Almshouse in this Town is hereby designated and provided as a suitable place for the detention of children who may be convicted of violating the laws in relation to truancy

ARTICLE VI — CEMETERIES

Sec 1.   No body of any deceased person shall be allowed to remain in any of the public receiving tombs in town for more than three days, from the first day of May to the first day of November in each year, and all bodies of such deceased persons deposited in such tombs during other months of the year shall be removed for burial on or before the first day of May in each year; and all bodies of deceased persons remaining in said tombs in violation of the provisions of this article, shall be immediately removed for burial by the officer in charge of said tombs, at the expense of the town.

ARTICLE VII

The Selectmen shall appoint annually three Police Officers, whose special duty it shall be to see that these By-Laws are duly enforced, and who shall discharge the duties of Truant Officers, as prescribed in Article VI of these By-Laws, if empowered to do so by a vote of the town, and who shall remain in Office until others are appointed in their stead, subject to removal however by the Selectmen, and they shall receive from the town such compensation for their services as the Selectmen may deem reasonable.

ARTICLE VIII

It shall be the duty of the Board of Selectmen, and they are hereby authorized to prosecute all suits in favor of the town, and defend all suits that shall be brought against the town, unless otherwise directed by a vote of the town.

ARTICLE IX.

No part of these By-Laws shall be amended or repealed except by a vote of the majority of the voters of the town, present and voting at a town meeting assembled by virtue of a warrant containing an article setting forth the substance of the proposed amendment or repeal

ARTICLE X

These By-Laws shall go into effect from and after their adoption, and their approval by the Superior Court within and for the County of Norfolk, or by some Justice of said Court, and thereupon all former By-Laws shall be repealed.

A true copy,   Attest   GEO. P. METCALF,
                                                          TOWN CLERK

ADDED TOWN BY-LAW.

"It shall be the duty of all constables, police officers and watchmen to disperse, and arrest if need be and put into the lock-up, such persons as congregate in or about the streets, or sidewalks, or public places, doors or steps of any public or private building, annoying others by idly gazing or staring at them, or in any way obstructing or occupying such places for idle gossip, or who use *loud, boisterous* or PROFANE *speech* or song, or in any way behave in a rude, indecent or disorderly manner in any such places or *elsewhere*, either by day or by night   And all such persons being duly convicted shall pay a fine, with costs of prosecution, of not less than one nor more than twenty dollars for each offence"

A true copy of Record — Attest.   O A MASON, Town Clerk.

Norfolk, ss. Superior Court, April Term.— To wit, May 7, 1874 the foregoing By-Law was approved by the court.

E. WORTHINGTON, Clerk.

AMENDMENT OF BY-LAWS.

At a meeting of the town April 1, 1878, voted to amend Sec. 4 of Art. 3 of the By-Laws of the town of Medway, by striking out the word December in the 3d and 6th lines, and inserting in place thereof the word November, and to strike out the word January in the 8th line, and insert instead the word December. Also to add the following: The compensation of the Collector of Taxes on all taxes committed to him for collection, shall be such a rate per cent. as the town shall vote at the annual meeting in each year, which shall be in full for all services and expenses, and he shall pay over to the Treasurer the amount of all taxes and interest accrued, committed to him, on or before the first day of February next following the commitment, except such as may be abated by the assessors, and he shall not be entitled to any compensation until the whole amount of taxes shall have been paid into the treasury as aforesaid.

A true copy. Attest: — O. A. MASON, Town Clerk.

Commonwealth of Massachusetts.

NORFOLK, SS. Superior Court, April Term, 1878, to wit: April 9, 1878. The foregoing amendments are approved by the Court.

ERASTUS WORTHINGTON, Clerk.

A true copy. Attest: —

ERASTUS WORTHINGTON, Clerk.

THE PUBLIC HIGHWAYS AND STREETS.

1713 — 1885.

The laying out of the most ancient highways has been sketched on previous pages. The public roads established and in use at the time the town was incorporated were the following:

A road from the Great Bridge to Dwight's Bridge. The Old Mendon or Country Road, laid out in 1670, from the Great Bridge to Bellingham. A road from the last named at the Abraham Harding place, to a highway near Dinglehole, which ran from the Old Mendon Road at a point near the ancient house of John Ellis, northward across Boggastow Brook, near the Upper Dam, to Sherborn. Another road from the Country Road not far from the house of Theophilus Clark, over Stony Plain, to the last named road at Bare Hill. A cross-road passing the house of John Richardson, to the road from the Abraham Harding place near the house of Peter Adams. Also a road from the last named northward over Long Plain, across Boggastow Brook at Hinsdell's mill, to Sherborn at "The Farms." Another road from the last named, not far from the house of John Rockwood, westward, across the Old Stone Bridge at the Neck, to the New Grant. These highways are indicated on the map of 1713. Subsequently other highways were projected from time to time, as seen from the town records. There were certain roads laid out which were never built, and on petition of citizens, in 1802, these road lands were sold.

THE HARTFORD AND DEDHAM TURNPIKE. 1807-1838.

In 1803 there was a petition by Captain Ezekiel Plimpton and others to the selectmen of the town as follows:

" April 6 1803 "

"TO THE SELECTMEN OF MEDWAY; — Gentlemen:

Please to insert the following article in your warrant for your next Town meeting, viz: To see if the Town will give their suffrage for a Turnpike road now contemplated by government to be laid out through our Town of Medway, on the most convenient route, that may best accommodate the Public, or act anything on the matter as may be thought best

In doing which you will oblige your

Hum^le Serv^ts·

Ezekiel Plimpton, Stephen Clark, Simpson Jones, Elihu Fisher, Elijah Bridges, Sylvanus Adams, Nathaniel Lovell "

This article was duly inserted in the warrant, but dismissed by the vote of the town. The next year a petition, dated January 23, 1804, and signed by sixty-nine citizens, largely from the easterly part of the town, was presented to the State Legislature of that year, asking that a turnpike road might be laid out and established, extending from near the house of Dr. Scammel, in Bellingham, through Medway, and Medfield to Dedham, to connect with the Dedham and Boston Turnpike The company to be called " The Hartford and Dedham Turnpike Corporation."

THE PETITIONERS FOR THE HARTFORD AND DEDHAM TURNPIKE, IN 1804.

Lewis Wheeler, Jeremiah Daniell, Jr , Nathaniel Lovell, Timothy Hamant, Joseph Lovell, Hope Lovell, Michael Lovell, Jasper Adams, Joseph Richardson, Moses Adams, Jr., Micah Adams, Silas Adams, Horatio Adams, Theodore Harding, Theophilus Harding, Phillips Clark, Sylvanus Adams, Benjamin Parnell, Stephen Harding, Bernard Partridge, Ezra Richardson, John Bullen, Josiah Blake, Thomas Harding, Abijah Richardson, Jr , Jeremiah Daniels, Oliver Ellis, Stephen Clark, Abijah Richardson, Silas Fairbanks, Timothy West, Jeremiah Curtis, Amos Rockwood, Elijah Bridges, Lewis Hill, Marcus Richardson, Nathan Jones, Abner Mason, Joseph Newell, Adam Bullard, Joshua Gould, Elihu Fisher, Hazeltine Taft, Darius Blake, Nahum Thayer, Benoni Morse, Jeduthan Bullen, Lemuel Daniels, Amos Daniels, Joseph Daniels, Joshua Whitney, Israel Daniels, Samuel Clark, Elisha Richardson, Zebina Kingsbury, Sabin Daniels, Moses Rockwood, Moses Rockwood, Jr., Simeon Partridge, Aaron Rockwood, John Hunting, Jr , Aaron Adams, Eliakim Adams, Moses Adams, Thaddeus Lovering, Elijah Partridge, Malachi Bullard.

There was a competing line from the same point in Bellingham through Franklin, North Wentham, and Walpole, to Dedham, petitioned for at the same time, but the Medway petitioners were successful, and " The Hartford and Dedham Turnpike Corporation " came into existence by an act of incorporation passed March 9, 1804. Among the corporators were Abijah Richardson, M D., Joseph Lovell, Willard Boyd, Elias Richardson, Jr., Benijah Pond, Abner Morse, and Artemas Woodward. An engineer's plan of the road, dated 1807, is filed with the papers in the office of the Secretary of State. " The Hartford and Dedham Turnpike " was constructed and opened to public travel in 1807 A toll-gate was placed near the " Hammond Place," afterward the railroad crossing in East Medway, and tolls were collected for many years The stock in this road sold in 1808 for fifty dollars per share, but in ten years it had declined to about ten dollars. The turnpike at length came to need expensive repairs, and the corporation decided to relinquish the care of it to the town, and accordingly, the County Commissioners were petitioned to lay it out as a public highway. After two or three years spent in negotiations, the town paid one hundred and sixty dollars into the county treasury, and the Commissioners, June 4, 1838, established the turnpike as a public highway. The road was at once repaired, and that portion of it lying through Black Swamp was placed under the care of William La Croix, Esq., as agent for the town, the other portions were assigned to the several highway districts. It is the longest highway in the town, and is called Main Street.

The Annual Report of the town for 1873 contains the names of the different roads and streets of the town, open to public travel at that date, which in all were one hundred and nine, making an aggregate of nearly one hundred miles of highway in the town.

PRINCIPAL STREETS LEADING EAST AND WEST.

MAIN STREET. The Old Turnpike from Medfield to Bellingham Town Lines.
VILLAGE STREET. The Old Country or Boston and Hartford Middle Road.
MILFORD STREET. From Highland Street, near the Second Church, to Milford line.

PRINCIPAL STREETS LEADING NORTH AND SOUTH.

SUMMER STREET. From Main Street, West Medway, to the Holliston line.
WINTHROP STREET. From the Baptist Meeting-house to Holliston line.
HOLLISTON STREET. From the Village Church to Holliston line.
EXCHANGE STREET. From Main, near the depot, East Medway, to Orchard.
ORCHARD STREET. From Holliston line, easterly and northerly, to Sherborn line.

STREETS IN EAST MEDWAY.

ASH STREET. From Prospect Street to house of Roger Shay.
AUBURN STREET. From Main Street, near the organ shop, to Ridge Street.
BIRCH STREET. From Village Street, near Asa F. Partridge's, to Forest Street.
BRIDGE STREET. From Main Street, at Elisha Adams's, to Dover Street.
CAUSEWAY STREET. From Holliston Street, by the Brick Yards.
CURVE STREET. From Ridge Street, by Henry Richardson's, to Union Street.
DOVER STREET. From Main Street, near Theodore Harding's, to the Great Bridge.
DWIGHT STREET. From the same point to Dwight's bridge, over the Charles River.
DYER STREET. From Village Street, near the new bleachery, to Pleasant Street.
EDEN STREET. From Main to Dover Street, to near the Jonathan Adams' estate.
FARM LANE. From Ridge Street to the Almshouse.
FOREST STREET. From Plain Street, near H. E. Hosmer's, by A. P. Lovell's.
FOREST LANE. From Forest Street to Caleb Blake's.
GROVE STREET. From Causeway Street to Orchard Street.
HAMMOND STREET. From Main Street, near the old Hammond place, to Farm Street.
ISLAND STREET. From Ridge Street, by the Island Road, to Dover Street.
MIDDLESEX STREET. From Orchard Street, northwesterly to Sherborn line.
PLAIN STREET. From Village Street, near George Harding's, to Exchange Street.
PROSPECT STREET. From the house of Lyman Adams, north to Holliston line.
RIDGE STREET. From the railroad cut, passing school-house, to Sherborn line.
RIVERSIDE PLACE. From Orchard Street to the old place of Captain Horatio Mason.
SPENCER STREET. From Acorn Street, passing Mr. Spencer's, to Pleasant Street.
SPRING STREET. From Main Street, at the organ shop, southerly to Village Street.
UNION STREET. From Main Street, near Theodore Harding's, to Ridge Street.
UNION LANE. From Union Street, near Deacon J. Phillips' house, to Ridge Street.
VINE PLACE. From Orchard Street to the house of Thaddeus M. Daniels.
WALNUT STREET. From Orchard to Prospect Street.

STREETS IN ROCKVILLE.

ACORN STREET. From Farm Street, southerly over Stony Plain, to Village Street.
BALTIMORE STREET. From Pleasant Street, near school-house, to North Wrentham.
CEDAR STREET. From Acorn Street, westerly to Main Street.
DEAN STREET. From James H. Ellis' saw-mill to Deanville.
GREEN STREET. From Village Street, near the Tyler place, to the Charles River.
MYRTLE STREET. From Green Street to Pleasant Street, in Rockville.
PLEASANT STREET. From Main Street, near James La Croix's, to Charles River.

SHORT STREET   From Myrtle Street to Pleasant Street, near the Rockville mill.
TURNER STREET.   From Charles River, in Rockville, to Baltimore Street.

STREETS IN MEDWAY VILLAGE.

BARBER STREET   From Village Street, near W H Cary's, to the Oakland Cemetery.
BROAD STREET.   From Village Street, near the hotel, to the railroad
CANAL STREET.   From Village Street, over Goose Island, to Edward Eaton's mill.
CHESTNUT STREET   From Oakland Street to railroad in "New City."
CHURCH STREET.   From Holliston Street to Broad Street, in the rear of the church.
COFFEE STREET   From Holliston Street, eastward to Main Street.
ELLIS STREET.   From Coffee Street, passing Simeon Ellis's, to Holliston Street.
FARM STREET   From Main Street, near Zachariah Lovell's, to Village Street.
HILL SIDE COURT.   From Village Street, near Albert Barton's.
JOHN STREET.   From Mansion Street to River Street.
KNOWLTON STREET.   From Oakland Street to North Street.
LOVERS' LANE.   From Village Street, near Alfred Brown's, to Holliston Street.
MANSION STREET.   From Sanford Street around the Sanford estate
MILL STREET.   From Sanford Street to the grist mill
NORTH STREET   From Holliston Street, near Patrick Conry's, to Oakland Street.
OAKLAND STREET.   From Village Street, northerly to Main Street.
PEACH STREET.   From Church Street, northerly to North Street.
PEARL STREET.   From Walker Street to Captain Paul's
PINE STREET   From Village Street, northerly, crossing Holliston and North streets.
POPOLATIC STREET.   From Walker Street to A. L White's
RIVER STREET.   From Sanford Street to Wilson's Creek
SANFORD STREET.   From Village Street, near the post-office, over Arch Bridge.
SCHOOL STREET.   From Village Street, northerly to North Street.
VILLAGE GREEN   The space westerly of the church
WALKER STREET.   From Village Street, at Eaton's Mill, to Franklin line.
WHITING STREET.   Private way from Village Street to Sanford Street.
WILSON'S LANE   From Village Street to Frank Neelan's house.
WINTER STREET.   From Broad Street to Barber Street, near the R R Station

STREETS IN WEST MEDWAY

ADAMS STREET   From Winthrop Street, near Partridge's mill, to Joseph Lovering's.
ALDER STREET   From West Street, towards Bear Hill, to Milford line.
ALLEN LANE.   From Hill to Seth Allen place
AWL STREET.   From Village Street to High Street
CAMPBELL STREET.   From Village Street to Charles Street
CAMPBELL'S LANE   From Village Street to the paper mill.
CHARLES STREET.   Parallel with, and between the railroad and Charles River.
CLARK STREET.   From Milford Street, near A Wight's, to Milford line.
COTTAGE STREET.   From Village Street, passing Evergreen Cemetery, to Main Street.
CORNER STREET.   From Clark Street to Milford line, towards Braggville
CROSS STREET.   From Village Street to Main Street, by Z. Brigham's.
CUTLER STREET   From Cottage Street to Lincoln Street.
ELM STREET.   From Main Street to Cottage Street
EVERGREEN STREET.   From Main Street, near Mrs Hastings', to Cottage Street.
FISHER STREET.   From the school-house, crossing Milford Street, to Braggville.
FRANKLIN STREET.   From Main Street, near the parish-house, to Franklin line.
GRANITE STREET.   From West Street, near Jonathan Pond's, to Bellingham line.
GUERNSEY STREET   From Cottage Street to Lincoln Street
HAVEN STREET   From Village Street to Charles Street.
HIGH STREET.   From Village Street, near Hunt's boot shop, to Main Street.
HIGHLAND STREET   From Main Street, passing the Common, to Summer Street.
HILL STREET   From Winthrop Street, near George Blake's, to Holliston line.
LINCOLN STREET.   From Village Street, near Hunt's boot shop, to Main Street.
LOVERING STREET   From Holliston Street, near Newell Adams', to Summer Street.

MAPLE STREET. From Winthrop Street, at Hollis Rice's, to Lovering Street.
MECHANIC STREET. From Main Street, passing A. P. Thayer's, to Willard Daniels'.
NORFOLK AVENUE. From Village Street to Main Street.
OAK STREET. From Mechanic Street, passing Mr. Stewartson's, to Highland Street.
PARTRIDGE STREET. From Winthrop Street, near the school-house, to Moses Pond's.
PHILLIPS STREET. From Guernsey Street to Cutler Street.
POND STREET. From Main Street, near Nathaniel Clark's, to Lovering Street.
SHAW STREET. From Village Street to Franklin line, at Plimpton's bridge.
SLOCOMB PLACE. From Main Street to the old school-house.
TEMPLE STREET. Near the Baptist Parsonage.
WARD LANE. From Partridge Street to Benjamin Ward's.
WELLINGTON STREET. From Cottage Street to High Street.
WEST STREET. From Main Street to Milford Street, near Alvin Wight's.

THE REPRESENTATIVES TO THE GENERAL COURT. 1726–1885.

The town, for several years after its incorporation, did not see fit to be represented in the Great General Court of Massachusetts. It was not until 1726 that her representative appeared in the halls of the State Legislature.

1726. Jonathan Adams.	1791. Moses Richardson.	1837. Eleazar Daniels.
1730. Jonathan Adams.	1792. Moses Richardson.	1838. Luther Metcalf.
1735. Edward Clark.	1793. Moses Richardson.	1839. Paul Daniell.
1736. Edward Clark.	1795. Eliakim Adams.	1840. Asa Cole.
1737. Samuel Metcalf.	1796. Eliakim Adams.	1841. Willard Daniels.
1738. Jeremiah Adams.	1797. Moses Richardson.	1842. Joel Hunt.
1739. Edward Clark.	1799. Abner Morse.	1843. Horace Richardson.
1741. Jeremiah Adams.	1800. Abner Morse.	1845. Horace Richardson.
1758. Jonathan Adams.	1801. Moses Richardson.	1846. Warren Lovering.
1760. Elisha Adams.	1802. Moses Richardson.	1847. Nathan Jones.
1763. Elisha Adams.	1803. John Ellis.	1848. Horatio Mason.
1765. Elisha Adams.	1804. Moses Richardson.	1849. Horatio Mason.
1766. Jonathan Adams.	1805. Abner Morse.	1851. Clark Partridge.
1767. Jonathan Adams.	1806. Jeremiah Daniels.	1853. Alpheus C. Grant.
1768. Elisha Adams.	1807. Jeremiah Daniels.	1854. Albert Thwing.
1769. Jonathan Adams.	1808. Abner Morse.	1855. Tisdale S. White.
1770. Jonathan Adams.	1809. Moses Richardson.	1856. Tisdale S. White.
1771. Jonathan Adams.	1810. William Felt.	1857. William B. Boyd.
1772. Jonathan Adams.	1811. Moses Richardson.	1858. William H. Temple.
1774. Jonathan Adams.	1812. Nathaniel Lovell.	1860. William H. Cary.
1775. { Moses Adams. { Jonathan Adams.	1813. Nathaniel Lovell.	1861. William H. Cary.
	1822. George Barber, Jr.	1863. William Daniels.
1776. Elijah Clark.	1823. Seneca Barber.	1864. William Daniels.
1777. Elijah Clark.	1824. George Barber, Jr.	1866. Anson Daniels.
1778. Elijah Clark.	1826. Warren Lovering.	1867. Leander S. Daniels.
1779. Elijah Clark	1827. Warren Lovering.	1869. James H. Ellis.
1780. Jonathan Adams.	1828. Joseph L. Richardson.	1870. George P. Metcalf.
1781. Jonathan Adams.	1829. Warren Lovering.	1872. Rev. Alexis W. Ide.
1782. Moses Adams.	1830. Warren Lovering.	1873. Edward Eaton.
1783. Moses Adams.	1831. { Warren Lovering. { Joseph L. Richardson.	1875. David A. Partridge.
1784. Joseph Lovell.		1877. David A. Partridge.
1785. Elijah Clark.	1832. Paul Daniell.	1878. Elijah B. Daniels.
1787. Moses Richardson.	1833. Paul Daniell.	1880. Joseph W. Thompson.
1788. Moses Richardson.	1834. Paul Daniell.	1883. Sewall J. Clark.
1789. Moses Richardson.	1835. George H. Holbrook.	
1790. Moses Richardson.	1836. Nathan Jones.	

The Town Clerks. 1713 – 1885.

1713.	John Rockwood.	1757.	Samuel Harding.
1714–15.	Edward Clark	1758–61.	Elisha Adams.
1716	John Rockwood.	1762–64.	Elijah Clark
1717–25	Edward Clark.	1765.	Elisha Ellis.
1726.	Jeremiah Daniell.	1766–68.	Elijah Clark.
1727.	Edward Clark	1769.	Elisha Adams.
1728.	Ebenezer Daniell	1770.	Timothy Clark.
1729–32.	Edward Clark	1771–78.	Elijah Clark.
1733.	Jeremiah Daniell.	1779	Henry Ellis.
1734–35	Edward Clark.	1780	Simon Fisher.
1736.	Jeremiah Daniell	1781–82.	Henry Ellis.
1737.	Edward Clark	1783–92.	Elijah Clark.
1738.	Jeremiah Daniell.	1793–94.	Theodore Clark.
1739	John Barber.	1795–'14.	Joseph Lovell.
1740	Jeremiah Daniell	1815–27.	Joseph L Richardson.
1741–42.	Jeremiah Daniell	1828–32.	Luther Metcalf, Jr
1743.	John Barber.	1833.	Joseph L Richardson.
1744–45	Samuel Harding	1834–36	Daniel Wiley
1746	Jeremiah Adams	1837–41.	Joseph L Richardson.
1747	Jeremiah Daniell.	1842–45.	Daniel Wiley
1748–49.	Samuel Harding	1846–48.	Luther Bailey.
1750–52	Jeremiah Daniell	1849–53.	Daniel C Fisher.
1753	Samuel Harding.	1854–67.	A. M B Fuller.
1754–55	Samuel Ellis.	1868–71.	George P. Metcalf.
1756.	Elisha Adams.	1872–85.	Orion A. Mason.

The Selectmen. 1713 – 1885.

1713 John Rockwood, Samuel Partridge, Jonathan Adams, Jonathan Adams, Jr.

1714 John Rockwood, Samuel Partridge, Jonathan Adams, Jr , Edward Clark, Theophilus Clark

1715. John Rockwood, Edward Clark, Ebenezer Thompson, Nathaniel Wight, Malachi Bullard, John Richardson.

1716. Jonathan Adams, Abraham Harding, John Bullard, John Clark

1717. John Rockwood, Edward Clark, Nathaniel Wight, Jasper Adams, Henry Guernsey.

1718 John Rockwood, Jonathan Adams, Edward Clark, Ebenezer Thompson, Abraham Harding.

1719 Edward Clark, John Bullard, John Partridge, Timothy Clark, Michael Metcalf.

1720. Samuel Partridge, Edward Clark, Ebenezer Thompson, Malachi Bullard, Jeremiah Daniell.

1721. Jonathan Adams, Edward Clark, Ebenezer Thompson, Malachi Bullard, Daniel Adams.

1722. John Rockwood, Jonathan Adams, Edward Clark, Theophilus Clark, Ebenezer Thompson

1723. Edward Clark, Ebenezer Thompson, John Bullard, Nathaniel Whiting, Ebenezer Daniell.

1724 Jonathan Adams, Jr., Edward Clark, Ebenezer Thompson, Jeremiah Adams

1725. Edward Clark, Jasper Adams, Jeremiah Daniell, Samuel Metcalf

1726. Ebenezer Thompson, Jeremiah Daniell, Nathaniel Whiting, Peter Balch, Thomas Harding.

1727 Edward Clark, John Bullard, Jonathan Adams, Eleazar Adams, John Barber.

1728. Jonathan Adams, Abraham Harding, Henry Guernsey, Ebenezer Daniell, Samuel Metcalf.

1729. Samuel Partridge, Edward Clark, Ebenezer Thompson, John Richardson, Ebenezer Adams

1730. Jonathan Adams, Edward Clark, Samuel Metcalf, Joseph Adams, Samuel Daniell.
1731. Edward Clark, Michael Metcalf, Jeremiah Daniell, Nathaniel Whiting, Eleazar Adams.
1732. Jonathan Adams, Jonathan Adams, Jr., Edward Clark, Jeremiah Daniell, Eleazar Adams.
1733. Jonathan Adams, Jr., Timothy Clark, Jeremiah Daniell, Eleazar Adams, John Adams.
1734. Jonathan Adams, Jr., Edward Clark, Jeremiah Daniell, Eleazar Adams.
1735. Edward Clark, Jeremiah Daniell, Nathaniel Whiting, Samuel Harding, Joseph Barber.
1736. Jonathan Adams, Jr., Jeremiah Daniell, Daniel Richardson, Benjamin Rockwood, John Barber.
1737. Jonathan Adams, Jr., Edward Clark, Nathaniel Whiting, Joseph Barber.
1738. Jonathan Adams, Jr., Jeremiah Daniell, Eleazar Adams, Benjamin Rockwood, Jonathan Partridge.
1739. Samuel Harding, Joseph Barber, John Barber, George Deming, John Harding.
1740. Jeremiah Daniell, Samuel Harding, Jeremiah Adams, Jonathan Adams, George Deming.
1741. Jonathan Adams, Jr., Jeremiah Daniell, Jeremiah Adams, Samuel Harding, George Deming.
1742. Jonathan Adams, Jr., Jeremiah Daniell, Joseph Adams, George Deming, Hugh Brown.
1743. Samuel Harding, John Barber, John Harding, Samuel Ellis, Nathaniel Whiting.
1744. Samuel Harding, Jonathan Adams, Jr., Timothy Clark, Jeremiah Adams, John Adams.
1745. Samuel Harding, John Barber, Ebenezer Daniell, Benjamin Rockwood, Nathaniel Cutler.
1746. Jeremiah Daniell, Thomas Harding, Michael Bullen, Henry Morse.
1747. Jeremiah Daniell, Jeremiah Adams, Eleazar Adams, Joseph Barber, Nathaniel Clark.
1748. Timothy Clark, Nathaniel Whiting, Samuel Harding, John Barber, Jonathan Adams.
1749. Timothy Clark, Nathaniel Whiting, Eleazar Adams, Samuel Harding, John Barber.
1750. Jeremiah Daniell, John Adams, Joseph Barber, Nathaniel Cutler, Jonathan Adams.
1751. Jeremiah Daniell, John Barber, Samuel Ellis, Nathaniel Cutler, Ephraim Partridge.
1752. Timothy Clark, Jeremiah Daniell, Sam'l Ellis, Nathaniel Cutler, Sam'l Fisher.
1753. Samuel Harding, Nathaniel Cutler, Jonathan Adams, Samuel Fisher, Elisha Adams.
1754. Samuel Ellis, Jonathan Adams, Samuel Fisher, Malachi Bullard.
1755. Joseph Barber, Samuel Ellis, Nathaniel Clark, Elisha Adams, Malachi Bullard.
1756. Elisha Adams, Jonathan Adams, Samuel Fisher, Malachi Bullard, Asa P. Richardson.
1757. Samuel Harding, Nathaniel Clark, Henry Daniels, Job Plimpton, George Barber.
1758. Jonathan Adams, Samuel Fisher, Elisha Adams, Job Plimpton, Uriah Morse.
1759. Jonathan Adams, Elisha Adams, Malachi Bullard, Job Plimpton, Eleazar Adams.
1760. Elisha Adams, Job Plimpton, Eleazar Adams, Moses Richardson.
1761. Elisha Adams, Eleazar Adams, Elijah Clark, Sam'l Hayward, Asa Richardson.
1762. George Barber, Eleazar Adams, Elijah Clark, Joshua Partridge, Daniel Ide.
1763. Eleazar Adams, Elijah Clark, Daniel Ide, Amos Turner, Jeremiah Daniels.
1764. Elijah Clark, Joshua Partridge, Elisha Ellis, Nathan Daniels, Thomas Adams.
1765. Jonathan Adams, Elisha Adams, Moses Richardson, Joshua Partridge, Thomas Metcalf.

Moses Richardson, Elijah Clark, Jeremiah Daniels, Ichabod Hawes, Nathan Whiting.

Eleazar Adams, Moses Richardson, Elijah Clark, Samuel Hayward, Henry Bullard.

Eleazar Adams, Elijah Clark, Samuel Hayward, Jeremiah Daniels.

Elisha Adams, Eleazar Adams, Jeremiah Daniels, Thomas Adams, James Penniman.

Eleazar Adams, Ichabod Hawes, James Penniman, Timothy Clark, Asa Daniels.

Uriah Morse, Eleazar Adams, Elijah Clark, Josiah Fuller, Daniel Bullen.

Elisha Adams, Eleazar Adams, Elijah Clark, Jeremiah Adams, Moses Adams.

Jonathan Adams, Eleazar Adams, Moses Richardson, Elijah Clark, Elisha Cutler.

Jonathan Adams, Eleazar Adams, Elijah Clark, James Penniman, Elisha Cutler.

Jonathan Adams, Eleazar Adams, Elijah Clark, Joshua Partridge, Elisha Cutler.

Jonathan Adams, James Penniman, Moses Adams, Joshua Partridge, Joseph Lovell, Asa Clark.

Jonathan Adams, Moses Richardson, Daniel Ide, Henry Bullard, Moses Adams, Joseph Lovell, Nathaniel Partridge

Jonathan Adams, Joseph Lovell, Henry Ellis, Simeon Fisher, Asa Clark.

Daniel Bullen, Moses Adams, Henry Ellis, Simon Cutler, Joseph Curtis.

Nathaniel Partridge, Simon Fisher, John Harding, Moses Thompson, James Morse.

Daniel Ide, Henry Ellis, Oliver Adams, Isaac Bullard, Moses Richardson.

Daniel Bullen, Joseph Lovell, Henry Ellis, Oliver Adams, Asa P. Richardson.

Daniel Bullen, Joseph Lovell, Nathaniel Partridge, Oliver Adams, Simon Clark.

Daniel Bullen, Elisha Cutler, Joseph Lovell, Nathaniel Partridge, Asa P. Richardson.

Daniel Bullen, Moses Adams, Joseph Lovell, Asa P Richardson, Daniel Pond.

Moses Adams, Joseph Lovell, Moses Richardson, Asa P Richardson, Nathaniel Partridge.

Moses Adams, Joseph Lovell, Asa Clark, Moses Richardson, Nathaniel Lovell.

Moses Adams, Joseph Lovell, Henry Ellis, Nathaniel Lovell, Eliakim Adams.

Moses Adams, Joseph Lovell, Henry Ellis, Nathaniel Lovell, Eliakim Adams

Moses Adams, Joseph Lovell, Henry Ellis, John Harding, Nathaniel Lovell.

Henry Ellis, Oliver Adams, Nathaniel Lovell, Eliakim Adams, Abner Morse.

Henry Ellis, Oliver Adams, Nathaniel Lovell, Eliakim Adams, Abner Morse

Henry Ellis, Abner Morse, Thomas Adams, Simeon Richardson, John Ellis.

Henry Ellis, Oliver Adams, Nathaniel Lovell, Eliakim Adams, Thomas Adams, Abijah Richardson

Henry Ellis, Oliver Adams, Eliakim Adams, Abijah Richardson, Joel Partridge.

Henry Ellis, John Harding, Eliakim Adams, Abijah Richardson, Abner Mason

Henry Ellis, Moses Richardson, Eliakim Adams, Jabez Shumway, Theodore Clark

John Harding, Thomas Adams, Theodore Clark, Nathan Jones, Micah Adams

Eliakim Adams, John Ellis, Amos Turner, Luther Metcalf, Jonathan Adams

Nathaniel Lovell, Abner Morse, Jabez Shumway, John Ellis, Abner Ellis

Eliakim Adams, Abijah Richardson, Jabez Shumway, Nathan Jones, Abner Ellis.

Nathaniel Lovell, Abner Morse, Nathan Jones, Luther Metcalf, Jeremiah Daniell

Theodore Clark, Nathan Jones, Luther Metcalf, Jeremiah Daniell, Thaddeus Lovering.

Theodore Clark, Nathan Jones, Luther Metcalf, Elijah Partridge, Sylvanus Adams.

Abner Morse, Theodore Clark, Jeremiah Daniell, Elijah Partridge, Jasper Adams

John Harding, Abner Morse, Theodore Clark, Jeremiah Daniell, Jasper Adams.

1807. John Harding, Nathaniel Lovell, Abner Morse, Theodore Clark, Ralph Bullard.
1808. Nathaniel Lovell, Jabez Shumway, Moses Richardson, William Felt, Seneca Barber.
1809. Jabez Shumway, Theodore Clark, Jasper Adams, Ralph Bullard, Calvin Cutler.
1810. Nathaniel Lovell, Moses Richardson, William Felt, Asa Daniels, Nathaniel Cutler.
1811. Nathaniel Lovell, Thaddeus Lovering, Moses Richardson, Asa Daniels, Nathaniel Cutler.
1812. Nathaniel Lovell, Amos Turner, Thaddeus Lovering, Sylvanus Adams, Nathaniel Cut'er.
1813. Nathaniel Lovell, Amos Turner, Thaddeus Lovering, Sylvanus Adams, Nathaniel Cutler,
1814. Nathaniel Lovell, Abner Morse, Amos Turner, Thaddeus Lovering, Sylvanus Adams.
1815. Nathaniel Lovell, Abner Morse, Amos Turner, Thaddeus Lovering, Sylvanus Adams.
1816. Abner Morse, Amos Turner, Thaddeus Lovering, Sylvanus Adams, Seneca Barber.
1817. Nathaniel Lovell, Abner Morse, Amos Turner, Thaddeus Lovering, Lewis Wheeler.
1818. Nathaniel Lovell, Abner Morse, Amos Turner, Thaddeus Lovering, Lewis Wheeler.
1819. Thaddeus Lovering, Seneca Barber, Lewis Wheeler, Simon H. Mason, Moses Rockwood.
1820. Thaddeus Lovering, Seneca Barber, Lewis Wheeler, Simon H. Mason, Simeon Partridge.
1821. Sylvanus Adams, Seneca Barber, Lewis Wheeler, Moses Rockwood, Aaron Adams.
1822. Thaddeus Lovering, Seneca Barber, Lewis Wheeler, Aaron Adams, Paul Daniell.
1823. Paul Daniell, Joseph L. Richardson, Joel Hunt, Moses Felt, Lemuel Clark.
1824. Joel Hunt, Moses Felt, Lemuel Clark, Thomas Harding, Elisha A. Jones.
1825. Thaddeus Lovering, Seneca Barber, Lewis Wheeler, Moses Rockwood, Amos Bullard.
1826. Sylvanus Adams, Seneca Barber, Paul Daniell, Joel Hunt, Christopher Slocum, Jotham Clark.
1827. Paul Daniell, Joel Hunt, Christopher Slocum, Jotham Clark, Sylvanus Adams.
1828. Simon H. Mason, Lemuel Clark, Luther Metcalf, Jr.
1829. Simon H. Mason, Lemuel Clark, Luther Metcalf, Jr.
1830. Simon H. Mason, Lemuel Clark, Luther Metcalf, Jr.
1831. Joseph L. Richardson, Joel Hunt, Cephas Thayer.
1832. Joseph L. Richardson, Cephas Thayer, Eleazar Daniels.
1833. Joseph L. Richardson, Eleazar Daniels, James Lovering.
1834. Christopher Slocum, Luther Metcalf, Jr., Eleazar Daniels.
1835. Christopher Slocum, Luther Metcalf, Jr., Eleazar Daniels.
1836. Christopher Slocum, Luther Metcalf, Jr.
1837. Paul Daniell, Joel Hunt, William Adams.
1838. Daniel Wiley, Asa Cole, Joseph Adams.
1839. Daniel Wiley, Asa Cole, Joseph Adams.
1840. Asa Cole, Joseph Adams, Orion Mason.
1841. Paul Daniell, Joseph Adams, Orion Mason.
1842. Joel Hunt, George Harding, Newell Lovering.
1843. Joel Hunt, George Harding, Newell Lovering.
1844. Christopher Slocum, Nathan Jones, William H. Cary.
1845. Joseph L. Richardson, Christopher Slocum, William Adams, Elisha Cutler, Horatio Mason.
1846. Milton M. Fisher, Albert Thwing, James Mann.
1847. Milton M. Fisher, Albert Thwing, Nathan C. Pond.

Joseph L. Richardson, Joel Hunt, Artemas Brown.
Joseph L. Richardson, Joel Hunt, Artemas Brown.
Eleazar Daniels, Clark Partridge, Joseph C. Lovering.
Horatio Mason, Elias Metcalf, Arnold Smith.
Horatio Mason, Elias Metcalf, Arnold Smith.
Christopher Slocum, Albert Thwing, Edward Eaton, James P. Clark.
Albert Thwing, James P. Clark, Simeon Fisher
Albert Thwing, James P. Clark, William Adams.
James P. Clark, William Adams, Alvin Wight.
James P. Clark, William Adams, Alvin Wight.
James P. Clark, Alvin Wight, Joel P. Adams.
James P. Clark, Alvin Wight, Joel P. Adams
Alvin Wight, Joel P Adams, William Daniels.
Simeon Fisher, Joel P. Adams, William Daniels.
Clark Partridge, Simeon Fisher, William Daniels
Clark Partridge, Simeon Fisher, William Daniels
Clark Partridge, Simeon Fisher, William Daniels.
Clark Partridge, Simeon Fisher, William Daniels.
Simeon Fisher, George W. Ray, James H. Ellis.
George W. Ray, James H. Ellis, Wales Kimball
George W. Ray, James H. Ellis, William H. Temple.
George W. Ray, James H. Ellis, A. M. B. Fuller.
James H. Ellis, Abram S. Harding, Joseph Bullard
Wales Kimball, Joseph Bullard, Willard P. Clark.
Wales Kimball, Joseph Bullard, Willard P. Clark.
Clark Partridge, Joseph Bullard, Willard P. Clark
Clark Partridge, Joseph Bullard, Willard P. Clark.
Edward Eaton, Joseph Bullard, Willard P. Clark.
Edward Eaton, Joseph Bullard, Willard P. Clark.
Willard P. Clark, David A. Partridge, Henry S. Partridge.
David A. Partridge, Moses C. Adams, Charles F. Daniels
Moses C. Adams, Charles F. Daniels, James M. Daniels.
Moses C. Adams, Charles F. Daniels, James M. Daniels
Moses C. Adams, Charles F. Daniels, James M. Daniels
William Everett, Edward Fennessy, George B. Thrasher.
David A. Partridge, Edward Fennessy, George B. Thrasher
David A. Partridge, Edward Fennessy, Elihu S. Fuller.
David A. Partridge, Edward Fennessy, Roswell P. Ross.

THE SCHOOL COMMITTEES. 1805-1885.

Abijah Richardson, M. D., John Ellis, Ezekiel Plimpton, Philo Sanford, Calvin
Cutler

Abijah Richardson, M. D., Philo Sanford, Nathan Jones, Amos Turner, Aaron
Adams.

Abijah Richardson, M. D., Amos Turner, Rev. David Sanford, Rev. Luther
Wright, William Green, Eliakim Adams, Joseph Lovell

Philo Sanford, Amos Turner, Rev David Sanford, Rev. Luther Wright, Joseph
Lovell, Lemuel Daniels, Abner Morse.

Abijah Richardson, M. D., Rev. David Sanford, Rev. Luther Wright, Joseph
Lovell, Abner Morse, Theodore Clark, Timothy Whiting.

Rev David Sanford, Rev. Luther Wright, Jeremiah Daniels, Seneca Barber,
Asa Daniels, Lyman Tiffany, Thaddeus Lovering

Abijah Richardson, M. D., Abner Morse, Seneca Barber, Sylvanus Adams,
Luther Metcalf

Abijah Richardson, M. D., Amos Turner, Rev Luther Wright, Sylvanus Adams,
Luther Metcalf, Aaron Rockwood.

1813. Abijah Richardson, M. D., Philo Sanford, Rev. Luther Wright, Seneca Barber, Joseph L. Richardson, Elijah Partridge, John Harding.

1814. Philo Sanford, Rev. Luther Wright, Lemuel Daniels, Seneca Barber, Joseph L. Richardson, Elihu Partridge.

1815. Rev. Luther Wright, Seneca Barber, Lyman Tiffany, Joseph L. Richardson, Elihu Partridge, Rev. Jacob Ide, Ralph Bullard.

1816. Rev. Luther Wright, Joseph L. Richardson, Rev. Jacob Ide, Timothy Hammond, Reuben Hill, Joel Hunt.

1817. Nathan Jones, Rev. Jacob Ide, Timothy Hammond, Joel Hunt, Rev. Luther Bailey, Sabin Daniels, Aaron Adams, Oliver Dean, M. D.

1818. Abijah Richardson, M. D., Seneca Barber, Joseph L. Richardson, Elihu Partridge, Rev. J. Ide, Rev. Luther Bailey, Christopher Slocum, Moses Felt.

1819. Abijah Richardson, M. D., Rev. Jacob Ide, Rev. Luther Bailey, Aaron Adams, Christopher Slocum, Eleazar Daniels, Elisha A. Jones, William Felt.

1820. Abijah Richardson, M. D., Abner Morse, Rev. J. Ide, Joel Hunt, Rev. Luther Bailey, Eleazar Daniels, Elisha A. Jones, Isaac Kibbe, Sewall Sanford.

1821. Seneca Barber, Rev. Jacob Ide, Joel Hunt, Rev. Luther Bailey, Eleazar Daniels, Calvin Cutler, Ezra Richardson, Luther Metcalf, Jr.

1822. Nathan Jones, Seneca Barber, John Harding, Rev. J. Ide, Rev. Luther Bailey, Christopher Slocum, Sewall Sanford, Lemuel Clark, James Lovering.

1823. Sylvanus Adams, John Harding, Rev. Jacob Ide, Rev. Luther Bailey, Aaron Adams, Luther Metcalf, Jr., Jasper Daniels, Nathan Grant, Joel Partridge.

1824. Christopher Slocum, Isaac Kibbe, Ezra Richardson, Silas Richardson, Moses Harding, John Bullard.

1825. Nathan Jones, John Harding, Joel Hunt, Aaron Adams, Oliver Dean, M. D., Elisha A. Jones, Amos Bullard.

1826. Philo Sanford, Sylvanus Adams, Christopher Slocum, Elisha A. Jones, Ralph Mann, Amos Cutler, Aaron W. Wight.

1827. Rev. Jacob Ide, Rev. Luther Bailey, Elisha A. Jones, Luther Metcalf, Jr., James Lovering, Lowell Bullen, Warren Lovering, Esq.

1828. Rev. Jacob Ide, Rev. Luther Bailey, Christopher Slocum, Elisha A. Jones, Luther Metcalf, Jr., Warren Lovering, Esq., Royal Southwick.

1829. Joseph L. Richardson, Rev. Jacob Ide, Rev. Luther Bailey, Christopher Slocum, Luther Metcalf, Jr., Warren Lovering, Esq., Royal Southwick.

1830. Joseph L. Richardson, Rev. Jacob Ide, Rev. Luther Bailey, Christopher Slocum, Elisha A. Jones, Luther Metcalf, Jr., Warren Lovering, Esq.

1831. Joseph L. Richardson, Rev. Jacob Ide, Rev. Luther Bailey, Christopher Slocum, Elisha A. Jones, Luthur Metcalf, Jr., Warren Lovering, Esq.

1832. Joseph L. Richardson, Rev. Jacob Ide, Rev. Luther Bailey, Christopher Slocum, Elisha A. Jones, Luther Metcalf, Jr., Warren Lovering, Esq.

1833. Joseph L. Richardson, Rev. Jacob Ide, Rev. Luther Bailey, Christopher Slocum, Luther Metcalf, Jr., Warren Lovering, Esq., Alex.L. B. Monroe, M. D.

1834. Rev. Jacob Ide, Rev. Luther Bailey, Christopher Slocum, Luther Metcalf, Jr., Abijah R. Wheeler.

1835. Rev. Jacob Ide, Rev. Luther Bailey, Alex. L. B. Monroe, M. D., Abijah R. Wheeler, Charles S. Cheever, Artemas Brown, M. D., Timothy Walker.

1836. Rev. Jacob Ide, Rev. Luther Bailey, Abijah R. Wheeler, Artemas Brown, M. D., Timothy Walker.

1837. Joseph L. Richardson, Rev. Jacob Ide, Rev. Luther Bailey, Artemas Brown, M. D., Rev. A. Haynes, A. G. Cheever, Wales Kimball.

1838. Rev. Jacob Ide, Rev. Luther Bailey, Artemas Brown, M. D., Rev. A. Haynes, Rev. Sewall Harding, Daniel Wiley.

1839. Rev. Jacob Ide, Rev. Luther Bailey, Rev. A. Haynes, Rev. Sewall Harding, Rev. David Sanford.

1840. Rev. Jacob Ide, Rev. Sewall Harding, Rev. David Sanford.

1841. Rev. Luther Bailey, Rev. David Sanford, Anson Daniels.

1842. Rev. Luther Bailey, Rev. David Sanford, Anson Daniels.

1843. Rev. Luther Bailey, Rev. David Sanford, Anson Daniels.

1844. Rev. Jacob Ide, Rev. Luther Bailey, Rev. David Sanford.
1845. Rev. Jacob Ide, Rev. Luther Bailey, Rev. David Sanford.
1846. Rev. Jacob Ide, Rev. Luther Bailey, Rev. David Sanford.
1847. Rev. Jacob Ide, Rev. Luther Bailey, Rev. David Sanford.
1848. Rev. Jacob Ide, Rev. Luther Bailey, Rev. David Sanford.
1849. Rev. Jacob Ide, Rev. Luther Bailey, Rev. David Sanford.
1850. Rev. Jacob Ide, Rev. Luther Bailey, Rev. David Sanford.
1851. Rev. Luther Bailey, Christopher Slocum, Milton M. Fisher.
1852. Anson Daniels, Milton M. Fisher, Rev. John O. Means.
1853. Rev. John O. Means, Rev. C. C. Messenger, Rev. George L. Cary.
1854. Rev. John O. Means, Rev. C. C. Messenger, Rev. George L. Cary.
1855. Rev. Luther Bailey, Rev. David Sanford, Andrew Washburn, Rev. A. W. Ide.
1856. Rev. Luther Bailey, Rev. David Sanford, Rev. Alexis W. Ide.
1857. Artemas Brown, M. D., Rev. David Sanford, Anson Daniels.
1858. Anson Daniels, Rev. C. C. Messenger, Asa Hixon.
1859. Rev. David Sanford, Anson Daniels, Asa Hixon.
1860. Rev. David Sanford, Anson Daniels, Asa Hixon.
1861. Rev. David Sanford, Willard P. Clark, Anson Daniels.
1862. Rev. David Sanford, Anson Daniels, Willard P. Clark.
1863. Rev. David Sanford, Anson Daniels, Willard P. Clark.
1864. Rev. David Sanford, Anson Daniels, Willard P. Clark.
1865. Rev. David Sanford, Anson Daniels, Rev. Jacob Roberts.
1866. Rev. David Sanford, Anson Daniels, Rev. Jacob Roberts, Charles H. Deans, Esq., Rev. Samuel Brooks.
1867. Rev. David Sanford, Rev. Jacob Roberts, Charles H. Deans, Esq., Rev. Samuel Brooks.
1868. Charles H. Deans, Esq., H. W. Brown, M. D.
1869. Anson Daniels, Milton M. Fisher, Charles H. Deans. Esq., Rev. Samuel Brooks, H. W. Brown, M. D., John S. Walker, O. A. Mason.
1870. Anson Daniels, Milton M. Fisher, Charles H. Deans, Esq., Rev. Samuel Brooks, H. W. Brown, M. D., John S. Walker, Elias T. Fisher, Lyman Adams, Jr., William A. Jenkes, Elbridge Smith.
1871. Anson Daniels, Milton M. Fisher, Charles H. Deans, Esq., John S. Walker, Elias T. Fisher, Lyman Adams, Jr., William A. Jenkes, Rev. Seth J. Axtell, Marcellus A. Woodward.
1872. Anson Daniels, Milton M. Fisher, Willard P. Clark, Charles H. Deans, Esq., Elias T. Fisher, William A. Jenkes, Rev. Seth J. Axtell, Marcellus A. Woodward.
1873. Anson Daniels, Milton M. Fisher, Willard P. Clark, Charles H. Deans, Esq., Elias T. Fisher, William A. Jenkes, Rev. Seth J. Axtell, Henry M. Daniels, Rev. E. O. Jameson.
1874. Anson Daniels, Milton M. Fisher, Willard P. Clark, Elias T. Fisher, William A. Jenkes, Rev. Seth J. Axtell, Henry M. Daniels, Rev. E. O. Jameson, Aaron Brigham.
1875. Anson Daniels, Elias T. Fisher, Rev. Seth J. Axtell, William A. Jenkes, Henry M. Daniels, Rev. E. O. Jameson, Aaron Brigham, J. Warren Clark, Waldo B. Hixon, Charles F. Daniels.
1876. Anson Daniels, Charles H. Deans, Esq., Elias T. Fisher, William A. Jenkes, Rev. Seth J. Axtell, Aaron Brigham, Waldo B. Hixon, Charles F. Daniels, Charles A. Bigelow.
1877. Anson Daniels, Charles H. Deans, Esq., Elias T. Fisher, William A. Jenkes, Rev. Seth J. Axtell, Waldo B. Hixon, J. Warren Clark, Charles A. Bigelow, Edward N. Clark.
1878. Anson Daniels, Charles H. Deans, Esq., Elias T. Fisher, William A. Jenkes, Rev. Ephraim N. Hidden, Waldo B. Hixon, Charles A. Bigelow, Frederic Swarman, Edward N. Clark.
1879. Anson Daniels, Charles H. Deans, Esq., Elias T. Fisher, Elbridge Smith, Charles F. Daniels, Edward N. Clark, E. A. Daniels, M. D., Rev. Ephraim N. Hidden, Frederic Swarman.

1880. Anson Daniels, Charles H. Deans, Esq., Edward N. Clark, Elias T. Fisher, Edwin A. Daniels, M. D., G. E. Sanderson, Frederic Swarman, Rev. Ephraim N. Hidden, Elbridge Smith.

1881. Anson Daniels, Charles H. Deans, Esq., Edward N. Clark, E. A. Daniels, M. D., G. E. Sanderson, Elias T. Fisher, Elijah B. Daniels, Elbridge Smith, Willard P. Clark.

1882. Anson Daniels, Willard P. Clark, Elias T. Fisher, Rev. E. O. Jameson, George E. Sanderson, Charles A. Bemis, M. D., George B. Towle, Dr. John S. Folsom, George E. Paul, Charles C. Lawrence.

1883. Anson Daniels, Willard P. Clark, Elias T. Fisher, Rev. E. O. Jameson, George B. Towle, Charles C. Lawrence, George W. Fallansbee, Charles S. Philbrich, Henry S. Partridge, Henry E. Bullard.

1884. Anson Daniels, Rev. E. O. Jameson, E. A. Daniels, M. D., Charles A. Bemis, M. D., Charles C. Lawrence, George W. Fallansbee, Henry S. Partridge, Edward Whiting.

1885. Charles H. Deans, Esq., E. A. Daniels, M. D., Charles C. Lawrence, Henry S. Partridge, Edward Whiting, George W. Follansbee, Rev. E. O. Jameson.

THE JUSTICES OF THE PEACE APPOINTED. 1736–1885.

Edward Clark	1736	William B. Boyd	1853
Elijah Clark	1775	William H. Cary	1853
Jonathan Adams	1791	Asa M. B. Fuller (d)	1853
Abijah Richardson	1792	Alpheus C. Grant	1854
Joseph Lovell	1800	Austin S. Cushman	1854
Eliakim Adams	1800	John S. Smith	1855
Aaron Adams	1806	James P. Clark	1857
John Ellis, Jr. (a)	1807	Charles H. Deans (d)	1858
Abner Morse	1808	Wales Kimball	1859
John Richardson	1810	Abram S. Harding	1859
Timothy Hammond	1815	Charles B. Whitney	1860
Amos Turner	1817	William H. Temple	1862
Joseph L. Richardson (b)	1819	William Daniels	1864
William Felt	1821	Amos H. Boyd	1866
Thaddeus Lovering	1821	Willard P. Clark	1866
Luther Metcalf	1822	Addison P. Thayer	1866
Warren Lovering (c)	1825	Edward Eaton	1866
Levi Adams	1829	Marcellus A. Woodward	1868
Luther Metcalf, Jr. (b)	1830	George P. Metcalf	1869
Christopher Slocum	1834	Alexander Fairbanks	1870
James Lovering	1836	Joel E. Hunt	1871
Joseph Adams	1837	Orion A. Mason	1871
Nathan Jones	1837	E. H. Tyler	1875
Joel Hunt	1843	Israel P. Quimby	1876
Artemas Brown	1843	David A. Partridge	1877
Elisha Cutler	1843	James H. Ellis	1878
John P. Jones	1843	Frederick L. Fisher	1879
Horatio Mason	1848		
Milton M. Fisher (c)	1848	(a) Also Associate Justice of County Court of Sessions.	
Seneca Barber	1849	(b) Also Justice of the Quorum.	
Clark Partridge	1852	(c) Also of the Peace and Quorum for the State.	
Charles H. Felt	1852	(d) Also Trial Justice.	

CORONERS. — Joseph Ware, 1794; Ralph Bullard, 1797; Zachariah Lovell, 1819; Valentine R. Coombs, 1855. MEDICAL EXAMINER. — Charles A. Bemis, M. D., 1877. NOTARY PUBLIC. — Hon. Milton M. Fisher, 1870.

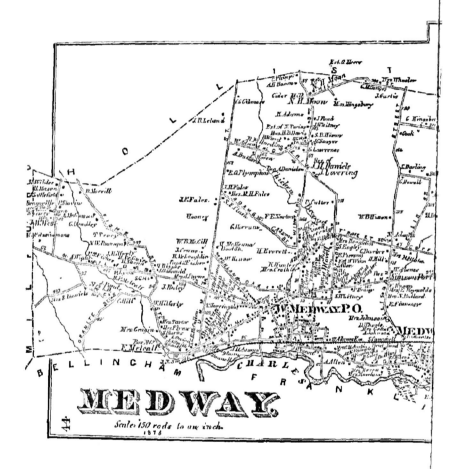

MEDWAY.

Scale: 150 rods to an inch.
1876

WAY, MASS.

THE CENSUS OF 1875.

POPULATION of the town, 4,242; males, 2,066, females, 2,176; males, married, 850, females, married, 852 — total married, 1,702; males, unmarried, 1,148, females, unmarried, 1,131 — total unmarried, 2,279; males, widowed, 64, females, widowed, 187 — total widowed, 251; males, divorced, 4, females, divorced, 6 — total divorced, 10; male natives of the town, 799, female natives of the town, 768 — total, 1,567; male natives of the state, 620, female natives of the state, 744 — total, 1,364; male natives of other states, 231, female natives of other states, 259 — total, 490; male foreigners, 366, female foreigners, 376 — total foreigners, 742; male unknown, 50, female unknown, 29 — total unknown, 79.

OCCUPATIONS.— Professional, 58; mercantile, 101; agricultural, 277; manufacturing and mechanical, (males, 859, females, 224), 1,083; domestic, 1,028.

SELECTED OCCUPATIONS.— *Males:* Engineers, 7; clergymen, 10; physicians, 5; expressmen, 6; teamsters, 13; clerks, 10; merchants and traders, 47; railroad employees, 10; farmers, 218; farm laborers, 59; brick makers, 9; boot-makers, 523; blacksmiths, 12; carpenters, 55; cotton mill operatives, 29; masons, 20; painters, 14; paper makers, 8; shoe makers, 18; straw workers, 36; tailors, 8; tinsmiths, 10; laborers, 20. *Females:* School teachers, 26; domestics, 62; housewives, 879; housekeepers, 11; house workers, 52; cotton mill operatives, 16; dress makers, 21; straw bonnet makers, 147; woolen mill operatives, 9.

VALUATION.— Personal, $363,200, real, $1,420,725 — total, $1,783,925.

PRODUCTS.— Agricultural, $149,419, manufacturing, $1,548,931 — total, $2,698,350.

STATISTICS OF THE CENTENNIAL YEAR, 1876.

Tax levied, $26,760; rate, $14 on a thousand.

Whole number of polls, 1,038.

Valuation, Personal, $329,695, real, $1,433,515 — total, $1,763,210.

Acres taxed, 12,977. Dwelling-houses, 740; horses, 393; cows, 658.

THE ECCLESIASTICAL REGISTER OF 1876.

The First Church of Christ, enrolled 136 members, 226 in Sunday School; the Second Church of Christ, enrolled 281 members, 200 in Sunday School; the Baptist Church, enrolled 109 members, 135 in Sunday School; the Evangelical Congregational Church, enrolled 232 members, 185 in Sunday School; the Methodist Episcopal Church, enrolled 95 members, 127 in Sunday School; the St. Joseph Roman Catholic Church enrolled 800 members; total Protestant Church members enrolled, 853; in Sabbath Schools, 873; total Roman Catholic members enrolled 800.

THE CENSUS OF 1880.

POPULATION. — 3,956. Males, 1,947; females, 2,009; native born, 3,299; foreign born, 657; white race, 3,956; both parents native, 2,440; both parents foreign, 1,323; one parent native and one foreign, 193; families, 901; dwellings, 816; natives of Massachusetts, 2,869; natives of other New England States, 339; natives of all other states, 91; natives of Ireland, 417; natives of Nova Scotia, 113; natives of ten other foreign countries, 127.

OCCUPATIONS. — All classes of occupation, 917; civil and professional, 50; domestic and official, 53; mercantile and carrying, 91; agricultural, 168; manufacturing and mechanical industries, 432; apprenticed and laboring, 123.

PRINCIPAL OCCUPATIONS. — Boot and shoe operatives, 160; farmers, 164; straw workers, 68; factory operatives, 47; carpenters, 45.

ILLITERACY. — Who cannot write, 10 years old and over, 212; natives, 22; foreign 190; who cannot read, 10 years old and over, 179.

THE CENSUS OF 1885.

Population after the division of the town, in Medway, ...	2,777
Population after the division of the town, in Millis, ...	683
Population after the division in both towns, ...	3,460
Population decreased since the Census of 1880, ...	496

THE ONE HUNDRED AND SEVENTY-SECOND ANNUAL REPORT OF THE TOWN OF MEDWAY, FOR THE YEAR ENDING FEBRUARY 1, 1885.

TOWN OFFICERS FOR 1884-5.

Selectmen — David A. Partridge, Edward Fennessy, Elihu S. Fuller.

Clerk and Treasurer — Orion A. Mason.

Assessors — Willard P. Clark, James A. Snow, Henry A. Walker.

Overseers of Poor — Samuel G. Clark, Isaac C. Greenwood, John W. Tuttle.

School Committee — One year — C. A. Bemis, E. O. Jameson, E. A. Daniels; two years — Henry S. Partridge, Charles C. Lawrence, George S. Follansbee; three years — Henry E. Bullard (*resigned*), Anson Daniels (*died*), Edward Whiting.

Engineers of Fire Department — Albert W. Barton, William Creasey, Marcellus A. Ware, Oliver A. Clark, William Colvin.

Auditor — James A. Snow.

Collector — James O'Donnell.

Constables — Malachi Brannon, Dennis W. Riordan, Frank A. Henry, John W. Tuttle, S. E. Howard, Wm. G. Cody.

Police — Malachi Brannon, D. W. Riordan, Frank A. Henry, John W. Tuttle, S. E. Howard, Wm. G. Cody, George H. Fiske, J. Emerson Morse, E. H. Rogers, Stephen B. Smith. *R. R. Police* — O. T. Mason, Ed. H. Rogers, Jeremiah Daniels.

Keepers of Lockup — Malachi Brannon, D. W. Riordan.

Board of Registration — John S. Folsom, Geo. E. Pond, Charles S. Mann, Orion A. Mason.

Measurers of Wood — George B. Fisher, Frederic Swarman, George A. Wiggin, George A. Parker.

Measurers of Lumber — Elijah Partridge, Jesse K. Snow, R. P. Ross.

Measurers of Leather — James M. Seavey, Lucius Pierce.

Pound Keeper — Putnam Clark.

Field Drivers — Alfred Johnson, Wm. B. McGill, Ezra Pierson.

Fence Viewers — Frank W. Cummings, W. P. Clark, Seth Partridge.

Public Weighers — George A. Wiggin, Elbridge G. Ware, Warren C. Mann, Jeremiah Daniels.

Sealer of Weights and Measures — William H. Cary, Jr.

Board of Health — Charles A. Bemis, M. D., Edwin A. Daniels, M. D.

Undertakers — Simon Whitney, James Kenney, Moses Richardson.

Highway Surveyors — District No. 1, J. A. Hutchins; District No. 2, L. F. Richardson; District No. 3, Samuel Huntley; District No. 4, R. P. Ross; District No. 5, Sewall Smith; District No. 6, Thomas Tracy; District No. 7, Edward Fennessy; District No. 8, Edward Fennessy; District No. 9, none.

STATISTICS OF VALUATION AND PERSONAL PROPERTY.

Valuation of real estate May 1, 1884, ...	$1,303,470 00
Valuation of personal estate May 1, 1884, ...	626,665 00
Total value of real estate and personal property taxed, . . .	$1,930,135 00

Gain in valuation of real estate since last year,	.	$ 17,930 00
Gain in valuation of personal estate since last year,	.	345,270 00
Net gain in valuation since last year,	. . . .	$363,200 00

Rate of taxation, . . $15 00   Poll tax, . . $2 00   Number of polls, . 992
Number of dwelling-houses, . . 766   Horses, . 417   Cows, . . . 762

Number of dogs licensed,	149
Number of school children between 5 and 15 years of age,	554
Number of persons in town liable to military duty,	466
Property exempt from taxation : Real estate,	$36,700 00
Property exempt from taxation : Personal estate,	5,000 00
Number of steam boilers in town,	29
Aggregate horse power of steam boilers,	594
Number of acres of land assessed Tillage,	3,206
Wood and sprout,	4,292
Pasture and meadow,	5,717
Area of town,	16,296 acres
Amount covered by water,	95 acres
Amount occupied by highways and railroads in town,	433 acres
Total length of highways and railroads in town,	89 miles

TOWN PROPERTY IN 1884.

Nine school-houses, land and fixtures	$28,000 00	Three safes.	600 00
Town farm and buildings	7,000 00	Book-cases and library	350 00
Personal property at almshouse	3,859 42	Gravel screens	25 00
Twenty acres of woodland	500 00	Weights and measures	100 00
Two lockups, fixtures and furniture	1,000 00	Town pound	50 00
		Three receiving tombs	1,100 00
Engine-houses and apparatus	13,000 00	Road scraper	217 75
Eight reservoirs	2,630 00	Total	$58,532 17

TOWN GRANTS IN 1884

Schools	$6,500 00	State tax		1,980 00
School incidentals	1,000 00	County tax		967 14
School books	500 00	Overlayings		930 11
Transportation of scholars	500 00	Deficiency		5,160 77
Support of poor	4,500 00			
Roads and bridges	2,500 00	Total		$32,038 02
Highland Street	500 00			
General incidentals	2,000 00	Deduct for bank and corpora-		
Debt and interest	2,000 00	tion tax estimate receipts		
Fire department	2,000 00	from the state		1,100 00
Snow bills	300 00			
Police	300 00	Total tax assessed		$30,938 02
Soldiers' aid	300 00	Tax on 992 polls at $2 00		1,984 00
Decoration day	100 00			
	$23,000 00	Tax assessed on property		$28,954 02

SUMMARY OF TOWN EXPENDITURES IN 1884.

	Expended.		Expended.
Roads and bridges	$2,996 76	Support of poor	$5,503 88
Snow bills	59 00	Soldiers' aid	377 00
Highland Street	562 65	General incidentals	2,429 55
Jennie P. Hewins vs. Medway	1,047 50	Police	573 50
Schools	7,324 84	Town history	26 44
School incidentals	1,107 55	Decoration Day	100 00
Transportation	562 76	Debt and interest	2,905 31
School book account	981 75		
Fire department	2,369 38	Total	$28,927 87

POPULATION AT DIFFERENT PERIODS.

1765	785	1810	1,213	1840	2,043	1875	4,242
1790	1,035	1820	1,525	1850	2,778	1880	3,956
1800	1,050	1830	1,756	1860	3,195	1885	3,460

CHECK LIST FOR 1885.

LIST OF VOTERS IN THE TOWN OF MEDWAY, MASS., qualified by the Constitution and Laws of Massachusetts to vote in the election of state, county, and town officers, and also in the election of representatives to Congress, as authorized by the Board of Registration, in said Medway, in the year 1885.

JOHN S. FOLSOM,
GEORGE E. POND, } *Board of Registrars.*
CHARLES S. MANN,

O. A. MASON,
Clerk.

A

Abbe, George A.
Abbe, Partridge
Ackley, George E.
Adams, Albert M.
Adams, Andrew J.
Adams, C. Albert
Adams, Chas. F., 1st
Adams, Chas. F., 2d
Adams, Charles T.
Adams, Daniel
Adams, Edward A.
Adams, Eugene E.
Adams, Frank P.
Adams, Horace
Adams, Horace W.
Adams, James T.
Adams, John M.
Adams, J. Sylvanus
Adams, Metcalf
Adams, Milton S.
Adams, Moses C.
Adams, Nathan
Adams, Nathaniel
Adams, Samuel B.
Adams, Stephen
Adams, Welcome
Adams, William H.
Adams, William M.
Allen, Alfred
Allen, Moses B.
Allen, Willard I.

Ambler, Warner A.
Andrews, George H.
Andrews, Robert L.
Andrews, Walter H.
Arbuckle, William J.
Armstrong, Albert
Ashworth, Chas. H.
Austin, Henry C.

B

Bacon, Abel H.
Bacon, Albert M.
Banks, Walter
Barber, Benjamin C.
Barber, Edson W.
Barber, George N.
Bartlett, George
Bartlett, George W.
Barton, Albert W.
Bean, Jesse M.
Bell, Harry J.
Bell, James M.
Bemis, Charles A.
Benjamin, Newell G.
Bickford, James L.
Bickley, John H.
Bigelow, Charles A.
Blake, Adin P.
Blake, Caleb
Blake, D. Newton
Blake, Edward H.
Blake, James

Black, Albert C.
Black, George
Blunt, Patrick
Boos, Fred E.
Bragg, Cyrus
Bragg, James H.
Brannan, Malachi
Brennan, William F.
Brigham, Aaron
Brooks, Joel W.
Brown, James
Brown, Thomas
Bruce, George W.
Bullard, Eleazar T.
Bullard, George W.
Bullard, Henry A.
Bullard, Henry E.
Bullard, J. Emerson
Bullard, Joel P.
Bullard, John
Bullard, John A.
Bullard, Joseph
Bullard, Joseph N.
Bullard, Maitland N.
Bullard, Timothy
Bullard, William B.
Bullock, Luther
Burke, John F.
Burns, Frank J.
Burns, Michael
Burns, Stephen
Burr, Charles E.

Burton, James L.
Burtt, John A.

C

Camp, Fred A.
Campbell, Samuel
Campsey, William H.
Carpenter, Asa H.
Cary, Erastus W.
Cary, Samuel B.
Cary, William H.
Cary, Wm. H., jr.
Casey, John
Casey, Michael
Cassidy, John
Cassidy, John J.
Cassidy, Philip
Cassidy, Terrence
Cauley, Dominick
Chadwick, Zelotes
Claflin, Hamlet B.
Claflin, James
Clancy, John
Clapp, David
Clark, Abijah
Clark, Albert H.
Clark, Asa D.
Clark, Charles S.
Clark, David
Clark, Edmund N.
Clark, Edward
Clark, Elbridge

Clark, Elijah
Clark, Erastus
Clark, Frank W
Clark, John A
Clark, Joseph D
Clark, J. Warren
Clark, John
Clark, Lemuel
Clark, Lewis
Clark, Oliver A
Clark, Putnam
Clark, Putnam R
Clark, Samuel G.
Clark, Sumner H
Clark, Willard F
Clark, Willard P
Clifford, Israel F
Clinton, Hugh
Clough, Alexander
Clough, Alvin E
Clough, Wilbur W
Cody, William G
Cole, Albert M.
Cole, Asa
Cole, Charles H.
Coleman, Frederic E
Coleman, John W
Collins, Michael
Collins, Michael, 2d
Collins, Michael H
Collins, Patrick
Colvin, William
Converse, Julius P.
Cook, Andrew T
Cook, Charles F
Cook, Frank E
Coombs, Eugene
Coombs, James
Cooper, Charles C
Cooper, Henry F.
Cooper, Henry F., jr.
Costello, James E.
Costello, Patrick
Covell, Daniel
Crane, John C.
Crane, John M
Creasey, Frederick E.
Creasey, Herbert N
Creasey, William E
Crimmings, Edwin B
Crimmings, John H.
Crimmings, J H, jr
Crockett, Gus. A.
Crooks, Joel A.
Crowley, Patrick
Crowther, James S.
Crusar, Henry
Cullen, John E.
Cummings, Edwin B.
Cummings, F. W.
Cummings, G. R
Curtis, Samuel H
Cushing, John
Cushing, John W.
Cutler, Alphonso D.
Cutler, Charles S.
Cutler, Joseph H.

D

Daley, Dennis F
Daly, Patrick
Daniels, Albert R
Daniels, Alfred
Daniels, Benjamin F
Daniels, Cyrus
Daniels, David
Daniels, Edwin A
Daniels, Elias S
Daniels, Francis H
Daniels, George H
Daniels, Henry M
Daniels, Hiram C.
Daniels, James M
Daniels, Jeremiah B
Daniels, J Willard
Daniels, Leander S.
Daniels, Noah
Daniels, Thad M
Daniels, William
Darling, Collins C.
Darling, Edwin A
Davenport, Nath W
Davis, Amos B
Davis, Charles L
Davis, Frank N
Deans, Charles H
Dearborn, Ebenezer
Dearborn, George H
Dearborn, Webster
DeCosta, Lucius
Desmond, Mathew F
DeWire, Richard
DeWire, Walter
DeWire, William H
Dickinson, Alfred C
Dillon, David J.
Disper, Charles M.
Disper, George E
Disper, James W
Disper, Joseph
Disper, Joseph H
Dodge, Tyler
Dowd, James
Dowd, Patrick O
Dowd, Patrick, jr.
Dowd, Peter
Drake, George R
Dunbar, Jonathan P
Dunbar, Shubael E.
Dunton, Charles H.

E

Ellis, Chester
Eliott, William S.
Engley, Sheperd
Estes, Charles W.
Everett, Isaac

F

Fales, Albert F.
Fales, James E.
Fales, John M.
Fales, Marshall
Fales, William A.
Farrington, Alfred

Ferry, Ralph
Finneran, James
Finnessey, Edward
Finnessey, James L.
Fisher, Elias T
Fisher, Frederick L.
Fisher, George B.
Fisher, Milton M.
Fisher, Simeon
Fish, Joseph
Fisk, George H
Fisk, Melville
Flaherty, Bryan
Flaherty, John J
Foley, Peter
Follansbee, Geo. W
Folsom, John S
Force, Emmons
Force, Horace E
Ford, Charles
Foskitt, Gilbert O
Fowler, Edgar R
Frink, Samuel H.
Frink, William
Fuller, Asa M B
Fuller, Charles W
Fuller, Elihu S
Fuller, Enoch B
Fuller, George W
Fuller, Israel D

G

Gaines, Charles
Gale, James A
Gallagher, James
Gallagher, John
Gallagher, Peter
Garland, Alonzo E
Gay, Alonzo H
Gay, Arthur S
Gay, Henry E.
Gay, William
Gay, William W.
Gilmore, Luman W
Gilpatrick, Wm. D
Gorman, James
Gormley, Charles F.
Gormley, Frank W.
Gormley, James
Gormley, John
Gormley, Owen
Grant, Alexander
Grant, Alpheus C
Grant, Alpheus O
Grant, Charles A
Grant, Charles A, jr.
Grant, James M.
Grant, William R
Gray, Louis J
Green, Charles E
Green, George K
Green, Matthew
Greenwood, Frank
Greenwood, H Sears
Greenwood, Isaac C.
Greenwood, John T.
Guild, George L.

Guild, George O.
Guild, Nathaniel H.
Guild, Waldo I

H

Hadley, John L.
Hagar, Frank
Haines, James H.
Haley, Arthur
Haley, James
Haley, James, jr.
Haley, James S, 3d
Haley, John, 1st
Haley, John 2d
Hall, Alanson A
Hall, Arthur H
Hall, Frederick
Hammond, Daniel
Harding, Clark P.
Harding, Edward S
Harding, George M
Harding, Thomas
Harding, William H
Harlow, Rufus K
Harrington, Chas D
Harrington, Thomas
Hart, Alexander L.
Hart, James
Hart, Lewis A.
Hart, Patrick
Hastings, Deming J.
Hawkes, Abijah
Heard, David H.
Heffron, John G.
Henry, Frank A
Henry, James, jr.
Henry, John
Henry, Thomas
Hickey, John
Higgins, Patrick
Hilferty, William
Hill, Cyrus M
Hitchcock, Justus C.
Hixon, Alonzo
Hixon, Clarence A
Hixon, George H.
Hixon, Herbert A
Hixon, Sewall B
Hixon, Willard J
Hodges, John S
Hodges, John W
Hodges, William B
Hodgson, Samuel
Holbrook, Edwin H.
Holbrook, Edwin L
Holbrook, Elmer E.
Holbrook, Frank W.
Holbrook, George F.
Holbrook, George V.
Holden, John
Honey, James
Hopkins, Walter P.
Hosley, German S
Hosmer, Alden A
Hosmer, Henry E
Houghton, Chas A.
Howard, Sylvester E.

Richardson, Lewis F.
Richardson, Moses
Richardson, Silas
Riordon, Dennis W.
Riordon, John
Riordon, John, jr.
Riordon, William H.
Roach, Henry S.
Robbins, Charles S.
Robbins, Sumner
Robinson, Squire
Robinson, Wm. H.
Robinson, W. H., jr.
Rockwood, Daniel
Rogers, Edwin T.
Rogers, Timothy
Rose, John L.
Rose, John O.
Ross, Eliakim H.
Ross, Peter
Ross, Roswell P.
Ruggles, Arthur L.
Russell, William
Ryan, Edward
Ryan, George S.
Ryan, John H.

S

Sanderson, George E.
Sanderson, Stillman
Sanford, Edmund I.
Sanford, Harlan P.
Saunders, Thomas J.
Savage, Robert E.
Sawyer, Judson C.
Schlief, William A.
Schofield, Edward
Scott, John
Scott, John, jr.
Seavey, Charles W.
Seavey, James M.
Shannon, Jere. H.
Shaughnessy, James
Shea, John
Sheehan, Thomas
Shields, Thomas R.
Shumway, Edmund
Simpson, George F.
Skahill, Peter
Slaven, Michael
Slaven, Patrick
Smith, Abner M.

Smith, Addison A.
Smith, Addison F.
Smith, Almond
Smith, Charles E.
Smith, Edgar M.
Smith, Elwyn
Smith, Frank A.
Smith, Fred
Smith, Jason
Smith, John C.
Smith, John S.
Smith, Marcus H.
Smith, Myron
Smith, Sewall
Smith, Stephen B.
Snell, Henry L.
Snow, James A.
Snow, Jesse K.
Sparrow, Curtis A.
Sparrow, Philip S.
Spellman, Michael
Spencer, Charles F.
Spencer, Henry G.
Springer, Otis S.
Stanley, Daniel A.
Stanley, Edward
Stanley, Jonathan C.
Stevens, Daniel G.
Stewart, Edward
Stewartson, Willie E.
Stockbridge, F. W.
Stone, Edward D.
Swarman, Frederick
Swarman, John H.
Sweeney, Augustus
Sweeney, John
Sweeney, Timothy J.

T

Tatten, Michael
Taylor, Lucius H.
Temple, George R.
Temple, William H.
Tevlin, James
Tevlin, John M.
Thayer, Addison P.
Thayer, Charles
Thayer, Luther
Thompson, Joseph
Thompson, J. R.
Thompson, J. Warren
Thompson, J. War. jr.

Thompson, Moses E.
Thrasher, George C.
Tobey, Willie S.
Touhey, James
Touhey, Thomas
Touhey, William
Towle, George B.
Tracy, James
Tracy, John
Tracy, Thomas
Tracy, Thomas B.
Treen, Benjamin
Tucker, Charles R.
Tuttle, Hiram
Tuttle, John W.

V

Vanness, Charles H.
Vanness, Henry
Vidette, Elmer L.
Vose, Alison A.
Vose, Stephen

W

Waite, Aldis L.
Waite, Arthur
Walker, Henry A.
Wallace, Richard W.
Wallace, William
Walsh, Peter H.
Ward, Daniel E.
Ware, Augustus L.
Ware, Elbridge G.
Ware, George H.
Ware, Marcellus A.
Warren, Varnum
Welch, John
Westcott, Jerome B.
Wheat, Henry
White, Elihu
White, Henry G.
White, William G.
Whiting, Edward
Whiting, George W.
Whiting, Joel W.
Whitney, Alfred A.
Whitney, Amos W.
Whitney, C. E. L. B.
Whitney, Henry L.
Whitney, Jason W.

Whitney, John F.
Whitney, Nathan
Whitney, Simon
Whooley, Daniel
Wiggin, George A.
Wight, Alvin
Wight, George A.
Williams, Asa
Williams, Caleb S.
Williams, Charles
Williams, Charles E.
Williams, John M.
Williams, Winfield S.
Wilmarth, Eugene S.
Wilmarth, Lewis A.
Wilson, Elihu C.
Wilson, Jason E.
Winslow, Elna. S.
Wiswell, David
Wiswell, Francis W.
Wiswell, George A.
Wood, Charles E.
Wood, Henry A.
Wood, James H
Wood. John, 1st
Woodman, Daniel S.
Woodman, Henry B.
Woodman, James
Woods, Amos R.
Woods, William, 1st
Woods, William, 2d

Y

Young, Robert O.

———

FEMALE VOTERS.

Adams, Susan F.
Bullard, Marion A.
Clark, Mary B.
Hill, Eliza A.
Hodges, Emma S.
Hosmer, Ann A.
Johnson, Nancy A.
LaCroix, Mary S.
McIntosh, Abbie M.
Richardson, E. B.
Sanborn, Kate
Spencer, Sarah E.
White, Marion A.
Wilson Mary E.

This concludes the account of the town and its doings in general, but some further mention of the acts of the town in educational, military, and religious affairs may be found on subsequent pages.

The Incorporation of Millis.

February 24, 1885.

After a municipal existence of one hundred and seventy-two years, marked by many changes, and a fair degree of prosperity, the time had come for the realization of an event, which for more than a hundred years at different times had been somewhat discussed, when Medway was to give up a part of her territory for the establishment of a new township.

The easterly part of Medway, embracing nearly all that was anciently known as the Old Grant, by the unanimous petition of its inhabitants, supplemented by the names of many residing in other parts of the town, without any serious opposition from any quarter, was incorporated February 24, 1885, and Millis took her place among the towns of the Commonwealth.

The new town was named for Lansing Millis, Esq., one of its most respected citizens. Mr. Millis had formed generous plans for the development and improvement of the new municipality, but suddenly died in a few weeks after its incorporation. His death was a great public loss, and deeply felt by the community and throughout New England. *Vid.* Biographies.

It is believed that this division of the town will prove no serious detriment to the part left as Medway, and will doubtless be to the great advantage of that part now Millis. Already a spirit of public improvement has been awakened both in the old and the new towns. The utmost harmony prevails, and each municipality has for the other only the kindliest feelings and best wishes for its largest prosperity.

THE CHURCHES.

1714—1885.

THE early inhabitants in that part of Medfield lying west of the river Charles, sought the incorporation of a new town that public worship might be established among themselves. And the Great and General Court secured to these early settlers the right to "have, exercise, and enjoy" all municipal privileges on the condition, "*That they procure and Settle a learned Orthodox Minister of good Conversation among 'em and make provision for an Hon^{able} support and maintainance for him.*" Accordingly, the town of Medway was incorporated October 25, 1713, and the people of the new town at once set about establishing the institutions of religion, as appears in the proceedings of their first town-meeting, which was held "November ye 23, 1713.

Voted, That John Rockett and Jonathan Adams, Jun. Serg^t Samuel Partridge and Serg't Jonathan Adams and edward Clark to be a comittee to take care to procure the meeting house built.

Voted, That abraham harding, Senr John partridge and Theophilus clark to procure and cary in a petition to the Town clerk of Medfield in order to the procuring of accommodations for the setting of the metting hous upon the place commonly called bare hills and procure some conven't accommodations for the ministry near ther abouts."

"1714 September ye 22nd Assembled the Enhabitants of Medway At the house of peter Adamses. John Rocket was chose moderator.

Voted, that the town will provide a minister for themselves for the time to come.

Voted, Capt. gorge fairbancks and John partridg and peter Adams and ensin John bullard and ser. Timothy Clarke is chosen a comitty to provide a minister for the Town untill the aniwall metting in march next following, and it is voted that ye town are to meet at the house of peter Adamses to attend the publick worship of God on the sabbath days and he haws given his consent to the same."

Arrangements were made and the first service of public worship in the new town was held October 7, 1714, in the house of Peter Adams, and was conducted by the Rev. David Deming, who continued to preach to the little congregation in Peter Adams's house for several months. Having secured some one to serve as a minister, it was needful to make provision for his support. Accordingly the first appropriation is thus recorded:

"Oct. ye 29 1714. Assembled the inhabitants of Medway at ye house of Peter Adams. Lt Theophilus Clark chosen for ye moderator for to cary on ye work of that day. Then and there by the vote of the Town was granted twenty and five pounds for the Ministry."

"Medway, April the 11th, 1715, at the house of Joseph Daniel, Sen. Then and there, Received the sum of 26 pounds of money of the Select-Men and Committee for preaching to the Town, which is in full discharge from the *seventh of October in the year* 1714 to the ninth day of April in the year 1715.

I say received by me, DAVID DEMING."

THE CHURCH OF CHRIST. ORGANIZED OCTOBER 7, 1714.

THE CHURCH OF CHRIST was organized after the method and simplicity of the New Testament, when the Christian believers met together in the house of Peter Adams, being assembled in one place for the worship of God. If there was anything more formal on the occasion of the dedication of the meeting-house, or the installation of the first pastor, the fact, with the records of the church during the pastorate of the Rev. Mr. Deming, has passed from knowledge.

The church doubtless was constituted largely of persons who had been members of the Church of Christ in Medfield, of which the Rev. Joseph

Baxter was then the pastor. There is no complete list of the names of those who were the original members, or of those who united with the church prior to 1724. But Peter Adams, Jonathan Adams, John Partridge, Ebenezer Thompson, Samuel Partridge, and Mrs. Susanna (Adams) Alexander, were among this number. The original name of the church was THE CHURCH OF CHRIST, but subsequently to the organization of another church in the westerly part of the town in 1750, it was designated THE FIRST CHURCH OF CHRIST. During the one hundred and seventy-one years of its existence, this church has received the ministrations of nine pastors, including one colleague pastor. The longest pastorate was that of the Rev. Nathan Bucknam, extending through a period of seventy-one years; the shortest pastorate was four years, that of the Rev. John O. Means

These nine pastorates constitute an aggregate of one hundred and sixty-one years, so that the church has been without a settled minister only eleven years during its entire history. The average length of its pastorates has been about twenty years.

THE FIRST PASTORATE.

1715 — 1722

"At a Town-meeting of the Inhabitants of the town of Medway, January 31st, 1715," of which John Rockwood was the moderator :

" It was proposed whether the town was ready to bring in their votes for a minister to settle amongst us. The votes were given in and sorted, and REV. DAVID DEMING was chosen to settle amongst us to carry on the work of the ministry."

" 1715 Sept ye 12 Assembled the inhabitants of Medway at the Meeting House to hear Mr. David Deming's answer. William Allin was chosen for Moderator to make proposals to the Town. And there was proposed to the town whether they would give Mr David Deming sixty pounds for his salary. And then and there was by vote of the town granted sixty pounds for his yearly salary, and upon the same day Mr. Deming accepted what ye Town voted for him "

" 1715 Assembled the inhabitants of Medway on Oct. 24th at the Meeting House to conclude upon the Ordaining of Rev. Mr. David Deming. Then was voted to ordain Mr. Deming on the third Wednesday in November." Accordingly, Mr. David Deming was ordained and installed, November 20, 1715, the first Pastor of Medway.

Meanwhile the new town had been busy in providing a meeting-house. At their first town-meeting, November 23, 1713, they fixed upon a location, and of a meeting held a few days later there remains this record

"Medway December ye 4th 1714. A proposall to the town whither the town will put out ye meeting house by ye gwab to som work man and the men that are to be imployed in the work to be hiered in this town this propsion fully granted A proposall — for the length and bredth of the meting house. The length to be thirty four foot and the bredth to be twenty and eight, and sixteen foot between ioynt and a rouf to rise four foot from the senter of the beame — voted for this for to be dimentions of the meeting house — this fully voted."

A proposal to the town that the meting house should be raised and couued and planked and claborded, and dors mad, and pulpit mad, and tabell mad, and seats mad, a pew mad, and stairs mad, and sealed with good boards from the seats to the plats all round with one teer of galriess — this proposition fully voted."

Pursuant of these votes of the town. "At a committee meeting held February ye 6th 1714 there were signed the articles of agreement made between John Richardson and ourselves for the building of the meeting-house."

"Medway June 7th 1714. At a meeting held by the committee who were chosen to take care to procure a Meeting house built, held at Daniel Richardson's the town reckoned with our Carpenter and have paid him thirty pounds and received a receipt from him acknowledging himself fully satisfied of the first payment." It appears that when the inhabitants on the west side aided in the building of the new meeting-house in Medfield it was agreed that when they came to build a meeting-house on the west side for themselves a certain part of the money paid should revert to their advantage in this matter. Hence, "June 14 1714. The select men of Medway assembled with the select men of Medfield to reckon and find out what was due to us from the town of Medfield for our helping them build their meeting house and upon the Reckoning was found by them and us to be 22lbs. 9s. 4d."

This amount was duly paid and received December 15, 1714. The work on the meeting-house was pushed forward, and sometime early in 1715 the building was completed, for we have this record:

"March 7 1715 Assembled the inhabitants of Medway at the Meeting House, it being their general Town Meeting."

THE FIRST MEETING-HOUSE.

1715 — 1749.

THE FIRST MEETING HOUSE stood on the west side of the old cemetery a little to the north of the public tomb. The engraving above was made from the exact measurements and description given in the ancient records. There were improvements made from time to time in their meeting-house by the vote of the town. About 1718 there was an appropriation of 25s. made, and Mr. John Richardson was instructed "to build another pew at the northeast end of the meeting-house next to the pulpit for the minister's family to sit in." Subsequently other pews were built by the more wealthy and honorable families at their own expense, permission being granted by the town. It was a current practice to have a committee chosen, men of good judgment, to seat the meeting-house, according to honorable standing by reason of years and wealth. The dedication of this house of God probably occurred on the same day as the installation of the first pastor.

In this small, unsteepled and unheated building worshiped the people of Medway for thirty-four years, until, January 18, 1749, it was destroyed by fire.

It is found that as a condition of Mr. Deming's settlement, the proprietors of the common lands made certain grants to his advantage.

"At a meeting of the Proprietors of common undivided lands within the towns of Medfield and Medway, held at the meeting-house in Medway upon April 20, 1715·

Granted To Rev⁴ Mr. David Deming, to him, his heirs and assignees forever twenty eight acres of land lying within the town of Medway, southward of Bare Hills, near the wood lots where their select men have marked out so much, being part swamp and part upland, bounded northward by wood land, and by common land on all other parts; provided he settle himself in Medway and continue with them as their settled Minister.

Granted To the Rev. Mr. David Deming a small parcel of land upon Bare Hill, near the burying place for to build on not exceeding two acres."

At this same meeting also was "*Granted* To the use of the ministry in Medway forever twenty acres of land in Medway at a place called black island being part swamp and part upland."

Voted that Abraham Harding Sen. John Richardson, Ebenezer Thompson be a committee to lay out said twenty acres for the Ministry." This grant is that known as The Parsonage Lot.

"Sept 13th 1722. In answer to the Rev Mr Deming's request that yᵉ Town would give him a total dissmission from his ministerial office," the selectmen ordered a town-meeting "to attend that business at yᵉ Meeting house on yᵉ 24th of the above said month at one o'clock afternoon."

Accordingly the inhabitants of the town assembled. Edward Clark was chosen moderator and "yᵉ Rev. Mr Deming renewed his request by writing to yᵉ town" After a vain attempt to adjourn and a lengthy debate upon the subject, "Then both Church and Town as a Town manifested their willingness by a vote to give Mr Deming his request, which did appear in the meeting he had been asking for more than for six weeks past at several times, and dismiss Mr Deming from his ministerial service amongst us" "The select men the same day by yᵉ desire of the Town acquainted Mr Deming that they had answered his request He accepted and manifested his thanks to them for the same"

"Oct. 16, 1722 The Church of Medway dismissed Mr Deming from his pastoral office over them by the advice of Council from the neighboring Churches"

The balance of Mr Deming's salary was receipted for as follows· "Received of Edward Clark, Town Treasurer the sum of thirty two pounds six shillings and a penny in full which was my due from the Town for carrying on the work of the Ministry in yᵉ year one thousand seven hundred and twenty two I say received by me this 29th January 1723. DAVID DEMING"

Thus closed the first pastorate in Medway. In the absence of church records it is impossible to learn much that it would be of interest to know of the church during these first seven years. The Rev. Mr. Deming doubtless removed from town soon after his dismissal, but to what place is unknown. *Vid.* BIOGRAPHIES.

Upon the termination of Mr. Deming's ministry, at a town-meeting held March 6, 1723, the town

"*Voted*, For a Committee to provide a minister for yᵉ Town who were Theophilus Clark, John Partridge, Nathaniel Whiting, Samuel Hill and Jeremiah Adams." Again,

November 4, 1723 the town was called together "To choose a Committee to provide a minister to supply the pulpit and proceeded as followeth :

Voted, Lieut. Rockwood for Moderator and Edward Clark, Ebenezer Thompson, Ensign Bullard, Joseph Daniell Sen., Col John Barber for a Committee to provide as afore said."

Being notified by warrant duly issued, "Assembled the inhabitants of this Town on Wednesday the 19th of February 1724.

Voted Capt Timothy Clark for Moderator. Then was proposed whether the Town were ready to give a minister a call.

Voted that they were ready. The votes were then called for to be brought in for a minister, when done and numbered it appeared to fall upon Mr. Green of Boston, very unanimously. Proposed what they would grant for Mr. Green's yearly salary. It appeared by the vote of the Town that they give Mr. Green if he settle with us 75 pounds for yearly salary. Proposed to the Town what they would give Mr Green for settlement and it appeared by the vote of the Town that they would give Mr Green if he settle with us ninety pounds for his encouragement and that Edward Clark, Ebenezer Thompson were chosen by the Town to acquaint Mr. Green with the Town's choice and proceedings."

It is evident that Mr. Green, of Boston, declined the call thus tendered.

The Second Pastorate.

1724 — 1795.

" Assembled the inhabitants of Medway on June the 11th 1724 by virtue of an orderly warning according to law, in order to make choice of a minister to settle in the work of yᵉ ministry, and proceeded." "When the votes came in and were numbered it fell unanimously upon Mr. Bucknam both Church and Town. And then was voted eighty pounds for the said Rev. Mr. Bucknam's yearly salary provided he take up to settle with us in the work of yᵉ ministry, then yᵉ Town voted one hundred pounds to encourage him, yᵉ said Bucknam to settle with us. Lastly voted, Lieut. Theophilus Clark and Lieut. John Bullard to treat yᵉ said Rev. Mr. Buckman upon settlement with us." August 26, 1724, additional salary was voted " as followeth To pay eighty pounds a year for the first three years after he settle with us in the work of the ministry then to rise five pounds more and after he has been settled with us in the work of the ministry six years rise five pounds more which will then make ninety pounds for his yearly salary."

Mr. Bucknam's acceptance of the call is found in the town records, as follows :

" *The Reverend Mr. Nathan Bucknam's Answer, Given October the* 25, 1724."

" To the Church and People of Medway :

"*Dearly beloved,*— Inasmuch as it hath pleased the Lord of the harvest, the King and Head of the Church, whose sole prerogative it is to send forth such Labourers into his vineyard, as seemeth Him meet, in his over-ruling and all wise Providence, so to order it, that you were directed at first to invite me to dispense the glorious Gospel of his Grace to you in this place, and to render my ministerial labors amongst you so pleasing and acceptable, and so to unite your hearts and affections to me, that you have so unanimously given me an invitation to settle with you in the Great Work of Gospel Ministry, for which I acknowledge with thankfulness his mercy and grace as well as your kindness to me. And whereas, He has in his Sovereign Provi dence so far drawn forth my heart in love towards you and has so enlarged your hearts, as that you have made me such offers, respecting my settlement and support amongst you, as that, I hope by His blessing with it I may, at present comfortably subsist. These, therefore, are to let you know, that, relying upon yᵉ Divine Grace, blessing, directing and assistance, and depending upon your kindness and generosity, that you will not let me want hereafter : but as God shall give you ability and my circumstances may require, you will further assist me. Upon serious consideration of, and good advice about, a matter of so great concern, as it so nearly relates to the glory of God, to your and my comfort here and happiness hereafter, I do now, here, openly, heartily and cheerfully embrace and accept of your invitation to settle with you in the work of yᵉ ministry at Medway Praying that the God of peace and love will continue our mutual love and more and more unite our affections to each other and yᵗ 'Grace mercy and peace' may be multiplied abundantly unto you all, and asking your joynt prayers and continual supplications to yᵉ God of all grace for me, that I may prove the infinite fullness that is in Christ, receive all the Grace yᵗ I shall stand in need of to enable me to behave myself wisely in the house of God, and faithfully and successfully discharging my duty amongst you, in all the parts of it so yᵗ I may not only save my own soul, but yours and all such as shall be committed to my trust, that we may all at length meet together, celebrate the praises of God and the Lamb, with the church triumphant in the everlasting joys of our Lord and Master to whom be Glory, Dominion and Power forever and ever. Amen."

The Rev. Nathan Bucknam was ordained and installed December 23, 1724 "This was an auspicious and happy day to the inhabitants of the town," says the Rev. Mr. Wright, in his Centennial Discourse in 1813 He also adds ·

"Although Mr. Bucknam was young and of slender constitution, he was mature in Christian knowledge and experience, and strong in the faith and hope of the Gospel At the time of his settlement he was deservedly considered as an able, pious, and promising young man ; and much was hoped, under God, through the instrumentality of his public and private labors. As to his religious sentiments they were Calvinistic He firmly believed in those doctrines which are usually called The Doctrines of Grace, or The Doctrines of the Reformation. These he faithfully and unequivocally preached."

The Rev. Mr. Bucknam was small in person, but a preacher of much pulpit ability. After the close of his active pastorate he still retained the pastoral relation, and received an annual salary until the time of his death, making the length of his pastorate more than seventy years.

When past eighty-two years of age, he arranged with the parish to settle a colleague, and terminated his active ministry in the sixty-second year of his pastorate, May 14, 1786. His Farewell Sermon was from the text: "*Thus saith the Lord, Stand ye in the ways, and see, and ask for the old paths, where is the good way, and walk therein, and ye shall find rest for your souls,*" Jeremiah vi., 16. The solemnity was closed by singing the 122d Psalm, from Tate and Brady's Hymn Book,

"*Oh, 'twas a joyful sound to hear,*" etc.

The Rev. Mr. Buckman was a man of quick impulses. Mr. Wright says "He sometimes spoke unadvisedly with his lips, under excited feelings, but was soon calmed and gave way to the dictates of sober reason and religion "

He must have been a man of great natural and acquired resources, and of wonderful administrative ability, to have retained such a hold upon the people, and to have led the church harmoniously through so many years of ministration. The deaths of the Rev. and Mrs. Bucknam are found recorded in an ancient diary, as follows: "The Revd Mr Bucknam Deceas^d on friday Evening the 6 of Feby 1795 in ye 92 year of his age. His funeral was attended on Thursday afternoon the 12th of the Same month with great Solemnity and Respect. The Procession Enter^d ye meeting house where Mr Haven made ye first prayer Mr Prentis Deliver^d a Discourse from 2^d Peter 1st 13 and 14 well adapted to the occasion. Mr Carrel prayed and Pronounced ye Blessing after which the Procession proceeded to ye Grave from thence to the Dwelling house again the chh walking before ye Procession.

N. B. Mr Bucknam Deceas^d in the 92 year of his age the 71 of his ministry and 67th year in a married state."

"M^d Bucknam Deceas^d Sunday Evening the 1st of May 1796 in the 91 year of her age her funeral was Attended the 5th day of the same month the Procession Entered ye meeting house where Mr Haven made ye Prayer and from thence to the tomb."

THE CHURCH RECORDS.

The earliest records of the church, extant, were kept by the Rev. Mr. Bucknam. The ancient record book is superscribed as follows:.

"MEDWAY CHURCH RECORDS since ye year 1724 December 23 Kept pr. me, Nathan Bucknam, Pastor of s^d church."

The covers of this book of records are much worn. They are inscribed with the recorded marriages solemnized by the Rev. Mr. Bucknam in his early ministry. The writing is legible only in part. The contents of this ancient church record are embraced under the following headings:

"*We must believe in the ability, authority and faithfulness of Baptism.*"
"*The names of those that have been received into Covenant and put themselves under ye watch and Care of this Church.*"
"*The votes and acts of ye Chh. of Christ in Medway.*"
"*A Record of ye names together with ye time of ye person admitted into ye Church of Christ in Medway since ye pastoral care of it was committed to me.*"

Under the first heading is an alphabetical registration of baptisms. This list embraces eight hundred and thirty-three names. Of these seventy-three are Daniell or Daniels, and one hundred and thirteen of them are Partridge; showing very plainly that young Daniels were more numerous than in Nebuchadnezzar's day, and that Partridges were not as scarce in the church at that period as they now are in Black Swamp. Among the entries made were the following:

"*Sept.* 16, 1739. I baptized London and Sambo, Negroes, the former, ye negro of Jasper Adams, ye latter, ye negro of Wm. Burges."

"*Nov. 29th*, 1741 I baptized Stephen and Charles, negroes, the former ye negro of Lieut. Timothy Clark, ye latter ye neg^ro of Capt. Nathl Whiting."

" *Dec. 20th*, 1741. Upon ye desire of Saml Harding and wife to have a negro child baptized w^h y^y had took in its infancy for y^ir own. It was put to the brethren, whether, they thought masters and mistresses might offer up ye servants that they had a property in, in their minority, and they had a right to baptism upon y^r account. It passed in the negative."

Under the second heading is the registration of those who entered into the Halfway Covenant. There appear one hundred and twenty-eight names, from 1725 to 1800, when the practice of receiving persons in this way was abandoned by the church.

Under the third heading are embraced the items of church business transacted in a period of seventy years. These items are all recorded on less than seven small pages of the old record book.

We are told of the choice of at least three generations of deacons, eleven or twelve in all, during this one pastorate, and of three or four cases of church discipline and a few other matters of church action.

Under the last heading is a registration of those who came into full covenant, and were admitted to the ordinance of the Lord's Supper. The whole number received during the Rev. Mr. Bucknam's ministry exceeded two hundred.

Perhaps there is no item of greater interest in these church records than a brief mention of an occasion which occured October 8, 1736. Almost the entire church assembled in the meeting-house, and after prayer was offered by the pastor, the Rev. Mr. Bucknam, all present renewed their vows to God and to one another by signing their names to the Church Covenant.

This was the original Covenant of the Church. It has recently come to light in a well-preserved copy, and is here printed for the first time.

" MEDWAY CHH. COVENANT: *Renewed by the major part of ye Chh. at a Chh. Meeting october* 8 1736.

WE THE MEMBERS OF THE CHH. OF CHRIST in medway that are in full Communion, having apprehended it Convenient & Even expedient for some reasons to renew Covenant with God & one another & being now assembled in the Holy presence of god, in the name of the lord Jesus Christ after humble Confession of our manifold Transgressions before the lord our god, & Earnestly Supplicating for pardoning mercy through the blood of Christ & deep acknowledgment of our great unWorthiness to be owned to be the lord's Covenant people to perform any Spiritual duty unless the lord Jesus does enable us thereunto by his Spirit dwelling in us & being awfully Sensible that it is a dreadful thing for Sinful dust and ashes personally to Transact with the infinitely glorious majesty of heaven, we do in humble Confidence of his gracious assistance & acceptance through Christ each One of us for himself and Jointly together Explicitly Covenant in manner and form following, viz.

1. We give up Ourselves to that god Whose name alone is Jehovah father Son & holy ghost the only true & living God, and to our blessed lord Jesus Christ & our only blessed Saviour phrophet priest & king over Our Souls, Only mediator of the Covenant of grace, promising by the help of his spirit & grace to cleave unto God as our chief good & to the lord Jesus Christ by faith & gospel Obedience as becometh his covenant people forever.

2. We do give up our ofspring to god in Jesus Christ, avouching the lord to be the god of our Children as well as our god & children with ourselves to be his people humble adorning the grace of god that we and our ofspring with us may be looked upon to be the Lord's.

3. We do give up ourselves to one another, in the love, and according to the will of god freely Covenanting & binding ourselves to walk Together as a particular Con-

gregational Chh. of Christ in all the ways of his worship according to the holy rules of yᵉ word of god promising in brotherly love to watch over one anothers Souls faithfully & to Submit to the government & discipline of Christ in his Chh. & duly to attend all those ordinances which Christ hath Instituted in his Chh. and Commanded to be attended by his people according to the order of the gospel & degrees of communion unto which we have attained, but promising after all & so that we will each of us do our part to uphold & maintain the word & worship of god & endeavor to transmit the same faithfully to posterity.

4. We promise & engage to walk orderly in a way of fellowship & Communion with all the Chhs. of Christ among us according to those rules of holy order which he hath appointed, that the lord may be one & his name one in all the Chhs. throughout all generations to his Eternal glory in Christ Jesus.

5. We do freely promise & engage as in the presence of god that we will, Christ helping us, Endeavor every one of us to reform our hearts & life by Seeking to mortify all our Sins & labouring to walk more Closely with god then ever yet we have done, and will worship god in publick private & secret, & endeavor to do it without formality & hipocricy & fully & faithfully discharge all covenant Duties one to another in Chh. Communion.

6. We promise and engage that we will walk before god in our houses with a perfect heart & that we will uphold the worship of god therein Continually according as he in word doth require both in respect of prayer & reading the Scriptures that so the word of god may dwell richly in us & will do what on us lies to bring up Our Children for Christ that they may be Such as those who have the name of Christ put upon them by a Solemn dedication to god in christ ought to be, & will therefore, as need Shall be Catechize exhort & Charge them to the fear of the lord, & endeavor to set a holy example before them & be much in prayer for their Convertion & Salvation.

7. We will endeavor to be pure from the sins of the times and in our places endeavor the suppression thereof & be careful So to walk as that we may give no occation to others to Sin or Speak evil of our holy profession. Now that we may observe & keep this Sacred Covenant & all the branches of it inviolable forever, we desire to deny ourselves & to depend wholy upon the power of the eternal Spirit of grace & on the free mercy of god & merit of Christ Jesus & where we shall fail thereto, wait upon the Lord Jesus for pardon, acceptance & healing for his names Sake."

This public renewal of the Covenant, by each one subscribing with his own hand, made the occasion one of deep solemnity. And to this act the Rev. Mr. Wright credits largely, the deepened spirituality that followed, which developed into a revival of religion in 1741, the most marked that had hitherto occurred in the history of the church, the results of which were the addition of some fifty persons to its membership.

There are many church papers not included in the book of records, which are quaint and deeply interesting, but which cannot have a place here. The Halfway Covenant, which was widely adopted by the churches of Massachusetts from the early date of 1662, the later Covenant of this church, and other documents may be found published in *A Historical Discourse of the First Church of Christ*, 1876.

Our fathers had their church troubles as well as those living now. Take for example, the matter of singing in the early days. It often was at the greatest remove from harmony.

THE OLD WAY OF SINGING was for the chorister to start the tune with the pitch-pipe, the congregation to follow each in his own fashion at his own tune, and no two persons singing alike, but singing with all their might, " like the voice of many waters."

The Westerly Precinct of Wrentham, now Franklin, June 26, 1738, voted, "To sing no other Tunes than are Pricked Down in our former Psalm Books which were Printed between thirty and forty years Agoe and To Sing Them as They are Prickt down in them as Near as they can."

This was a blow at the old way of singing, and March 8, 1739, that church voted not to sing in the old way, and near the close of that meeting the query was raised: "To see what notice the church will take of one of the brethren's striking into a pitch of the tune unusualy raised, February 18, 1739."

And it was voted,

"Whereas, our brother David Pond, as several of our brethren viz.: David Jones Ebenezer Hunting, Benjamin Rockwood Jr., Aaron Haws and Michael Metcalf apprehends, struck into a pitch of the tune on Feb. 18, in public worship on the forenoon raised above what was set, after most of the Congregation as is thought, kept the pitch for three lines and after our Pastor had desired them that had raised it to fall to the pitch that was set to be suitable, decent or to that purpose

"The question was put, whether the church apprehends this our brother David Pond's so doing to be disorderly, and it passed in the affirmative and David Pond is suspended until satisfaction is given"

David Pond afterwards applied to the Church of Christ, in Medway, for admission. Letters, which well illustrate the characteristics of the times, were exchanged by the two churches in regard to the case of Mr. Pond. It has been suggested that because of his uncommon height and muscular strength he pitched the tune too high. Whether this, or because of willfulness, others must determine; at any rate he was excommunicated from the church, but some years after made confession of fault, was restored to good standing, and became one of the founders of the Second Church of Christ, in Medway.

THE NOON-HOUSE.

Shortly after the Rev. Mr. Bucknam's settlement, it appears that, permission being given by the town, there was a subscription raised for the purpose as expressed, "To erect an house fifteen feet square in some convenient place near the meeting-house for our convenience on ye Sabbath between meetings." This subscription was headed by "Jonathan Plympton, £3."

This building was boarded on three sides, being open toward the south; in the centre was a large, flat stone, on which in cold weather a fire was kindled, there being an opening in the roof overhead for the smoke to escape; and all around were pine benches, where the people sat and ate their Sabbath lunch. This was called the Noon-house.

The FIRST MEETING-HOUSE was destroyed by fire January 18, 1749. How it took fire was unknown. Some surmised that it was set on fire by a certain negro, others, that a prominent desire among many persons to have a new meeting-house inspired the burning of the old; but, whatever the unknown facts, we see that burning meeting-houses is not a " new thing under the sun," and that the world has not yet outgrown a very old iniquity It seems that nothing was saved from the fire except the glass; this the parish, which began to exist about that time, voted should be sold, and accordingly sales were made from time to time, as opportunity offered, and the avails were appropriated to pay the incidental expenses of the parish, and for several years the income from this source was more than sufficient; so that, finally, from the unexpended receipts for the glass from the old meeting-house, ten shillings were appropriated to purchase a parish record book, five shillings for a latch to put on the pulpit door in the new meeting-house, and the balance, about four shillings, to compensate the parish clerk, Samuel Harding, Esq., for copying the minutes of the parish into the new and large record book. That old record book is still in existence; but what became of the five-shilling latch on the pulpit door is among the things unknown.

After the burning of the first meeting-house, public worship was conducted, for a time, in the dwelling-house of Captain Joseph Lovell, Esq. The people, however, took immediate steps to rebuild.

Hitherto the town had transacted the secular business of the church, but now, by a warrant issued under authority of King George II., in the twenty-second year of his reign, to one Samuel Harding, Esq., a meeting of the citizens of this part of the town was called, and the First Precinct in Medway was organized February 3, 1749. At this first meeting Samuel Harding, Esq., being chosen moderator and precinct clerk; it was "voted to build a meeting-house for the public worship of God." "Then voted to choose five men to be a committee to manage the affair of building said house, viz.: 1st, Samᶧ Harding; 2d, Dea. Thomas Harding; 3d, Lieut. Timothy Clark; 4th, Ensgⁿ Joseph Richardson; 5th, Jona. Adams, Juʳ. Voted 1600 pound old tenor to be assessed on polls & estates in said First Precinct, towards building said house." This sum was about £213 lawful money, or $1,000 in our currency.

"April 5, 1749, *Voted*, That yᵉ committee should build the meeting-house 42 feet long & 33 feet in width and twenty feet high between joynts." "*Voted* that the said meeting-house shall be raised about yᵉ width of yᵉ house, toward yᵉ North from yᵉ spot of land where yᵉ old meeting-house stood. *Voted*, that yᵉ provision that is to be made for yᵉ raising said meeting-house shall be by a free contribution, then voted that Samuel Ellis, Dea. Barbar, Joshua Partridge and Samuel Hill, shall take care that there shall be an equal or suitable quantity of Cyder, Rum & Beer brought to said house and a baiting bitt for the men before the Raising be finished."

The raising of this meeting-house came off on Thursday, April 27, 1749. The old house was burned the 18th of the previous January; and thus, in a little over three months, the trees that were standing in the forests were felled, drawn to the spot, hewn into timber, framed, and raised into a meeting-house, about a half larger than its predecessor. The 21st of May, following, just three weeks from the Sabbath next after the raising, the people gathered for public worship, and the Rev. Mr. Bucknam preached for the first time in the new meeting-house. But it was not finished; and while everything, so far, had gone on very harmoniously and with great dispatch, there was yet to come up quite a division of feeling and considerable delay before the house should be completed. The question arose, "whether yᵉ Precinct will have an Alley three feet and a half wide straight from the great double doors to the Pulpit " in their new house. At the first meeting of the precinct to consider this weighty matter, they voted *not* to have it. Another meeting was called, and they voted to have the alley. Then a meeting was called to reconsider. There was great excitement through the precinct; meeting after meeting was held; finally, at a crowded meeting, they polled the house. All in favor went to one side, all opposed, to the other, until counted; it was found that there was a majority of four in favor of the alley; thus, after a year's delay, great stir, much talk, and many meetings, it was decided; and the alley was made " from the great double doors straight to the pulpit."

THE SECOND MEETING-HOUSE.

1749 — 1816.

The second meeting-house stood some forty feet to the north of the site of the one destroyed. The spot of the front entrance to the new meeting-house is marked by the grave of Adam Bullard, Esq. The seating of people in the house of God at this date was a matter of grave importance, requiring the united wisdom of men whose good judgment was acknowledged.

In 1766 Moses Richardson, Elijah Clark, and Jonathan Adams, were instructed to " seat the meeting-house one pound of estate to a year's age as near as may be." About ten years after the house was built, the precinct appropriated " three pounds and eighteen shillings to be laid out in coloring and repairing the meeting-house." For some number of years they paid the Rev. Mr. Bucknam " for his negro woman keeping the meeting-house, 9s. 4d." In 1769 special seats were built for the negroes to sit in.

April 30, 1770 :

" *Put to vote*, to see if it be the minds of the Precinct, That the new seats built for the Negroes at each end of the Public meeting-house in said Precinct below, shall be the seats, and the *only seats*, in the s^d meeting-house for the Mulattoes, Negros, and Indians of this Precinct to sit in, in times of Divine Service, during the Precinct's pleasure. *Resolved* in the affirmative."

" *Put to vote* to see if it be the minds of the Precinct to prohibit the Mulattoes, Negros, & Indians of this precinct, sitting or standing in any of the allies or on the stairs of the s^d meeting-house in times of Divine Service. *Resolved* in ye affirmative."

" *Put to vote* to see if it be the minds of the Precinct to choose a committee of three men, to inform the masters of the Negros Mulattoes & Indians of this Precinct, of the above mentioned votes & resolves, and to desire them in the name of the Precinct to conform themselves thereunto and to order their servants into the seats built and provided for them. *Resolved* in yᵉ affirmative. Jonathan Adams Capt. Jona. Adams, and Isaiah Morse was unanimously chosen for the sᵈ Committee." . . .

" *Put to vote* to see if the Precinct will choose a committee of three men to prosecute the disobedience or non observance of the afore mentioned votes & resolves of this Precinct relating to the Mulattoes, Negros &c. *Resolved* in the affirmative."

" *Adjourned* to last Wednesday in May, 1770," at which time " Moses Richardson Oliver Adams and Jonathan Adams yᵉ 3d was chosen for the sᵈ committee. Then the sᵈ inhabitants granted the sum of 38£—os —od for the necessary charge of the sᵈ committee."

This second meeting-house continued to be occupied for sixty-seven years. Soon after the close of the Rev. Mr. Wright's ministry it was abandoned, a new and much larger house having been erected.

The Third (Colleague) Pastorate.

1788—1793.

The Rev. Benjamin Greene commenced preaching as a candidate for settlement in Medway, February 26, 1787. The church, and the parish also, were deeply impressed that to settle a minister was a grave responsibility, for such an event had not occurred for sixty-three years. The church called a special Day of Fasting and Prayer in view of it. And we find the parish in public meeting, March 29° 1787, voting as follows : " That we will join with the Church in this place, in setting apart a Day of Fasting and Prayer for direction in calling and settling a Gospel Minister in this place." That day was observed accordingly.

A call to settle was extended to Mr. Greene, June 13, 1787, but declined. It was renewed in August, and again declined. But the call being again renewed February 12, 1788, was accepted. The salary was £75, with a settlement of £200. Mr. Greene was ordained June 25, 1788, colleague pastor with the Rev. Mr. Bucknam. The Rev. Jacob Cushing, D. D., of Waltham, preached the sermon, taking for the text, "*For the Jews require a sign, and the Greeks seek after wisdom.*" 1 Cor. i., 22-24. This discourse was published. The Rev. Jonas Clark, of Lexington, delivered the charge to the pastor ; and the right hand of fellowship was given by the Rev. Elijah Brown, of Sherborn.

It is said that Joseph Lovell, Esq., entertained the council and learned gentlemen present on the occasion at his own expense, and that some two hundred persons sat down to dine at tables spread under the elm trees near his house. In 1885 these trees were still standing near the house of C. W. Emerson, M. D.

The Rev. Mr. Greene's ministry continued only about five years. He was dismissed at his own request, February 28, 1793, some two years prior to Mr. Bucknam's death. He preached his farewell sermon, March 17, 1793, taking for the text, "*But none of these things move me,*" etc., Acts xx., 24-27, 32. This discourse was printed and widely circulated.

On leaving Medway the Rev. Mr. Greene gave up preaching, and entered the legal profession, where he attained to eminence. He died in 1837, in Berwick, Me. *Vid.* Biographies, also Genealogies.

The Rev. Mr. Greene was a man of fine abilities and widely respected for his commanding talents and acquirements. It is narrated that a last and very important service to his old parish was rendered by the Rev. Mr. Greene years after his dismission. Being in Boston, he was met by his old friend, Joseph Lovell, Esq , who was there to appear in court for Medway in some case involving large interests. The lawyer engaged to attend to the case did not handle it successfully, and it was quite apparent that it would go against the town. At this juncture, Mr Lovell asked the Rev. Mr. Greene to appear and speak in its behalf, which he did, and the case, that all thought lost, was gained.

——————

The Fourth Pastorate.

1798—1815.

The Rev. Luther Wright, a recent graduate from Harvard College, Mass , preached his first sermon in Medway, Sunday, June 25, 1797 Subsequently he supplied the pulpit for three months with great acceptance. Afterward, while fulfilling an engagement of a few months in Brentwood, N. H., he received a call to return to Medway, and become their pastor.

This call to Mr. Wright was dated January 4, 1798, and the salary offered was $266.67, with a settlement of $666.67, to be paid within two years. Under date of April 29, 1798, the Rev. Mr. Wright returned an answer of acceptance, and was ordained June 13, 1798. At the time of his settlement he was unmarried, but about two years later the following appeared in *The Massachusetts Mercury* of January 3, 1800 : "At East Sudbury, on Monday, 23d ult., Rev. Luther Wright, of Medway, to Miss Nancy Bridge, daughter of the Rev. Josiah Bridge." It was on this day that the death of Washington, nine days after its occurrence, was first announced in Boston. Not long after their marriage the young minister and his bride arrived in Medway to receive the congratulations of his parishioners. Rev. and Mrs. Wright resided, during his ministry of some seventeen years, in the house recently the home of the late venerable Oliver Phillips, Esq.

The Rev. Mr. Wright, in person, was a short, thick-set man, of fair, full countenance, and is remembered by some persons still living He was devoted to his work, and while he met with some discouragements, he was loved by his people, and showed himself a man of ability and sagacity. Some fifty persons were added to the church, and during the first and last years of his pastorate, there were seasons of marked refreshing from the Lord. He was largely instrumental in bringing about the renewed fellowship of the First and Second Churches in the town, after an alienation of thirty-two years.

The Rev. Mr. Wright was a fine classical scholar, and fitted many young men for college. Students from Harvard College were sometimes placed for a season under his instruction. After a successful pastorate of seventeen years, his letter of resignation was read from the pulpit July 9, 1815 and he was formally dismissed, by advice of council, September 20, 1815.

The Rev. Mr. Wright preached his Farewell Discourse October 1, 1815, taking for his text, "*Men and brethren, let me freely speak unto you*" Acts ii , 29. On the same day he administered the Communion, and there were presented two children for baptism One was the son of Marcus Richardson, who received the name of Simon Hill, for the senior deacon of the church; and the other, the son of Samuel Seaver, was named Luther Wright, for the retiring pastor.

The Rev. Mr. Wright's printed sermons are: "A discourse preached May 25, 1806, at the funeral of Captain Cyrus Bullard," master of the brig Litteller, who died on his third voyage, April 13, 1806, of fever on the island of St. Thomas, at the age of twenty-six years. Captain Bullard was a young man of great promise. The text chosen was: "*Thou didst say, Woe is me now! for the Lord hath added grief to my sorrow: I fainted in my sighing and I find no rest.*" Jer. xlv., 3. "A centennial sermon of the town, preached November 4, 1813," the text being, "*This day shall be unto you for a memorial.*" Ex. xii., 14. The selectmen requested a copy for printing, and it was accordingly published.

The Rev. Mr. Wright continued to preach some years, and on retiring from the ministry removed to Woburn, Mass. He visited Medway on his eightieth birth-day and preached to his old people, taking this text, "*Lo! I am this day fourscore.*" Joshua xiv., 10. This was his last visit to the scene of his early labors in the Gospel ministry. *Vid.* Biographies.

THE THIRD MEETING-HOUSE.

1816 — 1850.

Early in 1813 a movement was started by Joseph Lovell, Esq., and others to build a new meeting-house. A vote of the parish was obtained the sixth of September following. The location selected was Bullard's Hill, somewhat to the southward of the old meeting-house. Some three acres of land were purchased of Mr. Adam Bullard, who gave one acre in addition, and small parcels of land adjacent were also given by Mr. Asa Darling, Timothy Hammond, Esq., and Mr. Jonathan Bullen, amounting in all to nearly five acres. These were liberal grounds for the purpose. The site chosen on which to erect the building was the very summit of the hill, obliging much labor and expense in so grading it as to make it accessible by carriage, or on foot. The ascent, after all, was very steep. These lands in later times were purchased of the parish by Major George Holbrook, and are still retained in possession by his descendants. The avails, $200, were expended in grading and fencing the grounds about the present meeting-house.

The building committee chosen were Joseph Lovell, Esq., Messrs. Theodore Clark, Comfort Walker, Moses Adams, and Thomas Harding. The building contractor was Malachi Bullard.

The plan of the new meeting-house made the dimensions fifty-three feet square, with a projection in front of thirty feet by fifteen. The posts were twenty-nine feet, and it was voted to build a "steeple instead of a cupola"; with this exception, and some other slight changes, it was to be built after the plan of the new meeting-house then building in West Medway. No church steeple, as yet, had been erected in the town, and the old East Parish said, "We must have a steeple to our new meeting-house." But alas! perhaps in rebuke of an undue pride, and certainly, to the grief of the builder, this first steeple had hardly pierced the skies, when the fearful gale of September 23, 1815, came, took it, while yet unfinished, completely off, hurled it to the ground, and broke it into a thousand fragments. However, the people came to the help of the contractor, and speedily the steeple was rebuilt.

This new house of worship was near completion when the first church-bell was cast in Holbrook's Bell Foundry. The happy thought seized the parish to purchase it; and, accordingly, it was hung aloft in the new church steeple, May 13, 1816, where it pealed forth its glad tones each Lord's Day for many years, reminding the people of the Sabbath and the worship of God in the sanctuary.

"THE EXPENSE OF BUILDING AND FINISHING the new meeting-house in East Parish in Medway (exclusive of the cost of the land whereon said house stands and the interest on money borrowed by the Treasurer of said parish to carry the same into effect) is as follows, viz.:

No. 1.	To cost of underpining said house, &c.,	$ 386 96
" 2.	To the first contract with Mr. Malachi Bullard by Bond,	6,500 00
" 3.	To the extra paid to Malachi Bullard,	134 00
" 4.	To the cost of dineing the men for raising said house,	39 50
" 5.	To the stepstones, transporting laying the same and cherry stuff,	296 21
" 6.	To the banasters, Scrapers Scrools and four Letters,	53 00
" 7.	To the Bell, Frame wheel yoke irons rope & ½ the risk of raising,	535 00
" 8.	To the committees services & sundry accounts,	99 09
	Total,	$8,043 76

No. 3, for extra paid to the Building Contractor, MALACHI BULLARD.

" The Committee for effecting the building a New Meeting house in the East parish in Medway to the subscriber Dr for Extra work on the New meeting house.

Scrool and Letters on the Vain,	$ 9 00
Mahogany for the banisters,	7 58
Window in the belfry,	28 00
Work on the front Door,	10 00
Window and side Lites to the front Door,	38 00
2 brass Latches for the pulpet,	02 00
Window over the inside Door,	09 00
For oil and Painting the third time,	25 00
For Plastering and finishing under the stairs,	06 00
Door under the stairs above the projections,	0 50
	135 08
For building Eight Pews in the Side Gallery,	025 00
For painting the floor,	16 00
To mending the windows in the belfry,	19 00
To puting up the pillers in the belfry,	1 75
	$196 83

I shall want the Pay when it becomes Due

MALACHI BULLARD.

MEDWAY June the 15, 1816.

CR.

By a Compromise with the Committee aforesaid to the amount of, . . $62 83

Balance due, . . $134 00

MALACHI BULLARD.

MEDWAY June 24, 1816."

" MEDWAY, June 28, 1816.

Received of the within mentioned committee one hundred and thirty-four dollars, being in full of the within account and all other accounts except a Bond.

MALACHI BULLARD.

Attest — ETHAN COBB."

The house completed, the pews were appraised, "except the First Pew at the right hand of the Broad Alley, which is to be left for the use of the Minister of the Parish." The sale of pews is thus attested:

" We, with the assistance of the Standing Committee of the aforesaid parish sold pews in the aforesaid new meeting house at public auction to the amount of eight thousand one hundred and eighty three dollars ($8,183.00): and have made out Deeds of conveyances of said pews to the purchasers, in behalf of the inhabitants of the said east parish in Medway; the considerations thereof made payable to Nathan Jones. Junr. Treasurer of the said east parish in Medway, or to his successor in that office agreeable to the conditions of the sale of said pews.

THEODORE CLARK, *Committee for effecting*
JOSEPH LOVELL, *the building a new*
meeting house in the east
THOMAS HARDING, *parish in Medway.* '

MEDWAY, Novr 11 1816."

" MEDWAY Ja^n 1817

We the subscribers a committee chosen by the East Parish in Medway to reckon with the committee chosen by s^d Parish to effect the building of a meeting house in said Parish do certify that the within acc^t is well avouched, rightly cast and correct.

ASA DANIELS
AMOS TURNER
ELISHA A. JONES."

Public worship was held in the new meeting-house for the first time September 8, 1816; the Rev. Mr. Holman, of Attleboro, Mass., preached the sermon. It was dedicated November 20, 1816, and continued to be occupied for worship until 1850, thirty-four years. It was then sold, taken down, removed to Rockville, re-erected, and, in 1885, stood bereft of its tall spire, emptied of its former glory, a gloomy, unoccupied building, with no token of its original sacredness. And nothing remains to remind the living of the consecrated sites occupied by the first three meeting-houses, where worshiped their fathers for more than a century. The hill on which stood the third meeting-house is now cut into two parts by the railroad, and the steam-car whistles on its iron way, thoughtless that once, just overhead, were the sanctuary and the pulpit, where the good parson preached his Gospel sermons and said his Sunday prayers.

THE FIFTH PASTORATE.

1816 — 1835.

Soon after the close of the Rev. Mr. Wright's ministry, while the church were looking for an under shepherd to go in and out before them as a pastor, there appeared one Sabbath morning in the pulpit as a candidate, a young man of fine personal bearing, but exceedingly tall, so that all marveled inwardly at his height, and some whispered, "Surely our pulpit has a minister in it to-day nearer Heaven in one respect than any one who ever stood in it before!" But by the time he had concluded the service, many thought that he must be nearer Heaven in another sense also, for he prayed and preached with no common unction and power. The Rev. Luther Bailey made a good impression on the people of Medway, and very shortly the church and the parish agreed in sending him an invitation to settle as their minister.

The annual salary was fixed at $600, and his settlement $200. Some correspondence passed between the parties, and the Rev. Mr. Bailey finally returned his answer of acceptance, dated August 14, 1816, Taunton, Mass.

The arrangements were completed to have the dedication and the ordination fall upon the same day. The day appointed was November 20, 1816. A large council was called, and the representatives of twenty-four churches met on the occasion. The examination of the candidate was highly satisfactory, and the council proceeded to the public services of the dedication and the ordination. The Rev. Daniel C. Saunders, D. D., of Medfield, preached the dedication sermon from the text, "*The glory of the Lord hath filled the house.*" 2 Chron. v, 14. The Rev. James Wilson, of the second church in Providence, made the dedicatory prayer. The Rev. Edward Richmond, D. D., of Stoughton, preached the ordination sermon. The text was, "*By this shall all men know that ye are my disciples if ye have love one to another.*" John xiii., 35. The Rev. Dr. Saunders made the ordaining prayer. The Rev. George Morey, of Walpole, gave the charge to the pastor, and the Rev. Jacob Ide, then recently settled over the Second Church of Christ in Medway, gave the right hand of fellowship.

These services fell on the one hundred and first anniversary of the settlement of the first pastor, the Rev. David Deming, which occurred November 20, 1715. The sermons preached were printed.

The Rev. Joshua Bates, of the First Church, in Dedham, was the scribe of this council, and his record of their doings concludes thus: "All things having been done recently and in order, the council was dissolved."

At the time of the Rev. Mr Bailey's settlement there were seventy-four members of this church. During his ministry there were added about a hundred and forty persons, mostly by confession of faith. The largest accessions were in the years 1827 and 1834. But no year of his ministry passed without some additions. He was a very faithful and laborious pastor, but met with some peculiar trials, owing to the great controversy which arose in the churches of Massachussetts about that time, in regard to the Person of Christ. And, although troubled at the division in his own Society near the close of his ministry, he bore himself with remarkable prudence, and retained the respect and confidence of his people, as a good man and devoted Christian minister.

About the time of the Rev. Mr. Bailey's settlement, the first Sabbath School in the town was organized. A little after, in 1822, a weekly prayer-meeting was started in Rockville on Saturday evenings by the efforts, principally, of two earnest Christian men living in that part of the parish, Mr. Timothy Walker, afterward a deacon of the church, and for many years the superintendent of the Sabbath School, and Mr. Matthew Brown, who afterward succeeded Deacon Walker as superintendent of the Sabbath School. Mr. Brown was quite tried, at first, as to what he should do. He was expected to be at his place of business at all hours of day and evening; and on Saturday night, of all other times, his patrons expected to find him at his shop. However, he decided to attend the prayer-meeting, and accordingly posted a notice, politely informing his customers, that for one hour, naming the time, on Saturday evenings, he should be engaged; at all other hours he should be happy to serve them. The result was, his business prospered even better than before, showing that it is not a vain thing to serve God, to be fervent in spirit as well as diligent in business.

This meeting was sustained for years with much interest and good result.

It was in 1822 that the parish hall was built, much to the accommodation of the young and prosperous Sabbath School, which occupied it for many years. In the year 1828 it was voted to hold the monthly Monday prayer-meeting, the object of which was to pray for Foreign Missions, which at that day was a new and exciting enterprise undertaken by the churches.

About the year 1834, there was a movement by some in the parish to set up another religious service, and procure "preaching of some other denomination"; and, for a time, those interested held an extra service in the parish hall by the courtesy of the First Parish. In 1835, near the close of the Rev. Mr. Bailey's pastorate, some more than forty members of the First Parish withdrew for the purpose of forming a new religious society. This new organization took the name of the "Third Congregational Society in Medway."

After a pastorate of nearly twenty years, the Rev. Mr. Bailey asked a dismission, which was granted, by advice of ecclesiastical council, December 29, 1835. In the result of the council this was adopted: "That the Council recommend the Rev. Luther Bailey, as a minister of the Gospel in good and regular standing, and they do hereby commend him as a faithful minister of Jesus Christ to the affection and confidence of the Churches."

The Rev. Mr. Bailey was still residing in the parish, and after hearing various persons, their meeting-house being completed, the new Society invited him to become their pastor. He accepted the invitation, and was installed December 7, 1836. After several years he retired from the public service of the ministry, but still resided in his old parish, and worshiped with the First Church of Christ. Several sermons preached by the Rev. Mr. Bailey were published. One was preached June 9, 1824, before the Norfolk County Education Society in Randolph, Mass.; another was preached on the Sabbath, October 17, 1830, at the funeral of Miss Betsey Adams, the text being, "*Lord, make me to know mine end and the measure of my days, what it is; that I may know how frail I am.*" Ps. xxxix., 4; and another was preached at the funeral service of Abijah Richardson Thayer and Asa Clark Thayer, two brothers, whose burial occurred at the same time, October 31, 1830.

The Rev. Mr. Bailey died December 19, 1861, at the age of seventy-eight years. He was "beloved and respected by all the people" among whom he had lived and labored for so many years. *Vid.* BIOGRAPHIES.

THE SIXTH PASTORATE.

1837 — 1851.

The First Church of Christ, under date of July 12, 1837, extended an unanimous call to the Rev. Sewall Harding, of Waltham, Mass., a native of Medway, offering a salary of $600 per annum. The invitation was accepted by letter, dated September 15, 1837, Waltham, Mass.

The Rev. Mr. Harding's installation occurred November 1, 1837. Ten neighboring churches were represented in the council. The Rev. David Long, of Milford, was chosen moderator, and the Rev. E. Smalley, scribe. The sermon of installation was preached by the Rev. Jacob Ide, D. D., of the Second Church; installing prayer by the Rev. Mr. Cummings, of North Wrentham; charge to the pastor by the moderator; the right hand of fellowship by the Rev. David Brigham, of Framingham; and the address to the people by the Rev. Elam Smalley, of Franklin.

At the opening of the Rev. Mr. Harding's ministry the church numbered one hundred and eighty-two: fifty-seven males, one hundred and twenty-five females. This is, probably, the largest living membership of the church.

During this pastorate of fourteen years, some sixty persons were added; about forty of them were received on confession of faith.

While the Rev. Mr. Harding was pastor, the slavery agitation commenced, and the Church of Christ in Medway, although in its early history even the minister held slaves, was true to Christian instincts and the progress of ideas. Decided anti-slavery views were taken, and published to the country and to the world, as appears in the following record: " On the second of September, 1842, the church voted unanimously the following:

PREAMBLE AND RESOLUTIONS.

Whereas, The Christian Church is established to be the light of the world, and the great instrument in the great work of the world's reformation. It is therefore

Resolved, That the Church ought to bear decided testimony against all sin, and especially reprove with all tenderness and fidelity those members of the Christian body who persist in open transgression.

Resolved, That the system of Slavery, as it exists in the United States, and as tolerated in many Churches in our land, is a violation of the letter and the spirit of the Gospel; inasmuch as it withholds from almost three millions of the human family their personal freedom, denies them generally the means of education, the privileges and protection of civil institutions, the sacred rights of matrimony, and the due reward of their labor, thus reducing them to and holding them in a state of oppression, ignorance, and moral degradation scarcely paralleled in the civilized world.

Resolved, That we feel constrained, in the spirit of meekness, to reprove and rebuke all professing Christians, ministers, and Churches who tolerate Slavery in word or deed, and that we cannot extend the fellowship of the Gospel to those who continue to enslave their fellow-men after the faithful admonition of their Christian brethren.

Resolved, That these resolutions be published in the Boston *Recorder*, the *New England Puritan*, and the *New York Evangelist*, signed by the Pastor and officers of the Church."

" The above resolutions were signed and published as above voted.

Attest,   SEWALL HARDING, Pastor."

By a communication, dated April 8, 1849, the Rev. Mr. Harding asked to be released from active service, and by advice of council the pastoral relation was dissolved December 3, 1851. *Vid.* BIOGRAPHIES.

THE FOURTH MEETING-HOUSE.

ERECTED IN 1850.

This HOUSE FOR PUBLIC WORSHIP was erected in pursuance of a vote of the First Parish, passed June 25, 1849. A new locality was chosen, and a site on spacious grounds given for the purpose by Henry Richardson, Esq.

September 10, 1849, Joseph L. Richardson, Jr., was chosen building committee; Messrs. Melvin and Page were the contractors. The cost was about $6,000, which was covered by the valuation placed upon the pews.

This house was dedicated November 13, 1850. The sermon on the occasion was preached by the Rev. Samuel Hunt, then of Franklin, afterwards the private secretary of the late Vice-President, Honorable Henry Wilson, of Natick. Since its erection, in 1854, the bell became damaged, and was exchanged for a new one from the foundry of Holbrook & Son. In 1857 the house was re-painted; and in 1867, thoroughly remodeled and enlarged at a cost of nearly $5,000. The gallery was lowered, a recess made in the rear of the pulpit, twenty pews added, the organ repaired, the audience-room neatly frescoed, and the building re-painted.

In 1882 it was again painted, and at the present time, 1885, important changes and improvements are being made in the vestry and church surroundings.

The Seventh Pastorate.

1851 — 1855.

The Rev. John Oliver Means was called September 4, 1851, to settle as pastor of the First Church of Christ. His salary was $800, with four weeks' vacation. The call was accepted by letter, dated Augusta, Me., October 15, 1851.

By advice of ecclesiastical council, December 3, 1851, Mr. Means was ordained and installed pastor of the church. The Rev. Benjamin Toppan, of Augusta, Me., moderator of the council, preached the sermon; the Rev. John Dwight, of North Wrentham, made the ordaining prayer; the Rev. J. T. Tucker, of Holliston, gave the charge to the pastor; the Rev. A. Swazey, of Brighton, the right hand of fellowship; and the Rev. Sewall Harding made the address to the people. The Rev. George H. Newhall, of Walpole, was the scribe of the council.

The pastorate of the Rev. Mr. Means was hardly four years in length. At its commencement the church numbered one hundred and thirty-two members. During his ministry, twenty-six were added, fifteen of these by confession of faith. The influence of this short pastorate was very great, not only in the church but in the whole community. A spirit of public improvement was inspired, and the name of the Rev. Mr. Means remained for many years peculiarly honored in the kindest remembrance of the people. His resignation took effect September 4, 1855. *Vid.* Biographies.

The Eighth Pastorate.

1856 — 1871.

By action of the First Church of Christ, taken April 21, 1856, an invitation was extended to the Rev. Jacob Roberts to become their pastor; the annual salary was $800, with a vacation of four Sabbaths. The Rev. Mr. Roberts returned a letter of acceptance, dated Fairhaven, Mass., June 12, 1856. He was installed, by advice of ecclesiastical council, October 9, 1856. The Rev. Sewall Harding was chosen moderator of the council, and the Rev. A. Bigelow, of Medfield, was the scribe. The sermon on the occasion was preached by the Rev. James A. Roberts, of Berkley, a brother of the pastor-elect. The text was, "*For the redemption of their soul is precious.*" Psalms xlix., 8. Installing prayer by the Rev. J. T. Tucker, of Holliston; charge to the pastor, by the Rev. Jacob Ide, d. d., of West Medway; right hand of fellowship, by the Rev. H. D. Walker, of East Abington, and the address to the people, by the Rev. S. Harding, of Auburndale. The Rev. Luther Bailey, the Rev. Sewall Harding, and the Rev. John O. Means, former pastors of the church, were present in the council.

The Rev. Mr. Roberts' ministry extended over a period of fifteen years, and was greatly blessed of God. Ninety-three persons were added to the church, about seventy of these on confession of faith. Over forty were added in the single year of 1866, the results of a revival. The Rev. Mr. Roberts' health failed, and he resigned October 14, 1870. *Vid.* Biographies.

THE NINTH PASTORATE.

1871.

The First Church of Christ, under date of September 26, 1871, extended a call to the Rev. E. O. Jameson to become their pastor, the parish offering a salary of $1,500, to which Mr. Jameson returned a letter of acceptance, dated October 5, 1871, Salisbury, Mass.

The installation of the Rev. Mr. Jameson took place on Wednesday, November 15, 1871. The Rev. Samuel J. Spalding, D.D., of Newburyport, was moderator of the council. The Rev. S. Knowlton, of West Medway, was the scribe. The venerable Rev. Sewall Harding, of Auburndale, the Rev. John O. Means, D. D., of Boston Highlands, and the Rev. Jacob Roberts, of Auburndale, former pastors, were present in the council. The Rev. Dr. Means preached the sermon; the Rev. J. M. R. Eaton, of Medfield, made the installing prayer; the Rev. Dr. S. J. Spalding delivered the charge to the pastor; the Rev. S. Knowlton gave the right hand of fellowship, and the Rev. Jacob Roberts, the retiring pastor, made the address to the people.

THE PARSONAGE. ERECTED IN 1872.

Early in the ministry of this pastor a desirable site was secured; a suitable house was erected, and for the first time in the history of the church and society, a period of more than one hundred and fifty years, they had a parsonage for their minister. This enterprise was started by a gift of twenty-five dollars from some unknown person, for building a Parsonage. A site was selected and land purchased nearly opposite the meeting-house. The work was pushed forward, and November 1, 1872, the house was ready to be occupied. Two years later a stable was erected. The entire cost of land and buildings was about six thousand dollars.

October 7, 1876, the church celebrated its one hundred and sixty-second anniversary, and the Sabbath School its sixtieth. The pastor, the Rev. Mr. Jameson, preached a sermon which was published by request.

The Official Register of the First Church of Christ.

The Pastors.

Rev. David Deming, ordained Nov. 20, 1715; resigned Oct. 16, 1722.
Rev. Nathan Bucknam, ordained Dec. 23, 1724; died Feb. 6, 1795.
Rev. Benjamin Greene, ordained June 25, 1788; resigned Feb. 28, 1793.
Rev. Luther Wright, ordained June 13, 1798; resigned Sept. 20, 1815.
Rev. Luther Bailey, ordained Nov. 20, 1816; resigned Dec. 29, 1835.
Rev. Sewall Harding, installed Nov. 1, 1837; resigned Dec. 3, 1851.
Rev. John O. Means, ordained Dec. 3, 1851: resigned Sept. 4, 1855.
Rev. Jacob Roberts, installed Oct. 9, 1856; resigned Nov. 15, 1871.
Rev. E. O. Jameson, installed Nov. 15, 1871.

The Deacons.

Jonathan Adams, elected ——; died Jan. 24, 1718.
Samuel Hill, elected ——; died March 24, 1723.
Peter Adams, elected ——; died Dec. 8, 1723.
John Partridge, elected Jan. 12, 1724; resigned Feb. 18, 1731.
Ebenezer Thompson, elected Jan. 12, 1724.
Peter Baulch, elected July 31, 1730; resigned 1732.
Samuel Partridge, elected Feb. 18, 1731.
John Barber, elected Sept. 22, 1732; died June 20, 1754.
Thomas Harding, elected ——: died Oct. 15, 1754.
Elisha Adams, elected Sept. 6, 1754; died March, 23, 1781.
Edward Clark, Jun., elected Dec. 27, 1754; died Feb. 7, 1799.
George Barber, elected Aug. 7, 1756.
Asa Daniell, elected Sept. 29, 1769; died Oct. 18, 1815.
Asa Ellis, elected ——.
Simon Hill, elected ——; resigned Aug. 4, 1814.
Asa Daniels, Jun., elected Nov. 21, 1805; resigned Nov. 3, 1829.
Josiah Blake, elected Sept. 29, 1814; died Aug. 3, 1858.
Timothy Walker, elected Dec. 7, 1827; resigned February, 1850.
Paul Daniell, elected Jan. 25, 1839; died Feb. 15, 1876.
Elbridge Clark, elected March 4, 1853.
James Mitchell, elected March 4, 1853; died Aug. 19, 1863.
Charles H. Fitts, elected March 4, 1864; resigned ——, 1864.
Milton Daniels, elected March 4, 1864; died March 3, 1871.
Horatio Jones, elected May 26, 1871.
William Daniels, elected May 26, 1871.

The membership of the church as recorded from its organization to the present date, February 24, 1885, including but a few names prior to 1724, makes a total of seven hundred and seventy-five members. There are now one hundred and eighteen members.

During the fourteenth year of the ninth pastorate, the easterly portion of Medway which was embraced in the First Parish, was incorporated February 24, 1885, as the town of Millis, so that the First Church of Christ in Medway will henceforth be known as The Church of Christ in Millis, Mass.

The Rockville Chapel. Erected in 1877.

For many years there had been a branch Sabbath School in Rockville, connected with the First Church of Christ, and a monthly religious service had been held in that part of the parish, but there was no suitable and permanent building for such purposes. In 1874 the teachers and scholars of the Rockville Sabbath School organized a society, called the Rockville Improvement Association. This society had for its object the raising of funds to erect a building in which the Sabbath School might be accommodated, and also other social gatherings and religious meetings.

The first contribution made towards the Rockville Chapel was a FIVE CENT NICKEL, with these accompanying words, "*For the Rockville Chapel, toward one of the towers thereof.*" The chapel was completed at a cost of $1,604.78, and it was finally dedicated, without debt, Thursday afternoon, July 26, 1877. The sermon was preached by the pastor of the First Church of Christ, the text being, Psalms xc., 16-17. Addresses of congratulation were made by other clergymen and gentlemen present.

This chapel is a beautifully located and a very well-arranged building for the purposes of its erection. The Rockville Sabbath School has a flourishing life, and numbers some one hundred members.

The EAST MEDWAY CIRCLE OF INDUSTRY connected with the First Church and Society celebrated, June 5, 1884, its semi-centennial anniversary. Address, by the pastor. Poem, by Deacon Anson Daniels.

THE MAIN STREET, WEST MEDWAY, IN 1885.

The Second Church of Christ.

1750 — 1885.

The West Precinct, as already mentioned, was incorporated December 29, 1748, with a view to the organization of a second church on account of the great distance to attend public worship.

A meeting-house was raised on Thursday, April 6, 1749, which was completed very soon after. It stood a little to the northwest of the old cemetery, and almost opposite the site where Dr. Ide afterwards erected his residence, in which he lived so many years. This first meeting-house of West Medway is described as a building "forty feet long and thirty-four feet wide, with posts twenty feet high between joints, without a steeple, and having two rows of windows and a gallery."

The Second Church of Christ was organized October 4, 1750. The day was memorable, being set apart as a day for fasting and prayer.

There were present with this little company of Christian believers, the Rev. Mr. Prentiss, of Medfield, and the Rev. Mr. Bucknam, pastor of the First Church of Christ, of whom it is recorded: "After the exercise ye Rev. Mr. Bucknam gathered a church, and pronounced them the Second Church of Christ in Medway." The Covenant was signed by thirty-four persons.

It is recorded that "The church were desired to meet on Monday, the 8th of October 1750. After, when met the church made choice of Capt. Nathaniel Whiting to be their moderator till they should have a minister ordained, Ezra Pond clerk and also voted to call Mr. Jonathan Derby to be their Pastor." At the end of three months Mr. Derby declined the call. They then invited Mr. Samuel Haven to settle with them in the ministry, but he also declined.

In February, 1752, the Rev. David Thurston, of Wrentham, Mass., was invited to become their pastor; he accepted the call, and was ordained June 23, 1752. The record reads: "The council being met, the church were called upon to renew their choice, whereupon they voted unanimously, upon which the council and church went to the meeting-house, and the business of the day was accomplished."

The Rev. Nathan Bucknam, of the First Church of Christ, preached the ordination sermon. The Rev. Mr. Dorr gave the charge, and the Rev. Mr. Webb extended the right hand of fellowship. Nathaniel Cutler and Joseph Holbrook had been chosen deacons, and soon after the ordination, Jonathan Metcalf was added, and, a few months later, Samuel Fisher. And May 7, 1753, Captain Nathaniel Whiting and John Pond were chosen ruling elders. They appear to have been the only persons who have held this office in the history of the church.

The Rev. Mr. Thurston, March 18, 1761, asked his dismission, "in consideration of the insufficiency of his support, and the repeated denials he had met with from the parish of any further support." The church voted not to grant the dismission, but to refer the matter of salary to the parish. But Mr. Thurston again asked, February 22, 1769, his dismission on account of impaired health from the "prosecution of constant study and preaching," and the church, "in consideration of his present indisposition," granted it.

Mr. Thurston was pastor of the church for seventeen years. After his dismission he retired from the ministry, and settled upon a farm in the town of Oxford; he subsequently removed to Auburn, and afterwards to Sutton, where he died May 5, 1777, at the age of fifty years.

During this first pastorate there were seventy-nine persons added to the church, and twenty-three came under the bonds of the covenant. In a brief biographical notice contained in the *History of the Mendon Association*, the Rev. Mr. Blake says: "No materials are in our possession for forming an opinion of Mr. Thurston's literary abilities. No writings of his are known to exist as an index of his attainments as a theologian, or skill as a preacher." At the close of Mr. Thurston's ministry there followed much discouragement and spiritual declension in the church. Few members had been added for many years. We have a hint of the state of things in a vote passed September 2, 1770, "to put off the administration of the Lord's Supper for the present, because of the uneasiness among some of the brethren." And April 11, 1771, was passed the following remarkable vote: "After prayer for direction and assistance, and some debate, *Voted*, to blot, cross, or wipe out sundry votes that are relative to unhappy differences and disturbances that have arisen in said church, and touch particular members of it, that so all things in the church and every member of it may now and forever hereafter, as far as possible, be as though these difficulties and disturbances had never been."

The church were now looking for a pastor, and October 11, 1771, held a meeting to confer with the Rev. Nathaniel Niles relative to his sentiments respecting the doctrines of the Gospel. Mr. Niles was present at the request of the church, and read a confession of his faith, which he appears to have prepared for the occasion. The church was satisfied, and gave him a call; but Mr. Niles declined. This was the second refusal; for Mr. Samuel Wales, who had been called the year before, after three months' consideration, declined. These refusals made an impression upon the church, for we again find them trying to reconcile differences, "with a view to the glory of God and the settlement of a Gospel minister." For this purpose they summoned the Rev. Mr. Bucknam and some other neighboring ministers to revise and "assist them in renewing church covenant one with another."

Soon after, having been destitute of a pastor almost four years, the church called the Rev. David Sanford, who accepted, and was ordained April 14, 1773. The Rev. Dr. West, of Stockbridge, preached the sermon, and the Rev. Samuel Hopkins made the ordaining prayer.

Mr. Sanford was a native of New Milford, Conn. He graduated at Yale College in 1755, commenced the study of divinity with the Rev. Dr. Bellamy, but completed it with the Rev. Dr. Hopkins, who was his brother-in-law. At the age of thirty-six he settled in Medway. During the Revolutionary War he was appointed Chaplain in the army. The Rev. Mr. Sanford died, April 7, 1810, in the thirty-seventh year of his ministry, and seventy-third of his life. "He was a man of fine personal appearance, with sharp, piercing eyes, a commanding presence, and a strong, clear voice. He was possessed of rare abilities, well learned in the Scripture, and usually preached without notes."

The church abolished, November 16, 1775, the practice of the Halfway Covenant, by which persons professing belief in the doctrines of the Gospel, placed themselves under the watch and care of the church by subscribing to the covenant, and thereby promising to perform the duties of religion and to seek for regeneration, and were permitted to be baptized and to have their children baptized. The church adopted, January 25, 1776, a written confession of faith. It appears that Deacon Samuel Fisher, Daniel Pond, and Samuel Hayward, and certain sisters of the church, had been dissatisfied with the pastor from the time of his settlement. At length they absented themselves from the ordinances of the church, and said, in self-justification, of the pastor that " (1) He denies imputative guilt; (2) He denies imputative righteousness; and (3) He makes God the author of sin." One of the sisters was not edified by the manner in which he taught the doctrine of free-will; and the other found the alteration of the covenant a stumbling-block. These reasons did not satisfy the church, but out of the discussion that ensued grew the necessity for a written statement of their faith, which was drawn up by the pastor and adopted by the church, only one member objecting. The dissatisfied ones, however, were not reconciled, and after many meetings and much debate they were placed under censure. They then sought for a Mutual Council, to advise respecting their difficulties, but the church refused to join with them, and they called an Ex-parte Council, which met at the house of Deacon Samuel Fisher. The record of which is as follows:

A Council at West Parish, Medway, Mass.

"November 11-12, 1777.

At an Ecclesiastical Council convened at Medway 2d Parish 11th of November 1777, composed of the Chh. of Christ in Walpole, the Chh. in Holliston and the Chh. in Dedham, the Chh. in Sherborn, and the Chh. in Medfield, at the request of Deacon Samuel Fisher, Mr. Daniel Pond and sundry sisters in said Parish, to advise them respecting some matters of uneasiness subsisting between them and the Pastor and Chh. in said Parish.

Voted 1st, The Rev. Mr. Phillips Payne, Moderator.

Voted 2d, Rev. Elijah Brown, Scribe.

And after solemn and devout Prayer for light and direction

Voted 3d, That a Committee wait on the Rev. Mr. David Sanford requesting that he and his Chh. would join with the aggrieved in calling a Mutual Council. Which request was not granted.

In the evening the Council received a message from the Rev. Mr. Sanford proposing, if it was the desire of the Council, said Chh. would by their Committee, wait on the Council when most agreeable. Accordingly by vote the Council desired their attendance at 8 o'clock next morning. To which time the Council adjourned.

Novemr 12th. The Pastor and Committee of said Chh. appeared before the Council in conformity to their agreement. When said Pastor & committee of the Chh. & aggrieved freely and fully rehearsed matters in which the Council were concerned.

And the Council entering upon a consultation of the matter laid before them came into the following result:

1st. That the Council mean not to infringe the right of private judgment that this Pastor and people have, on matters of religion, and wholly disclaim all dominion over their faith.

Yet claiming the same liberty to judge for themselves, which they allow to others, they are obliged to declare their disapprobation of several of the religious sentiments of the Rev. Mr. David Sanford which are matters of grievance to those persons at whose desire this Council was convened. And exercising equal tenderness for the consciences of the aggrieved, they cannot but say, they think their desire to enjoy Chh. privileges elsewhere, reasonable under such circumstances, justifiable upon the principles of Christian liberty, and accordingly they do not view their withdrawing a breach of covenant, & therefore not deserving the censure of the Chh. And in order that the harmony of this Chh. and the interest of Religion may be promoted in this place it is the opinion of this Council that the censure ought to be removed upon the aggrieved, complying with some articles of advice hereafter mentioned.

2nd. As to the charge of Hypocrisy & unfaithfulness exhibited by the said Chh. against Mr. Daniel Pond, the Council are sorry to find by the evidence produced a want of that simplicity and openness which the Gospel requires (in some part of his conduct) previous to the Ordination of Mr. Sanford, and though they charitably believe it arose from his particular situation at that time, and that fear of Men, that bringeth a snare. Nevertheless they judge it reasonable that he should ask the Christian candor & forgiveness of his brethren, who are offended with him on account hereof & accordingly advise him to do the same.

3d. Although in these unhappy disputes, there may have been some other things said and done on the part of the Chh. & the aggrieved, which have not savored so much of Christian Candor & meekness as could have been wished. Yet the Council imagine that the proper exercise of Christian love might be sufficient to remove all uneasiness and dissatisfaction thereby occasioned.

4th. The Council advise the aggrieved to apply to the Chh. in a Christian way to have the censure they have laid them under removed.

5th. Provided. The Chh. shall not upon the compliance of the aggrieved with the advice before given them, remove the censure, the Council judge them to stand fair to enjoy Christian privileges in other Churches to which they may apply for the same.

Finally the Council advise & exhort the aggrieved to endeavor to walk circumspectly, to cultivate a Christian temper, & to live in love and peace that the God of love and peace may be with them.

(Signed) Phillips Payson, Moderator, Joshua Prentice, Jason Haven, Elijah Brown, Tho. Prentice, Joshua Clapp, Aaron Phipps, Timothy Rockwood, Jonathan Metcalf, Benjamin Kendall, Benjamin Whitney, James Boyden, Daniel Perry."

"Sherborn, April *6th*, 1795.

A true copy — attest   ELIJAH BROWN."

Acting, as it appears, by the advice of this council, those concerned soon after requested that the censure of the church might be removed, preliminary to their asking for letters of dismission and recommendation to some other church ; whereupon the church voted to send a "second admonition, that should contain a suspension from all church privileges." They then applied to the First Church for admission without letters ; and in view of what the council had done, and after much inquiry and deliberation, the First Church received them. In consequence of this procedure, after some correspondence, this church withdrew fellowship from the First Church.

Although several attempts were made to restore harmony, this estrangement between the churches lasted for thirty-two years. At length, when all the members respecting whom the controversy originated were gone to appear at a higher tribunal, and the members of the churches were completely changed, by the efforts of the Rev. Mr. Wright, pastor of the First Church, and the assistance of Drs. Prentiss, of Medfield, and Emmons, of Franklin, the breach was healed. The case being submitted to these clergymen, they advised that, without concessions on either part, the churches embrace each other in church fellowship, in the spirit of love and tenderness. And the advice was mutually accepted.

The church seems to have been paralyzed by these trials, and diminished in numbers, until it had become "a small and feeble band, consisting of some eight or ten male members, with a proportionate number of females."

Immediately after the adoption of the written Articles of Faith, February

8, 1776, the church held a meeting for the confession of sins. This confession was drawn up in writing, and the church confessed the following sins:

(1) The Halfway Covenant; (2) The neglect of Christian watchfulness; (3) The neglect of the Discipline of the Church; (4) The neglect of the means of Grace. The influence of this meeting was most favorable. Subsequently several seasons of revival interest were enjoyed. In 1785 the church was greatly blessed, and as the result, eighty-five persons were received into the church, mostly on confession of their faith.

There are no records of the doings of the church for a period of thirty years prior to 1809; and only a few items are recorded until 1814.

After an interim of four years from the death of Mr. Sanford, and of seven years from the end of his active pastorate, the Rev. Jacob Ide, of Attleborough, was ordained pastor, November 2, 1814. Dr. Woods, of Andover, preached the ordination sermon, and the Rev. Mr. Wright, of the First Church, gave the right hand of fellowship. Mr. Ide was graduated from Brown University, in 1809; studied theology at Andover, where he graduated in 1812. Beside his pastoral labors, he was an editor, an author, and a teacher of theology, some forty persons having come under his instruction, in preparation for the ministry.

The period of an entire generation had passed since the last revival under his predecessor, with only rare and solitary additions to the church. The members of the church were few, and most of them advanced in age. Eighteen months before, they had discussed the subject of disbanding and returning to the First Church, so feeble and discouraged had they become. The people had contracted habits of neglecting worship and otherwise misspending the Sabbath. These circumstances rendered this an uninviting field. But the new minister soon brought a revived life into the church.

In 1832 Dr. Ide received repeated invitations to assume the chair of theology in the Bangor Seminary; but, although urged very persistently to accept the position, he finally concluded to remain with his people. He was pastor for fifty-one years, and his colleague successor was installed on the anniversary of his own settlement. In 1838, a portion of the members, with the approbation of the church, formed, with others, a new church at the Village, over which the Rev. David Sanford, grandson of the second pastor of this church, was installed, October 3, 1838.

The Rev. Dr. Ide preached a centennial discourse October 20, 1850, which the church voted to publish. The text was Psalms lxxiv., 2.

On the fiftieth anniversary of Dr. Ide's settlement, November 2, 1864, a commemorative service was held. A multitude gathered; more than could find seats or even standing-room, and many were obliged to retire. The pastor preached in the morning a historical sermon, in which he says: " I have attended one hundred and seventy-five ecclesiastical councils, have preached twenty-seven ordination sermons, five funeral sermons of ministers and four of ministers' wives," and enumerates other special and important occasions upon which he had been called upon to preach. Of his sermons he says: " I have printed about forty in pamphlet and other forms." He had solemnized four hundred and thirty-two marriages, administered five hundred and ten baptisms, and attended seven hundred and forty-three funerals within his own parish, besides a large number in neighboring towns and parishes. The afternoon was occupied with the recital of reminiscences, enlivened with anecdote and humor, by Dr. Ide's clerical friends. About seventy clergymen were present. Among the speakers were Professor E. A. Park, D. D., of Andover, Dr. A. L. Stone, Dr. Anderson, and Dr. Nehemiah Adams, of Boston, the Rev. J. T. Tucker, the Rev. H. D. Walker, and Charles Thurber, Esq.

The Rev. Dr. Ide lived to a great age. His ministry and life were a great power for good. *Vid.* BIOGRAPHIES.

The Rev. Stephen Knowlton was settled colleague pastor, November 2, 1865, and was the fourth pastor of the church. Dr. Park, of Andover, preached the ordination sermon, and Dr. Ide offered the prayer. Mr. Knowlton was an instructive preacher, and many were brought to receive Christ as their Saviour during his pastorate of seven years. He resigned November 20, 1872, in order to accept an invitation to New Haven, Vt.

The Rev. S. W. Segur, of Gloucester, Mass., was installed May 7, 1873, the fifth pastor. After a short and efficient ministry, he died, September 24, 1875, in the midst of great usefulness, universally beloved and lamented. His death occurred while on a visit to the place of his first pastorate, Tallmadge, Ohio. *Vid.* BIOGRAPHIES.

The Rev. James M. Bell, after successive pastorates in Ashby, Watertown, and North Hadley, covering a period of nearly twenty years, accepted a call to become the sixth pastor of this church, and was installed September 26, 1876. The Rev. Edwin B. Webb, D. D., of Boston, preached the sermon, and the installing prayer was by the Rev. Jacob Ide, Jun., of Mansfield, Mass. The Rev. Mr. Bell's ministry continued about nine years. He read his resignation May 3d, 1885, to take effect the first of the following July. He removed to Watertown, Mass., but continued to supply the pulpit of the church during the summer and autumn of that year.

A plan was adopted by the church, in 1815, for the public religious instruction of the children, who were divided into classes, according to their ages, and instructed by the pastor once a month. The Sabbath School was established in May, 1819. It was first placed under the care of Mr. Sewall Harding, then a theological student, afterward the seventh pastor of the First Church. The subsequent superintendents were Moses Felt, Daniel Wiley, Elihu White, Joshua Sevey, George S. Partridge, Charles H. Deans, the Rev. S. W. Segur, Warren E. Adams, and Addison A. Smith.

The present church edifice, the second built by this parish, was dedicated a few weeks before the ordination of Dr. Ide, in 1814. At that time there was but one dwelling in its vicinity. The change of location from the old site caused some dissatisfaction and unpleasant feeling for many years. In 1846, the spire, after standing thirty-two years, was re-built, and the body of the house much altered, externally as well as internally. It was newly seated throughout; the pulpit was re-constructed; the gallery was lowered and extended over the porch; the windows in the wall opposite the entrance were closed up, and blinds applied to those that remained; the ceiling and walls were frescoed by the generosity of Christopher Slocum, Esq., and the aisles for the first time carpeted. During the summer of 1873, it was again re-seated, the recess built for the platform, the present mode of warming adopted, and the interior greatly beautified. The next summer the chapel was built. The successful carrying out of these improvements was largely due to the taste and tact of the Rev. Mr. Segur.

By the sale of the pews, at the time the church was built, a fund of three thousand dollars was provided for the future use of the parish.

Levi Adams, Esq., a member of this church, who died in 1842, left in his will twelve hundred dollars for the purchase of a parsonage. With that sum and its accumulated interest the present parsonage was secured. He also left three hundred dollars for the supply of the communion-table.

Mrs. Charlotte Slocum bequeathed five hundred dollars, the income of which was to be expended in books for the Sunday School Library.

The Official Register of the Second Church of Christ.

The Pastors.

Rev. David Thurston, ordained June 23, 1752; resigned Feb. 22, 1769.
Rev. David Sanford, ordained April 14, 1773; died April 7, 1810.
Rev. Jacob Ide, ordained November 2, 1814; died January 5, 1880.
Rev. Stephen Knowlton, ordained Nov. 2, 1865; resigned Nov. 20, 1872.
Rev. S. W. Segur, ordained May 7, 1873; died Sept. 24, 1875.
Rev. James M. Bell, ordained Sept. 26, 1876; resigned July 1, 1885.

The Ruling Elders.

Nathaniel Whiting, elected May 7, 1753.
John Pond, elected May 7, 1753.

The Deacons.

Nathaniel Cutler, elected May 25, 1752.
Joseph Holbrook, elected May 25, 1752.
Jonathan Metcalf, elected July 2, 1752.
Samuel Fisher, elected May 7, 1753.
James Morse, elected—.
Moses Hill, elected—.
Jonathan Metcalf, elected—; resigned September 1, 1831.
Nathaniel Cutler, elected—; resigned September 1, 1831.
Daniel Wiley, elected September 15, 1831.
Daniel Nourse, elected October 13, 1831.
Ira Wight, elected August 28, 1845.
Anson Daniels, elected May 10, 1860.
Edmund Shumway, elected May 10, 1860.
Austin Metcalf, elected 1867.
Elias T. Fisher, elected 1877.
Stephen Adams, elected 1878.

The total recorded membership is one thousand and fifty-five; and the present membership, in 1885, is one hundred and sixty-nine.

THE BAPTIST CHURCH.

1832 — 1885.

THE FIRST BAPTIST residents of Medway, so far as is now known, were Eleazar Adams and Jonathan Partridge. On April 10, 1754, Mr. Adams was taken from his home and committed a close prisoner in jail because he had refused to pay the ministerial rates imposed by the standing order. He is described as " an ancient man, a substantial freeholder of Medway, a constant attender, and for several years past at the Baptist meeting in Bellingham." He probably resided on or near Summer Street. Mr. Partridge was a son of Deacon John Partridge, of the First Church of Christ in Medway. He was born in 1693. For some years, he had charge of the singing in the church to which his father belonged.

Some years later, two residents of the town, Abagail Partridge, wife of Timothy Partridge, and John Albee, were baptized at Bellingham. Still later, some became members at Medfield. But it was not until 1819, that a Baptist society was formed. Its organization was due to the unwillingness of some to be taxed for the support of preaching in which they did not believe, and to dissatisfaction in regard to the location of the meeting-house of the Second Church of Christ, erected in 1813.

The names of the constituent members were Simeon Partridge, Thaddeus Lovering, Moses Pond, Elihu Partridge, Ezra Richardson, Aaron Wright, Nathan Twiss, Barzilla Pond, Isaac Hixon, Asa Hixon, John Smith, Oliver Ellis, Simeon Holbrook, Samuel Clark, Samuel B. Blake, Newell Lovering, Moses Kimball, Moses H. Wight, Benjamin Ward, David Johnson. Among these were some of the wealthiest and most influential men of the town, but none of them was a member of a Baptist Church. There were only two Baptist professors in the town, two ladies, mother and daughter, both named Eda Richardson, members of the Baptist Church in Medfield. Others joined the society soon after its organization. Among them was Abner Morse, Esq., one of the most prominent citizens of the town, and of the parish from which he withdrew. Sixty-five times in twenty years he served as moderator of the town and of the parish. For many years he was one of the board of selectmen. He was a ready public speaker, and possessed a good knowledge of law. As a military man and a magistrate, he was greatly honored. He at once became a leader in the new society. He drew up its legal papers, and served as its clerk. His death in 1820 was then regarded as a great loss by his associates. Religious meetings were held by the society in the school-house in District No. 5. The first sermon was preached by the Rev. Charles Train, of Framingham. For the next two years Mr. Train and the Rev. William Gammell, of Medfield, encouraged the interest by their counsel and frequent presence. It was during these two years that Mr. Amasa Sanderson, a student of Mr. Train, spent considerable time here. In connection with these labors a goodly number became Christians, thirteen of whom were baptized into the Medfield Church. During this revival, and for more than thirty years afterwards, there was intense opposition to the Baptists.

The growing congregation found the school-house too small for its meetings. Accordingly, January 20, 1820, a call was issued for the members of the society to meet for consultation in regard to the erection of a house of worship. During the next few months meetings were frequently held to plan concerning the raising of money and the location of the house. Efforts were made to buy the land where the old Congregational Church had stood, and where most of the members of the society had attended meeting, but failing in this, the present site, nearly opposite, was chosen. Work on the house was commenced October, 1821. Early in the summer of 1822, there was a lack of funds. This was not caused by any lack of financial ability of the members of the society, but by their unwillingness to contribute for the erection of a house to be used exclusively, or even largely, by Baptists, for only one of the society had become a member of a Baptist Church. Accordingly, July 29, 1822, the society voted " to grant and give to all of whatever Christian denomination, that have subscribed, or shall hereafter subscribe and become proprietors of the meeting-house now erected on land purchased of Barzilla Pond, equal rights and privileges with ourselves in proportion to the property that they and we shall own, and be in possession of in said house." Again, on January 19, 1823, a confirmation of this vote was asked and granted. After this vote money was easily raised, and the house was finished. Among the largest contributions were those of Thaddeus Lovering, Moses Pond, Simeon Partridge, and Elihu Partridge.

The first sermon in the house was preached by Mr. Sanderson, whom the Baptists had hoped would become their pastor. But in this they were disappointed. Mr. Sanderson was ordained in 1823, in Littleton, Mass. He died in 1877 in Nashua, N. H. The vote, just mentioned, gave the control of the house to those not Baptists. The public services of dedication, on May 30, 1823, were conducted by Universalist preachers. For the next seven years people of this denomination occupied the house, not a Baptist preaching in it during all that time. Among their preachers were Hosea Ballou, Thomas Whittemore, Adin Ballou, and Lyman Maynard. The famous Matthew Hale Smith, when only seventeen years old, here preached his first sermon. Some of the society were Restorationists. Charles Hudson, afterwards a member of Congress, preached their doctrines. He had then, although a young man, become somewhat distinguished both as a preacher and an author.

In 1830 the Universalists, on account of a lack of interest, ceased to hold meetings, and the Baptists at once took possession of the house. Many of the Universalists attended the Baptist meetings. Among this number were Thaddeus Lovering, the wealthiest man in West Medway, who regularly contributed for the support of public worship until his death in 1850. From 1830 to 1833, the Rev. Moses Curtis, of Medfield, preached here once a month, and on other Sabbaths the pulpit was supplied chiefly by students from Newton Theological Institution. During the winter of 1831–32, a revival was enjoyed under the labors of the Rev. William Bentley, the Rev. Thomas Driver, and Mr. Ensign Lincoln. Thirteen were baptized. It now seemed that the number of Baptists in Medway was sufficient to warrant the formation of a church. Accordingly, November 15, 1832, a council was convened; the Rev. Charles Train, of Framingham, was chosen moderator, and the Rev. Moses Curtis, of Medfield, scribe. Recognition services were held the same day. Mr. Train preached the sermon, and Mr. Curtis gave the hand of fellowship The church numbered thirty-three members. The first pastor, the Rev. William Bowen, was publicly recognized August 21, 1833. He was a good speaker, and an excellent preacher The congregations upon the Sabbath were large, comprising some of the best citizens of the town. The Holy Spirit set the seal of his approval to the work. There were conversions and baptisms. But this season of prosperity did not continue. The pastor was an Englishman He could not adapt himself to the people like one "to the manner born." On the other hand, most of the church were young people, with but little experience in the management of church business. Troubles soon arose A council was convened for their settlement. The pastorate, so auspiciously commenced, terminated in less than three months. But little is now known here concerning the history of Mr. Bowen's life. It is impossible to ascertain either the time of his birth, or of his death He was a student at the school of the Rev. William Williams, at West Wrentham, of which place his wife was a native Before coming here he labored at Northboro. It is thought that he afterwards preached at Mansfield, Conn , and at Saratoga Springs, N. Y. Although during its first year the church received eighteen by baptism and eight by letter, yet during its second and third years it was in a divided state, and the congregation became small, but at the end of this period a brighter season dawned. Mr. Aaron Haynes, of Middletown, Vt , called December 20, 1835, was ordained pastor April 19, 1836. The Rev. Charles Train was moderator, and the Rev J. T. Massey, clerk. The sermon was preached by the Rev Thomas Driver. Mr Haynes was a bold and faithful preacher of the Gospel. He did not shun to declare "all the counsel of God " If his expressions in the pulpit were sometimes rough, lacking finish, it was because he thought more of saving his hearers than he did of winning their admiration During his pastorate of four years, twenty-six were added to the church by baptism, and twenty by letter After leaving here he was pastor in Vermont, in Southboro, Sutton, and South Braintree, in this state. In Southboro, he baptized, in three years, about one hundred and fifty converts. For years he engaged in secular business, during a portion of which time, it is said, that his interest in spiritual work waned. He manufactured the famous balsam bearing his name During the last of his life he labored as a colporteur in Pennsylvania. He died in 1880. For more than three years after his departure the church did not feel able to support a pastor. The pulpit was supplied six months by the Rev William Brown The Rev. John Holbrook, the Rev. Charles Train, and others, preached here. During this time another revival was enjoyed, and fourteen were baptized. In 1843, the members of the church became seriously divided on account of a difference of opinion concerning the second coming of Christ. Some had embraced the views of William Miller, which were opposed by others December 3, of this year, the Rev. David Curtis was called to the pastorate. The division continued increasing until it seemed that the church must soon become extinct. A council was convened for the settlement of the difficulties Mr. Curtis resigned his office September 6, 1845. While here he baptized three converts. He was born in East Stoughton, February, 1782. At the age of eighteen he became a Christian. He graduated at Brown University in 1808. He was pastor of seven churches, and the leader in forming as many more. Among the churches that he served as pastor were those in South Abington and West Harwich, in this state, and Coventry and Woonsocket, R. I. He is described as being "angular in character, and somewhat erratic," yet as "possessing a critical and logical mind." He loved his work, and earnestly desired to promote the progress of Christ's kingdom. Hence, rather than remain idle he would enter any field, however uninviting, and accept any compensation, however small. It was because of this self-sacrificing devotion to Christ's cause that Governor Briggs, in an address before the Massachusetts Baptist Convention in 1859, paid him a warm tribute of praise, and commended his example to the young ministers as worthy of imitation. In 1865 he visited each of the seven churches of which he had formerly been pastor, and bade the people farewell. He was at West Medway the first Sunday in December, and although he was then nearly eighty-four years old he preached twice, administered the Lord's Supper, and presided at the prayer-meeting in the evening.

He died September 12, 1869, at the home of his birth, and in connection with the church with which he first united, nearly seventy years before.

In the autumn of 1845 the Rev. Abner Mason was engaged to supply the pulpit "for the present." He found much to discourage him, so that he regarded his work as at the best but an experiment. The continued existence of the church seemed most precarious. But he quietly began his labors, visiting from house to house, and holding meetings during the week in different neighborhoods. Gradually the members of the church became not only humble, but completely broken down. They confessed their sins to God, and to each other. Dissensions ceased. Then the Holy Spirit wrought in power upon the hearts of the impenitent, and converts rapidly multiplied, of whom twenty-nine were baptized. Mr. Mason, on account of ill health, ceased to act as pastor, April 1, 1849. He was born in Medfield, in 1807. While residing in Lowell, in 1837, he became a Christian, and united with the Worthen Street Baptist Church. He studied at the Theological Institution, New Hampton, N. H., and, in 1843, became pastor of the Baptist Church, in Dunbarton, N. H. After closing his labors here, he became pastoral supply of the Baptist Church in Pocasset for one year and a half. He was employed for a short time in the cause of Sabbath Schools in Illinois. He died at his home here, December 11, 1864, soon after he had accepted an appointment from the Freedmen's Aid Society, to labor in Vicksburg. The funeral services were held at the church, the sermon being preached by his successor, the Rev. Mr. Messinger, from Psalms xxxvii., 37. To him was given, more than to most ministers of the Gospel, the power to win the hearts of the people. He could unite them not only in loving himself, but also in loving each other, while he was eminently kind and conciliatory, he was as eminently loyal to Christ and his truth. "To great gentleness of spirit he joined marked decision of character." His voice and his countenance indicated that he had a deeply sympathetic nature. He had a "passion for souls." The Rev. Edward Chase Messinger, April 1, 1489, was invited to supply the pulpit "for the present." He had preached for Mr. Mason since the second Sunday in December. Removing here, he bought the house that he occupied until his death. In 1850, the church began to consider different plans for securing a house of worship.

For twenty years they had enjoyed the free and unmolested use of the house dedicated in 1823, although but two of the proprietors had ever become Baptists. By gift and purchase, the property was obtained of the proprietors and their heirs. The old house was sold and removed, and the house now used by the church was dedicated May 27, 1852. The sermon was preached by the Rev. J. W. Parker, of Cambridgeport. The cost of the building was $2,800, of which Deacon J S Smith paid $500.

During Mr. Messinger's pastorate the congregations were good, and there were years when at the prayer-meetings, Sunday evenings, the vestry was thronged. Two revivals of religion were enjoyed—one in 1855, the other in 1858. The last time that Mr. Messinger preached at home, was the second Sunday in September, 1865. He exchanged, at West Dedham, the next Sunday. It was the last time that he ever preached. In November, he was present at one Sabbath service and offered prayer. His people never heard his voice in public again. He died peacefully and triumphantly, March 24, 1866. The sermon at his funeral was preached by the Rev. Isaac Smith, of Foxboro, one of his most intimate friends for thirty-three years. The closing prayer was offered by the Rev. Jacob Ide, D. D., then pastor of the Congregational Church. Mr Messinger baptized fifty-nine, and received forty-three by letter. He was born in Holliston, March 8, 1802. He was a lineal descendant of the Rev Henry M Messinger, pastor of the Congregational Church in Wrentham, from 1719 to 1750. In 1827, he became a Christian during a revival, and, in company with other young converts, united with the Congregational Church in his native town. Afterwards, as he prayerfully studied the Scriptures, he believed that the Holy Spirit revealed to him that while he had repented and believed on Christ, he had not been baptized. He could not live in the neglect of known duty. There was then no Baptist Church in Holliston, so he was baptized at Bellingham, and united with the church there. For some time he studied under the direction of the Rev Calvin Newton, of Bellingham. He was pastor of the Third Baptist Church, Middleboro, 1833–'37; South Abington, 1837–'45, East Brookfield, 1845–'47. He resigned this pastorate on account of ill health.

His sermons were sometimes entirely extemporaneous, and seldom fully written or greatly elaborated. He had good powers of analysis. He was an impressive speaker, and he possessed a warm and consecrated heart, so that his pulpit utterances were earnest and sometimes eloquent. He was a superior reader. He greatly excelled in public prayer. In the sick-room his ministrations were greatly prized. In the conducting of funerals, he had few equals and no superiors in this region. He was wise in the management of his secular affairs, and possessed qualities that would have probably rendered him successful in business. Blessed with an economical wife, who aided him in every department of his work, his house was better furnished, and he had more of the comforts of life than were enjoyed by most of his brethren in the ministry who received double the salary that was paid him. Unknown to most, he contributed to objects of benevolence, and sometimes more largely than his small salary seemed to warrant.

It is an interesting fact that Mr. Messenger's first sermon upon the Sabbath was preached at West Medway, and though fifty-two years have passed, there are some still living who distinctly remember the services of that day. They little thought that the young man who was preaching his first sermon, would, eighteen years afterwards, become their pastor.

From January until May, 1866, the Rev. John J. Bronson was pastoral supply. He labored earnestly, and his labors were crowned with the Divine approval. He baptized twenty-one converts. Eight more were baptized after his departure.

December 1, 1866, the Rev. Samuel Brooks became pastor. Needed improvements were soon made upon the meeting-house. The organ now used was bought by Deacon J. S. Smith and William Everett, who gave the church the use of it. The cost of the organ was $700, of which Deacon J. S. Smith paid $600. In 1869 the parsonage was erected

The thorough and critical scholarship of Mr. Brooks enabled him to render most efficient service to the public schools of the town, while by his gentlemanly manners and excellent spirit he quietly won the confidence and respect of all about him. He closed his labors here December 1, 1869, in order to accept a professorship at Kalamazoo College, Michigan. Dr. Brooks still occupies this place. He was born in Roxbury, now Boston. He was graduated at Brown University in 1852, where he was instructor in Greek, 1854–'55 ; graduated at Newton Theological Institution, in 1857 ; was pastor of the Second Baptist Church, Beverly, 1857–'60 ; instructor in Hebrew, Newton Theological Institution, 1860–'61. In 1862 he became pastor at South Framingham, where he remained until 1864, when he was compelled to resign on account of ill health

The Rev. Seth Jones Axtell, December 1, 1870, commenced his pastorate. Further improvements were made upon the church edifice. Mr. Axtell was a leader in the formation of the Framingham Association, and the Framingham Ministers' Conference He was also an active member of the school committee. He was an able and scholarly preacher. Several of his sermons and addresses were printed. He closed his pastorate April 1, 1878. *Vid.* BIOGRAPHIES.

The Rev. John Ezra Burr became pastor June 1, 1878. The following winter there was a pleasant work of grace. In 1879, a debt of $1,398 on the parsonage was paid. Of this Deacon Wales Kimball gave $478, and Deacon J. S. Smith, $470. During the week of prayer, January, 1882, a revival commenced, and continued for some months. Thirty converts were baptized, whose ages ranged from twelve to seventy-two years. During the summer of 1882, the house of worship was remodeled at an expense of $3.250.

November 15, 1882, was an important day in the history of the church In the morning the house was re-dedicated. The sermon was preached by the Rev. S. J. Axtell The prayer of re-dedication was offered by the Rev. F L. Batcheler. At this service a paper was read announcing the gift of the organ to the church by its owners, Deacon J. S. Smith and William Everett The semi-centennial services were held in the afternoon. The history of the church was given by the pastor, Mr. Burr, and a biographical sketch of its pastors was presented by the Rev. Lyman Partridge. Seven of the constituent members were present, viz , Deacon J. S. Smith and wife, Deacon Wales Kimball and wife, Alexander Grant and wife, and Mrs. Mary Smith Sears. Reunion services were held in the evening, presided over by the Rev S. W. Marston, D D.   The day was pleasant, and the attendance was large.

During the month of March, 1883, the health of Mr. Burr began to fail He preached for the last time on the first Sunday in April following   On the first Sunday in September he assisted in administering the Lord's Supper   The next Tuesday he started with his family for the home of his childhood, in Western Virginia, and when within about a hundred miles of his destination, he died on the railroad train, September 6, 1883, in Deer Park, Maryland.

During his pastorate, seventy-eight were added to the church, forty-nine by baptism

The Rev. Mr. Burr had clear views of Gospel truth.   His heart was in his work.   He lived for his people.   He had the gift of leadership.   He was constantly devising plans for developing and increasing the efficiency and strength of his church, and for saving souls.   It was largely through his efforts that the debts were paid, and the house was remodeled.   He excelled in the prayer-meeting in seasons of special religious interest, in his ability to bring the awakened sinner to an immediate decision to accept Christ.   A genial, faithful, conscientious man, he won the esteem and affection of his people.   They will never forget his pleasant smile, and cordial grasp of the hand   The Rev. Mr Burr was a native of Virginia

He was in the Union army from the spring of 1863 to the close of the war in 1865.   During the latter portion of the time he was in General Custer's division of Sheridan's Cavalry   He was wounded in battle.   He was graduated from Brown University in 1871, and from Newton Theological Institution in 1874   He was pastor of the Main Street Baptist Church, Fisherville, N H , 1874-'78.   *Vid.* GENEALOGIES.

The Rev. Mr Burr was succeeded by the Rev. B R Dow, of Fulton, N. Y , where he had served in the ministry one year.   Mr. Dow was a graduate of Madison University, and of Hamilton Theological Seminary, New York.   A few months after settlement, he married, June 4, 1883, Florence Horton, of Fulton, N. Y.

Frederick L. Bacheler, Adoniram J. Walker, Sylvester W. Marston, and Lyman Partridge, members of this church, have been licensed to preach the Gospel   In 1849, Anna Grant, daughter of Alexander Grant, became the wife of the Rev. Abner Mason ; the same year, Mary Kimball, daughter of Deacon Wales Kimball, was married to the Rev Harvey Goodell, then under appointment as a missionary to Canton, China.   She died suddenly, May 10, three days before the time arranged for their departure.

Several of the pastors have, in seasons of revival, been assisted by their brethren in the ministry.   Mention should be made of the Rev. Hervey Fittz, who labored here in 1847; the Revs. William C. Patterson, and H. F. Lane, in 1857, and the Rev William O Holman, in 1882.   In the period of seventy-one years, from November, 1832, to October, 1883, four hundred and seventy persons had been connected with the church.   Of these, thirty-three were constituent members, two hundred and seventy-four were added by baptism, and one hundred and sixty-three received by letter.   Eight of the church have served in the office of deacon.   Wales Kimball was elected 1833, resigned 1833, reelected 1858 ; J. S. Smith was chosen 1837, resigned 1845, reëlected 1867; H. C. Messinger was elected 1858; these three still serve; J. Eli Pond was chosen 1852, resigned 1865. The other four, Jesse New, Charles P. Gould, Samuel Leland, and Alfred Partridge, served for briefer periods.

The Sunday School has been connected with the church from the first, but no records were kept until 1859; from that year until 1883, the average attendance was eighty-five. The highest average was during 1860 and 1874, when it reached ninety-five. The largest attendance upon any one Sunday, was May 29, 1859, when 138 were present. The present membership of the church is one hundred and forty-two. This sketch, with slight changes, was approved by the church, October 4, 1883.

THE THIRD CONGREGATIONAL CHURCH.

1836 — 1865.

About the year 1834 there was a movement in the First Parish to set up another religious service, and procure "preaching of some other denomination"; and for a time those interested held an extra service in the Parish Hall by the courtesy of the First Parish. In 1835, near the close of the Rev. Mr. Bailey's pastorate, some more than forty members of the First Parish withdrew for the purpose of forming a new religious society, which was called "The Third Congregational Society in Medway." Soon after organization, they set about the erection of a meeting-house. Meanwhile, the Rev. Mr. Bailey had resigned, but was still residing in the parish. After hearing various persons, their meeting-house being completed, the new society invited their old minister to become the pastor. Soon after, eleven persons, members of the First Church, having requested dismission, "Wishing," as they say, "to associate in public worship with the 'Third Congregational Society in Medway,' agree and covenant together to be 'The Third Congregational Church.'" And they add, "We mutually agree to walk together in Christian fellowship and to adopt as our Church Covenant the Covenant used in the said First Church. Luther Bailey, Adam Bullard, Lewis Harding, Kezia Harding, Olive Harding, Sarah Harding, Mary Richardson, Kezia Harding, Eliza Adams, Dorcas M. Wright, Abigail Lovell."

In 1836 the church was recognized, and the Rev. Mr. Bailey installed their pastor, as seen from the following record:

"Agreeably to letters missive, an Ecclesiastical Council convened in East Medway on Wednesday, Dec. 7, 1836, at the house of Col. George H. Holbrook, & was organized by the choice of the Rev. Amos Clarke, as Moderator, . . . the Rev. James A. Kendall, Scribe.

After an examination of sundry papers submitted to them, the Council *Voted*. That they were satisfied with the proceedings of the Third Congregational Society in Medway, respecting their invitation given to the Rev. Luther Bailey to become their religious Teacher & Pastor, and his acceptance thereof. Also,

Voted. That they were satisfied with the measures adopted by the Third Cong Soc'y pertaining to the formation of a Society & Church, & were ready to proceed to assign the parts for the Dedication of the House of worship, & the Installation of the Pastor Accordingly, it was *Voted*. That the Introductory & Dedicatory Prayer should be offered by the Rev Mr. Sanger, Sermon by Rev. Mr. Ritchie, Installing prayer, Mr. White; Charge, by Rev. Mr. Clarke; Right hand of Fellowship, by Rev. Mr. Sanger; Concluding prayer, by Rev. Mr. Kendall

Attest,   JAMES A. KENDALL, Scribe."

This new church maintained service a number of years, and its membership increased, the Rev. Mr. Bailey being their minister; but, on his retirement, the organization gradually diminished, until public service was discontinued. Some of the members returned to the First Church, some removed from town, others died; so that the Third Congregational Church and Society became virtually extinct   Their meeting-house was removed to the opposite side of the street and known as St. Clement's Church.

THE REGISTER OF THE THIRD CONGREGATIONAL CHURCH.

PASTOR.—The Rev. Luther Bailey, installed December 7, 1836; died June 16, 1863.

DEACONS.—Adam Bullard, Amos B Davis.

MEMBERSHIP.—Fifty-one members recorded

THE EVANGELICAL CONGREGATIONAL CHURCH.

1838 — 1885

The growth of Medway "Factory Village," through its manufacturing industries, required religious privileges more accessible than either church in East or West Medway afforded   Occasional religious service was held in the school-house by the Rev. Dr Ide, of West Medway, and Sabbath School instruction was maintained previous to 1830   The increasing interest in these privileges, and their essential importance to this growing community, excited the citizens to the purpose of erecting and maintaining a place for public worship.

The site of the present meeting-house was given by David Whiting, of New York, a native of this village, by a deed of gift of one quarter of an acre, more or less, to Comfort Walker, dated April 21, 1836.   The same lot was conveyed by Mr. Walker, August 27, 1836, to the following persons, who became the original proprietors of the meeting-house property, divided into eighty-nine shares, to wit: Luther Metcalf, William White, Orion Mason, M. H. Sanford, ten each; James B. Wilson, and Comfort Walker, fifteen each; Dr. A. L. B. Monroe, six; Titus Bullard, three; and Wyman Adams, William Fuller, Charles Wheeler, and Collins Hathon, each two. They had become subscribers to a fund of $4,450, and they took forty-one pews in the meeting-house, to the value of $4,961.50, as follows: Comfort Walker, eleven pews, for $1,192; J. B. Wilson, six, for $818; L. Metcalf, four, for $580; William White, three, for $488; M. H. Sanford, four, for $451; Orion Mason, five, for $434; Dr. Monroe, two, for $280; J. O. Pond, one, $158; W. Fuller, one, $118; Charles Wheeler, one, $116; W. Adams, one, $126; Titus Bullard, one, $115; C. Hathon, one, $85; leaving nineteen pews, sold in part to other persons.

The consideration in the original deed of the land, was, "that a meeting-house shall be erected on these premises for the sole purpose of having public worship of the Evangelical Congregational order (preached and) maintained therein forever."

THE VILLAGE CHURCH.   ERECTED IN 1838.

Through the agency of Deacon M. M. Fisher, the grounds were much enlarged, and were conveyed by him, by deed, dated June 9, 1846, for the sum of three hundred dollars, with the stipulation that: "No building is to be erected upon the land, except to enlarge or rebuild the meeting-house. The grounds to be ornamented with shrubs and trees, and the society to have the use of all roads upon the place of said land." Slight changes have been made, by sale, to the Parson's estate, of some twenty feet in depth, and by exchange with the Hon. Clark Partridge. The enclosure of the grounds and the lawns, as they now are, was made by the liberality of Mr. M. H. Sanford, under the careful superintendence of the Rev. R. K. Harlow, pastor of the Village church in 1881.

The following persons were elected to act as a committee to contract for the building of the church, to wit: Luther Metcalf, J B Wilson, Wyman Adams, William White, and Milton H. Sanford, and they contracted with James Purrington to build the house. and William Page to do the stone work. The final cost of the whole, including the bell. was $5.829.57, and it was dedicated with appropriate ceremonies. June 15, 1838. The Rev. Joel Hawes, D. D., of Hartford, a native of the Village, preached the sermon of dedication.

A religious society was legally organized, and the meeting-house was committed to its use and care for public worship, May 25, 1838.

At the first meeting the following officers were chosen.

Milton H. Sanford, *Clerk*	A L. B. Monroe,	
Luther Metcalf,	Benjamin Smith,	*Assessors.*
Orion Mason,	William Fuller,	
J. B Wilson,	*Parish Com.* Comfort Walker, *Treasurer*	
Clark Partridge,	Charles Wheeler, *Collector.*	

The support of worship was wholly voluntary and not by any tax, as was the general practice at that time The salary was fixed at $600. with an expected donation party giving $100 to $200 annually

A church, called " The Evangelical Congregational Church of Medway Village," was organized September 7, 1838, consisting of thirty-four members. The organizing council was made up of representatives of the following churches: The Second Church of Christ in Medway, the Rev. Jacob Ide, D. D., pastor, Deacon Daniel Nourse. delegate ; Church in Franklin, Brother Caleb Fisher, delegate ; First Church of Christ in Medway, the Rev. Sewall Harding, pastor, Brother Paul Daniell, delegate ; Village Church, Dorchester, the Rev. David Sanford, pastor, Brother James Burt, delegate.

The First Pastorate.

1838—1871

The people from the first had their eye and heart upon the Rev David Sanford, a native of the Village, then settled at Milton Mills, Dorchester, for their pastor He accepted the call, and was installed, October 3, 1838. pastor of the Evangelical Congregational Church and Society of Medway.

The following ministers took part in the services: the Rev. D. J. Smith, of Sherborn, introductory prayer ; the Rev. J. Codman, D. D., Second Church, Dorchester, sermon ; the Rev. E Fisk, Wrentham, installing prayer ; the Rev. J Ide, D. D., West Medway, charge to the pastor ; the Rev. S. Harding, East Medway, fellowship of the churches ; the Rev. D. Long, Milford, concluding prayer

In 1846, the attendance at church was so large that the society erected galleries at a cost of $550, which were well occupied for several years, and until the introduction of foreign, instead of American, labor in the mills diminished the Protestant population. The congregation formerly numbered, at times, three hundred and fifty on the Sabbath.

The marble clock was presented by Mrs. John W. Richardson, in memory of her father, Elias Metcalf, who was a member of the church. The clock in the tower of the church was presented in 1850, by Pardon D. Tiffany, Esq., a native of the Village, then of St. Louis, Mo.

In 1850 the vestry of the church was finished at a cost of $341.16

In 1861 Mr. M. H. Sanford presented the society with the organ made by Mr. E. L. Holbrook, of East Medway, at a cost of $1,000, and the society enlarged the meeting-house to place the organ at the north end of the house, with singers' seats in front, with a platform and pulpit projecting into the main body of the house. This change was made at a cost of $566.25.

In 1870 repairs and changes were made at a cost of $1,991.45, and in 1874 the whole interior of the church was remodeled at a cost of about six thousand dollars. All these sums were raised by subscription.

Public worship was sustained until 1854 by voluntary subscription; since then the pews have been rented for its support.

During this pastorate four hundred and seven were added to the church.

THE SECOND PASTORATE.

1872

The Rev. David Sanford resigned the active duties of the pastorate, March 7, 1871, and the Rev. R. K. Harlow was installed colleague pastor, February 13, 1872. Sermon by the Rev. William B. Wright, of Boston; prayer of installation, by the Rev. D. Sanford; charge to the pastor, by the Rev. Isaiah C. Thatcher; right hand of fellowship, by the Rev. E. O. Jameson; address to the people by the Rev. Horace D. Walker.

The period represented by the pastorate of the Rev. R. K. Harlow, has been one of prosperity to the church and society. In addition to the improvement of the interior of the house of worship, and the adornment of its grounds, provision has been made, in part, for the future support of public worship, from the income of Sanford Hall, and from a legacy of $6,000, left by the late Edward Eaton, Esq. During the ministry of the Rev. Mr. Harlow, one hundred and sixteen have been added to the church.

THE OFFICIAL REGISTER.

PASTORS

Rev. David Sanford, installed October 3, 1838, died December 17, 1876.
Rev. Rufus Kendrick Harlow, installed February 13, 1872.

DEACONS.

Deacon Samuel Allen, ordained September 4, 1840, died January 15, 1866
Deacon George W. Hunt, ordained September 4, 1840, died March 24, 1870
Deacon Milton M. Fisher, ordained September 4, 1840.
Deacon John W. Richardson, elected November 1, 1867.

The total membership of the church to 1885 was five hundred and seventy-five. There are now two hundred and twenty-one members.

The St. Joseph's Church.

1850 — 1885.

Thirty-five years ago very few persons of the Catholic faith resided in Medway But these few, in 1850, gathered for religious service in the house of Walter De Wire, where mass was celebrated by the Rev. Father Callaher These services were held at irregular intervals until about 1857-8, when they were continued under the ministrations of the Rev. Father Cuddihy at the residence of John Kenny

The congregation gradually increased, and finally what was then known as the old straw shop was hired as a place of worship. This building stood upon the ground now occupied by the present St. Joseph's Church In 1863 the premises were purchased with funds raised by subscription among the members of the church, sixty-two in all, viz. :

Nicholas Lanigan.	Daniel Flynn.	Peter Phillips.	Walter DeWire
Laurence McGinnis	John Buckley	Francis Neelon	James Logan.
Patrick Conrey.	James Finneron.	James Toohey.	Patrick Hart.
Dennis Mawn.	Patrick O'Hara	James Brown	Barney Rooney
Owen Mawn	Peter Scales	Michael Sheehan.	Patrick McGullion.
Michael Casey	Thomas Casey	John Reardon	Michael Reilly.
James Jordan.	Patrick Keaney.	Hugh Keaney	Thomas Malloy.
Thomas O'Gara.	Francis Namarra	Edward Scofield	Edmund Hayes
Patrick McCormick.	Michael Haggerty	Andrew J Murphy.	Michael Costello
Edward O'Donnell	James O'Connors.	Patrick Keefe	John Gordon.
Francis McGullion.	Thomas Mullen.	William Wallace.	John Lanigan
Michael Cullen	John McGee.	Morris Kirby	John Woods.
James O'Hara	Anthony Gallagher.	Thomas McGullion.	Jeremiah Colbert.
Jeremiah Desmond.	Patrick Crowley.	Daniel Whooley.	Patrick Neelon.
Timothy O'Holloren	Michael Cleary	Patrick Phillips	James Reilley.
Thomas Kane	James Keaney		

To these subscribers may be attributed the real formation of the present St. Joseph's Catholic Church, of Medway During the period above named this church formed a portion of the Milford Parish, and was ministered to by the Rev Father Cuddihy, but in December, 1870, it was detached from the parish of Milford, and joined to that of Holliston, the Rev. Father Quinlan becoming the pastor. Shortly after assuming charge of the Medway Church, he started a subscription among the members for means for a new building, work on which was commenced in the spring of 1876. The basement of the edifice was occupied for the first service, August 12, 1877.

At this time a debt of $8,500 existed, and to reduce this amount the society held a fair, the proceeds of which netted some $3,000, which was not enough to finish the building, and, as a consequence, it has since then remained uncompleted, only the basement being available for public worship.

The care of both churches taxed the strength of Father Quinlan severely. Having asked for an assistant, the Rev Father Splain was appointed as such in 1879, being succeeded by the Rev. Father John Cummings, and later on by the Rev Father Campbell, who, not being possessed of a constitution of sufficient robustness to give the attention which he desired to so large a congregation, asked for his release, which, being granted, he was succeeded in June, 1885, by the Rev Father M. T Boylan.

The congregation having increased to some twelve hundred, the parish, with the incoming of Father Boylan, was made independent.

Upon the appointment of Father Boylan, a residence was purchased for him in Medway, and he at once commenced financial methods towards the completion of the house of worship, making a personal canvass in the parish, and by this means raising by pledge the sum of $2,500.

Father Boylan was educated by the Sulpitian Fathers, in Montreal College, Canada, his theological studies having been followed there in the Grand Seminary, an institution conducted by the Sulpitians, and his ordination to the priesthood occurred there December 19, 1874. His first ecclesiastical appointment was that of assistant pastor to the Rev Manasses Doherty, of St. Peter's Church, Cambridge, Mass., at which place he remained until his appointment, by Archbishop Williams, to the position which he now holds, as pastor of St. Joseph's Roman Catholic Church, of Medway.

THE METHODIST EPISCOPAL CHURCH.

1857 — 1885

There was no organized Methodist movement in this town previous to the year 1857. Meetings had undoubtedly been held and sermons preached by Methodist ministers, in school-houses and other places, before that date

In 1857, the Rev. William Jackson, formerly a Wesleyan minister, preached here, and such was the effect produced by his labors, that he located himself upon the hill, near the Congregational Church, and continued his ministry about two years, holding his meetings chiefly in a school-house. These labors resulted. July 19, 1857, in the organization of the "First Methodist Episcopal Church, of West Medway, Mass"

Mr. Jackson was much advanced in years, and a man of marked peculiarities His ministry could hardly fail to awaken the curiosity and interest of any community He had a wonderful knowledge of the Word of God, usually referring to the chapter and place of every verse used by him, and is mentioned by one of his successors, as a man of clear and quick understanding, faith in the Holy Ghost, bold as a lion, fearing not the face of clay. He was childlike, excitable, and sometimes imprudent; and while his manner awakened opposition and criticism, his wonderful knowledge of the Bible not only made him an intelligent and instructive preacher, but the writer of some useful books, *The Christian Legacy*, being, perhaps, the most useful of them

In December, 1858, the Rev. L. Crowell, then presiding elder, held the first quarterly meeting of the church, at the house of Mr. Jackson, where the last meeting under his ministry was held September 23, 1859. At that time there was no depot, the railroad was unfinished, and there were but few houses in that part of the town

Mr William Adams, a man of wonderful enterprise and public spirit, had become so far interested in Mr. Jackson and the Methodist movement, that he generously gave the land for a church and parsonage, and in many other ways helped on the struggling cause.

The ground was broken, walls laid, timbers and boards bought, the church raised and inclosed, but, although wonderful liberality characterized the few worthy people, the meeting-house was only partially completed.

Indeed, the society was so embarrassed by debts, that but for the timely aid of the Hon. Lee Clafflin, of Hopkinton, the house would have been sold, and the life of the society extinguished. But just at this crisis Mr. Clafflin was induced to loan the church $750, with which its obligations were met. The trustees gave him a deed of the property for that sum, which he generously deeded back at the end of three years for one-half that amount. From that time the church moved forward with renewed energy, the house being completed soon after.

In 1870 the excellent and commodious parsonage was built, largely through the generous and noble liberality of the lamented Thomas Campbell, who even in death loved and remembered the church. It should also be observed at this point, that Mr. Jackson's very excellent wife, and other members of his family, made most generous gifts to the church. The Rev. Mr. Jackson died distant from this place, and at his request was brought here, and buried near the Cottage Street gateway of our beautiful cemetery, and in close proximity to the church which he so much loved, and the spot so dear to his heart. Here mention should be made of others who took prominent part in the movement, viz.: Peter Ford, John Crowland, L. S. Whitney, Stephen Campbell, and several others, whose names do not appear in the records. Mr. Jackson was followed by the Rev. Mr. Tilton, of New Hampshire, who preached with acceptability for a short time, and was succeeded in 1860–1861, by the Rev Josiah Higgins, a local preacher, then living in Chelsea, being here only on the Sabbath. He was a man of true piety, warm heart, earnest and affectionate manner, very useful, and much beloved.

In 1861 the Rev. George Whitaker was appointed by the Conference, and became the first regular pastor of the church. This was his first appointment, having just graduated from Wesleyan University. He was without experience, but made many friends, and was successful in his work.

The Rev. T. C Potter was Mr. Whitaker's successor from 1863 to 1865. A good and true minister, but of whom little is known aside from his labors here. He subsequently removed from this Conference to other fields.

In 1866 the Rev. C. W Wilder, a modest, faithful, and useful man, was appointed to the charge, but went from Medway to the Vermont Conference, leaving before the close of the year, being followed for a short time by a young Mr Thayer, of Mendon.

The Rev. W. A Nottage, an educated, devoted, and faithful pastor, served the church the next two years.

In the spring of 1868 the Rev. W. P. Ray took the field, and served the church faithfully for three years. During Mr Ray's ministry the parsonage was built, and many were brought into the church.

He was succeeded by the Rev. William Merrill, a good, earnest, winning preacher, who served the church with great acceptability till the spring of 1873, though his labors were much embarrassed by illness, the last year.

Mr. Merrill was followed by the Rev. J. R. Cushing, who was with the church but one year. He was an active, earnest, social man, gifted as a singer, and a Sabbath School worker.

The pastorate for the next three years, from the spring of 1874 to the spring of 1877, was assigned to the Rev. L. Crowell, under whose administration as presiding elder, the church was first organized. Under his labors general prosperity prevailed. Seasons of revival were enjoyed, and about thirty persons were received into the church, making about one-third part of the whole membership at that time. During Mr. Crowell's term, $3,000 were expended in improvements on the meeting-house.

But in the midst of this prosperity there were some reverses. Many removed, mostly in consequence of depression in business. Twenty persons took letters, many of them permanent and valuable members, and other persons and families not members, but regular attendants, removed from the place. Mr. Crowell attended twenty-five funerals, six members of the church died, some of whom were aged and much honored and esteemed, and others helpful.

The Rev. W. N. Richardson was pastor in 1877–1879, and was succeeded by the Rev. J. C. Smith, whose labors covered a term of three years, closing in April, 1882, followed by the Rev. W. M. Hubbard, who remained three years, and was succeeded by the Rev. Mr. Dwight.

The full membership as reported in the minutes of the annual Conference of 1882, was one hundred and sixteen.

The board of trustees were Aaron Brigham, E. D. Stone, J. T. Greenwood, Charles Cole, S. J. Lawrence, Seth Partridge, William Creasey.

SAINT CLEMENT'S CHURCH AND SCHOOL.

1865 — 1871.

The Third Congregational Society lost its organization by the failure to hold annual and other business meetings. And their meeting-house, having been closed for some years, was fast going to decay.

A proposition was made June, 1865, by the Revs B I Cooley, pastor of the Episcopal Church, of Holliston, Mass., and B B Babbit, of Andover, to the pew-owners, who had become the owners of the church, that it should be, for a nominal sum, transferred to a board of trustees representing the Episcopal Church of Massachusetts, who agreed to repair and improve the property, and to maintain the services of the Protestant Episcopal Church forever. Unanimous consent having been obtained of the owners, the property was deeded to the Rev. Nicholas Hoppin, the Rev. Theodore Edson, and the Rev B. B Babbit Improvements were made, the whole building was repaired and enlarged, a chancel built, organ and bell, and fine furniture obtained, the clock on the tower repaired, and by means of funds contributed by wealthy and benevolent people in that denomination it became one of the best appointed churches in this vicinity. The church was named St Clement's Church in honor of St. Clement. The Rev Benjamin Cooley became the first rector. A few families in this section, who were attached to this service, gathered together and formed the nucleus around which a fine congregation gathered. The services were of the high ritualistic order, and very imposing. Every saint's day in the calendar was observed. The Holy Communion was observed weekly, and a large Sunday School was gathered. For several years the church prospered, though never self-supporting. Several members were added to the church by the active and faithful pastor. Gradually there arose a controversy between the pastor and leading men of the church, the latter protesting against the advanced ideas of the former, and declining to support the extreme ritualistic views and practices then performed by the rector This controversy, though conducted by both parties with dignity, prudence, and Christian spirit, was a blow which destroyed the usefulness of the active, faithful, and laborious pastor, who had collected the funds and built up the church, and he sorrowfully gave up his charge. Many retired from the church, and the life and force seemed gone out of it, and the field seemed very desolate and discouraging to the succeeding pastor, the Rev. Charles Kelley However, a small company rallied around him, more especially composed of young people, and services were continued until Sunday, February 5, 1871, the coldest day of the year, while the congregation were at worship the church took fire from the over-heated furnace, and in a few moments was entirely consumed, the congregation escaping by a rear door through the vestry. Services were suspended permanently. After several years the insurance was paid and a stone church was erected in Medway Village. *Vid* CHRIST CHURCH.

As soon as the church was well established, the zealous rector determined to locate here a school for the training of young men for the ministry. The Mansion House, formerly built for a boarding-school, and the building occupied by Adams Daniels, Esq., as a store, were purchased and fitted up as chapel and rectory. Mr Lewis Morris, late of New Haven, Conn., became the principal. Military drill, uniform, and discipline, were features of the institution A full course of instruction was adopted, and the school was opened by the Rt Rev. T M. Clark, Bishop of Rhode Island, assisted by other clergymen. The institution continued for several years, until the burning of their school building, which, with the church, was destroyed February 5, 1871. The rectory also was burned a few months later

THE CHRIST CHURCH. ERECTED IN 1871.

The erection of this beautiful stone structure, called CHRIST CHURCH, was commenced in 1874, but not completed for several years. It was largely the gift of a beneficent Christian gentleman of Boston. It was opened for divine service on Christmas Eve, 1881, by the Rev. J. S. Beers, missionary at large in the Diocese of Massachusetts.

The Rev. Samuel Edwards became officiating missionary under the Diocesan Board of Missions, on Sunday, January 8, 1882, and the church was formally dedicated, January 8, 1885. The dedicatory service was conducted by Bishop Paddock, of the Diocese of Massachusetts, who preached a sermon on the occasion. The Rev. J. B. Wicks is the rector in charge. The number of communicants is not far from twenty-five.

In conclusion, the town of Medway has always been, and still is, well furnished with religious institutions. There are five Christian denominations holding services on the Sabbath, having eight different places of public worship.

There have been twelve meeting-houses and one chapel erected within the town, of which seven and a chapel are now standing, and in constant use.

"Hitherto hath the Lord helped us."

1714.   1885.

THE SCHOOLS, AND OTHER INSTITUTIONS.

1713 — 1885.

IT has been said that wherever in New England a meeting-house was erected, the school-house sprang up beside it. So in Medway, as soon as a house for public worship was provided, the school-house soon followed. As early as 1671 the colonial government had decreed that every town containing fifty families should " forthwith appoint one within their towns to teach all such children as shall resort to him to write & read, whose wages shall be paid either by the parents or masters of such children, or by the inhabitants in general." It is recorded, May 13, 1717, that four pounds were voted " for building a pound & keeping a scool." How this was divided is not recorded, whether the cattle or the children received the larger share, we do not know. The next year two pounds were voted, thirty shillings for a writing-school, and ten shillings for a school at " ye bent of ye river." This was the origin of schools Nos. 1 and 2. Ruth Harding was paid nine shillings and eightpence, and Widow Partridge six shillings and fourpence, for keeping these schools. This was the day of small things, truly, yet it shows that the people of that time realized the importance of education, and were willing to make what was deemed suitable provision for it. The course of study must have been exceedingly limited, and the labors of these pioneer teachers could not have been very exhausting. Geography, astronomy, chemistry, and studies of that class were unknown in the common school. Books were scarce, newspapers and magazines seldom seen, so that a knowledge of reading, writing, and arithmetic, such as would be required in the ordinary transactions of life was perhaps all that was necessary to be added to the stock of common-sense that our fathers and mothers possessed.

In March, 1737, the town voted to build three school-houses, one at East Medway, one at the Bent, and one in the New Grant, and a committee of three from each part of the town was chosen to take the matter into consideration, and report at the May meeting; but as the town at that meeting refused to grant the necessary funds, their construction was probably delayed for a time.

THE OLD SCHOOL-HOUSE.

1737 — 1823.

THE FIRST SCHOOL-HOUSE was, doubtless, the one here represented, which was erected in East Medway; the exact date is unknown, but it stood not far from the dwelling-house of Deacon Peter Adams, where was held the first town-meeting, and where, also, was conducted, October 7, 1714, the first service of public worship. It is thought that this school-house was the same which, in 1823, was taken down to give place to the one of brick, mentioned elsewhere. This old school-house is still remembered by some persons living, as the place where, in early childhood, they went to school.

The first school district meeting, of which there is a record, was held February 11, 1801. "At a Legal School Meeting at the East Destrick the Committee open^d the Meeting. 1. Chose Major Jasper Adams, Moderator. 2. Chose Lewis Wheeler, Clerk. 3. past a vote for one months man school 4. Voted to have 4 months woman school. 5. Voted for the Committee to Provide A master and mistress for the future. 6. Voted the Committee provide four Cord of wood. 7. Put 2 Cord up at the highest Bider. Timothy Harding Bid the first 2 cord at 13s. 8d. per Cord. 9. 2 Cord More at 13s. 6d. pr Cord to Ezra Richardson."

The sum of $400 was granted by the town for schooling this year. At a meeting in January, 1823, it was voted to build a new school-house, and a committee, consisting of Sylvanus Adams, Moses Adams, Captain Lewis Wheeler, Zachariah Lovell, and Nathan Jones, were chosen to superintend the building, and "cause the spot to be suitably fixed whereon said house is to stand." Voted to build it of brick, and that it shall be not exceeding three rods from the old spot, and the sum of five hundred and fifty dollars was granted by the district. In 1883 the fire-place was replaced by an iron fire-frame, then considered a vast improvement on the old-fashioned brick fire-place. This house is standing, in 1885, and occupied as a dwelling.

The school-house erected in the westerly part of the town, the New Grant, stood in the neighborhood of the Baptist Church, near where the second church and cemetery were afterwards located. In 1745 the forty-five pounds granted were divided as follows: "twelve pounds for the school near Joseph Adams'; six pounds at the Widow Pratt's; twelve pounds at the Bent; eight pounds at the New Grant school-house; four pounds at Joseph Barber's house, and three pounds at the house of Job Plimpton." The wages of teachers at this time may be inferred from the record that Samuel Harding was paid three pounds lawful money for keeping school seven weeks.

In 1760, five schools were maintained. At East Parish, No. 1, the Bent, No. 2, the Neck, No. 3, the New Grant, No. 4, and the north part of New Grant, No. 5, and nine years after, in 1769, the school on the county line, No. 6, was added. The school money appears to have been divided in proportion to the valuation of property in the several districts, which was not deemed satisfactory by all the people, as in 1784 Simon Fisher and others petitioned the town to have the money divided in proportion to the number of scholars in each district; but it was not granted. The schools do not appear to have been in charge of a separate board; probably the selectmen had the general direction of them, and when in 1799, an article was inserted in the town warrant " to see if the town will choose a committee to inspect the schools," it was dismissed, and no further action appears to have been taken for several years.

THE FIRST SCHOOL COMMITTEE. Abijah Richardson, M. D., John Ellis, Ezekiel Plimpton, Philo Sanford. and Calvin Cutler, were chosen in 1805, a committee to inspect the schools. The same year the limits of the different districts were fixed, and the money divided according to a valuation to be made once in seven years.

There was usually a term of school during the summer, attended by the smaller scholars, taught by a female, and a term from ten to sixteen weeks in winter which included pupils of all ages, from four to twenty, and for this a male teacher was required. His qualifications were not necessarily very high in regard to learning, but he must be able to control the unruly element, hardly ever absent from the winter district school. Discipline must be maintained, or he would soon go to the wall. Solomon's maxims were then believed in and practised, and the rod was freely used on refractory backs. Some teachers acquired considerable notoriety for their skill in subduing unruly boys, and were much sought for by distracted committee-men, who had the oversight of " hard schools." The master taught in winter, and cultivated his farm or pursued his trade during the summer. In the Bent school in the early part of this century, Captain Seneca Barber taught for over twenty seasons. The studies pursued were Pike's Arithmetic, Morse's Geography without maps, American Preceptor for reading, and writing, including the art, now a lost one, of making and mending a quill pen. This was the usual course, but occasionally a bright scholar would pursue his studies beyond his class, and would perfect himself in surveying, or be sent away to college to become a minister, a lawyer, or a doctor.

Until 1816 the Village had belonged to district No. 4, but the population having increased considerably, owing to the various manufacturing interests which had been developed in connection with its water power, it was deemed advisable to form the new school district, No. 7. The record reads that it was determined that a school-house should be built " twenty six feet square, and that it should have a hip roof and belfry with a vane upon it, and that it should be finished inside after the same plan as the old Bent school-house." Such a house was accordingly built, under the direction of Nathaniel Clark, house-wright, at a cost of $500, and stood on the site between Sanford Hall and the Catholic Church. Many of the older citizens remember this room where they obtained their education. The floor contained a space of about ten by twenty feet, with a low seat running around it for the A B C scholars, back of this, on each side, were three rows of desks, each a little higher than the other; the stout oaken tops of these stiff, hard benches were able to resist the scholar's jack-knife, but the lower shelf of soft pine, seemed peculiarly fitted for this tool, and it bore marks of severe usage. A huge fire-place at one end of the room, and the teacher's desk at the other, completed the fitting-up. Maps, charts, and blackboards were but little used. In 1830 the house was enlarged by adding sixteen feet to its length, and putting another story upon it. This second story formed a fair sized hall, and was used for exhibitions, religious meetings, and other purposes, but was intended for, and used to accommodate, a school of higher grade. Such a school was taught at first by Mr. Abijah R. Baker, from Franklin, who was a recent college graduate. The school was very successful, and the grade of studies being much above that of the ordinary town schools, a large number of pupils from Medway and the surrounding towns were attracted to it, and for several terms the success of this school for higher branches was very gratifying to the citizens. But after a time it was given up, and succeeded by select private schools, taught at intervals of greater or lesser length. Among other teachers were Mr. George P. Smith, who afterwards was a clergyman in Worcester; the Rev. Samuel J. Spalding, D. D., now of Newburyport, who kept two terms in 1843-'44, and a year or two later the Rev. Harvey Adams, who afterwards went to the West, and was superintendent of Home Missions in one of the Western states. The wages of teachers at this period may be inferred from the following sums paid in No. 7: Mary Spurr, in 1824, was paid $25.50 for teaching twelve weeks; Sarah B. Phipps, in 1827, was paid $16 for teaching six weeks; Fanny Davis, in 1830, was paid $33 for teaching twelve weeks; Pardon D. Tiffany, in 1833, was paid $33 for teaching twenty-three days; M. M. Fisher, in 1836, was paid $82.50 for teaching two and a half months.

The town, in 1821, voted that two or more places should be provided where scholars might procure books at cost, and Gilbert Clark was appointed the first agent. The books to be kept were Alden's Spelling Book, Alden's Reader, Walker's Dictionary, Cumming's Geography, Murray's Grammar, and the New Testament.

About 1850, the population of the Village having increased considerably, there seemed to be an imperative necessity for more room than the old house afforded. The question of dividing the district, and erecting a building in the lower part of the Village was proposed and discussed, but at length it was determined to build one house in place of the old one, which would accommodate two hundred scholars. A lot of land was bought of the Medway Manufacturing Company, and a committee, consisting of J. C. Hurd, W. H. Cary, and Artemus Brown, M. D., was chosen, and in 1850-'51 the present house was erected at a cost of $7,362.75. It was quite expensive for those days. Great fault was found with the committee on account of the large outlay. It was deemed by many as very extravagant in cost, and too large in size. But it was soon filled with pupils, and was found to be too small, and after increasing its capacity, it is still crowded, and the need of further accommodations for the large number of scholars begins to be felt. Thus time exonerates and applauds those who have the moral courage, at the cost of popularity, to act for the public welfare.

THE HIGH SCHOOL HOUSE. ERECTED IN 1851.

On its completion the committee made the following report in December, 1851: "Your committee, appointed June 10, 1850, by school district No. 7, for the purpose of causing a school-house to be erected, would report that they entered upon their duties immediately after the site for the same had been purchased. They will waive a rehearsal of the opposition, as also the disappointments which have protracted the work until the present day, and enter upon the more agreeable duty of giving a general or detailed account of their expenditures, exclusive of any charge for expenses or time of your committee."

As already mentioned, the first school-house in district No. 4, West Medway, was located near the old church, in the vicinity of the burying-ground. It was afterwards moved up the hill to the northeast corner of the common belonging to the Second Church of Christ, where it was used until 1851 for the district school in connection with the parish house, the building now occupied by A. M. B. Fuller, Esq., where the select schools were kept. In 1831, Mr. Daniel Forbes, of Westboro', came to West Medway and established a school, which was very successful, calling in a large number of pupils from this and the surrounding towns. Mr. Forbes possessed a rare faculty for encouraging his pupils, and creating an enthusiasm for their works. The course of study was similar to that in academies of that time, including the languages and the higher branches of an English education.

In the autumn of 1838 Mr. Daniel J. Poor opened a school of a similar character, which was fully attended, but was not long continued. He afterwards taught an academy in Hopkinton, and later entered the ministry, and was for a short time settled in Foxboro', Mass.

The old school-house had become too small to accommodate the district, and in 1860 it was determined that a new one must be erected. The change was accompanied by the obstacles and trials that generally attend such changes. Some were in favor of rebuilding on the old lot; others were in favor of the Grove lot, the Sparrow lot, the Hunt lot, and the Sprout lot, and meeting after meeting was held, and finally, in September, it was determined to build on the Hunt lot; and a committee of three, William H. Temple, C. H. Deans,, and A. S. Chellis, was chosen, who contracted with W. L. Payson for the construction of the present house, which was built at a cost, including land and grading, of $6,963.61.

In 1849 it was decided to build a new school-house in district No. 1, larger, and more in accordance with modern ideas. The committee chosen were Adams Daniels, Michael Bullen, Amos B. Davis, George H. Holbrook, Hiram Kingsbury, John P. Jones, and William La Croix. This committee bought a lot of land on the turnpike, now Main Street, procured a plan, and contracted for the present house, which was stated by one of the committee to be a "model school-house," costing, with the land, $1,866. Unlike the building committee of No. 7, who, a few years later, were roundly censured for their services, this committee received a vote of thanks "for the faithful performance of the duties assigned them."

In 1868 an Episcopal Society was formed in East Medway, and in connection with it a school for boys, under the charge of the rector, the Rev. Mr. Cooley, was established, which was attended with considerable success for several terms. In the winter of 1871 the school building and church were destroyed by fire, followed soon after by the destruction of the rectory from the same cause. These were not rebuilt.

The present school-house in No. 2 was built in 1849 to replace the Old Bent school-house, which stood at the corner of the Stony Plain Road and Village Street. School-house No. 3, on The Neck, was built in 1858, at a cost of $1,484. School-house No. 5 was built in 1861, at a cost of $1,197.83. School-house No. 6 was built in 1870, a short distance north of the location of the old house. School-house No. 8 was formerly known as the Dry Bridge school-house; it stood on the north side of the turnpike a short distance west of the house of Mr. Henry S. Partridge. The present house was built in 1874, at a cost of $1,197. School-house No. 9 was built in 1873 to accommodate the growing population of that part of West Medway. It stands on Cutler Street; it cost $4.550. In 1850 Nathaniel Clark and others petitioned the town to build a town-house including a room for a high school upon a central and suitable lot on the old Hartford and Dedham turnpike, but this was not granted.

THE HIGH SCHOOL.

The necessity, however, for the establishment of a high school was every year forcing itself upon the attention of the town, as it had had for some years more than five hundred families, making it the legal duty of the inhabitants to support such a school, in which history, book-keeping, surveying, geometry, natural philosophy, and Latin should be taught. The additional expense entailed by this, rendered the tax payers somewhat reluctant to vote the necessary funds, but the threats of prominent citizens to cause the town to be indicted, which was, in fact, done, and the town cited to appear at Dedham to answer for its violation of the school laws, this, together with the feeling among a majority of the inhabitants that the law was a proper and just one, caused the town at its March meeting to grant the sum of $2,600: $1,100 for district, and $1,500 for a high school, and an additional $1,500 for a suitable building. This action was reconsidered at the next meeting and the town finally voted to leave the matter to the school committee to ascertain how the provisions of the law could be satisfied and to report at the next March meeting. The result was the establishment of a high school, to be kept one term in turn in the East and West parishes and in the Village. This rotary system was continued, although unsatisfactory, for three or four years. Mr. S. J. Sawyer was the first teacher at a salary of $500. In 1854 the school committee said: " there are two difficulties we meet with, one is the fact that we have several villages, distant from each other claiming equal importance and privileges, the other the reluctance of some to have any school. The difficulty arising from the fact that we have several villages is a serious one. It would be unjust to select one for the exclusive privilege of the high school. No one is so prominent as to justify this. There is not meekness and charitableness enough among the different sections to allow it if it were just. On the other hand it is impracticable at present to establish three yearly high schools" And they proposed the following plan : " That the appropriation for the high school be divided into three portions, and that one portion be added to the amount voted to the East parish district No. 1, one portion to the amount voted to the West parish district No. 4, and one portion to the amount voted to the Village district No. 7."

In 1869 the old district system was abolished, not without considerable opposition from the conservative voters of the town, who were opposed to any measure that seemed to take any power from the hands of the people and confer it on a central board. The school-houses were appraised as follows: No. 1, $2,062.91 ; No. 2, $1,657.43 ; No. 3, $1,602.15 ; No. 4, $6,627.42 ; No. 5, $1,218.03 ; No. 6, $345.50 ; No. 7, $5,776.00 ; No. 8, $1,035.50, and taken by the town. A committee of nine members instead of three, was chosen to take the entire direction of the schools, and from this time the old prudential committee of the district disappears.

The plan of three " high and grammar " schools, one in each part of the town, was adopted, and, with slight modifications, was continued for some ten years, until 1879, when the friends of advanced education in the town became convinced that while this arrangement might answer the requirements of the law, and was, on the whole, convenient for the three villages, yet there were serious objections to the system. A town of this size could not, of course, sustain three schools of a grade that would entitle them to be called high schools, and although they received that title they were, in reality, hardly more than grammar schools. The matter was fully discussed in town-meetings, and in 1880 the town adopted the present plan of having a single high school in the Village, of high school grade. As a compensation to those living at a distance, the town appropriated money to pay transportation to such pupils living in other parts of the town who were fitted to pursue the prescribed course of study. This change has been very beneficial, has given to Medway a good high school, and after a trial of several years it is considered a satisfactory arrangement, and probably will be continued.

The lower schools have been graded so that a scholar commencing at the age of five years in the primary, and passing through the intermediate and grammar, may graduate from the high school at seventeen with an education sufficient to fit him to enter college, or any of the ordinary pursuits in life.

The following estimate of the Medway high school is based upon the annual report of the school committee, issued in February, 1885:

The high school is in an excellent condition, and will bear comparison with other high schools in the Commonwealth. During the five years of its existence, from its graduates, three boys have entered the Institute of Technology; one, Amherst College; one, Amherst Agricultural College; one, Dartmouth College; and one, Olivet College. It has also sent three young ladies to Wellesley, one to Smith College, and two to the Boston University, while others are engaged in teaching.

The school, as it stands to-day, is a credit to the town. Any boy or girl who chooses to make use of its privileges, can lay the foundation for a liberal education; an advantage which otherwise would be beyond the means of many. A boy, no matter how poor, who has the spirit and ambition thoroughly to follow out the prescribed course of study, will generally find friends who will help him in the struggle to get a college education. Medway thus presents the opportunity to those of her boys and girls who are without means, but who have brains, to take rank with the eminent men and women of the future. Many boys, by the help of our free high school in obtaining the preparatory training, will be able to take a college course, who otherwise would be discouraged by the expense of this preliminary education away from home.

Furthermore, the road lying open before them, many will naturally undertake the journey who else might never think of its possibility. It seems to us, therefore, the duty of the citizens of Medway to sustain and strengthen our high school, which holds so commanding a place in the public attention and interest, as was especially manifested by the audience which filled to overflowing Sanford Hall, on the occasion of the last annual graduating exercises; as is shown, also, by the number of pupils gathered from all parts of the town, and some from other towns, in daily attendance to avail themselves of its privileges.

The broad and scholarly instructions given in the high school, render it most valuable for the higher education of those connected with it. As a fitting school for college, it has a good record and its rank is highly respectable. The Medway high school has sent out five classes, and the total number of its graduates at this date (1885) is thirty-seven.

The following statements and table of school statistics, taken from the town school report for 1884–5, will show items of interest in bringing to a close this account of the schools in Medway:

The appropriations for schools, $6,500; for school books, $500; for school incidentals, $1,000; for transportation, $500. Total amount raised, $8,500.

Other receipts for schools: from tax on dogs, $302.74; from the Massachusetts School Fund, $192.26; from pupils of other towns, $113.07. Total, $608.07.

Total amount for school expenditure, $9,108.07.

The number of schools, 18; teachers employed, 20; pupils enrolled, 805; pupils between eight and fourteen years, 481; average membership, 612; average daily attendance, 549; per cent. daily attendance, .897; high school year, 40 weeks;

grammar and No. 2 school year, 36 weeks; all other schools, 30 weeks; added at private expense, 15 weeks. Total, 589 weeks.

The aggregate of current monthly salaries, $708; the average monthly salary of male teachers, 1884-5, $105; the average monthly salary of female teachers, 1884-5, $32.21; cost to the town for the year ending February, 1885, for each pupil enrolled, including teachers' wages, fuel, care of school-houses, school books, and supervision, $10.83; cost to the town for each pupil enrolled as above, with amounts paid for transportation and school incidentals added, $12.91; cost to the town for each pupil enrolled, including all above items, with six per cent. interest on permanent investments ($28,000) added, $15.

A comparison of the State and town shows an average daily attendance in the State, .895; in the town, .897. The monthly pay of male teachers in the State, $108.02; in the town, $105; of female teachers, in the State, $44.18; in the town, $32.21. The average cost for enrolled pupils in the State, $19.34; in the town, $12.91.

SCHOOL STATISTICS, 1884-1885.

No. of School.	GRADE OF SCHOOL.	NAMES OF TEACHERS.	No. of Pupils enrolled.	No. of Pupils between 8 and 14 years.	Average Membership.	Average Attendance.	Per Cent. Attendance.	Monthly Salaries.
	High.	Geo. H. Rockwood, A. M., Prin. F. E. Brooks, A. B., Principal. Miss Emma Tate, Assistant. Miss Annie A. Allis, Assistant.	76	7	53.1	50.8	.95	$110 $100 $40 $40
1	Grammar.	Miss Susie E. McLane. Miss Hettie J. Richardson.	27	23	21.4	18.5	.86	$40 $36
1	Primary.	Miss Caroline C. Jameson. Miss Mary G. Russell.	40	25	25.7	24.1	.93	$32 $24
2	Mixed.	Miss Alice M. Duren. Miss Lelia S. Taylor. Miss Amy C. Jones, Assistant.	69	42	50.	38.	.76	$36 $36 $16
3	Primary.	Miss Minnie A. Park.	21	14	17.5	15.	.86	$32
4	Grammar.	Miss Effie E. Adams.	50	27	46.	42.5	.93	$40
4	SubGrammar.	Miss Nellie A. Warfield.	44	40	41.3	37.4	.96	$32
4	Intermediate.	Miss Melissa C. Gay.	28	28	23.4	21.5	.92	$32
4	Primary.	Miss Helen Z. Allen.	77	25	49.	46.	.94	$32
5	Mixed.	Miss Mary L. Rogers.	19	11	18.	16.3	.90	$28
6	Mixed.	Miss Sarah M. Keane.	31	22	21.6	18.8	.86	$32
7	Grammar.	Miss Emma A. Baker.	31	19	27.	21.	.78	$40
7	Intermediate.	Miss Caroline S. Cogswell. Miss Grace H. Wilder.	47	38	37.	34.	.92	$32 $32
7	Primary.	Miss Mary F. Wilder.	45	45	37.7	34.6	.92	$32
7	Sub Primary.	Miss Alma A. Knowlton.	84	17	55.3	48.8	.88	$32
8	Mixed.	Mr. George W. Wheat.	25	9	16.2	14.9	.92	$28
9	Intermediate.	Miss Ada E. Newton.	33	31	31.2	29.5	.95	$32
9	Primary.	Miss Susie A. Gardner.	58	58	40.6	37.4	.92	$32

The Graduates of the High School, 1881–1885.

1881.

ABBOTT, ADDIE C.
HOYT, FANNY B.

1882.

SMITH, ALBERT L.

1883.

COOMBS, ALVIN WIGHT.
CROOKS, CORA ESTHER.
DANIELS, ARTHUR HILL.
DEANS, ANNA LE BARON.
GARDNER, EVA SWIFT.
HIXON, LENA BRADFORD.
JAMESON, CAROLINE COGSWELL.
JENCKES, GRACE ADELLA.
KNOWLTON, JUNIUS CECIL.
MANN, HERBERT JAMES.
RUSSELL, MARY GRACE.
WHEAT, GEORGE WARREN.
WOODMAN, MYLA LILLIAN.

1884.

BICKFORD, MARY EVELYN.

BIRD, HERBERT STETSON.
JONES, ELLEN MARIA.
MANN, ARTHUR SIMONDS.
SPENCER, HENRY FRANCIS.
SWARMAN, ELMERA LILLIE.
THOMPSON, SANFORD ELEAZAR.
WALKER, MARY WHIPPLE.

1885.

CHILDS, HENRY THOMAS.
CLARK, EVA ESTELLE.
CLARK, GEORGE HAWLEY.
CONGER, ALBERT CRAIG.
DANIELS, CHARLES HENRY.
HOWE, FLORENCE ELIZA.
PARTRIDGE, MINNIE.
POND, ELEANOR DORCAS.
RICHARDSON, WILLIAM STEPHEN.
SCOTT, VIRGINIA.
STEVENS, ETTA SIBYL.
STEWART, FLORENCE ISABELLE.
WHITNEY, MAUD MILLER.

The Medway Graduates from Colleges, 1774–1885.

ADAMS, DANIEL. 1774, Harvard College, clergyman; died 1778.
ADAMS, JASPER, 1815, Yale College, clergyman; died 1841.
ALLEN, ALLDIS SAMUEL, 1827, Yale College, physician; died 1833.
ADAMS, EZRA, 1835, Amherst College, clergyman; died 1864.
ADAMS, EDWIN AUGUSTUS, 1861, Amherst College, clergyman.
ADAMS, GEORGE BURTON, 1873, Beloit College, clergyman; died 1881.
BAILEY, CHARLES, 1841, Brown University, physician.
BULLARD, JOHN, 1776, Harvard College, clergyman; died 1821.
BULLARD, ELI, 1787, Yale College, lawyer; died 1824.
BULLARD, AMOS, 1833, Amherst College, clergyman; died 1850.
BULLARD, MALACHI, 1841, Dartmouth College, clergyman; died 1849.
BULLEN, HENRY LEWIS, 1842, Dartmouth College, clergyman.
CARY, GEORGE LOVELL, 1852, Harvard College, clergyman.
CLIFFORD, JOSEPH CLARK, 1862, Amherst College, Captian U. S. A.
COLE, ARTHUR WELLS, 1877, Yale College; lawyer.
DANIELS, DAVID, 1776, Harvard College; died 1827.
DANIELS, DAVID, 1824, Brown University, merchant; died 1847.
DANIELS, HIRAM CLARKE, 1844, Dartmouth College, clergyman.
DANIELS, JOSEPH LEONARD, 1860, Yale College, clergyman.
ELLIS, FERDINAND, 1802, Brown University, clergyman; died 1858.
FAY, GILBERT OTIS, 1859, Yale College, clergyman.
FITTS, CALVIN RICHARDS, 1864, Amherst College, clergyman; died 1883.
HAMMOND, TIMOTHY, 1808, Harvard College, lawyer; died 1834.
HARDING, SEWALL, 1818, Union College, clergyman; died 1876.

HARDING, JOHN WHEELER, 1845, Yale College; clergyman.
HARDING, WILLIAM GREENOUGH, 1857, Williams College, manufacturer.
HAWES, JOEL, 1813, Brown University, clergyman; died 1867.
HIXON, ASA, 1825, Brown University, clergyman; died 1862.
HIXON, LLOYD WELLS, 1857, Dartmouth College, teacher.
HILL, CALVIN GRANT, 1867, Amherst College, clergyman.
HORTON, SANFORD JABEZ, 1843, Trinity College, clergyman.
IDE, JACOB, JR., 1848, Amherst College, clergyman.
JAMESON, ARTHUR ORCUTT, 1881, Harvard College; died 1881.
JAMESON, MISS KATHARINE STRONG, 1884, Smith College, teacher.
JENCKES, MISS MARY A., 1881, Wellesley College, teacher.
JONES, EDMUND ADAMS, 1865, Amherst College, teacher.
LOVELL, NATHANIEL, 1810, Harvard College, physician; died 1817.
LOVERING, WARREN, 1817, Brown University, lawyer; died 1876.
LOVERING, AMOS, 1828, Brown University, lawyer; died 1879.
METCALF, NATHANIEL WHITING, 1846, Brown University, teacher; died 1871.
MONROE, FRANCIS LE BARON, 1857, Williams College, physician.
MORSE, JOHN, 1791, Brown University, clergyman; died 1844.
MORSE, ELIJAH, 1809, Brown University, lawyer; died 1831.
MORSE, ABNER, 1816, Brown University, clergyman; died 1865.
MORSE, FREDERICK DANIELS, 1862, Amherst College, physician.
PARTRIDGE, MOSES, 1814, Brown University, clergyman; died 1824.
PARTRIDGE, LYMAN, 1863, Brown University, clergyman.
RICHARDSON, GEORGE LOVELL, 1862, Dartmouth College, teacher.
STEVENS, CHARLES PLIMPTON, 1884, Tufts College.
SANFORD, MOSES, 1800, Harvard College, lawyer; died 1830.
SANFORD, DAVID, 1825, Brown University, clergyman; died 1875.
THAYER, ADDISON SANFORD, 1881, Harvard College, physician.
TURNER, CHARLES, 1815, Brown University; died 1816.
WALKER, HORACE DEAN, 1841, Yale College, clergyman; died 1885.
WALKER, AUGUSTUS, 1849, Yale College, clergyman; died 1866.
WALKER, GEORGE FREDERIC, Amherst College, clergyman.

THE UNDER-GRADUATES OF COLLEGES, 1885.

DANIELS, ARTHUR HILL, 1887, Olivet College, Mich.
JAMESON, MISS CAROLINE COGSWELL, 1888, Smith College, Mass.
JENCKES, MISS GRACE ADELLA, 1888, Wellesley College, Mass.
KNOWLTON, JUNIUS CECIL, 1887, Amherst College, Mass.
POND, MISS ELEANOR DORCAS, 1889, The Boston University, Mass.
RUSSELL, MISS HELEN HALE, 1887, Smith College, Mass.
SPENCER, HENRY FRANCIS, 1888, The Boston University, Mass.
STEWART, MISS FLORENCE ISABELLE, 1889, The Boston University, Mass.

THE PUBLIC LIBRARIES.

THE DEAN LIBRARY ASSOCIATION was incorporated March 3, 1860, in Medway Village "for the purpose of maintaining a Library and a Reading-room and promoting public instruction by lectures or otherwise." The corporators named in the act were Messrs. Luther Metcalf, Clark Partridge, William H. Cary, John Cole, and A. L. B. Monroe, M. D.

The library originated in a conversation between Dr. Oliver Dean, of Franklin, and Mrs. Sarah B. Metcalf, the wife of the Hon. Luther Metcalf, during which Dr. Dean expressed a desire to aid in such an enterprise for the benefit of the Village where he once lived and practiced as a physician. He conferred with the Hon. M. M. Fisher as to the plan, and proposed to give at first $400, if a like sum were raised by the people. An association was formed whose capital stock was fixed at $1,000, divided into shares of $10 each. A sufficient number of shares were taken to meet the requirement of Dr. Dean, and the nucleus of a library was formed, to which additions have been made yearly until it consists of about three thousand volumes. The Hon. Luther Metcalf was the first President, and Orion A. Mason, Esq., has been from the first, Clerk and Treasurer. For the first ten years, the library was kept in Fisher's block. In 1872 it was removed to its present quarters in Sanford Hall building. In the agreement for the erection of this hall, it was provided that the association should have a suitable library and reading-room and the free use of the hall for lectures. By the will of Dr. Dean the association received a legacy from him in the stock of the Boston and Albany Railroad Company valued now at $4,375, the income of which is to be used for the purchase of new books. One share of stock at ten dollars constitutes a life membership *in perpetuum.* One dollar and fifty cents an equal right to the use of library for one year, or five cents for a week. One hundred volumes are usually taken out and returned each week. The library is open Saturday evenings and Wednesday afternoons. The reading-room every day and evening.

The present officers of the library are, the Hon. M. M. Fisher, *President;* O. A. Mason, Esq., *Clerk* and *Treasurer;* the Rev. R. K. Harlow, E. A. Daniels, M. D., and Frederick L. Fisher, Esq., *Library Committee;* the Rev. R. K. Harlow, Messrs. James M. Grant, William H. Cary, Jr., H. E. Mason, and E. C. Wilson, *Reading-room Committee;* Miss Mary E. Fisher and Mrs. M. C. Newell, *Librarians.*

THE CIRCULATING LIBRARY in East Medway was established by a society which was organized October 28, 1878, under the following resolution: "Feeling the need of a circulating library in our village, we have thought proper to form ourselves into a society for the accomplishment of this object." Accordingly, a constitution was adopted and officers were chosen, viz.: a president, a vice-president, a secretary, and a treasurer. The society was constituted of twenty-four ladies, and seventeen gentlemen. Funds were secured for the purchase of books by an annual tax upon the members, public entertainments given, and by the income from the loan of books. New volumes were added to the library yearly, and in 1883 a catalogue was published.

Soon after East Medway was incorporated as the town of Millis, the Library Society, by vote taken March 19, 1885, donated their library, together with such funds as were in their treasury, to the town of Millis, as the nucleus of a Free Public Library. The library consisted of 313 volumes, and the money in the treasury amounted to about forty dollars. The town of Millis, by vote taken March 23, 1885, accepted the gift, and tendered thanks to the donors.

The library was placed in the town office; the town clerk was appointed librarian, and the books distributed on Tuesday and Saturday evenings of the week, without charge, to the people of the town for reading. At their meeting for making the first annual appropriation, the income of the tax on dogs was appropriated by the town for the purchase of books for the Free Public Library of Millis.

The Newspapers.

The Medway Journal, a small semi-monthly sheet, 22 x 14 inches, printed on a hand-press, was the first newspaper issued in the town. It was edited, printed, and published, February 10, 1872, by Master Henry A. Bullard, of West Medway, a lad of seventeen years, who had never seen the inside of a printing-office. It was published as a semi-monthly until October 19, 1872 ; after that it was a weekly of six columns. The second volume began with January, 1873. The paper was purchased the last of February, 1873, by James M. Stewart, Esq., of Franklin, and continued under the same name, but issued from his printing-house in Franklin. After a few years the name was changed to *The Medway Courier*, and afterwards to *The Medway Magnet*, and issued under the management of the same editors and proprietors as *The Franklin Sentinel*. *The Medway Magnet* is still, 1885, issued by Edward D. Houston, Esq., editor and proprietor, and has a good circulation in the town. There also has been issued since January 29, 1874, *The Medway Gazette*, published by Messrs. Cook & Sons, editors and proprietors of *The Milford Journal*, and printed at their office in Milford, Mass. It had, in 1885, a circulation in town of 300 copies.

The Medway Savings Bank.

Incorporated February 20, 1871.

The Medway Savings Bank commenced receiving deposits March 30, 1871.

Amount of deposits May 1, 1885, $185,060.95.

THE POST-OFFICES.

There are four post-offices in the town, the oldest being that of the Village, which was established in the spring of 1803. This was on the middle road, as it was called, from Boston to Hartford, and at a convenient distance from Dedham on the east and Mendon on the west. The size of the settlement would otherwise have hardly warranted the establishment of an office, there being but eight dwelling-houses, a grist mill, a saw mill, and a store : the Simon Fisher house stood where E. C. Wilson now resides, a part of the Metcalf homestead was then built, the Hawes place where Mr. W. H. Cary's house now stands, the Bullen house opposite Thompson's boot shop, the Simon Fisher house, near Eaton & Wilson's batting mill, the Nathan Fisher house across the river, now the residence of Monroe Morse, Ichabod Hawes' saw mill just back of the boot shop, the Whiting grist mill and house near the present location of Sanford Mills, and the house and store of William Felt. The nearest office on the north was Marlboro, on the east, Dedham, on the south, Wrentham, and on the west, Mendon. Captain William Felt, a man of good business ability, was the first Postmaster, and his first quarterly return was made July 1, 1803, Gideon Granger being Postmaster-General. The office was kept in his store, near where the residence of Mrs. Hathon now stands. The amount of mail matter was very small, and was carried by a post-rider who went over the route once each week. The rates of postage were from six to twenty-five cents for each sheet without regard to weight, postage varying with the distance the letter was carried. Correspondence was not as universal as now, steel pens, envelopes, postage stamps, and postal cards were unknown, the daily paper was not established, and the weekly newspaper found its way to but few families. It has been said by an old resident, that probably there were not more than half-a-dozen newspapers left at this office : one or two copies of the *Hartford Courant*, the *Columbian Sentinel*, and, perhaps, the *Worcester Spy*.

A list of post-offices published this year shows that there were not quite thirteen hundred offices in the whole country. About 1812 a line of mail coaches from Dedham to Mendon, in connection with the Boston and Hartford line, was established by Ebenezer Clark, of Dedham, making two trips a week. This line was continued by others, and the number of trips increased to three each way, and for many years was owned and driven by Joseph Miller, who died a few years since in Medfield. About 1845 a cross-mail, intercepting the Woonsocket line at Rockville on alternate days, was established, giving the residents of the Village a daily mail.

Mr. Felt's successor was Warren Lovering, Esq., a rising young lawyer. He kept the Post-office a part of his term in the store of Gilbert Clark and a part in his law office, which stood where Mrs. Barns's house is located. Mr. Lovering, not being in sympathy with the administration under Jackson, was superseded, in 1829, and Mr. Sewall Sanford was appointed, and the office was removed to his store, where Dr. E. A. Daniels now resides, and remained there until Mr. Sanford's death in 1831. He was succeeded by James B. Wilson, and the office during his term and part of that of his successor, Clark Partridge, Esq., was kept where Mr. Partridge's house stands. It was removed in 1847 to Fisher's Block, where it remained twenty-six years under the charge of Captain Partridge, and Samuel W. Metcalf, Esq., who was succeeded, in 1858, by Collins Hathon, who kept it until 1861, when O. A. Mason., Esq., received the appointment, and, three years after, the present occupant, Mr. H. E. Mason, was appointed. The office was removed in 1873, to its present location in Sanford Hall.

The next office established was in East Medway, March 17, 1819, and Timothy Hammond, Esq., was the first postmaster. The mail was carried by the Mendon coaches, and the office was kept at the house of Adam Bullard, afterwards the residence of the late James La Croix, Esq. Mr. Nathan Jones, for many years sheriff in this town, and who died a few years since in Medfield, was the next incumbent. While he held the office it was kept in his store, on the site now occupied by the house of Mr. Stephen B. Smith. After him, George H. Holbrook, Esq., was appointed, and the office removed to his place of business, near the organ shop. After the erection of the meeting-house on its present site, the post-office was removed to the same vicinity, and Mr. Milton Daniels became the postmaster and kept it until his death in 1871, when he was succeeded by his widow, Mrs. Mariam Daniels, who held it until 1877, when the present postmaster, Mr. George B. Fisher, was appointed, and since that time the office has been kept at his store.

In 1832 petitions from Simeon Fuller and Christopher Slocum were made to the post-office department for the establishment of an office in West Medway. This was stoutly opposed by the people of the Village, who, in their remonstrance, urged as reasons: the small amount of postal matter for that section, being the previous year but $46.48 out of $312.75, and the close proximity of the two offices.

The post-office at West Medway was established September 19, 1834. Olney Foristall, who kept a hotel in a part of the building now occupied by Mr. James Coombs, was the first postmaster. Previous to this time the mail for that part of the town had come through the Village office, and Mr. Wilson, the postmaster, was accustomed, on Sunday, to carry a bundle of mail matter to the meeting-house to be distributed to the people as they came to church. The mail was carried tri-weekly by Miller's Boston and Mendon stage, going to the three Medway offices Monday, Wednesday, and Friday, and returning on alternate days.

Mr. Foristall was succeeded by Mr. Simeon Fuller, a trader, who kept the store now occupied by Mr. Coombs. After him came Deacon Daniel Wiley, another trader. Indeed, it seems to have been almost a necessity that in small villages the occupant of the office should be one whose place of business was always open to the public, and he must have some business for his support, in addition to the salary of the post-office.

The successors of Mr. Wiley have been as follows: Messrs. Levi P. Coburn, Stephen Partridge, Jason Smith, Gilbert Nourse, John Cushing, Lewis Clark, J. N. Tourtellotte, Mrs. Mary A. Tourtellotte, and Vincent Moses, Esq.

The fourth post-office in Medway was established in Rockville, February 23, 1838. As there were already three offices in town, and the village of Rockville was very small, the department was somewhat reluctant to establish it; but principally through the efforts of Dean Walker, Esq., who about that time came to Rockville, the application was successful.

Deacon Timothy Walker was the first postmaster, succeeded by Messrs. Eliab B. Blake, John S. Walker, Erastus H. Tyler, and Frederic Swarman, the present occupant.

THE ARRIVAL AND DEPARTURE OF THE MAILS IN 1885.

VILLAGE. Arrive, Boston 9.15 A. M., 5 P. M.; close 8.45 A. M., 3.30 P. M. Arrive, Milford 6 P. M.; close 8.45 A. M.

ROCKVILLE. Arrive 10 A. M., 5 P. M.; close 8.05 A. M., 3.15 P. M.

EAST MEDWAY. Arrive 9 A. M., 4.45 P. M.; close 8.50 A. M., 3.40 P. M.

WEST MEDWAY. Arrive, Boston 9.15 A. M., 5 P. M.; Milford 5.15 P. M.; Medway 9.30 A. M. Close, Boston, 8.40 A. M., 3.30 P. M.; Milford, 9.30 A. M.: Medway, 5.15 P. M.

THE RAILROADS. 1836 — 1885.

No enterprise has ever excited such genuine interest, or required so much time, persistent effort, and pecuniary expenditure, as the necessary means by which the three different sections of the town have secured railroad accommodations. Few of the people are aware that from the initial steps in this direction to the consummation of the work, twenty-five years elapsed.

From a very large mass of manuscript papers and printed matter left by the Hon. Luther Metcalf, who was very conspicuous in the movement, a very full history of the various schemes devised, the protracted struggles, and obstacles encountered, has been obtained.

The value and magnitude of the work and its results, alone justify the space given to this enterprise in the annals of the town.

The completion of the Boston and Worcester Railroad, in 1832, on the north, and of the Boston and Providence Railroad on the southeast, and the Blackstone River on the southwest, left a large triangular section of the State without railroad accommodation. The practical question among business men, living within this territory, was, how to bisect it in such a way as to secure the best railroad facilities.

The following statement, drawn up by Mr. Metcalf, and found among his papers, discloses the fact that the first public action upon the matter was had in his office, in Medway Village, very early in the history of railroads.

THE HON. LUTHER METCALF'S WRITTEN STATEMENT.

"The following statement was written March 8, 1872, from my recollections and memoranda in my possession:

THE FIRST MEETING of citizens interested in the project of a Railroad from Woonsocket to Boston was held at Medway Village on the thirtieth day of November, 1836, among whom were Dr. Fowler, Willis Cook, and some other persons from Woonsocket, Welcome Farnum, of Blackstone, Dr. Nathaniel Miller, of Franklin, Dr. Artemas Brown, Luther Metcalf, Warren Lovering, Wyman Adams, and others, of Medway, with other persons from some of the adjoining towns.

After a free and pretty full expression of the views of those persons present, it appeared to be the desire of all to have a survey made from Woonsocket along the valley of Peters River and Mine Brook through Bellingham and the northerly part of Franklin to Charles River, a little above Medway Village, thence in the valley of said river to Medfield and on easterly through West Dedham to the Dedham Branch of the Boston and Providence Railroad at the village in Dedham.

Accordingly it was voted to employ an engineer and commence a survey at once, and a subscription was opened to defray the expense of the same, a committee chosen to carry the vote into effect. The committee engaged R. S. Scott and S. B. Cushing, engineers, who commenced the survey of Woonsocket sometime in December and proceeded with the work as far as West Dedham when the deep snows of that winter prevented the completion thereof.

The next year, in 1837, the financial affairs of the country were in such a disturbed state that little was thought of any new railroad schemes or anything else that required much outlay.

Thus the matter remained until the autumn of 1844, when my mind was called to the numerous railroad charters that had been granted the past session of the Legislature — I thought it a proper time to renew the old project.

After a consultation with some of the former friends of the enterprise a second meeting was held at Medway Village and measures adopted to carry out the original plan.   LUTHER METCALF."

The surveys of Messrs. Cushing and Scott were not concluded till February 17, 1845. The first line surveyed commenced at Woonsocket Falls, running up the valley of Peters River, through Bellingham, and down the valley of the Charles River to Medway Village. From this place two routes were surveyed, one passing near Rockville, Medfield Village, and West Dedham; the other passing through a part of Franklin, North Wrentham, now Norfolk, and Walpole; each route terminating at the depot of the Dedham Branch Railroad.

E. S. Chesborough, Esq., surveyed the route from Walpole to Dedham. It was found that the distance by way of Medfield, from Woonsocket to Dedham was 25.85 miles, and the estimated cost, $500,299; and that the route via Walpole was 28.38 miles, and estimated cost, $553,689. A subsequent survey of a part of the route from Medfield to Dedham was found to increase the distance only $\frac{29}{100}$ of a mile, and to diminish the cost $42,766.49.

This was the beginning of surveys to give railroad facilities to any portion of the great triangle, and was supported by petition to the Legislature by persons resident in Woonsocket, Blackstone, Bellingham, Franklin, Medway, Medfield, Walpole, South Dedham, West Dedham, and Dedham. Dr. Nathaniel Miller, of " River End," in Franklin, was the first petitioner and it was called the Miller Route, in distinction from others that were soon afterward developed. A large committee of one or more from each locality was chosen to appear before the Legislative Committee and present the statistics of business, which had been very fully obtained and tabulated. The Hon. Luther Metcalf and the Hon. Warren Lovering went from Medway, and this petition, with others, was presented to the Legislature whose session began in January, 1846. At this session of the Legislature no less than ten petitions were presented for railroads, in some aspects distinct from each other, over portions of this triangular territory, including a Milford route which, it was foreshadowed that the Boston and Worcester Corporation would build as far as that town. These routes were designated by the name of their first petitioner. Beginning on the west there were the S. D. Armdown Route, F. Deane, Jr., Route, C. C. P. Hastings, or the Milford Route, the N. Dana Route, the Otis Pettee, or Central Air Line Route. The Nathaniel Miller Route, the G. R. Russell Route, the Willis Fisher Route, I. A. Gould Route, and the Martin Torrey Route.

The claims of these several routes were urged before the Railroad Committee of the Legislature of 1846. The statistics of business by freight and passengers and the feasibility and distances from Boston to and from other places were exhibited by the several petitioners and experts and by civil engineers, and the outcome and results of the whole examination which occupied several weeks appear to have been an agreement by the Railroad Committee to report unanimously in favor of the petition of I. A. Gould for the extension of the Dedham Branch to Walpole, and of Otis Pettee from Newton to Woonsocket, leaving Milford to be accommodated by a branch from Framingham, and of the Martin Torrey Route from Mansfield to Woonsocket which met with no opposition, was of no general importance, and never was built.

It was the understanding that the reports on the Pettee and Gould routes should be taken up and put along together, through the two Houses. In the Senate they both passed in due course of business, but, as it was said by many at the time, the bills were kept apart in the House by the skillful management of " Bird, of Walpole, and Bragg, of Milford," so that the Walpole Bill passed and the Woonsocket and Newton bill, or the Pettee Route, was defeated by a small majority of nineteen votes.

So this skillful adjustment of the competing schemes was defeated and all parties began at once to buckle on the armor for a decisive contest the next year.

In the contest of 1846, the project of a through line of railroad to New York, which had been incorporated in Connecticut and projected in Rhode Island, was but little mooted before the Massachusetts Legislature, although it was potent in the minds of leading men. Otis Pettee, Esq., of Newton, had more fully espoused this idea than other leaders, and openly adopted it as a part of his plan of operations for 1847. While the leaders in the Gould and Fisher routes put forward publicly only a road for local business.

In preparation for this great struggle, as reported in the *Boston Atlas*: "A large and highly spirited meeting of the friends of the proposed Boston and Woonsocket Railroad was held in Medway Village, on Wednesday the 17th inst.," *i. e.*, June 17, 1846. The object of the meeting was to combine the original friends of the Pettee and Miller routes and obtain the passage of the bill for the Boston and Woonsocket Road, defeated by the House in 1846. Otis Pettee, Esq., of Newton, was chairman and E. K. Whitaker, secretary.

The following gentlemen were chosen a committee to devise a plan of coöperation: Messrs. Sanger, of Dover, Arnold, of Bellingham, Wheeler, of Newton, Cook and Sprague, of Woonsocket, Whitaker, of Needham, Metcalf, Lovering, Holbrook, and Fisher, of Medway. The first resolution, by Mr. Fisher, of Medway, shows the animus and scope of the meeting:

" *Resolved*, That we hail, as an omen of triumphant success in this enterprise, the cordial union and effective coöperation of the leading friends of the 'Pettee and Miller routes,' both in the Blackstone Valley and along the whole line of towns in the western part of Norfolk County."

There were present, twenty-one delegates from Newton, thirty-eight from East Needham, twenty from Dover, twenty from Medfield, sixty-three from Medway, five from Bellingham, and twenty-four from Woonsocket. There were no delegates present from Franklin, as, on that day, June 17, 1846, the Emmons Monument was erected, with public ceremony.

The union, on the part of Dr. Miller and some others, was not completed, as the original Miller Route had an alternate route, between Medfield and Walpole, and Dr. Miller and his friends upon the latter line joined with the Willis Fisher Route in their petition for 1847. Similar meetings were subsequently held in Woonsocket and Newton Upper Falls, in the furtherance of the enterprise.

A large committee from the several towns was designated to sign the principal petition, and to prosecute the same before the legislature and its committee, consisting of the following gentlemen, whose names are attached to the general petition:

" *To the Honorable Senate and House, of Representatives of the Commonwealth of Massachusetts, in General Court assembled:*

THE subscribers, legal voters, a committee of other legal voters, residing in the towns and places below named, respectfully represent, that the public convenience and necessity demand the construction of a railroad from the city of Boston, in said Commonwealth, to the State line near to and in the direction of the village of Woonsocket, in the State of Rhode Island, Connecticut and New York, to the city of New York. And they earnestly request of your honorable body an act of incorporation for constructing and operating a railroad commencing from some convenient point in the said State line, near to Woonsocket, thence running through the towns of Blackstone, Bellingham, Franklin, Medway, Medfield, Dover, Needham, Newton, Brighton, and Brookline, entering said Medway by the valley of Charles River, thence passing down the banks of said river through Medway Village and through East Medway, Medfield, near to Dover Mills, East Needham, Newton Upper Falls, Newton Centre, and Brighton Centre, and near Corey's Hill in Brookline, to some convenient point in said city of Boston, with all the powers and facilities for constructing and operating a railroad upon improvements combining the greatest speed, safety, and public convenience; together with the right of constructing a branch road from some convenient point on said principal road, in Dover or Needham, to Dedham Village in the county of Norfolk.

October 20th, 1846.

Of Newton.

Otis Pettee,
Loring Wheeler,
Joseph L. Ellis,
Marshall L. Rice,
Samuel Langley.

Of Needham.

Edgar K. Whitaker,
William M. Stedman,
George Revere,
Daniel Kimball,
Thomas Kingsbury.

Of Dover.

Ralph Sanger,
Elijah Perry,

Calvin Richards,
Luther Eastman.

Of Medfield.

Joseph Miller,
Charles Harding,
Isaac Fiske,
Samuel Johnson.

Of Medway.

Luther Metcalf,
Warren Lovering,
Geo. H. Holbrook,
Joseph C. Lovering,
Wm. H. Cary,
M. M. Fisher,
William B. Boyd,

Nathan Jones,
John P. Jones,
Jos. L. Richardson,
Julius C. Hurd.

Of Franklin.

Erastus Rockwood,
S. W. Richardson,
Joel P. Adams.

Of Bellingham.

Noah J. Arnold,
James M. Freeman,
Asa Pickering,
John C. Scammel,
Ellery Thayer,
John Bates.

Of Boston.

Jabez Ellis,
Francis D. Ellis,
Samuel Wales, Jr.

Of Brookline.

Samuel A. Walker.

Of Woonsocket.

Edward H. Sprague,
David Daniels,
Willis Cook,
Oren A. Ballou,
Edward Harris,
Geo. C. Ballou.

The above is a true copy of the original petition to be presented to the General Court of Massachusetts to commence in January, A. D. 1847.

OTIS PETTEE."

This petition was supported by others from all the towns interested, and by more than six hundred of the leading merchants and business men of Boston. No matter, probably, ever engrossed the attention of the people nor required or exacted so much time and means from the men appointed to take charge of the petition as this question, upon which seemed to depend the future growth and prosperity of the whole town.

Some of the Medway committee were in Boston nearly all winter, and others were there much of the time. Nine of the eleven members in 1885 had passed away.

The result of the New York feature of the Pettee Route, afterwards adopted, and in competition with it, by the friends of the Russell Route, was to bring out the older railroad corporations having connections with New York by rail, wholly or in part, into strong and powerful opposition to both the Russell and Pettee routes.

Charles G. Loring, Esq., in his powerful argument before the committee for the Pettee Route, says: " But while sustained and encouraged by the vast numbers of petitioners and memorialists whom it is my honor to represent, and the great extent of commercial, manufacturing, and agricultural interests which I advocate, I am not unmindful of the formidable, and, seemingly, almost overwhelming opposition with which I have to contend. The united energies of the Western, Boston and Worcester, Boston and Providence, Norwich and Worcester Railroad Corporations, and numbers of wealthy capitalists in this state, and occupants of the palaces of the city, are arrayed against the project before the committee."

There was never before, and probably never has been since, so great an array of corporation influence combined, or so large a number of influential citizens and of professional men, lawyers, and civil engineers, engaged and interested in railroad legislation as on this occasion. A large delegation of leading men interested in the Pettee Route were present from Middletown, Conn.

No expenditure of money was spared by the " old corporations " to defeat the " Air Line " to New York. The highest professional talent was employed before the committee, and a large lobby influence maintained. The Hon. Rufus Choate, whose figures of rhetoric were more vivid, if not more accurate, than the statistics of the party he served, belittled on the one hand and exaggerated on the other, and if not convincing,

" Led to bewilder, and dazzled to blind."

Instead of the ten routes and petitions of 1846 they had been simmered down to four; two looking to New York connections, both coming through Medway, viz., the Pettee, and Old Russell, or Perkins, routes; two, viz., the Hastings, or the Milford and Framingham Route, strictly local, and the Norfolk County, or the Miller Route remodeled, nominally local, but with a concealed squinting at New York, with Blackstone as their western terminus.

After many and prolonged hearings before the committee, and much conference with each other, the committee reported in favor of the Norfolk County Route, with only one dissenting member, who favored the Perkins Route.

The legislature adopted the report of the committee, and Messrs. Welcome Farnum, Willis Fisher, Shadrach Atwood, and Jeremiah Blake were named as corporators.

If the rejoicings were great with the old railroad corporations and among the citizens of one tier of towns in Norfolk County over the success of their strenuous labors, the grief and disappointment among those who had originated the whole movement can hardly be described. There were charges of treachery to pledges and obligations, of weakness and want of tact and skill in the management of the case which embittered many minds, and continued for years afterwards. Although the friends of the " Pettee Route " were " cast down," they were not destroyed, as subsequent events proved.

In 1848 they came again with the same facts before the legislature, and the committee reported the withdrawal of the petition, one member only reported a bill in favor of a local road as far as Bellingham on the Pettee Route. But his report was not sustained. In 1849, not discouraged, Mr. Pettee presented a petition for a branch road, which was granted from Brookline to Dover, called the Charles River Branch Railroad. The corporators named were Messrs. Otis Pettee, Edgar K. Whitaker, and Elijah Perry.

In the same year the Southbridge and Blackstone Railroad was chartered as an extension of the Norfolk County and the Medway Branch to North Wrentham, as a sop to pacify the " original " promoters of the " Dedham Route," and the corporators named were Messrs. Samuel Frothingham, Eliab Gilmore, and Julius C. Hurd, of Medway.

The Norfolk County Railroad was opened for travel April 23, 1850. That year another off-shoot of the Norfolk County Road was incorporated, looking to an independent entrance into Boston, preparatory to their New York project, called the Midland Railroad, from the Norfolk County Road in South Dedham, to the foot of Summer Street, in Boston. The corporators named were Messrs. Marshall P. Wilder, Robert Codman, Welcome Farnum, and H. K. Horton.

In 1851, the Charles River Railroad was incorporated extending the Charles River Branch, from Dover, through Medway, to some convenient point in the northeasterly part of Bellingham, and the corporators named were Messrs. Luther Metcalf, Jonathan P. Bishop, and Noah J. Arnold. The Charles River Railroad was operated to Newton, December, 1852. The same year, the Bellingham Branch Railroad Company was incorporated to connect the Norfolk County Road with Woonsocket from Mill River.

The Medway Branch, opened in January, 1853, was discontinued in 1864, and the rails were taken up and removed in the night.

In 1853 the Wrentham Branch Railroad was incorporated to connect Wrentham Centre with the Norfolk County Road at North Wrentham, now Norfolk. This was never constructed. The Charles River Road was completed to Needham, and a celebration of the event occurred in that town, June 1, 1853. The Charles River Branch was united with the Charles River Railroad November 1, 1853, and both were merged, in 1855, in the New York and Boston Railroad.

In 1854 the East Walpole Branch Railroad was incorporated to extend from East Walpole station to East Walpole post-office, near the paper mills of the Hon. Frank

W. Bird. This line of road was a part of the original Walpole Branch, the first of the series incorporated in 1846, but which the Norfolk County Company refused to build, much to the regret of Mr. Bird.

Also, in 1854, the friends of the Pettee Route pressed their claims for the extension of their line to connect with the New York and Boston Route at the State line, in Bellingham. The railroad committee, reported a bill in favor of it. Pending this bill a large and enthusiastic meeting of its friends was held in West Medway. Appropriate resolutions were adopted which, with an account of the meeting, appeared in the *Boston Atlas*. This bill, reported by the committee, was not adopted by the legislature.

A sufficient amount of stock having been subscribed for the extension of the Charles River Road to Medway, no more exciting or interesting event ever occurred in the town than the Railroad Jubilee, July 4, 1854, in Medway Village. A full account of the occasion was prepared by the Hon. M. M. Fisher, and published July 15, 1854, in the *Dedham Gazette*.

After the great victory of the old railroads having a New York connection either by rail or water, and the defeat of the "Air Line" project in 1847, it had not been deemed wise "to beard the lion in his den," and ask the legislature for authority to extend the Pettee Route, or Charles River Railroad, from Bellingham to meet and connect with the New York and Boston Railroad, chartered in the States of Rhode Island and Connecticut, until the year 1855. This was the great "Know Nothing" year in Massachusetts politics. A new party, at one bound, elected Henry J. Gardner, Governor, by a large majority. All the former political leaders of both the old parties in the legislature were left at home, and new men with new ideas filled their places. This change gave encouragement to the friends of the old Air Line project, and no pains were spared to obtain such an organization of the Railroad Committee as would compensate, as far as possible, for the errors of the past, and prominent members of the legislature were "button-holed" in advance. It will be recollected by some that this committee came over the line of the road and spent the night at Hathon's Hotel, visited the straw shop in the evening, and were entertained by the young ladies with songs suited to the occasion, and everything done to make a favorable impression upon them. They soon reported a bill which made the last link in a chartered railroad connection of Boston with New York shorter by some thirty miles than by any other existing route. This closed the great struggle in the Massachusetts legislature to secure chartered rights to unite with the corporations in Rhode Island and Connecticut to construct this shortest line to New York.

As yet the road had only been constructed and opened to Needham. A large amount of stock must be subscribed and paid. The old Norfolk County Road had been built, and chartered extensions obtained, and financial circles had been thoroughly canvassed for sales of stock, and when calls were made for the construction of the Air Line it was found that the financial field had been thoroughly explored, and the means were nearly exhausted by the great panic of 1857. Slow progress was made, and it was found that funds must be raised largely upon the line of the road, and meetings were held to obtain pledges for stock in Medway and elsewhere.

At one of these meetings the Rev. Dr. Ide made a very effective speech, demonstrating his public spirit. He said in effect that the town better subscribe $100,000 and lose it all, if need be, rather than that the road should not be built, and then made a liberal subscription for the stock.

The following persons were original subscribers to the stock of the New York and Boston Railroad in Medway, or aided by the purchase of bonds for its construction, and probably there were others whose names are not known : Luther Metcalf and the Medway Cotton Manufacturing Company, William H. Cary, M. H. Sanford, M. M. Fisher, Allen Partridge, Joseph L. Richardson, Henry Richardson, Oliver Clifford, Amory Gale, A. P. Lovell, John Bullard, 2d, J. D. Richardson, Paul Daniell, H. F. Howard, Michael Bullen, Edward Adams, Nathan Jones, Michael Lovell, Elbridge Clark, John Clark, Asa D. Morse, Oliver Phillips, Horatio Mason, Lyman Adams, Henry Daniels, Lemuel Clark, George Harding, Cyrus Bullard, W. Battelle, Joseph Ingalls, Charles S. Wheeler, Lewis Wheeler, Cemetery Corporation, Richard Richardson, T. J. Baker, P. N. Spencer, Elisha Adams, Edwin Metcalf, T. M. Daniels, J. P.

Clark, T. H. Hall, Samuel Dudley, Theodore Harding, Jonathan Adams, William Adams, Stephen Campbell, Elisha Cutler, Samuel Rice, A. M. B. Fuller, George L. Pond, J. S. Smith, Simeon Fisher, Alvin Wight, Seth Inman, Cyrus Adams, Horace Hill, James Adams, Cephas Thayer, Timothy Partridge, Stephen Clark, Charles Clark, H. C. Bullard, William M. Adams, E. F. Pond, Stephen Smith, Elijah Partridge, Jotham Adams, Jr., Stephen Adams, A. L. Shaw, Cyrus M. Hill, William Everett, B. C. Barber, Edward Clark, Hawley Clark, Jr., Jerome Westcott.

The amount taken in stock in the New York and Boston Railroad was about fifteen thousand dollars, and nearly equally divided between the three parishes, while the amount in bonds cannot be well ascertained.

While the prospect for the completion of the " Pettee Route," as the " Air Line " was called, seemed doubtful, through the energy of Messrs. Daniels and Hurd, of Medway Village, the Medway branch to the Norfolk County Road, was pushed forward to completion. It is estimated that this enterprise cost them $40,000 in various ways which ultimately proved to be almost a total loss.

The Hon. John M. Wood, of Portland, was the contractor for constructing, and was the largest stockholder in the old Air Line Railroad, and was its first president.

It was completed and the cars began running to Medway in 1861, and reached the Blackstone River, at Woonsocket, in 1863. It was merged in the Boston, Hartford and Erie Railroad Company in 1865. Mr. E. C. Hawes was the first conductor, and continued upon the road until 1883. He deserves honorable mention for a long and faithful service. Messrs. Knapp, Monson, and Story will long be remembered by many passengers as courteous conductors. Mr. William Adams, of West Medway, became a large owner of stock and bonds in the road, and was a director for several years. The Hon. Luther Metcalf was the first president of the Charles River Railroad.

The financial condition of the country during the war, and the strong competition between the two roads from Boston to the Blackstone valley for means to construct and complete these roads and new connections, led to a proposition for a union of these corporations into the Boston, Hartford and Erie Railroad Company. This project was strenuously opposed by Mr. Wood, of the Air Line, and the result, it is said, hastened his death soon after.

All the money paid for both roads must either be considered a loss to the subscribers or a charitable donation to posterity. As an investment this road has never paid its original owners; but its existence has become a necessity to the town.

The following is the report of the Commissioner of the New York and Boston Railroad Company, or the old Pettee Route, when it was absorbed by the Boston, Hartford and Erie Railroad, as found in the *Massachusetts Railroad Returns*, for 1866:

" *The Annual Report of the Commissioner of the late New York and Boston Railroad Company, now merged into the Boston, Hartford and Erie Railroad Company, to the Legislature of Massachusetts.*

The undersigned, Commissioner for Massachusetts, being duly authorized and required by an Act of the Legislature, approved May 14, 1864, has this day examined the books of the Boston, Hartford and Erie Railroad Company, and hereby certifies that separate accounts of the expenditures of said Company in the several States of Massachusetts, Rhode Island, and Connecticut, have been duly kept, as required by law; and he finds that the following expenditures have been made in the several States upon that portion of the road of said Company derived from the New York and Boston Railroad Company, to wit:

Expended for construction in the State of Connecticut, . . .	$270,597 16
Expended for construction in the State of Rhode Island, . . .	408,939 16
Expended for construction in the State of Massachusetts, . . .	1,338,244 26
	$2,017,780 58
Total cost of the equipment of the road operated from Brookline, Massachusetts, to Woonsocket, Rhode Island, ...	82,880 25
	$2,100,660 83

12

As less than one mile of the road now in operation lies in the State of Rhode Island, and as the income of the road, as yet, does not exceed the expenditure, the Commissioner deems it unnecessary to make any apportionment of the cost of the equipment or of the current expenditures and receipts until this portion of the road is operated to a greater extent beyond the limits of this Commonwealth.

For general information the Commissioner would state that about one-fourth part of the receipts of the road now in operation is derived from Woonsocket, in Rhode Island. All which is respectfully submitted.

M. M. FISHER,
Commissioner of Massachusetts."

BOSTON, Jan. 3, 1866.

The Boston and Erie Railroad Company made a sad failure, and was finally re-organized, April 17, 1873, as " The New York and New England Railroad Company."

The Northern, or Woonsocket, Division of the road was neglected, and, in consequence, several accidents occurred to trains. Whereupon the selectmen of Medway petitioned the Railroad Commissioners to meet the citizens of Medway in Sanford Hall March 14, 1883, and a hearing was granted. The principal business men stated their grievances, and the Commissioners ordered new stations at Medway Village and West Medway, also the improvement of the track and better facilities for passengers and freight. The road is now in fair condition.

SUMMARY SHOWING THE AMOUNT OF FREIGHT AND PASSENGER BUSINESS TO AND FROM THE THREE STATIONS IN MEDWAY, FOR TWO YEARS ENDING JANUARY 31, 1883.

	1881.		1882.		AGGREGATES.	
	Total for Passengers.	Total for Freight.	Total for Passengers.	Total for Freight.	1881.	1882.
E. Medway........	$3,472 62	$1,635 12	$3,749 29	$1,752 75	$5,219 74	$5,500 04
Medway......	6,229 05	11,187 90	6,708 98	12,389 49	17,416 95	19,098 47
W.Medway.......	7,773 52	9,113 42	7,492 81	9,751 91	16,886 94	17,244 72
Total of each class of Receipts }	$17,475 29	$21,936 44	$17,949 08	$23,894 15	$39,521 33	$41,843 23

Total, both classes, East Medway, ... $10,719 78
Total, both classes, Medway Village, ... $36,515 42
Total, both classes, West Medway, ... $34,131 66
Total for two years, ... $81,366 68

THE SANFORD HALL MOVEMENT IN 1871.

The Village community having for more than thirty years occupied either the vestry of the church, or the hall of the district school-house, or the hall in the straw factory, for lectures and secular purposes, the need of a more capacious audience-room had long been felt. The young ladies, encouraged by the citizens, and especially by Mrs. Edena H. Sanford, began, by fairs and tea parties, to raise money for building a public hall, and in the autumn of 1871 the fund amounted to $500. This sum was increased by the generous donations of $5,000 from Milton H. Sanford, and $2,500 from his brother, Edward S. Sanford, of New York, for the benefit of the Evangelical Society of Medway Village. These were accepted at a meeting held on Monday, October 30, 1871, and it was *Voted:* " That the society gratefully acknowledge the generous donations of Five Thousand Dollars from Milton H. Sanford, and Twenty-five Hundred Dollars from Edward S. Sanford, toward the erection of a Public Building in this village for the benefit of this

Society and the Dean Library, and will make all reasonable efforts to comply with the conditions required. *Voted*, That the Plan of Subscription presented by M. M. Fisher, is hereby approved, and that a committee be appointed to carry the same into effect, and M. M. Fisher and E. C. Wilson were chosen to act as a committee for that purpose."

The following is the plan referred to :

" SUBSCRIPTIONS FOR A PUBLIC BUILDING, TO BE LOCATED IN MEDWAY VILLAGE.

Whereas, Mr. Milton H. Sanford having generously donated to the Evangelical Congregational Society of Medway the sum of $5,000, and Col. Edward S. Sanford the sum of $2,500, toward the erection of a Public Building for a Hall, Offices, Library-Room, and other purposes, to be located in Medway Village; to cost, including land, not less than $15,000; and whereas, the young ladies have raised the sum of $500 for the same object; — The undersigned hereby pledge ourselves to give on demand, or by installments, the sums against our names: *Provided*, that not less than $12,000 in the whole shall be pledged for the object. The balance, if any is required, may be raised by a loan or stock subscription.

The Dean Library Association shall have the free use of one room for their Library and for a Reading-Room, and the use of the Hall for public lectures.

The net income from the rents of said building shall be applied and given in such proportions to the Society aforesaid and the Association, as the sums given and designated by the donors for each shall bear to the whole amount donated.

The location, plan, construction, and management of said building shall be determined by a Board of Trustees, chosen by the subscribers, every ten dollars being a share, and entitled to one vote, and said Trustees shall be authorized to fill vacancies in their own Board occasioned by death, resignation, or removal from the town or the limits of the Society. NOVEMBER, 1871.

Milton H. Sanford,	$5,000	E. C. L. B. Whitney,	100
Edward S. Sanford,	2,500	Harding & Bassett,	1,000
Clark Partridge,	1,000	John Cole,	100
Edward Eaton,	1,500	R. O. Davis,	10
John A. Bullard,	1,000	Eli Darling,	5
E. Cutler Wilson,	500	D. Daniels,	10
M. M. Fisher,	500	M. A. Woodward,	25
Allen Partridge,	500	T. R. Fairbanks,	50
Mason & Brother,	150	W. A. Jenckes,	75
George W. Ray,	100	George Newell,	10
John W. Richardson,	20	Samuel D. Force,	10
George P. Metcalf,	25	Emmons Force,	10
J. P. Plummer,	25	Charles F. Daniels,	25
J. W. Thompson,	50	W. R. Parsons,	30
Joel P. Adams,	500	S. A. Metcalf,	10
Wales Kimball,	50	Alex. L. B. Monroe,	20
Henry F. Cooper,	25	J. R. Knowlton,	5
Stephen W. Richardson,	25	J. F. Adams,	5
Luther Metcalf,	250	Mrs. C. Hathon,	10
Daniel Rockwood,	10		
Jason E. Wilson,	25	Total,	$15,815
A. P. Phillips,	50	O. A. MASON, *Treasurer*."	

" NOTICE.—The subscribers to the Fund for erecting a Public Hall Building in Medway Village, and all who intend to become subscribers, are invited to meet at the Vestry of the Village Church, on Monday evening next, at Seven o'clock, to hear the Report of the Committee on Subscriptions, and to choose Trustees, agreeably to the terms of the subscriptions, and to transact any other business proper to be done at said meeting.

DECEMBER 7, 1871.

E. C. WILSON, } *Committee*."
M. M. FISHER, }

THE SANFORD HALL. ERECTED IN 1872.

On Monday evening, December 11, 1871, the subscribers met; Dr. Monroe, chairman, and Deacon Wales Kimball, secretary, and the following resolutions were unanimously adopted:

"*Resolved*, That as a memorial of the name of Sanford, a name associated with the dearest interests of this community through several generations, and in honor of the principal donors and especially of their venerated mother, Mrs. Edena H. Sanford, the Building shall be called the SANFORD HALL."

The following persons were elected the Board of Trustees: Messrs. Clark Partridge, M. M. Fisher, E. C. Wilson, Edward Eaton, A. S. Harding, O. A. Mason, and John A. Bullard.

A vote of thanks was passed to Mr. Oscar M. Bassett, of the firm of Harding & Bassett, for joining with the firm in a donation of $1,000.

It was also voted that copies of all proceedings antecedent to the construction of the building be engrossed, and other documents and mementoes be deposited under the corner-stone of the building, and they were so deposited under the northeast corner thereof.

An eligible location was found which contained 67,807 square feet. The land and the buildings standing thereon were purchased for $4,500, of Mrs. Patty Lincoln, of Holliston. Nearly one-half of the land was devoted, subsequently, to streets, and sold for other purposes.

Propositions for building the hall agreeable to a plan of Lewis Fales, of Milford, were received from the following persons: W. W. Douglass, of Walpole, $13,475; Holden & Sawyer, of Portland, Me., $12,174; Ross, Clark & Company, of Medway, $12,975; Corson & Verry, of Franklin, $11.557.60. The contract was given to the lowest bidder, to be executed on or before the 15th of November, 1872.

THE DEDICATION OF SANFORD HALL.

This Hall was dedicated on Tuesday evening, December 31, 1872, with appropriate exercises, a full account of which appeared in *The Medway Journal* of January 10, 1873.

The Hon. Milton M. Fisher, Chairman of the Board of Trustees, made an address of welcome, which was followed by prayer led by the Rev. Alexis W. Ide, and the singing of an original hymn. Theodore W. Fisher, M. D., of Boston, then delivered an historical address, in which he gave an account of Medway Village and its early inhabitants. From this address are taken the following extracts:

Nature evidently reserved the Village for what it afterward became, the cradle of that manufacturing interest which has since absorbed most of the enterprise of New England, and has carried the fame and fabrics of Massachusetts to the ends of the earth. The settlement and growth of this place has been due largely to the mechanical instincts of the Whiting family, transmitted from father to son for many generations. In tracing this branch of the family, we find an almost unbroken succession of millers. The records show that in 1638 the settlers of Dedham engaged in an engineering operation of remarkable magnitude for that period. Not finding sufficient fall on the Charles River they dug a canal across the country from the Charles to the Neponset, diverting water enough to turn several mills. Nathaniel Whiting, of Dedham, was interested in this artificial water-power, and was the first miller. His son John married Mary Billings and went, in 1688, to establish a mill in the then new town of Wrentham, where the Eagle Factory now stands. John Whiting's son Nathaniel was also a miller. He was born in 1691; married Margaret Mann, daughter of the Wrentham minister, in 1711, and came soon after to establish a grist mill at the foot of the hill in the rear of this building. He died in 1799, at the age of seventy-nine years. His son Nathaniel, also a miller, lived on the same spot, and died in 1779, forty-five years old, leaving two daughters. The older married Luther Metcalf, of Franklin, whose son Luther was also a miller and a manufacturer of cotton goods.

Let us endeavor to reconstruct the Village in imagination, as it existed ninety years ago, at the close of the Revolution. The present Village Street was then the Boston and Hartford Middle road, because it lay between one going north through Worcester, and another going south through Providence. On this road, commencing at the west, stood Simon Fisher's house, where Cutler Wilson's house now stands. This was of that old-fashioned style sometimes called the "saltbox house," with two stories in front, but sloping in the rear almost to the ground. It had a well with a sweep, a large barn, a row of elms, and a butternut tree. It also had an ell which contained a bakery and a store. Where the customers came from is a mystery. In this store was the following notice, worth repeating:

> "Pay to-day, trust to-morrow,
> May to-morrow never come."

The next house was a one-story frame building, just built for Luther Metcalf, of Franklin, a returned Revolutionary soldier. The carpenter who built it was afterwards concerned in a rebellion in Canada. This small house was moved away in 1792, and till recently, served as the Village bake shop. The present Metcalf house was built in part the same year and has been repeatedly enlarged.

The third house was Job Harding's, standing where the tavern now stands. This was also a new house in 1784, and was probably a small one. It grew, however, by various additions, so as to accommodate a store, kept first by Job Harding himself, and afterwards by Captain William Felt, and the first tavern, kept by William Fuller. The old tavern, as it appeared just before its removal northward twenty years ago, consisted of a two-story building with a long ell, and a low piazza in front and at the west side. A fine elm stood in front, under whose shade the mail coaches used to dash up in fine style to the door. The hay scales stood under this tree.

The fourth house stood still farther east, at the foot of the first part of the Village hill, where William H. Cary's house now stands. It was the Joel Hawes place, an old yellow two-story house with a row of dying poplars in front. Its chambers, once sacred to domestic uses, then resounded with the tintinnabulation of a tin shop.

Just below was the Samuel Bullen house. It stood on the cellar, still open, opposite William Parson's boot shop. It was at one time occupied by Asa Fuller, wheelwright and maker of spinning-wheels. Samuel Bullen and Asa Fuller died long ago; spinning-wheels are obsolete; and the old house itself is gone. Nothing remains but the cellar, choked with burdock and cellandine, good for a "lame back" and warts.

These five, with the old Whiting house under the hill, which was burned in 1811, make six houses, of which the Village proper was composed ninety years ago. They all faced south, standing at long intervals on the main road, surrounded with gardens and fields. Their exterior was humble, but their timbers were sound, and their frames bid fair to outlast the villas of to-day. What stories they could tell of old time Village life, and of individual history! Human life is seldom tame or uneventful. Goethe says, "grasp anywhere into the thick of it, and you will always find it interesting."

Take the old tavern, for instance, with its successive keepers, William Fuller, Colonel Ethan Cobb, Laban Adams, Elijah Thayer, Amos Fisher, Captain Luther Green, and Collens Hathorn, think of the sleigh-ride frolics, the militia suppers, the country balls, the stage coach arrivals before these days of steam, when staging was a business! Think of the queer customers accommodated; the strollers, the showmen, and the peddlers, and their stories round the bar-room fire! The bargains, the horse talk, and the village gossip! Here was life and variety, and 'tis no wonder the Village boys found a fascination in the tavern which was not wholly unreasonable nor dangerous.

Besides these six houses in the Village proper, was that of Nathan Fisher, grandfather of the late Amos Fisher, which stood in Franklin on the hill across the river, where Captain Paul's house now stands; in fact the present one may be the old house itself. At the extreme eastern limit of the present village was the Abram Harding house, where J. B. Peck lately resided, the Comfort Walker house, now owned by Edward Eaton, and the Timothy Clark house, kept by him in early times as a "house of entertainment," where Deacon Fairbanks now resides.

Cotemporary with these ten houses were the grist mill, a saw mill, built by Ichabod Hawes, where Eaton & Wilson's middle mill now stands, and at the same place a blacksmith's shop with a trip hammer worked by water and a machine for boring guns. There was no Franklin road, or bridge, and grist for the mill from the Franklin side of the river was brought down a bridle path on horseback and carried across a foot-bridge over the dam.

The year 1803 was signalized by the establishment of a post-office. Previous to this time the mail came through from Boston to Hartford once a week on horseback. Captain William Felt was the first postmaster, and to the office in his store in the old tavern building came letters for all the surrounding towns. In 1807 the turnpike was built, running through Black Swamp, extending from Dedham to the western limits of Medway, and directly connecting, for the first time, the east and west parishes. Candlewood Island road was laid out to meet it a little east of the boundary between the old and new grants. It was named from a patch of hard land in its route, covered with pitch pines. The Holliston road was soon after cut through in a straight line to the Village Street, and Lover's Lane fell into disuse, or rather into the use its name implies. There was a guide-board on an oak tree at the junction of the Holliston and Village streets, which read as follows:

> " The shortest run to Hollistoo!
> Come on, Daddy Niles,
> It's only five miles!"

There was also a picture of a man on horseback galloping towards Holliston. This bit of waggery, strange to say, was perpetrated by Deacon Samuel Allen, whose many noble traits of character are well remembered. The first stage from Boston to Hartford was put on in 1812 by Ebenezer Clark, of Dedham. It ran twice a week and was driven by Joseph Miller, one of the best men of his profession. Collens Hathorn and Anson White started the Providence and Framingham stage line in 1838.

Early in the present century the Village received a new impulse to its growth. The water privilege at the grist mill was seen to be available for a more profitable business. In 1806 it was proposed by Dr. Abijah Richardson, Major Luther Metcalf, and others, to build a cotton mill on the Franklin side of the river. The refusal of the town of Medway to lay out a street to it, if located on that side, induced its location on this side, and gave us the present Franklin Street. A wooden bridge was built over the river about this time, replaced in 1846 by a stone bridge of one large arch, which fell the night before Thanksgiving of the same year, and was at once rebuilt. The mill was set in operation in March, 1807, being the only cotton mill, except the Slater's, at Pawtucket, in the country. In 1809 the Medway Cotton Manufacturing Company was formed. It was the first corporation of the kind in the country, and consisted of Dr. Abijah Richardson, Major Luther Metcalf, Philo Sanford, Captain William Felt, Comfort Walker, Dr. Nathaniel Miller, John Blackburn, and Lyman Tiffany. The doctors in those days seem to have had money to spare, since, beside the two mentioned, Dr. Dean, to whom we owe the Dean Library, was afterwards a member of this corporation. On Sunday, October 20, 1811, the mill was burned, but was rebuilt the same year, and now stands, at the venerable age of sixty-one, waiting for some enterprising spirit to give it a successor worthy of its historical interest.

The new business of cotton spinning and weaving brought many families to the Village, and introduced an element of prosperity which was soon supplemented by the erection of mills at other points on the river. In 1813 William Felt and two brothers, by the name of Tufts, from Boston, Comfort Walker and George Barber, built a cotton mill lower down, on the site in the rear of William Parson's boot shop. This was afterwards owned by William H. Cary, and was burned in 1855, and re-built by J. B. Wilson.

George Barber at this time owned a small mill for dressing woolen cloth, built in 1795, by Job Harding, near the same site. In company with Alexander Wright, a native of Scotland, he went abroad and returned with a mechanic competent to construct and operate a power loom for carpet weaving. Here carpets were first woven by machinery in this country. Under their direction also, a loom for weaving coach lace was set up, the first in the country except one in New Jersey. They also made thread lace. In 1811 William Felt, Elias and Sanford Whiting built a cotton mill on the Flat. It was afterwards owned by George Daniels, and then by Hurd and Daniels. It was burned, and rebuilt for the manufacture of wadding, and is now owned by Eaton & Wilson. In 1816, Sewall Sanford built a thread mill where Eaton & Wilson's upper mill now stands. It was afterwards owned by J. B. Wilson, and was burned in 1839, but was at once rebuilt.

In 1815 a cotton mill was built by Major Luther Metcalf, Captain Luther Metcalf, Cephas Thayer, and Joel Hunt, a mile to the west. It was burned in 1844 and was rebuilt as a paper mill by the Campbell Brothers. Around this nucleus a village has grown up.

It is impossible in the time allotted to dwell upon the host of interesting personalities which crowd the memory. It would be pleasant to review the long line of sterling men, in all the professions and walks of life, who have lived here, or who have gone out from this village. I must, however, pay a passing tribute of respect to the members of my own profession, who have successfully filled the post of duty here. The Village has never lacked physicians, faithful, skillful, and generally eminent in their calling. Men equal to all emergencies, and qualified to fill positions more lucrative, perhaps, but not more honorable. That would be impossible!

We have fortunately been able to settle our quarrels so easily that the practice of law has not been particularly profitable. It is to be regretted that the Hon. Warren Lovering is unable to be present to represent his profession, and to give us a reminder of that vigor and eloquence of speech so well remembered by many.

I have thus far omitted allusion to the school and the church. In every New England community these agencies are taken for granted. Religion and education, as a matter of course, go hand in hand with material progress, each being a cause as well as an index of every kind of material prosperity. In Puritan times each new town was bound by its act of incorporation to provide for the establishment and support of a local orthodox ministry. For a people whose watchwords were "liberty of conscience" and "freedom to worship God" according to its dictates, this practical union of church and state in town affairs looks at first a little inconsistent. It is evident "liberty of conscience" then and now had two different meanings. But we need not criticise a policy which was a necessity of the age, and which gave a moral backbone to the colony, the stiffness of which is not yet entirely relaxed. This policy was the source of many sterling virtues of which we are the happy inheritors.

We need not dwell long on church matters here, not because of their small importance, but on account of their recent date. You have also heard them set forth in the thirtieth anniversary sermon of your late pastor. In 1834 the Universalists began to worship in the old school-house hall. In 1836 the Rev. David Sanford, then settled in Dorchester, began to agitate the question of establishing an Orthodox church and society here. In consultation with Comfort Walker, Luther Metcalf, Orion Mason, James B. Wilson, and others, the plan was pronounced feasible. The Universalists generously relinquished the field, and Dr. Ide, in conference with Mr. Sanford, acquiesced in the withdrawal of those of the Village who attended his church in West Medway, thus securing harmony at the outset between the new and the old societies. Milton M. Sanford circulated a paper, and the above-named parties and many others subscribed liberally, without regard to personal religious opinions. The financial crisis of 1837 delayed the completion of the meeting-house till June, 1838. On the 3d of October following, after much hesitation on account of his health, Mr. Sanford was installed as pastor. I am wholly unable to pay a just tribute to one whose life has been so radiant with Christian virtues, and whose long labors here have been the constant source of influences far-reaching and beneficent. Still less am I able to anticipate the advantages of the new pastoral relations this year so happily formed with the Rev. R. K. Harlow.

The children of the Village formerly attended at the district school-house, standing, till last year, when it was burned, beyond the Flat, near Bent Street. Afterwards a new district was formed, and a small house was built on the hill, opposite the tavern. This was, perhaps, a mistake in location, though the scholars, who found their minds pleasantly diverted by outside occurrences, did not think so. As the village grew, the school-house was enlarged, until the original structure became the woodshed to a large building with a projecting second story, supported on a row of wooden posts, making a very convenient shelter for rainy days. This building was metamorphosed into a Catholic Church when the new school-house was built, and is soon to undergo another change.

The old school-house holds a conspicuous place in the memory of every scholar who frequented it, and need only be mentioned to call up a long panorama of vivid recollections. For the benefit of the older inhabitants, I will remind them of an ambitious educational establishment which it once accommodated about the year 1832, known as the Medway Classical Institute, and kept by the Rev. Abijah Baker.

Some very good schools and some very bad ones were kept in the old school-house. I am inclined to attribute the success of the Rev. S. J. Spalding, of Newburyport, in his experience here, to his having lived in the factory village of Nashua, N. H., where he learned how to deal with factory boys. Other teachers distinguished themselves professionally afterwards.

For many years the old school-house furnished the only hall available for secular purposes. The hotel hall was used for balls and parties, and for a time the Odd Fellows' hall was devoted to the better class of lectures, concerts, and exhibitions, but the old school-house hall was our main-stay. Here the plank desks and benches, the green wooden chandelier stuck full of oil peg lamps, and the tin side reflectors, gave welcome to every sort of nondescript entertainment. Magic lantern shows, and displays of prestidigitation; lectures on phrenology, biology, physiology, and psychology, all equally delusive; administrations of laughing gas; exposés of Free Masonry, and the similar imaginary horrors of Catholic nunneries; Swiss bell ringers and cheap concerts, all spread their nets here for the hard-earned ninepences of the people.

These three halls have all been put to other uses, and the church vestry has suffered unwonted inroads on its sanctity. The need of a village hall has long been felt. The "town-meeting" by a long triennial "swinging round the circle" of parishes, had acquired such a rotary momentum that it was useless to ask for a town hall to be located here. Although the central one of the trinity of villages in Medway, we have never reaped much benefit from it in town affairs. If a high school house, a new engine, or a soldiers' monument is asked for by either of the town's three children, the unfortunate parent must refuse, or pay for three. I wonder we have allowed the East Parish its monoply of the poorhouse so long. These frequent triangular contests have been unfavorable to that concentration of effort and interest as important in town affairs as in larger spheres of government.

This building was in no sense intended as a memorial hall, and yet how eminently proper to place on its walls some tribute to the memory of those sons of the Village who gave their lives for freedom and union in the great Rebellion. That gift may seem to some remote in its relations to our local affairs, but let me say that without the noble devotion to duty, and the heroic self-sacrifice of our soldiers, this hall would not have been built. With their death the nation was born again to a new and healthy career of material prosperity.

But above these lower considerations arises the precious moral influence of their example. This cannot be estimated at the price of a paltry piece of marble. As a boy, and a student of American history, I often wondered if the scenes of the Revolution could ever be reënacted on our soil, if the common-place men I saw about me were capable of those patriotic emotions which animated their great grandfathers at Lexington and Bunker Hill. That question was soon answered for the whole country. The "spirit of '75" revived and ennobled the humblest citizen. Let us thank God that a higher opinion of human nature than once prevailed, is possible!

The following fact shows how history repeats its record. The town of Medway lost thirteen out of a population of eight hundred, in the Revolution; in the Rebellion, fifty-two out of about thirty-six hundred. The comparison of these proportions give no support to theories of modern degeneracy. Let us then perpetuate the names of our fallen heroes by a suitable mural tablet in this hall.

Then came the "Star Spangled Banner," performed by the band, after which the Rev. Horace D. Walker, of Bridgewater, read an original poem, composed expressly for this occasion. The following is an extract:

> The mother who cherished has sent out her call
>   To those who've forgotten her never,
> Where'er we had wandered we heard it, and all
>   Came shouting " Old Medway forever!"
>
> We're children once more, and in Memory's light,
>   Live over the bright blessed hour,
> When these hills were as grand as the Alps in their height,
>   And the Charles had the Amazon's power.
>   .   .   .   .
>
> This Hall binds the Future, and Present, and Past;
>   It gracefully owns the glad debt
> Of the living to-day, to the dead who stood fast,
>   And nobly their duty here met.
>
> Sanford Hall! where Future, and Present, and Past,
>   We greet on this eve of New Year!
> May never a shadow its brightness o'ercast;
>   The smile of the Lord ever cheer!

Then the audience sang, the band playing the accompaniment, an original hymn by the same author, as follows:

TUNE: *Auld Lang Syne.*

We're met as ne'er before we met,
  Our thoughts on days of old,
Here owning blessings God has given
  And asking grace to hold;
So here we come as brethren all,
  And feel as children true
Of dear old Medway's blessed soil,
  The old love burn anew.

To generations passed before,
  So wise to guard and gain
For us such goodly heritage
  We raise our grateful strain;
We come to bless their honored names,
  Who feared no toil nor ill;
To feel as ne'er we felt before,
  Their works shall praise them still.

Still may God's blessings crown this spot
  They loved and kept of yore,
And future years be brighter far
  Than all that went before.
Thanks that this Hall so clearly will
  In coming days declare
Our generation has not failed
  Our fathers' hearts to share.

And when our children here shall meet,
  To them may SANFORD HALL
Be full of memories as rich
  As those we now recall.
So e'er we part, as children true,
  We pledge our mother dear
To guard and swell her old renown
  Through each succeeding year.

At the conclusion of the singing, the Rev. Rufus K. Harlow, of the Village, delivered the

DEDICATORY ADDRESS.

Mr. President, Ladies and Gentlemen — Every structure man builds represents an idea, and better ideas are indicated by a better architecture.

Savage life wants occasional shelter, and the hut shows this. Civilization wants a home, and the comfortable dwelling is the response. Education needs its drill-rooms and arsenals, and schools, lecture halls, and libraries indicate the demand. The development of the æsthetic nature is discovered by art galleries. The awakening of the soul is revealed by the temples where it worships God. Man only a little higher than the brute is bewildered amid the appliances that satisfy the necessities of man a little lower than the angels. Show a savage the palace of Louvre and he is as unappreciative of its use as was Pat of the value of a trunk he was invited to buy. " Buy a trunk? And what would I do wid a trunk?" "Why, put your clothes in it, to be sure." "And go naked myself?" A man must own more than one suit of clothes before he can appreciate a trunk, and a community must feel the need of a hall, as we have, rightly to value this elegant structure. I have been invited to tell you how and why this building came to be.

It embodies many ideas, but a central one is developed in this beautiful hall which convenes us to-night. Our most sagacious citizens have for a long time felt the need of some place of assemblage for our people for secular purposes; a place for literary and social entertainment, for political debate, a halting house for our rotary town-meetings in their triennial revolutions. A citizen who has done more, perhaps, for our village than any other one man,— shrewdly caring for the living, and reverently providing a pleasant resting-place for the dead,— did more than confess and deplore the need, and set himself to devise means to meet it. The unsuccessful proposition made to one who has remembered us in another direction, opened the way for common talk about a hall. Our young ladies, true to the instincts that have somehow found a channel straight from mother Eve to every one of her daughters, when they saw that this hitherto forbidden fruit " was pleasant to the eye, and desirable to make people wise," determined to have it, and when a woman really determines anything, good or bad, who shall stop her? We gladly acknowledge that the very first money for this hall was raised by the hard and persistent labor of our young ladies. We will not detain you with the mention of the process that has made the project which some denounced as quixotic a certainty, we will only allude to that princely generosity of our citizens, and the sons of our citizens, that has made the gift of this building absolute — relinquishing all revenues that may accrue from it to the expenses of our religious societies and the replenishment of our library. The hall being a certainty, around that as a nucleus other ideas crystallized. A story underneath for the purpose of trade was suggested; worthier accommodations for our constantly increasing library were recommended; and then, as the plans for the building were drawn at a time when Mansard was an angel and his invention celestial, the trustees thought good to cover all in a storied roof, after the fashion of other cities, and forecasting the time when Medway shall be their peer. Alas! the angel has *fallen;* there are none now so poor as to do him reverence; his invention has gone down into a fiery furnace, and popular indignation consigns his memory to the same fate; and yet we have the roof — and it is just as celestial as ever to us, and we are glad to thank the much execrated inventor for the pleasant suite of rooms that over-top us, embracing a commodious parlor, where our ladies will devise liberal things, and a smaller hall with ante-rooms that would afford ample accommodations for a permanent organization. We understand that negotiations are pending between such an organization and the trustees for the rental of the place as a permanent home. If they do not seize upon this golden opportunity we shall deem them worthy of the adjective by which they designate their order, "Odd Fellows." Yes, we will give them the superlative of the adjective and vote them the oddest fellows we ever knew.

It is evident to you all that this building offers rare possibilities for the good of our people. This beautiful hall suggests courses of instructive and elevating lectures, entertaining and refining concerts. It answers the question, where? that has often stood between us and things harmless *per se*, but which are out of place in the sanctuary, the only place of concourse we have hitherto had. We hope to see this hall utilized; and for those purposes worthy of the name it bears and the elegance of its appointments. We hope its influence will be to lift our people up to worthier aspirations, so that the demand that always regulates supply, both as to quantity and quality, shall raise its standard by a continuous, if it must be gradual process.

If any of our friends present who have wealth, want to advance this work of education and culture, here is a grand opportunity. Give the trustees in charge the foundation of an annual course of lectures. By such a personal administration of one's estate, much satisfaction would be derived while living, and a first-class quarrel prevented when, after one's funeral, the heirs discuss the will.

Of the library, which now finds better accommodations, we can speak in the positiveness of experience. It is an advantage to our people. We are aware that many of the books are not of a very high order, and, perhaps, works of fiction show the hardest usage; but then we are creating a *taste* for reading, and the recipe for profiting people by reading is somewhat of the same character as the famous one for making hare soup: "First catch your hare." First get people to reading; teach them that books were made for something better than table ornaments or supports for open window sashes, then we can gradually improve the quality. Our librarian has told me that it is a noticeable fact that some who began with fiction, and would have nothing else, now will take more solid and profitable reading. Does not all literary interest begin at about the same point? Did not the driest theologian, the most abstract scientist, the profoundest statesman begin with *Mother Goose* and go through the *Arabian Nights, Gulliver's Travels,* and *Robinson Crusoe,* before they waded out into the deeper, bottomless waters.

We hope the time will come when the library will be free to every person who is known or can bring a voucher.

There is one thing I wish to say just here. We ought to keep the library room open at all suitable hours, and have it nicely warmed, lighted, and furnished with daily and weekly papers and a few of our best monthly magazines, making it a pleasant reading-room for any who choose to occupy it. The most persuasive argument that was urged upon the founder of our library was that our young people had no place for gathering but the bar-room, saloon, or stores, and no books except what they would borrow from one another. It was an argument, the bearing of which that practical philanthropist could appreciate.

Those who would preserve the morals of our youth ought to learn something from those who try to corrupt them. The devil always has furnished fire and light *gratis* — *always will* — where people find that they will go, especially in cold weather. Let us fight the devil with his own weapons; let us offer as good accommodations as he does; let us have a reading-room. Who will give light for a year? Who will give coal? Who a daily paper? Who will put his magazine upon the table after he has cut the leaves and read it? This will bring the dates just right, for in these fast days our magazines are a week old the day that they are born. In the language of the pulpit, " My hearers, this is the personal application of my subject."

We dedicate this building, then, first of all to its practical uses.

This spacious and elegant hall to that which shall make it a source of education, culture, entertainment, and accommodation to our people. We hope to see it often occupied by appreciative audiences, attracted hither by instructive lectures, elevating concerts, and rational entertainments; and we have confidence to believe that those to whose custody it is now committed by the donors will be more anxious to make it a blessing to our people than to make it simply a source of revenue; and by a wise discrimination will so conduct its affairs as to insure to us the benefits of a public hall without its common, and to be deprecated, evils.

We dedicate the story below us to the uses of legitimate business, and the whole structure to a worthy ministration to the inartificial wants of our community.

Lastly, we consecrate this building to its memorial uses. We are glad to call it after the name of those whose princely generosity secured it to us. We are happy to know that there are sons of Medway who are not only able but willing to make bequests by thousands for the benefit of our people. Large business success so often makes men miserly, selfish, oblivious of the place where the race of life began, forgetful of the boy friends who have not been able to keep up and in a score of years are far behind, that it is refreshing to have this tangible proof of an exception. We may not say of the living all we might wish. This we will say: The deed is worthy of the name, and the name is worthy of all honor and remembrance in our pleasant village. It has twined itself with interlacing memories amidst all that is noblest and best and most hopeful here. It shall bring to our remembrance the eldest living representative of the name — who is with us to-night, most deeply interested of any in these exercises — still fresh and useful in her feelings, like a green Christmas at the time when we naturally expect the cold and snow and dreariness of winter; linking four generations fast together, and standing to us younger people as a grand type of the sort of daughters with which the mothers of the Revolution blessed the world. She is, indeed, a mother in our Israel, " who loveth our nation and hath built us this synagogue," at least, by her instrumentality. It shall recall the children who loved their mother with a devotion as deserved as it is pleasant to see, and have remained loyal to their early home through decades of absence. Its mention shall bring to remembrance the servant of God whose history has been so identified with this people that they are all his family, so that their joys and sorrows find an echo in his heart — just like a father's quick response to a child's emotions. Neither this generation nor the next will need any reminder to preserve the name and memory. It is inseparably associated with the tenderest experiences of these families. But in the coming years, when Sanford Hall is venerable, linked with the name, parents shall repeat the tradition to their children that Goldsmith saw in prophetic vision our first village pastor, of whom he wrote in that inimitable poem :

> " A man he was to all the country dear,
> And passing rich with forty pounds a year;
> His house was known to all the vagrant train;
> He chid their wanderings but relieved their pain;
> Pleased with his guests the good man learned to glow
> And quite forgot their vices in their woe;
> Careless their merits or their faults to scan
> His pity gave ere charity began.
> Thus to relieve the wretched was his pride,
> And e'en his failings leaned to virtue's side;
> But in his duty prompt at every call,
> He watched and wept, he prayed and felt for all;
> And, as a bird each fond endearment tries
> To tempt its new fledged offspring to the skies,
> He tried each art, reproved each dull delay,
> Allured to brighter worlds, and led the way."

Beneath us is another memorial. The Library, founded by the munificence of the late Dr. Dean, of Franklin.

What a monument to *hold* a memory! Had the endowment been invested in marble it would have raised a noble shaft. But every year the friction of the rain, and hail, and hurricane (those harpies of our climate), would have claimed their dividends till in the reach of ages all would at last have perished. *This* monument is growing statelier every day; like a living thing its wear and tear and wastes are constantly replaced. It holds the secret of immortal youth. It was a rare bequest of one noted for shrewd investments.

The pleasant room above us has been called "Whiting Hall," in memory of one of our earliest families, whose descendants are still honored citizens. The name is now doubly identified with our public buildings. It underlies our church, and roofs this structure.

We value this building for its union of practical with memorial uses. With all its suggestions and hopeful possibilities we dedicate it to the uses of the present, to the demands of the future, conscious that it needs a future fully to utilize it. In the sentiment of one of the trustees, we have built with fifty years in view. We shall be disappointed if in less than one-half that time the wonder will not long have ceased why the builders laid the scale so large. Our facilities for business will not always be overlooked, our capable water privilege will not always rest content with the sound of the grinding so low. When the cheerful hum of many spindles shall waken hopeful echoes along our valley, when our many manufactories shall rival our neighbors on one side in caring for the head, on the other in caring for the feet, then this place of concourse will fully vindicate the foresight of the builders, and their generous and philanthropic policy, while embalming their memories, will stimulate their successors to like noble deeds.

The chairman then read various letters and called on gentlemen to respond to toasts which were given. The exercises of the evening closed by the audience singing "America," and as they retired the band played "Home, Sweet Home."

THE PARTRIDGE HALL. ERECTED IN 1876.

This building was located in the village of East Medway, giving accommodations for a residence, a store, the post-office, a public hall, and various ante-rooms. The builder and proprietor was Elijah Partridge, Esq. It was erected at a cost of about five thousand dollars, in the year of our NATIONAL CENTENNIAL.

THE FIRE DEPARTMENT.
1714—1885.

The early history of the Medway fire department is somewhat shrouded in obscurity, owing to its antiquity. The earliest records show that in 1714, Asahel Adams, Christian Pettibone, Claimwell Metcalf, and Justice Johnston were appointed fire watchers with the powers of " yᵉ tithing man " to provide buckets, hooks, and "yᵉ climbing poles" for the extinguishment of fires. Their duties consisted in watching at night in the villages or from the top of the village hill for signs of fire, and the alarming of the inhabitants thereof. They had powers to enter any settler's barn and take his cattle or horses " for yᵉ public weal," in case of fire.

About 1835 a fire-engine was brought to town by the cotton company, that then owned or run the " old white mill," which was torn down a few years ago to make room for the present Sanford Mills. A man named Mitchel, an Englishman, was clerk of this mill, and he seemed to have very decided ideas on fire matters. He purchased an engine, with buckets and tubes, for the protection of the mill and surroundings. He also caused to be constructed a lot of iron hooks on long poles, for pulling burning buildings to pieces, and was, in fact, the father of the present hook and ladder system.

The first regular suction-hose engine brought to the town was the old " Rapid engine," formerly belonging to Chelsea, which was purchased from Hunneman second hand. This old tub has a checkered record. From being champion of Chelsea, she took her place in Medway as the whole department, but in after years became the champion of the town, having wrested the honors from newer and younger sisters. She to-day is champion of hand-engines in the state of Maine, where she was sold when ungrateful Medway traded her off for a brighter namesake. The younger Rapid, however, has not disgraced its predecessor, as it still holds to the title of champion of the town. The first movement looking towards a permanent fire department was in 1855, by the appointment of the following gentlemen as a board of engineers: The Hon. Milton M. Fisher, chief engineer; William B. Boyd, first assistant; David A. Cheever, clerk; Samuel W. Metcalf, Addison P. Thayer, and Moses D. Richardson, engineers. November 6, 1855, this board adopted a code of regulations for the fire department, which was printed.

The department in 1885 consisted of six companies. The board of engineers comprises the following gentlemen, all of whom have served in the ranks, chosen May 1, 1884: Albert W. Barton, chief; William Colvin, first assistant; Oliver Clark, second assistant; and M. A. Ware, clerk.

The foremen of the companies are as follows: Torrent, No. 1, West Medway, W. J. Arbuckle; Rapid, No. 2, C. P. Harding; Union, No. 3, Rockville, J. H. Ingraham; Niagara, No. 4, East Medway, Louis LaCroix; Reserve, No. 5, West Medway, S. J. Clarke; General Taylor Volunteer Company, West Medway, H. A. Woodman.

In addition to the fire department, all the mills have force pumps, and in the Village the Sanford water works give additional security. Large reservoirs have been constructed by the town at eligible points.

THE TORRENT ENGINE HOUSE. ERECTED IN 1874.

THE TORRENT ENGINE COMPANY, No. 1, WEST MEDWAY, numbers fifty men.

OFFICERS.—William J. Arbuckle, Captain; Henry A. Bullard, Clerk.

EQUIPMENT.—350 feet hose (good); 250 feet hose (fair); 1 pump; 6 rubber coats; 2 pair runners; 5 belts with spanners; 2 suction spanners; 6 extra spanners; 1 wrench; 2 hose jackets; 1 5-gallon oil can; 2 axes; 2 ladders; 2 stoves; 1 bar; 3 lanterns; 2 jacks.

THE RAPID ENGINE COMPANY, No. 2, MEDWAY VILLAGE, has a vigorous organization of some fifty men.

OFFICERS.—C. P. Harding, Captain; Hugh Kenney, First Assistant; William Edwards, Second Assistant; George A. Abbe, Treasurer; Peter Phillips, Steward; Joseph D. Clark, Clerk.

EQUIPMENT.—600 feet hose (good); 200 feet hose (fair); 5 ladders; 2 jacks; 2 stoves; 2 wrenches; 2 pair runners; 6 rubber coats; 2 lanterns.

THE UNION ENGINE COMPANY, No. 3, ROCKVILLE, was organized some years since, and although it has a small number of men, it is a well equipped and effective organization.

OFFICERS.—John H. Ingraham, Captain; John H. Swarman, Steward; A. S. Clark, Clerk; ten men.

EQUIPMENT.—250 feet rubber lined hose; 100 feet linen hose; 2 ladders; 12 spanners; 1 axe; 1 wrench; 1 stove; 1 brake; 3 lanterns; 3 rubber coats.

NIAGARA ENGINE HOUSE. ERECTED IN 1879.

THE NIAGARA ENGINE COMPANY, No. 4, EAST MEDWAY, was organized about 1857. Elihu S. Fuller, Esq., served as captain of the company for twenty-five years; it embraced about forty men.

In 1879 the town granted $500 toward erecting a building for the accommodation of this fire company. The company and their friends purchased the site, put in the foundation, and furnished $175 toward the building, which cost $675.

Elijah Partridge, Esq., was the builder. *Vid. Town Report of 1880.* This company holds its annual meetings on the first day of May.

OFFICERS.— Louis LaCroix, Captain ; A. L. Ware, Esq., Clerk.

EQUIPMENT.— 300 feet hose (good) ; 200 feet hose (fair) ; 200 feet hose (poor) ; 2 stoves ; 4 lanterns ; 2 ladders ; 1 pump ; 5 rubber coats.

THE RESERVE ENGINE COMPANY, No. 5, WEST MEDWAY, has no records prior to April 4, 1874. The officers at that date were George R. Drake, Captain ; George McIntosh, First Assistant ; C. C. Lawrence, Second Assistant ; Lewis Goulding, Treasurer ; Stephen Vose, Steward ; Lewis Goulding, Clerk.

PRESENT OFFICERS.— Charles Gaines, Captain ; Matthew F. Desmond, First Assistant ; Joseph Fisk, Second Assistant ; Almond Smith, Treasurer ; William Russell, Steward ; Almond Smith, Clerk.

This company numbers forty-four men. Equipment: 150 feet hose (good) ; 550 feet hose (poor) ; runners for engine ; 2 stoves ; 2 ladders ; 1 jack ; 3 lanterns ; 2 belts and spanners ; 2 ladder hose straps.

THE MASONIC AND SECRET ORDERS.

CHARLES RIVER LODGE, F. & A. M., located at West Medway ; place of meeting, Masonic Hall, Bowen's Block ; organized March 9, 1870, and chartered, March 8, 1871 ; A. L. 5871. Officers: Clark P. Harding, W. M. ; George R. Temple, S. W. ; Edward S. Harding, J. W. ; Orville R. Kelsey, Treas. ; George W. Bullard, Sec'y ; Almond G. Partridge, Chap. ; Alonzo H. Gay, Marsh. ; George H. Daniels, S. D. ; George Harding, J. D. ; Edward S. Pond, S. S. ; James H. Wood, J. S. ; S. F. Metcalf, I. S. ; Albert

W. Barton, Tyler. PAST MASTERS: Alfred Ashton, James M. Seavey, William A. McKean, Roswell K. Colcord, Charles W. Seavey, George H. Daniels, Clark P. Harding. This lodge has a membership of fifty-three.

KNIGHTS OF HONOR. NORFOLK LODGE, No. 635. Instituted, May 31, 1877. Meets the second and fourth Thursday of each month in Odd Fellows' Hall. P. D., Albert W. Barton; Dic., George A. Abbe; V. D., George H. Daniels. Asst. D., John H. Bickley; Reporter, Frederick L. Fisher; Fin. Reporter, Charles W. Seavey; Treas., James M. Seavey; Guide, John H. Crimmings; Guardian, N. P. Noss; Sentinel, William H. Norton; Chap., Francis W. Cummings; Trustees, Frederick L. Fisher, Francis W. Cummings, Metcalf Adams. Thirty members.

THE EUREKA COUNCIL, No. 5, ROYAL ARCANUM, was instituted July 11, 1877. Officers: Albert W. Barton, R.; Edward S. Pond, V. R.; Millard Fuller, O.; Metcalf Adams, Sec'y; George H. Andrews, Coll.; Warren E. Blaisdell, Treas.; the Rev. J. E. Burr, Chap.; Nelson A. Bills, G.; George L. Pond, W.; William Colvin, S. Past Regents, William Colvin, Olney P. Newell, George L. Pond, and O. R. Kelsey. Thirty-four members. Regular meetings first and third Mondays of each month, at Mechanic's Hall, Main Street, West Medway.

I. O. G. T., MORNING STAR LODGE, No. 59. Regular meetings Friday evenings in Mechanic's Hall, West Medway. W. C. T., Alfred Daniels; W. V. T., Mrs. George Proctor; W. S., Jennie Scott; W. F. S., Lizzie Smith; W. Treas., Albert Smith; W. C., Mrs. Nathan Adams; W. M., Horace Force; W. O. G., Ernest Adams; W. I. G., Nathan Adams; P. W. C. T., Frank Greenwood; W. D. M., May Hunt; W. A. S., Willie Hitchcock; W. R. H. S., Ruth Adams; W. L. H. S., Libbie Rose; D. G. W. C. T., Isaac C. Greenwood.

I. O. O. F., MEDWAY LODGE, No. 163. Instituted October 17, 1873. Meets every Friday evening at Odd Fellows' Hall, Sanford Hall Building. N. G., Sumner H. Clark; V. G., Nelson H. Damon; Sec'y, Clark P. Harding; Permanent Sec'y, Samuel G. Clark; Treas., James H. Wood; Warden, George A. Abbe; Conductor, Erastus W. Cary; I. G., John H. Ingraham; O. G., C. Henry Richardson; Chap., John H. Crimmings; Sup. of N. G., Albert W. Barton, Alvin E. Clough; Sup. of V. G., James A. Snow, James H. Bragg; Scene Sup., George S. Ryan, Joseph T. Waite; S. P. G., Frederick L. Fisher; Trustees, Clark Partridge, Edward S. Harding, Henry S. Partridge.

THE SIXTY-SIXTH ANNIVERSARY OF ODD FELLOWSHIP IN AMERICA,

CELEBRATED APRIL 26, 1885.

FAITH, HOPE, AND CHARITY.

"All Institutions which tend to elevate, socially and morally, their members are worthy of support, and of more than a mere passing notice. Sunday last being the sixty-sixth anniversary of the introduction of the order of Odd Fellows into this country, it was deemed a fitting occasion by the members of Medway lodge No. 163, I. O. O. F., to make some public recognition of the event. The anniversary falling as it did upon the Sabbath day, was not observed in as brilliant a manner as it would have been upon a secular day, but the Medway lodge voted at their meeting to attend public worship at the Congregational church to listen to a sermon specially adapted to the occasion. The gentle rain of the morning prevented as large an attendance as was anticipated, and many of the venerable patriarchs of the order who had hoped to participate, were deterred from so doing by the inclemency of the weather.

"The lodge, together with many visiting brethren from Milford, West Medway, and Franklin, assembled at their rooms in Sanford hall, where, after certain ceremonies, known only to the initiated, they formed in line, and in full regalia, under the guidance of Grand Marshall Frank W. Cummings, marched to the church. They made a very imposing and impressive appearance during their march, and it afforded us much pleasure to see the active interest taken by so many of our well-known citizens. Zest was added to the occasion by the presence of Dist. Deputy Grand Master David H. Heard, of Milford, and other dignitaries who came especially for the event.

"After reaching the church they marched in, and taking the seats at the front and to the right of the pulpit, listened with earnest and intense interest to the pastor, the Rev. R. K. Harlow, who, at the beginning of his discourse, mentioned as his text: 'Then Jonathan and David made a covenant, because he loved him as his own soul'; 1 Samuel, xviii., 3, and after alluding to it as a beautiful picture of human fellowship, said this was indeed a model alliance, because the young men being of about the same age and having many traits in common, made the alliance not only natural but fitting.

"It was unselfish, strengthened by adversity, and was consummated in the true spirit of piety. The narrative of this covenant gives some suggestions which may be of use to us. It makes prominent the tendency among persons to band together, and this in itself is a fair measure of the degree of civilization, in any age, among any people, for civilization creates interdependencies and these naturally necessitate coöperation.

"The education, the pleasure, the work, the benevolence, as well as the social and moral redemption of the world, are all carried on and accomplished by persons in alliance. The preacher, quite at length, graphically and effectively developed the advantages resulting from these alliances, and then went on to speak of the motives that prompt such alliances, saying they were commonly made for mutual advantage and for self-interest, but that there is a type of alliance that rises above those motives, one that is projected in pure unselfishness and ratified in the sight of God, which brings men into fellowship, not from the consideration of what they themselves expect to get, but what in a spirit of disinterestedness they may be permitted to give.

"Such alliances are operated on the principle of self-sacrifice. Their sympathies are not limited by ordinary bounds. 'He who is in need is neighbor,' and, furthermore, their intentions are not only to benefit the bodies of men, but their souls as well; not only to look to the welfare of their physical condition, but also to their spiritual welfare; to redeem the whole man.

"There exists no organization which so conscientiously does this as the church of Christ, and so among all organizations the church stands preëminent; in fact, all that is best about these humanitarian associations has not only been inspired, but suggested by the presence of Christianity in the world.

"The speaker then addressed the representatives of the order, saying in substance : Three things now abideth ; Faith, through which are visible the glories of eternity ; Hope, by which our steps are directed toward them ; Charity, whose broad mantle relieves many ; and alluding to the principles and charitable works of the order, closed with two suggestions : *First*, that men will judge of the society more by the lives of its members than by their published principles ; *Second*, that Odd Fellowship, good as it may be, is not a substitute for personal piety. Membership in this order is not an equivalent for discipleship of Christ, nor can it offer the same comforts to the weary soul as can the true Christian religion."

PATRONS OF HUSBANDRY. EAST MEDWAY GRANGE, No. 112. Organized December 4, 1883. Meets first and third Wednesdays of each month at Partridge Hall, East Medway. Master, Louis La Croix ; Overseer, Moses C. Adams ; Lecturer, A. L. Ware ; Steward, George C. Thrasher ; Assistant, E. F. Lovell ; Chaplain, the Rev. E. O. Jameson ; Treasurer, H. E. Hosmer ; Secretary, Mrs. Jane A. Cook ; Gate keeper, G. W. Follansbee ; Ceres, Mrs. Laura S. Hosley ; Pomona, Mrs. Harriet La Croix ; Flora, Miss Winnie J. Lovell ; Lady Assistant Steward, Miss Eliza B. Richardson. There are about eighty members.

IMPROVEMENT ASSOCIATION, ROCKVILLE. President, Mrs. E. A. Jones ; Vice-President, Mrs. J. F. Springer ; Secretary and Treasurer, Miss Addie A. Clark ; Directresses, Mrs. J. F. Springer, Mrs. A. L. Waite, Mrs. J. Smith, Miss Sarah F. Clark.

THE HOME CIRCLE, ANCHOR COUNCIL, No. 75, organized January 18, 1884. Meets second and fourth Thursdays of each month in Partridge Hall, East Medway. Leader, Charles La Croix ; Vice-Leader, E. Eugene Adams ; Instructor, Lillian L. Fuller ; Past Leader, Moses C. Adams ; Secretary, J. B. Daniels ; Financier, Nelson Martin ; Treasurer, M. A. Ware ; Guide, Esther W. La Croix ; Warden, J. S. Adams ; Sentinel, J. W. Tuttle ; Trustees, A. F. Lovell, J. W. Tuttle, H. C. Hosmer.

C. L. S. C. This society meets alternate Monday evenings at the houses of the members in West Medway.

THE OFFICERS.— Vincent Moses, President ; George Wheat, Vice-President ; L. Metcalf Pierce, Secretary.

THE ZENOPHON BRANCH meets in the Rockville Chapel.

THE OFFICERS.— Mrs. S. F. Bucklin, President ; Miss Addie A. Clark, Vice-President ; Miss Amy C. Jones, Secretary ; Mrs. J. H. Ingraham, Treasurer.

THE GRAND ARMY OF THE REPUBLIC.

THE WILDER DWIGHT POST, 105, of the Grand Army of the Republic, was organized and had a vigorous life for several years; S. J. Clark, Commander. Subsequently there was instituted in its place

THE JAMES H. SARGENT POST, 130. This Post of the Grand Army of the Republic meets at its hall, in Bowen's Block, every Thursday evening. Commander, W. J. Arbuckle; S. V. C., Charles E. Burr; J. V. C., Emory Munyan; Chaplain, G. H. Greenwood; Adjutant, George Pond; Quartermaster, Justus C. Hitchcock; Sergt.-Maj., William G. White; 2d Sergt., Josiah Morse; Surg., P. A. Collins; O. D., Henry Purdy; O. G., Henry A. Wood. Delegates to Department Encampment, E. L. Videtto and H. A. Walker.

There have been various other societies and organizations formed in town, having an existence longer or shorter, all contributing to the better development of social life and public improvement.

The numerous temperance societies have done much to keep alive right sentiment and to aid in the suppression of the liquor traffic. The Washingtonian movement of forty years ago made such lasting impression on the people of the eastern part of the town, that from that day to this no place of sale has been tolerated, and scarcely a drinking man found among them. This part of Medway became Millis, and at their first annual town-meeting the question of " License " was submitted without a single vote cast in its favor.

The Old Apple Tree.

THE INDUSTRIES OF THE TOWN.

FARMS AND FARMING.

1714 — 1885.

THE founders of the town were owners of farms, and lived by farming. They submitted themselves with sweet content to the Divine regulation announced to Adam, " In the sweat of thy face shalt thou eat bread."

Their lands were not remarkable for fertility, although in some sections of the town the farms were very productive, and the poorer lands were often joined with more or less acres of meadow which yielded quantities of hay for the labor of the cutting. This was some compensation for lighter crops of corn. But nowhere in the town are the farms like the irrigated lands of Egypt, which yield three crops a year; yet, with a husbandry like that of the Chinese, which carefully enriches the soil, and suffers no weeds to grow, the farmers have always found their toil fairly remunerative. Of the more than sixteen thousand acres within the town, nearly six thousand acres are pasture and meadow, and somewhat more than three thousand acres are arable lands, and in a fair state of cultivation.

By the census of 1880 there were in the town one hundred and fifty-nine farms, giving employment to one hundred and sixty-four farmers, yielding a production valued at nearly sixty thousand dollars.

There are excellent farms in the western part of the town along Chicken Brook, where the earliest settlers of the New Grant located, but some of the best farms are situated in the easterly part of the town, and by the recent division are embraced in the town of Millis. These farms lie in the vicinity of Boggastow Brook, and among them are the Maplewood, the Evergreen Place, and the Oak Grove.

OAK GROVE FARM embraces several hundreds of acres of land, much of it in a high state of cultivation, and is devoted to the production of milk and high-bred stock. Its value and productiveness are being increased every year by a large outlay in improvements, and by bringing long neglected lands under cultivation.

THE SCYTHE AND EDGED TOOL FACTORY.

1784 — 1884.

COLONEL AMOS TURNER established a scythe and edged tool factory in Rockville soon after the War of the Revolution. He utilized a portion of the water-power belonging to Richardson's grist mill.

In 1818 Messrs. Comfort and Dean Walker, father and son, purchased of Colonel Turner's estate the privilege, and erected a cotton factory and machine shop. These works were enlarged from time to time, and for some years quite a business was carried on. In 1827 Mr. Dean Walker transferred his business to Baltimore, Md.

While in Rockville, Mr. Walker employed two Englishmen, one of them, French by name, a very skillful workman, the other, Bestwick, an operator of lace looms.

These men had so much to say of the lace manufacturing that upon French's assuring Mr. Walker that he could build a loom, he told him to do so at his risk and expense. The loom with its 1,260 shuttles was, in time, built, and thread imported for use. This machine was operated by Bestwick, and for years was one of the mechanical wonders of the region for miles around. Ladies, young and old, found pleasant and profitable employment in embroidering with it.

Deacon Timothy Walker, a son of Comfort and a brother of Mr. Dean Walker, came into the general management of the business. The grist mill was purchased and became subordinate to the thread, wadding, and batting interests of the factory, and Rockville became a flourishing little village. These mills were destroyed by fire in 1884.

Just below Rockville there was a slight fall which Moses Harding used for a cotton manufacturing establishment. This was called Baltimore, because Mr. Harding had talked of going to Baltimore before settling there.

THE CABINET MANUFACTURE.

1778 — 1878.

This industry was carried on for a hundred years but never on an extensive scale. Major Luther Metcalf was the first to set up the business in 1778. He had a shop in the Village and employed a few workmen. Cabinet making was then done entirely by hand, no machinery being used. Captain Eleazar Daniels carried on this business for some years in East Medway. The chair and communion table with which the new meeting-house, in 1816, was furnished were the work of his hands. In West Medway, Mr. Stephen Adams commenced cabinet making in 1826, and continued it until about 1878, when his age and failing health compelled him to relinquish all active labor. Mr. Adams was a deacon of the church for several years, and died in 1885, universally respected. These skilled workers in wood have no successors, so that cabinet making has ceased in the town.

THE MANUFACTURE OF STRAW BRAID AND BONNETS.

1805 — 1885.

The industrial applications of the straw of wheat for plaiting or braiding are very ancient. Plaiting straw was one of the oldest arts of the Egyptians, and is mentioned by Heroditus and other early writers.

The first account of it in Europe is found in the records of the reign of Mary, Queen of Scots, who observed that the peasants of Lorraine wore hats made of straw plait or braid, and that the manufacture was one of profit. About 1562 she introduced the manufacture of straw into Scotland, and later, her son, James I., introduced it into England. And it became an established branch of industry in Bedfordshire which has ever since been the great centre of the straw business.

The braid was first made of whole straw, but in the time of George I. split straw began to be used. By splitting the straw, desirable degrees of fineness were secured. Fine straw plaits can be made from only two kinds of wheat, viz., the White Chittim which is the best, and the Red Lammas.

The principal places of manufacture of fine plaits are Tuscany and Leghorn, in Italy, and Luton and Dunstable, in England. The manufacture of this straw braid and bonnets in these places in England employ over seventy thousand persons. Not long after the close of the Revolution this industry was introduced into America, but not until about 1825 did it come to be of much importance. For some years straw goods were made from straw raised and braid made in this country, but of late years fifty per cent. of the straw manufactured here is brought from Canton, China, while the Luton straw from England and the Leghorn from Italy are largely used. More than one-half the straw goods manufactured in America are made in Massachusetts, and of these Norfolk County produces the greater part.

The manufacture of straw braid was commenced about 1805, in the town of Wrentham, Mass., and it soon spread into the surrounding towns of

Franklin, Dedham, Foxboro, and Medway. Straw braid was made in the families, and sold and exchanged at the stores for goods. It was about 1810 that Captain William Felt, who kept a store in the Village, employed several young women to make the braid into bonnets, of whom Mrs. Edena (Holbrook) Sanford was one and Mrs. Sewall Clark was another. At a later period Mrs. Horace Richardson, in East Medway, did a thriving business. Mr. Charles Cheever, about 1830, began to weave imported straw from Tuscany, in Italy, and had many looms in private families, and erected a building to carry on the business on a larger scale, but did not for some reason achieve success. The building was afterward used as tenements, and was finally burned when occupied by the Hon. Clark Partridge as a boot shop. In 1837 there were 32,200 straw bonnets manufactured in Medway, valued at $40,400.

Mr. M. M. Fisher, in 1840, came from Westboro, where he had resided for four years, and established the straw goods manufacture in all its branches, substantially as now carried on. He occupied at first what is now the dwelling-house of Mr Lucius Taylor, which had recently been occupied by Milton H. Sanford as a boot shop, and who had gone to erect a mill at what is now Cordaville, in Southboro. This building was occupied for about four years, when the business was removed to what is now the dwelling-house of Captain David Daniels. In 1847 it was removed to what was then called the Odd Fellows' Hall, erected by Mr. Amos Fisher, and confined to the first story and basement of the building until 1857, when the whole building was used, to which three additions have since been made, which, with the boot shop building on Pine Street, and a stable, with nearly two acres of land, now constitute the Medway Straw Works. Mr. Elias Metcalf was a partner with Deacon Fisher from 1842, for about eight years. From 1850 to 1854 Deacon Fisher was out of health, but the business was carried on by George Richardson, Elias Metcalf, and David Daniels, afterward it was resumed by Fisher & Daniels. In 1857 Abram S. Harding was taken into partnership with Deacon Fisher, under the firm name of Fisher & Harding. Subsequently, Oscar M. Bassett came into the company, and in 1863 Deacon Fisher retired from the business, which was conducted by Harding & Bassett until 1878, when Mr. Bassett retired, and Mr. E. S. Harding was received as a partner with his father, under the firm name of A. S. Harding & Son, which continued till the unexpected and lamented death of his father occurred in June, 1882. During this period of forty years a very large number of persons have received remunerative employment from the industry, and a large amount of money has been distributed for labor in this and other towns in the vicinity.

Others have conducted this industry in town for short periods : John W. Partridge, at West Medway, removing from there to the city of Washington ; Samuel Metcalf and A. J. Snow used what is now the old Catholic Church for the straw goods business for two or three years from 1853, and George P. Metcalf succeeded them, and afterwards, in 1866, erected a fine building at the junction of Village and Holliston streets, upon the site of the dwelling-house of Samuel Hodgson, which was consumed by fire, December 15, 1868, at a loss of some $10,000, besides the law library, and other books and papers, belonging to the town.

THE VILLAGE STRAW FACTORY.

D. D. CURTIS, PROPRIETOR.

1885.

In 1854, as appears by the industrial statistics of the state, the number of straw bonnets made in Medway was 100,000, and employés, 200, and in 1874 the value of straw goods manufactured was $170,000, ranking in value next to the boot industry, which was $953,200.

As furnishing additional information in regard to the straw manufacture and the straw braid industry in their incipient history, a report is here inserted, made to the Norfolk County Agricultural Society, September, 1859, by a committee appointed to that service, of which the Hon. M. M. Fisher was chairman, as follows :

"REPORT ON STRAW MANUFACTURES. The committee on straw manufactures regret there were so few specimens of straw goods presented for premium or exhibition. At this season of the year it will always be impossible for manufacturers of bonnets to contribute many kinds of these goods without making a considerable sacrifice. The committee, however, hope that the liberal premiums offered by the Society will hereafter, as in some years past, secure large contributions from the bonnet manufacturers of the county, who, if they be 'men of straw,' are neither deficient in private enterprise or public spirit.

There was one bonnet in the exhibition this year eminently suggestive. It was made and contributed by Mrs. Betsey Baker, wife of Mr. Obed Baker, of West Dedham, now seventy-three years old. It was a *fac simile* of the first straw bonnet made in this country, made, too, by the same hands that plaited the first braid and sewed the first bonnet produced by American skill and labor. This bonnet deservedly attracted much attention, and is entitled to have its history stated in full in the volume of the *Transactions of the Society*.

The committee find in the *Transactions of the Rhode Island Society for the Encouragement of Domestic Industry* for the year 1858, pages 155 to 167, a 'Sketch of the rise of Straw Braiding for Ladies' Hats and Bonnets,' prepared by the Hon. W. R. Staples, Secretary of the Society.

Although Rhode Island claims to have given birth to the inventor of straw braiding, Norfolk County has given her a residence for nearly sixty years, and enjoys in herself, and exhibits to the world the fruits of her inventive skill to a greater degree than any other section of the country.

The origin of a branch of industry by which so many of our people subsist, ought to be more generally known, and the life or, at least, the name of one who has been such a public benefactor as Mrs. Baker, ought to be commemorated in the annals of this Society.

The committee would therefore recommend the insertion of the article referred to in the proceedings of this Society, and that to Mrs. Baker be awarded the Society's diploma for a '*Fac simile* of the Original American Straw Bonnet,' both being made by herself.   M. M. FISHER, *Chairman*."

From the sketch referred to in the above report it appears, so far as known, that the straw braiding business commenced in very early times in Tuscany, or one of the Italian states. At first bonnets and hats of straw were imported into England ; subsequently the braid was imported, and from England they were imported into this country, but the date is unknown. As early as 1798 Colonel John Whipple had in his store in Providence, R. I., Dunstable straw bonnets which his wife, Mrs. Naomi Whipple, trimmed to suit customers. There were residing in Providence at that date Joel Metcalf and family, recently come from Attleboro, Mass. Mr. Metcalf's daughter, Betsey Metcalf, born March 29, 1786, then a young miss of twelve years, greatly admired these bonnets of Dunstable straw, which she saw exposed for sale in the windows of Colonel Whipple's store.

Little Betsey Metcalf determined to have a Dunstable straw bonnet in some wise, even if she had to make it. She had never seen a piece of straw braid, but put her wits to work and experimented on oat straw that was grown on her father's farm and cut in June of 1798.

After much patient experimenting, splitting the straw with her thumb nail, she at length succeeded with seven straws to make the braid. To whiten it she put brimstone into a tin pan with coals of fire and held the braid in the smoke, which bleached it. Her first bonnet was of seven braids, open work, and lined with pink satin. It was much admired, and to Betsey Metcalf, afterward Mrs. Betsey Baker, the wife of Obed Baker, of West Dedham, Mass., belongs the honor of making the first straw braid and the first straw bonnet manufactured in America. She communicated her art to others and there sprang up this straw industry of the region, which has given to so many remunerative employment and made straw manufacturers rich. Mrs. Betsey Baker is to be remembered also for her devoted piety. It was her habit in receiving callers to have a season of prayer before they departed. In the year 1855, there were made in Norfolk County, 2,367,160 bonnets, and 1,580,000 hats, giving employment to over seven thousand persons. And in the thirty years that have since intervened, this has been one of the most thriving and profitable industries of the state, and has been one of the principal manufactures in Medway.

THE MANUFACTURE OF COTTON.

1807 — 1885.

Machines for the spinning of cotton were invented in England by John Wyatt, and patented in the name of his partner, Lewis Paul, as early as 1738, but Sir Richard Arkwright succeeded in constructing a machine for spinning cotton by means of rollers, which was patented about 1767, and a cotton mill was erected at Nottingham, operated by horse-power. This mode was found to be too expensive, and another mill was erected at Crawford on a larger scale, and operated by water-power. He afterwards invented a variety of machines and improvements for preparing the cotton for spinning, all of which were patented in 1775, and the world is indebted to him above any one else, probably, for the successful introduction of this important industry. He entered into partnership with Jedediah Strutt, of Derby, who established there an extensive manufacture of ribbed stockings, and in connection with Mr. Arkwright erected cotton works at Milford, near Belper. Samuel Slater was apprenticed to Mr. Strutt for six years, from the eighth day of January, 1783, to learn the art of a "cotton spinner." About the first of September, 1789, he took passage from London to New York. After a few weeks' employment in the New York Manufacturing Company, he engaged with Almy & Brown, of Providence, who had commenced the manufacture of various fabrics by hand-power, and had attempted the use of machinery by water which had failed of success.

Slater claimed to have a full knowledge of the business of Messrs. Arkwright and Strutt, and could make the machinery, and operate the works when erected. Though it appears he did not bring, as has been reported, any models or patterns concealed upon his person, he succeeded, from memory, in constructing machinery after the Arkwright patent, under a pledge that if he did not succeed he would have nothing for his services, but throw the whole of his work into the river at Pawtucket, where, in 1790, the first success was attained in America in spinning by water-power, as "*good yarn either for stocking or twist as any that was made in England at that time.*" Here was the beginning of a new and successful industry in the United States. It must be admitted, however, that in Beverly, Mass., a cotton mill was projected and managed by John Cabot and Joshua Fisher in 1787, and received the patronage of the state by a grant of land, but for want of ability and means to obtain the Arkwright patents they were obliged to abandon the enterprise, at a loss of $10,000, more or less.

After the success of Slater at Pawtucket had been established, cotton mills gradually sprang up in New England and elsewhere, until, in 1810, Albert Gallatin endeavored to secure the statistics of this industry, which had been extended into several of the states, and it appears at that time there were in the entire country 168 factories, with 90,000 spindles. Massachusetts had fifty-four, mostly small mills, with 19,488 spindles; Rhode Island had twenty-six factories, with 21,030 spindles; Connecticut fourteen, with 11,883 spindles. In 1813 the first mill in the world which united all the operations of converting the raw material into cotton cloth was erected in Waltham; and the American system of gathering around the mill the homes of the operatives, and providing them with means of intellectual and moral culture, was there established.

THE OLD COTTON MILL. 1811 — 1881.

Messrs. Luther Metcalf and Philo Sanford, who owned the old Whiting Mill on Charles River, associated, May 14, 1805, with Abijah Richardson, M. D., Nathaniel Miller, M. D., Messrs. William Felt, Comfort Walker, and John Blackburn, "for the purpose of carding and spinning, and manufacturing cotton in all its various branches," by a formal agreement. They contracted with one of their associates, John Blackburn, an English mechanic, who had been employed by Samuel Slater, to manage the business. The first mill erected was 60x30 feet, two stories high, and the machinery operated 820 spindles. When looms for weaving were first used in this mill is unknown. Mr. Blackburn's compensation was to be a good tenement house, with a garden, ten cords of wood annually for three years, and $2 per day until the machinery was completed, and $1.50 per day afterward, to superintend its operation.

The associates above named, including Lyman Tiffany, were incorporated by the general court as " The Medway Cotton Manufactory" by a special charter, approved March 4, 1809, and signed by Timothy Bigelow, Speaker of the House, H. G. Otis, President of the Senate, and Levi Lincoln, Governor. A true copy was furnished the corporation, and signed April 3, 1809, by William Tudor, Secretary of the Commonwealth.

On Sunday, October 20, 1811, this mill was destroyed by fire, but was rebuilt, substantially as at first, before the close of the year. It stood for seventy years, and was sold at auction August 17, 1881, for $1.50, to be removed within ten days. Lyman Tiffany was agent and treasurer of the corporation until 1819, when Oliver Dean, M. D., was elected, and served until 1826, when he was succeeded by Luther Metcalf, Jr., who held the position until the corporation was dissolved in 1864.

Before the organization was dissolved the real estate and machinery were sold to Messrs. J. P., J. G., and F. B Ray, of Franklin, who, after a brief ownership, and without operating the mill, sold the property to Mr. William A. Jenckes, of Woonsocket. Messrs. Jenckes and Joel A. Crooks operated the mill for the manufacture of flox, under the name of the Medway Flox Company, and August 10, 1881, the mill property, including one dwelling-house, was conveyed by deed of William A. Jenckes to the Sanford Mills Corporation for the sum of $15,000.

The early and complete success of the old corporation, and the manufacture of cotton machinery on the same premises, and afterward at West Medway, begun by Luther Metcalf, Jr., Joel Hunt, and Cephas Thayer, gave much importance to the town, and attracted young men desirous of engaging in manufacturing pursuits. In 1837 there were six cotton mills in operation along the river Charles, within the limits of the town.

Among those living in or attracted to Medway by these industries, and who laid here the foundations of their success and fortunes, achieved elsewhere, were John Blackburn, Lyman Tiffany, Oliver Dean, M. D., Royal Southwick, Peter Lamson, Duncan Wright, and his three sons, viz., Alexander Wright, Peter Wright, and John Wright, the Fisk brothers, Ephraim Stevens, Jacob Stevens, John Bestwick, Elias Whiting, Sanford Whiting, Gilbert Clark, John Smith, Mayo Pond, James W. Clark, and others. Here, in their infancy, carpet weaving by water-power, coach lace, bobinet lace, and cotton bleaching, were nursed until other fields invited them. Here cotton machinery was made for the first mills at Waltham, and for other places now recognized as manufacturing towns. Men graduated from these mills and shops in Medway to lay the foundations of Lowell and Manchester, and other large manufacturing cities.

The site of the old cotton factory, where Nathaniel Whiting built his saw and grist mill in the early days, is now occupied by a substantial brick factory for making woolen goods, known as THE SANFORD MILLS.

"THE COTTON MILL MORALIZED." This was a poem written by Walton Felch, of Medway, and published by Samuel Allen, in 1816. This poem was a literary curiosity. To it were appended a series of notes. The poetical effusion of the said Felch has been characterized as a "crude production," but the notes have been considered somewhat valuable as giving an idea of a cotton mill in Massachusetts in 1816, and as showing what mechanical devices were in use at that early date. These notes were published in an August number of the *Boston Journal of Commerce*, of 1885, to which persons interested are referred.

Among those who were identified with the early manufacturing in Medway were Mayo Pond, who subsequently was the able manager of the Schuylerville Mills near Saratoga, N. Y.; Royal Southwick, who was one of the earliest manufacturers in Lowell, accumulated large wealth, and was State senator from Middlesex County; the Fisk brothers, who, from the manufacturing of machinery on Chicken Brook, went to Dover, N. H., and established the Cocheco Mills; John Bestwick and his wife, who built and operated the first lace loom in America, and afterward removed to Andover; John Smith, who with his brother, Peter Smith, afterward carried on cotton manufacture in Andover, and who erected Brechen Hall Library, and gave so largely to Andover Theological Seminary; Oliver Dean, M. D., who was, in the early history of Manchester, N. H., the superintendent of the Amoskeag Manufacturing Company, and whose wealth founded Dean Academy in his native town, Franklin, Mass.; James W. Clark, of Framingham, for many years the senior member of a large wholesale manufacturing house in Boston.

The Lowell Carpet Manufacturing Company, known all over the world, was born on Chicken Brook, near the old Cutler place. THE OLD CARPET MILL, where the first woolen carpet was woven in New England, was torn down in 1860, by Timothy Partridge.

Almost the latest use this old mill was put to appears in the following incident: "In the winter of 1858, during a revival of religion, four or five young men were on their way home from meeting; some of them were deeply impressed, and it was suggested, as they passed by, that they go into the old mill for a season of prayer, which they did, and the result was the hopeful conversion of the whole number."

THE HOLBROOK BELL FOUNDRY.

1816 — 1880.

The business of manufacturing bells and church or town clocks, which, in former years gave employment to so many people, and contributed so much to the prosperity of the place, and which carried the name of the town to almost every habitable portion of the country, was established in 1816, by Major George Holbrook, who removed from Brookfield, Mass., where he first began the business in 1797. The reason of his removal from Brookfield was financial troubles caused by indorsing notes to a large amount for a supposed friend. Major Holbrook being obliged to meet these payments, was financially ruined. His successful business, and the beautiful home, famous among those of Worcester County for its elegance and generous hospitality, passed into the hands of strangers. Broken in health and spirits he returned to his native town, Wrentham, Mass. While residing there he was informed that a bell was wanted for the new meeting-house in East Medway, and he secured the contract to cast it. This bell was the first cast, and the first which ever hung in a church steeple in the town. It was cast in a shanty standing on the site of the present residence of E. L. Holbrook, Esq.

Through the assistance of many friends the shanty was built out of refuse lumber, and the melting furnace was built out of the condemned bricks of a neighbor's brick kiln. Major Holbrook did the greater part of the work himself. The bell was cast in the presence of almost the whole population of the vicinity, in fact, so great was the number of people, and so eager were all to see such an unusual sight, that the sides of the building were taken down and the space for the workmen roped around, in order that the people might see, and the bell makers might have room to work. This first venture of the bell business was successful. A finely cast, clear-toned bell, weighing 1,208 pounds was cast. This bell for many years called the good people of the parish together for the worship of God, and to all other public gatherings. The coming of Major Holbrook into the town had been opposed by very many good and well-to-do people, who objected to his becoming a citizen, for fear that he would become a pauper and a charge upon the town; but immediately upon his successful production of a bell which pleased them, and of which they were very proud, offers of assistance poured in from every side, and a large and successful business was established, one foundry after another being built, each larger and more complete than its predecessor. It is an interesting fact that Major Holbrook in early life had been an apprentice in the bell foundry and clock-making business to Paul Revere, of Revolutionary fame, for whom he entertained a warm friendship until his death.

The Holbrook bell foundry was in reality, though not legally, the successor of the famous Revere bell foundry, as during the years 1816–1820 it was the only establishment of the kind in America. The business was successfully carried on by four successive generations of the same family, until the year 1880, when the proprietor accepted a position offered to him in the Pension Office Department, Washington, D. C., and sold the valuable patterns and franchise to parties in San Francisco, Cal., who had long been endeavoring to secure the same. During the period of its existence, over eleven thousand bells were cast at this establishment and sent to all parts of the United States, British Provinces, Mexico, and the Sandwich Islands. As to the reputation of the Holbrook bells, they were everywhere celebrated. They were exhibited at the industrial exhibitions throughout the country, and came in competition with the bells of others, and always received the highest awards; and never, in a single instance, receiving any but the highest award. Among other awards was the grand gold medal from the Massachusetts Charitable Mechanics Association, of Boston, for general superiority and pure musical tone, and this on occasion when the proprietor of the principal rival in the business was President of the Association, and had many bells on exhibition at the same time. On another occasion the grand gold medal of honor of the American Institute, of New York, was awarded to the Holbrook foundry for undoubted superiority and general excellence, as compared with the productions of others, and for the pure and musical tones and extraordinary vibrations of their bells. In fact the very flattering testimonial from this association, which accompanied the medal, denominated the production of the Holbrook foundry as the standard bells of America, a declaration which the proprietors point to with no little pride, holding it, in their estimation higher than patents of nobility or of lordly birth. These complimentary testimonials were from leading musical men and mechanics of the country, among whom were Dr. Lowell Mason, Mr. George J. Webb, and Jonas Chickering, Esq., the famous piano manufacturer of Boston.

Major George Holbrook, who established the foundry, was a man who had great ingenuity, and could work his way out of any mechanical predicament, and could successfully plan and lay out the work for others, though he possessed no great faculty of doing the work himself. It is to his son, Colonel George H. Holbrook, who became an eminent musician, that is due the credit of improving the tone of the bells and changing them from noisy machines to musical instruments. This justly celebrated musician succeeded his father in the business, which he prosecuted until 1872. He was justly regarded as the foremost bell maker in America.

The business was for several years in charge of E. L. Holbrook, Esq., the son of Colonel Holbrook, until he entered the business of manufacturing church organs, which was more agreeable to him, and for which his superior musical education preëminently fitted him. Mr. E. H. Holbrook, a grandson of Colonel Holbrook, in 1868, became associated with his grandfather in the business, and in 1872 succeeded to the full ownership and control of the same, until it was relinquished in 1880. Very few business houses which were in existence in 1816, and which have been constantly carried on by the members of the same family, can now be found in the town or vicinity. Indeed very few people are now living in the town, who remember the establishment of this business in the place. Few families have ever associated in a business so long continued, so honorably conducted, and on which they can look back with so much to be proud of, and so little to regret, as the proprietors of the Holbrook Bell Foundry.

THE BOOT AND SHOE MANUFACTURE.

1828 — 1885.

The manufacture of boots was commenced in Medway by Mr. Willard Daniels at his home near Braggville, about the year 1828, giving employment to a few men. In 1832 he removed to West Medway, where, by his energy and industry, he established a large and successful business which has since become one of the leading industries, requiring more capital and employing more hands than any other in the town.

Mr. Daniels was succeeded by his son, Mr. Leander S. Daniels, who, with enlarged accommodations and improved machinery, is doing a very extensive and successful business.

Deacon John S. Smith moved from Holliston to Medway, and settled near the Baptist church in 1832, and began the manufacture of brogan shoes and boots, which he carried on successfully till about 1870, when he retired and was succeeded by his son, Mr. Abner M. Smith, who has made large additions to his factory and introduced improved machinery, giving employment to about one hundred and twenty-five men, and producing about nine thousand cases of goods annually.

Other manufacturers have carried on business here, prominent among whom were Mr. Joseph Bullard, who manufactured brogan shoes for the Southern trade as early as 1834, and was succeeded by his son, Mr. J. N. Bullard, who has continued the manufacture of boots and shoes to the present time. Among other prominent manufacturers in West Medway may be mentioned Messrs. Benjamin Ward, Elihu Partridge, George L. Pond, William H. Temple, Luther Daniels, Bullard & Brewer, C. F. Parker & Co., Fogg, Houghton & Coolidge, and David A. Partridge, Esq.

About the year 1835 Mr. Milton H. Sanford began the manufacture of russet brogans in the village, in connection with the store business, formerly conducted by his father, in the building which is now converted into the fine residence occupied by E. A. Daniels, M. D.

Soon afterward, Captain Clark Partridge joined him as an employé, and finally succeeded him in the store and brogan business, adding the manufacture of ladies' and children's shoes. The shop built by Mr. Sanford for the business was afterward, in 1841, occupied by Mr. M. M. Fisher, for the manufacture of straw goods, and is now a dwelling-house on Mansion Street, owned by Mrs. Jason E. Wilson.

Captain Partridge next occupied for a shop, one or both of the buildings now standing in the rear of Sanford Hall. In about 1840 he bought the residence and store of Mr. J. B. Wilson, standing where his family now reside, now occupied by Mr. J. W. Thompson, on Broad Street, and manufactured boots, using the barn, now Mr. Melville Fisk's paint shop, and a part of the house for this purpose. His business increasing from year to year, he contracted in 1847, with Mr. Elisha Cutler for a lease of a shop to be built, which now stands at the head of Pine Street.

Soon after, Mr. C. B. Whitney, a native of Milford, connected with the large boot and shoe house of Blacklock & Wheelwright, of Baltimore, removed to Medway, and was admitted as a partner in the business. They continued here together several years, and about 1854–'55, sold out to Mr. A. S. Harding. The firm of Partridge & Whitney opened a boot, shoe, and leather store in Boston, selling the goods made by Mr. Harding, until 1857, when Mr. Whitney repurchased the business of Mr. Harding, who entered into the straw goods business with M. M. Fisher, Esq. Mr. Whitney occupied the Cutler shop during the war and had profitable army contracts.

Captain Partridge, on giving up the Boston store, and the partnership with Mr. Whitney, bought the old Cheever straw shop, called the " Convent," standing near Noyes' new block on Broad Street, which was destroyed by fire in 1870. In 1863 he admitted to partnership, Mr. J. W. Thompson, under the firm name of C. Partridge & Company. After the fire of 1870 the firm resumed business in the Cutler shop which had been vacated by Mr. Whitney, who had erected a new shop, corner of North and Broad streets, where he first introduced steam-power to operate boot machinery.

The firm of C. Partridge & Company was dissolved in 1873, and Mr.

J. W. Thompson continued the business at the Cutler shop until 1875, when he removed to his present factory on Village Street, which had been built two years before for Messrs. Parsons & Seavey, by Eaton & Wilson. Messrs. Partridge, Whitney, and Thompson were all skillful and successful in their chosen life work as boot manufacturers. Mr. Whitney relinquished his business to his eldest son, Mr. C. S. Le B. Whitney, who, in company with Loring & Reynolds, of Boston, operated the Broad Street shop till that was consumed by fire in 1875, and it has never been rebuilt. Messrs. Mc-Ginnis & Tracy, in 1881, started a boot business in the old Barber mill building, which was continued till a fire in 1883 compelled a surrender.

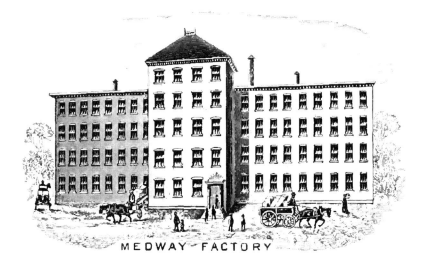

MEDWAY FACTORY

MESSRS. SEAVEY BROTHERS, PROPRIETORS AND MANUFACTURERS.

Messrs. Seavey Brothers in 1881 began work on boots for a Boston party, in the Cutler shop, and after a year's operation, the failure of the Boston house closed the shop for a year. They started again in the manufacture of fine goods, chiefly shoes, for Messrs. Field, Thayer & Company, of Boston, which proved so satisfactory as to justify the demand for greatly enlarged facilities, and in 1885, by the aid of Messrs. Field, Thayer & Company, and other citizens of Medway and Milford, they now possess the largest boot shop in this part of the country, sufficient to accommodate three hundred em-ployés.

THE MANUFACTURE OF CHURCH ORGANS AND ORGAN PIPES.

1837 — 1885.

THE HOLBROOK MANUFACTORY OF CHURCH ORGANS was established in 1837 by George H. Holbrook, Esq., and is at the present time the oldest establishment, with one exception, in that line in the United States. The first organ was built by Mr. Holbrook for his own use and as an experiment, not having had any experience in the business, or any practical knowledge of organs, as he had never seen many instruments of that kind. The proprietor manufactured his tools, patterns, made his own pipes, both of metal and wood, voiced and tuned the same, and succeeded in producing what in those days, passed for a fine organ. From that very humble beginning the business has increased until, at the present time, a large and complete factory stands where the little building stood, and organs of all sizes are manufactured, of fine musical quality and of beautiful design.

Mr. J. Holbrook Ware became associated with Mr. Holbrook, and the business was for many years carried on under the firm name of Holbrook & Ware. Mr. Ware was a skillful worker of wood, having learned the cabinet trade, and served several years in the celebrated Goodrich Organ Factory.

Mr. William G. Ware, under the direction of his father, became a thorough master of making the metal pipes, and after carrying on the business for many years disposed of the same to his brothers, Messrs. A. L. and M. A. Ware, who had become expert in the same manufacture. In 1850 the firm of Holbrook & Ware was dissolved by Mr. Ware's retiring. Mr. Holbrook disposed of the business to his son, E. L. Holbrook, Esq., then a teacher of music, residing in Bridgeport, Conn. This gentleman, who has since conducted the business, was particularly fitted for the same, on account of his superior musical education, his great mechanical skill and ingenuity, his knowledge of architecture and draughting, and his well-earned reputation, acquired at an early age, of being one of the foremost organists of New England. To accept this business, which he desired to make his life work, he left a position in a city near New York, where he had established himself as a teacher of music, and was rapidly acquiring fame and fortune. Contrary to the advice of his many friends, he abandoned one of the most promising positions ever occupied by a young musician, and returned to the old home, that he might live among his kindred and neighbors, and succeed his father in the business which he loved, and for which he was so well fitted. During his management of the business he built and sent to all parts of the country and Canada, many large and fine organs; and his organs are widely celebrated for the beautiful voicing, or pure and even tones. They have received very many severe trials, and highly complimentary testimonials from the leading organists of the country, among others Messrs. Whiting, Zrindell, Loretzy, Warren and Morgan.

THE HUNT MILLS AND PAPER MANUFACTURE.

1800 — 1885.

The privilege on Charles River, known as Hunt's Mills, was improved about 1800 by the erection of a saw and grist mill. Subsequently a factory was erected for the manufacture of cotton goods, and also for the building of machinery, which was carried on by Messrs. Thayer and Stevens. The premises were occupied by various parties till about 1850, when the factory was destroyed by fire. The property soon passed into the hands of Messrs. T. and G. Campbell, who erected a paper mill on the premises, which is now leased to Messrs. Morse and Somes for the manufacture of paper, giving employment to fifteen men, and producing about two tons of paper daily.

BARBER'S ACCOUNT OF MEDWAY IN 1837.

Mr. John Warren Barber, in his *Illustrated History of the Towns of Massachusetts*, gives a sketch of Medway which is accompanied with an engraving which he calls an "Eastern View of Factory Village, Medway." It reads as follows:

"This engraving shows the appearance of Medway, a Factory Village, as it is entered from the east upon the old Medfield road. The spire seen on the right is that of the Congregational Church. The building on the left with a small, low spire, is a four-story cotton factory, standing on Charles River. This village consists of thirty-seven dwelling-houses, three stores, three cotton and one woolen factories. The boot and shoe business is carried on to a considerable extent in Medway Village and in West Medway. In East Medway is a bell foundry (owned by Colonel George H. Holbrook), an organ manufactory, and a clock factory. This town is gradually improving in appearance, wealth, and population. There are in the limits of the town four churches: three Congregational, one of which is Unitarian, and one Baptist.

"Distance, twelve miles southwest of Dedham, and twenty southwest of Boston. Population, 2,050.

"In 1837 there were in the limits of the town, six cotton mills, 2,500 spindles; 428,200 yards of cotton goods manufactured, the value of which was $42,120; two woolen mills, three sets of machinery; 76,000 yards of cloth were manufactured, valued at $62,000.

"There were 38,494 pairs of boots, and 100,650 pairs of shoes, manufactured, valued at $149,774; males employed 198; females ninety-eight; there were 32,200 straw bonnets manufactured, valued at $40,000; there was also a manufactory for cotton batting, and another for cotton wadding."

THE CANNING BUSINESS.

1863 — 1885.

Mr. James La Croix was the pioneer in the canning business in this vicinity. He began by putting up a few cases of tomatoes yearly, doing the cooking in an ordinary kettle. From this small beginning the business enlarged, and a few years later he commenced the canning of corn, and afterward the canning of beans, squashes, and apples. Few hands were employed at first, but afterward there were more than a hundred and fifty names on his pay-roll. Recently, however, improved machinery has reduced the number of employés, and increased the amount of goods manufactured. From a business of $250, it has amounted to $40,000 per annum.

The cooking is done by steam boilers, and a one hundred horse-power engine is employed. This industry has greatly aided the farmers in the region, making the income from their cultivated lands much larger. These canned goods are sold by agents throughout the cities of New England, in Philadelphia, Penn., New Orleans, La., Savannah, Ga., Mobile, Ala., Minneapolis, Minn., San Francisco, Cal., Portland, Ore., and other large cities of the United States and Canada. La Croix's canned goods have a favorable reputation. Since the death of James La Croix, Esq., the business has been carried on by his son, Mr. Charles La Croix.

New England Awl and Needle Company.

The manufacture of awls and needles was established in June, 1869, the firm being Fenn, Daniels & Mann.

The New England Awl and Needle Company was incorporated in January, 1871. Its officers are Charles H. Deans, President; C. S. Mann, Treasurer and Superintendent. They employ about twenty-five or thirty men and women. These goods are sold all over the United States and Canada, and are rated as the best in the market. This company was the first to apply machinery to the manufacture of awls; also the first to make sewing awls in this country, and successfully compete with English manufacturers, who were enabled, by their cheap labor, to undersell, which difficulty was overcome by the aid of machinery, so that the English have been driven almost entirely from the American market.

The Batting and Wadding Manufactures.

Messrs. Eaton and Wilson, in 1869, united their interests, and became joint owners in all the water-power and mill property in the Village on Charles River, below the old white mill, comprising three separate mill privileges. It is now difficult to obtain the earliest history of these separate interests. Some accounts of operations just below the old mill dam of the original Whiting grist mill, would furnish material for a modern romance. There is, very evidently, a large mineral deposit in the underlying rocks of this locality. There is great variation of the magnetic needle. Traces of iron and other metals appear in the rocks cropping out, and workmen, employed in excavations for mill purposes, are so much diverted by the shining particles as to impair the value of their work to the employer. In the great silver mania that prevailed more than a century since, this region was examined, a company formed, and excavations were made here, and the crucible employed to test the metal, and, as the story goes, when one of the earliest tests was being made, a bystander dropped a silver coin into the melting mass, and, behold, the result disclosed a bonanza of wealth, and stimulated further search. One excavation, five or six feet square, and ten feet deep, was known as Captain Kidd's Hole, and has been filled by Mr. Wilson. The earliest industry in this locality was the manufacture of axes, scythes, and other products of iron, but was not of long continuance, and little is known of its history. The water of the river was diverted by a dam, which now exists, and a canal was dug, conveying the water for what was known as the Felt & Company's Mill, afterward owned by Mr. William H. Cary, and in part by George Barber, Esq. From this canal a square foot of water was taken to constitute a water-power for the thread mill of Mr. Sewall Sanford, afterward operated by his son, Mr. M. H. Sanford, then by Messrs. James B. Wilson and E. C. Wilson, then Messrs. Eaton and Wilson, and now by Messrs. Ray and Wilson. This mill was operated almost exclusively for the manufacture of thread, until Mr. E. C. Wilson made an addition of sheetings, and after his connection with Edward Eaton, Esq., it was, as now, wholly devoted to the wadding business. At the Felt, or Cary Mill, cotton yarns were first made, then cotton thread, cotton fabrics, and satinets, by Mr. William H. Cary. The mill was destroyed by fire about 1855. Mr. George Barber used a part of the power for his wool carding and cloth dressing business, occupying two buildings, situated on the canal, above the Felt Mill, one of which was destroyed by fire, being a boot shop, the other still stands, being used as a store-house by Messrs. Ray and Wilson.

After the fire this privilege was bought by Mr. J. B. Wilson, who erected the small shoddy picker mill, now owned by Ray & Wilson. The lower privilege was first taken up by a Scotchman, Duncan Wright, who erected a building for bleaching yarns, and between this and the Felt & Company's Mill, Mr. Comfort Walker erected a saw mill, which was, many years after, removed to the lower dam by Messrs. Hurd and Daniels. Messrs. Felt & Company succeeded Duncan Wright, and made yarns in the old bleachery. Messrs. Hurd and Daniels converted the mill into a batting mill, and did a very large and profitable business, but, unfortunately, invested too much in railroad enterprises. Mr. Edward Eaton succeeded them, and, in company with Mr. Alfred Daniels, continued the same industry until the death of Mr. Daniels. In 1869 Mr. E. C. Wilson became joint owner with Eaton in this, and all other mill property below Sanford Mills.

The batting and wadding business has been, and the latter now is, a large industry in this town. It has furnished the largest income of any other in town from freight to the railroad, amounting to some $8,000 per annum.

THE SANFORD MILLS. ERECTED IN 1882.

Efforts to inaugurate some new enterprise and utilize more fully the water power at this place, have been occasionally made, but without success until in the fall of 1880. At that time a letter, signed by the business men of the Village, was addressed and sent to Messrs. M. H. and E. S. Sanford, of New York, as follows :

"MEDWAY, Mass., Nov. 18, 1880.

"M. H. Sanford, Esq., and Col. E. S. Sanford.

"Dear Sirs:— Having had frequent and abounding evidence for many years of your deep and abiding interest in your native village, and acknowledging the same with many thanks, we are the more encouraged to address you in reference to a matter that now seriously affects our material interests and challenges our attention. Destruction by fire has, within a few years, taken from the number of our local industries a large tannery, a straw goods and boot factory, all giving employment to a large number of persons, and support to many families. Such has been the condition of the times that these works have not been rebuilt and some smaller industries have removed to other localities. The application of improved machinery to the business now existing among us has very much reduced the demand for mechanical and other labor. There is no demand for real estate offered for sale, and many tenements are now vacant. Our young men and women and some families are leaving and looking elsewhere for support, and unless soon checked this exodus will continue, to our great detriment.

"Our village, ' beautiful for situation,' and largely through your liberality, attractive and comely in its buildings and grounds, greatly needs business, and must have it or rapidly decline. It would now seem to be a favorable time to utilize the comparatively idle water-power of the river, if practicable, or to establish by steam-power, a new mill or business enterprise of some kind, to give employment to our surplus population and prevent further depletion.

"It is thought a woolen or hosiery mill upon the river, with steam added for dry seasons, with a power equal to eight or ten sets of woolen machinery would add from ten to twenty per cent. to the value of real estate generally, and that, under good management, it would be remunerative to its stockholders. We respectfully suggest whether you might not aid in such an enterprise, either personally or by enlisting others in it, or both, without any sacrifice, but even with pecuniary benefit to yourselves and family friends equally interested with us. Such are our circumstances as to age, pecuniary means, and business relations, that in such a work we can do but little, and without aid nothing can be done.

"Feeling that we cannot be mistaken as to your kindly interest in this community, and relying much upon your practical judgment as to means and methods, we submit this matter to your thoughtful consideration.

"Very respectfully yours,

"W. A. Jenckes, Wm. H. Cary, A. S. Harding, Clark Partridge, J. W. Thompson, M. M. Fisher, Eaton & Wilson, O. A. Mason, John A. Bullard, R. K. Harlow, A. P. Phillips, H. E. Mason, Wm. B. Hodges, Jesse K. Snow, M. E. Thompson, Richardson & Hopkins."

This letter proved to be the initial step. Milton H. Sanford, Esq., soon indicated his readiness to aid in almost any new enterprise in which Messrs. Eaton & Wilson, leading manufacturers, would invest their money and their talent. To utilize such a proposition it became necessary to find a party competent to manage a business that might be both beneficial as an investment, and incidentally promote the growth and prosperity of the whole community. An advertisement in the *Commercial Bulletin* brought a response from Mr. Samuel Hodgson, of Wales, Mass., which resulted in an agreement and a subscription to organize a corporation to be called the Sanford Mills, being so named for Mr. Milton H. Sanford, who subscribed $40,000 of the capital stock of $65,000 required by the agreement. The following is a copy of the agreement and subscription for stock of the Sanford Mills Corporation :

"Be it known that, whereas, it is proposed to organize a corporation under the laws of Massachusetts, to be known as the Sanford Mills, for the purpose of manufacturing cassimeres or other woolen goods, to be located in Medway, Mass., the amount of its capital stock to be $65,000, the number of shares thereof to be 650, and the par value of each share to be $100. Now therefore we, the subscribers, do mutually agree to take and pay for the number of shares of said capital stock hereunto set against our names respectively and immediately after the corporation is duly organized, or as a majority may decide."

William A. Jenckes, 75 shares; Eaton & Wilson, 50; John A. Bullard, 30; M. M. Fisher, 5; J. W. Thompson, 10; M. E. Thompson, 10; Clark Partridge, 10; C. S. Philbrick, 10; Samuel Hodgson, 20; J. P. Plummer, 10; M. H. Sanford, 400; O. A. Mason, 5; F. L. Fisher, 5; Edward Eaton, 5.

The corporation was organized by a meeting of the stockholders at the room of the Medway Savings Bank, July 9, 1881, by the adoption of by-laws and the choice of officers at that and an adjourned meeting, as follows:

President, Milton H. Sanford; Vice-President, Milton M. Fisher; Clerk and Treasurer, Orion A. Mason; Auditor, Fred. L. Fisher; Directors, M. H. Sanford, Edward Eaton, William A. Jenckes, Samuel Hodgson, E. C. Wilson. Mr. Sanford declined serving as president, and Mr. Edward Eaton was elected in his place; and E. C. Wilson was elected a director in place of J. W. Thompson, who declined.

The main building was a structure of brick, four stories above the ground, 106x55 feet, with a tower for stairways 18x18 feet, five stories. Brick ell, two stories, 53x40 feet. Stone ell, two stories, 40x36 feet. The foundation wall was laid of rough stone and cement, three feet in thickness, resting upon the native rock. The mill operated four sets of woolen machinery, and had a basement story for other purposes.

Mr. E. Eugene Adams, of East Medway, was the contractor for the labor of the mason work, the corporation furnishing the brick and the stones. Mr. P. J. Connolly, of Woonsocket, R. I., was the contractor for the other work, both for labor and materials. The mill, when completed, cost, as estimated, $20,000. Mr. Sanford donated $1,000 for improvement of the grounds and architectural ornamentation.

The laying of the corner stone took place September 10, 1881. The following were the deposits in a metallic box, placed in the stone at the northeast corner of the tower of the building, viz.:

An historical memorandum of the first occupation of the premises in 1711 by Nathaniel Whiting for a grist mill, brought down to the present time, and printed in *The Medway Magnet*, and the original manuscript. A crayon sketch of the old cotton mill by O. A. Mason; a distinct photographic view of the old mill and the arched bridge; *Medway Town Report for 1881*, and By-Laws and Circular of Committee appointed to publish the History of Medway; Medway Savings Book; Catalogue of Dean Library Association; Organization of Trustees of Sanford Hall, with account of dedication services, December 31, 1872, with the addresses of Dr. Theodore W. Fisher, the Rev. R. K. Harlow, and others, contained in a copy of the *Franklin Register* of January 10, 1873; the first number of the *Medway Journal*, February 10, 1872, by H. A. Bullard, with notice of the Installation of the Rev. R. K. Harlow; tenth number, of June 29, 1872, with a list of articles under the corner stone of Sanford Hall;

a copy of a newspaper printed for an entertainment April, 14, 1854, at Medway Village, called *Popped Corn;* services at the consecration of Oakland Cemetery, June 20, 1865; manual of the Village Church; anniversary of Village Sabbath School in centennial year, 1876; memoir of the Rev. David Sanford; a discourse, commemorative of Mrs. Edena Holbrook Sanford, by the Rev. R. K. Harlow, with heliotype likeness of Mrs. Sanford; photographs of citizens and their families, with some of the residences of those who have been or are interested in the business of the town; photograph of James A. Garfield, President of the United States, assassinated July 2, 1881, and removed in a critical condition to Long Branch, September 6, 1881; copies of *Medway Magnet, Medway Gazette, Dedham Transcript, Boston Daily Journal,* and *Woonsocket Patriot,* and various business cards.

As this corner stone was prepared and laid and its contents obtained at the expense of the Hon. M. M. Fisher, it was conceded that he may leave them as a legacy to his heirs, if any shall survive the "wreck of matter" in the mill, deeming this investment as remunerative to them in memories and associations of the past, if not financially, as shares in the incorporate stock.

The mill was leased for a term of years to Mr. Samuel Hodgson, one of the corporators, for the manufacture of cassimeres. No pains or expense were spared to render the mills perfect in all their appointments. They went into operation June 1, 1882, about eleven months after the commencement of the building, which was in July, 1881. The goods manufactured are of excellent quality and find a ready market.

MARBLE WORKS.

Mr. Joseph Cutler has invented and manufactured a patent machine for polishing granite, which is regarded as the best machine for that purpose.

Mr. Thomas Henry has a marble and granite factory in West Medway.

MEDWAY BUSINESS DIRECTORY IN 1884.

Auctioneers — F. W. Cummings & Co., Broad, W. M.

Awl and Needle Manufacturers — New England Awl and Needle Co., Awl, W. M.

Blacksmiths — Wm. J. Baker, Franklin, W. M.; John A. Burt, Wellington, W. M.; H. A. Green, Lincoln, W. M.; Timothy Ide, Lincoln, W. M.; E. T. Rogers, Pleasant, R.; G. S. Ryan, River, V.; J. H. Shannon, Exchange, E. M.

Bakers — Medway Bakery, Village, V.

Boot Manufacturers — Bullard & Temple, Main, W. M.; L. S. Daniels, Main, W. M.; McGinnis & Tracy, Main, W. M.; A. M. Smith, Main, W. M.; Seavey Bros., Pine, V.; J. W. Thompson, Village, V.; E. L. Pond & Co., Main, W. M.

Boot and Shoe Repairers — O. A. Clark, Pleasant, R.; I. D. Fuller, Main, E. M.; Frank W. Wiswell, Wellington, W. M.; Peter C. Wiswell, High, W. M.

Boot Heel Manufacturer — A. C. Grant, Village, W. M.

Box Manufacturers — S. G. Clark, Broad, V.; F. H. Metcalf, West, W. M.

Boots, Shoes and Rubbers — Hugh Clinton, and S. J. Lawrence, Village, W. M.

Bonnet Wire and Picture Cord Manufacturer — J. H. Haines. Myrtle, R.

Brick Manufacturers — G. N. Campbell, Village, V.; Dea. E. Clark, Causeway, E. M.; John Clark, Causeway, E. M.

Broom Manufacturers — Bay State Broom Co., Spring, E. M.

Canned Goods Manufacturers — Thomas Henry, Charles, W. M.; J. W. Hodges, and W. B. Hodges, Broad, V.; Charles La Croix, Main, E. M.

Wheelwrights — J. A. Burt, Wellington, W. M.; F. O. Philips, Exchange, E. M.

Carpenters and Builders — Albert M. Adams, Milford, W. M.; J. H. Bickley, Guernsey, W. M.; J. W. Brooks, Franklin, W. M.; Ralph Ferry, Village, W. M.;

A. H. Humes, Norfolk Ave., W. M.; Wm. Matthews, Cottage, W. M.; Capt. J. K. Snow, Barber, V.

Civil Engineer — H. S. Partridge, corner Main and Holliston, V.

Clothing and Gents' Furnishing Goods — S. J. Lawrence, Village, W. M.

Coal and Wood — A. J. Crooks, Sanford, V.; W. C. Mann, Village, W. M.; D. G. Marston, 101 Main, W. M.; M. E. Thompson, Broad, V.

Conveyancers — M. M. & F. L. Fisher, Village, V.

Custom Bootmaker — B. F. Daniels, Main, W. M.

Dentists — S. H. Curtis, Village, W. M.; J. S. Folsom, Exchange, E. M.

Dressmakers — Mrs. S. J. Bullard, Main, W. M.; Mrs. H. Collins, Cottage, W. M.; Mrs. J. J. Cunningham, Lincoln, W. M.; Mrs. S. J. Guild, Winthrop, W. M.; Hattie M. Hafferty, West, W. M.; Miss A. A. Hosmer, Plain, E. M.; Mrs. Alex. McDowell, Main, W. M.; Mary McGinnis, Village, V.; Mrs. Annie C. Pond, Main, W. M.; Mrs. Isabella Sizer, Barber, V.; Lottie D. Stewartson, Oak, W. M.; Mrs. F. White, Sanford, V.; Mrs. F. J. Williams, W. M.; Mrs. L. M. Mason, Curve, E. M.

Dry Goods — F. A. Bradford, Lincoln, W. M.; Hugh Clinton, Village, W. M.; James Coombs, Main, W. M.; S. J. Lawrence, Village, W. M.; Sumner Robbins, Main, W. M.; F. Swarman, Myrtle, R.; Thompson & Co., Village, V.; Varnum Warren, Cottage, W. M.; Geo. B. Fisher, Exchange, E. M.

Druggists — Adams & Co., Village, W. M.; N. G. Benjamin, Main, W. M.; W. W. Clough, Sanford Hall, Village, V.

Expresses — E. B. Fuller's Medway, 70 Main, W. M.; Hunter's Milford, Maple, W. M.; Marston's Boston, 101 Main, W. M.; Morean's Boston, 97 Main, W. M.

Fancy Goods — Hugh Clinton, 50 Village, W. M.; James Coombs, Main, W. M.; S. J. Lawrence, Village, W. M.; Sumner Robbins, Main, W. M.; F. Swarman, Myrtle, R.; Thompson & Co., Village, V.; Varnum Warren, Cottage, W. M.; Mrs. S. Whitney, 67 Main, W. M.; Geo. B. Fisher, Exchange, E. M.

Fish — E. Darling, Village, V.

Florists — C. Thompson Adams, Sunnyside, Main, W. M.; H. F. Cooper, John, V.; H. S. Partridge, Main, W. M.; E. H. Ross, Lovering, W. M.

Fruit and Confectionery — F. B. Hodges, Broad, V.

Furniture — Tuttle & Spencer, Main, E. M.

Granite Polishing, Jig Sawing and Wood Turning — J. H. Cutler, Haven, W. M.

Grocers — M. Brennan, High, W. M.; F. A. Camp, Lincoln, W. M.; James Coombs, Main, W. M.; Geo. B. Fisher, Partridge Hall, E. M.; I. C. Greenwood, Cottage, W. M.; Mason Bros., Village, V.; W. H. Norton, Village, V.; Sumner Robbins, Main, W. M.; R. P. Ross, High, W. M.; Frederick Smith, Main, W. M.; F. Swarman, Myrtle, R.; Thompson & Co., Village, V.; Arthur Waite, Pleasant, R.; E. G. Ware, Main, W. M.; Varnum Warren, Cottage, W. M.

Hairdressers — M. Boteilho, Village, W. M.; W. B. Kent, Main, W. M.; N. P. Noss, Sanford Hall, Village, V.

Harnesses — M. Livingston, corner Franklin and Main, W. M.

Hay, Etc. — Charles Ford, Cottage, W. M.; Sumner Robbins, Main, W. M.

Hotels — Stanley House, A. A. Whitney, Proprietor, Village, W. M.; Quinobequin House, A. O. Grant, Proprietor, Village, V.

Insurance — Hon. Milton M. Fisher, Village V.; F. L. Fisher, Village V.; S. J. Metcalf, Village, V.; T. J. Sanders, Auburn, E. M.

Knitting Machines — Leighton Wilder, Automatic Knitting Machine Company, corner Norfolk Ave. and Guernsey, W. M.

Lawyers — C. H. Deans, Main, W. M.; H. A. Walker, 4 Lincoln, W. M.

Livery Stables — C. W. Hill, Broad, V.; H. G. White, Main, W. M.; A. A. Whitney, Village, W. M.

Lumber — S. G. Clark, Broad, V.; Captain J. K. Snow, Barber, V.

Machinists — E. A. Adams & Co., Milford, W. M.; A. & E. Clark, Pleasant, R.

Mallet Manufacturers — West Medway Mallet Co., Main, W. M.

Marble Workers — H. C. Ross, Wellington, W. M.; J. Smith, 3 Evergreen, W. M.

Mason — E. E. Adams, Main, E. M.

Milk — N. H. Moon, Winthrop, W. M.; George F. Newell, Holliston V.; Varnum Warren, Cottage, W. M.

Millers — N. H. Guild, Winthrop, W. M.; M. H. Collins, Orchard. E. M.

Milliners — Mrs. E. E. Mann, Holliston, V.; Mrs. S. Whitney, 67 Main, W. M.

Music Teachers — Miss M. E. Bickford, Village, E. M.; Miss Emma C. Partridge, corner Village and Franklin, W. M.; Miss S. Etta Stewartson, Oak, W. M.

Newspapers — Medway Gazette, Milford; Medway Magnet, Franklin.

Notary Public — Hon. M. M. Fisher, Village, V.

Organ Manufacturer — E. L. Holbrook, Main, E. M.

Organ Pipe Manufacturers — A. L. & M. A. Ware, Spring, E. M.

Printer — H. A. Bullard, Main, W. M.

Paper Manufacturer — J. T. Greenwood, Village, W. M.

Painters — G. A. Crockett, Winthrop, W. M.; M. Fiske, Broad, V.; H. N. Langevin, Wellington, W. M.; Emory Munyon, Wellington, W. M.; George L. Myer, Island, E. M.; E. White, High, W. M.

Physicians — C. A. Bemis, M. D., Main, W. M.; James A. Gale, Main, W. M.; Miss Kate Sanborn, M. D., Sanford, V.; E. A. Daniels, M. D., Village, V.

Provisions — F. A. Camp, High, W. M.; E. S. Fuller, Main, E. M.; W. W. Gay, corner Main and Franklin, W. M.; William H. Purdy, High, W. M.; C. A. Sparrow, Main, W. M.

Medicines — A. A. Lawrence, Lincoln, W. M.; Luther Thayer, Williams, W. M.

Paper Stock, Etc. — A. E. Johnson, Holliston, V.; John Murphy, Orchard, E. M.

Real Estate Brokers — Erastus Clark, corner High and Village, W. M.; C. F. Daniels, Holliston, V.; F. L. Fisher, Village, V.

Straw Goods Manufacturers — D. D. Curtis & Co., Church, V.

Stoves, Tinware, Etc. — F. Hall, Village, V.; A. L. Ruggles, Lincoln, W. M.

Taxidermist — C. A. Houghton, corner Brigham and Williams, W. M.

Tailors — John Cushing, Main, W. M.; John Connell & Son, Village, V.

Teamster — C. L. Davis, 3 Evergreen, W. M.

Undertaker — Simon Whitney, 67 Main, W. M.

Watchmakers and Jewelers — N. G. Benjamin and A. M. B. Fuller, Main, W. M.

Woolen Goods Manufacturers — Samuel Hodgson, Sanford, V.; Ray & Wilson, Village, V.; Joseph T. Waite, Pleasant, R.

In concluding this brief account of the various industries of the town, it is proper to say that the materials for a complete history of the different industries could not be obtained. Some branches of business may not have received any mention, and others are very incompletely represented. This, however, becomes apparent, that for many years the manufacturing interests have far outgrown those of agriculture. That which in the early history of the town, furnished employment to nearly all, now receives the attention of but a small number of her citizens. The products of the farms are of small value in comparison with the products of manufacture. There is, however, an apparent revival of interest in agriculture within a few years, and more especially in the easterly part of the town, now Millis.

LANSING MILLIS PROPRIETOR

THE RECORD OF MILITARY SERVICE.

THE FRENCH AND INDIAN WARS.

1745 — 1760.

THE English and the French in constant war at home, contested through a period of nearly twenty years for the supremacy in America. The Indians usually took sides with the French. Hence, the English settlers were always in great danger, and in constant fear of their savage foes. The English government called upon her subjects in the colonies to go on various expeditions against the French in the provinces, and required them always to be ready to join in scouting parties against the Indians. They were sometimes called to go long distances, and to be absent from home several days, or perhaps weeks. This they were reluctant to do, so it became necessary to impress them into the service. Each taking his "turn," or part of a "turn," in scouting. The old lists of soldiers impressed into his Majesty's service against the Indians and the French, show opposite each soldier's name the amount of service, reckoned as "a whole turn," or "a half a turn," or "a quarter of a turn." It appears, also. that a "turn" had a money equivalent, *e. g.*, on one occasion we have this record: "Deacon Elisha Adams paid four Pounds Lawful money for Half a Turn." And again, in 1756, there was an "Impress" to Crown Point, and the record states: "After ye Impress, the Revd Mr Bucknam half a turne wanting five pound ould ten"; and then follows a list of twenty or more persons, opposite whose names is written some part of "a turne wanting," a sum of money varying from "two pound ten shillings ould tenor" to "fourteen pound five shillings ould tenor." The exact significance of these terms has apparently very much passed from knowledge, but the best authority consulted explains the word "turn" as meaning a scouting trip, which may have occupied several days. It was expected that each man would do his share of service, or pay a certain equivalent in money. The following statement shows some of the various occasions, and the number of men who were impressed and served:

The Inhabitant Soldiers in the French and Indian Wars.

"Impressed and Done service for his Majesty.

"Impressed by Capt. Whiting June the 17th 1745,"   .   .   .   sixty-five men.
"Impressed by Leat Nathaniel Clark March ye 1st 1754,"   .   .   .   two men.
"Persons that did Have turns to Crown forte,"   .   .   .   .   thirty-six men.
"Under the command of Edward Clark Capt in ye year 1754,"   .   twenty-two men.
"A gaine to Crown point in ye year 1756 Before the Impres,"   .   .   twelve men.
"After ye Impres,"   .   .   .   .   twenty-three men.
"Those men that ded in the Impres Sept ye 4th 1756,"   .   .   .   .   seven men.
"Medway April ye 3d 1758,"   .   .   .   .   forty men.
"May 2 1758,"   .   .   .   .   thirty-two men.
"May 23 1758" and "without date,"   .   .   .   .   .   twenty-two men.
"Y have Done Service under Lord Londen March 22 1759,"   .   twenty-one men.
The pay roll of 1759, ...   fifty-nine men.

"An account of the persons Impressed by Capt Whiting and Done Service for his Majesty June 17. 1745.

Samuel Hayward	Moses Thompson	Joseph Curtis	Henery Bullard
Nathan Adams	George Barber	James Clark	John Anderson
Thomas Metcalf	Amos Clark	Samuel Fisher	John Daniels
Henry Daniels	Samuel Hill, Junr	Eleazer Wight	Thomas Adams
Daniel Richardson	Henry Clark	David Wheten	Caleb Partridge
Joseph Lovel	Jonathan Wheeler	Hezekiah Rockwood	Jonas Fairbank
Nathan Whiting	Jeremiah Daniels, Junr	Seth Allen	John Ellis
Benjamin Rockwood	John Clark	Isaac Harding	Moses Daniels
Timothy Daniels	John Bullard	Malachi Bullard	Jonathan Underwood
Ichabod Haws	David Daniels	Isaac Adams	Samuel Daniels
Samuel Rockwood	Eli Partridge	Nathan Adams	Asa Daniels
Nathaniel Cutler	Eleazer Adams	John Harding	Hop Lovel
William Ellis	Job Harding	Timothy Rockwood	Jacob Parker
Uriah Morse	Joshua Harding	Seth Partridge	James Boydon
Ezekiel Mors	Joseph Harding	Job Plimpton	
Nathan Bullard	David Clarke	Ezra Daniels	
Phineas Adams	Edward Clark	Theophilus Clark	

NATHANIEL WHITTING *Sener.*"

"An account of the Persons Impressed by Leat Nathaniel Clark and Done Service for His Majesty March ye 1st 1754.

Joseph Barber   Malachi Partridge."

"Persons that did Have turns to Crown forte.

Asa Clark	abraham harding	Henery Ellice	John Hucker
Seth Ellice	Jonathan Ellice	Edward Clark	Daniel Bullen
David Clark	Moses Adams	Theop'lus Clark	Malachy Bullard
Nathan Daniels	Moses partridge	Nathaniell Partridge	Samuel Hill
John Bullard	Ebenezer Blake	Joseph Daniels	Deacon Elisha Adams
Timothy Clark	Nathan Danills	Thomas Jons	Jeams Wight
Stephen Adams	William Richardson	oliver Adams	John Boden
Nathaniel Clark, Junr	Hezekiah Rockwood	Jonathan Adams, Junr	Simeon Clark
Timothy forse	Jonathan Hill	Elisha Cutler	Asa Rockwood."

" An account of the persons that have Done Service for yᵉ King in Medway and under the command of Edward Clark Capᵗ in yᵉ year 1754.

Joseph Barber	Ebenezer Blake	Asa Clark	Stephen Adams
malachi partridge	Timothy forse	Nathan Danils	Silas partridge
Edward Clark	David Clark	Moses Adams	Henery Ellice
Theophˡ Clark	Joshuay partridge	Moses partridge	Seth Ellice."
John Bullard	Timothy Clark	Nathaniel Clark	
Abraham Harding	Jonathan Ellice	William Richardson	

" A gaine to Crown point in yᵉ year 1756, Before the Impres.

Oliver Adams	Joseph Danils	Nathaniel partridge	Josiah Rockwood
Jonathan Adams	Sam'll Hill	Elisha Cuttlear	Daniel Bullen
Tomous Jons	Jonathan Hill, junʳ	Nathan Harding	Jabez Bullen."

" After yᵉ Impres.

Revᵈ Mʳ Bucknam	Theodoʳ Harding	Jesse Adams	Ichaburd Harding
Dec. Elisha Adams	Asa Rockwood	Abel Smith	Elisha Ellice
Lef. Temo Clark	Timothy Ellice	Simeon Cuttlear	John Varney
John Hucker	Joseph farbanks	Moses Rockwood	Henery Morse
Simeon Clark	Joshuay Whitney	Daniel Wheeton	Joshua partridge
Timothy partridge	Nathaniel Allen	Jeams Wite	

" This I attest a true account of yᵉ originall, Errors Excepted per me,

EDWARD CLARK, Capt."

" Those men that ded in the Impres Sept yᵉ 4th 1756.

Nathan Richardson	Nathaniel Clark	William Rixford	Elisha Ellice."
Jonathan Adams	Elisha Bullard	Jese Carpenter	

" Medway April yᵉ 3d 1758.

James Clark	Samuel Cutler	george Barber	Abell Smith
Moses Partridge	Samuel Metcalf	Ezekiel Morse	Timothy Hill
Timothy Partridge	Jabez Bullen	Tem. Morse	John Harris
Asa Clark	John Alden	Ira Richardson	Moses Richardson
Nathaniel Clark	Thommas Adams	Wm. Daniels	Ezra Daniel
Simeon Clark	Elezer Adams	Elijah Clark	Jonathan Hill
Joseph Barber, Junⁿ	Samuel Jones	Samuel Ellis	William Williams
Joseph Curtice	John Melles	Joshua Partridge	Seth Ellis
James Penneyman	John Andey	John Carpenter	Nathan Daniel
John Ellis	Joseph Wheton	Daniel Bullen	David Clark, Junʳ."

" May 2, 1758.

Nathan Harding	John Hucker	Elisha Cutler	Jonathan Adams
Daniel Richardson	Stephen Adams	Joshua Wheten	Malachi Bullard
David Richardson	Jese Adams	James Boydon	Timothy Clark
Hozseiah Bullard	Samuel Richardson	Timothy Ellis	Henry Daniels
Samuel Haws	Abner Ellis	Jonathan Wheeler	Ichabod Harding
Lem'y Write	Theodʳ Harding	Henery Bullard	Joseph Rockwood
Silem partridge	Ebenezer Allen	John Clark	Asa Ellis
Jonas farbanks	William Rixford	Nathaniel partridge	Samuel Ellis."

" May the 23 1758.

John Harris	Jonathan Hill	Moses Rockwood	Sambow freeman.

" Without Date.

Erastus Harris	David Clark	John Mills	Moses Rockwood
Joseph follet	Joseph Whitney	Joseph Harris	Moses Thompson
Benjamin Cochs	Jonathan Hill	Jethro Jones	Ebenezer Hill."
Ezekiel Mors	Sambo Freeman	Jese Carpenter	
William Clemens	John Harris	William Williams	

"Medway March 22ᵈ 1759. The men Hereafter named yᵗ have Done Service in the Expedition under Lord Londen.

Nathan Whiting	Asa Richardson	Moses Thompson	Gershom Morse
Nathan Adams	George Fairbanks	Jeremiah Daniell Junʳ	Seth Harding
Willᵐ Grant	Henry Daniell	David Clark	Eleazer Adams
Simon Hill	Moses Richardson	Joseph Lovell	
James Partridge	John Harding Junʳ	Sergᵗ Seth Partridge	
Samuel Ellis	Ichabod Haws	Uriah Morse	
			JONATHAN ADAMS Capt."

" 1759.

Tho. Harding	Moses Rockwood	Henry Morse, Jn.	Samuel Jones
Abraᵐ Harding	Asa Rockwood	Jonathan Hall	Ensine Plimpton
Wᵐ Williams	David Wheaton	William Ellis	Nathan Bullard
Seth Partridge	Timᵒ Bullard	Nathan Adams	Daniel Richardson
Elisha Bullard	Samˡ Hill	Decⁿ Samuel Fisher	Henry Daniell, Junʳ
Elisha Ellis	Simon Hill	Seth Hixon	Theodʳ Harding
Moses Adams	Thoˢ Jones	John Varney	Jonʰ Wheeler
James Barber	Daniel Bullen	Nathan Richardson	Dea. Adams
John Mills	Henry Ellis	Benjamin Ellis	Joseph Baxter
Ichabod Haws	Ebenezer Ellis	Jonathan Hall	Oliver Adams
Nathan Whiting	Nathaniel Partridge	Samˡ Hayward	Nathan Adams
Joseph Perry	Timᵒ Metcalf	Uriah Morse	Jonathan Ellis
James Partridge	William Richardson	Jonah Clark	Lieut. Metcalf
Simon Cutler	Benjamin Whiting	Asa Daniell	Capt Jonᵃ Adams."
William Clemonds	Daniel Wheaton	Seth Rockwood	

THE WAR OF THE REVOLUTION.

1775 — 1783.

The alarm of April 19, 1775, roused to arms the patriots of Medway. Captain Joshua Partridge in command of " The First Military Company" of thirty-seven men, and Lieutenant Moses Adams at the head of " The West Medway Company" of thirty-six men, marched at once to Roxbury, ready for whatever service the hour of exigency and of peril might demand. And from that time onward, through all the years of a long and terrible struggle for national independence, the town of Medway bravely fulfilled its duty at home, in the camp, and on the field of battle. This is abundantly evidenced in the lists of her soldiers, and other documents and papers which have been preserved, some of which will be incorporated in this account as a memorial to the noble men whose names appear, and as a matter of family interest and pride to their descendants still living in the town. The patriotic spirit, which declared itself in the doings of the town-meeting long before the battle of Lexington, gave itself expression when the time came, in heroic service in the march and on the field of conflict. The military record of Medway in the Revolutionary period, as well as in the years of the War for the Union, may be a just occasion for congratulation to her citizens.

It has been judged best to introduce quite freely the original papers of the period, as reflecting better than any words of comment the noble part which the town took in the public and military affairs of those days which tried men's souls.

THE REVOLUTIONARY PAPERS.

"A Return of the Services Done by the First Company in the Town of Medway since April yͤ 19, 1775, to December, 1777.

	Men.	
April yͤ 20th 1775	37	That Marchᵈ in the Alarm and staid at Roxbury 7 Days.
April yͤ 27th 1775	19	That Marchᵈ and staid at Roxbury and Cambridge 8 Months.
Decᵐ yͤ 10th 1775	7	That Marchᵈ and servᵈ at Roxbury, 6 Weeks.
Janᵞ yͤ 1st 1776 .	19	That Marchᵈ and servᵈ in the Continental Service 12 Months.
Janᵞ yͤ 29 1776 .	13	That Marchᵈ and servᵈ at Roxbury and Dorchester 2 Months.
June yͤ 25 1776 .	13	That Marchᵈ and servᵈ at Ticondiroga 5 Months.
July yͤ 1st 1776 .	3	That Marchᵈ and servᵈ at Ticondiroga 5 Months.
July yͤ 29th 1776	3	That Marchᵈ and servᵈ at Dorchester Heights 4 Mos.
Augᵗ yͤ 8th 1776	3	That Marchᵈ and servᵈ at Nantasket 3 Months.
Sept yͤ 12th 1776	10	That Marchᵈ and servᵈ at New York 2 Months.
Decᵐ yͤ 1776 .	6	That Marchᵈ and servᵈ in the Jarseys 3 Months.
Decᵐ yͤ 8th 1776	33	That Marchᵈ and servᵈ in the Alarm at Provide 3 Weeks.
Decᵐ yͤ 29 1776	7	That were Draughted and servᵈ at Warwick 3 Weeks.
Janᵞ yͤ 1st 1777 .	16	That Marchᵈ into the Continental service for 3 years.
April yͤ 15th 1777	10	That Marchᵈ and servᵈ at North Kingstown 3 Weeks.
April yͤ 26 1777	3	That Marchᵈ and servᵈ at Providence 2 Months.
July yͤ 15 1777 .	1	That Marchᵈ to Boston for a store Guard 6 Months.
July yͤ 17 1777 .	7	That Marchᵈ to Brister and servᵈ There 1 Month.
July yͤ 22 1777 .	18	That Marchᵈ for the Alarm Post from Providence 2 Days.
Sept yͤ 24 1777 .	30	That Marchᵈ to Little Compton Private Expedition 1 Mo.
Novᵐ yͤ 2, 1777	3	That Marchᵈ to Cambridge for a Guard, Brit. Troops 5 Mos
Decᵐ yͤ 6 1777 .	2	That Marchᵈ to Boston for a Guard 3 Months.
Dec yͤ 15 1777 .	1	That Marchᵈ for a Store Guard 6 Months.
Decᵐ yͤ 27 1777	6	That Marchᵈ to North Kingston 3 Months."

" A Muster Roll of the first Military Company in Medway that marched in the Alarm April 19th 1775 under command of Capt. Joshua Partridge in Col. John Smithˢ Regiment.

Joshua Partridge Capt.	Henry Bullard Jr.	Private	David Hager	Private
Jeduthan Bullen 1st Lieut.	Simon Hill	"	Jonathan Adams	"
Stephen Clark 2ᵈ Lieut.	John Gould	"	Seth Mason	"
Theodore Clark Sergᵗ·	Denny Sheffield	"	Ozias Metcalf	"
John Wheeler Sergᵗ·	George Alerson	"	Isaiah Daniels	"
Hezekiah Bullard Corpˡ	George Fairbank Jr.	"	George Barber	"
Abijiah Fairbank Corpˡ	Asa Daniels Jr.	"	Ebenezʳ Ellis	"
Moses Pond Drummer	Samuel Demon	"	Moses Richardson	"
John Ellis Private	Daniel Richardson Jr.	"	John Whiting	"
Joseph Daniels "	Joel Morse	"	Ebenezer Nolton	"
Henry Daniels Jr. "	John Baker	"	Daniel Marrow	"
Nathan Fisher Jr. "	Jesse Richardson	"		
John Ellis Jr. "	Eliphalet Pierce	"		

" A Muster Roll of the West Medway Company that marched at the Lexington Alarm April 19th 1775 under the command of Lieut. Moses Adams under Majʳ I. Fuller in Col. John Smithˢ Regiment.

Moses Adams 1st Lieut.	Abner Adams	Private	Titus Adams	Private
Asa Clark 2ᵈ Lieut.	Benjⁿ Clark	"	Moses Thomson	"
Erastus Harris Seargent	John W. Fisher	"	Timothy Ellis	"
Isaac Bullard Seargent	John Harding 2ᵈ	"	John Allen	"
Job Manston Corpˡ	Eliab Adams	"	Amos Richardson	"
Isaac Kilbee Corpˡ	Joel Adams	"	Ichabod Harding	"
Nathan Partridge Private	James Barber	"	Thᵒ Adams	"
Seth Hixon "	Joseph Barber	"	Asa Fuller	"
Samuel Fisher "	Sam. Hayward	"	Samuel Partridge	"

John Kilburn	Private	Jotham Fairbank	Private	Moses Rockwood	Private
Jno Littlefield	"	Nathan Grout	"	Henry Morse	"
Seth Allen	"	Icabod Hawes Jr.	"	Nathan Smith	"

" A Muster Roll of the First Military Company in Medway that marched on the alarm of the 30th of April 1775 under the command of Capt. Hezekiah Bullard in Col. John Smiths Regiment.

Hezekiah Bullard Capt	Joseph Clark	Private	Joel Morse,	Private
Nathan Bullard 1st Lieut.	Joseph Daniels Jr.	"	Hezekiah Comacho	"
James Boyden Sergent	Josiah Bullard	"	John Richardson	"
Seth Mason Sergent	Daniel Richardson Jr.	"	Henry Ellis	"
Simeon Richardson Corpl	Levi Daniels	"	Albert Jones	"
Ozias Metcalf Corpl	Elisha Richardson	"	Simson Jones	"
Amos Turner Fifer	Elias Harding	"		

" The Muster Roll of Capt. John Boyds Co. of Foot in Continental Army At Fort No. 2, Oct. 5, 1775.

John Ellis	John Plympton	Ichabod Hawes	Joel Hawes
Jacob Bliss	Jeremiah Daniels	Theodore Mann	Timothy Lane
Obed Fisher	Saml Jones	Oliver Richardson	Samuel Partridge
John Hill	Francis Clark	Josiah Morse	Nathan Thayer."
Paul Holbrook	Porter Frost	Jotham Fairbanks	
Joseph Metcalf	Stephen Harding	Jonathan Graves	

" Upon Colony Service, Warrant of Col Wheelock.

" SIR :

The Committee of War the 17th Instant advised that Major General Lincoln order the Several Brigades of Suffolk, Essex, Middlesex & Plymouth, to hold themselves in readiness to march at the Shortest notice. And The Brigadier gave orders to me —

And agreeable hereto I direct that you immediately put your Company into such a state as to march upon sarvice at the shortest notice & I beg that there may be no delay in this business as the Enemy are daily expected upon our coast with a large Fleet & army. And also require you forthwith to make a return to me of the number of men in your company. And also of the quantity of Powder and Ammunition & of the Number of Arms & how they are equiped in each man's possession. And that each fourth man in your Company be immediately supplied according to Law. Given under my hand and seal at Medfield, this 24th Day of May, In the Year of our Lord 1776.

EPHRAIM WHEELOCK *Col.*

To Capt JOSEPH LOVEL."

THE WARRANT OF 1776.

" Suffolk ss.

Sir, you are hereby Required in connection with Capt Fuller, Forthwith, without Delay to Cause the Men of Medway Under Your Command, Both the Alarm and Training Band, to assemble and muster— And see that there Be Inlisted 26 men for the Continental Army Agreeable to a Resolve of the Grate and General Court of June 25th 1776.

And when these are Inlisted I will attend and muster and pay them their Bounty and Advance Pay Agreeable to the affore sd Resolve   Hereof fail Not.

Medfield June 29th 1776.

DANL PERRY, *Committee.*

To Capt JOSEPH LOVELL of Medway."

The Enlistment of 1776.

"Medway July 9 1776.

"We, the Subscribers being Sensible of the Necessity of Reinforcing the Continental Army at Canady Do hereby Promis to inlist Ourselves in the sd Reinforcment, Provided that we may have Justice & Impartiality executed in the appointment of the Commanding Officers of the Company to which this Town's Proportion of men are incorporated, And whereas Col Wheelock of medfield is appointed Chief Colonel of a Regiment for sd Reinforcment & as this Town Medfield & 2 other Towns are to be joined to make one Company in sd Regiment, we Apprehend that this Town may justly claim the first commission in sd Company And whereas we having heard much of ye Good Conduct of Mr Benju Bass, in the place & Rank of Lieut of a Company at Canady in the former war, Are desirous that he may Take the Command of the Company to which we may be joined.

Andrew Nelson	Theor Clark	Abijah Fairbank	John Gould
Simon Turner	Oliver Richardson	Ichabod Seaver	Francis Clark."

A Marching Warrant.

"To Capt Jos Lovil att midway

Sir, upon Receiving an express from Governor Cook of providence that the enemy had made an entrie in to these colonys therefore on sight of this you are required to start all the men under your command and march them to the Widow Whipple in Cumberland by six o'clock this after noon : given under my hand and seale this eighth Day of December 1776.

James Metcalf *Major.*

p. s. they are to bring their arms aminition & provision."

"The Pay Roll *of the Co. in Col. Wheelock's Regiment which marched from Medway to Warwick, R. I., On the Alarm Dec. 8 1776. Under command of Josiah Fuller.*

Josiah Fuller, Capt.	James Morse	}		Job Plympton,	}
Daniel Ide, 1st Lieut.	Eli Pond	} Sergts		Joel Partridge,	} Corprls
Henry Morse, 2d "	Amos Richardson	}		Obed Fisher,	}

Privates.

Jowell Hawes	Jeremiah Curtis	Moses Rockwood	Simon Cutler
Moses Adams	Seth Dixon	Silas Fairbanks	Eli Hawes
Eleakim Adams	Josiah Ide	Ichabod Harding	Elisha Cutler
Thomas Adams	Isaac Kibbe	James Barber	Asa Fuller
Philimon Adams	Jeremiah Littlefield	James Clark	James Perry
Elijah Allen	David Sanford	Nathaniel Partridge	Peter Wight
John Albee	John Whitney	Elijah Bullard	Moses Partridge
Joseph Barber	Jonathan Holbrook	Samuel Fisher Junr	Timothy Thompson.

Medway April 9 1777."

"Marching Orders, Decm ye 26 1776.

To Joshua Partridge, one of the Selectmen of Medway.

I have Recd orders from Capt Fairbanks to march with all the Men Draughted in medway and to be at David mans Inholder in wrentham on Monday the 30th Day of this Instant at Nine o'clock in the morning. There is a Carrage Provided to Carry the Soldiers' Packs to David Man's and is to be at your house to-morrow at 12 o'clock at noon and you are hereby Desired to Notifie the men Draughted in the East Company in Medway to appear at your house at the time above mentioned.

Medway December ye 28 1776.   Moses Thompson Lieut."

"*An Abstract of Wages & Travelling Fees Due to the Third Company of the Forth Regement of Militia in a Larram under the command James Metcalf Majr From the State of the Massachusetts Bay Commanded By Joseph Lovell Capn Warwick January ye 1st 1777.*"

The period of service from "Decem. ye 8, 1776 to Decm ye 29, 1776." The term of service rendered, from three to twenty-three days. The distanced traveled, from twenty-eight to thirty-nine miles. The number of officers, fourteen; privates, thirty-eight; total, fifty-two. The captain's wages and fees for the expedition, £5, 18s., 6d. Private's pay per day, 4s., 2d. The traveling fees £28, 16s., 10d. The wages £63, 10s. 5d. Total, £92, 7s., 3d.

OFFICERS.

Joseph Lovell, Capt.	Simon Hill Sergt.	Jeremiah Daniell Corpl
John Ellis 1st Lieut.	Samuel Bullen "	Stephen Harding "
Oliver Adams 2 Lieut.	Joshua Partridge "	Peter Frost, Drumr.
Asa Ellis Clerk	Simeon Richardson Corpl	Amos Turner, Fifer.
John Wheeler Sergt.	Abner Ellis "	

PRIVATES.

Jonathan Adams	Levi Daniell	Abraham Harding, Junr	Ozias Metcalf
Jeduthan Bullen	Joseph Daniell	Elias Harding	Benjamin Parnel
Amos Broad	Lemuel Daniell	Samuel Hill	Seth Partridge
Henry Bullard	Jesse Daniell	Moses Hill	Elisha Richardson
Eli Bullard	Samuel Deman	Thomas Jones	Ezra Richardson
Francis Clark	Ebenezer Ellis	Samuel Jones	Jabez Shumway
Elijah Clark	John Ellis	Abel Jones	Joshua Whitney
Stephen Clark	John Ellis, Junr	Ebenezer Knowlton	James Boyden."
Isaiah Daniell	Abel Ellis	Nathaniel Lovell	
Henry Daniell	Abraham Harding	Josiah Morse	

" MEDWAY, April ye 19th 1777.

We, the Subscribers Have Recd of Capt Joseph Lovell of Medway in Full of Our Wages Travelling Fees and Back allowances of Provisions and Sarse which was due to us upon the Alarm when in The State of Rhode Island Stationd at Warwick Decm ye 8th 1776.

We say Recd By us In Full as witness our Hands."

This was signed by fifty-one officers and men. The original document, with autographs, is still preserved.

" *An Abstract of Wages & Travelling Fees Due to an Independent Company Draughted from the Fourth Regiment of Melitia from ye State of the Massachusetts Bay, When at Warwick in the State of Rhoad Island Government, December ye 29, 7776 under the command of Capt. Joseph Lovell.*"

The time of service, from twenty to twenty-two days. The distance traveled, from thirty to forty miles. The amount of traveling fees, £18, 15s., 2d.; wages, £105, 0s., 6d.; total, £123, 15s. 8d.

OFFICERS.

Capt Joseph Lovell	Sergt Stephen Kingsbury	Corpl Obed Fisher
1st Lt Aaron Holbrook	Sergt Isaac Heaton	Drumr Charles Dupee
2d Lt Oliver Adams	Corpl Simeon Richardson	Fifer Samuel Brinton.
Sergt David Partridge	Corpl Cornelius Holbrook	
Sergt Jonathan Everet	Corpl Asa Kingsbury	

PRIVATES.

Jonathan Allen	Titus Adams	David McLane	David Harris
Nathan Coolidge	Simeon Partridge	Michael Metcalf	Jesse Day
Asa Clark	David Sanford	William Ray	Jason Richardson
Joseph Morse	Obediah Adams	Elias Craig	Jacob Hart
Nathan Turner	Samuel Wight	Timothy Cheaver	Billing Clap
Samuel Morse	Asa Blake	Cyrus Fisher	Jesse Smith
Jacob Turner	Josiah Lawrence	Obed Ware	Asa Robins
Ebenezer Lyon	Amos Lawrence	Daniel Ware	Jacob Boyden

Elias Harding	Luther Metcalf	James Kingsbury	Ebenezer Ferrington
Samuel Deman	Alexander Bragg	Zebulun Hodges	Calvin Gay
Jabez Shumway	Barzillai Pond	George Straten	Elihu Lawrence
Josiah Morse	Hanun Metcalf	John Hawes	Eliphaz Clap."
Benjamin Clark	Abijah Allen	Henry Holbrook	

The above pay-roll was made out March 26, 1777, and the several sums receipted for by the most of the soldiers as follows:

"MEDWAY, April yᵉ 20 1777.

"We the Subscribers Have Recᵈ of Capᵗ Joseph Lovell of Medway in Full of Our Wages, Travelling Fees & Back allowances of Provisions and Sarse which was Due to us Upon an Abstract Pay made up to us which were Draughted from yᵉ Fourth Regiment of the Militia when at Warwick in the state of Rhode Island Decᵐ yᵉ 29th 1776. We say Recᵈ by us in Full as Witness Our Hands."

To the above, fifty-one autographs were appended.

THANKS FROM COLONEL WATERMAN.

"WARWICK, HEAD QUARTERS Jan. 17, 1777.

Colˡ Waterman Returns his hearty Thanks to Capᵗⁿ Lovell and all the officers and soldiers under his command for their prudence and Civility since they have been in Camp at Warwick, also for their Zeal and activity on so Sudden Emergency to march into this State for the Defense Thereof he hopes they will be further Inspirᵈ with Bravery, Zeal and Perseverance in the Defence of our Country untill by the BLESSING of HEAVEN these united States are wholly Delivered from the unjust Tyranicall & Cruel oppressions of our Enemies.

JOHN WATERMAN Coˡˡ."

"*Pay Roll of Capᵗ Ebenʳ Battles Cᵒ. For travel to and from the State of Rhode Island, With Their Service in Col Joⁿ Titcomb's Regᵗ From May 8 1777 being 2 mos and a day.*

Corpˡ Elias Harden, 52 Miles,	£4- 6-9	Private Phineas Adams, 52 Miles,	£3-18-3
Private Eli Ellis, "	£3-18-8	" John Combey, "	£4- 1-4
" Reuben Adams, "	£3-18-8	" Ichabod Senor, "	£4- 1-4

"*Pay Roll of Capt. John Gay's Company from Medway.*

John Ellis Ensign	Matthew Hopkins
Seth Hixon Fifer	Abner Morse.
Joel Fairbanks	

"*An account of the Continental and State Services Don by the inhabitance and Residence Living within the Limits of the first Militia Company in the Town of Medway Since April yᵉ 19, 1775, to June 1777.*

Elisha Adams Esqr	£19	George Fairbanks	£ 5
Elijah Clark Esqr	5	Enoch Hill	8
Capt Jeremiah Daniels	10	Jonath Wheeler	10
Capt Timothy Hamant	5	David Clark	5
Capt Joseph Daniels	15	Thomas Harding	3
Capt James Penniman	3	Daniel Marrow	2
Lt Abraham Harding	11	Moses Daniels	13
Lt Joshua Gould	28	Asa pt Richardson	13
Lt John Ellis	13	Amos Broad	5
En. Daniel Bullen	8	John Morse	5

Theodor Harding. . . . .£ 4	Peter Frost. . . . .£ 9
Stephen Clark. 21	Amos Turner Junr. 6
Jeduthan Bullen. 13	John Ellis. 5
Thomas Jones. 2	Timothy Clark. 29
Asa Clark. 5	James Boyden. 5
Hezekiah Bullard. 8	Ebenezer Ellis. 7
Henry Ellis. 8	Joshua Bullard. 14-10s
Moses Pond. 8	Simpson Jones. 20
Seth Partridge Junr. 5	Joel Morse. 20
Jonathan Adams Junr. 8-10s	Jonas Brick. 10-15s
Timothy Bullard. 13-6s-10d	Elisha Richardson. 10
Samuel Jones. 8	Joseph Daniell Junr. 13
Samuel Hill Junr. 5	Abel Ellis. 12
Joshua Whitney. 4	Theodore Clark. 19-10s
Benjamin Parniel. 13	Elijah Clark Junr. 11
Henry Daniels Junr. 9-10s	Elias Harding. 6
Isaiah Daniels. 11	Abraham Harding Junr. 10
John Ellis Junr. 11	Abel Jones. 12-10s
Moses Richardson Junr. 11	Eli Bullard. 13
Samuel Bullen. 9	Jotham Fairbanks. 8
Simeon Richardson. 14	Silvanus Morse. 12
Samuel Partridge. 8	Jabez Shumway. 8
Joel Fairbanks. 6	Lemuel Daniell. 7
Henry Bullard Junr. 9-10s	Eli Ellis. 10
Moses Hill. 10	Ezra Richardson. 8
Adam Bullard. 3	Jesse Daniell. 6
Stephen Harding. 11	John Combs. 4
Jeremiah Daniels Junr. 9	Jonathan Bullen. 5
Oliver Richardson. 8	Ichabod Seaver. 5
Simeon Turner. 10	Josiah Morse. 4
Francis Clark. 9	Thomas Harding Junr. 5
Daniel Richardson Junr. 10	Levi Daniell. 8-10s
Nathan Hall. 10	Nathaniel Lovell. 12-10s
Samuel Demon. 10	Ozias Metcalf. 7-10s
Jedediah Philips. 20	Jotham Graves. 20
John Hill. 28	Paul Holbrook. 14
David Hoges. 20	Nathan Thayer. 28
Lt John Harding. 10	Joseph Clark. 20
Capt Samuel Harding. 10	Dening Sheffield. 28
Capt Jonathan Adams. 10	Hezekiah Commocbe. 20
Mr Daniel Adams. 10	Seth Maison. 20
Mr John Bullard. 5	Jonathan Ellis. 20
Mr David Daniels. 5	John Barber. 20
Moses Richardson. 10	Ashbel Bullen. 20
Nath'l Clark. 5	Jesse Richardson. 10
Joshua Partridge. 10	John Gould. 1-10s
Samuel Hill. 3	Andrew Nelson. 2
Samuel Cleaveland. 8	Nathan Fisher. 7-10s
Jesse Carpenter. 3	Jonathan Ralph. 5
Capt. Joseph Lovell. 17-15s	Robord Long. 5
Lt Oliver Adams. 12	Henry Bullard. 5
Asa Ellis. 9	John Anderson. 1
John Wheeler. 13-10s	William Stinner. 2
George Barber. 11	Uriah Morse. 2-10s
Simon Hill. 5-10s	Timothy Metcalf. 4
Joshua Partridge Junr. 10	Rev. Nathan Bucknam. 5
Abijah Fairbanks. 9	Matthew Hopkins. 3
Abner Ellis. 7	Isaac Harding. 3

" *Warrant for Store Guard, ye 10 of July 1777.*

" To CAPT. LOVELL :

Sir : Agree Able to Lawful Authority you are hereby Required to furnish one man as a Soldier Equipt^d as the Law Directs And to have him appear at the Court house in Boston Tuesday next at 2 o'clock P. M. it being Your Quoto to Compleat a Store Guard which is Now forming for the Term of six months Unless Sooner Discharg^d And to Be under the Direction of Major Gen^{ll} Heath. Pay and Subsistance the Same as the Continental Army.

Given under my hand and Seal att Wrentham this 10th day of July 1777.

To Capt Joseph Lovell.

Att medway.   BENJ^N HAWES, *Col.*"

" *Warrant 22 July 1777 Larram To March the Second Leut with Half the Larrum List and Half ye Militia to Providence.*

" SUFFOLK ss.

To Capt Joseph Lovell, agreeable to express orders from the Honorable Councils you are hereby Directed Immediately on Receipt hereof to Muster & order to March for Providence in the State of Rhond Island by nine o'clock Tomorrormorning your second Lieut. with one half of the Militia under your command both Trainingband & Alarm List will Direct them to the Alarm Post as soon as Possible there to Joyn Capt. Fuller's Company, you are to see your men are Equipped with arms & ammunition as the Law Directs with six days Provisions ; you will also inform your Selectmen that they are hereby Directed to follow such men as shall March with Provisions as by Law Directed ; you are Likewise Directed to notify the said half of the alarm List that they also to Proceed as the Law Directs & to march with the Rest to said alarm Post there to Joyn the Regiment ; of this you will not Fail as you value the Salvation of your Country.

Given under my hand and Seal this 22^d day of July 1777 at Wrentham,

BENJ^N HAWES, *Colo.*"

" *To Capt. Lovell & Fuller & The Select-men of the Town of Medway.*

Warrant 21st Sept. 1777.

To Capt. Fuller & Lovell for the Choice of Officers and the Draught of 47 Men for the Private expedition :

GENTLEMEN : You are in The Strongest terms called upon and are hereby Directed to assemble the militia of the town of medway, Both training and Band allarm List (Both Precents included) on Wednesday next at 8 o'clock in the morning. Each company on their own Parade for the Purpose of Electing one Capt & 2 Lieuts to each company as the Law Directs when one of the field officers will attend at time and Place and Preside as moderator.

N. B. Capt Fuller's Company to Parade at 12 o'clock at noon.

Furthermore you are Directed Emediately to Detach 3 Sub. 4 Ser 4 Cor and 47 Privates (viz.) from Capt Lovell 2 Sub. 2 Ser. 2 cor & 25 Privates from Capt Fuller 1 Sub. 2 ser. 2 cor & 22 Privates, from their Training Band and Alarm List. All of them to be able Bodyed Effective men on a Secret Expedition to be Ready to march on or Before the 25th Day of this Inst September. P: men to be completely Equiped with a Good firelock and Bayonet thereto Cartridge Box Knapsack & Blanket P.-men to continue in Service thirty Days from the first Day of October Next unless sooner Discharged. Their Pay and Subsistance to be the same as the Continental Army. Also over & above to the Non Commissioned officers and Private Soldiers shall be paid 2s-od. Per month, and the town is also Directed to furnish each soldier that is Unable with the Above accourtrements. And at marching the Select-men are to Pay if the Soldier requires it for milage and carrying their Packs to the Place of Destination 3^d pr mile Each, And Present their accounts to the Court for allowance and Payment You will hereby severally See to it that The afore said Detachment be Completely Equipted on or before the afore^{sd} 25th of Sept. Inst And that they be in actual Readyness to march at the shortest notice. Any person who shall Be Detached as afore^d

P. who shall not in twenty four hours after he is so Detached hire a man in his Room to the acceptance of the officer that Detached him or shall Refuse to Equip himself or march when ordered to by his Commanding Officer shall be considered as a Deserter and Punished Accordingly &c. Agreeable to a Resolve of the Genl Court of the 16th Day of this Inst — Sept.— 1777. Hereof fail not And make Return to myself on or Before the afor^sd 25 Day of Sept. of the names of the officers Elected and the officers detached together with the number So detached. Given under my hand and Seal at Wrentham this 21st Day of Sept. 1777.

BENJ^N HAWES *Col.*

To The Military Officers and Select-men of the Town of Medway."

Medway, 1st Precinct Assembled September 23, 1777. Elected,

Joseph Lovel Capt., Jonathan Gould 1st Lieut., John Ellis 2^d Lieut.

Medway, 2d Precinct, Assembled September 23, 1777. Elected,

Moses Adams Capt. ; Jonathan Holbrook 1st Lieut. ; Eli Pond 2^d Lieut.

" *Capt. Lovell's Return Medway Names of men Draughted to Little Compton, R. I. Sept. 24, 1777.*

" MEDWAY, Sept. 24, 1777.

Then we Assembled the Training Band and Laram men of the First Company in Medway and Drafted out the whole quoto of men According to orders from the warrant and the Return of their names viz. :

John Wheeler	Eli Ellis	Peter Froast
Abijah Fairbank	Ezra Richardson	Amos Turner, Junr
Samuel Jones	Jesse Daniels	Abel Jones
Oliver Richardson	John Combs	Henry Ellis
John Hill	Amos Broad	Benjamin Parnel
Daniel Richardson Jun.	George Sumner	Moses Hill
Joel Fairbank	Stephen Harding	Joseph Daniels
Abraham Harding Jun.	Ishmael Coffee	Simpson Jones
Jotham Fairbank	Elijah Clark Jun.	John Ellis
Lemuel Daniels	Eli Bullard	Ichabod Haws.

Attested By the Selectmen

Capt. LOVELL
1 Lieut. GOULD
2 Lieut. ELLIS

JONATHAN ADAMS
MOSES RICHARDSON
HENRY BULLARD."

" *Warrant Oct. ye 30 1777 5 Men to Guard The Prisoners Near Boston 5 Months.*
Maj^r Bullard.

To the Officers Selectmen and Committee of the Town of Medway. GENTLE :

Agreeable to Orders from Lawful authority you are required to Detach five able bodied Effective men from the Militia in your town to serve as a guard for the Prisoners, (Lately taken with Genl Burgoyne) at or near Boston to be at Genl Heath's head Quart^rs the third Day of November Next if Possible and to be under his Direction and to be on the same Establishment that the militia are upon now Doing Duty on the Fortress at or near Boston to serve During the stay of s^d Prisoners within the State.

You will see that the men so Detached are Equip^d with arms Ammunition and a Blanket as the Law Directs and have them at Doct^r Chenys Tavern in Walpole ye next monday at 10 o'clock in the forenoon where an Officer will be appointed to take the command of the men Detach^d from this Reg^t.

Hereof fail not and make return of this warrant with the names of the men Detached unto myself on or before the time of meeting at Doct^r Cheny's.

Given under my hand and seal at Walpole the thirtieth Day of Octob^r 1777.

SETH BULLARD Maj^r.

Officers Selectmen and Committee of Medway."

" *Warrant Dec^m 6th 1777, 2 Men to Guard at or Near Boston 3 Months.*

DEAR SIR : Agreeable to order from the general Court & Brigadier you are Required to Detach from your Company including the alarm List two able bodied men arm^d and accouterd as the Law Directs to serve as a guard at or near Boston, untill the first Day march next unless sooner Discharged to be under Direction of General Heath, their Pay & subsistance the same of the Continental army, the above men to Parade at Medfield at the House of Mr Seth Clark on wednesday Next at nine o'clock in the morning when they will Joyn the Detachment from my Regiment and Receive further orders : of this you will not fail & make Return of your Doings with the Names of the men so Detach^d to Maj^r man on or before Wednesday next, given under my hand & Seal at Wrentham the 6 Day of December A. D. 1777.

BENJ. HAWES Colo.

To Capt Lovell.

Order of Court Dec^m ye 2nd 1777."

" CAPT LOVELL. Sir : You are here by directed immediately to compleat your quota of men that was ordered to Cambridge as guards for the British Troops in Octr last, if there be any lacking. Also to compleat your deficiency (if any there be) of the late Draught which was made in consequence of a resolve of the 1st instant. Also you are directed to draught one man to serve six months unless sooner discharged; in a guard now raising for the Continental stores & Magazines in This State. To be under the direction of the Continental General of this State. Said man to be compleatly armed and accutred. And to parade at Mr Barachias Mason's in Medfield on the morning of the 29th Inst. Where the Detachment will receive further orders.

You will not fail to be punctual in this matter As the General is determined neglects in future shall not pass unnoticed. You will therefore make return to me of the names of the men that have marched upon the above named draught and the names of them that will not comply with orders also the name of the man draughted on the present guard to myself on or before the morning of the aforesaid 29th Inst. N. B. Penalty for either of the above for refusing to march £10 or hire a man in 24 Hours or be considered as a soldier and treated as such.

BENJ^N HAWESE, Coll.

After orders you will make return to on or before the fifth Day of January next of the Strength of your company including alarm List. Distinguishing them of the Alarm from the traning-Band : also that of the Alarm list that are above 60 years of age. Return to be made in Camp-form.

BENJ^N HAWSE Coll.

Wrentham Dec. 25 1777."

Regimental Orders.

"The Coll^o Directs that the Several Capt^s in his Reg^t Furnish the following Detachment Agreeable to Council & Brigade Orders viz : 1 Capt. 3 Sub^n 5 Serg^t 5 Corp^ls 1 Drum^r 1 Fife & 69 Privates able Bodied men to be completely equippt as the Law Directs to serve in the State of Rhode-island under the Command of Genl Spencer for the term of three Months from the first Day of January next unless sooner Discharged. The Detachment in the following manner, from Capt Metcalf Comp^y 1 Capt 1 Sub^n 1 Corp^l 6 privates Capt Claps Comp^y 1 Sub^n 1 Serg^t 1 Corp^l 11 Privates Capt Ellis Comp^n 1 Sub^n 1 Serg^t 8 Privates Capt Plimpton Comp^n 1 Serg^t 1 Drum 9 Privates Capt Fisher Comp^n 1 Serg^t 9 Privates Capt Cowels Comp^n 1 Serg^t 9 Privates Capt Lovell Comp^n 1 corp^l 1 fife 6 Privates Capt Adams Comp^n 1 Corp^l 6 Privates Capt Fairbanks 1 Corp^l 5 Privates.

S^d Detachment to Parade at Mr David Manns in Wrentham on Wednesday next at 10 o'clock in the morning where they will receive further orders. Each Capt will make Return of the Names of the officers and men that are Detacht, to myself on or Before s^d Wednesday.

BENJ^N HAWS Col^o

Wrentham Dec. 27, 1777."

"Order for Returns of Continental Soldiers.

" Pursuant to an Act of the great & General Court of this State of the Third of This instant Feb.y to me Directed you are hereby Required of the sixteenth instant to make Return unto myself on oath of all the men in the Company under your command that have Inlisted into the Continental army or that have bin hired in behalf of said Company expressing the Names of the men so inlisted or hired the Towns to which they belong the Town from which they enlisted or hired. The Cap.t under which they inlisted the Col.l under which they serve, the time when their engagements end, the state for which they inlisted: you are also to make return of all the men in said Company that were Draughted for Eight months that did not pay their fine or ware otherways cleared from said service, of this you will not fail. Given under my hand at Wrentham this Ninth Day of Feb.y 1778.

BENJAMIN HAWES, *Comttee.*

N. B. The form of the Return must be as followeth

The names of men engaged in Service	Town they belong to	Town for which they serve	Capt men which they enlisted	Col.l under which they serve.	Time when their engagement end	State for which they enlisted."

" A Return of the Continental Soldiers that Have Been Inlisted and Hir.d Either During the Present war or for three Years For and in Behalf of the First Company in the Town of Medway.

NAMES OF MEN.	TOWN FROM.	TOWN FOR.	CAPT.	COL.	TIME.
Ozias Metcalf	Medway	Medway		Crain	April 1780
Nathan Thayer	"	"	Fairfield	Wigglesworth	War
Joseph Clark	"	"	Whittington	"	"
Dening Sheffield	"	"		"	
Jonathan Graves	"	"	Forster	Graten	
Paul Holbrook	"	"	Sumner	"	Jan. 1780
Abijah Richardson	"	"		"	
Andrew Parkes	Unknown	"	Knap		War
Bishop Stanley	"	"	Rot Allen	Alden	June 1780
Sandy Sprague	"	"	"	"	" 1780
Jonathan Davis	"	"	Childs	Graten	May 1780
Samuel Cooledge	"	"	"	"	" "
Adonijah Rice	"	"	"	"	" "
Simon Hager	Boston	"	Stodhard	Paterson	" "
Ebenezer Kent	Unknown	"	G. Brown	H. Jackson	June 1780
John Welch	"	"	Jarvis	"	May 1780

Medway February y.e 12.th 1778.
Errors excepted —

Per M.e

JOSEPH LOVELL."

"FOR CAPT. LOVELL:

SIR: You are Hereby Directed to make Return to me by the 25 Day of Feb.y Instant of all the Services Done by your Company since y.e 19.th Day of April 1775. Expressing the Names of the Officers and the time and place they Served in. Also to compleat your Quota of Continental Souldiers, if not already Done and make Return to my self by the 16.th Instant. Given under my Hand att Wrentham this 12 Day of Feb.r A. D. 1778.

BENJ.N HAWES *Coll.*"

" Regimental Order Wrentham 25 1778.

I have this moment received intelligence from Gen.l Sullivan that the Enemy have taken Possession of Bristol and Warren and are on their March toward Slade's Ferrey.

You are therefore Directed to march immediately with the Company under your command to Landlord Dagget's at Attleborough there to secure further orders.

BENJ.N HAWES *Coll.*

After Orders you will also order the Detachments, for the men to parade at roxbury Old Meeting House next Thursday at 6 o'clock p. m. there to receive further orders. To Capt. Lovell.

BENJ^N HAWES Coll."

"To CAPT. LOVELL. Sir: You are hereby directed immediately to comply with and execute the orders contained in the resolve of Court of the 20 inst^t April that is to Furnish three men for the main army also two men for the North river. Equipage Term of Service, pay and subsistance as expressed in the aforesaid Resolve. Said men to be compleatly Ready for marching by the 12th day of May next and remain at a moments warning. Hereof fail not as you would avoyd the penalties set for the aforesaid Resolve and make return to myself of the Names of the men draughted Inlisted or hired to enter the Service in each Department on or before the 13th day of May next.

N. B. The above Equipage to be agreable to the melitia act.

Given under my hand at Wrentham this 29th day of April A. D. 1778.

BENJ HAWES Coll."

Regimental Orders.

"To CAPT. LOVELL. The Coll. Directs that the several Captains in his Regiment make Return of the Names of the men Draughted or Hired to compleat their Quota for the North River for the term of eight months if not all Ready Done.

Also that they cause the men from their Respective Companies so Raised to be Notified to appear at the House of Mr. Samuel Lathbridge in Frankling on Fryday Next at 2 o'clock afternoon Properly Equipt with Every article agreeable to the Militia Act. Given under my Hand at Wrentham this 5th Day of June A. D. 1778.

BENJ. HAWES, Coll."

Pay-roll of Selectmen.

"June 16, 1778.

Providence 21 Days. 14s. per man.

Abel Ellis	Jesse Daniell	Job Harding
Lemuell Daniell	Nathan Jones	Samuel Thompson.

21 days men. £1 5s. per man.

Joseph Daniell Junr	Zeba Partridge	Lieu^t Stephen Clark
Abraham Harding Ju^r	Eli Bullard	Jonas Brech
Jonathan Adams 3^d	Oliver Richardson	Asa Daniell Ju^r

27 days men. £1 5s. per man.

John Alden,	Eli Ellis	Jonathan Foster
Ezra Richardson	Henry Daniell J^r	John Coombs.
Asa Ellis Junr		

Bostonians. 12s. 6d. per man.

Stephen Clark	James Brick	Job Harding

Store-guard.

Amos Turner Ju^r ....£12-6 | Joshua Richardson............ .... £6-0

Guard of British Troops.

Daniel Richardson Ju^r .... | Asahel Fairbanks....................
Jonathan Adams 3^d .... |

Guard Boston.

Elijah Farrington........... .....£0-6-0 | Matthias Hopkins.............. ....£0-6-0

Providence. 7s. per man.

John Hill	Abraham Harding Ju^r	Nathan Hall
Ebenezer Ellis	Jabez Shumway	Cornelius Youngman."

" To the Officers, or Selectmen of the Town of midway.

GENTLEMEN: you are hereby ordered to detach indiscriminately from the Capts company of the town of midway one man to serve 6 months unless sooner Discharged as a guard now raising for the British Troops and Continental Stores in this State to be under the command of General Heath Said man to be Compleatly armed and accutered and to parade at the house of mr Barachias Mason in medfield on monday next at Eight o'clock in the morning then to receive further orders, and as encouragement they are to receive 5 pounds per month in addition to the Continental pay if any person (in the opinion of the Selectmen of ability) being detached by the Selectmen or Officers shall refuse, to pay a fine of ten pounds or procure an able bodied man in his room within 24 hours shall be held as a Soldier and treated as such, you will also make return of the name of the man so detach'd unto major Sabin man on or before the morning of the 6th of July next. You are also ordered to make return of all the names of the training band and alarm lists in your Town from 16 years old to 50 and from 50 to 65, also from 65 to 100 years. you will also view the Said Company and make return of their arms and every accoutrement as required by the militia acts you will punctually Comply with this order and make the above return to my self on or before the 20 day of July next.

Given under my hand Seal at Wrentham, this 30 day of June 1778

BENJAMIN HAWES *Coll.*"

Regimental Order.

" Capt Samuel Fisher,					1 Serj	1 Corp	13 privates		
Asa Fairbanks,	.	.	.	.	1 "	1 "	11	"	
Saml Cowell,	.	.	.	.	1 "	1 "	18	"	Capt
Joseph Lovell,	.	.	.	.	"	1 "	8	"	1 Drum
Amos Ellis,	.	.	.	.	1 "	1 "	7	"	1 " Capt
Adam Petos,	.	.	.	.	1 "	1 "	14	"	1 Fife
Oliver Clap,	.	.	.	.	1 "	1 "	13	"	
John Metcalf,	.	.	.	.	1 "	1 "	12	"	
Moses Adams	.	.	.	.	1 "		8	"	1 Fife Lieut 2

Said men to be Armd and Accourtred as the Law Directs to Parade at the House of Mr David Mans Innholder in Wrentham on Tuesday Morning Next at 8 of the clock in the Morning for 15 Days to be under General Sullivan at Providence the several Companys to be Ready to march at the shortest notice and make Return of the Names of the men so Detach'd. B. H. C.

Wrentham July ye 25 1778."

" Regimental Order. The Coll Directs that the Several Capt or Commanding officers of Company and where there is no officers organized to the Select-men and committee of the Fourth Regiment in the County of Suffolk Send in their Delinquents or at least Persuade them to go immediately to Coll. Hawse Quarters at Tiverton.

Capt Lovell 5 Delinquents.

Franklin August ye 4, 1778   J. METCALF *Lieut Coll.*

" To CAPT. JOSEPH LOVELL —*Sir :* You are hereby Directed immediately to detach from your company one Corporal one fifer & 8 privates, these men to be armed and accoutered according to Law & Parade at the Dwelling House of David man Inholder in Wrentham on monday Next at 8 o clock in the morning in order to march by the shortest Rout to the Island of Road island there to Do Duty under the command Major General Sullivan for the space of 27 Days after their arrival in camp unless sooner Discharged, and you are to make Return of the men so Detached with a List of their Names unto myself by the time above Perfixed hereof you are not to fail. Given under my hand at Franklin this 15 Day of august A. d 1778.

JAMES METCALF *Lieut Coll.*"

" Those that went on this Order.

Asa Ellis	Ezra Richardson	John Alden	Jonathan Fisher.
Eli Ellis	John Combs	Abraham Harding Jr"	

" FRANKLIN, August 19th, 1778.

" *To the militia Officers of the first military Company of foot in the town of Medway or to the Selectmen of the town of Medway.*

GENTLEMEN : I am obliged to Require you forthwith, without loss of time to Comply with the Reg't orders of the 15th Instant Except this Alteration, viz that you Detach the men to serve, During the Campaign on the Island of Rhodisland, And see that they are Compleatly Arm'd And Equipt, As the Law Directs.. And Cause them to march to the Island without Loss of time to join Capt. Peters of Col. Hawes Reg't; to the full Number of 1 Cor, 1 Dr and 8 Privates As Directed in the Aforesd orders of the 15th instant. you are also Required to Detach from the military Company Aforesaid 1 Ser, 1 Cor. And 10 Privats, And See that they are Compleatly Arm'd Acouterd and Equipt as the Law Directs and see them Boarded at the house of David mann, Innhoulder in Wrentham on Saturday Next at 10 o Clock A. M. Where they will Receive Orders to march the Island of Rhodisland And there Do Duty During the Campaign in R Island, and make Return to myself of your Doings together with the Names of the men Detach'd as Aforesd on or before the time of Parading, of which you will Not fail,— As you will Answer Your Default — Agreeable to An Order of Council. . . . &c.

JAMES METCALF, Lt. Coll.

N. B. You Are Requested to furnish 1 Person that has had a Commission to serve As A Lieut. Otherwise You Are Required to Detach Eleven Privates."

" *To the Selectmen in the Town of Medway.*

GENTLEMEN : You are Hereby Directed to Detach from the East Company in the Town of Medway two Privit Souldier armed and equipt according to Law to Guard the Sea Coast in this or the Neighboring States as the Council or General Court may thereafter order to Do Duty till the first Day of January Next unless sooner Discharged. Said men to hold themselves Ready to march at the shortest Notice & to Receive such pay as the General Court shall thereafter order. You are also Required Immediately to Compleat your Quota of men for ye six months service at Rhode Island, if not already Done. And make Return of the Names of the men so Detached to my self by the fifteenth Day of this Instant. Given under my Hand and Seal at Wrentham this Eleventh Day of September A. D. 1778. From Gentlemen,
yr Humble Servant

BENJN HAWES Coll."

" You are ordered to detach from your Company one Sergt one Corpl and nine Private Soldiers and see that Said men are armed and Equipt according to law and parade at the house of mr Headen in walpole on monday next at Eight o'clock in the morning in order to march to Boston and Continue in Service till the first day of January next unless Sooner Discharged and you will also make Return of the names of Said men by the aforesaid monday without fail.

BENJAMIN HAWES Coll.

WRENTHAM Sept. ye 22 1778.
CAPT. LOVELL & SELECTMEN."

"WRENTHAM OCT. 10, 1778.

DEAR SIR : You are Desired with your Subbalton to Attend at the House of mr Samuel Lathbridges in Franklin on Monday the 26th Instant at Eight o'clock in the morning In order to Consult and Determine Some matters in this Regiment if Agreable.   Your Humble Servant   BENJ. HAWES *Colo.*

CAPT JOSEPH LOVELL In Medway.
SIR be so Kind as to Notify your Subbalton of the time and Place."

" SIR, You are Derected Emediatly to make out a return of Number & State of your Company as Required Some time Past Expressing the Date of your first and Present Commission & all males above sixteen years of age that live in the Bounds of your Company are to be returned way on the other & none that are hired from other Towns or Companys.

Wrentham, Jan. 24, 1779

By order of COLL. HAWES, JOHN GUILD, *Lieut.*

Capt. LOVELL in Medway."

"DEAR SIR. you are hereby Notified to Attend on a Committee ordered by the General Court at the House of mr Seth Clark in medfield on Tuesday the 16 Day of march Instant at ten o'clock in the forenoon, where you may have opportunity to offer what you have to say Respecting the Ranks of your Company or any other Dificulty or Dispute of that nature — by order of Eleazer Brooks Chairman of Said Committee your Humble Servant.

BENJAMIN HAWES *Colo.*

WRENTHAM march ye 4th 1779
CAPTAIN LOVELL."

"Capt LOVELL. SIR·

You are Hereby Ordered to Detach from the East Company in the Town of Medway two able bodied Soldiers, armed and accoutred According to Law, to Do Duty in the State of Rhode Island till the first Day of July next unless sooner Discharged, to be under the same pay of the Continental Army, and Over & above to be paid by this State 12 pounds per month to each man and the Selectmen are Directed to pay to Each non Commisioned officer and Soldier one Shilling per mile for Travel & Transporting their Pack to Tiverton the Place of their Destination and Lay their Accounts before the General Court for Payment, Said men to Parade at the House of Mr David mann in Wrentham on Thursday the 13th Day of may Instant at Eight o'Clock in the morning in order to march to Tiverton you will make return of the Names of the men so Detached unto my self on or before said Thursday.

Given under my Hand and Seal at Wrentham this fifth Day of may A D. 1779·

BENJAMIN HAWES, *Coll.*"

"*A Copy of the Regulation of the Prices in the Town of Medway for Teaming Labour and Other Necessaries, agreable to a Resolve of a Late Convention held at Concord viz*

Wheet at	£8-10s	Ox work per day	£1- 1s
Rye at	5-10s	And other Teaming in Oour Owin Town in Proportion	
Indian Corn.	4		
Oats at	2	Carpenters work per Day	2- 8s
Barley at	4	Mason's ditto	3
Beef pr lb	4s	Raw Hides pr lb	3s
Mutton Beef & Lamb	2- 3s	Sole Leather ditto,	18s
Butter	10s	Good pair mens shoes	5- 8s
Fourmeal Cheese	5s	And all Other Shoes in Proportion	
Cyder per Barrel	3-10s		
Inholder for a Commons	12s	Good Bloom Bar Iron per cwt	25
Dinner	6s	Blacksmith work for Shoeing a Horse and Heating.	3-12s
and Other Vittels in Proportion			
Horse keeping by grass pr N	9s	And all other Smith work in Proportion and All other Articles that are Bought or Sold in This Town and all Mean Labour to be in Proportion to the above articles.	
Yoke of Oxen pr Night	13s-6d		
Best Sort of Sheeps wool	1- 2s		
Good Flax pr lb	11s		
Mans Labour at Haying per Day	2- 2s		
And other Labours in Proportion			

MEDWAY, August ye 24th, 1779.

Signed by Seven of the Committee."

"The Account of several Payments of money made of the Selectmen of medway to the militia of sd Town for Rations to support themselves and for the carriage of

Our Packs on their several marches hereafter mentioned to Reinforce the Army in the state of Rhode Island viz —

To men th^t marched by order of Council in the month of April to Providence 30 miles. To Brister in July 40 miles in July to Cumberland 20 miles in October to Little Compton 55 miles.

25 men to Providence.... 7s-6d £9-7s-6d	39 men to Cumberland... 5s £ 9-15-0
12 " Brister........10s 6-0 -0	55 " Little Compton.13s-9d 37-16-3

NAMES.

" John Ellis Ju^n	John Wheeler	Joshua Partridge	Joel Fairbank
John Combs	Abel Jones	Eli Bullard	Josiah Morse
Jabez Shumway	Jesse Daniel	Stephen Harding	Saml Damon
Job Harding	Jedediah Phillip	Ebenezer Ellis	Asa Ellis Ju^n
Ziba Partridge	Elias Harding	Benjamin Parnel	Simpson Jones
DanielRichardsonJu^n	Eli Ellis	Abraham Harding J^r	Abijah Fairbanks
Ichabod Seaver	Joseph Daniel	Samuel Jones	George Sumner
Oliver Richardson	Lemuel Daniel	Elijah Clark	Ishmael Coffee
Peter Frost	Moses Hill	Jonas Brick	Lt John Ellis
Francis Clark	John Hill	Amos Turner	Lt Joshua Gould
Jotham Fairbanks	Amos Broad	Cone^l Youngman	Joel Haws."
Ezra Richardson			

" *Pay Roll of Six Months Men Serving in Continental Army in the year 1780.*

John Alden	Henry Fleming	Bartholomew Fuller	Prince Brewster
Luther Cutler	Lovell Cushing	George Riley	Jeremiah Crocker
John Whiting	Dwight Allen	Elijah Ellis	Thomas Coffee."

" *A Return of the Continental Soldiers that have been enlisted and hired to enlist either during the present war or for 3 years for or in behalf the Town of Medway April 1780.*

Ozias Metcalf	Jonathan Graves	Nathan Thayer	Paul Holbrook."
Joseph Clark	Abijah Richardson	Dening Sheffield	

" *The following men served in Capt. Samuel Cowell's Co. in Col. —— Reg^t 2 months & 4 Days.—£4-5s-4d.*

Jonathan Holbrook	Elijah Clark	Elias Harding	Sylvanus Morse
Simeon Richardson	Simeon Partridge	William Ellis	Abel Ellis
Josiah Fuller	Joseph Daniels	Asa Fuller	Benjamin Clark
Fisher Adams	Eli Bullard	James Barber	Paul Ellis
Abner Morse	William Stinner	John Harding	Nathan Smith."

" *A List of Names of Men who Served at Fishkill from Medway.*

Phineas Adams	Isaac Boyden	Timothy Adams	Charles White."
Obadiah Adams	Ichabod Hawes		

" *The following men Served 8 mos. in Capt Jacob Mather's Co. in Col. Doolittle's Reg^t*

Hezekiah Bullard	Paul Ellis	Silas Fairbanks."

" *The following men Served in Capt. Joseph Morse's Co. in Col. John Patterson's Reg^t.*

Damon Clifford	Joseph Bullard."

Miscellaneous Revolutionary Notes.

"JONAS BRICK. Col. Whitcomb's Reg. Capt. Benj. Bullard's Company in Continental Service at Ticonderoga in the year 1777; brought home sick in Dec. 1776; charge against town £4-2s-6d; for Samuel Partridge man and horse 28 days in bringing him home, Doctor's Bill after his return 12s; all paid March 28 1778 by Joseph Lovell for Town.

ISHMAEL COFFEE. Served six months in Col. J. Greaton's Regiment; certified to by Col. Greaton Sept 26 1782.

NATHAN GROUT. Served nine months in 1779–80 in the Continental Army.

THOMAS MORSE. Served three years and gives his receipt in full May 20th 1781 for service in Continental Army.

WILLIAM LEE. receipts Dec. 15 1781 for £63 for *Bounty* for service three years in Continental Army of Medway.

SAMUEL NOBLE. receipts Dec. 7 1781 for £46 for *Bounty* for service During the war."

"MEDWAY April 20th 1781.

An account of the time of Inlistment of the three years Soldiers & the Agreement with them.

THOMAS MORSE. Inlisted May 20th 1781. To serve three years in the Continental Army for sd Town. For the sum of Ninety pound, in Gold or Silver, £30 Paid in hand & £30 more in one year, the other £30 in two years from the Date of his Inlistment. The above Thomas Morse has hired.

WILM DAMSEY, BENJN DAVIDSON, JNO DAVIDSON, ROGER CRAIN. Inlisted May 31st 1781. To serve three years in the Continental Army for sd Town For the sum of Eighty-four pounds Each 48 paid in hand & £36 more in Eight months from the Date of their Inlistment.

LOREING CUSHING, Inlisted May 30th 1781. For the Sum of Ninety pound, £30 paid in hand & £30 in one year & the remainder in two years.

BENJN PARNEL. Inlisted June 25, 1781, For the sum of Ninety pound £30 paid in hand & £30 in one year & the remainder in two years.

WILLM & JOSEPH SOUTHWORTH Inlisted August 16, 1781 to serve nine months in the Continental Army for sd Town for the Sum of Twenty five pound five shilling. Each paid in hand.

JOHN DICKERSON, JNO SILVESTER JOHNSON, & HENRY BURK. Inlisted Sept 4, 1781, to Serve three year for the Sum of Seventy five pounds Each, £36 paid in hand £24 in two months & 15 in 5 months to Each.

SAML NOBLE. Inlisted Decembr 7 1781. To serve Dureing the war with Great Britton in the Continental army for the Town of Medway for the sum of Forty-six pounds in Gold or silver.

WILLIAM LEE. Inlisted Decembr 7th 1781 To Serve three years in the Continental Army for the Town of Medway For the Sum of Sixty three pounds in Gold or Silver Twenty one pounds paid in hand, twelve pounds to be Paid in Six Months & Thirty pounds in twelve Months from the Date hereof."

" *The following sums of Money expended by the Town of Medway for hiring Soldiers to serve in the Continental Army in the year 1781, agreeable to Resolve of General Court Dec 2 1780.*

John Dickinson for 3 years	£70	Samuel Noble for 3 years	£70
Henry Bush "	70	William Southworth 2 years	70
William Lee "	70	Joseph Southworth 2 "	70

HENRY ELLIS ⎫ *Selectmen*
OLIVER ADAMS ⎬ *of*
JOSEPH LOVELL ⎭ *Medway.*

Medway, 30, 1783."

" JAREB PRESTON, receipts for £12 hiring four soldiers into the Continental service for 3 years, May 31 1781.

WILLIAM DEMSEY BENJ. DAVISON JOHN DAVISON RODGER CRAIN receipt May 31, 1781 for £90 for engaging themselves as soldiers in the Continental Army for the term of 3 years.

LORING CUSHING receipts, May 30 1781, for £30 for one year's service.

BENJ. PARNEL receipts for £90 as Bounty for three years service, June 25th, 1782.

JONATHAN PIERCE. Receipts Aug. 21st 1786, for £8·10·8 in full, for nine month's wages in the Continental Army in the year 1779–80."

"By virtue of An Act of the General Court, November y[e] 5th 1787.

A Return of Bountys and Hire Given by the Inhabitants of the Town of Medway.

Orders of Court of June and July 1776, to Ticonderoga

5 months to 28 men Hire Amount,	£432-13-4
Sept 1776 to 16 men to or near New York 2 months,	162
Nov[m] 1776 to 11 men to the Jarses for three months,	128
July 1777 to 12 men to Bristol in y[e] State Rhode Island,	48
Sept. 1777 to 56 men for the Private Exp[d] Rhode Island 1 month	224
Oct. 1777 to 5 men to Guard y[e] British Troops Cambdg 5 months,	70-10
Dec[m] 1777 to 4 men to guard y[e] store near Boston 3 months,	39
Dec[m] 1777 to 2 men to guard Continental stores 6 months,	39
Dec[m] 1777 to 14 men to y[e] State Rhode Island 3 months,	168
April 1778 to 6 men to fish Kill 9 months,	793
April 1778 to 4 men to North River 8 months,	360
June 1778 to 11 men State Rhode Island 21 Days,	120
June 1778 to 6 men State Rhode Island 6 months,	218-6
6 men Bountys for the Town £14 each,	84
June 1778 to 2 men Store guard in this State 6 months,	80
July 1778 to 20 men State Rhode Island 15 days,	280
August 1778 to 13 men State Rhode Island 27 days,	275-12
August 1778 to 14 men State Rhode Island During Seidge,	54-7
Sept. 1778 to 4 men to guard sea coast 3 months ½,	180
May 1779 to 4 men State of Rhode Island 6 weeks,	118
Sum Total,	£3,874-8-4
June 9 1779 to 6 men nine months (paper),	3,160
June 28 1779 to 2 men at or near Boston,	
July 24 1779 to 2 men. . . . near Boston,	126
August 11 1779 to 4 men State of Rhode Island one month	137-11
August 11 1779 to 3 men State Rhode Island one month	103
Oct. st 1779 to 2 men,	61
April 24th 1780,	
June 22, 1780 to 16 men for three months (paper),	22,680
March 1781 to 17 men to State Rhode Island N.E.,	70- 2-6
August 1781 to 9 men 3 months Standing Ac[t] (Hard Money),	121-10
Oct. 1782 to 2 men guard Nantasket, (Hard Mo.)	4-5-8"

THE REVOLUTIONARY PAPERS printed above were largely furnished by George Lovell Richardson, A. M., of Abington, Mass. Many of them were the original documents which had been preserved among the papers of Captain Joseph Lovell, of Revolutionary fame, who was the great-great-grandfather of Mr. Richardson.

THE INDEPENDENCE OF THE AMERICAN COLONIES was virtually achieved October 19, 1781, by the capture of Cornwallis and his army in Yorktown, but hostilities did not cease for some time after that event, and peace was not proclaimed until April 19, 1783, just eight years from the battle of Lexington.

THE WAR OF 1812.

THE UNITED STATES declared war against England June 19, 1812, the occasion being the seizure of American vessels and the impressment of thousands of American seamen into the British service. The town of Medway was represented in the army during this last war with Great Britain, but no complete list of the soldiers can be obtained from any official source. The statement is made that "In the settlement of the claims of Massachusetts upon the General Government growing out of that war the rolls were surrendered by the State and are held as vouchers by the United States Government. The State has not been permitted to have even copies of them. Some claim agents, a few years ago, made copies of a portion and sold them to the State. These are in the Adjutant-General's office in one large volume. But the rolls are simply lists of the men by companies without giving their residences. The only clue of their residence being the town in which the company was recruited. Neither do these copies contain all the organizations. The original rolls are in the Third Auditor's office, Washington, and the only method would seem to be to get copies from there, a matter of doubtful possibility."

The few names of soldiers in the War of 1812, which have been furnished by tradition, are the following: Captain Jeremy Daniels, Jotham Fairbanks, Leonard Fairbanks, Silas Fairbanks, and Charles Howard.

The last battle of the War of 1812 was fought January 8, 1815, in New Orleans, La., the United States winning a most decisive victory. Had the telegraph been in use at that time the great Battle of New Orleans would never have been fought, for a treaty of peace was signed December 24, 1814, fourteen days before, in Ghent, Belgium.

This treaty provided that all places captured by either army during the war should be restored to their rightful possessors. Provision was also made for the settlement of the northwest boundary of the United States, and the amicable arrangement of some other matters of minor importance. But the treaty was silent in regard to the impressment of American seamen, which was the great cause of the war. Nevertheless, England, from that day to this, has not impressed our sailors, so that the object of the war was practically attained.

The President issued a proclamation of peace February 18th, 1815, which was hailed with public rejoicings in all parts of the country.

The War for the Union.

1861 — 1865.

After a period of nearly half a century the national peace was again broken by the fire of Confederate rebel batteries, opened upon Fort Sumter. The first gun of the greatest civil war of modern times was fired at half-past four o'clock Friday morning, April 12, 1861. President Lincoln immediately issued a call for 75,000 troops, and there responded 300,000 volunteers, ready to defend the American flag.

The first blood of the war was shed in the streets of Baltimore, April 19, 1861, the eighty-sixth anniversary of the first blood shed in the War of the Revolution on Lexington Green. The Sixth Massachusetts Regiment, hurrying to the defense of Washington, was attacked in the streets of Baltimore and several soldiers were killed. A Union soldier, being fatally shot, turned about just before he fell lifeless, saluted the flag, and exclaimed: "ALL HAIL THE STARS AND STRIPES!"

The citizens of Medway were at once roused, and the old fire of patriotism kindled in their veins. They at first met together in a large informal assembly to listen to impromptu addresses, and to encourage the enlistment of volunteers. As soon as possible a warrant was issued and a regular town-meeting was assembled April 29th, 1861.

16

The Doings of the Town in Support of the War.

"April 29, 1861. The following committee of twelve was chosen by the town to recommend such measures as the emergency requires: Charles H. Deans, Wm. H. Cary, Wm. Everett, Wm. B. Boyd, David Daniels, Willard P. Clark, Jason Smith, A. C. Grant, M. M. Fisher, Horatio Mason, Abijah R. Wheeler, and Oliver Clifford, who presented the following RESOLUTIONS:

"*Whereas*, The people by certain conventions in the states of South Carolina, Georgia, Florida, Alabama, Mississippi, Louisiana, and Texas, in violation of their obligations to the other states of the Union and to the Federal Government, have declared themselves independent, taken forcible possession of the forts, arsenals, custom-houses, navy and dock yards, ships, and munitions of war, belonging to and in the lawful custody of the United States, confiscated the property, and cruelly tortured the persons, and even destroyed the lives of Northern citizens, living peaceably in their midst, and now threaten to expel the constituted authorities from the national capital, and possess or destroy the public archives at Washington, and

"*Whereas*, Large numbers in other states are in open sympathy or active coöperation with the rebel party in their designs to overthrow the American Union and to substitute a slave-holding oligarchy or a military despotism, rejecting entirely the principle of political equality and the right of a constitutional majority to govern,

"*Whereas*, In view of this great Rebellion, Abraham Lincoln, President of the United States, after long forbearance in the hope of returning reason, and submission to the Government, has issued his proclamation, calling upon the loyal states to furnish a sufficient force to defend the capital and to crush the Rebellion, and

"*Whereas*, John A. Andrew, Governor of this Commonwealth, the military authorities and forces thereof, have promptly responded to the call of the national executive, and the sixth regiment, through the energy and the prudent foresight of the Governor, became the first to enter the capital for its defense, the first to encounter danger and death in the city of Baltimore on the 19th instant, a day now twice rendered immortal in American history, and

"*Whereas*, The Governor has called upon the several towns and all good citizens to aid in defense of the constitution, the government and the enforcement of its laws, now be it

"*Resolved*, By the citizens of Medway in legal town-meeting assembled that we cherish with unalterable devotion the Constitution adopted by our fathers and will inflexibly support the Government of the United States, that we will contribute our full proportion of men and means to enable the President to prosecute the war invoked by a rebel force to a successful issue and to maintain its power at home and its honor abroad.

"*Resolved*, That we are not insensible to the evils and horrors of civil war, yet we regard civil government as an ordinance of God for the good of man, and especially deem it a duty to ourselves and to posterity to defend with life, if need be, that government which has given to us and to our fathers prosperity and peace, now that a traitor's hand is stretched forth to destroy it.

" *Resolved*, That it becomes all good citizens to practice a rigid economy in personal and family expenses, eschewing all luxurious and extravagant living in respect to diet, dress, furniture, and equipage, improving every opportunity to obtain more ample means for the support of government and all objects of public and private charity during the crisis now impending.

" *Resolved*, That a contingent military fund be established by the town, not exceeding in amount the sum of three thousand dollars.

" *Resolved*, That the treasurer is authorized to borrow on the credit of the town such sums of money not exceeding the above amount, as may be necessary to meet all payments duly authorized and drawn by the selectmen for military purposes.

" *Resolved*, That a military committee consisting of nine persons, including the selectmen and chairman of the board of overseers, be appointed with power to provide suitable clothing and uniforms, and all necessary equipments not furnished by the State, for any company of volunteer militia that may be raised in the town and vicinity and accepted by the Governor. To provide also a suitable armory for said company, and all other things needful to perfect them in military drilling and discipline preparatory to active service, and in case such a company be not organized, to make similar provisions for any citizens of Medway who may serve in any other company of volunteer militia.

" The committee are also authorized to pay such bounty to the members of said company, or to individual volunteers, that have or may enter into actual service and to make such provisions for the support of their families belonging to this town as they shall deem suitable or as the town may direct, not, however, incurring any expense beyond the amount of the military fund.

" *Resolved*, That the selectmen are hereby authorized and required to draw their warrant upon the town treasurer for all bills duly approved by the committee on military affairs.

" *Resolved*, That the military committee be authorized to confer with the proper authorities of other towns, and to make any joint arrangements with them for the raising and supporting a company of volunteer militia, or the families of any who may enter actual service, which they may deem lawful and proper."

The foregoing resolutions were adopted by the town, and the following military committee chosen: Messrs. Joel P. Adams, William Daniels, Simeon Fisher, David Daniels, Charles H. Deans, Horatio Mason, Jason Smith, William B. Boyd, and A. S. Harding.

" June 11. *Voted* to raise the sum of $3,000, to be expended under the direction of the above committee, for the families of the volunteers.

" September 23, 1861. *Voted*, That patriotism, no less than common humanity and natural affection, require that all suitable means be employed to recover the bodies of any of our citizen soldiers who may fall in battle or die in the service of their country, and to provide for their interment among their friends and fellow-citizens at home. That for this purpose the military committee be authorized to render such aid to the families of the volunteers from this town, as, in their judgment, the exigency of any case may require, and that the expense thus incurred shall be defrayed from the fund already provided in aid of the families of volunteers.

" January 3, 1862. *Voted.* That the selectmen be directed to prepare a suitable record of all volunteers from Medway. *Vid.* THE RECORD OF THE UNION SOLDIERS.

" March 3, 1862. The military committee reported that the sum of $5,277.37 had been paid during the year to the families of volunteers. Chose Messrs. William Daniels, Simeon Fisher, Clark Partridge, Chas H. Deans, and William B. Boyd a military committee for the ensuing year.

" *Voted,* That the committee be instructed to prepare a plan for future disbursements and present the same to the town for their action at the next April meeting, continuing the same plan as heretofore for the present month.

" April, 1862. *Voted,* That the committee be instructed to conform to the interpretation put upon statute by the state auditor in all cases of disbursement *Voted,* That the treasurer be authorized to borrow the sum of $5,000.

" July 19, 1862. *Voted,* That the selectmen are authorized to offer a bounty of One Hundred dollars, to be paid to each volunteer who shall enlist into the service of the United States, as a part of this town's proportion of volunteers, required of this state as indicated in General Order No. 26 of His Excellency Governor Andrew. and dated at Boston, July 8, 1862.

" That said sum be paid to each volunteer when he shall have been lawfully mustered into service and become also entitled to receive the bounty offered by the general government.

" That the town treasurer is authorized to borrow, upon the credit of the town, such sums of money as may be necessary to pay the bounty and such incidental expenses of recruiting as may be authorized by the selectmen, and that the faith of the town is hereby solemnly pledged to indemnify and save harmless all persons or corporations who may loan the treasurer, or in any way become liable for any sums of money loaned to the treasurer for the purpose aforesaid.

" That the selectmen, after having taken legal counsel, are instructed to petition the next legislature, if deemed necessary by them, to legalize the proceedings of this meeting

" That the selectmen, clergymen, and all good citizens, are earnestly solicited to encourage and stimulate, by public meetings and otherwise, the prompt enlistment of the requisite number of volunteers from this town, that our fellow-citizens already in the service may be cheered and sustained by accession of numbers and strength, the rebellion crushed, and peace and prosperity soon return to our common country.

" August 15, 1862. *Voted,* That the sum of one hundred dollars in addition to the sum already appropriated, be paid to all such as shall enlist to complete the quota of this town under the call for three hundred thousand volunteers for three years.

" That this additional bounty be paid to all such accepted volunteers as shall enlist on or before the day of draft.

" That the selectmen are authorized to pay a bounty of one hundred dollars to each volunteer when mustered into service for nine months, to the number that may be required of this town, under the order of the President of the United States for three hundred thousand of the militia for the several states, and dated August 4, 1862, provided that said volunteers shall enlist on or before the day of draft.

"That the selectmen be authorized to employ such persons as they may need to assist them in the service of recruiting the requisite number of volunteers.

"That the town recommend that the volunteers of this town for nine months, unite with others from adjoining towns to form an entire company, under such officers as they may elect, and to offer their services forthwith to the Governor.

"That the town treasurer is authorized to borrow money on the credit of the town to pay the aforesaid bounty, and such expenses for recruiting as may be ordered by the selectmen.

"September 13, 1862. *Voted*, That the town treasurer, under the direction of the selectmen, is hereby authorized to pay the bounty of one hundred dollars to each of the volunteers from this town now legally enlisted. That the volunteers for nine months be entitled to their bounty when mustered into the service of the United States.

"November 4, 1862. *Voted*, That the selectmen are hereby authorized to make such provisions for the support of dependent families of deceased volunteers from the town of Medway, or of such as may be discharged on account of sickness contracted, or wounds received while in actual service, as in their judgment may be necessary for their comfortable support.

"November 29, 1862. *Voted*, That a committee consisting of Messrs. M. M. Fisher, Charles H. Deans, and William Daniels, be chosen to confer with the authorities at the State House, and to ascertain if the quota assigned to this town of volunteers for nine months is correct, and to report at some future meeting.

"December 6, 1862. The committee chosen at the last meeting made a verbal report, which was accepted. And the town

"*Voted*, That all votes now upon the town records whereby bounties have been offered to nine months' men under the present call for 19,080 men, be, and are hereby repealed, and, further, that the selectmen of this town be directed not to accept any transfer of nine months' men.

"*Voted*, That the selectmen be authorized to recruit the quota of twelve men for which this town is liable, to serve for three years, by offering a bounty not to exceed the sum of two hundred and fifty dollars, and pay such agent as they shall find it necessary to employ, a reasonable sum as compensation, and, further, that they be authorized to pay the sum of two hundred dollars to all men who shall be drafted under the present call.

"July 20, 1863. *Voted*, That the selectmen be authorized to aid the families of each drafted man belonging to this town, who may, on due examination by the board of enrollment, be found liable to service, by the payment of three hundred dollars to the wife, child, parent, sister, or brother of such drafted man, on the following conditions:

"1st. That said drafted man shall actually serve, or furnish an accepted substitute, alien or non-resident.

"2d. That he shall give satisfactory security to the selectmen that his family, dependent upon him for support, shall require no further aid during his time of service.

"3d. That a sum equivalent to one hundred dollars for each man, whose family shall thus be aided, be raised by subscription among the drafted men and others, and paid into the town treasury.

" *Voted*, That the families of all drafted men entering the service personally, not provided for in the above conditions, shall receive such aid as the State allows.

" *Voted*, That the town treasurer be authorized to borrow such sums of money as may be required to carry the provisions of the above votes into effect.

" July 27, 1863. *Voted*, That the selectmen be authorized in accordance with Chapter 176 of the General Laws of 1863, to aid the dependent families of such persons as may be drafted, or become the substitutes of those drafted, to supply the quota of this town under the act of Congress, approved March 3, 1863, by an allowance of one dollar and fifty cents per week to each member of said families, not exceeding three. And the selectmen are further authorized to advance upon said allowance to such of said families as desire it, the sum of one hundred dollars whenever the aforesaid drafted men, or their legal substitutes, shall be duly mustered into service, and said advances shall be deducted from said weekly allowances in such a manner as the selectmen may deem best.

" November 28, 1863. A committee of seven to secure the enlistment of volunteers was chosen, viz.: Messrs. William Daniels, Simeon Fisher, Clark Partridge, D. J. Hastings, George L. Richardson, Jason Smith, and William B. Boyd. *Voted*, That the committee be authorized to expend such sums of money as they may deem necessary to fill the quota of this town, and that the committee be empowered to fill vacancies.

" February 29, 1864. *Voted*, That the selectmen, whenever they shall deem it lawful and expedient so to do, are hereby authorized to pay a bounty, not exceeding one hundred dollars, to any volunteer who has enlisted or may enlist as part of this town's quota under the last two calls of the President for five hundred thousand men, provided said volunteers receive no other than a state or national bounty. And they are also authorized as aforesaid to refund to George L. Richardson, treasurer of the citizens' bounty fund, such sums as may have been paid by him in behalf of any citizens as bounties to any volunteers as aforesaid, provided the sums so paid shall not in either case exceed a bounty of one hundred dollars to each volunteer.

" And the selectmen are further authorized to pay the amount of state aid to the families of all volunteers or drafted men.

" March 7, 1864. *Voted*, That the selectmen be authorized to grant such aid to the families of discharged volunteers as in their judgment the exigency of the case may require.

" April 4, 1864. *Voted*, To grant the sum of $5,000 toward the debt incurred on account of military expenses and interest thereon, and for recruiting purposes.

" April 25, 1864. *Voted*, To grant the sum of $2,000 for the purpose of filling the quota for the last call of the President, or any deficiency under the calls for 700,000 men, the amount not to exceed $125 per volunteer, and if there should be a balance remaining after filling such quotas, the same is to be applied to the payment of the town debt.

" June 7, 1864. *Voted*, To authorize the selectmen to pay the sum of one hundred and twenty-five dollars to each man who shall volunteer to fill the quota of this town. A committee of three was chosen to act with the selectmen, viz., Messrs. George L. Richardson, James M. Daniels, and Sumner Robbins.

"November 8, 1864, *Voted*, To abate the poll taxes of all soldiers who are or have been in the United States service the current year. The selectmen were also authorized to pay the sum of $125 to every person who enters the United States service and is accredited to this town on a future and expected call.

"April 3, 1865. *Granted*, The sum of $7,000 for paying state aid the current year.

"June 9, 1865. *Voted*, To pay and refund all sums of money contributed by individuals and expended by the selectmen for the purpose of obtaining volunteers to fill the quotas of this town in the year 1864, and that the whole amount be assessed and collected this year; and $6,700 was granted for this purpose.

"November 7, 1865. *Voted*, To abate the poll taxes of all soldiers from this town who have been in the United States service the present year."

MISCELLANEOUS NOTES AND COMMENTS.

The Military Committee, chosen April 29, 1861, immediately took in hand the business assigned them. At a meeting held on the evening of the same day of the town-meeting, the committee organized by the choice of Captain David Daniels as chairman, and Charles H. Deans, Esq., as secretary. There were sub-committees appointed to visit adjoining towns, to learn what course was being taken by them, and to invite volunteers to unite with our own townsmen in making up one or more companies. At subsequent meetings other matters were decided upon, which can only be stated from memory, as the records of the committee were afterwards accidentally destroyed by fire. A vote was passed to pay our volunteers for time spent in military drill. Satisfactory arrangements were also made for the support of their families and dependents, while in the service of the Government. The matter of uniforms and equipment was also taken into consideration. Meanwhile men were enrolling for service, and had commenced military drill under the instruction of Captain David Daniels, an experienced militia officer. There were those also, already in the service, who had enlisted under the first call of the President for troops for a three months' term. Early in May it was ascertained that by waiving their right to a choice of officers from among their own number, they could join a regiment, to be commanded by Colonel George H. Gordon. This they at once agreed to do, and at a meeting called for that purpose in the Village, they, by a unanimous vote, chose Samuel M. Quincy for Captain, William B. Williams for First Lieutenant, and O. H. Howard for Second Lieutenant, these being the men designated by Colonel Gordon. About May 11, 1861, the company, consisting of eighty men, fifty-four of whom were residents of Medway, left town for Camp Andrew, Brook Farm, in West Roxbury, and became Company E, Second Regiment Massachusetts Volunteers. In this camp of instruction they remained until July 8, 1861, when they marched by rail and steamer, via New York City, and through New Jersey and Maryland, to Northern Virginia, and became a part of the Army of the Potomac. It is not possible, within the limits here allowed, to give a history of their three years of field service. In addition to the brief biographical sketch of each soldier, which forms a part of this record, if any would know more of the weary marches, the hard-fought battles, and all the dangers and discomforts of army experience, they are referred to the *History of the Second Massachusetts Volunteers*, prepared by their Chaplain, the Rev. A. H. Quint, D. D., and also to a volume by the same author, entitled *The Potomac and Rapidan*.

But enlistments did not cease with the departure of the first company; men continued to volunteer, joining such branches of the service as suited their preference, until about thirty more had joined the army previous to the call of the President, dated July 2, 1862, for 300,000 additional men, to serve for three years, or the war. The quota of the town under this call was barely filled, when, on the 4th of August following, another call was issued for 300,000 men, to serve for nine months. This abbreviated term of service gave an impetus to enlistments. The quota of Medway, as first assigned, was rapidly filled, and more would have enlisted, had they been called for at the time. A subsequent revision of quotas throughout the state resulted in a call upon the town, later in the season, for twelve men more, under the same call, and for three years instead of nine months.

The nine months' men from Medway, with some from Medfield, Franklin, Bellingham, and Holliston, and a few from other places, made up a full company. This company was organized at Medway, on the 28th of August, 1862, by the choice of Joseph Stedman, of Medfield, Captain, David A. Partridge, of Medway, First Lieutenant, and Ira B. Cook, of Bellingham, Second Lieutenant. The sergeants were Joseph C. Clifford, George W. Ballou, Benjamin C. Tinkham, of Medway, T. M. Turner, of Medfield, and Albert L. Clark, of Medway; corporals, Fred D. Morse, of Medway, James B. Rabbit, of Wrentham, L. H. Turner, of Medfield, Edmund A. Jones, of Medway, Robert G. Lowey, of Sherborn, and Henry J. Daniels, of Medway. The company adopted the name of "The Adams Guard," in honor of the Hon. Charles Francis Adams, then United States Minister to England. On the 3d of September, 1862, they again assembled at Medway, preparatory to their departure for camp. Through the liberality of the citizens of the Village, they, with invited guests, partook of a bountiful dinner at the Quinobequin House, after which they marched to the church, where brief but stirring addresses were made by the several clergymen of this and adjoining towns, and by other distinguished citizens. Then a procession was formed, consisting of nearly a thousand persons, under command of the marshal of the day, A. Fairbanks, Esq., assisted by A. S. Harding and D. J. Hasting, Esqs., which escorted the " company to the station, where, amid cheers and tears, the train moved off with its precious freight." At the camp in Readville, Dedham, Mass., the company became Company B of the Seventy-second Regiment Massachusetts Volunteers. The regiment remained in camp until November 21, 1862, when it left for New York, to unite with the troops under General N. P. Banks, for an expedition to the gulf region. Their service was mostly in Louisiana. The company participated in two engagements, one at La Fourche Crossing, and the other at Brashear City. Owing to the exigencies of the service, the men were retained beyond their stipulated time, and did not arrive at home until nearly the middle of August, 1863. A large proportion returned suffering with malarial disease, of which several died, and the remainder recovered very slowly. Again, in 1864, at the call of the President for volunteers for one hundred days, many of the veterans of this regiment enlisted again, the ranks being filled up by new and younger men, about one-half the members of Company B being residents of Medway. During this term of service they were stationed at Alexandria and Great Falls, Md. The appended list of quotas contains the names of all who enlisted to the credit of the town under each call, from the beginning to the end of the war, with the amount of bounty paid to each, and the amount of state and town aid paid to families or dependents. There is also given an account of all the expenses of the town on account of the war, from April, 1861, to the close of December, 1865. It is certainly to the credit of the town, and worthy of mention, that at the close of the war the town had a surplus over all calls, of four men.

In June, 1863, a draft was ordered by the President for one-fifth of the first class enrolled. This class embraced all men between the ages of eighteen and thirty-five. For Medway, fifty-six were drafted. A copy of the provost-marshal's record appears on a subsequent page.

The acts of the town relating to the war, from 1861 to 1865 inclusive, already given, seem worthy of some comment. At a town-meeting held September 23, 1861, resolutions, prepared and presented by the Hon. M. M. Fisher, were unanimously adopted, authorizing the committee on military affairs to aid the families of any of our citizens who may fall in battle or die in the service of their country, to recover and bring home their remains. At a legal town-meeting, January 3, 1862, on motion of the same gentleman, the town voted unanimously, directing the selectmen to cause a record to be made of all volunteers from this town, or whose nearest kindred resided here, who have or may hereafter enlist in the service of the Government in the War for the Union. This is believed to have been the first act of the kind passed by any municipality in the Commonwealth. The Legislature of 1863 passed an act, a little more than one year later, requiring such a record to be kept by every town and city in the State. In the year 1864, when towns were prohibited by law from granting above a specified sum per man as bounty, the citizens subscribed to aid in filling the quotas of the town under the several calls for men, the sum of nearly seven thousand dollars. Afterwards, in 1865, under the provisions of a statute permitting the same, the town assumed and repaid these subscriptions to the amount of $6,700.

The ladies of the town, always ready for a good work, manifested from the first their interest in the comfort and welfare of our soldiers. The first company which left town, Company E, Second Massachusetts, carried many proofs of the thoughtful care of mother, wife, and sister, in conveniences indispensable to camp-life. The same care followed them, and Chaplain Quint, in his history of the regiment, speaks of special favors to the different companies by people of the towns from which they came ; alluding to Company E as experiencing particular kindness from Medway. But it was not to our own men alone but to others also that these supplies were sent. As the war progressed the call became more imperative. The sources of government supply had not expanded to keep pace with the necessities of such a vast army raised so suddenly. To meet these great needs, there were organized by the ladies in many towns and cities, Soldiers' Aid Societies. In this town the sewing circles of the day, better known then, perhaps, as "Ladies' Benevolent Societies," took up the work. At their large and frequent meetings a great amount of work was done. It would be gratifying if the amount and kind of work could now be stated. But no records can be obtained giving the interesting information. Suffice it to say that countless socks and mittens, under-flannels for soldiers' wear, clothing for hospital use, bedding, pillows for wounded limbs, lint and bandages were among the supplies. One lady says "the attic chests were ransacked, and grandmother's linen was none too good to be given." Fruit and delicacies for the sick were also donated and forwarded with the other supplies through the United States Sanitary Commission, or sent to the Chaplains of certain regiments.

A Complete Record of Men from Medway who served in the Army and Navy of the United States during the War for the Union, 1861 — 1865, with other Statistics of the Town relating to the War.

This Record was prepared under the direction of the Selectmen, pursuant of the Vote of the Town, and in accordance with the Acts of the State Legislature.

The Vote of the Town, passed January 3, 1862.

" Voted, That the Selectmen be directed to prepare a suitable record of all volunteers, from Medway and vicinity, attached to Co. E, 2d Reg't. Mass. Vols., and all others resident in this town, or whose parents or nearest kindred reside therein, enlisted or serving, or who may enlist and serve the Government in the war with the Rebel Confederacy; said record to give the names, ages, residence, nativity, date, and term of enlistment, term of actual service, date of their discharge, to what company and regiment attached, their rank, any action in which they may have been engaged, whether wounded, killed, or taken prisoner, also any important incidents connected with their service, together with the action of the town upon the war, votes passed, moneys expended, to whom, and for what paid, and all voluntary contributions in aid of the war, as far as practicable, said record to be made in a book provided for that purpose, and at the close of the war to be placed with other records of town in the clerk's office."

"THE COMMONWEALTH OF MASSACHUSETTS.

"An Act to Preserve a Record of our Soldiers and Officers.

"Approved March 7, 1863.

"Be it enacted by the Senate and House of Representatives, in General Court assembled, and by authority of the same, as follows:

"Section 1. It shall be the duty of the clerk of every city and town of the Commonwealth, as soon as may be after the passage of this act to make out a full and complete record of the names of all the soldiers and officers who compose his town's quota, of the troops furnished by the Commonwealth to the United States during the present rebellion, stating the place of residence, the time of enlistment of each, and the number and designation of his regiment and company; also the names of all who have resigned or been discharged, and at what time and for what cause, and all who have died in the service, and stating when practicable, at what time and place and the cause of death, whether by disease, accident, or on the field of battle, and the promotions of officers and from the ranks, and the date thereof; and the names of all absentees, if any; and all such other facts as may relate strictly to the military career of each soldier and officer.

"Sec. 2. It shall be the duty of the clerk of every city and town to procure a suitable blank book in which to make said record, and to preserve it among the other records of the town, and make such addition to the same as may be necessary, from time to time, to make said record perfect and complete. And said clerks shall be entitled to a reasonable compensation for their services and expenses in performing the duties devolved upon them by the provisions of this act, to be paid by their respective cities or towns.

"Sec. 3. This act shall take effect upon its passage."

"An Act in addition to 'An Act to Preserve a Record of our Soldiers and Officers.'

"Approved April 29, 1863.

"Be it enacted by the Senate and House of Representatives, in General Court assembled, and by authority of the same, as follows:

"Section 1. The first section of an act, entitled 'An Act to Preserve a Record of our Soldiers and Officers,' approved March seventh in the year eighteen hundred and sixty-three, is hereby so amended that the record required by the provisions of said first section, shall, as far as practicable, state the time and place of birth, names of parents, previous occupation, term of enlistment, time of entering the service, and whether married or single, of all such soldiers and officers.

"Sec. 2. The clerk of each city and town shall also keep a full and complete record of the names of all soldiers and officers residents of all such cities and towns engaged in the naval service of the United States during the present rebellion, which record, shall, as far as practicable, state the time and place of birth, names of parents, the date at which he entered such service, his previous occupation, whether he was married or single, the vessel or vessels on which he served, the battles or kind of service in which he was engaged, whether he resigned or was discharged, or deserted, and the date of such resignation, discharge, or desertion, the cause of such discharge or resignation, his promotion and the dates, occasions and nature of the same; and if he died in the service it shall state the date and cause of his death, and such record shall contain any and all other such facts as relate to the naval career of such seamen or officers during such rebellion.

"Sec. 3. The adjutant-general shall prepare suitable blank books in conformity with the requirements of this act, with proper blanks for marginal notes, and furnish the same to the several cities and towns at cost on the application of the clerk thereof.

"Sec. 4. All the expenses incurred in making said records, with the cost of the record books, shall be paid by the several cities and towns, and the records, when completed, shall be deposited and kept in the city and town clerk's office.

"Sec. 5. The second section of chapter sixty-five of the acts of the year eighteen hundred and sixty-three, is hereby repealed.

"Sec. 6. This act shall take effect upon its passage."

The Soldiers of the Union Army.

1861 — 1865.

The Volunteers under the first call of the President for three months' men, dated April 15, 1861.

	AID.		AID.
Amos L. Fuller	$36 00	Addison T. Hastings	
George W. Mahr		Egbert O. Hixon	
William S. Partridge		Francis L. B. Monroe	
William H. Dunbar			

The Volunteers under the second call of the President, and enlisted persons to July, 1862.

	AID.		AID.
Milton S. Adams	$498 17	George B. Everett	$
Sidney W. Allen	73 00	Charles H. Everett	
Henry W. Browne	130 75	Albert F. Fales	338 00
George F. Browne		John M. Fales	174 82
Albert A. Ballou	608 00	Emmons Force	
Edmund M. Bullen	444 30	Charles F. Fuller	230 00
George H. Barton	166 00	Thomas Flaherty	134 26
John W. Cass		James M. Grant	319 30
Albert H. Clark	338 00	Frank S. Grant	
Charles E. Cummings		Isaac C. Greenwood	664 00
Timothy Coughlin		George E. Greenwood	32 00
Charles E. Cary		Charles A. Grant	12 50
David Coates		John Gormly	
John Coad		Peter Harrington	
William A. Daniels		John Henry	
Charles M. Disper	71 00	Edmund W. Hill	126 00
Thomas Dudy		Alvin W. Houghton	155 00
Alonzo E. Dunton	178 50	Albert C. Houghton	
Charles H. Daniels	534 21	Alonzo Hixon	918 25
William D. Daniels	174 00	Edward Hogan	156 42

	AID.		AID.
Edward P. Hart	$103 00	Martin W. Phipps	$255 12
Moses Hill	330 26	Thomas Rollins	224 00
Edwin H. Hosmer	38 84	Benjamin F. Remick	266 85
Egbert O. Hixon	395 82	George H. Read	112 71
William Hawes		Michael Slaven	
George H. Ide		Herman S. Sparrow	
Daniel Inman	29 00	John H. Swarman	226 42
Charles C. Kimball		Frederic Swarman	456 80
Charles G. Kingsbury		Lewis A. Treen	195 00
Albert W. Mann	260 00	John A. Treen	
James B. May	384 00	William H. Turner	
Edward A. May		Charles H. Torrey	28 14
Daniel Mundon	172 00	Charles Whitney	518 00
Eleazar Morse	505 90	Henry Wheat	185 32
Lewis L. Miller		Alfred C. Wheat	
Milton H. Morse	22 57	George H. Williams	
Gilbert McCullom	33 00	George C. Webber	653 82
F. Le Baron Monroe		Horace J. Wilmarth	123 57
Michael O'Donnell		David S. Darling	29 00
Alfred Onion		George F. Simpson	
John O'Hara		William H. Dunbar	
William R. Parsons	267 62	George V. Partridge	
Jonathan Pitcher	98 00	Emory Richardson	
Asa D. Prescott	250 40	James McCowan	32 00

The Volunteers under the third call of the President, July, 1862, for three years' men.

	BOUNTY.	AID.		BOUNTY.	AID.
Daniel McAleyey	$200	$	John Harney	$	$95 42
Lord M. Ackert	200		John G. Hosmer	100	127 00
George Bancroft	100	25 42	Joseph H. Howard	200	
Aaron Brown	100	86 84	Albert M. Hayward	200	
Newhall Barber	100		Thomas J. Harrington	200	
Sylvanus Bullard	100		Gilbert H. Leland	100	
Edward C. Barrows	100		Amos B. Morse	100	423 60
William Hiram Chace	100	36 00	William M. Martin	100	263 20
Alexander M. Cushing	100	204 00	George L. Myer	100	
David A. Clark	100		Peter Mawn	200	290 80
Edmund N. Clark	100		George O. Pond	100	215 60
John Carr	100	239 60	Franklin Proctor	100	
Abram D. Craig	100		Brougham Roberts	100	
Charles Clark	100	148 56	George H. Stratton	100	
Alonzo M. Dain	100		Jeremiah Vose	200	
Francis T. Dodge	100		Henry A. Wood	100	130 42
Lewis L. Fisher	200	59 00	Albert H. Wiley	100	189 68
George O. Grant		68 20	John Whitman	100	
Joseph A. Greenwood		148 40	Charles Warden	100	

Volunteers under the fourth call of the President, August, 1862, for nine months' men.

	BOUNTY.	AID.		BOUNTY.	AID.
Charles A. Adams	$100	$	Albert E. Bullard	$100	$165 42
Erastus Adams	100	278 80	Robert W. Brown		134 80
George W. Adams	100		J. Warren Clark	100	
Stephen P. Adams	100		Sewall J. Clark	100	134 80
William Adams	100	48 70	Albert L. Clark	100	
Daniel Ackley	100	306 80	Joseph C. Clifford	100	11 00
Lewis Buffum	100	86 80	D. Frank Covell		14 00
George W. Ballou	100	186 80	Charles H. Cole	100	33 00

	BOUNTY.	AID.		BOUNTY.	AID.
Henry J. Daniels	$100	$	Edwin C. Pond	$100	$
James E. Fales	100	50 70	Edwin D. Pond	100	
Frank L. Fisher	100		George E. Pond	100	
George H. Fisher	100		Warren J. Partridge	100	
Willard P. Fisher	100	61 70	George S. Rice	100	48 70
Julius A. Fitts	100		Addison W. Richardson	100	
Theodore W. Fisher	100		Henry L. Snell	100	
George H. Greenwood	100	97 42	John F. Stratton	100	172 23
Edmund A. Jones	100		George S. Sanford	100	
Frank V. Mann	100	48 70	Benjamin C. Tinkham	100	87 20
James Mitchell	100	282 80	Lucius M. Turner	100	134 80
Frederic D. Morse	100		William H. Thomas	100	33 00
Robert T. Morse	100		John Willey	100	134 80
John Nolan	100	282 80	Lewis Wheeler	100	
David A. Partridge	100		Daniel S. Woodman	100	
George E. Pettis	100		Orson D. Young	100	134 80

Three years' men, enlisted under the same call. an additional number being required of the town by re-adjustment of quotas.

	BOUNTY.	AID.		BOUNTY.	AID.
William C. Hawes	$150	$226 00	John Watts	$150	
James Andrews	150		Charles Allen	150	
John Miller	150		Charles Murray	150	
John Winter	150		John Conly	150	
George F. French	150		John Thompson	150	
James Brown	150		Richard Searles	150	

Volunteers under the calls of the President, sixth, seventh, and eighth, October, 1863. February and March, 1864, for three years.

	BOUNTY.	AID.		BOUNTY.	AID.
Harrison G. O. Grant	$	$196 98	Charles Clark	$	$101 00
George G. Nourse	100	67 70	Alonzo E. Dunton		120 00
Aaron Brown	100	135 42	Charles H. Daniels		202 00
George W. Bullard	100	186 80	Horace J. Wilmarth		78 42
Joel P. Bullard	100		George H. Read		104 00
Warren A. Clark	100	8 00	Andrew Morse		136 00
Asa Clark	100	193 80	George H. Barton	165	166 00
Henry M. Rockwood	100	67 42	Asaph M. Bisbee	155	
Albert L. Vallet	100	96 80	Sheppard Davis	155	
James A. Gale	100	128 26	John H. Kendall	155	87 00
George H. Hixon	100	67 42	Marshall A. Bent	155	
Ezra Pierson	100	191 80	Henry Tibbets	155	15 00
Joseph L. Gould	100		George F. Leavit	155	
John Looby		233 00	John Farren	160	154 00
John A. Pierce	100	208 00	Martin M. Keith	185	
Robert O. Young	100	228 80	John H. Durgin	185	
Henry R. Dain	100	228 80	James Spellman	185	
Charles E. Burr		33 00	James G. Young	185	
Charles Magorty			David H. Benner	185	
Edmund J. Smith			Jeremiah Cassidy	185	
William Smith			Samuel P. Coffin	185	
Charles E. Whitney			Joseph Kersher	185	72 00
James Whitcomb			John Fendt	185	117 14
Timothy Daly		52 00	Thomas McKenna	185	
George Bancroft		59 42	Charles W. Bracket	190	
George A. Fuller			Andrew Fitzsimmons	190	
Willard P. Fisher	100	134 84	William Kirby	190	

	BOUNTY.	AID.
Matthew M. Sperry	$190	$
John McCann	190	
Alfred R. Bell	190	39 56
John B. Jones	190	
Arunah Ladd	190	
George Brown	210	
William W. Forman	285	130 84

	BOUNTY.	AID.
John F. O. Driscoll	$285	$212 40
Phillip O. Sparrow,		
George W. Mahr,	(Drafted men.)	448 20
George B. Hardy,		134 00
Shubael E. Dunbar,		
William H. Matthews (substitute)		

Volunteers for one hundred days, under the ninth call of the President, July, 1864.

Benj. C. Tinkham,	William O. Andrews,	Amos A. Dugan,	George S. Rice,
George W. Ballou,	Edwin H. Holbrook,	Edwin S. Davis,	Henry H. Rich,
George E. Fuller,	E. A. J. Adams,	Michael Fitzgerald,	Timothy Reardon,
Henry J. Daniels,	William Adams,	Edwin A. Grant,	Patrick Regan,
J. Warren Clark,	George H. Andrews,	Daniel Hammond,	George A. Stedman,
Alfred A. Cary,	Adln P. Blake,	James H. Heaton,	Lewis Wheeler,
Stephen P. Adams,	Samuel B. Cary,	Frank W. Kimball,	Edwin H. Hosmer,
Edmund W. Hill,	Charles H. Cole,	Geo. H. Kingsbury,	James S. Mitchell,
Sewall J. Clark,	Frederic F. Clark,	George L. Myer,	William A. Nolan,
Frank L. Fisher,	Alfred Clifford,	William F. Meritt,	George S. Sanford,
George E. Pond,	William B. Clark,	Stephen F. Purdy,	George H. Rich.

Volunteers under the tenth call of the President, July, 1864, for one, two, and three years.

	BOUNTY.	AID.
John Leonard	$	$87 00
Calvin Adams	325	44 00
Richard B. McElroy	325	122 80
Charles S. Clark	325	101 80
Wm. H. Dunbar	325	42 56
Albert Vallet	325	96 80
William Lilley	325	122 80
James G. Richards	325	
James E. Lawrence	325	138 80
Jesse Darling	325	101 80
Geo. W. Whitney	325	
Peter Foster	325	122 80
Isaac C. Greenwood	325	110 88
John T. Greenwood	325	
William M. Martin	325	110 90
Horatio T. Leonard	325	82 00

	BOUNTY.	AID.
Benj. F. Dexter	$325	$ 39 14
James F. Holmes	325	38 60
William Harold	325	22 00
Robert Hall	300	
James J. Treanor	300	
Charles E. Williams	325	24 00
Geo. A. Jacobs	300	37 84
Michael Schofield	325	
Chandler W. Sanders	325	50 12
John Higgins	325	110 80
John F. Stratton	325	109 60
Geo. C. Webber	325	123 20
John Monks (substitute)	125	33 00
George H. Allen		
William H. Pettis		29 00
Avery Sylvester		

Silas P. Adams	Navy		For one year.
William D. Newland	"		For four years.
James Fitzgerald	"		For four years.
George H. Hixon	"		For one year.
John O. Hara	"		Transferred from 18th Infantry.
Christopher Corrigan	$80		For one year	$52 00
James Murray	"		For one year	31 00

In addition to the above, there were assigned to the quota of Medway by the Navy Commissioners the following who had enlisted at large, that is, without naming any city or town as their residence.

Henry Clay,	John Donaphy,	Henry Callaghan,	Gustave Finck,
Rodman Carpenter,	Hugh Donnelly,	Thomas Farranty,	Alfred N. Fielder,
Daniel Cusick,	Michael Donovan,	Stephen Farrell,	Bernard Fitzpatrick,
Lucian R. Dorr,	Milton S. Dodge,	Ederic S. Fernald,	Joseph Fortis,
Thomas Donnivan,	Lysander W. Colson,	Albert Fisher (officer),	Willam Freeman,

Volunteers under the call of the President for one, two, and three years, dated December, 1864.

	BOUNTY.	AID.		BOUNTY	AID.
Frank B. Andrews	$130	37 70	John McCabe	170	
William P. Wyman	130		William F. Britton	170	
Charles H. Stewart	130		Edward H. Wheeler	170	
Edward L. Andrews	135	57 70	Jacob W. Butler	170	31 42
Charles H. Fisher	135		Patrick J. Donnovan	165	69 60
Michael Hart, Jr	135	33 70	James McLaughlin	145	87 42
Patrick Killaly	145	29 70	Timothy Coughlin	145	32 12
Silas Force	135		John Welch	165	6 00
James T. Higgings	145	32 70	Thomas Reese	165	
Henry S. Fisher	150	33 84	George W. Armitage	170	
Cornelius Keating	150	64 84	Charles Osborne	170	
William F. Kemp	175		John Hirl	170	
Hugh O'Brien	175		Melvin awyer	170	
Thomas O'Rourke	175		Edward G. Tutein	165	
William E. Pettingill	150		George W. Bartlett	125	28 00
Frank X. Sinzinger	170		Amos A. Dugan	125	
James F. Murphy	175		Henry Watts, (State Recruits.)	125	
Alpheus Proctor	175	31 84	James Wright, (State Recruits.)	100	
Patrick Raferty	160		James Hubbard, (State Recruits.)	100	
George W. Codding	165	44 98	Henry Ringold, (State Recruits.)	100	
Thomas Hacket	170		Alexander Scott, (State Recruits.)	150	
George F. Brown	165	69 20	John Lewis, (State Recruits.)	100	
George F. Marden	170		Nelson Neptune. (State Recruits.)	100	

Volunteers from Medway who were accredited to other towns but whose families received aid form this town.

John Crawford	Accredited to Milford	$157 60
Christopher McNemara	Accredited to Boston	51 70
John Scott	Accredited to Cambridge	326 00
Samuel B. Adams	Accredited to Orange	106 60
Henry Wheat	Accredited to Bridgewater	93 88
		$735 78

The Drafts Ordered and Made.

The first draft under the call of the President for one-fifth of the first class enrolled was made for this town July 15, 1863. The following is a copy of the Provost-Marshal's Record:

George H. Hixon. Exempted. The only support of his mother.
John F. Lesure. Exempted. Chronic inflammation, neck of bladder.
Joseph H. Disper. Exempted. Chest too small.
Addison A. Smith. Exempted. Natural feebleness of constitution.
George S. Lesure. Passed. Paid commutation, $300.
Otis Springer. Passed. Paid commutation, $300.
Asa A. Green. Exempted. Malformation of chest.
Thomas O'Sullivan. Exempted. Hernia, right inguinal.
Patrick Keith. Exempted. Over age.
William F. Carroll. Exempted. Over age.
Harlan P. Sanford. Drafted at Washington, D. C., and paid commutation there.

The Second Draft.

Henry E. Gay. Passed. Furnished a substitute. Paid $300.
Shubael E. Dunbar. Passed. Went into service.
Henry Cooper. Passed. Paid commutation, $300.

William W. Gay. Passed. Paid commutation, $300.
Elihu C. Wilson. Exempted. Chest too small.
Phillip O. Sparrow. Passed. Went into service.
Charles C. Kimball. Passed. Paid commutation, $300.
George H. Cummings. Exempted. Alien.
Andrew Partridge. Exempted. Insufficient teeth.
Joseph C. Claflin. Passed. Paid commutation, $300.
Oliver A. Clark. Exempted. Parents elect before the draft.
Henry M. Daniels. Passed. Paid commutation, $300.
Lewis L. Fisher. Exempted. Chronic diarrhœa.
Charles E. Wood. Exempted. Chest too small.

The Third Draft.

David A. Hixon. Exempted. Only son of infirm mother.
Nathaniel Adams. Passed. Paid commutation, $300.
Charles Morris. Exempted. Non-resident.
George A. Richards. Exempted. Hernia, left inguinal.
Charles F. Adams. Exempted. Hernia and natural feebleness of constitution.
Barney Rooney. Exempted. Alien.
Frank A. Lovell. Exempted. Insufficient teeth.
Byron Albee. Exempted. Old granular inflammation of eyelids.
George W. Mahr. Passed. Went into the service.
Charles S. Adams. Exempted. Hernia, left inguinal.
John A. Hutchins. Exempted. Hemorrhoids, ulcerated.
Matthew Mooney. A deserter. Never reported.
Walter D. Ray. Passed. Paid commutation, $300.
Charles S. Clark. Exempted.

The Fourth Draft.

Charles H. Torrey. Exempted. In service March 3, 1863.
Daniel Covell. Exempted. Only support of parents.
John W. Cass. Exempted. Decided feebleness of constitution.
Joseph S. Adams. Passed. Paid commutation, $300.
William B. Hodges. Exempted. Feebleness of constitution.
Nathan W. Davenport. Passed. Paid commutation, $300.
Willard P. Clark. Passed. Paid commutation, $300.
George Black. Exempted. Enlargement of the heart.
William H. Webb. Exempted. Malformation of chest.
Edward Cheeny. Exempted. Insufficient teeth.
Henry Wheat. Exempted. Insufficient teeth.
Silas P. Adams. In the navy.
William M. Adams. Exempted. Decided feebleness of constitution.
Charles McGuire. A deserter. Never reported.

The Fifth Draft.

George B. Hardy. Passed. Went into service.
Erastus H. Tyler. Exempted. Only support of mother.
Charles W. Seavey. Exempted. Chest too small.

SUMMARY.

Number drafted	56	Number went into service	4
Number exempted	35	Number drafted elsewhere	1
Number paid commutation	12	Number in naval service	1
Number put in a substitute	1	Number never reported	2

MILITARY EXPENSES OF THE TOWN, 1861 — 1865.

MAY, 1861, TO MARCH, 1862.

Paid to volunteers for drilling and outfit.................................$607 00
Paid George P. Metcalf, use of hall for drilling............................. 9 00
Paid sundry persons for expenses relating to volunteers...................... 44 69

17

Paid Military Committee for services to March 1, 1862, as follows

Abram S Harding........$ 5 00	William Daniels	$7 00	
David Daniels............ 20 93	Sundry bills by town		
Joel P Adams. 5 00	treasurer..............	8 25	$84 18
Jason Smith... ... . 6 00	Total expense for the year,		
Simeon Fisher. 5 00	aside from aid to fam-		
Charles H. Deans 27 00	ilies....		$744 87

MARCH, 1862, to MARCH, 1863

Paid Bounties to 35 three years' men... ....$4,300 00
Paid Bounties to 46 nine months' men 4,600 00
Paid Bounties to 12 three years' men 1,800 00

Total Bounties during the year....................$10,700 00

Miscellaneous Expenses.

Paid D J. Hastings for recovery of bodies of Ide and Sparrow. $41 00
Paid W D. Daniels toward expense of removal of body of W. A. Daniels 50 00
Paid sundry expenses........ .... 8 03
Paid Alfred A. Cary for attempt to recover the body of Charles E Cary 25 00
Paid A M B. Fuller, time and expenses recruiting 37 49
Paid William Daniels, 23 days and expenses 60 04
Paid Clark Partridge, 8 days and expenses..... .. .. 21 70
Paid Simeon Fisher, 4 days 6 00
Paid A P. & R O Forbush, board of recruits..... . .. . 13 00
Paid D. J. Hastings, telegram........... . ... 2 89
Paid Merrill & Son, printing posters 2 50
Paid Dr. A L. B Monroe, examining sixty-three recruits........ .... 31 50
Paid D A Partridge, assistance in recruiting 46 00
Paid music at funeral of W. A. Daniels 25 00
Paid special aid to Mrs. Caroline E Cushing 50 00

Total miscellaneous expenses paid $420 15

MARCH, 1863, TO MARCH, 1864.

Miscellaneous Expenses

Paid toward removal of body of C. E Cummings $46 00
Paid toward removal of body of George O. Pond.. ... . 50 00
Paid toward removal of body of D. F. Covell... .... 15 00

Total miscellaneous...... . ... $111 00

MARCH, 1864, TO MARCH, 1865.

Paid Bounties to 44 men, for three years, under calls of October, 1863, Feb-
 ruary and March, 1864 .... $ 7,005 00
Paid Bounties to 27 men for one year, call of July, 1864 .... 8,700 00
Paid J M. Daniels toward substitute................................... .. . 125 00
Paid one man in Navy, one year........ .... 80 00
Paid 39 men for one year, call of December, 1864 ... . 6,105 00
Paid for 7 state recruits. 725 00

Total....... .... $22,740 00

Miscellaneous Expenses.

Paid D. J. Hastings, money expended in recruiting $115 05
Paid D J. Hastings, 65 days, from December, 1863 to July, 1864...... . .... 130 00
Paid D J. Hastings, horse and carriage hire... .... 32 16

Paid Stacey and others for printing.. 9 37
Paid enrolled men to Worcester for exemption............................... 4S 8o
Paid board of 2d Heavy Artillery Band, 24 men, one day, and other expenses
    of recruiting meeting at the village............................. .... 46 oo
Paid W. Daniels, services, 46 days, @ $3.50, including expenses............. 161 oo
Paid for posters and circulars............ .... 5 5o
Paid V. R. Coombs, services and expenses...................... .... 8 oo
Paid C. Partridge, 7 days' services and expenses........................... 22 5o
Paid Daniel G. Marston, assistance in recruiting........... .... 25 oo
Paid D. J. Hastings, special services in securing credit for three years' men.. 375 oo
Paid for removal of body of Edwin A. Grant.......................... ..... 50 oo
Paid for removal of body of Gilbert McCullora............................. 4t oo

              Total miscellaneous expenses for the year.......$1,069 38

The Final Summary of Town Expenses for the War.

Paid for Bounties...$33,440 oo
Refunded by the State, 1863................................... 4,035 29
                             ————— $29,404 7t
Paid for the recovery of bodies............................. 318 oo
Miscellaneous expenses paid................................. 2,234 40
Paid State and Town aid to families and dependents, from May,
    1861, to December 31, 1865................................$27,150 65
Amount re-imbursed by the State 23,429 8o
                             ————— 3,720 85

           Total paid by the Town.............. $35,677 96

The Record of the Union Soldiers.

Lord M. Ackert was born in 1831, in New York City. He was recruited by Lieut. A. D. Sawyer, of the 2d Mass. Regt., and was mustered into the service of the United States for three years, Aug. 30, 1862, in Boston, Mass., and accredited to Medway. He was assigned to Co. H, 2d Regt. Mass. Vols. He was mustered out of the service May 28, 1864. He appears on the state record to the credit of Peru, Mass.

Daniel Ackley, son of Samuel and Eliza Ackley, was born Jan. 16, 1830, in Rumford, Me. He was mustered into the service of the United States for nine months, Sept. 13, 1862, in Camp Meigs, Readville, Mass., as a private of Co. B, 2d Regt. Mass. Vols. The regiment was in the Department of the Gulf. The only battle in which he was engaged took place June 23, 1863, in Brashear City, La. He was taken prisoner, paroled June 25, and mustered out of service Aug. 20, 1863, in Readville, Mass., his term having expired. Like many of his comrades he came home suffering with malarial disease, being for a long time incapacitated for labor.

Calvin Adams, son of Peter and Anna U. (Claflin) Adams, was born July 29, 1821, in Holliston, Mass., a part of that town now within the limits of Medway. He was mustered into the United States service Aug. 13, 1864, for one year, as a private of the 19th unattached Co., afterwards Co. C, 4th Regt. Mass. Heavy Arty. He served in the defense of Washington, D. C. He was mustered out of service June 17, 1865, at the close of the war.

CHARLES A. ADAMS, son of Gilbert and Sally (Seavey) Adams, was born May 18, 1845, in Holliston, Mass. He was mustered into the United States service, Sept. 13, 1862, for nine months, as a private of Co. B, 42d Regt. Mass. Vols., in Readville, Mass. He was mustered out of service in Readville at the expiration of his term, Aug 20, 1863. He enlisted a second time early in January, 1865, for one year, as a private of Co. K, 61st Regt. Mass Vols., and was accredited to the town of Bellingham. He was mustered out July 16, 1865.

CHARLES C. ADAMS was a lad who lived in West Medway, prior to the war. He enlisted in Boston, and served three years as a bugler in Co. G, 11th Regt. U. S. Inf Since the close of the war he has been in business in Boston He retains such an interest in the town where he lived in his boyhood, that he would gladly be accounted in the list of soldiers as a Medway boy.

ELIAKIM A. J. ADAMS, son of Eliakim and Elizabeth Adams, was born Sept 18, 1835, in Medway. Enlisted for one hundred days and was mustered into service July 22, 1864, as a private of Co. B, 42d Regt Mass Vols., stationed at Alexandria and Great Falls, Md He served in the defense of Washington, D. C., and was mustered out Nov 11, 1864

ERASTUS ADAMS, son of Walter and Mary (Dadmun) Adams, was born Jan. 3, 1842, in Union, Me He was mustered into the United States service Sept. 13, 1862, for nine months, as a private of Co. B, 42d Regt Mass. Vols , in Readville, Mass He was in the engagement at Brashear City, La., June 23, 1863, and was taken prisoner Paroled and liberated June 26, 1863. Mustered out of service Aug. 20, 1863, his term having expired. He removed several years since to Grafton, Mass , where he now resides

GEORGE W. ADAMS, son of William and Emeline Adams, was born Jan. 24, 1841, in Walpole, Mass. He was mustered into the United States service for nine months, Sept 13, 1862, in Readville, Mass., as a private of Co B, 42d Regt Mass. Vols He was mustered out of service by reason of the expiration of his term, Aug 20, 1863, in Readville.

MILTON S. ADAMS, son of William and Huldah Adams, was born Oct. 10, 1833, in Medway. He enlisted May 11, 1861, and was mustered into the service of the United States for three years, May 25, 1861, in Camp Andrew, West Roxbury, Mass , as Corporal of Co E, 2d Regt. Mass. Vols. He was in every battle and skirmish of the regiment during his term of service. The principal engagements were in Winchester, Va , May 25, Cedar Mountain, Va., August 9, Antietam, Md., Sept. 17, 1862, in Chancellorsville, Va , May 3, Beverly Ford, Va . June 9, Gettysburg, Penn., July 2 and 3, 1863 ; and in Resaca, Ga , May 15, 1864. He was mustered out of service May 28, 1864, his term of service having expired, and subsequently resided in Medway.

SAMUEL B ADAMS, son of Eliakim and Elizabeth Adams, was born July 2, 1840, in Walpole, Mass He was mustered into the United States service July 21, 1861, for three years, as a private of Co. A, 21st Regt. Mass. Vols , Col. Morse commanding Being at that time a resident of Orange, Mass , he was accredited to that town. He states that he was in the battles of Cedar Mountain, Aug 9, 1862, second Bull Run, August 29, Chantilly, about September 1 ; South Mountain, September 14 ; Antietam, September

17; Blue Springs in October, Lenons Station or Loudon Bridge in November, and at the siege of Knoxville, Tenn., from Nov. 17 to Dec. 5, 1863. He reënlisted Jan. 1, 1864, into Co. K, at Blairs Cross Roads, Tenn., for three years or the war, intending to be accredited to Medway, and so appears upon the elective vote, but by error in filling out the muster in roll he was again accredited to Orange. He was afterwards in the battle of the Wilderness, May 6, 1864, and at Spottsylvania, May 12, when he received a severe wound in the left hand. Transferred June 9, 1865, to Vet. Res. Corps, 131st Co., 2d Battalion. Discharged for disability July 10, 1865, from which date he has been a resident of Medway. He had twin sons born Jan. 11, 1864, during the war, who were named Edrick Jesse Butler and Edgar Samuel Burnside Adams. He received a pension.

SILAS P. ADAMS, son of Walter and Mary (Dadmun) Adams, was born July 24, 1843, in Lexington, Mass. He enlisted about July 24, 1863, for one year, in the United States Navy. Though at that time a resident of Worcester, he was accredited to the town of Medway, having been enrolled here on account of being a minor. He was assigned to the schooner "George Mangham"; rank, landsman. The vessel was first sent to the British Provinces. It was afterwards assigned to duty on the blockading fleet, and patrolled the coast from North Carolina to Florida. During his service he was under fire from Forts Wagner and Sumter during the siege of those works. He was discharged about Sept. 17, 1864, in Philadelphia, Penn.

STEPHEN P. ADAMS, son of Newell and Abigail (Blake) Adams, was born Aug. 29, 1842, in Medway. Was mustered into the United States service Sept. 13, 1862, for nine months, in Readville, Mass., as a private in Co. B, 42d Regt. Mass. Vols. He was mustered out of service at the expiration of his term, Aug. 20, 1863, in Readville. He reënlisted and was mustered into the United States service July 22, 1864, for one hundred days as 4th Sergt. of Co. B, 42d Regt. Mass. Vols.; was mustered out Nov. 9, 1864, his term having expired. Soon after the war he went through a course of study in the Commercial College of Poughkeepsie, N. Y. He then went to Augusta, Me., where he established a commercial school as principal and proprietor. This was broken up by the great fire which occurred soon after, and he then went to Plattsburgh, N. Y., where he opened a similar school, which he taught about seven months, when he was taken ill, and died Dec. 24, 1866.

WILLIAM ADAMS, son of Ira and Dolly (Morgan) Adams, was born Dec. 19, 1839, in Holliston, Mass. He was mustered into the United States service for nine months, Sept. 13, 1862, as a private of Co. B, 42d Regt. Mass. Vols., in Readville, Mass. He was mustered out of service by reason of the expiration of his term, Aug. 20, 1863, in Readville. He reënlisted, and was mustered July 22, 1864, for one hundred days, as a private of same regiment and company, and was mustered out Nov. 9, 1864.

CHARLES ALLEN enlisted and was mustered into the United States service December, 1862, for the term of three years, as a recruit for the 29th Regt. Mass. Vols. He was accredited to Medway but not a resident.

GEORGE H. ALLEN, son of Seth and Sarah (Curtis) Allen, was born June 21, 1829, in Medway. He enlisted and was mustered into the United States service Sept. 13, 1862, for nine months, as a private of Co. B, 42d

Regt. Mass. Vols. He was at that time a resident of Holliston and was accredited to that town. He was mustered out of service Aug. 28, 1863, his term having expired. He enlisted a second time and was mustered into service Dec. 7, 1863, as a private of Co. G, 2d Mass. Heavy Arty. He was taken prisoner at Plymouth, N. C., in April, 1864, and died Aug. 11, 1864, of hardship and starvation at the prison pen of Andersonville, Ga. On his last enlistment he was accredited to Medway. He was buried in the grave marked No. 5,334.

SIDNEY W. ALLEN, son of James W. and Jane (Whiting) Allen, was born Aug. 29, 1841, in Milford, Mass. He enlisted and May 25, 1861, was mustered into the service of the United States for three years, in Camp Andrew, West Roxbury, Mass., as a Private in Co. E, 2d Regt. Mass. Vols. He was in all the earlier skirmishes of the regiment, in the fight at Winchester, Va., May 25, and Cedar Mountain, Va., Aug. 9, 1862, when he was wounded in the hand by a buckshot, but returned to duty. and was in the battle of Antietam, Sept. 17, 1862, when he was severely wounded in the heel. He was sent to the hospital at Frederick, Md., afterwards to York, Penn., and subsequently to Convalescent Camp Hospital, in Baltimore, Md. He did not return to his regiment until March 1, 1864. He was under fire at the battle of Reseca, Ga., but not in the ranks, having been detailed as a servant to Lieut. Cook, of Co. E. He was mustered out of service May 28, 1864, his term having expired. He married Nov. 18, 1869, Sarah E. Martin, and resided in Medway. He became insane, was sent to the Worcester Asylum, and died Aug. 8, 1871.

EDWARD L. ANDREWS, residence Boston, was mustered into the United States service Nov. 21, 1864, to serve for one year, as a private of Co. G, 61st Regt. Mass. Vols. He was discharged for disability July 21, 1865, having been injured by sunstroke while on drill.

FRANK B. ANDREWS, residence Salisbury, Mass., was mustered into the United States service Oct. 25, 1864, to serve for one year as a private of Co. F, 61st Regt. Mass. Vols. He was a musician, and was mustered out of service July 16, 1865, by reason of the close of the war.

GEORGE H. ANDREWS, son of Albert A. and Cynthia (Mann) Andrews, was born March 3, 1847, in Medway. He enlisted and was mustered into the United States service July 22, 1864, as a private of Co. B, 42d Regt. Mass. Vols. He was mustered out at the expiration of his term, Nov. 9, 1864, having enlisted for one hundred days.

JAMES ANDREWS was mustered into the United States service, Dec. 13, 1862, to serve three years, as a private of Co. C, 2d Regt. Mass. Cav. He is reported as having deserted Dec. 28, 1862. Mr. Andrews was not a resident of Medway.

WILLIAM O. ANDREWS, son of Albert A. and Cynthia (Mann) Andrews, was born June 4, 1845, in Medway. He was mustered into the United States service July 22, 1864, to serve for one hundred days as a Corporal of Co. B, 42d Regt. Mass. Vols. He was mustered out Nov. 9, 1864, at the expiration of his term.

GEORGE W. ARMITAGE, age twenty-three, residence not known. He enlisted and was mustered into the United States service Dec. 13, 1864, for one year as a private of 26th unattached Co. Inf., and accredited to Medway. He was mustered out May 12, 1865, the war being ended.

ALBERT A. BALLOU was born in 1831, in Wrentham. He enlisted and was mustered into the United States service May 25, 1861, for three years, in Camp Andrew, West Roxbury, Mass., as a private of Co. E, 2d Mass. Inf. He was in the engagement at Winchester, Va., May 25, 1862, and was taken prisoner. He was paroled after a time, exchanged, and returned to duty Oct. 23, 1862. He was in the battle of Chancellorsville, May 3, 1863, and was mustered out May 28, 1864, by reason of the expiration of his term.

GEORGE W. BALLOU, son of Thurston and Caroline Ballou, was born May 15, 1832, in Cumberland, R. I. He enlisted and was mustered into the service of the United States, Sept. 13, 1862, for nine months, as a Sergeant of Co. B, 42d Regt. Mass. Vols. He was promoted to 1st Sergeant before the regiment left Massachusetts. In the engagement at Brashear City, La., June 23, 1863, being in command of a detachment of forty-six men of his regiment, which formed a part of the garrison at that place, he was severely wounded in the left fore-arm by a rifle shot. Finding themselves overpowered by numbers, the garrison made an attempt to escape, but were taken prisoners. The prisoners were paroled on the 26th of June, and set at liberty, Sergeant Ballou among them. He was mustered out of service Aug. 20, 1863, in Readville, Mass., his term having expired. He enlisted a second time, and was mustered into the United States service July 22, 1864, for one hundred days, as 1st Lieut. of Co. B, 42d Regt. Mass. Vols. He was mustered out at the expiration of his term, Nov. 11, 1864. Soon after the close of the war he removed to Wilmington, Del., and was engaged for several years in the business of millinery and straw goods. Suffering from the wound he had received he relinquished business, and retired, in 1875, upon a farm in Hubbardston, Mass. In 1883 he removed to, and now resides in, Franklin, Mass.

GEORGE W BANCROFT was born in 1828, in Blackstone, Mass. He was mustered into the United States service July 28, 1862, for three years, as a private of Co. E, 2d Regt. Mass. Vols. He was discharged Oct. 25, 1862, for disability in Camp Maryland Heights. He enlisted a second time, and was mustered into service Jan. 6, 1864, for three years, as a private of Co. C, 4th Mass Cav. He was again discharged for disability Oct. 5, 1864, and died March 31, 1865, of disease at home, in West Medway.

NEWELL BARBER, son of John H. and Sally Barber, was born May 1, 1848, in Medway. He enlisted and was mustered into the United States service, Aug. 17, 1862, as a private of Co I, 38th Regt. Mass. Vols. He was with his company in the engagement at Fort Bisland, La., April 13, 1863, and at Port Hudson, May 25 and 27, and June 14 of the same year. While before Port Hudson he was struck on the top of his head by a spent rifle ball. He died Aug. 14, 1863, of diphtheria, at the regimental hospital, Baton Rouge, La.

EDWARD C. BARROWS, son of Saben and Harriet Barrows, was born in 1844. He was mustered into the United States service Aug. 14, 1862, for three years, as a private of Co. I, 38th Regt. Mass. Vols. He resided in Sherborn, but was accredited to Medway. He deserted soon after the regiment left Massachusetts. State record says deserted Aug. 28, 1862, at Baltimore, Md.

GEORGE W. BARTLETT, son of George and Rebecca (Woodward) Bartlett, was born Dec. 26, 1846, in Canton, Mass. He enlisted and was mustered into the United States service Jan. 10, 1865, for one year, as a private of Co. K, 71st Regt., Mass. Vols. He was in the engagement before Petersburg, Va., April 2, 1865. He was mustered out of service July 16, 1865.

GEORGE H. BARTON, son of Willard and Susan M. (Spaulding) Barton, was born about 1848, in Medway. He first enlisted April 25, 1861, for two years, as a private of Co. E, 2d Regt. Maine Vols. While a member of this regiment he was in the battle of Bull Run, July 21, 1861, and was wounded in the left arm by a musket ball so as nearly to deprive him of the use of the left hand. He was discharged Feb. 27, 1862, for disability, at Halls Hill, Va. He enlisted a second time and was mustered into the United States service Dec. 28, 1863, for three years as a private of Co. G, 13th Regt. Vet. Res. Corps, and was accredited to the town of Medway. He was discharged by reason of general order from the War Department about Aug. 18, 1865.

ALFRED R. BELL was a resident of Kellysville, Md., and was mustered into the United States service May 10, 1864, for three years, as a private of Co. A, 20th Regt. Vet. Res. Corps. He was assigned to duty as a member of the regimental band.

DAVID H. BENNER was born in 1844. He was mustered into the United States Vet. Res. Corps, May 4, 1864, for three years, and accredited to Medway.

MARSHALL A. BENT, a private of the 13th Regt. Vet. Res. Corps, was mustered into the United States service April 30, 1864, for three years, and accredited to Medway. His family residence was Northfield, Mass. He was mustered out of service by reason of general order No. 155, Nov. 14, 1865.

ASAPH M. BISBEE, age twenty-one, residence unknown, was mustered into the 13th Regt. U. S. Vet. Res. Corps, July 11, 1863, for three years, and assigned April 30, 1864, to the credit of Medway.

AARON HENRY BLAKE, son of Solomon and Mary Ann (Rockwood) Blake, was born Oct. 2, 1836, in Bellingham, Mass. He enlisted in the spring of 1861, being then a resident of Dover, N. H. He first served three months in Co. F, 7th N. H. Vols. After the expiration of his term he again enlisted for three years, and served as a Corporal in the same regiment and company. From his letters it appears that he was in an engagement at or near Beaufort, N. C., when the rebels made an unsuccessful attempt to capture a fortification held by the Union troops. He also served in Florida, being stationed for a time at St. Augustine. He was in two of the bloody assaults on Fort Wagner, Morris Island, S. C., and was killed in the latter.

ADIN P. BLAKE, son of Caleb and Mary L. (Partridge) Blake, was born March 8, 1844, in Medway. He was mustered into the United States service Sept. 13, 1862, for nine months, as a private of Co. B, 42d Regt. Mass. Vols. He was at that time a temporary resident of Wrentham, and was accredited to that town. He was mustered out Aug. 28, 1863. He enlisted a second time from Medway, as a private of the same regiment and company for one hundred days; was mustered into United States service July 22, 1864, and mustered out Nov. 11, 1864, at the expiration of his term.

CHARLES W. BRACKETT, at the age of twenty-one, residence unknown, was mustered into the U. S. Vet. Res. Corps on the seventh day of May, 1864, for three years, and accredited to Medway.

WILLIAM F. BRITTON was mustered into the United States service Dec. 7, 1864, for one year, as a private of the 18th unattached Co. of Inf. Mass. Vols. He was accredited to Medway, though not a resident of the town. He was mustered out May 12, 1865, at the expiration of his term of service.

AARON BROWN, son of Stephen and Rachel Brown, was born May 28, 1833, in Milford, Mass. He enlisted and was mustered into the United States service July 28, 1862, for three years, as a private of Co. E, 2d Regt. Mass. Vols. He joined his regiment on the day previous to the battle of Cedar Mountain, Va., and was under fire there but without arms. He was discharged for disability, March 4, 1863. He enlisted a second time and was mustered into service Feb. 27, 1864, for three years, as a private of 14th Mass. Light Bat. He was detailed as a driver and was on duty with his battery in the engagements at Spottsylvania C. H. on the 9th, 10th, 12th, 16th, and 18th of May, 1864; at Tolopotomy Creek, June 1, at Bethesda Church, June 2 and 3; Cold Harbor, June 6 to 12, and at the siege of Petersburg, Va., from March 15, 1865, to the evacuation of the enemy's works, April 2, following. He was mustered out June 15, 1865, in Readville, Mass. He settled in Kansas, where he still resides.

GEORGE BROWN was enlisted and mustered into the United States service May 13, 1864, for three years, as a member of the 3d U. S. Artillery of the Regular Army, and accredited to Medway.

GEORGE F. BROWN, at the age of thirty years, a resident of Somerville, Mass., was mustered into the United States service Dec. 7, 1864, for one year, as a private of the 7th Mass. Light Bat., and was accredited to the town of Medway. He was mustered out May 29, 1865, at the end of the war.

GEORGE F. BROWN, son of Dr. Artemas and Patience M. (Bancroft) Brown, was born May 6, 1830, in Medway. He was temporarily residing in New York City at the outbreak of the Rebellion, and enlisted May 27, 1861, as a private of Co. B, 1st Regt. N. Y. Vols. He was soon after appointed Hospital Steward, which position he held until Aug. 11, 1861, when he was transferred, by order of General Butler, to the then squadron (afterwards 1st Battalion) Mounted Rifles, N. Y. Vols. Aug 16, 1861, he was appointed Assistant Veterinary Surgeon. October 1 he was appointed 4th Corporal of troop B. Jan. 22, 1862, he was appointed 5th Sergeant, troop B.; March 21, appointed Sergeant-Major of Battalion. He was afterwards commissioned 2d Lieut. He was discharged for disability Sept. 17, 1862, and died of disease December, 1882, in Washington, D. C. His remains were interred in Medway, Mass.

HENRY W. BROWN, son of Dr. Artemas and Patience M. (Bancroft) Brown, was born Nov. 27, 1832, in Medway. He enlisted early in May, 1861, and was mustered into the United States service May 25, 1861, for three years, as Sergeant of Co. E, 2d Regt. Mass Vols., in Camp Andrew, West Roxbury, Mass. He had just commenced the practice of medicine in Medway at time of enlistment. He was discharged for disability July 7, 1861. He enlisted a second time, and was mustered into service Nov. 27, 1861, for three years, as a private of Co I, 16th Regt. Mass. Vols. He was discharged by special order from the War Department, Aug. 19, 1863, to enable him to accept a commission as Assistant Surgeon of the 31st Regt. Mass. Inf. His commission was dated July 25, 1862, and he joined his regiment at New Orleans, La., in August, and was immediately detached to service in St. James's Hospital, of that city, where he remained until October, when he was ordered by General Butler to service on board the gun-boats "Estella" and "Kinsman." While on duty there he was in three engagements with the rebel steamer "Cotton," in a bayou, near Franklin, La., where the rebel steamer was finally destroyed. He was afterwards with the boats in an expedition planned for the destruction of the rebel salt-works at Iberville, La., which, however, proved unsuccessful. Early in January, 1863, he rejoined his regiment again at Fort Jackson. In February the regiment was ordered to Baton Rouge; and April 1 left that place for Port Hudson, where he was detached for service at Algiers, La., and afterwards at University Hospital in New Orleans, remaining there until Aug. 10, 1863, when he again joined his regiment. Sept. 12, 1863, he was promoted Surgeon of the 76th Regt. U. S. colored troops. From Sept. 13, 1863, to Feb. 28, 1864, he was Post Surgeon at Fort Jackson. During the summer of 1864 he was on duty at Port Hudson. In the spring of 1865 he took part in the siege of Blakely, Ala., being in the trenches before that place about three weeks before the final storming and capture of the works, April 9, 1865. He was mustered out of service Dec. 31, 1865. After the war he resumed his medical practice in Medway. Subsequently he removed to Hubbardston, Mich., where he still continues to practice his profession.

JAMES BROWN, residence unknown, was mustered into service January, 1863, for three years, as a recruit for the 29th Regt. Mass. Vols., and accredited to Medway.

ROBERT W. BROWN was born July 9, 1826, in Nova Scotia. He was mustered into the United States service Sept. 24, 1862, for nine months, as a private of Co. H, 42d Mass. Regt. He was a resident of Medway, but was accredited to the city of Chelsea, from which place he received a bounty. He first offered himself as one of the quota of Medway, but on examination by the surgeon here he was rejected. He subsequently enlisted at Camp Meigs and was mustered in as above. He was mustered out Aug. 20, 1863, at Readville, his term having expired. He died July 26, 1868, in Medway.

LEWIS BUFFUM was born in Salem, Mass. At the age of forty years he was mustered into the service of the United States Sept. 13, 1862, for nine months, in Camp Meigs, Readville, Mass., as a private of Co. B, 42d Regt. Mass. Vols. He deserted Jan. 4, 1863, but returned to duty again April 29, 1863. He was mustered out Aug. 20, 1863, his term having expired.

ALBERT E. BULLARD, son of Joseph and Susan (Clark) Bullard, was born Sept. 31, 1833, in Medway. He enlisted the last of August, 1862, and was mustered into the United States service Sept. 13, 1862, for nine months, as a private of Co. B, 42d Regt. Mass. Vols. He was in the engagement at Brashear City, La., June 23, 1863, and was taken prisoner. He was paroled, with other prisoners taken at the same time, on the 26th of June, and was mustered out of service Aug. 20, 1863, in Readville, Mass. He died April 26, 1865, of disease, evidently incurred in the service.

ELBRIDGE H. BULLARD, son of Appleton and Hephzibah (Harding) Bullard, was born Feb. 17, 1836, in Holliston, Mass. He was mustered into the United States service Aug. 22, 1862, for three years, as a private of Co. E, 38th Regt. Mass. Vols., and accredited to Boston. He did not reside in Medway. Was discharged Jan. 5, 1863, after a short term of service.

GEORGE W. BULLARD, son of Joseph and Sarah A. (Partridge) Bullard, was born May 24, 1841, in Medway. He was mustered into the United States service March 11, 1864, for three years, as a Corporal of the 16th Mass. Bat. Light Arty. He served mostly in the defenses of Washington, D. C., and was in no engagement. He was mustered out of service June 27, 1865, in Readville, Mass., and finally discharged July 13, 1865.

JOEL P. BULLARD, son of Joseph and Sarah A. (Partridge) Bullard, was born Oct. 18, 1845, in Medway. He was mustered into the United States service March 11, 1864, for three years, as a private of the 16th Bat. of Light Arty. Mass. Vols. The battery was employed mostly in the defenses of Washington, D. C., and was in no engagement. He was mustered out June 27, 1865, and finally discharged July 13, 1865.

SYLVANUS BULLARD, son of Cyrus and Eda (Partridge) Bullard, was born and resided in Medway. He enlisted as a private of Co. I, 38th Mass. Regt. He was rejected for disability at Camp Stanton, Lynnfield, before the regiment left camp for the war. He died at Medway, Oct. 27, 1866.

EDWARD M. BULLEN, son of Amos H. and Mary A. Bullen, was born March 17, 1833, in Medway. He enlisted early in May, and was mustered into the United States service May 25, 1861, for three years, in Camp Andrew, West Roxbury, Mass., as a private of Co. E, 2d Regt. Mass. Vols. He took part in the earlier services and marches of the regiment, and on the retreat of Gen. Banks, May 25, 1862, being sick in the hospital at Winchester, Va., he was taken prisoner, paroled May 31, and sent to Camp Parole in Annapolis, Md. He was exchanged and returned to duty in the regiment in December following, and in May, 1863, he was wounded through the left lung and arm. Removed to the rear by comrades and again removed as the Union troops fell back from the field, he was finally left for dead near a small stream of water. As the flow of blood became stanched he revived, and when the rebel forces came in possession of the field, he again fell into their hands. While lying near the stream he came near losing what little life still remained by drowning, from a sudden rise of the water after a rain. Removed from his perilous position by the captors, he was placed, with other wounded prisoners, in charge of a paroled Pennsylvania soldier, who pitched a tent over them and cared for them with great assiduity and kindness during the time he remained a prisoner. He was paroled and sent within the Union lines, May 13, and immediately sent to the hospital at Aquia Creek, Va., where he remained one month and was then removed to McKim's Mansion Hospital in Baltimore, Md. Slowly recovering from his wounds but unfit for further service, he was discharged at the hospital Aug. 26, 1863.

CHARLES E. BURR, son of Laban and Maria Burr, was born Oct. 11, 1842, in Bellingham. He enlisted Dec. 26, 1863, and was mustered into the United States service Jan. 5, 1864, for three years, as a private of Co. C, 4th Mass. Cav. He was in the engagement at John's Island, S. C., on the 2d and 5th of July, 1864, on the latter of which he was wounded through the right ankle. He was sent to the hospital in Beaufort, S. C., and afterwards to Readville, Mass., and subsequently to Worcester, at which place he was discharged, Oct. 20, 1864, for disability. He appears by the state record to be accredited to Bellingham, but he was at the time of enlistment a resident of Medway, and was accredited one of the quota of this town.

JACOB W. BUTLER, a resident of Chelsea, enlisted for and received a bounty from this town, and was mustered into the United States service Dec. 9, 1864, for one year, in Co. G, 61st Regt. Mass. Vols. He served with his regiment in Virginia and was mustered out July 16, 1865, as Sergeant.

JOHN CARR, son of John and Ann Carr, was born in Leitrim County, Ireland. At the age of forty-four years he enlisted in August, and was mustered into the United States service Sept. 3, 1862, for three years, as a private of Co. H, 40th Regt. Mass. Vols. He was discharged for disability after a brief term of service, April 2, 1863. He died Feb 5, 1884.

ALFRED A. CARY, son of Barnabas and Keziah Cary, was born Sept. 15, 1832, in Potsdam, N. Y. He enlisted, and was mustered into the United States service July 22, 1864, as 3d Sergeant of Co. B, 42d Regt. Mass. Vols. The regiment was stationed in the defense of Washington, D. C. He was mustered out of service Nov. 11, 1864, at the close of his term of one hundred days.

CHARLES E. CARY, son of Barnabas and Keziah Cary, was born Sept. 1, 1839, in Potsdam, N. Y. He enlisted in April, or early in May, 1861, and was mustered into the United States service June 26, 1861, for three years, as a private of Co. E, 12th Regt. Mass. Vols. He was in the battles of Cedar Mountain, Va., August 9; second Bull Run, August 30; South Mountain, September 14; and at Antietam, Md., Sept. 17, 1862, at which time he was instantly killed by the bursting of a shell from a Confederate battery. His remains were buried on the field. Immediately upon the receipt of the intelligence of his death, a brother, Mr. Alfred A. Cary, visited the battle-field for the purpose of securing and bringing home the body for interment, but though assistance was freely given him by those who had aided in burying the dead it was impossible to identify the remains.

SAMUEL B. CARY, son of Barnabas and Keziah Cary, was born Sept. 10, 1844, in Potsdam, N. Y. He enlisted and was mustered into the United States service July 22, 1864, for one hundred days, as a private of Co. B, 42d Regt. Mass. Vols. He was mustered out Nov. 11, 1864.

JOHN W. CASS was born in Boston, Mass. At the age of twenty-one years he enlisted early in May, 1861, and was mustered into the United States service May 25, 1861, for three years, as a private of Co. E, 2d Regt. Mass. Vols. He was discharged for disability Sept. 18, 1862.

JEREMIAH CASSIDY, at the age of twenty-two years, residence unknown, was mustered into the U. S. Vet. Res. Corps, May 4, 1864, for three years, and was accredited to Medway.

WILLIAM HIRAM CHACE, son of Mason and Laurania (Rounds) Chace, was born in 1826, in Medway. He enlisted July 23, and was mustered into the service of the United States July 28, 1862, for three years, as a private of Co. D, 35th Regt. Mass. Vols. He was injured while executing some rapid movements on drill, just previous to the battle of Antietam, and was discharged for disability Nov. 4, 1862. He died of disease Feb. 17, 1866.

CALVIN CLAFLIN, son of Hamblet B. and Betsey (Curtis) Claflin, was born Aug. 31, 1840, in Medway. He was mustered into the United States service Sept. 13, 1862, for nine months, as a private of Co. B, 42d Regt. Mass. Vols. He was at the time a resident of Holliston, and accredited to that town, though by state record he appears as from Medway. He died March 31, 1871, and was buried in Medway.

ALBERT H. CLARK, son of John C. and Eliza A. (Henderson) Clark, was born Oct. 26, 1834, in Medway. He enlisted early in May and was mustered into the United States service May 25, 1861, for three years, as a private of Co. E, 2d Regt. Mass. Vols. He was promoted Corporal, Feb. 24, 1862. He was in all the earlier engagements of his regiment. He was in the fight at Winchester, Va., May 25, 1862, and at Cedar Mountain, Va., August 9, where he was severely wounded in the leg and was sent to the hospital in Annapolis, Md. He was not fit for active service again till Aug. 15, 1863, when he rejoined his regiment at Kelly's Ford, Va. During this prolonged absence he was, on the 30th of December, 1862, reduced to the ranks. He was on duty with his regiment during the remainder of its term and was in the battle of Resaca, La., May 14 and 15, 1864. He was mustered out May 28, 1864, at the expiration of his term of service.

ALBERT L. CLARK, son of John and Marietta (Thompson) Clark, was born May 27, 1838, in Medway. He enlisted the last of August, and was mustered into the United States service Sept. 13, 1862, for nine months, at Camp Meigs, in Readville, Mass., as 3d Sergeant of Co. B, 42d Regt. Mass. Vols. He was at the time of enlistment a student of Williams College, having just completed the second year of his course. He served with his regiment in Louisiana, and was mustered out Aug. 20, 1863, his term having expired. He did not complete his college course, and for several years has been a resident of Franklin, Mass.

ASA CLARK, son of Sanford and Nancy Clark, was born Sept. 25, 1831, in Medfield. He was mustered into the United States service March 11, 1864, for three years, as a private of the 16th Mass. Light Bat. He served with his battery in the defenses at Washington, D. C., and was mustered out June 27, 1865, at the close of the war.

CHARLES CLARK, son of Nathaniel and Margery W. (Pond) Clark, was born Feb. 23, 1827, in Medway. He enlisted July 23, 1862, and was mustered into the United States service July 29, 1862, for three years, as a private of Co. H, 32d Regt. Mass. Vols. Though residing at the time in Ashland he preferred to be accredited to Medway, and received a bounty from the town. He was promoted Corporal about Dec. 20, 1862. He was promoted Sergeant March 1, 1863. He reënlisted, and was re-mustered Jan. 5, 1864, for the term of three years. He was discharged for promotion January 11, and mustered Jan. 12, 1865, as 2d Lieut. of 61st Mass. Inf. He was promoted to 1st Lieut., February 1. He states that he was in the following engagements: At Antietam, Md., Sept. 17, 1862, his regiment, however, being in the rear in support of batteries, and but little exposed; Fredericksburg, Va., Dec. 13, 1862, when the regiment was first thoroughly under fire; Chancellorsville, Va., May 1 to 3, 1863; skirmish at Aldie, June 22; Gettysburg, Penn., July 2 and 3; Rappahannock Station, November 7, under fire, but no losses in the regiment; Mine Run, Dec. 1, 1863; Wilderness, Va., May 5, 1864; skirmish at Todd's Tavern, May 8; Laurel Hill, May 10 and 12; Spottsylvania C. H., May 2; North Anna, May 23 and 25;

Tolopotomy Swamp, May 29 and 30; Bethesda Church, June 3; siege of Petersburg, Va., from June 18 nearly through July; Weldon R. R., August 18 to 21; skirmish at Hatcher's Run, October 27; and in the final charge at Petersburg, Va., April 2, 1865, as an officer of the 61st Regt. He was mustered out of service July 16, 1865. He died Dec. 23, 1874, in Milford, Mass.

CHARLES S. CLARK, son of Sanford and Nancy Clark, was born Aug. 27, 1830, in Medfield. He enlisted Aug. 23, 1864, and was mustered into the United States service on the same day, for one year, as a private of the 18th unattached Co., afterwards Co. B, 4th Regt. Mass. Heavy Arty. He was discharged for disability May 6, 1865. He continued to reside in Medway until his death, Aug. 2, 1882.

DAVID A. CLARK, son of John and Marietta (Thompson) Clark, was born Oct. 9, 1843, in Medway. He was mustered into the United States service Aug. 9, 1862, for three years, as a private of Co. I, 38th Regt. Mass. Vols. He was in the battle of Bisland, La., April 13, 1863, and was on duty with his regiment before Port Hudson, La., from the 25th of May until the surrender of the place on the 8th of July, during which time the regiment was under fire, and exchanged shots with the enemy nearly every day; he was in the fight at Cane River, La., April 23, 1864; and at the Plains of Mansura, May 16 following. On the 20th of July the regiment embarked on board the ocean steamer " Karmack," at Algiers, La., for the North, and he arrived at Washington, D. C., on the 30th, and was soon sent to the Shenandoah Valley. He then took part in the movements of his regiment and engagements with the enemy during the latter part of August and in September. At the battle of Opequan, September 19, he was taken prisoner with about three hundred others, and taken to Richmond, Va., where he was confined in the Libby Prison for four days, after which he was taken to Belle Isle, where he remained until paroled, Oct. 8, 1864. He arrived inside the Union lines on the next day, and was sent to Camp Parole at Annapolis, Md., remaining there till exchanged Dec. 14, 1864. He did not return to his regiment, but was detailed for duty on the provost-guard at Annapolis until the end of his term. He was mustered out June 14, 1865. Since the war he has been engaged in business, first in Baltimore, Md., afterwards, for a short time, in Savannah, Ga., and since then in Boston, as a member of the firm of Clark & Roberts.

EDMUND N. CLARK, son of Elbridge and Lydia (Newton) Clark, was born Aug. 19, 1840, in Medway. He was mustered into the United States service on the ninth day of August, 1862, for three years, as a private of Co. I, 38th Regt. Mass. Vols. He was in an engagement at Fort Bisland, La., April 13, 1863. He went with his regiment to Port Hudson, but before it became engaged he was taken sick and sent to Baton Rouge Hospital. He rejoined his regiment on its return to that place, Aug. 18, 1863. He was in the battle of Cane River, April 23, 1864, and in the skirmishes succeeding, his regiment forming the rear guard of the army in its progress towards Alexandria. Afterwards he was in the engagements on the return from Alexandria to the Mississippi, the principal of which was the battle at Mansura Plains, May 16, 1864. He was left at Morganzia, La., sick with chills and fever when his regiment started for Algiers, La., July, 3, 1864, to take conveyance for the North. Remaining unfit for service he was granted a furlough, and started for home, leaving New Orleans Aug. 16, 1864. His disability still continuing, he was discharged Dec. 14, 1864, in Boston.

FREDERICK F. CLARK, son of John and Marietta (Thompson) Clark, was born June 6, 1846, in Medway. He enlisted and was mustered into the United States service, July 22, 1864, for one hundred days, as a private of Co. B, 42d Regt. Mass. Vols. He was mustered out Nov. 11, 1864.

GEORGE EDMUND CLARK, son of Abijah and Ann C. (Sayles) Clark, was born Dec. 26, 1834, in Medway. He was mustered into the United States service Sept. 13, 1862, for nine months, as a private of Co. B, 42d Regt. Mass. Vols. He resided in Medfield at the time and was accredited to that town. He was in the engagement at Brashear City, La., June 23, 1863, and was severely wounded in the leg, and taken prisoner. He was paroled, and set at liberty June 26, 1863, and mustered out of service Aug. 20, 1863, by reason of the expiration of his term. He came home suffering from his wound as well as from malarial disease. After recovering, in a measure, his health, in April, 1865, he went West, and settled in Cobden, Ill., connecting himself with a firm in the hardware trade. Afterwards he removed to Marble Hill, Mo., and subsequently to Lutesville, where he still continues in the same business. He married, April 29, 1867, Eliza J. Walker, who died in December, 1884. Mr. Clark is a member of the School Board of Lutesville, occupying the position of the clerk of that body.

JAMES WARREN CLARK, son of James P. and Maria (Frost) Clark, was born Aug. 3, 1837, in Medway. He enlisted the last of August and was mustered into the United States service Sept. 13, 1862, for nine months, as a private of Co. B, 42d Regt. Mass. Vols. He was mustered out Aug. 28, 1863, in Readville, Mass., his term of service having expired. He enlisted again in the same regiment and company, and was mustered into the United States service July 22, 1864, for one hundred days, as 2d Sergeant. He was mustered out Nov. 11, 1864, the term of the regiment having expired.

SEWALL J. CLARK, son of Amos and Luthera Clark, was born Sept. 12, 1827, in Medway. He enlisted the last of August, and was mustered into the United States service Sept. 13, 1862, for nine months, as a private of Co. B, 42d Regt. Mass. Vols. He was in the engagement at Brashear City, La., June 23, 1863, and was taken prisoner. He was paroled and liberated June 26, 1863. He was mustered out Aug. 20, 1863, in Readville, Mass., the term of the regiment having expired. He enlisted a second time in the same regiment and company, and was mustered into the United States service July 22, 1864, for one hundred days, as a Corporal. He was mustered out at the expiration of his term, Nov. 11, 1864.

WARREN A. CLARK, son of John Craig and Eliza A. (Henderson) Clark, was born April 26, 1837, in Medway. He was mustered into the United States service Sept. 13, 1862, for nine months, as a private of Co. B, 42d Regt. Mass. Vols. He was at the time a resident of Bellingham and was accredited to that town. He was mustered out at the expiration of his term of service, Aug. 20, 1863. He enlisted a second time for the town of Medway, and was mustered into the United States service, March 11, 1864, for three years, as a private of the 16th Mass. Light Bat. He served with his battery in the defenses of Washington, D. C., and was in no engagement. He was mustered out June 27, 1865, by reason of the close of the war.

WILLIAM B. CLARK, son of Amos and Luthera Clark, was born April 10, 1825, in Medway. He enlisted for one hundred days, and was mustered into the United States service, July 22, 1864, as a private of Co. B, 42d Regt. Mass. Vols. He was mustered out Nov. 11, 1864, at the close of his term.

ALFRED CLIFFORD, son of Oliver and Elizabeth (Mann) Clifford, was born Feb. 11, 1845, in Medway. He enlisted July 22, 1864, and was mustered into the United States service for one hundred days, as a private of Co. B, 42d Regt. Mass. Vols. He was mustered out Nov. 11, 1864.

JOSEPH CLARK CLIFFORD, son of Oliver and Elizabeth (Mann) Clifford, was born Sept. 10, 1839, in Medway. He graduated in 1862 from Amherst College, Mass. He enlisted in August, married Sept. 10, 1862, Elizabeth Condit, daughter of Rev. U. W. Condit, of Deerfield, N. H., and was mustered into the United States service Sept. 13, 1862, for nine months, at Camp Meigs, Readville, as 1st Sergeant of Co. B, 42d Regt. Mass. Vols. He was promoted to 2d Lieut. Nov. 12, 1862. Served with his regiment in Louisiana, and was mustered out at the expiration of his term of service, Aug. 20, 1863. He taught school and studied law in New Hampshire, until the call for volunteers in 1864, when he took part in organizing a company of artillery, receiving a commission as 1st Lieut. He was mustered into the United States service Sept. 8, 1864, and served as 1st Lieut. of the 5th unattached Co. Heavy Arty. N. H. Vols., for one year in Fort Foote, Md., and in Fort Richardson, Va. He was detached from his company, and served on the staff of Gen. G. A. DeRussy, commanding the division south of the Potomac, and of Gen. J. A. Haskins, chief of artillery, 22d army corps. He was inspector of guards in Washington, on the night of the assassination of President Lincoln, and was one of five officers detailed as guard over the remains of the President while in the White House, before the funeral services. After the grand review of the Union Army at the close of the war he was mustered out of service with his regiment, 1st N. H. Arty., June 15, 1865. He was appointed June 9, 1865, 2d Lieut. in U. S. Regular Army Ordnance Department, promoted to be 1st Lieut. June 23, 1874, and to Capt. April 14, 1875. He was stationed at Fortress Monroe, Va., 1865 to 1868; in St. Louis, 1868 to 1871; in Benicia, Cal., 1871 to 1876; in Rock Island, Ill., 1876 to 1880; in West Troy, N. Y., 1880, and is now at Frankford Arsenal, Philadelphia, Penn. Captain Clifford has two sons, Charles Condit Clifford, born Feb. 17, 1866 in Fortress Monroe, Va., and Alfred Clifford, born Oct. 6, 1880, in West Troy, N. Y.

JOHN COAD, a resident of Medway, was born in Eastport, Me. At the age of thirty-three he enlisted and was mustered into the United States service Oct. 8, 1861, for three years, as a private of Co. H, 23d Regt. Mass. Vols. He was on duty with his regiment at the battle of Roanoke Island, N. C., Feb. 8, 1862, and at the battle of Newbern, N. C., March 14th following. He was discharged Oct. 7, 1862, for disability.

JOHN W. CODDING, at the age of twenty-four years, a resident of Attleboro, Mass., enlisted Dec. 7, 1864, and was mustered into service on the same day for one year, as a private of the 18th unattached Co. of Inf. Mass. Vols., and was accredited to Medway. He was mustered out of service May 12, 1865, at the expiration of his term of service.

SAMUEL P. COFFAN, at the age of twenty-four years, residence unknown, was mustered into the U. S. Vet. Res. Corps, May 4, 1864, for three years, and accredited to Medway.

CHARLES H. COLE, son of Asa and Mehitable (Fairbanks) Cole, was born April 11, 1839, in Medway. He enlisted the last of August, and was mustered into the United States service Sept. 13, 1862, for nine months as a private of Co. B, 42d Regt. Mass. Vols. He was mustered out Aug. 20, 1863, in Readville, Mass. He enlisted again and was mustered into service July 22, 1864, for one hundred days, as a private of the same regiment and company. He was mustered out Nov. 11, 1864, at the close of his term.

JOHN CONLY enlisted and was mustered into the United States service December, 1862, for three years, as a recruit for the 29th Regt. Mass. Vols., and accredited to Medway, though not a resident of the town.

TIMOTHY COUGHLIN was born in 1840, in Kerry County, Ireland. He enlisted in May, and was mustered into the United States service, May 25, 1861, for three years, as a private of Co. E, 2d Regt. Mass. Vols. Feb. 17, 1862, he left the regiment, having been detailed to gun-boat service on the Mississippi River. He was assigned to the gun-boat "De Kalb," and went on board at Cairo, Ill. He states that he was in the following engagements: at Island No. 10, March 16, Fort Pillow, May 10, off Memphis, Tenn., June 6, at St. Charles, up the White River, June 17, 1862; at Arkansas Port, Jan. 11, 1863; at the siege of Vicksburg, Miss.; in several engagements at Haines' Bluff, on Yazoo River; at Duvall's Bluff, on the White River; in a three days' engagement at Fort Pemberton; and at Yazoo City, Miss., July 13, 1863, at which time the "De Kalb" was blown up. In this last engagement he was wounded in the foot. He states that he was then transferred to the flag ship and afterwards to the receiving ship where he was discharged from the service Aug. 11, 1863. He enlisted a second time Dec. 13, 1864, and was mustered into the United States service the same day as a private of the 12th Mass. Light Bat., for the term of one year. During his service the battery was stationed at Port Hudson, La., and was in no engagement. He was mustered out July 25, 1865, at the expiration of his term.

DAVID F. COVELL, son of David and Lucy L. (Engly) Covell, was born May 1, 1846, in Medway. He was mustered into the United States service as a private of Co. G, 42d Regt. Mass. Vols. He first enlisted for Medway, but was rejected by the examining surgeon for want of proper age. He afterward enlisted in Camp Meigs, Readville, Mass., was accepted, and accredited to Boston, receiving a bounty from that city. He died April 22, 1863, of disease, at Bayou Gentilly, La. By the kindness of the members of his company enough money was raised among them to procure a metallic coffin and forward his remains to his home in West Medway. His name appears in the state record as Frank Covell.

CHARLES E. CUMMINGS, son of Benjamin and Lydia (Carey) Cummings, was born Dec. 19, 1832, in Franklin. He enlisted early in May, and was mustered into the United States service May 25, 1861, for three years, in Camp Andrew, West Roxbury, as a private of Co. E, 2d Regt. Mass. Vols. He was promoted Corporal Aug. 1, 1862. He was in all the earlier engagements of the regiment, and in the battle in Winchester on the retreat of General Banks, May 25; Cedar Mountain, August 9, and Antietam, Sept. 17, 1862. He died Jan. 19, 1863, in the hospital in Wash-

18

ington D. C., of chronic diarrhœa. His remains were brought to Medway for burial.

ALEXANDER METCALF CUSHING, son of Warren and Abigail (Adams) Cushing, was born March 25, 1823, in Newfane, Vt. He was mustered into the United States service July 28, 1862, as a private of the 2d Regt. Mass. Vols., and assigned to Co. E. He joined his regiment just previous to the battle of Cedar Mountain, Va., but took no part in the engagement. He died Nov. 24, 1862, of disease, in the hospital at Sharpsburg, Md., and his remains were buried there.

ALONZO M. DAIN, son of Rice O. and Mary Dain, was born Sept. 6, 1845, in Medway. He first enlisted at Camp Stanton, Lynnfield, and was sworn into the service for three years, as a private of Co. D, 35th Regt. Mass. Vols. Desiring to be transferred to the 2d Mass. Inf., he was sent to Camp Cameron, at Cambridge, by order of Col. Wild, and was there rejected. He enlisted again and was mustered into service Sept. 16, 1863, for three years, as a private of the 10th unattached Co., afterwards Co. F, 3d Regt. Mass. Heavy Arty. He served with his company until July 1, 1865, at which time he is reported by the state record as having deserted. There appears to have been a large number of desertions from the regiment about that time from some cause. He enlisted again about Dec. 10, 1866, in the 3d U. S. Cav., for five years, and served about one-half his time. He afterwards received regular discharge papers from the 3d Heavy Arty.

HENRY R. DAIN, son of Rice O. and Mary Dain, was born Feb. 8, 1831, in Royalston, Vt. He enlisted, and was mustered into the United States service, Feb. 26, 1864, for three years, as a private of Co. D, 3d Regt. Mass. Cav. He joined the regiment at Morganzia Bend, La., about the 1st of June, 1864. He died Sept. 14, 1864, of chronic diarrhœa, at Berryville Hospital, Va.

CHARLES H. DANIELS, son of Henry and Mary A. (Pike) Daniels, was born March 10, 1833, in Medway. He enlisted, and was mustered into the United States service July 2, 1861, for three years, as a private of Co. B, 16th Regt. Mass. Vols. He was promoted Corporal April 13, 1863. He was in the engagements at Fair Oaks, Va., June 18, 25, and 28; at Glendale, June 29; at Malvern Hill, July 1 and 8; at Briston Station, or Kettle Run, August 28; at 2d Bull Run, August 29 and 30; was under fire at Chantilly, September 1; at Fredericksburg, Dec. 13, 1862; at Chancellorsville, May 3, 1863; at Gettysburg, July 2 and 3; in a skirmish at Wapping Heights, or Manassas Gap, Nov. 27, 1863. About Aug. 1, 1863, he was detailed with some four or five others of his company as conscript guard, and was on duty at the conscript camp at Long Island, Boston Harbor, for several weeks, after which he again returned to his regiment. In February, 1864, he reënlisted for another term of three years. In his memorandum of February 15, is found the following : " Mustered into the U. S. service as a soldier for three years, or the war, at Division Head-quarters, by Capt. Williams, in the presence of Lieut. Lombard, the recruiting officer of the regiment. This is coolly done. My motto, ' Our Whole Country'; my prayer, 'God speed the right'; my platform, 'Honorable peace or perpetual war.' This thing must be put down, and it is the duty of those who believe rebellion to be wrong *to help put it down.* I can help most here in the army, so I must stay in the army as long as the war lasts, if I live so long." He was granted the usual veteran furlough, which he spent at home, and returning, joined his regiment near White Oak Church, Va., May 17, 1864. He was taken sick June 3, while the regiment was near Hanover C. H., and was sent to Finley Hospital, at Philadelphia, Penn. During his absence his regiment was mustered out, its term having expired, and the reënlisted men were transferred to the 11th Mass. Battalion. He returned, and was assigned to Co. E. He was in the engagement at Deep Bottom, Aug. 16, 1864, and in the following battles in the vicinity of Petersburg, Va. : one on the 19th of August, in front of that place ; near Fort Davis, Sept. 10 and 11 ; Poplar Grove Church, October 2 ; near Boydtown, Plank Road, October 27 ; near Fort Morton, a night attack by the enemy, November 5 ; took part in the destruction of the Weldon R. R., Dec. 9, 1864 ; and was again in front of Petersburg, Feb. 5, 1865. He was appointed 2d Lieut. of the U. S. colored Infantry by Maj.-Gen. E. O. C. Ord, March 10, 1865, and was discharged from the 11th Battalion for promotion March 28, and joined his regiment, and was mustered March 30, at Humphries Station, Va. He was first assigned to Co. A, but was transferred to Co. B, Oct. 26, 1865, and was in command of that company until Jan. 9, 1866. He was appointed Acting Regimental Quartermaster, March 1, 1866, and was commissioned R. Q. M. by the Secretary of War on the 1st of September following. With his regiment he took part in the final campaign in Virginia, which resulted in the surrender of General Lee. His regiment was afterwards ordered to Brazos Santiago, Tex., where it arrived on the 23d of June, 1865. It afterwards moved to White's Ranch, thence to Roma, where it remained until Jan. 30, 1866 ; again returning to White's Ranch, where it remained until September 13. During the stay at that place the regiment lost forty-five men by cholera. Returned to New Orleans, La., arriving there Sept. 25, 1866. He was on duty with his regiment in and about that city until Jan. 21, 1867, when the regiment started for Louisville, Ky., where the officers and men were finally discharged from the service, Feb. 7, 1867. Just before leaving New Orleans, in January, he was bitten on both hands by a dog of strange appearance, which was soon afterwards killed as a rabid animal. The wounds were slight, and soon healed, and it was hoped no harm would result. But these hopes were destined to disappointment, and we are left to wonder at that mysterious Providence which preserved him unharmed through a score of battles, and all the exposures of five and a half years of camp life, to fall so soon a victim to that terrible disease, the hydrophobia. He died June 6, 1867, in West Medway.

EDWARD DANIELS, son of Cyrus and Louisa (Whitney) Daniels, was born July 8, 1836, in Sherborn, Mass. He was mustered into the United States service June 27, 1861, for three years, as second-class musician in the band of the 11th Regt. Mass. Vols. He was in the first battle of Bull Run, July 21, 1861 ; the siege of Yorktown, April, 1862 ; Williamsburg, Va., May 5 ; and in the battles on the peninsula as follows : Fair Oaks, Savage Station, Glendale, and Malvern Hill. He was discharged at Harrison's Landing, Va., Aug. 8, 1862, by reason of general order in relation to the discharge of regimental bands. He enlisted a second time as a first-class musician in the band of Brigade 2d Division 2d Army Corps, July 10, 1863.

Served five months on Long Island, Boston Harbor. Joined his brigade at Brandy Station, Va., in December, 1863, and served in Virginia until the close of the war Being a musician, his duty during engagements was to assist in removing the wounded from the field. He was mustered out of service a second time, July 2, 1865, at Munson Hill, Va. He was a resident of Ashland, to which place he was accredited. Present residence Natick, Mass.

HENRY JASPER DANIELS, son of Jaazaniah B. and Cordelia (Ellis) Daniels, was born Jan. 16, 1842, in Medway. He enlisted the last of August, and was mustered into the United States service Sept. 13, 1862, for nine months, as a Corporal of Co. B, 42d Regt. Mass. Vols., at Camp Meigs, Readville, Mass He served with his regiment in the Department of the Gulf and was mustered out Aug. 20, 1863, his term having expired. He enlisted a second time for one hundred days, and was mustered into service as 1st Sergeant of the same regiment and company, July 22, 1864. He was mustered out at the expiration of his term, Nov. 11, 1864. He removed to Medfield, where he died Dec 9, 1870

JOSEPH LELAND DANIELS, son of Ellis and Sarah (Phillips) Daniels, was born December, 1834, in Medway. He was mustered into the United States service Aug. 13, 1861, as a private of Co. E, 16th Regt Mass Vols He was at the time a resident of Bellingham and was accredited to that town. Promoted Corporal September or October, 1862 He died of disease, Feb. 13, 1863, in camp, near Falmouth, Va., and his remains were buried there. His wife after his death came to reside in Medway.

WILLIAM A DANIELS, son of William D and Abigail H (Jones) Daniels, was born Jan. 21, 1840, in Medway. He enlisted early in May, and was mustered into the United States service May 25, 1861, for three years, in Camp Andrew, West Roxbury, as a private of Co E, 2d Regt Mass. Vols. He was in the engagement at Winchester, Va., May 25, 1862, and at Cedar Mountain, Va , August 9, when he was wounded in the leg and shoulder. He suffered amputation of the arm at the shoulder joint, and died Sept. 7, 1862, of hemorrhage, in the hospital in Washington, D. C. His remains were brought to Medway for burial

WILLIAM D. DANIELS, son of Jasper and Mehitable (Partridge) Daniels, was born Nov. 29, 1817, in Medway. He enlisted, and was mustered into the United States service Aug. 1, 1861, for three years, as a musician in the band of the 18th Regt. Mass Vols He was discharged at Harrison's Landing, Va., Aug. 11, 1862, by reason of a general order from the War Department, No. 151, relating to the discharge of regimental bands He died Oct. 31, 1863, in Medway.

TIMOTHY DALEY was born in Ireland, resided in Milford at time of enlistment, at the age of twenty-four years He enlisted and was mustered same day, Jan. 19, 1864, for three years, as a recruit of 38th Regt. Mass. Vols. He deserted July 10, 1864. He is reported to have been arrested as a deserter from some other regiment, Daley having been an assumed name.

DAVID S. DARLING, son of Nathan and Harriet B. (Leonard) Darling, was born April 14, 1844, in Medway. He enlisted, and was mustered into the United States service Feb. 16, 1862, for three years, as a private of Co. H, 31st Regt Mass. Vols He was in the expedition of Major-General Butler for the capture of New Orleans, La., and witnessed from on board the transport, the bombardment of Forts Jackson and St Philip by the fleet under Admiral Farragut. In taking possession of New Orleans his regiment was the first to land. He states that he was in the first advance before Port Hudson, La , from March 6 to 20 ; at Fort Bisland, April 12 and 13 ; again before Port Hudson from May 24 to June 17, and under fire nearly every day. On the 14th his regiment lay on the ground for many hours, without shelter, under a broiling sun, when to rise would have been to receive a rebel bullet. Dec. 19, 1863, his regiment was converted to cavalry. February 29, started on the Red River campaign   April 2 he was in a skirmish near Natchitoches ; April 8, in the battle of Sabine Cross Roads ; 9 and 10, battle of Pleasant Hill ; April 23, Cane River ; fight at Hudson's Plantation, May 1, and Governor Moore's Plantation, May 3 , Marksville, May 15 and 16 ; and at Yellow Bayou, June 18, 1864.   He states that he was mustered out of service Feb. 23, 1865, in New Orleans, La.

JESSE DARLING, son of Samuel and Sophia (Linnel) Darling, was born April 8, 1829, in Orleans, Jefferson County, N. Y. He enlisted, and was mustered into the United States service Aug. 23, 1864, for one year, as a private of the 18th unattached Co., afterwards Co. B, 4th Regt. Heavy Arty. Mass Vols. He served in the defenses of Washington, D. C., and was discharged for disability May 6, 1865.

AMOS FRANCIS DAVIS, son of Amos B. and Eleanor P. (Tyler) Davis, was born Jan. 6, 1843, in Medway. He was mustered into the United States service Aug. 23, 1861, as a private of Co. E, 39th Regt. Mass. Vols. He was at that time a resident of Somerville, and was accredited to that town. He was in an engagement at Mine Run, in November, 1863   Through the winter following he was on detail as Hospital Steward and Surgeon's Clerk. He was in the battle of the Wilderness, May, 1864 ; at Laurel Hill, where his regiment lost nearly fifty per cent in killed, wounded, and missing, at North Anna, Tolopotomy, and Bethesda Church. After the arrival of his regiment in front of Petersburg, he was detailed as clerk at brigade head-quarters, and remained in that position until the end of his term. He was mustered out near Washington, D. C., June 2, 1865, and finally discharged the last of June, in Readville, Mass.

EDWIN S. DAVIS, son of Amos B. and Eleanor P. (Tyler) Davis, was born March 2, 1848, in Medway. He enlisted for one hundred days, and was mustered into the United States service, July 22, 1864, as a private of Co B, 42d Regt. Mass. Vols.   He served in the defenses of Washington, D. C., and was mustered out Nov. 11, 1864, his term having expired. His regiment was stationed in Alexandria, Va., and Great Falls, Md.

SHEPPARD DAVIS, age twenty-seven, residence unknown, was mustered into the United States Vet. Res. Corps, 13th Regt., June 20, 1863, for three years, and accredited to Medway.   He was discharged for disability Sept. 11, 1864.

BENJAMIN F. DEXTER was born in Boston, and was a resident of that city at the time of his enlistment   He was mustered into the United States service Sept. 3, 1864, for one year, and was accredited to the town of Medway.   He held the position of 1st Sergeant of Co. B, while remaining in camp at Galloup's Island, 61st Regt. Mass. Vols. In October, 1864, when the 1st Battalion of that regiment left camp for the South, he was detailed

Acting Sergeant-Major, and was appointed to that position when the regiment was filled up. He was appointed 2d Lieut. April 3, 1864, and was mustered out of service June 4, 1865, by reason of the close of the war. Previous to his connection with the 61st Regt. he had held a 2d Lieutenant's commission in the 54th Regt. Mass. Vols.

CHARLES M. DISPER, son of Joseph and Lavina (Adams) Disper, was born Sept 27, 1841, in Medway He enlisted in May, and was mustered into the United States service May 25, 1861, for three years, as a private of Co. E, 3d Regt Mass. Vols He was in the engagements at Winchester, Va., May 25, and at Cedar Mountain, Aug. 9, 1862 He was discharged for disability, Feb 25, 1863

FRANCIS T. DODGE, son of Tyler and Addie (Wilkie) Dodge, was born Jan. 23, 1846, in Medway. He first enlisted at Camp Stanton, Lynnfield, Mass., and was sworn into the United States service about July 28, 1862, for the term of three years, as a member of Co D, 35th Mass. Regt. Desiring to be transferred to the 2d Mass. Inf., he was sent to Camp Cameron, by direction of Col. Wild of the 35th, and was there rejected by the recruiting officer He enlisted again in December following and was mustered into the United States service Jan 10, 1864, for three years, as a private of the 3d unattached Co., afterwards Co A, 3d Regt. Mass. Heavy Arty. He was transferred to the United States Navy Sept. 19, 1864.

PATRICK J. DONNOVAN, resident of Boston, enlisted and was mustered into the United States service, Dec. 10, 1864, for one year, as a private of Co. G, 61st Regt. Mass. Vols, and accredited to Medway. He was promoted Sergeant Dec. 14, 1864, and Commissary Sergeant March 1, 1865. He was mustered out of service June 4, 1865. He had previously served a term in Co H, 1st Regt Mass Vols

JOHN F. O. DRISCOLL, resident of Charlestown, Mass., enlisted and was mustered into the United States service, June 9, 1864, for three years, as a private of Co A, 6th Regt U S. Vet. Res. Corps, and was accredited to Medway. He was mustered out of service Nov. 18, 1865.

THOMAS DUDY was born in New Haven, Conn At the age of twenty-one years he enlisted in May, and was mustered May 25, 1861, for three years, as a private of Co. E, 2d Regt. Mass. Vols. He deserted July 6, 1861, from Camp Andrew, West Roxbury, Mass.

AMOS A DUGAN, son of William and Lucretia M. (Williams) Dugan, was born Oct 6, 1846, in Medway. He was mustered into the United States service as a private of Co. B, 42d Regt. Mass. Vols., July 22, 1864, for one hundred days. He was mustered out of service at the expiration of his term, Nov 11, 1864 He enlisted a second time, Jan 10, 1865, and was mustered into the United States service on the same day, for one year, as a private of Co. K, 61st Regt. Mass. Vols. He served with his regiment in Virginia, and was mustered out July 16, 1865.

SHUBARD E. DUNBAR, son of Charles and Patience Dunbar, was born Nov. 4, 1829, in Franklin, Mass. He was drafted into the United States service July 15, 1863, for three years, and was assigned to Co. G, 18th Regt. Mass. Vols. He joined his regiment at Beverly Ford, Va., about the middle of September, 1863, and was in the engagements at Rappahannock Station, November 7, and at Mine Creek, Nov. 30, 1863; at the Wilderness, May 5,

6, 7, Laurel Hill, May 9, Spottsylvania, May 23, skirmish at Shady Grove Road, May 30, Tolopotomy Swamp, June 1, Cold Harbor, June 3 to 5, skirmish at Sumner's Bridge, on Chickahominy River, June 7, and before Petersburg, Va., from June 19 to July 20, 1864, at which time the regiment was mustered out, the recruits and reënlisted men being organized as the 18th Battalion. He was afterwards engaged at Weldon R. R., August 21, and at Peeble's Farm, Sept. 30, 1864. The battalion was merged, October 26, in the 32d Mass. Inf., and took part in the destruction of the Weldon R. R. in December, and in the engagements before Petersburg, Va., in March and April, 1865. He was mustered out of service June 29, 1865.

WILLIAM H. DUNBAR, son of Charles and Patience Dunbar, was born March 28, 1835, in Franklin, Mass. He first served in the 2d R. I. Regt., in which he enlisted about June, 1861. He was in the first battle of Bull Run, July 21 of that year. He was discharged for disability in September, 1861. He also served in the U. S. Navy, having enlisted Jan. 22, 1862, in Boston. He shipped as landsman on board the gun-boat "Marblehead," which, during his service, was stationed off Charlestown, S. C. He was discharged for disability in May, 1863, from the Naval Hospital, Brooklyn, N. Y. He enlisted a second time, Aug. 23, 1864, and was mustered into the United States service, on the same day, for one year, as a private of the 18th unattached Co., afterwards Co. B, 7th Regt. Mass. Heavy Arty. He served in the defenses of Washington, D. C., and was mustered out of service June 17, 1865. He removed in 1879, and resides in Milwaukee, Wis.

ALONZO DUNTON, son of Joel and Lavina Dunton, was born June 10, 1840, in Franklin, Mass. He enlisted and was mustered into the United States service May 25, 1861, for three years, as a private of Co. E, 2d Mass. Regt. He was promoted Corporal Dec. 30, 1862, and Sergeant Feb. 22, 1863, which position he held until June 22, 1864. He reënlisted about Jan. 1, 1864, for three years. He states that he was in the battle of Cedar Mountain, Va., Aug. 9, 1862; at Antietam, Sept. 17, 1862; at Chancellorsville, May 3, 1863; at Gettysburg, July 2 and 3, 1863; at Cedar Creek, and in the battles on the Savannah River, under Gen. Sherman. He was also one of the party of sixty men under Capt. Cogswell, which crossed the Potomac to Shepardstown, Va., on a November night in 1862, and killed the noted guerilla, Burke, and took prisoners several of his men. He appears to have deserted Aug. 3, 1864. *Vid. The Potomac and Rapidan*, p. 231.

JOHN H. DURGIN, at the age of twenty-eight years, residence unknown, was mustered into the U. S. Vet. Res. Corps, May 4, 1864, for three years.

CHARLES H. EVERETT, son of William and Abby F. (Wiggin) Everett, was born Nov. 18, 1844, in Medway. He first enlisted Dec. 16, 1861, in Co. D, 5th Battalion R. I. Vols., and was discharged for disability, May 29, 1863. He enlisted a second time, December 1, and was mustered into the United States service Dec. 7, 1863, for three years, as a private of Co. H, 2d Regt. Heavy Arty. Mass. Vols. He was accredited to the town of Milford. He was taken prisoner at Plymouth, April 10, 1864, and confined at Andersonville, Ga., till about the middle of September following, when he was removed to Florence, S. C., where he remained in confinement until about March 1, 1865, when he was exchanged and sent within the Union lines. But hardship and starvation had done their work. He reached home in April, and died May 25, 1865.

GEORGE B. EVERETT, son of William and Abby F. (Wiggin) Everett, was born Aug. 21, 1840, in Medway. He enlisted in January, 1861, as a private of Captain Benison's Battery U. S. Light Arty., for the term of five years. This term was afterwards reduced to three years, and he was mustered out of service about January, 1864. He soon afterwards enlisted again in the 2d Regt. Mass. Cav., for three years, and was accredited to the town of Hanson. He was discharged from the regiment to enable him to accept a commission as 2d Lieut. in the 2d Regt. U. S. colored Cavalry. He was mustered out, February, 1866, in Brazos Santiago, Tex.

ALBERT F. FALES, son of James D. and Mary A. (Hill) Fales, was born Nov. 13, 1836, in Medway. He enlisted early in May, and was mustered into the United States service May 25, 1861, for three years, in Camp Andrew, West Roxbury, as a private of Co. E, 2d Mass. Inf. He was in all the earlier engagements of the regiment. At Winchester, Va., May 25, 1862, he was wounded through his arm, the ball, afterwards striking a comb in the pocket of his blouse, glanced off, thus averting a more serious, if not a fatal wound. At Cedar Mountain, Va., Aug. 9, 1862, he was wounded in the face by a pistol ball or buck-shot. At Antietam, Md., Sept. 17, 1862, he was severely wounded in the left hand. He was discharged Dec. 6, 1862, for disability, from the General Hospital, Harrisburg, Penn.

JAMES E. FALES, son of James D. and Mary A. (Hill) Fales, was born Feb. 5, 1828, in Franklin, Mass. He enlisted the last of August, and was mustered into the United States service Sept. 13, 1862, at Readville, for nine months, as a private of Co. B, 42d Regt. Mass. Vols. He served in the Department of the Gulf and was mustered out Aug. 20, 1863.

JOHN M. FALES, son of James D. and Mary A. (Hill) Fales, was born Jan. 27, 1835, in Bellingham, Mass. He enlisted early in May, and was mustered into the United States service May 25, 1861, for three years, in Camp Andrew, West Roxbury, as a private of Co. E, 2d Regt. Mass. Vols. He was detailed assistant in commissary department, and held the position of butcher through his term of service, exempt from duty in the ranks. He was mustered out at the expiration of his term, May 28, 1864.

JOHN FARREN, at the age of forty-five years, residence Boston, was mustered into the United States service Nov. 14, 1863, for three years, as a private of 13th Regt. Vet. Res. Corps. He was assigned to the credit of Medway, April 30, 1864, and mustered out Dec. 1, 1865, by reason of general order No. 155 of the War Department.

JOHN FENDT, at the age of thirty-one years, residence unknown, was mustered into the United States service May 5, 1864, for three years, as a Corporal of 1st Co., 2d Battalion. He was accredited to Medway.

CHARLES H. FISHER enlisted Nov. 21, 1864, and was mustered into service on the same day, for one year, in Co. G, 61st Regt. Mass. Vols. He was accredited to Medway, but was not a resident of the town. He served with his regiment in Virginia, and was mustered out July 16, 1865.

FRANK L. FISHER, son of Lewis and Betsey (Richardson) Fisher, was born Sept. 27, 1844, in Medway. He enlisted the last of August, and was mustered into the service of the United States, Sept. 13, 1862, in Readville, Mass., for nine months, as a private of Co. B, 42d Regt. Mass. Vols. He served with his regiment in Louisiana, and was mustered out Aug. 20, 1863, his term having expired. He enlisted again in the same regiment and company for one hundred days and was mustered into service July 22, 1864. He served in the defenses of Washington, D. C., and was mustered out Nov. 11, 1864. He resides in Pueblo, Col.

GEORGE H. FISHER, son of Timothy Fisher, at the age of eighteen years, enlisted and was mustered into the United States service, Sept. 13, 1862, for nine months, as a private of Co. B, 42d Regt. Mass. Vols. He was mustered out Aug. 20, 1863, his term having expired.

GEORGE S. FISHER, son of Simeon and Mary A. (Rockwood) Fisher, was born Sept. 13, 1828, in Holliston. He was a resident of Ashland, and was accredited to that town. He enlisted and was mustered into the United States service Sept. 16, 1862, for nine months, as a private of Co. E, 5th Regt. Mass. Vols. He served with his regiment in North Carolina. The regiment was engaged at Kinston, Whitehall, and Goldsboro', and in skirmishes at Hill's Point, Blount's Creek, and in a reconnoisance of rebel works at Mosely Creek, and subsequently in the capture of those works. He was mustered out July 2, 1863, at expiration of his term of service.

HENRY S. FISHER, son of John S. and Frances M. Fisher, resided in Malden, but was accredited to the town of Medway. At the age of sixteen years he enlisted and was mustered into the United States service, Dec. 1, 1864, for one year, as a private of the 12th Mass. Light Bat. He was mustered out July 25, 1865.

LEWIS L. FISHER, son of Ebenezer and Melatiah (Smith) Fisher, was born in Bellingham, Mass. He enlisted Aug. 20, 1862, and was mustered into the United States service on the same day for three years, as a private of Co. E, 2d Regt. Mass. Vols. He was discharged for disability, Feb. 19, 1863. He died July 4, 1866, an accidental death.

THEODORE WILLIS FISHER, son of the Hon. Milton Metcalf and Eleanor (Metcalf) Fisher, was born May 29, 1837, in Westboro, Mass. He was educated in the public schools of Medway, in Williston Seminary, East Hampton, and in Phillips Academy, Andover. He graduated, in 1861, from the Harvard Medical College in Cambridge, and was at once appointed to the position of Resident Physician for the city institutions in Boston Harbor. He was commissioned, Aug. 29, 1862, Assistant-Surgeon of the 44th Regt. Mass. Vols., and was mustered into the United States service Sept. 12, 1862, for nine months. He was at that time a resident of Boston, but preferred to be accredited to Medway. His regiment arrived in North Carolina, October, 1862. He was on duty in the Tarboro' Expedition, when his regiment took part in the engagement at Rawles' Mills, November 2, and also in the Goldsboro' expedition, when it was in the engagements at Kinston, December 14; Whitehall, December 16; and Goldsboro', Dec. 17, 1862. He was detailed Jan. 28, 1863, in charge of a section of Foster General Hospital, in Newbern, N. C. He obtained leave, Jan. 29, 1863, to go on the expedition to Plymouth, N. C., and on account of sickness did not return to the hospital till February 24 following. He was commissioned Surgeon of his regiment April 10, 1863, in place of Dr. Robert Ware, deceased, and rejoined his regiment at Washington, N. C., April 16, the day on which the siege of that place was raised. He was mustered out June 18, 1863, at the expiration of his term. In the

THEODORE WILLIS FISHER, M. D.

autumn of 1863 Dr. Fisher was appointed Assistant-Superintendent of the Boston Lunatic Hospital, which position he filled until 1869. During this period, in 1867, he traveled widely in Europe, making hospital construction and ventilation a special study. In 1869 he established himself in Boston as a specialist in the treatment of mental diseases. He was widely consulted, and testified as an expert in cases of insanity in courts throughout New England, and was a witness in the famous Guiteau trial. Dr. Fisher wrote many papers on insanity and mental diseases. In 1880 he was appointed Superintendent of the Boston Lunatic Hospital, which position he now fills. He is a member of numerous medical societies in the country. Dr. Fisher delivered an historical address Dec. 31, 1872, at the dedication of Sanford Hall, Medway. He married, Nov. 10, 1858, Maria C. Brown, daughter of Artemas Brown, M. D., of Medway. Mrs. Maria C. Fisher died July 28, 1860. Dr. Fisher married, Dec. 18, 1873, Ella G. Richardson, daughter of J. W. Richardson, Esq., of Boston, Mass. There are three children of the second marriage now living, viz., Willis R., Edward M., and Gertrude Fisher.

WILLARD P. FISHER, son of Simeon and Mary A. (Rockwood) Fisher, was born Oct. 2, 1842, in Holliston. He enlisted the last of August, and was mustered into the United States service, Sept. 13, 1862, for nine months, as a private of Co. B, 42d Regt. Mass. Vols. He was in the engagement at Brashear City, La., June 23, 1863, and was taken prisoner. He was paroled June 26, and was mustered out Aug. 20, 1863, in Readville, Mass. He enlisted a second time, and was mustered into service March 11, 1864, for three years, as a Corporal of the 16th Mass. Light Bat. He served in the defenses of Washington, D. C., and was mustered out June 27, 1865.

JULIUS A. FITTS, son of Charles H. and Emeline A. (Richards) Fitts, was born Nov. 12, 1843, in Medway. He enlisted in August, and was mustered into the United States service, Sept. 13, 1862, for nine months, as a private of Co. B, 42d Regt. Mass. Vols. He was detailed as an orderly to Lieut.-Col. Stedman, and was mustered out Aug. 20, 1863. He enlisted again from Holliston, Mass., for one hundred days, in the same regiment and company, and was mustered into service July 22, 1864, as 5th Sergeant. He served in the defenses of Washington, D. C., and was mustered out Nov. 11, 1864. He became a resident of Medfield, and engaged in mercantile business.

JAMES FITZGERALD, son of Edward and Mary (O'Connor) Fitzgerald, was born about September, 1840, in Kerry County, Ireland. He enlisted May 24, 1861, for four years, as a private of U. S. Marine Corps. He was first assigned to duty on board the United States steamer "Preble," Sept. 20, 1861. He was at the capture of Ship Island, Oct. 13, 1861, and in an engagement with the rebel ram, "Manassas" above the passes of the Mississippi River. He was in a slight engagement, April 3, with the rebel fleet under Admiral Buchanan, and June 29, 1862, at the capture of the steamer "Ann" at the entrance of Mobile Bay, bound for that port from Nassau, N. P., with harnesses, saddles, and artillery stores. He left the "Preble" Jan. 10, 1863, and was assigned to duty at the Pensacola Navy Yard, Fla., remaining there until December, when he went on board the United States transport "Bermuda." He was transferred, Feb. 17, 1865, to the United States steamer "Richmond," arrived at Charlestown Navy Yard, July 15, and was mustered out of service Aug. 1, 1865, his term having expired.

MICHAEL FITZGERALD, a resident of Medway, was mustered into the United States service July 22, 1864, for one hundred days, as a private of Co. B, 42d Regt. Mass. Vols. He was mustered out Nov. 11, 1864.

ANDREW FITZSIMMONS, residence Cambridge, Mass., was mustered into the United States service, May 7, 1864, for three years, as a member of unassigned detachment Vet. Res. Corps, and accredited to Medway.

JAMES BLAKE FLAHERTY, son of Thomas and Maria (Blake) Flaherty, was born May 15, 1848, in Ireland. He was a resident of Medway, but enlisted from Philadelphia, Penn., and was mustered into the United States service March 3, 1863, for three years, as a private of Co. H, 19th Regt. Penn. Cav. He took part in the battle of Nashville, Tenn., in December, 1864, and in many raids and skirmishes. He was mustered out May 12, 1866, at the expiration of his term of service, in New Orleans, La.

THOMAS FLAHERTY, son of Thomas and Maria (Blake) Flaherty, was born about 1846, in Ireland. He was a resident of Medway, but enlisted September 27, from Worcester, Mass., for three years, as a private of Co. K, 5th Regt. N. Y. Cav., and was mustered into service Oct. 15, 1861. He was afterward promoted Corporal. The service of his regiment was principally in Virginia. He took part, Nov. 12, 1862, in the movement by which the rebels were driven out of Stephensburg, Va., the Union troops occupying the rebel camp. March 28, 1863, he was in a raid under General Kilpatrick, resulting in the capture of a number of prisoners, and he was detailed one of the guards over them. On the 23d of March, in a skirmish with Moseby's cavalry near Chantilly, he was taken prisoner with thirty-four others of his regiment, and sent to Richmond, Va. He was paroled after three days, and sent to Camp Parole, at Annapolis, Md. When a prisoner on his way to Richmond, he was deprived of a part of his clothing by the rebel guards, and thus exposed, he took cold, which resulted in a fever, from the effects of which he never recovered. He was exchanged after several months, and returned to his regiment, but being unfit for service he was sent to the hospital, and in May, 1864, was removed to Lovell General Hospital, Portsmouth Grove, R. I. In October he returned to duty in the regiment, and took part in several skirmishes, and on one occasion, having his horse killed under him, he escaped capture only by mounting the horse of a comrade who had been killed. He was resolved, as he wrote to his mother, to be killed rather than be again taken prisoner. He was mustered out Nov. 14, 1864, at the expiration of his service. After being discharged his health continued to fail, and he died Dec. 21, 1865, in Medway.

EMMONS FORCE, son of Samuel and Relief (Hood) Force, was born July 5, 1834, in Westboro, Mass. He enlisted early in May, and was mustered into the United States service May 25, 1861, in Camp Andrew, West Roxbury, for three years, as a private of Co. E, 2d Regt. Mass. Vols. He was in the earlier skirmishes of the regiment and at the battle of Winchester, Va., May 25, 1862. Soon after he was sent to the hospital and was detailed as a mechanic. He was discharged Nov. 21, 1862, for disability.

SILAS FORCE, son of Samuel and Relief (Hood) Force, was born March 22, 1842, in Medway. He was mustered into the United States service Nov. 28, 1864, for one year, as a private of Co. A, 2d Regt. Mass. Vols. He remained on duty at Galloup's Island for one month after his enlistment; afterwards was some time at Hart's Island and did not join his regiment until April, 1865. He was mustered out July 26, 1865.

WILLIAM W. FORMAN, of Boston, enlisted and was mustered into the United States service June 9, 1864, for three years, as a private of Co. K, 10th Regt. U. S. Vet. Res. Corps, and was accredited to Medway.

GEORGE J. FOSTER, son of Appleton and Louisa A. (Bannister) Foster, was born June 23, 1845, in Medway. He was mustered into the United States service Aug. 25, 1862, for three years, as a private of the 3d N. Y. Light Bat. He was at the time a resident of New York City. He states that he was in some twenty or more engagements during his service. He was mustered out July 25, 1865, at the expiration of his term.

PETER FOSTER was born in Scotland, G. B. He enlisted May 20, and was mustered into service Aug. 24, 1861, in Co. I, 10th Regt. Mass. Vols., from Wrentham, Mass. He was discharged April 24, 1862, for disability. At the age of twenty-seven years he enlisted, Aug. 23, 1864, and was mustered into the United States service the same day, for one year, as a private of the 18th unattached Co., afterwards Co. B, 4th Mass. Heavy Arty. He served in the defenses of Washington, D. C., and was mustered out June 17, 1865.

WILLIAM B. FOSTER, son of Appleton and Louisa A. (Bannister) Foster, was born Dec. 19, 1842, in Medway. He was mustered into the United States service from Canton, Mass., Aug. 19, 1862, for nine months, as a private of Co. A, 4th Regt. Mass. Vols. He died April 1, 1863, in University Hospital, New Orleans, La., where he was buried.

GEORGE F. FRENCH, at the age of twenty-four years, enlisted in December, 1862, and was mustered into service for three years, as a private of Co. C, 2d Regt. Mass. Cav. He was accredited to Medway, though not a resident. By the state record he appears as mustered in March 17, 1863, and accredited to Middleton. He was discharged Nov. 16, 1863, for disability.

AMOS L. FULLER, of Medway, was mustered into the United States service May 19, 1861, for three months, as a private of Co. D, 3d Battalion Riflemen Mass. Vols. He was discharged July 23, 1861, for disability.

CHARLES F. FULLER, son of William and Mary (Henderson) Fuller, was born April 5, 1828, in Medway. He enlisted early in May, and was mustered into the service of the United States, May 25, 1861, for three years, as a private of Co. E, 2d Regt. Mass. Vols. He was discharged Jan. 8, 1862, for disability. He enlisted a second time as Frank C. Fuller, and was mustered into service May 13, 1862, for three years, as a private of the 7th Mass. Light Bat. He was transferred March 23, 1864, to the Vet. Res. Corps. He was assigned to the 31st Co., 2d Battalion, and afterwards transferred to the 32d Co., 2d Battalion Vet. Res. Corps.

GEORGE A. FULLER, son of Stephen B. and Mary A. (Christian) Fuller, was born Jan. 9, 1847, in Charlestown, Mass. He was mustered into the United States service Dec. 10, 1863, for three years, as a private of Co. G, 2d Regt. Heavy Arty. Mass. Vols. He was taken prisoner at Plymouth, N. C., April 18, 1864, and was sent to Andersonville, Ga., where he died in prison, August, 1864. He was buried in the grave marked No. 7,392.

GEORGE EDMUND FULLER, son of Elihu and Rhoda (Daniels) Fuller, was born March 3, 1826, in Medway. He enlisted and was mustered into the United States service, July 22, 1864, for one hundred days, as 2d Lieut. of Co. B, 42d Regt. Mass. Vols. He served in the defenses of Washington, D. C., and was mustered out Nov. 11, 1864.

GEORGE F. FULLER, son of Israel D. and Eliza (Barber) Fuller, was born March 8, 1841, in Medway. He enlisted from Brighton, and was mustered into the United States service Aug. 25, 1862, for nine months, as a private of 11th Mass. Light Bat. He was mustered out of service May 25, 1863, his term having expired.

JAMES A. GALE, son of Dr. Amory and Martha (Leland) Gale, was born Oct. 3, 1837, in Amherst, N. H. He enlisted in March, and was mustered into the United States service April 7, 1864, for three years, as a private of the 16th Mass. Light Bat. He served in the defenses of Washington, D. C., and was mustered out July 27, 1865, by reason of the close of the war. He removed to West Medway, and resumed his medical practice, which he still continues.

PATRICK GALLAGHER was born in Ireland. He resided in Medway, and at the age of nineteen years enlisted from Bellingham, and was mustered into service Dec. 27, 1864, for three years, as a private of Co. M, 4th Regt. Mass. Cav. He was found dead in his tent May 24, 1865, at camp, near

Richmond. Va., and is supposed to have been killed by the accidental discharge of his own carbine.

JOHN GLANCY, son of Owen and Margaret Glancy, was born June 24, 1841, in Ireland. He enlisted at Charlestown Navy Yard July 17, 1861, for four years, as a private of the U. S. Marine Corps. He was assigned to duty on the frigate " Congress," and was on board that ill-fated vessel when she was destroyed, March 8, 1862, by the rebel ram " Merrimac," at Hampton Roads, Va. He afterwards served on board the " San Jacinto," which was sent to the West Indies in pursuit of the pirate " Alabama." He was discharged, March 13, 1863, for disability.

JOHN GORMLY, on the rolls as John Gorman, was born in Tyrene County, Ireland. He resided in Medway. At the age of nineteen years he enlisted, in May, and was mustered into the United States service May 25. 1861, in Camp Andrew, West Roxbury, for three years, as a private of Co. E, 2d Regt. Mass. Vols. He was in the earlier skirmishes of the regiment; in the engagement at Winchester, Va., May 25, at Cedar Mountain, Aug. 9, 1862; at Chancellorsville, May 3, at Beverly Ford, June 9, and at Gettysburg, Penn., July 2 and 3, 1863. He was transferred Sept. 6, 1863, to the Vet. Res. Corps, and mustered out May, 1864.

JOSEPH H. GOULD was born in Nova Scotia. He was mustered into the United States service March 11, 1864, for three years, as a private of the 16th Light Bat. Mass. Vols. He deserted April 3, 1864, from Camp Meigs, Readville, Mass. He was a resident of Medway at time of enlistment.

CHARLES GRANT, born in Douglas, Mass., enlisted in Medway at the age of thirty-four years, and was mustered into service May 25, 1861, for three years, as a private of Co. E, 2d Regt. Mass. Vols. He was discharged, May 30, 1861, from Camp Andrew, West Roxbury, Mass.

CHARLES A. GRANT, son of Charles and Janette Grant, was born Jan. 3, 1849, in Medway. He enlisted and was mustered into the United States service, Jan. 5, 1865, for one year, as a private of Co. K, 61st Mass. Regt. He was at the time a resident of the town, but received a bounty from the town of Bellingham, to which place he was accredited. He was in the engagement at Petersburg, Va., April 2, 1865, and mustered out July 16, 1865.

EDWIN A. GRANT, son of Calvin and Eliza Grant, was born May 31, 1847, in Wrentham. He enlisted for one hundred days, and was mustered into the United States service July 22, 1864, as a private of Co. B, 42d Regt. Mass. Vols. He died Sept. 11, 1864, in Alexandria, Va., and was buried in Medway.

FRANK S. GRANT, son of Calvin and Eliza Grant, was born Aug. 18, 1844, in Wrentham. He enlisted in May, and was mustered into the United States service for three years, May 25, 1861, as a private of Co. E, 2d Regt. Mass. Vols. He was in the earlier skirmishes of the regiment: in the fight at Winchester, Va., May 25, at the battle of Cedar Mountain, August 9, Antietam, Md., Sept. 17, 1862; Chancellorsville, May 3, Beverly Ford, June 9, and at Gettysburg, Penn., July 2 and 3, 1863. At the latter engagement he was wounded through the knee, and was transferred Jan. 14, 1864, to the Vet. Res. Corps. He was mustered out of service at the expiration of his term, May, 1864, and died April 25, 1868, in Medway.

GEORGE O. GRANT, son of Calvin and Rebecca Grant, was born in 1841, in Medway. He enlisted, and was mustered into the United States service, Aug. 16, 1862, for three years, as a private of Co. B, 38th Regt. Mass. Vols. He was transferred Feb. 4, 1863, to the 1st Louisiana Cav., and was with that regiment in several skirmishes, and at the siege of Port Hudson, La., and afterwards at Carrion Crow Bayou, at which time he was wounded in the thigh, the ball lodging in the groin. He was discharged April 11, 1864, for disability arising from his wound. He enlisted again from Milford.

HARRISON G. O. GRANT, son of Calvin and Rebecca Grant, was born in 1838, in Medway. He enlisted in May, and was mustered into the United States service June 6, 1863, for three years, as a private of Co. D, 1st Bat. Heavy Arty. Mass. Vols. He served in the forts of Boston Harbor, and was mustered out of service Sept. 12, 1865, by reason of the close of the war. He became an inmate of Chelsea Soldiers' Home.

JAMES M. GRANT, son of Calvin and Eliza Grant, was born March 16, 1840, in Woonsocket, R. I. He enlisted early in May, and was mustered into the United States service May 25, 1861, for three years, as a private of Co. E, 2d Regt. Mass. Vols. He was in the earlier skirmishes of the regiment, and in the engagement at Winchester, Va., May 25, 1862, at which time he was taken prisoner. He was paroled, and sent to Camp Parole, in Annapolis, Md., from which place, after being exchanged, he returned, Oct. 23, 1862, to his regiment, then at Harper's Ferry, Va. In April, 1863, he was sent to the hospital, and remained there until the last of January, 1864, when he again joined his regiment, and was in the battle of Resaca, Ga. He was mustered out of service May 28, 1864, his term having expired.

JOHN P. GREEN, son of John P. and Martha Green, was born July 8, 1827, at Westford, Mass. He enlisted in Lowell, in Co. C, 30th Regt. Mass. Vols., and was mustered into service Oct. 2, 1861. He was discharged April 2, 1862, at Ship Island, Gulf of Mexico.

GEORGE E. GREENWOOD, son of George H. and Lydia E. Greenwood, was born July 20, 1842, in Franklin. He enlisted early in May, and was mustered into the United States service, May 25, 1861, for three years, as a private of Co. E, 2d Regt. Mass. Vols. He was promoted Corporal April 9, 1863, and Sergeant Dec. 30, 1863. During the winter of 1861–2 he was sick in the hospital at Frederick, Md., and remained there on detailed duty until August, 1862, when he returned to the regiment and was in the battle of Cedar Mountain, August 9, and at Antietam, September 17. In November he was one of a party of sixty men of his regiment who on a night excursion under Captain Cogswell, visited Shepardstown and killed the notorious Capt. Burke, a rebel guerilla, and took prisoners several of his men. He was in the battle of Chancellorsville, May 3, 1863, when he was wounded in the right arm and breast. He joined his regiment again August 18, at Alexandria, just as it was ready to leave for New York to assist in enforcing the draft. He continued on duty with his regiment, and in the battle of Resaca, Ga., May, 15, 1864, he was again wounded in the right arm. He was mustered out May 28, 1864, his term having expired. He married and settled in Frederick, Md., soon after the close of the war, where he still resides.

GEORGE H. GREENWOOD, son of Joseph and Betsey (Chenery) Greenwood, was born April 13, 1820, in Franklin. He enlisted the last of

August, and was mustered into the United States service Sept. 13, 1862, for nine months, as a private of Co. B, 42d Regt. Mass. Vols. He served with his regiment in Louisiana, and was mustered out Aug. 20, 1863.

ISAAC C. GREENWOOD, son of Joseph and Betsey (Chenery) Greenwood, was born May 2, 1822, in Holliston, a part of that town now within the limits of Medway. He enlisted early in May, and was mustered into service May 25, 1861, in Camp Andrew, West Roxbury, for three years, as a private of Co. E, 2d Regt. Mass. Vols. He was detailed July 1, 1861, to June 4, 1862, as hospital wagoner, after which he was in the ranks for a time, and took part, Aug. 9, 1862, in the battle of Cedar Mountain, Va. Soon afterwards he was detailed as a driver to the Division Ambulance Corps and continued in that service except for a very brief period until the end of his term. He was mustered out of service May 28, 1864. He enlisted a second time, Aug. 27, 1864, and mustered into the United States service on the same day, for one year, as a private of Co. B, 61st Mass. Vols. August, 1864, he was detailed as company cook to the end of his term of service. He was mustered out June 17, 1865.

JOHN T. GREENWOOD, son of Isaac C. and Sarah Greenwood, was born Jan. 15, 1846, in Medway. He enlisted Aug. 26, 1864, and was mustered into the United States service the same day, for one year, as a private of Co. B, 61st Regt. Mass. Vols. He served with his regiment in Virginia, and took part in the operations before Petersburg in March and April, 1865, but was not in the battle of April 2, having been detailed on special duty at the time. He was mustered out of service June 4, 1865.

JOSEPH A. GREENWOOD, son of Joseph and Betsey (Chenery) Greenwood, was born in July, 1829. He enlisted July 11, and was mustered into the United States service July 21, 1862, for three years, as a private of Co. B, 38th Regt. Mass. Vols. He deserted in December, 1862, from Stewart's Mansion General Hospital. He was returned to his regiment, and sentenced by a court-martial to serve out his term without pay. The sentence was subsequently remitted, and he was mustered out of service June 30, 1865, at the expiration of his term. He resides in Cliftondale, Mass.

THOMAS HACKETT, at the age of twenty-one years, residence Cambridge, Mass., enlisted and was mustered into the United States service Dec. 7, 1864, for one year, as a private of the 6th Mass. Bat. Light Arty., and accredited to Medway. He was mustered out Aug. 7, 1865.

ROBERT HALL, at the age of forty-one years, residence not known, enlisted Sept. 7, 1864, and was mustered into service the same day, for one year, as a private of Co. C, 61st Regt. Mass. Vols. He served with his regiment and was mustered out June 4, 1865.

DANIEL HAMMOND, son of Daniel and Mary E. (Tuttle) Hammond, was born March 3, 1822, in Salem, Mass. He enlisted and was mustered into the service of the United States, July 22, 1864, for one hundred days, as a private of Co. B, 42d Regt. Mass. Vols. He served in the defenses of Washington, D. C., and was mustered out Nov. 11, 1864.

GEORGE B. HARDY, son of Eliphalet D. and Eunice (Tyler) Hardy, was born in Medway. He was drafted into the United States service July 15, 1863, for three years, and was assigned to Co. C, 12th Regt. Mass. Vols. He was killed May 5, 1864, in the battle of the Wilderness, Va.

JOHN HARNEY was born in Roscommon County, Ireland, and resided in Medway. He was mustered into the United States service Aug. 4, 1862, for three years, as a private of Co. B, 38th Mass. Inf. He died June 4, 1863.

PETER HARRINGTON, son of Michael and Catharine (Jennings) Harrington, was born in 1839, in Roscommon County, Ireland. He enlisted early in May, and was mustered into the United States service May 25, 1861, for three years, as a private of Co. E, 2d Regt. Mass. Vols. He was in the earlier skirmishes of the regiment, and in the battles of Winchester, Va., May 25, and of Cedar Mountain, August 9; also at Antietam, Md., Sept. 17, 1862, when he was wounded in the elbow. He was discharged Dec. 6, 1862, for disability arising from his wound. On the night after the battle of Cedar Mountain, Harrington was detailed on the picket guard. The line ran through the woods not very far from the Confederate picket. In the darkness some one hailed him, and inquired the way to the head-quarters of a certain Confederate general. Taking in the situation at once Harrington's mother wit did not desert him, and he quickly replied, "Step this way and I will show you," and very soon thereafter the Confederate captain found himself disarmed, and under guard at the Union head-quarters.

THOMAS J. HARRINGTON, son of Michael and Catharine (Jennings) Harrington, was born March 29, 1831, in Roscommon County, Ireland. He was mustered into the United States service Sept. 3, 1862, for three years, as a private of Co. E, 2d Regt. Mass. Vols., but being a recruit, his term was to expire with that of the regiment. He joined his regiment before the battle of Antietam, and was there, but not engaged. At the battle of Chancellorsville he was detailed to duty on the supply train. He was transferred, Sept. 30, 1863, to the Vet. Res. Corps.

WILLIAM HARROLD, at the age of eighteen years, resident of Boston, enlisted Sept. 7, 1864, and was mustered into the United States service the same day, for one year, as a private of Co. C, 61st Regt. Mass. Vols., and was accredited to Medway, Mass. He was mustered out June 4, 1865.

EDWARD P. HART, son of Charles E. and Julia A. (Daniels) Hart, was born Jan. 31, 1843, in Medway. He was mustered into the United States service July 2, 1861, for three years, as a private of Co. B, 16th Regt. Mass. Vols. He was in the engagements at Fair Oaks, Va., June 18, 25, and 28; at Glendale, June 29; Malvern Hill, July 1 and 8; Kettle Run, August 27; and second Bull Run, Aug. 29, 1862. In the latter battle he was wounded in the hand, losing a part of the forefinger of his right hand. He was transferred to Vet. Res. Corps in July, 1863; assigned to Co. A, 14th Regt., of which company he was promoted July 20, Corporal. He took part in a few skirmishes on the invasion of Maryland and Pennsylvania by the rebels in 1863. He was mustered out of service July 2, 1864. He was a resident of Medway, but by the rolls is accredited to Holliston.

MICHAEL HART, JR., son of Michael and Margaret (Crowell) Hart, was born June, 1845, in Boston, Mass. He enlisted Nov. 23, 1864, and was mustered into the United States service the same day, for one year, as a private of Co. G, 61st Regt. Mass. Vols. He was with his regiment before Petersburg, Va., and in the final engagement, April 2, 1865. He was detailed during the latter part of his term as servant to Capt. Sutien, of Co. G. He was mustered out of service July 16, 1865.

19

ADDISON T. HASTINGS, son of Deming J. and Lucia (Daniels) Hastings, was born Feb. 22, 1842, in Medway. He enlisted and was mustered into the United States service about June 15, 1862, for three months, as a private of Co. B, 7th Squadron R. I. Cav. He was at the time of enlistment a student at the Military Academy at Norwich, Vt. He served in Maryland and Virginia, and was mustered out at the expiration of his term.

WILLIAM HAWES, son of Lewis and Irene Hawes, was born March 12, 1839, in Medway. He was mustered into the United States service July 18, 1861, for three years, as a private of Co. G, 20th Regt. Mass. Vols. He was with his regiment until June 30, 1862. At the battle of Ball's Bluff he was not engaged, having been detailed on some special service at the time, but is believed to have been on duty at the siege of Yorktown, Va., and at the battle of Fair Oaks, and also in some of the engagements after that battle, while on the retreat towards Harrison's Landing. Capt. O. W. Holmes, of Co. G, in a letter to the mother of Hawes, says, that " on the 30th of June, while on the retreat to James River, he fell behind the regiment, and was taken prisoner. He was reported by some of the men as sick, and some said wounded." Subsequently returned prisoners reported seeing him in prison in Richmond, Va. Since then nothing has been heard from him.

WILLIAM C. HAWES, son of John H. and Merriam (Clark) Hawes, was born Nov. 29, 1834, in Walpole, Mass. He enlisted from Milford, and was mustered into service May 30, 1862, for six months, as a private of the 8th Bat. Mass. Light Arty. He was in the following engagements : at Sulphur Springs, Va., August 22 ; Bull Run, August 30 ; Chantilly, September 1 : South Mountain, September 14 ; and at Antietam, Sept. 17, 1862. He was mustered out of service Nov. 29, 1862, his term having expired. He enlisted again about January 1, and was mustered into the United States service Jan. 6, 1863, for three years, as a Corporal of the 15th Bat. Mass. Light Arty., (state record says mustered February 13). He was detailed clerk of the battery, and for several months was Acting Adjutant. He was discharged from the battery Dec. 4, 1863, to enable him to accept an appointment as 2d Lieut. in the 162d Regt. N. Y. Vols. In relation to his character, his subsequent services, and his death, the following has been selected from an article prepared by a citizen of the town, and published June, 1864, in a local paper : " ANOTHER HERO GONE.—With sadness we record the death of another brave Medway volunteer, Lieut. William C. Hawes, who died at Alexandria, La., May 29, six days after receiving a mortal wound in the battle of Cane River." Lieut. Hawes, after joining his regiment, was in three hard-fought battles, at Mansfield, Mount Pleasant, and lastly at Cane River on the 23d of May, 1864, at which time he was wounded while charging up the wooded hill to which the enemy had been driven, and where they were strongly posted. In a letter to the wife of Lieut. Hawes, Capt. Seaman, his commanding officer, speaking of the manner of his being wounded, says, " He was struck by a ball and three buckshot. The ball entered at the left shoulder blade ; the buckshot entered the left shoulder, but did not pass through the body." He says, " our brigade was ordered to the front, and to charge up the hill. When nearly on the hill Lieut. Hawes ordered a rebel to surrender, and the man fired, the ball taking effect as above. The man that shot him was. fired at by our men three times, and severely wounded and taken prisoner, and had he not been hurried through our lines, would have been lynched by our men." He also adds, "allow me to say your husband had the kind feelings and sympathy of all who knew him. Since our acquaintance he has been my particular and intimate friend, and I deeply regret that I have to lose his society." After being wounded he was conveyed by ambulance and boat some fifty miles to Alexandria, where, in the hospital, under the charge of Dr. Andrews, of the 120th N. Y. Vols., he received the best of medical treatment, and was constantly attended by Mr. John Stephens, Jr., an agent of the sanitary commission, who, in a letter to his wife and mother, speaks in the highest terms of his fortitude and patience under all his sufferings. He says, " throughout all he was calm, and felt that perfect peace which cometh from nothing of earth." He was sustained by that comfort which Christ has promised to all his people. The night before he died he said, " I am dying, but tell mother I died happy, and in a good cause." After passing through the two previous battles unharmed, he wrote to his wife, " God has seen fit to spare my life thus far; though the bullets flew thick and fast all around me, yet I came out unharmed, and am extremely grateful to my Father in Heaven. I may fall in the next battle; if so, I freely offer my life for our noble cause." These were truly prophetic words. Lieut. Hawes was a young man of good education, temperate habits, correct and manly deportment, modest and unassuming, and wherever known bore an irreproachable character. In his diary, which he kept of each day's events, and which for purity of language, beauty of style, with minuteness of detail, to say nothing of superior penmanship, is a model composition, is found the following, which he seems to have adopted for his creed, and a better one in brief is rarely found: " Five facts: A living faith is the best divinity; a holy life is the best philosophy; a tender conscience is the best law; honesty is the best policy; and temperance the best physic." The temptations and vices of camp neither allured nor contaminated him, but the stern realities of war, the magnitude of the conflict, and its mighty results, gave breadth and expansion to his intellect, ennobled and purified his heart, and led to an entire consecration of himself to his God and his country. His death was full of consolation to his friends who mourned his loss. " HEADQUARTERS 15TH MASS. BATTERY, NEW ORLEANS, LA., DEPARTMENT OF THE GULF, May 30, 1864. Battery Order No. 36: 2d Lieut. William C. Hawes, late of Medway, Mass., while leading his company in the last battle of Cane River, received a wound of which he died some time last week. Lieut. Hawes enlisted as a private in this battery at its original formation, and served as clerk of the company till some time last fall, when he was promoted to a Lieutenancy in the 162d N. Y. Vols. He was an honest, faithful, and true soldier, a gentleman, and one of the best young men I ever met. In his death, the service loses an able officer, society, a bright ornament, and his family, a devoted husband, father, and brother, and we all, a sincere friend. While feeling deeply his untimely end, with proud satisfaction we can point to the fact that he fell wounded with his face to the enemies of his country. While we mourn his departure let us most sincerely sympathize with his dear friends who will miss him much. We shall ever remember 2d Lieut. William C. Hawes as a patriot. Per Order, T. PIERSON, Capt. 15th Mass. Battery, Commander." The degree of estimation at which he was held by the members of the battery appears in the letter of Capt Pierson to the sister of Lieut Hawes, in which he says: "When the preceding order was read to the company, many eyes were wet with tears when they remembered your dear brother." He also remarks, "he would have been promoted the next day if he had lived." It may be truly said he was promoted.

ALBERT M. HAYWARD, at the age of twenty-two years, residence not known, was enlisted by Lieut A. D. Sawyer of the 2d Mass. Inf, and was mustered into the United States service Aug. 30, 1862, for three years, as a private of that regiment.

JAMES H. HEATON, son of Samuel and Tirza (Carlton) Heaton, was born Sept. 1, 1831. in Franklin, Mass He enlisted for one hundred days, and was mustered into the service July 22, 1864. He served in the vicinity of Washington, D. C , and was mustered out of service Nov. 11, 1864.

JOHN HENRY was born in Sligo County, Ireland He enlisted in May, at Medway, and was mustered into the United States service, May 25, 1861, as a private of Co. E, 2d Regt. Mass Vols He states that he was in every engagement in which the regiment took a part, during his term of service except Gettysburg. He was at Winchester, Va., May 25; at Cedar Mountain, August 9; at Antietam, Sept 17, 1862, at Chancellorsville, May 2 and 3, 1863, when he was wounded in the breast. He returned to duty in the regiment again Aug 17, 1863. He was afterwards in the battle of Resaca, Ga., May 15, 1864 In November, 1862, he was one of the party under Capt. Cogswell, which visited Shepherdstown, Va., and killed the noted guerilla, Burke, and took several of his men prisoners. He was mustered out May 28, 1864, his term having expired.

JAMES T HIGGINS, at the age of thirty-eight years, a resident of Roxbury, but accredited to the town of Medway, enlisted, and was mustered into the United States service Nov. 29, 1864, for one year, as 1st Sergeant of Co. G, 61st Regt Mass. Vols. He had previously served a full term in the 1st Regt. Mass. Vols , from Roxbury, having been mustered out May 25, 1864, as 1st Sergeant of Co. K. He was discharged April 19, 1865, from Co. G, for promotion, and promoted 2d Lieut. Co. B, 61st Regt

JOHN HIGGINS, son of John and Catherine Higgins, was born June 24, 1836, in Limerick County, Ireland He enlisted Aug. 26, 1864, and was mustered into the United States service on the same day, for one year, as a private of Co. B, 61st Regt. Mass. Vols. He was in the battle of Petersburg, April, 1865, and was mustered out of service June 4, 1865. He removed to Hopkinton, where he died several years since.

EDMUND W HILL, son of Hiram and Clarissa (Henderson) Hill, was born Nov. 25, 1836, in Medway He enlisted in May, and was mustered into the United States service May 25, 1861, for three years. as a Corporal of Co E, 2d Regt. Mass. Vols. He was discharged Jan. 29, 1862, for disability. He enlisted a second time for one hundred days, and was mustered into the United States service July 22, 1864, as a Corporal of Co. B, 42d Regt. Mass. Vols. He was mustered out Nov. 11, 1864

LEWIS SOLON HILL, son of Lewis and Huldah (Randall) Hill, was born Nov. 23, 1844, in Medway His father continued to reside here for some years after. He enlisted in February, 1864, as a recruit to 28th Mass. Regt , and was assigned to Co. I. He was, at the time of enlistment, a resident of Framingham, and was accredited to that town. He was with his regiment, and took part in the engagements before Petersburg, Va., in the spring and summer of 1864. He died, November, 1864, in Washington, D. C.

MOSES HILL, son of Moses and Persis (Phipps) Hill, was born March 22, 1823, in Bellingham, Mass. He was mustered into the United States service Aug 21, 1861, for three years, as a private of the First Company of Sharpshooters, called "Andrew Sharpshooters." He first served on the upper Potomac, his company being attached to the command of Gen Lander during the winter of 1861-2. After the death of Gen. Lander it was transferred to the 15th Regt., with which it became connected in April, 1862, during the siege of Yorktown, Va. Lieut.-Col. Kimball of that regiment speaks of the company as having been of great service in that siege, with telescopic rifles, in silencing the enemy's batteries by picking off the gunners or compelling them to retire. He was subsequently in the battle of Fair Oaks in June, 1862, and in other succeeding engagements of the Peninsula Campaign. It was during the hardships and exposures of this campaign, that his health began to fail and he was finally sent to one of the hospitals in Washington, D C. There he continued to grow worse and at the request of his wife, Mr. Geo. L. Richardson of this town visited him, obtained his discharge on the 13th of October, 1862, and immediately accompanied him home, where he died Oct 29, 1862.

JOHN HIRL, at the age of thirty-five years, residence New Bedford, enlisted Dec. 13, 1864, and was mustered into the United States service on the same day, for one year, as a private of the 26th unattached Co. of Mass Vols. He was mustered out of service May 12, 1865, the war being ended.

ALONZO HIXON, son of Willard and Dorcas (Bartholomew) Hixon, was born Feb. 19, 1826. He enlisted in May, and was mustered into the United States service May 25, 1861, at Camp Andrew, West Roxbury, as a private of Co. E, 2d Mass. Regt. He was detailed as company cook in May, 1861, and occupied that position during his entire term, on which account he was generally exempt from duty in the ranks He was, however, in the ranks in the battle of Winchester, Va., May 25, 1862, and again May 15, 1864, at the battle of Resaca, Ga. He was mustered out May 28, 1864.

EGBERT OSWELL HIXON, son of Isaac and Persis (Adams) Hixon, was born in 1827, in Medway. He enlisted about April 15, 1861, for three months, as a private of Co. D, 8th Regt. Mass. Vols., and was accredited to Lynn. He was mustered out of service Aug. 1, 1861, his term having expired He enlisted again, and was mustered into the United States service, Aug. 15, 1861, for three years, as a private of the First Company of Sharpshooters, known as "Andrew Sharpshooters," He deserted about September, 1862, and afterwards enlisted in an Ohio regiment under an assumed name, and died in the service.

GEORGE H. HIXON, son of Elihu and Hannah Hixon, was born March 15, 1838, in Medway. He enlisted May 20, 1861, for one year, in the U. S. Navy, and shipped on board the steam frigate "Colorado." He served on board that vessel until April, 1862, when he was transferred to the sloop-of-war "Pensacola," at the mouth of the Mississippi River, for the expedition against New Orleans. He was at the bombardment of Forts Jackson and

St. Philip, engaged with the rebel fleet and earth works on the river above, encountered the fire rafts, and afterwards was in front of New Orleans when Gen. Butler took possession of the city. About the 1st of June he was returned to the " Colorado," and was discharged from that vessel about July 1, 1862. at Portsmouth, N. H., his term having expired He enlisted again, and was mustered into service March 11, 1864, for three years, as a private of the 16th Mass Light Bat. He served in the vicinity of Washington, D. C , and was mustered out June 27, 1865, the war being ended

EDWARD HOGAN, son of James and Margaret Hogan, was born Feb. 28, 1838, in Tipperary County, Ireland He enlisted, and was mustered into the United States service May 25, 1861, for three years, as a private of Co. E, 2d Mass Inf. He was promoted Corporal March 23, 1864. From August, 1861, to February, 1862, he was detailed for duty with the ordnance officer of the regiment. He states that he was in all the earlier skirmishes of the regiment, was in the battle of Winchester, Va., May 25 ; at Cedar Mountain, August 9, when he was wounded in the hand, but recovered so much as to return to duty Oct. 10, 1862 ; was in the battle of Chancellorsville, May 3 and 4, Beverly Ford, June 9; at Gettysburg, Penn., July 2 and 3, 1863, when the regiment lost in one charge, 137 out of 316 men engaged, and at the battle of Resaca, Ga., May 15, 1864. He was mustered out May 28, 1864.

EDWIN H. HOLBROOK, son of Edwin L and Abby D. (Hill) Holbrook, was born Oct. 30, 1846, in Medway. He enlisted for one hundred days, and was mustered into the United States service July 22, 1864, as a Corporal of Co B, 42d Regt Mass. Vols. He served in the defenses of Washington, D C , and was mustered out Nov 11, 1864, his term having expired. His regiment was stationed at Alexandria and Great Falls, Md. He was detailed as clerk of provost-marshal, at Alexandria, Va., during his term

JAMES T HOLMES, born in Nova Scotia, resided in Boston, enlisted Sept. 6, 1864, at the age of twenty years He was mustered into service on the same day, for one year, as a private of Co C, 61st Regt Mass. Vols. He was mustered out of service June 4, 1865, as Sergeant.

DENNIS HOSMER was born May 4, 1806, in Sterling, Mass He enlisted July 19, and was mustered into the United States service Aug 16, 1861, for three years, as a private of Co E, 21st Mass Regt His family resided in Medway, but he appears by the rolls to be accredited to the town of Holden, Mass He was discharged Dec. 7, 1861, for disability. As nothing is known of him since he is supposed to be dead.

EDWIN H. HOSMER, son of Dennis and Elmira Hosmer, was born Aug. 1, 1844, in Wrentham, Mass. He was mustered into the United States service April 4, 1862, for three years, as a private of Co E, 29th Regt Mass Vols He was with his regiment in the battles before Richmond, Va., in the summer of 1862 He was discharged Oct. 11, 1862, for disability. He enlisted again for one hundred days, and was mustered into the United States service July 19, 1864, as a private of Co. G, 60th Regt. Mass Vols., stationed at Indianapolis, Ind. He was mustered out of service Nov. 30, 1864.

JOHN G. HOSMER, son of Dennis and Elmira Hosmer, was born Jan. 25, 1846, in Wrentham, Mass. He enlisted July 23, and was mustered into service July 28, 1862, for three years, as a private of Co. D, 35th Regt

Mass. Vols. He states that he was in the following engagements : at South Mountain, Va., September 14; Antietam, Md., September 17; in a heavy skirmish at Sulphur Springs, the last of November; and at Fredericksburg, Va.. Dec. 13, 1862; afterwards he participated in the siege of Vicksburg, Miss., the last of June, 1863; and subsequently in the siege and capture of Jackson, Miss., in which his regiment took a prominent part, and was first to plant its colors within the city. After the latter engagements he was taken sick, and sent to the hospital at Camp Dennison, Ohio, and remained there four months, after which he was sent to Portsmouth Grove Hospital, R. I., from which place he paid a Thanksgiving visit home. He returned to Camp Dennison, and Feb. 1, 1864, was sent to Stevenson, Ala., where he was detailed as safe guard. September, 1864, he again joined his regiment at Petersburg, Va., and was in the battles on South Side R. R., Hatcher's Run, and at the capture of Petersburg. He was mustered out of service June 9, 1865.

ALBERT C. HOUGHTON, son of Abel S. and Anna Houghton, was born in Newton, Mass. He enlisted in Medway in May, and was mustered into the United States service May 25, 1861, in Camp Andrew, West Roxbury, for three years, as a private of Co. E, 2d Regt. Mass. Vols. He was promoted Corporal April 1, 1863. He was in all the earlier engagements of the regiment; at Winchester, Va., May 25; at Cedar Mountain, August 9; at Antietam, Sept. 17, 1862; and at Chancellorsville, May 3, 1863. In this last battle, he was struck in the leg by a round shot, nearly severing the limb and causing his death.

ALVIN W. HOUGHTON, son of Amos and Almira Houghton, was born June 5, 1843, in Swansey, N. H. He enlisted in Medway, in May, and was mustered into the United States service, May 25, 1861, for three years, in Camp Andrew, West Roxbury, as a private of Co. E, 2d Regt. Mass. Vols. During a larger part of his term of service he was detailed as officer's cook and forager. He was mustered out May 28, 1864. He afterwards enlisted again and served in the 16th Regt. N. H. Vols.

JOSEPH H. HOWARD, at the age of thirty years, residence unknown, was enlisted by Lieut. A. D. Sawyer, in Boston, and mustered into the service of the United States Aug. 30, 1862, for three years, as a private of the 2d Regt. Mass. Vols., and accredited to Medway.

GEORGE H. IDE, son of the Rev. Jacob Ide, D. D., and Mary (Emmons) Ide, was born Feb. 3, 1835, in Medway. He enlisted in May, and was mustered into the United States service May 25, 1861, in Camp Andrew, West Roxbury, as a private of Co. E, 2d Regt. Mass. Vols. He was promoted Corporal, July 7, 1861, and returned to the ranks Feb. 24, 1862. He was in the earlier skirmishes of the regiment, and in the engagements at Winchester, Va., May 25, and at Cedar Mountain, Aug. 9, 1862, at which time he was instantly killed. In this battle Herman S. Sparrow also fell, who was of the same company. They were among the first from the town to enlist in the service of the government and were also the first Medway men to fall martyrs to the Union cause in the War of the Rebellion. The news of the death of these young men brought not only deep grief to their families and relatives, but stirred our whole people, and gave us a more realizing sense of the stern realities of the terrible conflict in which we were engaged. Few subsequent events of the war affected all our people more deeply. In allusion to this feeling the Rev. D Sanford, in a funeral sermon, preached at the church of the Rev. Dr. Ide, on Sunday, August 24, said: " In the event of these two deaths, what sorrow! what anguish! what heart-stricken families! yea, what mourning and grief in the whole community ' and what a gloom has settled upon us The ordeal through which we are passing is full of instruction We are learning a lesson of great practical import. Our very calamity shows something of the terribleness of the war At this moment nearly or quite one hundred thousand homes in the loyal states are made desolate by the hand of death in the field or in the camp." But he adds · " This baptism of blood is the prelude to future triumphs These precious lives given up, will, with others, be the perpetual life and augmenting glory of the nation. In the future those who live will read the records of the present, and bless God for the patriotism, the self-sacrifice and devotion of the people now, as we bless Him for those who wrought deliverance and freedom for us." In a letter addressed to the chairman of the selectmen by Lieut. E. W. Patterson, who was in command of the company, Capt Quincy having been wounded and taken prisoner in the same engagement, he says . " Both Ide and Sparrow were shot through the head, and instantly killed. They were buried under the direction of our Chaplain. Please express to the afflicted ones in Medway the sympathy, not only of myself, but of the regimental commander, for their loss." In speaking of the company in the same letter, he says · " I cannot speak too highly of the courage and noble conduct of all the men There is not a single man who could have done better than he did " Says Chaplain Quint in a letter to the chairman of the selectmen · " Both Ide and Sparrow did their whole duty. Rely upon it they deserve the honor that Medway can give." In a letter to the Rev. Dr. Ide, he says : " Your son died fighting nobly and bravely, I can assure you His memory should have that record. You have given a son to a heroic death, where he never faltered in the midst of an overpowering and terrible fire." Immediately on the receipt of the intelligence of this death, the selectmen, acting under authority of a vote of the town, passed sometime previously, and at the request of the relatives, dispatched Mr. D. J. Hastings as an agent to secure and bring home for burial the bodies of the slain Before leaving Massachusetts he was furnished with a very earnest note from the Hon. Henry Wilson to the Secretary of War, which note was also approved by Gov Andrew, requesting that he might, if possible, be permitted to pass within the lines of Gen. Pope's army for the purpose indicated. Such, however, was the condition of affairs that his request could not be granted And so their remains where allowed to rest where comrade hands laid them down, " with green boughs placed over them lest the earth should press too rudely."

GEORGE A. JACOBS, at the age of twenty-one years, residence Boston, enlisted and was mustered into the United States service Sept. 12, 1864, for one year, as a private of Co. C, 61st Regt. Mass. Vols , and was accredited to Medway. He was mustered out June 4, 1865.

EDMUND A. JONES, son of Elisha A. and Rhoda (Ellis) Jones, was born Feb. 11, 1842. He enlisted and was mustered into the United States service Sept 13, 1862, for nine months, as a Corporal of Co. B, 42d Regt.

Mass. Vols. ; and was afterwards promoted 3d Sergeant, June 21, 1863 He was at the time of enlistment a student of Amherst College, having just completed his Sophomore year. After his discharge from the military service he returned and completed his course, graduating with the class of 1865. He served with his regiment in Louisiana, and in the engagement at Lafourche Crossing was wounded in the shoulder. He was mustered out with his company in Readville, Aug. 20, 1863 After his graduation at Amherst he was assistant in Lake Forest Academy, at Lake Forest, Ill., where he remained four years, the last year as principal. In 1869 he removed to Massillon, O., taking the position of superintendent of schools, which he has continued to hold to the present time, with the exception of an interval of two years, when he bore the same relation to the schools in Marietta, O. Mr. Jones is recognized as an educator of ability and prominence, not only in the city where he resides, but in the county. He is an active worker in the cause of temperance, and for some years has been the superintendent of a large Sunday School. He married, Dec 23, 1873, Flora Richards, the daughter of Warren C. Richards, Esq., of Massillon, O.

JOHN B JONES, at the age of nineteen years, residence unknown, was mustered into service May 9, 1864, for three years, in U. S. Vet. Res. Corps, and was accredited to Medway.

FRANK KANEY, son of James and Ann (Foley) Kaney, was born April 17, 1844, in Leitrim County, Ireland. He enlisted into the United States Navy for one year, and shipped on board the steamer " Mercidetta " March 31, 1863. The steamer was first assigned to duty in the West Indies, where it remained four months, after which it was stationed off Wilmington, N. C., until the end of his term. He was mustered out March 31, 1864.

CORNELIUS KEATING, at the age of thirty-eight years, resident of Medford, Mass , but accredited to Medway, enlisted Dec 2, 1864, and was mustered into the United States service the same day, for one year, as a private of Co. G, 61st Regt. Mass. Vols. He was mustered out July 16, 1865.

MARTIN M. KEITH, at the age of twenty-five years, residence Bridgewater, was mustered into the United States service May 4, 1864, for three years, as a private of 2d Bat. Vet. Res. Corps, and accredited to Medway.

WILLIAM F. KEMP enlisted, and was mustered into the United States service Dec 2, 1864, for one year, as a recruit of Co. B, 55th Regt. Mass. Vols., and accredited to Medway, though not a resident of the town. He was mustered out of service Aug 29, 1865.

JOHN H. KENDALL, residence Boston, enlisted, and was mustered into the United States service June 24, 1863, for three years, as a private of Co. I, 6th Regt. Vet. Res. Corps, and accredited to Medway He was discharged for disability in Cincinnati, O., Aug. 13, 1865, and died of disease on the 26th of October following.

JOSEPH KERSHER, at the age of thirty-nine years, family residence, Elgin, Kane County, Ill , was mustered into the United States service May 5, 1864, for three years, as a Corporal of the 3d Regt. Vet. Res. Corps, Co. G, and accredited to Medway. In the spring of 1865 he was transferred to 1st Co., 2d Bat. Vet. Res Corps. He was mustered out of service in Brattleboro, Vt., Nov. 14, 1865, by reason of general order 155, relating to the reduction of the army after the close of the war.

PATRICK KILLALEY, at the age of twenty-four years, residence Milford, Mass., enlisted, and was mustered into service Nov. 23, 1864, for one year, as a recruit of 1st Regt. Mass. Heavy Arty. He was assigned to Co. F, and was mustered out of service June 4, 1865, by reason of the close of the war. He was accredited to Medway.

CHARLES C. KIMBALL, son of Wales and Elizabeth (Blake) Kimball, was born Aug. 17, 1842, in Keene, N. H. He enlisted early in May, and was mustered into service May 15, 1861, for three years, as 5th Sergeant of Co. E, 2d Regt Mass. Vols. He was in the engagement at Winchester, Va., May 25, and also at the battle of Cedar Mountain, Aug. 9, 1862. He was discharged from the service Sept. 14, 1862, by order of the Secretary of War, to enable him to receive a commission as 2d Lieut. in another Mass. Regt , but upon being mustered out declined to be mustered in again.

FRANK W KIMBALL, son of Wales and Elizabeth (Blake) Kimball, was born Sept 4, 1846, in Medway. He enlisted for one hundred days, and was mustered into the United States service July 22, 1864 He served in the defenses of Washington, D C , and was mustered out of service Nov 11, 1864.

CHARLES G KINGSBURY, son of Charles and Miranda (Tyler) Kingsbury, was born March 20, 1837, in Medway He enlisted April 20, and was mustered into service June 26, 1861, for three years, as a private of Co. E, 12th Regt. Mass. Vols. He was detailed as wagoner, Dec 25, 1862, and was transferred to the Vet Res Corps, March 25, 1864, and mustered out of service June 28, 1864, his term having expired He enlisted again about the 25th of January, 1865, in Co. D, 39th Mass Inf., and at the battle of Five Forks, Va., on Saturday April 1. 1865, he was wounded through the body and died from the effects of the wound, May 29, 1865, in Washington, D. C His remains were brought to Medway for interment.

GEORGE H. KINGSBURY, son of Hiram and Charlotte (Wight) Kingsbury, was born May 25, 1846, in Medway. He enlisted for one hundred days, and was mustered, July 22, 1864, into the United States service. He was mustered out of service Nov. 11, 1864, his term having expired.

WILLIAM KIRBY, at the age of twenty-five years, residence unknown, was mustered into the service of the U. S. Vet. Res. Corps on the 7th of May, 1864, for three years, and accredited to Medway

ANNAH LADD, at the age of forty-four years, enlisted and was mustered into the United States service, May 7, 1864, as a member of Vet. Res Corps, for three years. He was accredited to Medway, but was not a resident.

JAMES E. LAWRENCE, son of Abijah and Elmira Lawrence was born Sept 2, 1827, in Medway. He enlisted and was mustered into the United States service Aug. 23, 1864, for one year, as a private of the 18th unattached Co. of Heavy Arty afterwards Co. B, 4th Regt. Mass Heavy Arty. He served with his regiment in the defenses of Washington, D. C , until April 24, 1865, when on account of ill health he was given a furlough of twenty days, and came home. He went to Camp Meigs, Readville, after the expiration of his furlough, and subsequently to the hospital at Worcester, Mass. He was mustered out July 14, 1865, in Boston.

GEORGE F LEAVITT, at the age of eighteen years, residence unknown, was mustered into the United States service, April 30, 1864, for three years, as a private of the 13th Regt Vet Res. Corps., and accredited to Medway.

GILBERT H. LELAND, son of Joseph and Betsey (Fisk) Leland, was born, 1835, in Sherborn, Mass. He was mustered into the United States service Aug. 14, 1862, for three years, as a private of Co. I, 38th Regt. Mass. Vols., and was accounted on the quota of Medway, though he appears, by the records at the Adjutant-General's office, to be accredited to Sherborn. He was in the engagement at Fort Bisland, La., April 13. 1863, and at Port Hudson. On the 27th of May he was detailed as guard for the company baggage, and did not return to the company, but was soon after sent to the hospital in Baton Rouge, sick, where he died June 3, 1863, of typhoid fever.

HORATIO T. LEONARD was born in Taunton, Mass., but resided in Medway At the age of twenty-five years he enlisted Sept. 3, 1864, and was mustered into service the same day, for one year, as a private of Co B, 61st Mass. Inf. He served with his regiment in Virginia, and was mustered out June 4, 1865, by reason of the close of the war.

JOHN LEONARD, at the age of twenty-seven years, residence Boston, enlisted June 24, 1864, and was mustered into the United States service on the same day as a member of Co I, 13th Regt. Vet. Res Corps. Mustered out June 24, 1866, at expiration of service. He had previously served in Co. A, 32d Regt. Mass. Vols., having been mustered into service Nov. 12, 1861, and discharged Feb. 19, 1863, for disability.

WILLIAM LILLEY, at the age of twenty-seven years, born in Union, Conn., enlisted and was mustered into the United States service Aug. 23, 1864, for one year, as a private of the 18th unattached Co., afterwards Co. B, 4th Regt. Mass. Vols. He served in the defenses of Washington, D. C., and was mustered out June 17, 1865.

JOHN LOOBY, at the age of thirty-one years, residence Lawrence, Mass., enlisted Nov 27, 1863, and was mustered into the United States service on the 7th of December following, as a private of Co G, 2d Regt Mass. Heavy Arty. He was discharged Aug. 13, 1865, for disability.

CHARLES MAGERTY, born in Ireland, at the age of twenty-eight years enlisted, Dec. 29, 1863, and was mustered into the United States service, Jan. 6, 1864, for three years, as a private of Co. E 4th Regt Mass Cav He served his term, and was mustered out Nov. 14, 1865, in Richmond, Va.

GEORGE W. MAHR, son of John and Betsey Mahr, was born Feb. 10, 1836, in Medway. He first enlisted for three months, and was mustered into the United States service April 16, 1861, as a private of Co. K, 1st Regt. R. I. Vols. He took part in the first battle of Bull Run, July 21, and was mustered out Aug. 2, 1861, at the expiration of his service He was drafted into the United States service July 15, 1863, and assigned to Co. I, 18th Regt. Mass Inf. He joined his regiment at Beverly Ford, Va., about the middle of September, and was in the battle at Rappahannock Station, November 7, and at Mine Run, Nov 30, 1863. May, 1864, he was taken prisoner at the Wildneress, Va. With other prisoners he was marched to a railroad station, about thirty miles from Richmond, where a large number of prisoners were put on board cars for Andersonville, Ga. They were crowded like cattle into box cars, there being some sixty-five in the car with him, nearly as many as could stand therein, and were there confined during the whole journey, lasting several days. For rations. a small allowance of corn meal was doled out to each. At Andersonville they were turned into the stockade prison like a herd of cattle to find such shelter as they could, none being furnished, and a larger part of their clothing being taken away, leaving them barely sufficient for a covering. The daily rations there were about two-thirds of a pint of corn meal, with, sometimes, a bit of bacon, but very rarely any vegetables. Their food they cooked as best they could. After a time, however, a cook house was built, and cooked rations issued, but still meagre and poor. After a few months of confinement he began to suffer with scurvy, and for several weeks was so sick as to be unable to walk, still slight care and little medicine were given him. Prisoners sickened and died in great numbers, sometimes a hundred per day, and each day a four-mule wagon would be drawn within the enclosure, the dead bodies piled on like logs of wood, and carried to trenches for burial. There, for nearly twelve months, he endured the privations of that prison, the very name of which will ever be a symbol of atrocity and barbarity. While there, no word from his family reached him, neither did they know what had become of him until the last of January, 1865, when a letter was received, dated "Prisoners' Camp, Andersonville, Ga., May 31," informing them that he had just arrived there, and was in good health. He was liberated at the close of the war, and reached home May 23, 1865. He was mustered out July 12, 1865, in Boston.

ALBERT W. MANN, son of Albert and Caroline S. (Pond) Mann, was born Aug. 14, 1836, in Wrentham, Mass. He enlisted early in May, and was mustered into the United States service, May 25, 1861, in Camp Andrew, West Roxbury, as 3d Sergeant of Co. E, 2d Regt. Mass. Vols. He was promoted 1st Sergeant July 13, 1861, Sergeant-Major May 10, 1862, 2d Lieut. of Co. C, March 31, 1863. He had a full share of all the marches and engagements of his regiment during his term of service. He took part in the movements in the Shenandoah Valley in the summer of 1861 and spring of 1862, and was in the battle of Winchester, Va., May 25, on the retreat of Gen. Banks, Co. E forming the rear guard. The regimental loss was sixty-four killed and wounded, and eighty-four missing, many of them prisoners. Capt. Quincy, of Co. E, in a letter written immediately after, speaks highly of the conduct of his men in this, their first battle. He was at the battle of Cedar Mountain, Va., August 9, when the regimental loss was one hundred and fifty-four in killed and wounded : of Co. E, Capt. Quincy wounded and taken prisoner, Ide and Sparrow, of Medway, killed, and W. A. Daniels mortally wounded. *Missing, none.* This latter fact, wrote Lieut. Patterson, "speaks highly for the company"; and he added, "all did their duty nobly." In August he was in a skirmish at Beverly Ford on the 21st, and under fire at Sulphur Springs on the 23d. He was at the battle of Antietam, September 17, when the regimental loss was sixty-seven in killed and wounded and two missing. April 21, 1863, he was in a skirmish at Germania Ford, where a force of rebels were building a bridge, one hundred and three of whom were captured ; and at the battle of Chancellorsville, May 2 and 3, where the regiment lost one officer and twenty-two men killed and eight men mortally, and eighty-six others more or less severely wounded, and eight taken prisoners, being thirty-three per cent. of its strength. He was at Gettysburg, July 2 and 3, where again the regimental loss was forty-four per cent., nearly all in a single charge, and again in a skirmish at Kelly's Ford, August 1. Soon after the regiment was ordered to New York to assist in enforcing the draft. He returned to the field early in September, and soon left Virginia for Alabama. In January, 1864, he was detailed with other officers of the regiment to accompany the reenlisted men home for their veteran furlough, with expectation also of obtaining recruits for the regiment, then reduced to less than three hundred men. But owing to the peculiar circumstances then existing, no recruits were secured. He returned to the regiment the last of January, and was in the advance towards Atlanta, Ga. May 15, 1864, he took part in the battle of Resaca, Ga., where the regimental loss was one killed and twenty-seven wounded, six of them mortally. His term having expired, he was mustered out of service May 28, 1864. Subsequent to his return he removed to Needham, afterwards to South Boston, and then to Saugus, Mass. He was a builder of the hotels at the Point of Pines and became superintendent of the grounds of this seaside resort. He died suddenly Aug. 28, 1881, and his burial was in West Medway.

FRANK V. MANN, son of Albert and Caroline S. (Pond) Mann, was born Sept. 10, 1840, in West Medway. He enlisted in August, and was mustered into service Sept. 13, 1862, for nine months, as a private of Co B, 42d Regt. Mass. Vols. He served in the Department of the Gulf and was mustered out Aug. 20, 1863, at the expiration of service.

GEORGE F. MARDEN, at the age of twenty-five years, enlisted on the 7th of December, 1864, and was mustered into the United States service on the same day for one year, as a private of Co G, 61st Regt. Mass. Vols. He was accredited to Medway, though not a resident of the town. He was mustered out of service July 16, 1865, as Sergeant of his company.

WILLIAM M. MARTIN, son of Gideon and Ruth Martin, was born March 24, 1821, in Chesterville. He was mustered into the United States service Aug. 6, 1862, for three years, as a recruit of the 2d Regt. Mass. Vols., but with the condition that he should be discharged when the term of that regiment should expire. He was in the battle of Resaca, Ga., May 15, and mustered out May 28, 1864. He enlisted again Aug 27, 1864, and was mustered into service the same day, for one year, as a private of Co. B, 61st Regt Mass. Vols. He served with his regiment in Virginia and was in the battle of Petersburg, April, 1865. He was mustered out of service June 4, 1865, by reason of the close of the war.

GEORGE E. MASON, son of Horatio and Julia (Adams) Mason, was born Oct. 3, 1837, in Medway. He enlisted December 2, and was mustered into the United States service Dec. 3 (Dec. 11, state record), 1863, for three years, as a private of Co I, 2d Regt. Mass. Heavy Arty., and being a resident of Holliston was accredited to that town. He served with his regiment in Virginia and North Carolina, and was in the engagements at Kinston and vicinity, in March, 1865. He was mustered out of service Sept 3, 1865, at Galloup's Island, Boston Harbor.

SIMON LEPRILETTE MASON, son of Horatio and Julia (Adams) Mason, was born Nov. 5, 1829, in Medway. He enlisted, and was mustered into service June, 1861, as a private of Co. I, 11th Mass. Regt., and being a resident of Charlestown was accredited to that city. He states that he was with his regiment in the following engagements: in the battle of Bull Run, Va., July 21,

1861 ; at the siege of Yorktown in April, 1862 ; at the battle of Williamsburg, May 5 ; Fair Oaks, June 25 ; Savage Station, June 29 ; Glendale, June 30 ; Malvern Hill, July 1 ; Bristow Station, August 27, 2d Bull Run, August 29 and 30 ; and Chantilly, about September 1   In the foregoing battles he served as a private in the ranks   Soon after he was detailed as a musician, a member of a band formed by detail from the several companies of the regiment, and continued in that position until the end of his term   He was constantly with or near his regiment in all the subsequent engagements to assist in removing the wounded or in their care at the corps hospital.   He was mustered out of service June, 1864, at the expiration of his term.   He enlisted again about October, 1864, in the 13th Regt. Vet. Res. Corps, and served at the conscript camp, Galloup's Island, Boston Harbor.   For several years past Mr. Mason has been a teacher of music in Boston.

THOMAS H. MATTHEWS was born in Wales, G. B.   At the age of thirty-six years he was mustered into the United States service, Aug 6, 1864, for three years, as a private of Co A, 1st Regt Mass. Cav.   He was a resident of Medway, but appears by the state record to be accredited to Lowell. He is reported to have been wounded in action, Oct 14, 1864, since which nothing is known of him

WILLIAM H MATTHEWS, at the age of twenty-three years, was mustered into the United States service Aug 11, 1863, for three years, as a private of Co. C, 28th Mass. Inf   He served as a substitute for Henry E. Gay, one of the drafted men from Medway.   He was mustered out June 30, 1865, at the expiration of his service.

PETER MAWN was born in Leitrim County, Ireland.   At the age of twenty-six years he enlisted, Aug. 12, 1862, and was mustered into the United States service on the same day, for three years, as a private of Co. E, 2d Regt Mass Vols.   At the battle of Chancellorsville, May 3, 1863, he was wounded in the leg, which was afterwards amputated above the knee.   He was discharged Aug 21, 1863, for disability, from the General Hospital at Washington, D C.   He removed to Milford, where he died in October, 1867

EDWARD A. MAY, son of James B and Juliette May, was born Aug. 17, 1843, in Attleboro, Mass.   He enlisted, and was mustered into service May 25, 1861, for three years, as a private of Co E, 2d Regt. Mass Vols. He was appointed regimental marker, and was in the engagement at Winchester, Va , May 25, and at Cedar Mountain, Aug 9, 1862.   He was discharged Dec 6, 1862, for disability   He enlisted again in the 2d Regt. Mass. Cav., Co D, mustered in Jan. 3, 1865, and discharged July 20, 1865. He was accredited to Holliston on the last enlistment.

JAMES B MAY, son of Elisha and Cynthia B May, was born June 12, 1822.   He enlisted in May, and was mustered into the United States service, May 25, 1861, for three years, as a private of Co. B, 2d Regt. Mass Vols. He was promoted Corporal Aug. 1, 1862.   In December, 1861, or in January following, he was detailed on recruiting service, and did not again join his regiment until the last of May.   In the battle of Cedar Mountain, August 9, he was severely wounded in the groin, and only escaped falling into the hands of the enemy by the assistance of a comrade, Peter Harrington.   His wounds proving so serious, he was discharged Dec. 22, 1862, for disability.

DANIEL McALEVEY was born about 1832, in England, (Chaplain Quint says Ireland). He enlisted Aug. 28, 1862, and was mustered into the United States service on the same day as a recruit of Co. H, 2d Regt. Mass. Vols. He was wounded in the hand at the battle of Chancellorsville, May 3, 1863, and was transferred to the Vet. Res. Corps, Oct 1, 1863. He was mustered out of service Aug 31, 1864.

JOHN McCABE enlisted on the 7th of December, 1864, and was mustered into service on the same day for one year, as a private of Co. G, 61st Regt. Mass. Vols. He was accredited to Medway, though not a resident of the town. He was mustered out July 16, 1865, as a Sergeant.

JOHN McCANN at the age of twenty-seven years, residence unknown, was mustered into service in the U. S. Vet. Res. Corps, May 7, 1864, for three years, and accredited to Medway.

JAMES McCOWAN was born about 1830, in Derry, Ireland. He enlisted at Medway in May, and was mustered into the United States service in Camp Andrew, West Roxbury, May 25, 1861, for three years, as a private of Co. K, 2d Regt. Mass. Vols. He was discharged Dec. 30, 1861, for disability. He enlisted again and was mustered into service for three years, as a private of Co. E, 2d Regt. Mass. Heavy Arty. By the state record he appears to be accredited to Milford. He died Oct. 5, 1864, of yellow fever, at Beaufort, N. C.

GILBERT McCULLOM, son of Granville E. and Agnes (Davidson) McCullom, was born Jan. 1, 1840, in Pawtucket, R. I. He was mustered into the United States service July 26, 1861, for three years, as a private of Co. I, 10th Regt. Mass. Vols. In December, 1862, he was taken prisoner near Fredericksburg, Va, and taken to Richmond, but was soon paroled and sent to Camp Parole at Annapolis, Md. He was exchanged and rejoined his regiment in the spring of 1864, about the time of the battle of the Wilderness, Va, and he was again taken prisoner and confined for a time at the infamous pen at Andersonville, Ga, and then removed to the equally notorious one at Florence, S C., where he remained until about the 1st of March, 1865. He was then taken to Wilmington, N C, and exchanged, but being too feeble to proceed further north was taken to Hospital No. 4, in that city, where he died March 11, 1865. His remains were subsequently removed and buried in West Medway.

RICHARD B. McELROY, son of Patrick and Margaret McElroy, was born April 2, 1831, in Albany, N. Y. He enlisted Aug. 23, 1864, and was mustered into service on the same day for one year, as a private of the 18th unattached Co, afterwards Co. B, 4th Mass. Heavy Arty. He served in the defenses of Washington, D. C, and was mustered out June 17, 1865, by reason of the close of the war.

THOMAS McKENNA at the age of thirty-seven years, residence unknown, was mustered into the United States service, Vet. Res. Corps, May 7, 1864, for three years, and accredited to Medway.

JAMES McLAUGHLIN, son of John and Lucy (Watson) McLaughlin, was born about A D. 1840, in Galway County, Ireland. He enlisted Dec. 13, 1864, and was mustered into the United States service on the same day, for one year, as a private of the 12th Mass. Light Bat. During his service the battery was stationed at Port Hudson, La., and was in no engagement. He was mustered out July 25, 1865, by reason of the close of the war.

CHRISTOPHER MCNAMARA was born in Philadelphia, Penn., resided in Medway. He enlisted and was mustered into the United States service Jan. 6, 1864, for three years, as a private of Co. A, 3d Regt. Mass. Cav, and accredited to Boston. He deserted Aug 23, 1865, from Fort Kearney, N T.

THOMAS MCNAMARA, born in Philadelphia, Penn, residence Medway, enlisted at the age of twenty-three years, and was mustered into the United States service March 19, 1864, for three years, as a private of Co A, 3d Regt. Mass Cav., was accredited to Boston, and mustered out July 20, 1865, at expiration of service. He had previously served in the U. S. Navy on board the ship "Clara Dolson," and was discharged July 31, 1862.

WILLIAM F MERRITT, son of William F. and Mary A. (White) Merritt, was born Feb. 26, 1846, in Ashland, Mass He enlisted for one hundred days, and was mustered into the United States service on the 22d of July, 1864 He served in the defenses of Washington, D. C., and was mustered out Nov. 11, 1864.

JOHN MILLER, at the age of twenty-seven years, residence unknown, was mustered into the United States service Dec. 15, 1862, for three years, as a private of Co. C, 2d Regt. Mass. Cav., and accredited to Medway. By the state record he appears to have deserted Dec 28, 1862.

LEWIS L. MILLER, son of Warren and Emily Miller, was born Aug. 17, 1840, in Franklin, Mass. He enlisted the last of April, 1861, but was not mustered into the United States service until June 26 following. He was a private of Co E, 12th Regt. Mass. Vols., and enlisted for three years. He was in the engagement at Cedar Mountain, Va., Aug. 9, 1862 ; at Rappahannock Station, August 25, and at the second battle of Bull Run, August 30, when he was wounded in the leg, and died, Oct 2, 1862, from the effects of the wound in the hospital in Washington, D. C. His remains were brought to Franklin for interment

DEA JAMES MITCHELL, son of Robert and Sarah (Begg) Mitchell, was born June 10, 1820, in Sherbrooke, Canada. He had been a resident of Medway for several years, and was an esteemed officer of the First Church of Christ. He first offered his services for three years, in July, 1862, but on examination at Camp Stanton, Lynnfield, he was rejected for physical disability. Still desirous of serving the country in its hour of need he enlisted and was accepted for the nine months' term, and was mustered into service Sept 13, 1862, as a private of Co. B, 42d Regt. Mass. Vol. Militia. His regiment was assigned to the Department of the Gulf, and performed most of its service in Louisiana. He was detailed during a considerable part of his term as hospital nurse, a service for which he was well adapted, and where such service was needed, sickness prevailing much among the men. The regiment was retained in service somewhat more than its stipulated term, probably on account of the protracted sieges of Vicksburg and Port Hudson, and Company K having been detached as pontooniers, took part in the siege of the latter place. It left New Orleans July 31, 1863, and arrived in Boston August 10, when the men were furloughed, and ordered to report at Readville on the 20th. Among the many who came home suffering with disease, was Dea. Mitchell, who was prostrate with an attack of camp dysentery. With strength hardly sufficient to enable him to reach home, he sank rapidly away and died Aug. 19, 1863.

JAMES S. MITCHELL, son of James and Elizabeth Mitchell, was born June 3, 1849, in East Medway. He enlisted for one hundred days, and was mustered into service July 16, 1864, (state record says mustered July 23,) as a private of Co. E, 60th Regt. He was mustered out Nov. 30, 1864, at expiration of service. His regiment was stationed at Indianapolis, Ind

JOHN MONKS, son of Matthew and Ann Monks, was born about A. D., 1838, in Kildare County, Ireland. He enlisted in Boston, and was mustered into the United States Navy Aug. 31, 1864, for three years, as a substitute for James M. Daniels, of Medway, an enrolled man. He shipped on board the U. S. steamer " Little Ada," Oct. 5, 1864, ranking as landsman.

ALEXANDER LE B. MONROE, son of Dr. Stephen and Susan (Le Baron) Monroe, was born May 3, 1807, in Sutton, Mass He had been for many years a practising physician and surgeon in Medway. During the summer campaign of 1862, there being a great demand for army surgeons, he offered his services as contract surgeon, and was sent to the Army of the Potomac by William J. Dale, Surgeon-General of Massachusetts, leaving home May 21, 1862, for his post. May 25 he was ordered to report for duty as Acting Assistant Surgeon in the General Hospital at White House, Va., by Charles S. Tripler, Surgeon and Medical Director of the Army. He gives the following as an item of his experience. " June 5, received the following order : ' GENERAL HOSPITAL, WHITE HOUSE, June 5, 1862. *To A. L B. Monroe, Ass't Surg., Gen'l Hospt.* Sir· You will immediately proceed to the R. R. station at White House, and strictly enforce the following order : ' HEAD-QUARTERS, June 2, 1862. To Brigade-Surgeon A. T. Watson. Please inspect carefully the cars as they arrive at White House, and send back every man who is not wounded, whether he be *sick* or *well,*— please see that the order to go back is obeyed. (Signed) S. WILLIAMS, Asst. Adj.-Gen. I have the honor to be your obt. serv't. ALEX. T. WATSON, Brig.-Surg'n., in charge of the hospital.' The next train of cars from the army brought down about three hundred soldiers. one already dead, three dying, who lived but a few hours, and over thirty likely to die, with the best of care ; the balance were more or less sick, but would probably recover with proper care. To send the sick men back to the swamps of the Chickahominy would be equivalent to dooming them to death, and inhuman to the last degree. I therefore determined to prevent it, if possible, and with that view called upon Mr. Olmstead, hoping that his influence would secure a countermand of the order. With great difficulty he prevailed upon Surgeon Watson to disregard it, and the poor fellows were brought to the hospital. How such a strange order should be issued from the head-quarters of the army was a mystery to me and others, which has never been explained. Dr. Watson was never disciplined for disregarding it June 22, ordered to report to Brig.-Gen. S. P. Heintzelman, 3d Corps, at Savage Station June 25 was assigned to temporary duty with 2d Regt. N. H. Vols , and in that position served through the Seven Days' Battle, and until the army arrived at Harrison's Landing, when I was sent to the hospital at Fortress Monroe, and discharged on account of sickness July 11, 1862 " Dr Monroe continued his practice in Medway until his death, Feb. 20, 1879.

FRANCIS LE BARON MONROE, son of Dr. A. L. B. and Louisa (Barber) Monroe, was born March 20, 1836, in Medway He first served as Assistant Surgeon of the 1st Light Mass. Bat., known as Boston Light Arty., commanded by Capt. Asa M. Cook. This was a three months organization. He gives the following brief account of his experience in the service. "Left Boston April 20, 1861, as Assistant Surgeon of Boston Light Arty.; ten days at Annapolis, six weeks at Relay House, occupied Baltimore with Gen. Butler. Gen. Banks next in command. Our battery was ordered into the city when he arrested the police commissioners. Mustered out August 2d, and returned home. Commissioned Assistant Surgeon of 1st Mass. Vol. Inf., Sept. 3, 1861. Joined the regiment at Bladensburg, belonged to Gen. Hooker's brigade, his first command; moved down to Budd's Ferry on the Potomac in October, 1861; spent the winter there. In the spring Hooker's division formed part of the 3d Corps; took part in the siege of Yorktown, battles of Williamsburg, Fair Oaks, Seven Days', Glendale, Malvern Hill, Harrison's Landing. Embarked at Yorktown August, 1862, to Alexandria, thence to Warrenton Junction — enemy in the rear — fought them at Bristow. Then with Pope's army at 2d Bull Run. Remained in camp at Fairfax Seminary until November 1, then marched to Fredericksburg, Gen. Sickles commanding division. Battle of Fredericksburg. Appointed Surgeon of 15th Mass. Vol. Inf., Dec. 29, 1862 The 15th was in Sully's brigade of Howard's division, Couch commanding 2d Corps. Was Acting Brigade Surgeon part of the winter, while we lay near Falmouth. In May, 1863, Gen. Hooker commanding the army, the battle of Chancellorsville occurred. The 2d Division 2d Corps, commanded by Gibbon, occupied the city of Fredericksburg, and cooperating with the 6th Corps, carried the Fredericksburg Heights about May 3; then in camp till June Marched to Gettysburg after the battle of that place, and was made medical inspector of 2d Corps, Warren commanding corps. In the campaign down to the Rapidan and back. Battle of Bristow; Mine Run. Wintered near Brandy Station Returned to my regiment in January, 1864 May, 1864, on the operating staff of the brigade, through Gen. Grant's campaign: battle of the Wilderness, after which, being left in charge of the wounded, was in the enemy's lines for two weeks; battle of Cold Harbor; Petersburg. Regiment came home, and was mustered out July 28, 1864 Sept. 11, 1864, was appointed Acting Assistant-Surgeon, U. S. Army, at Galloup's Island, Boston Harbor. May, 1865, made Past Surgeon of Draft Rendezvous at Galloup's Island until April 30, 1866, when I was formally discharged " He was subsequently commissioned Assistant Surgeon and Brevet-Major U. S Army, which position he held until June, 1876, when he resigned, and became a druggist in the city of Chicago, Ill

AMOS B. MORSE, son of Benoni and Abigail (Baker) Morse, was born Jan. 20, 1826, in Medway. He enlisted July 23, and was mustered into the United States service July 28, 1862, for three years, as a private of Co. D, 35th Regt. Mass Vols. He was in the battle of South Mountain, Va., September 14; at Antietam, Md, September 17; Fredericksburg, Va., Dec. 13, 1862; at the siege and capture of Jackson, Miss., in June, 1863, his regiment being the first to plant its colors in the city; at the siege of Knoxville, Tenn., November, 1863, on the Weldon R. R., July, 1864, Poplar Spring Church, September 30; Hatcher's Run, October 27, at Fort Sedgwick, in the vicinity of which his regiment remained from Nov. 27, 1864, to the last of March, 1865 ; and at Fort Mahone, April 2, 1865. He states that he was constantly on duty during his term of service and at the time of the battles of Campbell Station, Spottsylvania, North Anna, and Cold Harbor he was detailed on special duty at regimental head-quarters. He was mustered out of service at the expiration of his term, June 9, 1865, as a Corporal, to which rank he had been promoted Dec. 7, 1864.

ANDREW MORSE, at the age of twenty-two years, was mustered into the United States service Oct. 31, 1861, as a private of Co. I, 1st Mass. Cav. He was, at the time of enlistment, a resident of Medway, but appears by the state record to have been accredited to the town of Livermore, Me. He was transferred to Co. I, 4th Regt. Mass. Cav., and reënlisted in the field Jan. 1, 1864, for three years, and was accredited to Medway. He was in the battle of James Island, S. C., June 17, and at Pocataligo, Oct. 22, 1862, and was on duty at Morris Island during the siege of Fort Sumter in 1863, and in the Florida campaign in the winter of 1863 and 1864, and took part in the battle of Olustee. He was mustered out of service Nov. 14, 1865, by reason of the close of the war.

ELEAZAR MORSE, son of Eleazar and Polly (Adams) Morse, was born May 11, 1817, in Rutland, Mass. He was mustered into the United States service May 28, 1861, for three years, as a private of Co. G, 2d Regt. Mass. Vols. He was in the engagement at Winchester, Va., May 25, 1862, and at Cedar Mountain, August 9, of the same year. Much of the latter part of his term of service was spent in the hospital. He was discharged for disability March 10, 1864. Mr. Morse removed to Holliston, but at the time of his death, March 6, 1873, was stopping temporarily in Hopkinton. His remains were interred in West Medway.

FREDERIC DANIELS MORSE, son of Asa D. and Eliza (Hill) Morse, was born Dec. 25, 1838, in East Medway. He enlisted the last of August, and was mustered into the United States service Sept. 13, 1862, for nine months, as Sergeant of Co. B, 42d Regt. Mass. Vol. Militia. He was a student in Monson Academy, and graduated in 1862 from Amherst College, Massachusetts, having but just completed his course when he enlisted. He served with his regiment in Louisiana, and was in the engagement at Brashear City, La., June 23, 1863, at which time he was taken prisoner. He was paroled June 26, and mustered out Aug. 20, 1863, at the expiration of the service of his regiment. He afterwards studied medicine in the Rush Medical College, Chicago, Ill., from which he graduated in 1867, and commenced practice in Chicago, but in 1868 settled as a practising physician in Lawrence, Kan., where he still resides. Dr. Morse married, Oct. 19, 1869, Addie A. Smith, daughter of Alvin Smith, M. D., of Monson, Mass.

MILTON H. MORSE, son of John Morse, was born in 1842, in Milford, Mass. He was mustered into service July 27, 1861, for three years, as a private of Co. I, 18th Regt. Mass. Vols. He was discharged Jan. 4, 1862, for disability. He again enlisted and was mustered into service as a private of Co. I, 39th Regt. Mass. Vols., Aug. 25, 1862, and accredited to Natick, giving his name as Henry M. Morse. He was again discharged Sept. 12, 1863. He enlisted again for the third time and was mustered into service Nov. 17, 1863, as a recruit to Co. D, 1st Regt. Msss. Cav., and accredited to Milford. He was mustered out June 29, 1865, as absent.

ROBERT T. MORSE, son of Andrew and Margaret (Metcalf) Morse, was born Aug. 27, 1833, in Medway. He enlisted the last of August, and was mustered into service Sept. 13, 1862, for nine months, as a private of Co. B, 42d Regt. Mass. Vols. He died Oct. 4, 1862, of diphtheria.

DANIEL MUNDON, son of John and Sarah Mundon, was born Aug. 5, 1834, in Wareham, Mass. He enlisted at Medway early in May, and was mustered into the United States service in Camp Andrew, West Roxbury, May 25, 1861, for three years, as a private of Co. E, 2d Regt. Mass. Vols. He was detailed company cook June 23, 1861, to July 1, 1862, and afterwards as orderly of Lieut. Patterson of Co. E, by whom he was sent out for bread, while on the march from near Frederick, Md., over the South Mountain, towards Antietam Creek, Sept. 14, 1862, when he deserted.

CHARLES MURRAY, residence unknown, was mustered into the United States service December, 1862, for three years, as a recruit for the 29th Regt. Mass. Vols., and was accredited to Medway.

JAMES F. MURPHY, at the age of twenty years, enlisted and was mustered into the United States service on the 5th of December, 1864, for one year, and accredited to Medway, though he was not a resident of the town. He served as a private in the 6th Mass. Light Bat., and was mustered out Aug. 7, 1865, by reason of the close of the war.

GEORGE L. MYER, son of Henry and Nancy (Leonard) Myer, was born May 9, 1837, in Newark, N. J. He first enlisted at Camp Stanton, Lynnfield, Mass., and was sworn into service for three years, as a private of Co. D, 35th Mass. Inf. But before that regiment left camp he was sent, by direction of Col. Wild, to Camp Cameron, in Cambridge, to be transferred to the Sharpshooters, and was there rejected by the recruiting officer for being below the standard height. He enlisted again for one hundred days, and was mustered into the United States service July 22, 1864, as a private of Co. B, 42d Regt. Mass. Vols. He served in the defenses of Washington, D. C., and, Nov. 11, 1864, was mustered out.

WILLIAM D. NEWLAND, son of David and Sarah Newland, was born Jan. 3, 1841, in Boston. He entered the United States service as ordinary seaman in the navy, Feb. 20, 1862, and shipped on board the sloop of war, "Oneida." In April, 1862, he took part in the movements of the fleet under Capt. Farragut, for the capture of New Orleans. He was in the engagements at Forts Jackson and St. Philip, with the rebel fleet above the forts and the earth works below New Orleans, known as Fort Chalmette. Subsequently he was in engagements at Grand Gulf, and at the siege of Vicksburg and of Port Hudson, and with the rebel ram "Arkansas." Afterwards he was in the engagement, Aug. 5, 1864, at the passage of the fleet, under Commander Farragut, past Forts Morgan and Gaines at the entrance of Mobile Bay, and with the ram "Tennessee." He was wounded by a heavy fragment of shell, and discharged Oct. 27, 1864, for disability.

JOHN NOLAN, son of James and Mary Ann Nolan, was born July 6, 1826, in Boston. He enlisted in Medway the last of August, and was mustered into the United States service at Readville, Mass., Sept. 15, 1862, for nine months, as a private of Co. B, 42d Regt. Mass. Vols. He served in Louisiana, and when the regiment returned home he was left sick in the St. James Hospital at New Orleans, where he died Aug. 7, 1863.

JOHN NOLAN, son of John and Catherine Nolan, was born Aug. 17, 1849, in Boston. He enlisted and was mustered into the United States service, April 6, 1865, as a private of Co. B, 5th N. Y. Vols. He was mustered out of service Aug. 21, 1865.

WILLIAM A. NOLAN, son of John and Catherine Nolan, was born Aug. 11, 1847, in Boston. He was mustered into the United States service July 23, 1864, for one hundred days, as a private of Co. E, 60th Regt. Mass. Vol. Militia. He was mustered out of service Nov. 30, 1864, at the expiration of his term. He enlisted again, and was mustered into service April 6, 1865, as a private of Co. B, 5th Regt. N. Y. Vols. He was again mustered out Aug. 21, 1865.

GEORGE E. NOURSE, son of Gilbert and Betsey W. (Cargill) Nourse, was born July 14, 1842, in Medway. He enlisted Feb. 27, 1864, and was mustered into the United States service on the same day for three years, as a private of the 14th Mass. Light Bat. He was in the engagements at Spottsylvania Court House, from May 9 to the 18th, 1864; at Tolopotomy Creek. June 1; Bethesda Church, June 2 and 3; Cold Harbor, June 3 to 12; and at the siege of Petersburg, Va., from June 17 to the surrender, April, 1865. He was promoted Corporal in March, 1864, and was detailed Clerk of the Battery, May, 1864. He was mustered out in Readville, Mass., June 15, 1865, by reason of the close of the war.

HUGH O'BRIEN, residence unknown, at the age of twenty-seven years, was mustered into service Dec. 3, 1864, for one year, in Co. H, 1st Mass. Cav. He was mustered out as Sergeant, June 26, 1865, by reason of the close of the war.

MICHAEL O'DONNELL, son of James and Catherine (Welch) O'Donnell, was born Nov. 17, 1843, in Kilkenny, Ireland. He enlisted in Medway early in May, and was mustered into the United States service May 25, 1861, for three years, as a private of Co. E, 2d Regt. Mass. Vols., in Camp Andrew, West Roxbury. He was promoted Corporal Nov. 3, 1862; Sergeant Dec. 30, 1862; and 1st Sergeant May 1, 1863. He was in the battle of Winchester, Va., May 25, and at Cedar Mountain, Aug. 9. 1862, at which time he was wounded in the right arm. He returned to duty Sept. 17, 1862. He was in the battle of Chancellorsville, May 3; in the fight at Brandy Station, June 9; and at Gettysburg, July 3, 1863, when he was again wounded in the hip, after which he remained in the hospital until the expiration of his term. He was mustered out May 11, 1864.

JOHN O'HARA was born about 1839, in Ireland; resided in Medway, enlisted, and was mustered into the United States service July 26, 1861, for three years, as a private of Co. B, 18th Regt. Mass. Vols. He was with his regiment until detached, Nov. 16, 1861, to gun-boat service. He was in engagements on board the " Carondolet " at Island No. 16, in the spring of 1862, and afterwards in other engagements on the Mississippi River and its tributaries below. He was discharged for disability December, 1863, and died, Feb. 22, 1864, of disease, in Medway.

ALFRED ONION, (now known as Alfred Ashton), son of Lemuel and Sabra (Green) Onion, was born Sept. 28, 1844, in Medway. He enlisted and was mustered into the United States service, May 25, 1861, in Camp Andrew, West Roxbury, for three years, as a private of Co. E, 2d Regt.

Mass. Vols. Soon after the regiment arrived at the South and commenced its services in the field, he lost his voice. December, 1861, he was sent to barracks hospital, at Frederick, Md., and was detailed Commissary of the Hospital, in which position he continued to serve until the expiration of his term. He was transferred to the Vet. Res. Corps Jan. 23, 1864. He did not recover his voice till after his return North, at the expiration of his service. He was mustered out at Frederick, Md., the last of June, 1864.

THOMAS O'ROURKE, at the age of twenty-two years, residence unknown, was mustered into the United States service Dec. 3, 1864, for one year, in Co. H, 1st Mass. Cav. He was mustered out as Sergeant of his company, June 26, 1865, by reason of the close of the war.

CHARLES OSBORNE, at the age of twenty-one years, enlisted and was mustered into service Dec. 13, 1864, for one year, as a private of the 26th unattached Co. of Inf. Mass. Vols. He was accredited to Medway, though not a resident of the town, and mustered out of service May 12, 1865.

WILLIAM R. PARSONS, son of William and Agnes (Todd) Parsons, was born Oct. 8, 1825, in Lancashire, England. He enlisted in Medway, in May, and was mustered into the United States service May 25, 1861, for three years, as 1st Sergeant of Co. E, 2d Regt. Mass. Vols. July 13, 1861, reduced to rank of 3d Sergeant and made Ordnance Sergeant. Again appointed 1st Sergeant May 14, 1862. He was in the battle at Winchester, Va., May 25, and at Antietam, Md., Sept. 17, 1862, at which time he was wounded in the hand. He was discharged Nov. 29, 1862, for disability. He continued to reside in Medway, and was killed Feb. 13, 1875, by being thrown from a sleigh by a runaway horse.

DAVID ALLEN PARTRIDGE, son of Allen and Peggy J. Partridge, was born April 3, 1833, in Medway. He took an active part in recruiting Co. B, 42d Regt. Mass Vol. Militia, which was organized in Medway by the choice of company officers, on the twenty-eighth day of August, 1862, at which time he was elected 2d Lieut. He was mustered into the United States service in Camp Meigs, Readville, Mass., Sept. 13, 1862, for the term of nine months. His commission was dated Sept. 2, 1862. He was detailed, October 20, Assistant Adjutant-Gen. on the staff of Brig-Gen. R. A. Pierce, Commandant of the Camp at Readville, and remained on duty at camp after his regiment left for the South. Dec. 26, 1862, he was appointed Assistant Provost Marshal of Massachusetts, under Major Blake. Under these appointments he continued to serve till March 5, 1863, when he was discharged from the 42d Regt. and received the appointment of 1st Lieut. and Adj. of the 54th Mass. Inf., a colored regiment then being recruited at Camp Meigs. April 14 he was commissioned Captain of that regiment. He served with his regiment in the siege of Charleston, S. C., on James, Folly, and Morris islands. A failure of health compelled him to return North and he was discharged Jan. 19, 1864, for disability. Since the war Captain Partridge has taken an active interest in public affairs. He has twice represented the district very acceptably in the Legislature, and shown himself efficient as a town officer, having served for several years on the board of selectmen of which he is at present chairman. He is often called upon to preside over meetings of the town for which position he has an especial fitness.

GEORGE V. PARTRIDGE, son of Allen and Peggy J. Partridge, was born Nov. 9, 1842, in Harrington, Conn. He was mustered into service Sept. 23, 1861, for three years, as a private of Co. K, 1st Regt. Mass. Cav. This company was afterwards known as Co. K, 4th Regt. Mass. Cav. In April, 1862, he was on duty as a bearer of dispatches at the siege of Fort Pulaski on Cockspur Island, Savannah River. Afterwards he took part in many raids, skirmishes, and reconnoissances. April 2, 1864, in an engagement at Cedar Run, near Jacksonville, Fla., he was wounded, and died of his wound May 2, 1864, at Hospital No. 3, Beaufort, S. C., and was buried there in Lot No. 18, Grave No. 576.

WARREN J. PARTRIDGE, son of Allen and Peggy J. Partridge, was born Feb. 3, 1839, at Harrington, Conn. He enlisted in Medway, in August, and was mustered into service Sept. 13, 1862, for nine months, as a private of Co. B, 42d Regt. Mass. Vol. Militia. He was discharged for disability Oct. 22, 1862, from Camp Meigs, Readville, Mass.

WILLIAM S. PARTRIDGE, son of Allen and Peggy J. Partridge, was born April 30, 1841, in Harrington, Conn. He was mustered into the United States service April 16, 1861, for three months, as a private of Co. K, 1st Regt. R. I. Vols. He was in the battle of Bull Run, Virginia, July 21, 1861, and was mustered out of service Aug. 2, 1861, his term having expired.

WILLIAM E. PETTINGILL, at the age of twenty-one years, residence not known, enlisted Dec. 3, 1864, and was mustered into the United States service the same day, for one year, as a private of the 61st Regt., Co. G, and accredited to Medway. He was mustered out July 16, 1865.

GEORGE E. PETTIS, son of George and Sarah (Snelling) Pettis, was born Jan. 26, 1840, in Holliston. He enlisted in August, and was mustered into the United States service Sept. 13, 1862, for nine months, in Readville, Mass., as a private of Co. B, 42d Regt. Mass. Vol. Militia. He served with his regiment in Louisiana, and was mustered out Aug. 20, 1863, by reason of his term having expired. He married and settled in Medfield.

WILLIAM H. PETTIS, son of George and Sarah (Snelling) Pettis, was born July 5, 1841, in Holliston. He was mustered into the United States service Sept. 12, 1862, for nine months, as a private of the 44th Regt. Mass. Vol. Militia. He was, at the time of enlistment, residing in Sherborn, and was accredited on the quota of that town, though he appears by the state record to be accredited to Medway. He was mustered out of service June 18, 1863, his term having expired. He enlisted again, and was mustered into the United States service Dec. 7, 1863, for three years, as a private of Co. G, 2d Regt. Mass. Heavy Arty. He was taken prisoner at Plymouth, N. C., April 18, 1864, and carried to Andersonville, Ga., where, after suffering the rigors and privations of that filthy pen, he is reported to have enlisted in the rebel service to avoid starvation. Nothing further is known of him. On his last enlistment he was accredited to Medway.

JOHN A. PIERCE, son of John and Althea (Springer) Pierce, was born Aug. 20, 1831, in Milford, Mass. He enlisted and was mustered into the United States service Feb. 25, 1864, for three years, as a recruit of the 2d Regt. Mass. Vols. He was assigned to Co. E, and joined his regiment at Pumpkinvine Creek, La., the last of May, 1864. He was in but a single engagement during the advance upon Atlanta, Ga. Suffering from disease, he was sent to the hospital about the 10th of July, and afterwards to Convalescent Camp near Chattanooga, from which place he was detailed about October 1, as cattle guard and did not join his regiment again until the last of March, 1865. He was mustered out of service July 14, 1865, in Washington, D. C., by reason of the close of the war.

EZRA PIERSON, son of William and Mary Pierson, was born Jan. 19, 1831, in Yorkshire, England. He enlisted March 9, and was mustered into the United States service March 11, 1864, for three years, as a private of the 16th Mass. Light Bat. His term of service was passed principally in the defenses of Washington, D. C. He was mustered out at Readville, June 27, 1865, by reason of the close of the war.

JONATHAN PITCHER was born in Barnstable, Mass. At the age of forty-two years he was mustered into the United States service, Sept. 25, 1861, for three years, as a private of Co. K, 23d Regt. Mass. Vols. He was in the battle of Roanoke Island, N. C., Feb. 8, 1862, and at Newbern, N. C., March 14 of the same year. He was discharged May 23, 1862, for disability. He enlisted again and was mustered into service Sept. 15, 1863, for three years, as a private of Co. G, 24th Regt. Vet. Res. Corps. After a few months service he was again discharged for disability at Washington, D. C. He became an inmate of Soldiers' Home, Togus, Me.

EDWIN C. POND, son of Justin and Ruth D. (Perry) Pond, was born Sept. 10, 1834, in Franklin. He enlisted in Medway in August, and was mustered into the United States service Sept. 13, 1862, in Readville, Mass., for nine months, as a private of Co. B, 42d Regt. Mass. Vol. Militia. He served in Louisiana, and was mustered out at Camp Meigs, Readville, Aug. 20, 1863, his term having expired. He died, March, 1877, in Franklin.

EDWIN D. POND, son of Moses and Nancy Pond, was born Dec. 22, 1835, in Medway. He enlisted in Medway in August, and was mustered into the service in Camp Meigs, Readville, Sept. 13, 1862, for nine months, as a private of Co. B, 42d Regt. Mass. Vol. Militia. He served in Louisiana and was mustered out at Readville, Aug. 20, 1863, his term having expired.

ELMER H. POND, son of Jonathan and Eliza (Fisher) Pond, was born March 21, 1848, in Medway. He was mustered into the United States service Feb. 2, 1865, for one year, as a private of Co. K, 61st Regt. Mass. Vols. He was a resident of Medway, but received a bounty from Bellingham, and was accredited to that town. He was in the battle of Petersburg, April, 1865, and was mustered out July 16, 1865, by reason of the close of the war.

GEORGE E. POND, son of John and Charlotte (Wiswell) Pond, was born Jan. 27, 1841, in Medway. He enlisted in Medway in August, 1862, and was mustered into the United States service Sept. 13, 1862, for nine months, as a private of Co. B, 42d Regt. Mass. Vols. He served with his regiment in Louisiana. He was mustered out at Readville, Mass., Aug. 20, 1863, his term having expired.

GEORGE OTIS POND, son of Paul D. and Hilda (Hill) Pond, was born Sept. 22, 1829, in Franklin. He was mustered into the United States service Aug. 27, 1862, for three years, as a private of the 2d Co. of Sharpshooters. He was in the battle of Antietam, Md., Sept. 17, 1862, and at Fredericksburg, Va., Dec. 13, 1862. He died of disease Jan. 20, 1863, on board an ambulance near (state record says Falmouth, Va.) Strasburg, Va., while being removed from the field hospital to the General Hospital.

OSCAR A. POND, son of Jonathan and Eliza (Fisher) Pond, was born March 6, 1843, in Medway. He was mustered into the United States service Sept. 13, 1862, for nine months, as a private of Co. B, 42d Regt. Mass. Vol. Militia. He received a bounty from the town of Bellingham and was accredited on the quota of that town, but by the state record he appears as from Medway. He was mustered out Aug. 20, 1863, at the expiration of his service. While on duty in Louisiana he had an attack of typhoid fever, from which he never fully recovered. He died of dysentery September, 1863, in West Medway.

ASA D. PRESCOTT, son of John and Rhoda Prescott, was born January, 1835, in Phillips, Me. He enlisted May 3, and was mustered into service June 26, 1861, for three years, as a private of Co. B, 12th Regt. Mass. Vols. He was in the battle of Cedar Mountain, August 9; at South Mountain, August 14; and at Antietam, Sept. 17, 1862. In the latter engagement he was wounded through the thigh, and discharged in consequence, Jan. 13, 1863. His present residence is Boston, Mass.

ALPHEUS PROCTER, at the age of nineteen years, resident of Chelsea, Mass., enlisted Dec. 6, 1864, and was mustered into the United States service on the same day, for one year, as a private of Co. G, 61st Regt. Mass. Vols., was accredited to Medway, and mustered out July 16, 1865.

FRANKLIN PROCTER, son of Ezekiel and Martha Procter, was born Nov. 7, 1845, in Medway. He was mustered into the United States service July 28, 1862, for three years, as a private of Co. D, 35th Regt. Mass. Vols. He was discharged, Oct. 13, 1862, for disability. He continued to reside in Medway till his death, Sept. 19, 1879.

STEPHEN F. PURDY, at the age of twenty-three years, enlisted at Medway, and was mustered into the United States service July 22, 1864, for one hundred days. He was mustered out on the eleventh day of November, 1864.

PATRICK RAFERTY, residence unknown, enlisted Dec. 6, 1864, for one year, and was mustered into the United States service on the same day, as a private of Co. K, 61st Regt. Mass. Vols., and accredited to Medway.

GEORGE H. READ, son of George and Louisa (Fairbanks) Read, was born Feb. 12, 1841, in Medway. In April, 1861, he enlisted for three months, and was mustered into service April 15, as a Corporal of Co. H, 1st Regt. of R. I. Inf. He was at that time a resident of Providence, R. I. He served his full term with his regiment, and took part in the first battle of Bull Run, July 21, 1861. After his discharge he returned to Medway and again enlisted, and was mustered into service Oct. 31, 1861, as a private of Co. I, 1st Mass. Cav. This company was afterwards known as Co. A, Independent Battalion, and still later was transferred, and became Co. I, 4th Regt. Mass. Cav. He was in the battle at James Island, S. C., June 17, 1862, and at Pocataligo, S. C. He was on duty at Morris Island, S. C., during the siege of Fort Sumter, and afterwards took part in the Florida campaign in the winter of 1863-4, and was in the disastrous battle of Olustee, Feb. 20, 1864. Having reënlisted on 1st of January, 1864, for another term of three years, he received the usual veteran furlough, and visited home in March or April following. He afterwards returned to his regiment, but was suffering severely from the effects of a cold contracted during the exposure of the Florida campaign, and from which he never recovered. He was detailed as clerk of the Regimental Quarter-Master during the latter part of his term of service, and though suffering greatly from disease, he performed his duties unflinchly to the end. He was mustered out of service Nov. 14, 1865, by reason of the close of the war. After his discharge his disease made rapid progress, and he died Feb. 25, 1866, of pulmonary consumption.

TIMOTHY REARDON, (or Riordan), son of John and Julia (Wallace) Reardon, was born May 18, 1847, in Cork County, Ireland. He enlisted and was mustered into the United States service, July 22, 1864, for one hundred days, Co B, 42d Mass. Regt. He served with his regiment in the defenses of Washington, D. C., and was mustered out Nov. 11, 1864, his term having expired. He died March, 1880, in Milford, Mass.

THOMAS REISE, at the age of twenty-four years, residence unknown, enlisted Dec. 13, 1864, and was mustered into service the same day for one year, as a private of Co. K, 61st Regt Mass. Vols , and accredited to Medway. He was mustered out as Sergeant July 16, 1865.

PATRICK REGAN, at the age of nineteen years, enlisted for one hundred days, and was mustered into the United States service July 22, 1864, as a private of Co B, 42d Regt. Mass. Vols. He was mustered out Nov. 11, 1864, at the expiration of his term

BENJAMIN F. REMMICK, son of Benjamin and Eliza (Briggs) Remmick, was born Feb. 25, 1841, in Gardiner, Me. He was mustered into the United States service June 11, 1861, for three years, as a private of Co H, 2d Regt Mass. Vols. He was in the battles of Winchester and Cedar Mountain, Va , and at Antietam, Md. In the latter engagement he was instantly killed and was buried on the field.

GEORGE S. RICE, son of Hollis and Nancy (Abbe) Rice, was born April 24, 1840, in Medway. He enlisted at Medway in August, and was mustered into the United States service Sept. 13, 1862, for nine months, as a private of Co. B, 42d Regt. Mass. Vols. He served in Louisiana and was in the engagement at Brashear City, June 23, 1863, and was taken prisoner He was paroled June 25, and was mustered out of service Aug. 20, 1863, his term having expired. He enlisted again for one hundred days, in the same regiment and company, and was mustered into service July 22, 1864. He served in the defenses of Washington, D. C., and was mustered out Nov. 11, 1864, his term having expired.

GEORGE H. RICH, at the age of eighteen years, private of Co. B, 42d Regt. was mustered into service July 22, 1864, for one hundred days. He died Aug 14, 1864, from an accidental wound.

HENRY H RICH, son of Henry and Mary (Paine) Rich, was born July 30, 1842, in Truro, Mass. He enlisted for one hundred days and was mustered into service July 22, 1864. He served in the defenses of Washington, D C , and was mustered out Nov. 11, 1864, his term having expired.

JAMES G. RICHARDS, son of William and Nancy J. (Gilmore) Richards, was born Dec. 20, 1846, in Medway. He enlisted Aug. 23, 1864, and was mustered into service on the same day, for one year, as a private of the 18th unattached Co., afterwards Co. B, 4th Regt. Heavy Arty. Mass. Vols. He served in the defenses of Washington, D C., and was mustered out of service June 17, 1865, by reason of the close of the war

ADDISON WARREN RICHARDSON, son of Addison and Maria Richardson, was born June 14, 1843, in Medway. He enlisted for nine months, and was mustered into the United States service Sept 13, 1862, as a private of Co. B, 42d Regt. Mass. Vol. Militia. He served with his regiment in Louisiana, and was mustered out Aug. 20, 1863, at the expiration of his term.

EMORY RICHARDSON, son of Artemas and Deborah (Johnson) Richardson, was born Aug. 7, 1817, in Medway. He enlisted and was mustered into the United States service June 13, 1861, as a private of Co. F, 11th Regt. Mass. Vols., and having served his full term of three years was transferred June 24, 1864, to the 11th Battalion, by reason of having reenlisted. He was accredited to Medway, though he had not for some years been a resident of the town. State record says, on reenlistment, accredited to Weymouth, Mass., and mustered out July 14, 1865, at expiration of service.

HENRY S. RICHARDSON, son of Moses and Keziah (Fairbanks) Richardson, was born Dec. 25, 1833, in Medway. He was mustered into the United States service Sept. 13, 1862, for nine months, as a private of Co. B, 42d Regt. Mass. Vol. Militia. Being a resident of Dedham, he was accredited to that place. He was mustered out Aug 20, 1863, his term having expired. By the state record he appears as from Medway

JOSEPH H. RICHARDSON, son of Joseph L., Jr., and Sylvia (Partridge) Richardson, was born June 7, 1840, in Medway. He was mustered into the United States service July 2, 1861, for three years, as a Corporal of Co. B, 16th Regt. Mass. Vols He was in the battles of Fair Oaks, June 1; Peach Orchard, June 25; Glendale, June 29; Malvern Hill, July 1, Second Bull Run, August 29 and 30; Bristow Station, August 27, Fredericksburg, Dec. 13, 1862; Chancellorsville, May 2 and 3; Gettysburg, July 2, and Locust Grove, Nov 27, 1863. At Gettysburg he was wounded in the arm. He was also in the battle of the Wilderness and engagements succeeding, in May and June, 1864, when he states that his regiment was under fire more than fifty days in succession. He was a resident of Holliston at the time of enlistment and was accredited to that town. He was mustered out of service July 27, 1864, his term having expired.

BROUGHAM ROBERTS was born in London, England. He enlisted at the age of twenty-four years, in July, and was mustered into the United States service Aug. 9, 1862, for three years, as a private of Co. I, 30th Regt. Mass. Vols. He states that he was with his regiment until the last of March, 1863, when by an accidental wound in the foot he was compelled to go into the hospital. He was subsequently sick with the black-tongue fever and was not again fit for service until June 7, when he started to join his regiment at Port Hudson. Before reaching that place, however, he was sent back to Brashear City, by order of Gen. Emory, and was in the engagement at that place June 23, and taken prisoner. He was soon paroled with the other prisoners taken at that time, but he states that the paroles were considered of no force, not having been signed by an officer duly authorized to serve, and the men were immediately returned to service He joined his regiment again at Baton Rouge, July 30, and remained there through the succeeding winter, in camp, and was in the engagements in April and May following, during the Red River expedition of Gen. Banks. After the return of the regiment to Virginia he was in the engagements in the Shenandoah Valley in the autumn of 1864. The most important of these were at Opequan. September 19 ; Fisher's Mill, September 22, and Cedar Creek, October 19.   From December 11 to May, 1865, he was detailed as a clerk to Chief Quartermaster at Gen. Sherman's head-quarters.   He joined his regiment at Savannah, Ga., in May, but on account of an accidental injury he was sent to the Division hospital and did not return home with his regiment which started June 30. He was mustered out of service Aug. 13, 1865, in Boston.   He resides in New York City, where he has been engaged in business for several years.

HENRY M. ROCKWOOD, son of Martin and Julia M. Rockwood, was born March 6, 1842, in Bellingham.   He was mustered into the United States service March 11, 1864, for three years, as a private of the 16th Mass. Light Bat.   He served in the defenses of Washington, D. C., and was mustered out June 27, 1865, by reason of the close of the war.

THOMAS ROLLINS was born in Lancashire, England.   He enlisted at the age of twenty-five years, in Medway, and was mustered into the United States service in Camp Andrew, West Roxbury, May 25, 1861, for three years, as a Corporal of Co. E, 2d Regt. Mass. Vols.   He was promoted Sergeant, July 7, 1861.   He deserted July, 1862, from Winchester, Va.

CHANDLER W. SANDERS, son of Alexander R. and Fidelia Sanders, was born Sept. 11, 1843, in Upton.   He enlisted on the twentieth day of September, 1861, and was mustered into the United States service, for one year, as a private of Co. E, 61st Regt. Mass. Vols.   He was in the engagement before Petersburg, Va., April 2, 1865, and was mustered out of service June 4, 1865, by reason of the close of the war.   He is the overseer of boot manufactory in the State Prison, Providence, R. I.

GEORGE S. SANFORD, son of George and Sarah (Sanger) Sanford, was born April 10, 1842, in Medway.   He enlisted August 11, and was mustered into the United States service, Sept. 12, 1862, for nine months, as a private of Co. F, 44th Regt. Mass. Vol. Militia.   He was at that time a resident of Southboro, but preferred to be accredited to his native town of Medway.   He was in the battle of Rawle's Mills, on the Tarboro' expedition, November 2 ; at the battle of Kinston, N. C., December 14 ; at Whitehall Bridge, December 16, and at Goldsboro', Dec. 17, 1862.   He was discharged Jan. 23, 1863, for disability.   He enlisted a second time in Co. G, 60th Mass. Regt., for one hundred days, was mustered into service July 19, 1864, and mustered out Nov. 30, 1864, at the expiration of his term.

MELVIN SAWYER, at the age of twenty-one years, residence New Bedford, Mass., enlisted and was mustered into the United States service on the thirteenth day of December, 1864, for one year, as a private of the 26th unattached Co. of Inf. Mass. Vols., and was accredited to Medway.   He was mustered out of service May 12, 1865, by reason of the close of the war.

MICHAEL SCHOFIELD was born in Ireland.   He enlisted at the age of twenty-one years, Sept. 15, 1864, and was mustered into the United States service on the same day, for one year, as a private of Co. C, 61st Regt. Mass. Vols.   He was detailed as fifer during most of his term of service. He was in the engagement before Petersburg, April 2, 1865, and was mustered out at camp near Arlington Heights, June 7, 1865.

JOHN SCOTT, son of Samuel and Elizabeth Scott, was born Nov. 22, 1833, in Tyrone County, Ireland.   He enlisted as a substitute for James Doherty, of Cambridge, Mass., and was mustered into the United States service Aug. 25, 1863, for three years, and assigned to Co. K, 18th Regt. Mass. Vols. He joined his regiment at Beverly Ford, Va., about the 10th of September, and was in the engagement at Rappahannock Station, November 7; at Mine Run, Nov. 29 and 30, 1863; at the Wilderness, May 5, at Laurel Hill, May 10; at Spottsylvania, May 23; at Cold Harbor, June 3 to 5; and before Petersburg, Va., June 18, when he was struck in the leg by a solid shot and the limb so severely shattered that amputation became necessary, and his limb was removed Aug. 12, 1864. In September the term of the 18th Regt. having expired, it was mustered out of service and the recruits and reenlisted men were transferred to the 32d Regt. Being unfit for duty he never joined that regiment and was discharged March 1, 1865, for disability.

RICHARD SEARLES, residence unknown, enlisted and was mustered into the United States service, January, 1863, for three years, as a recruit for the 22d Regt. Mass. Vols., and accredited to Medway.

GEORGE T. SIMPSON, son of Hiram W. and Mary E. (Wendall) Simpson, was born Aug 14, 1838, in Boston. He enlisted May 21, 1861, in Capt. Thos. W. Clark's Co., afterwards a company of the 29th Regt., but during Simpson's service in it, attached to the 4th Mass Regt., a three months organization. While a member of this company he was in the battle of Big Bethel. He was discharged June 26, 1861 (state record, July 6), for disability. He enlisted again as a private of Co. K, 31st Regt., and was mustered into service Jan. 15, 1862. He was again discharged Dec. 9, 1862, for disability. He enlisted a third time as a private of Co. A, 3d Regt. Mass. Cav., and was mustered into service Feb. 29, 1864, for three years, and accredited to Boston. He was transferred to the Vet. Res. Corps in April, 1865, and was mustered out of service Nov. 21, 1865, by reason of General Order No. 116, Adjutant-General's Office, in Washington, D. C.

FRANK X. SINZINGER, at the age of thirty-two years, residence unknown, enlisted Dec. 5, 1864, and was mustered into the United States service on the same day, for one year, as a private of the 6th Mass. Light Bat He was mustered out of service Aug. 7, 1865, by reason of the close of the war.

MICHAEL SLAVEN, son of Philip and Bridget Slaven, was born in 1835, in Leitrim Country, Ireland. He enlisted in May, and was mustered into the United States service in Camp Andrew, West Roxbury, May 25, 1861, for three years, as a private of Co E, 2d Regt. Mass. Vols He says he was constantly on duty and in all the skirmishes and battles of the regiment during his term of service He was at the battle of Winchester, Va , May 25, 1862; at Cedar Mountain, August 9; Antietam, Sept. 17, 1862, Chancellorsville, May 3, Beverly Ford, June 9, Gettysburg, July 2 and 3, 1863, and at Resaca, May 15, 1864. He was mustered out of service May 28, 1864, his term having expired.

EDMOND J. SMITH, son of Jason and Lucy (Gay) Smith, was born June 20, 1846, in Medway. He enlisted Dec. 30, 1863, and was mustered into the service of the United States Jan. 6, 1864, as a private of Co. C, 4th Regt Mass Cav. He states that he was in many raids and skirmishes but the only engagement in which he took part was at Camden, S C., at which time he was wounded in the leg by a minie-ball. This fight occurred on the 17th of April, 1865. He was mustered out of service July 28, 1865, at the U. S. General Hospital, in Worcester, Mass.

WILLIAM SMITH, son of Jason and Lucy (Gay) Smith, was born March 2, 1846, in Medway. He enlisted Dec. 23, 1863, and was mustered into the United States service Jan. 6, 1864, for three years, as a private of Co. C, 4th Mass. Cav. He states that the only considerable engagement in which he took part was at Honey Hill, on the Charleston and Savannah R. R. He was in many raids and skirmishes, in one of which, at Davol's Neck, on the Charleston and Savannah R. R., he was wounded in the finger. For about six months of his term he was detailed as orderly first to Gen. Pattee, and afterwards to Gen. Van Wight. He was mustered out of service as a Corporal, in Richmond, Va., Nov. 14, 1865, by reason of General Order from the War Department, No. 144. He died Jan. 30, 1869, of consumption.

HENRY L. SNELL, son of Henry C. and Sibbel (Adams) Snell, was born Dec. 18, 1827, in Medway. He enlisted in Medway in August, 1862, and was mustered into the United States service at Camp Meigs, Readville, Sept. 13, 1862, for nine months, as a private of Co. B, 42d Regt. Mass. Vols. He served with his regiment in Louisiana, and was in the engagement at Lafourche Crossing, June 21, 1863. He was mustered out of service Aug. 20, 1863, his term having expired.

HERMAN SOLON SPARROW, son of Philip S. and Laura E. (Shepard) Sparrow, was born Feb. 14, 1841, in Medway. He enlisted early in May, and was mustered into the United States service at Camp Andrew, May 25, 1861, as a private of Co. E, 2d Regt. Mass. Vols. He bore a part in the earlier services of the regiment; he was in the engagement at Winchester, Va., May 25, and at Cedar Mountain, Aug. 9, 1862, when he was instantly killed, being shot through the head. Having been among the first to enlist, he was also one of the first from this town to fall in battle. Letters from regimental officers bear testimony to his manly qualities as follows: "He was a brave and good soldier, and never flinched from doing his duty. He was always at his post, let what would, come." "Calm, decided, faithful, accommodating, and affectionate, he won for himself the esteem of all." For more particulars see record of George H. Ide.

PHILIP O. SPARROW, son of Orlando and Tamson (Whitney) Sparrow, was born April 6, 1838, in Wrentham. He was drafted into the United States service July 15, 1863, for three years, and assigned to Co. A, 9th Regt. Mass. Vols. He was discharged Dec. 16, 1863, for disability.

JAMES SPELMAN, at the age of twenty-two years, residence unknown, was mustered into service May 4, 1864, for three years, in U. S. Vet. Res. Corps, and accredited to Medway.

MATTHEW M. SPERRY was mustered into service May, 1864, for three years, in U. S. Vet. Res. Corps, and accredited to Medway.

GEORGE A. STEDMAN, son of George and Elvira (Daniels) Stedman, was born in Holliston. He enlisted from Medway as a private of Co. B, 42d Regt. Mass. Vol. Militia, for one hundred days, and was mustered into the United States service July 22, 1864. He served in the defenses of Washington, D. C., and was mustered out Nov. 11, 1864.

CHARLES H. STEWART, at the age of thirty-eight years, residence unknown, enlisted Nov. 2, 1864, and was mustered into service on the same day, for one year, as a private of Co. F, 71st Regt. Mass. Vols. He was mustered out July 16, 1865.

GEORGE HERBERT STRATTON, son of John and Lucinda Stratton, was born Feb. 19, 1842, in Medway He enlisted July 23, and was mustered into the United States service July 28, 1862, for three years, as a private of Co. D, 35th Regt. Mass Vols He says he was in the following engagements : South Mountain, Va., September 14 ; Antietam, Md , September 17 ; at Sulphur Spring Va., last of November ; Fredericksburg, Dec. 13, 1862, when he was slightly wounded ; at the siege and capture of Jackson, Miss , in which his regiment took a prominent and highly honorable part. Soon after the capture of Jackson he was taken sick and sent to a hospital of which he was afterwards detailed Acting Quartermaster, and where he served out his time. He was mustered out November, 1865, in Boston.

JOHN S. STRATTON, son of John and Lucinda Stratton, was born April 18, 1834, in Sherborn. He enlisted in the United States Navy Oct. 10, 1861, on board the "North Carolina," and went to Fortress Monroe, when, on account of sickness he was sent back to the Naval Hospital at Brooklyn, N. Y., where he was discharged March 8, 1862, for disability. He enlisted in August, and was mustered into service Sept. 13, 1862, for nine months, as private of Co. B, 42d Regt. Mass. Vol. Militia He served with his regiment in Louisiana, and was mustered out of service Aug. 20, 1863, his term having expired. Again he enlisted and was mustered into service Aug. 30, 1864, for one year, as a private of Co. B, 61st Regt. Mass. Vols. He took part in the engagement before Petersburg, Va., April 2, 1865. He was mustered out June 4, 1865, by reason of the close of the war.

FREDERICK SWARMAN, son of Carson and Ann Swarman, was born June 6, 1839, in Boston, Mass. He enlisted April 29, and was mustered into the United States service at Fort Warren, Boston Harbor, June 26, 1862, as a Corporal of Co. E, 12th Regt. Mass. Vols , for the term of three years. He was in the battles of Cedar Mountain, Va , August 9 ; at Rappahannock Station, August 25 , Thoroughfare Gap, 2d Bull Run, August 30 ; Chantilly, September 1 ; and at Antietam, Sept. 17, 1862 , at which time he was wounded, having a leg cut off by a cannon shot. While he was lying on the field, the battle still raging, he was twice wounded, once in the arm and once in the head. He was discharged April 2. 1863, in consequence. He enlisted again Aug. 19, 1863, for three years, as a Corporal in the U. S Vet Res Corps. He was discharged Dec. 26, 1863, for disability. He is still a resident, and for several years has held the position of Postmaster in Rockville, Medway.

JOHN H. SWARMAN, son of Carson and Ann Swarman, was born April 7, 1837, in Boston. He enlisted in May, and was mustered into the United States service May 25, 1861, for three years, at Camp Andrew, West Roxbury, as a private of Co. E, 2d Regt. Mass. Vols. He was in the engagement, May 25, 1862, at Winchester, Va , and was taken prisoner. He was first kept a prisoner in Lynchburg, Va., and afterwards in Belle Isle, Richmond, until exchanged, Sept. 19, 1862. He again joined the regiment Oct. 23, 1862 , and was in the battle of Chancellorsville, May 2 and 3 ; engagement at Beverly Ford, June 9, and at Gettysburg, July 2 and 3, 1863 ; when he was wounded in the leg He was not again fit for service until November, when he was detailed for special duty as guard at Louisville, Ky., where he remained till the end of his term. He was mustered out May, 1864.

AVERY SYLVESTER, son of Ansel Sylvester, was born April 6, 1844, in

Etna, Me. He enlisted at the Provost Marshal's office in Worcester, Dec. 7, 1863, for three years, as a private of Co. G, 2d Regt. Mass. Heavy Arty. He appears by the state record to be accredited to Worcester, but he was understood to be accredited upon the quota of Medway. He was taken prisoner at Plymouth, N. C., April, 1864, and died in October following in the Confederate prison at Florence, S. C.

JOHN TEVLIN, son of Michael and Betsey Tevlin, was born about 1831, in Boston. He resided in Medway, but enlisted for the town of Bellingham, and was mustered into the United States service Dec. 27, 1864, for three years, as a private of Co. M, 4th Regt. Mass. Cav. State record says, "deserted Aug. 10, 1865."

WILLIAM H. THOMAS, at the age of nineteen years, enlisted in Medway August, 1862, and was mustered into the United States service Sept. 13, 1862, for nine months, as a private of Co. B, 42d Regt. Mass. Vols. He was mustered out Aug. 20, 1863, at the expiration of his service.

JOHN THOMPSON, residence unknown, enlisted and was mustered into the United States service December, 1862, for three years, as a recruit for the 29th Regt. Mass. Vols., and was accredited to Medway.

HENRY TIBBETS was mustered into the Vet. Res. Corps July 7, 1863, for three years.

CAPTAIN BENJAMIN C. TINKHAM.

BENJAMIN C. TINKHAM, son of Harvey and Jane (Cornish) Tinkham, was born Oct. 11, 1827, in Middleboro, Mass. He enlisted in August, and was mustered into service Sept. 13, 1862, for nine months, at Camp Meigs, as 2d Sergeant of Co. B, 42d Regt. Mass. Vol. Militia. He was promoted 1st Lieut. of the company, March 24, 1863. In the engagement at Lafourche Crossing, La , June 21, 1863, he was in command of a detachment of his regiment and was highly commended by his superior officer present, Lieut.-Col. Sawtelle for his coolness and bravery on the occasion. He was mustered out Aug. 20, 1863, at the expiration of his service. He enlisted again for one hundred days, and was mustered into service July 22, 1864, as Captain in the same regiment and company. He served in the defenses of Washington, D. C., and was mustered out Nov. 11, 1864, at the expiration of his service. Capt. Tinkham having completed his military career, returned to his former employment of railroad building. For two years he was engaged on the Dighton and Somerset road. Subsequently he was employed on the Boston water works and in railroad building in Connecticut. Meanwhile his family remained in Medway. In 1869 he removed to Boston Highlands, Mass., where he has since resided. He has been for some years a contractor and builder. Capt. Tinkham was a successful business man; for two years, in 1881 and 1882, he represented Ward 21 of the city of Boston in the State Legislature. He was an active and influential member of the Elliot Church, Roxbury, and for several years served as the treasurer of that society. He married, Jan. 3, 1849, Cynthia Perkins, of Middleboro, Mass. The children were: Nettie F., born Oct. 20, 1851; married June 21, 1876, the Rev. B. F. Hamilton, pastor of the Elliot Church, Roxbury. Idella, born March 19, 1857, and died Nov. 17, 1865.

CHARLES H. TORREY, son of the Rev. Charles T. and Mary (Ide) Torrey, was born Dec. 27, 1837, in Salem, Mass. He was mustered into the United States service Oct. 7, 1861, for three years, as a private of Co. D, 25th Regt. Mass. Vols. He was in the battles of Roanoke Island, N. C., Feb. 8, 1862, and Newbern, N. C., March 14, 1862. He was discharged March 16, 1863, for disability. He enlisted again, and was mustered into the United States service July 3, 1863, for five years, as Hospital Steward in the Regular Army, and was detached as a clerk in the office of the Surgeon General of the United States, in Washington, D C. He was mustered out Sept. 30, 1865, by reason of special order from the War Department, relating to the reduction of the army, consequent to the close of the war.

JAMES J. TREANOR was born in Ireland; resided in Boston; enlisted at the age of thirty years, Sept. 9, 1864, and was mustered into service on the same day, for one year, as a private of Co. K, 1st Regt. Mass. Heavy Arty., and accredited to Medway. He was mustered out May 29, 1865

JOHN S. TREEN, son of Joseph and Lucretia F. Treen, was born at Wallace River, N. S. He enlisted and was mustered into the United States service, May 25, 1861, for three years, as a private of Co. E, 2d Regt. Mass. Vols. He was with his regiment during the earlier service; at the battle of Winchester, May 25; at Cedar Mountain, August 9, and at Antietam, Sept. 17, 1862, when he was killed in action.

LEWIS A. TREEN, son of Henry and Sarah A. Treen, was born at Wallace River, N. S. He was mustered into the United States service, May 25, 1861, for three years, as a Corporal of Co. E, 2d Regt. Mass. Vols. He took part in all the earlier service of the regiment, and was in the fight at Winchester, Va., May 25, deserted, June 12, 1862, from Winchester, Va. In a letter to the chairman of the selectmen written soon after by Capt. Quincy, of Co. E, inquiring if anything was known here concerning Mr. Treen, he expressed the opinion that he must either have deserted or been taken prisoner. He could not believe the former without positive proof, for he regarded him as one of the best men in the company. But it is ascertained that Mr. Treen's course was mainly induced by domestic troubles at home. It was understood that he came to Massachusetts where he remained a considerable time, after which he enlisted again under an assumed name in Maj. P. A Taylor's Department of Signal Corps, U. S. Army, was enrolled on the 13th of March 1864, for three years or the war, and was honorably discharged on the 22d of August, 1865 Mr. Treen, after the war, settled in Olympia, Wash. Ter., and afterwards removed to Seattle, where he now resides. He is established with Mr. G. F. Raymond, under the firm name of Treen & Raymond, importer and manufacturers of boots and shoes He has been a member of the Territorial Legislature, and occupies an honorable position in business and social circles where he resides.

Lucius M. Turner, son of Samuel Turner, was born in Chester, Vt. He enlisted in Medway in August, and was mustered into the United States service Sept 13, 1862, for nine months, at Camp Meigs, Readville, as a private of Co. B, 42d Regt. Mass. Vol. Militia. He served in Louisiana, and was mustered out Aug. 20, 1863, at the expiration of his term.

William Henry Turner, son of Stephen and Polly M. (Williams) Turner, was born April 11, 1839, in Medway. He enlisted in Medway, in May, and was mustered into the United States service May 25, 1861, for three years, at Camp Andrew, West Roxbury, as a private of Co. E, 2d Regt. Mass Vols. He was in the engagement at Winchester, Va., May 25, at Cedar Mountain, August 9, and Antietam, Sept. 17, 1862. He was discharged for disability Jan. 24, 1863, and died June 3, 1863, of chronic diarrhoea, in Milford. Mass.

Edward G Tutein, at the age of twenty-four years, residence Chelsea, Mass., was mustered into service Dec 17, 1864, for one year, as Captain of Co. G, 61st Regt. Mass. Vols., and accredited to Medway. He was mustered out July 16, 1865, at the expiration of his service. He had previously served a full term of three years in the 1st Mass. Inf., first as Sergeant of Co. H, and from March 1, 1863, as 2d Lieutenant.

Albert Vallet, son of Brayton and Freelove Vallet, was born April 17, 1823, in Gloucester, R. I. He enlisted Aug 23, 1864, and was mustered into service on the same day, for one year as a private of the 18th Unattached Co., afterwards Co. B, 4th Regt Mass Heavy Arty. He served in the defenses of Washington, D. C., and was discharged April 25, 1865, for disability. He died of heart disease, Sept 1, 1880, in West Medway

Albert L. Vallet, son of Albert and Sarah Vallet, was born Aug. 2, 1847. He was mustered into the United States service March 11, 1864, for three years, as a private of the 16th Mass. Light Bat. He served in Maryland and Virginia, and was mustered out June 27, 1865.

John H. Vallet, son of Albert and Sarah Vallet, was born Jan. 12, 1841, in Medway. He was mustered into service of United States Feb. 8, 1864, for three years, as a private of Co. H, 4th Mass Cav He was mustered out May 30, 1865. He was accredited to Cambridge, though a resident of Medway.

JEREMIAH VASE, son of Stephen and Joanna (Bird) Vase, was born in 1835, in Northbridge, Mass. He enlisted Aug 21, 1862, and was mustered into service on the same day, for three years, as a recruit to the 2d Regt. Mass Vols., with the understanding that his term should expire with that of his regiment. In the battle of Chancellorsville, May 3. 1863, he was wounded in the neck. After his recovery, on his way back to the regiment, he was injured in the ankle by a railroad collision, so as to unfit him for service. He was mustered out May 20, 1864, and is now living, a farmer, in Nooksack Crossing, Wash. Ter.

JOHN WALCH enlisted Dec. 13, 1864, and was mustered into service on the same day, for one year, as a private of Co. K, 61st Regt. Mass. Vols. He was accredited to Medway, though not a resident of the town. He was mustered out July 16, 1865, as 1st Sergeant.

CHARLES WARDIN enlisted and was mustered in August, 1862, for three years, as a private of Co. D, 35th Mass. Inf. He deserted soon after receiving his bounty.

JOHN WATTS, residence unknown, enlisted and was mustered into the United States service, December, 1862, for three years, as a recruit for the 29th Regt. Mass. Vols., and accredited to Medway.

GEORGE C. WEBBER, born in East Douglas, Mass., enlisted at the age of twenty-six years, in Medway, and was mustered into service May 25, 1861, for three years, at Camp Andrew, as a private of Co. E, 2d Regt. Mass. Vols. He states that he was in the following engagements · Winchester, Va , May 25; Cedar Mountain, August 9; skirmish in Pope's retreat. August, 1862; Antietam, Sept. 17, 1862; Chancellorsville, May 2 and 3; Beverly Ford, June 9; Gettysburg, July 2 and 3, 1863, and Resaca, Ga., May 15, 1864 He was mustered out of service May 20, 1864, his term having expired. He enlisted again Aug. 23, 1864, and was mustered into service on the same day, for one year, as a private of the 18th unattached Co., afterwards Co. B, 4th Regt Mass Heavy Arty. He served in the defenses of Washington, D. C., and was mustered out June 17, 1865.

JAMES WELCH, son of James and Mary Welch, was born April 18, 1848 He enlisted as " John Blake," and was mustered into the United States service Jan. 23, 1865, for the term of three years, as a recruit to the 28th Regt. Mass. Vols. He was a resident of Medway, but was accredited to Dudley, Mass He was mustered out June 6, 1865, at the expiration of his service.

ALFRED C. WHEAT, son of Joel and Martha Wheat, was born Jan. 25, 1847, in Hancock, N. H. He enlisted in Medway in May, and was mustered into the United States service, May 25, 1861, at Camp Andrew, for three years, as a private of Co E, 2d Regt. Mass. Vols He was in the battle at Winchester, Va., May 25, at Cedar Mountain, August 9, at Antietam, Sept. 17, 1862; at Chancellorsville, May 2 and 3, at Gettysburg, July 2 and 3, 1863; and at Resaca, Ga , May 15, 1864. He was mustered out May 28, 1864, his term having expired. He enlisted again for the town of Bellingham, and was mustered into service for one year, as a private of Co. K. 61st Regt. Mass Vols. He took part in the first movements around Petersburg, Va , in the spring of 1865, and was mustered out July 16, 1865.

HENRY WHEAT, son of Joel and Martha Wheat, was born Jan 24, 1832, in Billerica, Mass. He enlisted in Medway in May, and was mustered into the United States service May 25, 1861, for three years, as a Corporal of Co. E, 2d Regt. Mass. Vols. He was promoted Sergeant May 14, 1862. He states that he was in a skirmish in the pursuit of Jackson by Shields in the spring of 1862, at the battle of Winchester, Va., May 25, 1862; at Cedar Mountain, August 9, and at the battle of Antietam, Sept. 17, 1862. In charging across the field of Antietam the regiment passed over the prostrate body of a rebel color bearer, lying upon his face, still grasping in one hand his colors and with the other a sword. Sergeant Wheat returned to him and the fallen man desired to be placed in an easier position and asked for a drink of water Gratifying his wishes Sergeant Wheat received his colors and sword, the latter of which he was permitted to retain as a trophy. The wounded man gave his name as Lieut Kidd, of the 11th Regt. Miss. Vols. Sergeant Wheat was discharged Dec. 11, 1862, for disability. He enlisted again for the town of Bridgewater, and was mustered into service Sept. 2, 1864, for one year, as a private of Co. C, 61st Regt Mass. Vols He was subsequently promoted 1st Sergeant. He was with his regiment in the engagements at Petersburg, Va., in March and April, 1865, and was mustered out of service June 4, and finally discharged June 17, 1865, in Readville.

EDWARD H WHEELER, at the age of eighteen years, residence Chelsea, enlisted Dec. 8, 1864, and was mustered into service on the same day, for one year, as a private of Co. M, 4th Regt. Mass Cav, and accredited to Medway. He was mustered out Nov. 7, 1865, at the expiration of his service.

LEWIS WHEELER, son of Abijah R. and Adaline (Jones) Wheeler, was born in Medway. He enlisted in Medway, in August, and was mustered into the United States service at Readville, Sept. 13, 1862, for nine months, as a private of Co. B, 42d Regt Mass Vol Militia. He served with his regiment in Louisiana, and was mustered out Aug. 20, 1863, his term having expired. He enlisted again and was mustered into service July 22, 1864, for one hundred days, as a private of the same regiment and company. He served in the defenses of Washington, D C., and was mustered out Nov. 11, 1864, at the expiration of his term. He resides in West Roxbury, Mass

JAMES WHITCOMB, born in Leominster, Mass., enlisted at the age of thirty-five years, Dec 29, 1863, and was mustered into service the same day, for three years, as a recruit to the 16th Regt. Mass Inf. He was assigned to Co. E, and transferred to the 11th Battalion, July 11, 1864, the term of the regiment having expired. He was mustered out May 29, 1865.

SAMUEL O. WHITE, born in Boston, enlisted at the age of twenty-six years, and was mustered into the United States service Aug. 12, 1862, for three years, as a private of Co. E, 16th Regt. Mass. Vols. He was a resident of this town at the time of his enlistment, but was accredited to the town of Sherborn. He was transferred Sept. 1, 1863, to the Vet. Res. Corps.

JOHN WHITMAN enlisted and was mustered in August, 1862, for three years, as a private of Co. D, 35th Mass. Inf., and accredited to Medway. He deserted soon after receiving his bounty.

CHARLES WHITNEY was born in Holliston, Mass He enlisted in Medway at the age of twenty-six years, in May, and was mustered into the United States service May 25, 1861, at Camp Andrew, for three years, as a

Corporal of Co. E, 2d Regt Mass. Vols. In the winter of 1861–2 he was detailed in company with James B. May for recruiting service in Massachusetts. He joined his regiment again soon after the engagement at Winchester, and was in the battle of Cedar Mountain, August 9, and at Antietam, Sept. 17, 1862; at Chancellorsville, May 2 and 3, at Gettysburg, July 2 and 3, 1863; and at Resaca, Ga., May 15, 1864. In the battle of Cedar Mountain he was hit on the breastplate and disabled for several days. He was mustered out May 28, 1864, his term having expired.

CHARLES E. WHITNEY, son of Nathan and Rosetta (Springer) Whitney, was born July 25, 1847, in Medway. He enlisted December 17, and was mustered into service Dec. 26, 1863, for three years, as a private of Co. A, 4th Regt. Mass. Cav. He states that he was in no general engagement, but took part in many raids and skirmishes. He was detailed for a considerable time as orderly to Brig. and Brevt Maj.-Gen Hatch. He was mustered out of service Nov. 14, 1865, in Richmond, Va., and finally discharged from Galloup's Island, Boston Harbor.

GEORGE W. WHITNEY, son of Charles B. and Mary Ann (Carey) Whitney, was born Feb. 18, 1844, in Milford. He enlisted Aug. 23, 1864, and was mustered into the United States service on the same day, for one year, as a private of the 18th unattached Regt. Mass. Heavy Arty. He served in the defenses of Washington, D. C., and was mustered out June 17, 1865.

ALBERT H WILEY, son of Daniel and Izanna E. (Hixon) Wiley, was born June 12, 1829, in Medway. He enlisted, and was mustered into the United States service, July 20, 1862, as a recruit of the 2d Mass. Inf., and was assigned to Co. E. He joined his regiment on the eighth day of August, and was under fire at the battle of Cedar Mountain, the next day, but without arms. He took part in the battle of Chancellorsville, May 2, 1863. On the 12th of June, 1863, he was detailed as servant to Lieut. Thomas, and continued in that position to the end of his term. Though he enlisted for three years, it was with the understanding that his term should expire with that of his regiment, and he was mustered out May 20, 1864. He removed to Medfield and died, March 26, 1880, of consumption.

JOHN WILLEY, born in Bartlett, N. H., enlisted, at the age of thirty-six years, in Medway, in August, and was mustered into the United States service, Sept. 13, 1862, at Camp Meigs, for nine months, as wagoner of Co. B, 12th Regt Mass. Vol. Militia. He served with his regiment in Louisiana, and was mustered out Aug. 20, 1863, his term having expired.

ALLEN T. WILLIAMS, son of Nathan A. and Esther B. Williams, was born Jan. 14, 1847, in Medway. He enlisted on the seventh day of September, 1864, and was mustered into the United States service on the same day, as a private of Co. A, 4th Regt. Mass. Cav. Though he appears from the state records as from Medway, of which town he was a resident, he is known to have been counted upon the quota of North Bridgewater. He served for a time as orderly to Gen. Terry. After the capitulation of Gen. Lee and his army, he served on the provost guard in Richmond, Va. He was mustered out June 26, 1865, by reason of the close of the war.

CHARLES E. WILLIAMS, son of Charles and Mary A. Williams, was born Feb. 27, 1829, in Franklin, Mass. He enlisted Sept. 10, 1864, and was mustered into service on the same day, for one year, as a private of Co.

C, 61st Regt. Mass. Vols. He took part in the engagements before Peters-burg, Va., in the spring of 1865. He was mustered out June 4, 1865.

GEORGE H. WILLIAMS, son of Nathan and Esther B. Williams, was born Dec. 26, 1837, in Wrentham. He enlisted in Medway in May, and was mustered into the United States service May 25, 1861, for three years, as a private of Co. E, 2d Regt Mass Vols. He states that he was constantly with his regiment during his service. He was in the engagement at Win-chester, Va., May 25 ; at Cedar Mountain he was not engaged, being pros-trated by a sun stroke, but took part in the battle of Antietam, Sept. 17, 1862. April 28, 1863, he was detailed as Company musician, and so continued to the end of his term. During the subsequent actions he was assigned to duty in the corps hospital, or to attend upon the Assistant Surgeon. He was mustered out May 28, 1864, his term having expired

HORACE J. WILMARTH, son of Horace and Julia Wilmarth, was born Sept. 27, 1844, in Medway. He was mustered into the United States ser-vice Aug. 24, 1861, for three years, as a private of Co G, 18th Regt Mass Vols. He was in the siege of Yorktown, Va., where his regiment was under fire nearly every day from April 11 to May 5, 1862. At the time of the second Bull Run he was sick in the hospital. He was in the battle of Antietam, September 17, Shepherdstown, September 20, Fredericksburg, Dec 13, 1862, where the regiment lost nearly fifty per cent. in killed, wounded, and missing, at Chancellorsville, May 2 and 3, 1863 ; at Gettys-burg he was not engaged, having been detailed as guard for the wagon train, and at Rappahannock Station, Nov. 7, 1863. Feb 8, 1864, he re-enlisted in the field, for another term of three years. At the battle of the Wilderness, May, 1864, he was detailed as provost guard, and continued in that position until the end of his service. Though his position was always in the rear, he was under fire in most of the engagements in which his regi-ment took part afterwards These were at Laurel Hill, May 9, Spottsyl-vania, May 23, skirmish at Shady Grove Road, May 30, Tolopotomy, June 1, Cold Harbor, June 3 to 5, and before Petersburg, from June 19 to July 20, at which time the regiment was mustered out, the recruits and reenlisted men being organized as the 10th Battalion. Afterwards was in the engage-ment at the Weldon Railroad, August 21, and at Peeble's Farm, Sept. 30, 1864. Soon after this the battalion was consolidated with the 32d Mass Inf., and was engaged at Boydtown Road, or Gravelly Run, and in other engage-ments in the vicinity of Petersburg, Va., in March and April, 1865. He was mustered out June 29, 1865, by reason of the close of the war.

JOHN WINTER, at the age of twenty-four years, residence unknown, en-listed, and was mustered into the United States service Dec. 12, 1862, as bugler of Co. C, 2d Regt. Mass. Cav., and accredited to Medway. By the state record he appears to have deserted Dec. 22, 1862.

EMORY WOOD, son of Levi W and Sophronia J. Wood, was born May 7, 1846, in Medway. He enlisted and was mustered into service March 15, 1865, as a private of Co. B, 1st Regt. R. I. Cav He was mustered out Aug. 3, 1865, by a special order from the War Department.

HENRY A. WOOD, son of George A. and Elvira H. Wood, was born July 3, 1843, in Walpole. He enlisted July 23, and was mustered into ser-vice July 28, 1863, for three years, as a private of Co. D, 35th Regt. Mass.

Vol. Inf. He was in the battle of South Mountain, Va., Sept. 14, 1862, when he was wounded in the arm, the ball lodging near the elbow joint. He was discharged in consequence, Jan. 23, 1863. He enlisted again in unassigned detachment Vet. Res. Corps, and was mustered into service Aug. 10, 1863, for three years. He was accredited to the town of Sandisfield, Mass., and discharged for disability Dec. 8, 1864, from Depot Camp, Vet. Res. Corps, Clifton, D. C.

LEVI PRESTON WOOD, son of Levi W. and Sophronia J. Wood, was born in 1838, in Medway. He was mustered into the United States service Oct. 9, 1861, as a private of Co. L, 1st Regt. Mass Cav. He was at the time living in the town of Westport, but was accredited to the town of Medford He died of disease Sept. 10, 1862, in Beaufort, S. C.

DANIEL S WOODMAN, son of James and Lydia D. Woodman, was born April 12, 1842, in Kennebunk, Me. He enlisted in Medway in August, and was mustered into service at Readville, Sept. 13, 1862, for nine months, as a private of Co. B, 42d Regt. Mass. Vol. Militia. He was in the engagement at Lafourche Crossing, La., June 21, 1863, and was dangerously wounded through the right lung and in the right hand. On the evacuation of the place, he fell into the hands of the enemy. The hospital was a rough building without beds, and he lay for four weeks with only a tent canvas upon the board floor, being compelled also by the nature of his wound to remain constantly upon the same side. His sustenance during this time consisted of corn bread and water. After the rebel forces withdrew, on the fall of Port Hudson, he was taken and cared for by a planter in the vicinity and received more considerate treatment. July 30 he was cheered by the appearance of Sergeant E. A. Jones, and Private A. E. Bullard, who had come in search of him and by whom he was conveyed to Algiers, and the next day started for Massachusetts, where he was mustered out Aug. 20, 1863 He is an efficient constable and collector of town taxes.

WILLIAM P. WYMAN, at the age of twenty-one years, residence unknown, enlisted and was mustered into service Oct. 31, 1864, for one year, as a private of Co. F, 2d Regt. Mass. Cav., and accredited to Medway. He was mustered out July 20, 1865, at the expiration of his service

JAMES G. YOUNG, at the age of twenty-three years, family residence Lebanon, Me., was mustered into the United States service May 4, 1864, for three years, as a Corporal of 21st Co., 2d Battalion Vet Res. Corps, and accredited to Medway. He formerly served in Co C, 16th Regt. Mass. Vols.

ORSON D. YOUNG, son of Nathaniel and Betsey (Palmer) Young. was born in Windsor, Vt. He enlisted at the age of thirty-seven years, in Medway, in August, and was mustered into the United States service Sept 13, 1862, for nine months, as a private of Co. B, 42d Regt. Mass. Vol. Militia. He was in the engagement at Brashear City, La., June 23, 1863, and was taken prisoner. He was paroled June 26, and mustered out of service Aug. 20, 1863, his term having expired. He removed to the West and settled in Oregon Territory where he now resides.

ROBERT O. YOUNG, son of Nathaniel and Betsey (Palmer) Young, was born Oct. 13, 1832, in Windsor, Vt. He was mustered into the United States service Feb. 26, 1864, as a private of Co. D, 3d Regt. Mass. Cav. He joined his regiment at Morganzia Bend, La., about June 1, 1864. He was in the battles of Opequan, Fisher's Hill, and Cedar Creek, besides many skir-mishes and raids. After the close of hostilities he was detailed for duty at Corps Head-quarters and so continued to the end of his term. He was mus-tered out Nov. 28, 1865, at Fort Leavenworth, Kansas. He had previously served a term of three months in Co. H, 1st R. I. Inf., being mustered into service April 17, and mustered out Aug. 1, 1861. He took part, July 21, 1861, in the first battle of Bull Run, Va.

THIS RECORD OF THE UNION SOLDIERS was prepared largely some years since, according to the vote of the town, by William Daniels, Esq., under the direction of the selectmen. To it some additions have been made in preparation for printing in this volume. This record concludes the military history of the town.

THE MISCELLANEOUS ITEMS.

THE FIRST BIRTH in the town of Medway occurred January 3, 1714; an infant son was born to John and Esther (Breck) Richardson, whom they named Samuel, doubtless hoping that he might be like the goodly son of Hannah of Bible history, whose name he bore. This Samuel Richardson must have been both very wise and very good if years are an index of such qualities, for he lived to be ninety-seven years old. He died February 10, 1811, in Wrentham, Mass.

WITCHCRAFT. The Rev. Joseph Baxter, of Medfield, on occasion went to reprove Goody Lincoln for the sin of practicing witchcraft. On his return home he felt a strange pain in his leg which was attributed to her evil influence.

THE MEDWAY POUND, in 1730, was at the north end of Long Plain.

THE SALE OF A SLAVE. The Rev. Nathan Bucknam, being hard pressed for money, and the town refusing to increase his salary, sold to one of his parishioners his slave, London, as appears by the following receipt:

"*Medway, June 18, 1736. Received of Jasper Adams the sum of one hundred and forty pounds for a negro boy named London, being in full.*

"£140-0-0. Per me,

"NATHAN BUCKNAM."

A SLAVE BUYS HIS LIBERTY. Caesar Hunt, *alias* Peter Warren, paid to Joseph Lovell the sum of £13, 6s., 8d. for his freedom, on condition that if, in the judgment of the selectmen of Medway, he be idle or prodigal of his time and interest so that there be danger of his becoming a burden on the estate he be remanded to the condition of servitude.

The following is a copy of the legal instrument of emancipation:

"Know all men by these Presents that I, Joseph Lovell of Medway in the County of Suffolk and Province of the Massachusetts Bay in New England yeoman for divers and good and valuable considerations me thereunto moving, as well as in consideration of the sum of thirteen pounds six shillings and eightpence paid me by Caesar Hunt *alias* Peter Warren a molatto slave, late the Property of my Father Joseph Lovell late of Medway afore[sd] deceased, and from him descended to me, have released and acquitted and discharged and by these Presents do freely fully and forever release the s[d] Caesar Hunt, *Alias* Peter Warren from my service and the service of my Heirs forever: so that neither I myself, my heirs, exec[tr] or any other Person or Persons for me or Them shall ever hereafter claim any Right, Title, Interest in the Person or the

Service of the said Molatto, Provided, nevertheless, that if the s^d Caesar Hunt, *alias* Peter Warren shall in the judgment of the Select Men of the town of Medway for the time being, at any Time hereafter become idle and prodigal of his Time and Interest so that there shall appear danger of his becoming a burden upon my estate or that of my heirs, I hereby reserve to myself and Heirs the Power at the advise and by the Direction of the Select Men of Medway for the time then being to remand s^d Caesar Hunt, *alias* Peter Warren to our service and to command Him in such a manner as to prevent his becoming an Incumbrance upon our estate, but during his good Behaviour in the opinion of the Select Men afores^d He is to all Intents and Purposes emancipated or set free from all obligations to me and mine forever by these Presents.

"In witness whereof I have hereunto set my Hand and Seal this . .   Day of . . . in the ninth year of the Reign of King George the Third Anno Domini 1769.   Signed Sealed and Delivered."

The above was duly executed and the said Caesar Hunt, *alias* Peter Warren, became a freedman and was never remanded to slavery. He removed to Medfield, where he died. Upon his tombstone is this honorable inscription: " *A respectable man of color* "

THE RELATION OF JAMES PENIMAN who was received to full communion Oct. 19, 1735

" I desire to be very thankful to the God of all grace y^t my Lot hath been cast in such a Place where I have enjoyed ye clear light of the Glorious Gospel, and have had it from time to time dispensed unto me, and altho I have reason to mourn, & be ashamed y^t I sate so long unprofitably under it, and was no more benefitted thereby, yet I have reason to be thankful y^t God hath as I hope been setting home his word, & sanctifying his Providences unto me, the Deaths of others have been awakening to me, and I have been brought thereby to consider how it would have been with me if I had been taken away when they were, and I have been brought to see ye necessity of my making hast to prepare for my own death   And those words were awakening to me in Prov 29. 1 He y^t being often reproved, hardeneth his neck shall suddenly be destroyed and that without remedy   And I have been awakened to see myself in a lost, undone, and perishing condition, & y^t I must unavoidably be destroyed forever without an interest in christ. I have had such a discovery of sin made unto me as y^t I think I can say y^t my sins are my greatest burden   And I have had such discoveries of christ made unto me in his beauty & glory in his fulness, and sufficiency as y^t I hope I prize him above every thing else, and hearing his gracious calls to sin burdened sinners to come unto him who saith in Matth 11 28 29. 30   Come unto me all ye y^t labor & are heavy Laden and I will give you rest, Take my yoke upon you & learn of me   for I am meek & lowly in heart & ye shall find rest unto your souls for my yoke is easie & my burden is light, and assures them y^t He will reject none of those who come to Him   John 6 37 Him y^t cometh to me I will in no wise cast out   I hope I have been made willing to come to him and accept of him on his own terms & commit my soul to him and put all my trust & confidence in him for salvation and put my neck under his yoke   and finding a need of more of X and of his benefits desire to wait on him in all ye ways of his appointment for communion with him, and communications of grace from him and therefore offer myself to this church with an humble dependence on the grace of christ to fit and prepare me to enjoy him aright in every ordinance y^t in ye way of his ordinances I may be prepared for the enjoyment of communion & fellowship with him in ye heavenly world forevermore.

THANKSGIVING DAYS. " 1743 Oct 13 Thanksgiving Day for ye Kings victory." " 1745 July 18 Thanksgiving Day for victory of Cape Briton."

THE MEETING-HOUSE BURNED. " Jan. ye 18 1748–9 the Medway Meeting House was Burnt " " 1749 ye 27 of April East Precinct Meeting House raised and 1749 ye 21st of May it was preached in."

FROM THE DIARY OF JOHN ELLIS. " May 19, 1780 extraordinary

darkness prevailed over the earth, which continued from 9 o'clock in the morning to 2 o'clock in the afternoon and no eclipse was known to intervene."

"Nov. 2, 1783 Rev. N Bucknam 80 years of age to-day."

"Dec. 9, 1786 a terrible snow storm in which 13 persons were cast away on Lovell's island, Boston Harbour. Several were from Wrentham, Franklin, and Sherborn. They were all frozen to death. Theodore Kingsbury of Franklin was not dead when found but died on Thursday, Dec. 21, in Boston and was brought to Franklin Dec. 25, 1786 for burial "

" June 2, 1789, Raised Medfield Meeting House to-day."

"REVOLUTIONARY CLAIM. I certify that in conformity with the Law of the United States of the 18th of March 1818 SIMPSON JONES late a private in the Army of the Revolution is inscribed on the Pension List, Roll of Massachusetts Agency, at the rate of eight dollars per month on the twenty-seventh day of April one thousand eight hundred and nineteen

"GIVEN at the War office of the United States this fourteenth day of July one thousand eight hundred and nineteen.

[SEAL]   (Signed) J C. CALHOUN, *Secretary of War.*"

MR. EDWARD FENNESSY, elected in 1882, was the first Irishman who ever held the office of selectman in the town of Medway

DRINKING AND DRUNKENNESS. About 1816 the Rev. Jacob Ide, pastor of the Second Church of Christ, requested the selectmen to canvass the town to ascertain the number of drunkards. The result showed that there were twenty-five men who would improve every opportunity to drink, and would become so drunk as to abuse their families. That there were forty-two men who would become intoxicated often, but not such beastly drunkards as the first class, and that there were eighty-four men in a fair way to become drunkards. These three classes making a total of one hundred and fifty-one men who were already or would soon become drunkards, out of a population of about fourteen hundred, including men, women, and children. Certainly seventy years have done something to cure intemperance.

A MONUMENT ERECTED TO THE MEMORY OF THE REV. DAVID SANFORD IN 1860 Upon the completion of this monument commemorative services were held, Tuesday, October 2, 1860, in the meeting-house of the Second Church of Christ in honor of the Rev. David Sanford who was for thirty-seven years, 1773–1810, the revered and beloved pastor of that church. There were present more than one hundred of the Rev. Mr. Sanford's lineal descendants out of the whole three hundred and more living, and also a large congregation gathered from the parish and the surrounding towns.

The Rev. Samuel H Smith, of New Jersey, a great-grandson of the honored dead, offered the prayer of invocation and read the Scriptures.

The Rev. Stephen Sanford Smith, of Warren, Mass., a grandson, offered the prayer preceding the address.

The Rev. Jacob Ide, D. D, the immediate successor of the Rev. Mr. Sanford, and in the forty-sixth year of his pastorate, made a most appropriate commemorative address.

The Rev. Abner Morse, of Boston, who in early life was a parishioner and hearer of the Rev. Mr. Sanford, gave some very interesting reminiscences of him and of the olden time

The Rev Henry M. Dexter, of Boston, offered the concluding prayer. After this service a procession was formed and marched to the cemetery and assembled near the monument where prayer was offered, an original hymn sung, and the benediction pronounced. The family connections then repaired to a hall in the Village and partook of a collation, after which brief addresses were made.

THE FIRST BURIAL in Oakland Cemetery was that of Mrs. Mary Darling who died October 26, 1865, at the age of 102 years, five months, and ten days, probably the oldest person who ever died in the town.

CENTENNIAL CELEBRATION, July 4, 1876, in Shumway's Grove, West Medway. Charles H. Deans, Esq , president of the day. Exercises : Prayer by the Rev. E. O Jameson. The reading of the Declaration of Independence by the Hon M. M. Fisher Oration by the Rev. S. J. Axtell. Music by the West Medway Band. After these exercises a collation was furnished, and in the evening there were fireworks.

A MEMORIAL SERVICE was held September 26, 1881, in Sanford Hall, commemorative of the death of PRESIDENT JAMES A. GARFIELD, which occurred September 19, preceding The following account of the occasion was published in the local paper of that date :

" Abram S Harding, Esq , president of the day, read the proclamation of Governor Long Hon. M M. Fisher, chairman of the committee on resolutions, then read the resolutions of the committee, which were unanimously adopted The Rev. John E. Burr of the Baptist Church of West Medway invoked divine blessing, which was followed by response by the choir, with E L Holbrook, Esq , of East Medway at the organ. The Rev John C Smith of the West Medway Methodist Church read from the Scriptures. A quartette, consisting of Mrs Dr Kelsey, Mrs G M. Richardson, Mr. James M Grant, and a gentleman from Middleboro, rendered a selection Addresses were then made by the Rev S J. Axtell, of New Orleans, formerly of West Medway, and the Rev. R. K Harlow of the Village Church, which were followed by singing by the congregation, of the funeral hymn, composed for the occasion by Dea. Anson Daniels, of West Medway, and sung to the tune of Hebron, as follows

" O God, beneath these autumn skies,
With heads uncovered, weeping eyes,
And banners trailing in the dust,
A nation stands before the Just.

" In all his nobleness he died;
His virtue, courage, patience tried :
The mighty head, the loving breast
Have ceased to throb at Thy behest

" No aid from human hands can come,
The mighty fall, the wise are dumb,
From North to South, from sea to sea,
Our yearning hearts still turn to Thee

" Walk Thou upon this troubled sea,
The ship of Freedom, keep it free,
And let Thy benediction fall
On widow, fatherless,— on all.

" The Rev James M Bell, of the Second Church of Christ, West Medway, offered prayer; singing by the congregation of "God save the State," tune "America " Benediction by the Rev Mr Shields, of West Medway.

" On the platform, besides those mentioned, were the committee on resolutions : Messrs. M. M Fisher, C. H. Deans, E H Holbrook, committee of arrangements . Messrs. M C. Adams, C. F. Daniels, J M. Daniels, selectmen, and Mr. Edward Fennessey. Mr. Henry B Woodman was marshal, and Messrs J. Tuttle, S E Howard, A. I. Fiske, and M Brennan, aids, the ushers were Messrs Clark P Harding, Edward S Harding, Frank W. Clark, and George W Whiting

" All those connected with the services wore black crape upon the left arm. The Rev. E. O Jameson, of East Medway, was expected to be present, but was detained at home by the illness of his only son, whose death occurred the following Friday "

WINTER BLOSSOMS.

The following lines were written by Miss Mary B. Richardson, of East Medway, during her last illness, which was long and painful, and terminated in her death, September 15, 1881. She endured her suffering with great fortitude and submission, patiently and cheerfully breathing ever this prayer, "God's will be done":

I looked from my window, the landscape was dreary,
　The brooklet was ice-bound, the orchard was bare,
The meadows and fields with pure snow-crystals glistened,
　But the beauty was lifeless, not a blossom was there.

The day was fast waning, the sun shone but feebly,
　There was chill in the air, there was frost on the pane,
And I wished as the sun sank behind a huge snowbank—
　I wished, how I wished it was summer again.

My chamber grew dark, as the soft winter twilight
　Slipped hurriedly down the horizon, as though
It, too, felt the chill of the landscape, and hastened
　To follow the sunshine and bask in its glow.

I turned with a moan on my pillow, and murmured,
　My life is all winter; its blossoms laid low;
Its brooklets of usefulness ice-bound; the meadow,
　The fields I would cultivate, covered with snow.

The winter of sickness has come to me early,
　Its pain and its suffering, like ice and like snow
Freeze from my heart the sweet bloom's rejoicing;
　Oh! might I the summer of health again know.

Through the darkness came a footstep,
　A gentle hand fell on my brow,
A voice in low and tender accents
　Asked "How's my little Mary now?"

Then a little talking followed:
　Trivial chats on subjects small—
As household matters, books, and papers.
　And stories we could both recall.

Trivial words and lightly spoken,
　But when left alone again,
Spring seemed near, the winter broken,
　Warmed with love the chilly pane.

And I thought, here is one floweret,
　Sister's love still blossoms sweet,
Then the love of father, mother,
　Rose this other love to meet.

Love of friends came crowding onward,
　Sympathy and tender care;
Kindly words from almost strangers;
　Gifts of flowers and viands rare.

Burdens borne for me by others,
　Self-sacrifice, though gladly given,
Making souls like spirit flowers, 　[ven.
　Which budding here, will bloom in Hea-

In my own heart now are budding,
　Flowers which may in time expand,
Gratitude and resignation
　Planted by a Father's hand.

Trust and love of human nature,
　Hope, which ever is a gain;
Praise the Lord for all the blessings
　Plucked in winter's cold and rain.

THE CEMETERIES.

"*Beneath those rugged elms, that yew tree's shade,*
Where heaves the turf on many a mouldering heap,
Each in his narrow cell forever laid,
The rude forefathers of the hamlet sleep."

THE OLD CHURCHYARD.

THE most ancient burial-place for the dead was located in the easterly part of the town. Some years before the incorporation of the town of Medway under date of March 4, 1700, the town of Medfield

"*Voted*, That the Inhabitants on the west side of Charles River shall have two acres of land for a burying Place whare they and a committee chosen by the selectmen for that end shall order it in any of the Town's Commons there." Not until some years after was anything further done. Under date of March 16, 1713, "The select men ordered Henry Harding and Alexander Lovell to lay out the two acres of land granted by the town to the inhabitants on the west side of Charles River in the year 1700 for a burying place there."

But before these gentlemen attended to this order of the selectmen of Medfield, the new town of Medway had become incorporated, and at a meeting of the legal voters of the town, October 29, 1714, at the house of Peter Adams, of which Theophilus Clark was moderator, it was

"*Voted*, That the buriing place should be upon Bare Hill sum whare within forty Rods of the meeting house and a commity was chos by the vote of the Town to joyn with the committy yᵗ Medfield have chosen to lay out the buring place who are cpᵗ george fairbanks and Zackri Partridge and John Richardson."

This was the first burying-place in the town, and for many years it remained the only one. It was merely a place to deposit the dead. No attempt was made to beautify or adorn it. It laid open and uncared for until, many years after, a committee was appointed to fence, clear up, and lay it out in lots with some regularity.

Early in the autumn of the year 1714 the plain, small, and humble meeting-house was erected on the western slope of Bare Hill. Following the good old English custom, the early inhabitants, when called upon to part with their dear ones, laid them to rest around their Sanctuary, and to this day their descendants continue to bury their loved ones within the hallowed enclosure, no longer a barren, dreary, and intimidating place, but covered with verdure, set with trees, adorned with flowers whose perfume fills the air ; and the morning carols and evening vespers of birds make vocal the hallowed abode of the silent dead. What spot so dear, so solemnly sacred, as the churchyard of our fathers? While wandering among the ancient tombstones one is impressed with the beauty of the place and the appropriateness of its selection. From this elevated spot the villages of Holliston, Sherborn, Medfield, and Norfolk can be seen, while away to the eastward appear the Blue Hills of Milton. On a pleasant Sabbath morning the mellow tones of the church bells of the surrounding towns can be plainly heard and their chimings are wafted gently and sweetly to the ear. The old houses of the town are visible, while to the westward appears the Village, and farther away towards the setting sun the spires of the churches of the New Grant are plainly seen. In a central position of this " God's acre," standing within a shaded avenue, is a tomb with a granite front, bearing the names " BUCKNAM & LOVELL, 1795."

This was erected by the Rev. Nathan Bucknam and Captain Joseph Lovell, of Revolutionary fame ; a slate-stone slab bears the date of the death of Mr. Bucknam, " Feb. 6 1795 Æ 92 years " Mrs. Margaret, his wife, "Died May 1st 1796 Æ 91 years." It is said that the tomb became filled and there was no room for other interments, and in the year 1845, under the direction of the Hon. Joseph Lovell Richardson, a grandson of Captain Lovell, it was opened, the remains were carefully collected and deposited in an iron box which was buried in the ground in the centre. The vault was repaired and afterward used by the Richardson family as a burial-place until November 10, 1880, when the remains of the Hon. Joseph Lovell Richardson, who died in his ninety-fourth year, the last of his generation in the family, were placed in this ancient tomb, and it was permanently sealed

There is another tomb near by, which was erected in 1797 by Captain Nathan Jones and Abijah Richardson, M. D., the former a prominent citizen, and the latter an eminent physician, and for a time a surgeon in the Revolutionary army. Surrounding these tombs on every side are a large number of mounds, each with its monument or headstone, marking the resting-place of citizens more or less prominent in their day, majors, captains, ensigns, and sergeants, deacons, elders, and good men, also the graves of good and true women, mothers in Israel, no less worthy than their companions Tablets long since covered with moss, and almost obliterated inscriptions record in verses quaint and queer the virtues of the deceased, and the hopes for their eternal welfare. Here is where the forefathers lie with their children, gathered together in family clusters. To this silent congregation the loved of the present generation are being added one by one, and the ancient churchyard becomes each year more and more hallowed by the remembrance of those who sleep beneath the turf,—a remembrance which serves to impress the living with the lessons of noble example.

In the year 1855 a number of citizens, desiring to provide additional land for burial purposes, petitioned and were incorporated under the statute law as an association for the purpose of legally holding land donated wholly or in part by Henry Richardson, located northeasterly of the churchyard and adjoining the same, for the purposes of a cemetery. The first meeting of the association was held under a warrant of John C. Jones, Justice of the Peace, in the vestry of the First Church on the twenty-eighth day of January, 1855. One hundred members signed the rolls and selected lots. A tomb of granite was erected by Henry Richardson, Esq., grounds were regularly laid out, lots surveyed and taken, avenues made, and shade trees set out. This burial-place is now known as THE OLD CHURCHYARD CEMETERY. Within these hallowed limits lie buried soldiers of the Revolution, and also twelve noble men who gave their lives for their country in the War for the Union, whose ashes within our home of the dead make sacred these grounds as a part of "The Nation's Field of Glory!" The names of these Union soldiers are WILLIAM DANIELS, THOMAS MUNYAN, GEORGE H. READ, GILMAN KINGS-BURY, WILLIAM DANIELS, 2d, JAMES MITCHELL, MOSES HILL, SYLVANUS BULLARD, WILLIAM FOSTER, ROBERT MORSE, LIEUTENANT CHARLES DANIELS, CAPTAIN J. D. STOCKBRIDGE

THE INSCRIPTIONS ON STONES IN THE OLD CHURCHYARD CEMETERY.

Captain Thomas Metcalf

"Your friend lies here bereaved of breath
Take warning from his sudden death
And hearken to God's voice to-day
Be ready now without delay
Your death is daily drawing nigh
As swift as wings of time can fly."

Mrs Mehitable Hill

"Imitate her virtues and follow her to glory."

Miss Betsey Richardson

"The time was once, that time is passed
When youth I bloomed like thee
The time will come tis coming fast,
When thee shall fade like me."

A Child

"Her days on earth sweet child were few
She passed away like morning dew
Take warning by her call in youth
And early seek the God of truth."

Mrs. Rebecca Bullen

"The pains of death are past
Labor and sorrow cease
And life long warfare closed at last
Her soul is found in peace"

Phinehas Allen.

"Behold and see as you pass by
As you are now so once was I.
As I am now so you must be
Prepare to die and follow me."

Stephen Harding

"Receive, O Earth, these faded forms
In thy cold bosom let them lie
Safe let them rest from every storm
Soon may they rise no more to die."

Colonel Amos Turner.

"The usefull friend and tender husband dear
With many of his children slumber here
Until the golden trumpet shall be blown
When one and all shall meet before the throne
When Christ descends with all his splen-did train,
The clods will burst our friends will rise again."

Mrs Mehitable Partridge

"While earthly friends stand here and weep
Her tears are ever dry
These sighs shall not molest her sleep
Her spirit rests on high"

Asa Turner, died at 20 years.

"We murmer not whatever is, is right
Yet still we mourn his so untimely flight
Look wistfull on his grave and deep de-plore
His early exit to return no more."

Mrs. Sibyl Lovell

"Time was I stood as thou dost now
And viewed the dead as thou dost me
Ere long thou'lt lie as low as I
And others stand and look on thee"

Captain Henry Ellis

" The church yard bears an added stone
  The fireside shows a vacant chair
Here sadness dwells and weeps alone
  And death displays his banner there
The life is gone the breath is fled
  And what has been no more shall be
The well known form the welcome head
  Ah where are they, and where is he."

Mrs. Cynthia Leland.

" Farewell my Mate
  My children fond and dear
Friends and Physicians could not save
  My Mortal body from the grave
Nor can the grave confine me here
  When Christ shall call I must appear."

Josephine M Adams   A Child.

" Rest little Josephine rest thee here
  Sweet Mortal bud a moment given
To show how bright those forms ap-
  pear
That only blush and bloom in Heaven.

" And tho' the melting tear drop starts
  From parents almost broken hearted
We hope to clasp thee to the heart
  Where tears are not nor friends are
  parted."

Mr. Simeon Hill.

" I with my offspring here securely rest
  God takes or leaves our comforts he
  sees best
Prepare my friends to meet me on
  that shore
Where sad bereavement will be felt no
  more "

Miss Lucretia Bullen

" Grieve not thou dear affianced friend
  That earths fond hopes so soon shall
  end."

Mrs Simeon Richardson.

" The sweet remembrance of the just
  Shall flourish tho' they sleep in dust "

Captain Amos Turner.

" Here lies in peacefull shades relieved
  from care
A Husband Father and Friend sincere
Benign to all a patern and a guide
The Poor who sought his aid were not
  denied
Here and forever his dust secure shall
  lie
Beneath the care of Heavens omnish-
  ent eye "

A Wife and Mother.

" Farewell my spouse and children dear
  I've left this world of pain
May Virtue be your practice here
  Till we do meet again
Farewell, my friends, dry up your tears
  My dust lies here till Christ appears "

Mrs Abigail Daniels.

" My youthfull days soon past away
  Old age comes at last
By slow decay I wore away
  And now my days are past "

Deacon Asa Daniels.

" Around this monumental stone
  Let friendship drop a sacred tear
The husband kind the Parent dear
  The upright man lies buried here."

Mrs Hannah Mellen.

" Decay ye tenements of dust
  Pillars of earthly pride decay
A nobler mansion waits the just
  And Jesus has prepared the way."

Mrs. Angeline Ware.

" Farewell dear friend again farewell
  Soon we shall rise to thee
And when we meet again no tongue can
  tell
How great our joy shall be."

Mrs Hannah Daniels.

" The months of affliction are o'er
  The days and the nights of distress
We see her in anguish no more
  She has found a happy release."

Mr Jesse Daniels.

" Afflictions sore I long endured
  Physicians proved in vain
At length God pleased to give me ease
  And free me from all pain "

John Harding, died, age 19 years

" Blooming youth had passed away
  Manhood's riper years had come
Longer here I thot to stay
  But alas the grave's my home "

Miss Caroline E. Munyan.

" She has gone to heaven before us
  But she turns and waves her hand
Pointing to the glories o'er us
  In that happy spirit land "

22

Miss Esther Lovell	*Mrs Abigail Hammond.*
" To Bliss and Life God's love hath surely borne thee Dear cherished one. Nor seek we to retain thee How much we loved how much we miss and mourn thee He knows alone, and blessed be his name God is Love "	" Humble and meek, a lowly path she trod And while she lived on earth she walked with God Good without show obliging without art Her speech the faithful language of her heart Her hope was grace and her delight was prayer Her aim was heaven O may we meet her there."

The Evergreen Cemetery.

The second burial-place in the town was laid out in West Medway.

At a meeting of the inhabitants of the West Precinct in March, 1749, a committee consisting of Eleazar Thompson, Nathaniel Cutler, and Henry Guernsey was chosen to consider and report on a suitable piece of land for a burying-place. At a meeting held April 12, 1750, the committee made a report which was accepted and the Precinct " Voted to lay out one half of an acre of land of Henry Guernsey next to that land he gave to this precinct. Said land to be for a burying-place, and the price to be £1 1s 4d lawful money "

In this place were interred the remains of many of the early residents of the West Precinct The names of Adams, Allen, Bullard, Clark, Hill, Harding, Partridge, and Plympton frequently occur on the stones that mark the ancient graves

This place was sufficient, with a small addition, to supply the needs of the community till within a few years, when some six acres of land were purchased of Mr. Simeon Cutler a little east of the former place. This tract was laid out into lots and soon sold for family burial places Small additions were made to this tract until more recently the entire tract lying between this and the old burial-place was purchased by an association which caused the same to be laid out with walks and avenues. To this purchase and all the former ground was given the name of " The Evergreen Cemetery "

The Oakland Cemetery.

After a church had been established, business increased, and the population had become numerous in the Village, it was felt that grounds should be secured for burial purposes. In 1860 terms were obtained for the Lily Pond Lot, on Oakland Street, but the purchase was not made, as the War for the Union came on and absorbed the interest of the people

In 1865, without conference with any one, a tract of land was bought by the Hon. M. M Fisher, with the view of appropriating a portion of it for a cemetery It was only after cutting out the dense undergrowth that it was seen by the public to be well adapted to such uses. The proprietor proposed to form an association to prepare the grounds and manage its affairs. Not meeting with a prompt and general response, upon the suggestion of Mr. Orion Mason, Sen., he assumed the burden alone. A petition to the town to allow a cemetery was drawn up and permission granted, and the sum of $300 was appropriated subsequently for a receiving tomb. The grounds were in part laid out and plans made by Mr. Herbert Fisher Keith, a civil engineer, and the cemetery was duly consecrated June 20, 1865, as the Oakland Cemetery, by appropriate religious services, as follows:

The singing of the following hymn:

We meet not now where pillar'd aisles,
  In long and dim perspective fade;
No dome, by human hands uprear'd,
  Gives to this spot its solemn shade.

Our temple is the hill and dale,
  It's shrines these grateful hearts of ours;
Our incense is the balmy gale,
  Whose perfume is the spoil of flowers

Yet here, where now the living meet,
  The shrouded dead ere long will rest,
And grass now trod beneath our feet,
  Will mournful wave above our breast

Here birds will sing their notes of praise,
  When summer hours are bright and warm;
And winter's sweeping winds will raise,
  The sounding anthems of the storm.

Then now, while life's warm currents flow,
  While restless throbs the anxious heart,
Teach us, Oh Lord, thy power to know,
  Thy grace, Oh Lord, our God, impart.

Then when beneath this verdant soil,
  Our dust to kindred dust is given;
Our souls, released from mortal coil,
  Shall find, with thee, their rest in Heaven

The reading of the Scriptures by the Rev. D. Sanford; a prayer of consecration by the Rev. Jacob Ide, D. D; an address by the Rev Jacob Roberts; the singing of a hymn written by the Rev. C. C. Sewall·

With the heart's uplifted prayer,
  And the voice of plaintive psalm
Rising softly on the air
  From an inward, holy calm;—

With a firm and joyful trust
  That our spirits cannot die,
We now consecrate the dust
  That shall o'er our loved ones lie.

Weep we not as they may weep,
  Who their dust to dust shall give
With no hope that from death's sleep
  They shall rise again to live.

Jesus, from his broken tomb,
  Hath ascended up on high,
And hath borne away the gloom
  Else would on the graveyard lie.

Here we calmly leave our dead,
  In the faith that angels keep
Watch around the lowly bed
  Where they unforgotten sleep.

Hope we may to meet again —
  Love and joy in every heart —
Where the saints in glory reign;
  Where the ransomed never part.

These services concluded with the Benediction.

The Messrs A. L B. Monroe, George W. Ray, and E. C. Wilson, were the committee of arrangements and of the appraisal of the lots.

Immediately after the devotional services the several lots were sold, agreeably to certain rules and conditions which were to be kept on file with the plan in the hands of the clerk of the Congregational society of the Village.

The first burial in the cemetery was that of Mrs. Mary Darling, who died October 26, 1865, aged one hundred and two years, five months, and ten days; interred in Lot No. 3, Section A, Wood Lawn Avenue.

The first monument erected was that of the proprietor, the Hon M M. Fisher, upon Lot No. 1, Section A, Auburn Avenue.

The remains of five children were removed from Evergreen Cemetery, April, 1866, and most of the early burials in the cemetery were removals of remains from the same place.

The price of lots has been so low that the enterprise has been far from remunerative to the proprietor, but, nevertheless, has been a source of much satisfaction to him and a great convenience to the public.

The Catholic Cemetery.

The town, in 1876, gave permission to Mr. James O'Donnell and others to lay out a cemetery on Oakland Street, which was accordingly done, and duly consecrated to burial purposes.

The various cemeteries of the town are all receiving from year to year increased attention, until they are fast becoming spots not only hallowed with the tenderest sentiments of remembrance and love, but made beautiful and attractive, and as resorts they preach to hundreds who traverse their avenues of the vanity of life here, save as devoted to usefulness and a preparation for the immortal life beyond.

William T Adams

BIRTHPLACE OF "OLIVER OPTIC."

THE BIOGRAPHIES.

WILLIAM T. ADAMS, ESQ.

To Medway belongs the honor of being the birthplace of this well-known author, whose *nom de plume*, "Oliver Optic," is a household word to the children of America. Mr. Adams is a writer of merit and popularity, having few equals even in these days when the writers of juvenile literature are as numerous

"As autumnal leaves that strew the brook in Vallombrosa."

WILLIAM T. ADAMS, son of Laban and Catherine (Johnson) Adams, was born July 30, 1822, in Medway, Mass. He descended from Henry Adams, immigrant, who came in 1632 to America from Devonshire, England, and settled in Quincy, Mass. Governor Samuel Adams, of the Revolutionary period, and the Presidents, John Adams and John Q. Adams, were of the same lineage. His more immediate ancestor was Edward Adams, one of the earliest settlers of Medfield, Mass., whose great-grandson was the grandfather of the subject of this sketch. Laban Adams, the father of Mr. Adams, first kept a public house in Medway, but removed about 1830 to Boston, Mass., and kept the Washington Coffee House, and subsequently the Lamb Tavern. In 1846 he erected the Adams House, which was named in honor of the Presidents. William T. Adams was educated in the public and private schools of Boston and vicinity, and when a mere lad showed a talent for writing. A school composition, which is a task to most pupils, was to him a delight. In 1841, at the age of nineteen, he published his first article in *The Social Monitor*, which was followed by others. For three years next succeeding 1842 Mr. Adams was the master of the Lower Road

School in Dorchester, Mass., where he won the reputation of a good teacher. In 1846 he resigned his position to assist his father and brother in the management of the new hotel, the Adams House, in Boston. This business was not suited to his taste, and was soon abandoned as the concern failed for the remarkable reason as given in court, " Because they kept too good a house." Mr. Adams resumed teaching in 1848 in the Boylston School, Boston, of which he became the master in 1860, and on the establishment of the Bowditch School he was transferred and held the position of master in that school until he resigned in 1865.

He then went abroad and traveled through the countries of Europe. From this time dates his career as an author. Mr. Adams' *nom de guerre*, " Oliver Optic," originated on this wise : he wrote a poem in 1851 for " The Boston Young Men's Total Abstinence Society," which was published in *The Flag of Our Union* under the heading "1951. A Poem Delivered before the Mutual Admiration Society, by Oliver Optic, M. D." The name Optic was suggested by a character in a drama at the Boston Museum, called Dr. Optic. To this Mr. Adams prefixed Oliver, with no thought of ever using it again. But not long after two essays appeared in *The Waverly Magazine* by " Oliver Optic," which were so well received that he continued to write under this pseudonym until it became impracticable to abandon it. From writing stories for newspapers the transition was easy to the writing of books. The following list embraces the different volumes he has written, in the order of their publication :

1853, *Hatchie, In Doors and Out;* 1854, *The Boat Club* , 1855, *All Aboard*, 1856, *Now or Never*, 1857, *Try Again*, 1858, *Poor and Proud, The Student and Schoolmate*, 9 vols (1858–1866), 1860, *Little by Little*, 1862, *The Riverdale Books*, 12 vols , 1863, *Rich and Humble, A Spelling Book, In School and Out*, 1864, *Watch and Wait, The Soldier Boy, The Sailor Boy*, 1865, *Work and Win, The Young Lieutenant, The Yankee Middy, Fighting Joe*, 1866, *Hope and Have, Haste and Waste, Brave Old Salt, Outward Bound, The Way of the World*, 1867, *Oliver Optic's Magazine*, 9 vols. (1867–1875), *Shamrock and Thistle, Red Cross, The Starry Flag, Breaking Away Seek and Find*, 1868, *Dikes and Ditches, Palace and Cottage, Freaks of Fortune, Make or Break, Down the River*, 1869, *Down the Rhine, Our Standard Bearer, Through by Daylight, Lightning Express, On Time, Switch Off*, 1870, *Brake Up, Bear and Forbear, Field and Forest, Plane and Plank;* 1871, *Cringle and Cross-tree, Desk and Debit, Bivouac and Battle, Up the Baltic*, 1872, *Northern Lands, Sea and Shore, Little Bobtail*, 1873, *The Yacht Club, Money Maker, Cross and Crescent*, 1874, *The Coming Wave, The Dorcas Club, Sunny Shores;* 1875, *Ocean-Born, Going West*, 1876, *Living too Fast, Vine and Olive;* 1877, *Out West, Just His Luck, Isles of the Sea, An Historical Sketch of Union Lodge, Dorchester;* 1878, *Lake Breezes*, 1879, *Going South*, 1880, *Down South, Our Little Ones*, 4 vols. (1880–1885); 1881, *Up the River, Robinson Crusoe* (edited) ; 1882, *All Adrift*, 1883, *Snug Harbor*, 1884, *Square and Compass;* 1885, *Stem to Stern.*

In all, more than one hundred volumes, the aggregate sale of which exceeds a million copies ! This has had no parallel in the annals of juvenile literature.

The elements of this author's popularity lie in his long and varied school experiences. At one time he had 1,200 scholars and twenty-five teachers under his immediate control ; for twenty years he was a teacher, and twelve years a superintendent of a Sabbath School. Few writers have been brought so directly in contact with the rising generation, or have enjoyed such varied observations of child-life. It is doubtless true, also, that Mr. Adams' books owe much of their interest and value to his quick and keenly appreciative mind. In a word, he appeals directly to the living, earnest sympathies of the young, his narrative is sprightly, his incidents true to actual life, and his moral pills are so well sugared that they are taken greedily by the young patient. He aims to impart the lessons of truth and morality, without creating in the mind a distaste for such reading.

It is evident from a perusal of his writings that he constantly aims to make goodness attractive and vice odious; he never allows an unrepentant bad character to appear in any other than a true light. His readers are taught to hate the mean and unworthy, and to love and strive for the good. He once gave, in conversation, as his motto in writing for the young, "First God, then country, then friends."

In 1867 Mr. Adams was elected a member of the school committee of Dorchester by every vote but one, which he cast himself; he served till the town was annexed to Boston, and was elected a member of the Boston School Committee in 1870. He was chairman of the Dorchester High School Committee six years. In 1869 he was elected a member of the Legislature for the town of Dorchester, but declined a re-nomination. In 1870 he went to Europe a second time, and traveled through all the countries of Europe not previously visited, and the books which he has since published show the result of his observations.

Industry and genius are seldom allied; the man of talent seldom plods; he who achieves a moderate success is only too apt to rest upon his laurels rather than keep hard at work for still higher ends, still greater renown. In briefly viewing the leading points in the life and labors of Mr. Adams, we find that he unites these unusual traits in a remarkable manner, and that to-day he is still the same untiring worker as when, a younger man, he had the great future before him, with talent, ambition, and industry as his threefold capital.

Mr. Adams, at the age of sixty-three years, is actively engaged in literary pursuits, his vigor as a writer unabated, and is still the favorite author of young readers in America and in Europe. *Vid. The Men of the Time.*

Rev. Jasper Adams, D. D.

Jasper Adams, son of Jasper and Anna (Rounds) Adams, was born Aug. 27, 1793, in East Medway. He fitted for college under the Rev. Luther Wright, and graduated in 1815 from Brown University, Rhode Island. Mr. Adams studied theology for two years in Andover Theological Seminary and taught in Phillips Academy. He was a tutor in Brown University in 1818–'19, and ordained to the ministry, Aug. 4, 1820, in the Episcopal Church. For five years prior to 1824, he was professor of mathematics and natural philosophy in Brown University, Rhode Island. Professor Adams married, May 16, 1820, Miss Mercy D. Wheeler, of East Medway, who died Nov. 11, 1821, while they resided in Providence, R. I. In 1824 he was called to the Presidency of the Charleston College, S. C., and soon after married Miss Mayrant, of that city. In 1826 he resigned his position to accept the Presidency of Geneva College, N. Y., which he held until 1828, when he resumed the Presidency of Charleston College, where he remained until 1836, when he was appointed chaplain and professor of ethics in the United States Military Academy at West Point, N. Y. In 1840, circumstances making it desirable for him to reside South, he resigned his position, purchased an estate in Pendleton, S. C, for his home, and preached in an Episcopal Church in that vicinity. He received the degree of D D. in 1827, from Columbia College, N. Y. He was a fine scholar and a writer of ability. He published a book on moral philosophy, and was recognized as a man of eminence in the literary world Several of his occasional addresses and sermons were printed. The Rev. Dr. Adams died after a brief illness, Oct. 25, 1841, at the age of forty-eight years. His sister, Mrs. Elizabeth (Adams) Bigelow, widow of Dea. Calvin Bigelow, of Dover, Mass, now resides with her son, Charles A. Bigelow. Esq., of Millis, in vigorous health, and in the full enjoyment of her mental powers, having passed her ninetieth birthday, Sept. 26, 1885. She is the last survivor of her father's family.

REV. EZRA ADAMS.

EZRA ADAMS, son of Ezra and Abigail (Partridge) Adams, was born Aug. 28, 1809, in West Medway. He graduated in 1835 from Amherst College, Massachusetts, and in 1838 from the East Windsor Theological Seminary, Connecticut. He was ordained to the Gospel ministry, and installed April 28, 1840, pastor of the Congregational Church in Surry, N. H. After a ministry of three years he removed to Roxbury, N. H., where he labored from Jan. 1, 1843, to 1850, when he commenced preaching in Gilsum, N. H., where he was installed, March 19, 1851, pastor of the church, in which office he continued until his death, which occurred at the age of fifty-four years, March 20, 1864. As a minister of the Gospel he has been spoken of as faithful and persevering in his work and discreet in all things, the crowning excellence of the man being his cheerful spirit and self-sacrifice for the Master. As a preacher he was clear and forcible, his sermons being the plain and practical presentations of the truth The pastorate of the Rev. Mr. Adams in Gilsum, N. H, continued through a period of nearly fourteen years. He was beloved by his people, much respected in the town as a wise counsellor and a man of tact in business affairs He was superintendent of schools for thirteen years. His ministry was one of usefulness, and his life a great public good. " Of few men could it as well be said ' Behold an Israelite, indeed, in whom is no guile'" Vid. *The History of Gilsum, N. H*

REV. EDWIN AUGUSTUS ADAMS.

EDWIN AUGUSTUS ADAMS, son of Newell and Abigail Fales (Blake) Adams, was born Oct. 21, 1837, in Franklin, Mass His parents soon after became residents of Medway. He graduated in 1861 from Amherst College, Massachusetts. In 1861-2 he was a teacher in West Boylston, Mass. Mr. Adams pursued his professional studies in Union Theological Seminary, New York, and in the Theological Seminary, Andover, Mass. He was ordained and installed, Sept. 3, 1868, pastor of the church in North Manchester, Conn. In 1872 he was appointed a missionary of the

American Board, and stationed in Prague, Austria, where he labored for ten years. He then returned to this country, and succeeded to the pastorate of Northboro', Mass., then recently made vacant by the death of his younger brother, the Rev. George B. Adams. He remained in Northboro' some two years, and then removed to Chicago, Ill., and became the pastor of a church of the Bohemians in that city.

Rev. George Burton Adams.

George Burton Adams, son of Newell and Abigail Fales (Blake) Adams, was born Oct. 4, 1841, in Medway, Mass. He graduated in 1875 from Amherst College, Massachusetts, and in 1876 from the Hartford Theological Seminary, Connecticut.

He was ordained and installed Nov. 19, 1879, pastor of the Congregational Church in Northboro', Mass. He married, Oct. 26, 1880, Emma C. Noble, daughter of James and Eliza Ann (Smith) Noble, of Hartford, Conn. He had entered upon a useful ministry, and was much beloved by his people, when he died Aug 25, 1881. He was succeeded by his elder brother, the Rev. Edwin Augustus Adams, recently returned from a mission to Prague, Austria.

Hon. Phinehas Adams.

Phinehas Adams, son of Phinehas and Sarah W. (Barber) Adams, was born June 20, 1814, in Medway.

His father was a manufacturer, and started, in 1814, the first power-loom in this country, in Waltham, Mass. Mr. Adams learned his father's business. In 1829, leaving school, he went to work in the Merrimack Mills, Lowell, Mass., where he soon held the position of an overseer. In December, 1833, Mr. Adams removed, and was an overseer in the mills of which his father was then the agent, in Hooksett, N. H. Subsequently he was an overseer in the mills in Pittsfield, N. H., and later he returned to Lowell, Mass., where he was for some time a clerk in the counting-room of the Merrimack Mills. In 1846 he left Lowell and became the agent of the Old Mills at Amoskeag Falls, N. H., and Nov. 6, 1847, he was appointed agent of the Stark Mills, Manchester, N. H. This position he held for more than twenty years. Mr. Adams was a director in several banking institutions in Manchester, also a director of the New England Cotton Manufacturers' Association. In 1872 he was elected a Presidential Elector for New Hampshire, and in 1872 and 1873 he was chief on the staff of Governor Straw, with the title of colonel. His only daughter married Daniel C. Gould, Esq., paymaster of the Stark Mills, Manchester, N. H., and his only son was Phinehas Adams, Jr., a partner in the cotton business of E. C. Bigelow, Esq., of Boston, Mass.

"Mr. Adams was a man whose life was based upon the highest ideas of right and wrong. Kindly and affable, of remarkable generosity, he was highly respected by all his fellow-citizens, and his personal popularity would have insured his election to any office in their gift, if he could have been induced to accept it." "His death was a great public loss." Vid. The History of Manchester, N. H.

Dea. Samuel Allen.

Samuel Allen, son of Abijah and Abigail (Maxcy) Allen was born March 15, 1778, in Franklin, Mass , the first male child born in the town after its incorporation. As a boy he developed great versatility of talent. Before twelve years of age he had constructed various articles for use or pleasure ranging from a windmill to a cheese press   His first invention of importance was a washing machine which was a curiosity, used for a time in the family of Dr. Nathaniel Miller.   During an apprenticeship of three years with Colonel George Hawes, of Wrentham, Mass., such were his habits of industry, with an aptitude for drawing, that in his leisure hours he acquired a knowledge of architecture, and fitted himself for a draftsman of the most intricate machinery.   In 1804 he moved to Newburyport and opened an office as an architect and building contractor, where he remained ten years, when on account of the death of his wife, losses by fire, and general depression in business he returned with his family to Franklin, Mass.   He was employed for a year in Medway Village, then for three years in West Medway in company with Captain William Green, manufacturing bass viols and other musical instruments.   Afterwards he turned his attention to machinery, manufactured cotton cards and other cotton machinery, and for many years had charge of this department of the Cotton Manufacturing Company in Medway Village, making some valuable improvements.   He was a great reader, drawing upon the town library for books of useful information, besides keeping himself posted with the current news.   He was a man of great self-control and uniform cheerfulness, made many friends, and seldom an enemy. He was not exhilarated by prosperity, nor depressed by adversity, but maintained a quiet, peaceful deportment through a long and useful life   He was a deacon in the Village church many years.   Deacon Allen died Jan. 15, 1866, at the house of his son-in-law, Darius D. Buffum. Esq , in Newport, R I

Aldis Samuel Allen, M D.

Aldis Samuel Allen, eldest son of Dea. Samuel and Sarah Wood (Aldis) Allen, was born Nov. 13, 1803, in Newburyport, Mass.   He pursued his preparatory studies with the Rev Dr. Jacob Ide, of West Medway, and in Phillips Academy, Andover, Mass.   He graduated in 1827 from Yale College, Connecticut, and studied medicine in New Haven, while teaching music, penmanship and gymnastics in a school for boys, under the charge of Dr. Sereno Dwight.   He practiced medicine three years in Bridgeport, Conn. He married Eliza M. Weeks, of Jamaica, L. I., and died Aug 9th, 1833, in Jacksonville, Ill.   He is remembered by those who knew him, for his musical talent, pleasing manner, social disposition, and Christian spirit.

Charles Coffin Allen, M. D.

Charles Coffin Allen, son of Dea Samuel and Sarah Wood (Aldis) Allen, was born Nov. 30, 1807, in Newburyport, Mass.   He inherited much of his father's mechanical ingenuity, and when not in school, was fond of working with tools in a machine shop in the Village.   Here he made a large brass clock, under the eye of his father, and completed it before he was eighteen years of age, which was placed upon the meeting-house in West Medway, where it gave correct time to the citizens for many years. When nineteen years of age he commenced the study of medicine while teaching school, afterwards attending lectures in New Haven, and graduated from the Medical College in Pittsfield, Mass. He practiced a short time in Uxbridge, but finding dentistry more congenial as well as more remunerative, he settled in 1835 as a dentist in Norwich, Conn. In 1840 he removed to New York City and took a high stand in his profession. He was the editor of *The Dental Recorder*, and a member of the Dental Society, of New York. He married in 1854, Mary Behean, and died May 24, 1857, leaving a widow and one daughter.

DR. ELIAB METCALF ALLEN.

ELIAB METCALF ALLEN, son of Dea Samuel and Julietta (Metcalf) Allen, was born June 16, 1818, in Medway. After leaving school he was a clerk for several years in Norwich, Conn , and in Worcester, Mass. Afterwards he studied dentistry with his brother, and in 1845 went to Georgia. He married, Aug. 5, 1847, Eliza C. Park, of Greensboro', Ga., and resided in Marietta, Ga. His only son was a dentist and died in 1877. His only daughter married and resided in Marietta, Ga.

DR. WILLIAM HENRY ALLEN.

WILLIAM HENRY ALLEN, son of Dea Samuel and Julietta (Metcalf) Allen, was born July 2, 1821, in Medway. In early youth he exhibited a desire to learn dentistry, and after receiving an academic education he entered the office of his brother, Dr. C. C. Allen, in Norwich, Conn., whom he succeeded in that city, and after Dr C C Allen's death, in 1857, he succeeded to his practice in New York City. He was a skillful operator and a high-minded man. He was one of the founders of the New York College of Dentistry, filling the chairs of president and professor, and was for several years president of the board of trustees of said college. He inherited an inventive and mechanical talent from his father, which served a good purpose in his practice. He married, May 10, 1853, Lizzie R Bently, of Norwich, Conn., who died, and he married, in 1872, a second wife, Linda M. Sangree. He died Oct. 23, 1882, leaving a widow, but no children.

DR. ALFRED WHITING ALLEN.

ALFRED WHITING ALLEN, son of Dea. Samuel and Julietta (Metcalf) Allen, was born July 25, 1825, in Medway. He spent his boyhood in Medway; prepared for a dentist with his brother, Dr. Charles C. Allen, in New York, and practiced several years in Attleboro and Foxboro, Mass. In 1853 he went to Georgia, and practiced in connection with his brother, Dr. E. M. Allen, for two years, and then in Norwich, Conn., until his brother, Dr. William H. Allen, required an assistant, when he went with him to New York, and remained until he died in 1869. When ten or eleven years old he suffered from a serious attack of brain fever, which so affected his memory that he forgot everything he had ever known, even the alphabet, all of which he learned again, but more rapidly than at first. This was one of the most remarkable instances of the loss and recovery of memory on record.

Rev. Seth J. Axtell.

Seth J. Axtell, son of Seth J. and Lucy B. (Stratton) Axtell, was born Dec. 18, 1841, in Worcester, Mass. He was descended from Thomas Axtell, who came from Burkhamstead, England, about 1642, to America, and whose brother was Colonel Daniel Axtell, a brave officer under Cromwell in command of the guards at the time of Charles I., and subsequently executed as a regicide, by Charles II. Thomas Axtell, immigrant, settled in Sudbury, Mass.; his son, Henry Axtell, was killed by the Indians April 21, 1676. Thomas Axtell, son of Henry Axtell, settled in Grafton, Mass. He is reported to have said of his two sons: "One was over much righteous and the other over much wicked." Seth J. Axtell, the subject of this sketch, from childhood was fond of books. Having passed through the public schools of Grafton he fitted for college at Pierce Academy, Middleboro, Mass., and graduated from Brown University in 1864. While a member of college he served one year as a soldier of the Union army in the 41st Regiment Massachusetts Volunteers. He pursued his professional studies in Newton Seminary, Mass., and was ordained to the work of the ministry Jan. 31, 1868, and installed over the Baptist Church in Monroe, Mich. He resigned and Dec. 1, 1870, settled as pastor of the Baptist Church in West Medway, where he remained until April, 1878, when he became President of the Leland University in New Orleans, La. He held this position several years, and then became pastor of the Baptist Church in Weymouth, Mass.

Rev. Luther Bailey.

Luther Bailey, son of Israel and Ruth (Fisher) Bailey, was born May 3, 1783, in Canton, Mass., and early united with the church of his native town. He graduated in 1808 from Brown University, Rhode Island. In 1811 he was the preceptor of Bradford Academy, and subsequently of Taunton Academy for some five years; while at Taunton, he preached for some time in Mendon and supplied other pulpits in the vicinity occasionally. In 1816 he became the pastor of the First Church of Christ in Medway, where he preached for many years, and resided until his death. The Rev. Mr. Bailey was a brother of the Hon. John Bailey who was a member of Congress from Massachusetts. Mr. Bailey married Anne Peck, daughter of Elisha and Rebecca Peck, of Providence, R. I. She was born April 16, 1785. After a long and useful life the Rev. Mr. Bailey died Dec. 19, 1861. His wife survived him a few years and died June 16, 1863. The children were Francis, who died in early life; Eliza A., married Horace Baker, resided in Boston, Mass.; Helen M., married Reuben E. Nichols, resides in Philadelphia, Penn.; Charles, married Caroline W. Goodrich, resides in Pittsfield, Mass.

Charles Bailey, M. D.

Charles Bailey, son of the Rev. Luther and Anne (Peck) Bailey, was born Sept. 2, 1821, in East Medway. He graduated in 1841 from Brown University, Rhode Island. He studied medicine and surgery with

Dr. Nathaniel Miller, and was, for a time, the partner of Dr. John Warren, of Boston. He attended his first course of lectures at Mason Street College, Boston, and subsequently had charge of Dr. Miller's hospital for two years, He acquired additional experience and practice at the Chelsea United States Marine Hospital, and finished his medical education with Dr. Henry II. Child, President of the Berkshire Medical College, Pittsfield, Mass., where he graduated in November, 1843, with the highest honors in a school of 175, and was chosen unanimously to deliver the valedictory address. He commenced practice in Springfield, Mass., the same year, in company with Dr. J. G. Holland, familiarly known as " Timothy Titcomb." He removed in four years to Holyoke, remaining there two and a half years. Then, on account of failing health, he was obliged to journey South. When his health was materially benefited he returned to Philadelphia, taking a course of lectures at the Filbert Street Homœopathic College, where he obtained a thorough understanding of homœopathy He then returned to Pittsfield in December, 1849, and commenced the practice which he still continues In May, 1846, he was married to Miss Caroline M. Goodrich, daughter of the late Levi Goodrich, of Webster, Mass. He had two sons, one of whom died while young, in Holyoke, the other is Dr. Edward L. Bailey, who is associated with his father in the practice of medicine. Dr. Bailey, when a boy, had a narrow escape from death by the premature discharge of a cannon with which he and a companion were firing a salute.

Rev. Abijah Richardson Baker, D. D.

Abijah Richardson Baker, son of David and Jemima (Richardson) Baker, was born Aug. 30, 1805, in Franklin, Mass. He pursued his studies in Medway, and graduated in 1830, from Amherst College. After graduating he opened a private classical school in Medway Village. He graduated in 1835 from Andover Theological Seminary, Massachusetts. The Rev Mr. Baker preached in Ware, Mass., West Hartford, Conn., and in Albany, N. Y. He was at length settled, April 25, 1838, in Medford, where he was greatly blessed in a ministry of ten years. He resigned his pastorate in 1849, and gave himself to literary, Sabbath School, and general Gospel work. He received the degree of D. D. in 1870 from Austin College. He labored for a while in the Gospel in South Boston, Mass. The Rev. Mr. Baker married, Oct. 1, 1835, Harriet Newell Woods, daughter of the Rev. L. Woods, D. D., of Andover, Mass. They had six sons, four of whom entered the ministry, one was a physician, and one died in infancy. The Rev Dr. Baker died April 30, 1876, at the age of seventy years.

Rev Joseph Barber.

Joseph Barber was born at the old homestead in West Medway, about a mile north of the Baptist Church. By his own unassisted efforts he prepared himself for the Gospel ministry and was ordained Dec. 5, 1861, the pastor of the Baptist Church in Brewster, Mass. Subsequently he was pastor of the churches in North Uxbridge, Mass., Southington, Conn., Bolton, West Bridgewater and Westminster, Mass, and in September, 1883, became pastor of the Baptist Church in Caryville, where he now ministers.

GEORGE BARBER, ESQ.

GEORGE BARBER, son of George and Bethia (Jones) Barber, was born Sept. 10, 1772, in Medway, Mass. Early in the present century he established himself in the Village, then a small hamlet, as a clothier and wool-carder, a calling that the modern improvements in machinery have entirely extinguished. At that time farmers very generally kept sheep, and the fleeces were spun and woven by the wife and daughters. It was found convenient to have the wool carded by machinery into rolls about three feet long, which were put up into bundles to be used on the spinning-wheel which was then found in most houses, and after being spun and woven, the cloth was taken to the clothier for dyeing, dressing, and finishing. Mr. Barber did his work in the old mill known as the McGinniss boot shop, destroyed by fire in 1883. His work was done partly by apprentices, of whom he ordinarily employed from six to ten, who lived in his family from the age of sixteen or seventeen, until they were twenty-one. These boys had the reputation which they probably deserved, of being a little wild, and if a practical joke was played off on the staid citizens, or a bit of mischief accomplished, it was usually laid to the " Barber devils." Mr. Barber was a kind master, and was respected by those whom he employed. He was interested in all efforts for the public advancement and improvement. Among those who served an apprenticeship with him were the Rev. Dr. Joel Hawes, of Hartford, Lewis

Thayer, of Worcester, Amos Fisher, Otis Nichols, Orion Mason, and Alfred Daniels. In connection with Dr. Oliver Dean, then agent of the Medway Cotton Manufactory, he built the large house, which he occupied until his death, at the corner of Barber and Village streets, afterward occupied by W. H. Cary, Esq., and later by the Rev. Father Boylan. During the latter part of his life he retired from active business, and devoted his attention to his farm, which extended north from Village Street half a mile, including what is now Barber, Broad, and North streets, and the land occupied by the railroad station, and Mr. Hodge's canning factory. In 1826 he visited England and Scotland, in company with Mr. Alexander Wright, who was one of the original members of the carpet company established in Lowell. Going abroad was not as common then as now and was considered a great undertaking. He passed a pleasant season in England and was never weary of recounting the scenes and incidents connected with his trip. He was a staunch member of the Masonic Fraternity, liberal in his religious belief, upright in his dealings, a friend of law and order, and his influence and example had much to do with the early character of the Village. Mr. Barber married Sally Orne, who lived but a few years. He afterward married Lois Whiting.

MRS. LOIS (WHITING) BARBER.

CHARLES ALBERT BEMIS, M. D.

CHARLES ALBERT BEMIS, son of Albert T. and Sarah H. (Hastings) Bemis, was born Sept. 22, 1843, in Ashburnham, Mass. He attended medical lectures in Harvard Medical School, Cambridge, Mass., and in 1872 graduated from the Jefferson Medical College, Philadelphia, Penn. After he had practiced his profession for two years in Spencer, Mass., he came to Medway, where he has had a successful and lucrative practice for twelve years. He has held the offices of Examining Surgeon for Pensions for the United States, Medical Examiner for the State, and served on the Board of Health and School Committee in the town. He married, Dec. 14, 1872, Lizzie Thompson, daughter of John and Ann (Lefferts) Thompson, of Philadelphia, Penn.

JOHN BLACKBURN, ESQ.

JOHN BLACKBURN, son of Henry Blackburn, was born March 10, 1777, in Bradford, England. By indentures now in existence, it appears that under date of May 1, thirtieth year of the reign of King George III., in the year 1790, he was bound an apprentice to James Hamsworth in the township of Shepley in the parish of Bradford, England, for a period of seven years, he then being thirteen years of age. About 1801 Samuel Slater wanted his younger brother, John Slater, to come to America and bring a machinist that understood building and working cotton machinery, and he prevailed upon Mr. Blackburn to come with him. He was in the employ of Mr. Slater for a year, who after obtaining all the information and benefit of his skill at a moderate compensation advised him to return to England. But not wishing to return he went to building a stone wall for a neighbor until employed by the Messrs. Jenckes, of Pawtucket, to build a mill for them, and put it into operation, which he did successfully. Afterward, on the fourteenth day of May, 1805, he entered into an indenture with others to build a cotton mill in Medway Village, of which an account is given elsewhere. Retaining an interest in the mill during his life, he settled in Walpole, June 11, 1811, and continued the construction of machinery and the manufacture of cotton yarn with his son, George Blackburn, until 1828, when their works were totally destroyed by fire. He then retired upon a farm, and died April 21, 1861, at the age of eighty-four years. He had six children, George and Hannah Battel, who were born in England, William born in Pawtucket. R. I., Mary, A., born in Medway, and John Henry, and one who died in infancy, born in Walpole, Mass. His son, Mr. John Henry Blackburn, resides in Walpole, Mass. He has in his possession the ancient indentures by which his father was bound out when a lad of thirteen years. He has also a watch and a large family Bible printed in 1777, which were brought by his father from England.

REV. ALVAN BOND, D. D.

ALVAN BOND, son of Deacon William and Sarah (Waters) Bond, was born April 27, 1793, in Sutton, Mass. He graduated in 1815 from Brown University, Rhode Island, and in 1818 from Andover Theological Seminary, Mass. He was ordained Nov. 29, 1819, and installed the pastor of Congregational Church in Sturbridge, Mass. He married, April 25, 1821, Sarah

Richardson, of East Medway. He was Professor of Sacred Literature in the Theological Seminary, Bangor, Me, from October, 1831, to April, 1835. May, 1835, he was installed pastor of the Second Congregational Church in Norwich, Conn., which office he filled for thirty years. In 1846 he received the degree of D. D., from Brown University, Rhode Island. The Rev. Dr. Bond resigned his pastorate in 1864. He edited an *Illustrated History of the Holy Bible* which was published in 1867. His death occurred July 19, 1882, in Norwich, Conn. A memorial address was delivered Oct. 22, 1882, by Professor Timothy Dwight, D. D., who, in early life, was one of Dr Bond's hearers. This memorial address was published, with a photograph of the Rev. Dr Bond, for private distribution.

Hon. Artemas Brown, M. D.

Artemas Brown, son of Benjamin Brown, Esq, of Lexington. Mass, was born sometime in 1789, in Winchendon, Mass. His father died at the age of forty-eight years, leaving a family of ten children, of whom Artemas was the youngest. His mother died soon after, and this loss, together with the straightened circumstances of the family at that time, doubtless helped to develop very early in life those marked traits of character which afterwards made him a useful and prominent man. By the force of his own energy, industry, and perseverance, he acquired a very good rudimentary education, and about the year 1813 he commenced the study of medicine with Dr George Holmes, of Athol, Mass, afterwards attending lectures in Boston, and finally, in 1817, took the degree of M. D. from the Harvard Medical School He also had the advantage about this time of spending a number of months with Dr. Francis Hayward, of Boston. as a student, and assisting him in his practice, and, under his supervision, having in charge patients in the city almshouse. All this proved of great advantage as preparatory to his professional life Dr. Brown was a man of vigorous intellect, sterling character, of noble form, great physical strength, and a devoted spirit.

He entered upon the practice of medicine in the spring of 1817 in Medway, assuming the place made vacant by the retirement of Oliver Dean, M. D. There are still in existence many most interesting letters written by Dr. Brown about this time in which are allusions to the place, the people, their habits of life, etc., and even to his own fluctuating hopes and fears as to his success in Medway, being a stranger in a strange place. In one letter, dated April 17, 1817, he writes: "My way lies through a wilderness beset by many dangers. I have too much confidence to despair, and too much knowledge of the world to suppose that I shall not meet with many disagreeable and discouraging circumstances in a profession where there is so much uncertainty, caprice, and rivalship"

Dr. Brown, however, rapidly gained the confidence and esteem of the people, his reputation as a careful and competent practitioner was soon thoroughly established, and before many months he had the satisfaction of being constantly employed, not only in Medway, but in many of the adjoining towns.

In September, 1817, Dr. Brown was married to Miss Patience Bancroft, of

23

Warwick, Mass., a very amiable and accomplished young lady, to whom he had been engaged for a long time.

Mrs. Brown brought to her new home a like energy, courage, and firmness of principle which had already established her husband in a successful professional career. For some years she had been a teacher of young ladies in a school in Northfield, Mass., and had attained a culture, combined with a generous piety, which made her not only a treasure to her husband but also an acquisition to the town. For forty years Dr. Brown pursued his profession in Medway and surrounding towns. He was an earnest worker in every good cause. He was a great force in raising the standard of education, an earnest advocate of temperance, and a practical Christian gentleman. His kindness to the poor was very marked. In his profession he devoted himself to toil, exposure, and expense for them, month after month, year after year, traveling over the long, dreary country roads, through summer's heat and winter's storms, administering to the necessities of the sick, unremitting in his care, soothing their pain, sympathizing with their sorrows, and in many cases supplying food and fuel and raiment from his own store, never expecting or hoping for any remuneration. In fact, one-fourth of his entire practice was at times devoted to those of whom he received no pecuniary compensation.

He was not without some personal eccentricities. He was at times somewhat brusque in his manner, and adhered to some old fashioned habits and customs. Not living in a place or at a period where apothecaries were near at hand, he carried his own jalop and ipecac, his "salts and senna" and squills in stout leather saddle bags, from which he compounded his own pills and powders, and paid for them out of his own pocket. He used to boast in his old age of having ridden in the same gig for over fifty years; though some younger members of the family declared that the gig had had in the mean time several new sets of wheels and a corresponding number of new bodies. But through all its transformations the gig still retained a peculiar rattle which was identified far and near by the doctor's friends and patients, and was often the welcome signal in the sick room of his approach long before his arrival.

Dr. Brown was a public spirited and patriotic man. He took enlarged views of civil and national affairs and entered with deep interest into whatever pertained to the welfare of our common country. By the votes of his fellow-citizens he was called to occupy a seat in the State Senate and after that to be a member of the convention to amend our constitution. Both of these important offices he filled with honor to himself, and with entire satisfaction to his constituents.

When the Rebellion broke out Dr. Brown was rejoiced that he had sons who could go for the country's defense. His eldest son was Second Lieutenant in a regiment of cavalry, and his youngest son was an Acting Surgeon of the Union Army during the war. *Vid. The Record of the Union Soldiers.* In the spring of 1855 Mrs. Brown suddenly died, which was a very great affliction to the surviving husband. Not long after, Dr. Brown was thrown from his carriage and injured seriously. Soon after came a second great sorrow, the death of his youngest daughter, and so the light went out of his earthly home. Dr. Brown lived several years but his strength of body and mind gradually failed until death came January, 1863, in the seventy-fourth year of his age, and the good man and beloved physician passed from the evils and sorrows of earth to the rest and joy of heaven.

Of the seven children of Dr. Brown only two survive. His second daughter, Mrs. E. D. Dickinson, of Watertown, Mass., and his youngest son, who is a physician in Hubbardston, Mich.

Rev. Edwin A. Buck.

Edwin A. Buck, son of James and Lydia (Treat) Buck, was born May 31, 1824, in Bucksport, Me. He graduated in 1849 from Yale College. New Haven, Conn., and in 1852 from the Theological Seminary, Bangor, Me. After supplying the pulpit in Pownal, Me., one year, he was ordained, and installed May 31, 1854, pastor of the First Congregational Church in Bethel, Me. After a ministry of some four years he was installed, June, 1858, pastor of the Congregational Church in Slatersville, R. I., where he remained nearly ten years, and was then called, November, 1867, to the work of a city missionary by the Central Church of Fall River, Mass., in which work he is still, 1885, engaged. The Rev. Mr. Buck married, Jan. 19, 1853, Rebecca Elmira Walker, daughter of Dean and Rebecca (Wright) Walker, of Medway, now Millis, Mass. Mrs. Buck died Feb. 16, 1877. There were seven children: Eliza Harding, born Nov. 12, 1853; Alice Lydia, born Aug. 6, 1855; Mary Rebecca, born July 18, 1857; N. Eveline, born March 2, 1860; Isabella Howard, born July 15, 1864, died Jan. 26, 1867; Augustus Walker, born Feb. 7, 1866; Clara Fay, born Dec. 29, 1868.

Rev. Nathan Bucknam.

Nathan Bucknam, second pastor of the Church of Christ, was born Nov. 2, 1703, in Malden, Mass. He graduated in 1721 from Harvard College, Cambridge, Mass., and almost immediately commenced preaching in Medway, at the age of nineteen years. Although urged to settle, he declined the invitation, not wishing to assume such responsibility until he was twenty-one years of age. He was ordained, and installed Dec. 23, 1824, pastor of the Church of Christ in Medway, where he fulfilled an active ministry of sixty-two years, and was continued in the pastoral office until his death which occurred Feb. 6, 1795. *Vid.* The Churches, also, The Genealogies

"*The Will of Nathan Bucknam.*

"In the Name of God. Amen. I, Nathan Bucknam, of Medway, in the county of Suffolk and Commonwealth of Massachusetts, clerk, being weak in body, having frequent monitors of my approaching dissolution, tho' sound in mind and memory, blessed be God therefor, do make and ordain this my last will and testament. And in the first place desire humbly and devoutly to commit my spirit to God who gave it; and commend my body to the dust from whence it was taken, there to be interred according to the discretion of my executor and executrix hereafter named, in the comfortable assurance of a resurrection from the dead, thro' Jesus Christ who is become the first fruits of them that sleep. And as touching the worldly estate, which by the blessing of God I am possessed of, I dispose of it in manner and form following, that is to say, it is my will and pleasure that all my just debts and funeral charges be paid as soon as conveniently can be after my decease.

" Furthermore it is my will and pleasure that Margaret, my beloved wife, have the improvement of the residue of my estate both real and personal, of whatever kind, and wherever found, during her natural life, she continuing my widow; and that the money for which the land was sold to Joseph Wood, lying in Sturbridge, purchased with her money before marriage, and the whole of the plate in the house be entirely at her disposal; and that the negro woman Flora serve her mistress during her natural life. But if that my wife should again enter into the marriage state, that she have no more than the improvement of one-third part of my estate, beside what is above specified to be at her disposal. Furthermore, My oldest daughter Anna Clarke, deceased, having received upon marriage, out of my estate, by estimation, the sum of fifty-three pounds, thirteen shillings and four pence, it is not my pleasure that her children, or any one on her behalf receive any more out of my estate during the life of my wife. Furthermore, My second daughter Margaret Ellis, having received out of my estate, the sum of fifty two pounds, ten shillings; my third daughter Elizabeth Luscombe, having received out of my estate, the sum of fifty three pounds, thirteen shillings and four pence; and my fourth daughter Catharine Dorr, having received fifty three pounds, thirteen shillings and four pence, out of my estate, it is not my will that they, either of them, receive any more out of my estate during the life of their mother. Then it is my will and pleasure, that my youngest daughter Lucy, upon marriage, receive out of my estate the sum of sixty eight pounds, thirteen shillings and four pence, in money or equivalent thereunto, the money being made as good to her as it was when her sisters received the sums above mentioned out of my estate, and whatsoever she may have in other things at the same price it was in silver currency.

"The reason I will her more than the other daughters is the service she has performed, in and for the family since she has been of age. And if she shall remain unmarried and shall choose to go from her mother and provide wholly for herself, it is my will that she receive the aforesaid sum as above specified out of my estate, but if she shall have a desire to abide with her mother and behave well and dutifully towards her, that she dwell with her in the mansion house that I may leave, during her natural life, and then the afore mentioned sum to be paid out to her. And with regard to my grandchildren, left by my son Nathan Bucknam, deceased, viz., Sarah, Margaret, Lucy, Anna and Mary Bucknam, it is my will and pleasure, that over and above what I have given to their father, or they have in any wise received, that, at my wife's decease, they receive out of my estate, each the sum of ten pounds, the sum to be paid to them severally be equal to silver currency. And with regard to my grandchildren, left by my daughter Clarke, viz., Samuel, Mary and Catharine, it is my will and pleasure, that over and above what I have given to their mother, or they have in any wise received, that they receive out of my estate their mother's part in equal proportion with my other daughters, and Samuel to have ten pounds more than either of the daughters, namely, his sisters to be paid by my executor at their grandmother's decease. And as to my negro woman Flora, it is my will and pleasure, that if she outlive her mistress, that she live with one of my children, which she shall choose, if the same can take her, and that there be a suitable allowance out of my estate for her comfortable support if she live to be chargeable, or her service should not answer for her maintenance. And at the decease of my beloved wife, Margaret, it is my will and pleasure that my estate which is not in any way above mentioned, given, or devised, be equally divided among my daughters, namely, Margaret, Elizabeth, Catharine and Lucy, and to be paid by my executor, hereafter named. And in case of the death of either of the daughters above named, before the aforesaid division, it is my will and pleasure, that my executor hereafter named, pay the above dividend to their surviving children in equal shares.

"And I do constitue and appoint Joseph Dorr, Esquire, my son-in-law, executor, and Margaret, my beloved wife, executrix, of this, which, revoking all others, I declare to be my last will and testament. In witness whereof I have hereunto set my hand and seal, this sixth day of October, in the year of our Lord, one thousand seven hundred and eighty-nine, and in the fourteenth year of the Independence of the United States of America. "NATHAN BUCKNAM.

[Seal.]

"Signed, sealed, and publicly declared, by the said Nathan Bucknam, to be his last will and testament, in presence of us:

"*Abijah Richardson,*
Timothy Hamant,
Elijah Clarke, Jun.   True copy: SAM'L HAVEN, *Reg't of Probate.*

"*A Codicil.*

"Be it known to all men by these presents, that I, Nathan Bucknam, of Medway, in the county of Suffolk, and Commonwealth of Massachusetts, Clerk, have made and declared my last will and testament, in writing, bearing date the sixth day of October, 1789. I, the said Nathan Bucknam, by this present Codicil, do ratify and confirm my said last will and testament; and do give and bequeath unto my daughter, Lucy Bucknam, my United States Loan Office Note, bearing date, 3d December, 1790, State of Massachusetts, No. 292, and said note declares that there is due to me the sum of one hundred and forty-four dollars, five cents, bearing interest at six per cent. per annum, from the first day of January, A. D. one thousand eight hundred and one, inclusively, &c., which said note is signed by Nathaniel Appleton, Commiss^n, to be paid unto her, my said daughter, Lucy Bucknam, by my executor, out of my estate. And my will and meaning is that this Codicil or Schedule be, and be adjudged to be part and parcel of my last will and testament; and that all things herein mentioned and contained, be faithfully and truly performed and as fully and amply in every respect, as if the same were declared and set down in my last will and testament.

"Witness my hand and seal this eleventh day of January, one thousand seven hundred and ninety-three.

"NATHAN BUCKNAM.

"Signed, sealed and publicly declared by the said Nathan Bucknam, to be a Codicil to his last will and testament, in presence of us

[SEAL.]

"*Abijah Richardson.*
Timothy Hamant,
Joseph Partridge.

"True copy on file in the Probate Office of the County of Norfolk.
"SAMUEL HAVEN, *Reg^r.*"

REV. AMOS BULLARD, A. M.

AMOS BULLARD, son of Amos and Abigail (Adams) Bullard, was born July 13, 1807, in Medway. He pursued his studies in Leicester and Hadley academies, graduated in 1833 from Amherst College, and in 1839 from the Theological Seminary, Andover, Mass. He was a tutor in Amherst College, from 1835 to 1837. Associate principal of Leicester Academy in 1840–'42, preached in Ware, Brimfield, and Fall River, Mass., in 1842–'43. He was ordained and installed Oct. 26, 1843, pastor of the Congregational Church in Barre, Mass., where he died Aug. 21, 1850. The Rev. Mr. Bullard married Dec. 30, 1839, Mary Ann Durant, daughter of William Durant, Esq., of Andover, Mass. There were four children.

REV. MALACHI BULLARD.

MALACHI BULLARD, son of Malachi and Dolly (Littlefield) Bullard, was born Nov. 4, 1816, in West Medway. He pursued his preparatory studies in Franklin Academy under the Rev. Mortimer Blake, D. D., and in 1837 entered Amherst College, Amherst, Mass. After two years he went to Dartmouth College, Hanover, N. H., where he graduated in 1841. In 1842 he was preceptor of the academy in Atkinson, N. H. He studied theology with the Rev. Jacob Ide, D. D., and was ordained Nov. 19, 1846, pastor of the Congregational Church in Winchendon, Mass. He died May 10, 1849. The Rev. Mr. Bullard married Nov. 11, 1846, Sabrina Bullard, daughter of Nathan and Nancy (Russell) Bullard. There was one child, Harriet Ellen Bullard, born March 19, 1848. The Rev. Mr. Bullard published a sermon on "Sinful Amusements."

Rev. Henry Lewis Bullen.

Henry Lewis Bullen, son of Lewis and Esther (Grout) Bullen, was born Aug. 17, 1820, in Medway, now Millis, Mass. He graduated in 1842 from Dartmouth College, Hanover, N. H. From that time to 1846 he engaged in teaching in Sherborn and West Newbury, Mass.; in Eatonton and Macon, Ga. He then was a student in the Theological Seminary, Andover, Mass., for a year or more, and afterwards taught two years in Holliston, Mass. He was ordained, and installed May 7, 1850, pastor of the Congregational Church in Byron, Ill., but very soon was called to the Professorship of Mathematics and Natural Philosophy in Iowa College. This position he filled for eight years, and resigned in 1858. In 1860 he was installed pastor of the Congregational Church in Durant, Ia., where he ministered for seven years. In 1871 he removed to Moline, Ill., where, in 1885, he resided. *Vid.* The Genealogies.

William Oscar Burdon, Esq.

William Oscar Burdon, (*Estes*[5], *Aaron*[4], *Jonathan*[3], *John*[2], *John*[1],) son of Estes and Abba A. (Warfield) Burdon, was born Aug. 30, 1840, in Slatersville, R. I. His great ancestor, John Burdon, immigant, son of John

Burdon, was born in 1685 in Durham City, England, and when a lad of fifteen years, in 1700, was impressed on board a man-of-war, and in 1704 was at the capture of Gibraltar. Subsequently he landed in America and settled in Danvers, Mass. He married Abigail Moulton of that town and was by occupation a tailor. Mr. Burdon's mother, Abba A. Warfield, (*Thurber⁶*, *John⁵*, *Elihu⁴*, *Elihu³*, *John²*, *John¹*,) daughter of Thurber Warfield, was born Nov. 25, 1815, and was descended from Dea. John Warfield, of Medfield, Mass. Mr. Burdon was educated at the academy in New London, N. H. In the fall of 1868 he was elected master of the High and Grammar School in East Medway. He was a successful and popular teacher for several years, but in the spring of 1874 he resigned and devoted himself to agriculture, and upon the decease of his father, he became the proprietor of the homestead farm in Blackstone, Mass.

WILLIAM HIRAM CARY, Esq.

WILLIAM HIRAM CARY, son of Barnabas and Phebe (Danforth) Cary, was born March 29, 1805, in Attleboro, Mass. In 1811 his father removed with his family to Rindge, N. H., and in 1818 they came to Medway, where his parents died at an advanced age. The family consisted of eleven children: four sons and seven daughters, of whom Mr. Cary and one sister, Mrs. Mary (Cary) Whitney, widow of Charles B. Whitney, are the only survivors.

Mr. Cary received his education in the public schools, and in Leicester Academy. He commenced his business career in the counting-room of the Messrs. William Felt & Co., manufacturers of cotton goods in Medway, and continued in their employment until the age of twenty, when he began trade in the Village store with the Hon. James W. Clark, now of Framingham, Mass., and continued with him for three years. He was afterwards in partnership with Mr. Charles S. Cheever, now of Cincinnati, O. Next he was appointed agent of Messrs. William Felt & Co., in the manufacture of satinet, whom he succeeded by purchase in 1837, and continued in business in the same mill until it was consumed by fire in 1854. Subsequently he bought of Mr. George Barber a mill property in Bellingham, which had been owned and operated by Mr. William White, which he rebuilt and enlarged, and erected three dwelling-houses on the premises. The Civil War depressed the cotton goods manufacture, and he sold the property in 1864 to Mr. F. B. Ray at a large sacrifice. Out of respect to the enterprise of Mr. Cary a post-office was established, and the village has ever since been known as Caryville. In 1866–7 he erected a brick mill on the site of the Eagle Mill in Wrentham, and afterward, in 1869, he purchased the Rockville Mills in East Medway, now Millis, making thread, yarn, and sheetings, and in 1871 he sold out to Messrs. Thayer and Jenkins, who manufactured cotton batting.

During sixty years of his active business life he was a leading manufacturer of various fabrics in this town and vicinity, and for more than thirty years to the value of from $75,000 to $100,000 per annum. He has held and managed a larger mill property and real estate for himself and as trustee for the Barber estate and others, than any other man in the community, and has been identified in promoting the industrial and other interests of the town. He was chairman of the committee charged with grading the famous Air Line Railroad from Dover, Mass., to Woonsocket, R. I. To this enterprise he devoted much time, and as a stockholder used his means freely. He was an active and liberal supporter of the Government in putting down the Rebellion, giving much aid to the Union soldiers and their families In 1861–2 he represented his district in the General Court of Massachusetts, and was called to serve on the important committees on banks and banking and manufactures. His experience and practical knowledge made him a wise and useful legislator.

He is justly entitled to the credit of suggesting the test by which the great question of drainages, considered for more than fifty years in the Legislature, and claimed for the flowage of the Sudbury Meadows by the Billerica Dam, was settled in favor of the dam owners. He was commissioned a Justice of the Peace, and served for twenty-five years, and has been a vice-president and trustee of the Medway Savings Bank from its establishment to the present time. In his later life he served the town in various municipal offices with great fidelity and acceptance. In his religious sentiments he was unsectarian, and a warm friend and liberal supporter of the religious institutions of the town At the age of eighty years he is sprightly in body and mind, and has the high respect of all with whom he has done business or with whom he has been associated.

Prof. George Lovell Cary.

George Lovell Cary, eldest child of William H and Lydia D (Lovell) Cary, was born May 10, 1830, in Medway. His earlier education was obtained in the schools, both public and private, of his native town. At the age of eighteen he entered Harvard College, his principal preparation having been made at Leicester Academy and Williston Seminary. Graduating in 1852, he spent the next two or three years in business, in company with his father, with a view to securing improved health by a temporary discontinuance of study. During a part of this time, he was a member of the school committee of the town In the autumn of 1856 he was appointed to the Professorship of Greek, in Antioch College, Ohio, then under the Presidency of the Hon. Horace Mann. The next year the chairs of Latin and Greek were united, and from that time to the suspension of the college in 1862, he had charge of both these departments. While meditating a residence at Cambridge, with a view to a more complete preparation for the Christian ministry, he was offered and accepted the chair of New Testament Literature in the Meadville Theological School, located in northwestern Pennsylvania. To this position were also attached the duties of instructor in metaphysics and some other academic branches. He has been constantly devoted to this work until the present time, with the exception of one year spent in Europe for the restoration of impaired health. He married March 12, 1854, Mary Isabella Harding, daughter of David and Mary M. (Daniels) Harding. She was born Dec. 27, 1834, in East Medway. They have one child, a daughter, Margaret Lovell Cary.

Capt. John Cole.

John Cole was born in Westmoreland, N. H. He was the fifth of a family of ten children. His father died when he was young and he was at a very early age obliged to work for his own support. A few winter terms in the district school was all the opportunity given him for an education. When eighteen years of age he went to Boston in search of employment, and after a few months, shipped in a merchant vessel sailing from that port. Before his return from a short voyage, he decided to follow the seas as a permanent business, and devoted himself to it with great energy. After a few voyages, he was promoted and before he was thirty years old, was in command of a fine whaling ship, with the reputation of being a superior navigator. His voyages were uniformly successful, and made without loss or accident, giving him, in a few years, a comfortable fortune. He studied navigation, and devoted a great deal of his time to general reading, so that, although deprived in early life of school privileges, he became in this way well informed in works of science and literature. On the sixth of March, 1838, he was married to Elizabeth Shaw, of Westmoreland, through whose faithful counsel and the study of the Bible, he had been brought to a serious consideration of his obligations to God, resulting in his conversion on a previous voyage. After taking one long voyage, he was strongly inclined to retire from the sea, and after a few months at Hartford and Boston, he moved to Medway, and made his home in the cottage under the hill, where he was to spend so many years of his life. Here he lived a few happy months with his family, before starting upon what he meant should be his last voyage. Soon after he sailed, his wife began to fail in health, gradually fading away with consumption, until her death, April 13, 1843. Mrs. Cole's sweet Christian spirit, her fortitude and serenity under the trying circumstances of her condition were wonderful, and her death triumphant.

There were three children; one little girl, Anna, died a single week before the mother, and was buried with her, leaving a twin sister, Ella A. Cole, and a brother, John Adams Cole, who are still living.

This affliction was deeply felt by the husband, when more than fifteen months after the sad event he received the tidings by the way of a passing vessel, while sailing the northern Pacific. Letters written to his pastor at this time show the depth of his grief and also the wonderful support he found in the Christian faith. He was through life an earnest student of the Bible. In 1845 he married Mary E. Wells and for the next ten years of his life resided most of the time in Walpole, N. H., where he had extensive interests and where he took an active part in the church, in temperance, and political affairs. He was a member of the convention that nominated Martin Van Buren as the Presidential candidate of the new Free Soil Party in 1848, and was always an ardent advocate of freedom. Many colored fugitives found a helper in him, when on their way to Canada. In 1854 he made another voyage accompanied by his wife, sailing around the Cape to San Francisco, suffering shipwreck off Cape Hatteras on his return the following year. Soon after, he returned to his old home in Medway, where he lived, until two or three years preceding his death which took place Jan. 6, 1875.

Michael Henry Collins, Esq.

Michael Henry Collins became a resident, in 1874, of Medway, now Millis, Mass. His residence on Orchard Street overlooks a beautiful sheet of water fed by the living flow of the ancient Boggastow Brook. His estate embraces lands once owned by Joseph Daniell and afterward by

THE RESIDENCE OF MICHAEL HENRY COLLINS, ESQ.

his son, Joseph Daniell. The preceding picture shows the site of the original Hinsdell Mill, which was burned by the Indians. The whole locality is full of historic interest. Mr. Collins, an Englishman by birth, has been identified with some of the most useful inventions.

He, in connection with another party, was the originator and inventor of the process of manufacturing what is known as granulated sugar; the author of the drawings of the Chase lozenge machine, from which large fortunes have been made by others; the inventor of a quartz-crushing machine which was of vast service in mining operations many years ago, and many of which were sold for $3,000 each, considered a fabulous sum in those days; the inventor of a system for the ventilation of buildings and which even now is widely used; the inventor of what has revolutionized our method of illumination, namely, the lamp "sun burner"; the inventor of a violin, or what is called the echolin. Perhaps his most valuable invention is the sun burner for the use of kerosene illumination.

At the time of the first use of kerosene, efforts were made by various scientific men, as well as inventors, to make a lamp burner which would avoid heating the chimneys to such a degree that they could not be handled, which would lessen the danger of explosion, and at the same time give the best illuminating power. Many of these men tried it and failed. Mr. Collins, with that originality which has always characterized him and his inventions, struck out into an entirely new field, and after years of experimenting upon and perfecting lamp-burners, produced the device known as the sun burner. It was patented in 1865, but as is usual with good things, his patent was immediately infringed upon, and although Mr. Collins has realized large amounts of money from the sale of his burner, yet the defending of his patent and the prosecution of the infringers thereon, has necessitated also the expenditure of large sums. An effort is being made to have the patent extended that he may yet reap some still more reasonable compensation for conferring so great a public blessing upon the world. Mr. Collins' latest perfected invention, after many years of experimenting, is the echolin, a musical instrument similar to a violin, which for depth of volume and exquisite richness of tone is a marvel. Several of these echolins have been tested by professional violinists who express themselves as being satis-

SOUTHERN VIEW OF THE RESIDENCE M. H. COLLINS, ESQ.

fied that they are, as is claimed for them by the inventor, the richest and purest toned instruments known to the musical profession. Mr. Collins has a most beautifully situated residence, the doors of which are always opened with a cordial and generous hospitality.

JOHN ADAMS COLE, ESQ.

JOHN ADAMS COLE, son of Capt. John and Elizabeth (Shaw) Cole, was born Dec. 16, 1838, in Westmoreland, N. H. He received his academic education in Kimball Union Academy, Meriden, N. H., studied his profession of civil engineering in Boston, Mass., where he practiced it for two years. From 1862 to 1865 he was Field Agent of the Christian Commission, and afterward Financial Agent of Howard University, Washington, D. C. Mr. Cole married, Dec. 15, 1870, Julia M. Alvord. For some years he has been a civil engineer and land surveyor in the city of Chicago, Ill.

ARTHUR WELLS COLE, ESQ.

ARTHUR WELLS COLE, son of Capt. John and Mary E. (Wells) Cole, was born March 2, 1856, in Westmoreland, N. H. He was a student in Phillips Academy, Andover, Mass., for three years, and graduated in 1873. He then entered Yale College, Conn., from which he graduated in 1877. In 1878 he was a member of the Harvard Law School, Cambridge, Mass., and the next year, 1879, was in a law office, and later went to California, where he remained until 1881, when he returned and became associated with his older brother in the study, and afterward in the practice of civil engineering, their office being Room 69, Ashland Block, Chicago, Ill.

JOHN MARTIN CRANE, ESQ.

JOHN MARTIN CRANE, son of the Rev. Dr. Silas A. and Mary E. (Martin) Crane, was born May 24, 1829, in Providence, R. I. He was educated in the schools of Greenwich, R. I., and in St. Paul College, Flushing, Long Island, N. Y. For several years he was a manufacturer of flour and lumber, being the proprietor of mills in Brainbridge, Ind., and in Davenport, Ia. In 1868 he returned to New England and settled upon a farm in East Medway, now Millis, where he still resides. Mr. Crane married Miss Laura Henshaw. She was a descendant of Joshua Henshaw, who was born in Lancashire, England, and who when a mere lad of ten years, in 1653, came to America and was brought up in the family of the Rev Richard Mather, of Dorchester, Mass. Mrs. Laura Crane died, and Mr. Crane married Miss Caroline S. Cogswell. She was a daughter of the late Rev. Prof. William Cogswell, D. D., of Dartmouth College and afterward President of the Theological Seminary, Gilmanton, N. H.

REV. PATRICK CUDDIHY.

PATRICK CUDDIHY was born March 17, 1809, in Clonmel, Tipperary County, Ireland. He was educated in the College of St. Isadore, Rome, attended lectures at the Roman University, and was ordained, in 1832, by Cardinal Zula. He spent twenty years in clerical labor in Waterford, Ireland, where he built a fine church. In this country he has built four churches.

He came to Milford in 1857, at which time he presided over the Catholic parishes of Milford, Hopkinton, Medway, Holliston, Ashland, Upton, and Westboro. During his stay there he built St. Mary's, a handsome granite church, and a fine residence adjoining, the grounds being tastefully laid out. He established a parochial school which has been a success.

Father Cuddihy was the first pastor of St. Joseph Church in Medway, and his ministry continued from 1857 to 1870. He has been thus described: "Father Cuddihy, in his splendid masculine quality, was a man sure to win strong affection. No one, who knew him at all, could know him in a lukewarm manner. His active life-memories ran through sixty years of stirring history. And he was never a dreamer or an idler. He was always deeply interested in the public movements, both of this country and Ireland. A patriot who was of man's estate before his co-religionists were entrusted with the franchise. He worked heartily with O'Connell in the repeal movement. He was a leader among the priests in Ireland forty years ago. He applied his experience, and his large natural ability, in judging of all the later Irish movements as they arose. When he differed from the earnest men who struggled, he always spoke his opinion, but he was never hasty to condemn. And defeat could not sap his hope and confidence. His sympathies were warm for the Land League. 'In Ireland,' he said, 'I upheld agitation and liberty, as I now uphold them in America And in my love for liberty I yield to no young American.' Father Cuddihy represents the grand old school of Irish priests of the early part of the century, men who were famous in all counties for learning, courtesy, and hospitality." On the fiftieth anniversary of his ordination, celebrated Dec. 28, 1882, there was not one of his many guests more erect and vigorous than he who so well knew the duty of a host. On this interesting occasion the Rt. Rev P. T O'Reilly preached a most eloquent and appropriate sermon.

Allusion was made to the work of Father Cuddihy in America, his zeal in the missions of Western Massachusetts, churches built, sacraments administered, religion upheld. Milford was appealed to as an evidence of his labors, the beautiful churches and especially the parochial school which the preacher regarded as his crowning work by which true education would be instilled into the hearts of the youth. The Bishop closed with a most eloquent address to Father Cuddihy in which he said: "Old Man, we have no triumphal car in which to carry you in triumph through the streets, there are no triumphal arches in your honor, there is no crown of laurel with which to deck your brow, but we crown you with the wreath of our love and best wishes for many more years of life to be useful to the Church and the people." Father Cuddihy rose as the Bishop addressed him and the scene was most impressive.

REV. CALVIN CUTLER.

CALVIN[6] CUTLER, (*Amos,[5] Calvin,[4] Jonathan,[3] Jonathan,[2] Jonathan,[1]*) son of Amos and Sarah (Topliff) Cutler, was born Feb. 19, 1833, in Holliston, Mass He pursued his preparatory studies at the Lawrence Academy, Groton, Mass., and graduated in 1856 from Dartmouth College, Hanover, N H. For two years he was the principal of the academy in St. Johnsbury, Vt.

He graduated in 1861 from the Theological Seminary, Andover, Mass. While in the seminary he was invited to become a tutor in Dartmouth College, but declined the appointment. He was licensed to preach Jan. 29, 1861, by the Norfolk Association in Randolph, Mass. Mr. Cutler was ordained, and installed, March 12, 1862, pastor of the Congregational Church in New Ipswich, N. H. He resigned, and was installed, May 9, 1867, pastor of the Auburndale Congregational Church in Newton, Mass., where he now resides. He was for several years one of the trustees of the Appleton Academy in New Ipswich; and for three years a member of the school committee of Newton. He published an article in the *Bibliotheca Sacra* for October, 1869, on "The Brethren of our Lord"; a sermon, "The Christian's Appeal"; and other sermons and articles in newspapers. He married into the family of the Rev. David Sanford, of Medway.

Daniel D Curtis, Esq

DANIEL D. CURTIS, son of Bracey and Eliza (Day) Curtis, was born Jan 19, 1830, in Kennebunk, Me At the age of twenty-one he left his home and went out into the broad world to look out for himself. He was for two years at work on a farm in Billerica, Mass In 1853 he became an apprentice in the manufacture of straw goods of Mr. Walter Jones, of Medfield, Mass After three years Mr. Jones took him into partnership, which continued for twelve years, when Mr. Jones died. From a very small beginning the business had grown so that in 1865 the concern manufactured some three thousand cases. Mr. Curtis, after the death of his partner, found a copartnership with Messrs H. A. Searle and G. F Dailey, of New York City, and managed the manufacture of the straw goods while his partners in New York conducted the sale of the same. It was the rule of this firm to do business only to the extent of their capital, and to avail themselves of all improved and labor-saving machinery. The business was profitable, and gradually extended until they employed some two hundred men and nearly a thousand women, and manufactured some two hundred thousand dozens of hats and bonnets annually. Mr. Curtis resided in Medfield, but in 1884 purchased the straw works in Medway in addition to his large factory in Medfield. Mr. Curtis died very suddenly of paralysis of the brain, on Monday, Dec 7, 1885. The event was widely felt, and the whole community mourned the loss of a respectable citizen and a man of eminent business ability and success. The funeral service was conducted by the Rev. J. J. Twiss, on Wednesday afternoon, Dec 9, 1885, in the First Parish Church, and the burial took place in Mt. Hope Cemetery, Medfield, Mass.

Rev. Samuel Chenery Damon, D. D.

SAMUEL CHENERY DAMON, son of Samuel and Alony (Chenery) Damon, was born Feb. 15, 1815, in Holden, Mass. His grandmother was Abigail Penniman, a daughter of James and Abigail (Clark) Penniman, of East Medway. He graduated in 1836 from Amherst College, Mass, and in 1841 from the Theological Seminary in Andover, Mass. He was ordained Sept. 15, 1841, and sailed as Chaplain of the Seaman's Friend Society to Honolulu,

Daniel D. Curtis

Sandwich Islands. This position he filled for forty years with great ability and usefulness. He was the "Father Taylor" of the Pacific. Early in his missionary life he established a monthly paper called *The Friend*, the first newspaper printed in the North Pacific, and at the present time an influential publication. The Rev. Dr. Damon died Feb. 8, 1885. He was held in high estimation in Honolulu, and his funeral was attended by many of the dignitaries, including the King and the Diplomatic and Consular Corps.

DEA. PAUL DANIELL.

PAUL DANIELL, son of Jeremiah and Pearlee (Richardson) Daniell, was born July 7, 1789, in the ancient Daniell homestead, and his life was spent in cultivating the ancestral acres which were cleared amid the primeval forests of two hundred years before by his great ancestor, Joseph Daniell, the second white settler within the limits of Medway, and whose dwelling was burned by the Indians in those savage days of the burning and massacre of Medfield in 1676. Mr. Daniell still clung to the ancient spelling of the name as well as to the productive lands of his ancestor. He was the last to write the name, Daniell, in this line of descendants of Robert Daniell, although the ancient spelling has been retained in other branches of the family. Dea. Paul Daniell was a man of excellent qualities of mind and heart, a public spirited citizen, and an active Christian. For more than forty years he was a faithful member, and for more than thirty years an honored deacon of the First Church of Christ in Medway.

Deacon Daniell filled many offices in the town and was three times, in 1834, 1835, and 1840, chosen to go to the General Court to help make the laws of the Commonwealth. Whatever position he filled, whatever business was entrusted to him, faithfulness always characterized his action. He was very much of a reader, full of wit, a good thinker, well acquainted with the writings of different theologians, and a great admirer of the Rev. Dr. Emmons. Deacon Daniell died Feb. 15, 1875, in the eigthy-sixth year of his age.

"Mark the perfect man and behold the upright for the end of that man is peace."

THE RESIDENCE OF DEA. PAUL DANIELL.

Mr. Paul Daniell married Eliza Breck, daughter of Daniel Breck, Esq., of Sherborn, Mass. Mrs. Daniell was a woman of rare quality and pious devotion. She survived her husband some ten years, and died suddenly, on the morning of June 16, 1885.

PROF. JOSEPH LEONARD DANIELS.

JOSEPH LEONARD DANIELS, son of Paul and Eliza (Breck) Daniell, was born Aug. 1, 1833, in East Medway. His father gave him the name Joseph in memory of his ancestor who lived on the same spot, and whose house was burned by the Indians just after the burning of Medfield, Feb. 21, 1676. His childhood and youth were spent with his father on the farm; his early education was in the "old brick school-house." He was a regular attendant in the winter but was early removed from the summer school because needed on the farm. He speaks of his early teachers gratefully, as faithful and enthusiastic in their work, and says: "I believe they were good instructors and laid the foundations well." When seventeen years old he was for two terms a member of the Hopkinton Academy, of which the Principal was then the Rev. Daniel J. Poor. At the age of seventeen he taught a district school in "the wild-cat district," in Milford, Mass. At the age of nineteen he entered Phillips Academy, Andover, in preparation for college.

Two years later found him teaching a winter school in Holliston, Mass. He returned the next year to Andover, finished his preparatory course, being assigned the Latin Salutatory at graduation. He entered Yale College in 1856, and graduated in 1860, taking the Townsend Prize and being elected class orator. He remained in New Haven until 1863, taking the theological course in the college, also attending one full course of medical lectures, meanwhile serving for two years as assistant librarian in the Yale College Library. In May, 1863, he was licensed to preach; in July he went from New Haven, taught a few weeks in the Lawrence Academy, Groton, Mass.; from there he was called to the position of principal of Guilford Institute, Guilford, Conn. This position he filled for two years. In April of 1865 he was called to the Professorship of Greek in Olivet College, Michigan, which he now fills, and is also the instructor in German. He was ordained to the Gospel ministry April 27, 1876, and has preached more or less on the Sabbath in the College Chapel, and in other pulpits in the vicinity. He spent from June to December of 1873 abroad in travel and study, chiefly in Germany and Italy. He married, Nov. 26, 1863, Miss Julia Burrage Allen, daughter of William T. and Mrs. Caroline (Gibson) Allen. Miss Allen was for two years prior to her marriage, a popular and successful teacher of a young ladies' school in Medway Village. The children are: Mira Allen, born Oct. 30, 1866; William Breck, born Nov. 25, 1868.

DEA. ANSON DANIELS.

ANSON DANIELS, son of Eleazar and Charlotte (Richardson) Daniels, was born July 8, 1813, in East Medway, now Millis, Mass. His father was a cabinet-maker, and held a captain's commission in the state militia. He pursued his studies in the public schools of his native place, and upon leaving the paternal roof he settled in the westerly part of the town, and devoted himself to art and literature. He was very successful as a painter of portraits, and was an apt writer of verse for occasions. He had a wonderful love for the beautiful in nature and in art. Many public and social occasions were enlivened by his ready lines of verse And many a home is gladdened by the life-like portrait on the wall of the loved whose presence is gone and whose voice is hushed forever. For twenty-eight years Deacon Daniels served as a valued member of the school committee and was in that office at the time of his death. He represented the town in 1866 in the State Legislature. For forty-two years he was a member of the Second Church of Christ, and for twenty-two years an honored Deacon in that body. He was a man who was worthy of, and received, honor and love in all the walks of life.

A citizen of the town who knew him intimately through a period of forty years, pays the following tribute to his gifts and character.

"I have occasionally visited his modest studio and invited friends with me, and always with high appreciation of the works of his art and great pleasure in his intelligent and critical judgment in matters pertaining to his profession. Knowing many of the persons whose portraits he painted, I am satisfied few artists have been more successful than he in reproducing life-like features and expressions on canvas

"In miscellaneous poems for every occasion he has far excelled many whose fame has been much wider. I betray no secret to some when I refer to a poem which has never yet been published, or even known to but few of his more intimate friends. It is of greater length than any which he has ever written, and when he read it to me I felt and said to him it would do honor even to Whittier, and is much in Whittier's style. It is due to the name of Deacon Daniels to publish this with many of his miscellaneous poems in a neat illustrated edition, to meet the demand of his numerous friends and acquaintances for some tangible memorial of his many virtues. But Deacon Daniels was more than poet or artist. He was a man of broad and generous culture, an intelligent and loyal citizen, and a Christian of a type both rare and beautiful. He possessed a discriminating knowledge of religious truth, and while strong in his own convictions he was tolerant of others. In spirit gentle and mild, he was conciliating without compromise of principle, or harsh in criticism of others' faults.

"If he lacked vigor and ambition to push forward, it was the result of temperament and not of mental or moral weakness. While not aggressive by nature he could stand firmly by his own convictions amid great opposition, and was seldom at fault in his judgment of others. His faults, if any, ' leaned to virtue's side.'   .   .   .   .   .

"The clock of the new year of 1884 had struck, when with a choice basket of flowers, the gift of friends, I made a New Year's call, and with the following lines from a lady friend, as a fit expression of our friendship and esteem for one who has since entered ' The garden beyond the iron gate ':

> " ' Where everlasting spring abides,
> And never fading flowers.'

" ' ERINNERUNG.'

" ' Gratitude is the memory of the heart '

"A New Year's greeting, cherished friend, we bring,
And while the merry bells ring out the hours,
We tune the lyre, our sweet songs we sing;
We strew the pathway with the choicest flowers.

" With grateful joy thine artist's skill we own;
Thine art divine, that spans the abyss of death,
Brings back to earth the faces we have known,
And makes them warm again with vital breath.

" From chapel walls the sacred canvas smiles
Sweet benedictions on the place of prayer:
Full many a grief thy glowing skill beguiles;
And fills the heart with angel's visions fair.

" We thank thee for thy generous gift of song;
For others' feasting thou has struck the lyre,
And now for thee we pour the strains along,
With praise too faint, yet warm with friendship's fire.

"Against cold winter's pallid cheek we lay
Our floral offering, bright as bowers of spring;
The good dwell ever in the balmy May,
Though ten times seven the birthday bells may ring.

" Thy spirit dwells in Beulah land afar;
Earth's wildest tempests die away at even;
Earth's clanging strifes no more discordant jar
Thy harp strings, tuned to harmonies of heaven.

" Sweet peace attend thee, and bright visions fair,
As down life's sunset slope thy footsteps stray,
May the good Father keep thee in his care,
Till glory's dawning ushers in the day."

Alas, ere the glad greetings of the next New Year were heard this gifted painter, poet, friend, had passed beyond the pearly gate. Deacon Daniels died Nov. 6, 1884, at the age of seventy-one years. At the time of his death he was a member of the committee appointed to prepare the History of Med-

THE RESIDENCE OF DEA. ANSON DANIELS.

way. To him the editor of this volume is much indebted for valuable contributions which were the result of his patient research and willing devotion of time and labor.

Alfred Daniels, Esq.

Alfred Daniels, son of Joseph and Orinda (Barber) Daniels, was born in East Medway. He learned the trade of a clothier of George Barber, Esq., and continued in that business several years. About 1836 he formed a co-partnership with Mr. Julius C. Hurd, and commenced the manufacture of batting which grew to be a large and prosperous business and both partners became wealthy. He built the house occupied by the late A. P. Phillips, Esq., and his partner a similar one at the opposite end of the Village. Unfortunately, as it proved, the firm became involved in the affairs of the Norfolk County Railroad, which ended disastrously in 1857. Afterwards he formed a business connection with Mr. Edward Eaton, and was in a fair way to retrieve his fortunes, when he died July 24, 1868. Mr. Daniels was a shrewd business manager, of a genial temperament, fond of a joke, a good citizen, who all his life possessed the esteem and confidence of his neighbors and those best acquainted with him. Mr. Daniels was the grandfather of Edwin Alfred Daniels, M. D., of Medway.

Rev. Hiram Clark Daniels.

Hiram Clark Daniels, son of Amos and Sarah (Pierce) Daniels, was born Aug. 10, 1815, in East Medway. He pursued his preparatory studies for two years, 1837-'39, in Worcester, Mass., and graduated in 1844 from Dartmouth College, N. H. He engaged in teaching a part of nearly every year from 1835 to 1845. He graduated in 1847 from Bangor Theological Seminary, and preached several years under the direction of the Home Missionary Society, in Kennebunkport, St. Albans, and Wilton, Me. On account of a severe bronchial complaint, with loss of voice, he was led to relinquish public speaking. He engaged in various agencies, was a bookkeeper, and had the management of a farm. The Rev. Mr. Daniels married, June 26, 1851, Miss Susan M. Cressey, daughter of John Cressey, Esq., of Rowley, Mass.

WILLARD DANIELS, ESQ.

WILLARD DANIELS, son of Japheth and Betsey (Ryder) Daniels, was born Sept. 10, 1803, in Holliston, now Medway, Mass. He was a lineal descendant of Robert Daniell, who settled as early as 1636 in Watertown, Mass., and of Joseph Daniell, who settled about 1648 in Medfield, Mass. Mr. Daniels was of an enterprising spirit, and while his early advantages for education were limited he seems to have put into active use his knowledge, and displayed a remarkable business ability. At the age of twenty-three years he married Mrs. Elizabeth Fisher, *née* Grant, and the same year, 1826, he commenced the manufacture of boots, being the first to engage in that business in the town. He had a small shop about twelve by fifteen feet square on the road leading from West Medway to Braggville. In this small way he started an industry which has proved the largest and most successful and lucrative of any in the town. In 1834 he removed to the village of West Medway, which consisted of a very few scattered dwellings. He erected a house and boot factory. The factory was thirty by fifteen feet and two stories high. Here he carried on the manufacturing of boots thirty years and more. The business increased so that in 1856 he made an addition of thirty by fifteen feet, to his factory, and in 1862 he made a still larger addition of fifty by thirty feet and employed about one hundred and fifty hands. It is no small credit to any man to start a new business and give to it growth and success. This honor belongs to Mr. Daniels. He was a man of great energy and remarkable industry. A day of sixteen hours of work was not too long, and all the working days in the year were none too many for him. He was interested in all public affairs, but declined the honors of office to which his townsmen would gladly have elected him, except in a single instance when he consented, in 1842, to be their Representative to the General Court, and served as a member of the State Legislature. Mr. Daniels did much to promote the growth of West Medway. His enterprise, energy, and great industry gave to him a prominence as a citizen, and he had the respect of all. He died March 25, 1874, at the age of seventy years. His son, Leander S. Daniels, Esq., now carries on the same business and in the same place.

LEANDER SLOAN DANIELS, ESQ.

LEANDER S. DANIELS, son of Willard and Mrs. Elizabeth (Fisher) Daniels, *née* Grant, was born May 8, 1834, in Medway. He was educated in the public schools of his native town, and commenced business at the early age of nineteen years. He was married in 1855, to Miss Elizabeth Hixon, who lived but a few years and died in 1859. Mr. Daniels married in 1861, Miss Adeliza M. Harding, of East Medway, who was a lady of remarkable loveliness of character and greatly beloved. Her death occurred in 1883, soon after a trip to Europe. For more than thirty years Mr. Daniels has conducted the manufacture of boots, in recent years on an extended scale, employing some two or three hundred hands. He inherited much of his father's enterprise, energy, and ability, and has had a very honorable and prosperous business career. Mr. Daniels has so conducted his business affairs as to have the universal confidence and respect of his townsmen and business associates. He was elected in 1867, Representative to the State Legislature, and served

L. L. Daniels

in the session of 1868, with credit to himself, and the approval of his constituents.

DEA. WILLIAM DANIELS.

WILLIAM DANIELS, son of Henry and Mary Ann (Pike) Daniels, and son-in-law of Dea. Paul and Eliza (Breck) Daniell, was born Feb. 3, 1825, in East Medway. Mr. Daniels received a good English education and was a teacher in the public schools. He settled on the farm of his ancestor, Mr. Henry Daniels, who was of the fourth generation of the name in America. He became a prominent citizen, filled all the important offices in the town, and served in the State Legislature two years, in 1863 and 1864, during the trying period of the War for the Union. He held the office of deacon in the First Church of Christ, and was for many years the superintendent of the Sunday School.

Charles F. Daniels.

CHARLES FISKE DANIELS, son of Luke and Jemima (Fiske) Daniels, was born July 19, 1817, in Franklin, Mass. For some years he was engaged in the straw goods business, being for a while a successful manufacturer of straw goods in Lowell, Mass. In later life Mr. Daniels became a real estate broker. He removed to Medway in 1867, and at once was recognized as a prominent citizen. He was chosen on the board of selectmen four years, on the board of school committee three years, and was a trustee

THE RESIDENCE OF CHARLES F. DANIELS, ESQ.

of the Medway Savings Bank. He was associated for many years in the sale of real estate, with the Hon. J. F. C. Hyde, of Newton, Mass. Mr. Daniels was a self-made man, and acquired a good property. His residence on Holliston Street was one of the finest in the town. He was esteemed a man of good judgment, and his death, Aug. 2, 1884, was a public loss.

Edwin Alfred Daniels, M. D.

Edwin Alfred Daniels, son of George and Amy A. (Jefferson) Daniels, was born in Medway, Mass. His father died when he was four years old, and he went with his widowed mother to live with his grandparents, in Uxbridge, Mass. When fifteen years of age he went to Woburn, Mass., entered the high school and graduated in 1870. He took the examinations and was admitted the same year to Harvard College, Cambridge, Mass. Subsequently he decided not to pursue the academic course and entered the Harvard Medical School, where he remained for a year and a half and then suspended his medical studies and taught school in Newton and in Woburn. But in 1875 he resumed his course in the Harvard Medical School, and in 1877 graduated, taking the degree of M. D. He then returned to his native town and Dec. 15, 1877, established himself in the practice of medicine as the successor of A. L. B. Monroe, M. D., who wished to retire from the duties of his profession. Dr. Daniels at once entered upon a good practice and has made for himself a favorable reputation for skill in the art of medicine and surgery. Dr. Daniels has the confidence and respect of his patrons and the medical profession. He is a member of the Massachusetts Medical Society, and for several years has served with great acceptance on the School Committee of the town.

Oliver Dean.

OLIVER DEAN, M. D.

OLIVER DEAN, son of Seth and Edna (Pond) Dean, was born Feb. 18, 1783, in Franklin, Mass. After learning the English branches in the town schools he studied Latin in Framingham Academy and Greek with the Rev. Dr. Crane, of Northbridge. He began the study of medicine with Dr. James Mann, of Wrentham, but completed it with Dr. Ingalls, of Boston, and received his degree of M. D. from the Massachusetts Medical Society in 1809. He practiced in Boston until 1812, when he removed to Medway, but his health broke down under his labors here and in 1817 he left his profession to assume the Agency of the Medway Cotton Manufactory which position he held nine years. In 1826 he was elected Superintendent of the Amoskeag Manufacturing Company, Manchester, N. H., and continued there for eight years. Having by skillful management accumulated a fortune he retired in 1834 to a small farm in Framingham, Mass. From 1844, until 1851, he resided in Boston, Mass. He next purchased a portion of the farm of the deceased Dr. Emmons and made Franklin his home till his death, which occurred Dec. 5, 1871. Dr. Dean devoted his last years chiefly to plans for the education of youth which resulted in the founding of the Dean Academy in Franklin, and which by his ample fortune is well endowed. He contributed largely to the endowment of Tufts College, to the Franklin Library, and to Grace Church, and will be long remembered in Medway as the founder and liberal patron of the Dean Library Association. Although of a different religious faith, he was an early and life-long friend of the Rev. Dr. and Mrs. Ide, of West Medway. While in Medway he was largely instrumental in the settlement of Dr. Ide, whose declining years he cheered with liberal tokens of his regard, and by his will provided largely for his future wants. Dr. Dean first married Caroline Francoeur, of Wrentham. She died Oct. 27, 1866, and in 1868 he married Mrs. Louisa C. Haines, of Wrentham, who still survives. He left no children. He was frugal and temperate in his habits, industrious and sagacious in business, intelligent and persistent in plan and purpose, and rarely failed in their accomplishment. He administered his own estate and has left enduring monuments of his skill and genius for business, and of his regard for knowledge and virtue as essential to all human progress. *Vid. The History of Franklin, Mass.*

CHARLES HENRY DEANS, ESQ.

CHARLES HENRY DEANS, son of Samuel and Hannah Le Baron (Wheaton) Deans, was born May 2, 1832, in Easton, Mass. He pursued a course of classical study in the academy in New Hampton, N. H., for four years, and entered, in 1854, the Sophomore class of Brown University, Providence, R. I. At the close of his Junior year his health failed, and he was obliged to leave college without graduating. His class graduated in 1857. Subsequent to leaving college he studied law with Samuel B. Noyes, Esq., and Ellis Ames, Esq., of Canton, Mass., and was admitted in 1858 to the Bar of Bristol County. He immediately opened an office in West Medway, where he has continued in the practice of his profession to the present time. Mr. Deans held the office of Trial Justice for twenty-one years. He has served on the school board for eighteen years, and is still a member. He was a Trustee of the Medway Savings Bank, and for fourteen years the President of the New England Awl Company. He was also the President of the Evergreen Cemetery Association.

Rev. David Deming.

David Deming, son of David and Mary Deming, was born July 20, 1681, in Wethersfield, Conn. He graduated, at the age of nineteen years, from Harvard College, Cambridge, Mass. He was the first pastor of the Church of Christ in Medway, his ministry extending from 1715 to 1722. *Vid.* The Churches. Nothing is known of his family beyond the following town record: "Jonathan Deming, the son of Mr. David Deming and Mariah his wife was born March 5, 1719." The Rev. Mr. Deming died in 1746, at the age of sixty-five years.

Edward Eaton, Esq.

Edward Eaton, son of Dea. Ebenezer and Amy (Walker) Eaton, was born Nov. 28, 1818, in Framingham, Mass., but came early in life to Medway, and lived with his grandfather until the death of Mr. Walker in 1840. He inherited the estate of his grandfather, where he afterwards resided. He engaged in the teaming and express business under the firm name of Baker & Eaton. Afterwards he engaged in the manufacture of batting with Mr.

RESIDENCE OF EDWARD EATON, ESQ.

Alfred Daniels until Mr. Daniels' death, when he formed a partnership with Mr. E. C. Wilson for the manufacture of batting and wadding, which was continued until his death, which occurred Aug. 31, 1883. He was a man of great activity and business energy, and became one of the most successful manufacturers. The Village had frequent occasions to acknowledge his liberality for religious and charitable interests as well as for other objects of public benefit. He was on the board of selectmen, and in 1873 represented the town in the State Legislature. He married, March 25, 1841, Sarah Ann Harding, daughter of Seth and Mary (Learnard) Harding. There were no children. Mr. Eaton's death was a great public loss.

REV. FERDINAND ELLIS.

FERDINAND ELLIS, son of John and Rhoda (Partridge) Ellis, was born June 16, 1780, in Medway. He graduated in 1802 from Brown University, Providence, R. I., where he was tutor from 1802 to 1805; afterwards he taught school for fifteen years in Exeter, N. H., and subsequently he became a Baptist clergyman and was settled as pastor of the Baptist Church, June, 1818, in Exeter, N. H. He resigned September, 1828. The Rev. Mr. Ellis was regarded as a fine scholar, a successful teacher, and an excellent preacher. He married Lydia Whitmarsh, of Providence, R. I. Mrs. Ellis died Feb. 22, 1838, and the Rev. Mr. Ellis died March 15, 1858.

REV. CHARLES WESLEY EMERSON, M. D.

THE EMERSON ARMS.

CHARLES WESLEY EMERSON, son of Thomas and Mary F. (Hewett) Emerson, was born Nov. 30, 1838, in Pittsfield, Vt. His father was for many years a teacher, and a man of great culture and fine literary taste. After leaving the public schools of his native town he was under the instruction of his father in higher English, scientific, and classical studies. This training was most thorough, the teaching being not merely a demand on memory but on the thinking and reflecting faculties. Mr. Emerson's paternal grandfather was a man remarkable for his knowledge of history and famous for his familiarity with the sacred Scriptures. His maternal grandfather was a Methodist minister, and is now living, at the good age of ninety-seven years. Mr. Emerson's grand-parents on his father's side lived to be ninety-three years old. He was remotely related to Ralph Waldo Emerson. His great ancestor, Thomas Emerson, immigrant, settled as early as 1638 in Ipswich, Mass., and was the progenitor of a race of ministers and learned men. Mr. Emerson graduated and took the degree of M. D. from the University in Philadelphia, Penn. He also passed through two departments of the Boston University, law and oratory, and completed a course of theological study under the Rev. Dr. Tyler, and was afterward ordained to the Gospel ministry by the Association of Congregational Ministers in Windham County, Vt. His first pastorate of three years was in Halifax, Vt. He was then settled for four years in Brookfield, Vt., and afterward preached for three years in Northfield, Vt. Subsequently he was installed pastor of the First Parish in Fitchburg, Mass., and for nearly five years was the popular preacher to a large and flourishing congregation. He then pursued the study of oratory under Professor Monroe, of the Boston University, preaching on the Sabbath in Chelsea, Mass. After about two years his health failed and he traveled in Europe. Upon his return he was elected one of the faculty of the Boston University School of Oratory. But after the death of Professor Monroe this department of the University was discontinued, and Dr. Emerson drew about him most of his associate professors in that department and opened a school of oratory of which he is the Principal, known as the Monroe Conservatory of Oratory, which for some years was in Pemberton Square, and recently removed to Wesleyan Hall, Bromfield Street, Boston. Soon after the incorporation of the easterly part of Medway as Millis, Dr. Emerson purchased the estate once owned by Capt. Joseph Lovell, of Revolutionary history, and is fitting up a fine residence which he will occupy as soon as completed. Dr. Emerson has already won the high respect of his new neighbors and townsmen by his urbanity of manner, his friendly interest in all, his scholarly habits, his eminent knowledge and commanding ability as a public speaker.

EDWARD HARVEY ELLIS, M. D.

EDWARD HARVEY ELLIS, son of James H. and Laura (Harding) Ellis, was born Feb. 6, 1856, in Rockville, Medway. He was educated in the public schools of his native town, and completed the course of scientific and classical studies in Dean Academy, Franklin, Mass., where he graduated in 1876. He pursued his professional studies in the Boston University School of Medicine, and received in 1879 the degree of M. D. He commenced the practice of medicine in Holliston, Mass., but after some six months, established himself in a wider field in Marlboro, Mass., where he has a successful and lucrative practice. Dr. Ellis married in November, 1879, Hattie Harding Bullard, daughter of Henry and Bethia (Wheeler) Bullard, of Holliston, Mass.

DR. GEORGE OTIS FAIRBANKS.

GEORGE OTIS FAIRBANKS, son of Otis and Sylvia (Fuller) Fairbanks, was born Feb. 14, 1815, in Medway. He was the oldest of nine children. In early youth he had the advantages of education then open to farmers' sons. When seventeen years old he began teaching school, and for several years was thus engaged in Upton, Canton, Dedham, Lowell, and Newburyport, Mass. Subsequently he studied dentistry, and in December, 1845, began to practice in Fall River, Mass., where he was for many years the leading member of his profession. Dr. Fairbanks took a deep interest in public affairs. In 1848 he was chosen a member of the general school committee, to which position he was reëlected. In 1852 and 1853 he was a member of the board of selectmen of the town. In 1861 he was elected to the common council, and upon its organization was chosen president of that body. In 1866 he was elected a member of the school committee for a term of three years, and on the organization of the committee was chosen chairman. In 1867 he was elected mayor, and was reëlected the following year. Dr. Fairbanks, during his administration, inaugurated and advanced to completion a large amount of important municipal work. As chief executive officer it was his desire to have the city take high rank in whatever would bring prosperity and happiness to the mass of the people. He was chosen representative in 1869 and was reëlected to that office in 1870, '71, '72, and '73, and again in 1875. During his second term in the legislature he was appointed on the committee on railroads, and continued on that committee during the remainder of his service in the house. After his return from the legislature, Dr. Fairbanks was appointed clerk of the overseers of the poor, which position he held for several years. He was re-appointed until failing health forced him to relinquish work. After a few weeks of confinement he died March 11, 1884. Dr. Fairbanks was married twice. His first wife died Feb. 2, 1849, and his second died April 27, 1860. Three sons and one daughter survive him.

Dr. Fairbanks came of good old Puritan stock, his ancestors being among the early settlers of Massachusetts. He was reared on a farm in a country town, and early imbibed those principles of domestic virtue and rectitude, together with the habits of industry which are so characteristic of the people who dwell remote from the cities. He was a great reader, an apt student, and was blessed with a retentive memory. He had great powers of observation with an intuitive mind, and could quickly grasp an idea or theory advanced by others. Hence, though his early advantages for securing an education in the scholastic sense were limited, yet his native intellect combined with perseverance and close application to studies brought to him at manhood a well-stored mind, and so thoroughly trained as to fit him for the work of teaching a public school, a profession in which he early engaged, and was very successful He was an acute thinker, a good reasoner, and was fond of argument. In his religious convictions he was clear and decided. Much of this was no doubt due to his early parental training, and the effects of the preaching of the Rev. Dr. Ide, of Medway, whose sermons were full of strong doctrinal truths, argumentative, and very closely reasoned. It was natural, therefore, that he should acquire a remarkable love for logical and able preaching Soon after he came to Fall River in 1845 during an extensive work of grace in the Central Congregational Church under the pastorship of the late Rev Dr Thurston, he made a public profession of religion and united with that church, retaining his membership with them until death. He was very constant in attendance upon the ministrations of the Gospel, whenever his health permitted He was a man of exceedingly generous nature, kind-hearted, and took great pleasure in administering to the necessities of the destitute. The poor were lavish in their praise of his kindness, and always remembered him with gratitude

EDMUND F. FARRINGTON, ESQ.

EDMUND F FARRINGTON, son of Asahel and Henrietta (Fisher) Farrington, was born Oct. 25, 1820, in the "southwest room of the old Otis Fairbanks house," which formerly stood on the road from West Medway to the Village. His maternal grand-parents, Leonard and Betsey Fisher, resided for years on the borders of Franklin. Their bodies rest in the old burying-ground in West Medway. They originally came from Wrentham, as did his paternal grand-parents. Mrs. Henrietta Farrington, his mother, resided, during the later years of her life, in West Medway, and became a member of the Congregational Church in that place, but died in 1846, in Warren, Mass. "Incompatibility of temper" caused an early separation between Asahel and Henrietta Farrington, and the guardianship of Edmund was assigned to his mother, who returned to her father's house. Asahel settled in one of the northern towns in New Hampshire, married again and became the father of nine sons and daughters He finally died at an advanced age in Lyndon, Vt. Some years before his death he became a Methodist lay preacher. Edmund Farrington in early life was frail in body, bashful and retiring in disposition, imaginative and unstable in mind. A few summers and winters in the district school and one term at Leicester Academy sufficed him for schooling in "book learning." The hand of poverty was ever upon him. In his tenth year he was "put out" on the farm of Sanford Ware, in Franklin After one season of farming we find him making cotton wadding with A. M. B. Fuller, in what is now known as Daniels' box factory, in North Franklin. Subsequently he worked for Hiram Metcalf, making stocking yarn in the same building, and a year or two more as card stripper and piecer in White's and Gills' factories. At the age of eighteen he began to learn the carpenter trade. He afterward worked for "Boss Daniels" at boot making, having been instructed by William H. Temple. Leaving Medway in 1839, he went on a whaling voyage from New Bedford, was left in the Azore Islands, shipped from there to the coast of Africa; thence to Brazil, and coming up to the West Indies, he ran away in San Domingo, whence, after a sojourn of several weeks, he shipped and worked his passage to Boston in the brig "Sea Eagle." Soon after his return from sea he joined the Fourier Association at Brook Farm, West Roxbury. Here he became acquainted with such men as Ripley, Dana, Parker, and Greeley, and became dimly conscious that he had a mind and a soul, and that there might be a place and a work for him in the world. At Brook Farm he learned last making, which he followed in Boston, Malden, Lynn, and Danvers, Mass., and in Gardiner, Me. In Lynn he edited for a time a paper called *The Forum*. He contributed also to various papers at different times and rode the "lecture hobby" with some success. He took up gas and steam fitting in Portland, and superintended gas works in Gardiner, Me. He married in 1847, in Lowell, Mass., Miss Emma A. Smiley, of Gardiner, with whom he led a happy life until her death in 1880. They had four children, but only a son and a daughter survive. In Lowell he assisted to build and fit up the large carpet mill, and afterward went to Chicago and engaged in building. He returned to Poughkeepsie, N. Y., where he remained for eighteen years, engaged mostly in contracting and building. He removed to New York and followed the same business, but failed in it during the first years of the war. While looking over a scrap of *The New York Herald*, in which a workman had brought a lunch, he saw an advertisement for a master carpenter on the Covington and Cincinnati suspension bridge. He answered this advertisement, was accepted and spent nearly three years in the position, mastering meantime all the mysteries of the business. He was next appointed superintendent of construction on the new suspension bridge at Niagara Falls, where he remained a year. He afterwards erected two suspension bridges over the Delaware River, between New York and Pennsylvania, at Hancock and Lordville. He was called to East River Bridge in 1870, and placed in charge of the wood work of that structure, to which was soon added the iron work, and finally the wire work, when he was installed master mechanic. He remained on this bridge twelve years and four months, when he retired July 31, 1882, on account of failing health. While on this work he went through the operations of sinking the caissons safely; got over all the temporary wire ropes and erected the foot-bridge after his own plans, and first crossed the space from one anchorage to the other in a "boatswain's chair," attached to the smallest of all the ropes. He erected the machinery for cable making, made the cables and suspended a large portion of the superstructure, and inspected and prepared the lumber for the roadway. No other individual had any previous knowledge of suspension bridge building except Col. W. A. Roebling, Engineer in Chief, and for nine years this gentleman was unable to visit the work, or to give it proper personal attention, so that the burden fell on Mr. Farrington. How well he bore it and how patiently, in face of the intrigues of place-seekers and the opposition of assistant engineers, arising from professional jealousy, the completed work and the encomiums of the public, who watched him in its daily progress testify. When he left the bridge, little remained but routine work to be done and men who had grown up under his instruction remained to do it. Mr. Farrington retired in 1882 to his native town to recuperate, where he remained until 1884, when he returned to New York to engage in new enterprises. Mr. Farrington's townsmen have reason to feel somewhat of pride and gratification in the success of one born among them who was a weak, friendless child, thrown on the world and his own resources at an early age, drifting for years on the tide without chart or compass, but who finally became an esteemed Christian, honored and even famous for his mechanical achievements.

Rev. Gilbert Fay.

Gilbert Fay, son of Otis and Mary (Morse) Fay, was born May 2, 1803, in Westboro, Mass. He graduated in 1826 from Brown University, and studied theology with the Rev. Dr. Ide, of Medway. He was ordained Oct. 6, 1830, as an evangelist in Westboro, Mass., and entered the service of the American Home Missionary Society, being stationed at Wadsworth, O., where he labored some five years without the loss of a single Sabbath from illness. But at the early age of thirty-two years, after a short and very useful ministry, he died Oct. 27, 1835. The little church of eleven members during his ministry increased to sixty members, and this is the record made : " He was much loved and lamented by his church and his brethren in the ministry." The Rev. Mr. Fay married, Sept. 11, 1831, Clarissa Walker, daughter of Comfort and Tamar (Clark) Walker. She was born Nov. 28, 1805, in Medway, and died Nov. 23, 1881. Their only son was Gilbert Otis Fay.

Rev. Gilbert Otis Fay, A. M., Ph. D.

Gilbert Otis Fay, (*Gilbert, Otis, David, David, Jonathan,*) son of Gilbert and Clarissa (Walker) Fay, was born Nov. 8, 1834, in Wadsworth, O. He pursued his preparatory studies in the schools of Medway and in Phillips Academy, Andover, Mass. He graduated in 1859 from Yale College, New Haven, Conn., and in 1862 from the Theological Seminary, Andover, Mass. He was licensed to preach April, 1862, by the Mendon Association. For four years next succeeding he was a teacher in the Ohio Institution for Deaf-Mutes in Columbus, O. From 1866 to 1880 he was the superintendent of the same institution. Since 1880 to the present time he has been a professor in the American Asylum in Hartford, Conn. Besides his other duties in these institutions he preached regularly to the deaf-mutes on the Sabbath, during the whole period of his connection with them. He received the literary degree of Ph. D. in 1880. Mr. Fay married, Aug. 25, 1863, Adelia Caroline Allen, daughter of William and Caroline (Gibson) Allen. Mrs. Adelia C. Fay died Jan. 11, 1867. Mr. Fay married, April 14, 1869, Mary Jane Jarvis, daughter of Edwin and Lydia (Gross) Jarvis. The children were : Adelia Clara, born Nov. 28, 1866; Elizabeth, born May 21, 1870; and Charles Jarvis, born Aug. 26, 1871. Dr. Fay was brought up in Medway, his father having died while he was an infant, and is regarded and beloved as a son of this good old town.

M. M. Fisher

Hon. Milton Metcalf Fisher, A. M.

Milton Metcalf Fisher, to whom the town of Medway is much indebted for its established industries and business enterprise, and who has contributed largely to the social, educational, and religious development of the place, was the son of Willis and Caroline (Fairbanks) Fisher He was born Jan. 30, 1811, in Franklin, Mass., and came of a godly and somewhat distinguished ancestry. *Vid The History of Franklin, Mass., The Published Works of Dr. Emmons*, and *The History of Norfolk County*. Mr. Fisher became a resident of Medway in 1840, when about thirty years of age. His manhood was fully fledged and he was well equipped for an honorable business career. In his earlier and preparatory life he had received the benefits of an education in the public, private, and classical schools of his native town and of Medway, and had had the training of two years in Amherst College, Amherst, Mass. Mr Fisher had had the experience, also, of several years as a teacher in the public schools, and had been in business and held official positions for a few years in the town of Westboro, Mass. All this qualified him to assume at once a prominence which for nearly half a century he has continued to hold, much to the welfare of the town, and with credit and honor to himself. Upon his settlement in Medway he became a manufacturer of straw goods, which business he vigorously pursued for a period of more than twenty years. In 1863 he retired from it and established an extensive Insurance Agency in which he is still active, his younger son, Frederick L. Fisher, Esq., being associated with him. He has had an official as well as business prominence during his residence in Medway rarely equaled by any citizen. As early as 1840 he was chosen a Deacon in the Village Church which office he still holds. His townsmen have repeatedly called him to fill the various municipal offices within their gift. He was appointed in 1856 to 1865 the State Commissioner for the New York and Boston Railroad and a State Commissioner to establish the line between Danvers and South Danvers. In 1859 and 1860 he was chosen to the Massachusetts Senate, and in 1863 he was elected Commissioner for Norfolk County. He continued in this office twelve years, until 1872, serving for three years as chairman of the board. In 1871 he brought about the establishment of the Medway Savings Bank of which he has been the only and honored President from then to the present, 1885. He was the one who set on foot measures which resulted in the erection of Sanford Hall the same year, and in 1881 he was prime mover in securing the building of the Sanford Mills. To a large extent he has been the moving spirit in the business and enterprise of the town for forty years. His connection with the development of the railroad facilities of the town was marked and full of interest. He was often upon the board of school committee. He held and advocated liberal and advanced views upon the subject of public education. He was a pioneer in the anti-slavery movement, and as a young man in college, startled the professors in their seats by his bold and fervid utterances in an oration before the college on the subject of "Human Freedom." He was a delegate in 1833 to the first anniversary of the American Anti-Slavery Society. He addressed public meetings, and wrote many articles for the press upon slavery and kindred topics of modern reform. In 1845 he prepared a petition, numerously signed, to the American Board of

Commissioners for Foreign Missions as to the matter of slavery in the churches under the patronage of that society. This petition led to the formation of the American Missionary Association Thus "Deacon Fisher," as he is familiarly known, has been a force for good in the town, the Commonwealth, and the nation, by his energy, his advanced sentiments, his earnest devotion and eminent ability, as a man, a citizen, a philanthropist, and a Christian disciple. On the seventieth anniversary of his birth, Jan 30, 1881, Sanford Hall, crowded with guests, and the air eloquent with laudatory greetings, manifested something of the wide public esteem in which the subject of this sketch was held

" The hall was tastefully decorated with bunting and evergreen Supper was served and the tables groaned under the load of viands prepared, consisting of all the solids and delicacies of the season About two hundred guests sat down to supper The Rev. Mr Cutler, of Auburndale, offered prayer, after which an hour was spent in discussing the viands The tables were cleared away, and then the Rev R K Harlow called the meeting to order, on behalf of the committee of arrangements Mr Harlow welcomed all to the occasion, and on behalf of the people assembled tendered the congratulations of the townspeople to Mr. Fisher, and in a humorous manner referred to his other days of like import When he celebrated his twenty-first birthday he doubtless thought that he was of considerable importance in the world Mr. Harlow paid a tribute to Mr Fisher's services, in both public and private life He read letters from relatives, and a telegram from George P Metcalf, Esq , of Framingham, who said ' Give my congratulations to the old Locofoco, and the sincere well-wishes of his kinsman ' Mr Wellington G H. Hunt, of Boston, was called upon, and responded in a felicitous manner. The Rev Alexis W. Ide, of West Medway, responded to a call in his earnest, happy way After Mr Ide's remarks the audience arose and sang one verse of Hebron—'Thus far the Lord hath led me on,' after which the Rev. E O Jameson, of East Medway, made remarks full of pleasant reminiscences of his intercourse and acquaintance with Mr Fisher, and tendered the congratulations of the old First Church in Medway Mr Jameson read a poem by the Hon Charles Hamant, of Medfield, appropriate to the occasion The Rev Dr. Spaulding, of Newburyport, related his early acquaintance with Medway and the honored guest of the evening, interpersing his remarks with illustrative anecdotes The Rev. James M Bell, of West Medway, in the absence of the author, after a few preliminary remarks, read the following poem, written for the occasion by Dea Anson Daniels

" THE GARDEN BEYOND THE IRON GATE

"Across life's road there's an iron gate,
Bolted and barred by the hand of fate,
Three score and ten are its iron bars,
Three score and ten are its rusty spars;
It is riveted thick, again and again,
And the number of rivets is three score and ten
Remorselessly shut on the human crew,
It noiselessly swings for only a few —
Only a few of the struggling crowd
Arrive at this portal, toil-worn and bowed,
With heads all white with the dust of the way,
Or a polished scalp above the gray —
Like a mountain dome above the pines,
Or a boulder, 'round which the snow reclines
Their eyes are dim with the constant strain,

Observing the scenes through which they came,
Far have they journeyed, far and long,
At first with a gay and hopeful throng
Who fell by the thousands, or one by one,
Dwindling away with each setting sun
All the long way there were flowers in bloom,
But the brightest group overshadowed the tomb,
And the sweetest perfumes of summer's breath
Were mingled and soiled by the odor of death,
And the soft, sweet voices that cheered the day,
And the eyes of love full of beauty's ray,

Were hushed and smothered in low mounds
by the way.
But they who have passed the narrow door,
Behold its repulsive side no more;
But looking back on the gate, behold
Three score and ten shining bars of gold,
Three score and ten bright rivets, like stars
Holding together the golden bars.
And all around is a garden fair,
Where the sunshine gilds the purple air,
And shining through the leaves overhead,
It flecks with light the ground they tread
'Tis the golden light of the afternoon
With the deeper tints, brown Autumn's
boon;
For the flowers and the grass that are
growing here,
And trees, have the hue of the closing year,
Golden, and brown, and crimson, and gray,
Like the woods on a soft October day
The paths are clean for the aged feet,
And under the trees there's a cool retreat,
There's a dreamy sound of the fountain's
play,
And the murmuring sigh of the breeze
alway;
And the chirp of the birds indistinct on the
ear,
And the soft, slow rhythm of footsteps
near;
All mingled in murmur soft and sweet,
That soothes the spirit and rests the feet
The bell from its tower, with sober tone,
Pronounces the name of the hour that's
gone,
From the great mad world of strife and sin
There comes but the hum of its ceaseless
din,
The boom of a gun, or the rumble of a
train,
Or shriek of a mill when its wheels start
again;
No more is heard of its worry and rage
In this garden of God, this home of old age.
And there in groups do the inmates sit,
As in early life they often met,
Some still ruddy and lithe and strong,
Ready to join in labor or song—
Others their thin hands lean on a staff,
With a wheezy voice and a creaky laugh,
Recounting the deeds of earlier years,
And laughing again till their eyes fill with
tears,
At some reminiscence of school-day fun,
Some narrow escape when the birch nearly
won.
Another recounts his earliest joy
When he first started out, a fisher boy,
With a stick and a string, a bent pin for
a hook,
He dabbled along in the edge of the brook,
And caught his first fish, a prouder prize
Than any that since has gladdened his eyes
Or he talks of his loves, of the Janes and
Bessies,
With radiant eyes and immaculate dresses—
How they flirted, and danced, and ban-
tered, and sung—

All the smiles he received and the hearts
that he won,
Remembering the joy of their weddings
and wooings —
Or they talk of more serious sayings and
doings ·
As what they have suffered for church or
state,
How often their vote was the fiat of fate,
How many elections they helped to carry,
What political foes they helped to bury,
What changes they've seen in nations and
men,
What reforms they have aided again and
again,
And with such reminiscence is mingled the
fear
That the true age of heroes will soon dis-
appear
Or they talk of the future, and try to fore-
cast
Its greatness and glory compared with the
past.
The sisters are there of these elderly broth-
ers,
Sweet, thoughtful women, and large-
hearted mothers,
With soft, quiet faces, white, ringleted hair,
And the warmth of affection that smiles
away care.
O' what were a garden all sunshine and
flowers —
Even Eden, if woman were not in its bow-
ers,
To join in its chatter, bring beauty and
grace,
Truth, purity, love, in the smiles of her
face?
There wait they the ferry across that river
On which the stars of eternity quiver,
And glance o'er waters so heavy and black
That the noiseless keel never leaves a track,
And never is heard the dip of an oar,
And they who step from the silent shore
Into the stillness, are never seen more
But beyond this dark and silent stream,
Figured afar in the evening's gleam,
Are the domes and spires in purple and
gold,
And glories too bright for the eyes to be-
hold,
Indistinct in the outline and soft as the
light,
And mixed with the purple and gray of the
night,
And those in this garden that linger and
stray,
May look on this vision of visions alway

May he who yesterday stepped through
the gate,
Find the joys that abound in this garden
of fate,
And be cheered by the music that floats
from the shore
Beyond the dark waters, where is life ever-
more."

25

DR. JOHN S. FOLSOM.

JOHN SANBORN[7] FOLSOM, (*John Tilton[6], Nicholas[5], Peter[4], Peter[3], Peter[2], John[1],*) son of John Tilton and Hannah Morrill (Sanborn) Folsom, was born Oct. 12, 1840, in Manchester, N H. He was a lineal descendant in the seventh generation from John Foulsham, now written Folsom, who set sail April 26, 1638, from the mouth of the Thames, England, in the ship "Diligent," of Ipswich, and on arrival in America settled in Hingham, Mass. *Vid. The Historical and Genealogical Register*, April, 1876; pp 207–231. His father, Dr. John T. Folsom, was for many years a successful and widely-known practitioner of dentistry in Gloucester, and afterwards in Boston, Mass John S. Folsom having spent his boyhood and youth in school, at the age of sixteen years entered his father's office, and devoted himself to the study and practice of dentistry under the careful instruction and experienced eye of his father, who designed to give his son the best advantages for this profession. After two or three years under the personal training of one of the best dentists in New England, he went to Baltimore and then to New York City, spending some two years in the offices of Drs. Stinson, Franklin & Sproul, Stratton, and other most eminent dentists in the country at that period. Dr. Folsom, about 1860, returned to his father's office in Gloucester, a well-read and skillful operator in dentistry. After some years he, with his father and uncle, N. T. Folsom, also a dentist, opened an office on Winter Street in Boston, where they had a large practice Meanwhile his uncle became the inventor of what was known as the "Folsom Dental Packing Ridge," patented Jan. 1, 1867, which became so important to dentistry everywhere that they all were engaged for a time in introducing this new invention, which yielded a very handsome pecuniary harvest Subsequently Dr. Folsom engaged somewhat in other business, but still doing more or less in his profession. He himself made some valuable inventions in saddlery and other hardware, which proved successful. Subsequent to 1873 he resided in the easterly part of Medway, which became Millis, Mass. After his father's death for some years he was in company with his uncle, N. T. Folsom, Esq., and had an office in Boston, where he gave attention to the sale of goods manufactured under their several patents, and devoted some time to his professional practice in the place where he resided He was a prominent citizen in Medway, and a leader in politics as a Jacksonian Democrat, being on the Democratic town committee, where he was a faithful and energetic worker. As a business man Dr Folsom had a good measure of executive ability, enjoyed the entire confidence of those who knew him, and among his business associates he was called a "square man," one whose word was considered as good as his bond. Dr. Folsom was a popular candidate in 1884 for Representative to the General Court of Massachusetts, receiving a heavy vote of his townsmen without respect to party lines In 1885, upon the incorporation of the town of Millis he was chosen a member of the first board of selectmen, and on the decease of Lansing Millis, Esq., Dr. Folsom became chairman of the board. He was a far-sighted, judicious, progressive and faithful town officer, a valuable and highly esteemed citizen of the new municipality. Dr. Folsom married, July 6, 1865, Marion Augusta Gould, daughter of Dr. James B. and Priscilla A. (Godfrey) Gould. She was born

RESIDENCE OF DR. JOHN S. FOLSOM.

Oct. 10, 1843, in New England Village, Mass. Mrs. Folsom was a lady of rare personal charms, attractive and graceful in manners, and of great loveliness of character. She died Feb. 17, 1883, in the very bloom of womanhood, and universally lamented.

REV. CALVIN RICHARDS FITTS.

CALVIN RICHARDS FITTS, son of Charles H. and Emeline A. (Richards) Fitts, was born Feb. 10, 1840, in West Medway. His youth was spent in Rockville, Medway. He pursued his preparatory studies in the academy in Monson, Mass., and graduated in 1864 from Amherst College, Massachusetts. His theological studies were pursued in the seminary in Chicago, Ill., from which he graduated in 1866. He ministered a few months to the Congregational Church in Harvard, Ill. Returning East he was ordained Sept. 5, 1866, in Medfield, and labored for a year with the Congregational Church in South Braintree, Mass. In 1868 he was installed pastor of the Second Congregational Church in Cohasset, Mass. He resigned in 1870 and removed to Slatersville, R. I., and ministered to the Congregational Church there for eleven years, until April 1, 1881. He then resided for a short period in West Quincy, and was called to the supply of the pulpit in Sudbury, Mass., in the spring of 1883, to which place he removed the 26th of September to minister permanently, when he was taken ill, and died suddenly Oct. 10, 1883. The Rev. Mr. Fitts married, Feb. 10, 1869, Helen F. Trask, daughter of Theodore Trask, Esq., of Quincy, Mass. The children were: Arthur Richards, born Dec. 23, 1869; Ernest Vinton, born

March 9, 1872 ; Charles Theodore, born April 4, 1875, died Nov. 6, 1878 ; Gertrude Augusta, born Dec. 21, 1876, died Jan. 9, 1880 , Walter Mansfield, born April 26, 1881.

Asa Metcalf Blake Fuller, Esq.

Asa Metcalf Blake Fuller, son of Asa and Hephzibah (Blake) Fuller, was born May 17, 1813, in Franklin, Mass. His early education was secured during about eight weeks of school yearly, until old enough to learn a trade. He first learned the cabinet trade in Holliston. Subsequently he learned the art of a jeweler, and from 1840 to the present, 1885, has prosecuted this business in West Medway. Mr. Fuller is one of the longest resident and most useful citizens of the town. He was for many years town clerk and treasurer. He also served as collector and selectman. He has ever taken a lively interest in public affairs, and for a long period has been a prominent member of the Second Church of Christ and devoted to its welfare. Mr. Fuller was a member of the committee appointed to prepare The History of Medway, and rendered valuable assistance to the editor.

Elihu Sanford Fuller, Esq.

Elihu Sanford Fuller, son of Elihu and Rhoda (Daniels) Fuller, was born May 25, 1824, in East Medway. Mr. Fuller was educated in the schools of his native town, where he settled and followed the business of a butcher for many years and was proprietor of a meat market. For twenty-seven years he was the Captain of the Niagara Fire Engine Company No. 4, and served two years on the board of selectmen of Medway, and was chosen, in 1885, to fill a vacancy in the first board of selectmen in the town of Millis

Rev. Amory Gale, M. D.

Amory Gale, son of Major Amory and Lucinda (Rich) Gale, was born Oct 15, 1800, in Warwick, Mass. His grandfather, Jonathan Gale, was a soldier in the War of the Revolution, and a man of sterling traits of character Major Amory Gale, his father, was a blacksmith and a manufacturer of edged tools, a man of intelligence and moral worth. His mother was a lineal descendant of Sir Richard Rich, Lord High Chancellor of England under Edward VI., and the Earl of Warwick. Mrs. Gale's father was a farmer, and owned a large grist mill. It is said of him that when a scarcity of coin prevailed, having a large quantity on hand, he declined to sell it to speculators at an advanced price, but allowed his townsmen to purchase it at the usual price of corn when it was plentiful, for he said : "I do not wish to enrich myself at the expense of my neighbors." The subject of this sketch had the advantages of an academic education, was for a time engaged in teaching, and then studied medicine with Dr. Taylor, of Warwick, and Dr. Batchelder, of Royalston, Mass. In the fall of 1823 he went to attend medical lectures in Hanover, N. H. The faculty considered him so far gone with consumption that they would not receive from him the usual matriculation fee, and plainly said to him. "Young man, you will be in your grave before the spring flowers blossom." But he was determined to disappoint them. He took to horse-back riding and vigorous exercise in the open air, and long outlived his medical teachers. He completed the course of lectures and attended a second course in the Medical School of Brown University, Rhode Island, where he received in 1824 the degree of M. D., his thesis at graduation receiving special mention for excellence. Prior to entering upon the study of medicine, Mr. Gale had a strong desire to enter the Christian ministry, but his ill-health forbade it. Dr. Gale married Martha Leland, of Warwick, Mass., whose mother was a native of East Medway. Mrs. Gale had been a teacher in the public schools for some years at the time of her marriage. Dr. Gale practiced medicine in Barre, Mass., in Amherst, N. H., and in South Scituate, Mass. He often gave lectures on scientific subjects. He was a pioneer in the temperance cause, and, by lecturing, by writing, and by personal appeals, did much to promote this reform. His principal purpose in locating at South Scituate was that he might study theology with the Rev. Samuel J. May, who was at that time pastor of the Unitarian Church in that town. He was ordained as an evangelist in Kingston, Mass. In 1844 he preached in East Bridgewater, Mass., Southington, Conn., and Pembroke, Mass., then became the pastor of the Unitarian Church in Norton, Mass., where for four years he labored with success. He then was called to Barnstable, Mass., and when about to remove his family to that place he was stricken with bronchitis, and was compelled to give up his chosen life work. He resumed medicine as a homœopathist, and had a large practice in Woonsocket, R. I. After a few years, worn by professional labors, in the autumn of 1853, he purchased a farm in East Medway to which he removed, and there spent the remainder of his life. The Rev. Adin Ballou, in writing of him " as a philanthropist and moral reformer," says. " The causes of temperance, anti-slavery, peace, and every movement in favor of human progress found his bosom open, warm, and responsive. He was among the pioneers of all these reforms, and breasted the storms of reproach which outspoken testimony in their behalf provoked in former times, with unflinching moral heroism. He was their devoted friend and advocate when it cost something to be so. The same characteristics marked his career in every development of progress which startled the popular prejudice His honest and manly nature demanded to know, not what was established in conservative public opinion or interest, but what was *true*, what was *right*. For this he searched fearlessly, and once convinced he had found it, bravely took his stand on its side." "As a physician," he adds, " he was remarkable for his intuitive insight into the causes and remedies of disease, for the soothing and inspiring influence which he carried with him into the sick chamber, and for the confidence which his benign sympathies and counsels excited in the minds of his patients He was physician both to their bodies and souls." It can truly be said of Dr. Gale that whatever he did, he did well. While always modest and unassuming in demeanor, and humble in his own esteem, he performed many acts of private benevolence and rare kindness, known only to those benefited by them. His long, busy life, full of faithful service to humanity, was fitly closed with brightest anticipations of the life above. He died Feb. 20, 1873, after a long and distressing illness, which he bore with great patience and resignation. He was buried in Warwick, Mass.

Mrs. Caroline R. James, eldest daughter of Dr. Gale, upon the death of her husband in 1874, prepared herself for the Gospel ministry, and was ordained in 1878, being the third woman ordained to the ministry within the Unitarian denomination. She was first settled as pastor of the Unitarian Church in Brooklyn, Conn., and continued there until 1881, when she took charge of a society in Francestown, N. H. Miss Martha L. Gale, the second daughter of Dr Gale, became a teacher in Clinton Seminary, Cooperstown, N. Y., and in Dean Academy, Franklin, Mass. She also wrote for the press, and gave private instruction in the French language.

Miss Mary K. Gale studied medicine and was a successful practitioner in Wollaston, Mass. James A. Gale, the only son of Dr. Gale, graduated in 1861 from the Homœopathic Medical College, Cleveland, O. He settled in West Medway and was a well known and skillful physician.

REV. JOHN HARPER GARMAN.

JOHN HARPER GARMAN, son of Joseph and Ann B. (Leach) Garman, was born Jan. 20, 1811, in Meredith Bridge, now Laconia, N. H. He married, March 1, 1840, Elizabeth Bullard, daughter of Nathan Bullard, of Medway. They taught a year in North Carolina and returned in 1842. He entered the Theological Seminary in Andover, Mass., from which he graduated in 1845. He was the acting pastor two years, 1846 and 1847, in Baldwin, Me. Nov. 3, 1847, he was ordained and installed pastor of the Congregational Church in Lemington, Me., where he remained until 1855 He then labored five years in Scarborough, Me., and was pastor from 1860 to 1865 in Lebanon, Me. He then removed to North Orange, Mass., where he ministered to the Congregational Church for eight years. He afterward preached in Shutesbury and Warwick, but in 1885 resided in North Orange, Mass. His ministry was greatly blessed to the churches where he preached and his labors were attended with many conversions. The Rev. and Mrs. Garman had three children: Mary E., born Feb. 25, 1849, married Dec. 1, 1868, Zina H. Goodell; Charles E., born Dec. 18, 1850, married Sept. 24, 1882, Eliza N Miner; Frederic H., born May 15, 1857. Charles E. Garman graduated in 1872 from Amherst College, Amherst, Mass., and in 1879 from Yale Theological Seminary. He was appointed Professor of Moral and Intellectual Philosophy in Amherst College, which position he now fills. The youngest son graduated in 1885 from Amherst College.

REV. AND HON. BENJAMIN GREENE.

BENJAMIN GREENE, son of Benjamin Greene, was born May 5, 1764, in Waltham, Mass. He graduated in 1784 from Harvard College, Cambridge, Mass., and entered the Gospel ministry. The Rev. Mr. Greene was settled as colleague pastor with the Rev. Nathan Bucknam over the First Church of Christ in Medway, where he continued five years. *Vid*. THE CHURCHES. He married Lydia Clark, a daughter of the Rev. Jonas Clark, of Lexington, Mass. It is said of the Rev. Mr. Clark that his Sunday public prayers were sometimes two hours long, his sermon never less than one hour, and sometimes three hours. Mrs. Greene's mother was a cousin of Gov. John Hancock, who, with Samuel Adams, was at her father's house on the morning of

April 19, 1775. After the retreat of the British on that day eight of her father's beloved parishioners lay dead on the ground directly under the windows of the meeting-house. Three of Mrs. Greene's sisters married ministers, viz., the Rev. T. Fiske, d d , the Rev. Dr. Harris, and the Rev. Dr. Ware. The Rev. Mr. Greene after leaving Medway resided for a few years in Marblehead, Mass., but removed in 1798 to Berwick, Me. For a time he was the Preceptor of the Berwick Academy. He then read law, was admitted to the bar, and was in the practice of his profession for some years. Subsequently he held the appointment of a judge and rose to eminence in the state. He was also United States Marshal for the District of Maine. His sons were educated and entered the professions of law and medicine. The Rev. and Hon. Benjamin Greene died in 1837, in Berwick, Me

CLARENCE E. GRIFFIN, Esq.

CLARENCE E. GRIFFIN, son of Enoch and Irene (Eaton) Griffin, was born Dec. 22, 1852, in Cornwallis, N. S. His parents were of a New England ancestry. His great-grandfather was Eli Griffin, of Stamford, Conn. In early boyhood Mr. Griffin worked on his father's farm in the summer and attended school in the winter. When eighteen years old he commenced teaching the winter term of school. Three years later he began to prepare for college, and September, 1875, entered Acadia College in Wolfville, King's County, N. S. He remained out one year, and graduated in 1880. He taught for a year, and in 1881 entered Harvard Law School, Cambridge, Mass., where he remained through the winter, and taught school in Franklin and Medfield while pursuing his legal studies under G. W. Wiggin, Esq., of Franklin He was admitted, Oct. 6, 1885, to the Norfolk County Bar, and opened a law office in Medway and in Franklin. Mr. Griffin by his scholarly attainments, his Christian character, and genial manners has already made certain the respect, the confidence and favorable opinion of the community, and his success in his chosen profession it is easy to predict.

REV. SEWALL HARDING.

SEWALL HARDING, son of Capt John and Beulah (Metcalf) Harding, was born March 20, 1793, in Medway, Mass. He pursued his preparatory studies somewhat under the instruction of the Rev. Luther Wright, and during this period he became a Christian and united, May 30, 1813, with the same church of which he was to become, twenty-five years later, the revered pastor. Mr. Harding graduated in 1818 from Union College, New York. He studied theology with the Rev. Drs. Emmons and Ide, and was ordained and installed Jan. 17, 1821, pastor of the First Congregational Church, Waltham, Mass. During his ministry in that town a division of the church occurred, and the Rev. Mr. Harding was pastor of the so-called Trinitarian Congregational Church. After a ministry in Waltham of sixteen years, the Rev. Mr. Harding was called and settled as pastor of the First Church of Christ in his native town, where he labored very successfully from 1837 to 1851, when he retired from the pastorate and became the Secretary of the Congregational Board of Publication, which office he filled until 1863, having his residence in Auburndale, Mass. The last fifteen years of his life he retired from public duties. His death occurred April 12, 1876, and his burial took place from the First Church of Christ in Medway, and he was interred in the old cemetery of his native town. The Rev. Mr. Harding was faithful, laborious, and successful in his profession, sprightly and social in his daily intercourse, a Hopkinsonian in theology, a very vigorous advocate of sound doctrine, an abolitionist in the very start of that movement, and a warm-hearted philanthropist. He cheerfully gave his two daughters to the work of Foreign Missions. Mrs. Harding was also a native of Medway ; she died Feb. 3, 1877, and was buried by the side of her husband.

REV. JOHN WHEELER HARDING.

JOHN WHEELER HARDING, son of the Rev. Sewall and Eliza (Wheeler) Harding, was born Oct. 12, 1821, in Waltham, Mass. He removed in 1837 to Medway, now Millis, when a lad, his father becoming the pastor of the First Church of Christ. He graduated in 1845, from Yale College, New Haven, Conn., and in 1848 from the Theological Seminary, Andover, Mass. The Rev. Mr. Harding was ordained, and installed, Jan. 1, 1850, the pastor of the Congregational Church, Long Meadow, Mass., where he is still fulfilling a long-continued and very useful ministry.

REV. RUFUS KENDRICK HARLOW.

RUFUS KENDRICK HARLOW, son of Branch and Lurany (Keith) Harlow, was born March 28, 1834, in Middleboro, Mass. He was educated in the schools and prepared for college in the Pierce Academy of his native town. In 1865 he graduated from Amherst College, and in 1868 from the Theological Seminary, Bangor, Me. Mr. Harlow was ordained to the Gospel ministry Oct. 15, 1868, in Middleboro, Mass. He was engaged as a stated supply by the St. Lawrence Street Church in Portland, Me., where he labored for more than a year. He then went to Belfast, Me., and was a stated supply for the First Congregational Church during some thirteen months, when he received a call to the pastorate of the Evangelical Congregational Church as a colleague pastor with the Rev. David Sanford. The call was accepted, and Mr. Harlow was duly installed Feb. 13, 1872. Under his ministry, which is still continued, the "Village Church," so called, has prospered, and the atttachments of pastor and people have become very strong. Mr. Harlow prepared various biographical sketches and discourses which were published. His ability as a preacher and fidelity as a pastor are universally acknowledged.

REV. JOEL HAWES, D. D.

JOEL HAWES, son of Ichabod and Keziah (Mann) Hawes, was born Dec. 22, 1789, in the old Barber house, on Village Street, which occupied the site of the late residence of William H. Cary, Esq. The house is now owned by Mr. William B. Hodges. The ancestors of Dr. Joel Hawes were among the early settlers of New England. They came from Lincolnshire, England, and settled in that part of Dedham which in 1673 became Wrentham, Mass. The Medway branch of the family came from Brookfield, Mass. The Rev. Dr. Hawes had a brother, Lewis Hawes, who lived and died upon the place now owned by Mr. Chadwick, on Village Street. He says of himself: "I was a wild, heady, reckless youth, delighting in hunting, fishing, trapping, and in rough athletic sports, which tended to invigorate my constitution, but added nothing to my mental or moral improvement." At the age of fourteen, his father returned to Brookfield. Here Joel had still fewer advantages for improvement, living three and a half miles from church and two from any school. He went in a few years to visit two uncles and seek his fortune in Vermont. He there learned the cloth dressing trade, and in 1806 he came back to Medway and was employed by Mr. George Barber, who had purchased the old homestead and was a clothier. He says he was here brought into bad company and spent much time in dissipation and card playing. He was, however, ambitious to earn money, and chopped wood by moonlight to increase his little store. He attended church for the first time in two years. The thought that he had desecrated the Sabbath awakened by that Sunday service, "pierced him like an arrow of the Almighty that drinketh up the spirit." Among his associates in Medway was Cyrus Kingsbury, afterward a missionary to the Choctaws, who was learning the cabinet maker's trade of Maj. Luther Metcalf. Young Kingsbury, while mowing on the Fairbanks lot, started a rabbit and rushing to catch him came in contact with his scythe and cut a main artery in one leg so that he came near bleeding to death. Hawes watched with him, and his pious resignation and conversation is supposed to have confirmed him in his purpose of a new life. He entered Brown University in 1809, and in 1810 taught school in Medway, at eighteen dollars per month. He kept a diary, and he writes Jan. 5, 1811: "Dined with Esquire Sanford by invitation and was very liberally received by him and Mrs. Sanford." He writes out in full the cards of invitation received and sent, which, though agreeable to fashion, were evidently not to his taste as he disliked all mere conventionalisms, as he then regarded them. He taught the next winter, and says his "residence in Medway has been pleasant and in many respects profitable." He was here in the midst of the great excitement occasioned by the introduction of cotton spinning and its attendant industries and he says, "the people are apparently in the very last stages of the hectic of avarice. They are rapidly increasing wealth and as rapidly do they grow in the love of it." He graduated in 1813 from Brown University, Rhode Island, studied theology in Andover, was duly licensed, supplied the pulpits in Newburyport, was afterwards called and ordained, March 4, 1818, pastor of the First Church in Hartford, Conn. He married, June 17, 1818, Miss Louisa Fisher, daughter of William C and Lois (Mason) Fisher, of Wrentham, who, upon her mother's side, was a descendant in direct line from John Mason, who came in the May Flower in 1620, from England. Dr. Hawes' pastorate continued forty-four years from 1818 to 1862, and added to his church 1,681 persons. Among them were thirty-seven candidates for the Christian ministry, seven of whom became missionaries, who with other lay workers from the church numbered in all thirty-five. The number of his printed publications were fifty-one. The other Congregational churches in Hartford were largely composed of colonists from his own. Whether Dr. Hawes was a great man or not is a question which some answer in one way and some in another. He made good proof of his ministry; was always a power in Hartford and accomplished great results, and has gone to his reward. He was always interested in Medway Village, and was much pleased to be invited to preach the sermon at the dedication of the Village Church, June 15, 1838. He remarked "that looking upon the hills over the river he was reminded of the wildness and wickedness of his youth." He was the reckless son of a rough, intemperate man. The Rev. Dr. Hawes continued pastor of the First Church in Hartford, Conn, until his death, which occurred June 5, 1867, in Gilead, Conn His monument, a horizontal sarcophagus facing the east and overlooking the city of Hartford, in Cedar Hill Cemetery, is inscribed as follows:

"REV JOEL HAWES, D D,

TENTH PASTOR OF THE CHURCH AND FIRST ECCLESIASTICAL SOCIETY OF HARTFORD.

Born at Medway, Mass., Dec 22, 1789

Died at Gilead, Conn, June 5, 1867 "

The most enduring inscription is in the traditions and upon the very hearts of the people of Hartford. Drs. Hawes and Bushnell were twin pillars upon which rested, for a generation, the religious life of Hartford.

REV. EPHRAIM NELSON HIDDEN.

EPHRAIM NELSON HIDDEN, son of Ephraim and Dorothy (Remick) Hidden, was born Aug. 28, 1810, in Tamworth, N. H. He was the eldest of four sons in a family of six children. When a lad of thirteen years his father met a sudden death by drowning. In this exigency great care and responsibility fell upon the oldest boy, and although a mere stripling he gave himself with unsparing energy to what seemed to rest on his young shoulders. Besides doing what he could for his family he prepared for college in Phillips Academy, Exeter, and graduated in 1836 with high classical honors from Dartmouth College, Hanover, N. H. Among his classmates were the Rev. E. E. Adams, D. D., the Hon. James W. Grimes, Governor of Iowa and United States Senator, Prof. Edward R Peaslee, M. D., the Hon. John Wentworth, of Chicago, the Rev. Samuel C. Bartlett, D. D., President of Dartmouth College, and many other men of honorable distinction Mr. Hidden ranked high in scholarship and upon graduation was appointed Principal of Gilmanton Academy, New Hampshire, which position he filled for four years, meanwhile pursuing his theological studies. He was ordained to the Gospel ministry, and installed, September, 1841, pastor of the Congregational Church in Deerfield, N. H. After a useful ministry of eight years he was called to a larger field of service. He was installed, Nov. 21, 1849, over the Congregational Church in Milford, N. H. His ministry in Milford was attended with large accessions to the church and his congregation was one of the largest in the State. Leaving Milford he labored in Derry, Candia, and Great Falls, N H. His last settlement was in Middleboro, Mass, although for five years, while resident in Medway, he statedly supplied the Congregational Church in Norfolk, Mass. He completed about forty years of Gospel service, closing his public ministry only with his death, which occurred Nov. 28, 1880. He preached on Sunday two sermons, returned home, and ere the coming of the morning sun he had gone to be with his blessed Lord. He had resided in Medway but a few years and in the retirement of a small farm, but had won all hearts to himself, so that his death was widely lamented. The youngest daughter and only surviving child, a young lady of rare gifts and intellectual culture, Emily Parsons Hidden, died April 1, 1882, and Mrs Hidden soon after removed to Chester, N. H.

REV. CALVIN GROUT HILL.

CALVIN GROUT HILL, son of George and Sylvia (Grout) Hill, was born May 10, 1842, in Elmore, Vt. He came to Medway in 1845, graduated at Medway High School, prepared for college in Andover and Wilbraham, was graduated at Amherst College, class of 1867, receiving the degree of A. B. From Amherst he went to Attleboro, Mass., as Principal of the East High School, in which he attained a good reputation as an instructor. Leaving Attleboro he entered the Theological Seminary, Bangor, Me , graduated in the class of 1871. During the last year of the seminary course he was "stated supply" of the Congregational Church in Dexter, Me., preached afterwards for nine months at Waterville, Me. ; declined a call there and accepted one at Hamilton, Mass., at which place he was ordained Sept. 5, 1872. From Hamilton he was called to Walpole, Mass. ; installed Sept 27, 1876. He remained pastor of this church somewhat more than five years, during four of which he was chairman of the board of school committee. Being dismissed from his pastorate in Walpole Aug. 1, 1881, he accepted a call to the First Evangelical Church in Milton, Mass., and was installed Feb. 8, 1882, where he has also been for a number of years a member of the board of school committee. Dec. 1, 1868, he married Miss Mary A. B. Reed, daughter of Dea. G. B. Reed, of Rehoboth, Mass. To them were born in Waterville, Nov. 16, 1871, a son, William Reed Hill, and at Hamilton, May 28, 1874, a daughter, Grace Annie Hill

DON GLEASON HILL, ESQ.

DON GLEASON HILL, son of George and Sylvia (Grout) Hill, was born July 12, 1847, in West Medway. In early youth he worked at the carpenter's trade, using the money thus earned to obtain his education. He fitted for college at the Wesleyan Academy, Wilbraham, Mass , graduating in 1865, the youngest of the class ; entered Amherst College, class of 1869, but for want of funds was obliged to leave college just before the close of the Sophomore year and go back to his trade, and soon after commenced the study of law, working during the day and studying evenings ; a short time, however, was spent in teaching, and during the winter of 1868-'69 he was assistant principal of Barre Academy, Vermont. He graduated at the law school of the University of Albany, N. Y., in May, 1870, receiving therefrom the degree of LL. B , and was at once admitted to the New York Bar Returning to Medway, he entered the law office of Charles H. Deans, Esq., but removed to Dedham in June, 1871, and entered the office of the Hon Waldo Colburn, now Judge of the Supreme Court of this State, with whom he continued his studies. He was admitted to the Norfolk Bar Sept. 25, 1871, on recommendation of Mr. Colburn, but still remained in his office until the appointment of Mr. Col-

Don Gleason Hill.

burn to the bench of the Superior Court, June, 1875, when Mr. Hill found a favorable time had come to "hang out his shingle," which he did at once from the same office. In October, 1875, a law partnership was formed with Charles A. Macintosh under the firm name of Hill & Macintosh, which continued several years. He was appointed a Justice of the Peace April 7, 1874, for seven years and re-appointed in 1881. Mr. Hill has given his attention principally to the study and practice of real estate law, and to the examination of real estate titles. In 1875 he was elected Attorney of the Dedham Institution for Savings and recently also of the Braintree Savings Bank. He is also frequently employed by the Quincy Savings Bank and other savings banks to examine their titles. Being located at the county seat his practice extends throughout the county. He is recognized as a thorough and careful conveyancer. In 1880 he was elected town clerk of Dedham, and in 1882 was elected also selectman, assessor, and overseer of the poor of Dedham, all of which, except the office of assessor, he still holds. He is also one of the trustees of the Dedham Institution for Savings, and, withal, rather a busy man, but finds time to interest himself in antiquarian matters; April, 1881, he was elected a member of the New England Historic Genealogical Society, and in February, 1883, of the Webster Historical Society, of Boston, and is also an officer in the Dedham Historical Society. Dec. 26, 1876, he married Miss Carrie Louisa Luce, of Dedham, and has four children, viz.: Carrie Frances Hill, born Sept. 27, 1877; Helen Florence Hill, born Jan. 20, 1880; Don Gleason Hill, Jr., born Aug. 26, 1883; and Maria Louisa Hill, born Jan. 11, 1885. Both Mr. Hill and his wife are members of the Congregational Church connected with the Allin Evangelical Society of Dedham, of which he is now one of the parish committee.

REV. GEORGE EDWIN HILL.

GEORGE EDWIN HILL, son of George and Sylvia (Grout) Hill, was born April 26, 1858, in Medway, and very early believing that he had been called to the ministry, began to prepare himself for that work, choosing the Methodist as his denomination, and he has already, although young, received several appointments, first at Mendon, afterwards at Savoy, then at Heath, and at Essex in this state. He is married and has one child.

WILLIAM FRANCIS HILL, ESQ.

WILLIAM FRANCIS HILL, son of George and Sylvia (Grout) Hill, was born Oct. 23, 1860, in West Medway. He pursued his studies in Boston and Wilbraham, and afterwards went to Dedham, where he was employed in his brother's law office until the spring of 1881. When the Dedham Water Company wished to employ a young man who would begin with the first laying of the pipes and grow up with the work, Mr. Hill was selected by the company and given a very responsible position, and through faithful attention to duties was, upon the completion of the works, at the early age of twenty-one years, made the superintendent thereof, which office he still holds; he is also clerk of the corporation. This company has over fifteen miles of main water pipes; an extension of over two thousand feet was made the past year under the personal direction of the superintendent. The important trusts committed to him by the directors show their confidence in his abilities and integrity.

REV. ASA HIXON.

ASA HIXON, son of Asa and Polly (Turner) Hixon, was born March 6, 1800, in Medway, Mass. At the age of nineteen years he began preparation for college under the instruction of the Rev. Mr. Ide, and completed his preparatory course at the academy in Bridgewater, Mass. He graduated from Brown University in the class of 1825, with the late Barnas Sears, D. D., of Boston, and the Rev. David Sanford, of Medway. Two years before graduation he chose the profession of the ministry, and pursuant to this choice took a theological course in the Theological Seminary, Auburn, N. Y. He was ordained to the Gospel ministry and installed Oct. 7, 1829, pastor of the Orthodox Congregational Church in Oakham, Mass. He married, June, 1829, Charlotte Baker, daughter of Capt. David and Jemima (Richardson) Baker, of Franklin, Mass. An illness of long standing soon compelled him to relinquish active labor, and he retired, hoping by a season of rest to rally, and again assume the duties of the pastorate. So unwilling were his people to sunder the relation, that for two years they continued to look to him as their pastor. In 1832 he removed to West Medway, and in 1845 to Franklin, Mass., where he resided for twelve years, coöperating, as he was able, with the pastor in religious work. In 1857 he returned to West Medway, where he resided until his death, Nov. 16, 1862. He was deeply interested in educational matters, and served for several years, as his health would permit, upon the school board of this town, and that of Franklin. He was a student throughout his life; and was constantly analyzing, treasuring up, and applying knowledge. He received some private pupils and took a profound interest in the case of one of naturally weak mental condition, with whom he made various original experiments in an attempt to teach simple mathematics. His life was not made brilliant by those achievements which attract the public gaze, but was nevertheless powerful in its influence upon a narrower circle, and illustrated the possibilities for good in the path of one seemingly cut off from an active service. David Baker Hixon, the only son of the Rev. Asa and Charlotte (Baker) Hixon, is a merchant in New York City, and resides in Brooklyn, N. Y.

WILLARD HODGES, ESQ.

WILLARD HODGES, a lineal descendant of the traditional three brothers who emigrated from England in the year 1635 or '40, was the second son of a father to whom was fulfilled the scriptural blessing of a "full quiver." He was born in 1792, in the town of Norton, Mass. In a genealogical record of the Hodges family, we read: "It will be found that, in the early history of New England it was considered quite honorable to aspire to commissions in the militia of this Commonwealth. The Hodges family have aspired to the commission of captain very generally, and whether qualified or not, they have been very successful in their aspirations. It has been remarked that in the towns of Taunton, Norton, and Mansfield, you may call every man you meet of the name, Captain Hodges, and you will be right about three-fourths of the time." Willard Hodges never aspired to any title save such as is due to an honest man; and his only inheritance was his name and the privilege of supporting his parents in their declining years. He resided in Taunton several years, and later in Walpole. In 1824 he was married to Hannah Smith Pond, of the good old Puritan family of the Ponds of Pondville, in Wrentham. They settled in Franklin where they resided over thirty years, leading a quiet, unassuming farmers' life. There they reared ten children. Becoming too feeble for the active duties of farm life, in 1859 he moved to Medway Village where he was only known as an old man, snowy headed, dependent on a cane. He always drove a good horse, and like General Taylor, deemed great occasions demanded strong language; but long after he could not hear a word of the services, he regarded the sacredness of the Sabbath by sleeping through Priest Sanford's sermons with a large red silk handkerchief spread carefully over his head. His characteristics were good common sense, a powerful will, a strong sense of justice, with rank intolerance of hypocrisy and vice. Ripe for the harvest, he fell asleep on the eighth day of August, 1876, aged eighty-four years, and awaits the resurrection in the Oakland Cemetery.

MAJ. GEORGE HOLBROOK.

GEORGE HOLBROOK, son of Daniel and Esther (Hall) Holbrook, was born April 28, 1767, in Wrentham, Mass. He received a limited education in the public schools, and while young was apprenticed to Paul Revere, of Revolutionary fame, to learn the machinist and clockmaker's trades. After serving his full time he began manufacturing bells in Brookfield, having learned the art from an old English Encyclopædia, was very successful and built up a large business. Meeting with financial troubles in 1812, he removed to Laconia, N. H., then Meredith Bridge, where he carried on a farm. Happening to be in East Medway in the year 1816, and knowing that a bell was wanted for the new church just completed, he agreed to cast it and did so in a shed standing where Mr. E. L. Holbrook's house now is. It was a novel thing and people came from many towns to see the sight. The bell was a good one, however, was raised on the church and served for many years. This was the first bell cast in Medway and is the date of the establishment of the Holbrook Bell Foundry in this place. Major Holbrook received his title as an officer of the State Militia. Mary Evalina Holbrook, daughter of Major Holbrook, was born Jan. 2, 1807, in Brookfield, Mass. She was a lady of great personal beauty and accomplishment. She had a musical education and a voice of great purity and sweetness. She was a leading singer in the Handel and Haydn Society, of Boston, Mass., and a great favorite among musical people. She married John Baker, Jr.

COL. GEORGE HANDEL HOLBROOK.

GEORGE HANDEL HOLBROOK, son of George and Mary (Wood) Holbrook, was born July 21, 1798, in Brookfield, Mass., attended town school, moved to Medway in 1816, became associated with his father in the manufacture of bells and church clocks, succeeded in 1820 to the entire business which he carried on until 1871, having at that time cast over ten thousand church and other bells. He married, Jan 1, 1824, Louisa Harding, daughter of Thomas and Keziah (Bullen) Harding. In 1837 he began building church organs, in company with his cousin, Mr. J. Holbrook Ware, until 1850, when the partnership was dissolved. Colonel Holbrook, a musician and a violinist of more than local reputation, was a member of the Handel and Haydn Society of Boston. He was, when young, offered the leadership of an orchestra in one of the theatres of Boston. He was very much interested in military service, and held every commission from ensign to colonel, declining the position of brigadier-general to which he was elected. He was postmaster at East Medway for over thirty-five years, and represented the town in 1835 in the Legislature. He was of a quiet, retiring disposition, though genial. His house was always open to musical and literary people, and he will be remembered for his liberality in providing musical entertainments of the highest order. The Handel and Haydn Society and Boston's most celebrated musicians often performed under his direction. Colonel Holbrook died March 20, 1875, aged seventy-six years. He was succeeded in the organ business by his son, Mr. Edwin L. Holbrook, and in the bell business by his grandson, Mr. Edwin Handel Holbrook.

Rev. Sanford Jabez Horton, D. D.

Sanford Jabez Horton, grandson of Dr. Nathaniel Miller, was born Sept. 24, 1817, in Franklin, Mass. He was, in his youth, engaged to learn the trade of a cabinet maker, to Maj. Luther Metcalf, of Medway. He early evinced a desire for knowledge, was fond of reading and study, and decided, if possible, to obtain a liberal education. He was encouraged by his friends in Medway and Franklin, and was subsequently assisted by Mr. Orion Mason. He graduated in 1843, at Trinity College, Hartford, Conn., and studied theology in Alexandria, Va. He became, in 1846, the rector of St. Andrew's Church, Providence, R. I. He was rector of Grace Church, New Bedford, from 1848 to 1852, and for ten years succeeding was rector of St. Paul's Church in Windham, Conn. In 1862 he was elected Principal of the Episcopal Academy, in Cheshire, Conn., which office he has held ever since. He received the degree of D. D. in 1869, from Trinity College. On his visits to Medway he has several times supplied the pulpit of the Village church, to the great pleasure of old friends. Dr. Horton has a practical talent, and in the management of a literary institution has achieved success.

Joel Hunt, Esq.

Joel Hunt, a young merchant, removed to Medway in 1811, and in connection with his father-in-law, Maj. Luther Metcalf, purchased what was called the "Garnsy farm" in the west precinct, consisting of eighty acres lying northerly of Charles River and west of Chicken Brook. They subsequently purchased the Richardson farm, easterly of Chicken Brook, and both sides of Charles River. Maj. Luther Metcalf, Joel Hunt, and Luther Metcalf, Jr., under the firm name of Metcalf, Hunt & Company, built in 1813, a factory on the site now occupied by Campbell's paper mill, and were early manufacturers of machinery and cotton goods. Some of the first machinery put in operation at Amoskeag Mills, Manchester, N. H., was built at this factory. The town and parish records for nearly forty years indicate Mr. Hunt to have been almost continuously in active office of selectman, assessor, over-

Joel Hunt

seer of the poor, etc. In 1842 he was elected to the Legislature and served the session of Governor Marcus Morton. He was an ardent Jeffersonian Democrat, and one of the only seven in town who cast a vote for Andrew Jackson. We append the following obituary, written by the Rev. Dr. Ide soon after his decease:

"JOEL HUNT, ESQ., died Sept. 1, 1852, aged seventy. He left behind him to mourn his loss, a wife and ten children. He was a kind husband and an affectionate and indulgent father. Few men would be more missed in their families than he. His good sense, his kind heart and social nature, made him a pleasant companion everywhere. A man of native talent, an independent thinker, a shrewd observer of the world, he had acquired a rich fund of practical information, which often served to render his conversation both instructive and entertaining. His store of anecdotes was inexhaustible. Something appropriate and striking from this source seemed instantly to occur to his mind on every subject and occasion on which he chose to speak. In this way, he could at pleasure excite a smile or draw a tear, illustrate a truth, or administer a reproof; compliment a friend, or retort upon an adversary. He was a useful citizen, much engaged in the business of the town, and of individuals who sought his counsel and his aid; and his accommodating spirit often led him to neglect his own business for the sake of giving aid to others. He was frequently elected to some of the most important offices in the gift of the town, and discharged the duties of these stations with credit to himself and satisfaction to his friends. He was good to the poor and afflicted; always on hand in the day of trouble. A friend to law and order and good morals, he exerted himself for the promotion of these in the community in which he lived. He was a cheerful supporter of the Gospel, and a regular attendant upon its institutions. He spoke freely, especially in his last illness, of the sanctity of the Sabbath, the value of the Bible as the word of God, and of the truth and importance of that religion which it inculcates. His death is deeply lamented, not only by his bereaved family and the religious society of which he had been a fast and active friend for forty years, but with sorrow by all who knew him." *Vid. The Hunt Genealogy.*

JULIUS C. HURD, ESQ.

JULIUS C. HURD, for twenty years one of the active business men of the town, came to Medway Village about 1836, and soon after formed a copartnership with Mr. Alfred Daniels, and began the manufacture of batting at the lower mill of the Village, afterward Eaton & Wilson, and buying and selling cotton waste. The business grew and prospered in their hands and their firm became the leading one in the Village. Mr. Hurd built the large house at the west end of the Village now occupied by Mr. M. E. Thompson, where he resided until he left the town. He and his partner became interested in the old Medway Branch Railroad, and furnished the larger part of the funds for its construction. Mr. Hurd also became one of the directors of the Norfolk County Railroad. This connection with the railroad was unfortunate and the affairs of the firm at length became so involved that in 1857 a suspension was the result. Mr. Hurd was a man of untiring energy and activity, and excellent business ability, a man of positive opinions, yet public spirited and liberal. During his active life when business success had given him a competence he retained a love for his early agricultural pursuits and the variety of fruits and flowers in his grounds showed the fondness of the owner for horticulture and kindred pursuits. He left Medway in 1858, and after a short residence in Dorchester, he returned to his early home in Bristol, Conn., where he has since resided. He was married in 1837, to Rebecca A. Robinson, of Smithfield, R. I.

REV. JACOB IDE, D. D.

JACOB IDE, son of Jacob and Lydia (Kent) Ide, was born March 29, 1785, in Attleboro, Mass. His father was a farmer in moderate circumstances. His mother was a daughter of Dea. Elijah Kent, of Rehoboth, Mass. The early years of his life were passed in hard labor on the farm, and the general expectation was that he would follow the occupation of his father. But at the age of seventeen he began to have strong leanings toward a public education. His thoughts were at Brown University. About this time he had a great desire to attend Commencement at that institution. His father said there was a field of corn whose stalks must be cut that day. So Jacob got up at three o'clock in the morning, and did a full day's work of cutting stalks, and then dressed and went on foot eight miles to Providence to attend Commencement. At length he gained the consent of his father that he might obtain a public education. He fitted for college with the Rev. Mr. Holman, pastor of the Second Church in Attleboro, who was well qualified to give classical instruction   It shows the earnestness of purpose which was in the young man, that his whole preparation for college was made in a year, and that, too, with many interruptions by reason of sickness, labor, and teaching, so that the period of solid study was hardly more than six months   At that time the candidates for admission to Brown University must be prepared to pass an examination in Æsop's Fables, eight books of Virgil's Æneid, eight orations of Cicero, and the four evangelists in the Greek Testament.   All this was done in the time specified, and the young man entered Brown University, went through the course of study and graduated in 1809, the valedictorian of his class.   After graduating he was engaged for a few months in teaching in Wrentham, and then went to Andover, entering the third class that passed through that institution.   Here he was brought into familiar acquaintance with that band of young men who had devoted themselves to the work of Foreign Missions, Judson, Mills, Newell, Hall, Richards, and Warren.   The thoughts that filled their minds were then freshly awakened, and the whole enterprise was new to the American churches.   During his stay at Andover the American Board was organized at Bradford, and some of these young men were commissioned to go forth and carry the Gospel to distant and idolatrous nations.   The impressions gained amid those scenes were never lost.   After graduating at Andover in 1812, he preached for a few Sabbaths at East Abington, and was then invited to Portsmouth, N. H., to preach as a candidate in the pulpit just made vacant by the death of the Rev. Joseph Buckminster   Here he had Ex-Governor Langdon for one of his constant hearers, and also Daniel Webster, then a young lawyer of great promise, and who was elected that same year, for the first time, Representative to Congress. After preaching for some months, in April, 1813, he received an unanimous call from the church to settle there in the ministry; but the parish did not concur.   From Portsmouth Mr. Ide came to Boston, and assisted Dr. Griffin for a few weeks, while he was preparing and delivering his famous "Park Street Lectures," Mr. Ide preaching in the morning, and Dr. Griffin in the afternoon and evening.   He preached also again at East Abington, and at York, Me.   Then his health failed, and for a time he was laid aside from labor, and grave doubts were felt whether he would be able to preach again.   But in 1814 he was so far recovered that he accepted a call from the church and society in West Medway to become their pastor, and there had a long ministry.   He was ordained Nov. 2, 1814, and for fifty-one years remained in full discharge of the duties of the pastorate.   After 1865 he was relieved of all ministerial responsibility, but continued senior pastor till his death   In 1815 he was united in marriage to Miss Mary Emmons, youngest daughter of Dr. Nathaniel Emmons, of Franklin, Mass.

In his long ministry, reaching considerably beyond the half century, he was a man of marked character and influence.   Of quiet and simple manners, without the slightest approach to the noisy and demonstrative, he had weight in all counsels, and was one in whom his fellow-men loved to confide and whom they found it safe to trust.   With little rhetorical power in the pulpit, and with no attempt whatever at oratorical display, he was an able and faithful preacher, kept a steady hold upon the respect and affection of his people, as few pastors are able to do, and was often called upon to exercise his gifts on public occasions abroad

Dr. Ide was a man of remarkable self-control. He had learned to rule well his own spirit. Those who came into his presence for the first time, seeing how meek and placid was his demeanor, how quiet and unpretending his manners, how silently and respectfully he listened to what a stranger had to say, might suppose for a moment that he was wanting in force of character and will. But a slight acquaintance would convince any one that he had an eye to see, as well as an ear to hear, that he had a mind of his own, a judgment eminently clear, incisive and decisive. He furnished a beautiful illustration of a truth, which we are sometimes slow to learn, that strength of will and purpose is more commonly the property of quiet and gentle natures than of noisy and blustering ones.

Dr Ide was early the friend of the slave. He embraced and proclaimed anti-slavery principles when it was an unpopular cause, and he was firm, steadfast, and influential therein. There were scenes in his life connected with this matter which were peculiarly trying, and which called for large wisdom and patience. But in this, as in other things, he bore himself faithfully and well. Few men pass away from earth with a record so clear and bright. Thousands of the living have seen him in his quiet and hospitable home, and many more have seen him in the pulpit and on public occasions. We have no fear that their verdict will not accord essentially with our own. He was a kind of model minister, and especially a model country minister. He loved the quiet and simplicity of country life. He was not a man for the noise, show, and excitement of a great city. He dwelt among his own people. He loved them and they loved him. There is something beautiful in the contemplation of such a life-long ministry as his. Such cases are growing rare among us. The picture of his long dwelling at West Medway is peculiarly attractive. The good which he has done will live after him. He will long be remembered in all that region as an able and successful pastor, and as a true and faithful preacher of the Gospel of Jesus Christ.

The following is a list of Dr. Ide's published writings.

Funeral Sermons — On the death of Miss Sarah J Fuller; Edmund I Sanford, Mrs. Hannah Miller, the Rev David Long, Milford, Dea. Daniel Wiley, Mr. James Partridge; the Rev Charles Simmons; Mr George Nourse, Mrs. Abigail Wright; the Rev Joseph Wheaton, Miss Lydia C Southwick.

Occasional Sermons — On Intemperance, Dec 14, 1817; at the ordination of the Rev David Brigham, at Randolph, Dec 29, 1818; before the Norfolk Education Society, June 13, 1821, at the ordination of the Rev Daniel J Poor, at Foxboro, March 11, 1840, on the fiftieth anniversary of the author's ordination and settlement, Nov 2, 1864; at the ordination of the Rev Sewall Harding, Waltham, Jan 17, 1821; at the ordination of the Rev. George Fisher, at Harvard, Mass, on the "Nature and Tendency of Balls, Seriously and Candidly Considered", on Fast Day, April 9, 1829, on "Character of John the Baptist", at the ordination of the Rev. Asa Hixon, Oakham, Oct 7, 1829, at the ordination of the Rev John M Putnam, Ashby, Dec. 13, 1820, at the ordination of the Rev. Samuel Hunt, Natick, July 17, 1839; at the installation of the Rev Samuel Hunt at Franklin, Dec 4, 1850, at the ordination of the Rev Charles T Torrey, March 23, 1837. One or two other discourses are lost.

Articles for the Christian Magazine.

Vol. 1. "Fasting Explained," p. 111, Obituary of the Rev M Partridge, p 376; Review of a sermon preached by the Rev Wm. B. Sprague, before the Bible Foreign

Missionary and Education Societies at Springfield, Aug. 28, 1823, p. 364; " Strange Thing," p. 266.

Vol. 2. Review of Dr Pond's Concert Lectures, p 107; "Ought a Wife to Refrain from Making a Public Profession of Religion in Consequence of being Forbidden by her Husband?" p. 137; "Total Depravity," p. 239.

Vol 3. "A's Answer to Discipulus," p 107; "Improper Instructions to an Awakened Sinner," p 149; "Deception or, Hypocrisy in Death," p 58; Review of the Rev Mr. Whitman's Sermon, pp 217, 243, 267, 309, 369; "The Criminality of Unbelief," p. 43, "Reply to Xanthus," p 142.

Vol 4. "Answers respecting Inquiries, Submission," pp. 50, 97.

Dr. Ide also edited *The Works of Dr. Emmons*, in seven volumes.

Dr. Ide retained to the last his characteristic dignity and gentle courtesy, thanking his attendants for the least service rendered. As he grew gradually weaker, he seemed conscious of the approaching end, and said to his oldest son, who had come from Mansfield for the final visit, with a tender pathos: "I am going away and shall be forgotten." The night but one before he died, when suffering from a sharp pain in his head, he arose and standing by his study desk, lifted up his hands and thus prayed with all the clearness of his pulpit utterance: "O Lord, when thou has kept us here on earth as long as it is thy will, be pleased to take us home to thyself." One night more had passed and the sun had just risen, when with gentle breathings, as of an infant's peaceful sleep, the good man's spirit was released.

REV. JACOB IDE, D. D.

" A hoary herald of the truth,
Who'd struggled with disease from youth,
But notwithstanding friendship's fears,
Had lived almost a hundred years,
With mind well trained and running o'er
With-wisdom's wealth and learning's lore,
With heart so tuned with Christ's to play,
He never feared the face of clay,
But feared, one inch to bow or bend,
If that would grieve his Heavenly friend
He preached the truth, without one thought,
If it would give offense or not,
And yet so calm and kind 'twas said,
Which showed the heart that prompted bled,
That guilt endowed with common sense,
Had been ashamed to take offense

A purer life has seldom been
Passed in this world so stained with sin.
He had his faults, as who has not?
And yet I ne'er discovered what

I've met him oft for many a year,
In many a phase of his career,
At home, abroad, and by the way,
Among the grave, among the gay,
When sweet repentance came to sue,
For one to tell it what to do,

Where sickness tossed its weary head,
And death was hovering o'er the bed,
Where guilt was suffering bitterer pangs
Than sickness shoots, from conscience's fangs,
In these and countless ways beside,
He was the same kind friend and guide,
And then his gems of wit would throng,
In places where such gems belong,
And make the moments spent, so sweet,
You'd wish such meetings to repeat,
And when Brown's fresh triennial came,
And brought me that old veteran's name,
And bore me to my native shore
And set me down before his door,
He wore the same mild gentle mien,
That I for years and years had seen.
But those purer powers, that made him strong,
And that he'd used so well and long,
The Master had in kindness come,
And picked them up to carry home,
And soon will come the happy day
When re-attuned they'll ever play

"O! if we ever are forgiven,
And by God's kindness enter heaven,
We shall behold close to his side,
That grand old veteran, Jacob Ide."

CHARLES THURBER.

A Hymn sung at the Funeral of Mrs. Mary Ide, July 3, 1880.

The hands that wrought for man and God
  Are folded on the breast of peace;
From toils for want, at home, abroad,
  These busy hands have sweet release.

The heart that beat is pulseless now,
  The heart that beat for human woe;
No more this heart will beat, or bow,
  Or pray for sufferers here below.

Her prayer to praise, her toil to rest,
  Is chang'd within the "Better Land,"
Where sorrow ne'er afflicts the breast,
  Nor sin defiles the heart or hand

Earth gives her up, though with a tear;
  Heaven greets on high the sainted one;
While living weepers round the bier
  Gather—TO TELL WHAT SHE HATH DONE !

W M. T

REV. AND HON JACOB IDE.

JACOB IDE, son of the Rev. Dr. Jacob and Mary (Emmons) Ide, was born Aug. 7, 1823, in West Medway He pursued his preparatory studies in the academy, Leicester, and graduated in 1848 from Amherst College, Amherst, Mass. He was a teacher of ancient and modern languages in Boston, and afterward taught two years in the academy, Leicester, Mass. He studied theology under his father's instruction, and after commencing to preach was one year a resident licentiate in the Theological Seminary, Andover, Mass He was ordained to the Gospel ministry and installed March 26, 1856, pastor of the Congregational Church in Mansfield, Mass., and is now filling out the thirtieth year of a useful ministry in that place The Rev. Mr. Ide married March 24, 1859, Ellen M. Rogers, daughter of the Hon. John and Eliza Ann (Williams) Rogers, of Mansfield, Mass. They had one son, John Emmons Ide, who was born Aug. 2, 1868. The Rev. Mr. Ide traveled in 1860 through the different countries of Europe In 1864 he was a member of the House of Representatives, and in 1866 a member of the Senate of the State of Massachusetts.

REV ALEXIS WHEATON IDE.

ALEXIS W. IDE, son of the Rev. Dr. Jacob and Mary (Emmons) Ide, was born Oct. 10, 1826, in West Medway. After a few years of business life he studied theology under the instruction of his father, the Rev Dr. Ide, who fitted many young men for the Christian ministry. He was ordained July 7, 1859, at Stafford Springs, Conn., where he fulfilled a successful pastorate of eight years He resigned July 2, 1867, and returned to his father's house, and with great fidelity and filial devotion he cared for his aged parents while they lived. The Rev. Mr. Ide was a member of the Legislature in 1872, and elected in 1874 Chaplain of the State Senate of Massachusetts. Since the death of his revered parents at very advanced ages, in 1880, the Rev. Mr Ide has continued to reside in the old homestead, giving himself to labors of beneficence and usefulness and preaching the Gospel as his services were demanded.

E. O. Jameson.

Rev. E. O. Jameson.

E. O. Jameson, son of Daniel and Mary (Twiss) Jameson, was born Jan. 23, 1832, in Dunbarton, N H. He pursued his preparatory studies in Gilmanton Academy, and graduated in 1855 from Dartmouth College, N. H. At the age of seventeen years he united, March 6, 1849, with the church in Chester, N. H. While a student he taught school in Dunbarton, Mont Vernon, Claremont, and Bristol, N. H. Mr. Jameson graduated in 1858 from the Theological Seminary, Andover, Mass. He was licensed to preach, Dec. 29, 1857, by the Middlesex South Association, in Framingham, Mass., and supplied the pulpits temporarily in Kennebunk, Me , Dracut, East Randolph, and Concord, Mass., and Concord, N H He was ordained and installed March 1, 1860, pastor of the East Congregational Church in Concord, N H In 1865 he was called to the Union Evangelical Church of Salisbury and Amesbury, Mass., where he was installed Nov. 9, 1865 He resigned and was installed Nov. 15, 1871, pastor of the First Church of Christ in Medway, now the Church of Christ, Millis, Mass. The Rev. Mr. Jameson married Sept. 20, 1858, Mary Joanna Cogswell, daughter of the Rev. Dr. William and Joanna (Strong) Cogswell. He was the author of a Memorial Sketch of the Rev. William Cogswell, D. D., which was published in the first volume of *Memorial Biographies of Deceased Members of the New England Historical Genealogical Society*. In 1884 he published *The Cogswells in America*, a volume of more than seven hundred pages, the results of many years of careful genealogical inquiry. He was chosen the editor and prepared for the press *The History of Medway, Mass* Mr Jameson pursued lines of historical research for recreation as some clergymen follow the trout brook, and a discovered name, date, or fact, was to him a thing of joy as much as the nibble of a hungry trout, or the living fish dangling at the end of a line to some of his professional friends.

Arthur Orcutt Jameson, A. B.

Arthur Orcutt Jameson, son of the Rev. E O. and Mary Joanna (Cogswell) Jameson, was born Nov. 25, 1859, in Concord, N. H He entered, in 1873, the Roxbury Latin School, Boston Highlands, Mass., and completed the course of study in four years, under the instruction of William C. Collar, A. M. He took the first rank in the Latin School, and graduated in 1881, the first scholar in his class, from Harvard College, Cambridge, Mass. After graduation he received an appointment as the teacher of classics and mathematics in the Arnold School, New York City But a few days before he was to assume this position he was taken suddenly ill, and died Sept. 30, 1881, at the age of twenty-one years His burial took place Oct. 5, 1881, in the Blossom Hill Cemetery, Concord, N. H. The spot overlooks the place of his birth and the Merrimac River, on whose banks much of his boyhood was spent. He was a young man as noble in character as he was brilliant in scholarship. He made a public confession of Christ at the age of sixteen years and united Nov 7, 1875, with the church of which his father was the pastor His early death was widely lamented, not only as a private affliction but as a loss to the world of one who gave promise of distinguished influence and usefulness. The following letter, received among many others by the afflicted family, from the Rev. George A. Gordon, then of Greenwich, Conn., and since pastor of the Old South Church, Boston, Mass , shows in what estimation Mr. Jameson was held by his fellow students :

"GREENWICH, Oct 8, 1881.

"MR AND MRS JAMESON.

"*Dear afflicted, though unknown friends* I have just learned with deep sorrow of the death of my admired and much respected classmate, Arthur Orcutt Jameson.   I am so much pained and shocked at the sad news that I cannot forbear offering you my sincere and sorrowful sympathy in your great grief   Mr Jameson and myself had in part the same elective studies for two years, and from what I saw of him in the classroom and elsewhere, I had acquired a profound admiration for his scholarship, and an affectionate appreciation of his elevated and manly character   I was always deeply interested in him and so knew him much better than he knew me.   His memory is and will be to me a constant inspiration in thought, principle, character, and devotion In accuracy and comprehensiveness of intellect, and in natural power of acquisition, I never knew his superior, scarcely his equal   At this moment as I think of his massive and serene face, now still in death, I am burdened with a personal sorrow, and cannot but feel, ' *How is the strong staff broken, and the beautiful rod* '

"Yours, with great respect and true sympathy,

"GEORGE A. GORDON."

NATHAN JONES, ESQ.

NATHAN JONES, son of Nathan and Sarah (Clark) Jones, was born Nov. 2, 1786, in East Medway   He was a farmer and lived at the corner of Main and Plain streets   Mr. Jones was called to fill many public offices.   He was appointed in 1837 a Justice of the Peace, elected in 1836 and 1847 a Representative to the General Court, and for more than twenty years served as the Deputy Sheriff for Norfolk County.   He was appointed June 22, 1841, special commissioner for five years, and as County Commissioner in 1847, holding the office for seven years   He removed in 1858, to Medfield, Mass., where he died Dec 8, 1870, at the age of eighty-four years.

ORVILLE R. KELSEY, M. D.

ORVILLE R. KELSEY, son of Robert and Judith (Batchelder) Kelsey, was born Nov. 17, 1841, in Danville, Vt   He married March 11, 1868, Abbie Augusta Shattuck, daughter of Samuel Farley and Abigail B. (Means) Shattuck   Mr. Kelsey was a Union soldier.   He enlisted Aug. 4, 1862, in Battery A, First Artillery, 11th Regiment Vermont Volunteers.   He was in thirteen battles, and wounded Sept 19, 1864, in the battle of Winchester, Va.   He received his discharge June 24, 1865.   Mr. Kelsey after the close of the war pursued his studies and received March 6, 1878, the degree of M. D. from the Boston University School of Medicine.   Dr Kelsey was Medical Examiner for the Norfolk Lodge, No. 635, R. A., for the Eureka Council, No. 5, the Mount Nebo Council, No 707, R. A., and for Medway Lodge, No. 42, A. O M. W.   He was District Deputy Grand Regent in the twenty-fourth R. A., District Massachusetts, and member of the Committee on Returns in the Grand Council, R. A. of Massachusetts.   Dr. Kelsey was a member of the Massachusetts Homœopathic Medical Society, and of the Massachusetts Surgical and Gynecological Society.   The children were . George W., born April 24, 1869; Samuel R., born Dec. 4, 1870   He resided in

Medway several years, but removed in January, 1883, to Waterbury, Conn., where he had an extensive practice.

REV. CALEB KIMBALL.

CALEB KIMBALL, son of Caleb and Elizabeth (Hammond) Kimball, was born June 3, 1798, in Ipswich, Mass. His father died when he was young, and at fourteen years of age he was apprenticed to a blacksmith in a neighboring town, where he remained until he was twenty-one years old. At the age of nineteen he became a Christian, with a strong desire to preach the Gospel. Failing in his effort to purchase his remaining time from his master, he toiled on till he was twenty-one, and the second day after started for Phillips Academy, Andover, to prepare for college. This was in 1819. He entered Dartmouth College in 1822, and graduated in 1826. In his preparatory course he was aided by the American Education Society, which aid he refunded after entering the ministry. In college his patron was a gentleman of his native town, who sought him out, and paid all his bills. In the autumn of 1826 he entered the Theological Seminary in Andover. Near the close of his first year there his eyes began to fail from a disease of the retina, attended with severe pain, and in the beginning of the second year, he was entirely disabled for study. In December, 1827, he entered the Eye and Ear Infirmary, Boston, where he remained six months, and obtained some relief. He returned to Ipswich, where he was confined to his room more than two years, and became totally blind. At the close of this period his eyes were free from suffering, and his heart so set on the work of the ministry, that he ventured to take a license to preach, and labored considerably in the revivals of 1831. Being too feeble to take charge of a parish, he was ordained in 1832, and under commission from the Massachusetts Home Missionary Society he labored in Gloucester Harbor, South Dennis, and Harwich, Mass. In the latter place he preached two years. Then his eyes again failed. He remained in Harwich four years, confined to a dark room and suffering intense pain. These four years of physical suffering were years of great spiritual enjoyment, and he spoke of them afterwards as among the shortest and happiest of his life. Then he returned to Ipswich, stopping in Boston three months at the Eye and Ear Infirmary, where he learned to write on the system of the blind, an invaluable blessing to him, as it enabled him to do his own writing. He soon began to labor again in revivals of religion, and some time after went to Portland, Me., to assist the Rev. Dr. Chickering in the great revival with which that city was blessed at that time. There he labored three months, amidst scenes of the deepest interest. On his return home, he stopped to preach one Sabbath at Biddeford. At the request of the people he consented to remain three months, if his health permitted, and he staid two years. On returning to Ipswich, at the request of a neighboring minister, he commenced writing and publishing some small books on religious subjects. With these he canvassed about half of New England, selling over one hundred and twenty thousand. In 1854 he married and came to Medway for a permanent home. Soon his health again failed, and he spent another year in a dark room. The last eleven years of his life he seldom left home. He died June 19, 1879. Mrs. Kimball survives him and resides in Medway.

REV. STEPHEN KNOWLTON.

STEPHEN KNOWLTON, (*Stephen, Smith, Jacob, Jacob, Thomas,*) son of Stephen Smith and Sally (Atwood) Knowlton, was born June 20, 1831, in Stockbridge, Vt. He prepared for college in the academies of Randolph and Ludlow, Vt., and graduated in 1857 from Middlebury College, Vermont. After graduation he taught for five years the Young Ladies' Seminary, in Castleton, Vt., which has since become the Castleton Normal School. Mr. Knowlton graduated in 1865, from the Andover Theological Seminary, and was settled Nov. 2, 1865, as colleague pastor with the Rev. Jacob Ide, D. D., over the Second Church of Christ in Medway. *Vid.* THE CHURCHES. He resigned this pastorate Nov. 20, 1872, to accept a call to settle with the Congregational Church in New Haven, Vt., where he remained nine years. He was again installed in 1881 in Greensboro, Vt., where he is still laboring in the Gospel. The Rev. Mr. Knowlton married, Aug. 25, 1858, Frances L. Kent, daughter of the Rev. Cephas Henry and Mary Abbie (Clark) Kent. Their only child was Kent Knowlton, born Aug. 14, 1872.

WILLIAM LA CROIX, ESQ.

WILLIAM LA CROIX, son of Frederick and Elizabeth (Cobb) La Croix, was born May, 1787, in Wrentham, Mass. His father came to this country in 1775, from the island of Gaudaloupe. The immediate occasion of his immigration was an insurrection of the slaves on the island. While here he married and after a few years returned to Gaudaloupe with his family, but soon died very suddenly. Mrs. La Croix then embarked for this country, and on the passage gave birth to a son, whom she named Frederick for her lamented husband. William La Croix went with his parents to Gaudaloupe and returned to Wrentham, Mass., with his mother. When a young man he learned the trade of carriage making, and established himself in business in Dedham, Mass. He married 1815, Lois Bullard, daughter of Adam and Lois (Richardson) Bullard, of East Medway, to which place he removed in 1818, and settled on the place of his father-in-law, Mr. Bullard. The house stood near the site of the residence of the Rev. Mr. Bucknam, the old minister. Mrs. Lois La Croix died February, 1825. Mr. La Croix married an elder sister, Jemima Bullard, and continued to carry on the farm, now known as the La Croix Fruit Farm, also doing something at his trade. Mrs. Jemima La Croix died February, 1857, and Mr. La Croix survived but a few years, and died suddenly, February, 1860. He was a man of generous impulses, and his life was upright and useful. Mr. La Croix possessed in combination an amiable and cheerful disposition, the sturdy virtues of a true New Englander, and the sprightly qualities of the French. He was an exemplary citizen, and his death was universally lamented.

JAMES LA CROIX, ESQ.

JAMES LA CROIX, son of William and Lois (Bullard) La Croix, was born Nov. 30, 1823, in East Medway. After his school days he went to Northampton and learned the tailor's trade, but his health being poor, having fulfilled his apprenticeship, he returned home and worked with his father on the farm. He married Mary Skinner Hodges, daughter of Willard and

Hannah Smith (Pond) Hodges, of Franklin, Mass., and settled down on the old homestead. Upon the death of his father he purchased the interests of the other heirs and established the business of manufacturing refined cider and vinegar. Subsequently he added the manufacture of canned corn, fruits and vegetables of various kinds. By careful and able management he developed a large business. The production of the first year was but five barrels of vinegar and some five thousand cans of fruits, while in 1882 the production reached three thousand barrels of refined cider and vinegar and some three hundred and seventy-five thousand cans of various fruits and vegetables.

THE RESIDENCE AND MANUFACTORY OF JAMES LA CROIX, ESQ.

In 1883 the manufacture of catsup was taken up successfully. The enterprise and courage of Mr. La Croix in establishing and enlarging this industry was a great benefit to the whole community. Not only was employment furnished to a large number of laborers, but the farmers in the vicinity were provided with a market for their products at home, and many thousands of dollars were thus distributed annually. Mr. La Croix was a man of great executive ability, naturally a leader among men, and for many years was a power in political circles and in the public affairs of the town. His health became broken by business cares, and being worn out by overwork he took a sudden cold and fell a prey to pneumonia, from which he died Sept. 6, 1883. Mr. La Croix was a citizen of prominence, a man of public spirit and of large business capacity, and his death was regarded as a great public loss.

LOUIS LA CROIX, ESQ.

LOUIS LA CROIX, son of James and Mary S. (Hodges) La Croix, was born Sept. 8, 1851, in East Medway. His education was obtained in the schools of Medway, and he gained the reputation of being an apt scholar and a thorough student. He was for some time engaged in business with his father, but abandoned manufacturing pursuits to become one of the tillers of the soil. He carried on quite an extensive farm in the northern portion of the town. Mr. La Croix was chosen, in 1885, the first Town Clerk and Treasurer of the town of Millis, Mass.

G. J. LA CROIX'S STUDIO, NO. 34 SCHOOL STREET, BOSTON, MASS.

GEORGE JAMES LA CROIX, son of James and Mary S. (Hodges) La Croix, was born Oct. 18, 1854, in East Medway. He was educated in the public schools of Medway and Worcester, Mass. Mr. La Croix early betrayed a gift for sketching, and having completed his education he devoted himself to learn the art of wood engraving. For some years he was in the office of Mr. William J. Dana, Tremont Temple Building, Boston. Mr. La Croix went into business for himself February, 1884, on School Street, Boston. He has won a good reputation and is constantly occupied in the work of engraving, the excellent quality of which is abundantly illustrated in this volume.

Hon. Warren Lovering.

WARREN LOVERING, son of Amos and Lucy (Day) Lovering, was born Feb. 21, 1797, in Framingham, Mass. In 1798, when Warren was about a year old his parents removed to Medway, Mass., where his life was spent, and his death occurred Aug. 21, 1876, in his eightieth year. Mr. Lovering was educated and fitted for college in the schools of Medway. At the age of sixteen years he entered Brown University, from which he graduated in 1817 with high honors, being one of the first six in his class. His classmate, Gov. Charles Jackson, of Rhode Island, referring in earlier years to his life in college, said: "Mr. Lovering lived an exemplary, moral life, and was a true gentleman; he was a born gentleman." After graduation he returned to Medway where he studied law, and was duly admitted to the bar by the County Court in Dedham, Mass. He opened an office in Medway Village in 1820. He soon acquired a high reputation as a lawyer in the county of Norfolk, which drew to him both clients and pupils. He was possessed of unusually varied acquirements in literature and history. Before he was thirty years of age he was chosen to represent the town of Medway in the Legislature of Massachusetts, and between 1826 and 1835 he was a member of six legislatures, and was afterwards a member of that of 1846. As a representative he soon attained an enviable position, and did much toward moulding and shaping the legislation of the State. In the years 1836-37 and '38 he was chosen by the people of the county, as the law then provided, a member of the Executive Council. The Hon. Edward Everett was at this time the Governor of Massachusetts, and with him he was in intimate personal relations. In 1839 he received from Governor Briggs an appointment as a member of the Board of Bank Commissioners for three years, an appointment which was renewed in 1842. He was also one of the commissioners for adjusting the boundary line between Massachusetts and Rhode Island. He was among the founders of the Whig party in Massachusetts, a member for many years of the State Central Committee, and one of the ruling spirits on that committee. He was chosen to represent his Congressional District in the National Whig convention which nominated Gen. William Henry Harrison for the Presidency, the other prominent name before the convention being that of the Hon. Henry Clay. It was said that to no one did Mr. Harrison owe more for his nomination than to the influence of Mr. Lovering in the convention. Subsequently Mr. Lovering visited Mr. Harrison in his home in North Bend, O., traveled with him through the West and was an intimate friend to the President, and had Mr. Harrison lived, Mr. Lovering would have filled some office under his administration. But with President Harrison's death the hopes of the Whig party were blasted, and Mr. Lovering's political influence commenced to wane. He was well entitled to a seat in Congress, and his name was frequently brought forward in the local conventions of the party, but he never secured a nomination. These repeated disappointments at length gave rise to a morbid melancholy, to which he is said to have been predisposed by his temperament, and this, though interrupted by occasional intervals of health and cheerfulness, at length blighted his prospects, both political and professional, and destroyed his happiness. He lost his interest in his profession and in public affairs, and allowed his estate gradually to pass into other hands. In 1851, at the age of fifty-four, he married Cornelia A. Phipps, of Holliston, Mass. At the age of sixty he retired from active professional and public service, and the last twenty years of his life were spent in an almost painful seclusion. He was without near kindred in this vicinity, the new generation that was about him knew little of his former prominence and ability, and almost forgotten and without friends and penniless, one of Medway's ablest and most eminent citizens died at the age of eighty years, Aug. 21, 1876, while the nation was celebrating the centennial of its marvelous history. "One lesson which the life of this gifted and cultured man teaches is that however popular and prominent men may become in public affairs, they may live to be forgotten and unappreciated by a whole generation. It teaches also, a lesson of the broadest charity in our judgment of men, especially those whose mental or moral vision has been clouded, either by disease, disappointment, or any providential event The funeral obsequies of Mr. Lovering were held in the Village church. The Rev. Mr. Jameson, of East Medway, conducted the service. His address left little that ought to have been said Appropriate musical selections were sung by the choir. The Masonic fraternity, of which the deceased in early life was a prominent member, attended the service, and performed the ritual for the dead at the tomb in the Oakland Cemetery."

" In Memoriam "

" Then I saw one — no, did not see —
Tears would gush out 'twixt him and me,
I'd known him long, I'd known him well,
And in his converse felt the spell,
And knew, full well he had a mind
Keen, accurate, polished and refined.
A Chesterfield in airs and dress,
Without one touch of his excess,
But tasteful dress and graceful air
Come not from special thought and care,
But blossoming or outer trace,
Of inner culture, power and grace.
His native state who knew him best,
For she'd applied full many a test,
Selected him from all her hosts,
For many of her highest posts,
And choicest honors freely shed,
On her accomplished servant's head,
And, in whatever station placed,
He filled, not only well, but graced;
And honors falling to his lot,
He wore as if he knew it not.
Not one of those who magnify
A humble post as if a high,
Or magnify a high, and then
Feel that they're wiser, bigger men.
Whate'er he gained, he gained because
He earned it with just what he was;
And having earned it felt no more

In worth's price current than before,
Yet notwithstanding all he'd done,
Positions gained and honor won,
All felt assured that he had not
Had all the honors that he ought,
Chicanery oft in friendship clad
Secured the prize he should have had
Books were his friends and played a part,
The nearest, dearest to his heart,
And every thought he read, he shrined
Within his memory and his mind.
My friend when I had met him last,
I hardly knew, he'd changed so fast.
That lofty spirit that had been,
At work so long and well within,
Had lost its fire, had lost its power,
Disarmed in its dismantled tower,
And soon, all helpless, had to come,
To die away from friends and home,
No kindred ear to hear his sigh,
No kindred hand to close his eye
Farewell, my friend, accept from me
This humble tribute paid to thee
I cannot think without a tear,
What sorrow thou didst suffer here.
But fondly hope and trust that thou,
Art free from care, and happy now.
Forget thee! with such memories frought,
Though all forget thee, I cannot "

C. T.

Hon. Amos Lovering.

Amos Lovering, son of Amos and Lucy (Day) Lovering, was born 1805, in Medway, Mass. He prepared for college in Day's Academy in Wrentham, Mass., and in 1828 graduated from Brown University, Rhode Island. After graduating, he studied law, and in 1832 settled for the practice of his profession in Louisville, Ky. At the end of a few years he removed to St. Joseph, Mo., and subsequently to Scott County, Indiana, where he served for several years as County Attorney, and was made a Justice of Common Pleas for Scott and Clark counties, a position which he held for ten years. In 1862 he removed to Nashville, Tenn. In 1869 he made his residence in Jackson, Miss., and was appointed a Judge in the Ninth Judicial District of that State. He was subsequently appointed by Governor Alcorn a member of a commission for codifying the laws of Mississippi. While engaged in this service, he contracted a malarial disease which affected the brain and wholly unfitted him for any subsequent labor. Thus disabled, he returned to Louisville in 1876, where he spent the closing years of his life. He died Jan. 28, 1879, at the age of seventy-four years, in Louisville, Ky. He was married in 1859 to Mary Shelby Pebworth, who with one son survived him.

Horatio Mason, Esq.

Horatio Mason, son of Simon Harding and Betsey (Leland) Mason, was born July 28, 1798, in East Medway, now Millis. He occupied the old homestead near Boggastow Pond, where his grandfather, Mr. Abner Mason, lived, the land first cleared within the territory of Medway by George Fairbanks. Mr. Mason was a much respected and prominent citizen of the town. He was appointed in 1848 a Justice of the Peace; and was elected two successive years, 1848 and 1849, a Representative to the General Court. He died May 11, 1868, at the age of seventy years.

Rev. John Oliver Means, D. D.

John Oliver Means, son of John and Sara Means, was born Aug. 1, 1822, in Augusta, Me. He graduated in 1843 from Bowdoin College. His collegiate course was marked by close application. He was a fine student, and exceedingly thorough in everything he undertook. His clear mind enabled him to grasp any subject, and this excellent trait followed him throughout his life and was the foundation for his success as a pastor. He ranked among the first in his class at the close of the course. After his graduation he spent a year in the Theological Seminary in Andover, Mass., and a part of the second year in the seminary at Bangor. He was principal for a time of the high school in Augusta, and spent the three or four succeeding years as purser in the United States Navy. He was stationed off the coast of Africa. Leaving the navy he studied for the ministry, and graduated in 1849 from the Andover Seminary. Mr. Means married Jane Chamberlain Strong, daughter of Dea. Elnathan and Jane (Chamberlain) Strong. He was ordained and installed Dec. 3, 1851, pastor of the First Church of Christ in Medway, where he remained about four years, when he resigned and traveled in Europe. After his return he became the pastor of the Vine Street

John O. Means.

Church in Roxbury, now Immanuel Church, Boston Highlands, Mass., where he labored for eighteen years, a successful and beloved minister of Christ. In 1875 he resigned to accept the position of Secretary of the Massachusetts Sunday School Publishing Society, but was soon called into a wider sphere of usefulness. After the death of the Rev. Dr. Treat, the American Board looked far and wide to find a man capable of filling the position of secretary They selected Dr. Means, and their choice proved to be an excellent one. He was congenial to his brethren, and a wise and efficient worker. Soon after his appointment, the Board received the large legacy from Mr. Otis, and in accordance with the oft-expressed wish of the testator, $250,000 were devoted to Africa. In this connection it may be interesting to know that Mr Otis had always manifested a great interest in the missionary work in that country, and in the many wills drawn up by him the legacy for this cause was always inserted. In his last will the amount to be devoted to this use was specified, but was afterward canceled and the total amount was given to the Board without any instructions. Dr. Means was given charge of this field, and in order to better prepare himself for the important work before him, he visited all the important countries in Europe and consulted every one from whom he could glean any information concerning Africa He spent many hours with the King of Belgium, who was a very large contributor to the support of Stanley's new exploration on the Congo. All the latest books and maps giving any light upon Africa were obtained and carefully studied. He thus mastered the whole subject of the geographical and political divisions of the country, gaining an accurate knowledge of the people and their customs. So intelligent was his understanding of the subject that his first paper read before the American Board was noticed in the English papers and was prized so highly that he was made an honorary member of the Royal Geographical Society. Throughout the term of his service as Secretary of the Board he was devoted to the work in Africa, and at the time of his death was engaged in an attempt to establish a mission at Bihe on the western coast and in Umzilla's kingdom on the eastern coast. His early knowledge of Africa and his earnest study of the country made him preeminently fitted to undertake the work of Christianizing the people. The Rev. Dr. Clarke, Foreign Secretary of the Board, once said· "There is probably not a man in America so well qualified to conduct Christian missions in Africa as Dr. Means."

Throughout his life Mr Means was an earnest student of matters in no way connected with his profession. A marked instance of this fact was noticed in an address on law delivered before the students of the college. On this occasion he delivered an oration in which he showed a knowledge of books of law acquired but by comparatively few of the legal fraternity. He was conservative in his religion. For many years he served on the Boston School Board, and at the time of his death he was President of the Roxbury Athenæum and also President of the Trustees of the Roxbury Latin School. In the spring, when his associates, Drs. Clarke and Alden, were sent to Constantinople to look after the interests of the missions in Western Turkey, Dr. Means took their work upon his shoulders, and in so doing brought upon himself the disease of the heart that proved fatal. His tireless energy and indomitable will overtaxed his physical system, but, notwithstanding his weariness and prostration, he would not desert his post until the steamer bearing his associates was announced in port. He then put his papers in order, locked his desk, and left the office never to return. This was in the summer. For three months he suffered the keenest anguish with heroic fortitude. When told that his painful illness must soon terminate in death he triumphantly exclaimed: "I didn't think of such good news so soon. Praise God!" The Rev. Dr. Means died Dec. 8, 1883. The funeral service was attended in the Immanuel Church on the following Wednesday, Dec. 12, 1883. The address on the occasion was made by the Rev. A. C. Thompson, D. D., which was published, with a portrait of this lamented servant of God. Mrs. Means survived her husband, and resides in Auburndale, Mass.

MICHAEL METCALF, ESQ.

MICHAEL METCALF, the immigrant ancestor of the Metcalf's in Medway, was born in 1587, in Tatterford, Norfolk County, England. He writes: "I was persecuted in the land of my fathers' sepulchres, for not bowing at the name of Jesus, and observing other ceremonies in religion forced upon me, at the instance of Bishop Wren, of Norwich, and his chancellor, Dr. Corbet, whose violent measures troubled me in the Bishops' Court, and returned me into the High Commissioners' Court. Suffering many times for the cause of religion, I was forced, for the sake of the liberty of my conscience, to flee from my wife and children, to go into New England; taking ship for the voyage at London, the 17th of September, 1636: being by tempests tossed up and down the sea till the Christmas following, then veering about to Plymouth, in Old England, in which time I met with many sore afflictions. Leaving the ship, I went down to Yarmouth, in Norfolk County, whence I shipped myself and family, to come to New England; sailed April 15th, 1637, and arrived three days before midsummer, with my wife, nine children, and a servant."

The above extracts we take from a copy of his letter, written in Plymouth, England, Jan. 13, 1636, on his voyage hither, directed: "To all the true professors of Christ's Gospel within the city of Norwich." In the postscript he remarks: "My enemies conspired against me to take my life, and, sometimes, to avoid their hands, my wife did hide me in the roof of the house, covering me over with straw."

History informs us that one of the charges brought against Bishop Wren, by a committee of Parliament, was, that during the term of two years and four months, while he held the See of Norwich, "3,000 of his Majesty's subjects, many of whom use trades, spinning, weaving, knitting, making cloth, stuff, stockings, and other manufactures of wool, some of them setting a hundred poor people at work," "transported themselves into Holland," and "other parts beyond the sea," in consequence of his superstition and tyranny.

Michael Metcalf was admitted a townsman in Dedham, July 14, 1637; joined the church in 1639, and was selectman in 1641. His name stands first on the committee chosen to "contrive the fabricke of a meeting house."

MAJ. LUTHER METCALF.

LUTHER METCALF, son of Joseph and Hannah (Haven) Metcalf, was born Sept. 1, 1756, in South Franklin, Mass. His father was a physician and a farmer. He had two brothers, Joseph and Calvin, who settled in Winthrop, Me. Luther Metcalf learned the trade of a cabinet-maker of Elisha Richardson, of North Franklin, Mass. In 1773 he crossed the river and settled in Medway Village, married Mercy Whiting, daughter of Nathaniel Whiting, Jr., the miller, and established the business of cabinet work, employed many apprentices, and carried on the business in connection with farming and cotton manufacturing till his death, which occurred Jan. 27, 1838. The Rev. Dr. Ide, in a published obituary notice of Major Metcalf, says of him: " In the death of this man the community has suffered no ordinary loss. He lived not for himself, but for the benefit of the public. In early life he listened to the call of his country and became a soldier of the Revolution. He entered the service in 1775, at the age of nineteen, and continued in it at different periods for nearly three years. He was a firm supporter of the principles and measures of Washington, and during a long life he cherished in his own breast and diffused among others, the principles of national liberty, and presented before the world an example of genuine patriotism. He was cheerful without lightness ; social without that familiarity which generates contempt, and dignified without austerity." He was a man of strict integrity, and remarkable for industry. The ample fortune which he possessed at his decease was acquired in a great measure by his own agency. He was truly a pious man, a liberal contributor to the support of the Gospel and the benevolent operations of the day. He was often called to stations of great responsibility in the town and the duties of these stations he discharged to the general satisfaction of the citizens. He was one of the original proprietors of the so-called " Old White Mill " Major Metcalf, under date of Sept. 7, 1832, made an application for a pension, in which occurs the following statement :

" I, Luther Metcalf, of Medway, this day seventy-six years of age, do testify that I removed from Franklin to Medway in the year 1773, and in the summer or autumn of 1774 I enlisted into a company of what we then called minute-men,' for the purpose of obtaining knowledge in military tactics, preparatory for an expected war with Great Britain We elected our officers as follows, viz.: John Boyd, Captain, Ebenezer Dean, Lieutenant, and Joshua Gould, Ensign Said company met from one to three times a week, for exercise, until April 19, (the date of the Concord and Lexington fight) on which day at 4 o'clock, P M, I was informed that hostilities had commenced Our company immediately met and marched to meet the enemy, and arrived at Roxbury about day-break, next morning I remained on duty in said company until May, when the officers above named were commissioned, and then enlisted under them for eight months as a musician, and remained on duty in said company until the first of January, following."

He reenlisted afterward, and served fifteen days in Tiverton, R. I., six months in Ticonderoga, N. Y., and marched on various expeditions until 1780, all amounting to some three years of service. He was subsequently commissioned as a Major of the State Militia.

Luther Metcalf

LUTHER METCALF, son of Major Luther and Mercy (Whiting) Metcalf, was born May 2, 1788, in Medway, Mass. After receiving his education in the local schools and at Day's Academy in Wrentham, Mr. Metcalf learned and worked at his father's trade of cabinet making until he was of age. In 1812 he began the business of making cotton machinery with John Blackburn. They made, by contract with Patrick T. Jackson and Francis C. Lowell, the first cotton machinery used in the Waltham cotton manufactory, and supplied mills in Lowell and other places. Mr. Metcalf afterwards became a manufacturer of cotton goods, a large owner in and agent of the Medway Cotton Manufacturing Company, which was the first incorporated company for the manufacture of cotton goods in Massachusetts. This corporation existed until 1864. He was elected in 1821, a director in the Norfolk Mutual Fire Insurance Company; he acted as agent and director until 1877. He was also at one time president of the company. During several years he was director of the Dedham bank; he was town clerk, collector, and treasurer for several years; and served eleven years on the school committee, and was the chairman of the board. In 1837 he represented the town in the House of Representatives, and in 1844 and 1845 he was a member of the Senate. Until 1856 he adhered to the fortunes of the Whig party, but in that year he voted for Fremont, and afterwards with the Republican party. He never missed voting in a Presidential election during his lifetime, and voted sixty-nine times for governor. He was appointed in 1830, a Justice of the Peace and Quorum by Governor Lincoln, and held a court for civil cases. Mr. Metcalf was one of the first to advocate a railroad from Boston to the valley of the Blackstone. The first meeting to promote this object was held in Medway, Nov. 30, 1837. Welcome Farnum, Dr. Ballou, Willis Cook, the Hon. Latimer W. Ballou, and Edward Harris, were early associated with him in this enterprise, which resulted in the present New York and New England Railroad. He was the first President of the Charles River Railroad, and broke ground with spade in hand to construct this link of the "Air Line," July 4, 1854. In 1838 he was very active and influential in the erection of the Village Church and the formation of a religious society, and suggested the calling and settlement of the Rev. David Sanford.

Before the days of railroads, no man was better known upon the highway between Medway and Boston than Mr. Metcalf. For nearly thirty years, in the same sulky in summer and the same cutter in winter, he passed over the road, in all something like a thousand times, and made the old Lamb Tavern, Washington Coffee House, or the Bromfield House, his head-quarters. He was a man of fixed habits and methods, and of great persistence of character, enjoying always remarkably good health. Regular and temperate in his habits, he rose and retired early, to which facts may be attributed the clearness of his faculties to the end of life. Some two years before his death he became a member of the Village Church. During the last year of his life he celebrated with his second wife the golden anniversary of their marriage. Mr. Metcalf reached a remarkable age, and his faculties were wonderfully preserved. The immediate cause of his death was an accidental fall by making a misstep. He died Feb. 16, 1879, being more than ninety years of age. His wife, two sons, and a daughter survive him. His death occurred early on Sunday evening, and his funeral was solemnized at the Congregational Church Wednesday afternoon, and a large concourse of friends and relatives

THE RESIDENCE OF THE HON. LUTHER METCALF.

attended to pay their last respects to this venerable man. The services were conducted by the pastor of the church, the Rev. R. K. Harlow, who was assisted by the Rev. E. O. Jameson, of East Medway, and the Rev. A. W. Ide, of West Medway. Mr. Harlow preached the sermon, and paid a high tribute to the deceased. The singing was of a special character, and the floral decorations profuse. The burial was in the family lot in Oakland Cemetery.

Nathaniel Whiting Metcalf, A. M.

Nathaniel Whiting Metcalf, son of the Hon. Luther and Lydia (Jenks) Metcalf, was born Aug. 24, 1819, in Medway. He graduated in 1846 from Brown University, Providence, R. I., and devoted his life to teaching in academies and high schools. He was thus employed in Pittsburgh, Penn., in New Marlboro and Medway, Mass. During the later years of his life he labored as a teacher among the freedmen. Mr. Metcalf died Oct. 16, 1871, in New Orleans, La.

Mrs. Caroline Cutler (Plimpton) Metcalf.

Caroline Cutler Plimpton was born July 21, 1809, in Medway. She married Sept. 25, 1835, Albert Metcalf, son of Dea. Jonathan and Mary (Pond) Metcalf. He was born Sept. 20, 1808, in Franklin, Mass. They resided in Auburn, N. Y., where he was the principal of a young ladies' school. Mr. Metcalf died Aug. 11, 1837, of consumption, at his father's house in Franklin, Mass.

Mrs. Metcalf became widely known as a teacher. In 1850 she was elected the Principal of the Wheaton Female Seminary in Norton, Mass., and continued in that position for twenty-six years, until her resignation in 1876. During this long period she presided over that institution with distinguished ability, and was recognized as one of the finest educators of young ladies in New England.

The Rev. Jacob Ide, of Mansfield, Mass., in his historical address on the occasion of the Fiftieth Anniversary of Wheaton Seminary, in 1885, which was printed, pays a very fitting tribute to the character and eminent service of Mrs. Metcalf in connection with that institution. Mrs. Metcalf was, indeed, one of the most distinguished daughters of Medway.

Lansing Millis, Esq.

Lansing Millis, son of William and Sallie (Holt) Millis, was born Sept. 3, 1823, in Lansingburgh, N. Y. His school days ended at the age of fifteen years, and he soon after made a confession of faith in Christ, and united with the church. He commenced trade when eighteen years of age, and was at first unsuccessful, but afterwards able to retrieve his losses and pay his creditors every dollar with interest. For some years he followed farming and mercantile business until in 1855 he came to Boston and commenced his career as a railroad agent and manager. In this business he was successful and at the end of thirty years he had won great prominence among the railroad managers of New England and the West, and was recognized as a man of superior judgment and great fidelity to responsibility and trust. He held also

an honored place in the respect of the religious circles of Boston for his Christian labors and large benevolence. In 1880 he purchased a farm in East Medway, and commenced improvements. He soon after added another farm by purchase, to the first, put up new buildings, and repaired the old. He fitted up a fine summer residence, and with a large outlay made Oak Grove Farm famous in the region. Early in 1885 the easterly part of Medway was incorporated a new town, and was named Millis, in honor of him who seemed by his social qualities, his interest in the place, and his Christian character, to win all hearts to himself. At the first meeting of the new town Mr. Millis was chosen the moderator, and subsequently elected chairman of the board of selectmen. But only a few weeks had passed when he was stricken with paralysis of the brain and died instantly April 6, 1885. The funeral services were largely attended, both at his residence and in Boston, where a large church filled at noonday in that city, principally of business men, showed how widely he was known and the universal respect in which he was held. His burial took place in his native town, Lansingburgh, N. Y. The death of Mr. Millis was a sad loss to the new town for which he had a great attachment, and to which his personal presence was a great inspiration. His family, since his death, continue to reside in the summer at Oak Grove Farm, and are carrying out his plans as far as known for the benefit of the town of Millis.

ALEXANDER LE BARON MONROE, son of Dr. Stephen and Susanna (Le Baron) Monroe, was born May 3, 1807, in Sutton, Mass. He graduated in 1831, from the Yale Medical College, New Haven, Conn., and the following year established himself as a physician in East Medway. He removed in 1833 to the Village, where he practiced his profession successfully for several years. In 1840 he removed to Chicopee, Mass., where he remained until 1843, when he located in Granby, Mass., where he remained ten years. In September, 1852, he returned to the Village in response to an earnest invitation of the citizens, where he continued in practice till failing health compelled him, in 1877, to retire from professional life. He was absent for a short time in 1862, serving as a surgeon in the Peninsula Campaign under General McClellan in the War for the Union, having volunteered in response to a call for extra medical service in an emergency.

Abner Morse

Dr. Alex. LeB Monroe was a well-read physician and greatly respected in his profession. He was also a man of devoted Christian character, and a valued helper in all departments of his Master's service. Dr. Monroe died Feb. 20, 1879, after a life of earnest usefulness. In a fitting memorial prepared by his pastor, the Rev. Mr Harlow, which was published, interesting mention is made of the religious experience of Dr. Monroe which enabled him to minister to his patients spiritually as well as physically. The writer says: "There are many households that will never forget his tender offices, as in the chamber made solemn by the approach of death, he committed the departing spirit of the loved one to the mercy of God, and commended those soon to be bereaved to the consolations of Divine Grace."

Rev. Abner Morse, A M.

Abner Morse, son of Abner and Mille (Leland) Morse, was born Sept. 5, 1793, in Medway, now Holliston, Mass. He prepared for college, and graduated from Brown University in the class of 1816. He preached in various places but devoted himself somewhat to lectures and other literary work He was a member of the New England Historic Genealogical Society, of Boston, Mass , and *The Morse Genealogy: or, The Genealogical Register of the Descendants of the Early Settlers of Sherborn, Holliston, and Medway, Mass* , is an enduring monument of his industry and patience as a pioneer in genealogical research which will perpetuate his name for generations. This volume is accounted exceedingly valuable as a book of constant reference to those engaged in tracing genealogy.

The Rev. Mr. Morse married twice, and had by his second wife four children. One of these is the Hon. Elijah Adams Morse, of Canton, Mass. The Rev. Mr Morse died May 16, 1865, in Sharon, Mass.

Rev. John Morse.

John Morse, son of Dea. James and Hannah (Daniels) Morse, was born March 24, 1763, in East Medway. He became a Christian in early life and was very active in the revivals of 1785, holding meetings in Holliston, Medway, and other towns. Having determined to enter the ministry, he prepared himself for college, and graduated in 1791 from Brown University, Providence, R. I. He studied theology with the Rev. Dr. Emmons and the Rev. David Sanford. Having completed his professional studies, he went to preach the Gospel in the then "far West," and was settled, in 1792, pastor of the Congregational Church in Green River, N Y, where he remained twenty-three years, and removed in 1816 to Otego, N. Y. He was installed over the Presbyterian Church in Otego, and labored there some twelve years. The last sermon he preached was on the occasion of President Harrison's death, he being at the time seventy-eight years of age. He died Jan. 3, 1844, in Otego, having spent over fifty years in the ministry. His ministrations were blessed and attended with seasons of revival. He preached the distinguished doctrines of Free Grace, which were his own comfort and support in his last illness and in death.

The Rev. Mr. Morse married, Feb. 4, 1793, Clarissa Sanford, daughter of the Rev. David and Bathsheba (Ingersol) Sanford. She was born Nov. 20, 1763, in Medway.

HON. ELIJAH ADAMS MORSE.

ELIJAH A. MORSE, son of the Rev. Abner and Hannah (Peck) Morse, was born May 25, 1841, in South Bend, Ind. He received his early education in the public schools of Boston, and under the instruction of the Hon. Charles Kimball, of Lowell, Mass. He very early betrayed a business turn of mind, and when a lad of fifteen years he manufactured stove polish on a small scale, and with his little stock in a carpet-bag he trudged from house to house to make sales of what he esteemed, and which has proved to be, a superior article. This polish was prepared according to a formula given to the lad by the eminent chemist, Dr. Charles Jackson, of Boston, who was a friend of young Morse's father. In 1860, Mr. Morse commenced to make this manufacture on a larger scale, but soon after the Rebellion broke out, and being of a patriotic spirit, he enlisted for three months in Company A, 4th Regiment Massachusetts Volunteers, and subsequently reënlisted in the same company, and was in active service for nine months. His term having expired, he settled, in 1864, in Canton, Mass., and rented a small room where he resumed the manufacture of stove polish, which has since become world renowned, grown into a colossal business, and made Mr. Morse, while a young man, the master of great wealth. Mr. Morse is an active Christian gentleman, a popular temperance lecturer, a man wide awake and of advanced ideas, prominent in the State, and everywhere greatly respected. In 1876 he served in the House of Representatives, and was elected Nov. 3, 1885, to the State Senate from the First Eighth Norfolk District, receiving a large number of votes in advance of the Republican ticket of that district, an index of the public esteem and honor in which Mr. Morse is held. His pleasing address, high Christian principles, popular abilities, devotion to human welfare, large wealth, and ready benevolence, render him a great power for good wherever his presence and influence are enjoyed.

ELIJAH MORSE, ESQ.

ELIJAH MORSE, son of Abner and Mille (Leland) Morse, was born Sept. 10, 1785, in Medway, Mass. He graduated in 1809 from Brown University, Providence, R. I., and studied law with Judge Thatcher, of Thomaston, Me., and with the Hon. Timothy Bigelow, of Boston, Mass. Having completed his legal studies he was admitted to the Suffolk Bar, and was associated with Judge Bigelow in the practice of his profession. He married Mary Jackson, daughter of Dr. Jackson, of Edinburgh, Scotland, whose father was one of the Aldermen of London, England. Mr. Morse represented ward seven, of Boston, in 1824–1825, in the Common Council. He was elected a Representative to the General Court of Massachusetts but declined a reëlection. Mr. Morse died Aug. 23, 1831, at the early age of forty-six years, in Boston, deeply lamented by a numerous circle of friends and acquaintances, and sincerely mourned by the profession which he so ably represented.

FRANCIS J. MORSE, M. D.

FRANCIS J. MORSE, son of Andrew and Margaretta (Metcalf) Morse, was born March 3, 1818, in East Medway, now Millis, Mass. His prepara-

Elijah A. Morse

tory course was in the public schools of Medway and in the Academy, Franklin, Mass. He graduated in 1844 from the College of Physicians and Surgeons, in New York. Having completed his medical studies he removed west, and settled, in 1845, in Constantine, Mich., where he continued in practice until 1878, when he returned east, and resided for a while in Woonsocket, R. I Dr. Morse died in 1883.

Vincent Moses, A. M.

VINCENT MOSES, son of Hiram and Betsey (Campbell) Moses, was born July 1, 1844, in French Creek, N Y. His parents were natives of Vermont. He fitted for college under Alanson Wedge, A. M., in Ripley and Mayville, N. Y., and graduated in 1866 from Amherst College, Masssachusetts. He then entered the Theological Institute in Hartford, Conn., but in the spring of 1867 came to Medway as the principal of the high school which at that time was kept in turn in the three parts of the town. After filling this position for three years, he returned to the seminary and graduated in 1871. He received a license to preach but was never ordained. For some years he was a teacher, but in 1876 he returned to Medway and engaged in business in West Medway, where he resides. He was appointed April 12, 1880, postmaster, and still holds that office. Mr. Moses married Aug. 25, 1874, Evelyn Alice Hazeltine, who died Aug. 6, 1875, and he married June 5. 1883, Mrs Lucasta Jane Thomas *née* Rogers, widow of Dr. John G. Thomas of Worcester, Mass. Mr. Moses traces his paternal descent through Hiram, Rufus, Elnathan, Benoni, John, John, to John Moses, immigrant, who came from England in 1630 and settled in Dorchester, Mass., and in 1636 removed to Windsor, Conn., where the family resided until 1777, when Elnathan Moses became one of the first settlers of West Rutland, Vt., and about 1800 Rufus Moses settled in Ticonderoga, N. Y.

Rev. Ezra Newton.

EZRA NEWTON, son of Ezra Newton, was born Sept 30, 1818, in Princeton, Mass. He was a student in the Academy, Monson, Mass., two years, and graduated in 1843 from Dartmouth College, Hanover, N. H. He pursued his theological studies with the Rev. Sewall Harding in East Medway. The Rev. Mr. Newton preached one year in Dighton, Mass., but declined a settlement. He was ordained and installed March 1, 1848, in Shutesbury, Mass., but resigned in a few years, on account of ill health. Subsequently he was for a season the agent of the New Hampshire Bible Society, and supplied the pulpit in Raymond, N. H. Being unable to preach he removed to Kingston, N. H.

Rev. Varnum Noyes.

VARNUM NOYES, son of Josiah and Mehitable (White) Noyes, was born July 1, 1804, in Acton, Mass. In 1821 he made a profession of his faith in Christ, and studied for the Christian ministry. He pursued his preparatory studies in the academies of Chesterfield, N. H., and Amherst, Mass , and in 1824 entered Dartmouth College, Hanover, N. H. During his Sophomore year he was prostrated by illness and left college. After his recovery he engaged in teaching, and then studied theology with the Rev. Dr. Ide, of West Medway. He was ordained Aug. 23, 1831, as an evangelist in Medway, and went west. He commenced preaching Oct. 2, 1831, in Guilford, O., where he was installed Sept. 21, 1836. He resigned his pastorate May 8, 1849, and labored a season in Wayne, O., but was invited to return to Guilford, O., where he died in 1852. The Rev. Mr. Noyes married, June 17, 1833, Lois Walker, daughter of Comfort and Tamar (Clark) Walker, of Medway.

Clark Partridge

CLARK PARTRIDGE, son of Joel and Sarah (Clark) Partridge, was born April 1, 1809, in Medway. He was reared upon a farm and educated in the schools of his native town. He began business in the Village, in a store and as a dealer in cotton thread, and established in 1837 the first boot and shoe manufactory in the place. He was early an active member of the State Militia and was elected captain, by which title he has always been familiarly called. He filled, by election and appointment, various civil offices, was Justice of the Peace, was sixteen years postmaster of Medway, and served upon the board of selectmen many years, holding this position during the War for the Union, and proved very efficient in filling the quota of the town with enlisted men. In 1852 he was a Representative to the General Court, and in 1868 he was a State Senator from the old Third Norfolk District. He made large investments in real estate in Chicago and vicinity, and in the second great fire was a loser. He had good financial ability, and was a director for many years of the Holliston National Bank, and a trustee of the Medway Savings Bank. He had been identified with various industrial and other interests in Medway; was an original member of the Village church, also contributing to the erection of other places of worship in the town. He was besides an active member of the order of Odd Fellows. He possessed unusual energy, persistence, and force of character, and had great influence in political and other circles in which he moved, and was liberal to the poor. In the latter part of his active life Joseph W. Thompson, Esq., was a partner, who succeeded him in the boot manufacture, Captain Partridge retiring in 1872 with a competency. He was a very companionable man, and his society was much sought by the young men whom he was always willing to encourage by his advice and counsel.

THE RESIDENCE OF THE HON. CLARK PARTRIDGE.

This residence was erected in 1869 at an expense of $15,000, including the site and furnishing, and was the finest private dwelling in the town. In the early morning of June 10, 1885, it took fire and was seriously damaged, while Captain Partridge and his wife had a narrow escape with their lives. A few months after the house was again ready for occupancy. Captain Partridge died Nov. 17, 1885. His death was much lamented as he had been a leading citizen in the town. His burial took place on the Friday following his decease, in Oakland Cemetery.

Rev. Lymam Partridge.

Lyman Partridge, son of Elihu and Maria (Paine) Partridge, was born Aug. 23, 1836, in West Medway. He prepared for college in Peirce's Academy, Middleboro, Mass., and graduated, in 1863, from Brown University, Providence, R. I. In 1866 he graduated from Newton Theological Institute. He was ordained to the ministry and installed in 1866 pastor of the Baptist Church, in Wales, Mass. In 1869 he resigned, and labored for two years in Wakefield, R I. The Rev. Mr Partridge was installed in 1872, pastor of the Baptist Church, in Sharon, Mass, where he remained ten years, and resigned in 1882. He supplied various churches, living at the time in West Medway, until he was installed, in 1883, pastor of the Baptist Church in Westminster, Mass. Several sermons and public addresses by the Rev. Mr. Partridge have been published.

Rev. John Pierce, D D.

John Pierce was born July 14, 1773, in Dorchester, Mass. He graduated in 1793 from Harvard College. Mr. Pierce was for a season after graduation an instructor in Leicester Academy, and afterward a tutor in Harvard College. He studied theology with the Rev. Dr. Tappan. He was ordained and installed March 15, 1797, in Boston, afterward Brookline, Mass. The Rev. Mr. Pierce married Abigail Lovell, daughter of Capt. Joseph and Jemima (Adams) Lovell, of Medway. Mrs. Abigail Pierce died July 2, 1800. The Rev. Dr. Pierce was descended of very humble parentage, but as by his own exertion and industry he won his way through college and into the Gospel ministry, so by his fidelity and power of character he maintained himself for half a century sole pastor of the church over which he was settled, meanwhile doing a large amount of literary work. He was a member of the Academy of Arts and Sciences, and of the Massachusetts Historical Society. He was for several years president of the Massachusetts Bible Society. In March, 1847, he published a half century discourse of Brookline, Mass. He died Aug. 24, 1849, greatly respected and deeply mourned by his people and the literary and ecclesiastical bodies to which he belonged. *Vid. Cyclopædia, McClintock and Strong.*

Alonzo Platts Phillips.

Alonzo Platts Phillips, son of Nathan and Lydia (Pingree) Phillips, was born May 2, 1804 in Rowley, Mass. His great ancestor, James Phillips, was born about 1700 in England. In early life he came to America and settled in Ipswich, Mass. His wife was Molly Lord of that town. Mr. Phillips was for many years a shoe manufacturer in Peabody, Mass, and the proprietor of a wholesale and retail boot and shoe store in Council Bluffs, Ia. He was a member of the Legislature in 1856, and became a resident of Medway Village in 1871, where he became a prominent citizen by reason of his intelligence and active interest in all public matters of the town and church. At the age of eighty-one Mr Phillips was vigorous in mind and took a lively interest in current events. His death occurred March 6, 1886.

REV. DANIEL POND.

DANIEL POND, son of John and Rachel (Fisher) Pond, was born May 13, 1724, in Franklin, Mass. He graduated in 1745 from Harvard College, and was ordained to the Gospel ministry, and settled, Dec. 10, 1755, in Templeton, Mass., which was then Narragansett Township, No. 6. The Rev. Mr. Pond resigned his pastorate August, 1759, and removed to Medway, where he resided for many years and fitted boys for college. He became a member of the Second Church of Christ in 1763, but subsequently being much opposed to the Hopkinsian theology of the pastor, the Rev. David Sanford, in 1778, with Dea. Samuel Fisher and four others, he united with the First Church of Christ, in the pastoral care of the Rev. Mr. Bucknam. This caused a rupture in the fellowship of the two churches which was not healed for thirty years His wife, Mrs. Lois (Metcalf) Pond, died March 17, 1787, in Medway. They had a daughter Miranda, who married Abner Merrifield, of Newfane, Vt The Rev. Mr Pond sold his estate and removed from Medway. Nothing further is known of his history save the tradition that he died in Otter Creek, Penn.

PHILIP CHESTER PORTER, M. D.

PHILIP CHESTER PORTER, son of Philip K. and Sarah (Carver) Porter, was born April 17, 1833, in Berkley, Mass. His father died when he was four years of age, and he went to live with his grandfather. He worked on the farm in the summer, and went to school in the winter. In 1850 his grandfather died, and he was encouraged by his pastor, the Rev. L. R. Eastman, to prepare for college, which he did, and graduated in 1855 from Amherst College, Massachusetts. For some ten years he engaged in teaching, and meanwhile studied medicine, and graduated in 1866 from the Pittsfield Medical College, Massachusetts. He practiced medicine for a few years in Lynn, Mass., but resumed teaching in 1873. Dr. Porter was elected principal of the High School in East Medway, in 1875, where he taught two years until ill health compelled him to resign. After regaining his health he again resumed teaching and is now Master of the High School in Sutton, Mass. Dr. Porter married, May 26, 1869, Marion J. Wood, of Jordan, N. Y. Their only child was born Feb. 8, 1873, and died the same day.

ABIJAH RICHARDSON, M. D.

ABIJAH RICHARDSON, son of Asa and Abigail (Barber) Richardson, was born Aug. 30, 1752, in East Medway, now Millis, Mass. He studied medicine and commenced practice in his native town. The Revolutionary War was inaugurated and Dr. Richardson offered his service and was appointed Surgeon on the staff of General Washington. He served some four years, and after the war settled on the place formerly owned by Ebenezer Daniell who was the grandfather of his wife, Mrs. Mercy Richardson. Dr. Richardson erected a fine residence of brick which is still standing, and occupied by Mrs. Lorana (Beals) Richardson, the widow of his youngest son. Dr. Richardson is described as a man of fine personal address, commanding figure, and with his military and medical reputation he at once became a prominent personage in the town. He was a member of the Society of Cincinnati, and

also of the Masonic Fraternity. He was a charter member of the Montgomery Lodge of Free Masons, formerly of Medway, but afterward removed
to Milford, Mass. Dr. Richardson was called to fill many positions of public
trust in the town. He was for many years on the school committee. He
was prominent in starting the manufacturing interests. His death occurred
May 10, 1822. The funeral service of Dr. Richardson was largely attended,
the audience-room of the church being filled to overflowing. There were
present large delegations of the medical profession, the military and Masonic
associations, and the citizens of the town were present *en masse* in respect to
his distinguished memory. Dr. Ebenezer Alden, in his address before the
Norfolk County Medical Society, said of Dr. Richardson : " Few physicians
pass their professional career more honored and beloved." He was a scientist, making botany a special study, and in many departments of science and
literature, he was an earnest student. He was possessed of a very retentive
memory and a good public speaker. He delivered a eulogy on Washington
on the occasion of his death, which was published. Dr. Richardson was
scrupulously exact in all transactions, benevolent and courteous ; he was an
honor to his profession, to the town and to his country.

HON. JOSEPH LOVELL RICHARDSON.

JOSEPH LOVELL RICHARDSON, son of Ezra and Jemima (Lovell) Richardson, was born March 29, 1787, in East Medway. He was educated in
the public schools and in the academy in Leicester, Mass. In early manhood
he suffered from ill health, but gradually became vigorous and strong. He

was a successful teacher, but after a few years settled down and devoted himself to farming. He was entrusted with much of town business and was often called to administer upon, and settle estates. He was appointed a Justice of the Peace and of the Quorum in 1819, was chosen on the board of selectmen and served as a member of the School Committee for several years. Mr Richardson succeeded, in 1815, his grandfather, Capt. Joseph Lovell, as Town Clerk. Captain Lovell had held the office for twenty successive years, and Mr Richardson continued to fill it for thirteen years next following He was elected Representative to the General Court in 1828 and in 1831 ; and in 1838 to the State Senate. He was one of the most prominent and honored citizens of the town through a long period. He survived to a great age. His death occurred Nov 8, 1880, when he was ninety-three years, seven months, and eleven days old.

George Lovell Richardson. A. M.

George Lovell Richardson, son of Joseph Lovell and Sylvia (Partridge) Richardson, was born March 9, 1838, in East Medway His early education was obtained in the public schools of his native town, and in the academy in Monson, Mass. He graduated in 1862 from Dartmouth College, Hanover, N. H. His life-work has been that of a teacher For nearly twenty years he has been the Principal of the High School in Abington, Mass. He has been called to fill various town offices

Marcus Richardson, Esq.

Marcus Richardson, son of Elisha and Sarah (Ellis) Richardson, was born Oct. 30, 1780. Mr. Richardson became, Oct. 5, 1803, a member of the Montgomery Lodge of Free Masons, at that time of Franklin, afterward of Milford, Mass. He married Prudence Hill, the daughter of Dea. Simon Hill, of Medway, where he resided for some years, but about 1820 he removed to Bangor, Me Mr. Richardson lived to the great age of one hundred years, and in 1880 visited his native town and spent his one hundredth birthday with his brother, Dea. Silas Richardson, who was about ninety years old. He was in East Medway from Oct. 28 to Nov 1, 1880, in the meanwhile riding over to Milford to be present at a reception tendered him by the Free Masons, of which order he was doubtless the oldest living member in the United States, having been connected with the organization for seventy-seven years. On the morning of Nov 1, 1880. he took the train from the East Medway station, reached Bangor, Me., November 2, was conveyed to the place of voting in a carriage drawn by six milk white horses, and voted for James A. Garfield for the Presidency. He reached his home in health and excellent spirits At this time he was in the full possession of all his faculties ; was sprightly in his conversation, wrote a firm, bold hand, read fine print without glasses, and his memory was excellent. For nearly sixty years he had resided in Bangor, Me., and his life had been quiet and useful. Not many days after his return he was taken ill, and died Jan. 13, 1881, at the age of one hundred years, two months, and fourteen days. His funeral was numerously attended.

28

DEA. SILAS RICHARDSON.

SILAS RICHARDSON, son of Elisha and Sarah (Ellis) Richardson, was born May 9, 1792, in East Medway, a younger brother of the centenarian, Marcus Richardson, Esq., of Bangor, Me. Mr. Richardson was a farmer, a man of devoted Christian character, and for many years a deacon in the Baptist church in Medfield, Mass. He survived all his children and in 1886, in his ninety-fourth year, is able to walk to the church in Millis where he has attended more or less in later years. Although a Baptist he is not sectarian, and feels at home and in fellowship with all the true disciples of Christ. John S. White, PH. D., of New York, a grandson of Mr. Richardson, as a memorial of his affection for his venerable grandfather contemplates placing a clock in the steeple of the meeting-house of the Church of Christ in Millis. The clock, it is expected, will be in position on or before May 9, 1886, the ninety-fourth birthday of Deacon Richardson, and the event will be duly celebrated.

REV. JACOB ROBERTS.

JACOB ROBERTS, son of Evan and Hester (Fussell) Roberts, was born in London, England. His ancestry were from Bala, North Wales. His mother was the daughter of James Fussell. She was born in 1769 near Frome, Somersetshire, England. Mr. Roberts was educated in Highbury College, London, England. He came to America in 1837, and was first settled in Fairhaven, Mass., and for fourteen years in East Medway. He resigned in 1871 and afterward resided in Auburndale, Mass.

REV. DAVID SANFORD.

DAVID SANFORD, son of David and Rachel (Strong) Sanford, was born Dec. 11, 1737, in New Milford, Conn. He graduated, in 1755, from Yale College, Connecticut, and on completing his theological studies, received a license to preach and was ordained and installed, April 14, 1773, pastor of the Second Church of Christ in Medway. The following mention of the Rev. David Sanford is copied from *Headley's Chaplains of the Revolution*·

"Previous to the commencement of hostilities he was an earnest advocate of the cause of the colonies, and when war actually began he launched at once and with all his heart, into the struggle. Mingling with the assemblies of the people, he took a leading part in every measure adopted for a vigorous defense against the encroachments of Great Britain. With a form almost perfect in its symmetry and majestic bearing, and a countenance of rare beauty and power of expression, his presence always arrested the attention of the beholder. But when the full, rich tones of his voice fell on the ear, now ringing clear, like the call of a bugle, and now melting into the sweetest and most plaintive accents, his hearers were held as by fascination. Impassioned, fearless, and knowing well how to use the rare gifts with which nature had endowed him, he mastered all who came under the spell of his eloquence. His high courage and strong will made restive under temporizing, timorous counsels, and when he arose to denounce them, his face was like a thunder cloud charged with wrath, and his powerful voice broke in startling accents on the audience. With such a man in every parish in the land, not a tory would have been found bold enough to have lifted his head in opposition. Patriotism became a passion with him, and when he called on his people to bear without murmuring their proportion of the expenses of the war, he showed them an example of self-sacrifice by throwing in his entire salary to swell the public treasury. But even this

D. Sanford

did not content him. Not only did he devote his rare eloquence and yearly stipend to the common cause, but as the sound of war rolled over the land, hastened to the army, and volunteered his services as a chaplain. He gave all he had to the service of his country, and no doubt if he had not been restrained by his profession would have been one of the most daring officers in the army. Indeed, nature had endowed him with rare gifts for a military leader. His commanding personal appearance, his impulsive, fearless spirit, and that power of expression in mere look which will carry men farther than words, eminently fitted him to be one. This power of the countenance can never be described any more than it can be resisted. Washington had it. As an illustration of it in Mr Sanford, he was once preaching to the troops in a somewhat dilapidated church, when a board, which had been placed in one of the shattered windows, blew down. The soldiers, in putting it back made so much noise that he was compelled to stop in his sermon. The board again being blown in, the soldiers the second time replaced it, arresting the services by the confusion they made. The third time it fell in; and the soldiers wishing to put it back, he thundered out 'Let that board alone.' One look at the pulpit and they slunk back to their places. After the services were over a citizen asked the commanding officer how he liked the eloquent preacher. He replied 'Very well, but I should have liked him better if he hadn't sworn so.' 'Sworn, captain,' exclaimed the man, 'I did't hear any oath.' 'Yes, he did,' replied the former, 'he said' (repeating the oath) 'let that board alone' 'You certainly are mistaken, he uttered no oath whatever.' 'Well,' replied the Captain, 'if he did not say those very words he *looked* them.' This became a by-word, and in after years whenever his brother ministers saw the frown of his displeasure darkening his open, manly brow, they would say good-naturedly 'don't swear so.' His features had the same power to express the softer emotions, and when moved with pity, or pleading with sinners, would melt the most stubborn heart. The soldiers not only reverenced him for his devoted piety, and loved him for his lofty patriotism, but they admired him for his personal presence. Not an officer in the brigade rode his horse with such incomparable grace and ease as he. His known inflexibility of purpose, abrupt and often stern manner also pleased them. These traits sometimes caused him to be charged with want of courtesy. Once a clownish, shabbily dressed licentiate asked him what system of divinity he would recommend him to study. He replied, with his stern expression of countenance 'Lord Chesterfield to *you*' So, on another occasion, a young preacher telling him that he had refused a call to a certain place on account of an extensive pine swamp in the vicinity, he turned upon him· '*Young man it is none of your business where God has put his pine swamps*'

"Notwithstanding these peculiarities he was a devoted minister and one who knew him well says 'His name was associated with early attempts to propagate the Gospel in the new settlements, and every fresh effort that was put forth for the promotion of Christianity, no matter on which side of the water, met his cordial and grateful approval' As counsellor he was sought after by the churches, and was not infrequently called away a great distance to aid in healing ecclesiastical divisions. In 1807 he was stricken with paralysis, from which he never recovered, and after languishing three years a suffering invalid, he died April 7, 1810, in the seventy-fourth year of his age."

Rev. David Sanford.

DAVID SANFORD, son of Philo and Lydia (Whiting) Sanford, was born Aug. 28, 1801, in Medway, Mass. He received a good common school education and afterwards fitted for Brown University with the Rev. Mr. Ide, of West Medway. He graduated in 1825, and was first settled in New Market, N. H., where he resided two years. For eight years he was the pastor of the church at Dorchester, Mass. He returned to Medway and organized the Congregational Church and society of which he was the honored and successful pastor for nearly forty years. He resigned as the active pastor in 1871, but continued as senior pastor, and the Rev. R. K. Harlow was installed as

THE RESIDENCE OF THE REV. DAVID SANFORD.

junior pastor. From time to time he continued to supply neighboring pulpits, until within two years of his lamented death.

LINES DEDICATED TO THE REV. DAVID SANFORD, JANUARY 1, 1845.

BY MISS BETSEY ADAMS.

"Hail! shepherd of this chosen flock,
The guide, the guardian of our youth,
The joy, the solace of old age,
Herald of righteousness and truth.

"We come, a happy, joyous band,
The schoolmates of thy earlier days,
Thy pupils, friends and kindred dear,
All come to join their cheerful lays.

"We come, a happy, joyous band,
To spread our pastor's festive board,
We come to join our hearts and hands
With him we love, for toils bestowed.

"Within these ancient, sacred walls
Thy reverend sires we once did see.
Their dust lies slumbering with the dead.
Their mantle now doth rest on thee.

"In those bright realms where angels swell
Their notes of everlasting praise,
They join in chorus loud and long
The humble song we now shall raise.

"Thou art our teacher, thou our friend,
Thou dost delight our joys to share;
When pressed with grief, our spirits bend,
Then too, we feel thy faithful care.

"Oft have we listened to thy voice,
As thou hast spoke with love sincere,
Those words which bid the heart rejoice,
Or start the penitential tear.

"And, pastor, dear, our warmest thanks
This night our offering shall be,
While grateful hearts breathe forth the prayer,
Heavens choicest blessings rest on thee.

"Gods guardian care thy path attend,
Long as on earth thy footsteps roam,
And when thy days below shall end,
May angels bear thy spirit home.

"O may to each a place be given
In blissful fields of light above,
All strike our harps of gold in Heaven,
And sing for aye, redeeming love."

M. H. Sanford.

Milton Holbrook Sanford, Esq.

Milton Holbrook Sanford, son of Sewall and Edena (Holbrook) Sanford, was born Aug. 29, 1813, in Medway. His father was a prominent business man and manufacturer in the town, and made the first cotton thread that was manufactured in America. Mr. Sanford was descended from the Rev. David Sanford, pastor of the Second Church of Christ, and his maternal ancestry is traced to Thomas Holbrook, of Broadway, England, who sailed March 20, 1635. for this country, and settled with his family in Weymouth, Mass. Mr. Sanford received a good education for one who so early in life assumed business responsibility. He was for a time in the Military School in Middletown, Conn., also in Andover and Bradford Academies. The death of his father when he was but seventeen years old, threw upon him the cares of business at an early age, and he became a very successful manufacturer, and accumulated a large property. He was a man of rugged and bold traits of character, softened and beautified by tender sensibilities, and of a ready beneficence. He did much for his native village to beautify and improve the place, where his only sister, Mrs. Edena Jane LeFavor, resides. After more than fifty years of business life, which was eminently successful, Mr. Sanford died on Friday, Aug. 3, 1883, in Newport, R. I. His burial took place on the following Monday in the family enclosure, in Medway. *Vid. The Obsequies of Milton Holbrook Sanford.*

THE RESIDENCE OF MRS. EDENA JANE (SANFORD) LE FAVOR.

JAMES HOVEY SARGENT, ASSISTANT SURGEON, U. S. A.

JAMES HOVEY SARGENT, son of Nathaniel and Abial H. Sargent, was born June, 1782, in York, Me. He was educated in Phillips Academy, Exeter, N. H., and studied medicine with Dr. Gilman of that town. He was appointed by President Thomas Jefferson, June 19, 1806, surgeon's mate, United States Army, his commission to date from March 6, 1806. For ten years Dr. Sargent belonged to the medical staff of Fort Independence, Boston Harbor. He was afterwards on duty in Fort Pickering, Salem, Mass., Fort Constitution, Portsmouth, N. H., Fort Preble, Portland, Me., Fort Trumbull, New London, Conn., Fort Aragon, Niagara, N. Y. While at the latter place, in 1846, he resigned, having been in the service forty years. Subsequently he came to reside with his daughter, Mrs. Francis J. R. Bullard, in Medway. Dr. Sargent married in 1812, Fanny Ruggles, who died Sept. 13, 1854. Their only child was a daughter who married Mr. Anson Bullard and resided in Medway. Dr. Sargent died Aug. 31, 1869, in Medway, and was buried in Mount Auburn Cemetery. He was a gentleman of fine presence and courtly manners. In recognition of his public service and in respect to his memory the Grand Army Post formed in Medway in 1882, was designated the JAMES HOVEY SARGENT POST.

STEPHEN SALISBURY, M. D.

STEPHEN SALISBURY, son of Samuel and Nancy Salisbury, was born Sept. 10, 1812, in Boston, Mass. " He was of an old and highly respected family of that city, and enjoyed, in early life, every advantage of careful and judicious training. He was prepared for college at the Boston Latin School, entered Harvard University at the early age of sixteen years, and graduated in the class of 1832. He immediately commenced the study of medicine, under the instruction of Drs. Jackson and Bigelow, and received his medical degree from Harvard in 1835. He was house surgeon of the Massachusetts General Hospital for a year, and then went to Paris to complete his studies in the schools and hospitals of that city.

" Soon after his return, he entered upon the active duties of his profession, in Medway, where he soon acquired a good and rapidly increasing practice. He was married, Jan. 2, 1844, to Miss Elizabeth P. Clark, of Walpole, Mass. In a few years his business had so increased that his physical strength was unequal to the demands made upon it by a widely scattered community, and therefore, about 1850, he removed to Brookline, Mass., hoping to be able to lead, amid a denser population, and in the near vicinity of the city, a life of less exhausting labor. Here, his upright character and professional fidelity, soon found ample recognition, and after twenty-five years of faithful and earnest labor in the profession for which he had an enthusiastic love, he died of Bright's disease, Sept. 12, 1875, respected by all, and mourned by a large circle of sincere friends. Dr. Salisbury was of a modest and retiring disposition, conspicuous for transparent sincerity and truthfulness, and scrupulously conscientious qualities by which Nature had endowed him, and which were broadened and deepened by his religious convictions and culture. A life-long student, he was always informed of the latest medical improvements and discoveries; kind hearted and sympathetic, his services were always at the command of the poor as promptly as of the rich and influential, tender and affectionate, he was idolized in his own home; leading a blameless Christian life, he was an ornament to the church of which he was a member; a good citizen, a staunch and loyal friend, a kind neighbor, he was, above all, the faithful, beloved physician."

Rev. Seth Willard Segur.

Seth Willard Segur, son of Dea. Joseph and Martha (Briggs) Segur, was born Dec. 24, 1831, in Chittenden, Vt. His mother was the daughter of Calvin Briggs, Esq., of Dighton, R. I., and was born March 30, 1798, in Williamstown, Vt. His father was the son of Elijah Segur, who was a Revolutionary soldier, and removed from Simsbury, Conn., to Philadelphia, now Chittenden, Vt., and died Feb. 8, 1851, in his ninety-seventh year, in Pittsfield, Vt. Dea. Joseph Segur was born Aug. 17, 1801, removed from Chittenden to Pittsfield, Vt., in 1832, where he died June 27, 1883. The subject of this sketch when a lad of twelve years experienced religion and at the age of fifteen, July 4, 1847, publicly confessed Christ and united with the Congregational Church of Pittsfield, Vt. He pursued his studies preparatory to college at Royalton Academy, Vermont, entered Middlebury College in 1855, and graduated in the class of 1859. After graduation he entered upon his professional studies in the Theological Seminary in Auburn, N Y. He was licensed to preach May 8, 1861, by the Royalton Association, Vermont, and ordained to the Gospel ministry by a council called by the church in Pittsfield, Vt., of which he was still a member. He commenced June 8, 1862, his ministry and was installed Feb. 6, 1867, as pastor of the Congregational Church in Tallmadge, O. During this pastorate there were received into the church one hundred and thirty-four persons, eighty-eight by confession of faith and fifty-six by letter. He administered the rite of baptism to eighty-nine children and to fifteen adult persons. By advice of ecclesiastical council, convened April 18, 1871, he closed his pastorate April 30, 1871, to accept a call to Gloucester, Mass.

He was installed, June 14, 1871, pastor of the Evangelical Congregational Church, in Gloucester, Mass. The Rev. Alexander McKenzie, D D., of Cambridge, preached the sermon. Here he did faithful service during a short pastorate, and resigned Feb. 15, 1873. He was installed, May 7, 1873, colleague pastor with the Rev. Jacob Ide, D. D, of the Second Church of Christ. The Rev Mr. Segur, in the little of life that remained to him, accomplished here a great amount of good. He inspired his people to effort, so that much was accomplished in various ways for the church and society who were so soon called to mourn the death of their beloved pastor

The Rev. Mr. Segur left home Sept. 6, 1875, for a little visit to his old parish in Tallmadge, O He was especially invited to come and be present at the semi-centennial of that church. He was taken ill soon after his arrival and in a few days died, Sept. 24, 1875, at the early age of forty-three years.

The funeral service was attended in Tallmadge, on Sunday, September 26, and on the same day in West Medway. By the very urgent request of his old parishioners, his grave is in the midst of his first church and people.

Funeral service was held also in Pittsfield, Vt., Oct. 3, 1875, the Rev. C. W. Clark preaching the sermon, and subsequently a memorial service was held, Oct. 31, 1875, in West Medway. The memorial discourse was preached from the text, "*I have fought the good fight, I have finished my course,*" etc.; 2 Tim. iv., 7-8, by the Rev. C. C. McIntire, of Rockport, Mass.

The Rev. Mr. Segur left a widow and an only son. Mrs. Segur resided some years in Andover, Mass., where Willard B. Segur, the son, fitted for college.

"Mr. Segur was a man of profound Christian spirit, and he won a way for truth. He harmonized discordant elements. He was a practical Christian worker. He took his place by the side of those who needed help, and gave them his hand in every possible way. He was an earnest temperance man, and knew how to help the intemperate. His preaching was full of the compassion of the Gospel, while compromising no sterner truth. His elocution was graceful and pleasant. He was deeply interested in sacred music, and was an excellent singer. He was a man of substantial worth, unassuming, consecrated, strong — a good man, and a good minister whom the people loved." The sentiment of his life and ministry was "I shall preach the truth whatever may be the consequences."

Several of the Rev. Mr. Segur's discourses were published at the request of his hearers. Among these were the following: *The Relation and Responsibilities of Pastor and People; The True Manhood; The Nation's Hope; National Blessings and Duties.*

Jabez Shumway, Esq.

Jabez Shumway, son of Amos and Ruth (Parker) Shumway, was born August, 1746, in Oxford, Mass. He came a young man, in 1767, to Medway, and was employed first by Capt. Nathaniel Whiting in his grist mill near the site of the present Sanford Mills in Medway Village. By prudence and economy, having accumulated a little money, he was negotiating for the purchase of a farm adjoining the "Arnold Factory" property in North Bellingham, when the Continental currency was repudiated, and he was thus deprived of the means to make the purchase. Discouraged, he returned to his native town, Oxford, Mass. Two years later, however, he came back to Medway and rented the farm of Seth Holbrook, Partridgetown, and in 1783 purchased the farm of William Ellis, which included what was known as Rabbit Hill and the land since occupied by his descendants, and known as the Shumway homestead. Mr. Shumway was a man of excellent judgment, and very systematic in his habits. He had the fullest confidence of his fellow-townsmen and was often called to the service of executor and administrator of estates and to fill offices in the town. There is a diary kept by Mr. Shumway now in the possession of a descendant, A. A. Shumway, Esq., of Philadelphia, which betrays, somewhat, the habits and the character of the man. In this journal he recorded brief notices of all extra religious gatherings, such as Fast and Thanksgiving days, ordinations, installations, etc., with the names of the preacher and a memorandum of the text, for example: "Bellingham, July 20, 1780 was State Fast on the reducion of Charlstown. Psalms lxxxv., 8. D. Sanford."

Important statistics and events that came under his observation were also chronicled "June 10, 1776 The number of men wimen and childeren in Medway 925."

"Bellingham May 19th 1780, this Day was remarkably Dark, it was at the darkest betwene one and twelve o'clock. It was so dark that I could not see to read." He served on one or more of the brief enlistments of "minutemen" which were made during the Revolutionary War upon special "alarms" and makes a note of one such instance in his diary: "Medway Dec. 8, 1776 was a Larrom for Provedence and Capt. Joseph Lovel marchet his company of 33 men and I came home the 19 day of December 1776."

Rev. Ethan Smith.

ETHAN SMITH, son of Dea Elijah and Sybil (Worthington) Smith, was born Dec. 19, 1762, in Belchertown, Mass. He was a soldier in the War of the Revolution and stationed at West Point at the time that post was betrayed by Arnold. He graduated in 1790 from Dartmouth College, entered the ministry, and was installed in 1792 pastor of the Congregational Church in Haverhill, N. H., where he remained eight years. He was then installed, March 12, 1800, pastor of the Congregational Church in Hopkinton, N. H., and resigned in 1818. The Rev. Mr. Smith was then pastor in Hebron, N. Y., from 1818 to 1821, and from Nov. 21, 1821, to December, 1826, in Poultney, Vt., from May 16, 1827, to June 2, 1832, in Hanover, Mass., and subsequently he was a city missionary, also agent of the Bible Society in Boston, Mass. The ministry of the Rev. Mr. Smith continued to the close of his life, and was one of great usefulness, marked by revivals of great power. During his pastorate in Hopkinton, N. H., one hundred and ninety-two persons were added to the church. He was the author of several published works besides sermons. Among these were: *View of the Trinity, Dissertations and the Prophecies, Lectures on Baptism, Memoirs of Mrs. Bailey, 1815, Key to Revelation, The Tribes of Israel in America, 1825,* etc The Rev. Mr. Smith married, Feb. 4, 1793, Bathsheba Sanford, daughter of the Rev. David Sanford, of West Medway. Mrs. Smith died April 5, 1835, at Pompey Hill, N. Y. The Rev. Mr. Smith died Aug. 29, 1849, in the eighty-seventh year of his age, at the residence of his son-in-law, the Rev. William A Sanford, of Boylston, Mass. He preached with great animation and impressiveness the Sabbath before the last brief illness which terminated his life The Rev. Mr. Smith had one son who was an eminent physician in Newark, N. J., three of his daughters married ministers and two sons were ministers. The Rev. Carlos Smith was for many years a pastor in Ohio, and the Rev. Stephen Sanford Smith was settled in Fayetteville, N. Y., in Westminster and Warren, Mass He spent his later years in Chicago, Ill. In 1871 he made a journey to the East, and died at the house of his sister, in Worcester, Mass. His last pulpit service was in Medway Village Church, on the Sabbath preceding his death, and he was expected to preach there the next Sabbath, but on Saturday while making preparations to leave Worcester for Medway, he suddenly died. He had selected his manuscript sermons for the next day and one of them was on this text: "*I shall be satisfied when I awake in thy likeness.*"

DEA JOHN SMITH.

JOHN SMITH, son of worthy parents, was born May 19, 1796, in Breckin, Scotland. His father was a carpenter, and his mother, one of the Middleton stock, was, as he said, an "honest, persevering, frugal, far-sighted woman, anxious for her children, and earnestly desiring that they might live to be good." At nine he was sent into the country to work on a farm, as a herd-boy, attending school only in winter. When thirteen, his father died, leaving five children, of whom John was the oldest, and for five years he worked as a mill-wright in Breckin. He embarked in August, 1816, for America. The passage took fifty-two days, and he narrowly escaped shipwreck, but landed finally at Halifax, N. S. He then shipped for Boston, Mass. After some years, about 1820, he went to Medway, where he remained a year and a half. Then he met Mr. Joseph Faulkner, of Andover, and Mr Warren Richardson, of Medway, with whom he formed a partnership, under the firm name of "John Smith & Company." They located at Plymouth, and began the manufacture of cotton machinery. He afterwards spoke of this as appearing to him the most important period of his life "I felt," he said, "that all the honor or dishonor would come on me, as my partners' names did not appear." From that time the strength and greatness of the man began to be developed.

The firm bought the Frye Village (Andover) water privilege, and located its business there in 1824 From 1831, both partners having died, Mr. Smith carried on the business successfully alone for three years. Meantime his brother, the late Dea. Peter Smith, had arrived ; and also the late Mr. John Dove. Mr. Dove proposed the manufacture of shoe thread and linen twine, and the Smith Brothers and Mr. Dove formed a firm, known for some thirty years as "Smith, Dove & Company," and since 1864 as the "Smith and Dove Manufacturing Company" Thus began one of the most successful business enterprises in the history of New England ; each partner amassed a large property and gave away liberal sums in benevolence.

Dea. John Smith died in Andover, Mass , Thursday, Feb 25, 1886, at the great age of eighty-nine years and nine months. But few men of his generation have grappled as earnestly with the great problems of the last half century. The story of his career is of great interest, and should be a source of inspiration to all men

REV. SAMUEL JONES SPALDING, D D.

SAMUEL JONES SPALDING, son of Abijah and Hannah (Eastman) Spalding, was born Dec 11, 1820, in Lyndeborough, N. H. He graduated in 1842 from Dartmouth College. Hanover, N. H., and in 1845 from the Theological Seminary in Andover, Mass. He was ordained, Oct. 28, 1846, pastor in Salmon Falls, N H. He resigned June 9, 1851, and was installed June 30, 1851, over the Whitfield Congregational Church in Newburyport, Mass., where he was pastor more than thirty years. He was Chaplain of the 48th Massachusetts Regiment, entered service Dec. 29, 1862, mustered out Aug. 30, 1863 Previous to his graduation from college he taught the public and also a select school in Medway Village, and June 27, 1848, he was married to Sarah Lydia Metcalf, of Medway, youngest daughter of Hon. Luther and

Saiah Brown (Phipps) Metcalf. She died Sept. 1, 1849, in Salmon Falls, N. H. The Rev Mr Spalding married, Sept. 16, 1851, Sarah Jane Parker Toppan, daughter of the Hon. Edmund and Mary (Chase) Toppan, of Hampton, N. H. The children were : Mary Toppan, born December, 1856 ; Annie Toppan, born March 23, 1860 ; Edmund Samuel, born Jan 5, 1865. *Vid. The Spalding Memorial.*

CEPHAS THAYER, ESQ

CEPHAS THAYER, son of Calvin and Abigail Thayer, was born Feb. 16, 1789, in Bellingham, Mass. At the age of sixteen he was apprenticed in the trade of cabinet making, to Maj. Luther Metcalf, of Medway. In 1813, he joined with Luther Metcalf, Jr., and Joel Hunt, in establishing the manufacture of machinery for cotton and woolen goods, at the Charles River water privilege in West Medway. Fourteen years later, Mr. Thayer bought the land surrounding the Chicken Brook privileges, and there, in 1840, with his son, Mr. Addison P. Thayer, built the machine shop which still goes by the name of " the stone mill." He served for a short time as a volunteer in the War of 1812, but always declined public office. As a citizen he was unobtrusive and thoroughly respected. He died April 16, 1882, in West Medway.

ADDISON PARSONS THAYER, ESQ.

ADDISON PARSONS THAYER, son of Cephas and Lavinia (Adams) Thayer, was born May 31, 1814, in Medway, Mass. While a young man, he found employment for several years in Boston and New York. In 1851 he traveled in Europe, and, not long after, spent two years in Iowa and other western states. For the greater part of the time since 1840, he has been engaged in this town in the manufacture of thread, of machinery for straw goods, and of raw-hide mallets. He was appointed, in 1866, a Justice of the Peace.

ADDISON SANFORD THAYER, A. M.

ADDISON SANFORD THAYER, son of Addison Parsons and Lydia Sanford (Partridge) Thayer, was born Aug. 5, 1858. He graduated, in 1877, from Phillips Academy, Andover, Mass., and in 1881, from Harvard College. Mr. Thayer was for two years a teacher in the High School in Portland, Me., and then devoted himself to the study of medicine.

GEORGE BREED THRASHER, ESQ.

GEORGE BREED THRASHER, son of Elkanah and Lydia (Codding) Thrasher, was born Jan 26, 1816, in Taunton Mass. He was the youngest of seven children, and commenced working out for wages in a brick yard, when nine years of age At first, all his wages, except enough to clothe himself scantily, went for the support of the family. He came to Medway at the age of eighteen years, to take charge of the brick yard of Capt. Simon H Mason, on the farm now owned by Patrick Crowley. He lived with Captain Mason for ten years, and then went to Dedham, where he carried on a farm one season, and held for a year the position of a turnkey in the county jail. He then returned to Medway, and commenced the manufacture of bricks on his own account, on the farm of Mr. Elisha Adams, which is now owned by C. K. Brackett, Esq.

After some two years he purchased five acres of land of Mr. Jonathan Adams, and in 1848, erected a house which was subsequently his home. Mr. Thrasher married, Oct. 13, 1847, Laura F. Ward, of Oxford, Mass. Mr. Thrasher was an industrious and thrifty business man, whose judgment was much sought and valued. He was genial, and always had a word of good cheer. In 1882 he was persuaded to accept the office of selectman, and fulfilled its duties with great acceptance. He was taken suddenly ill, and on town-meeting day, Monday, March 5, 1883, he died. On the very day of his death he was unanimously reëlected selectman. Mrs. Thrasher and a son, Mr. George C. Thrasher, survive him.

Rev. David Thurston.

David Thurston, son of Daniel and Deborah (Pond) Thurston, was born May 6, 1726, in Wrentham, afterwards Franklin, Mass. He graduated in 1751 from Princeton College, Princeton, N. J., and became the first pastor of the Second Church of Christ in Medway. After a ministry of seventeen years he resigned and removed to Oxford, Mass., where he settled upon a farm. Subsequently he removed to Auburn, N. Y., and afterwards to Sutton, Mass., where he died May 5, 1777, at the age of fifty years.

William Smith Tilden, Esq.

William S Tilden, son of Eleazar P. and Catherine (Smith) Tilden, was born April 4, 1830, in Medfield, Mass. Having completed his earlier education, he prepared himself for a teacher of music. He commenced in 1854 to teach evening classes in singing, and continued this until 1868. Since then he has been a director of musical instruction in the public schools in Salem, Norton, West Roxbury, Mass., and in other places. He is now in charge of the musical instruction of the State Normal School in Framingham, Mass. Mr. Tilden has been for eight years a member of the school committee of Medfield, where he resides. In 1879 he represented the Ninth Norfolk District in the Legislature of Massachusetts. He has devoted much time and labor in collecting materials for *The History of Medfield*, soon to be published. Mr. Tilden married, Nov. 6, 1853, Olive N. Babcock, daughter of Lowell and Thankful B. (Sanger) Babcock, of East Medway.

Aldis L. Waite, Esq.

Aldis L. Waite, son of Amos and Betsey (Stow) Waite, was born June 2, 1820, in Weston, Vt. In early manhood he engaged in business in Lowell, Mass. From 1844 for six years he was a grocer, and from 1850 to 1870 he was a wholesale produce dealer. He was married at the age of twenty-eight, and came to be widely known and much respected in the business, social, and religious circles in the young but enterprising city of Lowell where he resided. He was chosen a director in one of the city banks, and elected in 1861, a member of the Board of Aldermen; reëlected in 1862, with only three dissenting votes in the whole city, a rare honor. He was a valued member of the Kirk Street Church. Mr. Waite was a nephew of Mrs. Abigail (Stow) Abbe, widow of Amos Abbe, Esq., of Rockville, and in 1878 removed to

ALDIS L. WAITE, ESQ.

Medway to care for his aged aunt, who survived but a few years. Upon her
death he came into possession of a dwelling-house beautifully located on the

THE RESIDENCE OF ALDIS L. WAITE, ESQ.

bend of the Charles River. Mr. and Mrs Waite with her mother, Mrs. Gilman, have continued to reside in Medway. Although Mr. Waite's business is largely in Boston, he has taken much interest in the local affairs of his adopted place of residence, and after its incorporation became an active citizen of Millis

Rev Horace Dean Walker

Horace Dean Walker, son of Dean and Rebecca (Wright) Walker, was born Sept 15, 1815, in Framingham, Mass. He was in the seventh generation from Dea Philip Walker, who, with his brother James and their mother, came from England about 1632, and settled in Rehoboth, Mass. Mr. Walker pursued his preparatory studies in Wrentham and Leicester academies, and graduated in 1841 from Yale College, New Haven, Conn.

In the fall of that year he taught in East Medway for three months then studied theology with Dr Ide and graduated in 1843 from the Bangor Theological Seminary. He soon settled in the ministry in East Abington, Mass , where he continued for nearly twenty-five years. He accepted, in 1868, a call to Bridgewater, where he had a prosperous pastorate of twelve years. After closing his labors in Bridgewater, because of failing health, he purchased a residence in Palatine Bridge, N Y., which was his home at the time of his sudden death, Nov. 4, 1885. The Rev. Mr. Walker fulfilled a vigorous and useful ministry, extending over a period of forty years. He was an interesting preacher, an excellent pastor, a warm friend of the poor and unfortunate, and has been characterized as "a man of broad culture and literary attainments." On Saturday, Oct. 31, 1885, Mr. Walker met with a fall and received injuries which resulted fatally the following Wednesday The funeral services occurred Nov. 6, 1885, in Rockland, Mass. Tender commemorative addresses were made by the Rev. Messrs. J. C. Labaree, R. K. Harlow, and F. R Abbe, and the remains were deposited in Mount Vernon Cemetery, Abington, Mass.

Rev. Augustus Walker.

Augustus Walker, son of Dean and Rebecca (Wright) Walker, was born Oct. 30, 1822, in Medway. He graduated from Yale in 1849, and from the Theological Seminary, at Andover, in 1852, was ordained Oct. 16, 1852, and on the same day married Eliza M. Harding, of Auburndale, and soon after sailed as a missionary of the American Board, to Diarbeker, in Syria, where the remaining years of his life were chiefly spent. He was a devoted and earnest man, giving himself wholly to his work, and his death, which occurred Sept. 13, 1866, was felt to be a public loss both to his own people and the residents of the city where so much of his life was passed His wife and children, after his death, returned, in the spring of 1867, to this country, and have resided in Auburndale, where she has established a successful school for the training of missionary children sent to this country for their education.

Rev. George Frederic Walker.

George Frederic Walker, son of Dea Timothy and Louisa (Turner) Walker, was born May 31, 1825 He fitted for college in the academy in

Leicester, Mass., and graduated, in 1849, from Amherst College, Amherst, Mass. After graduation, he founded and became the Principal of the Mount Hollis Seminary, in Holliston, Mass. From 1855 to 1858 he was an assistant teacher in the Riverside Institute, Auburndale, Mass. Having studied theology under the instruction of the Rev. J. T. Tucker, D. D., of Holliston, he was licensed to preach, in 1863, by the Mendon Association. He was ordained and installed, July 3, 1863, as pastor of the Congregational Church, in Wellfleet, Mass. He resigned, was installed, and settled from June 30, 1867, to Aug. 1, 1872, in Little Compton, R. I., and from March 9, 1873, to Nov. 7, 1875, in Ashby, Mass. Subsequently he was acting pastor from April 9, 1876, to June 30, 1880, in Blackstone, and from Oct. 30, 1880, to the present time, in Freetown, Mass. The Rev. Mr. Walker married, Jan. 1, 1852, Esther Amelia Bullard, of Holliston, Mass. Mrs. Walker died Nov. 7, 1861, and Mr. Walker subsequently married Mary A. K. Atwood, of Wellfleet, Mass.

WILLIAM GOODRICH WARE, M. D.

WILLIAM G. WARE, son of Josiah H. and Huldah G. (Hale) Ware, was born Feb. 1, 1832, in East Medway, now Millis, Mass. His father was a church organ builder, son of Dea. Joseph Ware, of North Wrentham, now Norfolk, Mass. Dr. Ware was educated in the public schools and in 1849 entered Leicester Academy. In 1851 he began to turn his attention to the study of medicine, but not having the pecuniary means necessary, he resolved to devote himself to the organ business until he could command the funds to complete his medical education. He was married, Feb. 7, 1856, to Angeline E. Ellis, daughter of Henry and Jane Ellis, of Medway, who died a few weeks after, March 29, 1856, of consumption. He married, June 7, 1857, Mrs. Jane F. Daniels, widow of the late Francis P. Daniels, of Medway. In 1860 he commenced a more thorough study of medicine with C. Emory Morse, M. D., of Cambridgeport, Mass., and in the spring of 1866 graduated at the Western Homoeophathic Medical College of Cleveland, O., and soon after was elected member of the Hahnemannian Society of Cleveland. The following May he located in Medfield. In the spring of 1867 he removed to East Boston; but not liking the city and preferring a country residence, he removed, Nov. 1, 1867, to East Dedham, Mass. In 1868 he was admitted to membership in the Massachusetts Homoeopathic Medical Society, and in 1869 became a member of the American Institute of Homoeopathy. He has been very successful in his profession and won the confidence of the community where he lives as a faithful disciple of Hahnemann, who established the Homoeopathic law of cure: " *Similia similibus curantur.*"

JOHN S. WHITE, PH. D.

JOHN S. WHITE, son of the Rev. John S. and Anna (Richardson) White, and grandson of Dea. Silas and Mary (Carlton) Richardson, of East Medway, was born Feb. 3, 1847, in Wrentham, Mass. He graduated from the Chapman Grammar, English High, and Boston Latin schools, Boston, and was admitted June, 1866, to Harvard College, Cambridge, Mass. He took a high stand in scholarship, and his senior year on occasion of the inauguration of Prof. Charles W. Eliot as President of the college, he was selected by the faculty to deliver the Latin oration of welcome. Mr. White, on graduation, was elected Sub-Master of the Boston Latin School, and in a few months became Master by promotion. This position he filled for three years, when he resigned, in order to spend a year in Europe. Meanwhile he married, Feb. 28, 1871, Miss Georgie A. Read, of Boston, a graduate in 1870 of Mount Holyoke Seminary. While abroad Mr. White was a popular correspondent of the *Boston Daily Advertiser*. Upon his return he became, Sept 30, 1874, Master of the Brooks School in Cleveland, O., which under his management had a wonderful development and popularity. Mr. White resigned, and in 1880 established the Berkley School in New York City, of which he is the Head Master. Dr. White has had a most successful career as a teacher, and won an eminence in preparing students for college.

As a memorial of his affection for his grandfather, Dea. Silas Richardson, the oldest resident of the town, Mr. White has presented a clock to the Church of Christ in Millis, which is to be in position on or before the ninety-fourth birthday of his venerable and honored grandfather.

DUNCAN WRIGHT, ESQ.

DUNCAN WRIGHT was born in the year 1770, in Delmarkly, Argyleshire, Scotland. He married Janet Wilson, a sister of Alexander Wilson, the celebrated ornithologist. They had three sons, Peter, Alexander, and John. He came to America in 1812, intending to locate in Philadelphia, but was taken prisoner by the privateer "Yankee," James De Wolfe, owner, and taken into Bristol harbor. His business being that of a bleacher, De Wolfe secured his services in an establishment of which he was the owner, as superintendent of bleaching. He was the first person to establish chemical bleaching in America. In 1815 his wife and sons joined him in this country. He then located in Smithfield, R. I., where he remained two years. From there he went to Waltham, where he set up bleaching on his own account. After he had been there about three years, the Boston Manufacturing Company bought the site upon which his works were located. He then removed to Medway where he set up another bleachery near Charles River, living in the Amos Fisher house upon Paul's Hill. He resided here with his family five years. He afterwards had a bleachery in Milk Row, Boston. Then went to Fall River, and with his brother Daniel and two others, did the first calico printing in that city. He afterwards retired to a farm in Tewksbury, near Lowell, and died in 1837, at the age of sixty-seven years. His oldest son, Peter Wright, was employed in the Lowell Carpet Company factory until 1857, when he removed to Westminster, Mass., where he resided in 1882 at the age of eighty-four years. The second son was the Hon. Alexander Wright. John Wright, the youngest son, died in 1874 at Jamaica Plain, Boston, Mass.

HON. ALEXANDER WRIGHT.

ALEXANDER WRIGHT, son of Duncan and Janet (Wilson) Wright, was born in the year 1800, in Renfrewshire, Scotland. When a lad he attended school at Paisley, afterwards at a place near Glasgow, where he was considered the most prominent scholar, and always at the head of his class. When fifteen years of age he came to this country, his father, Duncan Wright, having come over some years earlier, and was employed as a bleacher at Smithfield, R I. He worked with his father in Waltham and in Medway at bleaching until he was twenty-one years of age, when he commenced, on his own account the manufacture of coach lace at Medway Village where the family lived until he began with Burdett the manufacture of carpets in West Medway, on Winthrop Street near the Cutler place, on Chicken Brook. This was the first carpet factory in Massachusetts and the second in America, the first being in Philadelphia, Penn. In a published pamphlet by the "Old Residents Historical Association" of Lowell, Mass., there is found mention of Mr. Wright in the following connection ·

"In 1800 a Frenchman named Jacquard invented a machine attached to looms at first for weaving silks and muslins and was found of great value in the fabrication of figured goods. Soon after a Mr. Morton, a Scotchman, applied it to a carpet loom and found it a great success. In the course of a few years small mills were started for the manufacture of carpets in the United States. One was located in Medway,—first owned by a Mr. Henry Burdett and Mr. Alexander Wright, who was the real manager.

"In 1825, Mr. Wright attempted to gain information by visiting a small mill in Philadelphia Failing in this, he went to Scotland and purchased looms, returning in 1826, with Claude and William Wilson, whom he employed to aid in operating.

"Narrowly escaping shipwreck as nearing the American shores, he soon began to operate his looms, in Medway, with success. He found the location not favorable to enlargement, and sold his interest to Mr. Burdett, who soon sold to Frederic Cabot and Patrick T. Jackson, of Boston, who organized the Lowell Manufacturing Company, Feb. 22, 1828. Cabot & Jackson sold the mill and machinery, in Medway, to the new company, which constituted the foundation of the great and world renowned carpet works in Lowell, Mass. Prior to the removal, Mr. Wright operated the machinery in Medway."

Peter Lawson was his designer, who afterward continued the same relation to the new company, and he and Mr. Wright became very prominent in business and public life in later years, in the city of Lowell.

The country probably owes as much to Mr Wright's skill and perseverance in perfecting the industry of carpet manufacturing, as to any other man.

The following is a duplicate bill of sale of a Medway carpet and rug:

	"MEDWAY. Jan 15, 1828	
"MISS SARAH B. PHIPPS	Bot of MEDWAY CARPET MANUF. Co	
25 yds. Superfine Carpeting, c. 7-6 per yd ,	. . . .	$31 25
1 Rug, ...		7 50
		$38 75
	"Received Payment,	
	"ALEXr WRIGHT, Agt."	

The Hon. Alexander Wright died in Lowell, on the 7th of June, 1852, suddenly, and was interred at Mount Auburn He was eminently social and intelligent, public spirited, naturally modest; was elected Alderman in 1836, to the Legislature in 1838, and though often urged, positively declined to accept the office of the mayor of the city.

Rev. Luther Wright.

Luther Wright was born in 1770 in Acton, Mass. He graduated in 1796 from Harvard College, Cambridge, Mass. In November, 1796, he united with the First Church of Cambridge, of which the Rev. Abiel Holmes was the pastor. Mr. Wright studied for the ministry and was settled in 1798 pastor of the First Church of Christ in Medway. He married, December 23, Nancy Bridge, daughter of the Rev. Josiah Bridge, of East Sudbury, Mass. His pastorate continued until 1815, when he resigned. He was installed, Jan. 29, 1817, over the Congregational Church in Barrington, R. I., where he labored some four years and was dismissed in 1821. Subsequently he supplied vacant pulpits in various places. He was the stated minister from 1825 to 1828 in Tiverton, R. I. The last twenty-five or thirty years of his life were spent in Woburn, Mass., where he died June 21, 1858. Mrs. Wright died Feb. 23, 1861. The Rev. and Mrs. Wright had no children. They were interred side by side in the cemetery in Woburn, Mass.

THE GENEALOGIES.

The Adams Family.

President John Adams erected a monument in the Old Burying-Ground in Quincy Mass., to the memory of his ancestor, Henry Adams, which bears this inscription:

"In Memory of Henry Adams, who took his flight from the dragon, persecution, in Devonshire, and alighted, with eight sons, near Mount Wollaston. One of the sons returned to England; and, after taking time to explore the country, four removed to Medfield, one of the neighboring towns; two to Chelmsford, one only, Joseph, who lies here at his left hand, remained here, who was the original proprietor of the Township of Braintree, incorporated in 1639."

Henry Adams, immigrant, with his eight sons, or, as some accounts have it, nine sons and a daughter, arrived, in 1632, in America. He settled in that part of Braintree which became Quincy, Mass. Four of his sons, Henry, Peter, Edward and Jonathan, were among the proprietors and the earliest settlers of Medfield, Mass. They drew land dividends on the west side of the Charles River. Their children and descendants were among the first, and have been numerous among the inhabitants of Medway. *Vid. The Adams Genealogy, The Morse Genealogical Register*, and *The New England Genealogical Register*, April, 1883.

[1] **HENRY**[1] **ADAMS** came, in 1632, from Devonshire, England, and settled in that part of Massachusetts Bay Colony which became Quincy, Mass. He died in 1646.

The children were: Henry [2], b. 1604. Samuel, res. in Chelmsford, Mass., d. 1666. Joseph, m. Abigail Baxter, res. in Braintree, Mass. Thomas, res. in Chelmsford, Mass. Peter [3]. Edward [4]. Jonathan [5]. John. Christopher, returned to England. Ursula.

[2] **HENRY**[2] **ADAMS** (Henry[1]), son of Henry [1] Adams, was born, in 1604, in England. He married, Oct. 17. 1743, Elizabeth Paine. They resided in Braintree, but removed, in 1649, to Medfield, Mass. Mr. Adams died Feb. 21, 1676, being massacred at his own door, by the Indians. Mrs. Adams died Feb. 29, 1676, from the effects of being shot by the accidental discharge of a gun, the bullet passing up through the ceiling, and producing a fatal wound, as she lay ill upon her bed, in the chamber overhead.

The children were: Eleazar, b. Aug. 5, 1644, m. Elizabeth ——, res. in Medfield, Mass., d. April 14, 1701. Jasper, b. April 23, 1647, unm., d. July 1, 1742. Elizabeth, b Nov. 11, 1649, m. Dec 16, 1668, Dea John Harding, *vid* JOHN, b July 14, 1652, m. Michal ——, d. April 11 1728 HENRY, b July 14, 1652, d. July 10, 1653. MOSES, b. Oct 26 1654, m Lydia Whitney, res. in Holliston, Mass, d 1724 HENRY [6], b. Nov. 15, 1657 SAMUEL, b Nov 2 1661, m. Mary ——, res in Medfield, Mass.

Memoranda Henry[2] Adams was a Lieutenant of the training band, Clerk of Writs, and Representative in 1659. 1665, 1674, and 1675, to the General Court. Jasper[2] Adams lived a bachelor to great age, his heirs were Sarah Rockwood, George Adams, Jonathan, James, and Stephen Partridge

[3] **PETER[2] ADAMS** (HENRY[1]), son of Henry [1] Adams, was born in England He married and settled in Medfield, Mass Mr. Adams died about 1690.

The children were PETER [7], b 1653. HANNAH, b. 1655 MARY, b. 1661 JONATHAN, b 1663. RUTH, b 1665 JOSEPH, b 1668, res in Canterbury, Conn. SAMUEL, res in Medfield, Mass HENRY, b. 1673

Memoranda. Peter[2] Adams drew land dividend in the New Grant, which was afterwards owned by Joseph Curtis Samuel[3] Adams was a physician.

[4] **EDWARD[2] ADAMS** (HENRY[1]), son of Henry [1] Adams, was born in England. He married Lydia —— They resided in Medfield, Mass.

The children were LYDIA, b. 1653, m [1]James Allen, m. [2]Joseph Daniell, *vid ;* d Dec 26, 1731 JONATHAN, b 1655 JOHN [8], b 1657. ELIZABETH, b 1658 SARAH, b 1660 JAMES, b 1661, res in Barrington, R. I HENRY, res in Canterbury, Conn ELISHA, b 1666, res in Bristol, R. I. EDWARD, b 1668, res. in Bristol, R. I. ELIASHIB, res in Bristol, R I BETHIA, b 1671, d. BETHIA, b. 1672. ABIGAIL, b. 1674 MIRIAM, b 1675.

Memoranda. Edward[2] Adams drew a land dividend in the New Grant, which was afterward occupied by his son John[3] Adams

[5] **JONATHAN[2] ADAMS** (HENRY[1]), son of Henry [1] Adams, was born in England. He married Elizabeth Fussell, daughter of John and Elizabeth Fussell. They resided in Medfield now Millis, Mass Mr. Adams died in 1692.

The children were ELIZABETH, b 1666, m 1688, John[2] Partridge, *vid ,* d Aug 14, 1719 SARAH, b 1667 An INFANT, b 1669, d JONATHAN, b 1670, d. JONATHAN, b 1671, d JASPER, b 1673 JONATHAN [9], b 1679. MARY, b 1681 LYDIA, b 1689

[6] **HENRY[3] ADAMS** (HENRY[2], HENRY[1]), son of Henry [2] and Elizabeth (Paine) Adams, was born Nov 15, 1657, in Medfield, Mass. He married Prudence Frary, daughter of John and Mrs Elizabeth (Harding) Frary, *née* Adams She was born Aug 30, 1662 They resided in Medfield, Mass. Mr Adams died September, 1773. Mrs Adams died Feb 20, 1750

The children were PRUDENCE, b. April 10, 1682, m. April 14, 1702, Capt Joseph Morse, res in Sherborn, Mass, d Feb. 23, 1772 HANNAH, b Oct 14, 1685, m June 9, 1703, Edward[3] Clark, *vid ,* d Oct 27, 1775 THOMAS, b May 21, 1688, m Mary ——, res. in Medfield, Mass , d March 31, 1763 JEREMIAH [10], b Jan 14, 1691 ELIZABETH, b. Jan 8, 1694, d. Nov 26, 1766 SARAH, b. Dec. 13, 1697, d April 1, 1725 HENRY, b. March 26, 1702, m Jemima Morse, res in Medfield, d Nov 3, 1782

[7] **PETER[3] ADAMS** (PETER[2], HENRY[1]), son of Peter [3] Adams, was born, 1653, in Medfield, Mass He married Experience Cook They resided in Medfield, now Millis, Mass Deacon Adams died Dec. 8, 1723 Mrs Adams survived him

The children were RACHEL, b 1680, m Jonathan Hill, *vid* JOSEPH [11], b 1682 PETER, b. 1684, res in West Wrentham, now Franklin, Mass EBENEZER, b. 1693 CATHARINE, m —— Ellis EXPERIENCE, b 1696, m. Dec. 6, 1718, Samuel[3] Daniell, *vid ,* d March 29, 1731 GEORGE [12], b 1699

[8] **JOHN[3] ADAMS** (EDWARD[2], HENRY[1]), son of Edward [4] and Lydia Adams, was born, 1657, in Medfield, Mass. He married [1]Deborah —— They resided in Medfield, afterward Medway. Mrs Deborah Adams died prior to 1695 Mr Adams married [2]Susanna Breck, daughter of Thomas and Mary (Hill) Breck She was born, May 10, 1667, in Sherborn, Mass Mr. Adams died March 1, 1751. Mrs Susanna Adams died May 28, 1744

The children were EDWARD, b 1682, res in Milton, Mass. JOHN, b. 1684, m. Judah ——, d. Nov. 20, 1759. DANIEL [13], b 1686 ELEAZAR [14], b. 1687 OBADIAH [15] JONATHAN [16]. THOMAS, b 1695, res in Amherst, Mass. SUSANNA, b 1697, m April 17, 1721, Nael Alexander, res in Killingly, Conn JEREMIAH, b 1799, res. in Brookfield, Mass. ABRAHAM, b 1701, res. in Brookfield, Mass. BETHIA, b 1702, m Feb. 27, 1728, Timothy Stearns, res in Framingham, Mass. PHINEHAS [17], b 1705 HANNAH, b 1707, m Jan. 1, 1730, [1]Timothy Ellis, vid , m May 21, 1739, [2]William Richardson, vid

[9] JONATHAN[3] ADAMS (JONATHAN[2], HENRY[1]), son of Jonathan [5] and Elizabeth (Fussell) Adams, was born 1679, in Medfield, Mass. He married Thamezin Sheffield, daughter of William and Hannah (Bullard) Sheffield She was born May 25, 1673, in Holliston, Mass. They resided in Medway. Mrs. Thamezin Adams died. Deacon Adams married Dec 12, 1717, Mehitable Chenery. He died Jan. 24, 1718

The children were. THAMEZIN, b 1699, m June 16, 1719, Joseph Ellis, vid HANNAH, b. 1701, m Jan. 25, 1727, Jonathan Jones, res. in Holliston, Mass EZEKIEL [18], b 1705 JONATHAN [19], b 1709

[10] JEREMIAH[4] ADAMS (HENRY[3], HENRY[2], HENRY[1]), son of Henry [6] and Prudence (Frary) Adams, was born 1691, in Medfield, Mass He married [1]Rebecca ———— They resided in Medway Mrs Rebecca Adams died. Mr Adams married [2]Elizabeth ————. He died Oct. 8, 1772. Mrs. Elizabeth Adams died Feb. 20, 1774

The children were ABIGAIL, b July 20, 1717 ELISHA [20], b Feb. 19, 1719. ELIZABETH, b Sept 29, 1728 ENOS, b June 9, 1733.

[11] JOSEPH[4] ADAMS (PETER[3], PETER[2], HENRY[1]), son of Peter [7] and Experience (Cook) Adams, was born in Medfield, Mass He married Mary ———— They resided in Medway

The children were MARY, b. 1705 JOSEPH, b. 1707 RACHEL, b 1709 HANNAH, b 1711 RUTH, b 1712 EXPERIENCE and ABIGAIL, b 1716

[12] GEORGE[4] ADAMS (PETER[3], PETER[2], HENRY[1]), son of Peter [7] and Experience (Cook) Adams, was born 1699, in Medfield, Mass. He married, March 13, 1723, Sarah Partridge, daughter of John[2] and Elizabeth (Adams) Partridge She was born, 1702, in Medfield, now Millis, Mass, where they resided, but removed to Wrentham, Mass

The children were SILENCE, b. April 17, 1724. ELIZABETH, b July 15, 1726. RACHEL, b. Jan 22, 1728 SARAH, b. Oct 4, 1730 EXPERIENCE, b July 11, 1732

[13] DANIEL[4] ADAMS (JOHN[3], EDWARD[2], HENRY[1]), son of John [8] and Deborah Adams, was born 1686, in Medfield, Mass He married Sarah ————. They resided in West Medway. Mrs. Adams died July 21, 1739

The children were BENJAMIN SARAH, b November, 1714, d April 1, 1716. DEBORAH, b. Feb 12, 1717 SARAH, b. March, 1719 ELIZABETH, b May 12, 1721 DANIEL, b. Jan 18, 1724, res. in Barre, Mass. THOMAS [21], b April 15, 1726 RUTH, b March 6, 1729, m May 17, 1750, Benjamin Rockwood, vid MOSES [22], b. Aug 4, 1731. ABIGAIL, b June 23, 1736, m. Feb 9, 1757, Abraham[5] Harding, vid TABITHA, b Nov 12, 1738, m June 27, 1754, John Littlefield, res in Holliston, Mass

[14] ELEAZAR[4] ADAMS (JOHN[3], EDWARD[2], HENRY[1]), son of John [8] and Deborah Adams, was born 1687, in Medfield. He married Margaret ———— They resided in Medway

The children were BENJAMIN, b Oct 13, 1715 MARGARET, b. Aug. 29, 1717, d. June 8, 1736. ELEAZAR, b. July 9, 1720, m March 6, 1745, Bathsheba Barber, res. in Holliston, Mass MARY, b Oct 7, 1722, m Oct 19, 1742, Jonathan Metcalf, res. in Rutland, Mass. JOHN [23], b Oct 27, 1724. LYDIA, b. Sept. 19, 1727, m April 9 1754, Simeon Daniell, res. in Franklin, Mass. SETH, b May 6, 1730. LOIS, b. May 25, 1732, m May 22, 1755, Ebenezer Allen

[15] OBADIAH[4] ADAMS (JOHN[3], EDWARD[2], HENRY[1]), son of John [8] and Deborah Adams, was born in Medfield, Mass He married, April 24, 1716, Christian Sanford. She was born in Mendon Mass They resided in West Medway. •

The children were DAVID b Nov. 18, 1716, res in Spencer, Mass. ABIGAIL, b Oct. 28, 1718, d. June 6, 1736 OBADIAH, b. Dec. 18, 1721, m. Dec. 8, 1744, Sarah Partridge, res. in Bellingham, Mass NATHAN [24], b Dec. 3, 1723 JESSE, b Sept. 10, 1727, m Thankful Watkins, res in Holliston, Mass., d April 12, 1797. STEPHEN [25], b Dec 27, 1729 CHRISTIAN, b. Aug. 8, 1732, m. Nov. 27, 1751, Moses Hill, res in Holliston, Mass. HEPHZIBAH, b March 31, 1735, m. Jan. 2, 1758, Stephen Metcalf, res. in Bellingham, Mass JEMIMA, b. March 24, 1737, m. May 1, 1757, William Fiske, res in Upton, Mass AMOS, res in Spencer, Mass.

[16] JONATHAN⁴ ADAMS (JOHN³, EDWARD², HENRY¹), son of John [8] and Deborah Adams, was born in Medfield, Mass He married Dorcas ——— They resided in Medway Mr Adams died May 12, 1744

The children were. DORCAS, b Dec 24, 1717, m Dec 9, 1736, John Fisher, res in Medfield, Mass ISAAC, b Oct 15, 1719 MARY, b May 6, 1722 KEZIA, b. Jan. 1, 1725, d June 18, 1733. SILAS, b Oct. 7, 1728, d Oct 24 1728 LYDIA, b Sept 9, 1731 JOEL, b Aug 6, 1733, d Aug 6, 1733 KEZIA b May 21, 1735 JONATHAN [26], b Aug 30, 1737

[17] PHINEHAS⁴ ADAMS (JOHN³, EDWARD², HENRY¹), son of John [8] and Susanna (Breck) Adams, was born, 1705, in Medfield, Mass. He married ¹Sarah Kingsbury She was born in Needham, Mass They resided in Medway Mrs. Sarah Adams died July 23, 1739 Mr Adams married ²Mehitable ———

The children were SARAH, b March 8, 1733, d Sept 14, 1733 MARY, b June 22, 1735 PHINEHAS [27] MOSES, b July 12, 1738 HANNAH, b Aug 7, 1742 JOHN, b July 2, 1744

[18] EZEKIEL⁴ ADAMS (JONATHAN³, JONATHAN², HENRY¹), son of Jonathan [9] and Thamezin (Sheffield) Adams, was born, 1705 in Medfield, Mass. He married, May 8, 1728, Bethia Parker They resided in Medway

The children were BENONI, b Feb 8, 1730, d Feb. 17, 1731. THAMEZIN, b June 20, 1731. EZEKIEL, b. June 29, 1735

[19] JONATHAN⁴ ADAMS (JONATHAN³, JONATHAN², HENRY¹), son of Jonathan [9] and Thamezin (Sheffield) Adams, was born 1709, in Medfield, Mass , afterward Medway. He married, April 30, 1732, Patience Clark, daughter of Edward and Hannah (Adams) Clark She was born May 3, 1710, in Medfield, afterward Medway Mrs. Adams died July 11, 1801 Mr Adams died Nov 4, 1804

The children were RACHEL, b Jan. 24, 1733, m Daniel Bullard OLIVER [28], b June 30, 1738 SARAH, b April 23, 1740, m Nov 1, 1759, Abel Smith.

[20] ELISHA⁵ ADAMS (JEREMIAH⁴, HENRY³, HENRY², HENRY¹), son of Jeremiah [10] and Rebecca Adams, was born Feb 19, 1719, in Medway He married. Nov 26, 1741, Rachel Daniell, daughter of Jeremiah and Hannah (Partridge) Daniell She was born Oct 30, 1714, in Medway, where they resided Mr Adams died March 23, 1781 Mrs Adams died Jan. 11, 1803.

The children were ABIGAIL, b Oct 4, 1744 DANIEL, b 1747, res in Watertown, Mass

Memoranda Daniel⁶ Adams, son of Elisha Adams, graduated in 1774 from Harvard College, Cambridge, Mass , studied for the ministry, and was ordained, 1778, in Watertown, Mass , where he soon after died, Sept 16, 1778 Daniel⁷ Adams, his son, was a lawyer, resided in Medfield, Mass , where he died in 1853 Horace⁷ Adams, another son of the Rev Daniel Adams, resided in East Medway on the place now owned by Mr Brackett, and was the grandfather of Elisha E Adams, Esq.

[21] THOMAS⁵ ADAMS (DANIEL⁴, JOHN³, EDWARD², HENRY¹), son of Daniel [13] and Sarah Adams, was born April 15, 1726, in Medway He married ¹Abigail ———. They resided in Medway Mrs Abigail Adams died. Mr. Adams married, Dec 27, 1748, ²Mary Partridge.

The children were DANIEL, b April 20, 1750, res in Rutland, Vt MARY, b July 13, 1751, m Jan 30, 1772, Nathan⁶ Adams, *vid* SYBIL, b Jan. 28, 1753 m. June 28, 1770, Abijah⁶ Harding, *vid*, d. Feb 6, 1813 ASA, b. March 26, 1757, res in Rutland, Vt THOMAS [29], b 1759.

[22] MOSES⁵ ADAMS (DANIEL⁴, JOHN³, EDWARD², HENRY¹), son of Daniel [13] and Sarah Adams, was born Aug 4, 1731, in Medway He married Rachel Leland, daughter of Daniel and Mary (Death) Leland. She was born, 1737, in Sherborn, Mass They resided in Medway Mrs Adams died 1826

The children were HEPHZIBAH, b Oct. 16, 1758, m May 29, 1777, Elisha Johnson, res in Holliston, Mass RHODA, b Feb 22, 1761, m June 7, 1781, John Plimpton, res in West Bloomfield, N Y MARY, b April 26, 1767, m Dea Jonathan Metcalf, res in Franklin, Mass RACHEL, b Sept. 25, 1769, m. Nov 3, 1790, Timothy Pond, *vid* RUTH, b April 7, 1772, m April 26, 1796, ¹Thomas Bacon, m Jan. 14, 1801, ²Joseph Whiting, res in Franklin, Mass AARON [30], b Sept 1, 1775

[23] JOHN⁵ ADAMS (ELEAZAR⁴, JOHN³, EDWARD², HENRY¹), son of Eleazar

[14] and Margaret Adams, was born Oct 27, 1724, in Medway. He married [1]——
Clark. They resided in West Medway Mrs Adams died. Mr. Adams married
[2]Zilpha Daniell, daughter of Ezia and Martha (Death) Daniell She was born Nov.
19, 1734, in Medway

The children were JOHN, JAMES, JOEL, JUDE, PHINEHAS, ELIAS, HEZEKIAH LYDIA,
PEGGY, PATTY, ELEAZAR,

[24] NATHAN[5] ADAMS (OBADIAH[4], JOHN[3], EDWARD[2], HENRY[1]), son of Obadiah [15] and Christian (Sanford) Adams, was born Dec 30, 1723, in Medway. He
married, May 9, 1750, Keziah Thompson, daughter of Eleazar and Hannah (Daniell)
Thompson. She was born Nov 17, 1730, in Medway, where they resided

The children were ISSACHAR, m. Millicent Alden, res in Hubbardston, Mass.
NATHAN, b. 1751, m Jan 30, 1772, Mary[6] Adams, res in Barre, Mass. OBADIAH [31],
b. 1758 REUBEN, b 1760, m. Azubah Jones, res in Hubbardston, Mass.

[25] STEPHEN[5] ADAMS (OBADIAH[4], JOHN[3], EDWARD[2], HENRY[1]), son of
Obadiah [15] and Christian (Sanford) Adams, was born Dec 27, 1729, in Medway.
He married Mary ——. They resided in West Medway

The children were SARAH, b. 1773, m Jesse Coombs, res in Bellingham, Mass
EZRA [32], b. 1775. STEPHEN [33], b. 1776 JOTHAM, b 1778 ELI, b May 26, 1779.
m. Esther Harding, res. in Readfield, Me , d Oct 21, 1832 MARY, b. 1781, m. Moses
Hill, res. in Bellingham, Mass. CHRISTIAN, b. 1783 LABAN [34], b Feb. 27, 1785

[26] JONATHAN[5] ADAMS (JONATHAN[4], JOHN[3], EDWARD[2], HENRY[1]), son of
Jonathan [16] and Dorcas Adams, was born Aug 30, 1737, in Medway. He married
Catherine Boyden. She was born in 1738. They resided in Medway Mr Adams
died March 21, 1818 Mrs. Adams died Dec 10, 1819.

The children were THANKFUL, b. 1760 MICAH [35], b. 1762. SILAS [36], b.
1765. CATHERINE, b. 1771, m Asa[6] Richardson, *vid* MOSES, b 1774, m. Persis
Cutler.

[27] PHINEHAS[5] ADAMS (PHINEHAS[4], JOHN[3], EDWARD[2], HENRY[1]), son of
Phinehas [17] and Sarah (Kingsbury) Adams, was born in Medway. He married,
May 3, 1781, Patience Pond, daughter of Moses and Patience (Carpenter) Pond She
was born June 10, 1762, in Wrentham, Mass They resided in Medway.

The children were ASAHEL, b 1781. PHINEHAS, b 1790, m Sarah W Barber,
removed to Waltham, Mass. PATIENCE, b March 30, 1792, m Amos[5] Shumway, *vid*.
WILLARD, b June 19, 1794 LOWELL, b Feb 21, 1796

[28] OLIVER[5] ADAMS (JONATHAN[4], JONATHAN[3], JONATHAN[2], HENRY[1]), son
of Jonathan [19] and Patience (Clark) Adams, was born June 30, 1738, in Medway He
married Elizabeth Adams, daughter of Henry[4] and Jemima (Morse) Adams She was
born Aug 1, 1736, in Medfield, Mass They resided in East Medway, Mrs Adams
died Dec. 11, 1822.

The children were JONATHAN, b 1761 OLIVER, b 1762. JASPER [37], b Feb
23, 1767. SYLVANUS [38], b. 1769 ELIZABETH, b 1773, m. Edward Cleveland, res
in Charlton, Mass. AMA, m 1795, Joseph[6] Richardson, *vid*

[29] THOMAS[8] ADAMS (THOMAS[5], DANIEL[4], JOHN[3] EDWARD[2], HENRY[1]),
son of Thomas [21] and Abigail Adams, was born 1759, in Medway He married
May 22, 1777, [1]Susanna Clark They resided in Medway, and removed, about 1803, to
Barre, Mass Mrs. Susanna Adams died Mr Adams married [2]Melatiah Partridge

The children were THOMAS, b 1779, m Sept. 29, 1803, Olive[5] Shumway. AMOS,
b. 1779 HANNAH, b 1781 SUSANNA, b. 1783 AVERY, b 1785. SYBEL, b. 1787 POLLY,
b 1789. PARTRIDGE, b 1791. BETSEY, b. 1793 AMOS, b 1794 NANCY, b 1797

[30] AARON[6] ADAMS (MOSES[5], DANIEL[4], JOHN[3], EDWARD[2], HENRY[1]), son of
Moses [22] and Rachel (Leland) Adams, was born Sept. 1, 1775, in Medway. He married, Nov 30, 1797, Catherine Adams They resided in West Medway Mr. Adams
died in 1824

The children were MOSES, b 1798, m. Catherine Partridge SILENCE b 1800 unm ,
d AARON, b. 1801, m Hannah W Skinner, res. in Dodgeville, Wis ELIZABETH, b.
1803, m. Jonas Fairbanks, res in Bellingham, Mass. JOANNA, b May 6, 1805, m April
7, 1830, Lyman[7] Adams, *vid*. CATHERINE, b. 1807 JEMIMA, m Abijah R. Wheeler,
vid LUTHER, m Caroline Baldwin. DANIEL, died young. MARION, m Feb. 14,
1842, James Willard[2] Daniels, *vid*

[31] OBADIAH[6] ADAMS (NATHAN[5], OBADIAH[4], JOHN[3], EDWARD[2], HENRY[1]), son of Nathan [24] and Keziah (Thompson) Adams, was born 1748, in Medway He married Abigail Harding. They resided in West Medway. Mr. Adams died Jan 1, 1823

The children were PERSIS, b 1780 KEZIAH, b 1783 m [1]Daniel Miller; m [2]Isaac Kibby ISRAEL, b. 1785, m Polly Johnson ABIGAIL, b 1787, m. Amos [5]Bullard, *vid* OBADIAH, b 1789, m Mary Johnson CANDACE, b 1792

[32] EZRA[6] ADAMS (STEPHEN[5], OBADIAH[4], JOHN[3], EDWARD[2], HENRY[1]), son of Stephen [25] and Mary Adams, was born 1775, in Medway He married Abigail Partridge, daughter of Joel and Waitstill (Morse) Partridge She was born Jan 9, 1777, in Medway, where they resided.

The children were · CYRUS [39], b Nov 4, 1800 STEPHEN [40], b Aug. 12, 1804 EZRA, b Aug 26, 1809, m Oct 16, 1839, [1]Abigail Bigelow; m. Oct 20, 1858, [2]Alice Melissa Ware, res in Surry, Roxbury, and Gilsum, N. H , d March 20, 1864 NANCY

[33] STEPHEN[6] ADAMS (STEPHEN[5], OBADIAH[4], JOHN[3], EDWARD[2], HENRY[1]), son of Stephen [25] and Mary Adams, was born 1776, in Medway He married Catherine Partridge, daughter of Joel and Waitstill (Morse) Partridge She was born April 1, 1779, in Medway, where they resided, but removed to Framingham, Mass.

The children were PARTRIDGE, m Julia Ann Richardson. LYMAN [41], b. March 25, 1803 ANN, m Elbridge Partridge, res in Worcester, Mass NEWELL, m. Abigail (Fales) Blake FRANCIS, m [1]—— Stone; m. [2]Nancy Richardson.

[34] LABAN[6] ADAMS (STEPHEN[5], OBADIAH[4], JOHN[3], EDWARD[2], HENRY[1]), son of Stephen [25] and Mary Adams, was born Feb 27, 1785 in Medway He married Catherine Johnson, daughter of David and Ede (Bullard) Johnson. She was born in Chester, Vt They resided in West Medway and Boston, Mass

The children were Two infants who died ELMIRA, b 1811, m Horace Baker, res in Boston, Mass., d. 1848 CATHERINE, b 1813, m Abraham Mitchell, res in Nashua, N H , removed to Chicago, Ill. ESTHER, b 1816, m Aquilla Jewett, res in Westbrook, Me , d. 1874 LABAN, b 1820, m Sarah Wheeler, d 1881 WILLIAM TAYLOR, b. July 30, 1822, m. 1846, Sarah Jenkins, res in Dorchester, Mass SARAH, b. 1824 m. William F Pope, res in Dorchester, d 1881

Memoranda. Mrs Sarah Adams, wife of William T. Adams, Esq , was the daughter of Edward Jenkins, of Dorchester, Mass She was born Oct 5, 1825, and died March 7, 1885 Mr and Mrs. William T. Adams had three children. The firstborn died in infancy. Alice Maria married Sol Smith Russell, Esq , an eminent comedian Emma Louisa married George W. White, Esq , a member of the Suffolk Bar. Mr and Mrs White reside in Charlestown, Mass

[35] MICAH[6] ADAMS (JONATHAN[5], JONATHAN[4], JOHN[3], EDWARD[2], HENRY[1]), son of Jonathan [26] and Catherine (Boyden) Adams was born 1762, in Medway. He married Mercy Penniman, daughter of James and Abigail (Clark) Penniman. She was born 1765, in East Medway, where they resided Mrs Adams died April 23, 1829 Mr Adams died April 1, 1842

The children were · JOEL, b Feb 3, 1791, d May 27, 1791. REBECCA, b. May 15, 1792, m Henry[6] Richardson, *vid* NABBY, b March 28, 1794, unm , d. Sept 29, 1881 EDWARD [42], b May 4, 1798 JOHN, b 1800, d Oct. 17, 1800 PATTY, b Aug. 20, 1804, d Feb 17, 1805 MARY, b Aug 14, 1807, d May 13, 1808.

[36] SILAS[6] ADAMS (JONATHAN[5], JONATHAN[4], JOHN[3], EDWARD[2], HENRY[1]), son of Jonathan [26] and Catherine (Boyden) Adams, was born 1765, in Medway Mr. Adams married [1]Patience Daniels, daughter of Henry[5] and Elizabeth (Harding) Daniels. She was born March 15, 1768, in Medway Mrs Patience Adams died Nov. 9, 1815 Mr. Adams married [2]Mary Harding, of Medfield, Mass. Mr Adams died June 21, 1849 Mrs Mary Adams died March 20, 1861.

The children were · JOSEPH, b. 1788. SILAS, b. 1794, m. April 20, 1817, Betsey Daby. JONATHAN [43], b. March 2, 1797. SAMUEL [44], b. April 10, 1805.

[37] JASPER[6] ADAMS (OLIVER[5], JONATHAN[4], JONATHAN[3], JONATHAN[2], HENRY[1]), son of Oliver [28] and Elizabeth (Adams) Adams, was born Feb. 23, 1767, in Medway. He married, Nov 22, 1792, Amy Rounds, daughter of the Rev Nathaniel and Elizabeth (Bowen) Rounds She was born July 27, 1764, in Rehoboth, Mass. They resided in East Medway. Mr. Adams died March 6, 1820. Mrs. Adams died Feb. 5, 1827

The children were· JASPER, b. Aug 27, 1793, m May 16, 1820, Mercy D Wheeler, *vid ,* res in Charleston, S C., d. Oct. 25, 1841. ELIZABETH, b. Sept 26, 1795, m. Nov. 11, 1819, Dea. Calvin Bigelow, res in Dover, Mass. BOWEN, b. April 6, 1798, m Dec. 18, 1823, [1]Fanny Cleaveland, m [2]Mrs. Clarissa Clark; m [3]Mrs Betsey Stratton, res. in Sherborn, Mass , d. Nov. 13, 1881. JULIA, b. Dec. 30, 1800, m. Dec. 6, 1821, Horatio Mason, *vid ,* d July 22, 1848 ANNA ROUNDS, b Nov 22, 1806, m Sept. 7, 1835, Lewis Hunting, res. in Southboro, Mass , d Oct 25, 1854.

[38] SYLVANUS[6] ADAMS (OLIVER[5], JONATHAN[4], JONATHAN[3], JONATHAN[2], HENRY[1]), son of Oliver [28] and Elizabeth (Adams) Adams, was born, 1769, in Medway. He married [1]Ruth Plympton, daughter of Silas and Esther Plympton. She was born in 1772. They resided in Medway. Mrs Ruth Adams died June 30, 1822. Captain Adams married, April 30, 1823, [2]Eliza Richardson, daughter of Dr Abijah and Mercy (Daniels) Richardson. She was born July 2, 1791, in Medway Captain Adams died May 31, 1838 Mrs Eliza Adams died Nov. 6, 1838

The children were. FANNY, b September, 1794, d. 1798. WALTER, b. 1799. JOSEPH [45], b. Oct. 15, 1804 SYLVANUS, b 1807. JOHN, b May 5, 1813, m. Abby Smith res in Worcester, Mass.

[39] CYRUS[7] ADAMS, (EZRA[6], STEPHEN[5], OBADIAH[4], JOHN[3], EDWARD[2], HENRY[1]), son of Ezra [32] and Abigail (Partridge) Adams, was born Nov 4, 1800, in West Medway He married, Jan 1, 1834, Mary Partridge, daughter of Job and Tamar (Partridge) Partridge She was born Jan. 18, 1807 They resided in Medway.

[40] STEPHEN[7] ADAMS (EZRA[6], STEPHEN[5], OBADIAH[4], JOHN[3], EDWARD[2], HENRY[1]), son of Ezra [32] and Abigail (Partridge) Adams, was born Aug. 12, 1804, in West Medway. He married, Sept 9, 1828, Julia Adams, daughter of John and Eunice (Mason) Adams She was born July 22, 1804, in Walpole, N. H. They resided in West Medway. Deacon Adams died July 26, 1885.

The children were JOHN MASON [46], b July 26, 1829 JULIA A , b Aug. 1, 1832 STEPHEN, b. Aug. 3, 1834, d Sept. 26, 1836. EUNICE, b Aug 3, 1834, d. Aug. 4, 1834. GEORGE STEPHEN, b. Dec 27, 1838, d June 4, 1842 CHARLES THOMPSON [47], b Oct 3, 1840

[41] LYMAN[7] ADAMS (STEPHEN[6], STEPHEN[5], OBADIAH[4], JOHN[3], EDWARD[2], HENRY[1]), son of Stephen [33] and Catherine (Partridge) Adams, was born March 25, 1803, in Framingham, Mass. He married, April 7, 1830, Joanna Adams, daughter of Aaron and Catherine (Adams) Adams She was born May 6, 1805, in West Medway. They resided in East Medway Mrs Adams died Jan 20, 1880. Mr. Adams died March 26, 1881.

The children were. JANE CATHERINE, b. May 28, 1831, d. Jan. 2, 1855 LYMAN [48], b March 23, 1836

[42] EDWARD[7] ADAMS (MICAH[6], JONATHAN[5], JONATHAN[4], JOHN[3], EDWARD[2], HENRY[1]), son of Micah [35] and Mercy (Penniman) Adams, was born May 4, 1798, in East Medway He married, Oct 4, 1829, Keziah Lovell Clark, daughter of Lovell and Mary (Bullen) Clark. She was born Oct. 30, 1804, in Milford, Mass They resided in East Medway Mr Adams died Sept 23, 1870

The children were: CHARLES EDWARD, b Nov 16, 1831, d Sept. 24, 1837 MERCY PENNIMAN, b April 26, 1834, m April 19, 1854, Francis Oliver Phillips, *vid.* MARY RICHARDSON, b Oct 24, 1838, m Jan. 19, 1866, George Horatio Wight, res in Medfield, Mass. EDWARD MICAH b Nov 17, 1840, d. Oct 12, 1849. MOSES CLARK [49], b. Nov. 16, 1843

[43] JONATHAN[7] ADAMS (SILAS[6], JONATHAN[5], JONATHAN[4], JOHN[3], EDWARD[2], HENRY[1]), son of Silas [36] and Patience (Daniels) Adams, was born March 2, 1797, in East Medway He married Feb 6, 1823, Esther Smith, daughter of Enos and Amy (Plympton) Smith. She was born Jan 29, 1798, in Medfield, Mass. They resided in East Medway. Mr. Adams died May 5, 1863. Mrs Adams died Aug 18, 1884.

The children were LOUISA, b June 27, 1823, m June 17, 1853, James Hawkes, WILLIAM, b. Sept 27, 1825, d Jan. 29, 1880 EDWIN SMITH, b Nov 24, 1828, d Aug 20, 1845. NATHANIEL, b. Sept 12, 1831. PATIENCE ELLEN, b Feb. 14, 1833, m. Sept 11, 1869, John L. Wyman, d Feb. 25, 1874 AMY PLYMPTON, b. Sept. 5, 1839

[44] SAMUEL[7] ADAMS (SILAS[6], JONATHAN[5], JONATHAN[4], JOHN[3], EDWARD[2], HENRY[1]), son of Silas [36] and Patience (Daniels) Adams, was born April 10, 1805

in East Medway He married, January, 1836, Mary Woods, daughter of Levi and Mary (Nevens) Woods. She was born Feb. 7, 1810. They resided in East Medway. Mr. Adams died March 2, 1882

The only child was MARY ELIZABETH, b May 5, 1837, m. March 30, 1863, William N. Allen, res in Hudson, N Y., d Oct. 25, 1870.

[45] JOSEPH⁷ ADAMS (SYLVANUS⁶, OLIVER⁵, JONATHAN⁴, JONATHAN³, JONATHAN², HENRY¹), son of Sylvanus [38] and Ruth (Plympton) Adams, was born Oct 15, 1804, in East Medway. He married, Nov 8, 1824, Mary Ann Mason, daughter of Simon Harding and Betsey (Leland) Mason She was born Jan 11, 1805, in East Medway, where they resided, Mr Adams died Dec. 15, 1847.

The children were RUTH P., b Oct 29, 1826, m Horace F. Howard, d Aug 23, 1881. JOSEPHINE MATILDA, b. May 29, 1834, d April 21, 1837 JOSEPH SYLVANUS [50], b. Oct. 12, 1838 ELIZA RICHARDSON, b Oct 7, 1840, d July 10, 1841

[46] JOHN MASON⁸ ADAMS (STEPHEN⁷, EZRA⁶, STEPHEN⁵, OBADIAH⁴, JOHN³, EDWARD², HENRY¹), son of Stephen [40] and Julia (Adams) Adams, was born July 26, 1829, in Medway. He married Sept. 10, 1850, Julia A. Hixon, daughter of Elihu H and Hannah (Putnam) Hixon. She was born May 9, 1830, in Hamden, Me They resided in Medway

The children were CASIE L., b. Dec 30, 1851, m Oct 25, 1871, Hiram F. Metcalf, *vid* NELLIE F , b Nov. 2, 1855, m. Nov 4, 1879, J Henry Adams, res in Warren, Mass LIZZIE D , b. April 23, 1860, d Oct. 5, 1860. CHARLES M , b Feb. 28, 1865 MINNIE L., b. May 27, 1867 JULIA F., b Sept. 5, 1872 LESLIE S , b May 10, 1875, d. July 31, 1877.

[47] CHARLES THOMPSON⁸ ADAMS (STEPHEN⁷, EZRA⁶, STEPHEN⁵, OBADIAH⁴, JOHN³, EDWARD², HENRY¹), son of Stephen [40] and Mary (Adams) Adams, was born Oct. 3, 1840, in West Medway. He married, July 24, 1864, Harriet Lucia Hastings, daughter of Deming Jarvis and Lucia (Daniels) Hastings. She was born Oct 2, 1840, in West Medway, where they resided

The only child was JASPER, b Aug. 17, 1867

[48] LYMAN⁸ ADAMS (LYMAN⁷, STEPHEN⁶, STEPHEN⁵, OBADIAH⁴, JOHN³, EDWARD², HENRY¹), son of Lyman [41] and Joanna (Adams) Adams, was born March 23, 1836, in East Medway He married, March 11, 1860, Annah Harding Gale, daughter of Dr. Amory and Martha (Leland) Gale. She was born July 26, 1840, in Canton, Mass They resided in East Medway Mr Adams died Jan. 5, 1872.

The children were JANE ANNA, b March 2, 1861, m March 3, 1878, Frank Edward Cook. CARRIE GALE, b. June 29, 1863

Memoranda. Mr. and Mrs. Frank E Cook have two children, viz. : Lyman Adams, b Feb 7, 1881, Emma Frances, b. Feb. 24, 1883. Mr. Cook was born Dec. 3, 1857.

[49] MOSES CLARK⁸ ADAMS (EDWARD⁷, MICAH⁶, JONATHAN⁵, JONATHAN⁴, JOHN³, EDWARD², HENRY¹), son of Edward [42] and Keziah Lovell (Clark) Adams, was born Nov. 16, 1843, in East Medway. He married, June 17, 1880, Abbie Henrietta Ellis, daughter of Warren and Louisa M (Cutler) Ellis She was born March 9, 1850, in Milford, Mass. They reside in East Medway

The children were· EDWARD ELLIS, b July 27, 1881. BESSIE K , b Sept. 30, 1883

[50] JOSEPH SYLVANUS⁸ ADAMS (JOSEPH⁷, SYLVANUS⁶, OLIVER⁵, JONATHAN⁴, JONATHAN³, JONATHAN², HENRY¹), son of Joseph [45] and Mary Ann (Mason) Adams, was born Oct 12, 1838, in East Medway. He married, Dec. 25, 1859, Abigail Maria Richardson, daughter of Addison and Abigail Maria (Richardson) Richardson She was born July 30, 1841, in East Medway, where they reside.

The children were ARTHUR C , b May 29, 1863. JESSIE MAY, b May 29, 1867

CHARLES FRANCIS ADAMS, son of Ezekiel and Susan (Fisher) Adams, was born April 2, 1838, in West Medway. He married Abby B Partridge, daughter of Job and Tamar (Partridge) Partridge. She was born April 27, 1837, in West Medway.

HORACE W. ADAMS, son of William and Emeline Adams, was born March 15, 1836, in Medway He married, March 9, 1862, D Rosina Babcock, daughter of Amos R and Rosina Babcock She was born Nov 5, 1846, in Boston, Mass They resided in West Medway.

The children were WILLIAM H , b. March 6, 1863. ERNEST A., b. July 13, 1866 CLIFTON C., b April 4, 1878.

JAMES T. ADAMS, son of Thomas B and Elizabeth (Adams) Adams, was born Oct. 16, 1844, in Holliston, Mass. He married, Nov 3, 1869, Eunice Rockwood. She was born Oct. 27, 1848, in Norfolk, Mass. They reside in Medway

The children were: EMILY M., b Aug. 23, 1870 GEORGE T., b Jan 16, 1873 WALTER R , b Feb 2, 1876. HARRY J., b Oct 8, 1879.

SAMUEL ALLEN, son of Abijah and Abigail (Mancy) Allen, was born March 15, 1778, in Franklin, Mass. He married, June 17, 1802, [1]Sarah Wood Aldis, daughter of Jotham and Mehitable (Aldis) Wood, niece and adopted daughter of Ebenezer and Hannah Aldis. She was born in Franklin, Mass. They resided in Newburyport, Mass., where Mrs. Sarah W Allen died Aug. 15, 1813 Mr Allen married, April 25, 1816, [2]Julietta Metcalf, daughter of Dea James and Abigail (Harding) Metcalf She was born 1792, in Franklin, Mass. They resided in Medway, where Mrs. Julietta Allen died Oct. 11, 1848. Deacon Allen married, December, 1851, [3]Rhoda Mason. She was born in Dedham, Mass. Mrs Rhoda Allen died April 15, 1862. Deacon Allen died Jan. 15, 1866

The children were ALDIS SAMUEL, b Nov 13, 1803, m. Nov. 2, 1831, Eliza M Weeks, res. in Bridgeport, Conn , d. Aug 9, 1833. CHARLES COFFIN, b Nov 30, 1807, m March, 1854, Mary Behean, res in Norwich, Conn , and New York City, d. May 24, 1857 ABIGAIL MANCY, b. April 21, 1809, m. Oct. 12, 1843, Jonathan Miller, res. in New Haven, Conn. SARAH ANN, b. Sept. 24, 1811, m. Nov. 16, 1837, Darius D. Buffum, res. in Newport, R I., d Dec. 18, 1880. ELIAB METCALF, b. June 16, 1818, m Aug 5, 1847, Eliza C Park, res in Marietta, Ga. WILLIAM HENRY, b July 2, 1821, m. May 10, 1853, [1]Lizzie R Bentley, m July 10, 1872, [2]Linda M. Sangree, res. in New York City, d Oct. 23, 1882. ALFRED WHITING, b July 25, 1825, m June 6, 1855, [1]Eliza J Lawcay, m December, 1853, [2]S. A. Simpson, res. in Newport, R. I , and New York City, d. Jan 8, 1869.

Memoranda. Mr. and Mrs Jonathan Miller had two sons and one daughter The daughter married Charles A. Edwards, a descendant of Pres Jonathan Edwards, D D Mr. and Mrs. Darius D. Buffum had two sons, one of whom resides in Providence, R I

SETH J [8] AXTELL (SETH J.[7], THOMAS[6], THOMAS[5], THOMAS[4], THOMAS[3], HENRY[2], THOMAS[1]), son of Seth J. and Lucy B (Stratton) Axtell, was born Dec. 18, 1841, in Worcester, Mass. He married, Aug 1, 1865, Mary C. Fletcher, daughter of Noah M. and Caroline E. (Chickering) Fletcher. She was born Nov. 25, 1841, in Grafton, Mass They resided in West Medway, and removed to Weymouth, Mass

The children were WILLIAM F., b. Aug. 12, 1869. ETHEL M , b Aug 10, 1872 HAROLD L., b. May 24, 1876

LOWELL BABCOCK, son of Col. Moses and Betsey (Leland) Babcock, was born March 18, 1801, in Sherborn, Mass. He married Thankful Sanger, daughter of Benjamin and Olive (Bullard) Sanger. She was born Dec. 1, 1803, in Medfield, Mass. They resided in Sherborn and removed to Medway in 1834, where Mr Babcock died Aug. 9, 1872 Mrs. Babcock removed to Medfield, where she died March 12, 1886

The children were ADELINE E., b May 14, 1821, m Dec. 22, 1846, Thaddeus R Haynes. ALBERT H., b. April 17, 1823, m. Urania Smith, res. in Charlestown, Mass BENJAMIN J., b. July 22, 1825, m. July 4, 1847, [1]Milletiah T. Johnson; m. in 1871, [2]Abby J. Colburn, res in Dedham, Mass. OLIVE M., b. May 22, 1835, m. Nov. 6, 1853, William S Tilden, res. in Medfield, Mass LOWELL, b July 31, 1837, m. 1859, Alfreda Bailey, res. in Medfield, Mass MARY A , b April 23, 1843, d Oct 3, 1861.

Memoranda Mr. and Mrs Haynes resided in Medway, Mass. Mr Haynes died June 29, 1860 Mrs Haynes removed to Medfield, Mass. The children were Mary E , Ella T , and Lowell

Mr Benjamin J Babcock had four sons Francis L , Albert J., William A , and Charles B. The eldest is Francis L. Babcock, M. D , a physician in Dedham, Mass

Mr and Mrs. Lowell Babcock had four children, viz : George G , Herbert W , Mary A , and Edward L The latter was drowned Aug 15, 1879

JOHN RICHARD BANNISTER, son of Henry Alexander Bannister, was born Oct 13, 1777, in Smithfield, England He married, May 2, 1803, Eliza Maria Bond, daughter of George and Eliza Maria (Davis) Bond, of New York Mr. Bannister died in 1809. Mrs Bannister died Oct 23, 1873, in East Medway, Mass.

The children were MATILDA ELIZA, b. June 3, 1804, m. Dec 25, 1836, Simeon L

Colburn, d 1874 HENRY ALEXANDER, b. Nov 13, 1807, d. April 19, 1845 LOUISE ANTOINETTE, b June 20, 1809, m March 20, 1834, Appleton Eames Foster, *vid.*

Memoranda Mr and Mrs Colburn had two children, viz Victoria Estella, b. November, 1837, m William Newman, d Feb. 2, 1875. Josephine, b. September, 1839.

[1] **GEORGE BARBER**, a Puritan, was born 1615, in England He came to America about 1635, and settled in Dedham, Mass Subsequently he became one of the original proprietors and settlers of Medfield, Mass. Mr. Barber married Elizabeth Clark His death occurred in 1685

The children were ELIZABETH, b 1641, d Feb 20, 1642 MARY, b. Aug 27, 1643, d Nov. 23, 1643 MARY, b Jan 31, 1644 SAMUEL [2], b Jan 6, 1646 JOHN [3], b. March 13, 1649 ELIZABETH, b April 1, 1651. HANNAH, b April 16, 1654. ZACHARIAH [4], b Sept. 29, 1656 ABIGAIL, b Oct 20, 1659

[2] **SAMUEL² BARBER** (GEORGE¹), son of George [1] and Elizabeth (Clark) Barber, was born Jan 6, 1646, in Dedham, Mass. He married ¹Maria ———, who died about 1675 Mr Barber married, Aug 7, 1676, ²Sarah Mullins They resided in Medfield, Mass Mr Barber died Dec. 29, 1736. Mrs Barber died Jan 11, 1721.

The children were MARIA, b Feb 20, 1675. SAMUEL, b Jan 7, 1677 JAMES, b Dec 25, 1680 HANNAH, b Sept 25, 1683, m Oct 18, 1706, Joseph³ Richardson, *vid* THOMAS, b July 4, 1686 MARIA, b May 28, 1693

[3] **JOHN² BARBER** (GEORGE¹), son of George and Elizabeth (Clark) Barber, was born March 13, 1649, in Medfield, Mass He married Abigail ———. They resided in Medfield, Mass

The children were JOHN, b. April 24, 1676. ABIGAIL, b April 26, 1679 ELIZABETH, b Nov 28, 1681. GEORGE, b. Dec 5, 1684 ABIAH, b Sept 12, 1689.

Memoranda George³ and Ann Barber had a son, John, b Aug 27, 1708, m. Sept. 8, 1725, Hannah Ellis. John and Hannah (Ellis) Barber had a daughter, Abigail, b Oct 31, 1736.

[4] **ZACHARIAH² BARBER** (GEORGE¹), son of George and Elizabeth (Clark) Barber, was born Sept 29, 1656, in Medfield, Mass He married, Aug 30, 1683, Abiah Ellis. She was born in Medfield, Mass, where they resided

The children were BENONI, b. Sept 9, 1684 ZACHARIAH [5], b Oct 19, 1685 JOSEPH [6], b Oct 4, 1687. ABIAH, b Oct. 4, 1691 JOHN [7], b Oct 12, 1693 RUTH, b March 5, 1695 THOMAS, b May 2, 1698 ELIZABETH, b July 5, 1700. MARY, b. May 26, 1703

[5] **ZACHARIAH³ BARBER** (ZACHARIAH², GEORGE¹), son of Zachariah [4] and Abiah (Ellis) Barber, was born Oct 19, 1685, in Medfield, Mass. He married Deborah ——— They resided in Medfield, Mass

The children were ZACHARIAH, b Feb 10, 1719 DEBORAH, b Nov 8, 1720 ELISHA, b Nov. 23, 1722, m Silence ———, res in Sherborn, Mass.

[6] **JOSEPH³ BARBER** (ZACHARIAH², GEORGE¹), son of Zachariah [4] and Abiah (Ellis) Barber, was born Oct 4, 1687, in Medfield, Mass. He married, May 19, 1726, Abigail Hawes. She was born in Medfield, Mass. They resided in West Medway Mr Barber died March 3, 1770

The children were· SAMUEL, b March 23, 1727, d Oct 28, 1728 MARY, b. April 2, 1729, m Oct 12, 1752, Peter Wight, res in Medfield, Mass JOSEPH [8], b April 23, 1731 ABIGAIL, b. March 27, 1732, m Jan. 15, 1755, Timothy Partridge, *vid.* SARAH, b Jan 27, 1736, m Jan. 20, 1762, Josiah Fisk, res. in Upton, Mass. JAMES [9], b May 4, 1738 ELIZABETH, b .Oct 30, 1740, m Jan 14, 1768, Jeremiah Littlefield

[7] **JOHN³ BARBER** (ZACHARIAH², GEORGE¹), son of Zachariah [4] and Abiah (Ellis) Barber, was born Oct 12, 1693, in Medfield, Mass He married ¹Mary ——— She was born 1683 They resided in Medway. Mrs Mary Barber died Sept. 12, 1747 Deacon Barber married, 1751, ²Mrs Mary Pond, widow of Samuel Pond. She was born in Wrentham, Mass Deacon Barber died June 20, 1754. Mrs Mary Barber died May 7, 1754

The children were ABIGAIL, b Aug 14, 1719, m Asa⁴ Richardson, *vid* BATHSHEBA, b April 7, 1722 GEORGE [10], b July 1, 1724

Memoranda John Barber held the office of deacon in the Church of Christ, Medway, from 1732 to his death in 1754 His son, George Barber, was elected to the same office Aug 7, 1756

[8] JOSEPH⁴ BARBER (Joseph³, Zachariah², George¹), son of Joseph [6] and Abigail (Hawes) Barber, was born April 23, 1731, in West Medway. He married, Dec 22, 1757, Rebecca ———. They resided in West Medway   Mr Barber died Jan. 12, 1812

The children were. Lois, b. June 29, 1759, m. Aug 4, 1779, Asa³ Clark, *vid* Samuel, b. Nov 23, 1761, d. May 31, 1766   Rebecca, b. Jan. 1, 1763, m. July 10, 1785, James Johnson, *vid.* Nabby, b. May 1, 1766, d. May 14, 1769   Joseph [11], b. Sept. 24, 1768.   Seth, b. Aug 16, 1772, d Aug 16, 1772.   Sarah, b May 13, 1775

Memoranda Mr. Barber was a soldier at Lexington   He was a grave-stone cutter, and many of the stones in the Evergreen Cemetery are the work of his hands

[9] JAMES⁴ BARBER (Joseph³, Zachariah², George¹), son of Joseph [6] and Abigail (Hawes) Barber, was born May 4, 1738, in West Medway, where he resided He married, March 3, 1762, Mrs. Rhoda Smith   She was born in Wrentham, Mass.

The children were: Daniel, b. Dec. 10, 1762   Asa, b. Oct 9, 1764   Nathan, b Jan. 3, 1766.

[10] GEORGE⁴ BARBER (John³, Zachariah², George¹), son of Dea John [7] and Mary Barber, was born July 1, 1724, in East Medway. He married Elizabeth Clark, daughter of Edward³ and Hannah (Adams) Clark.   They resided in East Medway

The children were· George [12], b. Dec. 21, 1743.   Mary, b. Oct 18, 1745, m. ¹Ebenezer Knowlton, ²Nathaniel Lovell, *vid ;* d Nov. 14, 1832   Zachariah, bapt Aug 28, 1748.   Triphena, bapt. Oct 27, 1750.   Elizabeth C , bapt. Oct 1, 1752   Elizabeth, bapt. Oct. 27, 1754   John, bapt. Nov. 28, 1756

[11] JOSEPH⁵ BARBER (Joseph⁴, Joseph³, Zachariah², George¹), son of Joseph [8] and Rebecca Barber, was born Sept. 24, 1768, in West Medway   He married ¹Chloe Haven   Mrs. Chloe Barber died.   Mr. Barber married, May 24, 1827, ²Keziah Partridge.   She was born in Franklin, Mass   Mr. Barber died Feb. 6, 1847.

The children were. Samuel, b July 21, 1792, m. Nov. 24, 1816, Sally White   Polly, b. Dec. 21, 1793, m. April 13, 1814, Reuben Hixon, *vid,* d. November, 1853.   Asahel [13], b. Feb. 2, 1796   Cyrus [14], b. Dec 21, 1797.   Sewall, b. June 2, 1799, d. Dec 12, 1799   John Haven [15], b May 5, 1801   Nancy, b Sept 5, 1802, m May 25, 1820, Benjamin Ward, d. Dec 26, 1862.

[12] GEORGE⁵ BARBER (George⁴, John³, Zachariah², George¹), son of George [10] and Elizabeth Barber, was born Dec. 21, 1743, in East Medway   He married Bethia Jones, daughter of Thomas and Bethia (Whitney) Jones.   She was born 1750   They resided in East Medway.   Mrs. Barber died Feb. 19, 1815.   Mr Barber died July 10, 1832.

The children were. Seneca [16], b. Nov 15, 1770   George [17], b. Sept. 10, 1772.   Calvin, b Oct 25, 1774   Lucinda, b. Oct. 19, 1776.   John, b July 15, 1778   Orinda, b. Oct. 4, 1780, m Jeremiah Daniels   Elial, b. July 1, 1782, m Sophia Ellis.   Achsah, b. July 24, 1784   Betsey, b Jan. 31, 1787   Mary, b. Sept 13, 1789, m. June 8, 1809, Josiah Blake, *vid*

[13] ASAHEL⁶ BARBER (Joseph⁵, Joseph⁴, Joseph³, Zachariah², George¹), son of Joseph [11] and Chloe (Haven) Barber, was born Feb. 2, 1796, in West Medway.   He married, Dec 3, 1818 Harriet Haven   She was born Nov. 13, 1796, in Liecester, Mass.   They resided in West Medway.   Mr. Barber died April 1, 1858   Mrs. Barber died April 10, 1882

The children were   Harriet Amanda, b. June 28, 1820, m. Dec 7, 1843, Anson B. Davis   Mary Ann, b. Nov. 6, 1822, d. June 5, 1848.   George N. [18], b Sept 16, 1824

[14] CYRUS⁶ BARBER (Joseph⁵, Joseph⁴, Joseph³, Zachariah², George¹), son of Joseph [11] and Chloe (Haven) Barber, was born Dec. 21, 1797, in West Medway.   He married Patty Smith   She was born in Framingham, Mass.   They resided in Medway   Mr Barber died July 22, 1867, in Ashland, Mass.

The children were· Ephraim O , b March 29, 1829, m 1850, Ann E. Thurber, d Nov. 30, 1882.   Joseph [19], b. July 19, 1831.

[15] JOHN HAVEN⁶ BARBER (Joseph⁵, Joseph⁴, Joseph³, Zachariah², George¹), son of Joseph [11] and Chloe (Haven) Barber, was born May 5, 1801, in West Medway.   He married, Nov. 29, 1825, ¹Eunice Smith   She was born in Framingham, Mass   They resided in West Medway.   Mrs Eunice Barber died May 13, 1838,

Mr. Barber married, April 10, 1839, [2]Mrs. Sally Newton, *née* Este   Mr Barber died Oct 20, 1878

The children were.   MARTHA S.,.b. April 26, 1826.   NEWELL, b. May 1, 1840, d. Aug. 14, 1863   EDSON W [20], b Dec 26, 1841

[16]   **SENECA[6] BARBER** (GEORGE[5], GEORGE[4], JOHN[3], ZACHARIAH[2], GEORGE[1]), son of George [12] and Bethia (Jones) Barber, was born Nov 15, 1770, in East Medway   He married Nancy Boyden.   She was born in Walpole, Mass.   They resided in East Medway   Mr Barber died Sept 30, 1856   Mrs Barber died March 26, 1866.

The children were: NANCY   JOHN   CHARLOTTE, b May, 1803, d Aug 29, 1876 ACHSAH, m April 3, 1828, Martin Barber   JOHN, m Dec 25, 1831, [1]Amanda Phillips   SUSAN, m Oct 24, 1833, George H Newell, res in Holliston, Mass   GEORGE, bapt June 6, 1813   ELIZA, m. Jan 10, 1839, Israel D Fuller, *vid*

[17]   **GEORGE[6] BARBER** (GEORGE[5], GEORGE[4], JOHN[3], ZACHARIAH[2], GEORGE[1]), son of George [12] and Bethia (Jones) Barber, was born Sept. 10, 1772, in East Medway.   He married, Nov 28, 1799, [1]Sally Orne, daughter of James and Esther (Everett) Orne   She was born in Attleboro.   They resided in Medway.   Mrs Sally Barber died Nov 25, 1803.   Mr Barber married [2]Lois Whiting, daughter of John and Lois Whiting   Mr Barber died Dec 28, 1850   Mrs Lois Barber died August, 1851.

The children were.   GEORGE W, b Dec 5, 1800, d Dec 23, 1823   SALLY ORNE, b May 6, 1803, m June 11, 1823, [1]Otis Nichols, d March 22, 1824   MARY ANN, b Sept 19, 1806 m Feb 14, 1828, James W Clark *vid*, d Sept 11, 1834   EMELINE, b July 9, 1808, d. Dec 39, 1827   HARRIET, b May 29, 1810, m Feb 28, 1830, [1]William White; m Sept 24, 1854, [2]William Hiram Cary, *vid*   LOUISA W, b Nov 21, 1813, m Oct 2, 1834, A L B Munroe, m D, *vid*, d June 2, 1836   MARIA, b. May 29, 1818, d Sept 23, 1827

[18]   **GEORGE N[7] BARBER** (ASAHEL[6], JOSEPH[5], JOSEPH[4], JOSEPH[3], ZACHARIAH[2], GEORGE[1]), son of Asahel [13] and Harriet (Haven) Barber, was born Sept 16 1824, in Medway   He married, Nov 15, 1848, [1]Mary A Fuller   They resided in Medway   Mrs Mary A Barber died March 4 1871   Mr Barber married, Nov 18 1872, [2]Anna V Holmes   Mrs Anna V Barber died Dec 9, 1876   Mr Barber married, Dec 26, 1880, [3]Mrs Sarah Partridge, *née* Bisbee, widow of Timothy Partridge

The children were   An INFANT, b Feb 13, 1852, d   ALICE M, b April 21, 1857, d Aug 3, 1859   MARY E, b Aug 14, 1860, d Sept 14, 1883   ELSIE F., b Oct 28, 1873, d Aug 11, 1877   GEORGE H, b Sept 7, 1875, d April 13, 1877

[19]   **JOSEPH[7] BARBER** (CYRUS[6], JOSEPH[5], JOSEPH[4], JOSEPH[3], ZACHARIAH[2], GEORGE[1]), son of Cyrus [14] and Patty (Smith) Barber, was born July 19, 1831, in West Medway   He married, Feb 13, 1861, [1]Julia A. Putnam   Mrs Julia A Barber died   The Rev Mr Barber married, Nov 27, 1870, [2]A Sophia Felton   They resided in Bellingham, Mass

The children were   MARTHA P, b July 9, 1864   ESTELLA, b Oct 29, 1874

[20]   **EDSON W[7] BARBER** (JOHN HAVEN[6], JOSEPH[5], JOSEPH[4], JOSEPH[3], ZACHARIAH[2], GEORGE[1]), son of John Haven [15] and Sally (Newton) Barber, *née* Este, was born Dec. 26, 1841, in West Medway   He married, June 15, 1867, Margaret Hunter daughter of William and Anna (Mills) Hunter   She was born Sept 5, 1836, on Goose River, Cumberland Co, Nova Scotia   They reside in West Medway

The children were   WILLIAM N, b. Jan. 24, 1869.   HENRY F, b Oct 17, 1870, d July 24, 1871   ESSIE M, b Nov. 22, 1872

[1]   **BENJAMIN C. BARBER**, son of Edmund Barber, was born in Townsend, Vt   He married, Aug 20, 1833, Miranda Cushing, daughter of Warren and Abigail (Adams) Cushing   She was born in Newfane, Vt   They resided in Townsend, Vt, and removed, in 1841, to West Medway, Mass

The children were   An INFANT   EDMUND C. [2]   FREDERIC M, m 1865, Julia McQuade, res in Bellows Falls, Vt   ABBIE M. m May 21, 1870, Sewall Holbrook, res in Milford, Mass.   ADDISON M, d May 4, 1854   LOTTIE A, m. May 2 1872, Arthur J Daniels, res in Southbridge, Mass

[2]   **EDMUND C. BARBER**, son of Benjamin C and Miranda (Cushing) Barber, was born in Townsend, Vt   He married, Jan 29, 1859, Eliza J Fuller   She was born in 1843   They resided in Medway   Mrs Barber died Nov 19, 1879

The children were: LIZZIE J, m Aug 23, 1879, Henry H Varnum.   ANNIE F. HATTIE J   Five other children died prior to 1884

HENRI[6] BATCHELDER (John[5], Odlin[4], Benjamin[3], John[2], John[1]), son of John and Emeline (Mason) Batchelder, was born Oct 4, 1842, in Holliston, Mass He married, Nov 18, 1868, Anna O. Messenger, daughter of Joel Messenger. She was born March 16, 1845. They reside in Medway.

The children were LAURA M , b Aug 16, 1869 ALICE E , b April 15, 1876.

Memoranda Mr Batchelder was in the United States Navy from 1861 to 1865. His father, grandfather, and great grandfather resided in Candia, N H , of which town the latter, Benjamin Batchelder, was first selectman He was also a soldier in the army of the Revolution, and a lieutenant in the French war. Benjamin Batchelder's father was born in Kensington, N H., and his grandfather was born in Reading, Mass

Mr. Batchelder's mother descended from Henry Leland, who was born in England in 1625, and was one of the earliest settlers of Sherborn, Mass

JAMES M [6] BELL (Thaddeus[5], James[4], Thaddeus[3], Jonathan[2], Jonathan[1]), son of Thaddeus and Eleanor (Yeoumans) Bell, was born Feb. 25, 1833, in New York City He married, Sept 14, 1858, Susan F Frye, daughter of Enoch and Mary B. (Foster) Frye She was born in North Andover, Mass.

The children were. John Frye, b Oct 4, 1859, d Aug 4, 1874 Harry James, b. Aug 19 1861, m Oct 11, 1882, Alice Carey Grace Lillian, b Dec 14, 1863, m April 5, 1880, Josephus W. Pratt, res. in Chicago, Ill Mary Gertrude, b Nov 30, 1869 Hattie Florence, b April 1, 1872, d Dec 11, 1876 Enoch Frye, b May 26, 1874 Sidney Eugene, b Feb 13, 1879

JAMES L. BICKFORD, son of Thomas and Sarah (Dearth) Bickford, was born in Sherborn, Mass He married, April 17, 1853, Maria A Harding, daughter of George and Keziah (Morse) Harding She was born Sept 17, 1828, in East Medway, where they reside

The children were Ida M , b May 4, 1855, m May 4, 1880, Addison H Hutchins George H , b. Jan 1, 1857, d. Sept. 19, 1858. James L , b Aug 9, 1861, d. June 23, 1862 Emma I., b Oct 4, 1863, m Nov 20, 1882, Charles W. Fuller Mary E , b Dec. 11, 1865, m. April 27, 1886, Nelson Lansing Martin, res in Cambridge, Mass

CHARLES A BIGELOW (Calvin, Converse, Josiah), son of Calvin and Elizabeth (Adams) Bigelow, was born July 11, 1830, in Dover, Mass. He married, Oct 4, 1860, Hannah F Thwing, daughter of Albert and Laura A (Fisher) Thwing. She was born June 23, 1826, in East Medway, where they reside

The children were Frank Wesley, b Sept 1, 1861, d. Jan. 10, 1862 Anna Laura, b. Oct 9, 1862 Albert Thwing, b Oct 12, 1865

WARREN H. BLAISDELL, son of Israel and Louisa V Blaisdell, was born Feb 21, 1849, in Westford, Mass He married, May 1, 1879 Georgia Tebbets, daughter of Baalis B and Hannah J. Tebbets. She was born Oct 7, 1854, in New Durham, N H They resided in West Medway

The only child was Baalis B , b June 19, 1880

[1] JOSIAH BLAKE, son of Dea Philip and Sarah (Allen) Blake, was born 1782, in Wrentham, Mass He married, June 8, 1809, [1]Mary Barber, daughter of George and Bethia (Jones) Barber She was born Sept 13, 1789, in Medway, where they resided Mrs Mary Blake died Mr Blake married, Nov 15, 1831, [2]Christiana Lincoln Mr. Blake died. Mrs. Christiana Blake died April 14, 1884

The children were Josiah Allen [2], b Jan 9, 1811 William, b Oct 20, 1812, d about 1832 James Partridge, b June 20, 1816, m Emeline Nelson, res in Poughkeepsie, N Y and in Waterbury, Conn Elial Barber, b May 24, 1818, m. Elizabeth Richardson, res in New York City.

[2] JOSIAH ALLEN BLAKE (Josiah, Philip), son of Josiah [1] and Mary (Barber) Blake, was born Jan 9, 1811, in Medway He married, April 27, 1836, [1]Sarah Plimpton, daughter of Wales and —— (Bullard) Plimpton She was born in Medfield, Mass They resided in Providence, R I Mrs Sarah Blake died Aug. 3, 1861. Mr Blake married, March, 1865, [2]Ellen Douglas Drowne

The only child was Sarah Ellen, b Nov 7, 1867.

[1] CALEB BLAKE (Darius, John), son of Darius and Elizabeth (Gould) Blake, was born Nov. 20, 1806, in Medway, Mass He married, Sept. 16, 1835, Mary L. Partridge, daughter of Adin and Mary (Leland) Partridge She was born Aug. 16, 1810, in Sherborn, Mass. They resided in Medway, Mass.

The children were MARY ELIZABETH, b July 6, 1836, d Oct 4, 1860 ELIZA ANN, b. April 5, 1838 ADIN PHILIP [2], b March 8, 1844, m. April 17, 1870, Phebe A Fry ALFRED ALEXANDER, b May 14, 1846, m Oct 28, 1871, Martha A Chickering

Memoranda. Mr. Blake's mother, Mrs Elizabeth (Gould) Blake, daughter of John and Esther (Clark) Gould, was born Aug 28, 1774, in Medway, Mass

[2] **ADIN P. BLAKE** (CALEB, DARIUS, JOHN), son of Caleb and Mary L (Partridge) Blake, was born March 8, 1844, in Medway, Mass. He married, April 17, 1870, Phebe Fry, daughter of Joseph W and Naomi (Harlow) Fry. They resided in Holliston, and in East Medway, Mass.

The children were ALICE MABEL, b. April 3, 1871, d Dec 22, 1876 HATTIE ELIZABETH, b March 23, 1873, d Dec 30, 1876 CHARLES ADIN, b Feb 14, 1874, d July 16, 1874 ALBERT FRANCIS, b March 4, 1875, d March 23, 1875 FREDERIC CALEB, b July 31, 1876, d Aug. 21, 1876. MABEL HATTIE, b. Oct 2, 1881 MAURICE ADIN, b Dec 1, 1882

ALVAN[7] BOND (WILLIAM[6], JOSIAH[5], JOSIAH[4], JONAS[3], WILLIAM[2], THOMAS[1]), son of William and Sarah (Waters) Bond, was born April 27, 1793, in Sutton, Mass He married, April 25, 1821, Sarah Richardson, daughter of Ezra[5] and Jemima (Lovell) Richardson She was born Sept. 24, 1796, in East Medway, Mass They resided in Sturbridge, Mass, and in Bangor, Me., where Mrs Sarah Bond died Aug 12, 1834 The Rev Alvan Bond removed in 1835, and died July 19, 1882, in Norwich, Conn

The children were SARAH ELIZABETH, b April 23, 1822, d Jan 27, 1846 ABIGAIL LOVELL, b. Oct 28, 1823, m Sept 17, 1862, William Adriance, res in Poughkeepsie, N Y WILLIAM CYRUS, b June 20, 1825, d Sept 25, 1826 ALVAN CYRUS, b Oct 18, 1826, d. Nov 12, 1847 WILLIAM, b April 9, 1828, m Feb. 11, 1863, Nannie E Day, res. in New York City FRANK STUART, b Feb. 1, 1830, res in New York City. HENRY RICHARDSON, b May 2, 1832, m March 10, 1858, Mary V Ripley, res. in New London, Conn LOUISA WATERS, b July 15, 1834, m Oct 7, 1862, Stephen B Meech, res in Norwich, Conn

Memoranda Thomas Bond, immigrant, was a son of Jonas Bond, of Bury St Edmunds, England, where he died in 1601.

[1] **WILLIAM B. BOYD** (WILLARD, JOHN), son of Willard and Betsey (Whiting) Boyd, was born Sept 25, 1800, in Franklin. He married, April 15, 1827, Emeline C Ackley She was born in Auburn, N Y. They resided in East Medway. Mrs. Boyd died Feb 8, 1868 Mr Boyd died July 27, 1883

The children were ELIZABETH, b June 29, 1828, d Oct 2, 1828 CORNELIA, b Aug 22, 1830, d May 14, 1837 ELLEN S, b April 21, 1833 SARAH I, b Dec 22, 1834, m July 13, 1864, [1]Erastus Tyler, *vid*, m Dec 27, 1883, [2]Benjamin Glidden, res in Beverly, Mass WILLIAM B, b Sept 30, 1839, d Oct 1, 1840 A CHILD, b September, 1840, d April 7, 1842. ISABELLA WALKER, b Nov 12, 1843, m 1872, William Brown Roberts, res in Medfield, Mass A CHILD, b Oct 28, 1848, d September, 1849

[2] **AMOS HAWES BOYD** (WILLARD, JOHN), son of Willard and Betsey (Whiting) Boyd, was born March 18, 1804, in Franklin, Mass He married, May 5, 1829, Rachel P Butler, of Manchester, Conn. They resided in East Medway, Mass Mr Boyd died Jan 26, 1872 Mrs Boyd died Dec 21, 1880

The children were MARY ANN PHELPS FRANCISCA MARIA. AMELIA BUTLER, b. Sept. 26, 1839, m Dec 6, 1864, George Lovell[3] Richardson, A M, *vid.;* res in Abington, Mass, d July 19, 1879 FRANCISCA DE WITT, b May 17, 1844, m May 23, 1871, John Adams[3] Richardson, *vid*

[1] **NATHAN BUCKNAM** was born Nov 2, 1703, in Malden, Mass He married, 1726, Margaret ——— She was born in 1706 They resided in Medway. Mr Bucknam died Feb 6, 1795 Mrs Bucknam died May 1, 1796

The children were ANNA, b Oct 16, 1728, m Oct 25, 1759, Edward Clark, d prior to 1789 NATHAN [2], b Nov. 26, 1730 MARGARET, b May 4, 1733, m May 30, 1753, Asa Ellis MARY, b May 13, 1736, m Oct 16, 1764, John Holmes, of Stoughton, Mass SAMUEL, b June 5, 1738, d Dec. 12, 1741. ELIZABETH, b. Feb 5, 1741, m. May 8, 1771, Robert Luscombe, of Taunton, Mass CATHERINE, b Feb 9, 1742, m Dec 24, 1767, Hon Joseph Dorr, of Mendon, Mass SARAH, b June 5, 1745, d Feb 20, 1770 LUCY, b Nov 23, 1748, m Dec 14, 1796, Dea David Davis, of Paxton, Mass

[2] NATHAN BUCKNAM, son of Nathan [1] and Margaret Bucknam, was born Nov. 26, 1730, in Medway. He married, and died prior to 1789.

The children were SARAH, MARGARET, LUCY, m Jan 1, 1778, Joshua Clapp; ANNA, and MARY.

There were four men of the name of Bullard who came, about 1630, from England to America. Robert Bullard and George Bullard had lands assigned them in 1637 and in 1644, in Watertown, Mass While John Bullard and William Bullard had lands assigned them in 1636 in Dedham, Mass

Benjamin Bullard, only son of Robert and Ann Bullard, of Watertown, his father dying April 24, 1639, and his mother marrying soon after a second husband, Henry Thorpe, was under the care of his uncle, John Bullard, in Dedham, where he was admitted a townsman, Jan 11, 1656. Benjamin Bullard married in 1659, Martha Pidge, and settled on the north side of Boggastow Pond, now Sherborn, Mass He was one of the petitioners for the incorporation of Sherborn in 1674, and subsequently became a large landed proprietor in Medfield and Holliston He married, 1677, a second wife, Elizabeth, and died Sept 27, 1689 From Benjamin Bullard have descended all of that name in the town of Medway.

[1] JOHN³ BULLARD (BENJAMIN², ROBERT¹), son of Benjamin and Elizabeth Bullard, was born March 7, 1678, in Sherborn, Mass. He married, Jan 7, 1702, Abigail Leland, daughter of Hopestill and Abigail (Hill) Leland. She was born Feb 17, 1683 They lived in Medway.

The children were· THANKFUL, m John Harding, *vid* JOHN [3], b. May 16, 1705 ABIGAIL, b Dec 4, 1708, m. Timothy Clark, *vid* HANNAH, b May 12, 1714, m 1733, Henry Daniels, *vid* MARY, b April 7, 1717, m Moses Harding, res in Medfield COMFORT, b. March 2, 1721, m. Jonathan Wheeler, *vid* HENRY [4], b. Oct 1, 1723

[2] MALACHI³ BULLARD (BENJAMIN², ROBERT¹), son of Benjamin and Elizabeth Bullard, was born March 8, 1685, in Sherborn, Mass He married, 1708, Bethia Fisher, daughter of Josiah Fisher They resided in Medway Mr Bullard died Nov. 15, 1726

The children were· MALACHI [5], b. April 27, 1710. KEZIAH, b Dec 2, 1711, m. James Partridge, *vid*, d. 1802 ELISHA [6], b. Aug 15, 1714. ELEAZAR, b Aug 15, 1714, d June 12, 1726 LYDIA, b June 25, 1726, d June 7, 1730

[3] JOHN⁴ BULLARD (JOHN³, BENJAMIN², ROBERT¹), son of John [1] and Abigail (Leland) Bullard, was born May 16, 1705, in Medway He married, Feb 20, 1733, Sarah Daniell, daughter of Joseph² Daniell. She was born May 1, 1707, in Medway

The children were. JOHN, b Dec 1, 1733, d young SARAH b Jan 1, 1736, m. David Fisk, of Holliston, Mass TIMOTHY [7], b March 21, 1740. NATHAN, b May 16, 1748, d young

[4] HENRY⁴ BULLARD (JOHN³, BENJAMIN², ROBERT¹), son of John [1] and Abigail (Leland) Bullard, was born Oct 1, 1723 He married, March 14, 1745-6, ¹Jemima Pond She was born in Wrentham, Mass They resided in Medway Mrs. Jemima Bullard died May 19, 1766 Mr. Bullard married ²Abigail Morse, daughter of Nathaniel and Sarah (Coolidge) Morse

The children were MARY, b Oct 14, 1746, m 1766, Timothy Hill, res. in Sherborn, d Feb. 18, 1825 HENRY [8], b April 29, 1749 ADAM [9], b Aug 10, 1752 JOHN, b. Nov. 28, 1756, m. Elizabeth Adams, daughter of the Rev Amos Adams, of Roxbury, Mass ELI, b Nov 16, 1758, m. 1794, Ruth Buckminster, res in Holliston, Mass ROYAL, b. April 21, 1762, m Ruth Penniman, d March 25, 1785 SAMUEL, b May 15, 1766, m. Abigail Bullard, res in Shrewsbury, Mass, d September, 1830 ABIGAIL, b April 11, 1773, d Sept 24, 1776. MARGARET, b. Nov 1, 1775, d Oct 11, 1776 LIBERTY, b Nov. 11, 1777, m Abigail Learned, res in New Salem, Mass, d 1848 AMOS [10], b Feb. 25, 1780. ABIGAIL, b. Aug. 11, 1783, m Thomas Burbank, res in Warren, Mass·

[5] MALACHI⁴ BULLARD (MALACHI³, BENJAMIN², ROBERT¹), son of Malachi, [2] and Bethia (Fisher) Bullard, was born April 27, 1710 He married Rachel Hill, daughter of Samuel and Rachel (Adams) Hill, of Medway.

The only child was. ISAAC [11]. b July 9, 1744

[6] **ELISHA⁴ BULLARD** (MALACHI³, BENJAMIN², ROBERT¹), son of Malachi [2] and Bethia (Fisher) Bullard, was born Aug 15, 1714, m April 9, 1736, Bathshela Fisher, daughter of Samuel and Mary (Rockwood) Fisher She was born May 4, 1714, in Wrentham, Mass

The children were LYDIA, b Nov 26, 1736, d Jan 4, 1741 MIRIAM, b Nov 24, 1739, d Jan 9, 1741 SAMUEL, b Oct 4, 1741, d Jan 25, 1741 SETH, b Feb 1, 1743 SAMUEL, b Oct 19, 1746, d April 24, 1754 DANIEL, b Dec 26, 1748 ELIJAH, b Jan 11, 1750-51, m Milcah ——, res in Holliston ELISHA, b March 26, 1752, m Rachel Rockwood MALACHI, b May 6, 1753, d Oct 1, 1756 JOHN, b Sept 12, 1755 ABEL, b Aug 29, 1757 BERIAH, b Dec 16, 1758, m April 24, 1778, Julietta Messenger

[7] **TIMOTHY⁵ BULLARD** (JOHN⁴, JOHN³, BENJAMIN², ROBERT¹), son of John [3] and Sarah (Daniell) Bullard, was born March 21, 1740 He married Rhoda Richardson, daughter of Moses⁴ and Abigail (Allen) Richardson She was born Oct 6, 1746, in Medway, where they resided Mrs Rhoda Bullard died May 19 1811 Mr Bullard died Jan 6, 1827

The children were GALIM, b. June 17, 1765, m Sarah Daniels, res in Sherborn, Mass, d 1853 RALPH [12], b Dec 10, 1766 ABIGAIL, b Aug 13, 1768, m Samuel Bullard, res in Shrewsbury, Mass RHODA, b Dec 25, 1770, m. Timothy⁵ Whiting.

[8] **HENRY⁵ BULLARD** (HENRY⁴, JOHN³, BENJAMIN², ROBERT¹), son of Henry [4] and Jemima (Pond) Bullard, was born April 29, 1749, in Medway He married Rebecca Richardson, daughter of Moses⁴ and Abigail (Allen) Richardson She was born April 3, 1751, in Medway, where they resided Mr Bullard died May 11, 1821 Mrs Bullard died June 15, 1838

The children were HENRY, b Feb 15, 1774, m Hannah Curtis, res in Holden, Mass, died March, 1831 REBECCA, b Aug 22, 1777, m Reuben Hill, *vid* MOSES, b Sept 20, 1779, m Elizabeth Clark, res in Princeton, Mass TITUS [13], b. March 15, 1783 JOANNA, b March 21, 1792, m Elias⁵ Whiting, *vid*

[9] **ADAM⁵ BULLARD** (HENRY⁴ JOHN³, BENJAMIN², ROBERT¹), son of Henry [4] and Jemima (Pond) Bullard, was born Aug 10, 1752 He married, 1777, Lois Richardson, daughter of Moses⁴ and Abigail (Allen) Richardson She was born Feb 1, 1749, in East Medway, where they resided Mr Bullard died March 8 1843

The children were PEGGY, b July 27 1778 m Aaron Thayer, resided in Hanover, Penn CYRUS, b March 6, 1780, d April 18 1806 JEMIMA, b Oct 26, 1781, m 1826, William La Croix, *vid*, d Feb 10, 1857 ADAM b Jun 27, 1783, d Oct 7 1809 LOIS, b June 12, 1787, m 1815, William La Croix, *vid*, d. Feb 11 1825

[10] **AMOS⁵ BULLARD** (HENRY⁴, JOHN³, BENJAMIN², ROBERT¹), son of Henry [4] and Abigail (Morse) Bullard, was born Feb 25, 1780, in Medway He married Abigail Adams, daughter of Obadiah⁶ and Abigail (Harding) Adams She was born in 1787, in Medway

The children were AMOS, b July 13, 1807, m Dec 30, 1839, Mary Ann Durant, res. in Barre, Mass, d Aug 21, 1850 MARY b Nov 21, 1808, m Stephen W Richardson, res in Franklin, Mass SYLVANUS [14] b Nov 26, 1810 CYRUS [15], b April 9, 1813 ELIZA, b Jan 7, 1816 m May 6, 1835 Stephen W Richardson, res in Franklin, Mass FREDERIC b Aug 25, 1817

[11] **ISAAC⁵ BULLARD** (MALACHI⁴, MALACHI³, BENJAMIN², ROBERT¹), son of Malachi [5] and Rachel (Hill) Bullard, was born July 9, 1744 He married Mary Fisher, daughter of Dea Samuel Fisher She was born Sept 4, 1741, in Medway She died March 12 1809 Mr Bullard died March 18, 1810

The children were SILAS, b Jan 12 1767 m ¹Thankful Adams, m March 15, 1797, ²Experience Orcutt, res in Wendell, Mass JULIA, b May 2, 1768, m Dec 4 1786, Elijah Clark, res in Wendell, Mass MALACHI [16], b Aug 13, 1770 RACHEL, b June 29, 1772, m Eli Thurston, res in Westboro Mass MARY b Dec 17 1774, d Aug 22, 1802 ISAAC, b Dec 26, 1776, m Peninah Fisher ACHSAH, b Aug 21, 1778, m Elihu White, res in Franklin, Mass ELIHU, b Jan 2, 1782, res in Wendell, Mass, d 1847 ELIAS, b May 15, 1785, d Feb 8, 1798 NATHAN [17], b May 19, 1787 VESTA, b Dec 21, 1789, d Nov 14, 1791

[12] **RALPH⁶ BULLARD** (TIMOTHY⁵ JOHN⁴, JOHN³, BENJAMIN², ROBERT¹), son of Timothy [7] and Rhoda (Richardson) Bullard, was born Dec 10, 1766. He married Amy Penniman, daughter of James and Abigail (Clark) Penniman

The children were JOHN [18]. b Dec 13, 1793 AMY, b 1809, m David Vinton, res. in Southbridge, Mass

[13] **TITUS[6] BULLARD** (HENRY[5], HENRY[4], JOHN[3], BENJAMIN[2], ROBERT[1]), son of Henry [8] and Rebecca (Richardson) Bullard, was born March 15, 1783, in Holliston, Mass. He married Esther Whiting, daughter of Elias[5] and Joanna (Bullard) Whiting She was born Oct 9, 1786, in Medway They resided in Holliston, Mass Mr Bullard died Jan 8, 1849

The children were. ADELINE, b. May 4, 1810 m Timothy Whiting. res in Cincinnati O., d. Dec 7, 1839 JOANNA, b Nov 4, 1812, m William Wight. res. in Holliston, Mass., d Oct 1, 1844 HENRY [19], b July 13. 1815 REBECCA, b Oct 4 1819, m. Nathaniel Whiting. res in Watertown, Mass JOHN A., b Oct. 31, 1822, m Frances J R Sargent. res in Watertown. Mass

[14] **SYLVANUS[6] BULLARD** (AMOS[5] HENRY[4], JOHN[3], BENJAMIN[2], ROBERT[1]), son of Amos [10] and Abigail (Adams) Bullard, was born Nov. 26 1810, in Medway He married, May 27, 1834 Mary F Morse, daughter of Andrew and Margarette (Metcalf) Morse She was born Sept 21, 1814, in East Medway. Mr Bullard died Dec 24. 1836 Mrs Bullard married Oct 30, 1850, [2]James Willard[8] Daniels *vid.*

The only child was FREDERICK F b Nov 30. 1836, d Sept 15. 1838

[15] **CYRUS[6] BULLARD** (AMOS[5], HENRY[4], JOHN[3], BENJAMIN[2], ROBERT[1]) son of Amos [10] and Abigail (Adams) Bullard, was born April 9 1813, in Medway He married [1]Ede Partridge Mrs Ede Bullard died June 14 1854 Mr Cyrus Bullard married, Dec 5, 1854 [2]Elvira A Cass, daughter of Luke and Lucy Cass, of Burke. Vt

The children were ABIGAIL A., b July 7, 1830 RHODA E., b July 12 1840. FREDERICK F, b Sept 15, 1841 m Oct 4, 1870, Marion Kingsbury SYLVANUS, b Oct 30, 1843, d Sept 27, 1866 AMOS E., b Oct 4, 1846, m June 1873, Betsey Newell JOANNA E., b Sept 12, 1846 CYRUS P, m May 15 1873,———Allen JACOB J CHARLES MARY R, b Aug 24. 1855, m May 6 1882, Herbert Williams EDF, b Jan 21, 1860. m Nov 15, 1881, George Willard, res in Wrentham, Mass LUCY C, b Sept 10. 1862 LIZZIE L, b July 24, 1864

[16] **MALACHI[6] BULLARD** (ISAAC[5] MALACHI[4], MALACHI[3], BENJAMIN[2], ROBERT[1]), son of Isaac [11] and Mary (Fisher) Bullard, was born Aug 13. 1770 He married Polly Littlefield, daughter of John and Tabitha (Adams) Littlefield. She was born Oct. 29, 1774.

The children were ELIAS, m Persis Daniels, res. in Holliston, Mass MALACHI, b Nov 4, 1816, m Nov 11, 1846, Sabrina Bullard, res in Winchendon Mass. d May 10, 1849 APPLETON HARTWELL, res in Wrentham, Mass.

[17] **NATHAN[6] BULLARD** (ISAAC[5], MALACHI[4], MALACHI[3], BENJAMIN[2], ROBERT[1]), son of Isaac [11] and Mary (Fisher) Bullard. was born May 19, 1787 He married, Nov. 16, 1814, Nancy Russell, daughter of Thomas Russell She was born Oct 19, 1794. in Oxford, Mass

The children were. ELIZABETH, b December, 1816, m March 1, 1840, the Rev John H. Garman SABRINA, b March 25, 1820, m Nov. 11, 1846, the Rev Malachi Bullard ELMIRA, b Sept 16, 1822, m Simeon M Cutler, res in Holliston, Mass

[18] **JOHN[7] BULLARD** (RALPH[6], TIMOTHY[5], JOHN[4] JOHN[3], BENJAMIN[2], ROBERT[1]). son of Ralph [12] and Amy (Penniman) Bullard, was born Dec 13. 1793, in East Medway. He married, about 1814, Chloe Partridge, daughter of Joseph and Chloe (Bullard) Partridge Mrs Bullard died April 13. 1861 Mr Bullard died Sept 27 1875

The children were · TIMOTHY [20], b Nov 29 1816 RHODA b February, 1819, d Oct 1, 1820. JOHN [21] b. Dec 7, 1823

[19] **HENRY[7] BULLARD** (TITUS[6], HENRY[5], HENRY[4], JOHN[3]. BENJAMIN[2], ROBERT[1]), son of Titus [13] and Esther (Whiting) Bullard, was born July 13, 1815, in Holliston, Mass He married Bethia Wheeler, daughter of Lewis and Betsey (Richardson) Wheeler She was born in East Medway They resided in Holliston, Mass.

The children were LEWIS HENRY, m Mary Freeman, res in Holliston, Mass ALICE REBECCA ALBERT, m Mary Brooks res in Newton Mass ELIZABETH, m Charles Adams, res in Dorchester, Mass. FRANCES, m Willis Kingsbury, res. in Holliston Mass. JAMES HOVEY res. in California. HARRIET B, m Edward H Ellis, M D, res in Marlboro Mass.

[20] **TIMOTHY**[8] **BULLARD** (John[7], Ralph[6], Timothy[5], John,[4] John[3], Benjamin[2], Robert[1]), son of John [18] and Chloe (Partridge) Bullard, was born Nov 29, 1816, in East Medway He married, Jan 25, 1838, Hannah Phillips, daughter of Oliver and Hannah (Richardson) Phillips She was born Nov 23, 1816, in East Medway, where they reside

The children were William Puffer, b Nov 11, 1842 Rhoda Damon, b March 8, 1845, m. Feb 25, 1886, John A. Hutchins Hannah, b. Feb 12, 1851, m. Aug 7, 1873, Walter H Andrews John Oliver, b Feb 21, 1853, d Feb. 1, 1883 Moses, b May, 1855

[21] **JOHN BULLARD** (John[7], Ralph[6], Timothy[5], John[4], John[3], Benjamin[2], Robert[1]), son of John [18] and Chloe (Partridge) Bullard, was born Dec. 7, 1823, in East Medway He married, May 29, 1845, Pearlee Daniels, daughter of Paul[5] and Eliza (Breck) Daniell She was born July 29, 1823, in East Medway, where they reside

The children were Harriet Partridge, b Oct. 20, 1846, m July 19, 1881, Louis La Croix, *vid* Luella Eliza, b Nov 4, 1849, m Dec 23, 1874, Louis La Croix, *vid*, d March 13, 1880 Sewall Harding, b. March 21, 1851, res in Sundance, Wyoming Joseph Daniels, b Sept 16, 1855, m May 13, 1878, Mary Emma Follansbee, res in South Framingham, Mass

[1] **JOSEPH**[6] **BULLARD** (Eleazar[5], Isaac[4], Isaac[3], Benjamin[2], Robert[1]), son of Eleazar[5] and Patty (Parker) Bullard, was born Oct. 4, 1816, in Holliston, Mass He married, April 25, 1839, [1]Clarissa Ann Williams She was born Sept 1, 1815 They resided in Medway Mrs Clarissa A Bullard died June 26, 1839 Mr Bullard married, June 14, 1840, [2]Sarah Ann Partridge, daughter of Joel[5] and Sarah (Clark) Partridge, *vid.* She was born Dec. 3, 1818, in Medway

The children were George Walton [2], b May 24, 1841 Clarissa Ann, b. March 31, 1843, d Sept 28, 1857 Joel Partridge, b Oct 18, 1845 Joseph Emerson, b Oct 20, 1848, m Jan 1, 1871, Mary Williams Edmund, b Oct 27, 1850, m Jan 1, 1872, Evie Hixon Sarah Ella, b Feb. 13, 1853, m Dec 25, 1877, Curtis A Sparrow Addison Eleazar, b March 7, 1855, m Sept 25, 1879, Lydia A. Metcalf Lizzie Louise, b July 10, 1857 Alida, b. April 22 1860, m Jan. 26, 1881, William Stewartson Charles, b Jan 22, 1864.

[2] **GEORGE WALTON**[7] **BULLARD** (Joseph[6], Eleazar[5], Isaac[4], Isaac[3], Benjamin[2], Robert[1]), was born May 24, 1841, in Medway. He married, June 28, 1860, Eleanor L Smith, daughter of James N and Sally P Smith She was born March 15, 1840, in Medway, where they resided

The children were Clara L , b Aug 25, 1860 Hattie L , b. April 6, 1862

SAMUEL BULLEN was a freeman in 1641, of Dedham, Mass All of this name who have lived in Medway are supposed to be his descendants

DAVID BULLEN married, Sept 5, 1718, Abigail Dana They resided in East Medway

The children were Abigail, b Oct 1, 1719 Judah, b May 3, 1821, d July 6, 1721 Judah, b May 6, 1722. Hannah, b April 12, 1824 Patience, b March 8, 1726, d March 9, 1826. Silence, b Nov 3, 1727, d. Nov 9, 1727. Submit, b Aug 16, 1731, d Aug 19, 1731 David, b March 10, 1733 Ebenezer, b May 13, 1734

[1] **MICHAEL BULLEN** married Lydia —— They resided in Medway. Mr. Bullen died Jan 28, 1747

The children were Elizabeth, b Dec. 15, 1727 Daniel [2], b Oct 27, 1729 John [3], b Sept. 8, 1732 Jabez, b Aug 4, 1734. Mary, b Oct 8, 1738 Benoni, b Sept 22, 1740. Joseph, b July 3, 1744.

Memoranda Jabez Bullen, son of Michael and Lydia Bullen, was crazed by disappointed love. He would not eat or speak They carried him into the church and prayed over him in the broad-aisle, that the dumb devil would come out of him, and he spoke at once!

[2] **DANIEL BULLEN**, son of Michael [1] and Lydia Bullen, was born Oct 27, 1729, in Medway He married Rachel —— She was born 1733 They resided in Medway Mr Bullen died Oct 28, 1801 Mrs Bullen died Jan 15, 1823

The children were Lydia, d July 18, 1780 Jonathan

[3] **JOHN BULLEN**, son of Michael [1] and Lydia Bullen, was born Sept 18, 1732, in Medway He married Elizabeth Adams Mr Bullen died Nov 28, 1817

There was a son Jeduthan [4], b Jan. 30, 1751

[4] JEDUTHAN BULLEN (John, Michael), son of John [3] and Elizabeth (Adams) Bullen, was born Jan 30, 1751, in Medway. He married, July 2, 1772, [1]Dolly Clark, daughter of David and Dorothy Clark. She was born in Medway, where they resided. Mrs Dolly Bullen died July 20, 1785 Mr Bullen married, Nov 9, 1785, [2]Bathsheba Daniels, daughter of Asa and Bathsheba (Fairbanks) Daniels She was born April 6, 1763, in East Medway Mrs Bathsheba Bullen died April 21, 1828 Mr Bullen died March 5, 1830

The children were· ELIZABETH, b Oct. 26, 1772 MARY, b Oct 24, 1774, m Lovell Clark. JEDUTHAN, b May 12, 1777, d Oct. 8, 1778 JOHN, b. March 21, 1779 DAVID, b March 24, 1782, m Patty Harding, res. in Union, Me JEDUTHAN, b Feb 7, 1784 OTIS HOLBROOK, b April 14, 1786, m. Nov 5, 1808, Jerusha Day, res in North Brookfield, Mass He was brought up by his grandfather and known as Otis Daniels, d Oct. 24, 1843 WALTER, b Aug 6, 1787, d June 14, 1788 LOWELL [5], b Oct. 8, 1789. ASA [6], b. June 19, 1791 SUSANNA, b Sept 7, 1792 BETSEY, b March 17, 1795, m Clark Holbrook, res Sherborn, Mass LEWIS [7], b April 10, 1798.

[5] LOWELL BULLEN (Jeduthan, John, Michael), son of Jeduthan [4] and Bathsheba (Daniels) Bullen, was born Oct 8, 1789, in Medway He married, 1808, Chloe Harding, daughter of Uriah Harding She was born in Medway, where they resided. Mrs Bullen died April 21, 1854 Mr Bullen died Nov 2, 1869

The only child was MARY MASON, b. March 27, 1809, m Feb 12, 1834, David Hoyt, res in Rochester, N Y.

Memoranda Mr and Mrs David Hoyt had eight children, viz· Lowell Bullen, b Feb 8, 1835, d July 24, 1836 George Harding, b April 18, 1837, m Oct 21, 1861, Hattie Hicks. Henry Bullen, b Oct 24 1839, m Nov 15, 1866, Libbie Morris Mary Adeline, b Oct 8, 1841. William Mason, b Aug. 21, 1843 David, b. Feb 18, 1846, m June 11, 1868, Mrs Elizabeth R Breck Charles Blake, b April 21, 1848 Frederick Edward, b April 17, 1851, d May 21, 1851 Mr. David Hoyt, Sen , d Dec 9, 1861

[6] ASA BULLEN (Jeduthan, John, Michael), son of Jeduthan [4] and Bathsheba (Daniels) Bullen, was born June 19, 1791, in East Medway He married, [1]Susanna Pike, daughter of Nathaniel Pike She was born 1788, in Hopkinton, Mass They resided in Medway Mrs Susanna Bullen died Jan 16, 1818 Mr Bullen married, Nov. 21, 1820, [2]Mary Littlefield, daughter of Pelatiah and Abigail Littlefield She was born June 19, 1793, in Hopkinton, Mass Mr Bullen died Feb 8, 1853 Mrs Mary Bullen died March 30, 1875

The children were SUSANNA, b Dec 30, 1817, m Nov 29, 1849, Alfred H Metcalf, res. in Norfolk, Mass MOSES DWIGHT, b Oct 16, 1821, m Dec 6, 1848, Mary Eliza Walker. MARY ANTOINETTE, b Nov 2, 1823, d May 7, 1826 GEORGE RUSSELL, b March 20, 1831, m April 13, 1859, Charlotte P Freeland, res in Worcester, Mass

[7] LEWIS BULLEN (Jeduthan, John, Michael), son of Jeduthan [4] and Bathsheba (Daniels) Bullen, was born April 10, 1798, in East Medway He married [1]Esther Grout, daughter of Elias Grout She was born 1789, in Framingham, Mass They resided in East Medway. Mrs Esther Bullen died Mr Bullen married [2]Mary Ann Mann, daughter of Ebenezer Mann She was born in Sherborn, Mass. Mr. Bullen died Mrs Mary Ann Bullen married [2] Jacob Pratt

The children were: HENRY LEWIS [8], b Aug 17, 1820. JOHN, res in Australia ANNA MARIA She died in early life MARY ANN, died young MARY

[8] HENRY LEWIS BULLEN (Lewis, Jeduthan, John, Michael), son of Lewis [7] and Esther (Grout) Bullen, was born Aug 17, 1820, in Medway He married, Nov. 28, 1844, [1]Mary Farrington, daughter of Nathaniel and Fanny (Gould) Farrington. She was born in Walden, Vt Mrs. Bullen died The Rev Mr. Bullen married, Oct 9, 1867, [2]Laura Day They reside in Moline, Ill

The children were· JOHN LEWIS, b. Dec 8, 1860 MARY E , b May 6, 1862. ALFRED T., b Nov. 7, 1865 LAURA D , b. Jan. 7, 1867. HENRY W , b Jan. 18, 1882.

JOHN EZRA[5] BURR (Elbridge G [7], John[6], Jonathan[5], John[4], John[3], Simon[2], Jonathan[1]), was born Feb 27, 1845, in French Creek, Upshur County, Va. He married, Sept 9, 1874, Emma Jane Goddard, daughter of Isaac and Mary A (Kingsley) Goddard, of Providence, R I The Rev. Mr Burr died Sept. 6, 1883. on the railroad train, at Deer Park, Md , on his way to his native place in West Virginia   Mrs Burr resides in East Providence, R I

The children were ALICE MABEL, b Aug 4, 1875   STELLA MALVINA, b April 26, 1878   FANNY KINGSLEY, b Oct 6, 1880

Memoranda   Mr Burr's great ancestor, the Rev Jonathan[1] Burr, was born in Redgrave, Suffolk County, England, in 1604   He emigrated to America in 1639, and was settled in 1640, as colleague pastor with the Rev Richard Mather, over the church in Dorchester, Mass , where he died very soon after, Aug 9, 1641   Mr Burr's mother was Mrs Emily Jane (Morgan) Burr, daughter of Ezra and Rhoda Morgan   She was born May, 1817, in Dunbarton, N H   His father was born May, 1811, in Worthington, Mass , but when six years old went with his parents to Buchanan, Va   *Vid The Genealogy of the Burr Family*

WILLIAM H CAMPSEY (HENRY, WILLIAM), son of Henry and Elizabeth (Lenox) Campsey, was born Nov 29, 1840, in Jamaica Plain Mass   He married, June 23, 1861, Abigail J Kingsbury, *née* Sargent, daughter of Moses and Sarah , (George) Sargent, and widow of Lowell A Kingsbury, of Medway. She was born in Rasburgh, Vt   They resided in West Medway

The children were   MABEL, b March 25 1866   FLORENCE S , b March 15, 1868 ANNIE M , b Aug 27, 1873

Memoranda. Mr and Mrs Lowell A Kingsbury had one child, viz , GEORGE A , b Oct 8, 1856

WILLIAM HIRAM CARY, son of Barnabas and Phebe (Danforth) Cary, was born March 29, 1805, in Attleboro, Mass   He married, Dec 8, 1828, [1]Lydia Daniels Lovell, daughter of Michael and Caty (Daniels) Lovell   She was born Feb 27, 1810, in East Medway   They resided in Medway   Mrs Lydia D Cary died Sept 11, 1853 Mr Cary married, Sept 24, 1854, [2]Mrs Harriet B White, *née* Barber, daughter of George and Lois (Whiting) Barber, and widow of William White   She was born May 29, 1810, in Medway

The children were   GEORGE LOVELL, b May 10, 1830, m March 12, 1854 Isabella Harding, res in Meadville, Penn   WILLIAM HIRAM, b Aug 22, 1835, m 1856, Maria B White, resided in Medway   CATHARINE ALICE, b Oct 17, 1840, d Oct 31, 1840   FRANCIS EUGENE, b Dec 11, 1842, d August, 1843   MARY ADELAIDE, b Oct. 3, 1846, m Dec 23, 1869, the Rev Channing Butler, res in Beverly, Mass   HENRY GRATTAN b April 16, 1850, m. July 7, 1863, Nora Wood, res in Milwaukee, Wis ALICE, b Aug 19, 1853, d Aug 19 1853

Memoranda. Barnabas Cary died Feb 4, 1834, in Medway, aged 75 years   Mrs Phebe Cary died Sept 8, 1843, in Medway, aged 76 years   Maria B White, daughter of William and Harriet (Barber) White, was born Nov. 30, 1835, in Boston, Mass Nora Wood, b May 15, 1854, in Milwaukee, Wis   The Rev Channing Butler was born Nov 4, 1843

JOSEPH CLARK, the ancestor of the Clarks of Medway and vicinity, came from Suffolk County, England, with his wife Mrs Alice (Pepper) Clark, in 1640, and settled in Dedham, Mass   The first mention of Joseph Clark appears as follows

"DEDHAM, ye 28 of ye 7 month called September 1640   Whereas, Edward Alleyen hath granted unto Joseph Clark one acre of ye land next Vine Brook towards the north for setting his house upon we do grant unto ye sayed Joseph one acre of ye land to adjoin thereunto for to make an house lot   And we do grant unto the sayed Joseph Clark six acres of planting ground to be beyond Vine Brook to be set off by the aforesaid men that we appointed to perform for Henry Wilson, provide that he subscribe to the town orders "

Ten years later Joseph Clark was one of the early proprietors and settlers of Medfield, and in his will bequeathed lands to his sons, on the west side of the Charles River, afterwards Medway

[1] JOSEPH CLARK was born in the County of Suffolk, England   He married prior to sailing for America in 1640, Alice Pepper   They resided in Dedham, and in Medfield, Mass   Mr Joseph Clark died Jan 6, 1684   Mrs Alice Clark died March 17, 1710

The children were JOSEPH, b Feb 27, 1642, m April 8, 1686, Mariah Wright, d Sept 4, 1702   BENJAMIN [2], b Feb 9 1643   EPHRAIM, b Feb 4, 1646, m March 6

1669, Mariah Bullen DANIEL, b Sept 29, 1647, was mortally wounded by the Indians and died April 7, 1676 MARY, b June 12, 1649 SARAH, b Feb 20, 1651, m Jan 7, 1673, John Bowers. JOHN [3], b Oct 28, 1652 NATHANIEL, b. Oct. 6, 1658, m May 1, 1669, Experience Hinsdell,.res. in Medfield, Mass REBECCA b Aug 16, 1660, m May 1, 1679, [1]John[2] Richardson *vid*, m. [2]John Hill, res in Sherborn, Mass., d Feb 17, 1738-9

[2] BENJAMIN[2] CLARK (JOSEPH[1]), son of Joseph [1] and Alice (Pepper) Clark, was born Feb 9, 1643, in Dedham, Mass He married, Nov 19, 1665, Dorcas Morse They resided in Medfield Mr Clark died Dec. 1, 1724. Mrs. Clark died July 14, 1725.

The children were HANNAH, b Oct 22, 1666, d Dec 14 1690 BENJAMIN, b Nov. 20, 1668, d. Feb. 7, 1688 THEOPHILUS [4], b Sept 25, 1670 TABITHA, b Dec 10, 1672 TIMOTHY, b Dec 19, 1674, d Sept 6, 1676 TIMOTHY [5], b. May 12, 1677 EDWARD [6], b Nov 11, 1679 EBENEZER, b May 12, 1682 d. Feb 14, 1683 REBECCA, b July 20, 1684, d Sept. 26, 1687 SETH, b May 1, 1687, m Dec 3, 1713, Abigail Metcalf, d. March 16, 1756 JONATHAN, d Nov. 16, 1690

[3] JOHN[2] CLARK (JOSEPH[1]), son of Joseph [1] and Alice (Pepper) Clark, was born Oct 28, 1652, in Medfield, Mass He married, Jan 9, 1679, Mary Sheffield, daughter of William and Hannah (Bullard) Sheffield She was born in Sherborn, Mass They settled, in 1681, on the west of the river Charles, the place now occupied by his descendants, Dea Elbridge Clark, and his brother, John Clark Mr Clark died Dec 14, 1720

The children were RACHEL ELSIE, m —— Brown RUTH, m. July 4, 1728, Jonathan Richardson, res in Brookfield, Mass NATHANIEL [7] JEREMIAH JAMES. JOHN, d 1709

[4] THEOPHILUS[3] CLARK (BENJAMIN[2], JOSEPH[1]), son of Benjamin [2] and Dorcas (Morse) Clark, was born Sept 25, 1670, in Medfield, Mass. He married [1]Rachel —— They resided in Medway Mrs Rachel Clark died Dec 1, 1717 Mr Clark married [2]Elizabeth ——

The children were DORCAS REBECCA, d Aug 13, 1718 BENJAMIN, d. Aug 24, 1716 THEOPHILUS, d Aug 28, 1716 Esther, b Jan 1, 1719 THEOPHILUS, b April 19, 1722, m. Experience Wheeler, res. in Holliston, Mass, d. Nov 24, 1760. BENJAMIN, b March 17, 1724

[5] TIMOTHY[3] CLARK (BENJAMIN[2], JOSEPH[1]), son of Benjamin [2] and Dorcas (Morse) Clark, was born May 12, 1677, in Medfield, Mass He married [1]Elizabeth ——. They resided in Medfield, afterward Medway. Mrs Elizabeth Clark died Sept 21, 1702. Mr Clark married [2]Sarah ——. Mr Clark died Aug 10, 1725

The children were JOSEPH, b. March 1, 1714. THEOPHILUS, b March 7, 1716 LYDIA, b April 11, 1719 MARIA b March 12, 1723. SILENCE, b Dec. 29 1725

[6] EDWARD[3] CLARK (BENJAMIN[2], JOSEPH[1]), son of Benjamin [2] and Dorcas (Morse) Clark, was born Nov 11, 1679, in Medfield, Mass He married June 9, 1703, Hannah Adams, daughter of Henry[3] and Prudence (Frary) Adams. She was born Oct 14, 1685 They resided in Medfield, afterward Medway. Mr Clark died July 3, 1746 Mrs Clark died Oct 27, 1775

The children were HANNAH, b July 28, 1704, m March 17, 1725, Jonathan Metcalf, *vid*, d Oct 24 1792 EDWARD, b Aug 18, 1707, d May 14, 1708 PRUDENCE, b March 16, 1709, m April 12, 1739, Joseph[3] Lovell, *vid*, d Sept. 18, 1789. PATIENCE, b May 3, 1710, m April 30 1732 Jonathan[4] Adams, *vid*, d July 11, 1801 EDWARD [8], b Nov 27 1712 DAVID [9], b April 23, 1714 BENJAMIN, b Jan. 6, 1717, d Dec 15, 1787 NATHANIEL, b March 16, 1718, d April 9, 1718. REBECCA, b Jan 21 1720, m James Knapp, d. March 23, 1786 ELIZABETH, b Oct 16, 1721, m June 21, 1743, George[4] Barber, *vid*, d July 7, 1759 SARAH b Aug 2, 1723, m Joshua Harding, d Aug 2, 1761. JOHN, b Feb 12, 1725, d Feb 15, 1801 ELIJAH [10], b Sept. 9, 1727 HENRY, b Sept 2, 1729

[7] NATHANIEL[3] CLARK (JOHN[2], JOSEPH[1]), son of John [3] and Maria (Sheffield) Clark, was born in Medfield, afterward Medway He married, June 21, 1732, Esther Whiting, daughter of Nathaniel[4] and Margaret (Mann) Whiting They resided in Medway

The children were BATHSHEBA b. June 29, 1734, unm JOHN, b Jan. 12, 1736

JEMIMA, b. Jan 10, 1738   SAMUEL, b April 30, 1739   MARY, b Jan. 12, 1740. Esther, b March 14, 1741, d. April 5, 1741   KEZIAH, b Oct 9, 1741   STEPHEN [11], b. March 21, 1743.   ESTHER, b. Oct 10, 1744, m June 8, 1769, John Gould.   WILLIAM P MIRANDA, m [1]——— Willey, m [2]——— Cobb.   CHARLES EMMA JANE, m. ——— Crother.

[8] **EDWARD⁴ CLARK** (EDWARD³, BENJAMIN², JOSEPH¹), son of Edward [6] and Hannah (Adams) Clark, was born April 23, 1714, in Medway.   He married, Jan. 5, 1735, Ann Nicholson   They resided in Medway   Deacon Clark died Feb 7, 1799

The children were   EDWARD, b Jan 25, 1736   ANN, b. Aug. 19, 1738   HANNAH, b. Dec 29, 1739   RACHEL, b Dec 9, 1741   NATHAN, b 1744   THEOPHILUS, b Jan 18, 1747   SAMUEL, b 1750   ELI, b 1752   SIMEON, b. 1754   MARY, b 1757

[9] **DAVID⁴ CLARK** (EDWARD³, BENJAMIN², JOSEPH¹), son of Edward [6] and Hannah (Adams) Clark, was born April 23, 1714, in Medway   He married Mehitable ——— They resided in Medway   Mr Clark died July 8, 1787   Mrs Clark died May 13, 1796.

The children were   DAVID, b Sept. 27, 1737   ELI, b Aug 31, 1739, d Sept 12, 1747   JONAH, b April 16, 1741   MARY, b 1743 d Sept 16, 1747   EUNICE, b 1745, m Stephen⁴ Clark, *vid*   SETH, b April 14, 1748.   MEHITABLE, b 1751   DOLLY, b. 1755.   SARAH, b 1763

[10] **ELIJAH⁴ CLARK** (EDWARD³, BENJAMIN², JOSEPH¹), son of Edward [6] and Hannah (Adams) Clark, was born Sept 9, 1727, in Medway.   He married, April 25, 1751, Bathsheba Harding, daughter of Isaac and Rachel (Hill) Harding   She was born Nov 29, 1731, in Medway, where they resided   Mr Clark died Oct 7, 1801   Mrs. Clark died Sept 14, 1819

The children were   THEODORE [12], b. April 20, 1752   EUNICE, b March 8, 1753, m June 3, 1778, Elisha Rockwood, res in Wrentham d. Sept. 28, 1838   ELIJAH, b Aug 30, 1756, m Dec 4, 1786, Julia Bullard, res. in Wendell, Mass., d May 30, 1805   HANNAH, b March 28, 1759, m Feb 2, 1786, John Metcalf, res in Wendell, Mass   JOTHAM, b Aug 23, 1761, d Feb 15, 1777.   BATHSHEBA, b. July 20, 1764, d Sept. 7, 1766.   PRUDENCE, b. July 21, 1766, m May 31, 1787, Isaac Smith, res in Holliston, Mass.   BATHSHEBA, b March 11, 1769, m Nov 7, 1793, John Littlefield, res in Hopkinton, d March 8, 1831   JOSEPH [13], b July 9, 1771.   ABIJAH, b July 24, 1775, d Sept 25, 1802

[11] **STEPHEN⁴ CLARK** (NATHANIEL³, JOHN², JOSEPH¹), son of Nathaniel [11] and Esther (Whiting) Clark, was born March 21, 1743, in Medway.   He married Eunice Clark, daughter of David⁴ and Mehitable Clark   She was born 1745, in Medway, where they resided   Mr. Clark died Jan 29, 1820

The children were   CHLOE, m. ——— Harding   JOHN [14], b June, 1769   ASENATH, b 1771, m Elkanah Haven, res in Leicester, Mass   STEPHEN, b 1776   EUNICE, b, 1779, m Ralph Mann, *vid*, d Feb 21, 1869   LEMUEL [15], b 1780   SARAH, b. 1785, m Feb 26, 1807, Joel Partridge, *vid*, d Nov 19, 1820   NATHANIEL, b 1788, m [1]———Adams, m [2]Margaret Pond, m. [3]Parmelia Pond   REBECCA, m Peres Coleman, res in Hubbardston, Mass

[12] **THEODORE⁵ CLARK** (ELIJAH⁴, EDWARD³, BENJAMIN², JOSEPH¹), son of Elijah [10] and Bathsheba (Harding) Clark, was born April 20, 1752, in Medway, Mass   He married, Nov 17, 1783, Sarah Clark, daughter of Timothy and Margaret Clark   She was born April 2, 1757, in Medway, where they resided   Mrs Clark died Dec 23, 1804   Mr Clark died Sept 16, 1827

The children were   IRENE, b May 20, 1784, m. Nov 27, 1801, Asa Ware, res in Leverett, Mass , d. May 7, 1864   JOTHAM [16], b Oct 24, 1785

[13] **JOSEPH⁵ CLARK** (ELIJAH⁴, EDWARD³, BENJAMIN², JOSEPH¹), son of Elijah [10] and Bathsheba (Harding) Clark, was born July 9, 1771, in Medway   He married, June 29, 1802, Lettice Walker, daughter of Comfort and Mehitable (Robinson) Walker   She was born Jan. 11, 1778, in Medway, where they resided   Mr Clark died July 31, 1826   Mrs Clark died Oct 3, 1836

The children were   MARIA, b Jan 1 1804, d. Sept 23, 1850.   ABIJAH [17] and ELIJAH [18], b Jan 28, 1806   SARAH ATHERTON, b Jan. 31, 1809, m. April 15, 1840, Ferdinand Fiske, res in Holliston, Mass   PRUDENCE, b July 6, 1811 m Aug 15, 1835, William Fuller   CALEB WALKER, b July 1, 1814, res in Carbondale, Ill   LOUISA, b July 7, 1816, d Nov 25, 1863 CHARLES TURNER, b. June 21, 1819, m Feb 5, 1842, Prudence Ann Crippin, res in Cincinnati, O AMY WALKER, b. Jan. 9, 1823, m Nov. 28, 1844, [1]Cyrus Warren ; m April 5, 1850, [2]Dea Martin Fletcher, res in Milford, Mass ; m. Dec 8, 1859, [3]Warren Miller, Esq , res in Holliston, Mass

[14] JOHN[5] CLARK (STEPHEN[4], NATHANIEL[3], JOHN[2], JOSEPH[1]), son of Stephen [11] and Eunice (Clark) Clark, was born June, 1769, in Medway He married [1]Sybil Penniman, daughter of James and Abigail (Clark) Penniman. She was born 1770, in Medway, where they resided Mrs Sybil Clark died March 29, 1840. Mr Clark married, March 5, 1855, [2]Polly Hammond. Mr. Clark died April 1, 1850. Mrs. Polly Clark died Nov 22, 1862.

The children were. JAMES PENNIMAN [19], b Dec 6, 1803 CHLOE, m. Oct. 3, 1831, Everett Clark.

[15] LEMUEL[5] CLARK (STEPHEN[4], NATHANIEL[3], JOHN[2], JOSEPH[1]), son of Stephen [11] and Eunice (Clark) Clark, was born 1780, in Medway He married Deborah Eliza Newton. She was born in Framingham, Mass They resided in Medway.

The children were. DAVID [20], b May 17, 1807. SARAH, b Oct 22, 1810, d. Oct. 27, 1857. ELBRIDGE [21], b. Sept. 11, 1812. JOHN [22], b Oct 2, 1816

[16] JOTHAM[6] CLARK (THEODORE[5], ELIJAH[4], EDWARD[3], BENJAMIN[2], JOSEPH[1]), son of Theodore [12] and Sarah (Clark) Clark, was born Oct. 24, 1785, in Medway He married, Dec 22, 1814, Eunice Rockwood, daughter of Elisha and Eunice (Clark) Rockwood. She was born June 14, 1793, in Wrentham, now Norfolk, Mass. They resided in Medway. Mr Clark died Sept 5, 1845. Mrs. Clark died Dec. 26, 1868.

The children (adopted) were AMY WALKER CLARK, b Jan. 9, 1823, daughter of Joseph and Lettice (Walker) Clark ISRAEL PUTNAM RICHARDSON, son of Oliver and Mrs Mary Stedman (Carroll) Richardson, *née* Fairbanks, b June 6, 1831 He took the name of PUTNAM RICHARDSON CLARK [23]. LOUISE ELIZABETH BANCROFT, m. 1860, Moses Cohen

[17] ABIJAH[6] CLARK (JOSEPH[5], ELIJAH[4], EDWARD[3], BENJAMIN[2], JOSEPH[1]), son of Joseph [13] and Lettice (Walker) Clark was born Jan. 28, 1806, in Medway He married, April 13, 1834, Anna Calista Sayles, daughter of Richard and Betsey Sayles. She was born March 1, 1810, in Wrentham, Mass. They resided in Rockville, Medway. Mrs Clark died July 18, 1880.

The children were. GEORGE EDMUND, b. Dec 26, 1834, m April 29, 1867, Eliza J. Walker, res in Cobden, Ill. ADELAIDE AUGUSTA, b June 4, 1842 CHARLES TURNER, b. Aug 26, 1844, d. Sept 14, 1844

[18] ELIJAH[6] CLARK (JOSEPH[5], ELIJAH[4], EDWARD[3], BENJAMIN[2], JOSEPH[1]), son of Joseph [13] and Lettice (Walker) Clark, was born Jan 28, 1806, in Medway. He married, Oct 8, 1835, [1]Mary Ann Kingsbury She was born May 25, 1813, in Franklin, Mass They resided in Rockville, Medway. Mrs Clark died Feb. 14, 1852 Mr Clark married, June 10, 1854, [2]Elizabeth Adams She was born June 11, 1812, in Medfield, Mass.

The children were MARY JANE, b Nov 22, 1837, d Aug 21, 1843. ELLEN MARIA, b Sept 9, 1840, d Dec. 10, 1875 SARAH FRANCES, b. Jan. 20, 1845 LOWELL ADDISON, b June 7, 1847, d Sept. 6, 1847. WILLIE EUGENE, b. April 22, 1850, d Aug 27, 1850.

[19] JAMES PENNIMAN[6] CLARK (JOHN[5], STEPHEN[4], NATHANIEL[3], JOHN[2], JOSEPH[1]), son of John [14] and Sybil (Penniman) Clark, was born Dec 6, 1803, in East Medway He married, Oct. 20, 1829, Maria Frost, daughter of William and Sarah Frost. She was born Sept 30, 1805, in Billerica, Mass Mr Clark died Sept 6, 1865. Mrs. Clark died May 14, 1883. They resided in East Medway.

The children were WILLARD PENNIMAN [24], b Dec 24, 1830 JAMES WARREN [25], b. Aug 3, 1837.

[20] DAVID[6] CLARK (LEMUEL[5], STEPHEN[4], NATHANIEL[3], JOHN[2], JOSEPH[1]), son of Lemuel [15] and Deborah Eliza (Newton) Clark, was born May 17, 1807, in East Medway. He married, Nov. 25, 1828, Huldah Barton, daughter of Caleb and Betsey (Lamb) Barton. They resided in East Medway Mrs. Huldah Clark died Nov 5, 1844. Mr Clark married [2]Harriet Danforth. Mrs. Harriet Clark died July, 1866 Mr. Clark married, Nov. 26, 1866, [3]Mrs Harriet Martha Lowe, *née* Mann,

32

daughter of Timothy and Susan (Doane) Mann, and widow of Samuel H. Lowe, of Fitchburg, Mass. She was born in West Medway.

The children were: DEBORAH ELIZA, b. March 4, 1830, m. James Fisher. ELIZABETH LAMB, m. Oliver Barber, res. in Sherborn, Mass. IRVING L., b. 1846, d. Nov. 4, 1854.

[21] **ELBRIDGE**[6] **CLARK** (LEMUEL[5], STEPHEN,[4] NATHANIEL[3], JOHN[2], JOSEPH[1]), son of Lemuel [15] and Deborah Eliza (Newton) Clark, was born Sept. 11, 1812, in East Medway. He married, November, 1835, [1]Lydia Church Newton, daughter of Ezra and Lydia (Howe) Newton. She was born July 18, 1814, in Princeton, Mass. They resided in East Medway. Mrs. Lydia Church Clark died May 31, 1869. Deacon Clark married, Nov. 30, 1871, [2]Mary Elizabeth Mansfield, daughter of John and Harriet (Rhodes) Mansfield. She was born Aug. 19, 1827, in Lynn, Mass.

The children were: MARY OPHELIA, d. June 6, 1843. EDMUND NEWTON [26], b. Aug. 19, 1840. LUCY JANE, m. Alvah Stone, res. in Medina, Mich. MARTHA OPHELIA. HARRIET LYDIA, m. Leander Day, res. in Taunton, Mass. ELBRIDGE WILLIAM, b. 1850, d. January, 1851. LEMUEL, b. Feb. 6, 1858.

[22] **JOHN**[6] **CLARK** (LEMUEL[5], STEPHEN[4], NATHANIEL[3], JOHN[2], JOSEPH[1]), son of Lemuel [15] and Deborah Eliza (Newton) Clark, was born Oct. 2, 1816, in East Medway. He married, May 24, 1837, [1]Marietta M. Thompson. They resided in East Medway. Mrs. Marietta M. Clark died Dec. 2, 1881. Mr. Clark married, March 8, 1883, [2]Abbie L. Russell. She was born in Medfield, Mass.

The children were: ALBERT L., b. May 27, 1838, m. Harriet Rice, res. in Franklin, Mass. JOHN ADDISON, b. Feb. 12, 1840, d. Feb. 19, 1842. SARAH LOUISA, b. Nov. 10, 1841, m. George B. Fisher, *vid.* DAVID ADDISON, b. Oct. 9, 1843, m. Rose Roberts, res. in Boston, Mass. FREDERIC FRANCIS, b. June 6, 1846, m. March 15, 1877, Florence E. Collins, res. in Philadelphia, Penn. RHODA ISABELLA, b. July 22, 1848, m. June 17, 1873, Charles Hamant Russell, res. in Medfield, Mass. JOHN EDWARDS, b. Sept. 16, 1850, d. July 1, 1854. MARY ADELINE, b. Dec. 17, 1852, m. Nov. 5, 1872, William Francis Harding, res. in Medfield, Mass. JENNIE MARIA, b. July 28, 1855, m. Sept. 24, 1874, Daniel Adams. ABBIE ELIZA, b. March 3, 1858, m. June 27, 1877, Francis Herbert Russell, res. in Boston, Mass. CARRIE F., b. Sept. 4, 1859, m. June 21, 1882, George R. Hill, d. July 25, 1884.

THE OLD CLARK HOMESTEAD.

THE RESIDENCE OF MR. PUTNAM R. CLARK.

[23] **PUTNAM RICHARDSON**[7] **CLARK** (JOTHAM[6], THEODORE[5], ELIJAH[4], EDWARD[3], BENJAMIN[2], JOSEPH[1]), son of Oliver and Mrs. Mary Stedman (Carroll) Richardson, *née* Fairbanks, and adopted son of Jotham [16] and Eunice (Rockwood) Clark, was born June 6, 1831, in East Medway. He married, March, 1852, Mary B. Perrigo, daughter of David and Hannah (Clark) Perrigo. They resided in East Medway.

The children were: OLIVER JOTHAM, b. Feb. 2, 1853, m. June, 1875, Alice S. Boos.

MARY JOANNA, b. Jan 1, 1855, m July 4, 1872, E F Plummer MARTIN FLETCHER, b Feb 11, 1857, d March 28, 1864 PUTNAM [27], b. Oct. 23, 1859. AMY JOSEPHINE, b Dec. 26, 1862, m July 21, 1883, Harry D. Hodges. FRANK R., b Oct. 27, 1869

[24] WILLARD PENNIMAN[7] CLARK (JAMES PENNIMAN[6], JOHN[5], STEPHEN[4], NATHANIEL[3], JOHN[2], JOSEPH[1]), son of James Penniman [19] and Maria (Frost) Clark, was born Dec. 24, 1830, in East Medway He married, Nov 8, 1854, [1]Susan Billings. She was born in Walpole, Mass They resided in East Medway Mrs Susan Clark died Nov 9, 1860 Mr Clark married, Nov 21, 1861, [2]Abbie Richardson Lovell, daughter of Asahel Plympton and Eliza (Stedman) Lovell She was born Aug. 26, 1834, in East Medway

The children were: JENNIE MARIA, b. May 6 1863 JOHN F, b. Aug. 11, 1868

[25] JAMES WARREN[7] CLARK (JAMES PENNIMAN[6], JOHN[5], STEPHEN[4], NATHANIEL[3], JOHN[2], JOSEPH[1]), son of James Penniman [19] and Maria (Frost) Clark, was born Aug. 3, 1837, in East Medway. He married, April 22, 1866, Lucinda Amelia Wallace, daughter of Ira and Keziah (Southwick) Wallace She was born in Dalton, N. H. They resided in East Medway

The only child was MARY A, b Nov 24, 1868

[26] EDMUND NEWTON[7] CLARK (ELBRIDGE[6], LEMUEL[5], STEPHEN[4], NATHANIEL[3], JOHN[2], JOSEPH[1]), son of Dea Elbridge [21] and Lydia Church (Newton) Clark, was born Aug 19, 1840, in East Medway He married, Jan 9, 1864, Tryphena Fisher, daughter of Lewis and Betsey (Richardson) Fisher. She was born Jan 17, 1841, in East Medway, where they resided.

The children were ERNEST NEWTON, b. Oct 8, 1868. ELSIE LYDIA, b Jan. 28, 1870. BETSEY FISHER, b Aug 25, 1871 ARTHUR LEWIS, b Feb 19, 1873, d. June 8, 1873 IRVING RICHARDSON, b Oct 24, 1874 FANNIE LOUISE, b Oct. 23, 1876

[27] PUTNAM[8] CLARK (PUTNAM RICHARDSON[7], JOTHAM[6], THEODORE[5], ELIJAH[4], EDWARD[3], BENJAMIN[2], JOSEPH[1]), son of Putnam Richardson [23] and Mary B. (Perrigo) Clark, was born Oct 23, 1859, in East Medway He married, June 7, 1883. Mary Eliza Lovell, daughter of Asahel Francis and Olive A. (Hartshorn) Lovell She was born March 1, 1864, in East Medway, where they reside

The only child was: SUMNER RICHARDSON, b June 2, 1884

SEWALL J. CLARK (AMOS, JOHN, ASA), son of Amos and Luthera (Johnson) Clark, was born Sept 27, 1827, in West Medway He married, April 30, 1856, Louisa Rice, daughter of Hollis and Nancy (Abbe) Rice They resided in West Medway.

The children were: EDMUND SEWALL, b June 21, 1857 CARRIE LOUISE, b. Jan. 7, 1862, m Dec. 21, 1881, Charles M Smith. FREDDIE H., b Sept. 5, 1868, d. May 15, 1872.

Memoranda. Mrs. Luthera (Johnson) Clark, a daughter of Benjamin and Esther Johnson, was born Feb. 21, 1803, in Hallowell, Me. Mr and Mrs. Charles M Smith have one child, Marion Louise, b Sept 6, 1882

JOHN CRAIG CLARK was born in Oakham, Mass. He married [1]Eliza Ann Henderson, daughter of Luther and Sylvia E Henderson They resided in Medway. Mrs. Eliza Ann Clark died Mr Clark married, May 11, 1843, [2]Betsey Daniels, daughter of Japheth[6] and Betsey (Ryder) Daniels She was born Sept 15, 1817, in West Medway

The children were. ALBERT H, m Lizzie McCaim WARREN A, m Ruth A Pond ERASTUS O, m. Lydia Armington ALICE C, m William H Rawson EMMA F.

JAMES W. CLARK (PETER, ASHERTON C., JOHN C, JOHN, HUGH), son of Peter and Elizabeth (Wilson) Clark, was born April 13, 1802, in Hopkinton, Mass He married, Feb 14 1828, [1]Mary Ann Barber, daughter of George and Lois (Whiting) Barber She was born Sept 9, 1806, in Medway. They resided in Medway, and in Boston, Mass Mrs Mary Ann Clark died Sept. 11, 1834 Mr Clark married, March 24, 1842, [2]Catharine Monroe March, daughter of Dr David and Catharine (Monroe) March. She was born in Sutton, Mass. They resided in Boston, Mass., until 1842, when they removed to Framingham, Mass., where they reside

The children were GEORGE BARBER, b Jan 15, 1833, d March 30, 1837. EDMUND SANFORD, b. May 1, 1843, m April 15, 1869, Mary Brainard. CATHARINE ELIZABETH, b July 23, 1844, d. Dec 15, 1849 EMILY J., b Dec 15, 1846, m April 3, 1872, Charles Dudley Lewis. FRANCES AUGUSTA, b. Sept. 12, 1848, d Feb 27, 1858

JAMES WILSON, b. Aug. 31, 1850, m. Jan. 16, 1873, Sibyl C. Fay. ARTHUR MARCH, b. Aug. 3, 1853.

Memoranda. Mr. James W. Clark was a resident of Medway for a period of about ten years, between 1819 and 1829, and was personally acquainted with many of the business men of that period, who afterward went elsewhere and became prominent, especially in the line of manufactures. Mr. Clark was a merchant in Boston, and became a man of large business and wealth. At the age of eighty-three years he was hale and sprightly, going to his counting-room daily, from Framingham to Boston.

ISRAEL F. CLIFFORD was born Aug. 24, 1834. He married, Jan. 1, 1862, Clara K. ———. They resided in East Medway.

The children were: SAMUEL A., b. Jan. 14, 1864, d. April 6, 1883. INEZ R., b. Nov. 4, 1866. FANNIE C., b. March 29, 1872.

[1] JOHN MARTIN CRANE (SILAS AXTELL, BENJAMIN, BERNICE, BENJAMIN), son of the Rev. Dr. Silas Axtell and Mary Elizabeth (Martin) Crane, was born May 24, 1829, in Providence, R. I. He married, Oct. 24, 1855, ¹Laura Matilda Henshaw, daughter of Charles and Matilda (Child) Henshaw. She was born April 15, 1819, in North Brookfield, Mass. They resided in Bainbridge, Ind., in Davenport, Ia., and in Medway. Mrs. Laura M. Crane died April 13, 1882. Mr. Crane married, Sept. 8, 1884, Caroline Strong Cogswell, daughter of the Rev. Dr. William and Joanna (Strong) Cogswell. She was born June 3, 1840, in Boston, Mass.

The children were: CHARLES HENSHAW, b. Aug. 30, 1857, d. May 1, 1862. HENRY AXTELL [2], b. Oct. 30, 1858. CLARENCE MITCHELL, b. June 7, 1862, in Northboro, Mass., m. Oct. 29, 1885, Bertha C. Bissett, res. in Sherborn, Mass.

[2] HENRY AXTELL CRANE (JOHN MARTIN, SILAS AXTELL, BENJAMIN, BERNICE, BENJAMIN), son of John Martin [1] and Laura M. (Henshaw) Crane, was born Oct. 30, 1858, in Bainbridge, Ind. He married, May 29, 1879, Ida Louise Mason, daughter of George E. and Lizzie M. (Foster) Mason. She was born Nov. 8, 1858. They resided in Natick, and in Sherborn, Mass.

The children were: ALICE MASON, b. June 27, 1881. LAURA HENSHAW, b. Sept. 25, 1882.

RICE O. DAIN, son of John and Sarah (Livingston) Dain, was born June 7, 1805, in New York. He married, May 3, 1828, Mary Durfee, daughter of Rufus and Clarissa (Perkins) Durfee. She was born April 18, 1806, in Royalton, Vt. They resided in Medway.

The children were: MARY J., b. Oct. 4, 1829, m. April 4, 1849, Dennison D. Dodge, d. Jan. 1, 1850. HENRY R., b. Feb. 2, 1831, m. Jan. 14, 1853, Susan Walker, of Canada; d. Sept. 14, 1864. ELIZABETH L., b. Dec. 27, 1832, m. Feb. 14, 1853, Robert O. Young, *vid.* CLARISSA M., b. Oct. 8, 1834, m. Oct. 4, 1853, Alfred Pond. LUCY W., b. June 21, 1837, m. May 17, 1856, Edmund L. Hill, d. Nov. 12, 1873. CAROLINE C., b. March 11, 1840, d. March 14, 1840. FRANCIS E., b. March 20, 1841, d. July 24, 1842. ALONZO M., b. Sept. 18, 1845.

DANIELS, in England and in the early history of this country, was spelled Daniell. In the *Encyclopædia of Heraldry* it occurs thirty-two times, and is spelled twenty-six times Daniell, five times Daniel, and but once Daniels. The persons earliest in America of this name were Robert Daniell, of Watertown, Mass., in 1636; William Daniell, of Dorchester, in 1648; and Joseph Daniell, of Medfield, in 1649. Their descendants down to a comparatively recent date, and in some lines to the present time, as appears by their autographs, have spelled the name Daniell. But the Medway branch of the family, for some years, have generally spelled the name Daniels, although the late Dea. Paul Daniell used the ancient spelling to his death, which occurred in 1876.

ROBERT DANIELL, the great ancestor of those of the Daniels name in Medway, came from England prior to 1636, and settled in Watertown, Mass. He was grantee of five lots, and purchased the "homestall" of Nicholas Jacobs, consisting of thirteen acres of land, situated not far from the present site of the United States Arsenal. He was admitted freeman March 14, 1639, in Watertown, Mass. His wife, Mrs. Elizabeth Daniell, died Oct. 2, 1643. In 1651 Mr. Daniell removed to Cambridge, Mass He married, May 2, 1654, [2]Reana Andrews Mr. Daniell died July 6, 1655.

The children were ELIZABETH, b. 1630, m. May 17, 1655, Thomas Fanning, d. Jan 27, 1722. SAMUEL, b about 1633, m May 10, 1671, Mary Grant, res in Medfield, Mass , d. 1695. *Vid The Daniell Family by Moses Grant Daniell, A M , of Boston, Mass* JOSEPH [1], b. about 1635 SARAH, b about 1640. MARY, b. Sept. 2, 1642, m June 14, 1660, Samson Frary, res. in Medfield, Mass.

[1] JOSEPH[2] DANIELL (ROBERT[1]), son of Robert and Elizabeth Daniell, was born about 1635, in Watertown, Mass He married, Nov 16, 1665, [1]Mary Fairbanks, daughter of George and Mary (Adams) Fairbanks She was born Sept. 10, 1647, in Dedham, Mass. They resided in Medfield, now Millis, Mass. Mrs Mary Daniell died June 9, 1682 Mr. Daniell married [2]Rachel Sheffield, daughter of William and Mary Sheffield. She was born March 24, 1660, in Braintree, Mass. Mrs Rachel Daniell died May 3, 1687. Mr Daniell married [3]Mrs Lydia Allen, *née* Adams, daughter of Edward[2] and Lydia Adams, and widow of James Allen. She was born in 1653, in Medfield. Mr Daniell died June 23, 1715, and Mrs Lydia Daniell died Dec. 26, 1731.

The children were JOSEPH [2], b. Sept 23, 1666 MARY, b July 14, 1669 SAMUEL, b Oct 30, 1671, m. 1694, Deborah Ford MEHITABLE, b July 10, 1674, d June 3, 1686 EBENEZER [3], b. April 24, 1677 ELIZABETH, b March 9, 1679, m. Joseph Mason, res. in Medfield, Mass. JEREMIAH, b. March 17, 1680, d June 16, 1680 ELEAZAR, b. March 9, 1681, res. in Mendon, Mass. JEREMIAH [4], b. Nov 3, 1684 RACHEL, b Oct 17, 1686 ZACHARIAH, b April 9, 1689, d May 2, 1689.

[2] JOSEPH[3] DANIELL (JOSEPH[2], ROBERT[1]), son of Joseph [1] and Mary (Fairbanks) Daniell, was born Sept 23, 1666, in Medfield, now Millis, Mass. He married [1]Rachel Partridge, daughter of John and Magdalen (Bullard) Partridge She was born in 1669 in Medfield, now Millis, Mass , where they resided. Mrs Rachel Daniell died. Mr. Daniell married [2]Bethia Breck, daughter of Thomas and Mary (Hill) Breck She was born Dec 20, 1673, in Sherborn, Mass Mr Daniell died Jan 14, 1739. Mrs. Bethia Daniell died Feb 3, 1754.

The children were SAMUEL [5], b Dec 25, 1693 JOSEPH [6], b. Dec 15, 1695 DAVID [7], b Feb. 21, 1698-9. HANNAH, b Sept 30, 1701, m Oct 27, 1725, Eleazar Thompson, *vid.* EZRA [8], b. March 10, 1704 SARAH, b May 1, 1707, m. Feb. 20, 1733, John Bullard, *vid* ABIGAIL, b March 15, 1715, d Dec. 14, 1718 TAMAR, b. March 17, 1717, m December, 1733, John Metcalf.

[3] EBENEZER[3] DANIELL (JOSEPH[2], ROBERT[1]), son of Joseph [1] and Mary (Fairbanks) Daniell, was born April 24, 1677, in Medfield, now Millis, Mass. He married, Dec 22, 1701, [1]Elizabeth Partridge, daughter of John and Elizabeth (Rockwood) Partridge. She was born in 1679 in Medfield, now Millis, Mass , where they resided Mrs. Elizabeth Daniell died April 25, 1706. Mr Daniell married [2]Mary Partridge, daughter of John and Elizabeth (Rockwood) Partridge. She was born in 1681, in Medfield, now Millis, Mass Mrs Mary Daniell died Jan. 20, 1725

The children were ELIZABETH, b Jan. 19, 1703 TRYPHENA, b June 12, 1704 MARY, b April 13, 1706 PHEBE, b Sept 5, 1709. MEHITABLE, b. Sept. 5, 1709. EBENEZER, b July 5, 1711. THANKFUL, b July 3, 1715 JEREMIAH [10], b Sept. 22, 1720 MOSES, b Jan 16, 1725, m Nov 4, 1751, Sarah Gould

[4] JEREMIAH[3] DANIELL (JOSEPH[2], ROBERT[1]), son of Joseph [1] and Rachel (Sheffield) Daniell, was born Nov 3, 1684, in Medfield. He married, May 7, 1713, [1]Hannah Partridge, daughter of John[2] and Elizabeth (Adams) Partridge. She was born in 1696, in Medfield, now Millis, Mass , where they resided Mrs Hannah Daniell died Oct 12, 1751. Mr. Daniell married, Jan 7, 1754, [2]Mrs Mehitable Wilson. Mr Daniell died Nov. 16, 1771, and Mrs. Mehitable Daniell died Oct 8, 1780

The children were. RACHEL, b Oct 30, 1714, m Elisha Adams, *vid* JEREMIAH [11], b. Sept 30, 1754. HANNAH, b. 1756, m. 1780, Amos Lawrence, res in Union, Me.

[5] SAMUEL[4] DANIELL (JOSEPH[3], JOSEPH[2], ROBERT[1]), son of Joseph [2] and Rachel (Partridge) Daniell, was born Dec 25, 1693, in Medfield, Mass. He married,

Dec. 6, 1718, [1]Experience Adams, daughter of Dea Peter[3] and Experience (Cook) Adams She was born 1696, in Medfield, Mass, afterward Medway, where they resided. Mrs Experience Daniell died March 29, 1731. Mr. Daniell married, Feb. 20, 1733, [2]Sarah Phipps, daughter of John Phipps She was born in Wrentham, Mass Her father was nephew and adopted son of Sir William Phipps, of London, England Mr. Daniell died 1789

The children were SAMUEL, b June 8, 1720, m Jan 7, 1743, Hannah Hill, res in Keene, N H. TIMOTHY, b Sept 6, 1722, m. Feb 6, 1754, Ruth Leland, res in Sherborn, Mass NATHAN [12], b Aug 20, 1727. JOHN [13], b Aug. 18, 1728 SIMEON, b. March 8, 1730-1, m April 9, 1754, Lydia Adams, res. in Franklin, Mass REUBEN, b Nov. 25, 1733, d Feb. 26, 1734 SARAH, b Jan 10, 1734-5, m. March 2, 1758, Timothy Force MARY, b April 23, 1736, m July 5, 1764, Jonathan Wiswell JAPHETH [14], b Feb 17, 1738, m March 17, Melatiah Hayward, res in Holliston, Mass, d March 3, 1805 ABIJAH, b July 27, 1740, m 1774, Hannah Dix, res in Milford, Mass

[6] JOSEPH[4] DANIELL (JOSEPH[3], JOSEPH[2], ROBERT[1]), son of Joseph [2] and Rachel (Partridge) Daniell, was born Dec 15, 1695, in Medfield, Mass. He married, Jan 28, 1726, Elizabeth Groce They resided in Medway. Mr. Daniell died May 23, 1751 Mrs Elizabeth Daniell married Samuel Holbrook, of Sherborn, Mass

The children were ASA [15], b Dec. 10, 1726 MOLLY, b Nov 7, 1729, d. Dec 30, 1729 JEMIMA, b Jan 25, 1731, m May 16, 1750, William Leland, res in Sherborn, Mass JOSEPH [16], b June 25, 1736 ELIZABETH, b. Jan. 3, 1742

[7] DAVID[4] DANIELL (JOSEPH[3], JOSEPH[2], ROBERT[1]), son of Joseph [2] and Rachel (Partridge) Daniell, was born Feb 21, 1698-9, in Medfield, Mass. He married Magdalen Partridge, daughter of Zechariah[2] and Elizabeth Partridge She was born Feb. 4, 1704, in Medfield, Mass They resided in West Medway, and about 1740 removed to West Wrentham, now Franklin, Mass. They both died about 1783

The children were HENRY, b May 8, 1731 SETH, b Oct 30, 1737, m Unity Thurston. ABIGAIL, b about 1740

Memoranda. David[4] Daniels [7] was the great great-grandfather of Waldo Daniels, Esq, of Franklin, Mass

[8] EZRA[4] DANIELL (JOSEPH[3], JOSEPH[2], ROBERT[1]), son of Joseph [2] and Rachel (Partridge) Daniell, was born March 10, 1673-4, in Medfield, Mass He married, Nov 8, 1726, Martha Death She was born in Sherborn, Mass. They resided in East Medway. Mr Daniell died June 8, 1778

The children were JEREMIAH, b May 6, 1727, d Sept 10, 1727 AARON [17], b March 2, 1728-9. SARAH, b Dec 10, 1731, d Oct. 7, 1745 ZILPHA, b Nov 19, 1734, m John Adams, *vid* MOSES [18], b Feb 8, 1736 LYDIA, b Jan 8, 1742, m Dea Asa Daniell, d Dec. 31, 1828 MARTHA, b Sept 30, 1744, d. Jan 25, 1754

[9] HENRY[4] DANIELL (JOSEPH[2], ROBERT[1]), grandson of Joseph [1] and Mary (Fairbanks) Daniell, was born 1708, in Medfield, now Millis, Mass. He married, 1733, Hannah Bullard, daughter of John[3] and Abigail (Leland) Bullard She was born May 12, 1714, in East Medway, where they resided Mrs. Daniell died March 27, 1792. Mr. Daniell died Nov. 28, 1806

The children were ABIGAIL, b April 17, 1734, d Aug. 15, 1740 RACHEL, b May 12, 1738, m Joseph Curtis, d March 4, 1810 HENRY [19], b Jan. 12, 1740 JESSE, b Nov. 24 1741, d July 23, 1756 ELIJAH, b Jan. 29 1747, d June 25, 1756 JEREMIAH, b. Nov 12, 1748, d March, 1753 ABIGAIL, b May 25, 1750. d. June 29, 1756 HANNAH, b July 1, 1756.

[10] JEREMIAH[4] DANIELL (EBENEZER[3], JOSEPH[2], ROBERT[1]), son of Ebenezer [3] and Mary (Partridge) Daniell, was born Sept. 22, 1720, in East Medway He married, Dec. 22, 1742, Mercy Clark, daughter of Timothy Clark She was born in Medway, where they resided Mr Daniell died May, 1806 Mrs Mercy Daniell died aged 93 years

The children were LYDIA, bapt April 17, 1743, m Henry Ellis, *vid* ISAIAH [20], bapt. April 2, 1744 MARY, bapt Sept 3, 1749, m Francis Hammond MERCY, b Dec 16, 1755, m 1772, Abijah[5] Richardson, M D, *vid*, d March 2, 1854 ABIGAIL, bapt July 30, 1758, m 1774, Moses[5] Richardson, *vid*

[11] JEREMIAH[4] DANIELL (JEREMIAH[3], JOSEPH[2], ROBERT[1]), son of Jeremiah [4] and Mehitable (Wilson) Daniell, was born Sept 30, 1754, in East Medway

He married, 1785, Pearlee Richardson, daughter of Moses[4] and Abigail (Allen) Richardson She was born July 17, 1758, in East Medway, where they resided. Mrs. Daniell died June 18, 1829 Mr Daniell died May 5, 1830.

The children were TIMOTHY, b Nov 7, 1785, m Ruth Death, res in Sherborn, Mass. ELEAZAR [21], b. Jan 30, 1788   PAUL [22], b July 17, 1789

[12] NATHAN[5] DANIELL (SAMUEL[4], JOSEPH[3], JOSEPH[2], ROBERT[1]), son of Samuel [5] and Experience (Adams) Daniell, was born Aug. 20, 1727, in East Medway. He married, March 17, 1746, Mary Adams, daughter of Jonathan[4] and Dorcas Adams She was born May 6, 1722, in East Medway. They removed to Franklin, Mass. Mrs Mary Daniels died Nov. 10, 1772   Mr Daniels died 1789.

The children were· NAPHTALI, b June 21, 1747. NATHAN [23], b July 12, 1748 ZEPHENIAH, b May 6, 1750, d March 8, 1754. SILAS, b Jan 11, 1752, d Sept 10, 1755. BENONI, b Nov. 5, 1754. ADAMS, b Sept 4, 1757, m Mary Smith, res. in Medfield, Mass ; d. 1804 SETH, b. July 3, 1760, d July 5, 1760. MARY, b Dec. 18, 1761. SILENCE, b. Aug 28, 1766

[13] JOHN[5] DANIELL (SAMUEL[4], JOSEPH[3], JOSEPH[2], ROBERT[1]), son of Samuel [5] and Sarah (Phipps) Daniell, was born Aug. 11, 1728, in East Medway. He married, June 6, 1753, Elizabeth Keith   They resided in East Medway, and prior to 1767, removed to Keene, N H

The children were RHODA, b March 4, 1754   JOHN, b Jan 4, 1755, d May 7, 1767. JAMES, b. April 16, 1761, d April 25, 1814. EZRA, b Jan 25, 1767. SAMUEL, b. March 31, 1770 SULLIVAN, b April 8, 1776

[14] JAPHETH[5] DANIELL (SAMUEL[4], JOSEPH[3], JOSEPH[2], ROBERT[1]), son of Samuel [5] and Sarah (Phipps) Daniell, was born Feb 17, 1738, in Medway He married, March 17, 1763, Melatiah Hayward She was born in Bellingham, Mass. They resided in Holliston, Mass Mrs. Daniell died March 11, 1797 Captain Daniell died March 3, 1805

The children were : CYNTHIA, b May 17, 1765, m May 9, 1780, Nathan Hayward ONESIMUS, b December, 1768. AMASIAH, b Nov 28, 1770, m Olive Ryder JAPHETH [24], b Aug 14, 1777 MELATIAH, b Nov 2, 1779

[15] ASA[5] DANIELL (JOSEPH[4], JOSEPH[3], JOSEPH[2], ROBERT[1]), son of Joseph [6] and Elizabeth (Groce) Daniell, was born Dec. 10, 1726, in East Medway. He married, May 20, 1752, [1]Bathsheba Fairbanks, daughter of George and Sarah (Harding) Fairbanks. She was born Oct. 7, 1724, in East Medway, where they resided. Mrs Bathsheba Daniell died Nov 25, 1774   Deacon Daniell married [2]Lydia Daniell, daughter of Ezra [8] and Martha (Death) Daniell. She was born Jan. 8, 1742 Deacon Daniell died Oct 18, 1815. Mrs Lydia Daniell died Dec 31, 1828

The children were ASA [25], b. May 6, 1753 LEVI [26], b Sept 30, 1755 DAVID, b. Nov 25, 1757, m ——— Shillaber, res in Danvers, Mass. JESSE [27], b April 10, 1760 BATHSHEBA, b. April 6, 1763, m Nov 9, 1785, Jeduthan Bullen, *vid.*

[16] JOSEPH[5] DANIELL (JOSEPH[4], JOSEPH[3], JOSEPH[2], ROBERT[1]), son of Joseph [6] and Elizabeth (Groce) Daniell, was born June 25, 1736, in East Medway He married, Feb. 3, 1757, [1]Deborah Keith. They resided in East Medway Mrs Deborah Daniell died Captain Daniell married [2]Sarah Learned Captain Daniell died Oct 16, 1823.

The children were : JOSEPH, b Dec 23, 1757, m. Thankful Penniman, res. in Worcester, Mass. LEMUEL [28], b Feb 9, 1759 BEULAH, b May 7, 1760, m May 6, 1778, Jotham Fairbanks, *vid.* ISRAEL [29], b June 19, 1763 NOAH [30], b 1770.

[17] AARON[5] DANIELS (EZRA[4], JOSEPH[3], JOSEPH[2], ROBERT[1]). son of Ezra [8] and Martha (Death) Daniell, was born March 2, 1728-9, in Medway He married, Feb. 25, 1753, Keziah Holbrook, daughter of Samuel and Keziah (Morse) Holbrook. She was born Aug 23, 1729 Mr Daniels died Jan 27, 1754, less than a year after the marriage at the age of twenty-four years

The only child was KEZIAH, b Dec 25, 1753, m Jonathan Hill, *vid.*

[18] MOSES[5] DANIELS (EZRA[4], JOSEPH[3], JOSEPH[2], ROBERT[1]), son of Ezra [8] and Martha (Death) Daniels, was born Feb 8, 1736, in East Medway He married Abigail Adams She was born in East Medway, where they resided Mr Daniels died Oct 20, 1800 He was drowned attempting to shut the water-gate at the upper mill on Boggastow Brook Mrs Daniels died Jan 1, 1822

The children were MOSES, b May 27, 1767, d Oct 20, 1767. ABIGAIL, b 1768, m Feb 21, 1791, Silas[5] Richardson, res in Leominster, Mass. LAVINIA, b Oct 15, 1770, d Nov 1, 1773 SARAH, b Jan 12, 1772 AMOS [31], b April 20, 1773 ELIAS [32], b Jan 11, 1775 LAVINIA, b. Jan 16, 1777, m [1]Israel Daniels, *vid.*, m Nov. 15, 1827, [2]Ezra Richardson, *vid* OBED, b Nov 28, 1778, res in Framingham, Mass EZRA [33], b Nov 24, 1780 MOSES [34], b. Oct 1, 1782 CATY, b Oct 30, 1784, m. April 27, 1808, Michael Lovell, *vid* OLIVE, b Nov 16, 1787, m. Sept. 27, 1808, Thomas Lawrence, res in Leominster, Mass

[19] HENRY[5] DANIELS (HENRY[4], JOSEPH[2], ROBERT[1]), son of Henry [9] and Hannah (Bullard) Daniell, was born Jan. 12, 1740, in East Medway He married Elizabeth Harding She was born 1745 They resided in East Medway. Mr. Daniels died Nov 11, 1815 Mrs Daniels died Jan 30, 1829

The children were PATIENCE, b March 15, 1768, m Silas[6] Adams, *vid* , d Nov 9, 1815 ELIZABETH, b Nov 18, 1770, m Zebina Kingsbury, d Aug 1, 1816 SABEN [35], b Nov 29, 1774

[20] ISAIAH[5] DANIELS (JEREMIAH[4], EBENEZER[3], JOSEPH[2], ROBERT[1]), son of Jeremiah [10] and Mercy (Clark) Daniell, was born April 18, 1745, in East Medway He married, 1768, Abigail Hill, daughter of John and Ruth Hill , She was born Feb 4, 1746. They resided in East Medway Mrs. Daniels died October, 1807

The children were JULIA, b 1769, m. Nathan Fiske, res in Holliston, Mass URSULA, b 1771, m Tisdell Puffer TRIPHENA, b 1773 ABIGAIL, b 1775, m Moses Felt, res in Medway JEREMIAH [36], b Nov 22, 1778 RHODA, m Timothy Fiske, M. D , res in Holliston, Mass.

[21] ELEAZAR[5] DANIELS (JEREMIAH[4], JEREMIAH[3], JOSEPH[2], ROBERT[1]), son of Jeremiah [11] and Pearlee (Richardson) Daniell, was born Jan 30, 1788, in East Medway He married [1]Charlotte Richardson, daughter of Joseph[3] and Anna (Adams) Richardson She was born February, 1797, in Medway, where they resided. Mrs Charlotte Daniels died Nov 17, 1840. Capt. Eleazar Daniels married, July 3, 1843, [2]Elizabeth Lovell, daughter of Michael[5] and Caty (Daniels) Lovell She was born Jan 7, 1816, in East Medway Captain Daniels died Nov. 2, 1858 Mrs Elizabeth Daniels died Oct 6, 1883

The children were ANSON [37], b July 8, 1813. MILTON, b Jan 9, 1816, m Feb. 19, 1852, Mariam Waite Cheney, d March 3, 1871 SAMUEL, b. April 11, 1827, d. May 4, 1827 CHARLOTTE LOVELL, b 1855, d. Feb 10, 1879

Memoranda Milton Daniels was a deacon in the First Church of Christ His wife was the daughter of Josiah and Sybil Cheney She was born June 29, 1820

[22] PAUL[5] DANIELL (JEREMIAH[4], JEREMIAH[3], JOSEPH[2], ROBERT[1]), son of Jeremiah [11] and Pearlee (Richardson) Daniell, was born July 17, 1789, in East Medway He married Eliza Breck, daughter of Daniel and Martha (Learned) Breck She was born in Sherborn, Mass They resided in East Medway Dea Paul Daniels died Feb 15, 1876 Mrs Daniels died June 16, 1885.

The children were PEARLEE, b July 29, 1823, m May 21, 1845, John Bullard, *vid*. MARTHA LEARNED, b Dec 20, 1825, m May 2, 1849, William[8] Daniels, *vid*. LUCY, b. Feb 24, 1828, d March 2, 1832 ELIZA, b Feb 2, 1831, m. Nov 8, 1854, Daniel Rockwood, *vid* JOSEPH LEONARD, b Aug 1, 1833, m. Nov. 26, 1863, Julia B Allen, res in Olivet, Mich ELIJAH BRECK [38], b Feb 17, 1836 LUCY CHARLOTTE, b Nov 11, 1841, m. Dec. 23, 1874, Calvin Bigelow, res in Boston, Mass

[23] NATHAN[6] DANIELS (NATHAN[5], SAMUEL[4], JOSEPH[3], JOSEPH[2], ROBERT[1]), son of Nathan [12] and Mary (Adams) Daniell, was born July 12, 1748, in East Medway. He married, June 22, 1775, [1]Elizabeth Partridge They resided in Franklin, Mass. Mrs Elizabeth Daniels died Mr Daniels married, Jan 23, 1786, [2]Sarah Smith, daughter of Seth and Ann (Hartson) Smith She was born Oct 17, 1758, in Walpole, Mass Mr Daniels died Nov 25, 1841.

The children were . ELIZABETH, b April 19, 1776, d April 19, 1776 CYRUS, b. Feb 9, 1778, m Polly Sawyer DORCAS, b. Oct 14, 1779, m Samuel Cushing DAVID, b Jan 12, 1782, d Aug. 8, 1782 EZRA, b Nov 1, 1786, m Abigail Woodward. LUKE [39], b. Jan 28, 1788 SALLY, b June 1, 1789, m. June 19, 1817, Samuel Ware NATHAN, b Aug 1, 1791, m Roxana Thayer OLIVE, b. Sept. 13, 1793, d Aug 24, 1882. BETSEY, b Oct. 19, 1795, d. Jan. 3, 1797

[24] JAPHETH⁶ DANIELS (JAPHETH⁵, SAMUEL⁴, JOSEPH³, JOSEPH², ROBERT¹),
son of Japheth [14] and Melatiah (Hayward) Daniell, was born Aug 14, 1777, in Holliston, Mass. He married, Feb 18, 1800, Betsey Ryder, daughter of Asa Ryder. She was born June 27, 1780, in Holliston, Mass , where they resided Mr. Daniels died Nov 10, 1851 Mrs. Daniels died June 1, 1858

The children were LAWSON [40], b Jan 3, 1801. WILLARD [41], b Sept 10, 1803 PEGGY J , b July 27, 1807, m. Dec 11, 1828, Allen Partridge, *vid*. HANNAH, b. Oct. 24, 1809, unm , d Oct 19, 1841. BETSEY, b Sept. 15, 1817, m. May 11, 1843, John Craig Clark, *vid*

[25] ASA⁶ DANIELS (ASA⁵, JOSEPH⁴, JOSEPH³, JOSEPH², ROBERT¹), son of Dea. Asa [15] and Bathsheba (Fairbanks) Daniell, was born May 6, 1753, in East Medway. He married Eunice Fisher, daughter Hezekiah and Abigail (Daniels) Fisher She was born in Franklin, Mass They resided in East Medway. Dea Asa Daniels died June 7, 1840. Mrs Eunice Daniels died July 3, 1846. Deacon Daniels succeeded his father in the office of deacon, and left some eight thousand dollars as a fund to the First Church of Christ, in Medway. There were no children.

[26] LEVI⁶ DANIELS (ASA⁵, JOSEPH⁴, JOSEPH³, JOSEPH², ROBERT¹), son of Asa [15] and Bathsheba (Fairbanks) Daniell, was born Sept. 30, 1755, in East Medway. He married Peninnah ———.

The children were· SIMEON, b Aug 27, 1784 PENINNAH, b. April 17, 1786. CHARLES [42], b Feb 16, 1790 BETSEY, b June 30, 1796.

[27] JESSE⁶ DANIELS (ASA⁵, JOSEPH⁴, JOSEPH³, JOSEPH², ROBERT¹), son of Dea Asa [15] and Bathsheba (Fairbanks) Daniell, was born April 10, 1760, in East Medway. He married, Dec. 16, 1784, Hannah Holbrook, daughter of James and Mary (Morse) Holbrook. She was born Oct. 8, 1763, in Wrentham, Mass They resided in Medway Mr Daniels died Jan 29, 1837. Mrs. Daniels died April 3, 1843

The children were HANNAH, b Sept. 23, 1785 MARY, b April 6, 1788, m April 22, 1819, James Leland, res. in Sherborn, Mass. SARAH, b June 19, 1799, m. April 13, 1820, Theodore Ware, res in Wrentham, Mass. CYNTHIA, b Jan. 9, 1804

[28] LEMUEL⁶ DANIELS (JOSEPH⁵, JOSEPH⁴, JOSEPH³, JOSEPH², ROBERT¹), son of Joseph [16] and Deborah (Keith) Daniels, was born Feb. 9, 1759, in East Medway. He married, Jan. 28, 1784, Priscilla Penniman, daughter of James and Abigail (Clark) Penniman She was born 1761, in East Medway, where they resided. Mrs Daniels died March 1, 1825 Mr Daniels died Oct 24 1848

The children were JASPER [43], b. Aug 2, 1788 JAMES [44], b Jan 2, 1794.

[29] ISRAEL⁶ DANIELS (JOSEPH⁵, JOSEPH⁴, JOSEPH³, JOSEPH², ROBERT¹), son of Joseph [16] Daniels, was born June 19, 1763, in East Medway. He married, June 7, 1787, Anna Parker, daughter of Solomon and Elizabeth Parker, sister of Mrs. Nathaniel Willis and the aunt of N. P Willis, the poet She was born Oct 2, 1766, in Holliston, Mass Mrs Anna Daniels died. Mr. Daniels married ²Lavinia Daniels, daughter of Moses⁵ and Abigail (Adams) Daniels She was born Jan 16, 1777, in East Medway Mr Daniels died Feb 8, 1822 Mrs Lavinia Daniels married, Nov 15, 1827, ²Ezra Richardson, *vid*

The children were. ANNA, b March 7, 1788, m Jan 20, 1808, Amos⁶ Daniels, *vid* RHODA, b Jan. 16, 1792, m. June 8, 1815, Elihu Fuller, *vid* DAVID [45], b Aug 4, 1799

[30] NOAH⁶ DANIELS (JOSEPH⁵, JOSEPH⁴, JOSEPH³, JOSEPH², ROBERT¹), son of Joseph [16] Daniels, was born 1770 He married Abigail Allen.

The children were JASON [46], b. Feb 26, 1793 THANKFUL, b 1795, m. Elisha Foster, res in Worcester, Mass NOAH [47], b Jan 23, 1814.

[31] AMOS⁶ DANIELS (MOSES⁵, EZRA⁴, JOSEPH³, JOSEPH², ROBERT¹), son of Moses [18] and Abigail (Adams) Daniels, was born April 20, 1773, in East Medway. He married, March 13, 1799, ¹Sarah Day. She was born in Walpole, Mass. They resided in East Medway. Mrs Sarah Daniels died Oct. 16, 1805 Mr. Daniels married, Jan 20, 1808, ²Anna Daniels, daughter of Israel⁶ and Anna (Parker) Daniels She was born March 7, 1788, in Medway Mrs Anna Daniels died April 28, 1809 Mr Daniels married ³Sarah Pierce, daughter of Jonas and Maria (Clark) Pierce. She was born May 20, 1787. in Weston, Mass. Mr Daniels died June 12, 1823 Mrs Sarah Daniels, *née* Pierce, married, March 30, 1831, ²Benjamin Hinds, of Sherborn, Mass

33

Mr Hinds died March 7, 1838 Mrs Hinds married, Feb 1, 1841, [3]Benjamin Bullard She died April 29, 1872

The children were CALVIN, b March 14, 1801, d. Sept 28, 1803. LEONARD, b March 3, 1803, m July 14, 1834, [1]Sophronia Bradley, res. in Hartford, Conn ANNA DAY, b. March 10, 1809, m. April 6, 1830, James Hosmer, *vid* MOSES, b. Oct 8, 1812, m. May, 1848, Julia Fairbanks, res. in Medfield, Mass , d Sept 20, 1859 MARTHA, b 1814, m April 29, 1841, Edwin Metcalf, *vid*. HIRAM CLARK [48], b. Aug 10, 1815

[32] **ELIAS[6] DANIELS** (MOSES[5], EZRA[4], JOSEPH[3], JOSEPH[2], ROBERT[1]), son of Moses [18] and Abigail (Adams) Daniels, was born Jan 11, 1775, in East Medway He married Betsey Derby. She was born in Harvard, Mass. They resided in East Medway Mrs Daniels died Nov. 16, 1850.

The children were BETSEY, b. June 9, 1804, m. June 7, 1821, Wyman Adams CYRUS [49], b April 5, 1808. SARAH H , b April 4, 1811, m. Nov. 19, 1834, Wyman Adams ALVIRA, b. June 21, 1816, m. George Stedman.

[33] **EZRA[6] DANIELS** (MOSES[5], EZRA[4], JOSEPH[3], JOSEPH[2], ROBERT[1]), son of Moses [18] and Abigail (Adams) Daniels, was born Nov. 24, 1780, in East Medway He married, Nov 13, 1800, [1]Esther Richardson. They resided in East Medway. Mrs. Esther Daniels died   Mr. Daniels married [2]Mary Richards   He died Aug. 2, 1834

The children were MELINDA, b Feb 19, 1801 ABIGAIL, b. Dec. 12, 1807, m Sept 6, 1827, James Boyden. SUSANNA, b. Feb. 4, 1812 OLIVE, b. Dec. 19, 1814.

[34] **MOSES[6] DANIELS** (MOSES[5], EZRA[4], JOSEPH[3], JOSEPH[2], ROBERT[1]), son of Moses [18] and Abigail (Adams) Daniels, was born Oct 1, 1782, in East Medway He married, Feb. 14, 1808, Mary Harding, daughter of Uriah and Chloe (Mason) Harding. They resided in East Medway. Mr. Daniels died June 12, 1816, in Warwick, Mass Mrs Daniels married, Oct. 9, 1828, [2]John Richardson, son of Moses[5] and Abigail (Daniels) Richardson, *vid*.

The children were : MARY MARTHA, b. April 16, 1811, m. June 28, 1832, [1]David Harding, m April 3, 1842, [2]Abner Johnson. OLIVE ADAMS, b. Jan. 2, 1814, m. Nov. 10, 1833, Lewis Blake, res. in Milwaukee, Wis. MOSES HARDING, b July 20, 1815, m September, 1840, Irene (Harding) Rhodes, res. in Montclair, N J

[35] **SABEN[6] DANIELS** (HENRY[5], HENRY[4], JOSEPH[2], ROBERT[1]), son of Henry [19] and Elizabeth (Harding) Daniels, was born Nov. 29, 1774, in East Medway He married, March 14, 1797, Hannah Ellis, daughter of Timothy and Sarah (Richardson) Ellis She was born May 31, 1775, in Franklin, Mass They resided in East Medway. Mr Daniels died July 18, 1848. Mrs. Daniels died Nov 16, 1864.

The children were HENRY [50], b. Aug. 30, 1799. MARINDA, b. March 12, 1801. CYRUS [51], b Jan. 23, 1803. HARDING [52], b Jan. 22, 1807. ELLIS [53], b May 15, 1809 ELIZABETH, b. May 17, 1811, m Nov. 13, 1834, Elisha R. Phillips, *vid*

[36] **JEREMIAH[6] DANIELS** (ISAIAH[5], JEREMIAH[4], EBENEZER[3], JOSEPH[2], ROBERT[1]), son of Isaiah [20] and Abigail (Hill) Daniels, was born Nov 22, 1778, in East Medway. He married, June 21, 1801, Orinda Barber, daughter of George and Bethiah (Jones) Barber. She was born Oct 4, 1780, in Sherborn, Mass., where they resided Mrs Daniels died Jan 1, 1869

The children were INDIANA, m Isaac Smith. ALFRED DANIELS [54], born Nov. 18, 1803 LUCINDA, b July 12, 1805, m. Benjamin F. Bachelder, res. in Holliston, Mass ORINDA, b Aug. 24, 1806, married Benjamin Chenery, res. in Medfield, Mass. ABIGAIL, b. Oct. 30, 1807, m John Boyden GEORGE. JOSEPH.

[37] **ANSON[6] DANIELS** (ELEAZAR[5], JEREMIAH[4], JEREMIAH[3], JOSEPH[2], ROBERT[1]), son of Eleazar [21] and Charlotte (Richardson) Daniels, was born July 8, 1813, in Medway. He married [1]Harriet Lovering, daughter of James and Lavina (Edson) Lovering. She was born in West Medway, where they resided. Mrs Harriet Daniels died 1851. Mr. Daniels married, May 2, 1853, [2]Josephine M. Daniels, daughter of Jaazaniah B and Cordelia (Ellis) Daniels. She was born March 24, 1833, in Medway. Dea. Anson Daniels died Nov. 6, 1884.

The only child was JAMES MILTON, m Harriet Cordelia Daniels.

[38] **ELIJAH[6] BRECK** (PAUL[5], JEREMIAH[4], JEREMIAH[3], JOSEPH[2], ROBERT[1]), son of Paul [22] and Eliza (Breck) Daniels, was born Feb. 17, 1836, in East Medway. He married, Dec. 1, 1860, Roxa Boyden, daughter of Porter and Mary (Richards)

Boyden. She was born Nov. 2, 1836, in Dedham, Mass. They resided in First Medway Mr Daniels died Dec. 20, 1881

The children were· JERRY BOYDEN, b. May 25, 1862. ARTHUR HILL, b Oct 19, 1865. CHARLES HENRY, b Nov. 4, 1867.

[39] LUKE[7] DANIELS (NATHAN[6], NATHAN[5], SAMUEL[4], JOSEPH[3], JOSEPH[2], ROBERT[1]), son of Nathan [23] and Sarah (Smith) Daniels, was born Jan. 28, 1788, in Franklin, Mass. He married Jemima Fiske, daughter of Leland Fiske They resided in Franklin, Mass.

The children were· JEMIMA LELAND, m. Joel Daniels. CHARLES FISKE [55], b. July 19, 1817 ELIZA JANE, m. Horace Morse.

[40] LAWSON[7] DANIELS (JAPHETH[6], JAPHETH[5], SAMUEL[1], JOSEPH[3], JOSEPH[2], ROBERT[1]), son of Japheth [24] and Betsey (Ryder) Daniels, was born Jan 3, 1801, in Holliston, Mass. He married, March 29, 1822, Clarissa N. Pond.

The children were· CLEMENTINA, b April 28, 1824, m Alvin Collins, res. in Milford, Mass., d. May 30, 1869. CLARISSA P, b. April 28, 1824, m. Marshall Collins, res in Milford, Mass, d. July 30, 1858 NEWELL, b. Aug. 31, 1828, m Isabel O Stone LORINDA, b June 24, 1831, m. Dec 6, 1849, Ethan Adams, *vid.*; d. Aug. 2, 1860. CHARLES, b 1834, d. 1865. SABRA, b 1836, m. 1860, Henry Fairbanks GEORGE S, b. 1839, d. 1841. HELEN M, b. 1842, m 1861, Edwin Washburn GEORGE S., b 1844, d 1844 GEORGE EUGENE, b 1846, m. 1867, Ellen L. Adams.

[41] WILLARD[7] DANIELS (JAPHETH[6], JAPHETH[5], SAMUEL[4], JOSEPH[3], JOSEPH[2], ROBERT[1]), son of Japheth [24] and Betsey (Ryder) Daniels, was born Sept 10, 1803, in Holliston, now Medway. He married, March 27, 1826, Mrs. Elizabeth Fisher, *née* Grant, daughter of Noah and Sally (Whittem) Grant, and widow of Nathan Fisher She was born July 2, 1803, in York, Me. They resided in West Medway. Mrs. Daniels died Feb 15, 1862. Mr. Daniels died March 25, 1874.

The children were· SARAH NARCISSA, b Feb. 12, 1827, m July 4, 1852, Almon Chellis, d Feb 22, 1862. LEANDER SLOAN [56], b May 8, 1834 ELIZA JANE, b. April 27, 1838, m April 27, 1854, George W. Ballou, res in Franklin, Mass LUTHER, b April 25, 1842, m. May 4, 1870, Annie Longfellow, res. in Boston, Mass LAURA, b April 25, 1842, m July 18, 1867, Mowry S Smith, res in Hackensack, N J

[42] CHARLES[7] DANIELS (LEVI[6], ASA[5], JOSEPH[4], JOSEPH[3], JOSEPH[2], ROBERT[1]), son of Levi [26] and Peninnah Daniels, was born Feb 16, 1790, in Medway He married, April 3, 1811, Sarah Phillips, daughter of Jedidiah and Sarah (Bullen) Phillips. She was born March 3, 1791, in East Medway, where they resided, and afterward removed to Westboro, Mass.

The children were LEVI P, b. Dec. 17, 1818, died June 11, 1820 SARAH E., b Aug 11, 1822

[43] JASPER[7] DANIELS (LEMUEL[6], JOSEPH[5], JOSEPH[4], JOSEPH[3], JOSEPH[2], ROBERT[1]), son of Lemuel [28] and Priscilla (Penniman) Daniels, was born Aug 2, 1788, in East Medway He married, March 24, 1808, Mehitable Partridge, daughter of Samuel and Mehitable (Allen) Partridge. She was born Dec. 20, 1788, in Rockville, Medway. Mr. Daniels died May 23, 1876. Mrs Daniels died Nov 7, 1880.

The children were. JAAZANIAH BUSSEY [57], b May 1, 1809. WILLIAM DAMON [58], b. Nov 29, 1817

[44] JAMES[7] DANIELS (LEMUEL[6], JOSEPH[5], JOSEPH[4], JOSEPH[3], JOSEPH[2], ROBERT[1]), son of Lemuel [28] and Priscilla (Penniman) Daniels, was born Jan 2, 1794, in East Medway He married, June 28, 1815, Rhoda Richardson, daughter of Simeon[5] and Elizabeth (Jones) Richardson. She was born 1793, in East Medway, where they lived. Mrs. Daniels died Feb 24, 1882 Mr Daniels died July 28, 1882.

The children were: JAMES WILLARD [59], b April 2, 1817 RHODA R, b. Aug 31, 1821, d. Nov. 13, 1831 ABIGAIL P., b. March 16, 1829, d. Dec. 3, 1831.

[45] DAVID[7] DANIELS (ISRAEL[6], JOSEPH[5], JOSEPH[4], JOSEPH[3], JOSEPH[2], ROBERT[1]), son of Israel [29] and Anna (Parker) Daniels, was born Aug 4, 1799, in East Medway He married, June 6, 1820, [1]Keziah Hill, daughter of Reuben and Rebecca (Bullard) Hill. She was born Dec. 20, 1800, in Medway, where they resided. Mrs. Keziah Daniels died May 23, 1875 Mr Daniels married, Feb 13, 1879, [2]Mrs Mary E. Glines, *née* Forbush. She was born in Hallowell, Me.

The children were: FRANCIS PARKER [60], b. March 17, 1823. DAVID HILL [61], b March 11, 1826. ELIZABETH BULLARD, b. Aug 5, 1834, m. May 6, 1858, George Metcalf, *vid*

[46] JASON[7] DANIELS (NOAH[6], JOSEPH[5], JOSEPH[4], JOSEPH[3], JOSEPH[2], ROBERT[1]), son of Noah [30] and Abigail (Allen) Daniels, was born Feb 26, 1793, in Medfield, Mass He married, 1816, Julia Morse, daughter of Thaddeus and Cynthia (Clark) Morse. She was born May 4, 1792, in Medfield, Mass They resided in East Medway. Mr. Daniels died Sept 8, 1866 Mrs Daniels died July 13, 1868.

The only child was THADDEUS MORSE [62], b Nov 17, 1818

[47] NOAH[7] DANIELS (NOAH[6], JOSEPH[5], JOSEPH[4], JOSEPH[3], JOSEPH[2], ROBERT[1]), son of Noah [30] and Abigail (Allen) Daniels, was born Jan 23, 1814 He married, March 24, 1839, [1]Sarah Hill, daughter of David and Sally (Crooks) Hill They resided in East Medway Mrs Sarah Daniels died June 20, 1859 Mr Daniels married, Sept 26, 1861, [2]Nancy E. Hawes, daughter of Lewis and Elizabeth (Smith) Hawes She was born March 31, 1834, in Medway

The children were LAURA, b March 1, 1841, d Sept. 13, 1850. ANNIE L , b Dec 5, 1842, d. Aug 3, 1864 KEZIAH HILL, b March 8, 1845, d Nov 5, 1867. JOSEPH L , b. Sept. 15, 1849, d Sept 15, 1849 ABBIE ELIZABETH, b Jan 12, 1863, m Nov. 24, 1881, [1]William Jones, m April 22, 1884, [2]Alvin E. Clough ALMOND L. and ALFRED H., b. Oct 22, 1867. IDA ISABEL, b Sept. 15, 1869 WILLIAM PERCY, b. July 15, 1874 JASON NOAH, b June 18, 1877

[48] HIRAM CLARK[7] DANIELS (AMOS[6], MOSES[5], EZRA[4], JOSEPH[3], JOSEPH[2], ROBERT[1]), son of Amos [31] and Sarah (Pierce) Daniels, was born Aug 10, 1815, in East Medway He married, June 26, 1851, Susan Cressey, daughter of John and Susan (Jewett) Cressey. She was born July 2, 1826, in Rowley, Mass. They resided in East Medway

The children were MARY ELLA, b. Jan 8, 1857, d May 28, 1868 ABBIE FRANCES, b Feb 21, 1859 LEONARD CRESSEY, b. Sept 29, 1863, res. in Hartford, Conn.

[49] CYRUS[7] DANIELS (ELIAS[6], MOSES[5], EZRA[4], JOSEPH[3], JOSEPH[2], ROBERT[1]), son of Elias [32] and Betsey (Derby) Daniels, was born April 5, 1808, in East Medway He married, April 8, 1835, [1]Rebecca Adams, daughter of Elijah Adams She was born July 20, 1809, in Medfield, Mass They resided in East Medway Mrs. Daniels died Mr Daniels married, 1871, [2]Jane E Robinson He died Jan 5, 1884.

The children were. HARRIET R., b. Oct 24, 1836, m Newell Hunt, res. in Holliston, Mass ALBERT ROBBINS [63], b June 4, 1842.

[50] HENRY[7] DANIELS (SABEN[6], HENRY[5], HENRY[4], JOSEPH[2], ROBERT[1]), son of Saben [35] and Hannah (Ellis) Daniels, was born Aug. 30, 1799, in East Medway He married, Nov. 20, 1823, Mary Ann Pike, daughter of Elijah and Sarah (Clark) Pike. She was born June 30, 1801, in Framingham, Mass They resided in East Medway Mrs Daniels died July 19, 1882 Mr. Daniels died Dec. 5, 1883

The children were WILLIAM [64], b Feb. 3, 1825 CAROLINE ELIZABETH, b. Nov 5, 1829, m April 8, 1842, Thomas P. Howard, d July 6, 1870 CHARLES HENRY [65], b March 10, 1833. MARY ANN, b Feb. 5, 1840, d. Feb. 16, 1840. MARY ELEANOR, b Aug 3, 1842

[51] CYRUS[7] DANIELS (SABEN[6], HENRY[5], HENRY[4], JOSEPH[2], ROBERT[1]), son of Saben [35] and Hannah (Ellis) Daniels, was born Jan 23, 1803, in East Medway. He married, Nov. 29, 1827, Louisa Whitney, daughter of James and Lois (Blodgett) Whitney She was born July 6, 1804, in the Mohawk Country, New York They resided in East Medway Mrs Louisa Daniels died Jan 6, 1886

The children were· HANNAH, b March 23, 1829, m Jan. 8, 1852, Horace R [8] Richardson, *vid*, res in Cambridge, Mass HENRY MARTYN [66], b May 16, 1832 EDWARD, b July 8, 1836, m July 5, 1859, Nellie Spooner, res in Natick, Mass

Memoranda Mr and Mrs Edward Daniels had four children, viz . Nellie S , b. March 11, 1864, d 1877 Bertha J , b October, 1866 Lillian G , b December, 1871. William E , b October, 1883

[52] HARDING[7] DANIELS (SABEN[6], HENRY[5], HENRY[4], JOSEPH[2], ROBERT[1]), son of Saben [35] and Hannah (Ellis) Daniels, was born Jan. 22, 1807, in East Medway He married, April 28, 1830, Abigail Stedman, daughter of Josiah and Keziah (Richardson) Stedman. Mr Daniels died Dec 20, 1849 Mrs Daniels died July 12, 1864

The children were HARRIET, b Jan. 28, 1831, m April 17, 1866, Charles Edward Simpson, res. in Holliston, Mass RHODA ABIGAIL, born March 26, 1833, d April 8, 1854 MARIA STEDMAN, b Oct 5, 1839, m. June 26, 1864, Joseph Henry Morse, res. in Milford, Mass

Memoranda Mr and Mrs. Charles E Simpson had six children, viz Hattie Maria, b Jan. 31, 1867. Arthur Willot, b April 24, 1869 Charles Hovey, b Sept. 23, 1870 Grace Winnifred, b Aug 2, 1872 Nellie Augusta, b Nov 6, 1874. Annie May, b March 28, 1877

[53] ELLIS[7] DANIELS (SABEN[6], HENRY[5], HENRY[4], JOSEPH[2], ROBERT[1]), son of Saben [35] and Hannah (Ellis) Daniels, was born May 15, 1809, in East Medway. He married, 1834, [1]Sarah Phillips, daughter of Oliver and Hannah (Richardson) Phillips. She was born Sept 13 1813, in East Medway, where they resided Mrs Sarah Daniels died July 3, 1844 Mr Daniels married, Jan. 1, 1847, [2]Mrs Rhoda (Smith) Bole, *née* Smith, daughter of Samuel Smith. She was born Dec. 16, 1819 They resided in Milford, Mass. Mrs. Rhoda Daniels died March 25, 1880.

The children were JOSEPH LELAND, b December, 1834, m 1860, Adelaide Despeaux, d. Feb. 13, 1863. SARAH, b. Nov 19, 1836, d Nov. 19, 1848 AMANDA, b April 23, 1842, d Nov 29, 1867 HANNAH, b. March 11, 1844, d Aug 21, 1844 GEORGE E., b March 30, 1848, d Oct. 30, 1855 FRANK E, b April 24, 1850, m. March 18, 1875, Eva F Harrington, res. in Milford, Mass. NELSON S, b. May 18, 1852, d Aug 18, 1855. SAMUEL O., b. March 10, 1854 GEORGE N, b. Aug. 3, 1856, d Dec 5, 1856 CLARA M., b March 24, 1858 ADOLPHUS, b. July 7, 1861.

[54] ALFRED[7] DANIELS (JEREMIAH[6], ISAIAH[5], JEREMIAH[4], EBENEZER[3], JOSEPH[2], ROBERT[1]), son of Jeremiah [36] and Orinda (Barber) Daniels, was born Nov. 18, 1803, in East Medway. He married, Aug. 4, 1825, [1]Daty N Nickerson She was born Sept. 19, 1806, in Dennis, Mass. They resided in Medway Village. Mrs. Daty Daniels died August, 1851. Mr Daniels married, April, 17, 1853, [2]Myra Ann Nickerson, daughter of Levi and Myra Nickerson Mr Daniels died July 24, 1868.

The children were: GEORGE ALFRED [67], b. April, 1826 EMILY DATY, b June 24, 1829, m Capt Luther Nickerson, res in Meadville, Penn EMELINE LOUISA, b. June 7, 1831, m William Alden, res in Hartford, Conn EVELINE FRANCES, b. March 27, 1833, m. John F Wheeler, res in Meadville, Penn ELLEN MARIA, b March 29, 1835, m George B Eaton, res. in Revere, Mass. ALBERT HARRISON, b Aug 15, 1851 EDWIN NICKERSON, b Sept 8, 1843 d Oct 2, 1843 ALICE E, b March 18, 1857, m. November, 1876, Charles Levi Hathaway, res. in Newton, Mass JESSE, b Feb. 7, 1860. ALFRED, b Oct 23, 1861 HAROLD BARBER, b. June 5, 1864 JENNIE ORINDA, b Feb. 11, 1867.

[55] CHARLES FISKE[8] DANIELS (LUKE[7], NATHAN[6], NATHAN[5], SAMUEL[4], JOSEPH[3], JOSEPH[2], ROBERT[1]), son of Luke [39] and Jemima (Fiske) Daniels, was born July 19, 1817, in Franklin, Mass He married, Oct. 20, 1841, Eliza Phipps, daughter of William and Fanny (Moulton) Phipps She was born Sept 23, 1820, in Franklin, Mass They resided in Medway. Mr. Daniels died Aug 2, 1884. Mrs Daniels removed to Millbury, Mass.

The children were JEROME STARKWEATHER, b May 5, 1845, m Oct 26, 1865, Sarah Allen, res in Somerville, Mass JANETTE PHIPPS, b July 31, 1850, m. Dec 25, 1872, George J Dudley, res in Millbury, Mass. GARDNER FISKE, b Aug 15, 1855, m. Nov 8, 1882, Louisa M Gillis, res in Somerville, Mass

[56] LEANDER SLOAN[8] DANIELS (WILLARD[7], JAPHETH[6], JAPHETH[5], SAMUEL[4], JOSEPH[3], JOSEPH[2], ROBERT[1]), son of Willard [41] and Mrs Elizabeth (Fisher) Daniels, *nee* Grant, was born May 8, 1834. He married, Oct 18, 1855, [1]Elizabeth P. Hixon, daughter of Elihu and Hannah (Perry) Hixon They resided in West Medway Mrs. Elizabeth P Daniels died Oct. 25, 1859 Mr. Daniels married, Oct 18, 1861, [2]Adeliza M Harding. daughter of Nathan and Keziah (Adams) Harding. She was born April 29, 1840, in East Medway. Mrs Adeliza M Daniels died Oct 28, 1883 There were no children.

[57] JAAZANIAH BUSSEY[8] DANIELS (JASPER[7], LEMUEL[6], JOSEPH[5], JOSEPH[4], JOSEPH[3], JOSEPH[2], ROBERT[1]), son of Jasper [43] and Mehitable (Partridge) Daniels, was born May 1, 1809, in Medway. He married, Dec 1, 1831, Cordelia Ellis, daughter of Capt Henry and Azubah (Kingsbury) Ellis She was born September,

1809, in Medway, where they resided. Mr. Daniels died Aug. 26, 1852. Mrs. Daniels resides in Malden, Mass.

The children were: JOSEPHINE M., b. March 24, 1833, married, May 2, 1853, Dea. Anson[8] Daniels, *vid.* ELLEN CORDELIA, b. March 24, 1835, d. Sept. 28, 1836. EDMUND BUSSEY, b. Jan. 8, 1837, d. Feb. 20, 1837. HARRIET CORDELIA, b. Dec. 15, 1839, m. James Milton[7] Daniels. HENRY JASPER, b. Jan. 16, 1842, m. Agnes Ord, res. in Medfield, Mass., d. Dec. 9, 1870. ARTHUR JAAZANIAH, b. Oct. 12, 1845, m. [1]Alice Wight; m. [2]Charlotte Barber, res. in East Brimfield, Mass. ELLEN AZUBAH, b. Sept. 6, 1848, m. Henry Austen Ferns, res. in Malden, Mass.

[58] **WILLIAM DAMON**[8] **DANIELS** (JASPER[7], LEMUEL[6], JOSEPH[5], JOSEPH[4], JOSEPH[3], JOSEPH[2], ROBERT[1]), son of Jasper [43] and Mehitable (Partridge) Daniels, was born Nov. 29, 1817, in Medway. He married, April 4, 1839, Abigail Jones, daughter of Capt. Elisha Adams and Hannah (Richardson) Jones. She was born Aug. 23, 1818, in Medway, where they resided. Mr. Daniels died Oct. 31, 1863.

The children were: WILLIAM ADAMS, b. Jan. 21, 1840, d. Sept. 7, 1862. SAMUEL PARTRIDGE, b. Oct. 3, 1841, m. Aug. 31, 1862, Mary Alexander, res. in Pawtucket, R. I. FRANCIS HAMMOND [68], b. June 7, 1844. GEORGE HERBERT, b. Jan. 1, 1847, m. Jan. 31, 1872, Carrie Nolan, res. in West Medway. ABBIE JONES, b. Dec. 21, 1852, m. Nov. 3, 1875, Eugene Wilmarth, res. in West Medway.

THE MAPLEWOOD FARM.

THE RESIDENCE OF JAMES WILLARD DANIELS, ESQ.

[59] **JAMES WILLARD**[8] **DANIELS** (JAMES[7], LEMUEL[6], JOSEPH[5], JOSEPH[4], JOSEPH[3], JOSEPH[2], ROBERT[1]), son of James [44] and Rhoda (Richardson) Daniels, was born April 2, 1817, in Medway. He married, Feb. 24, 1842, [1]Marion Adams, daughter of Aaron[8] and Catherine (Adams) Adams. She was born in West Medway. They resided in East Medway. Mrs. Marion Daniels died March 24, 1849. Mr. Daniels married, Oct. 30, 1850, [2]Mrs. Mary F. Bullard, *née* Morse, daughter of Andrew and Margarette (Metcalf) Morse, and widow of Sylvanus Bullard, *vid.*

The children were: RHODA A., b. Dec. 4, 1842, d. April 2, 1860. MARION JANE, b. Feb. 23, 1849. MARY A., b. Oct. 1, 1851, d. Feb. 21, 1856.

[60] **FRANCIS PARKER**[8] **DANIELS** (DAVID[7], ISRAEL[6], JOSEPH[5], JOSEPH[4], JOSEPH[3], JOSEPH[2], ROBERT[1]), son of David [45] and Keziah (Hill) Daniels, was born

March 17, 1823, in Medway. He married Jane F. Ellis, daughter of Henry Ellis. Mr. Daniels died June 18, 1853

The only child was FRANCES JANE, b Oct 9, 1853, m Dr. Babcock

[61] **DAVID HILL⁸ DANIELS** (DAVID⁷, ISRAEL⁶, JOSEPH⁵, JOSEPH⁴, JOSEPH³, JOSEPH², ROBERT¹), son of David [45] and Keziah (Hill) Daniels, was born March 11, 1826, in Medway. He married, Dec 31, 1853, Sarah H. Mellen, daughter of Michael and Sarah (Holden) Mellen. They resided in Brookline, Mass

The children were: FRANK WILLIS, b. Feb. 24, 1859. NELLIE M., b. May 15, 1863

Memoranda. David H Daniels was educated in the Normal School in Bridgewater, Mass., and in Wilkesbarre, Penn. He was a teacher in West Wrentham, Cohasset, Medway, and Brookline, Mass. Since 1880 he has been the Superintendent of Public Schools in Brookline, Mass.

[62] **THADDEUS MORSE⁸ DANIELS** (JASON⁷, NOAH⁶, JOSEPH⁵, JOSEPH⁴, JOSEPH³, JOSEPH², ROBERT¹), son of Jason [46] and Julia (Morse) Daniels, was born Nov. 17, 1818, in Worcester, Mass. He married, Nov 8, 1841, ¹Sarah Wight, daughter of Dr. Moses H and Dorcas M (Gladden) Wight. She was born Aug 31, 1822, in East Medway, where they resided. Mrs Sarah Daniels died Nov. 1, 1842. Mr. Daniels married, Dec. 25, 1844, ²Anna Armsby, daughter of Willard Armsby. Mrs. Anna Daniels died Nov. 8, 1851. Mr. Daniels married, July 7, 1853, ³Ellen S. Lovell, daughter of Zachariah and Sibbel (Plympton) Lovell. She was born Jan. 13, 1828, in East Medway. Mrs. Ellen S Daniels died Sept 12, 1879

The children were: FRANCIS THADDEUS, b. April 20, 1847, m April, 1870, Mary I Neale, res in Sherborn, Mass. ANNIE FRANCES, b. Oct 17, 1854, m March 19, 1873, Elisha Eugene Adams.

Memoranda. Mr and Mrs. Adams reside in East Medway. The children are: Edna Gertrude, b Aug. 26, 1874. Grace, b. Nov. 7, 1876.

[63] **ALBERT ROBBINS⁸ DANIELS** (CYRUS⁷, ELIAS⁶, MOSES⁵, EZRA⁴, JOSEPH³, JOSEPH², ROBERT¹), son of Cyrus [49] and Rebecca (Adams) Daniels, was born Jan 4, 1842, in East Medway. He married, April 14, 1866, Ama Frances Richardson, daughter of Addison and Maria (Richardson) Richardson. She was born June 5, 1846, in East Medway, where they reside

The only child was EVA ALBERTINE, b. Sept 17, 1867.

Memoranda. This family of the Daniels name were millers for seven generations.

[64] **WILLIAM⁸ DANIELS** (HENRY⁷, SABEN⁶, HENRY⁵, HENRY⁴, JOSEPH², ROBERT¹), son of Henry [50] and Mary Ann (Pike) Daniels, was born Feb. 3, 1825, in East Medway. He married, May 2, 1849, Martha Learned Daniels, daughter of Deacon Paul and Eliza (Breck) Daniels. She was born Dec. 20, 1825, in East Medway, where they reside. Mr Daniels owns the farm called The Evergreen Place.

The children were ERWIN AUGUSTUS, b Aug 19, 1850, m. Oct. 7, 1873, Alice M Lovell, res. in Holliston, Mass. FREDERIC MILTON, b. Feb 14, 1872.

[65] **CHARLES HENRY⁸ DANIELS** (HENRY⁷, SABEN⁶, HENRY⁵, HENRY⁴, JOSEPH², ROBERT¹), son of Henry [50] and Mary Ann (Pike) Daniels, was born March 10, 1833, in Medway. He married, May 30, 1854, Lucretia Woodbridge, daughter of Dudley and Mary (Jameson) Woodbridge. She was born July 31, 1832, in Andover, Mass. They resided in West Medway. Mr. Daniels died June 6, 1867.

The children were ADA FRANCES, b May 6, 1855, m. Nov 25, 1874, Harry E Underwood, res. in Holliston, Mass., d. Oct 11, 1884. EMMA LUCRETIA, b Feb 25, 1858, m Nov 30, 1881, Charles A. Gardner, res. in Holliston, Mass. LIZZIE AUGUSTA, b. May 1, 1860, m. May 22, 1885, George A. Omstead, res in Holliston, Mass

[66] **HENRY MARTYN⁸ DANIELS** (CYRUS⁷, SABEN⁶, HENRY⁵, HENRY⁴, JOSEPH², ROBERT¹), son of Cyrus [51] and Louisa (Whitney) Daniels, was born June 18, 1832, in Sherborn, Mass. He married, Nov. 25, 1858, Catharine Maria Miller daughter of Joseph and Catharine (Guild) Miller. She was born Nov. 7, 1837, in North Wrentham, Mass. They reside in East Medway.

The children were: LEWIS E, b Sept 9, 1859, m. June 2, 1885, Ada Presby, res in Cambridge, Mass. GEORGE M, b. Aug 24, 1861, m. May 13, 1885, Jessie F. Cate, res. in Somerville, Mass. FLORA ETTA, b. Jan. 11, 1864. SARAH J., b. Jan. 7, 1866. CORA MARIA, b May 4, 1872

[67] **GEORGE ALFRED⁸ DANIELS** (ALFRED⁷, JEREMIAH⁶, ISAIAH⁵, JERE-

MIAH[4], EBENEZER[3], JOSEPH[2], ROBERT[1]), son of Alfred [54] and Daty (Nickerson) Daniels, was born April 23, 1826, in Medway   He married Amy A Jefferson, daughter of Joseph and Susan (Congdon) Jefferson   She was born in Uxbridge, Mass   They resided in Medway.   Mr Daniels died July 11, 1857

The children were   EDWIN ALFRED [69]   ELLEN, died in infancy

[68]   FRANCIS HAMMOND[9] DANIELS (WILLIAM DAMON[8], JASPER[7], LEMUEL[6], JOSEPH[5], JOSEPH[4] JOSEPH[3], JOSEPH[2], ROBERT[1]), son of William Damon [58] and Abigail (Jones) Daniels, was born June 7, 1844, in Medway   He married, Dec 23, 1874, Lizzie J Hill, daughter of James N and Jane (Whitney) Hill. She was born Nov 5, 1848, in Sherborn, Mass. They reside in Medway.

The only child was   JENNIE WHITNEY, b. Feb 21, 1877.

Memoranda   Mr and Mrs Daniels reside in an old homestead being the fifth generation Joshua Partridge, the first settler, cleared the land in 1740   He was a great hunter.   There are in the house to-day, deer's horns which belonged to the deer which Joshua Partridge shot on the place when he was clearing the lands   There is also a huge bear's trap preserved in the attic

[69]   EDWIN ALFRED[9] DANIELS (GEORGE ALFRED[8], ALFRED[7], JEREMIAH[6], ISAIAH[5], JEREMIAH[4], EBENEZER[3], JOSEPH[2], ROBERT[1]), son of George Alfred [67] and Amy A. (Jefferson) Daniels, was born in Medway   He married, June 15, 1880, Caroline Thompson LeFavor, daughter of Richard and Edna Jane (Sanford) LeFavor   She was born in Boston, Mass   They reside in Medway

The only child was   RICHARD HOLBROOK, b June 8, 1881

[1]   ASA DARLING (SAMUEL), son of Samuel and Sarah (Burr) Darling, was born July 18, 1783, in Bellingham, Mass   He married, June 10, 1810, Julia Thayer, daughter of Nathaniel and Susan Thayer   She was born Aug 7, 1786, in Franklin, Mass   They resided in East Medway   Mr Darling died July 16, 1819   Mrs Darling died March 24, 1879, in the ninety-third year of her age, in the house where she had resided for sixty-six years

The children were   COLLINS COURTNEY [2], b Feb 18, 1811. ASA THAYER, b. Jan. 24, 1813 m Dec 3, 1838, Sylvia L Leland, d April 10, 1876   FRANCIS DAVIS, b. Aug 3, 1818, m Oct 14, 1844, Caroline C Choate, res in Boston, Mass.

Memoranda   Mr and Mrs Francis D Darling had three children · Caroline Louisa, b. 1846, d Sept. 9, 1878. Mary Greenleaf, b 1847. Herbert Choate, b 1852, d 1877

[2]   COLLINS COURTNEY DARLING (ASA, SAMUEL), was born Feb 18, 1811, in East Medway   He married, May 29, 1845, Miriam P. Thayer. She was born, in Bellingham, Mass. They resided in East Medway.

The children were. EMMA M , b May 27, 1846. WILLIAM R , b Oct 18, 1852, d Oct 24, 1852   JULIA E , b Dec. 19, 1854, d Nov 12, 1884   JENNIE A , b. Jan 9, 1860

CHARLES HENRY DEANS (SAMUEL, ELIJAH), son of Samuel and Hannah Le Baron (Wheaton) Deans, was born May 2, 1832, in Easton, Mass   He married, Nov 21, 1861, Mary M Harris, daughter of Rufus and Elvira G (Goss) Harris   She was born Dec 1, 1834, in Westboro, Mass   They resided in West Medway

The children were · HARRIS WHEATON, b Oct 29, 1862   ANNA LE BARON, b. March 21, 1865   HARRIET ELIZABETH, b Feb 27, 1869   GERTRUDE AGNES, b. Nov 1, 1871   MARY ELVIRA, b July 16, 1877.

[1]   JOHN ELLICE, the first of the name to settle west of the Charles River, lived on the old Mendon Road or Village Street, near where it is crossed by Pleasant Street.   He married, April 7, 1698, Mary Hill, of Sherborn, Mass   Mr. Ellice died Nov 14, 1716. Mrs Ellice died March 3, 1729

The children were   JOSEPH [2]   SAMUEL [3]   JOHN [4]. TIMOTHY [5]

[2]   JOSEPH ELLIS (JOHN), son of John [1] and Mary (Hill) Ellice, was born in Medfield   He married, [1]Elizabeth ——   They resided in Medway. Mrs Elizabeth Ellis died Jan 14, 1718   Mr Ellis married, June 16, 1719, [2]Thamezin Adams, daughter of Jonathan[3] and Thamezin (Sheffield) Adams. She was born in 1699

The children were   JOSEPH, b Jan 5, 1718. BENONI, b July 29, 1720, d July 29, 1720   WILLIAM, b June 14, 1722   THAMEZIN, b April 18, 1725   ELISHA, b April 22, 1729   JONATHAN, b. Feb 27, 1731. ELIZABETH, b Dec 1, 1732. LYDIA, b. Feb 19, 1734   HENRY, b Nov 10, 1737   HANNAH, b June 13, 1741

[3] SAMUEL ELLIS (JOHN), son of John [1] and Mary (Hill) Ellice, was born in Medfield He married Dorothy —————— She was born in 1700 They resided in Medway. Mr. Ellis died Aug 14, 1769 Mrs Dorothy Ellis died May 13, 1790

The children were: DOROTHY, b June 27, 1721, m Job Harding JOHN [6], b Oct. 28, 1723 SAMUEL, b Feb 15, 1726 EBENEZER [7], b July 17, 1729 MARY, b. Oct. 7, 1731. BENJAMIN, b March 29, 1734 HENRY [8], b. June 7, 1736. HANNAH, b March 31, 1740.

[4] JOHN ELLIS (JOHN), son of John [1] and Mary (Hill) Ellice, was born in Medfield He married Mary ——————. They resided in Medway Mrs. Ellis died Oct. 25, 1732. Mr. Ellis died June 27, 1745

The children were: ASA, b Nov 11, 1727, d December, 1727. LYDIA, b. Nov. 13, 1728. SETH, b Sept. 28, 1731, m Phebe ——————, d Dec. 27, 1806. Mrs Phebe Ellis d. Nov. 27, 1815 MARY, b. Dec 20, 1739

[5] TIMOTHY ELLIS (JOHN), son of John [1] and Mary (Hill) Ellice, was born in Medfield He married, Jan 1, 1730, [1]Hannah Adams, daughter of John[3] and Susanna (Breck) Adams. She was born in 1707. They resided in West Medway Mr. Ellis died Mrs. Hannah Ellis married, May 21, 1739, [2]William Richardson, *vid.*

The children were HANNAH, b Sept 28, 1731, m Moses[5] Rockwood. MARY, b. Sept. 29, 1733 TIMOTHY, b June 4, 1735 LYDIA, b Nov. 29, 1736, m. Moses[5] Rockwood.

[6] JOHN ELLIS (SAMUEL, JOHN), son of Samuel [3] and Dorothy Ellis, was born in East Medway He married Sarah Harding They resided in East Medway.

The children were: JOHN [9], b 1754 ABEL, res in Sutton, Mass. ABIJAH, res in Hopkinton, Mass. ELI. SARAH, m 1773, Elisha Richardson, *vid*, d Jan 31, 1843

[7] EBENEZER ELLIS (SAMUEL, JOHN), son of Samuel [3] and Dorothy Ellis, was born July 17, 1729, in Medway He married Sarah Richardson They resided in Medway Mrs Sarah Ellis died Nov. 17, 1800. Mr. Ellis died Aug. 28, 1819

The children were: CATY, b. 1751, d Dec. 1, 1828. HANNAH, m. Joseph Abbe. OLIVE. SARAH, b. 1760, d Nov 1, 1824

[8] HENRY ELLIS (SAMUEL, JOHN), son of Samuel [3] and Dorothy Ellis, was born June 7, 1736, in Medway. He married Lydia Daniels, daughter of Jeremiah[4] and Mercy (Clark) Daniels They resided in East Medway Mr. Ellis died Oct 3, 1822. Mrs. Ellis died July 8, 1836.

The children were: SAMUEL, m. Mary Smith. HENRY [10]

[9] JOHN ELLIS (JOHN, SAMUEL, JOHN), son of John [6] and Sarah (Harding) Ellis, was born 1754, in Medway. He married Rhoda Partridge, daughter of Joshua[3] and Elizabeth (Kingsbury) Partridge. She was born Feb. 3, 1759, in Medway, where they resided

The children were: FERDINAND [11], b. June 16, 1780. MOSES [12], b November, 1782. ALEXANDER. RHODA, m [1]Moses Harding, *vid*, m [2]Orion Ellis.

Memoranda. Col. John Ellis was in the Revolutionary army and six years a Senator in the General Court of Massachusetts

[10] HENRY ELLIS (HENRY, SAMUEL, JOHN), son of Henry [8] and Lydia (Daniels) Ellis, was born 1776 in Medway He married Azubah Kingsbury. She was born 1775, in Foxboro, Mass. They resided in Medway Captain Ellis died March 26, 1832 Mrs. Ellis died March 22, 1858

The children were: LYDIA, m. James Fisher. HENRY, m Dec 4, 1822, Jane Thayer. ORION, m Mrs. Rhoda Harding, *née* Ellis. CHARLES, m Oct 5, 1826, Maria Holbrook WILLARD K [13], b. April 3, 1808 CORDELIA, b September, 1809, m Dec. 1, 1831, Jaazaniah B[5] Daniels, *vid* ANGELINA, d. at the age of thirteen years.

[11] FERDINAND ELLIS (JOHN, JOHN, SAMUEL, JOHN), son of John [9] and Rhoda (Partridge) Ellis, was born June 16, 1780, in Medway, Mass He married Lydia Whitmarsh. She was born in Providence, R. I They resided in Exeter, N H Mrs. Ellis died Feb. 22, 1838 The Rev Mr. Ellis died March 15, 1858

The children were: FERDINAND CHARLOTTE. LYDIA ELIZA, m —————— Knight JAMES SARAH, m. —————— Flagg RHODA, res in Exeter, N H ANNA, m. Dr Ordiorne. JOSEPH W, res. in Mt Vernon, Mo

[12] MOSES ELLIS (JOHN, JOHN, SAMUEL, JOHN), son of John [6] and Sarah

(Harding) Ellis, was born Nov 17, 1782, in Medway He married, Jan. 18, 1816, Almera Woodward She was born Oct 15, 1784, in Franklin, Mass. They resided in Medway Mrs Ellis died June 18, 1843. Mi Ellis died Nov 25, 1860

The children were RHODA, b April 6, 1820, m April 29, 1840, Elisha Adams Jones, *vid*, d Sept 27, 1873 MOSES H, b Jan 30, 1821, d March 28, 1822 JAMES HARVEY [14], b Sept. 12, 1823 JOHN PRESTON, b March 8, 1828, d Feb. 8, 1845

[13] **WILLARD K. ELLIS** (HENRY, HENRY, SAMUEL, JOHN), son of Henry [10] and Azubah (Kingsbury) Ellis, was born April 3, 1808, in Medway He married, April 24, 1831, Amy Smith, daughter of Enos and Amy (Plimpton) Smith. She was born Sept 25, 1809, in Medfield, Mass They resided in Medway Mr Ellis died November, 1878.

The children were ANTOINETTE L, b Aug 27, 1833, m. Nov. 24, 1853, Horatio Jones, *vid* WILLARD SMITH, b Jan 2, 1837, d. March 1, 1837 CATHARINE ELIZABETH, b. June 28, 1841, m. Oct 24, 1883, Lewis Wheeler, ies in West Roxbury, Mass ELLEN M, b Feb 11, 1848, d July 12, 1865

[14] **JAMES H ELLIS** (MOSES, JOHN, JOHN, SAMUEL, JOHN), son of Moses [12] and Almera (Woodward) Ellis, was born Sept. 12, 1823, in Medway. He married, Nov 18, 1843, Laura Ann Harding, daughter of Natnan[7] and Keziah (Adams) Harding She was born Oct 25, 1825, in East Medway, where they resided Mr. Ellis died Nov 15, 1875

The children were ALMERA FRANCES, b Sept 19, 1844, d. Nov 25, 1861. GEORGE A., b. July 25, 1849, m Nov 20, 1872, Maria M Keep, res in Franklin, Mass. ESTELLA A., b April 26, 1852, m Jason M Hawkes, res. in Valley Falls, R. I EDWARD HARVEY, b Feb 6, 1856, m 1879, Hattie Harding Bullard LAURA, b. July 27, 1859, m Sept 1, 1876, Charles Fiske, res. in Chelsea, Mass RHODA E., b. June 27, 1864, m Nov 19, 1882, Arthur Waite.

THOMAS ELLIS, of Medfield, received a grant of land in West Medway, which he conveyed to his son, Samuel Ellis, who deeded it to his son, Timothy Ellis, Aug 18, 1725 In 1792 Timothy Ellis deeded it to his son, Oliver Ellis, who, in 1832, deeded it to his son, Simeon Ellis, and Simeon Ellis conveyed it, in 1862, to his youngest son, David G Ellis

[1] **TIMOTHY ELLIS** (SAMUEL, THOMAS), was born in Medway

The children were OLIVER [2]. PAUL SARAH RACHEL

[2] **OLIVER ELLIS** (TIMOTHY, SAMUEL, THOMAS), son of Timothy [1] Ellis, was born in Medway

The children were SIMEON [3] SYLVIA, m Luther Henderson

Memoranda Oliver Ellis was one who shouldered his musket and marched to put down the Shay Rebellion

[3] **SIMEON ELLIS** (OLIVER, TIMOTHY, SAMUEL, THOMAS), son of Oliver [2] Ellis, was born in Medway. He married Mercy A. Grover, daughter of David Grover. She was born April, 1788, in Mansfield, Mass

The children were, CHESTER [4] MARTHA B DAVID G

Memoranda Simeon Ellis served in the War of 1812, and was stationed at Fort Warren. For this service he drew a pension.

[4] **CHESTER ELLIS** (SIMEON, OLIVER, TIMOTHY, SAMUEL, THOMAS), son of Simeon [3] and Mercy A (Grover) Ellis, was born March 27, 1816, in Medway He married, Feb 18, 1841, Clarissa Richardson, daughter of Artemas and Deborah (Johnson) Richardson She was born in Medway, where they resided.

The children were ALVIRA R, b. Sept 2, 1844. ANNIE C, b. June 26, 1848, m. Dec. 27, 1865, George E Pond, *vid*

WILLIAM EVERETT (JOEL, ISAAC), son of Joel and Catherine (Smith) Everett, was born Jan. 3, 1817, in West Dedham, Mass He married, Nov 14, 1839, [1]Abby D. Wiggin They resided in West Medway Mrs Abby D Everett died March 10, 1854 Mr Everett married, Jan. 3, 1855, [2]Mary P Blake. Mrs. Mary P. Everett died Sept 3, 1856 Mr Everett married, Nov 26, 1857, [3]Betsey Goodale. Mr. Everett died Oct. 31, 1882.

The children were GEORGE L, b Aug 21, 1840. MARY F., b. Sept 5, 1842, m Edwin A. Mann CHARLES H, b Nov 18, 1844, d May 25, 1865 ELLEN A., b July 6, 1847, m Edward Belcher. ABBY M., b. June 26, 1850, m. James Mott WILLIE W., b Feb 9, 1854, died Jan. 9, 1879 He was killed by the Indians. DAVID E., b. July 25, 1856, d. Oct. 14, 1856.

Memoranda Mr Everett's early life was one of trials, and his opportunities for an education were very limited. He was a self-made man, and under the favoring control of a Divine Providence which he recognized, he won his way to prominence as a citizen, and at the time of his death was a member of the Board of Selectmen of the town. *Vid. The Dedham Transcript* for Dec 2, 1882

[1] GEORGE FAIRBANKS, the first settler, came with his wife and five children about 1657 from Dedham, Mass He married, Aug. 26, 1646, Mary Adams. Mr. Fairbanks died Jan 10, 1682 Mrs Fairbanks died about 1703

The children were MARY, b Sept 10, 1647, m. Nov. 16, 1665, Joseph Daniell, *vid.*, d. June 9, 1682. GEORGE [2], b. March 26, 1650 SAMUEL, b Aug 28, 1652, d. Nov. 20, 1676. ELEAZAR, b April 8, 1665, m. Martha Bullard, and settled in Sherborn, Mass. JONAS, b. Dec. 23, 1656, d Nov 28, 1676 JONATHAN, b. May 1, 1662, m Sarah ———, res. in Sherborn, Mass. MARGARET, b. June 27, 1664.

[2] GEORGE² FAIRBANKS (GEORGE¹), son of George [1] and Mary Fairbanks, was born March 26, 1650 He married ¹Rachel ———. They resided in the homestead. Mrs Rachel Fairbanks died May 12, 1678 Mr Fairbanks married ²Susanna ——— Mrs. Susanna Fairbanks died Mr Fairbanks married ³Sarah ——— Captain Fairbanks died May 5, 1737

The children were RACHEL, b. Sept 29, 1672. MARIE, b Jan 5, 1675 SUSANNA, b March 24, 1680 SUSANNA, b March 17, 1682, m. ——— Whitney DOROTHY, b. Nov. 6, 1683, m Ebenezer Thompson MARGARET, b Jan 5, 1685. JONAS, b. Feb 15, 1687-8, d. Nov 10, 1690. SARAH, b Nov. 16, 1690 GEORGE [3], b. Oct 2, 1694 JOHN, b Oct 9, 1697. HANNAH, m. Joseph Curtis

[3] GEORGE³ FAIRBANKS (GEORGE², GEORGE¹), son of George and Sarah Fairbanks, was born Oct 2, 1694, in Medfield, afterward Medway. He married Sarah Harding, daughter of Abraham² and Sarah Harding. They resided in Medway.

The children were JOHN, d Dec 14, 1714 PHEBE, b May 16, 1716, m. 1759, Abraham Cousins JOHN, b. Feb. 5, 1719, d. May 3, 1719. JONAS [4], b. Oct. 20, 1720 GEORGE [5], b. Dec 12, 1722 BATHSHEBA, b Oct 7, 1724, m May 20, 1752, Asa Daniels, *vid.* SILENCE, b. Feb. 26, 1727, m. Elisha Barber. ELIJAH, b April 29, 1729, d. Oct 1, 1746. DAVID, b July 10, 1731, d Oct 8, 1746 JOHN, b Oct 27, 1733. JOSEPH, b Dec. 8, 1735, m Abigail Coolidge. SARAH, b April 4, 1738 ELIZABETH, b Dec. 29, 1740, d. Aug 20, 1744.

[4] JONAS⁴ FAIRBANKS (GEORGE³, GEORGE², GEORGE¹), son of George [3] and Sarah Fairbanks, was born Oct 20, 1720 He married, 1745, Experience Leland, daughter of Hopestill and Mary (Bullard) Leland She was born June 21, 1725, in Sherborn, Mass They resided in Medway.

The children were MIRIAM, b. March 9, 1745-6, d Oct 21, 1779. DEBORAH, b. June 2, 1747, m Nov 29, 1769, Job Partridge, res. in Bellingham, Mass. SARAH, b. Jan. 4, 1748-9 MARY, b June 4, 1751. ELIJAH, b. March 21, 1753. EXPERIENCE, b April 19, 1755, m. Jabez Whitney HOPESTILL, b March 4, 1757 RUFUS, b Dec 8, 1758 JOSEPH, b. Feb 22, 1761, m Mary Metcalf, res. in Bellingham, Mass ; d Jan. 5, 1835.

[5] GEORGE⁴ FAIRBANKS (GEORGE³, GEORGE², GEORGE¹), son of George [3] and Sarah Fairbanks, was born Dec 12, 1722, in Medway. He married Jerusha ———. They resided in Medway. Mr. Fairbanks died Sept 29, 1795. Mrs Fairbanks died Jan 9, 1796.

The children were ABIJAH, b Jan 21, 1745-6, m Mary Clark. JOEL, b Jan 26, 1747, m Mary ———, res. in Oxford, Mass ELIZABETH, b. Aug 11, 1749 GEORGE, b. July 12, 1751, m. Cally Boyden, res. in Wrentham, Mass SILAS [6], b Sept. 29, 1753. JOTHAM [7], b. April 6, 1757. ASAHEL, b June 2, 1761. ADAM, b. Dec. 1, 1763.

[6] SILAS⁵ FAIRBANKS (GEORGE⁴, GEORGE³, GEORGE², GEORGE¹), son of George [5] and Jerusha Fairbanks, was born Sept. 29, 1753, in Medway. He married Mary Day. They resided in the old homestead Mr. Fairbanks died June 11, 1823. Mrs. Fairbanks died June 21, 1827.

The children were: POLLY, b March 14, 1785, m. Feb. 8, 1807, Moses Pond, *vid.*

CHARLES, b. Sept. 30, 1787. SILAS, m. Mille Plimpton. JAMES. BETSEY, m. Baruch Perry. NANCY, b. 1796, m. [1] —— Bullard; m. [2] Moses Pond, *vid.* CHARLOTTE.

[7] **JOTHAM FAIRBANKS**, son of George [5] and Jerusha Fairbanks, was born April 6, 1756, in Medway. He married, May 6, 1778, Beulah Daniels, daughter of Joseph [5] and Deborah (Keith) Daniels. She was born May 7, 1760, in Medway, where they resided. Mr. Fairbanks died May 24, 1834. Mrs. Fairbanks died May 29, 1853.

The children were: JOTHAM, b. Oct. 19, 1778. LEONARD, m. Nov. 30, 1823, [1]Abigail Harding; m. [2]Keziah Harding; m. [3]Lydia Abbe, d. May 21, 1874.

OTIS FAIRBANKS married Sylvia Fuller, daughter of Asa and Melatiah (Metcalf) Fuller. She was born Oct. 9, 1791, in Medway, where they resided. Mrs. Fairbanks died July 4, 1835.

The children were: GEORGE OTIS, b. Feb. 14, 1815, res. in Fall River, Mass. MELATIAH. CATHARINE. HARRIET. ELIZA. MARY ANN. HEPHZIBAH. ABIGAIL M. ELEANOR M.

THE FISHER COAT OF ARMS.

THOMAS FISHER, of Winston, Suffolk County, England, was the first man of this name who came to New England in the great Puritan immigration of 1630. He, with his wife Elizabeth, and their children, Samuel, Thomas, and Constance, settled in Cambridge, in 1634, and removed to Dedham in 1637. In that year ten more of the same name came to Dedham from Syleham, and in 1640 two more, making seventeen immigrants of the same kindred. The English ancestor of those who came in 1637 and 1640 was Anthony Fisher; This family group consisted of Anthony, Jr., wife Mary, children, Anthony, Cornelius, Nathaniel, Daniel, and Lydia. With them came two nephews of Anthony, sons of Amos, named John and Daniel, and another nephew, Joshua, son of Joshua, who, with his second wife, Mary Luson, joined their son Joshua and their other kinsfolk at Dedham in 1640. These twelve men and five women soon gave their name to a large posterity which gradually, and quite early, spread through the county, especially in Dedham, Wrentham, Franklin, and Medfield. Nearly all who bear the name in the Northern, Eastern, and Western States, trace their ancestry to those seventeen pioneers in Dedham, Mass.

There were a few persons who bore the name of Fisher in the early settlements at Jamestown, Va., and in Pennsylvania. Some of the latter were Quakers.

The English coat of arms of this family appears to be the same with the Dauphin of France, but how the coincidence happened is not known. The name being that of a common employment, is found in nearly all nations. In German it is Fischer, in French it is Pechéur. The German name is common in New York and in Brooklyn, N. Y. *Vid. The History of Franklin, Mass.*

The Fisher coat of arms, doubtless of French origin, used in this country by Joshua Fisher, Sen., of Medfield, and Capt. Ebenezer Fisher, of Dedham, is the same as is described in *The History of Norfolk County, England,* with notices of Richard and Edward Fisher "Gentlemen," "Richard Fisher, Chaplain 1442, John Fyshere, 1449, burgess of Thetford, the Rev. William Fisher, a Public Benefactor," and of Mrs. Mary Fisher, "who died and went to Heaven in a hurricane."

Joseph Fisher married Susa Fisher, daughter of the Hon. Jabez Fisher, of Franklin, Mass. Their son, Willis Fisher, married Caroline Fairbanks, of Franklin, Mass. These were the parents of the Hon. M. M. Fisher, of Medway, among whose ancestry are the names of Fairbanks, Metcalf, Haven, Coburn, Adams, Ellis, Snow, Heaton, Faxon, and Fiske. In England the Fishers intermarried with the Briggs, Buckingham, and Locke families. The celebrated John Locke was of this kindred.

[1] **MILTON METCALF**[8] **FISHER** (WILLIS[7], JOSEPH[6], BENJAMIN[5], COR-

NELIUS[4], CORNELIUS[3], ANTHONY[2], ANTHONY[1]), son of Willis and Caroline (Fairbanks) Fisher, was born Jan 30, 1811, in Franklin, Mass. He married, Aug 22, 1836, Eleanor Metcalf, daughter of the Hon. Luther and Lydia (Jenks) Metcalf. She was born Sept. 1, 1813, in Medway, Mass. They resided in Westboro and in Medway. Mrs. Fisher died March 13, 1885

The children were. THEODORE WILLIS, b May 29, 1837, m. Nov. 10, 1858, [1]Maria C. Brown, who died July 28. 1860, m. Dec. 18, 1873, [2]Ella G. Richardson, res in Boston, Mass CHARLES HAVEN, b. July 20, 1839. d. July 20, 1839 LYDIA CAROLINE, b. May 29, 1841, d. Oct. 9, 1846. MARY ELEANOR, b Dec 5, 1844. ELLENA METCALF, b April 2, 1843, d Oct 7, 1843 SARAH FAIRBANKS, b. April 13, 1846, d Sept. 16, 1846. FREDERICK LUTHER [2], b. Jan 12, 1853 HELEN FRANCES, b May 12, 1854, m. Oct 26, 1876, Walter V. Hawkes, res in Saugus, Mass MILTON ARTHUR, b. May 10, 1856, d Nov. 26, 1856.

[2] **FREDERICK LUTHER[9] FISHER** (MILTON METCALF[8], WILLIS[7], JOSEPH[6], BENJAMIN[5], CORNELIUS[4], CORNELIUS[3], ANTHONY[2], ANTHONY[1]), son of Milton M. [1] and Eleanor (Metcalf) Fisher, was born Jan. 12, 1853, in Medway, Mass He married, May 23, 1876, Caroline Pamelia Lyon, daughter of George and Sally Barber (Nichols) Lyon, of Boston, Mass. She was born Aug 22, 1851, in Boston, Mass

The only child was HARRIET LYON FISHER, b. Aug. 23, 1880

Memoranda. Frederick L. Fisher graduated in 1873 from the Massachusetts Institute of Technology, in the department of civil engineering. He was an agent for insurance in Medway and Boston, and was appointed a Justice of the Peace in 1878

[1] **LEWIS FISHER**, son of Simeon Fisher, was born Feb 15, 1771, in Medway He married, Oct. 5, 1797, Hannah Thayer, daughter of Capt Elias and Hannah (Ellis) Thayer She was born Nov 11, 1775, in Bellingham, Mass. They lived in Medway.

The children were HEPHZIBAH A , b March 24, 1799, d May 23, 1825 SIMEON [2], b. Jan 6, 1801 HANNAH, b. Dec 15, 1802, d July 3, 1826. LAURA ANN, b. Oct. 31, 1804, m. Albert Thwing, d November, 1867. OLIVIA, b. Oct. 19, 1807, m. October, 1842, Chandler Pratt PAULINE, b Oct 20, 1809, m Robert Mowry LEWIS [3], b Nov 15, 1811. ELIAS T. [4], b. March 25, 1814. EBENEZER H , b July 21, 1816, m. Milly W. Smith, d. Dec. 15, 1851

Memoranda Simeon Fisher, Sen , was born in 1733, and died Sept. 10, 1818.

[2] **SIMEON FISHER** (LEWIS, SIMEON), son of Lewis [1] and Hannah (Thayer) Fisher, was born Jan. 6, 1801, in Holliston, Mass. He married, 1824, [1]Mary Ann Rockwood She was born Feb. 8, 1805, in Medway, where they resided Mrs. Mary Ann Fisher died Sept. 30, 1867. Mr. Fisher married, April 29, 1869, [2]Matilda G Mason, daughter of Simon Harding and Betsey (Leland) Mason She was born Aug. 9, 1813, in East Medway.

The children were. CAROLINE R , b March 19, 1825, m Oct. 17, 1843, Mellen C. Bragg, d Sept. 12, 1849 GEORGE S , b. Sept 13, 1828, m Nov 22, 1852, Mira A Babcock ELIAS T., b. Aug 13, 1835, d. March 8, 1837. MILLE A., b. Nov 24, 1837. LEWIS L., b. Aug. 19, 1839, d. July 4, 1866 IRVING A., b. March 28, 1841. WILLARD P , b Oct. 2, 1842, m. Jan. 27, 1862, [1]Mary L Hastings, who died Jan 21, 1868, m 1869, [2]Clara Bancroft. FANNY S , b. April 13, 1845, d July 28, 1850

[3] **LEWIS FISHER** (LEWIS, SIMEON), son of Lewis [1] and Hannah (Thayer) Fisher, was born Nov 15, 1811. He married, March 27, 1838, Betsey Richardson, daughter of Abijah and Olive (Pond) Richardson. She was born Sept 13, 1818, in East Medway.

The children were. ABIJAH RICHARDSON, b March 14, 1839, d Jan. 22, 1841. TRYPHENA RICHARDSON, b. Jan. 17, 1841, m Jan 9, 1867, Edmund Newton Clark, *vid* BESSIE ADELAIDE, b Oct. 28, 1842, d. July 24, 1860 FRANK LEWIS, b Sept 7, 1844, m. Emeline Wheeler, res in Rye, Col ASA O , b May 24, 1846, m. Mrs. Addie Steele, res in Bismark, Dak. OLIVE MARIA, b. March 16, 1848, m. Dwight Bagley, res. in Rye, Col. IRVING AUGUSTUS, b. Feb. 15, 1850 CHARLES THURBER, b. Feb. 16, 1852, m. Helen Bagley, res. in Pueblo, Col. ALBERT THAYER, b May 3, 1854, m. Emma ———. FANNIE L., b. Oct. 3, 1856, d. Nov 17, 1871. MARY ABBIE, b Nov. 16, 1858, m. William Dewey. LEWIS ROBERT, b Nov 5, 1862, res. in New Mexico.

[4] **ELIAS THAYER FISHER** (LEWIS, SIMEON), son of Lewis [1] and Han-

nah (Thayer) Fisher, was born March 25, 1814, in Holliston, afterward Medway. He married, May 21, 1841, ¹Martha B Ellis, daughter of Simeon and Mercy (Green) Ellis She was born Jan 30, 1818, in West Medway, where they resided. Mrs Martha B Fisher died July 19, 1852 Deacon Fisher married, June 16, 1853, ²Sarah H Blackmer, daughter of John and Esther (Bartlett) Blackmer. She was born April 5, 1826, in Plymouth, Mass.

The children were JENNIE O , b March 12, 1842, m March 4, 1869, Julius M Jones, res in Webster City, Ia MARTHA B , b. Feb 14, 1846, d Aug 26, 1846 MARY E , b Aug 17, 1848, m Aug 28, 1876, Watson J Cosil, res in Webster City, Ia CHARLES S , b July, 1852 EMMONS E , b Oct, 10, 1854, d. July 29, 1873 MARTHA M , b Aug 4, 1856, m. Oct 16, 1883, Herbert A Eames, res in Webster City, Ia. JOHN B , b March 24, 1860 LILLIAN S , b. May 19, 1863 ANNIE MAY, b. June 12, 1865

GEORGE BRAYTON FISHER (WILLARD, JOHN, JOHN), son of Willard and Olive (Brayton) Fisher, was born April 9, 1841, in Killingly, Conn He married Sarah Louisa Clark, daughter of John and Marietta (Thompson) Clark She was born Nov 10, 1841, in East Medway, where they resided.

The children were HERBERT CLARK, b. Oct 21, 1869 GEORGE KELSEY, b Feb. 5, 1872. ETHEL LOUISE, b Oct 26, 1878 ERNEST BRAYTON, b May 16, 1883

Memoranda Mr Fisher entered the Union army in 1861, reënlisted after three years, and continued in the service until the close of the war He was wounded through the right lung at the siege of Petersburg, Va Subsequently he was a merchant, and filled the office of postmaster several years in East Medway.

APPLETON EAMES FOSTER married, March 20, 1834, Louise Antoinette Bannister, daughter of John Richard and Eliza Marie (Pond) Bannister, of New York They resided in Medway, Mass Mr Foster died May 23, 1859

The children were ELIZABETH MATILDA, b. March 24, 1835, m Nov 1, 1857, George E Mason, *vid* HENRY APPLETON, b. Sept 6, 1836 LOUISE ANTOINETTE, b Jan 8, 1839, m June 8, 1865, William C Loring, res. in Boston, Mass. WILLIAM BANNISTER, b Dec 19, 1842, d April 21, 1863. GEORGE JONES, b June 23, 1845. ALICE JOSEPHINE, b. Aug 15, 1850, d July 9, 1855

[1] **ASA FULLER** (AMOS), son of Amos and Esther Fuller, was born Sept. 20, 1752, in Needham, Mass He married, June 1, 1780, Melatiah Metcalf, daughter of Jonathan and Bathsheba (Pond) Metcalf She was born Aug 19, 1756, in West Wrentham, now Franklin, Mass They resided in Medway Mr Fuller died Aug. 11, 1836 Mrs. Fuller died Feb 13, 1837

The children were ASA, b Dec 26, 1781, m April 4, 1811, Hephzibah Blake, res in Franklin, Mass , d March 2, 1872 ABNER, b Aug 30, 1783, m Lydia Rogers, d Aug 3, 1866 MELATIAH, b. Nov 29, 1785, d. Feb 7, 1796 ELIHU [2], b. April 19, 1788 SYLVIA, b Oct 9, 1791, m Otis Fairbanks, *vid.*, d July 4, 1835 NEWELL, b Feb 19, 1795, m. Jane Davis, res. in Harvard, Mass , d April 18, 1863.

[2] **ELIHU FULLER** (ASA, AMOS), son of Asa and Melatiah (Metcalf) Fuller, was born April 19, 1788, in Medway. He married, June 8, 1815, Rhoda Daniels, daughter of Israel and Anna (Parker) Daniels She was born Jan 16, 1792, in Medway, where they resided Mr Elihu Fuller died Sept. 17, 1852 Mrs Rhoda Fuller died Nov. 10, 1881.

The children were ISRAEL DANIELS [4], b April 5, 1816. RHODA A P , b. Oct 22, 1817, m June 1, 1836, William H Hunting, *vid* , d March 23, 1845 ELIHU SANFORD [5], b May 25, 1824 GEORGE EDMUND [6], b March 3, 1836

[3] **ASA METCALF BLAKE FULLER** (ASA, ASA, AMOS), son of Asa and Hephzibah (Blake) Fuller, was born May 17, 1813, in Franklin, Mass He married, May 25, 1847, ¹Nancy D Forbush, daughter of Ephraim and Polly (Stowe) Forbush She was born Aug. 16, 1820, in Upton, Mass. They resided in West Medway. Mrs. Nancy D Fuller died Dec 21, 1854 Mr Fuller married, Jan 25, 1859, ²Mrs Mary A K Ingraham, *née* Tarleton, daughter of Matthew Tarleton, and widow of Adolphus Ingraham, of Newport, N H. She was born June 18, 1823, in Deerfield, N H

The children were. CHARLES METCALF, b Oct. 18, 1854, m. Feb 2, 1880, Mrs Lilla Johnson, *née* Bates, res in Medfield MARY LOUISA, b. April, 1861, d. 1861. GEORGE ARTHUR

Memoranda. Charles M Fuller was a physician in Medfield, Mass   Mrs. Polly (Stowe) Forbush was an aunt of Prof. Calvin E Stowe, D D , of Hartford, Conn

[4] **ISRAEL DANIELS FULLER** (ELIHU, ASA, AMOS), son of Elihu [2] and Rhoda (Daniels) Fuller, was born April 5, 1816, in Medway   He married, Jan 10, 1839, Eliza P. Barber, daughter of Seneca and Nancy (Boyden) Barber.   She was born in East Medway, where they resided

The children were   GEORGE I , b. Nov 8, 1841, res in Springfield, Mass   EMMA E., b. May 12, 1849, m Oct 30, 1872, Edwin Handel Holbrook, *vid.,* res in Washington, D. C   ANNA B , b Aug 14, 1850, m. May 20, 1874, William G White, d June 29, 1883   RHODA D , b Aug 3, 1856, m Dec 6, 1882, George F Holbrook, *vid*

[5] **ELIHU SANFORD FULLER** (ELIHU, ASA, AMOS), son of Elihu [2] and Rhoda (Daniels) Fuller, was born May 25, 1824, in East Medway.   He married, Sept. 20, 1848, Caroline Ellis, daughter of John and Virtue (Parkhurst) Ellis.   She was born Jan 16, 1830, in Milford, Mass.   They resided in East Medway

The children were   FRANCES ELNORA, b April 18, 1849.   MILLARD ANSON, b Sept. 22, 1850, m. Dec 29, 1871, Hattie J Baker, res. in Chicago, Ill   CARRIE JOSEPHINE, b Jan 13, 1858, d Aug 16, 1878.   ELIHU, b March 12, 1862, d Dec 17, 1876.

[6] **GEORGE EDMUND FULLER** (ELIHU, ASA, AMOS), son of Elihu [2] and Rhoda (Daniels) Fuller, was born March 3, 1826, in East Medway   He married, Sept. 3, 1850, Ellen M. Winslow, daughter of Elnathan Sampson and Clarissa (Roberts) Winslow.   She was born Sept. 3, 1834, in Ellsworth, N Y.   They resided in East Medway and removed to Arlington, Mass

The children were : GEORGE E , b. April 2, 1854, m. Nov. 5, 1875, Florence O Hurd.   EDMUND W., b. Nov 20, 1858   NELLIE A., b. Nov 7, 1862, m. June 10, 1885, Frank A Marden   FRANK SHERIDAN, b Oct 4, 1867, d Dec 8, 1884

[1] **AMORY GALE** (AMORY, JONATHAN), son of Amory and Lucinda (Rich) Gale, was born Oct 15, 1800, in Warwick, Mass.   He married, 1825, Martha Leland, daughter of Perley and Hannah (Harding) Leland.   She was born June 3, 1800, in Holliston, Mass   They resided in East Medway.   Dr. Gale died Feb 20, 1873.

The children were   CAROLINE LELAND, b 1828, m. 1874, Alfred James, res. in Weymouth, Mass   MARTHA LELAND, b 1832, res in Boston, Mass.   MARY KENDALL, b. 1835, res. in Wollaston, Mass.   JAMES AMORY [2], b 1837   ANNAH HARDING, b. July 26, 1840, m March 11, 1860, Lyman[s] Adams, *vid*

[2] **JAMES AMORY GALE** (AMORY, AMORY, JONATHAN), son of Dr Amory and Martha (Leland) Gale was born 1837   He married Jemima Adams Wheeler, daughter of Abijah Richardson and Jemima (Adams) Wheeler.   She was born in East Medway.   They reside in West Medway.

The children were   LELAND AMORY LEWIS.   ANNA ADAMS   HATTIE WHEELER.

HENRY E. GAY (JOSEPH, JOSEPH), son of Joseph and Jane (Rugg) Gay, was born Oct 15, 1830, in Natick, Mass   He married, July 1, 1863, Sarah E. Adams, daughter of Thomas B and Elizabeth (Adams) Adams   She was born in Holliston, Mass   They reside in Medway.

The children were : EMMA D , b May 20, 1866, d Nov. 16, 1866   HATTIE A , b May 1, 1869   EDITH L , b. Feb. 16, 1872, d Nov 13, 1880.

WILLIAM GAY (PETER, PETER), son of Peter and Elizabeth (Merriam) Gay, was born Jan 19, 1812, in Farmington, Me   He married, March 26, 1840, Catherine Williams, daughter of William and Betsey (Springer) Williams, of West Wrentham, Mass   They resided in Medway, Mass.

The children were : MARY ELIZABETH, b. Nov. 18, 1841, d Dec 8, 1847   PHILANDER AUGUSTUS, b July 25, 1846   CHARLES SALISBURY, b Oct 24, 1847, d. Aug 13, 1850   MARY ELIZABETH, b. March 8, 1849, d Aug 21, 1850   MELISSA CATHERINE, b. March 31, 1851.   ARTHUR SUMNER, b. June 17, 1859

ALPHEUS C. GRANT (RHODES, EBENEZER), son of Rhodes and Martha (Cook) Grant, was born Jan. 24, 1812, in Wrentham, Mass.   He married, July 2, 1834, [1]Hannah A Wiggin, daughter of Joshua and Mary Wiggin, of South Berwick, Me   They resided in Medway.   Mrs Mary Grant died March 23, 1849   Mr Grant married, March 23, 1857, [2]Hephzibah B. Jackson, daughter of William and Mary Jackson.   She was born in England.

The child en were · ALPHEUS ORVILLE, b Aug 23, 1842, m Nellie Lovitt, res. in Milford, Mass WILLIAM RHODES, b. Jan 24, 1861. FRANKLIN P , b. April 29, 1865

Memoranda EBENEZER GRANT, Mr. Grant's grandfather, was born in 1714, in Ken-. nebunk, Me , and married Mary Bull, who was born in 1733, in Marblehead, Mass. He died 1799, in Wrentham, Mass. She died in the same place in 1822

RHODES GRANT, Mr. Grant's father, was born in 1780 in Wrentham, Mass , and died Dec. 30, 1852, in Franklin, Mass His mother, Mrs. Martha (Cook) Grant, was born in 1783, in Cumberland, R. I , and died Jan. 18, 1857, in Franklin, Mass

BENJAMIN COOK, Mr Grant's maternal grandfather, born in Salem, Mass , was a cordwainer by trade, at which he worked after he was one hundred years old He died at the age of one hundred and five years, in Cummington, Mass. His wife, Mrs. Abbie Cook, died in the same town at the age of ninety-five years Their married life was nearly eighty years

[1] ABRAHAM[1] HARDING, of Braintree, Mass , became, in 1650, a proprietor of Medfield, Mass. His parentage is unknown. Perhaps he was a son of John Harding, of Weymouth, Mass Mr Harding married Elizabeth Adams They resided in Medfield, Mass Mr Harding died May 22, 1655 Mrs Harding married, 1656, [2]John Frary

The children were MARY, b May 1, 1653 ABRAHAM [3], b Aug 15, 1655

[2] JOHN[1] HARDING, probably a brother of Abraham [1] Harding, settled in Medfield, Mass He married, Nov 26, 1665, [1]Hannah Wood, daughter of Nicholas and Mary (Williams) Wood She was born in Sherborn, Mass. Mrs Hannah Harding died Feb 23, 1667 Mr Harding married, Dec 16, 1668, [2]Elizabeth Adams, daughter of Lieut. Henry and Elizabeth (Paine) Adams. She was born Nov. 11, 1649, in Medfield, Mass. Dea John Harding died March 4, 1720

The children were HANNAH, b Feb. 13, 1667, d. May 26, 1667. ABRAHAM, b Feb 6, 1668, d April 5, 1670 JOHN, b Sept 11, 1669, d May 16, 1670 JOHN, b. Feb 21, 1671, d June 8, 1672 HENRIE, b June 7. 1673. m July 7, 1698, Marie Allen, res in Medfield, Mass ICHABOD, b Nov 23, 1675, m. 1699, Abigail Barbour, d Feb 2. 1730, res. in Medfield, Mass. MARIE, b June 22, 1681, d Jan. 12, 1682. ABRAHAM [4], b Dec 27, 1683. HANNAH, b Oct 16, 1686, d Jan 13, 1718 JOHN, b Sept 23, 1691, d. Jan 16, 1693

[3] ABRAHAM[2] HARDING (ABRAHAM[1]), son of Abraham [1] and Elizabeth (Adams) Harding, was born Aug 15, 1655, in Medfield, Mass He married [1]Mary ——— They resided in Medfield, afterward Medway, Mass Mrs Mary Harding died Mr Harding married [2]Sarah ———.

The children were MEHITABLE, b Oct 17, 1684 MARY, b Aug 25, 1687, m Daniel ——— ELIZABETH, b Jan 1, 1689, d. April 15, 1708 ABRAHAM [5], b. April 5, 1691 THOMAS [6], b Dec 15, 1692 JOHN [7], b April 6, 1694 SARAH, b Feb 22, 1696, m George Fairbanks, *vid* SAMUEL [8], b. May 15, 1698. HANNAH, b Jan. 18, 1699 LYDIA, b Dec 14, 1701, m March 22, 1728, Ephraim Partridge BATHSHEBA, b. Feb 12, 1703, d Jan 18, 1722 ISAAC [9], b. Feb. 16, 1705. ELIZABETH, b July 25, 1708 JOSEPH, b March 22, 1710, d Dec. 31, 1732

[4] ABRAHAM[2] HARDING (JOHN[1]), son of Dea John [2] and Elizabeth (Adams) Harding, was born Dec. 27, 1683, in Medfield, Mass He married, 1706, Mary Smith They resided in Medfield, afterward Medway Mr Harding died May 4, 1741 Mrs Harding died Jan 22, 1749

The children were MOSES, b Dec 23, 1707, m Mary Bullard, res in Medfield, Mass MARY, b. 1709 ELISHA, b April 11, 1711. JOHN, b April 19, 1713 CAIEB, b. Nov 26, 1714 STEPHEN, b May 26, 1717, d July 29, 1717 SIMON, b April 11, 1719. m [1]Patience———; m 1752, [2]Mary Gardner OLIVE, b Sept 4, 1722. JABEZ, b. June 28, 1726, m. 1754, Miriam Wells, res. in Sturbridge, Mass , d February, 1800

[5] ABRAHAM[3] HARDING (ABRAHAM[2], ABRAHAM[1]), son of Abraham [3] and Sarah Harding, was born April 5, 1691, in Medfield, Mass He married Ruth ——— They resided in Medway

The children were RUTH, b. Nov. 2, 1716, d Jan. 18, 1717. SETH, b. Dec. 1, 1717, m March 19, 1743, Experience Hill JOB, b Oct 25, 1719 ICHABOD, b May 31, 1722 DEBORAH, b Oct 1, 1724 RUTH, b Nov. 16, 1726. RUTH, b July 13, 1728. ABRAHAM [10], b Dec 7, 1730.

[6] THOMAS³ HARDING (ABRAHAM², ABRAHAM¹), son of Abraham [3] and Mary Harding, was born Dec. 15, 1692, in Medfield, afterward Medway. He married Hannah ———. They resided in East Medway. Mrs Harding died Sept 15, 1739. Deacon Harding died Oct. 15, 1754

The children were: HANNAH, b June 25, 1719, m David Lovell, res. in Medfield, d 1785 THOMAS [11], b May 13, 1722 JOSHUA, b May 25, 1726, m. Sarah Clark, res in Sturbridge, Mass DOROTHY, b. March 23, 1729 ELIJAH, b. Oct. 15, 1730, res in Sturbridge, Mass PRESERVED, b Sept 29, 1734.

[7] JOHN³ HARDING (ABRAHAM², ABRAHAM¹), son of Abraham [3] and Mary Harding, was born April 6, 1694, in Medfield, afterward Medway He married Thankful Bullard, daughter of John³ and Abigail (Leland) Bullard. They resided in Medway

The children were. JOHN [12], b. Jan 20, 1724 ABIGAIL, b Sept 22, 1726, m February, 1745, Nathan Fiske THANKFUL, b Dec. 17, 1733, m Dec 3, 1755, James Boyden. MERCY, b Dec 9, 1735, m Oct. 9, 1760, Seth Partridge, res. in Wrentham, Mass.

[8] SAMUEL³ HARDING (ABRAHAM², ABRAHAM¹), son of Abraham [3] and Sarah Harding, was born May 15, 1698, in Medfield, afterward Medway. He married Mary ——— They resided in Medway. Mrs. Harding died October, 1778. Mr. Harding died February, 1780

The children were SAMUEL, b. Sept. 21, 1723, d Oct 30, 1723. MARY, b. March 19, 1725. SAMUEL [13], b Jan 7, 1727 JOSEPH, b April 23, 1728 NATHAN [14], b. Oct 1, 1731 STEPHEN, b Oct. 23, 1732. ELIZABETH, b Feb 14, 1738.

[9] ISAAC³ HARDING (ABRAHAM², ABRAHAM¹), son of Abraham [3] and Sarah Harding, was born Feb 16, 1705, in East Medway. He married, March 27, 1728, Rachel Hill, daughter of Samuel and Hannah (Twitchell) Hill. She was born Dec. 12, 1703, in Medfield. They resided in Medway. Mr. Harding died Oct 5, 1779. Mrs. Harding died March 16, 1786

The children were. BATHSHEBA, b Nov. 29, 1731, m. April 25, 1751, Elijah Clark, vid.; d. Sept 14, 1819 SARAH, b. June 12, 1734. THEODORE [15], b July 24, 1736. LOIS, b. July 15, 1739 HANNAH, b. July 8, 1743

[10] ABRAHAM⁴ HARDING (ABRAHAM³, ABRAHAM², ABRAHAM¹), son of Abraham [5] and Ruth Harding, was born Dec. 7, 1730, in Medway He married, Feb. 9, 1757, Abigail Adams, daughter of Daniel⁴ and Sarah Adams She was born June 23, 1736, in Medway, where they resided Mr Harding died March 3, 1819

There was a son SETH [16]

[11] THOMAS⁴ HARDING (THOMAS , ABRAHAM², ABRAHAM¹), son of Thomas [6] and Hannah Harding, was born May 13, 1722, in Medway. He married Susanna Cummings They resided in East Medway

There was a son: THOMAS [17]

[12] JOHN⁴ HARDING (JOHN³, ABRAHAM², ABRAHAM¹), son of John [7] and Thankful (Bullard) Harding, was born Jan 20, 1724, in Medway He married Kezia Pond. She was born in Wrentham, Mass. Mr. Harding died Sept 7, 1809

The children were KEZIA HANNAH, m David Leland. ABIJAH, m June 28, 1770, ¹Sybil Adams; m March 3, 1814, ²Mary Smith, res in Barre, Mass MARY, m Jeremiah Leland, res. in Holliston, Mass. JOHN [18] ALPHEUS, died young.

[13] SAMUEL⁴ HARDING (SAMUEL³, ABRAHAM², ABRAHAM¹), son of Samuel [8] and Mary Harding, was born Jan. 7, 1727, in East Medway. He married and resided in East Medway

There was a son. STEPHEN [19].

[14] NATHAN⁴ HARDING (SAMUEL³, ABRAHAM², ABRAHAM¹), son of Samuel [8] and Mary Harding, was born Oct 1, 1731, in Medway, where he settled.

There was a son ASA [20]

[15] THEODORE⁴ HARDING (ISAAC³, ABRAHAM², ABRAHAM¹), son of Isaac [9] and Rachel (Hill) Harding, was born July 24, 1736, in Medway. He married Lois Clark, daughter of Timothy and Abigail Clark. She was born 1737, in Medway, where they resided Mrs Harding died Sept 28, 1817 Mr Harding died Dec. 18, 1817.

The children were. RHODA, b 1755. SILAS, b. 1756. ELIAS, b 1758. URIAH, b. 1760. LOIS, b 1762. TIMOTHY, b 1764 THEODORE, b. 1767 ABIGAIL, b 1769

35

THEOPHILUS [21], b June 3, 1771   HANNAH, b 1773.   RACHEL, b. 1777.   MARTHA, b. 1779

[16] SETH[5] HARDING (ABRAHAM[4], ABRAHAM[3], ABRAHAM[2], ABRAHAM[1]), son of Abraham [10] and Abigail (Adams) Harding, was born in Medway   He married Mary Learned, daughter of Edward and Sarah (Pratt) Learned   She was born in Sherborn, Mass.   They resided in Medway   Mr. Harding died (was drowned) Jan 28, 1825   Mrs. Harding married, September, 1834, [2]Comfort Walker, of Medway.

The children were. MARY ANN. ABIGAIL, b Oct 24, 1808, m Nov 26, 1829, [1]William J. Partridge, *vid*, m March 25, 1835, [2]Clark Partridge, *vid*, res in Medway. MARY, b March 17, 1811, m April 6, 1830, Clark Partridge, *vid*, d. March 23, 1834   SARAH ANN, b Nov. 23, 1815, m. March 25, 1841, Edward Eaton, *vid.*, d Aug. 28, 1882   ABRAHAM S., m Harriet L Clark, d. May 31, 1882   ADELIZA H., m Francis W Clark, res in Medway   EDWARD L   HARRIET M , m. 1853, Timothy Daniels, res in Holliston, Mass

[17] THOMAS[5] HARDING (THOMAS[4], THOMAS[3], ABRAHAM[2], ABRAHAM[1]), son of Thomas [11] and Susanna (Cummings) Harding, was born in Medway   He married Keziah Bullen   They resided in East Medway

The children were· HENRY [22] LYMAN. SUSANNA, m Charles Howard. LEWIS. A SON. KEZIAH, m. Leonard Fairbanks, d April 25, 1823   ABIGAIL, m Nov 30, 1823, Leonard Fairbanks, d April 17, 1824   LOUISA, m Jan 1, 1824, George H Holbrook, *vid*

[18] JOHN[5] HARDING (JOHN[4], JOHN[3], ABRAHAM[2], ABRAHAM[1]), son of John [12] and Kezia (Pond) Harding, was born in Medway   He married Beulah Metcalf, daughter of the Hon Stephen Metcalf   She was born March 26, 1762, in Bellingham, Mass   They resided in Medway.   Mr Harding died March 11, 1833   Mrs. Harding died March 20, 1839

The children were· HEPHZIBAH, b March 7, 1785, m Alexander Leland, res. in Holliston, Mass   ALPHEUS, b April 20, 1789, m Abigail Chamberlain   BEULAH, b. July 23, 1790, m Lemuel Littlefield, res. in Holliston, Mass   SEWALL [23], b March 20, 1793

[19] STEPHEN[5] HARDING (SAMUEL[4], SAMUEL[3], ABRAHAM[2], ABRAHAM[1]), son of Samuel [13] Harding, was born in Medway   He married [1]Ruth Greenwood.   They resided in Medway, now Millis, Mass   Mrs. Harding died Jan 9, 1819   Mr. Harding married, July 1, 1819, [2]Mrs Sarah Bullen, widow of Jonathan Bullen   She was born in Medfield.

The children were PLINY   PHINEHAS, res in Boston, Mass. GEORGE [24], b June 20, 1799   PATTY, m David Bullen

[20] ASA[5] HARDING (NATHAN[4], SAMUEL[3], ABRAHAM[2], ABRAHAM[1]), son of Nathan [14] Harding, was born in Medway   He married Keziah Jones, daughter of Thomas and Bethiah (Whitney) Jones   She was born in East Medway

The children were. ASA   NATHAN [25], b. Feb 7, 1797   LYDIA, m Dec. 25, 1834, Elias N Tyler.

[21] THEOPHILUS[5] HARDING (THEODORE[4], ISAAC[3], ABRAHAM[2], ABRAHAM[1]), son of Theodore [15] and Lois (Clark) Harding, was born June 3, 1771, in East Medway   He married, Dec 5, 1798, [1]Abigail Clark   She was born in East Medway   Mrs Abigail Harding died Sept 28, 1817   Mr. Harding married, Feb 4, 1819, [2]Mrs Polly Atwell.

The children were. PHILIP CLARK, b Dec. 13, 1799, res. in Brighton, Mass , d. 1882   BETSEY, b July 8, 1802, m Nov 18, 1833, John Cook, res in Watertown, Mass. JULIA, b. Sept 11, 1806, m Sept 11, 1827, Owa Pratt, res in Natick, Mass   THEODORE [26], b Dec 10, 1809   ABIGAIL, b 1816, m Adin Partridge, res in Philadelphia, Penn

[22] HENRY[6] HARDING (THOMAS[5], THOMAS[4], THOMAS[3], ABRAHAM[2], ABRAHAM[1]), son of Thomas [17] and Keziah (Bullen) Harding, was born in East Medway, Mass , where he resided   He married Sally Pickering, of Salem

The children were WILLIAM, m Ruth C. Sherley. ELIZABETH, m Joseph Nute, res in Charlestown, Mass. THOMAS, m Sarah Bacon. MARY ADELAIDE

[23] SEWALL[7] HARDING (JOHN[6], JOHN[5], JOHN[4], JOHN[3], ABRAHAM[2], ABRAHAM[1]), son of John [18] and Beulah (Metcalf) Harding, was born March 20, 1793, in

Medway He married, Nov. 2, 1820, Eliza Wheeler, daughter of Lewis and Betsey (Richardson) Wheeler. She was born in Medway. They resided in Medway, Mass The Rev Mr. Harding died April 12, 1876 Mrs Harding died Feb 2, 1877.

The children were JOHN WHEELER [27], b. Oct 12, 1821. SEWALL BRIGHAM, b Dec. 25, 1823, d. Sept. 19, 1834 ELIZA MERCY, b Dec. 24, 1826, m. Oct. 13, 1852, the Rev Augustus Walker, *vid* GEORGE LEWIS, b Jan. 9, 1830, d Aug. 24, 1849 WILLIAM GREENOUGH [28], b. Aug. 5, 1834 HARRIET BETHIAH, b. Sept. 15, 1836, m April 15, 1857, the Rev. William F Williams, d Dec 25, 1857.

Memoranda. The Rev William F Williams, who married the youngest daughter of the Rev. Sewall Harding, was a missionary of the A. B. C. F. M Mrs. Williams died soon after her arrival on missionary ground.

[24] **GEORGE[6] HARDING** (STEPHEN[5], SAMUEL[4], SAMUEL[3], ABRAHAM[2], ABRAHAM[1]), son of Stephen [19] and Ruth (Greenwood) Harding, was born June 20, 1799, in East Medway He married, Jan. 13, 1825, Kezia Morse, daughter of Benoni and Polly (Hobbs) Morse. They resided in East Medway Mr. Harding died March 24, 1883

The only child was MARIA A , b Sept. 17, 1828, m. April 17, 1853, James L Bickford, *vid ,* res in East Medway, now Millis.

Memoranda. Chester Harding, Esq , an eminent artist, was a descendant of Samuel[4] Harding, grandfather of Stephen Harding, Esq He painted the portraits of several of the Presidents of the United States, and also of the Dukes of Norfolk, Hamilton, Sussex, and many of the nobility of England *Vid Harding Genealogy.*

[25] **NATHAN[6] HARDING** (ASA[5], NATHAN[4], SAMUEL[3], ABRAHAM[2], ABRAHAM[1]), son of Asa [20] and Kezia (Jones) Harding, was born Feb. 7, 1797, in East Medway. He married, April 10, 1825, Keziah Adams, daughter of Elijah and Lydia (Smith) Adams She was born Jan. 25, 1799, in Medfield, Mass. They resided in East Medway. Mr Harding died May 30, 1854 Mrs Harding died Sept. 21, 1882

The children were LAURA ANN, b Oct 25, 1825, m Nov 18, 1843, James H Ellis, *vid.,* ADDISON A , b. Dec 2, 1830, d August, 1832. ELVIRA A , b. March 2, 1833, m. John A. Hutchins, *vid,* d. April 11, 1884 TRYPHENA MELVINA, b Sept. 6, 1837, m. Nov. 25, 1854, Frederic Swarman. ADELIZA MARIA, b. April 29, 1840, m. Oct. 18, 1861, Leander S Daniels, *vid ,* d. Oct. 27, 1883.

[26] **THEODORE[6] HARDING** (THEOPHILUS[5], THEODORE[4], ISAAC[3], ABRAHAM[2], ABRAHAM[1]), son of Theophilus [21] and Abigail (Clark) Harding, was born Dec. 10, 1809, in East Medway. He married [1]Nancy Clark She was born in Milford, Mass. They resided in East Medway. Mrs. Nancy Harding died Nov. 10, 1857. Mr. Harding married, Dec 19, 1861, [2]Mrs Abigail Adams Crosby, *née* Lovell, daughter of Michael and Caty (Daniels) Lovell, and widow of George Crosby. She was born Oct 25, 1818 Mrs Abigail A Harding died Dec 23, 1870 Mr Harding married [3]Harriet Conant Mr Harding died March 9, 1883.

The children were SARAH PRATT, b May 8, 1835, m L J Brown, res in Fitchburg, Mass MARY FLIZABETH, b. Nov 1, 1836, m. J. M. Batchelder, res. in Holliston, Mass JOHN CLARK, b. Dec 9, 1838, m Fanny Estabrook, res in Philadelphia, Penn BETSEY MARIA, b. April 14, 1841, m Edward A. Brown, res. in Worcester ABIGAIL ELIZA, b. March 7, 1843, res in Fitchburg, Mass. CHARLES THEODORE, b Aug 31, 1845, m. [1]Ella Josephine Haines; m. [2]Ellen Lane, res in Fitchburg, Mass. GEORGE LEWIS, b Sept 3, 1848, m. Augusta ———, res in Utah. WILLIAM FRANCIS, b June 24, 1851, m. Mary Clark, res in Medfield, Mass. SYLVIA ANNA, b Jan. 29, 1854, d Dec 19, 1873

. [27] **JOHN WHEELER[7] HARDING** (SEWALL[7], JOHN[6], JOHN[5], JOHN[4], JOHN[3], ABRAHAM[2], ABRAHAM[1]), son of the Rev Sewall [23] and Eliza (Wheeler) Harding, was born Oct. 12, 1821, in Waltham, Mass. He married, Dec. 29, 1852, Mehitable Pratt Lane, daughter of Jenkins and Mehitable (Pratt) Lane She was born in Abington, now Rockland, Mass They reside in Long Meadow, Mass.

The children were WILLIAM COLT, b June 24, 1854 GRACE, b. Aug 19, 1857, m. June 26, 1884, William B. Medlicott JOHN PUTNAM, b. April 26, 1861 MARY, b. April 17, 1865 PAUL, b. Oct 27, 1870, d Oct. 1, 1871.

[28] **WILLIAM[9] GREENOUGH HARDING** (SEWALL[7], JOHN[6], JOHN[5], JOHN[4], JOHN[3], ABRAHAM[2], ABRAHAM[1]), son of the Rev. Sewall [23] and Eliza (Wheeler)

Harding, was born Aug 5, 1834, in Waltham, Mass. He married, June 27, 1861, Nancy P Campbell, daughter of George and Matilda (Jenkins) Campbell. She was born in Pittsfield, Mass , where they resided.

The children were HATTIE, b Aug 8, 1862 ISABEL, b. July 30, 1864. GEORGE CAMPBELL, b May 18, 1867 MALCOLM CAMPBELL, b. Aug. 11, 1869, d. Nov. 5, 1874 HOPE CAMPBELL, b. Aug 24, 1871, d Nov 8, 1874

THOMAS J. HARRINGTON (MICHAEL, PETER, THOMAS), son of Michael and Catharine (Jennings) Harrington, was born in Parish Kiltoma, County of Roscoe, Ireland. He married, April 5, 1858, Mary Donovan, daughter of Thomas and Dora (Cleary) Donovan They resided in West Medway.

The children were CATHARINE, b. Dec 28, 1859, m November, 1881, Thomas McCan JOHN, b Feb 7, 1861, d June 7, 1882 MARY SUSANNA

EPHRAIM NELSON HIDDEN, son of Ephraim and Dorothy (Remick) Hidden, was born Aug 28, 1810, in Tamworth, N H He married, Aug 28, 1840, Mary Elizabeth Parsons, daughter of Josiah and Judith (Badger) Parsons. They resided in East Medway The Rev Mr. Hidden died Nov 28, 1880.

The children were. FANNY MARTHA, b Dec 20, 1841, m Aug 28, 1865, Benjamin Greely Page, d. Oct. 28, 1870 MARY E , b Sept 29, 1843, d April 17, 1847. EMILY PARSONS, b. Dec 28, 1846, d April 1, 1882

DEMING J. HASTINGS, son of Benjamin and Sally (Jarvis) Hastings, was born March 10, 1818, in Boston, Mass He married, Nov 28, 1839, Lucia A Daniels, daughter of Lyman and Hyrena (Payne) Daniels She was born May 28, 1817, in Mendon, Mass

The children were. HARRIET LUCIA, b Oct 2, 1840, m July 24, 1864, Charles Thompson Adams, *vid.* ADDISON T , b Feb 22, 1842 MARY LAMB, b Jan. 27, 1844

MOSES HILL, son of Moses and Persis Hill, was born March 22, 1823, in Bellingham, Mass. He married, Feb 26, 1846, Eliza A Arnold, daughter of Nathan and Rosina Arnold. She was born in Cumberland, R. I. They resided in East Medway Mr Hill died Oct 29, 1862

The children were LUSINA M , b June 2, 1848, m Frank Howe, res in Medfield, Mass. GEORGE R., b. Nov 26, 1858, m. June 21, 1882, Carrie F Clark, res in Holliston, Mass

Memoranda Mrs Hill's father, Nathan Arnold, was born Sept 18, 1787, in Cumberland, R. I. He was a manufacturer, and died Oct. 31, 1848 Her mother, Mrs Rosina Arnold, was born Dec 2, 1783, in the same town, and died Dec 6, 1825

[1] SAMUEL[5] HILL (SAMUEL[4], SAMUEL[3], SAMUEL[2], JOHN[1]), son of Samuel and Mary Hill, was born May 10, 1736, in Medway He married [1]Abigail ——. They resided in Medway Mrs Hill died Mr. Hill married [2]Kezia —— Mrs. Kezia Hill died Oct 27, 1810. Mr. Hill died May 25, 1815

The children were SAMUEL, b Dec 5, 1767, d Feb. 4, 1802 REUBEN [2], b. 1774.

[2] REUBEN[6] HILL (SAMUEL[5], SAMUEL[4], SAMUEL[3], SAMUEL[2], JOHN[1]), son of Samuel Hill, was born in East Medway He married Rebecca Bullard, daughter of Henry[5] and Rebecca (Richardson) Bullard. She was born Aug 22, 1777. They resided in East Medway. Mr Hill died Aug 12, 1830 Mrs Hill died Sept 25, 1852

The children were DAVID [3], b Oct 11, 1798 KEZIAH, b. Dec 29, 1800, m. June 6, 1820, David Daniels, *vid*

[3] DAVID[7] HILL (REUBEN[6], SAMUEL[5], SAMUEL[4], SAMUEL[3], SAMUEL[2], JOHN[1]), son of Reuben and Rebecca (Bullard) Hill, was born Oct 11, 1798, in East Medway He married, Dec 2, 1819, Sarah Crooks. She was born in Hopkinton, Mass Mr. Hill died Oct 25, 1839 Mrs. Hill died July 24, 1849

FISHER HILL (SIMON[5], SAMUEL[4], SAMUEL[3], SAMUEL[2], JOHN[1]), son of Simon and Prudence (Lovell) Hill, was born Jan. 17, 1784 He married, April 19, 1818, Clarissa Partridge, daughter of Samuel[4] and Mehitable (Allen) Partridge. They resided in Medway Mr Hill's maternal grand-parents were Joseph and Prudence (Clark) Lovell His mother, Mrs. Prudence (Lovell) Hill, was born Oct. 3, 1743

The only child was. CLARA P , born Feb 13, 1819.

Memoranda. Simon Hill, brother of Samuel [1], was born July 17, 1738 They had a sister, Mary, born Feb. 15, 1734, and a brother, Timothy, born Dec 16, 1740

CHARLES HILL, son of Samuel and Mary (Partridge) Hill, was born Sept. 27, 1796, in Sherborn, Mass He married, July 11, 1824, Nancy Jones, daughter of Simpson and Abigail (Hammond) Jones She was born July 29, 1797, in East Medway, where they resided Mr Hill died Aug 2, 1874

The children were. SAMUEL FRANCIS, b. March 20, 1826, d Sept 29, 1826. MARY PARTRIDGE, b July 13, 1827, m. Elijah Partridge, *vid.* ABBY HAMMOND, b March 1, 1830 PHEBE AUGUSTA, b Dec 13, 1831, d Aug 19, 1877. CHARLES IRVING, b. May 18, 1839, d. November, 1840 HARRIET ELIZA, b Sept. 3, 1841, m May 1, 1867, Edward Southworth, res. in Quincy, Mass.

[1] "WALTER HIXON, of Stoughton, Bricklayer," was the earliest known ancestor of the Medway Hixons He was born June 15, 1705 Walter Hixon was a volunteer in the quota of Massachusetts in the expedition sent by the British Government against the Spanish dominions in America, especially Cuba. Only fifty men of the five hundred whom the state sent out, survived to return. It is probable that Mr. Hixon was among those who lost their lives. He married Mary ————.

The children were EBENEZER, b. June 17, 1729, d. Oct. 5, 1733. MARY, b. Oct 3, 1731 EBENEZER, b. Feb 19, 1733 SETH [2], b 1734 ELKANAH H, d. March 19, 1740 EZRA, b March 19, 1741.

[2] SETH HIXON (WALTER), son of Walter [1] and Mary Hixon, was born 1734 He married Bethiah Partridge, and settled in Medway about 1759.

The children were· SETH, b. June 21, 1759, d. May 19, 1770. JOTHAM, b May 29, 1761, d Oct 4, 1764 ISAAC [3], b Oct 18, 1762. REUBEN, b June 9, 1765. ASA [4], b April 9, 1768

[3] ISAAC HIXON (SETH, WALTER), son of Seth [2] and Bethiah (Partridge) Hixon, was born Oct 18, 1762, in Medway He married ¹Elizabeth Harding. They resided in Medway Mrs. Elizabeth Hixon died Mr Hixon married ²Persis Adams. Mr Hixon died March 18, 1852

The children were WILLARD [5], b Oct 16, 1788 ELIAS [6], b July 19, 1791 ELIHU [7], b April 18, 1796 ISAAC [8], b January, 1799 ABRAHAM, b March 3, 1802, m Jemima Gould JACOB, b April 17, 1804. ELIZABETH, b June 11, 1812, m Henry Field, res in Dayton, O. ALFRED, b Jan 3, 1815 IRA [9], b. April 23, 1817 EGBERT OSWALD, b Aug 1, 1824

[4] ASA HIXON (SETH, WALTER), son of Seth [2] and Bethiah (Partridge) Hixon, was born Sept 9, 1768, in Medway. He married Polly Turner. Mr. Hixon died March 18, 1852

The children were AMOS T, b June 7, 1792, d Oct 25, 1815. MARY, b May 9, 1799,· m. Zebina Bullard, d May 26, 1856. SETH [10], b. Aug 22, 1799 ASA [11], b March 6, 1800. ISANNA E., b. March 23, 1804, m Dea. Daniel Wiley, d March 18, 1855.

[5] WILLARD HIXON (ISAAC, SETH, WALTER), son of Isaac [3] Hixon, was born Oct. 16, 1788, in Medway He married Dorcas Bartholomew. Mr Hixon died Jan 12, 1851.

The children were EDWIN, b June, 1809, res in Uxbridge, d January, 1880 ANSON, b. Dec. 9, 1812, m Eliza C. Fuller. JOTHAM, b. Feb. 8, 1815, m Lavinia Pickering FRANCIS [12] JULIANA, b Dec. 18, 1818 ELIZABETH, b March 24, 1820, m H Wilmarth, d Sept 19, 1880 SUSANNA, b April 25, 1822, d. March 17, 1832 JOSEPH W [13], b Feb 3, 1824 ALONZO [14], b Feb 17, 1826 PEMBROKE [15], b May 18, 1828. ABRAHAM, b Aug 3, 1829, d. April 12, 1835

[6] ELIAS HIXON (ISAAC, SETH, WALTER), son of Isaac [3] Hixon, was born July 19, 1791 He married Zebiah Learned Mr Hixon died Oct 25, 1864.

The children were· HARRIET, m Jerome S Peck GEORGE, b. Nov 14, 1818. GILBERT, b. April 24, 1822.

[7] ELIHU HIXON (ISAAC, SETH, WALTER), son of Isaac [3], was born April 18, 1796 He married Hannah Putnam. Mr Hixon died Oct 12, 1852.

The children were. LUCY A, b June 11, 1828, m Joel Baker. JULIA A, b. May 9, 1830, m. John M Adams. ELIZABETH P., b. March 20, 1832, m Oct 18, 1855, Leander S Daniels, *vid.*, d. Oct. 25, 1859 BENJAMIN F., b. Feb 24, 1834, d. Aug 30, 1840 HELEN M, b. July 7, 1836, d. Oct. 16, 1837 GEORGE [16], b. March 15, 1838.

[8] ISAAC HIXON (ISAAC, SETH, WALTER), son of Isaac [3] Hixon, was born Jan. 18, 1799 He married Sally Perry Mr Hixon died Dec. 14, 1860

The children were MARIANNA, b. March 2, 1823, m. Daniel Bullard, res in Sherborn, Mass CALVIN P., b Oct 9, 1825, res in Iowa WILLIAM, b. June 14, 1827, d March 26, 1850 GILBERT, b Aug 3, 1829, res in Union City, Penn. EDWARD, b. March 23, 1832, res in Southville, Mass ANDREW J , b March 26, 1834, m Kate E. Harvey, res in New York City SARAH T., b July 16, 1837, m. [1]C. L. Coolidge, m. [2]Lucius Pierce. EUGENE F., b. Jan 7, 1844, d in infancy

[9] IRA HIXON (ISAAC, SETH, WALTER), son of Seth [3] Hixon, was born April 23, 1817 He married Caroline Cargill. Mr Hixon died in 1847

The children were ADELAIDE, b Dec 30, 1840, m Samuel P Moody ADELIZA, b Dec 30, 1840. ALBERT W , b Sept 26, 1844

[10] SETH HIXON (ASA, SETH, WALTER), son of Asa [4] and Polly (Turner) Hixon, was born Aug 22, 1799 He married Mehitable Barton He died July 28, 1873

The children were. JULIA M , b Feb. 20, 1825, m [1]James E Leach; m [2]Dea N P Chapin, res. in Brooklyn, N Y C DANA, b March 28, 1827, d. Jan. 12, 1848 OPHELIA A , b. July 1, 1830, m. Elbridge Smith, res in Walpole, Mass. SOPHIE A , b. July 9, 1839, d Oct 2, 1860 WALDO B [17], b Nov 22, 1842, m Sarah Lincoln, d March 12, 1879

[11] ASA HIXON (ASA, SETH, WALTER), son of Asa [4] and Polly (Turner) Hixon, was born March 6, 1800 He married Charlotte Baker The Rev Mr. Hixon died Nov 16, 1862.

The only child was DAVID B [18], b Feb 22, 1843

[12] FRANCIS HIXON (WILLARD, ISAAC, SETH, WALTER), son of Willard [5] and Dorcas (Bartholomew) Hixon, was born March 9, 1816 He married Betsey Greenwood

The children were CAROLINE F , b Jan 10, 1847, m Charles C Greenwood HENRY A., b. Sept. 16, 1848 ZACHARY T , b March 10, 1850 AMY A , b Nov 25, 1851 MARY E , b Oct 13, 1852 ORIELLA, b Feb 23, 1854 FLORIBELLE, b Sept 10, 1855 BENJAMIN C , b Oct 24, 1858 ELSIE, b April 25, 1860 CHARLES G , b Dec 11, 1863

[13] JOSEPH W. (WILLARD, ISAAC, SETH, WALTER), son of Willard [5] and Dorcas (Bartholomew) Hixon, was born Feb 3, 1824 He married [1]Rhoda A Phipps Mrs. Rhoda Hixon died Mr Hixon married [2]Marianna Mason

The children were EDGAR L FANNIE CHARLES M.

[14] ALONZO HIXON (WILLARD, ISAAC, SETH, WALTER), son of Willard [5] and Dorcas (Bartholomew) Hixon, was born Feb 17, 1826 He married [1]Caroline Greenwood, who died, and Mr. Hixon married [2]Susan Maynard

The children were ESTHER A HERBERT A. ELLEN F. GEORGE F. EGBERT A WILLIAM I

[15] PEMBROKE HIXON (WILLARD, ISAAC, SETH, WALTER), son of Willard [5] and Dorcas (Bartholomew) Hixon, was born May 15, 1828 He married [1]Mary E Andrews Mrs Mary E. Hixon died Mr Hixon married [2]Annie Brown

The only child was ALICE M

[16] GEORGE HIXON (ELIHU, ISAAC, SETH, WALTER), son of Elihu [7] and Hannah (Putnam) Hixon, was born March 15, 1838 He married [1]Mary E Green, who died Mr. Hixon married [2]Hannah E Coombs

The children were HERBERT N , b April 16, 1877 CATHERINE, b June 7, 1881.

[17] WALDO B HIXON (SETH, ASA, SETH, WALTER), son of Seth Hixon, was born Nov. 22, 1842 He married Sarah Lincoln Mr Hixon died March 12, 1879

The children were LENA B , b May 15, 1866 CHARLES D , b. May 7, 1868

[18] DAVID B HIXON (ASA, ASA, SETH, WALTER), son of the Rev Asa [11] and Charlotte (Baker) Hixon, was born Feb 22, 1843 He married, Jan 24, 1866, Carrie P Shumway, daughter of Amos and Patience Shumway They reside in Brooklyn, N Y

The children were HERBERT S , b. Aug 18, 1867. NELLIE S , b Jan 11, 1870

[1] GEORGE[6] HOLBROOK (DANIEL[5], DANIEL[4], ELEAZAR[3], THOMAS[2], JOHN[1]), son of Daniel[5] and Esther (Hall) Holbrook, was born April 28, 1767, in Wrentham,

Mass He married [1]Mary Wood, daughter of Thomas and Nabby (Bannister) Wood. They resided in Brookfield, Mass., and removed, in 1815, to East Medway. Mrs Mary Holbrook died Jan 22, 1834 Mr. Holbrook married [2]Roxanna Hills. She was born in Haddam, Conn. Major Holbrook died Sept 30, 1846

The children were GEORGE HANDEL [2], b July 21, 1798 MARY EVALINA, b. Jan 2, 1807, m Jan. 27, 1825, John Baker, res. in Boston, Mass EDWIN.

[2] GEORGE HANDEL[7] HOLBROOK (GEORGE[6], DANIEL[5], DANIEL[4], ELEAZAR[3], THOMAS[2], JOHN[1]), was born July 21, 1798, in Brookfield, Mass. He married, Jan. 1, 1824, Louisa Harding, daughter of Thomas and Keziah (Bullen) Harding She was born Sept 28, 1800, in East Medway, where they resided Col George H. Holbrook died March 20, 1875

The children were· EDWIN L. [3], b. October, 1824 MARY L, res in Dedham, Mass., d Nov 15, 1833 ELLEN, res in East Medway, now Millis.

[3] EDWIN L.[8] HOLBROOK (GEORGE HANDEL[7], GEORGE[6], DANIEL[5], DANIEL[4], ELEAZAR[3], THOMAS[2], JOHN[1]), son of George Handel [2] and Louisa (Harding) Holbrook, was born October, 1824, in East Medway. He married, Nov. 12, 1845, Abigail Davis Hills, daughter of Seneca and Maria (Richardson) Hills. She was born in East Medway, where they resided

The children were: EDWIN HANDEL [4], b Oct 30, 1846 LOUISA MARIA, b. Jan. 12, 1851, m. Sept 4, 1872, Lowell A Mann MARY EVELYN, b March 1, 1856, m. March 1, 1880, George E Stanniford, res. in Salem, Mass GEORGE FRANCIS [5], b. March 8, 1858, m Dec 6, 1883, Rhoda D. Fuller. ABBIE LOVELL, b. July 2, 1860, m. June 6, 1881, Edward R. Davis, res. in Boston, Mass. JESSIE FLORENCE, b. Feb 1, 1862, m Sept 18, 1882, Metcalf F. Pond, res. in North Adams, Mass.

[4] EDWIN HANDEL[9] HOLBROOK (EDWIN L[8], GEORGE H.[7], GEORGE[6], DANIEL[5], DANIEL[4], ELEAZAR[3], THOMAS[2], JOHN[1]), son of Edwin L.[8] [3] and Abigail Davis (Hills) Holbrook, was born Oct 30, 1846 He married, Oct. 30, 1872, Emma E. Fuller, daughter of Israel Daniels and Eliza (Barber) Fuller She was born May 12, 1849, in East Medway. They reside in Washington, D C.

The children were HARRY M, b. June 2, 1875, d Sept 8, 1875 WESLEY FULLER, b Aug 22, 1878

[5] GEORGE FRANCIS[9] HOLBROOK (EDWIN L[8], GEORGE H[7], GEORGE[6], DANIEL[5], DANIEL[4], ELEAZAR[3], THOMAS[2], JOHN[1]), son of Edwin L.[8] [3] and Abigail Davis (Hills) Holbrook, was born March 8, 1858. He married, Dec. 6, 1882, Rhoda D. Fuller They reside in East Medway.

The only child was HARRY FRANCIS, b in 1883

GERMAN S HOSLEY (SAMUEL, DAVID), son of Samuel and Polly (Remington) Hosley, was born in Brooklyn, Vt. He married, Feb 24, 1863, Laura S. Ingalls, daughter of William and Sophia Ingalls. She was born in Vernon, Vt. They resided in East Medway.

The children were MORGIANNA, b May 2, 1879, d March 27, 1881 LULA R, b Dec. 2, 1880.

JAMES HOSMER, immigrant, son of Stephen and Dorothy Hosmer, was born 1605, in Hawkhurst, Kent, England He came to America in 1634 He died in 1685, in Concord, Mass

JAMES[6] HOSMER (JOEL[5], EPHRAIM[4] STEPHEN[3], STEPHEN[2], JAMES[1]), was born 1802, in Acton, Mass He married, April 7, 1830, Anna Day Daniels, daughter of Amos and Anna (Daniels) Daniels She was born March 10, 1809, in Medway, where they resided Mr. James Hosmer died Oct. 29, 1861.

The children were ANN AUGUSTA, b 1831 ESTHER MARIA, b 1834, d 1857. MARSHALL EDMUND, b 1835, d 1857 HARRIETTE ELIZABETH, b. 1839, d. Feb 14, 1851. HENRY EDWARD, b 1842 ALDEN ABIEL, b. 1845.

ENOCH HUNT was the first of the name in this country. The English records make mention of the name of Hunt as early as the twelfth century. The name is of Norman descent, and had its origin in the sports of the chase, i. e, " to pursue " Enoch Hunt settled in 1633, in Weymouth, Mass.

WILLIAM HUNT arrived from Halifax, Yorkshire, England, with his wife, four sons, and two daughters, in 1635, and settled in Concord, Mass From him descended the first of the name in Medway.

JOEL[6] HUNT (DANIEL[5], ABIJAH[4], ISAAC[3], ISAAC[2], WILLIAM[1]), son of Daniel and Mary (Phillips) Hunt, was born Nov. 27, 1782, in Milford, Mass He married, June 3, 1807, Clara Metcalf, only daughter of Luther and Mary (Whiting) Metcalf She was born Feb 7, 1784, in Medway, to which place they removed in 1811, from Milford, Mass Mr. Hunt died Sept. 1, 1852. Mis Hunt died Dec. 3, 1853

The children were GEORGE WASHINGTON, b. March 14, 1808, m May 1, 1833, Nancy Adams, res. in Lawrence, Kan LUTHER METCALF, b. Aug 4, 1809, m Dec 20, 1832, [1]Phebe Force; m June 1, 1844, [2]Abby H. Partridge, m Jan 13, 1850, [3]Fanny C. Draper, res. in Milford, Mass. CLARA AMELIA, b July 19, 1811, m March 25, 1856, Cephas Thayer, *vid*. JOEL EDWARD, b June 19, 1813, m November, 1839, Emelia Knapp MERCY MARIA, b Aug 17, 1815, m Enos Goss WELLINGTON L. G., b Oct. 31, 1817, m Oct. 28, 1845, [1]Caroline A Fisher; m Oct. 2, 1848, [2]Hephzibah A. Watts, res. in Boston, Mass HARRIET SOPHIA, b. Jan 18, 1820, m. April 19, 1847, Charles Hamant, res in Medfield, Mass FRANCIS ALPHONZO, b March 20, 1822, m June 26, 1845, Henrietta Heard, res in Denver, Col CAROLINE, b. July 6, 1824, m. Oct 30, 1845, John W Partridge, res in Franklin, Mass ELIZABETH MINERVA, b April 14, 1827, m Nov 30, 1854, John N Brown, res. in Candia, N H.

WILLIAM HENRY HUNTING (RICHARD, DANIEL), son of Richard and Margaret (Kingsbury) Hunting, was born May 9, 1814, in Boston, Mass He married, June 1, 1836, [1]Rhoda A. P Fuller, daughter of Elihu and Rhoda (Daniels) Fuller She was born Oct 22, 1817, in East Medway, where they resided Mis Rhoda A P Hunting died March 23, 1845 Mr Hunting married, Nov. 17, 1853, [2]Sarah A Phipps, daughter of Nathan Phipps Mrs Sarah A Hunting died June 17, 1861 Mr. Hunting married, May 12, 1867, [3]Julia A Jepson. Mr Hunting died May 17, 1880

The children were SARAH MARIA, b Aug 25, 1838 RHODA DANIELS, b. Nov 26, 1840, m Albert F Fales. OPHELIA, b May 31, 1843, m Charles H Bickford, res in Sherborn, Mass.

JACOB IDE, son of Jacob and Lydia (Kent) Ide, was born March 29, 1785, in Attleboro, Mass He married, April 13, 1815, Mary Emmons, daughter of the Rev Dr Nathaniel and Martha (Williams) Emmons She was born Dec. 3, 1790, in Franklin, Mass. They resided in West Medway The Rev. Dr Ide died Jan 5, 1880. Mrs Mary Ide died June 30, 1880

The children were. ISABELLA TAPPAN, b Feb 6, 1816, d Nov 18, 1863 MARY, b. June 29, 1817, m March 29, 1837, Charles T Toirey, d Nov 6, 1869 HENRY, b Oct. 23, 1818, d Jan. 30, 1819 ERASTUS, b Jan 10, 1820, d. Feb. 20, 1821 NATHANIEL EMMONS, b Aug. 28, 1821, d July 29, 1847 JACOB, b. Aug. 7, 1823, m March 24, 1859, Ellen M Rogers, they resided in Mansfield, Mass. SARAH WILLIAMS, b. Aug 17, 1825, d Jan 20, 1826 ALEXIS WHEATON, b. Oct. 10, 1826 CHARLES W, b Jan 20, 1829, d Aug 9, 1829 GEORGE HOPKINS, b. May 10, 1830, d July 10, 1831 GEORGE HOMER, b. Feb 3, 1835, d Aug. 9, 1862.

ARMS.

EPHRAIM ORCUTT[4] JAMESON (DANIEL[3], DANIEL[2], HUGH[1]), son of Daniel and Mary (Twiss) Jameson, was born Jan 23, 1832, in Dunbarton, N H He married, Sept 20, 1858, Mary Joanna Cogswell, daughter of the Rev. Dr. William and Joanna (Strong) Cogswell. She was born June 6, 1832, in Boston, Mass They resided in Concord, N H, Salisbury, Mass, and removed in 1871, to East Medway, now Millis, Mass

The children were ARTHUR ORCUTT, b. Nov 25, 1859, d Sept, 30, 1881 KATHARINE STRONG, b Sept. 15, 1861. WILLIAM COGSWELL, b. Jan 2, 1865, d. Jan. 7, 1865 CAROLINE COGSWELL, b Feb 7, 1866 MARY, b Jan 10, 1868

[1] WILLIAM[1] JONES, immigrant, was born about 1587 He came to America and was one of the earliest settlers of Charlestown, Mass. His death is thus recorded " Old Father Jones, near ninety, died March 8, 1677."

There was a son THOMAS [2]

[2] THOMAS[2] JONES (WILLIAM[1]), son of William [1] Jones, was born about 1645, in Charlestown, Mass. He married, 1669, Sarah Couch, of Charlestown, Mass. Mr. Jones died Nov. 28, 1679. Mrs Jones died Dec 11, 1704

The children were. SARAH, b April 24, 1670, m Jonathan Smith. MARY, b May 13, 1672. THOMAS [3], b July 3, 1674 WILLIAM, b. Oct. 4, 1676

[3] THOMAS³ JONES (THOMAS², WILLIAM¹), son of Thomas [2] and Sarah (Couch) Jones, was born July 3, 1674, in Charlestown, Mass. He married, April 30, 1701, Elizabeth Bullard Mr. Jones, prior to 1695, settled in Sherborn, that part which since 1723 is Holliston, Mass. Mr Jones died May 25, 1729

The children were JONATHAN, b Dec. 13, 1701, m Jan 25, 1727, Hannah Adams, res in Holliston, Mass. ELI, b. Dec 5, 1704. m. May 15, 1729, Mercy Underwood. THOMAS [4], b. May 27, 1706. ELIZABETH, b May 27, 1711 AARON, b. April 11, 1713, m. Elizabeth Bullard, res in Holliston, Mass

[4] THOMAS⁴ JONES (THOMAS³, THOMAS², WILLIAM¹), son of Thomas [3] and Elizabeth (Bullard) Jones, was born May 27, 1706, in Sherborn, now Holliston, Mass. He married, May 27, 1728, Esther Richardson, daughter of John and Esther (Breck) Richardson. She was born Jan 2, 1707, in Medfield, afterward East Medway, where they resided. Mr Jones died June 23, 1734 Mrs Esther Jones married, Jan. 31, 1735, ²Lieut Nathaniel Clark. She died March 24, 1770

There was a son THOMAS [5], b. May 29, 1730.

[5] THOMAS⁵ JONES (THOMAS⁴, THOMAS³, THOMAS², WILLIAM¹), son of Thomas [4] and Esther (Richardson) Jones, was born May 29, 1730, in East Medway He married Bethia Whitney. of Uxbridge, Mass. They resided in East Medway. Mr Jones died Feb 7, 1802. Mrs Jones died July 22, 1822.

The children were. SIMPSON [6], b April 7, 1756 NATHAN [7], b. April 4, 1762. KEZIAH, m Asa⁶ Harding, *vid*

[6] SIMPSON⁶ JONES (THOMAS⁵, THOMAS⁴, THOMAS³, THOMAS², WILLIAM¹), son of Thomas [5] and Bethia (Whitney) Jones, was born April 7, 1756, in East Medway He married, June 22, 1780, Abigail Hammond, daughter of Timothy and Abigail (Adams) Hammond She was born Oct. 29, 1761, in East Medway, where they resided Mrs Abigail Jones died Aug 3, 1816. Mr. Jones married, Nov. 18, 1819, Mrs. Mercy Hill, *née* Holbrook, of Mendon, Mass Captain Jones died June 28, 1825 Mrs Mercy Jones died 1841.

The children were: ELISHA ADAMS [8], b April 11, 1781. HORATIO, b. June 2, 1786, d Jan 6, 1825. NABBY, b. October, 1790, m Dec 12, 1824, Thomas Munyan, res in Providence, R I, d March 4, 1872 NANCY, b July 29, 1797, m July 11, 1824, Charles Hill, res in Sherborn, Mass., but removed to East Medway.

[7] NATHAN⁶ JONES (THOMAS⁵, THOMAS⁴, THOMAS³, THOMAS², WILLIAM¹), son of Thomas [5] and Bethia (Whitney) Jones, was born April 4, 1762, in East Medway. He married, Aug 22, 1782, Sarah Clark.

There was a son. NATHAN [9], b. Nov. 2, 1786.

[8] ELISHA⁷ ADAMS JONES (SIMPSON⁶, THOMAS⁵, THOMAS⁴, THOMAS³, THOMAS², WILLIAM¹), son of Simpson [6] and Abigail (Hammond) Jones, was born April 11, 1781, in East Medway He married, Feb. 11, 1810, ¹Hannah Richardson, daughter of Asa Partridge and Hannah (Hill) Richardson. She was born March 1, 1780, in East Medway, where they resided Mrs Hannah Jones died Jan. 19, 1838. Mr. Jones married, June 25, 1840, ²Amy Richardson, daughter of Joseph and Ama (Adams) Richardson She was born 1799, in Medway. Captain Jones died Feb 16, 1860 Mrs Amy Jones died July 12, 1866

The children were: HARRIET, b. Dec 12, 1811, m June 8, 1838, Matthew Brown, d. Dec. 20, 1849 ADELINE, b. Jan. 12, 1814, m. Jan. 20, 1841, Abijah R. Wheeler, d. July, 1848. EMELINE, b Jan 12, 1814, d April 8, 1875. ELISHA ADAMS [10], b Oct 23, 1815 HORATIO [11], b Sept 1, 1823.

[9] NATHAN⁷ JONES (NATHAN⁶, THOMAS⁵, THOMAS⁴, THOMAS³, THOMAS², WILLIAM¹), son of Nathan [7] and Sarah (Clark) Jones, was born Nov. 2, 1786, in East Medway. He married, April 21, 1808, Jemima Richardson, daughter of Ezra and Jemima (Lovell) Richardson. She was born Nov. 30, 1788, in East Medway, where they resided. Mrs. Jones died Feb 12, 1868. Mr Jones died Dec. 8, 1870

The children were· JOHN P SARAH, m ——— Thurston. FRANCES B, d. Jan 12, 1827. THOMAS, d. Feb. 21, 1832

[10] ELISHA ADAMS⁸ JONES (ELISHA ADAMS⁷, SIMPSON⁶, THOMAS⁵, THOMAS⁴, THOMAS³, THOMAS², WILLIAM¹), son of Elisha Adams [8] and Hannah

36

(Richardson) Jones, was born Oct 13, 1815, in East Medway He married, April 29, 1840, [1]Rhoda Ellis, daughter of Moses and Almera (Woodward) Ellis She was born April 6, 1820, in Medway, where they resided. Mrs Rhoda Jones died Sept. 27, 1873 Mr Jones married, Jan 25, 1877, [2]Mrs Melinda G. Walker, *née* Whipple, daughter of Jonathan and Melinda (Grout) Whipple, and widow of John S Walker, *vid* She was born March 5, 1831, in Grafton, Mass

The *children were* ELLEN ALMERA, b. Feb. 14, 1841, d. Feb. 19, 1841 EDMUND ADAMS, b Feb 11, 1842, m Dec. 23, 1873, Flora Richards, res. in Massillon, O

[11] HORATIO[8] JONES (ELISHA ADAMS[7], SIMPSON[6], THOMAS[5], THOMAS[4], THOMAS[3], THOMAS[2], WILLIAM[1]), son of Elisha Adams [8] and Hannah (Richardson) Jones, was born Sept 1, 1823, in East Medway He married, Nov 24, 1853, Antoinette L. Ellis, daughter of Willard and Amy (Smith) Ellis She was born Aug 27, 1833, in East Medway, where they resided.

The *children were* HARRIET LOUISA, b Aug 23, 1854, m July 6, 1882, Edward J Keith, res in Norfolk, Mass WILLARD ELLIS, b July 8, 1856 ELISHA ADAMS, b Oct 17, 1858, m Lessie Brown, res. in Philadelphia, Penn AMY CATHARINE, b. April 6, 1862 ELLEN MARIA, b Dec 9, 1868 CLARENCE HORATIO, b Nov 1, 1874.

JAMES KENNY (FRANCIS, FRANCIS), son of Francis and Ann (McGuire) Kenny, was born Jan. 30, 1814, in Leitrim County, Ireland. He married, Feb 20, 1840, [1]Ann Foley She was born 1824, in Ireland Mrs Ann Kenny died April 21, 1847 Mr Kenny married, June 25, 1854, [2]Mary O'Hurne She was born Dec. 25, 1827 Mr Kenny immigrated, Aug 24, 1849, to Medway

The *children were* PATRICK E , b April 5, 1841 FRANCIS J , b April 17, 1844, m 1864, Catherine Beigen HUGH C , b Jan 22, 1856. THOMAS, b Dec 4, 1858, d July 20, 1868 ANN L , b Nov 8, 1860. JAMES M , b March 5, 1862 ROSA M., b Sept 14, 1865 MICHAEL I , b Sept 30, 1868 JOHN, b Sept 21, 1870

PETER KENNY, son of William and Catherine (Dolan) Kenny, was born June 29, 1843, in Ireland He married, Nov. 5, 1872, Mary Henry. She was born in Canada, Feb 18, 1845 They resided in Medway

The *children were* WILLIE, b. Sept 15, 1873 JAMES, b Nov 8, 1878 PETER JOSEPH, b. June 28, 1881.

HUGH KENNY, son of William and Catherine (Dolan) Kenny, was born July 15, 1849, in Ireland He married, Nov 5, 1875, Catherine Henry, daughter of James and Susan (Keenan) Henry She was born in Canada They resided in Medway.

The *children were*. WILLIAM JAMES, b June 8, 1878 SUSIE, b Feb 26, 1879

FREDERICK LA CROIX, immigrant in 1775, from the island of Gaudaloupe, was of French nationality He married Elizabeth Cobb She was born in Wrentham, Mass , where they resided

The *children were* WILLIAM [1], b May, 1787. MILLIE, m. —— Holden, res in Worcester, Mass FREDERICK, b 1790, m Abigail Stanley, res. in Winthrop, Me.

[1] WILLIAM[2] LA CROIX (FREDERICK[1]), son of Frederick and Elizabeth (Cobb) La Croix, was born May, 1787, in Wrentham, Mass He married, 1815, [1]Lois Bullard, daughter of Adam and Lois (Richardson) Bullard. She was born in East Medway, where they resided Mrs. Lois La Croix died Feb. 11, 1825 Mr La Croix married, 1826, [2]Jemima Bullard, an older sister of his first wife. Mrs Jemima La Croix died Feb 10, 1857 Mr La Croix died Feb 20, 1860

The *children were* WILLIAM, b 1816, d April 30, 1840 EMILY, d Oct. 19, 1819 FREDERICK, d June 18, 1861 LAURA, b. 1820, d Aug 7, 1844. LOUIS, d Oct 28, 1844 JAMES [2], b Nov 30, 1823 EDWARD, m Eliza Felton, res in Lynn, Mass

[2] JAMES[3] LA CROIX (WILLIAM[2], FREDERICK[1]), son of William [1] and Lois (Bullard) La Croix, was born Nov 30, 1823, in East Medway, Mass He married, June 24, 1849, Mary Skinner Hodges, daughter of Willard and Hannah S. (Pond) Hodges. She was born in Franklin, Mass They resided in East Medway. Mr La Croix died Sept 6, 1883 Mrs. La Croix removed in 1885, to Cambridge, Mass

The *children were* LOUIS [3], b Sept 8, 1851. GEORGE JAMES, b Oct 18, 1854, res. in Boston, Mass CHARLES [4], b Oct 18, 1856 EDWARD, b May 30, 1867, res. in Cambridge, Mass.

[3] LOUIS LA CROIX (JAMES[3], WILLIAM[2], FREDERICK[1]), son of James [2] and Mary S (Hodges) La Croix, was born Sept. 8, 1851, in East Medway. He mar-

ried, Dec. 23, 1874, [1]Luella Eliza Bullard, daughter of John and Pearlee (Daniels) Bullard. She was born Nov. 4, 1849, in East Medway, where they resided   Mrs. Luella Eliza La Croix died March 13, 1880. Mr La Croix married, July 19, 1881, [2]Harriet P. Bullard. sister of his first wife. She was born Oct. 20, 1846

The children were· LOIS BULLARD, b Oct 11, 1875   CHESTER, b. July 11, 1879.

[4] CHARLES LA CROIX (JAMES[3], WILLIAM[2], FREDERICK[1]), son of James [2] and Mary S (Hodges) La Croix, was born Oct 18, 1856, in East Medway   He married, Jan 9, 1883, Esther W Bullard, daughter of Hinsdale F. Bullard. She was born in Medfield, Mass. They resided in East Medway.

The children were   JAMES, b. Nov. 3, 1884   LAURA, b. Nov 21, 1885, d Feb. 25, 1886.   ANNA, b Nov 21, 1885

[1] ALEXANDER[1] LOVELL may have been the son of Robert Lovell, who was admitted a mason in 1635, in Roxbury, Mass. He married, Oct. 30, 1658, Lydia Albie, daughter of Benjamin and Hannah Albie. They resided in Medfield, Mass.

The children were· NATHANIEL [2].   ALEXANDER [3].   LYDIA, m Joseph Ellis SARAH.   DEBORAH, m Samuel Ellis

Memoranda   Alexander Lovell's will, made Aug 15, 1701, provides, "That if any of my sons-in-law shall quarrel, or molest my said two sons, then they and their wives shall have but twelve pence apiece. '*Concordat cum originale* '"

[2] NATHANIEL[2] LOVELL (ALEXANDER[1]), son of Alexander [1] and Lydia (Albie) Lovell, was born in Medfield, Mass   Mr. Lovell died March 16, 1731.

The children were· MICHAEL [4], b 1700   HOPESTILL [5].   NATHANIEL, b. 1715, d Sept 29, 1736

[3] ALEXANDER[2] LOVELL (ALEXANDER[1]), son of Alexander [1] and Lydia (Albie) Lovell, was born in Medfield, Mass   He married Elizabeth ———.   They resided in Medfield, Mass   Mrs. Lovell died 1747   Mr. Lovell died Aug 25, 1751.

The children were· JOSEPH [6]   DAVID JONATHAN.   HANNAH, m. David Smith. MARY, m. ——— Clark.   MEHITABLE, m Jonathan Boyden.   RACHEL, m. Nathaniel Ames   LYDIA, m James Plimpton.   DEBORAH.

[4] MICHAEL[3] LOVELL (NATHANIEL[2], ALEXANDER[1]), son of Nathaniel [2] Lovell, married Mary ———.   They resided in Medway

The children were: MICHAEL, b. July 5, 1728.   EBENEZER, b March 25, 1730. MARY, b. Feb. 10, 1732.

[5] HOPESTILL[3] LOVELL (NATHANIEL[2], ALEXANDER[1]), son of Nathaniel [2] Lovell, married ——— ———.

The children were   NATHANIEL [7], b. 1747   MOSES, b. 1750.

[6] JOSEPH[3] LOVELL (ALEXANDER[2], ALEXANDER[1]), son of Alexander [3] and Elizabeth Lovell, was born July 26, 1708, in Medfield, Mass   He married, April 12, 1739, Prudence Clark, daughter of Edward and Hannah (Adams) Clark   She was born March 16, 1709, in Medfield, Mass.   They resided in East Medway.   Mrs. Prudence Lovell died Sept 17, 1789.   Mr Lovell died May 14, 1759

The children were. BENONI, b. June 30, 1740, d June 30, 1740   JOSEPH [8], b. Aug. 28, 1741.   PRUDENCE, b Oct 3, 1743, m. Simon Hill, d Oct 8, 1807.   ELIZABETH, b. July 31, 1746, m Abel Clark, d Sept. 24, 1777

[7] NATHANIEL[4] LOVELL (HOPESTILL[3], NATHANIEL[2], ALEXANDER[1]), son of Hopestill Lovell, was born in 1747.   He married Mrs. Mary Knowlton, *née* Barber, daughter of George[4] and Elizabeth (Clark) Barber, and widow of Ebenezer Knowlton.   She was born Oct. 18, 1745, in East Medway.   Mr Lovell died June 29, 1829   Mrs. Mary Lovell died Nov 14, 1832.

The children were   HOPESTILL, m Prudence Clark, res in Medfield   MICHAEL [9], b July 15, 1779   ZACHARIAH [10], b Nov 2, 1783   NATHANIEL, d May 21, 1817.

[8] JOSEPH[4] LOVELL (JOSEPH[3], ALEXANDER[2], ALEXANDER[1]), son of Joseph [6] and Prudence (Clark) Lovell, was born Aug. 28, 1741, in East Medway.   He married, Sept 27, 1764, [1]Jemima Adams, daughter of Henry and Jemima (Morse) Adams She was born April 11, 1740, in Medfield, Mass   They resided in East Medway   Mrs Jemima Lovell died Oct 27, 1814   Captain Lovell married, June 11, 1817, [2]Mrs. Elizabeth (Wheeler) Leland, *née* Partridge, daughter of Joshua[3] Partridge, *vid* Captain Lovell died Oct. 2, 1827   Mrs. Elizabeth Lovell died April 13, 1833.

The children were: JOSEPH, b. Dec 23, 1765, d. March 31, 1766.   JEMIMA, b. June

5, 1767, m 1786, Ezra Richardson, *vid*, d Oct 3, 1826. ELIZABETH, b June 17, 1769, m. the Rev Stephen Baxter, d Oct 11, 1852 SARAH, b May 29, 1772, d April 27, 1775 ABIGAIL, b. Jan 20, 1775, m the Rev John Pierce, d. July 2, 1800 KEZIAH, b March 2, 1778, d. May 7, 1797 SARAH, b Oct. 31, 1783, d Sept 10, 1786

[9] MICHAEL[5] LOVELL (NATHANIEL[4], HOPESTILL[3], NATHANIEL[2], ALEXANDER[1]), son of Nathaniel [7] and Mrs Mary Knowlton, *née* Barber, was born July 15, 1779, in East Medway. He married, April 27, 1808, Caty Daniels, daughter of Moses[5] and Abigail (Adams) Daniels. She was born Oct 30, 1784, in East Medway, where they resided. Mrs Lovell died Sept 25, 1857.

The children were. LYDIA DANIELS, b Feb 27, 1810, m Dec. 8, 1828, William H. Cary, *vid*, d Sept 11, 1853 CATHARINE, b. Dec 8, 1813, m Jan. 1, 1839, Gilman Cary, res. in Medfield, Mass ELIZABETH, b. Jan. 7, 1816, m July 3, 1843, Eleazar[5] Daniels, *vid*, d Oct. 6, 1883 ABIGAIL ADAMS, b Oct 25, 1818, m Jan 1, 1839, [1]George Crosby; m Dec 19, 1861, [2]Theodore Harding, d Dec. 23, 1870 LAVINA, b Dec 14, 1820, m Jan 28, 1847, Willard Battelle, res. in Taunton. MARY BARBER, b. Oct. 22, 1824, res in Medfield.

[10] ZACHARIAH[5] LOVELL (NATHANIEL[4], HOPESTILL[3], NATHANIEL[2], ALEXANDER[1]), son of Nathaniel [7] and Mrs Mary (Knowlton) Lovell, *née* Barber, was born Nov. 2, 1783, in East Medway. He married [1]Sibbel Plimpton, daughter of Capt Ezekiel and Esther Plimpton Mrs. Sibbel Lovell died Jan. 20, 1828. Mr. Lovell married, Jan 1, 1829, [2]Mrs. Abigail Thayer, *née* Richardson, daughter of Dr Abijah and Mercy (Daniels) Richardson, and widow of Asa Thayer Mrs Abigail Lovell died July 22, 1864 Mr Lovell died Feb 24, 1875

The children were MARY, b Feb 24, 1808, m. Charles Cheever, res in Cincinnati, O, d Jan 2, 1883 ASAHEL PLIMPTON [11], b. Feb 4, 1811 WILLIAM, b Feb 28, 1813, res. in Quincy, Wis EDWARD, b March 4, 1816, res. in Savannah, Ga MARIA, b July 31, 1817, m Alfred Baker, res in West Dedham, Mass NATHANIEL, b. March 19, 1820, m Hopestill Neale, res in Savannah, Ga. ESTHER P., b Jan 28, 1825, d Nov 22, 1844 ELLEN SIBBEL, b Jan 13, 1828, m Sept 7, 1853, Thaddeus M Daniels, *vid*, d Sept. 12, 1879 FRANCIS ALEXANDER, b. June 5, 1830, m. Laura A. Twing, res in Holliston, Mass

[11] ASAHEL PLIMPTON[6] LOVELL (ZACHARIAH[5], NATHANIEL[4], HOPESTILL[3], NATHANIEL[2], ALEXANDER[1]), son of Zachariah [10] and Sibbel (Plimpton) Lovell, was born Feb 4, 1811 He married, Dec 15, 1831, Eliza Stedman, daughter of John and Mercy (Richardson) Stedman They resided in East Medway Mrs. Lovell died April 12, 1875

The children were SIBBEL PLIMPTON, b Oct. 6, 1832, m June 19, 1853, Daniel G Stevens ABBY RICHARDSON, b. Aug 26, 1834, m Nov. 21, 1861, Willard P.[7] Clark, *vid*. ASAHEL FRANCIS [12], b. Dec. 28, 1836.

[12] ASAHEL FRANCIS[7] LOVELL (ASAHEL PLIMPTON[6], ZACHARIAH[5], NATHANIEL[4], HOPESTILL[3], NATHANIEL[2], ALEXANDER[1]), son of Asahel P. [11] and Eliza (Stedman) Lovell, was born Dec 28, 1836, in East Medway. He married, June 9, 1861, Olive A. Hartshorn, daughter of Edmund and Susan M (Ware) Hartshorn. She was born July 16, 1839, in Franklin, Mass

The children were EDMUND FRANCIS, b. Dec 25, 1862 MARY ELIZA, b. March 1, 1864, m June 7, 1883, Putnam Clark, *vid*. WINNIFRED JENETTE, b April 14, 1868 WALLACE DEAN, b. April 14, 1868, d. Sept 14, 1869 SUSAN WARE, b. Feb 10, 1873 FREDDIE STEDMAN, b. July 1, 1877, d July 24, 1877

ALBERT[5] MANN (VARNUM[4], THEODORE[3], SAMUEL[2], WILLIAM[1]), son of Varnum Mann, was born in Medway He married Susan Pond.

The children were ALBERT. WATSON LOWELL ABIJAH, m. Sept 4, 1872, [2]Louisa Maria Holbrook FRANK VARNUM HORACE WALDO

Memoranda. William[1] Mann, immigrant, was born 1607, in the county of Kent, England He came to America and settled in Cambridge, Mass His only son, the Rev Samuel Mann, born in 1647, was the first settled minister in Wrentham, Mass

ROBERT MASON, who settled in Roxbury about 1633, and died there in 1667, was the ancestor of the Medway Masons Thomas Mason, son of Robert, came from England with his father and was one of the original settlers of Medfield, and was killed by the Indians in the attack on that town in 1675. Ebenezer Mason, son of

Thomas, succeeded his father, and died in 1754   Ebenezer Mason, son of Ebenezer, succeeded to the paternal homestead, and died in 1787. About 1778, Abner Mason, son of Ebenezer, Jr., came across the river and settled in East Medway.

[1] ABNER³ MASON (Ebenezer⁴, Ebenezer³, Thomas², Robert¹), youngest son of Ebenezer and Dorothy (Morse) Mason, was born Feb. 26, 1741, in Medfield, Mass. He married Phebe Harding, daughter of Simon Harding   She was born July 23, 1746, in East Medway, where they resided. Mrs Mason died April 3, 1810   Mr. Mason died Nov 7, 1825

The children were. ALPHEUS [2], b Nov 27, 1772   SIMON HARDING [3], b July 25, 1774. OLIVE, b Dec. 25, 1776. RUTH, b March 17, 1779   JOSEPH DANIELS, b May 29, 1780   WALTER, b Nov 6, 1781, d March 7, 1844   HORATIO, b. Jan 4, 1784   ABNER, b April 24, 1786, res in Medfield, d March 7, 1825.

[2] ALPHEUS⁶ MASON (Abner⁶, Ebenezer⁴, Ebenezer³, Thomas², Robert¹), son of Abner [1] and Phebe (Harding) Mason, was born Nov. 27, 1772, in East Medway   He married Judith Leland, daughter of Adam and Prudence (Leland) Leland   She was born, 1775, in Sherborn, Mass. They resided in East Medway. Mrs. Mason died in 1848.

The children were. OLIVE, b 1797, d. 1824   ORION [4], b 1799

[3] SIMON HARDING⁶ MASON (Abner⁵, Ebenezer⁴, Ebenezer³, Thomas², Robert¹), son of Abner [1] and Phebe (Harding) Mason, was born July 25, 1774, in East Medway   He married, May 4, 1797, Betsey Leland, daughter of Moses and Mercy (Twitchell) Leland   She was born May 17, 1777, in Sherborn, Mass   They resided in East Medway   Mr. Mason died Oct. 7, 1860. Mrs. Mason died July 8, 1865.

The children were   HORATIO [5], b. Feb. 28, 1798. LARKIN, b March 11, 1800, d. Oct. 2, 1803. MATILDA, b Aug 3, 1802, d May 1, 1808   MARY ANN, b. Jan. 11, 1805, m. Nov. 8, 1824   JOSEPH ADAMS, *vid*   EMELINE, b. July 20, 1809, m Dec. 15, 1828, John Batchelder, res in Holliston, Mass, d July 7, 1883. MATILDA GOULDING, b Aug. 9, 1813, m April 29, 1869, Simeon Fisher, *vid.*

[4] ORION⁷ MASON (Alpheus⁶, Abner⁵, Ebenezer⁴, Ebenezer³, Thomas², Robert¹), son of Alpheus [2] and Judith (Leland) Mason, was born, 1799, in East Medway. He married, April 27, 1824, ¹Elmira Walker, daughter of Comfort and Tamar (Clark) Walker. She was born Oct 27, 1803, in Medway, where they resided. Mrs Elmira Mason died. Mr Mason married, Aug 7, 1828, ²Tamar Walker, an older sister of his first wife. She was born Dec. 13, 1797, in Medway   Mr Mason died July, 1865.

The children were   ORION A [7], b. April 5, 1825. OLIVE, b June 1, 1827, d Sept 28, 1827. HENRY, b. Aug. 27, 1829, d. Aug 13, 1831   HENRY E [8], b May 27, 1833   WILLIAM F., b. Aug 1, 1835, d Dec. 11, 1837   ELMIRA L, b Jan. 26, 1840, m. Dec. 4, 1862, John W Richardson, of Franklin, d. May 18, 1875   MARIA J., b Sept 7, 1841, d Oct 11, 1841.

Memoranda. Mr. Orion Mason, in 1815, became an apprentice to George Barber, clothier, whose mill is now used as McGinnis' boot shop. Here he remained until he was of age, and continued to follow the trade for several years. He afterwards engaged in cotton manufacturing. He was one of the founders of the Village Congregational Society, and was for two years on the board of selectmen of the town.

[5] HORATIO⁷ MASON (Simon Harding⁶, Abner⁵, Ebenezer⁴, Ebenezer³, Thomas², Robert¹), son of Simon Harding [3] and Betsey (Leland) Mason, was born Feb. 28, 1798, in East Medway   He married, Dec. 6, 1821, ¹Julia Adams, daughter of Jasper and Amy (Rounds) Adams. She was born Dec. 30, 1800, in Medway. They resided on the old homestead of his grandfather, Abner Mason, in East Medway. Mrs Mason died July 22, 1848   Mr Mason married, Dec 16, 1850, ²Almira F Coolidge, daughter of Daniel and Hannah (Frost) Coolidge. She was born in Marlborough, N. H. Mr. Mason died May 11, 1868   Mrs Almira Mason removed to Framingham, Mass

The children were   MERCY ADAMS, b. Feb 18, 1823, m. Jan 21, 1844, the Rev. Horace Dean Walker, *vid ,* res. in Palatine, N Y. LARKIN LELAND, b Dec. 6, 1825, d. Jan. 3, 1829. SIMON LEPRELETTE, b. Nov 25, 1829, m 1853, Lizzie N. Shute, res. in Boston, Mass. GEORGE E [9], b Oct. 23, 1837. ANNIE MATILDA, b. Oct 11, 1857, res. in Framingham, Mass.

[6] ORION A.⁸ MASON (Orion⁷, Alpheus⁶, Abner⁵, Ebenezer⁴, Ebenezer³, Thomas², Robert¹), son of Orion and Elmira (Walker) Mason, was born April 5, 1825, in Medway He married, Dec. 31, 1857, Mari Graves She was born in Agawam, Mass They resided in Medway There were no children.

Memoranda Orion A Mason, Esq , was much identified with the mercantile business of the town for many years, being in trade with his brother, Henry E Mason, Esq. Mr Mason has been treasurer of the Medway Savings Bank from its incorporation, in 1871 He has been the clerk and treasurer of the town for many years.

[7] HENRY E.⁸ MASON (Orion⁷, Alpheus⁶, Abner⁵, Ebenezer⁴, Ebenezer³, Thomas², Robert¹), son of Orion [4] and Tamar (Walker) Mason, was born May 27, 1833, in Medway He married, March 11, 1858, Sarah M Thomas. She was born in Winthrop, Me They resided in Medway.

The children were Orion Thomas, b April 4, 1865 Mary S , b. Jan 22, 1869.
Memoranda Henry E Mason, Esq , has been postmaster since 1874

[8] GEORGE E.⁸ MASON (Horatio⁷, Simon Harding⁶, Abner⁵, Ebenezer⁴, Ebenezer³, Thomas², Robert¹), son of Horatio [5] and Julia (Adams) Mason, was born Oct 23, 1837, in East Medway He married, Nov 1, 1857, Elizabeth M Foster, daughter of Appleton Eames and Louise Antoinette (Bannister) Foster. She was born March 24, 1835, in East Medway, where they resided

The only child was Ida Louise, b Nov 8, 1858, m. May 29, 1879, Henry Axtell Crane, *vid* , res in Sherborn, Mass.

GRANVILLE McCOLLUM was born June 6, 1806, in Glasgow, Scotland He immigrated to this country in 1830, and took up his residence in Pawtucket, R I , afterward removed to Medway He married Agnes Davidson

The children were . Alice, m E B Drake Eliza, m James H Welch Gilbert, b Jan 1, 1840, d March 11, 1865

GEORGE McINTOSH was born March 6, 1838, in Medfield, Mass He married, Nov 29, 1866, Abbie M Morse, daughter of Josiah E and Salome (Manley) Morse. She was born Sept 30, 1848, in Medway, where they resided

The children were Lillie S , b Jan 31, 1869. Abbie R , b Aug. 26, 1870. Josiah C., b May 24, 1875 Mary B , b Aug 17, 1877

Metcalf is a name derived from the following traditional exploit, which, it is said, occurred in 1312, in Chelmsford, County of Essex, England "On a certain day his Majesty, Edward II , with many lords and gentlemen were in his Majesty's park, where was a wild bull that they feared to encounter, but when he encountered with Mr. John Armstrong he was killed with his fist, and when Armstrong came to his Majesty, says he to Mr. Armstrong, 'Have you seen the mad bull?' 'And please your Majesty,' (says he), 'I met a calfe and knocked him down and killed him with my fist,' which, when it was known to be the bull, Mr Armstrong was honored with many and great honors. And in token of this notable exploit he was made a Knight, and his name was changed to Metcalfe " *Vid The History of Milford, Mass.*

The Metcalfs of Medway descended from the Rev Leonard Metcalf, born in 1545, and Rector of Tatterford, Norfolk County, England Michael Metcalf, his son, came to this country and was admitted freeman July 14, 1637, in Dedham, Mass

[1] LUTHER⁶ METCALF (Joseph⁵, Michael⁴, Eleazar³, Michael², Michael¹), son of Dr. Joseph and Hannah (Havens) Metcalf, was born Sept 7, 1756, in Wrentham, now Franklin. He married, April 5, 1781, Mercy Whiting, daughter of Nathaniel and Lydia (Partridge) Whiting. She was born March 14, 1763, in Medway where they resided Mrs Mercy Metcalf died Oct 31, 1825 Major Metcalf married, Sept 28, 1826, ²Mrs Hannah Fisher, *née* Hill, daughter of James and Grace (Jones) Hill, and widow of John Fisher She was born April 28, 1774, in Sherborn, Mass Mr Metcalf died Jan 27, 1838. Mrs Hannah Metcalf died Sept 24, 1863.

The children were · Clarissa, died in infancy Clara, b Feb. 7, 1784, m June 3, 1807, Joel Hunt, *vid* , d. Dec. 3, 1852 Luther [3], b May 2, 1788

[2] DANIEL⁷ METCALF (Philip⁶, Barnabas⁵, Michael⁴, Eleazar³, Michael², Michael¹), son of Philip and Anna (Knowlton) Metcalf, was born March 4, 1791, in Framingham. He married, Sept 26, 1816, Clarissa Twitchell, daughter of John and Catherine Twitchell. She was born Oct 5, 1792, in Medway. They resided

in Medway, now Millis, Mass   Mrs Metcalf died April 15, 1855.   Mr. Metcalf died Oct. 27, 1855

The children were: EDWIN [4], b Sept 21, 1817   DANIEL, b. June 13, 1819, m April, 1845, Eliza Houghton. JOHN, b. Jan 8, 1821, m May 20, 1847, Mary Bullard. WILLIAM, b. Oct. 4, 1822, m. Ellen Johnson   SARAH P , b. Sept. 10, 1824, m. Aug. 18, 1848, Albert Wiley, res in Medfield, Mass. CATHERINE, b Oct 15, 1826, d April 20, 1845   ELLEN E , b November, 1833   GEORGE, b July, 1836, m. Lydia Boyden.

[3] LUTHER [7] METCALF (LUTHER[6], JOSEPH[5], MICHAEL[4], ELEAZAR[3], MICHAEL[2], MICHAEL[1]), son of Luther [1] and Mercy (Whiting) Metcalf, was born May 2, 1788, in Medway   He married, May 12, 1812, [1]Lydia Jenks, daughter of Stephen Jenks   She was born May 13, 1793, in Pawtucket, R I   They resided in Medway.   Mrs. Lydia Metcalf died Dec. 16, 1826.   Mr. Metcalf married, Jan 14, 1828, [2]Sarah B. Phipps, daughter of Sylvanus and Anna (Winch) Phipps   She was born Nov. 25, 1803, in Framingham, Mass   The Hon. Luther Metcalf died Feb 16, 1879

The children were   ELEANOR, b Sept 1, 1813, m Aug 22, 1836, Milton M. Fisher, *vid* STEPHEN JENKS [5], b. April 9, 1816   NATHANIEL WHITING, b Aug 24, 1819, m. July 10, 1850, Caroline Henshaw, d. Oct 16, 1871   LUTHER HAVEN, b Oct. 26, 1826, m Sept 5, 1850, Sarah C. Smith, of Potsdam, N Y., d March 17, 1878   SARAH LYDIA, b. Aug. 3, 1829, m. June 27, 1848, the Rev. Samuel J. Spalding, d Sept 1, 1849   GEORGE PHIPPS, b May 17, 1834, m. May 6, 1858, Elizabeth Daniels, res in Framingham, Mass

[4] EDWIN[8] METCALF (DANIEL[7], PHILIP[6], BARNABAS[5], MICHAEL[4], ELEAZAR[4], MICHAEL[2], MICHAEL[1]), son of Daniel [2] and Clarissa (Twitchell) Metcalf, was born Sept 21, 1817, in Sherborn, Mass   He married, April 29, 1841, Martha Daniels, daughter of Amos and Sally (Pierce) Daniels   They resided in East Medway   Mr Metcalf died July 6, 1885

The children were · EDWIN W , b Dec. 26, 1848, d. Sept. 24, 1874   SARAH JENNIE, b Nov. 18, 1852, m. Jan 12, 1876, Appleton Phipps, res in Hopkinton, Mass., d. Feb. 18, 1880   GEORGE H , b, July 17, 1859

Memoranda. Mr. and Mrs Phipps had one child, Harry J., b Feb 18, 1880

[5] STEPHEN JENKS[8] METCALF (LUTHER[7], LUTHER[6], JOSEPH[5], MICHAEL[4], ELEAZAR[3], MICHAEL[2], MICHAEL[1]), son of the Hon Luther [3] and Lydia (Jenks) Metcalf, was born April 9, 1816, in Medway.   He married, May 21, 1840, M. Caroline Child, daughter of John Weld and Sally (Richards) Child.   She was born Jan. 15, 1818, in Roxbury, Mass   They resided in Medway   Mrs. M. Caroline Metcalf died July 26, 1840   Mr Metcalf married, Feb. 10, 1842, [1]Esther M Child, daughter of John Weld and Sally (Richards) Child   She was born May 12, 1819, in Roxbury, Mass.

The children were · M CAROLINE, b Nov 23, 1842, m Oct 29, 1868, Daniel W. Newell.   STEPHEN C., b. Feb 8, 1848, d Jan. 7, 1856.   MARY C., b. March 3, 1852, m. June 30, 1881, Leonard E Taylor

LANSING MILLIS, son of William and Sally (Holt) Millis, was born Sept 3, 1823, in Lansingburg, N Y.   He married, April 27, 1843, Harriet P. Lavender, daughter of John and Elizabeth (Burt) Lavender   She was born in Sandhurst, County of Kent, England.   They resided in Lansingburg, N. Y , Concord, N. H , Boston, Mass., and came to East Medway in 1880   Mr. Millis died April 6, 1885

The children were   HATTIE E b Oct 3, 1846, m April 27, 1868, Frederick C. Dow, Esq , res in Manchester, N H   HELEN E., b. Sept. 25, 1848, m June 2, 1869, Livingston B Van Kleeck, res in New York City.   CHARLES W., b Nov 26, 1851, d. Feb. 4, 1852   HENRY LANSING, b. Jan. 2, 1855, m. Dec 15, 1880, Annie C Russ, res. in Millis, Mass.

Memoranda. Mr. and Mrs. Dow have two children, viz : Irving F., born April 2, 1871.   Lansing M., born March 13, 1875   Mr and Mrs. Van Kleeck have one (adopted) son, viz   Walter B , born Sept. 10, 1872.   Mr and Mrs Henry L Millis have two children   Violet B , born July 18, 1883   Lansing, born April 24, 1886

[1] ALEXANDER LE BARON MONROE (STEPHEN, NATHANIEL), son of Dr. Stephen and Susanna (Le Baron) Monroe, was born May 3, 1807, in Sutton, Mass. He married, Oct. 2, 1834, [1]Louisa W Barber, daughter of George and Lois (Whiting) Barber.   She was born Nov 21, 1813, in Medway, where they resided.   Mrs. Louisa W. Monroe died June 2, 1836.   Dr. Monroe married, Nov 30, 1837, [2]Mrs. Miriam H.

Hawes, *née* Clark They resided in Chicopee and Granby, Mass , and returned to Medway in 1852, where they continued to reside. Dr. Monroe died Feb. 19, 1879 Mrs. Miriam H. Monroe died Nov. 20, 1881.

The children were FRANCIS LE BARON [2], b March 20, 1836. ALEXANDER, d 1842. SARAH LOUISA, m Wm. C Huntington, Esq

Memoranda Susanna Le Baron was the daughter of Lazarus and Susanna (Johonnot) Le Baron She was born Dec 17, 1767, in Sutton, Mass Her ancestry is traced back to Dr. Francis Le Baron, who was born in Rochelle, France, in 1668. The Monroes came from Scotland Nathaniel Monroe, Dr Monroe's grandfather, was born in 1712, and resided in Bristol, R I

[2] FRANCIS LE BARON MONROE (ALEXANDER Le B , STEPHEN, NATHANIEL), son of Dr. Alexander Le Baron and Louisa (Barber) Monroe, was born March 20, 1836, in Medway He married, Jan 7, 1873, Tamson Lavinia Barrows, daughter of John J and Lydia C (Smith) Barrows. She was born Nov 29, 1845, in Vineyard Haven, Mass They resided in Medway, and removed to Chicago, Ill

The children were ALEXANDER LE BARON, b Jan. 19, 1875, d. Jan 21, 1875 MIRIAM CLARK, b Nov 28, 1881

Memoranda. Francis Le Baron Monroe, M D , entered Yale College, Conn., in 1853, and graduated, 1857, from Williams College, Mass He pursued his medical studies at Bowdoin and Harvard Medical Schools, and graduated in 1861, from the latter. He was a Surgeon in the army during the War for the Union, and until 1876, when he resigned his commission and engaged in the drug business in Chicago, Ill.

[1] JOSEPH MORSE, who led the early patriot settlers of Sherborn and Medfield against the Indians, was the son of Joseph Morse, of Medfield, and a nephew of Colonel Morse, of Oliver Cromwell's army. He married, Oct. 17, 1671, [1]Mehitable Wood, daughter of Nicholas and Anna (Babcock) Wood. She was born July 22, 1655, in Sherborn, Mass , being the first white child born in that town Mrs Mehitable Morse died Nov 12, 1681 Captain Morse married, April 11, 1683, [2]Hannah Babcock She was born in Milton, Mass Mrs. Hannah Morse died Nov 9, 1711 Captain Morse married, May 17, 1730, [3]Mrs. Hannah Dyer, the widow of Capt Joseph Dyer, of Weymouth, Mass Capt Joseph Morse died Feb 19, 1718, and lies buried in the Morse Lot, Holliston Cemetery, Mass Mrs Hannah Morse died Sept 4, 1727

The children were. MEHITABLE, b April 25, 1673, d in early life JOSEPH, b April 3, 1676, d. June 12, 1676. ELISHA, b Dec 12, 1677, d. young JOSEPH [2], b March 25, 1679. MEHITABLE, b Nov 2, 1681, m. John Breck, res in Sherborn, Mass. JAMES, b. July 1, 1686, m Ruth Swain, res. in Sherborn, Mass , d June 5, 1725 HANNAH, b April 5, 1689, m Isaac Coolidge, Esq , res. in Sherborn, Mass., d Dec 11, 1774 SARAH, b April 12, 1692, m William Barrows, res. in Sherborn, Mass. DAVID, b Dec 31, 1694, m Sarah Dyer, res. in Natick, Mass , d Jan. 7, 1773 ISAAC, b Sept. 14, 1697, m Elizabeth Drury, res. in Worcester, Mass , d. 1750 KEZIAH, b June 30, 1700, m Sept 4, 1718, Samuel Holbrook, res. in Sherborn, Mass , d. Feb 18, 1754. ASA, b Aug 24, 1703, m Mary Rider, res in Natick, Mass , d. Oct 7, 1770

[2] JOSEPH MORSE (JOSEPH[1]), son of Capt Joseph [1] and Mehitable (Wood) Morse, was born March 25, 1679, in Sherborn, Mass He married Prudence Adams, daughter of Henry and Prudence (Fraiy) Adams She was born April 10, 1683, in Medfield, Mass They resided in Sherborn, Mass. Mr Morse died April 18, 1754 Mrs Morse died Feb. 23, 1772

The children were HENRY [3], b June 14, 1703 JOSEPH, b. Nov 15, 1705, m Experience Morse, res in Sturbridge, Mass SETH, b Sept 12 1708, m Abigail Battle, res in Hopkinton, Mass ELISHA, b April 13, 1715, d. unm JACOB, b. Sept 12, 1717, m Mary Merrifield, res in Douglas, Mass , d March 30, 1800 JUDITH, b Oct. 13, 1720, m. Capt Caleb Leland, res. in Sherborn, d Oct 26, 1774 JOHN, b. Dec 31, 1724, d 1725

[3] HENRY[a] MORSE (JOSEPH[2], JOSEPH[1]), son of Joseph [2] and Prudence (Adams) Morse, was born June 14, 1703, in Sherborn He married Sarah Kibby They resided in West Medway on land granted to his great-grandfather, John Frary, of Medfield, in 1659, southeast of Winthrop Pond. Mr. Morse died April 5, 1766

The children were ABIGAIL, b April, 1726, d. Dec 18, 1759 EZEKIEL [4], b. Oct 1, 1727 SARAH, b Dec. 1, 1729, m. Joseph Rider, res in Holliston, Mass , d.

1804   HANNAH, b March 2, 1732, m William Andrews, res in Hopkinton, Mass., d
Nov 20, 1817   HENRY, b. Dec 2, 1734, m. Abigail Bullen, d. June 23, 1807.   LYDIA,
b June 13, 1736, d young   THANKFUL, b June 19, 1740, m Andrew Watkins, res in
Holliston, Mass, d March 19, 1810   JAMES [5], b Sept 5, 1742   OBADIAH, b
March 9, 1745, d young   ABNER, b. Feb. 13, 1747, d. September, 1756

[4] EZEKIEL⁴ MORSE (HENRY³, JOSEPH², JOSEPH¹), son of Henry [3] and
Sarah (Kibby) Morse, was born Oct 1, 1727, in Medway   His father carried him fully
five miles on foot to church for baptism when an infant of a few days   He married
Rebecca Cozzens. She was born March 24 1729, in Ashland, Mass   They resided in
West Medway   Mr. Morse died March 24, 1778   Mrs Morse died Nov 19, 1807.

The children were   LYDIA, b April 4, 1751, d. Oct. 1, 1756.   ELIZABETH, b Oct
8, 1753, m. Elijah Adams, res. in Hubbardston, Mass , d. Dec. 31, 1833.   WAITSTILL,
b March 6, 1755, m Joel Partridge, *vid*, d March 8, 1825   LYDIA, b Sept 12, 1757,
d March 18, 1773   ABNER [6], b. Oct 11, 1759.   SARAH, b Dec 21, 1761, m Isaac
Cozzens, res. in Holliston, Mass , d July 31, 1839   ABIGAIL, b June 16, 1765, d
March 18, 1773   MERCY, b. Dec 26, 1772, m David Eames, res in Hopkinton, Mass.

[5] JAMES⁴ MORSE (HENRY³, JOSEPH², JOSEPH¹), son of Henry [3] and Sarah
(Kibby) Morse, was born Sept. 5, 1742, in West Medway   He married Hannah
Daniels. They resided in Medway   Deacon Morse died July 19, 1808

The children were   OBADIAH, b 1761, d. 1766   JOHN, b March 24, 1763, m Feb.
4, 1793, Clarissa Sanford, res in Otego, N Y., d Jan. 3, 1844.   HENRY, b April 25,
1766, res in Paxton, Mass , d about 1851   RUTH, b 1768, m Joel Howard, res in
Milford, Mass , d Jan 3, 1844   RHODA, b 1768   POLLY, b 1769, m. Daniel Elliot,
res in Sutton, Mass.   CATHERINE, m. Nathaniel Fletcher, res. in Carlton, Mass.

[6] ABNER⁵ MORSE (EZEKIEL⁴, HENRY³, JOSEPH², JOSEPH¹), son of Ezekiel
[4] and Rebecca (Cozzens) Morse, was born Oct 11, 1759, in West Medway.   He married Mille Leland, daughter of Asaph and Beulah (Littlefield) Leland   She was born
1761, in Holliston, Mass   They resided in West Medway   Mr Morse died March 11,
1821. Mrs Morse died 1821.

The children were   NABBY, b 1783, m Uriah Cutler, res in Holliston, Mass.
ELIJAH, b 1785, m Mary Jackson, res. in Boston, Mass   MILLE, b. 1789, m. Alexander
H. Jones, res in Framingham, Mass   CHLOE, b. 1791, m. Lemuel Leland, res in
Sherborn, Mass   ABNER, b September, 1793, m Oct 1, 1832, ¹Sarah Ann Voorhees,
who died Sept 27, 1833, m. Oct 15, 1836, ²Hannah Peck, who died Aug 29, 1842, d
May 16, 1865.   BETSEY, b 1796, m Seneca Wright, res. in Bellingham, Mass.
THOMAS J, b 1801, m Lucy Leland, res in Sherborn, Mass.   LUCRETIA, b 1804, d
1828

ANDREW⁶ MORSE (ANDREW⁵, ANDREW⁴, SAMUEL³, JONATHAN², DANIEL¹),
son of Andrew and Lois (Smith) Morse, was born July 10, 1789, in Sherborn, Mass.
He married, Sept 10, 1810, Margarette Metcalf, daughter of Titus and Peggy Metcalf
She was born Sept 12, 1791, in Franklin, Mass   They resided in East Medway   Mrs
Margarette Morse died Feb 22, 1879   Mr. Andrew Morse died April 16, 1884

The children were   ASA DANIELS, b. Nov. 23, 1811 d. March, 16, 1812.   ASA
DANIELS, b Jan. 30, 1813, m. Sept 21, 1836, Eliza Hill.   MARY F, b Sept. 21, 1814,
m May 27, 1834, ¹Sylvanus Bullard; m Oct 30, 1850, ²James Willard Daniels, *vid*.
METCALF, b March 31. 1816, m Aug 13, 1843, Lucinda Maxwell, d Feb 22, 1854.
FRANCIS JUDSON, b. March 3, 1818, m Jan. 4, 1848, ¹Ellen Burnell, m ²Mrs. Letitia
McCall, *née* Carpenter, res in Constantine, Mich , d June 24, 1883   JULIA A b June
9, 1823   J AMORY, b Oct 9, 1826, m Susan Keith, d Sept 4 1855   ROBERT G.,
b. Aug 27, 1833 m. Sept. 4, 1855, Olive Merrifield, d Oct 4, 1862

[1] BENONI⁷ MORSE (BENONI⁶, JOSIAH⁵, JEREMIAH⁴, JEREMIAH³, JOSEPH²,
SAMUEL¹), son of Benoni and Mariam Morse, married, 1785, Polly Hobbs.   They
resided in Medway   Mr Morse died Dec. 23, 1836   Mrs. Morse died April 6, 1843

The children were. AMASA, b July 26, 1788, m Susan Bullen   POLLY, b Dec. 9,
1790, m Joseph Green.   URIAH, b Dec 10, 1792   ELIZA, b Aug. 26, 1794   LUCY,
b June 14, 1796   MELINDA, m William Bacon   JOSIAH [2], b May 15, 1801   BENONI,
b May 22, 1803, m Oct. 30, 1825, Abigail Baker.   KEZIAH, b. July 7, 1805, m. Jan. 13,
1825, George Harding, *vid*   CHLOE, b. Sept 18, 1807

[2] JOSIAH⁸ MORSE (BENONI⁷, BENONI⁶, JOSIAH⁵, JEREMIAH⁴, JEREMIAH³,

37

Joseph[2], Samuel[1]), son of Benoni [1] and Polly (Hobbs) Morse, was born May 15, 1801, in Medway. He married [1]Caroline Williams. She was born June 27, 1801, in Medway, where they resided. Mrs. Caroline Morse died Jan. 15, 1836. Mr. Morse married [2]Sylvia Littlefield. She was born Feb. 18, 1812. Mrs. Sylvia Morse died March 31, 1855. Mr. Morse married [3]Emeline Wilson. She was born Oct. 21, 1812. Mr. Morse died July 9, 1885, in Norfolk, Mass.

The children were: Josiah E. [3], b. Nov. 2, 1823. George A., b. Feb. 2, 1826. Caroline M., b. Feb. 14, 1827. Angenette M., b. Nov. 4, 1830, d. April 2, 1842. Lucy A., b. Oct. 12, 1833, d. Nov. 8, 1851. Sylvia A., b. June 9, 1842, d. Oct. 27, 1851. Charles H., b. June 4, 1845. Clarissa A., b. July 30, 1848, d. Feb. 19, 1851. Laura F., b. April 7, 1853.

[3] **JOSIAH E.[9] MORSE** (Josiah[8], Benoni[7], Benoni[6], Josiah[5], Jeremiah[4], Jeremiah[3], Joseph[2], Samuel[1]), son of Joseph [2] and Caroline (Williams) Morse, was born Nov. 2, 1823, in Medway. He married Salome Manley. She was born March 2, 1823, in Medfield, Mass. They resided in Medway.

The only child was: Abbie Manley, b. Sept. 30, 1848, m. Nov. 29, 1866, George McIntosh, *vid.*

JESSE NEW (James, John), son of James and Annie (Perry) New, was born July 13, 1793, in Grafton, Mass. He married, Oct. 22, 1815, [1]Sarah Winter. They resided in West Medway. Mrs. Sarah New died May 29, 1822. Mr. New married, Aug. 12, 1827, [2]Martha Eager, daughter of John and Betsey (Marble) Eager. Mr. New died Feb. 20, 1865. Mrs. Martha New died Dec. 26, 1878.

The children were: James, b. July 29, 1816. Adoniram Judson, b. June 28, 1820. Mary E., b. July 11, 1829, d. June 16, 1874. Martha A., b. Sept. 22, 1830, d. March 28, 1854. Irving Drover, b. Nov. 4, 1833, d. July 29, 1836. Sarah J., b. May 29, 1836, m. July 9, 1855, John P. Jones. Rebecca A., b. Feb. 16, 1838, m. Sept. 16, 1861, Charles H. Mitchell. John Q. A., b. Feb. 13, 1840, m. March 18, 1863, Vienner Follansbee. Enos S., b. June 25, 1842, m. March 4, 1869, Martha A. Claflin, d. June 29, 1873. Anna M., b. June 30, 1844, d. March 25, 1846.

JAMES K. P. NOURSE (Gilbert, Daniel), son of Gilbert and Betsey W. (Cargill) Nourse, was born March 30, 1845, in West Medway. He married, May 29, 1867, Nellie J. Blake. She was born Nov. 26, 1847, in South Natick, Mass. They resided in West Medway.

The children were: Louis E., b. May 12, 1868. Albert H., b. May 26, 1870. James G., b. Jan. 28, 1873. George F., b. May 30, 1877. Charles C., b. April 12, 1880.

[1] **JOHN[1] PARTRIDGE** was an original proprietor of the town of Medfield, Mass. His parentage is unknown. He may have been the son of William and Ann Partridge, of Salisbury, Mass., and grandson of John Partridge, of Olney, Buckinghamshire, England, who was a descendant of Richard de Pertriche, of Wishanger Manor, Gloucestershire, England. He married, Dec. 18, 1655, Magdalen Bullard, daughter of John and Magdalen Bullard, of Dedham, Mass. They resided in Medfield, Mass.

The children were: John [2], b. Sept. 21, 1656. Hannah, b. April 15, 1658. Eleazar, b. 1664. Abiel, b. 1667. Experience, b. 1669, and Rachel, b. 1669, m. Joseph Daniell, *vid.* Samuel [3], b. Feb. 22, 1671. Zachariah [4], b. 1674. Elizabeth, b. 1678.

[2] **JOHN[2] PARTRIDGE** (John[1]), son of John [1] and Magdalen (Bullard) Partridge, was born Sept. 21, 1656, in Medfield, Mass. He married, 1678, [1]Elizabeth Rockwood, daughter of Nicholas and Margaret (Holbrook) Rockwood. She was born April 3, 1657, in Medfield, Mass. They resided in Medfield, now Millis. Mrs. Elizabeth Partridge died 1687. Mr. Partridge married, 1688, [2]Elizabeth Adams, daughter of Jonathan[2] and Elizabeth (Fussell) Adams. She was born 1666, in Medfield, Mass. Mrs. Elizabeth Adams died Aug. 14, 1719. Mr. Partridge married, April 17, 1721, [3]Hannah Sheffield, daughter of William and Mary Sheffield, of Sherborn, Mass. Mr. Partridge died Dec. 9, 1743. Mrs. Hannah Partridge died July 19, 1754.

The children were: Elizabeth, b. 1679, m. Dec. 22, 1701, Ebenezer Daniell, *vid.* Mary, b. 1681, m. Ebenezer Daniell, *vid.* John, m. 1708, Ann Pond, res. in Wrentham. Benoni [5], b. 1687. Jonathan [6], b. 1693. Hannah, b. 1696, m. May 7, 1713, Jeremiah Daniell, *vid.* Deborah, b. 1698, m. Israel Keith, res. in Uxbridge, Mass , d. Aug 30, 1740. JAMES [7], b October, 1700. SARAH, b 1702, m March 13, 1723, George Adams, *vid.* STEPHEN [8], b. April 16, 1706. ANNA, b 1709

[3] SAMUEL[2] PARTRIDGE (JOHN[1]), son of John [1] and Magdalen (Bullard) Partridge, was born Feb 22, 1671, in Medfield, Mass He married Hannah Mason, daughter of Robert and Abigail Mason She was born Sept 3, 1676

The children were· HANNAH, b. April 6, 1702 THANKFUL, b. Aug 7, 1703 SAMUEL, b. Nov 6, 1704 EBENEZER, b May 29, 1706 ABIGAIL, b Nov 7, 1707 BENJAMIN and SILENCE, b March 13, 1709. MEHITABLE, b. July 6, 1710 JOSHUA [9], b July 27, 1713 CALEB, b May 27, 1716, d. Feb. 20, 1755. SILENCE, b March 5, 1719, m. Dec. 23, 1742, Stephen Kingsbury, res in Holliston, Mass.

[4] ZACHARIAH[2] PARTRIDGE (JOHN), son of John [1] and Magdalen (Bullard) Partridge, was born, 1674, in Medfield, Mass. He married Elizabeth ———. They resided in Medfield, afterward Medway Mr Partridge died Sept 23, 1716

The children were· MARY, b. 1702, m. Benjamin White, res. in Dudley, Mass. MAGDALEN, b Feb 4, 1704, m. David Daniell SARAH, b. 1706, m. Joseph Green. ZECHARIAH, b. 1709, d Aug. 31, 1718 ASA, b 1712 PHEBE, b Aug 27, 1714, m William Tweed, res. in Ashuelot, Mass.

[5] BENONI[3] PARTRIDGE (JOHN[2], JOHN[1]), son of John [2] and Elizabeth (Rockwood) Partridge, was born 1687, in Medfield, Mass. He married, 1709, Mehitable Wheelock They resided in West Medway. Mrs Partridge died Jan. 20, 1761 Mr Partridge died Dec 26, 1769.

The children were PRESERVED, b. 1709, m. 1737, Katharine Armstrong, res. in Holliston, Mass THOMAS, b. 1711 SETH, b. 1713, m. Sarah ———, res in Medfield, Mass. JOSEPH, b. Aug 22, 1715. DAVID, b May 21, 1718. MEHITABLE, b April 24, 1720, d. Aug. 4, 1741 SAMUEL, b June 24, 1722, d. Sept 7, 1741. SARAH, b Sept. 27, 1724, m. 1744, Obadiah Adams, res. in Bellingham, Mass TIMOTHY [10], b. Jan 18, 1727. ELI, b June 3, 1729, res in Holliston, Mass. MOSES [11], b. Aug 28, 1733

(6) JONATHAN[3] PARTRIDGE (JOHN[2], JOHN), son of John [2] and Elizabeth (Adams) Partridge, was born 1693, in Medfield, afterward Medway. He married, Nov 13, 1717, [1]Elizabeth Learnard She was born in Framingham, Mass They resided in Medway. Mrs Elizabeth Partridge died April 23, 1738 Mr. Partridge married, January, 1739, [2]Ann Phipps

The children were MATTHEW, b March 16, 1718. ELIZABETH, b Aug 17, 1720 HULDAH, b. July 18, 1722 JONATHAN, b July 16, 1724, m. Oct 12, 1748, Abigail Lovet, res in Sherborn, Mass. MARY, b July 19, 1726, m 1747, Abner Ellis. EDE, b Dec 4, 1727, m 1750, Nathan Bullard HANNAH, b Feb 12, 1729. JASPER, b April 15, 1732 LEARNARD, b. Feb. 7, 1735. SILAS, b July 22, 1737, m Abigail ———, res in Peru, Mass. THADDEUS, b. Nov. 28, 1739, m Thankful ———, res in Barre, Mass REUBEN, b. Nov. 21, 1741, m Mary Perry, res in Gardiner, Me JABEZ, b. Nov 21, 1741 RHODA, b Feb. 11, 1743. JOHN, b. Oct 28, 1746, m Phebe ———, res in Barre, Mass

[7] JAMES[3] PARTRIDGE (JOHN[2], JOHN[1]), son of John [2] and Elizabeth (Adams) Partridge, was born October, 1700, in Medfield, now Millis He married, Jan. 27, 1729, Keziah Bullard, daughter of Malachi and Bethiah (Fisher) Bullard She was born Dec. 2, 1711. They resided in Medway. Mr Partridge died 1769. Mrs Partridge died July 25, 1799

The children were JAMES, b Oct 10, 1730, m 1759, Abigail ———, res in Boylston, Mass. MALACHI, b. Nov. 30, 1731, res in Sturbridge, Mass. KEZIAH, b Nov. 12, 1733, m Moses Thompson ASA, b March 6, 1735. LOIS, b Sept 20, 1736, m. July 29, 1756, Benjamin Pond, res in Wrentham, Mass. BETHIAH, b Nov 22, 1738, m. March 15, 1759, Seth Hixon, res in Stoughton, Mass ELEAZAR, b April 19, 1740, m 1764, Lois R Rockwood, res in Wrentham, Mass, d 1826 LYDIA, b Dec 6 1743, m. Samuel Bullard, res. in Holliston, Mass, d 1840 STEPHEN, b. June 10, 1746. JOEL [12], b. Feb. 19, 1748 EUNICE, b. July 26, 1749 NATHAN [13], b March 26, 1751. HANNAH, b Sept 19, 1753, d. Dec. 25, 1756 ELIZABETH, d. Sept. 18, 1818 CHLOE, b. April 11, 1756

[8] STEPHEN[3] PARTRIDGE (JOHN[2], JOHN[1]), son of John [2] and Elizabeth (Adams) Partridge, was born April 16, 1706, in Medfield, Mass He married, April

7, 1737, Mary MacCanne. They resided in East Medway. Mr. Stephen Partridge died March 10, 1742. Mrs. Mary Partridge married [2]Abner Ellis.

The children were: MARY, b. June 20, 1738, m. Joseph Baxter. AZUBA, b. April 16, 1742, m. Dec. 25, 1765, Aaron Gardner, res. in Sherborn, Mass.

[9] **JOSHUA**[3] **PARTRIDGE** (SAMUEL[2], JOHN[1]), son of Samuel [3] and Hannah (Mason) Partridge, was born July 27, 1713. He married, Dec. 23, 1742, Elizabeth Kingsbury.

The children were: ELIZABETH, b. Sept. 28, 1743, d. Jan. 3, 1744. JOSHUA [14], b. April 20, 1745. ELIZABETH, b. March 20, 1747, m. [1]Ira Richardson; m. [2]John Wheeler, *vid;* m. Asaph Leland; m. [4]Joseph Lovell, *vid.* ICHABOD, b. Aug. 13, 1749. SAMUEL [15], b. Dec. 26, 1752. RHODA, b. Feb. 3, 1759, m. John Ellis, *vid.*

[10] **TIMOTHY**[4] **PARTRIDGE** (BENONI[3], JOHN[2], JOHN[1]), son of Benoni [5] and Mehitable (Wheelock) Partridge, was born Jan. 18, 1727, in Medway, Mass. He married, Jan. 5, 1755, Abigail Barber, daughter of Joseph Barber. She was born in Medway, where they resided. Mr. Partridge died Sept. 8, 1787. Mrs. Partridge died Feb. 22, 1809.

The children were: SAMUEL, b. March 18, 1756, res. in Paxton, Mass. EUNICE, b. March 15, 1758, m. March 6, 1783, Ralph Mann, res. in Walpole, Mass. ELIJAH [16], b. April 4, 1762. ZILLAH, b. March 15, 1764, d. Oct. 22, 1783. DAVID, b. Dec. 30, 1765, d. Sept. 25, 1783.

[11] **MOSES**[4] **PARTRIDGE** (BENONI[3], JOHN[2], JOHN[1]), son of Benoni [5] and Mehitable (Wheelock) Partridge, was born Aug. 28, 1733, in Medway. He married, Sept. 9, 1755, Rachel Thayer. They resided in Medway. Mr. Partridge died Oct. 6, 1804. Mrs. Partridge died Sept. 6, 1812.

The children were: FREELOVE, b. Feb. 11, 1757, m. June 29, 1778, David Pike, res. in Rockingham, Vt. DEADAN, b. Feb. 14, 1759, d. Feb. 14, 1759. SIMEON [17], b. Feb. 28, 1760. BEULAH, b. July 5, 1762, m. Dec. 18, 1782, [1]Elias Hayward, who died Oct. 22, 1783; m. June 26, 1788, [2]Daniel Fiske, res. in Upton, d. March, 1858. TABITHA, b. April 30, 1765, m. July 5, 1781, James Johnson, d. soon after. CLARISSA, b. June 14, 1775, m. Jan. 11, 1795, [1]Gregory Ide, who died Aug. 6, 1798; m. Oct. 23, 1799, [2]Asa Childs, res. in Pittsburgh, Penn.

[12] **JOEL**[4] **PARTRIDGE** (JAMES[3], JOHN[2], JOHN[1]), son of James [7] and Keziah (Bullard) Partridge, was born Feb. 19, 1748, in Medway. He married Waitstill Morse, daughter of Ezekiel and Rebecca (Cozzens) Morse. She was born March 6, 1755, in Medway, where they resided. Mr. Partridge died Feb. 13, 1823. Mrs. Partridge died March 8, 1825.

The children were: EZEKIEL, b. July 1, 1775, m. Deborah Harding, res. in Worcester, Mass. ABIGAIL, b. Jan. 9, 1777, m. Ezra[6] Adams, *vid.* CATHERINE, b. April 1, 1779, m. Stephen[8] Adams, *vid.* TAMAR, b. Aug. 8, 1781, m. Job[8] Partridge, res. in Bellingham, Mass. JOEL [18], b. March 1, 1784. JERUSHA, b. May 2, 1787, m. David Mann, of Westboro, Mass. EDE, b. June 25, 1789, m. Nathaniel Clark. JAMES, b. Sept. 3, 1793, d. April 26, 1816.

[13] **NATHAN**[4] **PARTRIDGE** (JAMES[3], JOHN[2], JOHN[1]), son of James [7] and Keziah (Bullard) Partridge, was born March 26, 1751, in Medway. He married Melatiah Holbrook, daughter of Dea. Joseph Holbrook. She was born Feb. 28, 1755, in Bellingham, Mass. They resided in Medway. Mr. Partridge died May 25, 1785. Mrs. Partridge married [2]Capt. Thomas Adams, of Barre, Mass.

The children were: LOVINA, b. Jan. 8, 1777, d. July 10, 1782. NATHAN, b. Dec. 27, 1778, m. Isabella Fessenden, res. in Barre, Mass. SUSANNA, b. Nov. 30, 1783, m. Capt. Asa Fiske, res. in Holliston, Mass.

[14] **JOSHUA**[4] **PARTRIDGE** (JOSHUA[3], SAMUEL[2], JOHN[1]), son of Joshua [9] and Elizabeth (Kingsbury) Partridge, was born April 20, 1745, in Medway. He married Hannah Cutler. They resided in Medway.

The children were: JOSEPH, b. April 26, 1768, m. Chloe Puffer, d. Oct. 26, 1822. PRISCILLA, b. June 14, 1774, d. Aug. 12, 1774. DAVID, b. Sept. 20, 1775, m. 1804, Miriam Partridge, res. in Brimfield, Mass. HANNAH, b. Oct. 3, 1780, d. Sept. 1, 1810. SABRA, b. Aug. 5, 1783, d. Nov. 29, 1793.

[15] **SAMUEL**[4] **PARTRIDGE** (JOSHUA[3], SAMUEL[2], JOHN[1]), son of Joshua [9] and Elizabeth (Kingsbury) Partridge, was born Dec. 26, 1752, in Medway. He

married Mehitable Allen. She was born in 1753. They resided in Medway. Mrs. Partridge died Jan. 15, 1829. Mr. Partridge died Feb. 17, 1842.

The children were: ELIZABETH, b. April 8, 1776, m. [1]Simon Hill; [2]Jeremiah Pratt. MATILDA, b. May 9, 1778, m. [1]Oliver Richardson; m. [2]——— Wheeler. RHODA, b. Dec. 20, 1780, m. Elisha Fisher. VESTA, b. Sept. 22, 1782. MIRIAM, b. August, 1785, m. David[5] Partridge. MEHITABLE, b. Dec. 20, 1788, m. March 24, 1808, Jasper Daniels, *vid.;* d. Nov. 7, 1880. CLARISSA, b. May 13, 1791, m. April 19, 1818, Fisher Hill, *vid.*

[16] **ELIJAH[5] PARTRIDGE** (TIMOTHY[4], BENONI[3], JOHN[2], JOHN[1]), son of Timothy [10] and Abigail (Barber) Partridge, was born April 4, 1762, in Medway. He married [1]Keziah W. Curtis. They resided in West Medway. Mrs. Keziah Partridge died Jan. 16, 1795. Mr. Partridge married [2]Catherine Clark. She was born in Medway. Mr. Partridge died Sept. 9, 1805. Mrs. Catherine Partridge married [2]Moses[5] Pond, *vid.* Mrs. Catherine Pond died June 18, 1834.

The children were: RACHEL, b. Dec. 7, 1785, m. Daniel Leland, Jr., of Sherborn, Mass. LEAH, b. Jan. 7, 1788, d. Jan. 9, 1788. TIMOTHY [19], b. March 14, 1789. CLARK, b. May 16, 1799. CATHERINE, b. Feb. 6, 1801. ELIJAH [20], b. Jan. 29, 1805.

[17] **SIMEON[5] PARTRIDGE** (MOSES[4], BENONI[3], JOHN[2], JOHN[1]), son of Moses [11] and Rachel (Thayer) Partridge, was born Feb. 28, 1760, in Medway. He married, 1784, Jerusha White. She was born in Franklin, Mass. They resided in Medway. Capt. Simeon Partridge died Jan. 9, 1832. Mrs. Jerusha Partridge died March 23, 1834.

The children were: LYMAN, b. Nov. 21, 1785, d. Aug. 12, 1805. ELIHU [21], b. Sept. 28, 1787.

[18] **JOEL[5] PARTRIDGE** (JOEL[4], JAMES[3], JOHN[2], JOHN[1]), son of Joel [12] and Waitstill (Morse) Partridge, was born March 1, 1784, in Medway. He married, Feb. 26, 1807, [1]Sarah Clark, daughter of Stephen and Eunice (Clark) Clark. She was born in 1785. They resided in Medway. Mrs. Sarah Partridge died July 19, 1820. Mr. Partridge married, Nov. 16, 1820, [2]Joanna Sanford. Mr. Joel Partridge died Aug. 19, 1852. Mrs. Joanna Partridge died April 25, 1853.

The children were: REMEMBRANCE, b. April 18, 1808, d. May 1, 1808. CLARK [22], b. April 1, 1809. STEPHEN [23], b. March 12, 1811. JOEL GILBERT [24], b. May 22, 1813. SARAH ANN, b. Dec. 3, 1818, m. June 14, 1840, Joseph Bullard, *vid.* EDMUND JAMES, b. April 6, 1827, d. May 31, 1828. LYDIA SANFORD, b. Sept. 11, 1830, m. April 12, 1853, Addison P. Thayer, *vid.*

[19] **TIMOTHY[6] PARTRIDGE** (ELIJAH[5], TIMOTHY[4], BENONI[3], JOHN[2], JOHN[1]), son of Elijah [16] and Keziah W. (Curtis) Partridge, was born March 14, 1789, in Medway. He married Charlotte Adams, daughter of Jonathan Adams. They resided in Medway. Mr. Partridge died June 13, 1827. Mrs. Partridge died Dec. 4, 1834.

The children were: SEWELL, b. May 25, 1812, m. June 6, 1838, Sarah G. Mann, res. in Holliston, Mass. CHARLOTTE, b. April 24, 1815, d. April 10, 1838. ELIZA, b. April 9, 1817, m. Dec. 31, 1839, Jotham Adams, Jr., d. Oct. 25, 1844. TIMOTHY A., b. Feb. 29, 1820, m. Nov. 24, 1864, Sarah Bisbee, d. April 6, 1875. ELIJAH [25], b. Aug. 7, 1822. HARRIET, b. Jan. 23, 1825, m. June 4, 1845, Jotham Adams, Jr., d. Aug. 20, 1846. EDMUND, b. July 27, 1827, d. Jan. 18, 1852.

[20] **ELIJAH[6] PARTRIDGE** (ELIJAH[5], TIMOTHY[4], BENONI[3], JOHN[2], JOHN[1]), son of Elijah [16] and Keziah W. (Curtis) Partridge, was born Jan. 29, 1805, in Medway. He married, Dec. 11, 1839, [1]Ruth Adams, daughter of Jotham Adams. She was born Aug. 19, 1811. Mrs. Ruth Partridge died Jan. 29, 1856. Mr. Partridge married, Oct. 3, 1867, [2]Lucy G. Dodge. She was born March 25, 1832, in Burnham, Me.

The only child was: RUTH E., b. Oct. 21, 1868.

[21] **ELIHU[6] PARTRIDGE** (SIMEON[5], MOSES[4], BENONI[3], JOHN[2], JOHN[1]), son of Simeon [17] and Jerusha (White) Partridge, was born Sept. 28, 1787, in Medway. He married, Nov. 7, 1810, Charlotte Wight, daughter of Dr. Aaron and Jemima Wight. She was born June 17, 1788, in Medway, Mass., where they resided. Mrs. Charlotte Partridge died March 2, 1833. Mr. Partridge married, March 13, 1834, Maria Paine, daughter of Capt. William Paine, of Wellfleet, Mass. Mr. Elihu Partridge died Oct. 13, 1848.

The children were · LYMAN WIGHT, b. Nov 23, 1811, d April 18, 1812. ELIHU [26], b March 28, 1813 SIMEON, b. Oct. 6, 1815, m. Betsey Maria Adams, d. Jan. 20, 1882. JERUSHA WHITE, b. May 6, 1822, m. Amos Whitney. LYMAN, b Aug 23, 1836, m June 28, 1870, Julia O. Elliott, res in Westminster, Mass.

[22] CLARK⁶ PARTRIDGE (JOEL⁵, JOEL⁴, JAMES³, JOHN², JOHN¹), son of Joel [18] and Sarah (Clark) Partridge, was born April 1, 1809, in Medway He married, April 6, 1830, ¹Mary Harding, daughter of Seth and Mary (Learned) Harding. She was born March 17, 1811, in Medway, where they resided. Mrs Mary Partridge died March 23, 1834 Mr Partridge married, March 25, 1835, ²Mrs Abigail Partridge, *née* Harding, daughter of Seth and Mary (Learned) Harding, and widow of William Partridge She was born in Medway, where they resided The Hon Clark Partridge died Nov 17, 1885

The only child was MARY HARDING, b. March 14, 1834, m David Parsons Wilder, Esq , res in Chicago, Ill

Memoranda David Parsons Wilder was born in Westfield, Mass. He graduated in 1851 from Harvard College and in 1855 from the Cambridge Law School. Mr. Wilder practiced law in Chicago, Ill , and attained eminence in his profession He died March 18, 1872, in the very prime of life Subsequently, Mrs. Wilder, with her family, removed to Medway, where they reside The children were Clark Partridge. Mary Faustina Grace Harding. Gertrude Parsons. Lothrop Bertha Frances. David Parsons

Clark Partridge Wilder was of the firm of Wilder & Parker, Chicago, Ill.

[23] STEPHEN⁶ PARTRIDGE (JOEL⁵, JOEL⁴, JAMES³, JOHN⁴, JOHN¹), son of Joel [18] and Sarah (Clark) Partridge, was born March 12, 1811, in Medway He married, Oct 23, 1833, Fidelia Allen. They resided in Medway Mr. Partridge died Oct. 15, 1885

The children were ABIGAIL ELLEN, b May 22, 1835, d. June 9, 1836 ABIGAIL MARIA, b April 28, 1838, m Nov 25, 1863, Asa Adams FIDELIA, b April 5, 1840, m Oct 2, 1859, John Frank Lesure, d June 7, 1864. EDSON, b June 6, 1842 ADELIZA, b Nov 3, 1843, d Oct 23, 1862 ALMOND G [27], b July 18, 1847. JOEL CLARK, b Aug 24, 1852, m April 1, 1874, Mary A Davis

[24] JOEL GILBERT⁶ PARTRIDGE (JOEL⁵, JOEL⁴, JAMES³, JOHN², JOHN¹), son of Joel [18] and Sarah (Clark) Partridge, was born May 22, 1813, in Medway. He married, Nov 19, 1835, ¹Emeline Richardson They resided in Medway Mrs Emeline Partridge died April 20, 1840. Mr. Partridge married, Oct. 6, 1841, ²Roxana Richardson Mr Partridge died Feb 18, 1846

The children were SARAH C., b Aug. 3, 1836, m. June 5, 1862, Edward Clark HARRIET M , b Aug. 17, 1837, m. November, 1863, Payson Goodell, d May 5, 1868. GEORGE H , b. February, 1839, d Oct. 12, 1839 EMELINE, b Oct 9, 1842, m. November, 1863, Elbridge Hill CHARLES W , b March 6, 1844

[25] ELIJAH⁷ PARTRIDGE (TIMOTHY⁶, ELIJAH⁵, TIMOTHY⁴, BENONI³, JOHN², JOHN¹), son of Timothy [19] and Charlotte (Adams) Partridge, was born Aug 7, 1822, in Medway. He married, Jan 19, 1859, Mary Partridge Hill, daughter of Charles and Nancy (Jones) Hill She was born July 13, 1827, in Sherborn, Mass They reside in East Medway

The children were WILLIAM HERBERT CHARLES HILL, b Sept 30, 1869

[26] ELIHU⁷ PARTRIDGE (ELIHU⁶, SIMEON⁵, MOSES⁴, BENONI³, JOHN², JOHN¹), son of Elihu [21] and Charlotte (Wight) Partridge, was born March 28, 1813, in Medway He married, Nov 25 1841, Olive Shumway, daughter of Amos and Patience (Adams) Shumway She was born Jan 15, 1815, in West Medway, where they resided Mr. Partridge died Oct 10, 1875.

The children were LOUISA F., b. July 20, 1846, d Feb 23, 1847. SARAH F , b Oct 17, 1849, d Nov 2, 1874. EMMA C , b. Feb 28, 1856.

[27] ALMOND G. PARTRIDGE (STEPHEN⁶, JOEL⁵, JOEL⁴, JAMES³, JOHN², JOHN¹), son of Stephen [23] and Fidelia (Allen) Partridge, was born July 18, 1847, in Medway. He married, Nov 28, 1872, Nellie L. Kingsbury, daughter of Hiram and Charlotte (Wight) Kingsbury She was born in East Medway. They reside in West Medway

The only child was JOEL EVAN, b Feb. 4, 1878

BERNARD PARTRIDGE, son of Edward and Hannah (Legg) Partridge, was born Nov 1, 1773, in Oakham, Mass. He married Mary Phillips, daughter of Jedidiah and Sarah (Bullen) Phillips. She was born Feb 3, 1779, in East Medway, where they resided. Mrs. Mary Partridge died Dec. 30, 1861.

The children were ELIZABETH MARY ANN, m Charles Newell, res in Medfield, Mass DANIEL, m Mary Plaisted ASA CHARLOTTE, m George Allen HIRAM. ADEN, b. Sept 13, 1812, m Abigail Harding, res in Philadelphia, Penn ; d. Aug. 20, 1859 EDWARD, b. May 18, 1814, m. [1]Susan Brooks, m. [2]Minerva Jackson, res. in Philadelphia, Penn CATHARINE. CHARLES D., b. Sept. 2, 1817, m April 27, 1845, Nancy L. Reid, res in Philadelphia, Penn , d Dec 11, 1877 ARTEMAS, b Jan. 17, 1820, m. April 12, 1849, Grace A Warner, res in Philadelphia, Penn ANDREW

JAMES PENNIMAN, son of James Penniman, was born 1726, in Medfield, Mass He married, 1755, Abigail Clark, daughter of Timothy and Abigail (Bullard) Clark She was born Sept 30, 1732 They resided in East Medway. Mr Penniman died March 17, 1804 Mrs Penniman died Dec. 13, 1831

The children were· AMY, m. Ralph Bullard, *vid* OLIVE, b. Feb 24, 1751, m. March 29, 1775, Jabez Shumway, *vid.*, d. Sept 17, 1823 ABIGAIL, b 1755, m. 1779, Samuel Damon, res in Holden, Mass , d March 18, 1842 THANKFUL, m Joseph Daniels, res. in Worcester, Mass PRISCILLA, b. 1761, m. Jan 28, 1784, Lemuel Daniels, *vid.*, d March 1, 1825 REBECCA, b 1763, d Feb 10, 1844 MERCY, b 1765, m. Micah Adams, *vid.*, d April 23, 1829 SYBEL, b 1770, m John Clark, *vid.*; d March 29, 1840.

CHARLES SUMNER[8] PHILBRICK (JOSEPH[7], JOSEPH[6], ABNER[5], THOMAS[4], SAMUEL[3], THOMAS[2], THOMAS[1]), son of Joseph Philbrick, was born July 19, 1846, in Seabrook, N. H. He married, Sept 21, 1876, [1]Emily R Bullard They resided in Medway. Mrs. Emily R. Philbrick died Jan 13, 1877 Mr Philbrick married, May 28, 1879, [2]Annie Maria Crooks, daughter of George Crooks, of Chelsea, Mass

The children were ARTHUR LLOYD, b. March 19, 1880. ROSCOE HUNTER, b. Sept 1, 1881.

Memoranda. Thomas[1] Philbrick, immigrant, with his wife and six children came from Lincolnshire, England, in company with Gov. John Winthrop and Sir Richard Saltonstall. They arrived in Massachusetts Bay, June 12, 1630, " after a tempestuous seventy-six days' passage." They attempted a settlement where Salem now is, but in July, with Sir Richard Saltonstall and others, they went to Watertown, Mass., where they remained until 1645, when Mr. Philbrick with his family removed to Hampton, N H., to which place his son, John Philbrick, had gone in 1639, and settled Thomas[1] Philbrick died 1667, in Hampton, N H.

Thomas[2] Philbrick, son of Thomas[1] Philbrick, was born in England in 1624, and died Nov. 24, 1700, in Hampton, N H Samuel[3] Philbrick, born March 19, 1660, and died Feb 22, 1694, Thomas[4], born 1684, died Feb. 15, 1747; Abner[5], born Jan 21, 1708, died May 2, 1790, Joseph[6], born Dec 7, 1755, died May 8, 1831; Joseph[7], born May 11, 1796, died Sept. 19, 1863; all died in Hampton, now Seabrook, N. H. Charles Sumner· Philbrick, born July 19, 1846, came to Medway in 1876.

REV. GEORGE PHILLIPS, son of Christopher Phillips, was born about 1593, in Rainham, St Martins, County of Norfolk, England. He graduated in 1613, and received the degree of A. M. in 1617, from Gonville and Caius College, Cambridge. He was settled in the ministry in Suffolk County, but on account of persecution embarked for America, April 12, 1630, on the ship Arbella, with his wife and two children. On board the same ship were Gov John Winthrop, Sir Richard Saltonstall, the Rev John Wilson, Isaac Johnson, Simon Broadstreet, and others They landed June 12, 1630, in Salem Mass., where his wife soon died and was buried by the side of Lady Arbella Johnson The Rev Mr Phillips was settled not long after as pastor of the church in Watertown, Mass , where he remained a beloved minister of Christ until his death, July 1, 1644 His son, the Rev. Samuel Phillips, was settled in 1651, as colleague with the Rev Ezekiel Rogers, in Rowley, Mass., and his great grandson, the Rev. Samuel Phillips, was the first pastor of the "Old South Church," in Andover, Mass.

Ebenezer Phillips, of Southboro', the ancestor of Jedidiah Phillips, of East Medway, was doubtless descended from the Rev George Phillips, of Watertown, although the line of descent has not been traced

[1] JEDIDIAH PHILLIPS (Samuel, Ebenezer), son of Samuel and Martha (Newton) Phillips, was born Dec 20, 1754, in Southboro, Mass. He married [1]Sarah Bullen, daughter of Jonathan Bullen. They resided in East Medway Mrs Sarah Phillips died Mr Phillips married [2]Charlotte Bacon She was born in Franklin, Mass Mr Phillips died Jan 25, 1847 Mrs Charlotte Phillips died Nov 27, 1849

The children were. John, b July 12, 1775. d Nov 22, 1857 Mary, b Feb 3, 1779, m Bernard Partridge, *vid*, d. Dec. 30, 1861 Lydia, b June 3, 1781, d July, 1857 Rachel, b. Aug 9, 1783, m Joshua Leland, d 1862 Oliver [2], b June 10, 1786. Josiah [3], b. Aug 8, 1788 Sarah, b March 3, 1791, m April 3, 1811, Charles[7] Daniels, *vid*, d March 3, 1871 Catherine, b June 8, 1793, d April 13, 1795 Jedidiah, b March 2, 1796, d March 2, 1800

[2] OLIVER PHILLIPS (Jedidiah, Samuel, Ebenezer), son of Jedidiah [1] and Sarah (Bullen) Phillips, was born June 10, 1786, in East Medway He married, Dec 1, 1808, [1]Hannah Richardson, daughter of Elisha and Sarah (Ellis) Richardson. She was born Nov 23, 1787, in East Medway, where they resided Mrs Hannah Phillips died Jan. 27, 1855 Mr Phillips married [2]Mrs Irene (Turner) Hawes, *née* Richardson, daughter of Simeon and Elizabeth (Jones) Richardson, and widow of [1]Obed Turner, and [2]Lewis Hawes She was born April 14, 1796, in East Medway. Mrs Irene Phillips died March 1, 1875 Mr Phillips died March 14, 1880

The children were Amanda, b March 31, 1809, m Dec 25, 1831, John Barber, *vid.*, d. July 18, 1834 Elisha Richardson [4], b April 5, 1811 Sarah, b Sept 13, 1813, m 1834, Ellis Daniels, *vid*, d July 3, 1844 Hannah, b Nov 23, 1816, m. Jan 25, 1838, Timothy Bullard *vid* Oliver Francis [5], b Jan 8, 1829

[3] JOSIAH PHILLIPS (Jedidiah, Samuel, Ebenezer), son of Jedidiah [1] and Sarah (Bullen) Phillips, was born Aug 8, 1788, in East Medway He married Sally Morse She was born in North Wrentham, Mass They resided in East Medway Dea Josiah Phillips died Nov. 14, 1857

The children were Sarah B, b Jan 18, 1812, m Nov 27, 1830, Dea John Staples Smith, *vid* Josiah Emerson, b March 20, 1815, d June 20, 1838. Martha A, b. Jan 22, 1817, m Brainard Rockwood, res. in Milford, Mass

[4] ELISHA RICHARDSON PHILLIPS (Oliver, Jedidiah, Samuel, Ebenezer), son of Oliver [2] and Hannah (Richardson) Phillips, was born April 5, 1811, in East Medway He married, Nov 13, 1834, Elizabeth Daniels, daughter of Saben and Hannah (Ellis) Daniels She was born May 17, 1811, in East Medway, where they resided Mr Phillips died Aug 27, 1852

The children were Elizabeth, b Jan 25, 1837 Amanda M, (adopted) daughter of Ellis and Sarah (Phillips) Daniels, b April 23, 1842, d Nov 29, 1867

[5] OLIVER FRANCIS PHILLIPS (Oliver, Jedidiah, Samuel, Ebenezer), son of Oliver and Hannah (Richardson) Phillips, was born Jan 8, 1829, in East Medway He married, April 19, 1854, Mercy Penniman Adams, daughter of Edward and Keziah L. (Clark) Adams. She was born April 26, 1834, in East Medway, where they resided

The children were Edward Adams, b Jan 30, 1857. Mary F, b Nov 15, 1861, m Feb 16, 1881, Stuart McLees, res in Norfolk, d Nov. 19, 1881

ALONZO PLATTS[5] PHILLIPS (Nathan[4], James[3], James[2], James[1]), son of Nathan and Lydia (Pingree) Phillips, was born May 2, 1804, in Rowley, Mass He married, April 15, 1830, [1]Louisiana Dodge, daughter of Phineas and Mercy Dodge She was born in Rowley, Mass They resided in Peabody, Mass Mrs Louisiana Phillips died Sept 28, 1863 Mr. Phillips married Oct 12, 1865, [2]Mrs. Irene F Proctor, *née* Upton, daughter of Elisha C and Irene F Upton, and widow of Aaron C. Proctor. She was born in Danvers, Mass They resided in Medway Mr Phillips died March 6, 1886

The children were Oscar, b July 27, 1833, m Sept 18, 1855, Irene Trask, res in Worcester, Mass. Elizabeth Mercy, b. June 12, 1837, d Dec 17, 1881. Lydia Maria, b Sept. 6, 1839, d Aug 29, 1840 Lydia Maria, b. Jan 3, 1842, d May 24, 1883 Lucy Dodge, b Oct. 6, 1844, d April 11, 1871

DANIEL POND settled in Dedham as early as 1652, where he died Feb. 4, 1698

Robert Pond, son of Daniel Pond, of Dedham, was born in that town Aug. 5, 1667. He became an owner of land in Wrentham, Mass., on the "Mine Brook," and became possessed of considerable property in that vicinity. Robert Pond died July 3, 1750, in Wrentham, Mass.

EZRA POND, son of Robert Pond, was born in Wrentham, Mass. He purchased several tracts of land in Wrentham and in Medway, and resided in that part of Wrentham which became Franklin, not very far from West Medway. He was parish clerk for many years, and was one of the founders of the Second Church of Christ in Medway. He died prior to 1782.

MOSES POND, the eighth son of Ezra Pond, was a soldier in the French and Indian wars, and at Ticonderoga in 1758. At the alarm at Concord, April 19, 1775, he served as drummer in the company that marched under the command of Capt. Joshua Partridge from Medway. He served also in one campaign of the Revolution under Capt. Samuel Cobb.

[1] **MOSES⁴ POND** (Ezra³, Robert², Daniel¹), son of Ezra Pond, was born April 16, 1737, in Wrentham, Mass. He married, March 12, 1760, Patience Carpenter. They resided in Wrentham, Mass., and after 1769, in Medway. Mr. Pond died Nov. 5, 1832.

The children were: Patience, b. June 10, 1762, m. May 3, 1781, Phinehas Adams, *vid.* Betsey, b. Sept. 26, 1764. Matilda, b. Nov. 1, 1769. Catherine, b. Nov. 1, 1779. Moses [2], b. March 16, 1782.

[2] **MOSES⁵ POND** (Moses⁴, Ezra³, Robert², Daniel¹), son of Moses [1] and Patience (Carpenter) Pond, was born March 16, 1782, in Medway. He married, Feb. 8, 1807, ¹Polly Fairbanks, daughter of Silas³ and Mary (Day) Fairbanks. She was born March 14, 1785, in East Medway. They resided in West Medway. Mrs. Polly Pond died April 23, 1811. Mr. Pond married ²Mrs. Catharine Partridge, *née* Clark, daughter of James Clark, and widow of Elijah⁵ Partridge. Mrs. Catharine Pond died June 18, 1834. Mr. Pond married, Oct. 29, 1834, ³Mrs. Nancy Bullard, *née* Fairbanks, daughter of Silas³ and Mary (Day) Fairbanks, and widow of Almoran Bullard. She was born 1796, in East Medway. Mr. Pond died Jan. 3, 1856. Mrs. Nancy Pond died Feb. 1, 1865.

The children were: John [3], b. Oct. 13, 1808. Mary, b. Dec. 23, 1809, m. April 6, 1832, Charles Wight, res. in Medfield, Mass. Moses, b. Aug. 12, 1812, m. Nov. 19, 1838, Zelpha Thayer Clark, res. in Holliston, Mass. Martha, b. June 29, 1816, m. Nov. 4, 1835, James N. Smith, d. April 3, 1838. Sally P., b. April 12, 1818, m. Jan. 1, 1839, James N. Smith. Edwin Day, b. Dec. 22, 1835, m. ¹Eliza Curtis; m. March 12, 1867, ²Caroline A. Ware, res. in Holliston, Mass.

[3] **JOHN⁶ POND** (Moses⁵, Moses⁴, Ezra³, Robert², Daniel¹), son of Moses and Polly (Fairbanks) Pond, was born Oct. 13, 1808, in West Medway. He married, March 31, 1840, Charlotte Augusta Wiswell. They resided in Medway.

The children were: George E. [4], b. Jan. 27, 1841. Ruth Augusta, b. Aug. 17, 1845, m. April 11, 1866, Warren A. Clark, *vid.;* d. Feb. 25, 1867. Mary Coolidge, b. Sept. 12, 1848, d. Nov. 18, 1863. Moses Warren [5], b. Sept. 12, 1848. Charlotte Wiswell, b. Dec. 6, 1850, m. Dec. 21, 1869, Henry W. Parker.

[4] **GEORGE E.⁷ POND** (John⁶, Moses⁵, Moses⁴, Ezra³, Robert², Daniel¹), son of John [3] and Charlotte A. (Wiswell) Pond, was born Jan. 27, 1841, in Medway. He married, Dec. 27, 1865, Annie C. Ellis, daughter of Chester and Clarissa (Richardson) Ellis. They resided in Medway.

The children were: Moses Wallis, b. Dec. 7, 1866. Selma E., b. June 15, 1879.

[5] **MOSES WARREN⁷ POND** (John⁶, Moses⁵, Moses⁴, Ezra³, Robert², Daniel¹), son of John [3] and Charlotte A. (Wiswell) Pond, was born Sept. 12, 1848, in Medway. He married, April 2, 1879, Cora M. Thompson. She was born in West Medway, where they resided.

The only child was: Elmer Freeman, b. Jan. 4, 1880.

HOLLIS⁷ RICE (Seth⁶, Edmund⁵, Seth⁴, Edmund³, Samuel², Edmund¹), son of Seth and Lydia (Stevens) Rice, was born June 26, 1803, in Marlboro, Mass. He married, Nov. 1, 1825, Nancy Abbe. They resided in Medway. Mr. Rice died Nov. 26, 1868. Mrs. Rice died Dec. 1, 1871.

The children were: Urania B., b. Oct. 5, 1826, d. Aug. 7, 1850. Albert, b.

Oct 24, 1828, m Dec 11, 1864, Lizzie A Lombard, res. in Marlboro, Mass GILBERT, b. Jan 2, 1831, m. Dec 31, 1857, Mary P Clark, res in Holliston, Mass LOUISA, b May 24, 1834, m April 30, 1856, Sewall J Clark, *vid* EDMUND HOLLIS, b Jan 6 1837, d Oct 15, 1843 GEORGE SELWYN, b April 24, 1840, m Sept 23, 1862, [1]Mary E Adams, m Nov 25, 1874, [2]Lizzie Dunn

JOHN RICHARDSON appears among the early inhabitants of Watertown, Mass The exact date of his arrival from England in America is not known, but he probably embarked July, 1635, at London, in the ship Assurance, for Virginia, but arrived in New England as did many in that period who embarked ostensibly for Virginia

John Richardson, immigrant, received a giant in 1636-7, of one acre of land in the Beaver Brook Plowlands, of Watertown, which is now embraced in the town of Waltham, Mass He probably left Watertown in 1638, as a follower of the Rev. John Wheelwright, for John Richardson, doubtless the same person appears in Exeter, N. H , in 1642, whose wife was Hannah Truair. Apprehensive that Exeter, N H., would come under the jurisdiction of Massachusetts, the Rev Mr. Wheelwright purchased several hundreds of acres of land in Webhannet, afterwards Wells, Me , and established a church of which he was the pastor, and John Richardson probably was one of the Rev Mr Wheelwright's little flock. He was doubtless the father of John[2] Richardson who appears in Medfield, and married, in 1679, Rebecca Clark This is made almost certain by the fact that the sons of John[2] Richardson, Joseph and Benjamin Richardson, held lands in Wells, Me , which they sold in 1751 These lands came probably by inheritance from their grandfather, John[1] Richardson, who, as we have seen was one of the early settlers of that town *Vid The Richardson Memorial*

[1] JOHN[2] RICHARDSON (JOHN[1]), son of John and Hannah (Truan) Richardson, was born about 1650, in Wells, Me. He married, May 1 1679, Rebecca Clark, daughter of Joseph and Alice (Pepper) Clark She was born Aug 16, 1660, in Medfield, Mass They resided in Medfield, afterward East Medway Their estate was handed down from father to son, and in 1886, is owned and occupied by a lineal descendant, Moses[7] Richardson, Esq Mr Richardson died May 29, 1697 Mrs Richardson married [2]John Hill, of Sherborn, Mass , where she died Feb 17, 1738-9

The children were JOHN[3] [2], b Aug 25, 1679 ELIZABETH, b Sept 20, 1681, d prior to 1711 DANIEL [3], b Aug 31, 1685 JOSEPH, b in 1687, m Oct 18, 1706, Hannah Barber MEHITABLE, b June 16, 1689 REBECCA, b in 1693 BENJAMIN [4], b Feb 28, 1697, m Aug 18, 1712, Eleazar Hill, res in Douglas, Mass

[2] JOHN[3] RICHARDSON (JOHN[2], JOHN[1]), son of John [1] and Rebecca (Clark) Richardson, was born Aug 25, 1679, in Medfield, afterward Medway He married, about 1699, Esther Breck, daughter of John and Mehitable (Morse) Breck She was born 1679, in Medfield, Mass They resided in Medfield, afterward Medway Mr Richardson died May 19, 1759. Mrs Richardson died Aug 17, 1774

The children were SARAH, b April 25, 1700, m. David Pond, of Wrentham, Mass JOHN, b Oct 22, 1701, m May 5, 1730, Jemima Gay, res in North Wrentham, now Franklin, Mass DAVID, b. June 19, 1703, d March 9, 1724 JONATHAN, b Feb 1, 1704, m. July 4 1728, Ruth Clark, res in Brookfield, Mass ESTHER, b Jan 2, 1707, m May 27, 1728, [1]Thomas Jones, *vid* , m. Jan 31, 1735, [2]Nathaniel Clark, res in Wrentham, Mass , d March 24, 1770 MARY, b Sept 9, 1709, m June 4, 1736, James Boyden, Jr , d prior to 1759 JOSEPH, b April 3, 1711, m Abigail ———, res in Uxbridge, Mass. SAMUEL, b Jan 3, 1714, the first birth recorded in the town of Medway , m April 2, 1734, [1]Mary Allen, m [2]Sarah Clark, res. in Wrentham, Mass , d Feb. 10, 1811 SOLOMON, b April 21, 1716, m Rebecca Mann, res in Brookfield, Mass , died November, 1771 MOSES [5], b Feb 8, 1717-8 ASA [6], b. Oct 16, 1720 DAVID, b Dec. 6, 1724, m Esther Smith, res in Barre, Mass , d. 1777.

[3] DANIEL[3] RICHARDSON (JOHN[2], JOHN[1]), son of John [1] and Rebecca (Clark) Richardson, was born Aug 31, 1685, in Medfield He married, 1709, Hannah Underwood, daughter of Joseph and Elizabeth Underwood She was born in Watertown, Mass They resided in Medfield, afterward Medway Mr Richardson died Aug 28, 1748 Mrs. Richardson survived her husband

The children were WILLIAM [7], b Feb 3, 1710 HANNAH, b Dec. 25, 1718, m. June 15, 1739, Jonathan Underwood, res in Westford, Mass DANIEL [8], b. June 26, 1721

[4] BENJAMIN[3] RICHARDSON (JOHN[2], JOHN[1]), son of John [1] and Rebecca (Clark) Richardson, was born 1693, in Medfield, Mass. He married Elizabeth ———. They resided in Medway. Mr Richardson died April, 1761.

The children were BENJAMIN, b March 9, 1739, res in Braintree, Mass. ELIZABETH, b. Dec. 20, 1740, m. William Penniman, res in Braintree, Mass EZEKIEL, b April 3, 1744. JOB, b. April 15, 1745, m Eunice ———, res. in Hubbardston, Mass. JEREMIAH, b Nov 25, 1748, res in Sutton, Mass CATHARINE, b April 9, 1753, m 1762, ——— Partridge

[5] MOSES[4] RICHARDSON (JOHN[3], JOHN[2], JOHN[1]), son of John [2] and Esther (Breck) Richardson, was born Feb 8, 1717 He married, March 17, 1740, Abigail Allen, daughter of James and Rebecca Allen She was born Nov 9, 1716. They resided in East Medway. Mr. Richardson died April 6, 1797. Mrs. Richardson died June 10, 1807.

The children were: MOSES [9], b. Oct. 27, 1740. ABIGAIL, b. Feb. 12, 1742, d. young SIMEON [10], b June 27, 1744. RHODA, b Oct 6, 1746, m. Timothy[5] Bullard, *vid* LOIS, b Feb. 1, 1749, m 1777, Adam[5] Bullard, *vid* REBECCA, b April 30, 1751, m. Henry[5] Bullard, *vid*, d June 15, 1838 OLIVER [11], b Sept 10, 1754. KEZIA, b. July 26, 1756, m. ——— Hall, res in Oxford, Mass. PEARLEE, b. July 17, 1758, m. 1785, Jeremiah[4] Daniels, *vid.*, d June 18, 1829

[6] ASA[4] RICHARDSON (JOHN[3], JOHN[2], JOHN[1]), son of John [2] and Esther (Breck) Richardson, was born Oct 16, 1720, in Medway, now Millis, Mass He married Abigail Barber, daughter of John[3] and Mary Barber. She was born Aug 14, 1719, in Medfield, Mass They resided in Medway Mr Richardson died about 1764 Mrs Richardson survived her husband

The children were: MIRIAM, b. July 4, 1742, m Samuel Slocum, res. in Hubbardston, Mass. ABIGAIL, b. Jan 24, 1744, m ——— Cutler, res. in Nova Scotia. ASA PARTRIDGE [12], b about 1746 ELI, b Aug 4, 1749, d Oct 2, 1752. ABIJAH [13], b. Aug 30, 1752. HEPHZIBAH, b. Jan. 30, 1755, d Sept. 23, 1759. MARY, b Nov 14, 1757, d Sept 17, 1759 EZRA [14], b. March 17, 1760.

[7] WILLIAM[4] RICHARDSON (DANIEL[3], JOHN[2], JOHN[1]), son of Daniel [3] and Hannah (Underwood) Richardson, was born Feb 3, 1710-11, in Medfield, Mass. He married, May 21, 1739, [1]Mrs Hannah Ellis, *née* Adams, daughter of John[3] and Susanna (Breck) Adams, and widow of Timothy Ellis, *vid* She was born in 1707. They resided in Medway Mrs. Hannah Richardson died. Mr. Richardson married, 1759, [2]Abigail Curtis.

The children were: MARY, b Feb. 17, 1739-40, m ——— Stacey, d prior to 1795. AMOS, b May 8, 1742, m. Mrs. Ede Johnson, *née* Bullard. NATHAN, b September, 1746, d Jan 2, 1747. DANIEL, b September, 1746, d Dec 24, 1746 SARAH, b. April 8, 1748, m. Ebenezer Ellis, *vid*, d Nov 17, 1800

[8] DANIEL[4] RICHARDSON (DANIEL[3], JOHN[2], JOHN[1]), son of Daniel [3] and Hannah (Underwood) Richardson, was born June 26, 1721, in Medway. He married Judith ———. They resided in Medway Mr. Richardson died Dec. 23, 1779 Mrs Richardson died Dec. 22, 1788.

The children were BATHSHEBA, b. April 21, 1743, d April 25, 1827. ELISHA [15], b. Jan 25, 1745. HANNAH, b Jan 30, 1747, d. Jan. 22, 1795. SALLY, b. Dec. 24, 1748. ABIGAIL, b Nov 13, 1750, d. June 11, 1830. DANIEL, b. Feb. 10, 1752, d 1831 JUDITH, b Feb. 2, 1754 PATIENCE, b. Feb. 18, 1756, d Nov. 24, 1792. JOSHUA, b April 22, 1760, m Aug 2, 1781, [1]Sarah Morse; m 1800, [2]Mrs Polly Babbit, res in Charlton, Mass ; d June 17, 1823 SILAS, b. Jan 12, 1762, m. Feb. 21, 1791, Abigail Daniels, res. in Leominster, Mass , d June 15, 1833. MARY, b Sept 12, 1764, d. Oct 31, 1778.

[9] MOSES[5] RICHARDSON (MOSES[4], JOHN[3], JOHN[2], JOHN[1]), son of Moses [5] and Abigail Allen Richardson, was born Oct 27, 1740, in Medway. He married, 1774, Abigail Daniels, daughter of Jeremiah and Mercy (Clark) Daniels She was born in Medway, where they resided. He kept a public house on the old Mendon road, where George Washington dined on his way to Cambridge, Mass., in 1775. Mr. Richardson died Sept. 6, 1826.

The children were MOSES, b. April 3, 1776, m 1797, Patty Wight JABEZ, b.

April 15, 1778 JOHN, b Feb 9, 1782, m Oct 9, 1828, Mrs Mary Daniels, *née* Harding, widow of Moses⁶ Daniels, *vid.*

[10] SIMEON⁵ RICHARDSON (MOSES⁴, JOHN³, JOHN², JOHN¹), son of Moses [5] and Abigail (Allen) Richardson, was born June 27, 1744, in East Medway He married Elizabeth Jones, daughter of Thomas⁵ and Bethia (Whitney) Jones She was born Nov 9, 1753, in East Medway, where they resided Mrs Richardson died Nov 21, 1822 Mr Richardson died May 4, 1825

The children were ABIGAIL, b July 24, 1774, d Sept 17, 1778 ELIZABETH, b July 22, 1776, d Sept. 18, 1778 MATILDA, b Nov 18, 1778, d Jan 29, 1785 KEZIA, b Jan 17, 1781 SOLOMON, b March 8, 1783, m Olive Morse, res in Brookfield, Mass ELIZABETH, b Nov 12, 1785, m ¹Lowell Coolidge; m ²Samuel Sanger, res in Sherborn Mass. HENRY [16], b March 30, 1788 PEARLEE, b June 22, 1790, m June 20, 1811, Joseph Lovell⁶ Richardson, *vid* RHODA, b Jan 12, 1793, m June 28, 1815, James⁷ Daniels, *vid* ORINDA, b April 14, 1796 IRENE, b April 14, 1796, m Jan 23, 1817, ¹Obed Turner, m March 10, 1835, ²Lewis Hawes, m ³Oliver Phillips, d March 1, 1875 SIMEON, b March 16, 1799, m Abigail Richardson

[11] OLIVER⁵ RICHARDSON (MOSES⁴, JOHN³, JOHN², JOHN¹), son of Moses [5] and Abigail (Allen) Richardson, was born Sept 10, 1754 He married Vashti Ramsdell She was born in Medway, where they resided Mrs Richardson died May 3, 1833 Mr Richardson died July 4, 1845

The children were PRISCILLA, b Dec. 2, 1775, m ¹Daniel Allen; m ²——— Manning, res in Lexington, Mass OLIVER, b March 16, 1778, m Matilda Partridge. CHARLES, b. May 26, 1780 IRA, b. Dec. 27, 1782 ABIGAIL, b May 30, 1786, m Joel Brown, res in Brookfield, Mass.

[12] ASA PARTRIDGE⁵ RICHARDSON (ASA⁴, JOHN³, JOHN², JOHN¹), son of Asa [6] and Abigail (Barber) Richardson, was born about 1746 He married Hannah Hill, daughter of John and Ruth Hill She was born Oct 16, 1741, in Sherborn, Mass Mrs Richardson died Sept 8, 1813 Mr Richardson died July 2, 1837

The children were ASA, b. July 12, 1768, m ¹Catharine Adams, m ²Betsey Dexter, d July 30, 1813 PERSIS, b Nov. 27, 1769, m 1790, Paul Metcalf, res in Franklin, Mass. CHARLES, b March 22, 1777 HANNAH, b March 1, 1780, m Feb 11, 1810, Elisha Adams Jones, *vid*, d Jan 19, 1838 SILENCE, b March 1, 1780 LEWIS [17], b Nov 23, 1785 WARREN, res in Andover, Mass

[13] ABIJAH⁵ RICHARDSON (ASA⁴, JOHN³, JOHN², JOHN¹), son of Asa [6] and Abigail (Barber) Richardson, was born Aug 30, 1752, in East Medway He married Mercy Daniels, daughter of Jeremiah and Mercy (Clark) Daniels She was born Dec 16, 1755, in East Medway, where they resided Dr Richardson died May 10, 1822 Mrs Richardson died March 2, 1854

The children were BETSEY, b April 2, 1773, m 1793, Lewis Wheeler, *vid* JOSEPH [18], b April 24. 1775 ABIJAH [19], b Nov 21, 1781 MERCY, b May 2, 1783, m John Stedman, res in Holliston, Mass CHARLOTTE, b July 28. 1785, d Oct 5, 1795 ABIGAIL, b July 31, 1787. m ¹Asa Thayer, m. Jan 1, 1829, ²Zachariah Lovell, *vid* MARY, b March 29, 1789 ELIZA, b July 2, 1791, m April 30, 1823, Sylvanus⁶ Adams, *vid* TRYPHENA, b. June 9, 1794, m Joseph Perry Leland, res in Sherborn, Mass , d July 5, 1837 JEREMIAH DANIELS [20], b April 13, 1796

Memoranda Mr and Mrs. Asa Thayer had two sons, viz.. Abijah Richardson, b Jan 3, 1811, entered Amherst College in 1826, d Oct. 24, 1830 Asa Clark, d the following day, Oct 25, 1830

[14] EZRA⁵ RICHARDSON (ASA⁴, JOHN³, JOHN², JOHN¹), son of Asa [6] and Abigail (Barber) Richardson, was born March 17, 1760, in Medway He married, 1786, ¹Jemima Lovell, daughter of Joseph and Jemima (Adams) Lovell She was born June 5, 1767, in East Medway, where they resided. Mrs Jemima Richardson died Oct 31, 1826 Mr Richardson married, Nov 15, 1827, ²Mrs Lavinia Daniels, *née* Daniels, daughter of Moses and Abigail (Adams) Daniels, and widow of Israel Daniels She was born Jan. 16, 1777, in East Medway Mrs Lavinia Richardson died Sept 7, 1838 Mr Richardson died Feb 2, 1843.

The children were JOSEPH LOVELL [21], b March 29, 1787 JEMIMA, b Nov

2, 1795 SARAH, b. Sept. 24, 1796, m. April 25, 1821, the Rev Alvan Bond, *vid* ELI, b March 20, 1800, d 1800.

[15] ELISHA[5] RICHARDSON (DANIEL[4], DANIEL[3], JOHN[2], JOHN[1]), son of Daniel [8] and Judith Richardson, was born Jan. 25, 1745, in East Medway. He married, 1773, Sarah Ellis, daughter of John and Sarah (Harding) Ellis. She was born in Medway, where they resided Mr Richardson died Aug 17, 1810. Mrs Richardson died Jan 31, 1843

The children were ELISHA, b Feb 4, 1779, d March 16, 1779 MARCUS, b Oct. 30, 1780, m Prudence Hill, res in Bangor, Me., d Jan 13, 1881 SARAH, b March 19, 1785 HANNAH, b Nov 23, 1787, m Dec. 1, 1808, Oliver Phillips, *vid* AMA, b. Oct. 7, 1789 AARON, d Nov. 3, 1803 SILAS [22], b May 9, 1792

[16] HENRY[6] RICHARDSON (SIMEON[5], MOSES[4], JOHN[3], JOHN[2], JOHN[1]), son of Simeon [10] and Elizabeth (Jones) Richardson, was born March 30, 1788, in East Medway He married, Jan 6, 1814, Rebecca Adams, daughter of Micah[6] and Mercy (Penniman) Adams She was born May 15, 1792, in East Medway, where they resided Mr. Richardson died Oct 20, 1870. Mrs. Richardson died Dec 26, 1871

The children were JASON, b. Sept 12, 1814, d Sept 12, 1814. MARY A., b. March 5, 1816, d July 22, 1837 MOSES [23], b July 25, 1819 BETSEY, b. Aug 9, 1822, m Dec 10, 1845, Elial B Blake, res in New York City, d. April 23, 1852 ABIGAIL, b Sept 24, 1825, d Dec 4, 1833

[17] LEWIS[6] RICHARDSON (ASA PARTRIDGE[5], ASA[4], JOHN[3], JOHN[2], JOHN[1]), son of Asa Partridge [12] and Hannah (Hill) Richardson, was born Nov. 23, 1785, in East Medway He married, March 29, 1829, Abigail Mann Tyler, daughter of David and Abigail (Mann) Tyler She was born Dec 5, 1793. They resided in Medway. Mr Richardson died May 19, 1872 Mrs Richardson died Feb 13, 1882.

The children were ABIGAIL MARIA, b Feb 17, 1822, m April 19, 1840, Addison[7] Richardson, *vid* HANNAH AMELIA, b. June 5, 1824, m. Joseph C Plimpton. LEWIS FITZLAND [24], b Dec 30, 1826. ELMIRA FRANCES, b. Jan 29, 1831, res in Grafton, Mass ELMEDA LUCRETIA, b March, 1834, m. November, 1855, Hartwell J. Chickering, res in Grafton, Mass, d Oct 5, 1883.

[18] JOSEPH[6] RICHARDSON (ABIJAH[5], ASA[4], JOHN[3], JOHN[2], JOHN[1]), son of Dr Abijah [13] and Mercy (Daniels) Richardson, was born April 24, 1775, in East Medway. He married, 1795, Ama Adams, daughter of Oliver[5] and Elizabeth (Adams) Adams She was born 1777, in East Medway, where they resided

The children were HORACE [25], b Sept 23, 1795. CHARLOTTE, b February, 1797, m Eleazar Daniels, *vid*; d. Nov. 17, 1840. AMY, b 1799, m June 25, 1840, Elisha Adams Jones, *vid* MARIA, m. Seneca Hills, res in Franklin, Mass RICHARD [26], b September, 1802 MERCY, m Horace Underwood. JOSEPH OLIVER ADAMS, m Mary Bingham, res in Boston, Mass.

[19] ABIJAH[6] RICHARDSON (ABIJAH[5], ASA[4], JOHN[3], JOHN[2], JOHN[1]), son of Dr. Abijah [13] and Mercy (Daniels) Richardson, was born Nov 21, 1781, in East Medway He married Olive Pond, daughter of Dr Elisha and Olive (Dean) Pond She was born Feb. 1, 1782, in Franklin. They resided in East Medway. Mrs Richardson died March 5, 1873.

The children were FANNY, m Joel Brooks. BETSEY, b Sept 13, 1818, m March 27, 1838, Lewis Fisher, *vid* ASA, who died young TRIPHENA, who died in early life. OLIVE, who died young. ABIJAH [27], b Aug 12, 1825

[20] JEREMIAH DANIELS[6] RICHARDSON (ABIJAH[5], ASA[4], JOHN[3], JOHN[2], JOHN[1]), son of Dr Abijah [13] and Mercy (Daniels) Richardson, was born April 13, 1796, in East Medway He married, Lorana Beals, daughter of Asa and Olive (Cheney) Beals She was born May 24, 1801, in Milford, Mass They resided in East Medway. Mr Richardson died March 17, 1875

The children were. FRANCIS DANIELS [28], b May 1, 1821 CLARISSA HAWES, b July 13, 1824 m June 28, 1847, William Wallace Leland, res. in Sherborn, Mass. CHARLES LEWIS, b May 14, 1838, res. in Boston, Mass.

[21] JOSEPH LOVELL[6] RICHARDSON (EZRA[5], ASA[4], JOHN[3], JOHN[2], JOHN[1]), son of Ezra [14] and Jemima (Lovell) Richardson, was born March 29, 1787, in East Medway He married, June 20, 1811, Pearlee Richardson, daughter of Simeon and Elizabeth (Jones) Richardson She was born June 22, 1790, in East Medway, where

they resided   Mrs. Richardson died Dec. 5, 1865   The Hon Joseph L Richardson died Nov. 8, 1880.

The children were: ELIZABETH, b Aug. 14, 1812, m. June 11, 1832, Adams Daniels, d Oct 15, 1833. JEMIMA, b. March 20 1814, m April 3, 1838, Lyman Beecher Larkin, d June 21, 1850 JOSEPH LOVELL [29], b July 11, 1815 STEPHEN BAXTER [30], b July 15, 1818 JOHN PERLEY, b March 18, 1824, d Jan. 12, 1827

[22] SILAS[6] RICHARDSON (ELISHA[5], DANIEL[4], DANIEL[3], JOHN[2], JOHN[1]), son of Elisha [15] and Sarah (Ellis) Richardson, was born May 9, 1792, in East Medway   He married, Dec 22, 1811, Mary Carlton   She was born April, 1792, in Sutton, Mass   They resided in East Medway   Mrs Richardson died March 11, 1873

The children were   AMA, b. Nov. 20, 1812, m the Rev John S White, res in Everett, Mass , d April 5, 1885   ADDISON [31], b Oct 27, 1816.

[23] MOSES[7] RICHARDSON (HENRY[6], SIMEON[5], MOSES[4], JOHN[3], JOHN[2], JOHN[1]), son of Henry [16] and Rebecca (Adams) Richardson, was born July 25, 1819, in East Medway   He married, Oct 30, 1842, [1]Kezia A Fairbanks, daughter of Leonard and Abigail (Harding) Fairbanks   She was born March 29, 1824, in East Medway, where they resided   Mrs. Kezia A Richardson died Dec 6, 1858   Mr Richardson married, April 8, 1863, [2]Martha M. Fussell, daughter of Jonathan F. and Martha (Roberts) Fussell   She was born Nov 30, 1830, in Old Street, London, England

The children were   HENRY SIMEON, b Dec. 25, 1843, m Dec 8, 1867, Emma Howard, res in Dedham, Mass   MARY ABIGAIL, b Dec 18, 1845, m April 23, 1868, Henry Augustus Roberts, res in Newton, Mass   JOHN ADAMS [32], b Oct. 1, 1848. HESTER JENKYN, b June 16, 1865   EVAN FUSSELL, b March 9, 1867   EDITH MARIA, b Sept 26, 1870

[24] LEWIS FITZLAND[7] RICHARDSON (LEWIS[6], ASA PARTRIDGE[5], ASA[4], JOHN[3], JOHN[2], JOHN[1]), son of Lewis [17] and Abigail M (Tyler) Richardson, was born Dec 30, 1826, in East Medway, Mass   He married, April 14, 1854, Hester Roberts, daughter of Jonathan and Judith (Hall) Roberts   She was born Oct 16, 1831, in Rome, Me

The children were   ELMER, b April 7, 1855   ANNIE FRANCES, b. April 14, 1857, m Aug 4, 1879, Arthur C Mundon, res in Boston, Mass.   HESTER AMELIA, b Dec. 18, 1863, m June 7, 1885, Frederic R Chadwick, res. in Attleboro, Mass

[25] HORACE[7] RICHARDSON (JOSEPH[6], ABIJAH[5], ASA[4], JOHN[3], JOHN[2], JOHN[1]), son of Joseph [18] and Ama (Adams) Richardson, was born Sept. 23, 1795, in East Medway   He married Catharine Draper. She was born in 1800, in Dedham, Mass   They resided in Medway   Mr. Richardson died Dec 25, 1856   Mrs Richardson died June 1, 1861

The children were   GEORGE   JOSEPH   HORACE ROBBINS [33]   EMMA, m. ——— Prentice, res in Chicago, Ill.

[26] RICHARD[7] RICHARDSON (JOSEPH[6], ABIJAH[5], ASA[4], JOHN[3], JOHN[2], JOHN[1]), son of Joseph [18] and Ama (Adams) Richardson, was born September, 1802, in East Medway   He married [1]Eliza Bullard, daughter of John Bullard   She was born in Sherborn, Mass   They resided in East Medway   Mrs Eliza Richardson died Dec 5, 1844   Mr Richardson married [2]Elizabeth Baker, daughter of John and Mary E (Holbrook) Baker   She was born in Boston, Mass   Mr Richardson died June 2, 1884

The children were   ELIZA B   MARY B , d Sept 15, 1881

[27] ABIJAH[7] RICHARDSON (ABIJAH[6], ABIJAH[5], ASA[4], JOHN[3], JOHN[2], JOHN[1]), son of Abijah [19] and Olive (Pond) Richardson, was born Aug. 12, 1825, in East Medway   He married, Nov. 20, 1844, Frances Maria Manning, daughter of Jonas and Mary Wright Manning   They resided in East Medway and in Lawrence, Mass

The children were   ABIJAH FRANCIS, b Nov. 12, 1845, m 1869, Margaret Fitzpatrick, res in Boston, Mass , d Dec. 16, 1872.   ALVAN MANNING, b April 23, 1848, m October, 1876, Clara M Bullard   MARY ALICE, b Jan. 28, 1850, m Nov 15, 1875, Arthur D Marble, res in Lawrence, Mass.   BENJAMIN COOLIDGE, b. March 13, 1852, d Aug 31, 1873

[28] FRANCIS DANIELS[7] RICHARDSON (JEREMIAH DANIELS[6], ABIJAH[5], ASA[4], JOHN[3], JOHN[2], JOHN[1]), son of Jeremiah D [20] and Lorana (Beals) Richardson, was born May 1, 1821, in East Medway   He married, Nov. 21, 1842, [1]Betsey Fisher

Bullard, daughter of Elijah Bullard She was born Dec 10, 1820, in Medfield, Mass
Mrs Betsey F. Richardson died May 4, 1854, in Oakland, Cal Mr Richardson married, June 7, 1856, [2]Mrs Laura Ann Abbott, née Bullard They reside in Woodside, Long Island, N Y

The children were· EDWARD FRANCIS, b Oct 17, 1843, m Maggie Lawrence, res. in Corona, L I JEREMIAH DANIELS, b Dec 4, 1845, m. Wilhelmina Augusta Ward, res in Corona, L. I. ABBOTT, b. June 3, 1852, d. Jan. 16, 1853

[29] JOSEPH LOVELL[7] RICHARDSON (JOSEPH LOVELL[6], EZRA[5], ASA[4], JOHN[3], JOHN[2], JOHN[1]), son of Joseph Lovell [21] and Pearlee (Richardson) Richardson, was born July 11, 1815 He married Sylvia Pond Partridge, daughter of Eleazar and Mary (Fisher) Partridge She was born in Franklin, Mass They resided in East Medway. Mr. Richardson died Feb. 13, 1885

The children were· GEORGE LOVELL [34], b March 9, 1838. JOSEPH HENRY [35], b June 7, 1840. ELLEN MARIA, b May 3, 1842, m. Casper Lavater Russell, d March 5, 1873

[30] STEPHEN BAXTER[7] RICHARDSON (JOSEPH LOVELL[6], EZRA[5], ASA[4], JOHN[3], JOHN[2], JOHN[1]), son of Joseph Lovell [21] and Pearlee (Richardson) Richardson was born July 15, 1818, in East Medway He married, June 21, 1842, Laurette Newton Howe, daughter of George and Lydia (Perry) Howe They resided in Nashua, N H.

The children were: JANE ELIZABETH, b. Oct. 27, 1847, m Jan. 15, 1880, James E. Muir INFANT SON, b. Nov 2, 1851, d. Nov. 3, 1851. CHARLES ADDISON, b Nov 21, 1856, d. Sept 9, 1857. LAURA ALICE, b Feb. 19, 1859, m July 17, 1883, George H Moulton, res. in Dorchester, Mass

Memoranda Mrs Laura Alice Moulton furnished the engraving of her grandfather, the Hon. Joseph Lowell Richardson *Vid* p 424

[31] ADDISON[7] RICHARDSON (SILAS[6], ELISHA[5], DANIEL[4], DANIEL[3], JOHN[2], JOHN[1]), son of Silas [22] and Mary (Carlton) Richardson, was born Oct 27, 1816, in East Medway He married, April 19, 1840, Abigail Maria Richardson, daughter of Lewis[8] and Abigail (Tyler) Richardson She was born Feb 17, 1822, in East Medway, Mass. Mr. Richardson died March 28, 1883

The children were: ABIGAIL MARIA, b July 30, 1841, m Dec 25, 1859, Joseph S[8] Adams, *vid* ADDISON WARREN, b. June 14, 1843, m. Harriet A Brown, res in Boston, Mass ALBERT EDGAR, b. Dec 13, 1844, m. Josephine A Brown, res. in Boston, Mass ANNA FRANCES, b. June 5, 1846, m. April 14, 1866, Albert Robbins[6] Daniels, *vid*. ALIDA LILLIAN, b. July 9, 1850 ARTHUR CARLTON, b. Dec. 28, 1858, d Sept 20, 1862. ARTHUR CLARENCE, b. Oct 19, 1861, d Sept 23, 1862

[32] JOHN ADAMS[8] RICHARDSON (MOSES[7], HENRY[6], SIMEON[5], MOSES[4], JOHN[3], JOHN[2], JOHN[1]), son of Moses [23] and Kezia A. (Fairbanks) Richardson, was born Oct. 1, 1848, in East Medway. He married, May 23, 1871, Francisca De Witt Boyd, daughter of Amos Hawes and Rachel P (Butler) Boyd. She was born May 17, 1844, in East Medway. They reside in West Medway.

The children were ALICE K, b Aug 19, 1873. LOUIS B., b. April 30, 1876 ISABEL B., b. June 8, 1877 IRVING L., b. Dec 10, 1882 JENNIE M, b June 5, 1884, d March 25, 1885.

[33] HORACE ROBBINS[6] RICHARDSON (HORACE[7], JOSEPH[6], ABIJAH[5], ASA[4], JOHN[3], JOHN[2], JOHN[1]), son of Horace [25] and Catherine (Draper) Richardson, was born in Medway. He married, Jan 8, 1852, Hannah Daniels, daughter of Cyrus and Louisa (Whitney) Daniels She was born March 23, 1829, in Medway, now Millis They resided in Cambridge, Mass

The children were HORACE, b May 16, 1856 LOUISA, b Sept 17, 1862.

[34] GEORGE LOVELL[8] RICHARDSON (JOSEPH LOVELL[7], JOSEPH LOVELL[6], EZRA[5], ASA[4], JOHN[3], JOHN[2], JOHN[1]), son of Joseph Lovell [29] and Sylvia Pond (Partridge) Richardson, was born March 9, 1838, in East Medway. He married, Dec 6, 1864, [1]Amelia Butler Boyd, daughter of Gen. Amos Hawes and Rachel (Butler) Boyd She was born Sept 26, 1839, in Franklin, Mass. They resided in Abington, Mass Mrs. Amelia B Richardson died July 19, 1879 Mr. Richardson married, Dec 21, 1881, [2]Alice Amelia Giles, daughter of Jesse Howard and Louisa (Ford) Giles She was born in Abington, Mass.

The children were JOSEPH LOVELL, b Nov 5, 1865. FRED BOYD, b. Sept. 1, 1870.

[35] JOSEPH HENRY[8] RICHARDSON (JOSEPH LOVELL[7], JOSEPH LOVELL[6], EZRA[5], ASA[4], JOHN[3], JOHN[2], JOHN[1]), son of Joseph Lovell [29] and Sylvia Pond (Partridge) Richardson, was born June 7, 1840, in East Medway. He married, Dec. 6, 1866, Annie Eliza Tucker, daughter of the Rev. Dr. Joshua Thomas and Mary Oland (Stibbs) Tucker She was born July 7, 1839, in Rushville, Ill They resided in Chicago, Ill , and in East Medway Mrs Richardson died Oct 11, 1882

The children were MARY LOUISE, b May 23, 1868, d May 23, 1868 EDITH ROSS, b Nov 16, 1869 o Feb 22, 1871. HARRY TUCKER, b Dec 26, 1871.

JACOB ROBERTS (EVAN, LEWIS), son of Evan and Hester (Fussell) Roberts, was born in London, England He married, May, 1844, Mary Augusta Church, daughter of Nathan Church She was born in Fairhaven, Mass They resided in Fairhaven, East Medway, and Auburndale, Mass.

The children were. HENRY AUGUSTUS, b 1845, m April 23, 1868, Mary Abigail Richardson, res. in Newton, Mass WILLIAM BROWN, b. 1847, m 1872, Isabella Walker Boyd MARY AGNES, b 1851, d. 1853. GEORGE HERBERT, b. 1854, m Sept. 16, 1880, Mrs Elmira M Harding, *née* Harding, res in Auburndale, Mass HELEN OLIVIA, b 1856 JOSEPH ARTHUR, b 1860

RICHARD[1] ROCKWOOD was a planter in 1636, in Dorchester, Mass The exact date of his arrival in America is unknown He probably came from Weymouth, Dorsetshire, England He was twice married Mrs Agnes Rockwood, his first wife, died May 9, 1643, in Braintree, Mass. Mr Rockwood died in 1660, and his second wife, Mrs Ann Rockwood, died in 1664

[1] NICHOLAS[2] ROCKWOOD, son of Richard and Agnes Rockwood, was born as early as 1628 He married [1]Jane Adams. They settled in Braintree, Mass Mrs Jane Rockwood died Dec 15, 1654 Mr Rockwood married, July 16, 1656, [2]Margaret Holbrook They removed to Medfield prior to 1666, and settled in that part which became Medway Mrs Margaret Rockwood died April 23, 1670 Mr. Rockwood married [3]Silence ——, who died Nov 9, 1677 Mr Rockwood died Jan 26, 1680.

The children were SAMUEL, m Dec 15, 1671, [1]Hannah Ellis, m. [2]Sarah ——, d Dec 1728 BENJAMIN, b Sept 8, 1651, d Dec 5, 1747, in Wrentham. JOSIAH, m. May 9, 1677, Mary Twitchell, res in Mendon, Mass. ELIZABETH, b April 3, 1657, m 1678, [2]John Partridge, *vid* JOSEPH, b 1659, m April 2, 1679, Hannah Partridge res in Swansea, Mass , d July 21, 1693 JOHN [2], b Feb 12, 1662 NATHANIEL, b. Feb 23, 1665, res in Wrentham, Mass , d Sept 24, 1721 ISAAC, b July 22, 1667, d Oct 11, 1677.

[2] JOHN[3] ROCKWOOD (NICHOLAS[2], RICHARD[1]), son of Nicholas [1] and Margaret (Holbrook) Rockwood, was born Feb 12, 1662, in Medfield, Mass. He married, July 19, 1688, Bethia Twitchell, daughter of Benjamin Twitchell She was born in Dorchester, Mass They resided in Medfield, afterward Medway. Mrs Bethia Rockwood died Jan. 1, 1706-7 Mr Rockwood married [2]Sarah Adams, daughter of Jonathan[2] and Elizabeth (Fussell) Adams The Rev John Rockwood died Dec. 16, 1746 Mrs Sarah Rockwood died May 17, 1758.

The children were BETHIA, b Aug 26, 1689, m. Aug 25, 1712, William Burgess JOHN, b October, 1690, d. April 16, 1703 JOSEPH, b Nov. 15, 1692, m. Hannah ——, res in Oxford, Mass ; d October, 1774 SAMUEL [3], b April 15, 1695 BENJAMIN [4], b Nov 19, 1697 DEBORAH, b April 7, 1700 HEZEKIAH [5], b March 1, 1702 JOHN, b Dec 26, 1706, m Hannah Fisher, res in Hopkinton, Mass

[3] SAMUEL[4] ROCKWOOD (JOHN[3], NICHOLAS[2], RICHARD[1]), son of John [2] and Bethia (Twitchell) Rockwood, was born April 15, 1695, in East Medway. He married Mary White She was born in Mendon, Mass They resided in West Medway, on land assigned to George Barber in 1659, a half mile southeast of Winthrop Pond Mr. Rockwood died Jan 18, 1754

The children were. SAMUEL, b May 3, 1724, m Nov. 7, 1750, Sarah Pierce, she was esteemed a witch. TIMOTHY, b May 23, 1727, m Elizabeth Perry, res. in Holliston, Mass ASA, b. Dec. 28, 1734, m. Sybil Littlefield, res. in Holliston, Mass MOSES [6], b May 19, 1737 NATHAN, b. Nov 15, 1739 AARON, b. March 8, 1743, d. in the Revolutionary Army, near Ticonderoga

[4] BENJAMIN[4] ROCKLAND (JOHN[3], NICHOLAS[2], RICHARD[1]), son of John

[2] and Bethia (Twitchell) Rockwood, was born Nov 19, 1697, in Medfield, Mass. He married Rachel Morse, daughter of Benoni and Rachel (Bullard) Morse She was born May 30, 1702, in Medfield, Mass They resided in Medway and removed to Grafton, Mass

The children were BENJAMIN, b. Nov. 18, 1723, m May, 1750, Ruth Adams. RACHEL, b. July 5, 1737.

[5] HEZEKIAH[4] ROCKWOOD (JOHN[3], NICHOLAS[2], RICHARD[1]), son of John [2] and Bethia (Twitchell) Rockwood, was born March 1, 1702, in Medfield, afterward Medway He married Esther ———. They resided in Medway, on what is now known as the Oak Grove Farm, Millis, Mass Mr Rockwood died Mrs. Esther Rockwood married, May 7, 1767, John Wilson, res in Dedham, Mass

The children were· JOSIAH, b. April 7, 1733. d Oct 20, 1762 SETH, b April 10, 1737, d Sept. 15, 1761 AMOS, b. May 22, 1739 d Feb. 26, 1747

[6] MOSES[5] ROCKWOOD (SAMUEL[4], JOHN[3], NICHOLAS[2], RICHARD[1]), son of Samuel [3] and Mary (White) Rockwood was born May 19, 1737, in West Medway. He married [1]Lydia Ellis, daughter of Timothy and Harriet (Adams) Ellis. She was born Nov 29 1736, in Medway. They resided in West Medway Mrs. Lydia Rockwood died Mr Rockwood married [2]Hannah Ellis, a sister of his first wife

There was a son MOSES [7]

[7] MOSES[6] ROCKWOOD (MOSES[5], SAMUEL[4], JOHN[3], NICHOLAS[2], RICHARD[1]), son of Moses [6] and Hannah (Ellis) Rockwood, was born in West Medway. He married, July 1, 1798, Lois Johnson, daughter of Joseph and Mercy (Cozzens) Johnson. She was born June 3, 1767, in Holliston, Mass Mr Rockwood died Feb 4, 1825

The children were. SIMEON, b. Sept. 21, 1799, m. Melatiah Clark JOHNSON, d. young HANNAH ELLIS, b Dec 11, 1802, m George Blake. CALVIN, m Elizabeth Marsh, res in Holliston, Mass ELIZA, m Newell Lovering MOSES, b March 24, 1809, m Adeline Johnson, res in Holliston, Mass

DANIEL[7] ROCKWOOD (PETER[6], ELISHA[5], BENJAMIN[4], NATHANIEL[3], NICHOLAS[2], RICHARD[1]), son of Dea Peter and Sabra Parnell, was born in Medfield, Mass He married, Nov. 8, 1854, Eliza Daniels, daughter of Dea. Paul and Eliza (Breck) Daniell. She was born Feb 2, 1831, in East Medway. They resided in Medway.

THOMAS SANFORD, son of Anthony and Jane Sanford, of Stowe, Gloucestershire, England, came to America, and arrived in Boston between 1631 and 1633, being of the "John Winthrop Colony" He received lands in Dorchester, Mass, both in 1634 and 1635, and became freeman March 9, 1637 In 1639 he removed to Milford, Conn, where his name appears in the earliest records as prominent among the founders of that town. He was associated with Governors Treat, Lute, Buckingham, and other leading men of those times His second wife, Mrs. Sarah Sanford, died May, 1681, and a few months later, October, 1681, Mr. Sanford also died

EPHRAIM SANFORD, the youngest son of Thomas and Dorothy (Meadows) Sanford, was the progenitor of the Sanfords in Medway Ephraim Sanford married, Nov. 16, 1669, Mary Powell, daughter of Thomas Powell, Esq , of New Haven, Conn. They had a son, Samuel Sanford, who married, 1695, Hannah Baldwin, daughter of Nathaniel Baldwin, of Milford, Conn Samuel Sanford was very wealthy David Sanford, son of Samuel and Hannah (Baldwin) Sanford, married in 1730, Rachel Strong, daughter of Elnathan Strong David and Rachel (Strong) Sanford were the parents of the Rev David Sanford, pastor of the Second Church of Christ, in Medway

[1] DAVID SANFORD (DAVID[4], SAMUEL[3], EPHRAIM[2], THOMAS[1]), son of David and Rachel (Strong) Sanford, was born Dec 11, 1737, in New Milford, Conn. He married, Aug 14, 1757, Bathsheba Ingersol, daughter of Moses and Catherine Ingersol She was born June 5, 1738, in Great Barrington, Mass The Rev Mr Sanford died April 7, 1810 Mrs Sanford died

The children were. DAVID, b Jan 6, 1760, res in Great Barrington, Mass., d July 19, 1841 PHILO [2], b Sept 7, 1761. CLARISSA, b Nov 20, 1763, m Feb. 4, 1793, the Rev John Morse, res in Green River, N. Y , d March 15, 1850, in Pompey Hill, N Y ELIHU, b Jan 28, 1766, m [1]Hannah Metcalf , m [2]Betsey Fisher, res. in Oxford, Mass ICHABOD, b. Oct 18, 1768, res in Belchertown Mass BATHSHEBA, b. Feb 14, 1770, m. Feb. 4, 1793, the Rev. Ethan Smith, res in Haverhill, N. H., d.

April 5, 1835. STEPHEN, b. March, 1773. MOSES, b. Nov. 7, 1775. ELECTA, b. March 13, 1778. SAMUEL, b. Jan. 29, 1780, m. Betsey Wight.

Memoranda. Mrs. Bathsheba Sanford was a sister of Mrs. Hopkins, the wife of the Rev. Samuel Hopkins, D. D.

The Rev. Ethan and Bathsheba (Sanford) Smith had several children who died in infancy. Those who lived to maturity were: Myron, b. 1794, d. 1818. Lyndon Arnold, b. Nov. 11, 1795, m. Nov. 20, 1823, Frances L. Griffin, res. in Newark, N. J.; d. Dec. 15, 1865. He graduated from Dartmouth College in 1817, and was a physician. Stephen Sanford, b. 1797, res. in Westminster and Warren, Mass.; d. Oct. 28, 1871. He was a minister. Carlos, b. 1799, graduated 1822, from Union College, N. Y.; pastor for many years in Ohio. Grace Fletcher, b. 1803, m. J. H. Martyn; d. 1840. Sarah Towne, m. 1841, the Rev. J. H. Martyn. She was an authoress of much repute, d. 1879. Harriet, b. 1807, m. 1830, the Rev. William H. Sanford, pastor of the Congregational Church in Boylston, Mass. Ellen Chase, b. 1812, m. 1837, the Hon. Charles B. Sedgwick, res. in Syracuse, N. Y.; d. 1846.

[2] **PHILO[6] SANFORD** (DAVID[5], DAVID[4], SAMUEL[3], EPHRAIM[2], THOMAS[1]), son of the Rev. David [1] and Bathsheba (Ingersol) Sanford, was born Sept. 7, 1761, in West Medway. He married Lydia Whiting, daughter of Nathaniel and Lydia (Partridge) Whiting. She was born Aug. 22, 1764, in Medway, where they resided. Mr. Sanford died 1835. Mrs. Sanford died.

The children were: NATHANIEL WHITING, m. Hannah ———, res. in New York City. PHILO, m. Martha Druce, res. in Newark, N. J. DAVID [3], b. Aug. 28, 1801. CLARISSA, m. Aug. 16, 1826, the Rev. Levi Packard, res. in Spencer, Mass. SEWALL [4], b. 1791. JOANNA, m. Nov. 16, 1820, Joel Partridge, *vid.* LYDIA, m. the Rev. Mr. Eaton. BATHSHEBA, m. Horace Holden, Esq., res. in New York City. STEPHEN, m. Maria Fisher. EDMUND.

[3] **DAVID[7] SANFORD** (PHILO[6], DAVID[5], DANIEL[4], SAMUEL[3], EPHRAIM[2], THOMAS[1]), son of Philo [2] and Lydia (Whiting) Sanford, was born Aug. 28, 1801, in Medway. He married, July 22, 1828, [1]Sarah Parkhurst Daniels, daughter of Obed and Sarah (Parkhurst) Daniels. She was born in Holliston, Mass. They resided in New Market, N. H., Dorchester, Mass., and Medway. Mrs. Sarah P. Sanford died Jan. 6, 1860. The Rev. Mr. Sanford married, March 19, 1861, [2]Mrs. Adeline P. Patrick, *née* Davis, daughter of Isaac and Polly (Rice) Davis, and widow of John Patrick, of Warren, Mass. The Rev. Mr. Sanford died Dec. 17, 1875. Mrs. Adeline P. Sanford removed to Northboro, Mass.

The children were: HARRIET NEWELL, m. July 11, 1856, Eleazar Thompson. DAVID BRAINARD, m. Dec. 10, 1855, Nancy J. Allen. HENRY MARTYN, d. May 14, 1836. HARLAN PAGE. SARAH DANIELL, m. Sept. 9, 1862, the Rev. Calvin Cutler, res. in Auburndale, Mass., d. May 11, 1873. MARY CODMAN, m. Sept. 7, 1870, the Rev. Richard Winsor. EDMUND INGERSOLL, m. Aug. 18, 1875, MARTHA ELIZABETH, m. Aug. 18, 1875, the Rev. Calvin Cutler, res. in Auburndale, Mass. NATHANIEL EMMONS.

[4] **SEWALL[7] SANFORD** (PHILO[6], DAVID[5], DAVID[4], SAMUEL[3], EPHRAIM[2], THOMAS[1]), son of Philo [2] and Lydia (Whiting) Sanford, was born 1791, in Medway. He married, 1812, Edena Holbrook, daughter of Joseph and Amelia (Fisher) Holbrook. She was born Dec. 25, 1786, in Bellingham, Mass. They resided in Medway. Mr. Sanford died April, 1831. Mrs. Sanford died Jan. 7, 1876.

The children were: MILTON HOLBROOK, b. Aug. 29, 1813, m. 1836, [1]Anna T. Davenport; m. [2]Cordelia Riddle, res. in New York City, d. Aug. 3, 1883, in Newport, R. I. EDWARD SEWALL, b. March 17, 1817, m. Mary Downing, res. in New York City, d. Sept. 9, 1882, in Glenolden, Penn. GEORGE FRANCIS, d. 1852. EDENA JANE, m. 1842, Richard M. LeFavor, res. in Medway.

PETER SHUMWAY was the earliest of the family in this country. The tradition current in the family from early date is that the first immigrant in America, of the name of Shumway, was a Huguenot exile from France. His name appears in the earliest records of Essex County, Mass., and is spelled Shamway, which corresponds so nearly in sound with the French name " Chamois," pronounced Shamwah, that support is given to the traditional nationality of the name. Peter Shumway settled about 1660, in Topsfield, Mass. Mention is made of him in the ancient records as doing service in the Narragansett war. He was at the taking of the Indian fort, Dec.

19, 1675, in Rhode Island. His son, Peter² Shumway, removed in 1713, to Oxford, Mass. Amos³ Shumway, the youngest son of Peter² Shumway, was born in 1722, and Jabez⁴ Shumway, the eldest son of Amos³ Shumway, was the first of the name to settle in Medway.

[1] **JABEZ⁴ SHUMWAY** (Amos³, Peter², Peter¹), son of Amos and Ruth (Parker) Shumway, was born Aug. 15, 1746, in Oxford, Mass. He married, March 29, 1775, Olive Penniman, daughter of James and Abigail (Clark) Penniman. She was born Feb. 24, 1751, in East Medway. They resided in West Medway. Mr. Shumway died June 30, 1821. Mrs. Shumway died Sept. 17, 1823.

The children were: OLIVE, b. Nov. 22, 1777, d. March 4, 1778. ABIGAIL, b. Feb. 20, 1780. OLIVE, b. Feb. 28, 1783, m. Sept. 29, 1803, Thomas Adams, d. Sept. 25, 1881. AMOS [2], b. March 27, 1787. RUTH, b. Feb. 4, 1793, m. Nov. 29, 1815, William Adams.

[2] **AMOS⁵ SHUMWAY** (Jabez⁴, Amos³, Peter², Peter¹), son of Jabez [1] and Olive (Penniman) Shumway, was born March 27, 1787, in West Medway. He married Patience Adams, daughter of Phinehas and Patience (Pond) Adams. She was born March 30, 1792, in Medway. They resided in West Medway. Mr. Shumway died Aug. 21, 1871. Mrs. Shumway is living, in 1886.

The children were: WILLARD A., b. March 20, 1811, m. May 25, 1837, Susan Parker, d. April 19, 1860, in St. Augustine, Fla. AMOS PENNIMAN, b. Oct. 31, 1812, d. 1850, in New Mexico. OLIVE, b. Jan. 15, 1815, m. Nov. 25, 1841, Elihu Partridge, *vid.* SEWALL, b. Sept. 5, 1817, m. March 10, 1852, ¹Laura Bradley; m. Nov. 29, 1860, ²Anna B. Bussier, res. in Philadelphia, Penn. ABIGAIL, b. Aug. 29, 1820, m. Oct. 8, 1847, Asa Partridge, res,, in Philadelphia, Penn. ALBERT, b. Jan. 22, 1824, m. Nov. 27, 1856, Sarah J. Reynolds. EDMUND, b. Jan. 22, 1826, m. March 26, 1850, Clara A. Kelsey. WILLIAM WARREN, b. Sept. 26, 1830, m. Nov. 24, 1857, Susan E. Davis. ASAHEL A., b. June 3, 1833, m. Oct. 4, 1859, Fannie M. Shaw. CAROLINE P., b. May 28, 1836, m. Jan. 24, 1866, David B. Hixon, *vid.;* res. in Brooklyn, N. Y.

JOHN STAPLES SMITH (John, Isaac, John), son of John and Mary (Chamberlain) Smith, was born Feb. 17, 1809, in Holliston, Mass. He married, Nov. 27, 1830, Sarah B. Phillips, daughter of Josiah and Sally (Morse) Phillips. She was born Jan. 18, 1812, in East Medway. They reside in West Medway.

The children were: SARAH JANE, b. Oct. 17, 1831, d. Jan. 25, 1835. JOHN EMERSON, b. April 1, 1833, d. Sept. 4, 1834. JOHN MILTON, b. Jan. 25, 1837, d. Sept. 27, 1837. SYLVIA ALTHEA, b. Aug. 27, 1838, d. April 16, 1842. LEANDER BRAYTON, b. Jan. 31, 1841, d. May 4, 1842. MARTHA ANN, b. Aug. 31, 1843, m. March 30, 1862, Chandler Sanders. WARREN MASON, b. Jan. 21, 1845, m. Oct. 29, 1862, Frances Vose. CLARA ANGERETT, b. Dec. 7, 1848, m. Aug. 5, 1868, Charles C. Sumner. ALICE MARIA, b. Aug. 30, 1847, m. July 21, 1869, Nathan Adams. GEORGE EMERSON, b. Oct. 5, 1850, d. Sept. 17, 1851. SARAH LOUISA (adopted), b. Aug. 10, 1840, m. Nov. 8, 1852, James Boyden.

ADDISON A. SMITH (Arnold, Enos), son of Arnold and Jerusha (White) Smith, was born Nov. 8, 1831, in West Medway. He married, March 30, 1854, Mary A. R. Wight, daughter of Seth and Mary Ann (Richards) Wight. She was born Oct. 29, 1832, in Bellingham, Mass. They reside in West Medway.

The children were: ADDISON S., b. Dec. 24, 1856. MARY A., b. June 24, 1860, m. Sept. 9, 1881, Willard I. Allen. ALICE M., b. March 24, 1871.

Memoranda. Mr. Smith's mother was a descendant of Peregrine White.

JAMES A. SNOW (Jesse K., Joseph, Solomon), son of Jesse K. and Eliza S. (Atkins) Snow, was born April 21, 1848, in Boston, Mass. He married, June 30, 1869, Lucy T. Crosman, daughter of David and Mary W. (True) Crosman. She was born in Durham, Me.

The children were: MARY E., b. April 11, 1870, d. Oct. 30, 1878. EDITH E., b. Nov. 27, 1871, d. Oct. 21, 1878. PEARL B., b. March 1, 1875, d. Oct. 29, 1878. LUCY C., b. Oct. 13, 1881.

JOHN¹ SPENCER, immigrant, the son of Robert Spencer, was born near Berwick-on-Tweed, Scotland, where his father, Robert, his grandfather, John, and great-grandfather, Robert Spencer, lived and died. While in college he was drafted to enter the army, and came over to Quebec with General Wolfe, and was under his command at the taking of that place   Subsequently he came to Massachusetts and settled in the town now bearing his name   He married Hannah Bishop, of Leicester, Mass   Mr Spencer was in the battle of Bunker Hill   There is still in the possession of his descendants a part of the gun he carried in that battle. He removed from Spencer to Keene, N H , and from there to Croydon, N. H , where were born his three sons, John, Asa, and Robert   From Croydon, N H., he removed to Marshfield, Vt., where he died at the age of one hundred years   His son John married Persis Jones, of Croydon, N H , and resided in Marshfield, Vt.   They had nine children, who settled in different parts of the country   He lived to be seventy-eight years of age

[1] **PHINEHAS N.³ SPENCER** (JOHN², JOHN¹), son of John and Persis (Jones) Spencer, was born July 15, 1800, in Newport or Croydon, N. H.   The house being partly in one town and partly in the other leaves in some uncertainty which was his native town   He married, Oct 6, 1824, Fanny A Williams, daughter of Guilford and Mary (Deans) Williams, of Taunton, Mass , where they resided until 1833, when they removed to Medway   Mr Spencer died Sept 27, 1884   Mrs Spencer died Oct 9, 1884   Their married life extended over almost sixty years

The children were   EMORY and EMILY, b 1825, d 1825   PHINEHAS FRANCIS, b 1826, d 1826   ADELINE F , b October, 1827, m July 3, 1853, Alfred Cutler, res in Medfield, Mass , d Jan 4, 1863   ALLEN P , b. April, 1830, m 1852, Abby J Clark   HENRY G [2], b April 1, 1833   CHARLES F , b April 1, 1833, m May, 1866, Eleanor J Adams

[2] **HENRY G ⁴ SPENCER** (PHINEHAS N³ , JOHN², JOHN¹), son of Phinehas [1] and Fanny A (Williams) Spencer, was born April 1, 1833. in Taunton, Mass   He married, Nov 29, 1855, Sarah E Wood, daughter of George A and Eliza H (Robbins) Wood   She was born June 27, 1836, in Walpole, Mass

The children were   FANNIE A , b Sept 9, 1856, m Dec 21, 1876, Herbert Prescott Kingsbury, res in South Framingham, Mass   ELIZA, b Nov 23, 1858. HENRY FRANCIS, b Aug 6, 1868

DANIEL G STEVENS, son of Phinehas K and Mary S (Wardwell) Stevens, was born Jan 14, 1826, in Rumford, Me   He married, June 19, 1853, Sibbel Pimpton Lovell, daughter of Asahel P and Eliza (Stedman) Lovell   She was born Oct 6, 1832, in East Medway, where they resided

The children were   MARY E , b Dec 3, 1856, d Jan 31, 1858   CHARLES P , b Nov 14, 1860   ABBY A , b Aug 27, 1862, m June 25, 1884, George C Thrasher, *vid* ROSABELLE W , b Nov. 4, 1865   ETTA S , b Aug 11, 1867   JOSEPHINE S , b Aug 8, 1873

FREDERIC SWARMAN, son of Carson and Ann (Haverstock) Swarman, was born in Boston, Mass   He married, Nov 25, 1854, Tryphena M Harding, daughter of Nathan and Keziah (Adams) Harding   She was born Sept 6, 1837, in East Medway, where they reside

The children were   IRVING H , b June 6, 1858   ANNE E , b Aug 15, 1859. ALMEDA L , b. Sept. 15, 1865   ELMERA L , b Sept 15, 1865   KEZIAH H , b. Feb 25, 1870. WESLEY A , b May 6, 1882, d Sept 10, 1882

[1] **CEPHAS THAYER** (CALVIN, EBENEZER), son of Edwin and Abigail, (Pike) Thayer, was born Feb 16, 1789, in Bellingham, Mass   He married, Aug 5, 1813, ¹Lavinia Adams, daughter of Titus and Anna (Johnson) Adams   She was born in Barre, Mass   They resided in West Medway   Mrs Lavinia Thayer died Sept 6, 1855. Mr Thayer married, March 25, 1856, ²Clara Amelia Hunt, daughter of Joel and Clara (Metcalf) Hunt   She was born July 19, 1811, in Medway   Mr Thayer died April 16, 1882

The only child was   ADDISON P [2], b May 31, 1814

[2] **ADDISON P THAYER** (CEPHAS, CALVIN, EBENEZER), son of Cephas and Lavinia (Adams) Thayer, was born May 31, 1814, in West Medway   He married, April 12, 1853, Lydia Sanford Partridge, daughter of Joel and Joanna (Sanford) Partridge   She was born Sept 11, 1830, in Medway   They resided in West Medway

The children were   ADDISON SANFORD, b Aug 5, 1858   CLARA LOUISA, b Jan. 30, 1862. SARAH EMMA, b Jan 8, 1865

GEORGE C THRASHER (GEORGE BREED, ELKANAH), son of George Breed and Laura F (Ward) Thrasher, was born in East Medway   He married, June 25, 1884,

Abby A. Stevens, daughter of Daniel G and Sibbel P. (Lovell) Stevens. She was born Aug 27, 1862, in East Medway, where they reside

The only child was · SIBBEL PLIMPTON, b July 29, 1885.

ERASTUS TYLER (ELIAS N , DAVID), son of Elias N. and Lydia (Harding) Tyler, was born Dec 5, 1835, in Medway. He married, July 13, 1864, Sarah Isabel Boyd, daughter of William Bradbury and Eveline C. (Ackley) Boyd. She was born Dec. 22, 1834, in Medway, where they resided Mr. Tyler died Dec. 9, 1881 Mrs Tyler married, Dec 27, 1883, [2]Benjamin Glidden, and removed to Beverly, Mass

The children were · FRED W , b Jan 15, 1867 EVELINE H., b Sept. 27, 1868.

Memoranda. David Tyler was born Sept 10, 1771 He married Abigail Mann She was born July 23, 1774 Their children were: Abigail Mann, b Dec. 5, 1793 Eunice M , b Nov 21, 1796 Miranda, b. July 22, 1799. David S , b March 22, 1802 Elias N , b Nov 20, 1804 Eleanor P , b Jan. 17, 1810

ALDIS L. WAITE, (AMOS, JOHN, JOHN), son of Amos and Betsey (Stow) Waite, was born June 2, 1820, in Weston, Vt He married, Feb. 28, 1848, Sophia Dudley Gilman, daughter of Jacob and Betsey (Dudley) Gilman. She was born June 6, 1818, in Lyndon, Vt They resided in Lowell, Mass , and after 1878 in Medway.

Memoranda Mrs Betsey (Stow) Waite, daughter of Abner (*Abner, Samuel, Samuel, Thomas, John,*) and Eunice (Goldsbury) Stow, was born Oct 31, 1779, in Grafton, Mass *Vid The History of Grafton*

[1] **COMFORT[5] WALKER** (COMFORT[4], CALEB[3], EBENEZER[2], PHILIP[1]), son of Comfort and Mehitable (Robinson) Walker, was born Jan 18, 1765, in Rehoboth, Mass He married, Nov. 24, 1789, [1]Tamar Clark, daughter of Timothy and Tamar (Plimpton) Clark She was born July 30, 1770, in Medway, where they resided. Mrs Tamar Walker died May 28, 1813 Mr Walker married Dec 2, 1813, [2]Peggy Whiting She was born Aug 3, 1769 Mrs Peggy Walker died Jan. 29, 1834. Mr Walker married, September, 1834, [3]Mrs Mary Harding, *née* Learned, daughter of Edward and Sarah (Pratt) Learned, and widow of Seth[5] Harding, *vid* She was born in Sherborn, Mass. Mr. Walker died July 31, 1840

The children were AMY, b Oct 9, 1790, m Jan 9, 1817, Ebenezer Eaton, res. in Framingham, Mass DEAN [2], b Feb 25, 1793. CLARK [3], b March 11, 1795 TAMAR, b. Dec 13, 1797, m Aug 7, 1828, Orion Mason, *vid* TIMOTHY [4], b April 26, 1801. ELMIRA, b. Oct. 27, 1803, m April 27, 1824, Orion Mason, *vid* CLARISSA, b Nov 25, 1805, m Sept 11, 1831, the Rev Gilbert Fay, res. in Wardsworth, O MARY, b Sept 17, 1808, m September, 1835, Charles Wheeler, res in Mexico, N. Y. LOIS, b Aug 6, 1810, m. June, 17, 1833, the Rev. Varnum Noyes

Memoranda Comfort Walker came to Medway in 1790, from Killingly, Conn , and settled on the place afterward occupied by his grandson, Edward Eaton, Esq. He was a manufacturer of spinning wheels used in spinning flax He was also a millwright and erected numerous saw mills in Medway and vicinity Later in life he was engaged in company with his sons in the manufacture of cotton in Framingham, Mass , and in Rockville where they erected a mill in 1831. Mr Walker entered heartily into the work of forming a religious society in Factory Village, Medway, and was a liberal contributor for the building of a meeting-house there. He was of a genial disposition, temperate in his habits, and a declared foe to tobacco in every form. By frugality and industry Mr Walker accumulated a large property for those days. In his later life he was familiarly known as "Uncle Comfort"

[2] **DEAN[6] WALKER** (COMFORT[5] COMFORT[4], CALEB[3], EBENEZER[2], PHILIP[1]), son of Comfort and Tamar (Clark) Walker, was born Feb. 25, 1793 in Medway. He married, Nov 29 1814, [1]Rebecca Wright, daughter of Henry and Sally (Newhall) Wright. She was born Oct 10, 1793, in Boston, Mass They resided in Baltimore, Md , and in Medway, Mass Mrs Rebecca Walker died April 29 1864 Mr Walker married, May 3, 1865, [2]Mrs Susan Symonds, *née* Symonds, daughter of Thorndike and Elizabeth (Girdler) Symonds, and widow of John Chapman Symonds She was born Jan 27, 1803, in Salem, Mass Mr Walker died March 25, 1875. Mrs Susan Walker died Feb 3, 1878

The children were HORACE DEAN [5], b Sept 15, 1815. WILLIAM, b. Sept 7, 1817, d April 7, 1819, WILLIAM F b Nov 12, 1819, d Dec. 11, 1822 AUGUSTUS [6], b Oct 30, 1822 JOHN SAVAGE [7], b Sept 4 1824 REBECCA ELMIRA, b. Dec

9, 1827, m Jan. 19, 1853, the Rev. Edwin A Buck, res in Fall River, Mass   ARA-
BELLA, b Dec 8, 1830, m June 19, 1860, Frederic L. Church, res in Andover, Mass
ISABELIA, b Dec 8, 1830

Memoranda   Dean Walker inherited his father's activity and industry   He engaged in the manufacture of machinery and was successful in business   He established, in connection with others, a cotton manufactory near Baltimore, Md , where
he spent several years   He returned to Rockville, Medway, about 1835, where he
lived until his death, March 25, 1875

Frederic L. Church, Esq , of Andover, was cashier for many years of the Old
Boston Bank, Boston, Mass

[3] CLARK⁶ WALKER (COMFORT⁵, COMFORT⁴, CALEB³, EBENEZER², PHILIP¹),
son of Comfort [1] and Tamar (Clark) Walker, was born March 11, 1795, in Medway. He married, Jan 5, 1819, Sarah Lovering, daughter of Amos Lovering   She
was born Dec 3, 1799, in Medway, where they resided, and afterward removed to Killingly, Conn

The children were   SARAH, b Aug 9, 1820, m May 18, 1848, Augustus Bassett, res
in Killingly, Conn   TIMOTHY CLARK, b. May 22, 1823, m June, 1852, Mary Smith,
res in Gardiner, Me   ELLEN FRANCIS, b. Aug 14, 1835   ANNE AUGUSTA, b Nov. 11,
1839, d July 18, 1850

[4] TIMOTHY⁶ WALKER (COMFORT⁵, COMFORT⁴, CALEB³, EBENEZER²,
PHILIP¹), son of Comfort [1] and Tamar (Clark) Walker, was born April 26, 1801. He
married, April 29, 1824, Louisa Turner, daughter of Colonel Amos and Rachel Turner
She was born Aug 26, 1801, in Medway, where they resided until 1850, when they removed to Holliston, Mass   Mrs Louisa Walker died   Mr Walker married, Feb
4, 1867, ²Mrs Sarah E Warfield, *née* Nichols. They resided in Holliston, Mass

The children were   GEORGE F , b. May 31, 1825, m Jan 1, 1852, ¹Amelia Bullard,
m. May 2, 1864, ²Mary A Atwood, res in Freetown, Mass   LOUISA A , b April 21,
1834, m June 10, 1862, Edward G Plimpton, res in Holliston, Mass

[5] HORACE DEAN⁷ WALKER (DEAN⁶, COMFORT⁵, COMFORT⁴, CALEB³,
EBENEZER², PHILIP¹), son of Dean [2] and Rebecca (Wight) Walker, was born Sept
15, 1815, in Framingham, Mass. He married, Jan 21, 1844, Mercy Adams Mason,
daughter of Horatio and Julia (Adams) Mason   She was born Feb 18, 1823, in
Medway   They resided in Abington and Bridgewater, Mass , and in Palatine Bridge,
N Y. The Rev Mr Walker died Nov 4, 1885

The children were   WILLIAM MASON, b March 9, 1845, m. Feb 2, 1869, Lydia
Maria Reed, res. in Nebraska   HORACE DEAN AUSTEN b Aug 6, 1847, d Oct. 24,
1848   ANNA MATILDA, b Jan 2, 1850, d Jan 10, 1852   ELLEN AUSTEN, b. Nov 23,
1851, m. Dec 12, 1878, Gov. Marcellus L Stearns, res in Florida   PHILIP AUGUSTUS,
b Sept 8, 1853, d Aug 22, 1854   SOPHIA ANTOINETTE, b June 22, 1855, res in
Palatine Bridge, N Y.   EDWARD AUGUSTUS, b June 22, 1860, m March 14, 1883,
Mary Weeks Torrey, res in Boston, Mass

[6] AUGUSTUS⁷ WALKER (DEAN⁶, COMFORT⁵, COMFORT⁴, CALEB³, EBEN-
EZER², PHILIP¹), son of Dean [2] and Rebecca (Wight) Walker, was born Oct 30,
1822 He married, Oct 16, 1852, Eliza Mercy Harding, daughter of the Rev Sewall and
Eliza (Wheeler) Harding   She was born Dec 25, 1826, in Waltham, Mass   They re-
sided in Diarbekr, Asia Minor, where the Rev Mr Walker died Sept. 13, 1866   Mrs
Walker returned to America in the spring of 1867, and resided in Auburndale, Mass

The children were   SEWALL HARDING, b Oct 16, 1854, d Jan 7, 1856   FREDERIC
WILLIAMS, b. Jan 10, 1858   DEAN AUGUSTUS, b Feb 3, 1860   DWIGHT RIGGS, b
Jan 19, 1862, d Aug. 25, 1862.   HARRIET ELIZA, b Aug 12, 1863   NELLIE BUCK, b
Feb 9, 1867

[7] JOHN SAVAGE⁷ WALKER (DEAN⁶, COMFORT⁵, COMFORT⁴, CALEB³,
EBENEZER², PHILIP¹), son of Dean [2] and Rebecca (Wright) Walker was born Sept
4, 1824, in Savage Factory Village, Md   He married, Jan 30, 1850, ¹Ellen M Hoyt.
She was born Jan 30, 1824   They resided in Medway. Mrs Ellen M. Walker died
Dec. 9, 1851   Mr. Walker married, April 28, 1853, ²Melinda G Whipple, daughter of
Jonathan and Melinda (Grout) Whipple   She was born March 5, 1831, in Grafton,
Mass   Mr Walker died Oct 26, 1871   Mrs Walker married, Jan 25, 1877, ²Elisha
Adams Jones, *vid.*

The children were DEAN HOYT, b May 20, 1851   ELLEN M., b June 3, 1854, m May 10, 1876, Frank D Bullard   HENRY WHIPPLE, b Oct 12, 1863, res, in California   MARY WHIPPLE, b Sept. 18, 1866

Memoranda. John Savage Walker was an upright, public-spirited, and earnest Christian man   For some years he was the efficient Superintendent of the Sabbath School of the First Church of Christ in Medway   He was a manufacturer, and died at the early age of forty-five years, universally respected, and deeply lamented by the whole community

[1] JONATHAN WHEELER, born in 1718, the tradition is, in Rhode Island, came to Medway and purchased the place of Abner Ellis which is now the summer residence of Mrs Lansing Millis   He married Comfort Bullard, daughter of John[3] and Abigail (Leland) Bullard   She was born March 2, 1721, in Medway, where they resided.   Mr. Wheeler died April 23, 1796

There was a son· JOHN [2], b 1742.

[2] JOHN WHEELER (JONATHAN), son of Jonathan and Comfort (Bullard) Wheeler, was born 1742, in East Medway   He married Mrs Elizabeth Richardson, *née* Partridge, daughter of Joshua and Elizabeth (Kingsbury) Partridge, and widow of Ira Richardson.   She was born March 20, 1747, in Medway, where they resided.   Mr Wheeler died Nov. 20, 1788.   Mrs. Wheeler married [2]Asaph Leland, and after his death married, June 11, 1817, [3]Capt Joseph Lovell, *vid*   Mrs Lovell died April 13, 1833

The children were LEWIS [3], b. November, 1767   JOHN, b 1779, m [1]Mary Scammell, m [2]Bethiah Scammell, m. [3]Mrs Ann Balch, *née* Clapp, res. in Boston, Mass   There were several children who died young.

[3] LEWIS WHEELER (JOHN, JONATHAN), son of John [2] and Mrs. Elizabeth (Richardson) Wheeler, *née* Partridge, was born November, 1767, in East Medway   He married, 1793, Betsey Richardson, daughter of Dr. Abijah[5] and Mercy (Daniels) Richardson   She was born April 2, 1773, in East Medway, where they resided   Captain Wheeler died Nov 7, 1842   Mrs Wheeler died March 24, 1852

The children were JASON, b August, 1794, d. October, 1795·   ELIZA, b August, 1797, m Nov 2, 1820, the Rev Sewall Harding, *vid*, d. Feb. 3, 1877.   MERCY DANIELS, b May, 1799, m May 16, 1820, the Rev Jasper Adams, *vid*, d Nov 11, 1821.   JONATHAN b. April, 1801, d Dec. 11, 1817.   He was in college.   LEWIS, b. August, 1803, m. May, 1828, Catherine Adams, res in Cambridgeport, Mass   He was a physician, d Sept 9, 1872.   BETSEY RICHARDSON, b. February, 1805, m January, 1828, Willard Fisher, res in Franklin, Mass, d July, 1847   ABIJAH RICHARDSON [4], b June, 1807   JAMES, b. February, 1809, d February, 1809   ABIGAIL ANN, b March 1813, m Oct 28, 1835, Paul Baxter Clark, res in Franklin, Mass   BETHIA SCAMMELL, b October, 1815, m December, 1840, Henry[7] Bullard, *vid*, res. in Holliston, Mass

[4] ABIJAH RICHARDSON WHEELER (LEWIS, JOHN, JONATHAN), son of Lewis [3] and Betsey (Richardson) Wheeler, was born June, 1807, in East Medway. He married, June, 1837, [1]Jemima A Adams, daughter of Aaron[8] and Catherine (Adams) Adams   Mrs Jemima A. Wheeler died Oct 3, 1839   Mr Wheeler married, Jan 20, 1841, [2]Adeline Jones, daughter of Elisha Adams Jones   She was born Jan. 12, 1814, in East Medway   Mrs Adeline Wheeler died July, 1848   Mr Wheeler married [3]Mary Bryant   They resided in East Medway.   Mr. Wheeler died April 16, 1878   Mrs Mary Wheeler removed to Hyde Park, Mass

The children were JEMIMA ADAMS, m James Amory Gale, M D., *vid*   AMY, m Albert H Thwing, res in Holliston, Mass   LEWIS [5], b Nov. 21, 1844   EVELINE F, m Frank E. Fisher, res. in Pueblo, Col   AN INFANT, b 1848, d 1848.   ADDIE M, m Oct. 29, 1874, Henry L. Whitney, d Aug 7, 1875   NELLIE E, m July 23, 1874, Edwin H Ellis, res in Medfield, Mass   JENNIE L., m July 31, 1878, Horace Kern, res. in Connecticut.   BESSIE, m Charles Alden, res in Hyde Park, Mass.   JOHN, res in Dedham, Mass   MARTHA, m Irving Mahr, res in West Roxbury, Mass

[5] LEWIS WHEELER (ABIJAH RICHARDSON, LEWIS, JOHN, JONATHAN), son of Abijah Richardson [4] and Adeline (Jones) Wheeler, was born Nov 21, 1844, in East Medway.   He married, Feb 28, 1868, [1]Julia E. Raybold, daughter of James and Elizabeth (Collins) Raybold.   Mrs Julia E Wheeler died   Mr Wheeler married, Dec 29, 1879, [2]Mrs Mary F. Westfall, *née* Burton, daughter of Isaac and Mary Bur-

ton   Mrs Mary F Wheeler died   Mr. Wheeler married, Oct 24, 1883, [3]Catherine E Ellis, daughter of Willard K and Amy (Smith) Ellis   They reside in West Roxbury, Mass.

The children were ARTHUR JAMES KIRBY, b March 10, 1869, d. March 7, 1872   LOUISE MARIA, b May 16, 1870   GRACE AMY, b Oct 15, 1871   FLORENCE ADELINE, b April 10, 1874   WILLIAM HARDING, b June 25, 1876   ALBERT THWING, b Aug 15, 1878, d Sept 13, 1878

[1] NATHANIEL[3] WHITING (JOHN[2], NATHANIEL[1]), son of John[2] and Mary (Billings) Whiting, was born Feb. 2, 1691, in Wrentham, Mass   He married, April 18, 1710, Margaret Mann, daughter of the Rev Samuel and Esther (Ware) Mann   She was born Jan 24, 1693, in Wrentham, Mass   He established a mill on the Charles River soon after marriage.   Mr. Whiting died 1769

The children were   ESTHER, m. June 21, 1732, Nathaniel[3] Clark, *vid*   MARGARET, b Oct. 8, 1715   NATHANIEL [2], b. Dec 22, 1725   NATHAN [3], b Dec 22, 1725

[2] NATHANIEL[4] WHITING (NATHANIEL[3], JOHN[2], NATHANIEL[1]), son of Nathaniel [1] and Margaret (Mann) Whiting, was born Dec 22, 1725, in Medway. He married Lydia Partridge.   She was born March 14, 1736, in Medway, where they resided.   Mr Whiting died 1779

The children were   MERCY, b March 14, 1763, m. April 5, 1781, Maj Luther[6] Metcalf, *vid*   LYDIA, b Aug 22, 1764, m Philo Sanford, *vid*   LOIS, b March 5, 1766

[3] NATHAN[4] WHITING (NATHANIEL[3], JOHN[2], NATHANIEL[1]), son of Nathaniel [1] and Margaret (Mann) Whiting, and twin brother of Nathaniel[4] Whiting, was born Dec 22, 1725, in Medway   He married Mary ———.   They resided in Medway

The children were.   NATHAN, b Feb 25, 1749-50   DAVID, b. Jan. 17, 1753   ELIAS [4], b Jan. 17, 1753   JOEL, b Aug 15, 1755   MARY, b. Nov. 9, 1758   ABIGAIL, b May 19, 1760   JOHN, b. Sept 9, 1762   NATHAN, b Feb 1, 1765   TIMOTHY [5], b Aug 5, 1767   NATHAN, b Feb 1, 1770

[4] ELIAS[5] WHITING (NATHAN[4], NATHANIEL[3], JOHN[2], NATHANIEL[1]), son of Nathan [3] and Mary Whiting, married Joanna Bullard, daughter of Henry[5] and Rebecca (Richardson) Bullard   She was born March 21, 1792   They resided in Medway.

The children were   DAVID, b Jan 6, 1782   SUSANNA, b July 8, 1783.   POLLY, b Nov 28, 1784   ESTHER, b Oct 9, 1786, m Titus[6] Bullard, *vid*   ELIJAH, b Aug. 30, 1793   PATTY JUDSON, b Jan 23, 1798

[5] TIMOTHY[5] WHITING (NATHAN[4], NATHANIEL[3], JOHN[2], NATHANIEL[1]), son of Nathan [3] and Mary Whiting, married Rhoda Bullard, daughter of Timothy and Rhoda (Richardson) Bullard   She was born Dec 25, 1770, in Medway, where they resided

There was a son   TIMOTHY, b April 11, 1797

GEORGE WALLACE WHITING (JOEL WARE, DEXTER, JOHN), son of Joel Ware and Harriet Joanna (Ware) Whiting, was born Dec 14, 1855, in Medway, Mass   He married, May 28, 1878, Allethina Carol Leland, daughter of Abner Adams and Phebe (Coggeshall) Leland   She was born in Milford, Mass

The children were.   ALICE MAUD, b Jan. 14, 1880   LELAND KENDRICK, b Nov 18, 1884

JAMES B. WILSON was born Aug 23, 1795, in New Braintree, Mass.   He married, Dec 23, 1824, [1]Sally N Cutler   They resided in Medway   Mrs Sally N Wilson died.   Mr Wilson married, 1854, [2]——— Pond   He died Nov 27, 1857

The children were   JANE LAVINIA, b March 10, 1827, m Nov 28, 1853, Gilbert E Daniels   JAMES R., b April 16, 1829, d Dec 20, 1851   ELIHU CUTLER, b June 26, 1831   CHARLES E, b Oct 15, 1835, d Aug 25, 1836   HELEN M, b July 1, 1838, d. Sept 30, 1838   ISABELLA B, b Oct 29, 1841   JASON E, b Sept 4, 1843

Memoranda   James B. Wilson came to Medway in 1818   He was engaged in trade and manufacturing.   Mr Wilson was for several years postmaster, and held a high position in the Masonic fraternity.   He contributed much to the enterprise and growth of the Village, and was succeeded in business by his son, Elihu Cutler Wilson, Esq., who was for some years the partner of Mr Edward Eaton, and still continues a large and prosperous manufacturing establishment.

ROBERT O. YOUNG, son of Nathaniel and Betsey (Palmer) Young, was born Oct. 13, 1831, in Windsor, Vt. He married, Feb. 14, 1853, Elizabeth L. Dain, daughter of Rice O. and Mary (Durfee) Dain. She was born Dec. 27, 1832, in Royalston, Vt. They have resided since 1859 in Medway.

The children were: IDA L , b. 1853, d. Nov. 27, 1860. SANFORD L., b. Nov. 22, 1855, m. July 7, 1876, Emma L. Palmer. She was born Feb. 5, 1857, in Nova Scotia. ORION R., b. Nov. 16, 1858, m. May M. Coolidge. She was born May 31, 1859, in Medway.

Memoranda. Mr. and Mrs. Sanford L. Young had one child, Robert L., b. March 24, 1877. Mr. and Mrs. Orion R. Young had two children : Herbert E., b. Feb. 24, 1880. Grace E., b. March 16, 1881.

THE ERRATA.

Page 26, line 6.   For Mary A. Harris, *read* Mary Adams.
Page 141, line 34.   For Dec. 17, 1876, *read* Dec. 17, 1875.
Page 374, line 23.   For Nov. 28, 1805, *read* Nov. 25, 1805.
Page 456, line 32.   For Emeline C. Ackley, *read* Eveline C. Ackley.
Page 457, line 32.   For d. 1802, *read* July 25, 1799.
Page 458, line 22.   For April 3, 1751, *read* April 30, 1751.
Page 459, line 58.   For Harriet B., m., *read* Harriet H., m. Nov. 30, 1881.
Page 464, line 41.   For Nov. 19, 1820, *read* July 19, 1820.
Page 482, line 24.   For m. 1879, *read* m. Nov. 30, 1881.
Page 500, line 1.   For d. Oct. 3, 1826, *read* d. Oct. 31, 1826.

THE MEDWAY GENEALOGIES given in the preceding pages are necessarily incomplete, but may furnish the basis of still further research, and suggest the preparation of a book of the genealogies of these and other families of the town more complete than the limits of this volume will allow.

THE INDEX.

LaVergne, TN USA
02 March 2011
218644LV00003B/51/P